*Cultural Pasts*

# Cultural Pasts

## *Essays in Early Indian History*

Romila Thapar

OXFORD
UNIVERSITY PRESS

OXFORD
UNIVERSITY PRESS

YMCA Library Building, Jai Singh Road, New Delhi 110001

Oxford University Press is a department of the University of Oxford. It furthers the University's objective of excellence in research, scholarship, and education by publishing worldwide in

Oxford New York

Athens Auckland Bangkok Bogota Buenos Aires Calcutta
Cape Town Chennai Dar es Salaam Delhi Florence Hong Kong Istanbul
Karachi Kuala Lumpur Madrid Melbourne Mexico City Mumbai
Nairobi Paris Sao Paolo Shanghai Singapore Taipei Tokyo Toronto Warsaw
with associated companies in Berlin Ibadan


Published in India
By Oxford University Press, New Delhi



ISBN 019 564050 0

Typeset in Charter 10 pts
By Rastrixi, New Delhi 110070, New Delhi
Printed at Saurabh Print-o-Pack, Noida
Published by Manzar Khan, Oxford University Press
YMCA Library Building, Jai Singh Road, New Delhi 110 001

*. . . Included in this land were fruit-yielding trees, water, lands, gardens, all up-growing trees and down going wells, open spaces, wastes in which calves graze, the village site, ant hills, platforms built around trees, canals, hollows; rivers and their alluvial deposits, tanks, granaries, fish-ponds and deep ponds, clefts with bee-hives; and everything else on which the iguana runs and the tortoise crawls; and taxes such as the income from places of justice, the taxes on betel leaves, the cloths from looms . . . everything that the king could take and enjoy . . .*

Anbil Copper Plate Grant of
Sundara Chola c. AD 960

# *Preface*

The papers and lectures that comprise this volume were written at different times over the past thirty years or so and have appeared earlier within diverse journals, pamphlets, books. I was asked to pull them together into a single volume by Oxford University Press who — as they persuasively put it — were certain that 'a fulsome selection of your best essays will interest a large number of historians and general readers.'

I have arranged the essays thematically and not chronologically because that makes for more interesting reading. As a consequence, a certain level of overlap in the subjects discussed is more noticeable than it might otherwise have been, but editing out the overlap would probably have truncated lines of thought within each essay and perhaps made each seem less unified and readable.

No substantial revision has been made to these essays, therefore, except here and there in order to correct dated information. A little more than such minimalist revision was required in those essays that appeared in an earlier form in my collection titled *Ancient Indian Social History: Some Interpretations*, but here again I have taken care to preserve the essays' original argument and unity.

Fortunately, major changes in perspective within the study of early Indian history take time getting established! My present views on some of the themes within this present volume have marginally altered, but I feel there is much to be said for retaining the flavour of the separate periods in which these essays were originally written.

I am aware that the terms 'culture' and 'cultural' have had many meanings and connotations, ranging from an interest in literature, the arts and philosophy to the sophisticated analyses of those who work in 'cultural studies'. Nevertheless, the choice of title for this book derives from my preference that culture be defined as 'a pattern of life'. In this sense, historical analysis — where it is not an arid recounting of dates and events — inevitably refers to the culture of a society, or to a segment of that society.

I would like to thank Venkatesh Nayyar and Avinash Kumar for help with the nitty-gritty of preparing this book.

New Delhi, 1999 ROMILA THAPAR

# Contents

# *List of Illustrations*

(between pp. 692–3)

# I

# *Historiography*

The first theme of the historiographical section attempts to sketch some of the historical perceptions which have influenced the writing of early Indian history. An earlier version of the first paper, 'Changing Interpretations of Ancient Indian History,' was published in the journal *History and Theory* in 1968. The first three papers are essentially looking back at these perceptions. D.D. Kosambi's writings mark a water-shed in that he not only introduced new perspectives but also demonstrated the need to interweave varieties of source material keeping in mind their contextual particularities.

Regional history has come into importance during the last few decades with the constant discovery of new evidence and the projections of the self-perception of social groups drawing on regional identities. I have attempted to suggest ways of looking at regional history from a comparative perspective as well as its integration into the history of larger areas.

The last three papers discuss aspects of traditional historical writing. This is an area which has been ignored in the past because of the assumption that historical consciousness was absent in Indian societies. These essays attempt to explain why this assumption took root and to present an alternate view. A discussion of notions of time and how they were related to perceptions of the past is the theme of an independent publication, *Time as a Metaphor of History: Early India*.

1. Ideology and the Interpretation of Early Indian History (1974)
2. Durkheim and Weber on Theories of Society and Race Relating to Pre-colonial India (1980)
3. The Contribution of D.D. Kosambi to Indology (1977)
4. Early India: An Overview (1983)
5. Regional History: The Punjab (1972)

6. Regional History with Reference to the Konkan (pub. 1996)
7. Society and Historical Consciousness: The *Itihāsa-purāṇa* Tradition (1986)
8. Historical Consciousness in Early India (1995)
10. Antecedents, Religious Sanctions and Political Legitimation in the Ladakh Chronicles (1978)

# 1

# *Ideology and the Interpretation of Early Indian History**

It is some times said that the interpretation of the ancient periods of history has little historiographical interest, since they refer to times too distant for an ideological concern to have much meaning for contemporary society, and that the sparseness of the evidence does not provide much margin for ideological debate. This view would not however be valid for the interpretation of early Indian history, where both the colonial experience and nationalism of recent centuries influenced the study, particularly of the early period of history.

In Europe, post-Renaissance interests, which initiated the extensive study of the ancient world, brought to this study the ideological concerns of their own times.[1] These concerns are also reflected in the historiography of India,[2] if not of Asia. The interpretation of Indian history from the eighteenth century onwards relates closely to the world view of European, and particularly British historians, who provided the initial historiographical base. The resulting theories frequently reflected, whether consciously or not, the political and ideological interests of Europe — the history of India becoming one of the means of propagating those interests. Traditional Indian historical writing with its emphasis on historical biographies and chronicles was largely ignored. European writing on Indian history was an attempt to create a fresh historical tradition. The historiographical pattern of the Indian past, which took shape during the colonial period in the eighteenth and nineteenth centuries, was probably similar to the patterns which emerged in the histories of other colonial societies.

Investigation into the Indian past began with the work of the

* Lecture delivered at Cornell University, 1974.

Orientalists or Indologists — mainly European scholars who had made India, and particularly Indian languages, their area of study. The majority of the Indologists, and certainly the great names among them such as Jones, Colebrooke and Wilson, were employed by the East India Company in various administrative capacities. Trained as many of them were in the Classical tradition of Europe, they were also familiar with the recent interest in philology and used the opportunity to acquire an expertise in a new area. As administrators they required a specialized knowledge of traditional Indian law, politics, society and religion, which inevitably led them to the literature in Sanskrit and Persian. Thus, scholarly and administrative interests coalesced.

The nineteenth century saw the development of not only these studies in India, but also the introduction of courses in oriental languages at various European universities and elsewhere.[3] The term Indologist now came to include those who had a purely academic interest in India and who were intellectually curious about India and the Indian past. The study of Sanskrit language and literature not only gave shape to the discipline of comparative philology, but also became the source material for the reconstruction of ancient Indian society. Vedic Sanskrit, the language of the Vedic literature in particular, was used extensively in the reconstruction of both Indian and Indo-European society, since the linguistic connection between the two had been established. It was now possible for scholars of Sanskrit to attempt wide-ranging interpretations of what was believed to be the beginnings of Indian history, with little or no personal experience of the Indian reality. One of the most influential of such scholars in his time was Max Müller, whose full and appreciative descriptions of contemporary Indian village communities would hardly have led one to suspect that he had never visited India. Inevitably those who were sympathetic to Indian culture tended to romanticize the ancient Indian past. These interpretations carried the imagery and the preconceptions not only of the sources, but also of those interpreting them.

By far the most influential theory to emerge from Indological studies in the nineteenth century was the Theory of Aryan Race. The words *airiia* and *ārya* from the Iranian Avestan and Vedic Sanskrit texts were given a racial connotation, as referring to the race of the Aryans. They were described as physically different from the indigenous population and their cultural distinctiveness was apparent from the fact that they spoke an Indo-European language. It was held that large numbers of Aryans, described as a branch of the Indo-European race and language group, invaded northern India in the second millennium BC, conquered the indigenous peoples and established the Vedic Aryan culture which became the foundation of Indian culture.

The identification of language and race was seen to be a fallacy even during the lifetime of Müller.[4] Although in his later writings he clarified his views on this identification, it was by then too late, and the idea had taken root. It is curious that Aryan should have been interpreted in racial terms since in the texts it refers merely to an honoured person of high status and in the Vedic context, this would be one who spoke Sanskrit and observed the caste regulations and rituals. The racial connotation may have been due to the counterposing of *ārya* with *dāsa*, in the *Ṛg Veda*, and it was argued that the *dāsa* is described as physically dissimilar to the *ārya*.[5] This was interpreted as representing two racial types with the *āryas* evolving later into the three upper castes and the *dāsa* remaining the lowest, included in the *śūdra* caste; the racial identity of each being preserved by forbidding intermarriage between the castes. The pre-eminence of the *ārya* was explained as due to the successful conquest of the *āryas* over the *dāsas*. The term *varṇa*, etymologically associated with colour and occurring as a technical term referring to the caste organization of society, was used as yet another argument to support the Aryan theory of race. It was believed to provide a 'scientific' explanation for caste, namely, that the four main castes represented major racial groups, whose racial identity was preserved by forbidding intermarriage and making birth the sole criterion for caste status. The latter half of the nineteenth century in Europe was concerned with the discussion on race in the theories of Gobineau and the growing interest in social evolution. Some of the Indologists were by no means unfamiliar with this debate.[6] The distinction between Aryan and non-Aryan, and the polarity of Aryan and Dravidian suggested by them for the Indian scene, echoes to a degree which can hardly be regarded as coincidental, the Aryan-non-Aryan distinction and the Aryan-Semitic dichotomy based on language and race, in the European context. The suggested social bifurcation is also remarkably similar; the upper castes were the Aryans and the lower castes were the non-Aryans.

The belief in the Indo-European origins of both European and Indian societies intensified the interest in Vedic Aryan sources, since these were seen as the earliest survivals of a common past. The village community of Vedic society was looked upon as the rediscovery of the roots of ancient European society. It was described as an idyllic community of gentle and passive people given to meditation and other-worldly thoughts, with an absence of aggression and competition.[7] Possibly some of these scholars, well disposed towards India, were seeking an escape into a utopia distant in time and place, perhaps fleeing from the bewildering changes overtaking them in their own times. Others were defending Indian society from its critics. Eventually the theory of Aryan race gave way to what has come to be called the Aryan Problem, namely, the historical role of the Indo-Aryan speaking people and their identification in early Indian sources.

But the early nineteenth century saw a new direction in the attitude of the administrator-scholars of the East India Company towards Indian history. Some, although they did not romanticize the ancient Indian past were nevertheless sympathetic in their interpretations. Others, in increasing number, became critical of what they called the values of ancient Indian society. This was in part due to the mounting problems of governing a vast colony, with an unfamiliar, if not alien culture. The nature of the relationship between Britain and India was also undergoing change, for trading stations were being substituted by colonial markets. The major intellectual influence, however, was that of English Utilitarian philosophy. James Mill, its first ideologue in the context of Indian history, completed his lengthy *History of British India* in the early decades of the nineteenth century. Mill's *History* claimed to be a critical investigation of the traditional institutions of India. These, by the standards of nineteenth century Utilitarianism, were found to be static, retrogressive and conducive to economic backwardness. He recommended a radical alteration of Indian society, to be achieved by imposing the correct legal and administrative system in India. Both the analysis and the solution suggested by Mill suited the aims and needs of imperial requirements His *History*, therefore, became a textbook on India at the Haileybury College, where the British officers of the Indian Civil Service were trained.

Further intellectual support for this view of the pre-modern history of India was found in writings of the more eminent philosophers of history of the time. Hegel, for example, remarked on the absence of dialectical change in Indian history, and consequently dismissed Indian civilization as being static, despotic in its orientation, and outside the mainstream of relevant world history.[8]

Central to this view of the pre-modern history of India, and implicit in Mill's *History*, was the theory of Oriental Despotism.[9] The genesis of this theory probably goes back to the Greco-Persian antagonism, with references in Greek writing to the despotic government of the Persians. To this was added the vision of the luxuries of the oriental courts, a vision built partly on the luxury trade with the east from early times, and partly on the fantasy world of oriental courts as described in the accounts of visitors to these regions, such as those of Ktesias at the Persian court and Megasthenes at the Mauryan court in India. The Crusades and the ensuing literature on the Turks doubtless strengthened the fanciful notion of the all-powerful, despotic, oriental potentate. When interest in the notion was revived in the eighteenth century as an explanation for continuing empires in Asia, the focus was shifted from the doings of the despot to the nature of the despotic state. Given the concerns of eighteenth century France and England, the central question was seen as that of private property in land, and the state ownership of land.[10] Once again, the accounts of ambassadors and visitors to Mughal India such as Roe and Bernier were quoted, and they maintained that there was an absence of the right to private property in land.[11] Some, such as Montesquieu, accepted the theory of oriental despotism; others, such as Voltaire, doubted the correctness of its assumptions. By the mid-nineteenth century it had such currency in Britain that again the standard text on the traditional economy of India used at Haileybury College was that of Richard Jones, who endorsed the theory. Inevitably, the major historians of the late nineteenth century in India, who also happened to be the administrators, assumed the correctness of the theory as a precondition to their understanding of the Indian past. Even Marx, despite his concern for dialectical movement, was not averse to the idea with its emphasis on a static society and an absence of change, and worked the theory into his model for Asian society — that of the Asiatic Mode of Production.[12]

The absence of private property in land was central to this model of social and economic structure. The structure was seen in the form of a pyramid, with the king at the apex, and self-sufficient, isolated village communities at the base. The surplus was collected from the cultivators by the bureaucracy, and the process of redistribution led to its being appropriated, substantially, by the king and the court — hence the fabulous wealth of oriental courts. Control over the peasant communities was maintained by the state monopoly of the irrigation system — or the hydraulic machinery, as a more recent author has called it[13] — the control over which was crucial in arid lands dependent on artificial irrigation. The subservience of the peasant communities was ensured not only by extracting the maximum surplus from them, but also by investing the king with absolute powers and divinity. The isolation of social groups was made more complete by the absence of urban centres and effective networks of trade.

The idealization of the village community from one group of scholars was now juxtaposed with the starkness of those supporting the other interpretation. This historical kaleidoscope was readjusted when a third perspective was introduced at the start of the twentieth century. The authors of this were Indian historians, using the current methodology but motivated ideologically by the national movement for independence; scholars who have been referred to in recent writings as the nationalist historians.[14] Of the two major theories, the theory of Aryan race had their approval, whereas that of Oriental Despotism was opposed for obvious reasons. The former was believed to be based on the most up-to-date philological evidence. Its supposed 'scientific' explanation for caste was gratifying, in view of the general condemnation of caste society from the stalwarts of egalitarianism. *Homo hierarchicus*, if one may borrow the phrase, stood exonerated. The depiction of Aryan society in glowing terms was soothing to the sensitivities of Indian scholarship. There was also an appeal to some middle-class Indians that the coming of the English represented 'a reunion of parted cousins, the descendants of two different families of the ancient Aryan race'.[15]

Nationalist historical writing took up the theme, among other things, of the importance of religion to Indian society. The bipolarity of the spiritual content of Indian culture and the materialist basis of western culture was seen as an essential and inherent difference. This was in part a reaction to the earlier view, that religion was such a central factor in traditional Indian society that it obstructed progress — the latter being defined as social and economic change. This view had been eagerly taken up both by Christian missionaries anxious to proselytize among the more enterprising Indian social groups, as well as by those who were looking for a single factor which would explain the backwardness of India as a colonial society.[16]

The nationalist historians concerned themselves with those ideas which were necessary to nationalist polemics. They questioned individual items of historical interpretation, rather than examining the validity of a theory as a total pattern of interpretation. Nor did they attempt to replace the existing theories by new ones, fundamentally different from what had gone before. In a sense, nationalist ideology delimited the nature of their questions. However, in spite of these weaknesses, the impact of the nationalist school was both considerable and necessary. The role of ideology in historical interpretation was recognized with the highlighting of the ideological content of earlier interpretations. Above all, it prepared the way for questioning the accepted theories.

This has been of necessity an over-simplified sketch of the main ideological trends in modern interpretations of early Indian history. I would now like to consider at greater length the two main theories to which I have referred. In selecting the Aryan problem and Oriental Despotism for further analysis, in the light of new evidence and methods of enquiry, my purpose is not merely to indicate the inapplicability of the theories, but also to suggest the nature of possible generalizations which arise in the reexamination of accepted theories.

The questioning of the Aryan theory is based on the work in recent years from three different disciplines, archaeology, linguistics and social anthropology. The discovery and excavation of the cities of the Indus civilization has pushed back the beginnings of Indian history to the third millennium BC, and the Indus civilization has replaced the Vedic Aryan culture as foundational to Indian history. The cities of the Indus pre-date the Vedic culture by at least a millennium, since the decline of the cities dates to the early second millennium and the diffusion of Sanskrit as a part of the Vedic culture is believed to have begun at the end of the same millennium.[17] The Indus cities epitomize a copper-bronze age urban civilization, based on commerce both within the north-western area of the sub-continent as well as West Asia. The earliest of the Vedic texts, the *Ṛg Veda*, reflects a pastoral, cattle-keeping people unfamiliar with urban life. If the Aryans had conquered north-western

India and destroyed the cities, some archaeological evidence of the conquest should have been forthcoming. In only one part of one of the cities is there evidence of what might be interpreted as the aftermath of conquest and even this has been seriously doubted.[18] The decline of the Indus cities is generally attributed to extensive ecological changes. The repeated flooding of the Indus, the rise of the water-table and salination of the land under cultivation, the change in the course of the Sarasvatī river with a consequent encroaching of the desert and major sea-level changes affecting the ports along the west coast, seem more convincing explanations for the decline of the cities.[19] Palaeo-botanical analyses are suggesting a change in climatic conditions from humid to dry.[20] Unlike conquest, ecological change was more gradual and as the cities declined there were migrations out of the cities as well as small groups of squatters moving in from the neighbouring areas. Recent evidence from excavations in western India and the Indo-Gangetic divide is pointing toward some continuity from the Indus civilization into later cultures.[21] There is little doubt now that certain facets of the Indus civilization survived into the second and first millennium cultures, in spite of the decline of the cities. The earlier hiatus between the Indus civilization and the Vedic culture is no longer acceptable, and the Indus civilization has now to be seen as the bedrock of early Indian culture.

Recent linguistic analyses of Vedic Sanskrit have confirmed the presence of non-Aryan elements, especially Proto-Dravidian, both in vocabulary and phonetics.[22] Consequently it has been suggested that Proto-Dravidian could have been the earlier language of northern India, perhaps the language of the Indus civilization, although this awaits the decipherment of the Indus script, and that Vedic Sanskrit as the language of a particular social group, slowly spread across the northern half of the sub-continent, with a possible period of bilingualism, in which Vedic Sanskrit was modified by the indigenous language.[23] It is significant that some of the Proto-Dravidian loan words in Vedic Sanskrit refer to agricultural processes. We know from archaeological evidence that plough agriculture was practised by the Indus settlements[24] and from the *Ṛg Vedic* hymns it is apparent that pastoralism and not agriculture was the more prestigious profession among the early Aryan speakers.

Anthropological studies of Indian society have encouraged a reappraisal of the social history of early periods. The insistence on the precise meaning of words relating to social categories in the sources has been all to the good. The valid distinction between *varṇa* as caste in the sense of ritual status, and *jāti* as caste in the sense of actual status is again a help to the social historian. The most useful contribution, however, has been in the study of the formation of castes, which has made it apparent that caste society does not require the pre-condition of different racial entities, nor the conquest of one by the other. It does require the existence of hereditary groups determining marriage relations, which groups are arranged in a hierarchical order and perform services for one another. The hierarchy is dependent on occupation, on certain beliefs of purity and pollution, and on continued settlement in a particular geographical location. The formation of a new caste has therefore to be seen in terms of the historical change in a particular region. Thus, a tribe incorporated into peasant society could be converted into a caste.[25] Occupational groups often acquired a caste identity through the corporate entity of the guild or through hereditary office in administration.[26] Religious sects, frequently protesting against the caste hierarchy, often ended up as castes themselves. Possibilities of social mobility and variations in status were linked to the historical context of time and place. Social attitudes were often set; nevertheless, the opportunities for social change were exploited, and the historian can no longer dismiss the social dimension by merely referring to the unchanging rigidity of caste society. In this context the theory of Sanskritization has been a breakthrough in the study of social history.[27]

The combination of new evidence and fresh perspectives from all these sources raises a host of new questions with reference to the Vedic period. Evidently it was not a purely Indo-Aryan assertion over Indian culture and has to be seen as an amalgam of the Indo-Aryan and the existing culture, which in turn requires a clearer definition of each. Since the spread of Sanskrit, certainly in the Ganges valley if not in the north-west as well, appears to have occurred through a process of diffusion and less through conquest, the motivation for the diffusion would have to be sought. One of the possibilities suggested is that it coincided with the arrival of a new technology at the start of the first millennium BC. This is apparent in the use of iron in preference to copper and the introduction of the horse and the spoked wheel, both new to India.[28] The ambiguity of the word *ayas*, copper or iron in Sanskrit, creates some difficulties in an immediate acceptance of this idea. Vedic Sanskrit is closely connected with priestly groups and the belief in ritual may have accelerated the diffusion, particularly as it seems that Vedic ritual was closely associated with knowledge of the solar calendar providing, among other things, a more effective control over agricultural processes. The diffusion of a language does not require the physical presence of large numbers of native speakers. It can often be done more effectively by influential groups in the population adapting the new language and using the traditional networks of communication. The spread of Sanskrit might be more meaningfully seen as marking a point of social change, apart from merely a change of language.

The notion of historical change, other than changing dynasties, was curiously unacceptable to nineteenth century thinking on the Indian past. The unchanging nature of society is central to the theory of Oriental Despotism. The span of Indian history was seen as one long stretch of empire with an occasional change of dynasty. Yet in fact, empires were of short duration and very infrequent. There was only one empire in the early period, the Mauryan empire, lasting from the end of the fourth to the early second century BC, which would even approximately qualify as an imperial system. It was not until the historical writing of the twentieth century that some concession was made to change, and imperial golden ages were interspersed with the dark ages of smaller kingdoms.[29]

In re-examining Oriental Despotism it is not new evidence which provides an alternative analysis, but the more careful questioning of existing sources. It is surprising that references to private property in land should have been overlooked. The socio-legal texts, the *dharmaśāstras* and the early text on political economy, the *Arthaśāstra*, list and discuss the laws and regulations for the sale, bequest and inheritance of land and other forms of property.[30] More precise information comes from the many inscriptions of the period after AD 500, on stone and on copper-plates, recording the grant of land by either the king or some wealthy individual to a religious beneficiary, or alternatively, by the king to a secular official in lieu of services rendered to the king.[31] These inscriptions were deciphered in the nineteenth century, but read primarily for the data which they contained on chronology and dynasties. In the last few decades, however, they have become the basic source material for the study of the agrarian structure of the first millennium AD.[32]

Since these were the legal charters relating to the grants, the transfer of the land is recorded in detail. In areas where the land granted was already under cultivation, the person from whom the land was acquired and the person to whom the property was transferred are mentioned, together with the location of land, the authority of the officials under whom the transfer was completed and the consent of the village within whose jurisdiction the land lay.

Not only do these inscriptions provide evidence of the categories of ownership of land, but where they refer to waste land it is possible to indicate the gradual extension of the agrarian economy into new areas. This information is of some consequence, not merely to economic history, but also to those concerned with the history of religion; for the extension of the agrarian economy was generally accompanied either by Buddhist missions or by nuclei of *brāhmaṇa* settlements, through which Sanskritic culture was introduced into the new areas and the local culture of these areas was assimilated into the Sanskritic tradition.[33] The interplay of these two levels of belief systems was a necessary process in the delineation of Indian culture. The stress so far has been on the high culture of the Sanskritic tradition which is inadequate for understanding the historical role of cultural forms.

Many of these records provide information on the rise of families of relatively obscure origin to high social status, usually through the channels of land ownership and administrative office.[34] Those who became powerful had genealogies fabricated for themselves, bestowing on the family *kṣatriya* status and, if required, links with royal lineages as well. Such periods of historical change demanded new professions, which professions finally evolved into castes. For example, administrative complexities relating to grants of land on a large scale needed professional scribes. Not surprisingly the pre-eminent caste of scribes, the *kāyastha*, are first referred to in the sources of this period.

The importance given to a centralized bureaucracy in the model was perhaps a reflection, among other things, of the nineteenth century faith in the administrator as the pivot of the imperial system. For the bureaucratic system of early India was rarely centralized, except in the infrequent periods of empire. Recruitment was impersonal, and most levels of administration were filled by local people. And it was at the more localized levels that the effective centres of power were located. In periods of empire, the surplus did find its way into the hands of the royal court. But during the many centuries of small kingdoms, the income from revenue was distributed among a large number of elite groups, which in part explains the regional variations and distribution in art styles, where the patron was not a distant emperor but the local king. This tendency towards political decentralization was accentuated from the post-Gupta period c. AD 600 when grants of revenue and later grants of land became the mechanism of renumeration.

Bureaucratic control over the economy, such as it was, derived from control over revenue collection. The hydraulic machinery played only a marginal role. Large-scale, state-controlled irrigation was rare. In the main, irrigation aids consisted of wells and tanks, built and maintained either by wealthy landowners or through the co-operative effort of the village. The more relevant question is not that of the state ownership of the hydraulic machinery, but the variation in irrigation technology and the degree to which irrigation facilities gave an individual or an institution a political edge over others.

The other mechanism of control according to the theory was a belief in the divinity of kingship, which gave the king a religious and psychological authority additional to the political. The attribution of this quality of divinity to kingship was probably the result of earlier studies on kingship and divinity in the ancient Near East. The interrelation between divinity and political authority was never absolute in ancient India. Divinity was easily bestowed, not only on kings, but on a variety of objects, both animate and inanimate. Far from emphasizing divinity, the kings of the Mauryan empire were patrons of the heterodox sects, which denied the existence of any god and ignored the notion of divinity. Divinity was appealed to initially in the rise of monarchy as a political form, in the first millennium BC.[35] But, the maximum references to kings as either incarnations or descendants of the gods coincide with the period of the rise of obscure families to kingship and the fabricated genealogies, suggesting that the appeal to divinity was a form of social validation and its significance was largely that of a metaphor. A particularly subtle aspect of the Indian notion of authority which has not so far received adequate attention has been the interaction of political authority with what may be called the moral authority of the renouncer. Time and again, the renouncer has returned to society and whilst still not fully participating in it, has played a significant role outside the realms of conventional political authority. Whereas political authority (*rājadharma*) derives in part from the power of coercion (*daṇḍa*) and religious authority from ritual and formulae (*yajña*, *pūjā* and *mantra*), the derivation of the authority of the renouncer is difficult to ascertain, combining as it does elements of the psychological, the social, the moral and the magical.

One of the more striking refutations of an aspect of Oriental Despotism has been that involving the absence of urban centres. The evidence for an early continuous urban economy has been pinpointed by archaeological excavation. This, combined with literary sources, suggests significant variations in the nature of urbanization. That the literary sources were not fully utilized was largely because the details of urban society occur first in the Pāli Buddhist texts, and these were not given the attention which they deserved by those using Sanskrit sources. The cities of the Indus civilization were smaller concentrations of population as compared to those of the second urbanization, linked with iron technology and which evolved in the Ganges valley in the first millennium BC. This had as its economic base trade within the subcontinent. The widespread use of coins and other adjuncts to extensive trading relationships, such as letters of credit and promissory notes, not only extended the geographical reach of trade but considerably increased the volume of trade. Steps towards the growth of exchange are apparent in the Buddhist literature relating to the cities of the Ganges valley; but this is less evident in the growth of the cities of maritime south India at the end of the first millennium, where archaeology has corroborated the literary references to a lucrative trade with the Roman empire.

At another level attempts have been made to correlate certain religious movements to the needs of urban groups. The work on the rise and spread of Buddhism and Jainism in relation to the mercantile community has inspired a wider debate on aspects of the *bhakti* movements as being in part the religion of urban groups with elements of dissident thought or, for that matter, the investigation of the Hindu temple as an economic entrepreneur.[36] The outcome of such studies is likely to lead to a rather radical revision of Max Weber's thesis on the social and economic role of religion in India.

In suggesting that these two theories — the Aryan theory and

Oriental Despotism — emanating from ideologies pertinent to nineteenth century Europe, are now no longer tenable, it may appear as if I am tilting at windmills. Yet, it is surprising how deeply rooted these theories are, both in India and elsewhere, and how frequently they are revived for reasons of academic study as well as in political polemics. The theory of Aryan race has not only served cultural nationalism in India but continues to serve Hindu revivalism and, inversely, anti-brahmin movements. At the academic level, the insistence on ascribing Indo-European roots to all aspects of Vedic culture has acted as a restraint on the analysis of mythology, religion and cultural symbols from the historical point of view. The intellectual history of a period as rich as that of the *Upaniṣads* and early Buddhism, approximately the mid-first millennium BC, has been hemmed in by the constraints of seeing it in terms of an internal movement among dissident Aryans, rather than from the more meaningful perspective of a period of seminal change. The perennial search for 'the Aryans' continues apace, with archaeologists still attempting to identify a variety of archaeological cultures as Aryan.[37]

Oriental Despotism was revived a few decades ago in Wittfogel's assessment of bureaucratic systems and in association with an oblique critique of the Soviet system. The reincarnation of the theory as the Asiatic Mode of Production has had, I believe, an even fuller transfusion in recent Soviet assessments of the Chinese past, as it has from time to time at the academic level in more general economic analyses of historical change in Asia.

That the interpretation of ancient Indian History was subject to the polemics of political ideology was inevitable. Colonial situations tend to play on the political content of historical interpretation. The sanctity of ancient culture as seen through a nationalist vision made it sensitive to historical analysis. This is not to deny, however, that over the last two centuries, at the level of the discovery of evidence, the scholarship has been both meticulous and extensive. Earlier theories of interpretation have not been replaced as there is now a concern with the need for clearer definitions of historical concepts based on a larger body of precise evidence. This is most apparent in the current debate on the periodization of Indian history. Nevertheless, for a while there was a disinclination to move away from the subject of polemics.

Symbolic of this disinclination was the consistent overlooking of one significant aspect of historical interest: the traditional Indian understanding of its own past. It has long been maintained that the Indians were an a-historical people, since there was no recognizable historical writing from the Indian tradition similar to that from Greece and China. This was in part because the Indian historical tradition — the *itihāsa-purāṇa*, as it is called — was in a form not easily recognizable to those familiar with Greek historical writing. Another reason may have been the inability of modern scholars to perceive and concede the awareness of change, so necessary to a sense of history, in the *itihāsa-purāṇa*, and this precluded them from seeing the historical basis of the tradition.

The early Indian historical tradition which is now receiving the attention of historians and is being analysed in terms of its ideological content does reflect a distinct image of the past, and its concerns are different from those of modern interpretations of the past.[38] For instance, the unit of history is not the empire but the *janapada*, the territory settled by a tribe, which later evolves into a state, generally a kingdom. References are made to emperors as universal rulers, the *samrāṭ* and the *cakravartin*, but these are at the abstract level. Reality revolves around the kings of smaller kingdoms. The genealogical sections of the tradition explain the settlements of tribes, and with the emergence of states, the association of dynasties.[39] But the past was not recorded as a succession of political events, for the legitimation of political authority was more important and it was to this that the historical tradition gave precedence. The records of these early genealogies were used from the first millennium AD onwards for legitimizing new dynasties who were given links with the ancient royal lineages. Recent work in social history has shown that political power was a relatively open area in early Indian society and the social antecedents of the founders of dynasties were rarely questioned, as long as they complied with the procedures necessary for legitimizing political authority.

In the Buddhist tradition the unit of history was the Saṅgha or Buddhist Saṅgha and monastic chronicles formed the core of the tradition. These were not merely the history of the Elders of the Church, for the monastery as an important socio-religious institution played an active political role and its relationship with political authority is apparent from these chronicles.[40]

Cyclic time and the change implicit in the movement of the cycle was the cosmological reflection of the consciousness of change. Even more interesting is the evolution in the form and style of the historical tradition itself, in the latter part of the first millennium AD, when the record includes details of events relating to political authority — in short, the kind of literature which is easily recognizable as historical writing, consisting of biographies of rulers and statesmen and chronicles of dynasties.[41] This new development in the tradition coincides with actual historical change, characterized by small kingdoms generally conforming to the geographically nuclear regions. These were based on a decentralized administration and economic structure, with an extension of patronage to local cultures and the emergence of the devotional religion — the *bhakti* movement — which, through its appeal to a large cross-section of social groups and its use of the regional language, strengthened the regional focus.

Yet the link with the mainstream of the tradition was not broken. Into the early history of the region or the dynasty is woven, quite deliberately, the mythology and lineages of the earlier tradition. The network of Sanskritic culture at least at the upper levels of society was a more real bond between people and places than the mere inclusion of these within the confines of an empire.

The perspective of the ancient Indian historical tradition when seen in juxtaposition with the more recent analyses of early Indian history, apart from its inherent intellectual interest, can suggest the ideological concerns of the pre-colonial period. These might provide to the historian of early India a clearer vision of the priorities of the Indian past than have been provided by the polemics of more recent times.

## Notes and References

1. A. Momigliano discusses some of these in his *Studies in Historiography*, New York, 1966.
2. C.H. Philips (ed.), *Historians of India, Pakistan and Ceylon*, London, 1961, pp. 92–3; Thapar, 'Interpretations of Ancient Indian History', *History and Theory*, 1968, 7 (3), pp. 318–35. For a comparative study, see D.G.E. Hall (ed.), *Historians of South-East Asia*, London, 1961; Soedjatmoko (ed.), *An Introduction to Indonesian Historiography*, Ithaca, NY, 1965.
3. J.F. Staal (ed.), *A Reader on the Sanskrit Grammarians*, Cambridge, Mass., 1972.
4. J. Leopold, 'British Applications of the Aryan Theory of Race to India, 1850–70', *The English Historical Review*, 1974, 89 (352), pp. 578–603.

For various interpretations of the term *ārya*, see H.W. Bailey, 'Iranian *Arya* and *Daha*', *Transactions of the Philological Society*, London, 1959, pp. 71–91; P. Thieme, *Der Fremdling im Rigveda*, 1938, who has argued that the term refers to 'foreigner/stranger'.

5. *Ṛg Veda*, 1.130.8; 1.101.1; 10.65.11.
6. L. Poliakov, *The Aryan Myth*, New York, 1974.
7. M. Müller, *India, What Can It Teach Us?*, London, 1883, pp. 101ff.
8. F. Hegel, *Lectures on the Philosophy of History*, London, 1974.
9. R. Koebner, 'Despot and Despotism: Vicissitudes of a Political Term', *Journal of the Warburg and Courtauld Institutes*, 1951, 14, pp. 275–80; F. Venturini, 'Oriental Despotism', *Journal of the History of Ideas*, 1963, 24, pp. 133–42.
10. D. Thorner, 'Marx on India and the Asiatic Mode of Production', *Contributions to Indian Sociology*, 1966, 9, pp. 33ff.
11. F. Bernier, *Voyages de F. Bernier . . .*, Amsterdam, 1699. T. Roe, *The Embassy of Sir Thomas Roe to India, 1615–19*, London, 1926.
12. R.A.L.H. Gunawardana, 'The Analysis of Pre-colonial Social Formations in Asia in the Writings of Karl Marx', *The Indian Historical Review*, 1976, 4.
13. K. Wittfogel, *Oriental Despotism*, New Haven, 1957.
14. Such as for example, K.P. Jayaswal, *Hindu Polity*, Calcutta, 1924; R.K. Mookerji, *Harsha*, London, 1926; H.C. Raichaudhury, *The Political History of Ancient India*, Calcutta, 1923, among others.
15. *Keshab Chunder Sen's Lectures in India*, Calcutta, 1923, p. 323.
16. M. Weber, *The Religion of India*, 1958. Glencoe, is the culmination of a range of such views over the nineteenth century. For a discussion of the Christian missionary position, A. Embree, *Charles Grant and the Evangelicals*, London, 1962.
17. R. and B. Allchin, *The Birth of Indian Civilisation*, Harmondsworth, 1966; R.E.M. Wheeler, *The Indus Civilisation*, Cambridge, 1968.
18. G.F. Dales, 'New Investigations at Mohenjo-daro', *Archeology*, 1965, 18 (2), p. 18.
19. H.T. Lambrick, 'The Indus Flood-plain and the Indus Civilisation', *Geographical Journal*, 1967, 133 (4), pp. 483–95; R.L. Raikes, 'The End of the Ancient Cities of the Indus', *American Anthropologist*, 1964, 66 (2), pp. 284–99; 'Kalibangan: Death from Natural Causes', *Antiquity*, 1965, 39 (155), pp. 196–203; 'The Mohenjo-daro Floods', *Antiquity*, 1965; A.V.N. Sarma, 'Decline of Harappan Cultures: A Relook', in *K.A.N. Sastri Felicitation Volume*, Madras, 1971.
20. G. Singh, 'The Indus Valley Culture (seen in the context of post-glacial climate and ecological studies in North-West India)', *Archeology and Physical Anthropology in Oceania*, 1971, 6 (2), pp. 177–89.
21. As for example, in the co-existence of the Black-and-Red Ware culture with the late Harappan in western India and that of the Ochre Colour

Pottery culture and Painted Grey Ware in the Indo-Gangetic divide and the Ganga-Yamuna Doāb.

22. A.L. Basham, *The Wonder That Was India*, London, 1954, p. 387; T. Burrow, *The Sanskrit Language*, London, 1965, pp. 373ff; M.B. Emeneau, *Collected Papers*, Annamalainagar, 1967, pp. 148, 155.
23. M.B. Emeneau, *Collected Papers*, Annamalainagar, 1967.
24. B.B. Lal, 'Perhaps the Earliest Ploughed Field so far Excavated Anywhere in the World', *Puratattva*, 1970–71, 4, pp. 1ff.
25. N.K. Bose, 'The Hindu Method of Tribal Absorption', in *Cultural Anthropology and Other Essays*, Calcutta, 1953; D. Mandelbaum, *Society in India*, Berkeley, 1970.
26. R.S. Sharma, *Changes in Early Medieval India*, New Delhi, 1969, Devraj Chanana Memorial Lecture.
27. M.N. Srinivas, *Religion and Society among the Coorgs of South India*, Oxford, 1952.
28. R. Thapar, 'The Study of Society in Ancient India', in *Ancient Indian Social History: Some Interpretations*, New Delhi, 1978, pp. 211–39.
29. V. Smith, *The Oxford History of India*, Oxford, 1919.
30. P.V. Kane, *History of Dharmaśāstra*, Poona, 1942, vol. 3, pp. 490ff; 574ff.
31. e.g. B. Morrison, *Political Centres and Culture Regions in Early Bengal*, Tucson, 1970.
32. R.S. Sharma, *Indian Feudalism*, Calcutta, 1965.
33. This is clearly reflected in the origin myths of ruling families for instance, even in areas as seemingly remote as Chota Nagpur. The origin myth of the Nāgabansis is clearly derived from Purānic sources but also incorporates local mythology.
34. As for example, the Maitrakas of Valabhī, during the fifth and sixth centuries AD.
35. J. Spellman, *Political Theory of Ancient India*, Oxford, 1964.
36. B. Stein, 'Social Mobility and Medieval South Indian Hindu Sects', *Comparative Studies in Society and History*, 1968, suppl. 3, pp. 78–94.
37. e.g. B.B. Lal, 'Excavations at Hastinapura . . . ', *Ancient India*, 1954–1955, 10 and 11, pp. 5–51.
38. Publications on this tradition are F.E. Pargiter, *The Ancient Indian Historical Tradition*, London, 1922; V.S. Pathak, *Ancient Historians of India*, London, 1966 and A.K. Warder, *An Introduction to Indian Historiography*, Bombay, 1972.
39. R. Thapar, 'Genealogy as a Source of Social History', op. cit., 1976, pp. 326–60.
40. L.S. Perera, 'The Pāli Chronicle of Ceylon', in Philips (ed.), op. cit., 1961, pp. 29ff.
41. Such as Bānabhaṭṭa's *Harṣacarita*, Bilhaṇa's *Vikramānkadevacarita*, Kalhaṇa's *Rājataraṅginī* and various *vaṃśāvalis*.

# 2

# *Durkheim and Weber on Theories of Society and Race Relating to Pre-colonial India**

This paper is concerned with the ideas of Durkheim and Weber in relation to pre-colonial India. An attempt is made to examine the colonial comprehension of India, and its influence on these two sociologists — a comprehension which included both early and contemporary India. Such a projection from one historical period onto another was, in many ways, a characteristic of eighteenth and nineteenth century European studies of India. Whatever seemed alien to the European perspective of contemporary India was often visualized as a survival from earlier times and the presumed continuity was imbued with historical authenticity. More frequently the social institutions from the past were believed to persist virtually unchanged into the present and made it legitimate for those studying contemporary Indian society to concern themselves with the texts of earlier periods. Such chronological glissandos were played by both evolutionists and functionalists.

As far as India was concerned, the focus of study was on caste which was seen as the distinctive feature of Indian civilization. This in turn required analyses of Indian religion and the racial composition of the Indian people, since religion and race were seen as essentials of caste. Both Durkheim and Weber tended to concentrate on the former as the more important factor, but this did not preclude a discussion on the latter.

Unlike Weber, Durkheim has written little directly on India.

* Published in Marion O'Callaghan (ed.), *Sociological Theories: Race and Colonialism*, Paris, 1980, 93–116.

I am grateful to my colleague Dr Satish Sabarwal for his helpful criticism of an earlier draft of this paper.

The impact of his thinking is more apparent in the works of his disciples — the sociologists Marcel Mauss, Henri Hubert and Célestin Bouglé — and to some extent on a number of Indologists such as G. Held, G. Dumézil and P. Masson-Oursel. Nevertheless, Durkheim occasionally used the existing studies on Indian civilization to highlight some of his generalizations. The most often quoted example of this is his argument that the definition of religion cannot be restricted to a belief in gods since Theravada Buddhism, widely accepted as a religion, did not postulate a belief in gods. Durkheim's concern with the origins of moral and social systems and the dichotomy of the sacred and the profane would have lent itself admirably to an analysis of the interrelations between caste and religion in India, but this clearly was a region with which he felt himself to be unacquainted.[1]

Marcel Mauss and Henri Hubert published a pioneering study on the ritual of sacrifice, *Sacrifice : its nature and function*, in which the Vedic literature with its wealth of detail on the central ritual of Vedic life, the *yajña* (sacrificial ritual) provided the authors with what was until then comparatively new data among sociologists. Earlier studies had centred on Tylor's evidence as discussed in *Primitive Culture* and that of Robertson-Smith's work in *The religion of the Semites*. These studies were based in part on observation (not always of a very systematic kind) with descriptions which were patchy and not nearly as meticulous in detail as were the Vedic texts. Above all, the Vedic texts were sacrificial manuals *per se*. Frazer's attempt to universalize the theories on sacrifice had complicated the process of analytical investigation. Hubert and Mauss were attempting to apply Durkheim's theories to a new area of evidence, a procedure which was to be repeated in some of the essays in the collections published as, *Mélanges d'histoire des religions*, and more specifically by Mauss in *Essai sur le Don*. Subsequently Masson-Oursel in his chapters in the collection entitled *Ancient India and Indian Civilisation* has tried to separate the magical elements from the rational in the structure of early Hinduism and has posed the problem of the expectation of worldly success in the performance of religious rituals. These ideas have been further developed by Heesterman in a study on the ancient Indian sacrificial ritual, *The Ancient Indian Royal Consecration*. Held has used the Durkheimian method more directly in an analysis of the *Mahābhārata* basing himself on a statement from Marcel Mauss,

'Le Mahābhārata est l'histoire d'un gigantesque potlatch'.[2] In *The Mahābhārata*: *An Ethnological Study*, Held argues that the Kauravas and the Pāṇḍavas were two phratries and that dicing and war were both part of the symbol of potlatch competitions; that the mythology of the epic revolves around notions of early classifications, such as the constant use of the number five and the cyclic concept of cosmic movement; and that the text distinguishes between the sacred act (*karma*) and sacred knowledge (*jñāna*) particularly in its didactic sections. More recently Dumézil has acknowledged the influence of Durkheim in his studies of Indo-European society and mythology. He argues that all Indo-European societies reflect a three-fold social division (the priest, the warrior and the commoner, what he calls the tripartite function) in the arrangement of their mythologies relating to the deities they worshipped. This in a sense overarches the religious and racial perspective.

Among the nineteenth and early twentieth century analyses of caste in India, Bouglé's work, deriving as it did from Durkheim's ideas of community, religion and stratification, introduced a new dimension and shifted the focus from race and occupation to new categories of stratification. It is unfortunate that his book *Essays on the Caste System* remained untranslated from the French for half a century; certainly its impact on studies of caste would have had a greater significance. Both Mauss and Bouglé were interested in the Indian data largely because it provided new source material on a society which had not been extensively investigated by sociologists. They were interested in the difference *per se* between Indian society and those with which they were already familiar. Caste society was for Bouglé a contrastive study in a wider area of sociological concern — the study of egalitarianism:[3] a trend which has continued until recent times as is demonstrated by Louis Dumont's *Homo Hierarchicus*.

Weber had a more clearly defined purpose in using the Indian material. He was setting up a model of Indian society in order to prove a series of theses regarding modern European society. The non-European tradition was essential to his analysis not only as a contrastive study but more specifically in order to explain the absence of the emergence of capitalism in areas other than western Europe. His study of Asian religions (India and China) focused on the intermeshing of religion and economic life. Weber was among those who subscribed to the critique of Marx by pointing to what he thought were the inadequacies of Marxist explanation. Capitalism, therefore, was not the result of an historical evolution but a unique development which had its roots in seventeenth-century western Europe. In order to demonstrate his analysis, he had to use contrastive models from traditions other than the European. A precondition to his analysis was the assumption that there were factors in the European situation which made it significantly different from all others and by implication substantially more effective in terms of world history. Weber's interest in the non-European past was not therefore in the essential difference with the European, but in testing and proving a hypothesis concerning the European past.

The choice and comprehension of the Indian material was to some extent conditioned by the use which these sociologists wished to make of it. The reliability and the range of the source material which was available to them by the end of the nineteenth and early twentieth centuries when they were writing is another question which has to be considered. By this time the Indian pre-colonial past had been interpreted by a large number of sophisticated ideologues who, under the guise of the newly-found objectivity of the nineteenth century, were supporting a variety of preconceptions or what they believed were definitive models. In most cases the interpretations were highly coloured by the intellectual preconceptions current in Europe at the time.

The problem of source material operated at two levels. One was that those who were not professional Indologists had to use the sources in translation. This was crucial to the question of interpretation. Terms relating particularly to social organization could only be translated and interpreted in the light of current research. Those for example who were reliable scholars of Sanskrit were not necessarily acquainted with the nuances of social forms and stratification. Consequently, the translation of concepts could result in misunderstandings. For example, the notion of race was embedded in the European intellectual consciousness in the nineteenth century. The universality of the concept was sought to be proved by translating various words as 'race' from the literatures of non-European societies even where the concept of race did not exist. Thus Monier-Williams, an undoubtedly outstanding Sanskritist and the compiler of the standard Sanskrit dictionary, refers to race as lineage and proceeds to translate a series of terms essentially connected with descent groups and kinship relations as 'race' — *vaṃśa, kula, jāti, gotra, jana, varṇa.*[4] None of these words could today be translated as race. Similarly, the frequently used term, *ñāti*, in the Pāli texts, now often translated as phratry or as extended kin-group, was also earlier translated as race. The understanding of caste as described in the *Dharmaśāstra* of Manu would naturally take on a strange coloration if references to *varṇa* and *jāti* were translated as race. This particular example is interlinked with the fact that most nineteenth century theories explaining the origin of caste saw it primarily as a system of demarcating the identities of various racial groups and maintaining separation.

At the other level, the sources of India available to those who were not professional Indologists were generally limited. The primary data on caste was taken from the Census Reports and the Imperial Gazetteers for the contemporary period and from the translations of the *Dharmaśāstras*, the socio-legal texts, for earlier times. The former category was compiled by officials of the Government of India and naturally reflected the conceptual biases then current on the pre-colonial Indian past among British administrators who were also, in the main, the scholars in the field. For the religions of India there were again the translations of the texts and the works of Indologists such as Zimmer, Oldenberg, Fick, Hopkins or historians such as Vincent Smith and Grant Duff.

The investigation of Indian society by European scholars had begun in a systematic way in the late eighteenth century. A major strand in the early interpretations was what became well known in the nineteenth century as the Aryan Theory. It derived academic sanction from the work of comparative philologists such as Max Müller, Auguste Pictet and Christian Lassen, ideological sanction from the essays of the Comte de Gobineau and political sanction by the end of the nineteenth century from the competing imperialism of the West European nations. The basis of the theory was the equation of language with race. In Europe the major dichotomy was seen as between Aryan and Semitic and in India it became Aryan and Dravidian, with the upper castes viewed as the descendants of the Aryans. The association of the theory with India had its genesis in the philological relationships noticed between Sanskrit and Greek, Latin and other European languages.

The Aryans it was argued were implicitly superior to the non-Aryans as they were the initial conquerors who had founded civilizations in Europe and Asia. In India, the arrival of the Aryans was associated with the compilation of the *Ṛg Veda* and this was believed to be the bed-rock of Indian civilization, the excavation of the Indus cities not as yet having taken place. By the late nineteenth century, the fallacy of equating language with race had been clearly demonstrated. Nevertheless, the theory remained established in European thought with reference to India. It also became acceptable to the new middle-class élite in India as it could call itself Aryan, differentiate itself from the lower castes believed to be non-Aryan and even seek a connection with the British rulers who represented European aryandom.[5]

Caste society was explained as being based on racial segregation with the Aryans forming the higher castes. The system was defended as a scientific division of society based on racial grouping, where the identity was preserved by rigid laws of marriage. The linking of caste society with racial segregation grew, in part, out of a linguistic misapprehension. The two most frequently used Sanskrit words referring to caste are *varṇa* and *jāti*. The latter quite clearly refers to descent and derives from the root *jan* — to be born. *Varṇa* on the other hand, which is used to categorize the four groups (*brāhmaṇa*, *kṣatriya*, *vaiśya* and *śūdra*), has been derived from a root meaning colour. This was immediately interpreted as a reference to human pigmentation and colour in the racial sense by the early translators of the texts. That the racial connotation is the suggestion of the translators is clear from the entry under *varṇa* in the Monier-Williams dictionary.[6] From the texts it would seem that the connotation of colour is symbolic since the four colours associated with the groups are white, red, yellow and black.[7] Social differentiation symbolized in colours is not unusual in the traditions of many early societies. Additional support for the racial basis of caste was sought from the references in the *Ṛg Veda* to the initial division of society into the *ārya-varṇa* and the *dāsa-varṇa* wherein the latter is described as being constituted of short-statured and dark-complexioned people,[8] but the description of the former is vague.

Apart from the rather simplistic racial dichotomy, other aspects were introduced gradually as caste came to be seen as the foundation of Indian social structure. Earlier, Max Müller in *Chips from a German Workshop* had argued that the racial factor was not a sufficient explanation for the evolution of caste although the most significant, and had added two more: conquest and political formation and professional or occupational groups. To these, Alfred Lyall had added a fourth, the religious sectarian factor, arguing that religious sectarian movements could also evolve into castes and this evolution was the reflection of the divisive tendencies inherent in Indian society.[9] Ibbetson took the argument further and suggested that three factors were important: the creation of guilds founded on hereditary occupation, the exaltation of the sacerdotal function and the importance attributed to heredity. Caste was consolidated by a series of laws regulating marriage alliances, the purity of food and intercaste relations. The consolidation was largely within the framework of *brāhmaṇa* authority and power. Nesfield argued that occupation was the dominant causative factor. He favoured an evolutionary pattern from tribe to caste where marriage rules and behaviour taboos reflect tribal forms in caste and the occupation taken up by the tribe on the decline of the tribal form identified its caste status. Status was largely determined by whether the occupation was of a pre-metal working society and therefore low or of a post-metal working society and therefore high. The *brāhmaṇa*, however, remained always the highest caste.

Risley revived the racial theory in *The People of India* (1908). He argued that there was a tribal genesis to caste, a memory of which is retained in the exogamous groups such as the *gotras*. But this soon gave way to primarily ethnological distinctions, the germ of which lies in the enmity of the white and black races as expressed in the *ārya-varṇa* and the *dāsa-varṇa* of the *Ṛg Veda*. The segregation was maintained by carefully worked out endogamous laws. He took very literally the Brahmanical idea that all low status castes are necessarily the product of interbreeding. The hierarchy of caste was based on an ethnological distinction between the Aryans retaining their purity as the highest castes and the aboriginal inhabitants of India being clustered at the lower end. Risley maintained that race was the generating principle and he used ethnographic measurement, particularly the nasal index in an attempt to prove his theory.

A rather different point of view was put forward by Senart in his *Les Castes dans l'Inde* (1896). He was dissatisfied with the racial theory. He felt that the emphasis on occupation as the crucial variable was exaggerated since caste distinctions were known even among people in the same profession. Senart sought the answer to the origins of caste in the constitution of the family. Caste has the same rights over individuals as do early families in other ancient societies such as the Greeks and the Romans. Endogamous laws were also fundamental to these societies (e.g. the *jus connubii* of Rome). Laws of commensality in caste were intended to exclude the aliens from sacrifices and religious feasts since a meal signifies sharing and equality. Even the fear of impurity and defilement has analogies from Greco-Roman parallels. The origin of caste requires a multi-causal explanation. He accepted that there was initially a conflict between the Aryans and the dark-skinned race of inferior civilization which resulted in a strengthening of the exclusiveness of the Aryans. Gradually however there was an admixture of races and apart from the extensive family groups which developed into castes, function-based groups of a mixed origin also developed into castes. The sacerdotal power strengthened itself and worked out the ideal caste system — the *varṇa* system. Notions of purity made the exclusion more rigid and prevented absorption into the indigenous population. As in the case of the Greeks, it also preserved the higher castes from performing manual labour. The unending justification of social distinctions was endorsed by the concept of metempsychosis. The continuity of caste was largely due to the absence of a political authority to cut across these divisions and unify them.

The theory of the absence of political authority derived in part from the current notion that the Indian village community contributed to the consolidation of caste since it subsumed common territory, kin and jurisdiction. It was an organic and integral unit which managed to maintain its autonomy from the political superstructure. Max Müller had described it in glowing terms as an idyllic community[10] and it became one of the tenets of nineteenth-century colonial sociology. The village community was also seen as the root of Indo-European life and it was thought that in the Indian village community Europe had rediscovered its origins. Less romantically, Marx argued that the Indian village community was one of the causes of the stagnation of Indian society.[11] Henry Maine saw it as a point along the linear form of the social growth of society from a kin-organized system to a commercial-industrial society.[12] Lyall took the argument of an absence of political authority still further and argued that India was at 'an arrested stage of development'. According to him, the evolutionary stage of the tribe was still prevalent (as in parts of Rajasthan) which was a survival from an earlier social form. The absence of political stability was due to an absence of the political institutions required to counterbalance monarchical power.

The notion of Indian society reflecting an early, if not a primitive, stage in social evolution or demonstrating a form of arrested growth was also implicit in another widely-accepted theory which pertained more closely to the nature of political and economic forms in Asia — the theory of Oriental Despotism. Its main postulates were, the existence of isolated, self-sufficient village communities, superimposed upon which was the despotic ruler and his court who creamed the surplus off the peasantry through a very efficient bureaucratic machinery. The latter was not only the mechanism for revenue collection but also ran the state-controlled irrigation system upon which all cultivation was dependent. The divine origin of the king also helped to create the appropriate distance. Since it was believed that there was no private property in land, it was argued that there were no intermediary groups between king and peasant nor, therefore, any political institutions to counterbalance the monarchy. The economic autarchy of the village community allowed it a political autonomy except for the mechanism of revenue collection which impinged on the autonomy. There was also an absence of urban centres specializing in the production of commodities for a market which, had they existed, might have been the basis for a political check on despotism and might have encouraged economic change.

The theory, partially subscribed to by historians such as James Mill in the early nineteenth century, gained ground in England over the decades and by the middle of the century was axiomatic to the understanding of Indian society and politics. Inevitably, it was reflected to a greater or lesser degree in the reports compiled by British administrators working in the districts. Others too were not left untouched. Marx in his discussion on colonialism in India used this theory to explain what he regarded as the political stagnation and economic backwardness of India which facilitated the British conquest. The Indian village community was for Marx a survival from the past and, consequently, an anachronism which had to be done away with if the condition of arrested growth were to cease.

The assumption in these theories was that there is a contrastive difference between the Indian and the European experience. This difference can be explained by locating its causes. The methodological approach was to assume that the Indian experience had failed since Indian society had not evolved to a capitalist form and it was important to try and discover why it had failed. Basic to this assumption was the notion that Indian society reflected a stepping off, as it were, from the escalator of social evolution. This in brief was the intellectual background to the views current in Europe on Indian society. Even where these views were questioned or discarded, the rejection has to be seen in terms of the prevalent ideas. The inability of certain societies to evolve into a capitalist form became a major characteristic in differentiating various societies. This distinction also lay at the centre of sociological thought for many decades and was expressed in a variety of supposed oppositions — *gesellschaft*: *gemeinschaft*, folk: urban, status: contract and, ultimately, tradition: modernity.

Marx had earlier brought to a head the question of the primacy of ideas or social facts. The question arose repeatedly in later writing not only as part of the critique of Marxism but as a controversial issue in itself. Durkheim moved gradually from a position of regarding ideas and beliefs as a derivative of a subsect of social facts towards suggesting that symbolic thought is a condition of, and explains society.[13] Durkheim's ideas on the sociology of religion were important in the analysis of Indian society since religion was often regarded as the crucial variable which gave a particular direction to Indian society, a point of view more fully elaborated by Weber. That the essential elements of religious thought are to be found in seminal form in primitive religion or at any rate, 'it is easier to see the forms at an early stage', is suggestive of an element of evolutionism in Durkheim's argument. There was a tendency to classify religio-social phenomena into two categories: one pertaining to pre-literate societies and the other to literate societies. The Durkheimian interest was essentially in the former with its emphasis on totemism, magic, matrilineal society, the overarching deity and pre-logical thinking, which makes this imperative as a starting point. Religion was pre-eminently a social phenomenon. Although the factual correctness of his use of interrelationships between totem and clan and his reliance on dubious ethnography have been criticized,[14] nevertheless his views on religion have been used to correlate religious forms and social realities in Indian society, which have further strengthened the hypothesis of the particular role of religion in Indian society. Since Durkheim's views were largely limited to the religion of primitive societies, their application to Indian data was mainly in the form of recognizing primitive survivals in religious rites and beliefs of the early historical period. Few attempts have been made to apply them to the religious systems of 'tribal India' current even today. The application of his views to more advanced forms of religion in India were limited owing partially to his own initial hesitations in extending his ideas to more complex religious forms.

Durkheim's own analysis did not pertain centrally to Indian religion and even where he uses the absence of deity in Buddhism to point up his definition of religion he is not concerned with any detailed understanding of Buddhism. He argues that the turning in of man upon himself in the process of meditation allows the absence of a deity, a point made by earlier Indologists such as Oldenberg and Barth.[15] Nevertheless, Buddhism is a religion since it admits of the existence of sacred things. Buddhism, Jainism and Hinduism enter the discussion again when Durkheim argues that altruistic suicide is a form of sacrifice arising out of a sense of duty and not unrelated to pantheistic beliefs. Durkheim's division of religious phenomena into beliefs and rites reappeared in later studies of the Vedic sacrifice.

Hubert and Mauss analysed the ritual of sacrifice in some detail with frequent reference to the texts on the early Vedic sacrifices. They asserted that the ritual implied the consecration of a common object to a religious plane and that it symbolized the separation of the sacred and the profane. This separation is inherent all the time but can only be actualized through the mediation of religious agents. The separation is apparent at many levels: the area where the sacrifice takes place is demarcated as sacred, the priest communicating with the god is sacred in the sacrificial context as also is the sacrifiant and the mundane animal now consecrated as the sacrificial victim. Outside of a sacred place immolation is murder. As the texts put it, he who performs the sacrifice, 'passes from the world of men into the world of gods'.[16] The preparation for consecration is as elaborate as that of desacralisation. The sacrificer purifies himself by being in a condition of sanctity and redeems himself by substituting the victim in his place. Sacrifice therefore also becomes a procedure of communication between the sacred and the profane worlds. Mauss elsewhere develops the argument with reference to *dāna* (gift giving) which is generally treated as a purely religious action, but he views it as a form of gift-exchange. Using the lengthy discussion on the ritual of *dāna* as stated in the Anuśāsanaparvan of the *Mahābhārata* as his data, Mauss argues that a routine action of making a gift can become a sacred rite depending on the donor, the recipient, the place and the intention with which the gift is made, all of which are listed in the text as important factors in the process of *dāna*. Alternatively, the same ritual can be seen as establishing the secular relationships implicit in a gift- exchange.

The bipolarity of the sacred and the profane in the Vedic sacrificial ritual can be seen as embodying social representations in as much as it can be argued that this was also germinal to the idea of purity and pollution with reference to caste groups. The purity of the *brāhmaṇa* was partly derived from his condition of sanctity at the time of the *yajña*, and the exclusion of the other castes may have been measured in terms of their social distance from the sacrificial enclosure. Thus, the *kṣatriya* was frequently the *yajamāna*, he who has the sacrifice performed, and could therefore be admitted as a participant. The other castes were at best observers from a distance.

Clearly, this was but one aspect of caste differentiation and for Bouglé it was by no means the central. Closer to his interest was Durkheim's distinction between mechanical solidarity and organic solidarity underlying which was the notion of pre-industrial and industrial society. The morphological structure of the first which Durkheim characterized as the segmental type — a clan-based society moving to territorial identity — was to be a repeated feature in the discussion on caste. Such societies according to Durkheim, were not based on a division of labour and lacked a fusion of markets and the growth of cities both of which were noticeable in organic solidarity. Other characteristics of the first category were the relatively weak interdependence between the segments, rules with repressive sanctions and the prevalence of penal law and absolute collective authority with little room for individual initiative. Such a society also placed a premium on values relating to society as a whole in its ethical forms, manifested a highly religious conscience and emphasized the transcendental. The transformation from mechanical solidarity to organic solidarity was for Durkheim the central focus of social change with its attendant social integration.[17]

Bouglé examined caste in the light of the definition of mechanical solidarity. He began by investigating whether caste was indigenous to Hindu society alone or was common to all societies at some stage. He includes among the characteristics of caste the following four: hereditary specialization; hierarchy and the inequality of rights; a clear opposition between elementary groups which isolate themselves through a series of taboos relating to food, contact, clothing etc., and which resist unification; and the incidence of mobility being collective rather than individual. When considering the roots of the system, Bouglé disagrees with the explanation that the *brāhmaṇas* were the originators of caste using it to divide and control society which he felt laid too great an emphasis on religion. The theories of some Indologists who saw caste evolving out of industrial guilds and therefore gave prominence to hereditary specialization were also unacceptable to Bouglé, for this would require an equation of caste with economic function and occupation, and such an equation is thwarted by a series of overlapping relations in caste. Senart had listed three groups among the *āryas*: the sacerdotal who had appropriated the sacrificial ritual, the aristocracy founding itself on heredity, and the common people. These three divisions provided the impetus for further divisions and the separation of the Arya from the non-Arya. Senart was looking at the origins of caste with reference to *varṇa*. For Bouglé the prototypes of caste were not the *varṇas* but the *jātis* which were lineage descendants and indicated the dominance of ancient familial exclusivism. Such exclusivism was not specifically Aryan; tribal societies are known to have had rigid rules of exogamy and commensality and fraternity taboos are also to be found among the Semites.

The pre-eminent status of the *brāhmaṇa* was not secured from the start, but was gradually usurped by the *brāhmaṇa* after an initial competition for status between the *brāhmaṇa* and the *kṣatriya*. Bouglé argued that since the *brāhmaṇa* caste could not accumulate riches its essential strength lay in religious power which it exploited and in this was encouraged by an absence of political organization. The prestige of the *brāhmaṇa* arose out of many factors. The racial superiority of the Aryans who conquered the Dravidians was partly responsible since the *brāhmaṇas* salvaged what they could of their Aryan inheritance by careful marriage regulations. However, he qualified this by stating that it could not be based on physical types but on the perception of differences among ethnic groups. In addition, the *brāhmaṇas* had become the guardians of the sacrifice and as such were in a perpetually consecrated condition (a view rather similar to Hubert and Mauss) which was reiterated by an emphasis on avoiding pollution through food and touch, all of which strengthened the exclusivity of the *brāhmaṇa*.

Caste therefore resulted from a concurrence of spontaneous and collective tendencies subject for the most part to the influence of ancient religious practices. The closed cult of the first familial groups prevented castes from mingling and the respect for the mysterious effects of sacrifice finally subordinated them to the castes of priests. The ideas which generated the caste system argued Bouglé, are not peculiar to the Hindus or to the Aryans, but were the common patrimony of primitive peoples. They survived in India because they managed to resist the influence of any unifying forces cutting across the exclusive groups. Thus, Hindu civilization is characterized by an arrested social development. Indian society has moved in an inverse direction and has continued to divide, specialize and hierarchize whereas other societies have unified, mobilized and levelled. Thus, caste society had the same roots and origins as egalitarian societies, but unlike the latter, which underwent changes in the egalitarian direction, caste society deliberately remained inegalitarian.

The lack of social and historical change is specifically noted by Bouglé who uses this as a partial explanation as to why there are neither historians nor historical records in pre-colonial India. He maintains that superficially political forms have changed and there have been administrative monarchies and feudal politics, but beneath this the caste structure has preserved a constant form. Even religion does not succeed in destroying caste since religious sects take on the characteristic identities of castes. The only exception to this was Buddhism and significantly Buddhism did not survive in India. Its disappearance was not due to Hindu intolerance, since intolerance requires political dogmatism which was lacking in India. Rather it was the abstracting of the Buddhist community from social life which prevented it from denting the caste system and furthermore the monastery was closed to those in opposition to authority. Philosophies of detachment and inaction are not conducive to change and the theory of transmigration encourages neither reform nor revolt nor change.

On the question of race Bouglé did not totally discard racial identities in caste although he was unsympathetic to the theories of Risley and anthropometry, arguing that castes are not pure races and are racially mixed. To correlate caste and race in accordance with Brahmanical theory (of course assuming that this *was* in fact Brahmanical theory) is to superimpose the theory on observed data. Further, hereditary specialization has not deposited essentially different properties in different castes, as was occasionally suggested by other commentators on Indian society. Bouglé was of the view that the philosophy of race remains unproven, although castes as strictly enclosed groups may have preserved primitive repulsions of a racial nature.

In his discussion on law and caste Bouglé appears to have relied heavily on Durkheim's description of mechanical solidarity. Bouglé maintains that rules relating to behaviour are governed by notions of purity and are therefore largely ritual prescriptions. Unlike western law which is restitutive, the *dharmaśāstras* of India in which the laws are coded, are repressive. The legal system did not seek to cut across caste distinctions and instead supported the hierarchy of castes and the stress on inequality by assuming an ascending scale of punishment. Hindu law was able to preserve its religious colouring because no political power arose to counterbalance the power of the priestly caste nor did economic life change caste. Caste did not obstruct economic production — if anything it assisted in perfecting the dexterity of the craftsman based on hereditary specialization and the intensive practice of skills. But caste did obstruct economic change in that it retained the primitive clan character of society and mechanical solidarity could not give way to organic solidarity. In the terminology of Henry Maine, status repels contract. Since caste is essentially divisive and separatist, economic groups could not arise which would cut across caste boundaries and the organization of authority left little place for the institutions of liberty. There was never a body of towns large enough and numerous enough for the production and circulation of wealth and at the same time the production and circulation of ideas acting as the necessary centres of co-ordination. Centres of production were associated with political capitals and were therefore transitory. Commerce was never predominant in law, action and style. The city requires a unity among citizens to safeguard its independence, but this was inimical to caste. Guilds were rooted in caste since they could not adopt new members or associate socially among themselves. Thus, there was an arrested development of economic formations, a generalization on which Weber was to expand.

Some of Bouglé's views on India are shared by Weber. His focus was not on caste however but on the absence of the emergence of capitalism. European capitalism was seen as the watershed or the divide separating pre-capitalist from capitalist societies and the dichotomy was emphasized by many theorists at the time such as Tönnies, Simmel and Maine.[18] Marx saw it as a stage in historical development, but Weber saw it as a totality, as a 'civilization'. Central to this totality was the role of rationality in western capitalism which made it a unique experience in world history.[19] This was not to deny the rationality of other civilizations but to point to the generally more static role of rationality in these as compared to its dominant role in western capitalism. Weber tended to pose rationality and irrationality as bipolarities which are present in every situation. Rationality permeated the whole of capitalist culture. It dominated science, law (a written constitution regulating political activity), music, architecture and above all economics, where it is evident not only in the more obvious technological basis of industrialization, but also in the separation of industrial from household economics and the precise analysis of cost and profit which lies at the core of capitalist enterprise. All these in turn tend to impersonalize relationships and conduct (and perhaps even dehumanize certain segments of society). In addition to rationality, there was also the historical factor of the simultaneous emergence of free labour without any land and the industrialist who had accumulated capital through the mercantile activities of the pre-capitalist world.[20] This was a major element in the rise of capitalism which Weber conceded to the Marxist model. The third factor which Weber stressed was the Protestant religion which he felt embodied the spirit of capitalism. Weber's emphasis was on the role of Protestantism in developing capitalism rather than on Protestantism reflecting the rise of capitalism.[21] Weber did not accept the possibility of establishing laws of social development and thereby predicting social change as had been proposed explicitly by Marx and suggested implicitly by Durkheim. He rejected evolutionary theories and maintained that the best analysis was based on categories and 'ideal-types'. The social scientist was also not in a position to make a representation of reality. Methodology was merely a means of understanding — hence the exaggeration implicit in his 'ideal type' was deliberate in order to highlight differences and clarify the model.

Weber's explanation for the absence of capitalism in India required a detailed examination of religion in India, the two being intertwined. But, apart from examining the religions of Asia, he also argued for certain historical situations in Europe having provided some base for the growth of capitalism. His attempt to locate the latter was by discussing the absence of capitalism in antiquity. It was from this perspective that he viewed the historical development of the pre-capitalist world, both the agrarian structures of ancient civilizations and the rise of the medieval city.

Weber's discussion on the absence of capitalism in antiquity appears to be somewhat anachronistic and arises no doubt from his refusal to make concessions to alternate forms of historical evolution. Yet at the same time he does speak of stages in the social organization of agricultural societies. These he describes as the walled settlements of household and village, the fortress, the aristocratic city-state, the authoritarian liturgical state, the hoplite polis and the democratic citizen polis.[22] The initial stage was characterized by a distinction between free members and slaves and the emergence from among the former of princely clans, their justification being based on division of spoils, voluntary gifts and special allotments of land enhanced by divine legitimacy. The second stage sees the emergence of the king and greater dependence on rent from land. The aristocratic city-state emphasized the status of those who owned land and debt slaves (often peasants who could not pay rents). The feudal nobility of the fortress stage became the urban community, although Weber does not explain the emergence of either. The fifth stage refers to the power of the state and its imposition of duties on the subject. The hoplite polis, a derivative of the aristocratic polis, was subject to the domination of the clan and was characterized by a self-equipped citizen army dependent on ownership of land. This, in turn, gave way to the final stage of the democratic citizen polis where land ownership was closely regulated but at the same time separated from military service. Communal forms of land ownership were abolished and rent alone remained. This led to the rise of capitalism since slaves were not debt slaves but purchased. Sharecroppers and slave agriculture gave way to yeomanry and mercenary armies replaced the hoplites. Ultimately city-states declined and were replaced by monarchical state systems with their major structural unit in the manor, channelling land relations, taxes and military recruitment. Weber saw the large empires of Asia such as the Assyrian and the Persian as conglomerates of urban and manorial areas. Yet at the same time he accepted the theory of the absence of private ownership of land in Asian civilization. He argues that, whereas in Europe the pattern of settlement moved from cattle breeding to agriculture and private ownership of land emerged on the basis of communal grazing grounds, in Asia it changed from nomadism to horticulture and the notion of private ownership was thus by-passed.[23]

Weber argues against the possibility of a capitalist economy emerging in the ancient past because the cities were centres of consumption rather than production. The urban economy of cities was limited since they were dependent on grain imports, their export articles were based on high labour inputs which required the purchase of slaves and their policies were solely determined by commercial interests. The development of capitalism was not based on rent from land but on commodity production. Slave agriculture could be regarded as capitalist although here Weber would be subjected to the same criticism as that made of Rostovtzeff's views on capitalist agriculture in Greco-Roman antiquity.[24]

In his study *The City*, with particular emphasis on the medieval city, Weber moves away from earlier theorists who had emphasized religion, legal structure replacing kinship, contract replacing status and economic institutions providing the theoretical basis of the city. Weber argues that it is the evolution of the urban community as an institution which characterizes the basis of the city. Above all that the urban community is typical of Occidental society and is virtually absent in the Orient (except in the ancient Near East). It is based on the dominance of trade-commercial relations and characterized by the presence of fortifications, a market, a court reflecting partially autonomous law, association of city members with partial autonomy and administration by authorities in whose election the burghers participate. With reference to India, Weber argued that only guilds and castes developed courts and special legal structures but even here trial by law and courts were absent. Autonomous administration was virtually unknown. The Indian urban dweller remained a member of the caste, guild or city-ward, but not a citizen of the city. There was no joint association representing the city and this was prevented by the segregating necessities of the system. Endogamous castes with their exclusive taboos were an obstacle to the fusion of the city dwellers into a status group enjoying social and legal equality and the ban on commensality among castes prevented the display of solidarity and fraternity of those sharing a common table. The only exceptions to this were that in periods of salvation religions, guilds could sometimes cut across town loyalties if they subscribed to the religion; and in the periods prior to the rise of bureaucratic kingdoms there were autonomous cities governed by clan elders. Indian cities were essentially royal centres or political capitals with market places and fortifications.

Medieval Occidental cities (and especially those north of the Alps) were strikingly different from Asian cities. They grew as a result of immigration so that local ties were eroded and the city became an administrative district within which all inhabitants irrespective of differences shared the same administration. Taboo barriers of totem, caste and clan were absent. On the contrary, the *conjuratio,* the oath-bound fraternity of burghers, broke through some of the earlier tendencies towards separation. Weber's rather glowing account of the medieval Occidental city tends to blur the distinctions within the citizens where both fraternity and autonomy tended to belong to limited groups. For Weber, the most important aspect of the city, namely civic development, emerged neither in the Asian city nor in the medieval European city. It emerged later in the West European city. He gives among possible reasons for its absence the lack of city fraternization which encourages the growth of the urban community. Clans and castes were mutually exclusive. There were no urban military interests and the burgher was not a military man. The guilds in the cities of India and China could bring pressure on royal power, but could not oppose it in a military manner. In the later European cities the guilds could not only combine and assert civic power, but the *conjurationes* could take up arms independently of the king. It was this ability to unite as citizens, demonstrate independence and defy royal power which made the difference. The legalization of privileges encouraged political autonomy. In Weberian terms traditional domination gradually gave way to legal domination. The occurrence of a charismatic figure was not precluded, but the potential for a reciprocal relationship so necessary to the theory of domination would be reduced in a society built on legal domination and the bureaucracy.

Charismatic leadership was more apparent in the role of the

prophet in early societies.[25] Here Weber differentiates between the exemplary and the ethical prophet. The Buddha typifies the first where there is no divine mission, the prophet merely showing his followers the path to salvation. Moses as an ethical prophet highlights the claim to communion with God and demands obedience as an ethical duty. The exemplary prophet is common in India and China because of the absence of a personal transcendental and ethical god and also because the rationally regulated world had its point of origin in the ceremonial order of sacrifice. The difference between Asia and Europe is spotlighted by another fundamental notion, that of predestination. In Europe, predestination strengthened the idea of vocation and gave the Christian a justification for his activity as being ordained. Success was a sign of God's blessing. Whereas in Asia it provided a negative impulse where salvation lay not in vocation but in escape from the sufferings of the terrestrial world. Similarly, there were basic differences in the nature of asceticism. Christianity culminated in asceticism of the inner-worldly category not the contemplative withdrawal of the world-rejecting type in Asia. Man had to ethically justify himself before the Christian God and not submerge himself. Christian monasteries placed a premium on labour and work rather than on meditation and the bureaucracy of the Christian church required an involvement in life. Some of these contrasts filled out the dichotomy which Weber was posing between Europe and Asia, a dichotomy which he analysed at greater length in his detailed studies of religion in China and India.

It is evident from looking at the sources which Weber consulted in writing *The Religion of India* that he was influenced by the current theories of nineteenth century Indologists and historians, relying as he had to on secondary works.[26] Weber's analysis of the social structure of India was a background to his understanding of both the orthodox doctrines of Hinduism and the heterodox doctrines of Buddhism together with the influence of popular religion on these. Caste and religious beliefs were therefore linked and, ultimately, he was concerned with the impact of religious beliefs on the secular ethic of Indian society. Weber sees caste as a status group with rigid rules of intermarriage and social intercourse and with pollution acting as a discriminatory factor between castes.

According to Weber, the spread of caste society was brought about by three agencies: conquest, the conversion of tribes into castes, and the sub-division of castes. As a result of conquest racial differences led to segregation and prevented intermarriages, although Weber did not believe that racial differences were inherited. Whereas for Weber race was not the basis of caste as Risley had argued, the juxtaposition of racial differences were significant for the development of caste in India. The conquerors claimed rights in land and the conquered became subservient and lost their rights. Weber makes much of the difference between what he calls 'guest' and 'pariah' people without realizing than many 'guest' peoples were not given the lowest status in caste as he assumes. The conversion of tribes into castes was a commonly held theory among the ethnographers of the time. Tribes and castes had a totally opposite structure and the gradual conversion began with the assimilation of ruling groups among tribal societies into Hindu society generally by their being given *kṣatriya* status.[27] It was also said that food-gathering tribes who had lost their land as a result of the expansion of the agrarian economy were sometimes assimilated *en masse* as a single caste, usually that of peasants. The sub-division of castes meant that a new caste could branch off from an existing one by migration, a change in ritual duties, entry into a new religious sect, inequality of property possession where the better-off would imitate high caste social norms or a change of occupation arising out of economic or technological change. A difference of caste was established with the denial of connubium and commensalism by the original caste and the renunciation of ritual duties by the new caste.

Weber argued that the formation of castes was fundamental to the Indian social order which is based on clan charisma. Even feudal state formation did not rest on land grants but derived from sib, clan, phratry and tribe. The historical evidence however indicates that it was the making of land grants from the first millennium AD that broke the clan charisma. This evidence was available to Weber in the translations of epigraphical data but he, like the historians of the time evidently overlooked this. In the absence of genuine feudalization he argued that there was a prebendalization of the patrimonial state.

The *śūdras* as craftsmen, he described either as helots of single villages receiving a fixed wage, or artisans in self-governing villages selling their products directly or through traders, or artisans settled by the kings, the temple, the landlord and, whether bondsmen or free, subject to servitude, or, finally, independent artisans settled in well-defined parts of the city and working as wage earners. For the *vaiśyas* the caste of traders and merchants, Weber drew his information from the description given by Baden-Powell, and maintained that they could not struggle against the patrimonial prince because of the caste system as well as the pacifism preached by the salvation religions. The stress on pacifism degraded the status of the peasant and inhibited the traders from creating an urban militia. Caste had a negative effect on the economy since it was anti-rational and traditionalistic. Ritual laws stood in the way of economic and technical revolutions. The trader remained a merchant, incapable of using a new form of labour power and of diverting his wealth into capitalist forms. Neither was there any chance of cross-caste associations leading to the autonomy of the city nor was there any fraternization of castes as in European guilds followed by the seizing of political power. Caste emphasized distance rather than association. Cities were fortresses rather than urban centres with a weak market nucleus.

Enveloping the social totality was the theory of *saṁsāra* and *karma* (transmigration and rebirth) which developed into a system for the first time in Buddhist thought. Although Buddhism denied the existence of the soul and merely postulated the continuity of consciousness through a cycle of rebirths, it nevertheless related the ethics of rebirth to caste and this became axiomatic to both Hindu and Buddhist social philosophy. *Karma* transformed the world into a strictly rational, ethically determined cosmos, representing the most consistent theodicy ever produced in history. But it also required the strict fulfilment of caste obligation. Ethnic and economic factors were no doubt significant to caste structure, but *karma* reinforced it at the ethical level. There was no universally valid ethic but a compartmentalization of private and social ethic with each caste having its own ethic and therefore, men were forever unequal. The absence of ethical universalism led to striving for individual salvation based on attempts to escape the wheel of rebirth. Even asceticism was a striving for personal, holy status where gnosis and ecstasy were sublimated to personal salvation as also were the natural sciences. Rational methods of asceticism were directed towards irrational goals. Yogic and ascetic techniques had two purposes: they had to accommodate the holy through the emptying of consciousness and they sought gnostic knowledge through meditation and techniques conducive to meditation. The salvation doctrines within which Weber included Buddhism, Jainism and the Bhāgavata and Bhakti aspects of Hinduism, showed scant interest in the ethic for life on a temporal plane. For them reality consisted of the eternal order of the universe and the rebirth of souls.

Weber described Buddhism as the polar opposite of Islam and Confucianism: it was an unpolitical and anti-political status religion of wandering and intellectually schooled mendicants. It was a salvation religion — an ethical movement without cult or deity and centred on the personal salvation of the single individual. Above all, it advocated that the will to life has to be destroyed in order to achieve *nirvāṇa*. Although Buddhism did have a levelling, democratic character, it nevertheless did not attempt any rational method in life-conduct. Weber explains the schisms in Buddhism from the fourth century BC onwards as being due to a lack of strong roots in society, its marginal demands on the laity and its essentially monastic and itinerant way of life. When the monks became materialist minded and accepted gifts and proselytized, the religion declined. This decline was helped by the antagonism of secular rulers to Buddhist monasteries and the rising power of the town guilds. The Brahmanical restoration as Weber saw it continued to emphasize irrational ends. Ritualistic activities were strengthened because the *brāhmaṇas* wished to protect their fees and prebends. Instead of a drive towards the rational accumulation of capital, Hinduism created irrational accumulation chances for magicians, mystagogues and the ritually oriented strata. Brahmanism was supported by rent from land and fees for religious services which were inheritable and given in perpetuity. This encouraged a bifurcation of religious and secular authority and led to the weakening of the latter. In addition, local autonomy was strengthened as against a centralized system. The absence of a secular ethic was particularly apparent from an equal absence of the characteristics of European Protestantism. There was no devotion to a calling in Calvinistic terms with its attendant economic success nor could a rational transformation of the world be postulated as an act of Divine Will. The other-worldliness of Indian religion did not diminish an interest in this world, but the aim of this interest was different. Therefore, even if people were materialistic by nature, they were influenced by non-materialistic ideology into channelling their materialism to ineffective ends.

Perhaps the most frequently used word in Weber's analysis of the religion of India is 'absence' — reflecting a sharp distinction in his mind between the characteristic features of the Occidental civilization and their absence in the Asiatic/Oriental. To this extent he was echoing a common belief among nineteenth-century European thinkers for whom the dichotomy between Occidental and Oriental was very real. This was enhanced by the supposed duality between materialist and spiritualist civilizations, a duality which was to play an even more dominant role in the ideology of Asian nationalism in the twentieth century. The stress laid by Weber on the rationality of developments in Europe came under attack and such analyses were seen as part of a larger racial framework in which ideologues other than Weber attached value judgements of *a priori* superiority to the rationality. This was of course quite apart from the question of whether rationality was the prime motive in the development of European capitalism, a question which has been legitimately raised by some of those examining the place of Weber's thought within the European ideological tradition.[28]

Weber's understanding of capitalism has its own limitations. He fails to distinguish between the two major phases of capitalism — merchant capitalism and industrial capitalism. Thus, the characteristics of the first tend to get extended into the second. Hence the stress on the Protestant ethic, which undoubtedly was significant in the crystallization of the first phase but of only marginal significance to the second phase. What was central to the second phase was colonialism; both in its early form resulting from the colonization of Latin America and industrialization in the second phase dependent on the colonization of Asia and Africa. The ploughing in of the profits of colonialism into the development of European capitalism made a qualitative difference to the nature of capitalism. This not only accelerated industrialization but provided to capitalism precisely the kind of momentum which made it of consequence to world history and more than just a localized European phenomenon. Had the latter been the case, sociological theory in nineteenth-century Europe would not have regarded capitalism as the great divide in the classification of societies. Up to a point this reflects the inadequacies of the understanding of the process of industrialization and capitalism current in Europe at the time. Weber's ideal-type draws on the second phase, but he seeks to explain it by reference to the characteristics of the first phase. The uniqueness of western capitalism became apparent to him when the consequences of the second phase were being felt in Europe. The advance of Europe against the arrested growth of Asia was an established postulate in European thought in the nineteenth century. It was the nature of colonialism which was seen as the historical manifestation of the advance. The initial inadequacy of Weber's theory is the absence of any reference to the role of colonies in the development of capitalism. Even if seen as a unique civilization, Weber's analysis of capitalism was restricted to its nascent phase and to that extent it was incomplete. His dismal prognostications for the future as envisaged in bureaucratic systems, tended to jump from the nascent to the mature without adequately examining the intervening phases.

It is doubtless Weber's refusal to concede historical evolution which led him to inquire into the possibility of capitalist forms in antiquity, both European and Asian. His historical probings would have been more apposite had he analysed non-European history during periods immediately prior to the rise of capitalism in Europe. This he was probably prevented from doing as he did not visualize historical change in Asian societies. Weber was clearly influenced by the concept of Oriental Despotism and, although he does not elaborate on this point, he saw Indian society basically as a static society. Whereas he does see at least three faces to the form of Modern Europe in Judaism, Greco-Roman antiquity and medieval Europe, in the case of India and China, he views them almost as faceless monoliths. This leads to his underplaying, even though aware of it, the change within religious movements or social groups as, for example, his repeated references to Buddhist monks as itinerant mendicants even for periods when some were well-settled and monasteries were property owners. This weakness also relates to the discrepancy in the source material which he consulted for Europe and India. In the former case his generalizations are based on data recorded by the actual groups under discussion but in the Indian case he uses the media of Brahmanical texts for virtually all his major generalizations.

Weber accepts the primacy of religion above all other facets in Indian society. This is perhaps what prevented him from examining the more clearly-defined economic aspects at the root of capitalism in his study of Indian society. Whereas the availability of free labour and the existence of accumulated capital is a prior requisite for the emergence of capitalism, he nowhere attempts to assess the availability of these in India. To this extent Weber subscribed to the current lack of interest in the economic institutions of Indian society. Indian civilization was defined as Hindu and Buddhist with a sprinkling of Jainism. Yet it was precisely in the period of what has recently been called incipient capitalism in India, i.e. the seventeenth and eighteenth centuries, that the Islamic ethic, both religious and political was an important factor. A study of merchant capitalism in India would have involved the need to look at Islam in India, particularly at communities such as the Bohras and Khojas of Guajarat and the west coast, of for that matter even non-Islamic communities such as the Parsis. The exclusion of Islam stemmed from the nineteenth-century tendency to identify religions with their areas of origin and therefore Islam was limited to West Asia. To search for the roots of capitalism in the religious ethic of India during the first millennium BC and the first millennium AD is, to say the least, an anachronistic exercise.

Weber's study of India was a by-product of his main thesis and it would be unfair to be too critical of his theories, particularly as he was relying on secondary material for data. It is strange, though, that he should not at any point have questioned the contextual bias of his sources. One can only assume that his faith in the rationality of contemporary scholarship was as axiomatic to him as his faith in the rationality of capitalism. One cannot criticize him for the limitations of his source material but only for accepting unquestioningly the current interpretations and for not applying his own methodology to these sources — an accusation which can equally well be levelled at Marx in his writings on Asia.

In their analyses of caste both Bouglé and Weber were basing themselves on the existing theories without questioning too closely the premises of these. That the argument was often circular did not seem to matter too much, as for instance, in the Census Reports where the model of caste often related to the Brahmanical *Dharmaśāstras*. It has however to be remembered that they were writing over half a century ago with no access to the more recent insights into the social and economic history of India. Early models without the advantage of detailed research tended to result in over-simplification. Thus, in spite of arguing quite correctly that caste formation often took the form of the conversion of a tribe into a caste, there was all the same an acceptance in Weber's writing of the racially distinct character of upper and lower castes.

Caste is seen as divisive and separatist, but it can be maintained that at another level it is associative and this is expressed for example in the uniformity of certain cultural patterns over extensive geographical areas. This aspect is not analysed. The horizontal perspective played a significant role in the spread of 'Hindu civilization' at the élite levels, and was crucial to the extension of caste society. It was again the associative character of caste which was fundamental to major social and economic changes from the late first millennium AD onwards, particularly in periods of state formation. It could be argued that the nature of caste underwent a fundamental historical change during this period — a change which has not been fully recognized by historians and sociologists.[29] So strong was the preconception of the unchanging character of Indian society that generalizations based on the sources of the Vedic period (1000 BC) were considered adequate for the pre-colonial period up to the eighteenth century AD. For example, the status of the *brāhmaṇa* is rightly linked with his control over the sacrificial ritual in the Vedic period. However, with the extensive granting of property to the *brāhmaṇa* in livestock, in gold and ultimately in land there was a qualitative change in the status of the *brāhmaṇa* by the end of the first millennium AD as also in the sacrificial ritual. Far from abstracting a community from social life, the monasteries (the Buddhist *vihāras* and the Hindu *maṭhas*) were also to take on the role of social institutions with substantial political and economic functions. These institutions became parallel seats of power. Alienation from society would have been one reason for joining the monastery but accelerated social and political mobility could as well have been another. The renouncer rapidly acquired both social status and charisma and frequently built on it a worldly ambition. The 'this-worldly' role of the renouncer seems to have been missed by these sociologists.

From the monastic centres, both Hindu and Buddhist in their time and later even Islamic, there arose the foci of sectarian and political orthodoxy as well as heterodoxy and opposition which led them into varying relationships vis-à-vis political authority. Such religious centres often doubled for networks of trade and were therefore in close contact with merchants and guilds. The nature of the relationship between guilds and political authority was earlier believed to be one of subservience from the former towards the latter, but this view requires re-examination with the availability of more specific and local source material relating to the seventeenth and eighteenth centuries. The jockeying for power between political authority and merchant interests in India during this period suggests a more complex relationship than had been supposed earlier. The crucial question may remain the same as the one posed by Weber, namely, the inability (real or seeming) of the merchants to make an open bid for political power. The answers to such questions lie perhaps less with caste as the crucial variable and more with the role of the European trading companies in Asia. It is curious that Weber did not examine the sources for this period in detail. Had he done so his analysis may have been sharper. But perhaps this would have required of Weber too great an emphasis on historical perception.

From the perspective of the limitation of source materials perhaps the greatest injustice is done to the analysis of Buddhism. Theravada Buddhist sources composed in Pāli were generally regarded by Indologists as somehow not as reliable as Brahmanical, Sanskrit sources. The former were assumed to be *parti pris* but strangely enough not the latter. Since Buddhism had died out in India, Buddhist texts were not given the same importance even though at the time of their composition or soon after, Buddhism was as important, if not more so, as Brahmanism. Had Weber looked more fully at Buddhist sources he would have seen a different epistomology with an emphasis on the universal ethic within which the caste structure was adjusted (and not just the absence of the former and an insistence only on the caste ethic), a movement from a pristine utopia to a well-defined future in terms of a trajectory of time, a strong sense of sectarian historiography impinging on political history of a more secular nature and a monastic life deeply embedded in a society of lay-followers. The three major characteristics as defined by Weber seem doubtful since Buddhism was often closely associated with political authority, at the level of popular support it assimilated local cults and far from advocating a destruction of the will to life it endorsed a programme for the householder and lay-followers which precluded monasticism. Many of the sectarian splits within Buddhism arose because of its having to adjust to changing social mores as it spread across India and Asia. The decline of Buddhism in India had more to do with the changing role of the monastery as an institution, together with competition from other religious sects and a decline in patronage with the decrease of trade in the middle of the first millennium AD.

Weber makes a distinction between early Buddhism, a religion of salvation-striving monks and the later phase with the emergence of what he calls monastic landlordism. The salvation-striving monks were from the start part of a monastic order and the monasteries were segments of what might be called parallel societies. The development of monastic landlordism is seen by Weber essentially in terms of change within the Buddhist structure and to a lesser degree as the interplay between Buddhist institutions and the other institutions of society. Monastic landlordism tends to take on a static form which does not conform to the historical evidence; nor is the emergence of monastic landlordism merely the result of extensive support from the laity since the nature of the institution was such that it made demands both on political authority and the economy. When, even the forest-dwelling monks, theoretically seeking isolation were willing to accept royal patronage and become the nuclei of political centres, the role of such monasteries takes on various political dimensions.

It is not the intention of this paper to attempt to refute the interpretations of Bouglé (as linked to Durkheim) and Weber. Both studies have been seminal to much that is new and meaningful in the sociology and social history of India. A more serious concern with the validity of these interpretations would undoubtedly result in still newer areas of research and analysis. Its intent was to suggest that both Bouglé and Weber in their studies on India were influenced by the prevailing preconceptions about India, which preconceptions they surprisingly tended to accept without too much questioning. One wishes that Weber had applied some of his more innovative categories of thought to the pre-colonial Indian past as he did to the European past.

## Additional Bibliography

Baden-Powell, B.H., *The Indian Village Community*, New Haven, 1957. (originally published in 1896)

Bendix, R., *Max Weber, An Intellectual Portrait*, London, 1960.

Dumezil, G., *Mythe et Epopée*, I and II, Paris, 1968, 1971.

Dumont, L., *Homo Hierarchicus: The Caste System and Its Implications*, New York, 1972.

Durkheim, E., *The Division of Labour in Society*, New York, 1964 (reprint and trans).
—— *Primitive Classification*, Chicago, 1963 (reprint and trans).
—— *The Elementary Forms of Religious Life : A Study in Religious Sociology*, London, 1915 (reprint and trans).
Heesterman, J.C., *The Ancient Indian Royal Consecration*, The Hague, 1957.
Held, G.J., *The Mahabharata : An Ethnological Study*, London, 1935.
Hubert H., and M. Mauss, *Sacrifice : Its Nature and Function*, London, 1964 (reprint and trans).
—— *Melanges d'histoire des Religions*, Paris, 1909.
Mill, J., *History of British India*, London, 1818–1823.
M. Müller, *Chips from a German Workshop*, I and II, London 1867–75.
D. Kantowsky has edited a collection of papers entitled, *Recent Research on Max Weber's studies of Hinduism*, London 1986, in which he argues that many scholars working on Weber's theories on India have misunderstood Weber because the translation of his study on the religion of India has misrepresented the original German text. This may well be. One expects therefore a more correct translation to be made available.

A recent and important addition to some of the discussion in this paper is T.R. Trautmann, *The Aryans and British India*, Delhi, 1997.

## Notes and References

1. E. Durkheim, 'De la definition des phenomenes religieux', *L' année Sociologique*, II, Paris, 1899, pp. 1–28.
2. M. Mauss, *Essai sur le Don*, Paris, 1925, p. 143 (trans., *The Gift*, New York, 1967).
3. C. Bouglé, *Essays on the Caste System*, Cambridge, 1971, p. vii (Originally published 1908 in French).
4. M. Monier–Williams, *A Sanskrit-English Dictionary*, New York, 1976, p. 652.
5. *Keshab Chunder Sen's Lectures in India*, p. 323.
6. M. Monier–Williams, *A Sanskrit-English Dictionary*, New York, 1976, p. 924 qv. *varṇa*.
7. *Mahābhārata*, 12.181.5ff. refers to the four *varnas* as symbolized by the colours white, red, yellow and black, the differentiation of which comes about after a preliminary period when all *varnas* were identical. The same sequence of colours is used in connection with the four epochs (*yugas*) 3.148.5–37.
8. *Ṛg Veda*, 1.130.8; 5.29.10; 9.41.1.
9. A. Lyall, *Asiatic Studies*, London, 1889; D.C.J. Ibbetson, *Report on the*

*Census of the Punjab Taken on 17th February 1881*, Calcutta, 1883; J.C. Nesfield, *Brief View of the Caste System of the North-western Provinces and Oudh, Together with an Examination of Names and Figures Shown in the Census Report, 1882*, Allahabad, 1885; H.H. Risley, *The People of India*, London, 1908. These were all officials involved in the administration of India and contributed to the collection of census data and studies of castes and tribes in British India during the late nineteenth and early twentieth centuries. In contrast to the British writing on this subject which came mainly from administrators, French studies on society and religion in India came largely from professional scholars of Sanskrit and from sociologists.

10. M. Müller, *India, What Can It Teach Us?*, London, 1883, pp. 15, 101.
11. K. Marx and F. Engels, *On Colonialism*, Moscow, 1968, p. 41.
12. H.S. Maine, *Village Communities in the East and West*, New York, 1974 (reprint), pp. 22ff.
13. S. Lukes, *Emile Durkheim: His Life and Work*, London, 1973, pp. 235ff.
14. Ibid., pp. 477ff.
15. H. Oldenburg, *The Buddha*, London, 1922, pp. 214ff; M. Weber, *The Religion of India*, Glencoe, 1958, p. 146; Quoted in W.S.F. Pickering, *Durkheim on Religion*, Boston, 1975, pp. 80ff.
16. *Śatapatha Brāhmaṇa*, 1.1.1.1ff.
17. It has been suggested that Durkheim understated the degree of interdependence and reciprocity in mechanical solidarity and overstated the role of repressive law. Lukes, op. cit., pp. 159ff.
18. S. Hughes, *Consciousness and Society*, New York, 1961.
19. J. Freund, *The Sociology of Max Weber*, London, 1968, pp. 5ff.
20. J. Lewis, *Max Weber and Value-Free Sociology*, London, 1975, p. 67.
21. R.H. Tawney, *Religion and the Rise of Capitalism*, Harmondsworth, 1961, pp. 89–142.
22. M. Weber, *The Agrarian Sociology of Ancient Civilisations*, London, 1976, pp. 69ff.
23. Ibid., pp. 37ff. Horticulture implies a mixture of food-gathering and primitive food production requiring neither technological innovations nor substantial changes in demographic structure and land-rights as were necessary in the transition from cattle breeding to agriculture.
24. M. Reinhold, 'Historian of the Classic World: A Critique of Rostovtzeff', *Science and Society*, 1946, 10, pp. 361–91.
25. *The Sociology of Religion*, London, 1965, pp. 46ff.
26. Ibid., pp. 344ff.
27. E.W. Hopkins, 'The Social and Military Position of the Ruling Caste in Ancient India as Represented in the Sanskrit Epics', *Journal of the American Oriental Society*, 1899, 13, pp. 57ff.
28. S. Hughes, op. cit., pp. 330ff.
29. Romila Thapar, *The Past and Prejudice*, New Delhi, 1975.

# 3

# The Contribution of D.D. Kosambi to Indology*

It has recently been argued that a revolution in scientific knowledge comes about not through the accumulation of data alone but through a change in the paradigm.[1] When the framework of explanation or the hypothesis is altered or a new set of questions are posed only then can there be a breakthrough in scientific knowledge. This applies as much to history and the social sciences. The accumulation of data is of course a necessary first step and includes the deriving of fresh data from new sources, but an advance in knowledge is dependent on using the data to present new formulations.

Histories of the Indian sub-continent, such as were to become germane to the perception on the Indian past, have subscribed to three major changes of paradigm. The first comprehensive history was James Mill's *History of British India*[2] published in the early nineteenth century, where he set out his theory of Indian history evolving out of three civilizations, the Hindu, the Muslim and the British. The first two of these he described as backward, stagnant and ahistoric. His theory was to become axiomatic to the periodization of Indian history and is with us still, though sometimes in a disguised form. A change came about with Vincent Smith's *History of India*[3] published in 1919, which tried to avoid the sharpness of Mill's value judgements. Smith concentrated more on a chronological overview which was in any case less charged with colonial and anti-colonial sentiment and argued for the rise and fall of dynasties as being crucial to the study of Indian history. By the early twentieth century chronological data had accumulated to the point where such a treatment of history was possible. Where

* Lecture delivered at the Asiatic Society, Bombay. Published in *Journal of the Asiatic Society of Bombay*, 1977–78, n.s. 52–3, 365–84

Mill's assessment was seeking to justify the British conquest of India, Smith was justifying colonial rule. The infrequency of explicitly negative value judgements on the pre-British period was largely an indication of his awareness of Indian national sentiment in the matter. Nationalist historians writing on early India reversed the value judgements but adhered to the paradigm of dynastic and chronological concerns.

Kosambi's first book, *An Introduction to the Study of Indian History*[4] published in 1956, was a major shift in the paradigm. He had little use for a chronological narrative since he argued that chronology for the early period was too obscure to be meaningful. For him history was the presentation in chronological order of successive developments in the means and relations of production.[5] Because of the absence of reliable historical records he argued that Indian history would have to use the comparative method.[6] This meant a familiarity with a wide range of historical work and his own familiarity with classical European history is evident in his writing; it also meant the use of various disciplines and interdisciplinary techniques to enable the historian to understand the pattern of social formations. His definition of the comparative method required the historian to be an inter-disciplinary creature in himself with the ability to use a large number of investigative techniques. This ability he demonstrated to the full in his writings on Indology. Added to this was his conviction that the historian in India was in a particularly happy position since so much of the past survives in the present. As he puts it, '. . . the country has one tremendous advantage that was not utilised till recently by the historians: the survival within different social layers of many forms that allow the reconstruction of totally diverse earlier stages.'[7] For him, this amply made up for the absence of reliable historical records.

Kosambi's acknowledged status as an Indologist was all the more remarkable, in that by profession he was a mathematician. Indology to begin with was a subsidiary interest, perhaps inherited from his father, a scholar of Pāli and Buddhism who taught at various centres in India, apart from a period at Harvard. The older Kosambi walked the countryside in an effort to relate the texts to their original milieu, an approach which was followed by his son. A quick perusal of the younger Kosambi's many publications, points to a telling trend. His earliest papers in the 1930's are mainly on various aspects of mathematics. In the 1940's his interest in Indology become apparent in the form of occasional papers. (This was also the period when he wrote on Soviet contributions to mathematics and genetics and was enthusiastic about the Soviet attempt to build a socialist society). He was appointed to a Mathematics Chair at the Tata Institute of Fundamental Research in Bombay, in 1946. During the 1950's however and until his death in 1966, most of his publications were on Indology and early Indian history although his mathematical interests remained constant.

Given that Indology is now seen as essentially rooted in a colonial perception of the past, and since Kosambi's writing challenged this perception, it would be more appropriate to refer to him as a historian, the field in which lay his major contribution. But he was prolific and researched into other related areas as well, hence the continuing use of the label, Indologist. His first venture into early Indian sources was a critical assessment of Bhartṛhari which can be regarded as a model for such analysis.[8] At a later stage he edited, jointly with V.V. Gokhale, the Vidyākara *Subhāṣita-ratna-kośa* for the Harvard Oriental Series.[9] Apart from applying the norms of higher criticism to such texts he also tried to place them in historical context not merely through a chronological analysis but by referring them to the society from which they emanated. He argued that from the first millennium AD Sanskrit should be seen as a measure and expression of upper class unity when it replaced Prākrit in the royal courts and was patronized, particularly in the initial stages, by foreign rulers. This is of course evident in the change from Prākrit to Sanskrit as the language of royal inscriptions between the Mauryan and the Gupta periods. He stressed the feudal background of many Sanskrit texts which brought him into a lively controversy with one of his closest friends, the Harvard Sanskritist, Daniel Ingalls. Kosambi maintained that Sanskrit was deliberately kept restricted to a small number of people, even though the excellent early grammar of the language by Pāṇini, commented upon by Patañjali, converted it into an orderly and systematic language, open to anyone who was taught it properly. However he felt that it froze in the hands of what he called, 'a disdainful priest class',[10] and much of the real world was bye-passed in the courtly literature.

The relation of text to context was examined at greater length in his papers on the *Bhagavad Gītā* where he attempted to relate ideology to society.[11] He argued that the *Gītā* in propounding the concept of *bhakti* laid emphasis on unquestioning faith in, and personal loyalty and devotion to, a deity, and these values were in conformity with the ideology of feudalism which also required a chain of unquestioning loyalties. The text emphasized caste functions and the requirement to do one's ordained duty as a member of a particular caste which he saw as a message in support of caste society and the conservatism which such a society entails; a message propounded by the upper castes to keep the rest of society passive. He further suggests that religious sects supporting a synthesis of gods and of tolerance are expressions of a period of a social surplus, when wealth was more widely distributed; whereas the ideology of *bhakti* is more frequent in periods of crisis, but that it nevertheless acted as a means of inter-relating the scattered religious beliefs of a region. It could be argued however that the *bhakti* endorsed by the *Gītā* is not identical with that which was taught by later *bhakti* teachers. Whereas the single minded devotion to a deity is retained, the social content changes substantially and is expressed in a concern with a universal ethic which echoes that of the Buddhists and Jainas and which permits the *bhakti* movements to become powerful mobilizers of various social groups. There is an almost apparent contradiction between the emphasis on caste-duty in the *Gītā* and the universal ethic of the later *bhakti* movement.

Kosambi uses Buddhist texts mainly to draw out data on social and economic life and much of his discussion on early trade, for instance, is based on these sources. This was not new as such data had earlier been extracted from these sources by scholars of Buddhism such as Rhys Davids[12] and Fick.[13] Kosambi co-related this data with evidence from Sanskrit sources but also from archaeological excavations and contemporary inscriptions and brought the Buddhist material into the wider orbit of reconstructing the history of the late first millennium BC. The fact that the Buddhist sources do at times contradict the brahmanical tradition was for him a particularly important aspect of the Pāli texts and invested them with the kind of authenticity which he found invaluable. The recognition of this feature he owed to his father's work on the Buddhist texts.[14]

His knowledge of Sanskrit led Kosambi to a series of etymological analyses which he used to great effect in reconstructing the social background, particularly of the Vedic period.[15] Thus he argued that the names of many of the established *brāhmaṇas* in Vedic literature and the Purāṇic tradition clearly pointed to their being of non-Aryan origin. Some were given the epithet, *dāsī-putra* (such as Dīrghatamas) or else their names suggested totems, as for instance, Ajīgarta or Kaśyapa. Further, that the original seven *gotras* of the *brāhmaṇas* were of mixed Aryan and non-Aryan priests. His analysis of the *gotras* led him into a debate with John Brough.[16] From the study of the *gotras* he went on to the logical point that the language of the Vedic texts could not have been pure Aryan and must have had an admixture of non-Aryan elements reflecting the inclusion of non-Aryans as *brāhmaṇas*. This theory is now more acceptable to those who have worked on Indo-Aryan linguistics, on the basis of the linguistic analyses of the texts and language which clearly indicates non-Aryan structures and forms both in syntax and vocabulary.[17] Kosambi's own use of linguistic analyses bears the stamp of philology and he was evidently less familiar with the changes in linguistic practices of the mid-twentieth century. His etymological reconstruction of Sātakarṇi as Indo-Austric is an example of this where he makes no attempt to support his argument by providing other Austric links.[18] The same problem arises with his attempt to equate the Hittite *khatti* with the Sanskrit *kṣatriya* and the Pāli *khettiyo*.[19]

An area in which he successfully utilised his mathematical knowledge was Indian numismatics and more especially in the one coinage system on which he worked in great detail, namely, the punch-marked coins which were in circulation between c. 500–100 BC. These were coins cut from a sheet of silver, each coin bearing a set of symbols but generally with no legend. Hence their chronology and the agency which issued them was an enigma. Kosambi wished to demonstrate the application of scientific methods for obtaining information from numismatic evidence. He worked initially on a statistical analyses from one hoard with a meticulous weighing of each coin to ascertain loss of weight by wear and tear and with a careful analysis of their fabric and alloy. By arranging the coins in accordance with their weight and their set of symbols he hoped to provide a chronological sequence of the coins and believed that this would in turn provide a clue as to the source of their issue.[20] For the method to be ultimately successful the coins to be used as control had to come from stratified excavations. These could be tested against coins from hoards provided they were free from encrustations. His analyses revealed that the average weight decreases when the symbols on the reverse increase. From this he argued that coins in constant circulation would also be the ones to be weighed and valued more frequently. He maintained that they were originally issued by traders but were ratified by the kings' valuers and marked with the kings' symbols. The next step was the identifying of particular symbols as the marks of particular kings. Whereas the statistical analyses of the coins is generally accepted, the identifications of certain symbols with royalty remain controversial with some numismatists still arguing that the coins may not bear any royal marks. It does seem curious that with major changes in the nature of the state and of royalty during this period, the coins, if connected with royalty, should have remained without any appreciable change in style. It seems implausible that the Mauryan kings would not have issued special coins and would have been content to merely ratify those issued by traders, for, if nothing else they would at least have imitated the Persian and Greek coins which were circulating in West Asia and with which area Indian kings and traders were in contact. It seems more likely that the coins continued to be issued and ratified by guilds as legal tender, a suggestion which has been linked to the occasional legend of *negama* (from *nigama*?) on some issues from Taxila. The evaluation of coins by the king's valuer as described in the *Arthaśāstra* would doubtless have applied to all coins irrespective of where they were issued.

Kosambi's use of archaeology was in part to reconstruct the prehistoric period where he literally walked the stretch around Pune in an effort to record the archaeological data. On the basis of his extensive fieldwork on microlithic sites and through his typology of microlithic artefacts he was able to suggest the routes which herders, pastoralists and incipient traders would have taken across the western Deccan in the pre-historic period.[21] Relating to a more developed culture, he looked for continuities of archaic artefacts and sought to explain these in their fullest function, for example, the function of the saddle-quern which he explained both with reference to those found in archaeological excavations and as well as those in current use.[22] By the term 'use' he meant not merely the technological function but also the role of the object in religious ritual. He was also among the earliest scholars to recognize the significance of the megalithic material and the potentialities which it held in the discussion on the origins of many institutions.

Added to the fieldwork was an intelligent understanding of geo-morphology and topography. In many cases his assessment of the historical importance of a site was based on the logic of geography. This he felt should indicate to the historian where to look for sites and the likely nature of the sites. This approach is demonstrated in what can only be called a brilliantly insightful discussion of the trade routes from the west coast upto the plateau and across the *ghats* in the western Deccan.[23] Geographical considerations were partially responsible for the location of urban centres and Buddhist monasteries in this area during the first millennium AD with a continuity of Maratha forts and British railway links in the second millennium.

It was the recognition of cultural survival which led Kosambi to weave so much material from ethnology and anthropology into his historical narrative. This is perhaps best demonstrated in the pages of his *Introduction to the Study of Indian History*, where he describes what he sees in the vicinity of his house in Pune.[24] Here we have history virtually on the door-step, what with the encampment of a nomadic group, the presence of a tribe which had once given rise to a *jāti*, and of another which became a quasi-guild. He noticed trees and sacred groves, stones marking a sacrificial ritual, caves and rock shelters which may have been occupied successively by prehistoric men, by Buddhist monks and later by practitioners of Hindu cults. Such places have a remarkable continuity as sacred centres and often provided a greater historical continuity both in object and ritual than many written texts. These for him were primary areas for archaeological and historical investigation. It is important to clarify that Kosambi was not arguing that religion played a more significant part in Indian culture than has been the case in other cultures, as has been the stand of those who maintain the greater spirituality of the Indian past; but rather, Kosambi's position is that there was a greater survival of the archaic in religious ritual than in other areas of Indian life suggesting a certain conservatism, but which at the same time makes it worth investigating historically. This perspective on culture is again demonstrated in the discussion on the probable Harappan religious forms and their continuity into later periods.

Kosambi had little use for physical anthropology. For him, both the measuring of nasal indexes and the theories on the racial identities of India derived therefrom, were worthless.[25] At a wider anthropological level he maintained that one of the clues to understanding the Indian past was the basic factor of the transition from tribe to caste, from small, localized groups to a generalized society.[26] This transition was largely the result of the introduction of plough agriculture in various regions which changed the system of production, broke the structure of tribes and clans and made caste the alternative form of social organization. This process he traced in part from the evolution of clan totems into clan names and then into caste names. The agency through which plough agriculture was introduced would therefore become the major factor of control in caste society. This agency he saw as the brahmanical settlements in various parts of the country. These led to an assimilation of local cults into the brahmanical tradition as is evident from the various *Purāṇas* and *Māhātmyas*. But equally important it led to the sanskritization of local folk cults with the incorporation of *brāhmaṇa* priests and rituals, the association of epic heroes and heroines, and by the inclusion of such cults in Sanskrit mythology.

The interpretation of myths is essential to any study of early cultures and Kosambi's work is peppered with such interpretations. In a detailed discussion of the story of Purūravas and Urvaśī which he traces through its many varients in the texts,[27] he dismisses the simplistic nature-myth interpretation of Max Müller and his contemporaries who saw the disappearance of Urvaśī as symbolic of the vanishing dawn on the rising of the sun. Kosambi attempts a functional anthropological analysis in which he argues that it reflects the institution of sacred marriage in prehistoric societies as well as the ritual sacrifice of the hero by the mother goddess.[28] One of the frequent strands in his explanations of myths was related to his belief that societies were matriarchal in origin and many gradually changed to patriliny and that myths therefore reflect the transition from the one to the other. This view was largely derived from the writings of F. Engels[29] and what one might call the 'mother-right school of anthropology.'[30] He applied the same argument to explain the *kumbha* symbol or birth from a jar of certain *brāhmaṇa gotras* and of the Kauravas in the *Mahābhārata* where the jar has an obvious symbolic equation with the womb. Bride-price is also for him a survival of matriliny.[31] The insistence on a transition from matriarchy to patriliny in every case is not now acceptable since many societies are known to have been patrilineal from the beginning. It is curious that the structural study of myths was known at that time but Kosambi shows little interest in it.

I have tried to indicate the various ways in which Kosambi contributed to Indological studies in his handling of the various sources and data. That his scholarship ranged over a variety of aspects was in conformity with the best Indological tradition which required a many faceted scholar who could claim familiarity with different source materials. What distinguished Kosambi from other scholars was that his ultimate concern was with an overall theoretical frame-work, into which, not only was his scattered research directed, but which he propounded as an attempt to comprehend the totality of Indian history. His first book, *An Introduction to the study of Indian History*, drew together the many themes on which he had researched in earlier years and which he had published as papers in various journals of Oriental Studies. This book was to prove his claim not merely to being a historian but to changing the paradigm for early Indian history.

For Kosambi, Marxism provided the clue to understanding the past and he identified his method unambiguously with Marxism. Kosambi would doubtless have accepted the judgement of Jean Paul Sartre that Marxism is the 'necessary' philosophy of our time, by which Sartre meant that even if Marx's particular conclusions are un-acceptable, the method of analysis which he had worked out is virtually unavoidable in the social sciences. Many among the non-Marxist and anti-Marxist historians in this country tried to dismiss the book with the predictable critique of all Marxist histories, that the author was forcing the facts to fit a preconceived theory: a critique which is applied *ad nauseam* to many versions of knowledge which are intellectually uncomfortable for those who are incapable of changing the paradigm and who are fearful of scholars attempting to do so. A few among the more intellectually gifted realized that what Kosambi was doing was not forcing the facts to fit the received Marxist pattern on Indian history, but was instead using a Marxist methodology to investigate a possible pattern and suggest a new framework; that in fact he was using the method creatively. As he himself states elsewhere, Marxism was not being "proved" or "justified", but simply being used as a tool of professional investigation. And this was also part of the reason why he was regarded with suspicion by the then Marxist political establishment in this country, the people whom he has referred to in his writings as the OM—the Official Marxists![32] Enthusiastic support came to him from intellectuals interested in Marxism and in history and from liberal intellectuals in Europe and America. It is significant that Kosambi was invited to give a series of lectures on the history of Hinduism at London University and to lecture at the Oriental Institute in Moscow in 1955, and this was before any Indian University took such a step.

I would like now to consider his approach to early Indian history with which he was centrally concerned. In the context of his general argument of the transition from tribe to caste, socio-economic formations were his primary interest. He draws his evidence on tribal forms both from literary sources as well as from the survival of such groups into recent centuries and from their interaction with peasant groups. The earliest of such transitions occurred in the Indus valley; hence Kosambi's concern with agrarian technology at that time.[33] He assumed that it was a culture without the plough, that the river bank was cultivated with a harrow and that the seasonal flood water was utilized for irrigation with dams and embankments helping in retaining this water and the river silt for a longer period. The decline of the Indus civilization is attributed to the Aryans who destroyed the agricultural system by breaking the embankments, which action he maintains, is symbolically referred to in the Ṛgvedic descriptions of Indra destroying Vṛtra, and releasing the waters. Kosambi was of the opinion that the plough was brought by the Aryans [i.e. the speakers of Indo-Aryan] who thereby changed agricultural technology. Recent evidence on the Indus civilization makes it clear that plough agriculture was practised even as early as the pre-Harappan period and that the plough was known to the non-Aryan since the more commonly used word for the plough in Vedic literature is of non-Aryan etymology.[34] The theory of the destruction of the embankments is conjectural and may have greater application to dams built to prevent the flooding of the cities rather than for agricultural purposes. Nevertheless the question posed by Kosambi as to why the agrarian base of the Harappan culture declined and was unable to support an urban civilization in the later stages still remains a valid one and is now sought to be answered by evidence of a far reaching ecological change with which Harappan technology could not cope and which at a later time resulted in the location of new urban centres in the Ganga valley.

Although he had no use for any theory of an Aryan race, Kosambi did support the idea of the Aryan speaking peoples having settled in north-western India and spreading gradually into the Ganges valley, in both cases initially as conquerors.[35] Such a theory of conquest had been questioned by those working in Indo-Aryan linguistics and it is now being proposed that conquest should be replaced by considering the possibility of migrations and technological changes being responsible for the arrival and the dominance of the Aryan speakers, the resulting long period of co-existence between them and the indigenous peoples being suggested by the evidence of bi-lingualism. Even the archaeological data which was once put forward to support the destruction of the Harappan cities by invaders is now discounted.[36] The new evidence however tends to strengthen the more important point made by Kosambi that much of the Indian tradition from the earliest Vedic texts is already an amalgam of Aryan and non-Aryan as indeed are even those of the highest caste.

Plough agriculture and iron technology when it was introduced into the Ganges valley led ultimately to the growth of urban centres as well as the recognizable forms of caste. Recent views would include as causal factors in this development, the role of a change in crop patterns with a dependence on rice agriculture, the diversity of irrigation systems, the use of labour in the new technologies and the range of control over these factors by different social groups. This is a fleshing out, as it were, of Kosambi's argument by extending the span of causal factors. Analyses of the structure of caste at this time in terms of the theoretical form given to the actuality, gives further rein to the question implicitly raised by Kosambi, namely, the degree to which ideology and social structure are inter-connected.

The Mauryan monarchy which controlled the Indian subcontinent was a feasible political system according to Kosambi because of the expansion of the village economy through *śūdra* agriculturalists being settled on state lands and by the deportation of prisoners-of-war who were used for the same purpose.[37] He argues against the use of slavery in production in early India and prefers the theory of *śūdra* helotage, although he does not develop this theory in detail. The decline of the Mauryan empire is attributed to an economic crisis, the details of which are debatable. His argument that the currency was debased devolves from his own chronological interpretation of the coins, which as we have seen, is not entirely acceptable, as also the argument that double cropping indicated an economic crisis, for we now know from archaeological sources that double cropping was an established practice even in earlier centuries.[38] However, that the inability of the Mauryan polity to survive must be attributed to causes which in part were economic, cannot be doubted. A more plausible analysis would be to examine the nature of the Mauryan polity in terms of whether the existing man power and agricultural resources were conducive to such a system. Equally important is the question of whether the polity was as centralized as has been made out in historical studies.

Kosambi's treatment of the rise of the Buddhist, Jaina and other sects of that time links them to major technological changes and to urbanism. But above all he maintains that they reflect a situation of detribalization in which they attempt to reach out across castes to a wider social range through their universal ethic. He argues forcefully in support of a mercantile patronage extended to these sects which rooted them in society more firmly than did the help they received from royal patronage. The punch-marked coins are for him an indication of developed commodity production[39] which provided a high status for artisans and traders as members of urban society and their link with religions propagating a universal ethic would not be surprising. This link was demonstrated in his discussion of the post-Maurya period where he examines the role of guilds and artisans as donors to the Buddhist *saṅgha* in the light of the expansion and diffusion of trade. The emergence of occupational *jātis* in urban areas can frequently be associated with this development.

An evident departure from the orthodox Marxist pattern of historical periodization is Kosambi's refusal to apply either the Asiatic Mode of Production or the Slave Mode of Production to early Indian history without modifications of a major kind. For Karl Marx the Indian past conformed, by and large, to what he called the Asiatic Mode of Production characterized by a static society, an absence of private property in land, self-sufficient villages, a lack of a commercial economy and by a state control over the irrigation system. Although he and Engels recognized deviations from this pattern, they saw this pattern as a contrast to that prevalent in Europe and argued that historical stagnancy in India was broken by the coming of colonialism. This was not altogether acceptable to Kosambi, for whom the key to the Indian past in the advance of plough agriculture over tribal society made a static history impossible. Of the notion of the self-sufficient village economy he writes, '. . . acute and brilliant as these remarks are, they remain misleading nevertheless . . . '.[40] The dependence of the village on external sources for salt and metals would automatically preclude self-sufficiency. Elsewhere he has argued for the existence of the tenant and of the landowning peasant.[41] He did however concede that from the end of the Gupta period there was a relative increase in self-sufficiency and this brought with it a static mode of production which was not the Asiatic mode for it came about during a period of feudalism.[42] He also argued that the lack of a sense of history and the power of myth further reduced individuality. A static mode of production could not have co-existed with a form of feudalism since the latter breeds its own contradictions. Perhaps if he had been questioned on this ambiguity he may have modified his position to argue that the degree of self-sufficiency increased, but not to the extent of the static mode of production becoming the dominant feature.

Elaborating his views on the Asiatic Mode of Production he wrote

> The real difficulty here (not in China) is the misleading documentation. Ancient Indian records derive from the brahman caste and those who read them pay no attention to the function of caste in ancient — (as well as modern and feudal) Indian society. Indian history is, to me, a very fine example of Marxist theory working very well in practice. Unfortunately, Marx had only the solitary report of Buchanan-Hamilton on Karnatak villages, not even the *Foral* of 1640 by the king of Portugal guaranteeing the rights of Goa village communities, which existed in a much more primitive form, and which could not be called 'hydraulic', in view of the torrential rainfall. The Goan organisation (which I have studied elsewhere, *Myth and Reality*, Chapter V) was actually the model for the Karnatak settlement, and survived almost to this day.
>
> It follows that 'Oriental Despotism' has to be looked at from some other points of view than Wittfogel's hydraulic social aberrations. It seems to me that the two main Marxist considerations are: (1) The incidence of commodity production (per head) with the relative ease of food-gathering. This becomes vital when you consider Africa. By the way, the Pharoah's main function was not regulation of water or irrigation, but distribution of the numerous materials which had all to be imported from a long distance, including wood, metals, and so on. Henri Frankfort has a very neat answer to Toynbee, where he brings

this out, in contrast to Mesopotamian development of numerous warring cities. (2) The need to use overriding force to compel the people (in an environment where food-gathering was, however irregular, always possible) to change over to food-production i.e. agriculture with the plough. In Egypt food-gathering was different except in the delta, but the cultivator had to be kept at his work. You will find that the British had to impose a poll-tax in Africa in order to get cheap labour for the mines and the white man's farms.

If you grant this, then it follows that despotism, even of the so-called oriental type, was a tool (however disgusting) used to bring a more productive form of society into existence. But during this very process, there came into being a class of state servants, state nobility or administrators — at times priests, who reduced the need for violence and helped develop the back-lands (as did my own ancestors in Goa and the Buddhist monasteries in China as well as in the Deccan). This class then used the absolute, despotic monarchy and the more or less passive substratum for its own purposes. Hence the changeless appearance of the country, seeing that the actual tools of production need not become more efficient. Under such circumstances, feudalism is a special development used to keep the rule in the hands of a ruling warrior caste-class, often conquerors. Don't be misled by the supposed Indian *kshatriya* caste, which was oftener than not a brahmanical fiction . . . .[43]

His rejection of the Slave Mode of Production as applicable to the Indian past arose from a hesitation in applying the accepted Marxist periodization of European history. Marx had suggested that primitive communism gave way to a slave mode of production predominant in Greco-Roman antiquity and this in turn gave rise to feudalism in Europe from which evolved the capitalist mode of production. Kosambi was averse to the mechanical application of this model to India as had been done by various historians in Soviet Russia and in India, as for example, by S.A. Dange. Kosambi was caustic in his evaluation of Dange's book, *From Primitive Communism to Slavery*, which he said followed the Russian analysis and which analysis, '. . . saves a certain type of "left intellectual" the trouble of reading anything else or thinking for himself.'[44] Kosambi's analysis differed from any existing model. He maintains that the statement of the Greek ambassador Megasthenes (of the fourth century BC) that there was an absence of slavery in India was correct because Megasthenes makes a comparison with Sparta which suggests helots instead of slaves.[45] Kosambi states that at this period the *śūdras* were essentially helots. He does not however discuss in greater detail the nature of *śūdra* helotage. Whereas the origin of the *śūdra* caste could perhaps be traced to a form of helotage, the classification cannot hold for the entire past. At the ideological level it would be clearly contradicted by the early *Dharmaśāstra* exposition of the *varṇa* theory where the origin of the *śūdra* is attributed to mixed caste marriages including those involving the upper castes. Such a theory even if not based on actuality would have undermined the notion of helotage. The possibility of a Slave Mode of Production in early India is problematical since it is difficult to assess the ratio of slaves to other forms of labouring men nor is there a clear distinction between slaves in domestic employ or in agricultural and craft production. Doubtless these numbers would also have varied in the *gaṇa-saṅgha* chiefships where they were probably higher and in the kingdoms where with a diversity of labour, slavery for production may have been smaller. It would also be important to consider the degree of unfreedom of the *dāsa* in relation to the *karma-kāra, bhṛitaka* and *śūdra* which would involve questions of the legal status of these categories.

Kosambi accepts the Feudal Mode of Production as relevant to pre-modern Indian history, although even here he makes his own distinction between what he calls, 'feudalism from above' and 'feudalism from below', and which he regards as the peculiar features of Indian feudalism. Feudalism from above was his characterization of the changes which came about in the late first millennium AD subsequent to the Gupta period.[46] Incidentally he has little time for the Gupta period and is justifiably contemptuous of the nationalist historians who described it as the golden age of Hindu revivalism. His contempt is summed up in the sentence, 'Far from the Guptas reviving nationalism, it was nationalism that revived the Guptas.'[47] Recent research has not only tarnished some of the golden quality of this age, but has on occasion even revealed that a part of it was mere tinsel. The changes noticeable in the post-Gupta period were mainly those of an increase in the granting of land with a greater frequency of transition from tribe to caste through the introduction of plough agriculture, a decline in trade and commodity production which adversely affected the growth of urban centres, the decentralization of the army and a concentration of wealth at local courts. With this was associated the spread of *bhakti* cults whose emphasis on loyalty and devotion he saw as a characteristic feature of feudal society. In a discussion on private property in land, central to the concept of the Asiatic Mode of Production, he argues that it should be viewed in the Indian context which implies, firstly, that actual cultivators were ex-tribals who still regarded land as territory deriving from kinship rights, and secondly, the holding of a field was proof of membership of a community rather than ownership of land and thirdly, that in a non-commodity producing village or one located near waste land, land would have no sale value. The only conditions were the regular payment of taxes to either the grantee or the king. These arguments read more like an attempt to somehow salvage the notion of the absence of private property without a willingness to admit the pattern of the Asiatic Mode of Production as an explanatory model. Nor are these arguments wholly convincing because although in some areas the cultivators were recent converts to peasantry in others they were peasants of long standing since many of the grants of land were made in villages of well-established cultivators. The statement that land had no sale value in newly settled areas is contradicted by inscriptional evidence in some areas where, in Bengal for example, land is sold and the price is stated in districts which were regarded as being on the edge of waste land.[48] Part of the problem with his analysis of the two phases of feudalism, and this is a problem of which he is well aware, is that no generalization can cover the entire sub-continent since the changes varied from region to region.[49]

In his discussion on feudalism from below he draws his evidence mainly from Kashmir and Rajasthan and depicts a more clearly recognizable form of feudalism but with specific Indian features.[50] This phase is characterized by political decentralization accompanied by a low level of technology with production for the household and the village and not for a market, and the holding of land by lords on a service tenure who also have judicial or quasi-judicial functions in relation to the dependent population. The Indian features were the absence of demesne farming on the lord's estate by forced labour where in many cases, slaves were used instead, leading to an increase in slaves; there was also an absence of guilds and of any organized church. The backwardness of technology allowed of an easy conquest of northern India by those with a more advanced military technology. Changes in the ruling class did not substantially affect the nature of feudalism in India and it continued until the coming of colonialism.

Kosambi's definition of feudalism would today find its critics and its general applicability to the sub-continent would be debated. On the latter point one would have to consider whether other systems prevalent in other parts of the sub-continent would seriously subtract from the generalization.[51] The nature of control over land was different in parts of the peninsula as also was the condition of trade, where the rise of powerful guilds was characteristic of this period. The increase in the number of slaves was not such as to constitute a Slave Mode of Production and as Kosambi maintains quite correctly there was no slave economy of the Roman kind to initiate the institution of the manor. The existence of serfdom has also been suggested for many areas. Although there was no organized church nevertheless there is what Max Weber has called 'monastic landlordism' both among Buddhist and Hindu sects, which at some levels was a parallel system to that of church lands in Europe. The monastic centres of this period were opulent and powerful. Kosambi argues that religious sects frequently failed to provide the ethical and religious values by which they had once held the society, but he does not consider the monastic institution as the foci of political and economic control, a role which it often played at this time.[52]

It is curious that Kosambi takes as his model feudalism in England and shows no familiarity with the classic work on feudal society by Marc Bloch which would have been far more pertinent to his analyses. (His facility in French would have enabled him to have read Marc Bloch in the original). In a sense, this points to something of a narrowness in his wider historical reading. Although far from being an orthodox Marxist he nevertheless showed little interest in schools of analyses other than the Marxist as far as interpreting early societies was concerned. He does not for example indicate any familiarity with the works of those who were critical of Lewis Morgan and Frederick Engels inspite of using Marxist analyses as a starting point for the study of early societies, such as Karl Polanyi. It is also curious that inspite of his interest in French scholarship (arising out of a concern with French colonial activities in Vietnam and North Africa) he was not introduced to the writings of French historians such as Fernand Braudel with which, one suspects, he would have found a rapport. Whereas his respect for the works of Gordon Childe and George Thomson is evident in his own studies, his acquaintance with Moses Finley's work on the Greeks came later[53] and one wonders whether he would have analysed the Indian epics in a manner similar to Finley's analysis of the Greek epics. Convinced as he was of the correctness of one methodology, Kosambi seems to have found the debate on methodology unnecessary. His utilization of Indian anthropological literature was more as a source of ethnology and a study of survivals and indigenous forms rather than as a means of examining the validity of any anthropological method. Possibly this limitation may also have been due to the tendency among Indian Marxists at that time to confine themselves to the writings of British Marxists, which can perhaps be explained as a curious reflection on the limitations of colonial scholarship where, even in radical circles the intellectual metropolis remained British with occasional forays into the writings of Soviet scholars. This is in striking contrast to more recent years in which the translations of European Marxist writing and that from other parts of the world are as widely read as the works of British Marxists.[54] A more mundane explanation may be the paucity of new books at that time and Kosambi was very conscious of this lack of availability of up-to-date research. In his personal correspondence with scholars in fields other than Indology he makes repeated requests to be kept informed of new studies since such information was not available in India. Where he could obtain such works he read them with great thoroughness and commented at length on them, as for example, on Maurice Godelier's views on early societies, many of which views he endorsed. That the deepest intellectual influence on Kosambi came from the writings of Frederick Engels is evident from both his books on Indian history.[55]

Such limitations, as these may be, are marginal to the serious quality of Kosambi's work, a quality which is enhanced by the intellectual honesty with which he justifies his use of Marxist methodolgy. His was a mind which by any standards would be considered outstanding. He combined in himself the best of a rigorous Indian intellectual tradition and rejected the facile revivalism and cultural chauvinism which in recent decades have emasculated Indian thinking. In changing the paradigm Kosambi presented a view of Indian history which sought answers to the fundamental questions of how and why Indian society is what it is today. He provided a new theoretical framework which was not a mechanical application of theories derived from elsewhere but was hammered out by his proficiency in handling a variety of sources and the intellectual perceptions and originality of thought which he brought to bear on his explanations. Fresh evidence may well lead to a reconsideration of the answers which he gave to these questions but his questions and his concerns still remain valid. Even in this reconsideration we are often dependent on the leads which he initially gave and which he indicated were worth pursuing. Kosambi raised the debate on early Indian history from variations in narrative to contending theoretical formulations.

Above all he was concerned with the contemporary relevance of his understanding of the past. But he insisted that the relevance was never to serve any doctrinaire purpose;[56] rather, it should stem from what he thought was the natural function of the historian. I can only conclude with what he himself quoted as the summation of the role of the historian. E.H. Carr writes: 'The function of the historian is neither to love the past nor to emancipate himself from the past, but to master and understand it as the key to the understanding of the present. Great history is written precisely when the historian's vision of the past is illuminated by insight into problems of the present . . . . The function of history is to promote a profounder understanding of both past and present through the interrelation between them.'[57]

NOTES AND REFERENCES

1. T. Kuhn, *The Structure of Scientific Revolutions*, Chicago, 1970.
2. J. Mill, *History of British India*, London, 1918–23.
3. V. Smith, *The Oxford History of India*, Oxford, 1919.
4. D.D. Kosambi, *An Introduction to the Study of Indian History*, Bombay, 1956. Henceforth *ISIH*.
5. Ibid., pp. 1ff.
6. Ibid., pp. 5ff; 'Combined Methods in Indology', *Indo-Iranian Journal*, 1963, VI, pp. 177–202.
7. D.D. Kosambi, *The Culture and Civilisation of Ancient India in Historical Outline*, London, 1965. Henceforth *CCAIHO*.
8. 'Some Extant Versions of Bhartṛhari's *Śatakas*', *JBBRAS*, 1945, XXI, pp. 17–32; *The Śatakatrayam of Bhartṛhari with the commentary of Rāmarṣi*, ed., in collaboration with Pt. K.V. Krishnamoorthi Sharma, Anandāsrama Sanskrit Series No. 127, Poona, 1947; *The Southern Archetype of Epigrams ascribed to Bhartṛhari*, Bharatiya Vidya Series, 9,

Bombay, 1946; 'The Quality of Renunciation in Bhartṛhari's Poetry', in *Exasperating Essays,* Poona, 1857, pp. 72ff.

9. Harvard Oriental Series No. 44, Cambridge, Mass., 1956.
10. *ISIH*, p. 266.
11. 'The Avatāra Syncretism and possible sources of the Bhagavad Gītā', *JBBRAS*, 1948–9, XXIV–XXV, pp. 121–34; 'Social and Economic Aspects of the Bhagavad Gītā', in *Myth and Reality*, Bombay, 1962, pp. 12ff.
12. *Buddhist India*, London, 1903.
13. *The Social Organisation in North East India in Buddha's Time*, Calcutta, 1920.
14. *ISIH*, pp. 174, f.n.1.
15. 'Early Brahmans and Brahmanism', *JBBRAS*, 1947, XXIII, pp. 39–46; 'On the Origin of the Brahman Gotra', *JBBRAS*, 1950, XXVI, pp. 21–80. 'Brahman Clans', *JAOS*, 1953, 73, pp. 202–8.
16. J. Brough, *The Early Brahmanical System of Gotra and Pravara*, Cambridge, 1953; D.D. Kosambi, 'Brahman Clans', *JAOS*, 1953, 73, pp. 202–8.
17. T. Burrow, *The Sanskrit Language*, London, 1965; B.M. Emeneau, *Collected Papers*, Annamalai University, 1967; M.N. Deshpande and P. Hook, *Aryan and Non-Aryan in India*, Ann Arbor, 1979.
18. *ISIH*, pp. 229–30.
19. *CCAIHO*, p. 77.
20. 'Study and Methodology of Silver Punch-Marked Coins', *New Indian Antiquary*, 1941, 4, pp. 1–35 and 49–76; 'The Effect of Circulation upon Weight of Metallic Currency', *Current Science*, 1942, XI, pp. 227–30; *ISIH*, pp. 162ff.
21. 'Pilgrim's Progress: A Contribution to the Prehistory of the Western Deccan', in *Myth and Reality*, pp. 110ff.
22. *ISIH*, pp. 43ff.
23. Ibid., pp. 246ff.
24. Ibid., pp. 24ff.
25. *Sovetskaya Etnografia*, Ak. Nauk USSR, No. 1, 1958, pp. 39–57.
26. *ISIH*., pp. 24ff.
27. 'Urvaśī and Purūravas', in *Myth and Reality*, pp. 42ff.
28. 'At the Crossroads: A Study of Mother Goddess Cult Sites', *Myth and Reality*, pp. 82ff.
29. *The Origin of the Family, Private Property and the State*, London, 1946.
30. e.g. R. Briffault, *The Mothers*, New York, 1927; O.R. Ehrenfels, *Mother Right in India*, London, 1941.
31. *ISIH*, p. 27. In his letters to Professor Pierre Vidal-Naquet dated 18.9.1965 and 27.9.1965 he provides further examples of this in the wealth paid by Bhīṣma for the marriage of Pāṇḍu to Mādrī, the Madra princess, *Mahābhārata*, I.105.1. and also in the form of the marriage

of Arjuna to Subhadrā, of the Yadu tribe. I am grateful to Professor Vidal-Naquet for showing me this correspondence.

32. In the introduction to *Exasperating Essays*, Poona, 1957, pp. 3–4 and on p. 18. He says of them, 'These form a decidedly mixed category, indescribable because of the rapidly shifting views and even more rapid political permutations and combinations. The OM included at various times several factions of the CPI, the Congress Socialists, the Royists and numerous left splinter groups . . . The OM Marxism has too often consisted of theological emphasis on the inviolable sanctity of the current party line, or irrelevant quotations from the classics.'
33. Ibid., pp. 62ff.
34. Romila Thapar, 'The Study of Society in Ancient India', in *Ancient Indian Social History: Some Interpretations*, New Delhi, 1978 pp. 211ff. *See* chapter 14 in this volume.
35. *CCAIHO*, p. 41.
36. Romila Thapar, op. cit.
37. *ISIH*, pp. 176ff.
38. K.A. Chaudhuri, *Ancient Agriculture and Forestry in Northern India*, Bombay, 1977.
39. *CCAIHO*, p. 125.
40. *ISIH*, p. 244.
41. *CCAIHO*, p. 101.
42. *ISIH*, pp. 244ff.
43. Letter to Pierre Vidal-Naquet dated 4.7.1964.
44. Ibid., p. 6; see also, 'Marxism and Ancient Indian Culture'. *ABORI*, 1949, 29, pp. 271–7. Kosambi's views on his relations with the Communist Party of India over his review of Dange's book and his relations with Dange are described in his letters to Vidal Naquet dated 22.11.1963 and 4.12.1963.
45. *ISIH*, p. 187.
46. Ibid., p. 275.
47. Ibid., p. 291.
48. B. Morrison, *Political Centres and Culture Regions in Early Bengal*, Tucson, 1970.
49. *CCAIHO*, pp. 177ff.
50. *ISIH*, pp. 326ff.
51. R.S. Sharma had argued for a substantial similarity in many parts of northern India, *Indian Feudalism*, Calcutta, 1965.
52. An example of the analysis of this role can be found in H. Kulke, *Jagannatha Kult und Gajapati Konigtam*, Wiesbaden, 1979.
53. M. Finley, *The World of Odysseus*, was first published in 1954. The fact that he was initially working in the United States would at that time have made his books less easily available in India. Kosambi refers

to his study *Ancient Greeks* as being most stimulating, but not to his more acclaimed work on the Greek epics.

54. The easy availability of English translations has helped in this, such translations resulting mainly from the interest in Neo-Marxism on the part of American radicals and academics. It is significant that some of the most stimulating debates on precapitalist societies emanating from new Marxist writing are to be found in the issues of the last fifteen years of *Current Anthropology* and *American Anthropologist*.
55. A view put forward in the course of a conversation by Charles Malamoud (who translated *CCAIHO* into French) and with which view I am in agreement. In a letter to Vidal-Naquet dated 4.6.1964 Kosambi writes, 'I learned from these two great men [Marx and Engels] what questions to ask and then went to fieldwork to find the answers, because the material did not exist in published books'.
56. *CCAIHO*, p. 24.
57. *What is History?*, pp. 20, 31, 62.

4

# Early India: An Overview*

The scope of ancient Indian history is undergoing modification and the erstwhile ancient period, which stretched from Harappan times to the early second millennium AD is now being subdivided into the ancient and the early medieval period. The nomenclature 'early medieval' does little towards either explaining itself or the subsequent medieval period: but the differentiation between pre-Gupta and post-Gupta history is a necessary and welcome change as also is the continuity between the late first millennium and the second millennium AD.

Harappan society remains enigmatic. There have been few attempts at detailed reconstruction from the archaeological evidence. This is in part because the variety of data required from studies such as palaeo-botany, ecology and hydrology remains limited for such a reconstruction and partially also because there are few archaeologists working on India willing to attempt a theoretical reconstruction in which the use of concepts from other disciplines such as anthropology, demography and statistics would be a prerequisite.[1] Such a reconstruction is especially required with the fading of the so-called 'dark age' between the Harappa Culture and subsequent societies.[2] The question as to how far Vedic society is entirely Indo-Aryan or draws on the Harappan tradition in language, ritual and institutions becomes even more apposite than before.[3]

It is in the study of the many sub-periods within the broad boundaries of the ancient period that fundamental questions arise, providing scope for wide-ranging discussion. For a better definition of these sub-periods and in the interests of historical clarity a considerable refining of concepts and theories becomes necessary.

* General President's Address — Indian History Congress. Burdwan, 1983. Published in Proceedings of the Indian History Congress, 1–22.

Many of the crucial terms used in the definitions have been applied to such diverse social forms that they cease to have a specific meaning and tend to mask the diversities. This sharpening of focus becomes particularly necessary with the growing interest in social and economic history. It will also help in understanding the process of historical mutation over time. Although there is now a rich literature describing segments of the period, the explanation of change from one to the next and the linkages between these require a fuller consideration. A creatively critical discussion is called for on the terms used to translate categories mentioned in the sources since much of the interpretation depends on such discussion.

The nineteenth century was the age of the grand edifices of historical explanation and theoretical construction. While some of these edifices still stand firm, others are tottering. Even those which still stand often require repair and renovation, sometimes of a structural kind, in the light of new knowledge and fresh theories. The refining of concepts and theories therefore becomes a necessary part of the historical exercise and is particularly incumbent on those who, as conscientious historians, build their explanations on the basis of theoretical frameworks.[4] It is of this need for the refining of concepts that I would like to speak.[5]

Among the early sub-periods, Vedic society has been described as tribal. The term 'tribal', which we have all used in the past, has rightly come in for some questioning.[6] In its precise meaning it refers to a community of people claiming descent from a common ancestor. In its application however, it has been used to cover a variety of social and economic forms, not to mention claims to biological and racial identities; and this tends to confuse the original meaning. Even as a convention it has lost much of its precision. The more recently preferred term, lineage, narrows the focus. Although the economic range remains, lineage does emphasize succession and descent with the implication that these are decisive in determining social status and control over economic resources. It also helps differentiate between chiefships where lineage dominates, and kingship, which as a different category, evokes a larger number of impersonal sanctions. The concept of *vaṃśa* (succession) carries a meaning similar to lineage and is central to Vedic and epic society with its emphasis on succession even as a simulated lineage. Thus *vaṃśa* is used to mean lineage or descent group among the *rājanyas* and *kṣatriyas* but is also used in the list of Upaniṣadic teachers where succession does not appear to be by birth but by the passing on of a tradition of knowledge.[7] Lineage also becomes important in the structure of each *varṇa*, defined by permitted rules of marriage and kinship and by ranking in an order of status, the control over resources being implicit. In this sense the emergence of the four *varṇas* is closely allied to the notions of a lineage-based society.[8]

In a stratified society the reinforcing of status is necessary. But where there is no recognized private property in land and no effective state such reinforcing has to be done by sanctions which often take a ritual or religious form. In the absence of taxation as a system of control in the society of the Vedic corpus, sacrificial ritual functioned as the occasion for renewing the status of the *yajamāna*, initially a *rājanya* or a *kṣatriya*. Apart from its religious and social role sacrificial ritual also had an economic function. It was the occasion when wealth which had been channelled to the *yajamāna* was distributed by him in the form of gifts to the *brāhmaṇa* priests which strengthened their social rank and ensured them wealth. The ritual served to restrict the distribution of wealth to the *brāhmaṇas* and the *kṣatriyas* but at the same time prevented a substantial accumulation of wealth by either, for whatever came in the form of gifts and prestations from the lesser clans, the *viś*, to the ruling clans, the *kṣatriyas*, was largely consumed in the ritual and the remainder gifted to the *brāhmaṇas*. Generosity being important to the office of the chief, wealth was not hoarded. The display, consumption and distribution of wealth at the major rituals such as the *rājasūya* and the *aśvamedha*, was in turn a stimulus to production, for the ritual was also seen as a communication with and sanction from, the supernatural. Embedded in the sacrificial ritual therefore were important facets of the economy. This may be a partial explanation of why a major change to the state system and a peasant economy occurred initially in the mid-first millennium BC not in the western Ganga valley but in the adjoining area of the middle Ganga valley. This change was occasioned not only by an increase in economic production and a greater social disparity but also by the fact that the prestation economy associated with the lineage-based society became more and more marginal in the latter region and in some areas was altogether absent.

The term 'peasant economy' is frowned upon by some scholars as an imprecise concept.[9] However it is of some use as a measurement of change. The label of 'peasant' has been applied to a variety of categories some of which are dissimilar. The use of a single word as a portmanteau description confuses the categories and therefore a differentiation is necessary. Eric Wolf at one point defines peasants as:

> . . . rural cultivators whose surpluses are transferred to a dominant group of rulers that uses the surpluses both to underwrite its own standard of living and to distribute the remainder to groups in society that do not farm but must be fed for their specific goods and services in turn.[10]

This definition seems to me inadequate even in terms of Wolf's study of peasants. The important point is not merely the existence of a surplus but the mechanism by which it is transferred and it is to this that I would relate the emergence of a peasant economy. That the recognition of an incipient peasant economy in various parts of India is significant to the study of social history hardly needs stressing, since, concomitant with this is also the establishing of particular kinds of state systems, variant forms of *jātis* and new religious and cultural idioms in the area.

For the early period of Indian history the term peasant has been used to translate both the Ṛgvedic *viś*[11] as well as the *gahapati* of Pāli sources. But some distinction is called for. The Vedic *viś* was primarily a member of a clan although this did not preclude him from being a cultivator as well. The transferring of surpluses, in this case the voluntary prestations of the *viś* to the *kṣatriya*, points to a stratified rather than an egalitarian society and the simile of the *kṣatriya* eating the *viś* like the deer eating the grain[12] would indicate greater pressures for larger prestations. But the transfer was not through an enforced system of taxation. In the absence of private ownership of land, the relationship of the *viś* to the *kṣatriya* would have been less contrapuntal with little need of an enforced collection of the surplus. The context of Vedic references to *bali*, *bhāga* and *śulka* (the terms used in later periods for taxes) suggest that they were voluntary and random although the randomness gradually changed to required prestations, particularly at sacrificial rituals. However the three major prerequisites governing a system of taxation — a contracted amount, collected at stipulated periods by persons designated as tax collectors — are absent in the Vedic corpus. The recognition of these prerequisites in the post-Vedic period and the collection of taxes from the cultivators by the state would seem decisive in registering the change from cultivators to peasants in which the existence of an economy based on peasant agriculture becomes clear.

The introduction of taxation presupposes the impersonal authority of the state and some degree of alienation of the cultivator from the authority to whom the surplus is given, unlike the lineage-based society where prestations are more personalized. Taxation reduced the quantity of prestations and became the more substantial part of what was taken from the peasant, but prestations were not terminated. The sanction of the religious ritual becomes more marginal and that of the state more central, the change occurring gradually over time. The formation of the state is therefore tied into this change. For the cultivator land becomes property or a legal entity and the pressures on cultivation have to do not only with subsistance but also with a provision for ensuring a surplus. This highlights the difference between appropriation in the earlier system and exploitation in the latter.

The Vedic *viś* was more a generalized term in which herding, cultivation and minimal crafts adequate to a household were included. Such groups were germane to the later peasant household. In effect, because the relationship with the dominant *kṣatriya* was based on gifts and prestations rather than on taxes, these cultivators would seem part of a lineage society in which their subservience to a dominant group arises more out of the exigencies of kinship or the ordering of clans than out of exploited labour, although the latter can be seen to increase in time.

The gradual mutation which took place becomes evident from the frequent references in the Pāli sources to the *gahapati*. The existence of the *gahapati* focuses more sharply on the presence of what might be called a peasant economy. But to translate *gahapati* as peasant is to provide a mere slice of its total meaning. Derived from *gṛhapati*, the head of the household, the term *gahapati* includes a range of meanings such as, the wealthy *mahāśālā-brāhmaṇas* addressed as *gahapatis* by the Buddha,[13] who had received as donations extensive, tax-free, arable land as well as those who paid taxes — the wealthy land-owners who cultivated their large farms with the help of slaves and hired labourers (*dāsa-bhṛtaka*).[14] Those at the lower end of the scale who either owned small plots of land or were professional ploughmen are more often referred to as the *kassakas*.[15] An intermediate group is also implied in one of the *Dharmaśūtras*.[16] The *Arthaśāstra* mentions tenants as *upavāsa* and also refers to another category, the *śūdra* cultivators settled by the state on cultivable or waste land on a different system of tenure from the above; as also the range of cultivators employed on the state farms supervised by the overseers of agriculture, the *sītādhyakṣa*.[17]

*Gahapati* with reference to agrarian society, therefore, is perhaps better translated as the landowner of some substance who would generally pay taxes to the state except when the land which he owned was a religious benefice. Private land ownership and the payment of taxes demarcates this period as one in which a peasant-based economy is evident. Traces of the lineage based society continued in the marking of status by *varṇa* and the performance, although by now of marginal economic significance, of the sacrificial rituals.

That the *gahapati* was not even just a landowner but more a man of means is supported by the fact that it was from the ranks of the *gahapatis* that there emerged the *seṭṭhis* or financiers.[18] The two terms are often associated in the literature and this is further attested in the votive inscriptions recording donations to the *saṅgha* in central India and the western and eastern Deccan from the late first millennium BC.[19] *Gahapati* fathers have *seṭṭhi* sons as well as the other way round. It would seem that *gahapati* status was acquired through the practice of any respectable profession which provided a decent income, although the most frequent references are to land-ownership and commerce.

This is not to suggest that trade originated with the land-owning groups but rather that the large-scale commercialiaztion of exchange was tied to the emergence of the *gahapati*. In examining the origins of trade it is necessary to define more clearly the nature of the exchange involved. Broadly, there are some recognizable forms of exchange which can either develop into commercialized exchange or supplement it. There is evidence of luxury goods exchanged by ruling groups as a part of gift-exchange. Marriage alliances between *kṣatriya* families involved an exchange of gifts. Thus when Bharata visits his maternal kinsmen, he returns with gifts.[20] This is not an exchange based on need but is a channel through which status and kinship is confirmed. It may in addition lead to other forms of exchange. The major royal sacrifices required tributes and gifts and the *rājasūya* of Yudhiṣṭhira provides an interesting inventory of valued items.[21] The more ordinary sacrificial rituals involved the giving of gifts such as cattle, horses, gold, *dāsīs* and chariots by the *yajamāna* to the priests.[22] These gifts became part of a distribution and exchange of wealth which in the lineage based societies formed the salient part of the wealth of those who ruled, whereas in the change to an economy based on peasant agriculture, they were merely a part of the wealth accumulated by the ruling families and the more wealthy *gahapatis*.

Less spectacular but more essential was another form of exchange, that of raw materials and commodities brought by itinerant groups such as smiths and pastoralists. It has been argued that the itinerant metal smiths formed a network of connections between villages.[23] Metal, particularly iron, was also a major item of regular trade. The role of pastoralists in trading circuits is now coming in for considerable attention particularly with reference to those groups which had a regular pattern of transhumance.[24] Exchange through sources of itinerant professionals was probably the starting point of the beat of pedlars which is a continuing feature of one level of exchange in India.

Yet another category is what might be called exchange between one settlement and the next. This is a useful basis for plotting the gradual diffusion of an item, as for example, the better quality varieties of pottery from excavations. Such an exchange provides evidence not only on local trade but also on the geographical reach of intra-regional contacts. Some of these settlements may then have come to play the role of local markets, the equivalent perhaps of what the Pāli texts refer to as *nigama*. These in turn are likely to have been the nuclei of urban growth as in the case of Rājagṛha and Śrāvastī.[25]

Distinct from all these is the familiar picture of trade which dominates the scene in the post-Mauryan period. This is the commercial exchange between two or more centres, processing and producing commodities specifically destined for trade. The organization of this more complex form involved a hierarchy of producers and traders some of whom were sedentary while others were carriers of the items traded but of a different order from pedlars and pastoralists. The picture of commercialized exchange emerges from Buddhist texts and by the time of the *Arthaśāstra*, it is regarded as a legitimate source of revenue for the state. The question then arose of the degree of state interference and control which would be conducive to increasing the finances of the state.[26] The major artefact in this trade (other than the commodities) is coined metallic money, providing evidence of the degree of complexity and the extent of such trade and trading circuits. These early coins in some instances were issued by the *nigama* and in other cases may have been issued by local authorities or possibly by ruling families. In the post-Mauryan period dynastic issues gain currency, a clear pointer to the importance of commercialized exchange. However even in this period local issues remain in circulation suggesting multiple levels of exchange.

With such commercialized exchange the control of trade routes becomes a significant factor in political policy and military annexations. A recent analysis of the Silk Trade, involving a variety of levels of exchange from gift-exchange to sophisticated emporia, in the context of political relations between tribal groups and established centres of political power, suggests ways in which the complicated question of trade, often treated as a uniform monolith by historians of ancient India, may be investigated.[27] The trade between the Roman empire and India, as is clear from both commodities and the function of money, also spans a similar range. Diverse forms of exchange suggest the coexistence of various economic levels within larger trading systems and sharpen the social contours of the groups involved.

The analysis of trade also requires locating those involved in these exchanges in the social hierarchy of the time. In the production of goods for exchange, artisans, whether individuals or in guilds, relate to merchants and financiers in forms as diverse as the various categories of cultivators to land-owners. The role of the *śilpìn* (artisan) and the *śreṇī* (guild) is quite distinct from the *seṭṭhi*. Their presence registers a change in the nature of the trade as also does the differentiation between categories of professionals such as the *vānija*, the *seṭṭhi* and the *sārthavāha*. Clearly there is a sea change when commercialized exchange becomes active. The investment required for an elaborate trade can only be provided by a well-endowed social group which can invest its surplus in risk-taking ventures. The obvious category was the *gahapati* who could fall back on land if the venture failed. That it turned out to be highly successful is clear from the fact that not only did the *seṭṭhis* emerge from the ranks of the *gahapatis*, but, by the post-Mauryan period, had an independent identity as financiers and gradually superceded the *gahapatis*.[28] The wealth of the *seṭṭhis* became in turn an avenue to power, for some of them were known to be the financiers of kings and obtained in return rights to collect revenue, perhaps the prototype of what was later to become the regular form of emoluments to administrative officers.[29] On the manifestations of trade, Buddhist and Jaina sources together with epigraphic and archaeological evidence provide a useful counterpoint to the *Dharmaśāstra* literature.

The link between agriculture and commerce is important for understanding the changes in the subsequent period. The opulence of those involved in commerce was poured into the adornment of religious monuments, monasteries and images and in the conspicuous consumption which is associated with the wealthier town-dwellers of these times. This tends to obscure the agrarian scene where one notices less of *mahāśālā* landowners and large estates and more of those with small holdings. Small plots of land could be purchased and donated to religious beneficiaries and it seems unlikely, as has been argued, that such sales were restricted to religious donations.[30] Smallholdings together with the alienation of land could point to some degree of impoverishment among peasants. The inclusion of debt bondage (*āhitaka* and *ātma-vikreta*), as a regular if not frequent category of slavery,[31] as well as the increasing references to *viṣṭi* (forced labour or a labour tax), suggest a different rural scene from that of the preceding period. That oppressive taxation had become a recognized evil is explicitly mentioned in various texts.[32]

This mutation was endemic to the evident change in the post-Gupta period. Where trade flourished there the resources of the urban centres and the trade routes bouyed up the system; but this period points to a declining trade in some areas.[33] Internal commercialized trade requires the ballast of agrarian settlements and where lineage based societies could be converted into peasant economies there the agrarian support to trade would be strengthened. Earlier networks of exchange had permitted an easier co-existence with lineage based societies. Their resources, generally raw materials such as timber and gem-stones could, as items of exchange, be easily tapped by traders through barter and direct exchange without disturbing the social structure to any appreciable degree. On the other hand because of the requirement of land and labour, state systems more heavily dependent on a peasant economy had to absorb these societies and convert them into peasant economies in order to extract the benefits. Where trade declined or where new states were established the need to develop the agrarian economy became urgent. The granting of land appears to have been the mechanism adopted for changing the agrarian situation. The reasons for this change in the post-Gupta period need more detailed investigation particularly at a regional level.[34] In the very useful work done so far substantial data has surfaced. What is now required is a sifting and classifying of the data to provide more precise answers and to evoke fresh questions.[35]

It is curious that there is little resort to the policy recommended by the *Arthaśāstra* and other texts of establishing colonies of cultivators on land owned by the state so as to extend agriculture and thereby increase the revenue.[36] Was the state unable to do so because it lacked the administrative infrastructure or was it because it did not have the power to implement such a policy? Instead the state increases the grants of land to religious beneficiaries and later to administrative officers in lieu of a salary. This points to a need for an evaluation of the nature of 'early medieval' states with the possibility that their formation and structure were different from the previous ones. Was this type of state attempting to restructure the economy to an extent greater than the previous which appear to have been more concerned with revenue collecting functions, judging by the model advocated by Kauṭilya? Did the system of granting land predominate (perhaps initially) in areas where lineage based societies were prevalent so as to facilitate their conversion to a peasant economy (where lineage could also be used for economic control) and to a *varṇa* and *jāti* network? The identification with *varṇa* status would have acted as a bridge to a peasant economy and prevented a rupture with the lineage system. Elements of lineage have often continued even in some areas where peasant agriculture became the norm.

Religious benefices were on the pattern of earlier grants and were not strictly an innovation except that now grants were made increasingly to *brāhmaṇas* and ostensibly in return for legitimizing the dynasty and for acquiring religious merit.[37] These were the stated reasons for the grant but were not sufficient reasons. Grants of this nature, as has been pointed out, were a channel of acculturation. They could also be used as foci of political loyalty.

If the grants were made initially from state-owned lands they amounted to a renouncing of revenue. If some states had problems with administering the extension of agriculture, did they introduce the system of grants to encourage settlements in new areas where the grant was of waste land, or alternatively, of cultivated lands, to stabilize the peasantry and induce increased production? Given the fact that slaves were not used in any major quantitative degree in agricultural production at this time, was the system of grants an attempt at converting the peasantry into a stable productive force through various mechanisms of subordination and a chain of intermediaries? Interestingly the term *gahapati/gṛhapati* drops out of currency for the system had changed and terms incorporating *rājā*, *sāmanta* and *bhogin* become frequent. The recipients of land grants had the right to receive a range of taxes and dues previously collected by the state and were soon given administrative powers as well. This permitted them to act as a 'back-up' administration where the grant was in settled areas and to introduce the system where new settlements were being established. It may in origin have been a fiscal measure but in effect became the means of controlling the peasantry. The apparent increase in debt bondage and the fear of peasant migration would point to this being one of the functions of the large-scale grants. That the possibility of peasant migration to alleviate discontent was being slowly stifled is suggested by the fact of peasants taking to revolt as well from the early second millennium onwards.[38] A rise in brigandage may well have been a possibility for this period.[39] A qualitative change occurs when the state begins to grant villages or substantial acreages of land already under cultivation; a change which reflects both on the economy and on the nature of the state.

The need to fetter the peasantry would seem an evident departure from the earlier system and this in turn introduced a change in the relationship between the cultivator and the land now riveted in legalities and liabilities, with tax or rent no longer being the sole criterion of a peasant economy. The *karṣaka* of this period found himself in a different situation from the *kassaka* of earlier times. The term 'peasant' therefore cannot have a blanket usage or meaning since the variations within it have to be distinguished.

The secular grantees were part of a hierarchical system in which they mirrored the court at the local level. This is evident from their attempts to imitate the courtly style as depicted in the art and literature of the time. Grants of land to the *brāhmaṇas* as the major religious grantees rehabilitated them to a position of authority and their anguished invocation of Kalki as a millennial figure becomes less urgent.[40] A new religious ideology gained popularity focusing on the image and the temple and asserting an assimilative quality involving the cults and rituals of Purāṇic Hinduism and the genesis of the *bhakti* tradition. Ideological assimilation is called for when there is a need to knit together socially diverse groups. It is also crucial when there is an increase in the distancing between such groups as well as the power of some over others and the economic disparity between them. The significance of these new cults and sects may lie in part in the focus on loyalty to a deity which has a parallel to the loyalty of peasants and others to an overlord. But it would be worth examining the rudiments of each sect in its regional dimension, its grouping towards a *jāti* status and the use of an ostensibly cultural and religious idiom to express a new social identity. Were these also mechanisms for legitimizing territorial identities drawing on sacred geography and pilgrimage routes with the temple as the focal point?[41] The egalitarian emphases of the devotees in the eyes of the deity has rightly been viewed as the assertion of those lower down the social scale in favour of a more egalitarian society. But its significance grows when the social background to this belief is one of increasing disparity. Movements of dissent which had religious forms were often gradually accommodated and their radical content slowly diluted. The move away from community participation in a ritual to a personalized and private worship encourages the notion of individual freedom, even if it is only at the ideological level.

In the justifiable emphasis on social and economic history there has been too frequently a neglect among historians of the analysis of ideology. To study ideology without its historical context is to practice historical hydroponics, for ideas and beliefs strike roots in the humus of historical reality. To restrict the study of a society to its narrowly social and economic forms alone is to see it in a limited two-dimensional profile. The interaction of society and ideology takes a varied pattern and to insist always on the primacy of the one over the other is to deny the richness of a full-bodied historical explanation.

Ideas are sometimes analysed as a response to social pressures and needs. This is particularly pertinent for those dealing with social history. Some of the more important literature is suffused with a theoretical representation of society even in symbolic or ideational forms. Meanings very often do not stem from just the vocabulary but require familiarity with the cultural context of the word. Examples of this would be the levels of meaning of words such as *varṇa* and *jāti* as they travel through time in texts such as the *Dharmaśāstras*. The ideological layers in the latter as codes of behaviour have to be peeled in order to obtain a better comprehension of their ordering of society.

Central to any concern with ideology in the ancient past is the critique of religious thought (as distinct from religious practice or organization). Some analyses of the *Upaniṣads* for instance, can provide an interesting example of this. One of the major strands in Upaniṣadic thought is said to be a secret doctrine known only to a few *kṣatriyas* who teach it to select, trusted *brāhmaṇas*.[42] Even the learned among the latter, the *mahāśālā mahāśrotriyāḥ*, are described as going to the *kṣatriyas* for instruction.[43] The doctrine involves the idea of the soul, the *ātman* and its ultimate merging with the *brahman* as well as metempsychosis or the transmigration of the soul: in fact a fundamental doctrine of this age which was to have far-reaching consequences on Indian society. That it should have been secret and originally associated with the *kṣatriyas* raises many questions, some of which have been discussed by scholars.[44] It is true that the *brāhmaṇas* and the *kṣatriyas* were both members of the 'leisured classes' in Vedic society and could therefore indulge in idealistic philosophy and discourse on the niceties of life after death. But this is only a partial answer and much more remains to be explained. Was the ritual of sacrifice so deeply imprinted on the *brāhmaṇa* mind and so necessary to the profession at this point that it required non-*brāhmaṇas* to introduce alternatives to salvation, other than the sacrificial ritual? The adoption of meditation and theories of transmigration had the advantage of releasing the *kṣatriyas* from the pressures of a prestation economy and permitting them to accumulate wealth, power and leisure. Alternatively, was the accumulation of these already present in the fringe areas, described as the *mlecha-deśa* (impure lands) in the Vedic corpus, where the sacrificial rituals for various reasons had become less important? Thus Janaka of Mithilā, Aśvapati Kaikeya and Ajātaśatru of Kāśī could reflect on alternative ways to salvation. This also places a different emphasis on the function of the *kṣatriya* who had now ceased to be primarily a cattle-raiding, warrior chief.

These are not the only kinds of connections relevant to a history of the period. Upper and lower status groups or even classes treated as monolithic, belie social reality. The tensions within these should also be noticed where the evidence suggests this. The competition for status between *brāhmaṇas* and *kṣatriyas* and the separation of their functions, as well as their mutual dependence, is symbolized in the sacrificial ritual which becomes a key articulation of the relationship. The new belief was the reversal of the sacrificial ritual in that it required neither priests nor deities but only self-discipline and meditation. At another level, the transmigrating of the soul through the natural elements and plants to its ultimate rebirth, carries an echo of shamanism which may have remained popular outside priestly ritual.

There is in the new belief the first element of a shift from the clan to the individual in as much as the sacrificial ritual involves the clan but meditation and self-discipline, perhaps in opposition to the clan, involves only the individual. It symbolizes the breaking away of the individual from the clan. It also introduces an element of anomie which becomes more apparent in the later development of these beliefs by various sects. These reflections were seminal to what became a major direction in Indian thought and action, the opting out of the individual from society and where renunciation is a method of self-discovery but can also carry a message of dissent.[45] That the new ideas were attributed to the *kṣatriyas* and yet included in a brahmanical text was probably because for the *brāhmaṇas* to author a doctrine openly questioning the sacrificial ritual would, at this stage, have been an anomaly. That the doctrine stimulated philosophical discussion would in itself have required that it be recorded. But its inclusion may also partially have been motivated by the fact that when the doctrine was appropriated by heterodox teachers such as the Buddha, it could be maintained that even the roots of heterodoxy stemmed from the Vedic tradition. This was to become yet another technique by which orthodox theory in subsequent centuries sought to disguise ideas contradicting its own position. The Buddha not only democratized the doctrine[46] but also nurtured the idea of *karma* and *saṃsāra* and related it, among other things, to social inequities. But his negation of the soul (*ātman*) introduces a contradiction of the doctrine as visualized in the *Upaniṣads*. Such theoretical contradictions were current at this time.[47] The positing of a thesis and an anti-thesis becomes a characteristic feature of philosophical debate and is reflected both in empirical disciplines such as grammar as well as in more abstract analysis.[48]

The relating of ideology to historical reality can result not only in new ways of examining a historical situation and be used to extend or modify the analysis from other sources but can also help in confirming the reality as derived from other sources. (It might also stir the still waters of contemporary interpretations of early Indian thought). Such a study, incorporating elements of deconstruction, would sharpen the awareness of concepts and theoretical frameworks. Historical explanation then becomes an enterprise in which the refinements of concepts and theories are a constant necessity, not only because of the availability of fresh evidence from new sources but also because of greater precision in our understanding of the categories which we use to analyse these sources. It is a bi-focal situation where the frame of reference provided by the analysis of ideology remains the distant view while the historian's use of a theoretical explanation of the data indicates the closer reading.

## Notes and References

1. An exception to this is the recent study of Harappan and West Asian trade by Shereen Ratnagar, *Encounters: The Westerly Trade of the Harappan Civilisation*, Delhi, 1981. A primary requirement relating to ecology and hydrology would be a series of studies along the lines of those Robert MacAdams on Mesopotamia, particularly *The Heartland of Cities*, Chicago, 1981. Evidence from other disciplines can be utilized more effectively through a larger input of scientific techniques into excavation and analyses as well as data gathered from such disciplines. This may well happen in the near future now that archaeology the world over is drawing increasingly on scientific sources and less on the study of the classics. This calls for a little more theoretical daring on the part of archaeologists working on India and a concern with questions relating to the nature of Harappan society. The decipherment of the Harappa script, still a long way off, would of course be a help and would involve using the more conventional techniques of linguistics and cultural symbols. But the reconstruction of Harappan society could be met half-way by an approach which tries to intelligently reconstitute the society on the basis of material remains, environment and ecology. That the interest in ecology and environment does not have a relevance limited to archaeological data

alone is clear from the recent Harris-versus-Heston debate on why the cow is sacred in India. M. Harris, 'The Cultural Ecology of India's Sacred Cattle', *Current Anthropology*, 1966, 7, pp. 51–60; A. Heston, 'An Approach to the Sacred cow of India', *Current Anthropology*, 1971, 12, pp. 191–209; S. Odend'hal, 'Energetics of Indian Cattle in their Environment', *Human Ecology*, 1973, I.I. pp. 3–22.

2. Archaeological continuities are being discovered between Harappan and post-Harappan societies, as for example, in the repeated occurrence of the Black-and-red Wares from Harappan to proto-historic times and more recently the overlap in the Punjab between Late Harappan and the Painted Grey Ware culture (associated by some with Vedic society) J.P. Joshi and Madhubala, 'Life During the Period of Overlap of Late Harappan and PGW Cultures', *Journal of the Indian Society of Oriental Art*, 1977–78, NS, IX, pp. 20–9.
3. Romila Thapar, 'The Archaeology of the Agnicayana', in F. Staal (ed.), *AGNI — The Vedic Ritual of the Fire Altar*, vol. I, Berkeley, 1982. *See* chapter 15 in this volume.
4. In the refining of concepts and theories the comparative method can be a useful tool. This involves an awareness of the historical analyses of other cultures and the use of specific categories of explanation which may not be directly applicable to early Indian history, but which would nevertheless generate questions and comparisons which can in turn assist in fresh analysis. It is to be deeply regretted that serious expertise on the ancient history of areas outside the Indian sub-continent is generally unavailable in Indian centres of research.
5. I have elsewhere analysed in greater detail some of the themes which I am touching upon here. Questions relating to lineage-based societies, the sacrificial ritual and the peasant economy were considered by me in *From Lineage to State*. A summary of these ideas was contained in a paper, 'State Formation in Early India', *International Social Science Journal*, 1980, XXXII, no. 4, pp. 655–69.
6. M.H. Fried, *The Notion of Tribe*, Menlo Park, 1975.
7. *Bṛhadāraṇyaka Upaniṣad*, II.6.1ff; IV.6.1ff; VI.5.1ff.
8. Romila Thapar, *From Lineage to State*, pp. 37–69.
9. J. Ennew et al., 'Peasantry as an Economic Category', *Journal of Peasant Studies*, 1977, IV, 4, pp. 295–322; M. Harrison, 'The Peasant Mode of Production in the work of A.V. Chayanov', *Journal of Peasant Studies*, 1977, IV, 4, pp. 323–36; Utsa Patnaik, 'Neo-Populism and Marxism: The Chayanovian View of the Agrarian Question and its Fundamental Fallacy', *Journal of Peasant Studies*, 1979, VI, 4, pp. 375–420.
10. E. Wolf, *Peasants*, New Jersey, 1966, pp. 3–4.
11. This was popularized through A.A. Macdonell and A.B. Keith's *Vedic Index of Names and Subjects*, 1912. The technical term for the cultivator

was *kīnāśa* and the root *kṛṣ* is used more frequently in association with cultivation.

12. *Śatapatha Brāhmaṇa*, VIII.7.1.2; VIII.7.2.2; IX.4.3.5.
13. e.g. *Majjhima Nikāya*, I.401.
14. As for example the *gahapati* Meṇḍaka, *Mahāvagga*, VI.34.
15. *Dīgha Nikāya*, I.61; *Saṁyukta Nikāya*, I.172; III.155; IV.314; *Aṅguttara Nikāya*, I.241; 229; 239.
16. The *Baudhāyana Dharmasūtra*, III.2. 1–4 refers to householders of the upper *varṇas* who can in some cases be tenants and who cultivate six *nivartanas* (*bīghās*) of land. These were not poor peasants for they are also described as *śālina*, living in well-to-do homes, and would probably constitute an intermediary category between the *gahapati* and the *kassaka*. That this was a recognized category seems evident from their mode of subsistence being described as *ṣannivartana* (six *nivartanas*).
17. III.10.8; II.1.1.
18. *Aṅguttara Nikāya*, IV.282; VIII.1.16.
19. *Epigraphia Indica*, X.1909–10. Lüders List Nos 1056, 1062, 1073, 1075, 1121, 1127, 1209, 1281, etc. The inscriptions are later than the Pāli texts and may indicate the repetition of a process which had occurred earlier in the Ganga valley.
20. *Rāmāyaṇa*, VII.90.1–5. Among the gifts were horses, probably imported from Gandhāra which was close enough to the Kekeya territory. The trade in horses from the north-west would doubtless have been accelerated by such forms of exchange. Romila Thapar, 'The *Rāmāyaṇa*: Theme and Variation', in S.N. Mukherjee (ed.), *India History and Thought*, Calcutta, 1982, pp. 221–53. *See* chapter 30 in this volume.
21. *Mahābhārata*, Sabhā Parvan, 47.5; Romila Thapar, 'Some Aspects of the Economic Data in the Mahābhārata', *ABORI*, Poona, 1977–8, LIX, pp. 993–1007; 'The Historian and the Epic', *ABORI*, 1979, LX, pp. 199–213. *See* chapter 29 in this volume.
22. Romila Thapar, '*Dāna* and *Dakṣinā* as Forms of Exchange', *Ancient Indian Social History: Some Interpretations*, pp. 105ff. *See* chapter 24 in this volume.
23. D.D. Kosambi, *Introduction to the Study of Indian History*, Bombay, 1956. pp. 11, 91.
24. Apart from the question of whether or not the Ṛgvedic Aryan speakers introduced iron technology to northern India, it would be worth examining whether as pastoralists there were patterns of movement which permitted them to maintain a symbiotic relationship with pre-existing agricultural communities. This would perhaps explain the factor of bi-lingualism in Vedic Sanskrit.

25. N. Wagle, *Society at the Time of the Buddha*, Bombay, 1966, p. 22.
26. *Arthaśāstra*, IV.2.
27. M.C. Raschke, 'New Studies in Roman Commerce with the East', in H. Temporim and W. Haase (eds), *Aufsteig und Niedergang der Romischen Welt*, Berlin, 1978. The Silk Trade spanning Central Asia, northern India and the eastern Mediterranean drew on a variety of exchange systems and Raschke's discussion on the role of silk as part of the exchange of gifts in Central Asia provides a new perspective on that section of the trade. An almost graphic representation of the varieties of exchange comes from the recent discoveries of rock engravings and inscriptions, the latter from the Kuṣāna period onwards along the Karakorum Highway in Gilgit. K. Jettmar, *Rock Carvings and Inscriptions in the Northern Areas of Pakistan*, Islamabad, 1982; A.H. Dani, *Chilas*, Islamabad, 1983.
28. I. Fiser, 'The Problem of the Seṭṭhi in Buddhist Jātakas', *Archiv Orientali*, Prague, 1954, XXII, pp. 238–66.
29. Ibid., p. 261.
30. The *Arthaśāstra* refers clearly to the sale of land. II.1.7; III.9.3, 15–17; III.10.9.
31. *Arthaśāstra*, III.2.; Nārada, I.128; V.29; Manu, XI.59.
32. *Viṣṇu Purāṇa*, IV.24; *Mahāsupina Jātaka* No. 77; *Mahābhārata* Aranyaka Parvan, 188.18ff; Śānti Parvan, 254. 39ff.
33. That the external trade — the Silk Trade and the Roman trade — played a significant role in northern India is also clear from the negative evidence. Areas where trade declined as in the Ganga valley shows a decline in the urban economy which has been pointed out by R.S. Sharma. Areas on the northern borders of the sub-continent, arterial to the Central Asian trade flourished in the post-Gupta period as did those in peninsula India.
34. A comparative regional analysis has become necessary with the recognition not only of regional environmental differences but also variations in the processes of change and the nature of change, particularly the fact that not all changes coincide chronologically and completely in form. This makes the study of regional history significant not only in terms of regional variations but also as a prerequisite to broader generalisations about the history of the sub-continent.
35. This work ties in with the debate on feudalism in India, and studies of this period such as those of D.D. Kosambi, R.S. Sharma, B.N.S. Yadava, B.D. Chattopadhyaya, D.N. Jha and H. Mukhia, in addition to many detailed regional studies of the post-Gupta period, too numerous to list here.

Much of the argument on the debate on feudalism in India so far has been of a generalized form. Perhaps what is required at this stage is comparative regional views which could better cope with the areas of investigation which call for analysis. Initially a few selected regions could be analysed in depth for both the urban and the agrarian aspects of the economy, but a start could be made with the agrarian. A tabulation of the data might sharpen the focus. Grants in a region could be classified in accordance with the type of grantee and the nature of the grant. Categories could be defined such as grants of waste land or cultivated land, grants converting lineage-based societies into peasant economies where the grant would be made to the lineage chief, or grants of state-owned lands already cultivated where cultivators were transferred along with the land, and other such categories where data is available. The chronological order and quantum of each would be useful information. Proprietory rights could also be part of this tabulation. At another level the analyses of the titles of grantees and changes therein might provide clues. The question of whether the peasantry was free hinges not only on the technical and legal definitions but also requires a discussion of the actual status of the peasant. Rights, obligations and dues of the grantees vis-à-vis the peasants would need to be tabulated in detail. These would provide some indications of the essentials of the prevailing system.

A worms's eye view of agriculture also needs to be investigated since some aspects of the debate involve questions relating to soil fertility and control over water resources. Some of these questions could be better handled through inter-disciplinary research if historians were to work jointly with specialists in soil analysis, and hydrology. The expertise of a wide range of agricultural scientists has entered into debates on the archaeological evidence relating to agriculture, but curiously has not been invited by agrarian historians into their domain. Now that the study of these subjects has become so specialized this reluctance as well as the absence of field studies is to be regretted. Considering that the data from survivals of various forms would be much richer for medieval history than for the ancient period one only hopes that a trend in this direction will develop soon. An increase in data of the technical kind can assist the quality of theoretical analysis. Questions more specific to the history of agriculture relate to investigating cultivation techniques, crop patterns, crop rotation, irrigation systems and water cesses, the percentage of arable land available in an area which would condition decisions about starting new settlements or intensifying existing agriculture, variations in the system of fallow for particular crops, the size of holdings in relation to the quality of the soil and the crops, the subsistence level of the peasant, labour input into land and crops and other similar questions. Many of these questions would involve extrapolating back from revenue records as well as considerable field work in the area under study, in order to sharpen the questions and gain insights into possibilities for an earlier period. It is not for nothing that R.H. Tawney is believed to have said that the first essential of research into agrarian history is a pair of stout boots.

36. Some grants are given of waste land and this would be a case of extending the area under cultivation, but the revenue from this goes to the grantee and not to the state, which makes it different from the situation described in the *Arthaśāstra*. *Śūdra* cultivators are mentioned but in some cases as labourers of land-owners, e.g. Manu, IV.253.
37. Legitimacy was necessary where the dynasty was of obscure origin or was described as having served the previous one e.g., F.E. Pargiter, *The Purana Texts of the Dynasties of the Kali Age*, Oxford, 1913, pp. 38, 45, 47, 55, 56.
38. Instances of such revolts are mentioned in R.S. Sharma, *Indian Feudalism*, Delhi, 1980, pp. 127, 220; cf. N. Karashima, *South Indian History and Society*, New Delhi, 1984. Prior to this the more common form of protest was peasant migration which is referred to in the *Jātaka* literature and which is held out as a threat to a king who demands excessive taxes. Romila Thapar, 'Dissent and Protest in the Early Indian Tradition', *Studies in History*, 1979, I. No. 2, pp. 189ff. *See* chapter 11 in this volume.
39. The increasing frequency in hero-stones commemorating a heroic act in defence of a village would point to uncertain conditions in certain areas. These tend to be in the interstices between kingdoms and between settled and forested areas. Romila Thapar, 'Death and the Hero', in S.C. Humphreys and H. King (eds), *Mortality and Immortality*, London, 1981. *See* chapter 31 in this volume.
40. *Viṣṇu Purāṇa*, IV.24; *Mahābhārata*, Śānti Parvan, 254.39ff.
41. This appears to have become important in a later period judging from the Jagannātha cult at Puri and the Viṭhobā cult at Pandarpur. H. Kulke, *Jagannātha-kult und Gajapati Königtum*, Wiesbaden, 1979; G.A. Deleury, *The Cult of Viṭhobā*, Poona, 1960.
42. S. Radhakrishnan, *The Principal Upaniṣads*, London, 1953. Introduction.
43. *Chāndogya Upaniṣad*, V.11.1ff.
44. P. Deussen, *The Philosophy of the Upanisads*, Edinburgh, 1906, pp. 17ff; A.B. Keith, *Religion and Philosophy of the Vedas*, HOS, 1925, pp. 495ff; D.P. Chattopadhyaya, *Indian Philosophy*, New Delhi, 1964, pp. 85ff.
45. Romila Thapar, 'Renunciation: The Making of a Counter-Culture?', *Ancient Indian Social History: Some Interpretations*, pp. 63ff. *See* chapter 40 in this volume.
46. S. Radhakrishnan, op. cit.
47. K.N. Jayatilleke, *The Buddhist Theory of Knowledge*, London, 1963, pp. 49ff.

48. S.D. Joshi (ed.), *Patañjali's Vyākaraṇa Mahābhaṣya*, Poona, 1968, pp. i–xiv. At the more abstract level it is evident in the Brahmajālasutta in the *Dīgha Nikāya*, I.1. The method of *pūrvapakṣa-uttarapakṣa-siddhānta*, although reminiscent of Hegel's dialectic should not be taken as an equivalent as it appears to have been limited to categories of logical analysis.

# 5

# *Regional History: The Punjab**

The initial interest of Indian historians in regional history grew out of nationalist historical writing. It was motivated to some extent by a search for new source materials, a search which has resulted in an abundance of sources — archaeological, epigraphic, historical literature, religious literature, archival records and family papers — all of which have added to the body of information available on the history of many regions of the subcontinent. It is however at the interpretational level that the interest in regional history assumes greater historiographic potential, a potential with which we are perhaps as yet not altogether fully familiar.

The historical interest in regions such as south India, Bengal and Maharashtra, coincided with the new sources providing information particularly on what came to be regarded as the inter-empire periods of Indian history, or, alternatively, complementing the information available from records outside the region. It began to be seen that the supposed 'dark ages' stressed by the historiography of the nineteenth century were far from dark and that the lacunae could be eliminated by using local source material. Further, that it was in these inter-imperial periods that the nature of historical change at the regional level could be seen more clearly. Regional history thus became a corrective to the earlier tendency to generalize about the subcontinent from the perspective of the Ganga Valley.

The spread of nationalism into the various states increased the interest in regional history. This brought its own perspective with the emergent professional groups who participated in the national movement and at the same time sought for an identity from the past; a process which has continued into the post-independence period. It might be argued that historical writing often takes the form of a desire to establish an identity on the part of the social

* Address to the Punjab History Conference, Patiala, 1976.

group to which the historian belongs. Thus, Ganesh Das writing his *Char Bagh-i-Punjab* in 1849, was, as a member of the social elite, projecting the known history of the *khatris* of the Punjab, a form of legitimation of the *khatri* status. Groups in power, therefore, sometimes tend to see the history of their community as the history of the region or even of the nation. This is further emphasized in contemporary historical writing by the equating of the present-day state boundary as the boundary of the region; and this is held to be viable for all periods of history.

These trends are in many ways parallel to those of nationalist historical thinking in the early decades of this century. As such there are both the negative and the positive sides of the impact of nationalist historical thought. Of the former, I would like to draw attention in particular to three trends. There is, the all-too-ready acceptance of the conventional periodization of Ancient, Medieval and Modern. Periodization does not merely imply time-brackets; it also involves historical assumptions (which is why the nomenclature at least was changed from the earlier Hindu, Muslim and British). The acceptance of this periodization imposes assumptions on the historical data from regional sources, and it seems to me that the evidence from the Punjab supports neither the assumptions nor the time-brackets. Admittedly there is a certain convenience in this periodization but a convenience should not be allowed to become an intellectual truth.

Certain theories current in earlier historical writing and believed to be almost axiomatic are endorsed even for regional history. For example, the theory of the Aryan origin of culture and of social stratification is projected even where it is obviously untenable. In the Punjab the social stratification based on the four-caste division presents its own problems. *Brāhmaṇas* rarely play a dominant role in the society of this region, the *kṣatriyas* fade out after a while and the *khatris* who have recently laid claim to being *kṣatriyas* are invariably associated with professions more akin to the *vaiśya*. Clearly there is a deviation from the prescribed norm and this deviation can only be explained by investigating the actual caste stratification at various historical times.

There is the almost inevitable search for a golden age, often identified as the period to which the currently dominant group traces its roots, and it is painted in the glowing tints of cultural resurgence. The protagonists of this age became the heroes of history and act as eponymous ancestors to those in power. In ancient historiography the golden age was generally in the distant past, in the beginnings of time; so distant and so mythological that none could question the historicity of the age and it was imbued with whatever values the historian wished to propagate. Gradually the utopias were brought forward into historical times and eventually into recent periods, when the social and political function of history became more important. Golden ages have to shift as new social groups come to the fore and they have the disadvantage that they focus on a particular series of historical events often to the near exclusion of others of equal importance.

Enfolded in the writing of regional history is also the positive side. Nationalist historians of the early twentieth century, succeeded in generating a debate on the historical assumptions of previous historians concerning the nature of the Indian past: a debate which has opened up many new dimensions. Regional history in the context of Indian history could play a similar, catalytic role. This however does not mean the substituting of the concerns of nationalist Indian ideology by those of regional ideology. On the contrary it would require the analysis of the historical patterns of the region and the relating of these patterns to the generalizations of Indian history. Here again, I do not mean the acceptance of the theories of Indian history and their application to the region, but, rather, the juxtaposing and comparing of the analysis of the regional patterns which would indicate the generalizations required to be made at the wider level. The testing of these generalizations would involve the understanding of the patterns of historical change at the regional level.

I would like at this point to consider some of these patterns for they give rise to the problems which I spoke of earlier.

One might begin with the historical point at which the awareness of being a region, and having a history, is first expressed. In the case of the Punjab it has been suggested as having evolved during the Mughal period. The historian's interest lies in analysing the roots of this consciousness — whether they result from an administrative or political coherence, or from linguistic or religious urges or a combination of many factors. In analysing this consciousness it is equally imperative to consider that which preceded it and that which came subsequently. In order to do this we arrive at the second important problem, namely, what were the geographical boundaries of the region.

The question of boundaries has its own complexities since man-made boundaries change frequently and rapidly with each political change. The only stable boundaries are geographical and even these are liable to be substantially modified by ecological changes. The definition of a region requires the correlation of many facets in the study of historical evolution, as is amply demonstrated in the Punjab.

On the face of it the Punjab is easy enough to define. It is the land of the five rivers and the inter-fluvial regions, the Doābs. Yet the coinciding of this geographical definition with a political and cultural entity has occurred only for a brief period of its history. Prior to that the area contained more than one political and social identity. What seems significant, therefore, is not just the brief period when the larger frontiers coincided, but the investigation of the interaction and relationship between the sub-regions and this constitutes a major part of the history of this region.

The sub-regions within the larger area can be listed as follows: firstly, the Potwar plateau and the Salt Range constituting the northern part of the Sind-Sagar Doāb, the southern half being mainly desert; secondly, what I shall refer to as the Upper Doābs, those of the Chaj, Rachna, Bari and Bist, lying at an elevation of 200–500m and stretching into the sub-montane tracts and with which the Potwar area had close contacts; thirdly, the upper reaches of the rivers leading into the hill valleys at the forefront of the Himalayas; and fourthly, the Lower Doābs forming the hinterland of Multan. Both the plain of Peshawar and the watershed of the Indo-Gangetic divide, although historically very significant, remain geographically marginal to the main area. Even though the sub-regions can be approximately demarcated, their historical interaction has been complex and any history of the Punjab will have to take both the interaction and the complexities into account. The pattern of relationships has not been consistent and similar through time. One of the more obvious reasons for these changes has been the extreme hydrographic disturbances, such as those involving the Sarasvatī, the Sutlej-Beas and the Rāvi. But the complexities are also due to other reasons.

Evidence of settlement in this area during the third and second millennia BC show a distribution of pre-Harappan and Harappan sites along the Indus (particularly the trans-Indus region) and in the Bari Doāb and along the Sutlej and Hakra. Archaeological explorations in Pakistan and India point to a concentration of population in these areas. The upper reaches of the Hakra have been identified by some with the Vedic Sarasvatī. The concentration of population was further down in Bahawalpur and Cholistan. It has been plausibly argued that there were major ecological changes in this area during the second millennium BC which appear to be accompanied by a decline in settlements in Cholistan and a concentration in the Indo-Gangetic divide. References to the occupation of the Upper Doābs, as for example the *janapadas* of the Kekeyas and the Madras, come from sources of the first millennium BC. Was there a migration of people from the gradually desiccated regions to the Upper Doābs? A slow ecological change would encourage migration. If Harappan agriculture was based on inundation irrigation then hydrographic changes would virtually necessitate a migration. However, the discovery of a pre-Harappan ploughed field at Kalibangan in northern Rajasthan, not too far south from the Hakra, would point to a different agricultural technology. Or, were the new areas settled by fresh migrants from elsewhere? The distribution of the Painted Grey Ware culture suggests that the settlers, may have moved along the Sutlej and Sarasvatī valleys. The further distribution of this culture extends from the Indo-Gangetic divide to the upper Ganga valley, the link between the two areas having been previously established through the Ochre-Colour Pottery Culture. In subsequent centuries the people of the Ganga valley regarded those of the Upper Doābs of the Punjab with some disdain. The Madras are accused not only of forsaking brahmanical rites but of unconventional behaviour and the breaking of social taboos. For the orthodox of the *madhyadeśa* this region was always on the brink of the social pale if not actually outside it. It is also worth remembering that for some centuries two linguistic systems seem to have had currency since Vedic Sanskrit carries evidence of the assimilation of some Dravidian elements.

More precise information on the condition of the Punjab comes to us from the accounts of Alexander's campaign in the late fourth century BC. Alexander's route was from the Peshawar plains across the Doāb — rich, fertile lands supporting monarchical kingdoms such as those of Āmbhi, Pūru and Saubhūti, and a relatively sophisticated culture. In contrast to this was the stark, primitive habitat of the Śibi in the Shorkot region. Further south in the Bari Doāb, the oligarchies of the Mālava and the Kṣudraka presented a more cheerful picture. It seems that the Lower Doābs were not as prosperous as the Upper Doābs, nevertheless, the agricultural base of the latter was not substantial enough to support a single powerful state. That the desiccation in the Lower Doābs was spreading seems probable from the fact that by the first couple of centuries AD the Mālava (among others) had migrated to Rajasthan and Avanti.

For the Mauryas the significance of the Punjab seemed to focus further to the north-west on Taxila which became the administrative seat and commercial centre of the northern province of Gandhāra. This, in a sense, introduces a new dimension to the patterns discussed so far. Taxila was the meeting point, on the one side, of the royal highway and the trade route running from the Ganga valley via the watershed and through the Upper Doābs and, on the other, the route from west Asia via the Khyber Pass as well as the recently discovered route from central Asia through Gilgit and Chitral. Mountain passes accentuate communication and the Khyber has always been the route of migration, trade and invasion, with cities such as Taxila and Begram flanking either end of the pass and giving way in time to other cities (ultimately Peshawar and Kabul), but always in the same vicinity.

The role of invasions in the history of the Punjab is mentioned so often that it hardly bears repeating. But it might be as well to consider also some of the other factors contributing to the history of this region, as, for instance, trade. One easy index to the growth of trade is an increase in the number and size of towns. Sources such as Ptolemy list a large number of towns in the Upper Doābs, far exceeding those in the Lower Doābs. Can it be argued that the prosperity of the Upper Doābs was based primarily on trade rather than on agriculture? Is it possible that the peak periods of affluence coincided with the political control of this region extending its reach into Afghanistan and possibly Kashmir, since Kashmir also had links with central Asian trade routes? The earliest references to Taxila as a commercial and cosmopolitan centre relate to the period when Gandhāra was included as a satrapy in the Achaemenid empire in the mid-first millennium BC. Post-Mauryan dynasties in this region frequently straddled the Khyber Pass and this period also saw a sharp rise in trading activities and commercial income. One has only to compare the Mauryan settlement of Bhir Mound at Taxila with the post-Mauryan city of Sirkap at the same place to see the difference. Whereas the former has an organic growth indicatiing the gradual evolution of an urban centre, the latter is a planned city based on earlier urban experience, perhaps from elsewhere. The political importance of Śākala during this period may also have been due to its location on the trade route. The attempt of empire builders from the Mauryas to the Mughals, who, if their empires included the Punjab, tried to annex eastern Afghanistan as well, may in part have been motivated by the wish to control not only the strategic entrances into the subcontinent, but also the trade routes.

Gupta rule appears to have made scant impression on the Punjab in spite of Samudragupta claiming to have uprooted the oligarchies of the Mālavas, Yaudheyas and Ārjunāyanas in Rajasthan and the watershed and the Madrakas in the Upper Doābs. If the control of the trade route involved the conquest of the Potwar plateau and beyond and if the Upper Doābs were not agriculturally very developed, this might have acted as a disincentive to further conquest in the region. It would seem that effective Gupta control stopped at the watershed which in later times, as suggested by the place name Sirhind, was the frontier to the Ganga valley. The persistence of oligarchies in this region, despite the Mauryan and Post-Mauryan conquests, suggests a relative autonomy from interference by strong political powers which interference would have been inevitable had it been a rich, agricultural region. Interestingly, some of these oligarchies are said to have provided soldiers in lieu of revenue, in the true frontier tradition. The Indo-Gangetic divide seems more frequently to have been drawn into the vortex of the Ganga valley. Harṣavardhana, although originating from Thanesar, moved the centre of his kingdom into the Ganga valley rather than up into the Punjab.

Hsüan Tsang, visiting India in the seventh century AD, travelled from Taxila through the towns of the Upper Doābs to Thanesar and the Ganga valley. It is significant that when he visited Multan he approached it from Sind, suggesting that its accessibility and association with Sind was stronger. Multan itself was a commercial centre of great importance, but its hinterland to the north and to the east called for little attention. In his description of the Upper Doābs, Hsüan Tsang refers mainly to towns, some of which are surrounded by fertile country. But his more glowing references are to fields of grain and fruit orchards in the submontane areas and the hill valleys fanning out along the mountain reaches of the rivers.

One of the most puzzling problems in the latter part of the first millennium AD is the surprising absence of land-grant inscriptions from the Punjab plains. If agriculture was of primary importance in this region, then there would have been some record either of the bringing of waste land under cultivation or of the granting of cultivated land to religious or secular grantees. The absence of these records would either suggest a low priority for agriculture or else an agrarian and administrative system which did not require the kind of changes taking place in neighbouring regions. Land-grant inscriptions are available from the hill areas, as for example from Kangra, as early as the seventh century and from Chamba a little later. The extension of agriculture into the hill valleys must have taken place in the latter half of the first millennium AD to allow of the granting of land during this period. Does this reflect a migration from the Upper Doābs into the hills and the creation of the hill states? Or was this due to a natural migration caused by shortage of land and an increasing population? The pressure of revenue collection was probably not a causal factor as this would have led to agrarian changes in the plains. If insecurity resulting from invasions was the cause, then the accusation of creating this insecurity would have to be levelled against the Hūnas rather than the Turks, since the migration to the hills predates the Turkish invasions by a few centuries. Alternatively, one may have to argue that, given the existing agricultural technology, cultivation was easier in the hill valleys. Access to these higher valleys also introduced new commodities and trade connections especially with the increasing use of mountain passes into Kashmir, Ladakh and Tibet. The proximity of the main trade route of the plains to the hill states doubtless facilitated these connections. Absence of evidence is not a conclusive argument but it is indeed strange that records of land grants should be a rarity in the Punjab plains when such records are available for many other regions of northern India. This would also imply a corresponding rarity of at least one aspect of such grants, the instituting of *agrahāras* and brahmanical settlements and endowments to temples. Hsüan Tsang refers to 'deva' temples in the cities of the Upper Doābs but none as spectacular as the one at Multan. There are few early temples in the Punjab plains and one wonders whether their lack of survival was due to insufficient endowments or to the conventional explanation of Muslim invasions destroying temples. The sub-montane and hill areas however, which were also at the receiving end of such invasions, although admittedly not on the direct route, do have surviving examples of early temples, many of which were well-endowed. The absence of land-grants would have further implications not only for the role of brahmanism as a religion of the area but also for the pattern of caste formation and caste structure, given that the acculturating role of brahmanical settlements noticed in certain other parts of the subcontinent was less common. Brahmanism never seems to have had a deep social root in the plains. But in the hill states it had a firm foothold and the process of acculturation is more evident.

It has been suggested that, at the end of the first and in the early half of the second millennia AD, there appears to have been a population movement with the Jats of Sind settling in the Punjab mainly in the area between the Chenab and Sutlej rivers, as also in the watershed and extending further into eastern Rajasthan and western Uttar Pradesh. This was not merely a population movement for the Jats had converted from pastoralism to agriculture; and crucial to the change was that they brought with them the technology of the Persian wheel. This resulted in a rapid extension of agriculture, particularly in the Upper Doābs. The *Ain-i-Akbari* records the presence of Jat *zamindār* castes and well-irrigation in the Doābs of the Punjab. Had there already been a large agricultural population in these areas, such a movement would have created a massive unrest; but for this there is no evidence: unless one argues that the migration into the hill states had something to do with this movement. The Jat migration was probably a slow movement not causing much displacement. The hinterland of Multan was in any case sparsely populated. At most, the Jats may have pressurized the cultivators of the Upper Doābs and the sub-montane area to move further up into the mountain valleys. By the time of Akbar, the Subah of Lahore is described as agriculturally very fertile and yielding a healthy revenue. One has the impression that agriculture was more in evidence now with possibly more land under cultivation than before, judging by the relatively infrequent references to agriculture in this region from pre-Mughal sources. The numerically larger *zamindār* castes included the Jats, Bhattis, Rajputs and various others.

The *zamindār* castes were however distinct from the trader and administrator caste, that of the *khatris*. The references to *khatris* associated with land are very few. The post-Gupta period is seen as one of a decline in trade in northern India. However a modicum of commercial activity must have continued, as is suggested by the ninth century inscription from Pehoa, which refers to a body of horse-dealers some of whom were *brāhmaṇas* coming from various places and agreeing to contribute to a donation to temples at Pehoa and Kannauj from every sale of their animals. The emergence of the *khatris* as major traders seems to coincide with the period of the Turkish invasions, perhaps because the invasions had the supplementary effect of opening up the trade routes to central Asia which were under the control of Mahmud of Ghazni. His armies certainly marched through the towns of the Upper Doābs, but his prize targets were cities elsewhere — Multan, Kannauj, Thanesar and Somanath.

Agricultural technology was perhaps to play a further role in historical change in the Punjab. It is somewhat startling to read in the *Ain-i-Akbari* that the Bet Jalandhar Doāb in the *sarkar* of Dipalpur yielded a very high revenue, until one remembers that Firuz Tughlaq built a canal in this region in 1354. The upper Bari Doāb becomes a key area of the Punjab from the seventeenth century. Was this also related to the canal built by the Mughal administration in this period? The Multan area was sought to be controlled by the administration of Ranjit Singh in the early nineteenth century through the building of inundation canals. The British policy of canal networks and canal colonies in the underdeveloped areas of the Lower Doābs had its antecedents. The extension of agriculture in the Punjab made it possible to extend the natural frontier northwards.

Whatever the reasons, whether involving agricultural technology, new commercial possibilities, invasions and migrations, there appears to be, in the Mughal period, a change in the relations between the sub-regions of the Punjab. The upper Doābs and the hill states impinge on each other to a greater degree than before. Lahore and Multan seem to be in closer contact, although not always well-disposed towards each other. The ambitions of the Governors of Lahore extended in their geographical reach to more distant areas such as Kabul and Kashmir, doubtless motivated by the trading network.

Evidence of a more general economic stabilization, probably due to the extension of agriculture, is apparent from the appearance of land-grants and endowments to various religious sects. The sects are largely heterodox, irrespective of whether they are included in the Hindu or Islamic tradition. The core of the religious tradition comes from groups of renouncers, such as the Nāthpanthis, Bairāgis, Sufis. The earlier groups of renouncers, the Buddhists, had also once been important in this region. Although they had now disappeared, possibly some of the earlier social requirements which had led to the support of Buddhism may have been remanifested in the support for the renouncers of this later period. The creation and diffusion of the Punjabi language is also linked with religious sects. They adopted the language of the towns-people and villagers in preference to that of the courtly elite, and gave both form and status to the language.

A variety of sects were recipients of land-grants. The Upper Bari Doāb furnishes examples of such grants (as for instance, the Jogis of Jakhbar and the Vaiṣṇavas of Pindori). They appear to have had fairly easy access to revenue-free land, exemption from irrigation cesses and a variety of perquisites. Their patrons changed over the centuries but the status of the patrons remained the same. They were all members of the ruling order — the Rajput rulers of the hill states who patronized the shrines, the Mughal emperors who endowed them with land, the governor of Lahore and later the Sikh rulers of the kingdom of Punjab and the British. In spite of the sharp differences in the religious persuasions of this cavalcade of rulers they were all making grants to these and similar sects. The documents of the Punjab kingdom refer to the grants as being in accordance with the practice of the times of the Mughal rulers: a strange continuity among those whom we today project as being antagonistic to each other on religious grounds. Doubtless, most believed that they were acquiring religious merit by making these grants, but one wonders if other more mundane reasons did not encroach upon the decision. Perhaps such endowments would help to stabilize the area politically since the sects would develop into centres of political loyalty as long as the grant was forthcoming. Some of the documents of the later period describe the location of the land granted and judging by the continuity of the villages it would seem that the Upper Bari Doāb was by now well populated. The continuity of the grants from the Mughal period by later rulers may also have been regarded as a status symbol. Many of these sects had a network of connections via itinerant members and monastic establishments over large geographical areas. The Nātha sect was well distributed in northern India by now. These connections could also have served as trading networks, as they were known to do, for instance, with the Gosain sects of other parts of northern India. It is interesting that eventually market centres develop on some of the lands thus endowed. Gradually the religious institution evolved into a body of landowners. Income from the endowments was spent on the maintenance of the institution and the order. Often this involved investing the income in land or commerce. Thus the renouncers came to perform administrative and entrepreneurial functions, assisted by secular agents. Perhaps the religious teaching of such sects did not remain unchanged and took on the nuances of their new role in society.

Did the acquisition of the new status breed political ambition among these religious groups? The hostility between them was not invariably over religious differences though this may have been presented as the apparent cause. Hostility could equally well arise from a competition for patronage or from the need to protect property which in part explains the organization of para-military sections among such sects.

Popular support for religious sects involves the question of the link between them and the various castes. This is crucial not merely to the history of a religious movement but also to the social pattern of the region. It is often said that the initial support for Guru Nanak came from the *khatris* but that gradually Sikhism drew greater support from the Jats. This may suggest that the evolution of Sikhism be seen in two phases, since the social base would differ in each case. At the same time it would be relevant to examine why the initial *khatri* leadership gave way to the increasingly effective Jat participation. Urban groups may find universalistic teaching more acceptable. Peasant groups would require the assimilation of their own cults into the new religion. Would this in part explain Guru Govind Singh's tendency to use Hindu symbols, particularly those relating to the Śakti tradition? Does it also reflect political concerns, either hostile or friendly, between the Hinduized hill states and the Sikhism of the plains? It has been suggested that the Jats, as a low status group, were drawn to use this for improving their social status. Such a group would, on consolidating its position, tend to introduce a hierarchical separation between itself and others. Is it a coincidence that it was also at this time that the demarcation between the *sardar* and the *mazhabi* Sikhs enters the movement?

The emergence of the kingdom of the Punjab was not a sudden development of the eighteenth and nineteenth centuries. It has, as I have tried to show, a long gestation period. It incorporates in its development the various connections which I have referred to: the changing links between the sub-regions where the changes are indirectly man-made or directly so; the two economic thrusts of agriculture and trade, and of technology as a factor in these; the emergence of caste relations; the growth of religious sects; and the crystallization of political identities. The contribution which regional history can make is in seeking to connect these elements at a more precise level. If the focus on the pattern of historical change in the region can be sharpened it contributes to the quality of generalizations at the broader level as well as makes for more valuable comparative studies with other regions. In terms of comparative studies mention is often made of the kingdoms of the Punjab and the Marathas. They are said to have been motivated by an anti-Muslim sentiment which helped them to be rid of central, imperial authority. As a mono-causal explanation this can be traced to communal historiography where the tension between imperial authority and regional pressures was seen at the single plane of religious differences. A careful examination of the mainsprings of these developments however suggests a multitude of factors, not least of them the crisis within the Mughal empire itself. Comparative studies would suggest the similarities within the two regions, thereby enabling a wider generalization. Dissimilarities would indicate the particular regional factors and would lead to the modification of the broader generalization.

I began with the suggestion that there are three trends in regional history which need to be reconsidered. I have tried to show that the accepted periodization on the large scale seems to be inapplicable to the Punjab. Medievalism, with its attendant social and economic changes, would have to be placed later than is normally done. To date the modern period to the mid-eighteenth century would create its own problems in the history of the Punjab. The assumptions on which this periodization is based would in any case require serious reconsideration. The deviation from the standard picture of caste society also needs careful investigation. With the search for a golden age, one treads on soft ground, for this is also tied up with the attempt to suggest a regional periodization, but without changing the assumptions of the existing periodization.

Thus the history of Maharashtra is equated with the rise of the Maratha kingdom, that of Rajasthan with the emergence of Mewar and Marwar, that of the Punjab with Sikhism and that of Tamil Nadu with the Chola polity. I have attempted to suggest that even a movement as powerful as that of Sikhism and the emergence of the kingdom of the Punjab can become a viable historical study only in the context of the totality of the history of the Punjab. Historical events are not isolated phenomena, suspended in space and time, and the historical matrix in which they are embodied is as important as the events.

# 6

# *Regional History with Reference to the Konkan*[*]

I would like in this paper to consider regional history with reference to western India, and specifically, the Konkan. I have not specialised in the history of this area and am therefore interested in the broader implications of regional history which I hope to place before you.

A pertinent historiographical question relates to the point at which regional history becomes significant. The answer to this is in part connected with the definition of a region. It can be variously an area of the subcontinent such as western India, or that which constitutes a present-day state — in this case Maharashtra, or the geographically nuclear area which is a part of the larger unit — in this case, the Konkan. The definition of a region therefore has to do with how we, as historians, look at a region.

The history of a region becomes important either because of the discovery of source material in plenty which gives a new understanding to its past, or, as is more frequent, when there is a search for a historical identity among people of that region which encourages research into its history. The seeking of an identity is dependent on people seeing themselves as distinct within a region. This is often the case where it has been a core region in the past. Core regions are important historically as nuclei of power, of relatively more advanced economies and as centres of administrative and cultural control. Such areas often have a more homogeneous cultural identity which becomes a point of reference and is exploited by contemporary groups for a variety of reasons. Frequently this trend is associated with a community coming into prominence,

* Keynote Address, History of Maharashtra Conference, Pune. Published in A.R. Kulkarni et al. (eds), *Medieval Deccan History*, Bombay 1996, 19–29.

although this may not invariably be the case. In such a situation regional history in a precise sense should be a history of the region and not just of that particular community — a caution which is becoming increasingly necessary in view of various uses to which such histories are put.

At the historiographical level, the importance of regional history needs no bush. It encourages the search for and often the discovery of, new sources, ranging from archaeology to archival data. This inevitably leads to new questions which raise the study from information to fresh interpretations. This in turn helps us to redefine the pattern of the region. Frequently in the past regional histories have been viewed from the perspective of the subcontinent and this perspective obviously differs from that of the region. The redefinition of the region and the purpose of regional history can also lead to a reconsideration of the pattern of Indian history, as a fresh assessment of periodisation, change, continuity and a variety of factors which go into the making of a larger pattern. There is therefore a tandem relationship between the two which makes them interdependent. Such a redefinition derives from the degree to which the historical information on the region has already been collected and studied and which study then enables historians to take the next step of attempting to draw out patterns from its past.

For the history of the Konkan we are fortunate that it has attracted the interest of both our predecessors and our peers, which interest has been expressed in some fine field work and study of source material. Even if some of these studies do not focus on the Konkan itself we can at least use a large body of work which is linked to its history. I shall therefore attempt to view the area in what might be called its formative period in historical terms and suggest some patterns which seem to me to be of significance to its history. I shall however be concentrating on only a small part of the Konkan, which has already been worked upon, and shall try to look at the evidence in terms of integrating the region to the larger whole.

The geographical definition of a region forms the starting point and provides features which give some character to the region. In the case of Konkan it is obviously the coastal strip which constitutes what I would call the primary hinterland. This is an area of varying fertility but has two consistent features, namely, creeks and estuaries on the coastal side and passes in the ghats on the elevated side. The strictly geographical definition is a narrow one sketching out the physical features; historical geography extends the parameters to include the potential of links and connections with other areas.

The coastline provides harbours for shipping and exchange, both conducive to trade. The multiplicity of these encourages a variety of economic networks. One consists of a looping trade with a localised exchange from harbour to harbour or a cluster of these. The other links major harbours to long distance trade involving mid-ocean voyages. In assessing the role of trade therefore it is important to keep in mind the diverse networks. The looping trade, as has been suggested, perhaps goes back to Harappan times when the string of ports along the Sind and Gujarat coastline appear to have been active. Such a system would be useful to people in search of resources. The tracking down of reserves of timber and semi-precious stones could account for a gradual opening up of the coast from Gujarat southwards. The looping trade along the Konkan coast probably developed in post-Harappan times since the Harappan settlements in northern Maharashtra tend to go into the interior and not along the coast. Although it is likely that the looping trade precedes long distance trade, the former did not die out with the development of the latter, as is evident even to this day. Communication along the shore assumes greater importance in areas where the rivers flowing east to west make longitudinal contacts overland, difficult.

The Western Ghats as a topographical feature seemingly act as a barrier. Yet, as in every case of mountains bordering on plains the passes in the mountain become crucial both as passages for trade as well as prime points for defence. This is very clear from the many passes in the ghats (Thalghat, Nanaghat, Bhorghat, etc.) which were the ancient trade routes as well as the placement of Shivaji's forts along these and overlooking the coastal plain as points strategic to the defence of both the plain and the plateau. The passes also gave access to sources of timber, ivory and semi-precious stones. Pockets of fertile areas on the plateau would also have provided agricultural produce. The demand for these would have encouraged communications between the coastal area and the plateau.

So much for the secondary hinterland, albeit something of a climb from the coast to the ghats. Fanning out from this were other links going further afield. From Nasik and Paithan, routes traversed the Tapti and Narmada valleys to Ujjain, Mathura and the north and to Vidiśā, Pāṭaliputra and the east. The plateau of the western Deccan was also the source of rivers flowing north-west to south-east with goods and traffic following in these directions to the edge of Karnataka and Andhra Pradesh. These links were not only between commercial centres but also between the variant cultures evolving in these regions. This territory fanning out becomes important to the historian looking not only at economic history but also at cultural history. The suggested links between the western Deccan and Karnataka in the discussion on the origins of the Viṭhobā cult is a case of the historian's use of geography having to span the narrower boundaries of cartography where they are based on administrative and political units. What I have referred to as the secondary and tertiary hinterlands of the Konkan, when viewed from the coastal area, take on magnified proportions but these hinterlands cannot be ignored. Nevertheless they should not be permitted to shroud the activities of the coast. This is not to suggest that the history of the Konkan cannot be studied without looking at the entire history of western India, but rather that in certain specific aspects of the history of Konkan it is necessary to look beyond the immediate hinterland.

The neolithic and chalcolithic sites of the western Deccan tend to remain on the plateau. Sites such as Daimabad, Prakash, Bahal, Nasik, Jorwe, Nevasa and Inamgaon suggest that it was the plateau ecology which was most suitable to the kind of cultures which evolved at this time. The Mula-Mutha has been described as the meeting point of the Jorwe people moving southwards and the Krishna valley people moving to the north. The direction of movement forged the routes of later periods on the plateau. The megalithic settlements tend to skirt both the Konkan coast and the western edge of the plateau and keep to the interior. It would seem that the routes from the plateau to the coast developed during the early historical period and probably arose because of a strong pull from the coast, a pull involving trade.

The start of what may be termed historical evidence goes back to the Mauryan period. The question of why the Mauryas conquered the Konkan has to do with resources and commerce. There is no evidence of any major power in the region prior to their arrival. The Aśokan inscriptions refer to the Bhoja, Āndhra and Pitinika, probably on the plateau. The chalcolithic settlements and even the possible reach of the megalithic cultures into this area, even if not of settlements, would point not to an established state but more likely to chiefships controlling a tribal society, or what I have preferred to call, a lineage society. The Mauryan armies doubtless followed the route established by previous settlements. Coming from the Ganga valley to the Malwa plateau and central India, across the Narmada and Tapti, they continued to the western Deccan and from there to the coast. The location of NBP and punch-marked coins along this route are pointers to this as also the Aśokan edicts at Sanchi, Hoshangabad and Sopara. The latter inscription underlines the importance of Sopara as a port. It has the distinction of being the only port on the west coast with a major Mauryan inscription. Its importance seems to indicate that there was at least one significant link between the coast and the plateau in the period just prior to the Mauryan, probably via the Thalghat to Nasik and Paithan. This may have been due to the fertility of the Ulhas basin or to the coastal trade using Sopara as a port for tapping the resources of the plateau hinterland. However had the trade been limited to a coastal trade it would still not explain why Sopara was singled out. The limited Buddhist remains found at the site do not offer a sufficient explanation. Inevitably the possibility of long distance trade with the arrival of the Mauryans has to be considered. Logically long distance trade with the Gulf would have been better handled by Bhṛgukaccha also under Mauryan control with Sopara perhaps as a subsidiary alternative. Nevertheless it is useful to consider the possibility of long distance trade between Sopara and southern Arabia, which had links with the Red Sea and Egypt, and which might account for the importance of Sopara in the Mauryan period. Close relations between the Mauryas and the Ptolemies and the coming of the ambassador from Ptolemy Philadelphus to the Mauryan court, as reported by Pliny, would suggest that contacts with the Red Sea ports could be dated to an earlier period than is generally assumed. That the Mauryan emperor Aśoka should mention Magas of Cyrene as one of the five Greek kings to whom he had sent emissaries does seem strange unless the Mauryans had fairly direct relations with the Ptolemies, since Cyrene was not part of the circuit of the Seleucid court in West Asia. Cyrene adjoined Egypt to the west, and Magas and Philadelphus were related through a marriage. Greek sources refer to a powerful medicinal herb which was among the main products of Cyrene — the silphium plant. They also mention that the Mauryas were interested in herbs and aphrodisiacs brought by ambassadors from the west. Admittedly journeys from Egypt and Cyrene could have been undertaken overland and through the domains of the Seleucids with whom the Mauryans had even closer relations, but if that was the case then the importance of Sopara remains enigmatic. A more extensive exploration and excavation of the site may provide clues to its earliest date. The importance of Sopara therefore raises the question of the chronology of long distance contacts between the Red Sea and Konkan. As part of coastal voyaging Sopara may have been an extension of the contacts with the Gujarat coast. But the possibility of mid-ocean contacts needs to be re-examined. Although the Greek record of the use of the monsoon is attributed erroneously to Hippalus at a later date, it has been argued that the winds could have been known to Arab navigators of earlier periods. The importance of Sopara may support this theory.

The nature of Mauryan interest in the area relates to a wider question which can be asked of many parts of the Mauryan empire. Since it was an area with an availability of natural resources, were the Mauryans satisfied with tapping these resources and obtaining a revenue from them or did they attempt to restructure the economy of the region introducing new resources such as the conversion of waste land to agriculture? In a sense this question can best be answered by looking at the post-Mauryan situation since the evidence in this region for the earlier period seems limited. The earliest organized state in the region was that of the Sātavāhanas evolving out of the declining Mauryan power. The presence of the state is suggested by the evidence of political control and the use of an administrative structure. References to units of administration and of what appear to be official designations point to a monarchical system. The title of *mahāmātra* is suggestive of the Mauryan designation. The *mahābhoja* and *mahārathi* as officials may in origin have been associated with high status in the clans and made the transition to administrative office when the requirements of the state demanded it. The constituents of the seven limbs of state, the *saptānga*, are reflected in these and other indications such as the reference to Sātavāhana armies in action against the *ksatrapas*, to allies and enemies, to the treasury from the existence of Sātavāhana coins and revenue collection, to the capital from references to

Pratisthāna and finally to the recognition of territory under Sātavāhana control.

A dramatic indication of change under the Sātavāhanas comes from the excavations of urban centres such as Ter and Bhokardan providing evidence of urbanisation and active commerce. This is reflected in objects covering a wide range from beads to coins, Indian and Roman type pottery, terracotta figurines, ivory carving and a variety of well-constructed structures, some residential and others perhaps workshops. Had there been no other evidence for trade this in itself would have forced historians to look for it. In the production of these items the reach of the towns had to extend into interior districts involving the question of relations between those who provided the raw material and those responsible for producing the item.

The commercial and urban economy was more evident but this did not preclude the agrarian side. Large scale states often rise on the basis of land revenue and the study of agriculture becomes important. In this area the role of trade providing such a use has also to be considered. Agrarian history can be examined at various levels. The foremost is that of agriculture literally on the ground. The thesis of the emergence of the state, dependent on a combination of wet rice cultivation, the iron ploughshare and tank and canal irrigation, would of course not hold in relation to the western Deccan. There would be a need to look afresh at soil conditions, crop patterns, cultivation techniques and the type of irrigation required, and for much of this the historian would have to work with the agronomist and the hydrologist. At another level there would be a need to enquire into the ownership and control over land. Here the epigraphic data provides evidence of small-scale landowners, *gahapatis* with larger holdings and also state ownership of land in the context of land grants.

In some inscriptions, *gahapatis* and *seṭṭhis* are jointly referred to in the same family with the *gahapati* in one generation and the *seṭṭhi* in another. The context would indicate perhaps that well-to-do landowners invested some of their wealth in trade. The term *gahapati* requires a more detailed analysis since its meaning ranges over references to heads of households, landowners and generally wealthy people. Were some of the *gahapatis* originally local chiefs, who, when clan lands were changing to private ownership came to be regarded as heads of extended households?

The existence of women donors is an interesting feature in the light of statements in the contemporary *Manu Dharmaśāstra* where a woman's position is subordinate and a woman's access to wealth is only to her *strīdhana*. According to the votive inscriptions some women as wives of *gahapatis* and *seṭṭhis* did have access to their husband's wealth. Possibly Buddhism gave a freer and more responsible status to women than the authors of the *Dharmaśāstras* or else the latter were exaggerating the subordinate status to make the point. What is even more interesting is that the *bhikkhunīs* also made donations. It is unclear whether this was from their *strīdhana* or from gifts received from their families even after they became nuns. An allied question is why women from wealthy families became nuns. The theory that nunneries were the refuge of widows may hold in cases where sons are mentioned, but in other situations the nuns were unmarried women. Would it be an exaggeration to argue that there might have been a demographic imbalance which led to unmarried women becoming nuns; or were there links between property, inheritance and marriage patterns which resulted in some women remaining unmarried? Customary law and kinship rules of the region would have to be considered. There has been perhaps too great a reliance on theoretical texts and we have not been sufficiently careful to correlate these with other sources of evidence in our assessment of social questions. That monks and nuns made donations, sometimes quite substantial, may also be explained by their participation in commercial enterprise, in spite of being renouncers, either as individuals or on behalf of the *saṅgha* and donating their earnings to the enrichment of the *saṅgha*.

Grants made to the Buddhist *saṅgha* reflect on its social role and in the case of royal grants, on its relation to the state. Monasteries were corporate organizations and investments by the state in them had a larger impact than royal donations to individuals. In some cases money was invested by royalty in guilds, as in the case of the potter's guild and the interest was given to the monastery for the performance of a ritual, or the maintenance of an oil lamp. This created a nexus between political power, the commercial economy and the religious institution. The link between the first two is further supported by some aspects of Sātavāhana coinage. The authority issuing punch-marked coins remains puzzling and continues to be a point of debate among historians.

That the issuing of coins was taken over in this area by the Sātavāhanas was an indication of a spurt in trade to a degree which made it worthwhile for the state to intervene by controlling the medium of exchange. The symbol of the ship on other issues makes an even more pointed reference to maritime trade. The hostility accompanying the diverting of Greek shipping to Sopara would have had a political dimension as well.

The linking of the state with religious institutions encouraged further roles for the monastery. It could become a centre of loyalty to the state. This was particularly important in frontier regions through which trade routes would often have to pass. The monastery could act as a channel of acculturation introducing the culture of the urban centres and the royal courts to the countryside. The fact of royal donations, earlier prevalent in relation to Buddhist institutions became an accepted pattern and when Buddhism declined and the donations took the form of *brahmadeya* and other similar grants to the non-Buddhist institutions, the pattern continued. It would be worth examining the changes which occurred at the local level, apart from the evident one of the change in religion. The monasteries also became linked to trade. They were located along the major routes and in the vicinity of centres of commerce or strategically at the major passes linking the plateau with the coastal region. Interestingly they are frequently found on the plateau side of the ghats. A major exception is Kanheri lying close to the ports of Sopara and Kalyana and in the relatively fertile Ulhas basin. It is pertinent that many of the donations at Kanheri are in money rather than in kind. It would be appropriate to examine this phenomenon in the light of transportation facilities. Caravans traversing the plateau routes would have to halt at the edge of the ghats and perhaps reload their goods on to pack animals for the steep descent. The halt at these points, if this was the case, perhaps resulted in a change in transportation technology, such as the building of roads through passes, and this would have had a somewhat adverse effect on the prosperity of the monasteries. This would not preclude other reasons for the decline of trade in this specific area, such as the silting up of the approach to Sopara.

The excavation of towns such as Ter and Bhokardan assumes considerable importance when one is looking for the origins of such centres. Commercial centres sometimes grow from a nucleus of production such as textiles at Ter and bead making and shell and ivory cutting at Bhokardan and Ter. Horizontal excavations in particular would be useful in observing the evolution of urban centres and the significance of commerce to the economy of the region. Centres of exchange involve questions of levels of exchange. This concerns the obtaining of raw materials, the production of items for trade either through individual craftsmen or through guilds and the distribution of goods by merchants, not to mention the financing of trade as well.

The analysis of these exchanges could benefit from a detailed study of the identity of the merchants involved in the trade. One may well ask whether *gahapatis* jointly functioned as merchants or whether some members of the *gahapati* families referred to as *seṭṭhis* functioned separately as merchants and financiers. In this connection the references to Yavanas in the inscriptions remains intriguing. It is generally assumed that they were Hellenised west Asians who came from families settled in northern India and that they migrated to the new trade centres which expanded in the western Deccan. That they gave donations to the *saṅgha* and had Buddhist names would indicate that they came from families which had been associated with Buddhism.

It is however also plausible to argue that some of them might have come from families of Greek and Levantine merchants from the eastern Mediterranean whose involvement with the western Indian trade went back a few generations, and who were associating themselves with the predominant religion of the traders of this area. At least one Yavana is described as belonging to Gata. This is usually taken to be Trigarta or the region of Jullundar in northern India. An alternative reading could be that Gata was the Prākrit for Koptos in Egypt. On the analogy of Candragupta/Sandracottos, Coptos would be rendered as Gopto or Gapta in Sanskrit, the vowel sound being less meticulously observed, and the latter in turn could be Gata in Prākrit. In a census list of the district of Arisone in Egypt dating c. AD 72, mention is made of four adults of Greek descent who live outside Egypt and one of these is said to be resident in India. Such Yavanas may well have become Buddhists. These Yavanas from the eastern Mediterranean would have maintained close relations with the existing Yavana traders of northern India some of whom may have participated in the western Indian trade. Their contact with things Indian may have come from Indian traders settled in the Egyptian and Red Sea ports and referred to in Greek and Latin sources, as for example in the oration of Dio to the Alexandrians in Egypt. The recent find of potsherds with Tamil Brāhmī inscriptions which have been read as proper names at the site of Qushehr on the Red Sea would support this possibility. It would be logical to find Indian traders living in the ports along the shores of the Red Sea and the Arabian Sea given the possibility that prior to the participation of Roman shipping it was mainly Indian and Arab shipping which carried cargoes from western India to the ports of west Asia. That some Yavana merchants were Buddhists is not surprising. The donations of the Yavanas, wherever they may have come from, to the Buddhist *saṅgha* were doubtless pious expressions of religious faith. But it should also be remembered that such donations would have brought them closer to the local *seṭṭhis*, a closeness which may have facilitated trade.

The prominent status of the *seṭṭhi* and *gahapati* at this time presents yet another contrast to the ordering of society in accordance with *dharmaśāstra* regulations. Social historians in the past have assumed that the *varṇa* model was the actuality and even when not conformed to fully it remained the framework within which society functioned. But the reality appears to have been rather different. The high status families according to the inscriptions would have been those with a *varṇa* ranking of *kṣatriya* and *vaiśya*. The *mahārathi* and the *mahābhoja* and perhaps some *gahapatis* would belong to the former and the *seṭṭhis* would be ranked as *vaiśyas*. These were the groups which in actual fact held the position of the elite in society. The lower sections were the artisans and hired labourers. Social distance would then be measured by the status of the *gahapati* on the one hand and the *karmakāra* or *bhṛtaka* on the other.

It could be argued that the inscriptions emanate from a Buddhist context in which *varṇa* distinctions were not so important and emphasis is given to *jāti* distinctions, which were in any case the more essential units of social functioning. Yet the *varṇa* distinctions are not ignored in brahmanical sources. Perhaps the function of *varṇa* was the legitimation of status. Thus royal families claiming to be *kṣatriyas* had to perform the required sacrifices and make the appropriate gifts to *brāhmaṇas* accompanied by the ritual observances required of their status. This did not however prevent them from making lavish donations to the Buddhist *saṅgha* reflecting a combination of religious and political sensitivity.

This pattern persisted into later centuries. The difference however was that after the decline of Buddhism in this region, no doubt in part tied to the decline of the west Asian trade, the donations to *brāhmaṇas* and to temples began to replace donations to the *saṅgha*, and strengthened the *varṇa* hierarchy. As in the case of Buddhism, the new form of Hinduism was also partially an import from the tertiary hinterland and partially the result of the internalising of this import in the plateau and coastal regions. The study of this process is still new and may ultimately suggest some worthwhile avenues of research. The process of internalising cultural forms or what may also be called acculturation can be examined for different segments of society although the evidence as we have it so far relates mainly to elite groups. I would like to touch briefly on one of these.

This process of acculturation is quite forcefully demonstrated in the cult of the hero-stone, which has only recently begun to receive attention of an appropriate kind from historians. This cult spans the frontiers of the region under discussion and manifests modifications clearly tied to the local environment. An impressionistic view of the location of hero-stones suggests that they occur frequently in the frontier regions between states or in politically disturbed regions and on the boundaries of villages and unsettled areas. A detailed mapping of find spots in a chronological series would either confirm or contradict this hypothesis. Given the fact that in the absence of cartography the boundaries of states were not clearly demarcated, some areas would have functioned as frontier regions. These were generally inhospitable areas, often mountainous or forested or arid, not settled by agriculturalists and sometimes given over to pastoralism. Such areas would have a rather ambiguous relationship with the more developed core regions which formed the nuclei of well-defined states and would change political loyalty frequently depending on which of the states in the vicinity happened to be more powerful. The defence of such settlements was frequently in the hands of local chiefs who protected the settlement from predators, both human and animal.

The earlier memorials were simple depictions of the hero with perhaps just a suggestion of a cause for action: a cattle-raid, sea piracy, brigandage or a man-eating tiger. Gradually when such heroes acquired status the cult became more elaborate. Towards the late first and early second millennia AD the hero-stone became almost a small shrine depicting not only the hero in action and in worship but also being carried, often by celestial maidens, to the heaven of Indra and the association of the symbols of eternity, the sun and the moon. The concept of the hero being carried to heaven was of course crucial to all hero cults. This was a different eschatology from that of *karma*, *saṃsāra* and rebirth, for the hero's reward had to be immediate.

What is equally interesting is the social use made of hero-stones. In some cases the memorial came to be worshipped as a deity, as has been argued by scholars examining the origins of the Viṭhobā cult. In others the memorial became a social marker. In the village of Bedsa at the foot of the hill which houses the Buddhist complex there is evidence of both, an early form of what seems to be a hero-stone and a group of the much later and more elaborate ones. The former is located in the part of the village inhabited by those regarded as low in the social hierarchy and is worshipped with rituals involving animal sacrifice and libations of alcohol. The more elaborate memorial stones are placed in the vicinity of the upper caste inhabitants and their worship is in accordance with brahmanical ritual. In such situations the historical evidence acquires a double function: one relating to its original purpose in the past and the other to what it symbolises in the present. Both aspects are invaluable to the historian. Such evidence is more easily available in the study of regional history and can provide fresh perspectives on the general understanding of a historical pattern. The cult of the hero-stone is an interesting example of a cultural phenomenon which spans the three hinterlands which I had referred to at the beginning.

Needless to say I have used the term hinterland not in its purely geographic sense but with a degree of historical license. This is perhaps permissible in an attempt to define a maritime area such as the Konkan. The economy and the society of such an area draws naturally on maritime trade; but in the case of the Konkan, inspite of the barrier to the coastal strip in the form of the ghats, the trade of the area was linked to the plateau and beyond. The question then arises as to the extent to which the Konkan was dependent on these hinterlands and the degree to which this dependence varied over time and in relation to other historical changes. Another question would relate to whether the Konkan was largely confined to the role of being an outlet for the plateau or whether it had an independent maritime economy based on both coastal and mid-ocean routes.

In the play between the regional and the supra-regional factors, the history of coastal areas becomes particularly pertinent. I have touched upon only a small segment of the Konkan. Being a long coastal area its hinterlands varied from north to south. The variations in themselves form an additional dimension to the complex subject of regional history and its co-relation with the larger geographical area of the country; and the complexity in this case is increased by the further dimensions of the Arabian Sea and the Indian Ocean.

# 7

# *Society and Historical Consciousness: The Itihāsa-purāṇa Tradition**

The expression of historical consciousness, it has often been assumed, takes the form of historical writing, clearly recognizable as a genre of literature. More frequently, however, the geological analogy of a particular vein embedded in rock seems more apposite, in that such consciousness is not always visible and has to be prised from sources which tend to conceal it. Within the vein lies information purporting to relate to events of the past, and enveloping this vein is the commentary which arises from concerns of the present. The form it takes tends to reflect the kind of society from which it emanates.

Historical consciousness, therefore, can change over time. Historians tend to view historical writing as conforming almost entirely to the format and pattern familiar from the last couple of centuries, or from models borrowed from particular societies such as ancient Greece and China. The more important but neglected aspect is the search for historical consciousness, irrespective of how immediately recognizable or evident it may be, in its literary form. This perhaps requires a distinction between what might be termed 'embedded history' — forms in which historical consciousness has to be prised out — and its opposite, 'externalized history' — which tends to bring embedded consciousness into the open, as it were, and to be more aware of its deliberate use of the past. The need for such a deliberate use suggests a changed historical

* S. Bhattacharya and R. Thapar (eds), *Situating Indian History*, Delhi, 1986, 353–83.

I am grateful to my colleagues Satish Saberwal and B.D. Chattopadhyaya for comments on an earlier draft of this essay.

situation. This distinction can be apparent not only between societies but also within the same society as it undergoes change. The attempt in this essay is not to analyse historical consciousness in relation to society as a whole, but in relation to a more restricted view of its expression among those who successfully aspired to power. It relates therefore only to historical writing in terms of changing forms in the perception of power.

Each version of the past which has been deliberately transmitted has a significance for the present, and this accounts for its legitimacy and its continuity. The record may be one in which historical consciousness is embedded: as in myth, epic and genealogy; or alternatively it may refer to the more externalized forms: chronicles of families, institutions and regions, and biographies of persons in authority. There is no evolutionary or determined continuum from one form to the other and facets of the embedded consciousness can be seen as a part of the latter, whether introduced deliberately or subconsciously. The degree to which forms change or overlap has a bearing on dominant social formations. Similarly, major social and political changes influence the form of historical consciousness even though there is no mechanical correlation between the two.

Evident historical texts such as chronicles of families, institutions and regions often incorporate mythical beginnings which act as charters of validation. The tracing of links with established lineages through genealogical connections, and frequently with epic heroes, plays the same role of drawing upon embedded history. I shall consider some forms of embedded history, such as the prevalent myths in the *itihāsa-purāṇa* tradition, which encapsulate features of what might be seen as historical experience; the eulogies and hero-lauds which were gradually expanded into epic literature; the genealogical sections or *vaṃśānucarita* of the Puranic texts which, by implication, carry a commentary on the social status of ruling families.

In contrast to these the more externalized forms draw upon the embedded but have other primary concerns and carry a different type of historical information. Thus historical biography or the *carita* literature has as its germ the hero-laud and the epic hero. Family chronicles and *vaṃśāvalīs* assimilate myth and genealogy to other events. Chronicles of institutions and regions maintain a variant form of mythology and genealogy, and are aimed at recording the history of the institution or the area. The distinction made between the two forms is not arbitrary; I am arguing that the embedded form is closer to what have been called lineage-based societies and the externalized form to state systems incorporated in monarchies. Or, to put it in another way, the existence of the state requiring its own validation encourages the creation of an externalized historical consciousness.

In the articulation of historical consciousness in early north-Indian society the truly embedded forms are evident in the literature of the lineage-based society characterized by an absence of state formation, and the more free-standing or externalized forms emerge with the transition to state systems. The terms 'lineage society' and 'state systems', used here as a short-hand, represent not merely a change in political forms but a multiple social change. Thus the term 'state' would refer to a society registering political polarities, an increasingly vertical hierarchy of authority, social inequalities, differentiated economies and distinct ideological identities; not that these characteristics are completely absent in lineage societies, but there are endemic differences between the two. Sometimes these differences are blurred in the texts. Lineage society derives its validity from different sources of authority as compared to state systems, with which we are in any case more familiar.[1] The central role of lineage in the earlier society has reference to more than just the ordering of kinship for it dominates virtually every aspect of activity.

## I

The deepest layer of the embedded form is myth. Events are assumed to have happened, and time is almost proto-chronos since it involves gods and the supernatural in an active role with humans and animals. The significance of myth to the historian lies more in its being the self-image of a given culture, expressing its social assumptions. The role of myth in this context is often explanatory. Origin myths are concerned with cosmogony and the start of events such as the Flood myth.[2] The *Śatapatha Brāhmaṇa* version of the Flood myth carries obvious traces of association with the Mesopotamian Flood myth. Manu, when performing his morning ablutions, finds a fish in his cupped hands and rears the fish until it reaches an enormous size. The fish explains the intention of the gods to drown the earth in a deluge and, wishing to save Manu and the seven *ṛṣis* (in whom vests all knowledge) from this disaster, it orders Manu to build a boat for this purpose. This is tied to its horn and it swims through the deluge. The boat and its passengers remain safely on a mountain until the flood subsides, after which they return. By means of sacrifical rites Manu creates a series of sons for himself and one androgynous daughter, his children being the founders of the various lineages. The eldest son, Ikṣvāku, establishes the Sūryavaṃśa or Solar lineage, and the androgynous daughter, Iḷā, establishes the Candravaṃśa or Lunar lineage.

The *Matsya Purāṇa* version links the fish with the incarnation of Viṣṇu, thus bringing the gods more directly into the story, and at the same time using what was obviously a familiar myth to demonstrate the power of the new god, Viṣṇu. Manu, as the name suggests in its association with *mānava* (mankind), is the primeval, archetypal man who is the eponymous ancestor of all the lineages. The emphasis on origins is again stressed in the deluge, where the flood is seen as a time-marker. Floods tend to wipe away earlier conditions and society can start afresh.[3] The survival of Manu and the *ṛṣis* links the new creation with the old, in spite of the deluge washing away the old, since Manu is the seventh in a succession of pre-Flood Manus. The link is important to the genealogical records. The status of the earlier Manus is conveyed through it to the new lineages. All the eponymous ancestors of the lineages are the children of Manu.

Other myths provide social sanctions, one such being the Puruṣasūkta story in the *Ṛg Veda* describing the origin of the four castes.[4] The Puruṣasūkta hymn occurs in a late section of the *Ṛg Veda* and describes the sacrifice of the god Prajāpati, from whose body the four *varṇas* are said to have sprung: the *brāhmaṇas* from his mouth, the *kṣatriyas* from his arms, the *vaiśyas* from his thighs and the *śūdras* from his feet. The symbolism of each bodily part relates to the ritual status and function of the particular *varṇa*. That the origin and hierarchy go back to a ritual occasion underlines the nature of the ranking. The evolution of *varṇa* stratification is rooted in the lineage-based society of Vedic times. In a sense the *brāhmaṇa* and the *kṣatriya varṇas* were to evolve as distinct lineages with their separate rules of marriage and descent: exogamy in the *brāhmaṇa gotras* and the more frequent endogamy of the *kṣatriyas*. The *śūdra varṇa* is excluded by its very origin, which is a denial of lineage since it is said more often to include groups identified by the status of the two parents.

Some myths legitimize a changed social and political condition, as is apparent from the much repeated story of Pṛthu.[5] The various versions of this story begin by referring to the wickedness of Veṇa who had to be killed by the *ṛṣis* because of his unrighteous rule. From his left thigh they churned a successor, Niṣāda, who was inadequate and was expelled to the forest as a hunter-gatherer. From the right arm of Veṇa they churned another successor, the righteous *rājā* Pṛthu, who introduced cattle-keeping and agriculture and bestowed so many benefits on the earth, that she in gratitude took his name Pṛthivī. Veṇa was wicked because he ceased to perform the sacrificial ritual and had to be killed by the *ṛṣis* (and not expelled by his subjects), who alone had the right to depose a ruler. The dark, short, ugly Niṣāda became the prototype of all forest-dwelling people. The myth sought to legitimize the expulsion of such groups when land was cleared and settled by agriculturists.

In each of such cases an attempt is made to explain social origins and assumptions which are significant to historical reconstruction. Myth was transmitted orally in its earliest phase. With the evolution of a more heterogeneous and stratified society, myths were questioned and explanations sought. Some myths were replaced with new or different versions and others added to and embellished, often to such a degree that the original myth became almost opaque. That myths in some ways mirrored society was not their sole function, but for our purposes this aspect is significant.

Myths of descent often serve to integrate diverse groups by providing common origins. Among competing groups a myth can be used for the reverse process of distinguishing one from the other. Origin myths posit beginnings authoritatively and are therefore central to embedded history. The degree to which myths reflect different social assumptions can be demonstrated by a comparison of origin myths from the *Ṛg Veda* and from Buddhist sources, a comparison which also demonstrates the degree to which historical consciousness is embedded in myth.[6] The origins of the Śākyas, Licchavis, Mallas and Koliyas are all described in stories which have a common format, which format suggests a tradition deviant from the brahmanical origin myths. The clans are of the Ikṣvāku lineage, are said to be of the families of *rājās* (which could mean royal descent but more likely refers to families of lineage chiefs) and are often the exiled children of such families, thus suggesting a lineage migration or fission. The new settlement is in a forest clearing with a town as its nucleus. The name of the lineage is frequently associated with an object such as the *kol* or *śaka* tree. More interestingly, the original founders have a system of sibling marriages and in each case sixteen pairs of twin children are born: it is from these that the lineage expands. Sibling incest, since it is never actually referred to as prevalent, would point to a symbolic concern with purity of lineage, a demarcation between the families of the *rājās* who owned land and the rest of the people, by the assertion of origins otherwise taboo; or perhaps an endorsement of cross-cousin marriage, which, because it was prohibited by brahmanical codes referring to northern India, may have been seen as a form of sibling incest. That the origin myth was of some consequence is evident from its inclusion in the history of every lineage and by the considerable emphasis given to it in the biographies of the Buddha. There is an absence of any reference to ritual status.

## II

Apart from myth, other embedded forms are associated with various fragments of literature moving towards the emergence of the epic. The evolution is traceable via the *dāna-stuti* (eulogies on gift-giving), *gāthā*, *nārāśaṁsī* (eulogies on heroes) to the *ākhyāna* and the *kathā* (cycles of stories generally involving heroes). The *dāna-stuti* hymns scattered throughout the *Ṛg Veda* are eulogies on chiefs and deities who act as would chiefs bestowing generous gifts on grateful bards and priests.[7] The prototype of the gift-giver was the god Indra. The Indra-*gāthās* express the gratitude of the *jana* (tribe) whom he has led successfully in a cattle-raid and subsequently in distributing the wealth bestowed, much of it on the priests. The same was expected from the ideal *rājā* (chief) in a society where raids were a major access to property and where wealth was computed in heads of cattle and horse, in chariots, gold and slave girls. The *dāna-stutis* mentioned the names of their patrons, who were doubtless actual chiefs, but, equally important, the hymns indicated the purpose of the gift and the items of wealth. They were not only eulogies of past actions but also indicators of what was expected from the chiefs.

The *ākhyānas*, commemorating *rājās* and heroes, were the cycles of stories recited at the time of the *yajñas* (sacrificial rituals).[8] Some heroes underwent a metamorphosis in time and came to be remembered for reasons quite different from those of the earliest stories. Thus Purūravas in the *Ṛg Veda* is a mortal who loves a celestial woman, Urvaśī; in the *Śatapatha Brāhmaṇa* he is shown as aspiring to become a celestial being himself in pursuit of his love; and finally in the *Mahābhārata* he is not only a celestial being but is among the more important ancestors of the Candravaṃśa lineage.[9] The protagonists in these stories are members of the chiefly families (*rājanyas* and *kṣatriyas*); the stories narrate their lives and activities and incidentally provide information on the lineages as well. An example of the latter is the transformation of single lineages into confederacies of tribes — the Bharatas and the Pūrus of the *Ṛg Veda* confederating with others into the Kurus of later times. The genealogies tend to be shallow and activities centre around the lineages rather than the succession of hereditary status.

A common feature of these many embedded forms is that they are linked to the ritual of sacrifice, the *yajña*. This imparts sanctity to the story and ensures it a continuity coeval with the performance of the ritual; it also imbues it with what were believed to be transcendental powers associated with the accurate and precise performance of the ritual. Even if the events were limited to the activities of the *kṣatriyas*, the audience was much wider and incorporated the entire tribe. Apart from the obvious ritual and religious function of the *yajña* its relevance also lay in its being the occasion for the redistribution of wealth, both from cattle raids and from agricultural production. Up to a point certain rituals had elements of a potlatch in which wealth was not merely redistributed but was also consumed. Both the redistribution as well as the destruction of wealth were directly concerned with claims to status.[10]. When the ritual was enlarged to include representation from other *janas*, either in the form of honoured guests or as tribute bearers, its function as a potlatch gradually gave way to its symbolizing status on a grander scale. The claims of individual lineages or their segments as descent groups could be established on such occasions, as for example the famous *rājasūya* sacrifice of Yudhiṣṭhira[11] which raises a complex set of problems concerning the status of various lineages, not least among them that of Kṛṣṇa as the chief of the Vṛṣṇis. The *yajña* therefore stated, as it were, the ranking order of the lineages. The stories which related to these lineages became social charters recording status *vis-à-vis* other lineages, or changes of status, as for example from segment to confederacy, or the migration and fissioning off of a segment from a lineage, as in the case of the Cedis migrating from the western Ganga valley to central India.[12] The record of such migrations was crucial not only to territorial claims but also to genealogical links with established lineages by those newly formed. The *yajña* was a conduit of gift-exchange as well where the wealth of the lineage brought as *bali* or tribute (initially voluntary and later less so) by the *viś* (clan) to the *kṣatriya* or the *rājā*, or else the wealth captured in a raid would be ceremonially used in the ritual and what remained of it would be gifted to the *brāhmaṇas* performing the *yajña*. The exchange was at many levels. Wealth was offered to the gods in return for the success and well-being both of the *kṣatriya* and the *viś*, the well being guaranteed by the *brāhmaṇas*. Tangible wealth moved from the household of the *kṣatriya* to that of the *brāhmaṇa*. Such a limited exchange was economically non-productive in the sense that it was self-perpetuating with little chance of breaking through to new social forms. But its actual significance lay in its being an operative process in maintaining the lineage society.

III

It was doubtless these fragments of eulogies (*praśastis*) on the heroes and the cycles of stories which led to the first gropings towards epic forms in India, referred to as the *kathā*. Both the *Mahābhārata* and the *Rāmāyaṇa* had their earlier and perhaps more truly epic versions in what have been referred to as the *Rāma-kathā* and the *Bhārata*[13] or *Jaya*. In their later forms, as we have them now, each of the two epics has a distinct locale and the narrative is woven around one of the two main lineages. Thus the *Mahābhārata* focuses on the western Ganga valley, referred to as *madhya-deśa* in the literature, and is concerned with the Aila lineage. The *Rāmāyaṇa* as the epic of the Ikṣvāku lineage has its nucleus in the middle Ganga valley, in Kośala and Videha, and is concerned with migrations southwards into the Vindhyan region, with Dakṣina Kośala perhaps providing the clue to the area of exile.

The epic continued to be recited, initially on ritual occasions; the *Mahābhārata* is said to have been recited at the *yajña* in the Naimiśa forest and the *sarpa-yajña* of Janamejaya, the *Rāmāyaṇa* by Lava and Kuśa in the Vālmīki-*āśrama*. But it also became the stock for court poetry, the *kāvya*, in the newly emerging courts of the monarchies of the late first millennium BC, or for that matter in more elaborate literary fashions in the courts of the various kingdoms of the first millennium AD.

The epic form carries within it the germs of a more conscious and less embedded historical tradition.[14] Its historicity lies in the fact that it is a later age reflecting on an earlier one, the reflections frequently taking the form of interpolations interleaved among the fragments of the oral, bardic tradition. When epic literature ceases to be a part of the oral tradition and is frozen into a written form, reflections begin to tail off. The pastoral-agricultural society of the world of the heroes structured around lineage gives way to the more clearly agrarian societies and to the rise of urban centres controlled by what is visibly emerging as a state system — which in the Ganga valley at this time was mainly monarchical.

Many of the seeming contradictions in the stances and configurations characterizing the epics can perhaps be explained by these texts (and particularly the *Mahābhārata*), reflecting something of a transitional condition between two rather different structures, the societies of the lineage-based system and that of the monarchical state. Idealized characters are seldom the gods but rather the heroes who occupy the centre of the stage and the gods remain in the wings. Sometimes the earlier deities even come in for a drubbing.[15] The importance of the heroes is further endorsed by their being almost the terminal descendants in the major lineages of the past, a matter of some despair for their death is seen as the wrapping up and putting away of the lineage society, which, in certain areas, was being replaced by monarchies. However, some elements of the lineage society did persist and among them was the continuation of *varṇa* ranking. In many areas outside the *madhya-deśa*, lineage society continued for longer periods and the transition to monarchical states was a gradual process. Nevertheless the change to monarchy meant a substantial alteration of social configurations.

Unlike myth, epic does not attempt to explain the universe or society. It is sufficient that the problems of society are laid bare, and even solutions are not sought since the ultimate solution is the dissolution of the system. Societies experiencing greater stratification require an overall authority to maintain the cohesion of lineage and strata. When such an authority comes into being and is eulogized, that eulogy becomes the dirge of a truly epic society. In laying bare the conditions in the transition from lineage society to state systems, a number of bi-polarities are reflected in the literature which give an added edge to the image of the past and the contours of the present. Thus *grāma* (settlement) is contrasted with *araṇya* (forest), the kingdom with exile; the orderliness of the *grāma* is opposed to the disorder of the *araṇya*; the kingly ethic arises out of governing a people and claiming land, the heroic ethic emerges from war and confrontation. The monarchical state is seen as the superior and is the successor to lineage society, irrespective of whether this is clearly spelt out — as in the conflict between the kingdom of Kośala and the *rākṣasas* in the *Rāmāyaṇa* — or whether it is left more ambiguous — as in the diverse assumptions of the narrative and didactic sections of the *Mahābhārata* where the Sabhāparvan, encapsulating the essence of a lineage society, stands in contrast to the Śāntiparvan with its rhetoric on the monarchical state. The new ethic is sustained in part by the popularizing of new sources of authority. Among them and significant to the political arena were the king, the *brāhmaṇa* and the *ṛṣi*. None of these were entirely new in that the chief, the priest and the shaman were dominant figures in lineage society. But it is the tangible authority of the king based on land as the source of revenue, or of the *brāhmaṇa* as the sole performer of and manual on rituals, and of the *ṛṣi* and *saṁnyāsi* as symbolizing an intangible moral authority almost as a counterweight to that of the first two, which gives a fresh dimension to their role and their interrelations. The changed situation is reflected in a shift in the kind of authority exercised. From a more diffused, equitable authority there is a movement towards a hierarchical, vertical authority.[16] This was mitigated somewhat by the countervailing presence of the renouncer and the charisma attached to renunciation.

The epic as the literature of one age looking back nostalgically on another can become a literature of legitimation. Interpolations are often the legitimation of the present but are attributed to the heroes of the past. The bards were perhaps providing the models of what patrons should be like. But, more important, it is the kingdoms looking back on an age of chiefships: where recently founded dynasties were seeking ancestry from the *kṣatriya* lineages through actual or, more often, imagined genealogical links; where such ancestry would also bestow social legitimacy and validate kingship. That legitimacy and validation are essential to the epic is clear from the central event of the narrative, namely the legitimacy of succession, involving elder and younger sons and the problems of disqualification.[17] Legitimacy also relates to using the past to explain the present. Perhaps the most dramatic example of this is the series of explanations in favour of accepting the strangeness of Draupadī marrying five brothers, fraternal polyandry not being a commonly practised form of marriage. Among the explanations is predictably a reference to an earlier birth of Draupadī.[18] Fortunately the doctrine of transmigration, referring to events and situations in a previous birth, makes the use of the past more plausible. The interplay of the past and the present is thus not only part of the implicit epic idiom but is made more explicit by recourse to the theory of transmigration. At another level the past validates the present in the long discourses on what constitutes good government or the correct functioning of the *kṣatriya* as king: perhaps best exemplified in the dying Bhīṣma delivering the lengthy *mokṣadharma* perorations, lying on his bed of arrows. Legitimacy makes the claim to historicity more feasible and the association with myth is weakened.[19]

## IV

The gradual prising of historical consciousness becomes visible in the compilation of what came to be called the *itihāsa-purāṇa*.[20] The phrase remains difficult to define, veering between the perceived past and historicity. It is described as the fifth Veda but was an oral tradition for many centuries until it was compiled in the form of the *Purāṇas* in the mid first millennium AD. The genealogical sections of the *Purāṇas* were a reordering of the earlier material in a new format. The lesser and multiple *Purāṇas* borrowed the format of the earlier major *Purāṇas*, although their contents differed. The *Purāṇa* was to become a recognized literary form. To the extent that it recorded history, it was initially transitional from embedded to externalized history. It was linked to the bardic tradition, where the *sūta* and the *māgadha* are said to have been its earliest authors.[21] In the Vedic texts the *sūta* has a close relation with the *rājā* and was of high status, but by the time of the Manu *Dharmaśāstra* the *sūta* had been reduced to the level of a *sankīrṇajāti* or mixed caste. Doubtless by now the tradition had been appropriated by the literate *brāhmaṇas* who had also seen the potential value of controlling oral information on the past and recording it in a literary form relevant to emergent contemporary requirements.

There is evidence to suggest that the Purāṇic texts were translated from the oral Prākrit to the literate Sanskrit.[22] The structure of the *Purāṇas* was an attempt to provide an integrated world view of the past and present, linking events to the emergence of a deity or a sect, since each *Purāṇa* was dedicated to such a one, the *Viṣṇu Purāṇa* being regarded as the model. The historical epicentre of the *itihāsa* tradition was the *vaṃśānucarita*, which, as the name suggests, was the genealogy of all the known lineages and dynasties upto the mid-first millennium AD. It was not a parallel tradition to the earlier *kathās* and *ākhyānas* since it incorporated many of these forms of embedded history. The genealogical core pertaining to those who were believed to have held power in the past was carefully preserved after it had been worked out into a systematic pattern. This was because it not only purported to record the past but was also later to become essential to future claims to lineage status, and was therefore linked with historical writing. Evidently there was a need for a recognizable historical tradition at this time. In the transition from lineage to state, which was occurring in many parts of north India, monarchy had emerged as the viable political form.

The major dynasties recorded in the *Purāṇas* upto the mid-first millennium AD start with descendants of recognized *kṣatriya* lineages, but by the mid-first millennium BC begin to refer to families of non-*kṣatriya* origin. Some are specifically said to be *śūdras*, such as the Nandas and possibly the Mauryas. Others, judging by their names, were *brāhmaṇa*, such as the Śuṅgas and Kāṇvas. The lesser dynasties dating to the early centuries AD are stated to be *vrātya-dvija*, *śūdra* and *mleccha*, and this is explained as resulting from the inevitable degeneration of all norms in the Kaliyuga. Successor dynasties are frequently referred to as the *bhṛtyas* or servants of the previous ones, suggesting that the founders of dynasties may often have been administrators, high in the hierarchy of office who overthrew weak kings. This may well account for the rise of *brāhmaṇa* dynasties. The gradual increase in references to *śūdra* rulers would indicate that political power, although in theory restricted to *kṣatriyas*, was infact open to any *varṇa*. It required force and administrative control to establish a dynasty. Claims to territory were established through strength of arms. Legitimation through brahmanical ritual was evidently not required since some dynasties are described as not conforming to Vedic rites. This may well have been due to the influence of Buddhism and Jainism at this time. The Brahmanical refusal to bestow *kṣatriya* status on such families may have been in part due to their being patrons of non-brahmanical religious sects. Buddhist and Jaina literature on the other hand insists on the *kṣatriya* status of some of these dynasties. Thus the Mauryas are not only listed as *kṣatriyas* but are linked to the clan of the Buddha, the Śākyas, which would automatically have related them to the prestigious Sūryavaṃśa as well.[23] The absence of proper status in the brahmanical sources did not detract from the importance of these families. If anything it points to the relative independence of the state as a political form from the clutches of traditional validation during this period. The need for legitimation through lineage status was apparently not required at this time.

The encroachment of foreign rulers in the post-Mauryan period led to some indigenous families having to recede into the background. Claims to power and to actual status were conceded to the Indo-Greeks, Śakas, Parthians and Kuṣāṇas, but claim to *varṇa* status was denied them and they continued to be called *vrātya-kṣatriyas* (degenerate), having no indigenous land-base in the subcontinent nor being able to claim kinship links with earlier established lineages.[24] This was despite the fact that some among them did claim *kṣatriya* status in their own inscriptions.[25] The lack of genealogical connections was a form of exclusion, effective in a society where ritual status still drew heavily on the values of a lineage-based social organization and where genealogical links had played a crucial role.

Although dynastic status was not confined to any particular *varṇa*, those who succeeded to kingship from the mid-first millennium AD onwards often observed the formality of claiming *kṣatriya* status, or at least of participating in a common *kṣatriya* past as embodied in the *itihāsa-purāṇa* tradition. The question may well be asked as to why such a practice becomes more necessary during this period, and the answer covers a range of possibilities. The making of land grants to *brāhmaṇas* and the consequent spread of Sanskritic culture provides an obvious reason. But it would be as well not to overlook the reality on the ground, as it were, and examine the actual process of state formation at a time when it related to secondary (if not tertiary) states, or new states emerging from association with established states. Land grants of a substantial size to non-religious grantees would have provided the base for the grantee establishing a network of political control over the area through his lineage connections.[26] The partial *brāhmaṇa* ancestry of some ruling families as given in their genealogies would suggest that even *brāhmaṇa* grantees were not averse to participating in this process. Where unoccupied land was still available and the migration of peasants feared, political control would be less effective if dependent on force and more effective if drawing its strength from legitimacy. The expression of power in the sense of controlling resources and seeking compliance through persuasion, influence and support[27] would be better achieved by legitimacy than by force. The legitimation of lineage origins therefore became a necessity.

The granting of land, apart from its other functions, served also to incorporate areas under lineage systems into the society dominated by the state. Lineage-based agrarian activity was assimilated into the new economy and erstwhile clansmen or else their chiefs were converted into tax-paying peasants. Lineage traditions continued up to a point and could be adjusted to the *varṇa* framework, which acted as a bridge between the earlier society and its later form.

It would be worth investigating whether the process of state formation in the late first millennium AD provided a different emphasis from that of the earlier period. The overlap between lineage and state continued, but the political form was perhaps not so reliant on institutions of the state and included a more substantial dependence on lineage. Would it then be correct to argue that the post-Gupta state did not attempt to uproot the *kṣatriyas* (to use the phrase of the *Purāṇas*) and reduce the importance of lineage societies, but rather that it attempted to encourage the emergence of a new role for lineages through which it sought to extend its control?

With the kaleidoscopic formation of states in the post-Gupta period, new ruling families relied heavily on genealogical links, fabricated genealogies providing them with claims to being *kṣatriyas*: claims which were carefully stated in the then legal charters, i.e. the inscriptions recording the grants of land by these families to *brāhmaṇas* and other grantees. Such claims became even more crucial in a situation of competition for status by horizontal marriage alliances among the 'new' *kṣatriyas*. Matrimonial links sealed the claims to status. Thus the possible tribal Gond and Bhil associations of the Candella and Guhilot ruling families did not eventually stand in the way of their claims to *kṣatriya* status, which were backed not merely by land-ownership but also by claims to genealogical links with the Candravaṃśa and the Sūryavaṃśa: the claim being recognized with marriage into other established *kṣatriya* families.[28] The sixteenth century marriage of a Gond *rājā* into the Candella family is an interesting example of how the system worked. The acceptance by other competing families of the origin myth and of the genealogy of the family successfully installed in power was largely because political power was relatively open and individual families were concerned with succeeding to power, not with altering the framework within which status was conferred. The narrowing down of legitimation to one family meant that others could aspire to the same power in changed circumstances.

The earlier states from the Mauryan to the Kuṣāṇa tended to develop administrative structures in which local regions were left relatively untampered as long as they provided the required revenue.[29] When revenue requirements became oppressive, peasants could threaten to migrate from the state and establish new clearings in the forest and on waste land. Migration was the alternative to peasant revolt and kings are cautioned against oppressive taxes lest peasants migrate. From the Gupta period onwards there was a gradual and increasing tendency to intensify the revenue demands and tie down the peasantry.[30] The economic restructuring of the local region was regarded as part of the state's legitimate right to revenue. The ability of the peasant to migrate was hampered, and even though there is little apparent evidence of peasant revolts the earlier flexible relationship between peasants and the state would have changed — with the intermediate grantees playing the difficult role of keeping the peasants tied since it was not only the revenue demands of the state but also their own revenue rights which were at stake. This points towards an urgent need on the part of grantees and landowners and clan chiefs, the potential ruling families, to not only insist on their high status but to be able to prove it whenever necessary. An emphasis on status, with the insistence on service by the lower orders inherent in the formulation of *varṇa*, became in some areas an adjunct to coercion by those who had succeeded in rising to higher levels of political power. The *itihāsa-purāṇa* tradition became one of the means of legitimizing status and the *vaṃśānucarita* sections had to be carefully preserved.

Lists of succession (*vaṃśa*) — whether of teachers as in the Vedic texts, or of Elders in the *sangha*, or of descent groups as in the case of the Sūryavaṃśa and the Candravaṃśa, or of dynasties — encapsulate perceptions of the past. Genealogy as a record of succession lay at the core of the epic tradition and linked epic to embedded history as well as to the *itihāsa-purāṇa* and later historical forms. Genealogy is used by new groups in the ascendant to legitimize their power and claim connections with those who were earlier in power. Links were therefore sought in the post-Gupta period by new ruling families with the Sūryavaṃśa and the Candravaṃśa. The epics embodying the stories of these lineages were thus assured continuity, quite apart from the infusion of a religious dimension through the theory of epic heroes being *avatāras* of Viṣṇu. The less obvious information from genealogical data indicates kinship patterns, marriage forms, geographical settlements and migration.[31]

The pattern or structure of a genealogy is often indicative of social integration where competing groups are shown through a listing of descent. Among these the successful ones claim a larger share of the genealogical structure, parallel to their claim to inheritance and power. In the Aila genealogy, for example, the Pūrus and the Yādavas claim the major part of the genealogy and the lines of Turvaśa, Anu and Druhyu peter out fairly soon. The ideological function of the genealogy is to legitimate those who have succeeded to power or to subvert the claims of those who for various reasons are unacceptable. That genealogy was of considerable consequence is indicated not only by the *Purāṇas* but also by other sources.[32]

The *vaṃśānucarita* section has three distinct constituent parts.[33] The first is the mythical section of the rule of the seven Manus, which is wiped away by the action of the Flood. This is followed by the detailed listing of the generations in each of the two major lineages. The Ikṣvāku is the senior and more cohesive. Descent is recorded only from eldest son to eldest son with a tight control over a well demarcated territory, indicative of a stronger tendency towards monarchy and primogeniture. The Aila lineage is more akin to the pattern of a segmentary system with a wide geographical distribution involving northern, western and central India. Possibly it reflects a more assimiliative system in which the segments are less the result of branching off or migrating away from the main lineage and more a record of alliances with existing clans. The spread of the Haihaya group in central India would suggest this. It might also be the result of an element of the 'tidying up' of lineages by the authors of the *Purāṇas*. Two sub-lineages among the Candravaṃśa are given pre-eminence, those of the Pūrus controlling the western Ganga valley and the more diffused Yādavas migrating to western and central India. The segments are all treated as *kṣatriyas*, even though at times this status conflicts with the status assigned to some of them in other sources.[34] Thus the genealogy was a method of legitimizing all those who had held power. However, they had to have performed the brahmanical sacrificial ritual in order to be included in the *itihāsa-purāṇa*, for those who were lax in this matter were either dropped altogether, such as the Licchavis, or like the Śākyas were merely mentioned *en passant*.[35]

The *Mahābhārata* war acts as another time-marker and brings to the battlefield virtually all the lineages of the Candravaṃśa, and a few others as well, and marks the death of the lineages. That it was a terminal event is reflected in the switch to the future tense after the war, suggesting a prophetic form, and is followed by details on dynastic succession in the kingdom of Magadha, an area which emerged in fact as the most powerful kingdom of the Ganga valley. Descent lists now become king lists mentioning historically attested dynasties — Nandas, Mauryas, Śuṅgas, Kāṇvas, Āndhras, and so on, as well as the regnal years of kings. The genealogical record thus indicates a change to monarchies during this period, a change which was of considerable historical importance. Those dynasties which did not claim links with earlier descent groups such as the Indo-Greeks, Śakas, Kuṣāṇas and Kṣatrapas receive short shrift at the hands of the genealogists. The Yavanas as a generalized term are described as the descendants of the Turvaśa, who, as a segment of the Candravaṃśa, become relatively insignificant fairly early in the genealogical listing.[36] The entry of *śūdras* as kings, be they Indian or foreign, was of course seen as the inevitable consequence of social imbalances foretold for the Kaliyuga. The *vaṃśānucarita* section therefore becomes a preservation of the record of social and political relations as perceived at a crucial historical moment, and incorporates much of what was believed to be historically accurate. This is put together in a distinctive structure which not only gives form to the past but also becomes a charter of sanction for existing social institutions as well as a potential charter for future claims to legitimacy and status.

Purāṇic literature, in the sections other than the *vaṃśānucarita*, reflects facets of change which impinged upon the historical tradition. It comprises essentially assimilative texts where the Sanskritic tradition and the local tradition are sought to be intermeshed. This was inevitable in a situation where those of a Sanskritic cultural milieu received grants of land and settled in areas where the exposure to Sanskritic culture had been relatively sparse, if at all. Some degree of mutual interchange was required, even if for no other purpose than that of establishing dominance. The Purāṇic texts with their various sub-categories are facets of this development. The culture of the dominant and of the subordinate remained distinct, but proximity and some degree of absorption smoothened the edges of an otherwise angular relationship in many areas. The rhetoric of the Great Tradition and the systematizing of substratum cultures, both of which are reflected in the *Purāṇas*, made the literature acceptable to the audience and useful in mobilizing social and political action.[37]

## V

A more clearly recognizable historical tradition is evident in the post-Gupta period, linked in part to the historical changes of the early and mid first millennium AD. The states of this period were territorially not as large as the Mauryan and the Kuṣāṇa, for example. There was a multiplicity of state formation, particularly in areas hitherto regarded as peripheral or marginal and often characterized by a lineage society. Many of these new states emerged as a consequence of the changes in agrarian relations in the earlier established states, when the system of making grants of land became current. These changes required new processes of authority, law and revenue collection in areas which earlier were either outside the state system or on the edge of it. The change was not limited to the political arena but also introduced new forms of a wider social mobility. There was a growth of sectarian religious groups, some of which professed a doctrinal cult (*bhakti*, narrowing in on an individual's devotion to a particular deity); others which attempted to systematize more earthly cults of fertility and magic; and still others which remained loyal lay supporters of the Buddhist and Jaina *saṅgha*. It was also perhaps in part a reaction to this last group which motivated the increasing interest in an *itihāsa-purāṇa*. Both the Buddhists and the Jainas had shown a sense of centring their sects in avowedly historical events which imparted a certain historicity and added to the intellectual strength of their institutions. The historicity of the Buddha and Mahāvīra was emphasized, major events in the history of the respective *saṅgha*s were linked to political events and personalities, chronology was often calculated on the basis of the date of the death of the Buddha and of Mahāvīra. This point was not missed by other groups and in the latter half of the first millennium AD when Vaiṣṇava and Śaiva sects competed for royal patronage, they not only established monastic institutions but also introduced a historical dimension into the discussion on the evolution of the sect. It can be argued that Buddhist and Jaina sects arose as a part of a counter-culture and therefore as groups in dissent had a clearer sense of their historical purpose.[38] This is a partial explanation of a far more complex question: why Buddhism has a more recognizable sense of externalized history — a question which cannot be discussed in this brief essay. Be it said in passing that apart from considerations of eschatology and epistemology, all of which have their own significance, it is as well to consider also that Buddhism and Jainism were quite early on institutionally based and moved fairly soon to becoming property holders on a considerable scale. As such the records of their evolution did not merely narrate the life of the Buddha and the history of the *saṅgha* (with its various divergent sects, each claiming status and authenticity), but also described the building of monasteries, the amassing of property and the rights to controlling these — rights which became complex and competitive with the fissioning off of sects from the main stems. The sense of the historicity of the sect becomes evident even in Śaiva and Vaiṣṇava sects when they begin to locate themselves in *āśrama*s and *maṭha*s and become immensely wealthy property holders, and when intensified competition for patronage has to be supported by claims to legitimacy — which require a substantial input of historically phrased argument.

Implicit in the genealogical form is the notion of time and chronology. The arrangement of events in a chronological order is less precise for earlier times and only when sequential causation becomes important does chronological precision enter the focus of history. Genealogical generations indicate time periods, as also do regnal years. The latter move from fanciful figures to more credible ones as the dynastic lists approach historically attested time. Thus the chronology given for the Śiśunāga, Nandas, Mauryas and other dynasties is feasible. The arrangement of chronological order becomes more important as historical memory becomes less embedded. The cosmological time of the *mahāyuga* and the start of the Kaliyuga gives way to historical time.[39] The accuracy of historical time increases by the reference to dateable eras — the Kṛta (c. 58 BC), Śaka (AD 78), Gupta (AD 319–20), Cedi (c. AD 249), Harṣa (AD 606), and so on: and by the very precise dates recorded in era, regnal year, season, month, lunar fortnight and day in the inscriptions. The era, apart from commemorating an event, can also be seen as a capturing of time, symbolic of an articulation of power in a context where time is viewed as part of an eventual point of destruction. The word for time is *kāla* from the root *kal* 'to calculate', which suggests a meaning indicative of measurement. Perhaps because of the cyclical theory it was also associated with destruction in the sense of the end of time.

The inevitability of time is strengthened by the use of prophecies in genealogies, for time is the ultimate destroyer, *mahākāla*. Cosmological time is distinct from historical time not only by its mathematical pattern and the spatial form in its description, but also by its total orderliness, an orderliness which emphasizes its unreality. This in part might also explain the marginality of chiliastic and millenarian movements in such a pattern as compared to the Judaeo-Christian tradition in which they play a distinctive role. The coming of Viṣṇu as Kalkin arises out of an anxiety relating to the present — the wish to terminate the inequities of the Kaliyuga through Viṣṇu yet again being incarnated as a saviour figure. But such a termination is predetermined by the length of the cycle and will in any case lead to the ultimate ending of the cycle. It is more to the weakness of the eschatology that the marginality of millenarian movements can be attributed. The interplay of cosmological and historical time in the brahmanical tradition can perhaps be explained partially by the *yajña* and *varṇa* requirements which were part of the process of legitimizing families and cults. Cyclical time it has been argued, goes counter to an eschatology which would point to a historical change towards a directed goal.[40] Yet within the *mahāyuga* there is an emphasis on change. It is change rather than repetition which is inherent in the concept, and within this the explanation of change is also implicit.[41]

The notion of change is even more central to the Buddhist concept of time.[42] Because of the claim to the historicity of the Buddha there is a single, central point to which all events relate chronologically, namely the Mahāparinirvāṇa, the death of the Buddha. Buddhist eschatology envisages the extinction of consciousness in *nirvāṇa*, which, although seemingly negative, is the aim of human endeavour since it is a release from rebirth. Change within cosmological time is emphasized further by the cyclic movement of time taking the form of a spiral, in that the cycle never returns to its point of origin: and a spiral if fully stretched can become a wave, if not a linear form. The rise and fall within the cycle purports constant change and even the fall carries within it the eventual upward swing of the cycle, and this is conducive to the idea of a coming millennium, an idea envisaged in the Buddha Maitreya. This in turn is paralleled by decay carrying within it the seeds of regeneration.

The precision of historical time as recorded in inscriptions probably derived from the more widespread use of the solar calendar from the first millennium AD. But it also had to do with the legitimacy of the individual in authority, for the inscription was frequently a legal charter. Not only was the authority of the king time bound in such charters, but so also was his claim to the property which he was donating in as much as later kings could revoke these grants in spite of the insistence in the inscriptions that they were given in perpetuity. An additional factor was the influence of the idea that all actions are conditioned by the auspiciousness of the moment when they are carried out, and in the case of donations and grants this would be particularly apposite.[43] The multiple use of historical time focused on the individual and gave sharper definition to the individual as a figure of authority: an idea by no means unfamiliar by now in the historical consciousness of the period. A fuller exposition of this idea had come from Buddhist sources. Aśoka Maurya, as a patron of Buddhism, acquired an accretion of legends, some of which were gathered in the *Aśokāvadāna*. The attempt was to give historicity to the Buddhist *sangha* by linking it to a powerful political personality, a notion which was not alien to the emergence of much of the other non-Buddhist *carita* literature. The need to write the biography of the Buddha, *buddha-carita*, had been felt since the time of the early monastic movement and the first missions. It changed from being a part of the canonical texts to a separate genre of literature.[44] Gradually the idea of biography was extended to the 'hero' in a wider context. A historical background is also helpful to organized missionary activity in new areas where antecedents have to be explained; this was useful to the entry of Buddhism into Asia, as indeed it was useful to brahmanical centres in the more remote parts of the Indian subcontinent. The *carita* tradition doubtless also drew on the *praśastis* incorporated in a number of early inscriptions, such as that of Khāravela at Hāthigumphā and Rudradāman at Junagadh; a style which became more elaborate in time as evidenced by the Udaipur *rāj-praśasti*.[45]

## VI

Those in authority seek validation from the past, and this validation was the starting point of a new category of texts, the *vaṃśāvalīs* and the *caritas* of the post-Gupta period. The *vaṃśāvalīs* were the histories of the ruling families in specific geographical regions, the latter often coinciding with the new kingdoms and states in areas previously either unoccupied or settled by groups of tribes. As a genre they lay between the lineage lists of the *Purānas* and the historical biographies of individual rulers. The *carita* or historical biography was a complement to the *vaṃśāvalī* and focused on the king, who was seen as the centre of authority in a more radial state system. Bānabhatta's *Harṣacarita* led off the biographical form and was followed by a large number of others.[46] Most of the better known ones were written between the eighth and twelfth centuries AD, but as a form *carita* literature continued into later times, in each case commemorating the rise of new kings. The *carita* was unashamedly the eulogy of the patron, but the persons chosen were those who had a special status and function in the ruling family and were contributors of a more than ordinary kind, not only to their own families but also to the consolidation of kingdoms and kingship. The rhetoric of eulogy when deconstructed would doubtless reveal multiple relationships within a courtly edifice of norms and actions, and despite the ambiguity in presenting hard historical data much of the subtlety of historical nuance can be gathered from these biographies. *Carita* literature also focuses on other aspects of the individual in society. Cyclic time carries a certain inevitability but the individual can opt out of it, and on a lesser level this is demonstrated in biographies where the *karma* of the individual may play a larger role than the inevitability of the time cycle: and the individual *karma* and its historic role was central to the doctrine of Buddhism as well as the ideology of the *bhakti* tradition.

On occasion the subjects of the biographies were younger brothers who had come to rule (as for example, Harṣavardhana and Vikramāditya VI), and their legitimacy over other claimants had to be established. The royal patron was linked with the major lineages of the *itihāsa-purāṇa* or with a new lineage which had acquired status since then, such as the Agni-kula among Rajputs or the Nāgavaṃśa among certain central Indian dynasties. The *carita* was essentially a literary form in origin and thus a far cry from the bardic fragments of epic times. The most sophisticated courtly tradition found expression in this literature and the courtly values of chivalry, heroism and loyalty were at a premium.[47] Two obvious characteristics of this form were the depiction of the king as the focus of the court and a clear awareness of a well-defined geographical area which constituted the kingdom and was identified with the dynasty. Obeisance is made to the lineage but it plays a secondary role in relation to the king who is now most clearly the figure of formal political authority in both state and society.

Political decentralization inherent in the granting of land on a large scale encouraged a competition among families aspiring to dynastic status. Dynasties survived through an assertion of power, legitimacy and recourse to marriage alliances with ambitious feudatories. Attempts to restructure the economic potential within certain areas of the state and to balance the intricate relationship between royal power, brahmanical authority and the dominant religious cults of the region become a further support to power. The emphasis on territory had again to do with the jostling of new states and with the legitimizing of the economic and administrative changes which the system of land grants introduced into the kingdoms.

The *vaṃśāvalī* was the chronicle of a dynasty, and inevitably also the chronicle of the territory controlled by the dynasty. The *vaṃśāvalī* therefore used as source material the various local

*Purāṇas* as well as the oral tradition.[48] It became the characteristic literature of the new states in various parts of the subcontinent in the early second millennium AD. This is indicative of some elements of similarity in historical change, which in turn reflects a degree of cultural uniformity. These elements do not indicate the influence of one dominant regional culture over the others, but rather the expression of a similar historical situation, which, formulated in a certain kind of literature, was common to many regions.

The structure of the *vaṃśāvalī* was almost identical in all these regions. The earliest section narrated the origin myths pertaining to the region and the dynasty. In this there was a recording of local lore as well as a borrowing from the *itihāsa-purāṇa* tradition. Attempts were made to link local history with themes from the *Purāṇas* incorporating the myths and the genealogies of the Great Tradition with local persons and places. The *Purāṇas* were the prototypes and local personalities were the protagonists. This required the continued availability of the *Purāṇas* as sources from which the *vaṃśāvalīs* could draw. The major part of the text, however, dealt with more contemporary events, and a history of the ruling dynasty was narrated giving its genealogy and referring to important events associated with the dynasty. The veracity of this information can often be ascertained by comparing it with the evidence of inscriptions, since many of the grants of land were recorded on copper plates or on temple walls. Whereas the need for a *vaṃśāvalī* was motivated by the acquisition of power, the historically authenticated section would appear to coincide with the constitution of power, often articulated in the taking of royal titles such as *mahārājādhirāja*. Concomitant with this was the acceptance of responsibilities of power by the family. The authors of the *vaṃśāvalīs* were court poets and officials and were therefore familiar with political and administrative concerns. The *vaṃśāvalīs* would also be important to those who received grants of land in vouching for the legitimacy of the granting authority.

The *vaṃśāvalī* differs from the earlier tradition in that it legitimates a particular family and not an entire lineage, and to that extent the legitimation of lineage is indirect. The family was not seen merely as a household of agnatic and affinal kinsfolk but was the hub of power. It drew its strength both from claims to high descent as well as to property. Marriage alliances were controlled because dowry and inheritance were a part of the property structure. Such forms of the legitimation of families in power and of regions was of more immediate necessity to newly risen families in small states. The *vaṃśāvalī* therefore was by its very nature not a record of expansionist states. The major dynasties of the past, such as the Nandas and Mauryas, were not the models and only the very early lineages were considered possible sources of status. The appeal was not to the political system of the state but to sources of power which could back up the economic reality of aristocratic families with visions of dynastic ambition. It is significant that the *caritas* and the *vaṃśāvalīs* take up the narrative, as it were, from where the major *Purāṇas* leave off. The Purāṇic accounts of the ruling dynasties come to a close soon after the Guptas. The dynasties listed prior to these are mainly of the core regions of the Ganga valley and western and northern India. That the account was not continued in these *Purāṇas* was probably because there was a bigger distribution of centres of power in the post-Gupta period, and in each of such areas local *Purāṇas* and chronicles of various kinds began to be maintained. These texts often incorporate both the Purāṇic tradition and the local tradition, as is exemplified in those cases where legitimation is sought by reference to local myths of descent — as in the case of the Agni-kula Rajputs and the Nāgavaṃśis of central India.

As a form the *vaṃśāvalī* was not restricted to dynastic chronicles and was adapted to the history of other institutions as well. Some of these were monastic institutions where not only was the succession of elders chronicled but also their relations with political authority. This dynastic and political information pertained either to royal patrons of the institution or recorded relations between the institution and political authority, generally in the context of the institution establishing its own legitimacy. An early expression of this relationship is evident from the Buddhist tradition where monastic chronicles were a regular part of the historical tradition.[49]

In attempting to establish the legitimacy of the dynasties or institutions whose history they are recording, chronicles stress the uniqueness of historical events relating to the origin and history of the subject of the chronicle, with indications of its growth and change. Actions are directed towards a goal, often resulting in the success of the subject. Chronicles are therefore compiled when a dynasty or institution has established itself and is recognized as powerful. The chronicle helps to establish its claims to authority over competing groups, especially those which are politically important. The borrowing from the *itihāsa-purāṇa* tradition suggests continuity and also stresses legitimacy, for the new group is seen as being related to those who were in power in the past and can also claim antiquity by maintaining these connections with earlier lineages. The chronicle is again the statement of the successful group and manages to deflect if not erase the presence of competitors. This becomes a particularly useful aspect of the chronicle in a society where not only dissent but even protest often takes the form of opting out or migration away, in preference to confrontation.[50]

If changing forms in the expression of historical consciousness symbolize historical change, and if changes in the political forms of society are reflected in the nature of historical expression, then the *itihāsa-purāṇa* tradition would point to three phases in the unfolding of early Indian history. Initially, in lineage societies, historical consciousness was embedded, and it recorded the perception of the ordering of lineages. With the evolution of states in northern India the second phase was inaugurated, focusing on dynastic power and the supremacy of the state as a system which in the political arena seems to have overridden caste ordering. The post-Gupta period saw a change in the structure of the state, accompanied by the need in many cases for the legitimation of status of ruling families.

Historical consciousness in early India took a form which grew out of embedded history. Part of the explanation for this may lie in the fact that the *varṇa* ordering of society, which never fully coincided with a clearly defined socio-economic stratification, carried a large element of the lineage-based structure and therefore also the embedded history of that structure. Where *kṣatriya* legitimation became necessary, the *itihāsa-purāṇa* tradition was strengthened with a drawing upon embedded history for origins. In such cases the past in relation to political power became a *kṣatriya* past. But at the same time it did not remain embedded. Although the origin myths of the dynasties recorded in the *vaṃśāvalīs* become something of a *mantra* or a formula, this should not hide the fact that despite the continuing idiom from the past there is a substantial historical core in the *vaṃśāvalī* which is distinguished from the embedded section, and which is therefore a break from the past and takes the form of historical consciousness expressed as externalized history.

## Notes and References

1. I have discussed these differences as they pertain to early Indian society, specifically to Vedic and post-Vedic times prior to the rise of the Mauryan state, in *From Lineage to State*, Delhi, 1984). The term 'lineage' is used in preference to the more commonly employed term 'tribe', as lineage whether fictive or real is central to such societies, is more precise and points to the crux of such societies where descent and birth are in fact the major focus of social ordering.
2. *Śatapatha Brāhmaṇa* I.8.1.1–10; *Mahābhārata*, Sabhāparvan, 185; *Matsya Purāṇa*, I.11–34; Romila Thapar, 'Puranic Lineages and Archaeological Cultures', in *Ancient Indian Social History: Some Interpretations*, New Delhi, 1978 (hereafter referred to as *AISH*), pp. 240ff.
3. M. Eliade, *The Myth of the Eternal Return*, Princeton, 1971.
4. *Rg Veda*, x.97.
5. *Mahābhārata*, Śāntiparvan, 59: *Viṣṇu Purāṇa*, I.13; *Matsya Purāṇa*, x.4–10.
6. *Sutta Nipāta*, 420ff; *Sutta Nipāta Commentary*, I.352ff; *Sumaṅgalavilāsinī*, I, pp. 258–60; Romila Thapar, 'Origin Myths and the Historical Tradition', *AISH*, pp. 294ff.
7. *Ṛg Veda*, VI.63; V.27; V.30; VI.47; VIII.1; VIII.5; VIII.6.
8. Both the terms *ākhyāna* and *kathā* have the meaning of recitation or oral narration, and the purpose of the form is clear from these words. Some of the bardic fragments in the form of stories are also to be found in the *Jātaka* literature.
9. *Ṛg Veda*, X.95; *Śatapatha Brāhmaṇa*, XI.5.1.1ff; *Mahābhārata*, Ādiparvan, VII.70–1.
10. Romila Thapar, '*Dāna* and *dakṣiṇā* as forms of exchange', in *AISH*, pp. 105ff.
11. *Mahābhārata*, Sabhāparvan, 30ff; 34ff.
12. *Mahābhārata*, Ādiparvan, 57.
13. V.S. Sukthankar, *On the Meaning of the Mahabharata*, Bombay, 1957; 'Epic Studies', *ABORI*, XVIII, pp. 1–76; C. Bulke, *Rāma-kathā*, Allahabad, 1972; H. Jacobi, *The Ramayana* (trans. S.N. Ghoshal), Baroda, 1960. It is a moot question as to how much of the original epic persists in the now heavily inflated and interpolated versions, which, despite the critical editions of both texts, still require substantial pruning to be brought anywhere near the original. The interpolations have been both of substance and form: hence the reference to the *Rāmāyaṇa* as a *kāvya* or literary poem and to the *Mahābhārata* as *itihāsa*, more closely approximating history, although the historical content remains difficult of access.
14. This is in part reflected in the perennial search by archaeologists for 'epic ages'. The financially flourishing 'Ramayana archaeology', even

though without any tangible results, continues to be discussed seriously in some archaeological and historical circles, despite the near absurdity of the idea. That epic archaeology is an almost non-existent category becomes clear from a discussion of the encrustations which go into the making of an epic. E.W. Hopkins, *The Great Epic of India: Its Character and Origin*, New York, 1901; V.S. Sukthankar, *Prolegomena* to the Critical Edition of Adi Parvan, Poona, 1933; Romila Thapar, *Exile and the Kingdom: Some Thoughts on the Rāmāyaṇa*, Bangalore, 1978; 'The Historian and the Epic', *Annals of the Bhandarkar Oriental Research Institute*, 1979, vol. LX, pp. 199–213; B.D. Chattopadhyaya, 'Indian Archaeology and the Epic Tradition', *Puratattva*, VIII, 1975–6, pp. 67–71.

15. The treatment of Indra in the epics, for example, records a sea change from the Indra-*gāthās* of the *Ṛg Veda*. Indra is now subservient not only to the rising status of Viṣṇu but is unequal even to the superior power of the *ṛṣis*. Leaving aside the deliberate incarnating of Viṣṇu as the epic heroes Rāma and Kṛṣṇa, there is little doubt that the epic heroes are now more central than the Vedic gods.
16. Cf. W.B. Miller, 'Two Concepts of Authority', *American Anthropologist*, April 1955, vol. 57, pp. 271–89.
17. J.A.B. van Buitenan refers to the problem of the 'disqualified eldest' in his introduction to the translation of the Ādiparvan. The *Mahābhārata. The Book of the Beginning*, Chicago, 1973, p. xviii. The problem goes back to earlier antecedents. Thus the Candravaṃśa lineage starts with the replacement of Yadu, the eldest son of Yayāti, by his youngest son, Pūru. The *Mahābhārata* war, which involves virtually all the *kṣatriya* lineages and becomes the last heroic act of a lineage society, is again motivated by the problem of succession where physical ailments further complicate the question. The exile of Rāma is over the issue of succession, which, in spite of the heavier emphasis on primogeniture, is still subject to the whims and wishes of the parents.
18. *Mahābhārata*, Ādiparvan, 189.
19. Romila Thapar, 'The *Rāmāyaṇa*: Theme and Variation', in S.N. Mukherjee (ed.), *India: History and Thought*, Calcutta, 1982, pp. 221–53.
20. The *itihāsa-purāṇa* is referred to in the *Arthaśāstra*, 1.5. Its literal meaning is 'thus it was' — *iti-ha-āsa*. The events of the past were to be so related as to link them with the goals and purposes of the tradition which was being historicised.
21. The *sūta* and the *māgadha* are said to have arisen from the sacrifice of Pṛthu, and immediately on appearing began a *praśasti* of the *rājā*. *Atharvaveda*, 3.5.7; *Taittirīya Brāhmaṇa*, II.4.1. In texts such as *Gautama*, IV.15; *Manu*, X.11, 26; *Nārada*, 110, the status of the

*sūta* has changed. This change is made explicit in the *Mahābhārata*, Ādiparvan, 122.4ff and 126.15ff, in which the *sūta* is inferior to the *kṣatriya*.

22. F.E. Pargiter, *The Ancient Indian Historical Tradition*, London, 1922, pp. 77ff; *Dynasties of the Kali Age. . .* , 1913 (reprint, Delhi, 1975), pp. 77ff.
23. *Mahāvaṃsaṭīkā*, pp. 180ff.
24. *Viṣṇu Purāṇa*, IV.21–4: *Manu*, X.43–5.
25. *Epigraphia Indica*, VIII, pp. 59, 86; E.J. Rapson (ed.), *The Cambridge History of India*, vol. I, *Ancient India*, Cambridge, 1935, p. 577.
26. For a later period, cf. R.G. Fox, *Kin, Clan, Raja and Rule*, Berkeley, 1971.
27. Miller, op. cit.
28. J.N. Asopa, *Origin of the Rajputs*, Delhi, 1976, pp. 102ff, 208ff; J. Tod, *Annals and Antiquities of Rajasthan*, vol. I, London, 1960, pp. 173ff. Asopa argues that 'Guhila' means a forest and that it is to be located in the area between Guhila-bala and the Mahi river. See also B.D. Chattopadhyaya, 'Origin of the Rajputs: The Political, Economic and Social Processes in Early Medieval Rajasthan, *The Indian Historical Review*, July, 1976, vol. III, no. 1, pp. 59–82. Claims to *ksatriya* status were also made by ruling families and politically powerful groups in south India. Thus the Colas claimed to be Sūryavaṃśi, the Pāṇḍyas Candravaṃśi, and the *vel* chieftains sought Yādava descent.
29. Romila Thapar, 'The State as Empire', in H. Claessen and P. Skalnik, *The Study of the State*, The Hague, 1981, pp. 409ff.
30. R.S. Sharma, *Indian Feudalism*, Delhi, 1980.
31. Romila Thapar, 'Genealogy as a Source of Social History', *AISH*, pp. 326ff.
32. Pliny in *Natural History*, VI.21.4–5, quotes Megathenes as stating that the Indians count 154 kings upto the time of Alexander. Genealogical data is also contained in the seals and in most land-grant inscriptions from the Gupta period onwards, e.g. Sonpat Copper Seal of Harshavardhana, in J.F. Fleet (ed.), *C.I.I.*, vol. III, Inscriptions of the Early Gupta Kings, Varanasi, 1970, p. 231: Ralanpur Stone Inscription of Jajalladeva I, V.V. Mirashi (ed.), *C.I.I.*, vol. IV, Inscriptions of the Kalacuri-Cedi Era, Ootacamund, 1955, p. 409; the Lakhamandala inscription, *Epigraphia Indica*, I, 1892, pp. 10ff.
33. Romila Thapar, op. cit.
34. Pargiter, *The Ancient Indian Historical Tradition*, pp. 109ff; *Manu*, X.8, X.23 refers to the Āndhras and Sātvats as *śūdras*. The Āndhras are identified with the Andhaka of the Andhaka-Vṛṣṇi group and the Vṛṣṇis married the Sātvats. Pāṇini, II.2.95 and VI.2, 34, refers to the Andhaka and the Vṛṣṇis as being *kṣatriya gotras*. The events of the

*Mahābhārata* suggest that the Vṛṣṇis were of a lower status, judging by the objection of some of the *kṣatriyas* present to giving Kṛṣṇa the status of the honoured guest. Sabhāparvan, pp. 33.26ff; 34.1ff.

35. *Viṣṇu Purāna*, IV.22.
36. *Mahābhārata*, Ādiparvan, 80.1ff.
37. Examples of such adjustments extend even to the literal Sanskritization of non-Sanskrit names, and to the story which relates the event, e.g. the Śailodbhava dynasty in its origin myth relates the story of how a *brāhmaṇa* was requested to create a man out of chips of rock, and thus the ancestor of the Śailodbhavas was created, the story evidently explaining the Sanskritization of a non-Sanskrit name. R.G. Basak, *History of North-eastern India*, Calcutta, 1967, pp. 211ff.
38. Romila Thapar, 'Renunciation: The Making of a Counter-culture?', in *AISH*, pp. 63ff. *See* chapter 40 in this volume.
39. Cosmological time moves in the Mahāyuga of 4,320,000 years and the complete cycle is then divided into four *yugas*: the Kṛta of 1,728,000 years; the Tretā of 1,296,000 years, the Dvāpara of 864,000 years and the Kaliyuga of 432,000 years, the size of the *yugas* declining in arithmetical progression. The Kaliyuga is crucial and there is a regular reduction by subtracting the length of the Kaliyuga from each preceding *yuga*, an orderliness which is basic to the concept. The numbers used are quasi-mathematical, a mixture of magic and astronomy. Numbers such as 3,7,12 and 72 are considered magical and constitute the fractions in the figures. Thus $432{,}000 = 60 \times 7200$, and this further introduces the sexagesimal unit of 60, frequently used in ancient West Asia as well as in south Indian astrology. The Babylonian tradition also uses 72,1,200 and 432,000 for its chronology (J. Campbell, *The Masks of the Gods*, vol. II, New York, 1959, pp. 128ff) and the *Jyotiṣa-vedāṅga* shows a familiarity with Babylonian astronomy and mathematics. (D. Pingree, 'The Mesopotamian Origin of Early Indian Mathematical Astronomy', *Journal for the History of Astronomy*, 1973, IV, pp. 1–12). The figure of 72 years is taken to calculate the processional lag moving over one degree and 432,000 is the basis of calculating the epicycle. Was cosmological time the earlier and more popular astronomical knowledge which was deliberately preserved in this manner, as distinct from the mathematics and the solar-based astronomy of the period reflected in the more formal writings of astronomers and mathematicians. As a contrast to these majuscule dimensions there are also the minuscule fractional parts of time listed in Jaina texts of the late first and the early second millennia AD. Interestingly, the description of the *yugas* and *kalpas* is spatial, e.g. *Saṁyutta Nikāya*, XV.1.5–8.
40. M. Eliade, *Cosmos and History*, New York, 1959.
41. Kalhaṇa, *Rājataraṅginī*, V.21.

42. A.L. Basham, *The Wonder That Was India*, London, 1964, pp. 272–3; *Dīgha Nikāya*, III, pp. 75ff.
43. Some of the dates for inscriptions were provided by astrologers, and these include astronomical details. However they are not always correct. D.C. Sircar, *Studies in Society and Administration of Ancient and Medieval India*, vol. I, Calcutta, 1967, pp. 171–2. It is worth noting that apart from the legal charters, another sphere of life in which time was very precisely recorded was the horoscope. As a corollary to this it is interesting that an almost exact counterpart to the careful record of time in inscriptions is to be found in discussions on the precise time for conducting a *yajña*, where the time is again indicated in terms of the year, season, month, lunar fortnight, constellation, date and time of day.
44. This change is reflected in the difference between the *Suttas* and the *Vinaya*, where the life of the Buddha is part of canonical scripture, and Aśvaghoṣa's *Buddhacarita*, which is a biography *per se*.
45. D.C. Sircar, *Select Inscriptions*, second edition, Calcutta, 1965, pp. 213–19, 175–80; *Epigraphia Indica*, vol. XXIX, 1951–2, parts 1–5, pp. 1–90.
46. Such as Vākapati's *Gauḍavāho* on Yaśovarman of Kannauj; Bilhaṇa's *Vikramānkadevacarita* on Vikramāditya VI, the Cālukya kin; Sandhyākaranandin's *Rāmacarita* on Rāmapāla; Jayānaka's *Pṛthvīrājavijaya*; Nayacandra Sūri's *Hammīra-mahākāvya*; Someśvaradeva's *Kīrtikaumudi*, a biography of Vastupāla, who, although not a king, was a person of great political importance; and Hemacandra's *Kumārapālacarita*.
47. V.S. Pathak, *Ancient Historians of India*, Bombay, 1966, pp. 21ff.
48. The sources drawn upon by the authors of the *vaṃśāvalīs* included the *sthala-purāṇas*, *upa-purāṇas*, *tīrtha-purāṇas*, caste *purānas* and *māhātmyas*, all of which were texts recording the past and the evolution of places, sects and deities, locations of pilgrimage, dominant castes and local history. Such texts were part of the larger Purāṇic tradition and, although conforming to the major *Purāṇas* in sprit if not in form, included a large amount of local and regional data. The oral sources consisted of bardic fragments and ballads on local heroes and events of significance, not to mention the genealogies and marriage alliances of land-owning families, for the bardic tradition was still alive, as it remains to this day. It has been argued that Kalhaṇa's *Rājataraṅginī*, a fine example of a *vaṃśāvalī*, was a unique document in that it was the only genuine piece of historical writing from India (A.L. Basham, 'The Kashmir Chronicle', in C.H. Philips, *Historians of India, Pakistan and Ceylon*, Oxford, 1961, pp. 57ff). Yet the *vaṃśāvalī* form occurs in various parts of the country — from the neighbouring Chamba *vaṃśāvalī* (Vogel, *The Antiquities of Chamba State*,

Calcutta, 1911, *A.S.I.*, vol. 36 to the most distant *Mūṣakavaṃśa* or chronicle of the Ay dynasty in Kerala. Gopinath Rao, 'Extracts from the Mūṣakavaṃśam . . . ', *Travancore Archaeological Series*, 1916, II.1, no. 10, pp. 87—113; See also M.G.S. Narayanan, 'History from Muśakavaṃśa-kāvya of Atula', *P.A.I.O.C.*, Jadhavpur, 1969. Curiously in both cases the founder is born in a cave (*guhā*) and is associated with a *mūṣaka-vaṃśa* (literally: 'mouse lineage'). A better known cave association is of course that of the Guhilots of Mewar (J. Tod, I, pp. 173ff). For further lists of *vaṃśāvalīs* see A.K. Warder, *Introduction to Indian Historiography*, Bombay, 1972, and J.P. de Souza and C.M. Kulkarni (eds), *Historiography in Indian Languages*, Delhi, 1972.

49. The *Mahāvaṃsa*, as the chronicle of the Mahāvihāra monastery in Sri Lanka composed in the mid first millennium AD, is primarily concerned with establishing its legitimacy both as the fount of the pristine teaching of the Buddha as well as in its interaction with political authority. Thus the Theravāda sect, which was established in the Mahāvihāra monastery, is said to have originated from the schism at the Council of Pāṭaliputra, called at the initiative of Aśoka Maurya, and was established in Sri Lanka largely through the patronage of Devānampiya Tissa. Buddhist chronicles do tend to show a greater degree of historical determinism. Sri Lanka is predestined for the establishment of Buddhism. Events move towards proclaiming the primacy of the *saṅgha*. L.S. Perera, 'The Pali Chronicles of Ceylon', in C.H. Philips, pp. 29ff. This is further emphasized by the notion of causality and contract so central to Buddhist ethics, and by the historical role of the missionaries who propagate Buddhism in new areas.

50. Romila Thapar, 'Dissent and Protest in the Early Indian Tradition', *Studies in History*, 1979, vol. I, no. 2, pp. 177–95. *See* chapter 11 in this volume.

# 8

# *Historical Consciousness in Early India**

The eighteenth and nineteenth centuries in Europe were centuries when history as a discipline was being established. It was argued that every discipline has a history, the understanding of which was one of the ways of systematising knowledge. Inevitably therefore in the colonial encounter between Europe and Asia, there was a search for indigenous histories which would provide an avenue to comprehending these new and different cultures. However the definition of history remained that which emerged out of the European tradition. The equivalent of Herodotus and Livy were sought in other civilisations and not surprisingly such equivalents were not always available. It has taken us many decades to realise that societies in the past wrote their histories in ways appropriate to their own needs. Therefore historical writing does not follow a single pattern.

My intention in this lecture is initially to consider why, from the perspective of colonial historiography, there was an insistence that early Indian society lacked historical consciousness. I would then like to discuss a few categories of those texts which have come to us from the early Indian past and which from their own perspective claim to be narrating the past. Such narratives take divergent forms. My concern is not with the historical accuracy of the data presented in these texts but with the manner in which they perceived the past and the relation of that past to their present.

The search for histories of early India began in the eighteenth century. But European scholars, conscious by now of historical literature as a distinct category, could not locate such literature from the Sanskrit tradition. Indian culture, and particularly the

* Lecture delivered at Orientalists Conference, Kyoto, 1995. Reprinted with the kind permission of Toho Gakai.

Sanskrit articulation of Hindu culture, came to be defined therefore, as ahistorical. William Jones, the leading Indologist of the late eighteenth century, working at Calcutta, suspected that some texts, even if including the myths and legends of the Hindus, probably contained the core of a history.[1] Most scholars tended to dismiss them as entirely fanciful as they showed little concern for an accurate record of the past. It was agreed that the only exception was the *Rājataraṅginī* of Kalhaṇa, a twelfth century history of Kashmir, regarded as atypical among Sanskrit texts.

A century later MacDonell's searing remark that, 'early India wrote no history because it never made any',[2] was modified by Rapson, who subscribed to the general view, although he added, 'But this is not because the people of India had no history . . . We know from other sources that the ages were filled with stirring events; but these events found no systematic record.'[3] Comparisons with the Chinese chronicles of Ssu-ma-ch'ien and the writings of the Arab historian Ibn Khaldun, or even the Biblical genealogies, strengthened if only in contrast, the axiom of Indian society denying history.

In the supposed absence of a systematic record the premises of the reconstruction of early Indian history by European scholars was drawn from contemporary European historiography. This marked a change of approach towards the past from what it was prior to the Renaissance. Awareness of evidence, interest in causation, and a premium on chronology together with sequential narrative were features of the Renaissance sense of the past. These were a departure from the historiography of medieval times with its focus on the Christian Church.[4] The European perception of the Indian past created a break with whatever may have been the historical traditions of earlier times. These included the Islamic historical tradition in India which had sought to link the history of local Muslim dynasties with the wider framework of Islamic historiography. No link was even possible between what might have been seen as a sense of history in Sanskrit sources with the new colonial reconstruction of Indian history, for the presuppositions of the relevance of the past to the present were, far too different.

Attempts were made to reconstruct early Indian history focussing on chronology and sequential narrative. The acclamation given to the identification by William Jones of Sandracottos with Chandragupta thus linking him with Alexander, shows the concern with chronology.[5] Chronology in Indian sources was said to have been so disguised by the fantasy of the *brāhmaṇas* that it was almost impossible to unravel it. But the attempted co-relations with Biblical genealogies had turned out even more fanciful than the theories of the *brāhmaṇas*.[6]

The officers of the East India Company constituting the larger number of scholars working on India at the time, had as their informants, learned *brāhmaṇas*. They emphasised the centrality of the texts important to Brahmanism and to a lesser extent the texts of others such as the Buddhists which they regarded as second order knowledge. This was partly because there were no Buddhist monks in India to introduce the texts to European scholars and partly because they were regarded as inferior branches of Hinduism. Therefore they could not form a mainstream of information. That these could earlier have been interacting systems of knowledge was hardly conceded.

The tendency to give primacy to Hinduism was conditioned by a variety of factors. European attitudes to Indian Islam were mediated by the perspective of its being a Semitic religion with a heritage common to Christianity, and by the experience of the Crusades, when Islam was viewed as the enemy. Having been the erstwhile power in India, Islam was again seen as a political rival. But from both curiosity and the requirements of governing India as a colony, Hinduism presented the more formidable challenge. Doubtless the exotica and the incomprehension of a religion so totally different from the Semitic must also have been intriguing — as perhaps it still is. This would be one reason why attempts were made to try and induct it into a recognisable framework and to provide it with the kind of history which would make it less alien and therefore easier to comprehend or to confront. The texts were mainly read for information on law and religion, the latter defined as Hindu deities, cults, sects and philosophical schools. What this scholarship brought into prominence was largely an upper caste, text-based Hinduism, thereby presenting a limited view. The more essential feature of its history, namely, the evolution of sects or their relations with particular castes, was of lesser interest. This was relegated to the concerns of ethnographers.

By the latter half of the nineteenth century, the reconstruction of early Indian history was based on a new set of premises. Theories of historical origin and explanation precluded the need for historical writing in the indigenous tradition. The new scholarship drew its inspiration from European ideological debates and perceptions which were then applied to Indian data. Thus a familiarity with the intellectual history of Europe in the nineteenth century becomes a precondition to understanding these interpretations of the Indian past.

The first history of India written independently by a European was James Mill's *History of British India* published between 1818 and 1823. This was to become the standard history in the nineteenth century, dominating the understanding of the Indian past. In Mill's view Indian history was divided into the Hindu and Muslim civilisations and the period of British rule. He viewed Hindu civilisation as irrational, backward and unchanging and Muslim civilisation only marginally better, if at all. The despotic state was thought to be the only form known to Indian society. Its static character was to be broken by British administration legislating change. These views were in part a reflection of the debate on current colonial policy,[7] a debate which introduced corresponding interpretations of the Indian past.

The insistence on Indian society being static eliminated the need to look for points of change and to that extent for histories which may have registered this change. In the absence of change one of the functions of using the past, namely, to legitimise the present, becomes irrelevant. From Mill's perspective the elimination of the past lends support to despotic power, for, it then cannot be questioned even from the point of view of violating tradition, nor can any appeal be made to thwart despotism in the name of the past.

The debate on the nature of Indian society and history was in many ways an exercise in theory. It drew upon current European controversies and the history of India was largely an arena for trying out ideas derived from European concerns.[8] The present of India was viewed as the past of Europe within the general format of social evolutionism. There was less intrinsic concern among these theorists with the society being studied. For some scholars such societies provided a form of exotica and permitted a play of fantasy. There were curious anomalies in these attitudes. Scholars who worked as officers in the East India Company in India, read Sanskrit texts with their *brāhmaṇa* informants. There was however little attempt at discourse on the wider context of the texts or the society which produced them. Although the Asiatic Society in

Calcutta was founded in 1784 and was the fulcrum for Indological research, it remained closed to Indian participation until 1829, almost half a century later. Then too the interest seems to have been largely in encouraging wealthy Indians to make a financial contribution, which the latter gladly did, seeing this as a means of acquiring status.

Colonial attitudes to knowledge pertaining to their colonies, assumed on occasion that such knowledge was a form of control. This is perhaps best summed up in the statement of Lord Curzon that the intellectual discovery of the Orient was 'the necessary furniture of empire.'[9] This attitude would be enhanced if it could be maintained that the colonial society had no awareness of its past and that even this awareness had to be provided by the colonial power.

The most influential theory of origins in the interpretation of early Indian history was the theory of Aryan race.[10] It postulated an invasion by a racial group identified as the Aryans and speaking an Indo-European language which took the form of Indo-Aryan. The argument drew on comparative philology and the affinities between Indo-European languages as well as similarities in mythology and social institutions. The idea of invasion was based on references in the *Ṛg Veda* to hostilities against the *dāsas*, believed to be the indigenous people where the victorious *āryas*, the successful conquerors, were the authors of the texts. The entirely different Puranic version of historical beginnings was ignored on the ground that the *Purāṇas* were of less importance and compiled at a later date. The upper castes and particularly the *brāhmaṇas* were seen as lineal descendents of the Aryan race and the lower castes and untouchables were regarded as the indigenous non-Aryans. Caste as a social system was traced back to the notion of racial segregation, where at an early stage, stratification was frozen so effectively that there was little or no social change.

The initial identification of language with race, was rapidly accepted and few paused to make a demarcation, although later it was cautioned against even by Max Müller. It was assumed therefore that the early history of India was to be viewed as the spread of the Aryan race over the subcontinent using the Aryan derived languages as the guage for this expansion. History lay in starting with the foundations of Aryan culture in the Vedic texts and proceeding with its development and establishment in northern India.

This was then projected as a pattern to explain the beginnings of civilisation in various parts of the Indian subcontinent.

This processing of knowledge about India derived in part from an almost obsessive concern with seeing the Orient necessarily as 'the Other' from the perspective of western Europe. The two most influential statements on such 'otherness' are to be found in Karl Marx and Max Weber. In both cases the starting point was the question as to why Asian societies did not develop capitalism. This exploration was conditioned by the rather fragmentary nature of historical knowledge, and by the centrality given to theories about Asian societies even if they conflicted with empirical data, a predilection for which has not been altogether discarded even now. The construction of the reality of 'the other' was derived not from trying to understand a culturally different perception of the world, but from noting the absence of European characteristics in this perception. Marx emphasised the lack of change and therefore of dialectics and of history.[11] Weber's emphasis on what has been called the *karma* theodicy, the tying in of one's actions with birth into a specific caste, supported the view that this would prevent any innovation or defiance of caste rules. This would make caste a significant factor in the failure of economic rationalism.[12]

The discovery of data for the reconstruction of Indian history continued apace with the earlier attempts of the Asiatic Society being pursued further by officers involved in the administration of India. Painstaking and meticulous scholarship yielded rich results. James Prinsep deciphered inscriptions in the Brāhmī script, the major break-through being what were later identified as those of the Mauryan king, Aśoka. Alexander Cunningham followed the itinerary of the seventh century Chinese pilgrim Hsüan Tsang and located a number of Buddhist sites mentioned in his text. Numismatics helped not only in the deciphering of scripts by the reading of bi-lingual coin legends, but the coins of the Indo-Bactrian Greeks linked Indian history with Hellenistic history. Underlying all this activity was the conviction that the Indian past had to be wholly reconstructed through contemporary scholarship.

An adjunct to this scholarship was the interest in bardic literature. James Tod had a romantic vision of Rajput clans whom he viewed in the light of Scottish clans, and argued that his sources, collected from bards and Jaina monks, constituted historical records.[13] Tessitori, in the early twentieth century made a systematic attempt to collect bardic material and to co-relate it with inscriptions, also with a view to treating these as possible historical documents.[14] But there was little dialogue between those who were interested in such documents and others who were reconstructing what they perceived as an impersonal narrative of the early history of India, using what they regarded as the more reliable brahmanical sources.

By the early twentieth century many Indian historians had come under the influence of the prevailing nationalist ideology. This tended to direct the focus of historical interpretation to the intellectual concerns of India, but even then not fully so. Indian nationalist historians were inclined to accept parts of the general reconstruction. The theory of Aryan race for example was attractive because it was thought to link early India with the roots of European culture. It also endorsed the special status of the upper castes. Although the concept of Oriental Despotism was rejected, Mill's periodisation of Indian history was not questioned. The Hindu period of three thousand years was projected as one of sustained prosperity, an argument which effectively conceded the absence of major historical changes in that period.

Alternative theories of explanation came with later scholars, using both data and methods drawing on a variety of disciplines and new theories of analysis. This was a change in paradigms. In the last four decades this has acted as a point of departure for a number of analyses of the nature of society and of social reality. Such analyses also have a bearing on the question of how a society views its own past.

The recognition that Indian society was not static and did undergo change and that the nature of such change was not uniform in time and space, constituted a radically different view of the Indian past. This perspective was introduced by Indian historians writing in the post-nationalist phase, using a broad spectrum of analyses — some Marxist and some not so — and recognising the validity of evident social and economic change in early India.[15] The so-called Hindu period stretching from the Harappan civilisation of the third millennium BC to the establishment of the Delhi Sultanate in the thirteenth century AD is no longer seen as an unbroken continuity but as registering periods of major change within this time span. The urban Indus civilisation was succeeded by a series of pastoral and agricultural chalcolithic cultures. The mid-first millennium BC saw some of these societies moving towards what has been called the second urbanisation, this time in the Ganga valley. Associated with this was the emergence of territorial units, the *mahājanapadas* which began as chiefdoms and some changed into kingdoms. The variations in political forms were closely related to environmental factors, the nature of economic resources and their social distribution, and to belief systems and ideologies.[16]

The rise of monarchical states shifted the focus of political forms to dynastic rule as a characteristic feature. State power under the Mauryas in the fourth century BC was earlier described as bureaucratically centralised but is now being viewed as centralised more in intent than in practice.[17] Successor states to the Mauryas reflect the dominance of monarchy and were associated with substantial efforts at drawing revenue from agriculture and trade.

The period from about the eighth to the twelfth centuries AD saw a multiplicity of small states competing for power, some of which emerged as major kingdoms. Even those that attained this status were centred more recognisably on regional foci, adopting a new pattern of mobilising social groups through a system of making grants of land to those high in administrative office and to *brāhmaṇas*. The frequency with which evidence for this is available in various parts of the country suggests that it relates to a different social and economic landscape from the one known before.[18]

The picture which emerges is that in the early period of Indian history there were variant societies which in some areas were sequential and in others, over-lapped. The evidence for historical change is clear. That such change may express itself in historical consciousness makes it viable to search for a sense of history. But changes in society are not the sole reason for the development of historical consciousness. There is also the wish to articulate a particular perspective on the past for political and social reasons and these reasons would emerge from the situation in the present. This may require either taking over an existing tradition, or maintaining a dialogue with other traditions or, creating a tradition for specific purposes. Elements of all these features are present in what is referred to in the early texts as, the *itihāsa-purāṇa* tradition.

The two terms in Sanskrit which are associated either separately or conjointly with traditions relating to the past are, *itihāsa* and *purāṇa*. The literal meaning of *itihāsa* is 'thus it was' and has come to be used now to mean history, but earlier it was not history in any modern sense of the term. *Purāṇa* means that which belongs to ancient times and includes events and stories believed to go back to early periods. Later, in the first millennium AD this term was applied to a specific body of texts, the *Purāṇas* which were in essence the literature linked to emerging socio-religious sects and what has been called Puranic Hinduism. The conjoint term *itihāsa-purāṇa*, referring to that which was believed to have happened in the past is mentioned in an *Upaniṣad* as the fifth *Veda*, which makes it an important but separate branch of knowledge.[19] Promotion to the status of a fifth *Veda* is sometimes given to texts whose subject matter is initially outside the interests of Vedic Brahmanism. In this case it may have been because *itihāsa-purāṇa* was central to the *kṣatriya* tradition, the tradition of the ruling clans.[20] From the perspective of Vedic Brahmanism it tended initially to be seen as second order knowledge, perhaps because it did not incorporate ritual and normative texts. Doubtless this ambiguity about the importance of the *itihāsa-purāṇa* tradition also assisted in creating the impression that a concern with the past was unimportant to Indian civilisation.

It has recently been argued that a historical tradition in early India did exist but that it was a weak tradition, and given the intellectual interests of Indian society, it is curious that historical writing received little attention.[21] This has been attributed to various factors: to the decentralised nature of political institutions, to the role of the priestly elite in fabricating genealogies for rulers of low caste whose status could not be openly disclosed, and to the exclusive control by the *brāhmaṇas* over the transmission of the tradition. Another view points to the bifurcation of the keepers of the state records, where some were scribes and others *brāhmaṇas* and from the latter a critical intellectual assessment might have been expected.[22] But there is evidence to the contrary in relation to all these explanations. The cyclic concept of time was also seen as obstructing history,[23] but as I hope to show, the treatment of time in the *itihāsa-purāṇa* tradition draws on notions of both cyclical and linear time but the latter is the more functional. It would seem therefore that a more detailed exploration of the texts which claim to incorporate historical perspectives, is necessary.

An analysis of the *itihāsa-purāṇa* tradition requires examining whether in its view of the past it reflects socio-political changes and emphasises what the authors of this tradition took to be significant; and where the texts take variant forms, whether there is a resonance with historical change. This is possible because historians are now turning to themes which had been earlier precluded from history. There is for example, an increasing interest in the oral traditions of societies without literacy, and therefore, by the earlier definition said to be without history. It is also realised that communities have their own versions of their history, as for instance, the histories of many castes, and that although some of these may be fanciful they reflect a particular perception of their past. Even a fabricated version claiming to be historical tells us much about a society, for fabrication may be used as a rhetoric of change or as the basis of innovation.

What is required therefore is not to look for Greco-Roman, Arab or Chinese models of historical writing from the Indian past. It is perhaps more pertinent to analyse the forms in which Indian society has chosen to record its past. This is likely to tell us more about the community which accepts these versions as perspectives of the past. Thus one predictable feature of the *itihāsa-purāṇa* tradition in early India would be indications of the introduction of caste as a form of stratification, as also the legitimation of the ruling caste. Another related feature would be the transformation of pre-state systems into monarchies and of these into more complex forms. Every society has many pasts and this is especially so in a society constituted of multiple social segments. The records of these many pasts would vary and there would be some which may conflict or others which may confirm. A comparative analysis of variant forms might clarify the motivations behind a particular form.

A view of the past is increasingly pertinent at times of transition when the past can either be rejected or become a model or can be used to legitimise the changing present. One of the functions of history has been to legitimise those in power. Much of the historical writing which survives from early periods is in the form of statements of the elite. What others had to say has often to be extrapolated from these statements. Attempts at legitimation were not fraudulent given that the rules of the game were well-known and the texts have to be decoded according to these rules. This also requires that historical traditions be comprehended in terms of their social and political identity. Texts which purport to relate to the past have also to be placed in their contemporary context. The ordering of time concepts therefore takes on an added dimension.

Perceptions of the past and historical consciousness are found in varied forms.[24] A part of this consciousness lies in an embedded form — veins within the larger structure of texts and therefore requiring to be prised out. These consist of origin myths, compositions in praise of heroes, or legendary material in what are said to be the genealogies of ancient descent groups. In as much as myths and legends encapsulate social assumptions, they are significant to the recollection of the past. Other texts have a more externalised historical form in that they are biographies of rulers and those in authority, written in a recognisable format. There are also chronicles, the latter occurring both as literary texts or more concisely in inscriptions, where inscriptions become the official version of the narrative. The reading of inscriptions in the last hundred years has tended to overlook the fact that some of them do draw on an evident consciousness of past events, such as in the inscription at Girnar recalling specific renovations of a dam by various administrators over many centuries.[25] These more apparent forms of historical record seem to coincide with the strengthening of the monarchical state as the ultimate form of political authority and high culture.

The embedded forms tend to be scattered. The earliest are the *dāna-stutis* of the *Ṛgveda*, hymns in praise of gift-giving where the more generous heroes were lauded as model patrons. On other occasions some eulogies are said to be exaggerated, thus hinting at an actual happening. The *ākhyānas*, often recited as part of the more elaborate sacrificial rituals, are narratives of ancient heroes. The inclusion of the narratives in the sacrificial ritual gave them greater credence as well as ensuring continuity. Some of these narratives were modified, elaborated upon and reconstructed to suit the requirements of later times. Not least of these are the epics, the *Mahābhārata* and the *Rāmāyaṇa*. Variant versions introduce new features into the story, for the appeal to the past can also be to fix a precedent for action in the present.

This was part of the raw material which was incorporated into later categories of texts. Thus the encapsulation of the past in the form of varied genealogical patterns in the early *Purāṇas*, drew on this material but also interestingly reformulated it and sometimes stretched out the generations. A cursory glance at the genealogies would suggest that they are in part fabricated, all except the last section which carries traces of some historical authenticity. But an analysis of the various patterns through which the genealogies are incorporated into the description of successions, points to distinctive time periods and indications of socio-political changes.[26]

Let me illustrate this by reference to the chapter on succession, the *vaṃśānucarita* of the *Viṣṇu Purāṇa* composed in the earlier part of the first millennium AD. The initial section relating the story of the various Manus who ruled in remote antiquity, is mythological and is associated with huge cycles of time. In one of these cycles there occurs the Flood which also acts as a time marker. The ruling Manu is saved in the fashion of the Mesopotamian version and of Noah, where he takes refuge in a boat which the god Visnu in the form of a fish, tows safely through the flood waters. On returning to dry land Manu becomes the progenitor of the descent groups to which the various heroes of the *kṣatriya* lineages belong. His eldest son is the ancestor of the Sūryavaṃśa or Solar lineage and the younger, androgynous child is ancestress to the Candravaṃśa or Lunar lineage. The symbolism is replete with many layers of meaning. Interestingly, the *Rāmāyaṇa* and the *Mahābhārata* are narratives of the last few generations of these lineages. In later times many families wishing to legitimise themselves as royalty claimed descent from one of these two lines. In the succession of heroes and ruling clans, reckoning is by generations and therefore time is linear although within the framework of the overall cyclic ages — the *yugas*. Kinship relations within the larger genealogical form take different patterns suggesting that differences in social organisation were being registered and these were important to the way in which the past was seen. The second time marker is the great war described in the *Mahābhārata* in which nearly all the clans are said to participate and meet their end. It is as the texts say, the end of the age of the *kṣatriya* heroes.

Subsequent to this, the text changes from the past to the future tense and claims to be predicting the events which are described. Descent groups give way to dynasties and generalised time reckoning by generation gives way to regnal years. Dynasties, historically attested from other sources, are referred to. Some of these are known to have ruled from about the fourth century BC to the fourth century AD. This is a very different kind of past from that of the heroes and we are now involved in the computations of royal families ruling monarchical states. It is emphasised that this is not the age of the noble *kṣatriyas*, the born heroes, but the age of upstart, *śūdra* families and foreign degenerate *kṣatriyas* such as the

Yavanas or Indo-Greeks. It is in some ways quite remarkable that through the idiom of genealogical patterns there is so much that relates to how the past was perceived.

Another category of texts grew out of the courtly ambience and looked briefly back at the past. These are biographies of kings which become a significant genre of literature in the period after the seventh century AD.[27] The seminal forms of royal biographies are to be found in inscriptions dating to the turn of the Christian era, such as that of Khāravela at Hathigumpha giving a thumb-nail sketch of his activities or a Sātavāhana queen-mother's summary of her son's achievements inscribed at Nasik.[28] The first historical biography, reflective of this new genre, was Bānabhaṭṭa's *Harṣacarita*, the early life of Harṣavardhana of Kannauj, written in the seventh century. A spate of biographies emerged from the tenth to the thirteenth centuries such as Bilhaṇa's *Vikramānkadevacarita* on the Cālukya king of the Deccan and Sandhyākaranandi's *Rāmacarita* on Rāmapāla, a king of eastern India.

The biographies were often contemporary with the rulers, but each narrated a brief history of the dynasty and then proceeded to record the important events of the patron's life. A brief history of the author's family was also included to provide the author with appropriate credentials. Royal families of obscure origin required legitimation through the intervention of a deity. This was particularly important where there was a contested succession as was often the case and where the biography was justifying the patron's right to rule. Although couched in the literary style of court poetry, where fantasy had poetic licence, nevertheless the biography often centred on actual events crucial to the political authority of the patron, such as Harṣa establishing himself as the king of Kannauj or the Pāla king defeating the Kaivarta revolt.

This was also the period which saw the composition of a large number of *vaṃśāvalīs* or chronicles of ruling families.[29] The *vaṃśāvalī* is literally the path to succession. These are either narratives of a dynasty, recorded and maintained by a family of court poets, or else in summary form, they occur as royal inscriptions. These chronicles are charters of validation of the family and of the region constituting the kingdom. Inscriptions came to be engraved after the family had established itself, since such inscriptions, being official statements were regarded as a mark of authority. An example of this would be an inscription of the Candella dynasty composed in the tenth century AD which describes the previous seven rulers, each associated with actions which helped strengthen the power of the dynasty. Subsequent to this there is a long eulogy to the ruling king's father and then to the king himself who was the patron of the temple where the inscription is located.[30] Many such inscriptions were engraved at temples since temples when built and endowed by royalty or by the elite, were statements of power. Families of obscure origin such as the Candellas required an origin myth invoking divine connections and providing them with high status. Particular mention is made of a marriage alliance with an established *kṣatriya* ruling family which provides a clue to the point in time when the Candellas came to be accepted as *kṣatriyas* by other ruling families, many of whom had been through the same process. Political power appears to have been fairly open to those who were bold enough to aspire to it. The complaints of the earlier authors of the *Purāṇas* that royalty would come increasingly from low status groups seems to be reflected in these claims. Mention is made of campaigns and battles and of generous endowments to *brāhmaṇas*, endowments which ensured the fabrication of genealogies for the ruling family frequently linking them to the Solar or Lunar line and endorsing the origin myth.

Occasionally there are other documents from other ruling families which contradict the official version as related in an inscription. Thus the epic on an important Chauhan ruler, the *Pṛthivīrāja-rāso*, written a few centuries later, contradicts the origin myth of the Candellas and makes them out to be upstarts and adventurers and socially rather unacceptable. An oral epic of the same period, but recorded later, the *Ālhā-khaṇḍa*, is also suspicious about Candella origins.[31] In this the local hero emerges as the defender of the Candella domain and his battles against the enemies of the kingdom, put the contemporary Candella ruler to shame.

The longer *vaṃśāvalīs* or chronicles maintained by bards and court poets often set the history of the dynasty in the context of the region. They include a perceived history going back to earlier times. Thus the chronicle of the kingdom of Chamba in the northern Himalayas, weaves a narrative from which it is possible to observe the gradual transformation of clan territories into a kingdom.[32] The narrative of early rulers is linked to some of the heroes of the Puranic genealogies. This provides the appropriate status. More realistic connections with the kingdom of Kashmir introduce the ancestors of later ruling families. The genealogy of rulers appears to be a seamless construction but in effect there are major changes recorded in variant family names and the locating of families in a dispersed geography. The expansion moves from a small, high valley to a larger valley to a bigger territory. The descendents of lesser chiefs begin to take royal titles indicative of a change in the nature of authority. A capital is established as the royal centre. Roving religious sects and ascetics of earlier times yield place to recognised Vaiṣṇava religious sects and temples adorn the capital. At this point marriage alliances become important to status and there is also much mention of campaigns and endowments. Some of the personalities of these chronicles are also known to us from the inscriptions which they issued, often recording the details of donations.

The *itihāsa-purāṇa* tradition came to constitute the core of one kind of historical thinking. This included the variations in the working over of the tradition which moved from a heroic to a courtly phase, although the former was frequently incorporated into the latter and the complexity of social forms encouraged this incorporation. There were of course other parallel traditions reflecting a historical consciousness but taking a different form. One example was that of the Buddhist monastic chronicle. In some cases when focussing on the history of the Saṅgha, it inevitably included a substantial segment of the history of the period. A case in point are the two chronicles from Sri Lanka, the *Dīpavaṃsa* and the *Mahāvaṃsa*, both composed in the mid-first millennium AD but narrating events from an earlier period.[33]

The *Dīpavaṃsa* is a history of the island where the focus is on the narrative of the coming of Buddhism to Sri Lanka and the establishment of the Buddhist *saṅgha*. The *Mahāvaṃsa* covers the same themes but also highlights the history of the important Mahāvihāra monastery, to which the author belonged. The political inter-relations of the *saṅgha* and the Sri Lankan state are described which introduces a substantial excursis into the history of the Nandas and Mauryas as well.

Monasteries as the institutional centres for preserving the historical tradition as seen from the Buddhist and Jaina perspective, maintained chronicles of monastic and sectarian activities. These texts carry the imprint of a perspective which touches on the question of historicity. A number of reasons could be suggested for this perspective, differing partially from the *itihāsa-purāṇa* tradition. Among them would be the historicity of the founders, the breaking away from what has been regarded as orthodoxy and orthopraxy, and the importance of an eschatology more conducive to a historical worldview. Equally significant was the social background of the patrons of these sects and the urban and literate milieu of the early teaching. With the institutionalisation of the sects as orders, the need to maintain versions of sectarian conflicts among these orders as well as their property relations and the interplay between the religious order and political power became necessary. There is some awareness of the Brahmanic perception of the past among Buddhist authors as also some borrowing, but the differences are more marked. The awareness of alternate views and traditions could not have been overlooked. The patrons of each are projected as separate and distinct subjects of the history as recorded by the various sects.

The arrival of the Arabs, Turks, Afghans and Mughals did not terminate the importance of the *itihāsa-purāṇa* tradition. Although no longer dominant at the capitals of the major kingdoms, it was still fostered in those where legitimation from the past was culled from earlier historical traditions. A few desultory attempts were also made to trace the ancestry of the Sultans to *kṣatriya* lineages or to link the origins of local dynasties to Islamic historiography. The introduction of European concepts of historical writing marked the termination of earlier traditions.

In attempting to analyse what might be called the expression of historical consciousness in early India, let me emphasise that it has not been my intention to try and reinstate what might be viewed as an indigenous version of Indian history. This would be historically untenable given the methodology and purpose of present-day historical writing. I have attempted instead to describe colonial views of the Indian past and to explain why the idea of an absence of historical consciousness in early India, became axiomatic. I have then juxtaposed various categories of texts purporting to represent the past. My concern has been not with the historicity of their contents but rather to observe the ways in which they perceived the past and demonstrated a historical consciousness. Since the supposed absence of the latter was largely argued on the premise that early Indian society was a static society, registering no change, the constant underlining of change in various forms in these texts becomes fundamentally different from the received view. So also does the question of the nature of historical change as apparent from these texts. The use of the past to legitimise the present is the starting point for the recognition of various ways of representing historical consciousness. To see the earlier tradition as a coherent whole seems to me to be relevant as also to perceive its relation with the society from which it emerged; and above all, to recognise the nature of historical consciousness which in any society is meaningful to the understanding of its culture.

## Notes and References

1. *Asiatic Researches*, 4, p. xvii.
2. A.A. MacDonell, *A History of Sanskrit Literature*, London, 1900, p. 11.
3. E.J. Rapson, *The Cambridge History of India*, I, 1922, p. 57.
4. P. Burke, *The Renaissance Sense of the Past*, London, 1969.
5. D.P. Kejriwal, *The Asiatic Society of Bengal and the Discovery of India's Past*, Delhi, 1988.
6. W. Jones, 'On the Chronology of the Hindus', *Asiatic Researches*, 1, pp. 345ff and 2, pp. 88–113. F. Wilford, 'On the Chronology of the Hindus', *Asiatic Researches*, 1808, 5, pp. 241ff.
7. J. Majeed, *Ungoverned Imaginings*, Oxford, 1992.
8. J. Majeed, op. cit.
9. Quoted in E. Said, *Orientalism*, London, 1978, p. 215.
10. Romila Thapar, 'Society in Ancient India: The Formative Period', in *Ancient Indian Social History: Some Interpretations*, New Delhi, 1978, pp. 211–39. *See* chapter 14 in this volume. 'The Archaeological Background to the Agnicayana Ritual', in F. Staal (ed.), *Agni*, II, Berkeley, 1983, pp. 1–40. *See* chapter 15 in this volume. 'Archaeology and Language at the Roots of Ancient India', *Journal of the Asiatic Society of Bombay*, 1989–91, 64–6, n.s., pp. 249–68.
11. R.A.L.H. Gunawardana, 'The Analysis of Precolonial Social Formations in Asia in the Writings of Karl Marx', *Indian Historical Review*, 1976, II, 2, pp. 365–88. B. Hindess and P. Hirst, *Pre-Capitalist Modes of Production*, London, 1975.
12. M. Weber, *The Religion of India*, Glencoe, 1958. J. Heesterman, *The Inner Conflict of Tradition*, Chicago, 1985, pp. 194ff. Romila Thapar, *Interpreting Early India*, New Delhi, 1992, pp. 23ff.
13. J. Tod, *Annals and Antiquities of Rajasthan*, London, 1829–32.
14. L.P. Tessitori, 'A Scheme for the Bardic and Historical Survey of Rajputana', *Journal of the Asiatic Society of Bengal*, 1914, 10, pp. 373–86; 1919, 15, pp. 5–79; 1920, 16, pp. 251–79.
15. The most influential of these was D.D. Kosambi who introduced a high level of intellectual discussion into the interpretation of Indian history and particularly of early India. Apart from papers of a

specialised kind, see *An Introduction to the Study of Indian History*, Bombay, 1956 and *The Culture and Civilisation of Ancient India in Historical Outline*, London, 1965.

16. Romila Thapar, *From Lineage to State*, New Delhi, 1984.
17. Romila Thapar, *The Mauryas Revisited*, Calcutta, 1988. *See* chapter 23 in this volume. G. Fussman, 'Central and Provincial Administration in Ancient India: the Problem of the Mauryan Empire', *Indian Historical Review*, 1987–88, 14, 1–2, pp. 43–72.
18. This has been described by some as a form of Indian feudalism, but it remains a controversial issue. R.S. Sharma, *Indian Feudalism*, Delhi, 1980; H. Mukhia, 'Was there Feudalism in Indian History', *Journal of Peasant Studies*, April 1981, 8, 3, pp. 273–310; B.D. Chattopadhyaya, *The Making of Early Medieval India*, New Delhi, 1994. The debate has been extended to the history of south India, N. Karashima, *South Indian History and Society*, Delhi, 1984, *Towards a New Formation*, Delhi, 1992; K. Veluthat, *The Political Structure of Early Medieval South India*, Delhi, 1993.
19. *Bṛhadāraṇyaka Upaniṣad*, 2.4.10; *Chāndogya Upaniṣad*, 7.1.2.
20. F.E. Pargiter, *Ancient Indian Historical Tradition*, London, 1922.
21. C.H. Philips (ed.), *Historians of India, Pakistan and Ceylon*, London, 1961.
22. H. Kulke, 'Geshchichtschreibung und Geshchichtsbild in Hinduistechen Mittelalter', *Secculum*, 1979, 30, pp. 100–13.
23. M. Eliade, *The Myth of the Eternal Return*, Princeton, 1971.
24. Romila Thapar, 'Society and Historical Consciousness: the Itihasa-purana Tradition', in S. Bhattacharya and Romila Thapar (eds), *Situating Indian History*, New Delhi, 1986, pp. 353–83. *See* chapter 7 in this volume.
25. Junagadh Rock Inscription of Rudradāman, *Epigraphia Indica*, 8, 36ff. Junagadh Rock Inscription of Skandagupta, J.F. Fleet, *Corpus Inscriptionum Indicarum, III*, Varanasi, 1970, reprint, 56ff.
26. Romila Thapar, 'Genealogical Patterns as Perceptions of the Past', *Studies in History*, 1991, 7, 1, pp. 1–36. *See* chapter 33 in this volume.
27. V.S. Pathak, *Ancient Historians of India*, Bombay, 1966.
28. Hathigumpha Cave Inscription of Khāravela, D.C. Sircar, *Select Inscriptions . . .*, Calcutta, 1965 (2nd ed.), 213ff. Nasik Cave Inscription of Balaśrī, E. Senart, *Epigraphia Indica*, VIII, pp. 60ff.
29. A.K. Warder, *An Introduction to Indian Historiography*, Bombay, 1972.
30. Inscription of Yaśovarman, *Epigraphia Indica*, 1, pp. 122ff.
31. G. Grierson, *The Lay of Alha*, Gurgaon, 1990 (reprint).
32. Ph. Vogel, *The Antiquities of Chamba State*, Calcutta, 1911.
33. L.S. Perera, 'The Pali Chronicles of Ceylon', in C.H. Philips (ed.), *Historians of India, Pakistan and Ceylon*, London, 1961, pp. 29ff.

# 9

# *Antecedents, Religious Sanctions and Political Legitimation in the Ladakh Chronicles**

Chronicles of the second millennium AD from the lesser states of the Indian subcontinent, are characterised by a concern with origins relating to the dynasty and often by extension, to the kingdom. The discussion on origins links those in political power with the established clans and lineages of earlier times and the links are often sanctioned through a religious connection. It would seem that political legitimation, essential to the furtherance of the notion of the state, drew both on social status through lineage connections and on ideological backing through religious support. An attempt will be made here to examine this in relation to the Ladakh Chronicles.

The Ladakh Chronicles relate the history of the area called La-dvags, identified with the Indus furrow and the valleys leading off it.[1] The Chronicles were put together from approximately the middle of the second millennium AD onwards. The authors drew on a large body of sources which included well-known Buddhist texts such as the Vasubandhu *Abhidharmakośa* and the *Lalitavistara* and the histories of Buddhism in Tibetan as well other sources such as the Gesar epic, the annals, the genealogies, the biography of Senge Namgyal by his son and possibly the *vaṃśāvalīs* of the Himalayan hill states. Variant manuscripts of the Chronicles of Ladakh from diverse sources have been collated by modern scholars.[2] The chronicles of lesser chiefdoms which went into the making of the state of Ladakh were also used and where these exist as separate minor chronicles as in the case of Zanskar, Guge, Chigtan, Sod, they can be seen as similar

* Paper given at a Seminar on Ladakh, CSRD, JNU. 1978.

and constituent forms. Since many of the earlier authors of the Chronicles were in the main lamas, the history of the state and that of Buddhism in the area came to be treated virtually as a single entity. It is likely that some of the monastic chronicles were also used as sources of data. This paper is not an attempt to verify the historical accuracy of the Ladakh Chronicles but rather to examine their historical perceptions.

The Chronicles follow a pattern which is familiar from the *vaṃśāvalīs* of the Indian *itihāsa-purāṇa* tradition and also reflect the influence of the Tibetan chronicles. The imprint of the *itihāsa-purāṇa* tradition may not have been direct and may well have come via Tibetan or other traditions, nevertheless it is significant that Indian origins and links were believed to be of considerable consequence. There are broadly three sections to the text. The first deals mainly with cosmology, mythology and the emergence of Buddhism. The second section discusses the history of Tibet by way of a link and an introduction to the history of Ladakh and the final section is a reasonably reliable record of the major dynastic events in Ladakh, set in a genealogical framework.

The earliest section[3] inspite of being largely a recitation of myths, is not without its own significance, in that mythology can be regarded as a clue to the social assumptions and symbolic high-points of a culture. The cosmology carries the impress of Bon elements, this being the substratum culture in many parts of Tibet, the Himalayan borderlands and the area under discussion. Inspite of the formal antagonism of Buddhist monks to Bon practices there is here a concession to the earliest culture being Bon. The creation of the continents with a focus on Jambudvīpa and the rising of the central mountain Sumeru, is evidently derived from Indian sources as it is familiar from the *Purāṇas*. The geographical perspective is however significant. Among the list of kingdoms mentioned some importance is given to Persia, Samarkand, Swat, Kashmir, Mandi, Guge, Nepal, Lop Nor, Koko Nor and Amdo, an indication of the areas with which there was communication and contact.

Reference is made to the people of India and in this connection the myth of the emergence of the four castes is related. We are told that they emerged from the body of primeval man, the *rājanyas* from his top-knot, the *brāhmaṇas* from his neck, the *kṣatriyas* from his heart and the *śūdras* from his feet, and they were differentiated by their colours, white, red, yellow and black. The borrowing of many ideas from Indian sources is evident: the *puruṣasūkta* hymn of the *Ṛg Veda*[4] describing the origin of the four castes from the body of Prajāpati; the association of colour as a distinguishing mark and the listing of the colours as given in the *Mahābhārata*.[5] The pre-eminence of the *rājanya* reflects a Buddhist preoccupation where the early Buddhist sources frequently placed the *khattiya* as higher than the *brāhmaṇa*. The substitution of the *vaiśya* by the *kṣatriya* is curious, particularly in a society in which trade played such an important part. It may however suggest that the *varṇa* classification was more normative than actual and conformity demanded the listing of four status groups, the names and the order being less important; or alternatively, that inspite of the importance of trade to the area, a separate category of traders was not recognised, or that the heads of clans were also traders.

The distribution of tribes is then described and lineage ties are associated with territory. The major theme is the story of Mahāsammata which as in other sources elsewhere, is used to legitimise the dynasty. The story in the Chronicles follows in essentials the Buddhist tradition. In times long past, the initial egalitarian utopia gave way to a society based on differences of colour and together with the growth of families, houses and the ownership of fields, all of which emerged largely through the sin of desire and pride, the differences were accentuated. Civil strife then became so intense that it was necessary to elect a 'lord of the fields', a Mahāsammata, who formulated laws and divided men into four classes according to the work which they performed. In this classification, the *brāhmans* and the *kṣatriyas* are given almost equal status and are described as virtuous and clean. The next two were of mixed virtue and were looked down upon. The references to these two points of stratification are of some interest. It would seem that whereas on the first occasion the stratification was largely a symbolic distinction in which colours were used to identify groups, the second refers to the specific conditions of caste society. Whereas the first precedes the utopian beginnings, the second is the outcome of a situation of social competition and strife.

Mahāsammata is then treated as the eponymous ancestor of a large distribution of lineages, his descendents being the virtuous wheel-turning kings of the various *kalpas*. This is in keeping with the historiography of some schools of Buddhism, such as the Theravāda.[6] The descent of the Śākyas is linked to that of Mahāsammata and their history is related through many generations of kings until the time of the Buddha. The Śākyas are described as a prosperous people with an abundance of sugarcane and rice and other crops which grew without the need for ploughing, again indicative of utopian beginnings. The family of the Buddha is also called Ikṣvāku and Sūryavaṃśa in keeping with the *itihāsa-purāṇa* tradition and early Buddhist sources. Interestingly, the etymology of Ikṣvāku is derived as in the Mahāyāna tradition, from *ikṣa*/sugarcane,[7] and not in association with Okkāka as is more common in the Theravāda tradition and which is sometimes explained as deriving from, . . . *kathamakāle ukka viya mukhato pabha niccharati* . . .[8]

The origin myth of the Śākyas is given as in other Buddhist sources with the exiling of the princes and princesses who settle near the *āśrama* of the sage Kapila. The princes are permitted by the *ṛṣi* to marry their step-sisters, i.e. their mother's sister's daughters, unlike the earlier versions of the story which refer to sibling incest and cross-cousin marriage.[9] Their ability to marry in this fashion, *śākyam*, gives them their name, Śākya. The section concludes with the birth of the Buddha and the four contemporary princes, Bimbisāra of Magadha, Praśenajit of Kośala said to be a kinsman of the Buddha, Udayana of Vatsa and Pradyota of Avanti. The story is rounded off with the marriage and renunciation of the Buddha, the birth of Rāhula and his being ordained as a monk.

The details on the Śākyas were necessary since the kings of Ladakh also claimed Ikṣvāku origins, doubtless to link themselves to the highest in status, namely, the family of the Buddha.[10] Some refer to Śuddhodana, the father of the Buddha, as their ancestor. This reflects the continuing importance of lineage connections even after the establishment of the kingdom of Ladakh and was doubtless used to emphasise the sovereignty and divine connections of the royal family.[11] Incidentally the Ceylon Chronicles, the *Dīpavaṃsa* and the *Mahāvaṃsa*, go to great lengths to build a kinship connection between the Śākyas and the Mauryas, so that Mahinda the son of Aśoka Maurya, who led the first Buddhist mission to Ceylon could be described as a descendent of the Buddha.[12]

The Chronicle then moves to the history of Tibet[13] in order to introduce the Tibetan link. The kings of Tibet are traced back to the third son of Praśenajit of Kośala who was of the same kingroup as the Buddha according to the Chronicles, although other Buddhist sources would place the Kośalan royal family a notch lower in the social scale.[14] (In the Bon tradition the ancestor of the kings of Tibet is identified with Karṇa, the son of Kuntī, thus suggesting a link with the *Mahābhārata*[15] but curiously with a person of almost inverted status). The story of the Kośalan prince founding a kingdom in Tibet carries the stereo-types of similar stories from elsewhere.[16] The child had peculiar physical features and was therefore sent away and brought up by a hunter. Thus when he finally won his way to becoming the overlord of Yarlung, the nucleus of what was to become the kingdom of Tibet, he was believed to have come from the sky, so uncertain were his origins; this story also satisfied the theory of kingship from heaven. His descendents were the kings of the Khri Dynasty each named after his mother. To one of his descendents is attributed the discovery of charcoal, iron, the plough and the yoke, irrigation canals and bridges, suggestive of a period which saw the extension of agriculture and the smelting of metals. Not surprisingly the arrival of Buddhism is subsequent to this development since the establishment of monasteries requires a fairly developed agricultural economy and trade networks. The new religion is also believed to have been introduced in the form of a basket carrying the teachings which came down from the sky, doubtless a garbled symbolism involving the Tripiṭaka and heaven!

The most eulogised of the early Tibetan kings is Sron-btsam-gam-po of the seventh century AD. His reign was a watershed in early Tibetan history since he attempted the consolidation of clan territories into a state, extended the frontier of Tibet to the Mānasarovara area, introduced a script which some scholars link with that of Kashmir and others Khotan, and patronised Buddhism by both inviting Indian teachers and supporting the new religion in Tibet. The patronage to Buddhism derived from personal inclination but also had the function of helping consolidate the state since as a religion it could be used across lineage ties and was not limited to localised cult groups. Networks of monasteries acted as a means of linking areas. An attempt was made to weld chiefships into a single political unit sustaining the power of the state through marriage alliances and the use of Buddhism as a unifying religion. The eighth century saw a further development of this trend and specific mention is made of the invitation to Padmasambhava from Uḍḍiyāna. Other Indian Buddhist teachers were invited to teach and to help in the translation of Buddhist texts. The number of monasteries seem to have increased quite sizeably since in the ninth century it was stipulated that groups of seven households were to support one lama, thus linking the monastery to the economy of the villages in its vicinity. Equally interesting is the statement that weights and measures were made identical with those used in India, a pointer to growing trade connections. Yet it is the Tibetan calender which was adopted in Ladakh presumably because the monastic annals were kept in accordance with Tibetan time reckoning. The use of a script would emphasise literacy acting as a factor of change which made record keeping precise, orderly and continuous. Literacy may also have acted as a divider separating the literate monks from those who still maintained an oral tradition.

Patronage to Buddhism also meant a decline in the earlier Bon religion which was to have disastrous consequences for Buddhism during the reign of Glang-dar-ma. Many of the nobles still observed Bon practices with an emphasis on family cults and animism. As such they were suspicious of Buddhism and possibly some of their opposition derived from the threat to their status posed by political centralisation which centralisation was strengthened by patronage to Buddhism.[17] The Bon religion rooted in shamanism was not capable of providing the kind of ideological support which Buddhism could give to consolidating state systems.[18]

We are told that four *brāhmaṇaś*, jealous at the success of Buddhism in Tibet, arranged to be reborn as demons and organised the attack on the Buddhists.[19] It is again significant that at the root of the persecution of Buddhism lay the *brāhmaṇas*, an antagonism which went back to early times in the history of north India. Glang-dar-ma, ruling in the ninth century gave political support to this attack making it into a major persecution of the Buddhists. Although Buddhism was eventually to revive, the form it took in the subsequent period had even closer political connections which safe-guarded it from another persecution even though these connections introduced innovations into the religion. The persecution of the Buddhists was a turning point in the history of Ladakh. The Chronicles state that the grandson of Glang-dar-ma fled from Tibet and married the daughter of the king of Purang and on inheriting the kingdom extended its boundaries from Mar-yul and the Mānasarovara region into Guge, Spiti, Zanskar and Ladakh.

The contemporary scene in neighbouring areas was one in which after the seventh century AD a number of 'hill states' emerged in the upper reaches of the river valleys cutting across the sub-Himalayan

route from Lamayuru met the Indus near one of the major fordable points at Khalatse where a bridge and a customs house was maintained. By now Ladakh was being brought into the circuit of the central Asian trade with the competition between the Tibetans, the Chinese, the Turks and the Mongols for control over at least some sectors of the route through central Asia. Alchi would have linked Zanskar with the route upstream via Khalatse to Skardu and Gilgit. Spituk and Nyar-ma dominated the wide valley of the Indus near the Leh fan. In terms of location the monasteries were parallel to the garrison forts controlling the routes along the Indus furrow. Doubtless they also acted as halting points along the route when trade developed.

The attraction of the trade drew merchants, the armies of those wishing to control the routes, and religious missions. Judging by the inscription of a Nestorian Christian at Tankse,[21] it would seem that the western oases of the Takla Makan were important trading points. It was these western oases that were continually disturbed in attempts to oust the Chinese from their control over the trade.[22] The disturbances in this region may well have required the search for an alternate route. With the growing importance of Khotan there would have been a tendency for the route to have shifted eastwards and possibly it was at this time that the Indus furrow began to be regarded as a viable alternative. At the same time the Tibetan control over the southern oases of the Takla Makan increased during the eighth century and for a while even Tun-huang was under Tibetan control.[23] This may also have encouraged the use of the Khotan-Leh connection which, given the Tibetan occupation of Ladakh would have meant a major and secure route in Tibetan hands. The Indus furrow would have linked Khotan with Kashmir and further west. This link may have been some compensation for the loss of Tibetan participation in the control of the area to the west of the Pamirs and the extension of interest into the Tarim basin.

Not surprisingly by the mid-second millennium AD the Indus furrow had become the bone of contention between Kashmir and Tibet with the use of the Zoji-la as an entry point. Thus we are told that in the fourteenth century the Bhauṭṭa Rincana attempted to disrupt the political power of Kashmir.[24] In the sixteenth century, Mirza Muhammad Haider took a Mughal army to the Zoji-la and won a victory. Familiarity with the territory held by the Bhauṭṭas increases in the later Kashmir Chronicles of Jonarāja and Śrivara of the fifteenth century. The latter[25] speaks of a Great and Little Bhuṭṭa-deśa when referring to Ladakh and Baltistan.

Kashmir and Baltistan were not the only areas with which Ladakh had political relations. An attempt was made to build up links between Ladakh and Bhutan with an invitation from the ruler of Ladakh for a *siddha* of the 'Brug-pa order from Bhutan to come to Ladakh. This link could be seen as an assertion of independence *vis-à-vis* Tibet and need not be unexpected if viewed as following the route along the Himalayan borders parallel to the Tsang-po river. Communication along the borders may also be suggested by the stamp of Nepalese craftsmanship in the art of Ladakh. This doubtless had its origin in the close relations between Tibet and Nepal in the seventh century AD and it has been argued that the style was diffused through the spread of Tibetan art. It is equally possible that connections were extended along the Himalayan borders with states such as Guge, Mar-yul, Nepal and Bhutan maintaining their own contacts as well. The Indo-Tibetan style as some have termed it is evident in the earlier monasteries of Ladakh.[26]

The first spurt of monastery building in Ladakh seems to have coincided with the emergence of the kingdom of Ladakh suggesting a period in which power was stabilised into a state system which probably absorbed a variety of earlier forms some of which could well have been chiefships centred on the main valleys. The Buddhist monastery in such a system would not only act as a halting point along routes but would also become the nucleii of power in the limited fertile tracts of valley areas. Ultimately each of the monasteries came to be 'landlords' in these tracts and were inevitably situated in areas where some sizeable cultivation was possible. The monastery would act as an agency of acculturation introducing and extending the Buddhist systems as described by the various sects. Where its relationship with royalty was close it would act as a representative of political authority. Some of the early monasteries were built in the vicinity of forts. In some instances, such as Chendey, the fort was taken over by the monastery.

The second significant phase in the history of Ladakh was the sixteenth century by which time both the monastery and political authority were well-established. The fifteenth century had seen the invasion of Ladakh by Zain-ul-Abadin, a reflection of the growing importance of the Indus furrow as a trade corridor. The unsuccessful hold of Kashmir encouraged further consolidation in Ladakh with the emergence of the Namgyal dynasty. Monasteries were built at Tiktse, Phyi-dbang, Stakna and Hemis indicating a shift eastwards to the neighbourhood of Leh. Shey became the main political centre. It had a good agricultural base using canals drawn off the Indus and it was also connected with the Changchenmo route to Yarkand. The monastery at Shey carries an imprint of central Asian forms among what appear to be donor figures. Even more strikingly central Asian are the frescoes at the monastery at Miru beyond Upshi and also of the same period. However, the proximity of Kashmir continued to be felt as is demonstrated in the distinctly Mughal style of dress of Tashi Namgyal[27] and the connection continued, although often discrete.

The consolidation of the state presupposes certain other changes in society which seem to have occurred during this period. In the establishing of the suzerainty of the dynasty, hostages and tributes were taken from the chiefs and the Chronicle states that the king placed his own men in their castles to emphasise his overlordship. Significantly, the minor chronicles from different areas included in the kingdom are largely in the form of genealogies suggesting the continuance of chiefships even under the sovereignty of the ruler of Ladakh.[28] The Chronicle informs us that Guge paid a tribute of three hundred *zo* of gold together with silver, sheep and one horse.[29] The tribute was by no means vast, but the fact of political suzerainty was important.

The continuance of chiefships even with the rise of an overarching state would not be strange in a society where the major form of identity remained the clan. Where the clan rights and identities would tend to produce vertical social divisions, Buddhism would have acted as a horizontal ideology cutting across these divisions. This in part explains the significance of Buddhism as a parallel to political authority and state formation. The two are inter-linked in a relationship of exchange; patron and recipient, with each playing both roles in the exchange of donations for legitimacy and merit.

The clan provided membership to the three strata which characterised society in Ladakh, the chiefly families or the aristocracy, the monks who in the process opted out of the clan and the peasants who were either independent landholders or were assigned to the monasteries and the chiefly families. Smiths, carpenters and musicians were ascribed a status which was low and excluded, presumably because they were itinerant groups and had no clan moorings. They are sometimes included in the category of Mons and are referred to as the indigenous population with Bon survivals.[30] But the anthropology of this area needs to be examined afresh.

Taxfree grants were made to certain categories of officials such as the village headman and to monasteries. Landholders rarely made grants of land since ownership was vested in the male members of the family. Since it was stipulated that one son would go to the monastery from each family, the monastery had some indirect hold over the family, and could on occasion claim a share in the movable property. The possibility of the subdivision of holdings was reduced by fraternal polyandry which although not the exclusive marriage system was fairly prevalent and which eliminated the growth of nuclear families as claimants to property. With the woman entering the clan of her husband's family on marriage, her separate identity was largely annulled. In an area of limited agricultural land such arrangements were inevitable. Irrigation works were also jointly owned by landholders and water-rights shared. This is again not strange in an area where hill-side aqueducts or *kuls* were the major form of irrigation.

In addition to agriculture an equally important source of revenue for the state was the tax on items of trade. It is likely that the monasteries also had a system of collecting such revenue from passing traders other than the regular donations. There is however an absence of commercially based towns until the rise of Leh as a commercial centre. Trade appears to have been more in the nature of a direct exchange of commodities at various levels without the controls of even an approximate market system. Each of the major monasteries, developed over time, a system of branch monasteries in other areas from which they derived additional wealth. This also required qualified monks to look after the administration and revenue records and collect the dues, which introduced a range of secular functions which the monks had to perform.

The Tibetan connection was further endorsed by a series of events which took place in the late sixteenth and early seventeenth century. A Balti invasion threatened both the Namgyal dynasty and Buddhism in Ladakh but the threat was diverted with a marriage alliance. The most renowned of the Ladakhi kings, Senge Namgyal had a Balti princess for his mother.[31] Ladakh was now placed in the awkward position of facing the Turks and the Mongols in Kashmir and Baltistan, and at the same time tight-rope walking in relations with Tibet. To add to the complication, Senge Namgyal was a supporter of the 'Brug-pa sect which was looked upon with some disfavour by the Dalai Lama who upheld the dGe-lugs-pa sect founded by Tsong-kha-pa.

Senge Namgyal is said to have invited the Bhutanese to send a *siddha* to Ladakh to strengthen the 'Brug-pa order. The famous sTag-tshang Ras-pa arrived after extensive travels in the western Himalayas, Uḍḍiyāna and Zanskar. The monasteries of Hemis, Stakna and Chendey were built and the Chronicles list the lavish gifts bestowed on sTag-tsang.[32] The relationship between the monk and the monarch is compared to that between the moon and the sun and the reign of Senge Namgyal is remembered for the closeness between the king and the Buddhist Order. The monasteries were the recipients of large grants including many estates.

The prosperity of Ladakh is indicated in its being 'full of yaks and sheep', a pastoralists paradise.[33] This flush of prosperity was obviously not due to merely the tribute gathered from subordinate chiefs. It was also linked to profits of trade which in turn made Ladakh a lucrative prize in the eyes of its neighbours. This is made apparent later in the seventeenth century when Ladakh was forced to draw up treaties with both Kashmir and Tibet. The main items in both treaties relate to trading areas, monopolies over goods traded, prices and access to markets.[34] Kashmir was given a monopoly over importing fine wool and soon after this Kashmiri merchants are established in Ladakh. In addition horses, yak-tails and musk was supplied to Kashmir in return for rice. It is worth noting that the agricultural base of Ladakh was perhaps not adequate to meet the demands for rice.

The treaty with Tibet was more stringent. Territory ceded included Guge and Ru-thog, the latter giving access to the gold-producing areas on which the Tibetans had their sights. The Tibetans fearing the annexation of Ladakh by Kashmir, kept it as a sphere of influence. Among trade items, gold and musk was to be sent to Tibet and in return Ladakh received brick tea. The increasing influence of Tibet had meant the gradual conversion of many of the monasteries of Ladakh to the dGe-lugs-pa persuasion, a conversion which became more evident now. The acceptance of dGe-lugs-pa symbolised both the importance of Tibet as well as, more indirectly, the appeasement of the Mongols, given the particular relationship which the Dalai Lama had with the Mongols.

By the end of the eighteenth century the Namgyal dynasty had declined. But now Balti and Kashmiri traders had also gained footholds in Ladakh. There was enough motivation for frequent incursions into Ladakh.

The Ladakh Chronicles are concerned essentially with the second millennium AD, a period which is also central to the growth and development of Buddhism in Ladakh. The Chronicles are by no means entirely reliable but even a cursory investigation of their pre-suppositions reveals an aspect of the history of Ladakh which is worth considering. There is a close co-relation between the founding and the growth of the monasteries with forms of change in political authority and economic activities. The growth of the monasteries coincides with the extension of sovereignty and the attempts to establish a powerful authority over and above the chiefs; this further coincides with the location of the monasteries in the potentially and actually cultivable areas of the Indus furrow as well as the exploitation of a number of trade routes, particularly the one linking Leh with Khotan and Yarkand. Baltistan, Kashmir and Tibet all sought control over this route when its potential was actualised and the competition became intense from the sixteenth century. Tibet, with its reach into central Asia had the maximum to gain by this control since it gave access to the markets of the north Indian plains. For Kashmir too the annexation of Ladakh meant the tapping of a lucrative trade and access to raw materials.

The inter-locking of the three areas is symbolised in the nature of Buddhism as it evolved in Ladakh and in the cultural symbols used in the Ladakh Chronicles. The attempt to fuse the northern Indian Buddhist tradition with Tibetan historiography may be seen both as an attempt at political adjustments as well as the reality of Buddhism in Ladakh. What does remain significant is that a characteristic of the relationship between Buddhism and political authority which is the main thread of the Chronicles, results here as elsewhere in similar texts, in the history of the state being virtually indistinguishable from the history of the religion. Ultimately for the authors of the Chronicles what was primary was the history of Buddhism in Ladakh.

The Ladakh Chronicles emphasise antecedents and origins, using

Tibetan and Indian sources to endorse the highest status for the ruling families. The endorsement of kinship links was necessary for purposes of political sanction. State formation which can be the precondition to or accompaniment of monarchy, cuts across lineage ties but nevertheless the ties remain important. This would seem even more necessary in areas where the state had not converted the existing system into full subordination to central authority with a restructuring of the economy, either in the form of intensive agriculture or trade directly under the control of the central political authority.

The religious sanction is linked to the infrastructure of the state. In places where Buddhism was introduced, not as a movement of dissent or an alternative belief system (which characterised it in India at the time of its early history), but as part of the established structure of the state, it was likely to take on a supervisory role from the start. Where the establishment of the Buddhist monastery coincided with state formation it acted as an adjunct of the state, the networks of sectarian centres providing a parallel network of control. Literate monks were in a position to maintain records both of the monasteries and of the state. In distant areas the monastery would function as an administrative centre, collecting revenue and maintaining law and order. In some parts of the kingdom the monastery could also have had a para-military function. This is particularly noticeable in sparsely populated mountain areas, along passes and in frontier regions. Such active participation in local life precludes the categorising of the monastery as a non-productive and entirely parasitical institution.

The religious sanction was further reinforced by the demarcation of sacred space on a permanent basis. Unlike religions with purely sacrificial rituals in which sacred space could shift in accordance with the location of the sacrificial ritual, religions with institutional bases required permanent locations. This provided a territorial dimension to sacred space. The boundary between sacred and profane space was clearly demarcated and the ordering of sacred space became the right of the religious hierarchy. This is turn underlined the duality of sacral and temporal authority but with an interlocking of the two. Although the Buddhist *śāsana* was independent of the *cakravartin* there was simultaneously much interdependence.[35]

The importance of antecedents and religious sanctions in the process of political legitimation is also linked to the pattern of historical movement as viewed in Buddhist historiography. The central purpose of historiography being to record the establishment of the religion, there is some similarity in the unfolding of this pattern in different areas. The introduction of the religion is usually attributed to a dominant political personality, preferably at the conjunction of historical change from small political formations to a large state. Thus the reigns of Devānampiya Tissa in Ceylon and Sron-btsam-gam-po in Tibet are recognised as historically appropriate points for the introduction of Buddhism. The initial enthusiastic support of the religion gives way to a period of persecution, either of Buddhism itself as in the case of Tibet, or of the more orthodox sect, the Theravāda, as in the case of Ceylon. Ultimately the persecution dies down and there is a stronger re-establishment of the religion or sect. If the historical pattern has as one of its aims the final triumphal outcome of this re-establishment, then it has to be accompanied by both social antecedents of the highest order and a religious sanction which tends not to be questioned.

## Notes and References

1. It is thought that references to the area, probably to the north of the furrow, go back to Herodotus (III.98–106) who mentions the gold-digging ants of the region said to burrow in the ground and throw up earth containing gold dust. This was then collected and seived by the inhabitants and became an important item in the tribute paid by the satrapy of Gandhāra to the Achaemenid emperor. The story of the gold-digging ants is repeated in Megasthenes (Frag. XXXIX, Strabo XV.1.44) and Pliny (VI.C.19). The area producing the gold dust seems to have been more likely the Nubra and Shyok Valleys and the Chang Tang plateau known for their gold dust in later periods, as well as Baltistan (the Byltae of Ptolemy — XIII.3.) Megasthenes describes the area as inhabited by the Derdai who are referred to in other sources as Dardae and Daradai, almost certainly the people referred to as Dards in the area today. The *Mahābhārata* refers to the same region as the source for gold, when at the *rājasūya* of Yudhiṣthira are brought basketfuls of gold dust obtained from the *pipīlaka* ants (II.48.3–4)

   khaśā ekāśanājyohāḥ pradarā dhīrghavenavaḥ
   paśupāśca kunindāśca tangaṇāḥ paratangaṇāḥ
   te vai pipīlikam nāma varadattam pipīlikaih
   jātarūpam dronameyamahārṣuh puñjaśo nṛpāḥ

Possibly the ants were the marmots which are found in large numbers in these valleys and are known to heap up earth near their burrows and which perhaps was what Megasthenes meant when he thought that they were wild foxes. The epic states that the men of the mountains also bring yak-tails, sweet honey and herbs from Uttara Kuru and from near Kailāśa. The Khaśas are believed to have occupied the adjoining region and were probably separated from these areas by the Pir Panjal range.

Some occupation of the area in the early centuries AD is indicated by the discovery of Kusāna period inscriptions in the vicinity of Khalatse, but the texts are extremely brief, often illegible and therefore do not provide much evidence. The best preserved of them mentions the year 184/7 of an unknown era and the second line reads, *mahārājasa uvima kavthisasa*, probably indicating the reign of Vima Khadphises. (S. Konow, Kharosthi Inscriptions, *Corpus Inscriptionum Indicarum*, vol. II.1, pp. 79–81, Varanasi (reprint), 1969).

The suggestion that the Indus furrow may have been a route of communication with central Asia prior to the second millennium AD is doubtful. It would seem that the Zoji-la came to be used fairly late. There is no clear reference to this in the itineraries of the early Chinese Buddhist pilgrims and those coming from Tibet. Fa-hsien refers to Kie-chha which James Legge has identified with Ladakh but which most other scholars identify with Kashgar and Skardu. The journey as described by Fa-hsien would point to a route from the western Takla Makan to Baltistan and Swat, bye-passing the Indus furrow. Hüan Tsang's route clearly goes from Badakshan to Kashgar via Gilgit and no further east. (J. Legge, *Fa-hsien's Record of Buddhist Kingdoms*, Oxford, 1886, pp. 16–31; S. Beal, *Buddhist Records of the Western World*, II, London, 1884, pp. 306ff).

For the Chinese pilgrims India began with the Indus river and this is mentioned as soon as it is met with. In neither case do they refer to the Indus except in the proximity of Swat and the north-western part of the subcontinent. Had they met it in Ladakh they would certainly have referred to it. An eighth century Chinese visitor, Ou-k'ong seems to make an indirect reference to Ladakh when he mentions a route going eastwards from Tibet to Kashmir which Stein takes as the route across the Zoji-la. (M.A. Stein, *Memoir on Maps Illustrating the Ancient Geography of Kashmir*, Calcutta, 1899, p. 19).

From the Kuṣāṇa period onwards there were close links between Gandhāra (including Begram and Taxila), the Swat valley and Kashmir. The route to Uḍḍiyāna if it is identified with Swat, lay through Kashmir. But even before it became a sacred land of Tibetan Buddhism, the area witnessed a major change in the history of Buddhism with the schism leading to the emergence of the northern Mahāyāna school as distinct from the southern Hīnayāna. The early centuries AD were in any case a period of extensive patronage to Buddhism and it was towards the middle of the millennium with the coming of the Hūṇas that the patronage declined. This may have encouraged Buddhist missionaries to establish themselves in adjoining areas. The establishment of centres at Lahul, Spiti and Zanskar may well have dated to the latter half of the first millennium AD.

The *Rājataraṅginī* refers to Mihirakula re-establishing the *dharma* in lands over-run by the Bhauṭṭas (I.312–16).

> ākrānte dāradairbhauṭṭairmlecchairaśrucikarmabhiḥ
> vinaṣṭadharme deśasmin puṇyācāra pravartanam

Stein has argued that the references to the Bhauṭṭas is to the Tibetan populations of Dras and Ladakh. Stein's argument that the Zoji-la should be taken as the ethnographic frontier between Kashmir and Ladakh seems reasonable. The reference to the Bhauṭṭas though could also refer to Zanskar. Later in the text (IV.168) Kalhaṇa refers to the campaign of Lalitāditya of the eighth century AD against the Tibetans. The list of Lalitāditya's conquests is a conventional panaegyric, but the conquests in the neighbourhood may have been correctly reported. The Ladakh Chronicles do not refer to such an early association of the area with the Tibetans, but there may well have been small populations settled in the valleys. The Chinese T'ang Annals quote Lalitāditya's claim and also mention that Chinese forces were sent to assist the king in dispelling the Tibetans from Baltistan. Possibly the Buddhist sculptures at Dras and Mulbek may point to a thrust from Kashmir in the direction of the Indus furrow. It is significant that when referring to events of the twelfth century, Kalhaṇa in a reference to the area uses the term *Bhuṭṭarāṣṭra*, indicating in the use of the word *rāṣṭra* that he was referring to a state and not to an ethnic group.

> kālakṣepekṣamatvam cedbhuṭṭarāṣṭrādhvanādhunā
> tvāntarnidadhmo bālinastrillakasyopaveśane (VIII.2887)

2. The two basic editions of the Ladakh Chronicles are, A.H. Francke, *Antiquities of Indian Tibet*, part II, New Delhi (reprint), 1972, which contains the text and a translation with additional notes by Karl Marx (the latter being a Moravian missionary and not to be confused with his better-known name-sake!); and L. Petech, *A Study of the Chronicles of Ladakh*, Calcutta, 1939.
3. Francke, op. cit., pp. 63ff.
4. *Ṛg Veda*, X.90.
5. *Mahābhārata*, XII.181.v.15ff.
6. *Dīpavaṃsa*, III.

7. S. Beal, *Romantic History of Buddha*, London, 1907, pp. 18ff.
8. *Sumaṅgalavilāsinī*, I.248.
9. G.P. Malalasekera, *Dictionary of Pali Proper Names*, II, London, 1960, p. 970.
10. Francke, op. cit., p. 76.
11. Petech, op. cit., p. 17.
12. *Dīpavaṃsa*, IIIff; *Mahāvaṃsa*, Vff.
13. Francke, op. cit., ch. IV, pp. 76ff.
14. *Majjhima Nikāya*, II.110, 127.
15. Petech, op. cit., p. 19.
16. O. Rank, *The Myth of the Birth of the Hero*, New York, 1959.
17. H. Hoffman, *The Religion of Tibet*, London, 1961, pp. 13–28. D.L. Snellgrove, *The Nine Ways of Bon*, London, 1967; L. Petech, op. cit., p. 62.
18. The Bon religion seems initially to have been a form of shamanism with the ibex and the reversed *svāstika* as frequent symbols. It had a wide distribution in the mountainous areas along the northern borders of the Indian subcontinent. There are curious parallels to practices elsewhere, such as the association of the number 108 with things magical, and dietary prohibitions, such as the ban of the eating of garlic and onions. In the best shamanistic tradition, hallucinatory visions were not excluded and some of this tradition might well be reflected in the Tibetan Book of the Dead, the *Bardo Thodol*.
19. Francke, op. cit., p. 90.
20. J.Ph. Vogel, *Antiquities of the Chamba State*, Calcutta, 1911.
21. O.H.K. Spate, *India and Pakistan*, London, 1964, p. 393.
22. M.A. Stein, *Ancient Khotan*, Oxford, 1907, vols I and II.
23. A. Rona Tas, 'Social Terms in the List of Grants of the Tibetan Tun-huang Chronicle', *Acta Orientalia*, Hung. V.1955, pp. 249–70, Facs. 3.
24. M.A. Stein, *Kalhaṇa's Rājataraṅginī*, II, pp. 408, 490.
25. III.445, *sūkṣmabṛhad bhuṭṭadeśau*.
26. D.L. Snellgrove, *The Cultural History of Ladakh*, Warminster, 1977, pp. 16ff.
27. Ibid., p. 83.
28. Francke, op. cit., pp. 151–79.
29. Ibid., VII, p. 105.
30. Francke, 'Notes on a Language Map of Western Tibet', *JASB*, LXXIII, p. 362.
31. Francke, *Antiquities of Indian Tibet*, II, p. 106.
32. Ibid., pp. 108ff.
33. Ibid., pp. 108–9.

34. Ibid., VII, pp. 115–16.
35. S.J. Tambiah, *World Conqueror and World Renouncer*, Cambridge, 1976.

# II

# Social and Cultural Transactions

Arguing for social change in the past draws on evidence of change in essential perceptions through a series of historical processes. The nature of some of this change is seen in the form of social transactions, a process which has been continuous and is not specific to early India. The explanation of social disjunctures relates to various dichotomies and categories such as donors and donees, the oral and the written, dissenters, barbarians, but the dichotomies are not always evident and may be disguised or may be different from the obvious.

A further discussion of this theme is included in *Cultural Transaction and Early India: Tradition and Patronage*, published in *History and Beyond*, OUP, 2000.


1. The Oral and the Written in Early India (1988)
2. Dissent and Protest in the Early Indian Tradition (1979)
3. The Image of the Barbarian in Early India (1971)

# 10

# The Oral and the Written in Early India*

I would like in this lecture to consider some of the ways of the transmission of knowledge in early Indian society relating to elements of the oral and written traditions. Let me state at the outset that the areas of knowledge are perforce selective and further, that my interest is largely in raising a few questions relevant to our understanding of this transmission in what are now referred to as 'traditional forms'. I might add that we need to investigate this process from the past not out of intellectual curiosity alone, for it has a bearing on how we transmit knowledge today, as well as on the broader question of the degree to which we use familiar forms or else introduce new ones. In speaking of tradition we should perhaps keep in mind that although it appears to be a process of deliberate continuity, in fact it is a continual selection of desired elements, often arising out of contemporary concerns and defined by existing social relations. To the extent that education organises and carries tradition it includes a selection of such desired knowledge.

Discussions on the transmission of knowledge generally concentrate on the products of high culture expressed in forms involving literacy. It would seem though that if looked at analytically, parallel forms were used. Knowledge is now being defined as the ways in which people organise their everyday experience of the social world. Thus the sociology of knowledge would include not only ideologies, philosophies and belief systems, but also everyday concerns. The organisation of experience as abstract understanding is one among such forms and knowledge as the practice of a technique is another. The latter should especially not be disregarded as it is an essential

* Basu Memorial Lecture, CIE, Delhi University, 1988.

dimension of knowledge. This is particularly so when literacy is not universal and techniques have to be practiced, improved upon and handed down as part of an oral tradition. The point at which such an oral handling of knowledge is converted to a literate form has its own historical importance.

It is sometimes assumed that with the coming of literacy there is a shutting out of the oral tradition and that if both co-exist there is an antagonism built into the relationship. Yet methods of transmission referring to the oral and the literate involve three situations: firstly, the oral pre-literate tradition; secondly, the interface between the oral and the literate where the relevant question is why the oral tradition was continued when literacy was current and was not necessarily antagonistic to the other but complementary;[1] and thirdly the use of literacy. In a society such as ours where the second of these, the oral-literate interface, continues to be current, the relevance of analysing these relationships can hardly be ignored. I would like therefore to look a little more closely at this link and its articulation in the early Indian past.

In an oral culture there are clearly perceptible mnemonic patterns intertwining serious thought with systems of memorising.[2] These may be expressed as formulaic phrases, as has been so effectively demonstrated in the analysis of epics by Parry and Lord,[3] or even as pictorial representation as has been suggested by Frances Yates in her study of the theatre of memory.[4] It has also been argued that oral thought is situational rather than abstract,[5] but this argument should perhaps not be stretched too far.

Within the oral tradition in India there was a demarcation between a carefully preserved oral tradition and a relatively free oral tradition, a difference which was maintained even when the composition took a literate form. The oral tradition therefore cannot be taken as a single uniform system. It is necessary to classify the varieties within it since their presuppositions, functions and form differed. This is clearly illustrated in the two dominant oral traditions of the first millennium BC which were converted to a written form in subsequent centuries, the Vedic texts on the one hand and the epics on the other.

Vedic hymns were composed and handed down orally over many centuries. Even after writing became current in the third century BC these compositions continued to be recorded orally for some time as they are even to this day in some places. The composers of these primarily ritual texts were priests. The meticulous oral preservation was backed by the theory that the sound was of fundamental importance and therefore a mispronunciation could render the purpose of the ritual ineffective. It has therefore been maintained that the preservation was entirely oral and so it may have been. Yet priestly training in literate societies assumes a knowledge of literacy and the *brāhmaṇas* were no exception. The mnemonic devices used for memorising the hymns, such as the *padapāṭha*, could have been entirely oral but could have included a reference to literacy, for example, in the breaking down of the verse into syllabic segments and the memorisation of these in various patterns. The working out of these mnemonic patterns would probably have been easier if there was a written text as the basis. There is an on-going debate on whether the oral transmission of Vedic compositions was based on reference to a written text.[6] The important point however is that, as ritual texts, the attempt was to freeze the composition in memory. Large scale memorisation is known to literate societies. It is therefore of greater interest to recognise that inspite of literacy there was a premium on oral recording and that the two continued alongside each other. The continuance of the oral in this case was doubtless largely to insist on the correctness of the sound when recited, which is the stated aim. The unstated aim was to limit the availability of the texts, for oral memorisation was closed to those whom the priests wished to exclude. *Śūdras* are therefore prohibited from even accidentally hearing the Vedic hymns.[7] Here the control is less on the fact of the transmission being oral and more on the power of what is being transmitted and the control of those concerned with the transmission. Correct speech was considered the hallmark of the *brāhmaṇa* and power lay in the sound of the recitation.[8] The association of literacy with power belongs to a later time.

In contrast to this was the freer oral recording of the epics, the *Mahābhārata* and the *Rāmāyaṇa*. These were originally composed by bards, the *sūtas*, before they were taken over by *brāhmaṇa* authors, and the Bhṛgu *brāhmaṇas* in particular, who probably recorded them in a written form. The bards wandered from place to place reciting their compositions at the large sacrificial rituals conducted by the *rājās* or at their gatherings.[9] The *Mahābhārata* was recited at the snake sacrifice of Janamejaya. The *Rāmāyaṇa* is said to have been recited by Kuśa and Lava again on a public occasion. (Incidentally, the compound phrase *kuśīlava* came to have the technical meaning of bards).[10] Fragments were composed for special patrons and these were then strung together and tidied up into the longer epics. The bards lived in the present and the requirement of the moment led them to adding on or sloughing off, what they thought was relevant or irrelevant either to themselves or their patron. When the bardic authors were dispensed with and the *brāhmaṇas* took over, changes of other kinds were introduced: the hero became an incarnation of the deity in the *Rāmāyaṇa*, or long passages on the duties of the king declaimed by Nārada; or the elaborate discourse on creation, ethics and liberation from rebirth by Bhiṣma in the *mokṣa-dharma* section, were interpolated into the *Mahābhārata* so that the text became more appropriate to the needs of the monarchies of the time and the new religious sects. The change to a literary form, extended the social function of the composition.

Interpolations into the texts, particularly when they were transcribed gave authority to the new idea, and although it suggests the centrality of literacy, it also points to legitimation for the new idea being sought from what was regarded originally as the more prestigious oral tradition. The major variant versions of the *Rāmāyaṇa* also reflect the incorporation of particular needs.[11] Thus the Buddhist *Dasaratha Jātaka* retells the story of the Ayodhyā-kāṇḍa, with the major difference that Rāma and Sītā are brother and sister, in conformity with the Buddhist origin myths of the Śākyas and other high-ranking clans. In the Jaina Rāmāyaṇa of Vimalasūri, the *Paumacariyam*, the picture of exile changes, for the vast forest in the area of exile often recedes and is replaced by kingdoms, the urban and the courtly culture being more familiar to the adherents of Jainism.

The interface between the oral and the literate is further demonstrated in the institution of learning known as the *guru-śiṣya paramparā*. Here again it is popularly associated with a retreat in the forest where primitive living conditions are combined with sophisticated learning in Sanskrit. It is as well to remember that the same institution prevailed even for applied knowledge, except that there were some differences when the knowledge consisted of formal learning and when it was intended as the learning of a technique towards a profession. Boys of the upper castes who were sent to *gurus* for formal education went through a process of decontextualisation when they left home. But the training was to fit them for functioning in the upper caste professions. In the forest hermitage the training was largely oral although it included familiarity with the major texts as well as practical training. When the *Rāmāyaṇa* speaks of those who are learned it refers to them as *bahuśruta*[12] that is, well-versed in oral learning. The theory of the four stages of life, the *āśramas*, in which the period of studentship was followed by that of the householder, brought the functional aspect back into the life of the trainee. In the case of boys learning a craft, the degree of decontextualisation was far less if at all, since this training was either in the house or in the guild, which was not an unfamiliar environment.

The *guru-śiṣya paramparā* was in origin an oral training. It would be interesting to visualise the change when it turns to literacy. In the dialogue between the teacher and the pupil there would be the intervention of the text which may have become the third participant in a trilogue. Does the text take the form of an alternative authority as an embodiment of knowledge? Does the crystallisation of knowledge into a text make it so sacrosanct that it cannot be challenged? Or is the interpretation of the text by the teacher to the pupil the continuation of a dialogue, in which the text plays a minor role? An analysis of the pedagogy of this tradition, a tradition which still obtains in many centres of Sanskrit learning would be very revealing in explaining the transmission of knowledge. The persistence of oral memorising of certain branches of knowledge or the dichotomy of what is taught orally and what through literacy and why, would be of significance.

The change from oral to literate is reflected even in indirect ways such as in what constituted authoritative predecessors. In the *Upaniṣads* the legitimacy of the teacher is established by reciting the *vaṃśa* or succession of teachers. This provides depth in time as well as status and does not have to be factual as is clear from the anomalies in the succession lists. But the emphasis is heavily on the teacher. With the establishment of literacy there is a shift to include together with the list of teachers various categories of texts, as is indicated in the opening section of Kautilya's *Arthaśāstra*.

The location of learning also gradually shifts. The *āśramas* of the *guru* became more elaborate settlements often on the edges of towns and villages in touch with everyday society. The towns were also centres of literacy where many of the patrons of formal learning resided. By the late first millennium AD, when learned *brāhmaṇas* were recipients of handsome grants of land from royalty, the centres of learning were often concentrated in such settlements characterised by wealth and prestige. The *agrahāras* of these times were different in nature and function from the forest settlements of earlier periods. Here there was a different kind of institutionalising of knowledge with much that concerned abstract thought, sophistry and language as the articulation of the subtle mind. This was not accidental in a situation where brahmanical learning in many parts of the country was at a premium even for the seemingly mundane affairs of legitimising political power, controlling economic resources and maintaining the social hierarchy. The growth of large and wealthy temples of the same period introduced the institutions where the educating of priests became a more systematic process. By this time the oral and the literate tradition were complementary at one level, but at another, the literate tradition was regarded as the more prestigious.

Literacy it is maintained is the product of cities. It arises from a need for record keeping in the institutions of urban life. The records related to property both individual items and generalised property. Writing was also used for identifying persons at far remove, whether by designation and status or by a corporate group: the identity being necessary in the process of exchange.

The earliest Indian script is of course the as yet undeciphered Harappa script, generally described as pictographic. The pictographic nature could suggest that it catered to more than a single language group and this would not be unusual in a situation where a script is used primarily in commercial enterprise. Its frequency on seals identifying goods, on jars used for storage and transport with some indication of measure and identity, and infrequently on amulets, points to a largely commercial use.

There is so far no acceptable evidence to provide a link between the Harappan script and the earliest Indian alphabetic-phonetic script, Brāhmī. The Aśokan inscriptions dating to the third century BC provide the earliest evidence of the use of the Brāhmī script. Allowing for at least a half century of literacy prior to the inscriptions, it can be pushed back to the fourth century BC. The evolution of the Brāhmī script is best seen in the context of the Iranian Aramaic and the South Semitic script with which it has affinities and its emergence seems tied to trade. The adoption of a common script strengthens ethnic and linguistic ties and an alphabetic script pegs down the phonetics of a language. Just after the script was introduced we also have the extraordinary text of Pāṇini, systematising the grammar of currently spoken Sanskrit. Pāṇini refers to a script[13] and presumably the reference is not merely to Aramaic but to a script used for Sanskrit as well. If a written form is a requirement for a detailed grammar then one can assume that Sanskrit had such a form by the early fourth century, the date generally assumed for Pāṇini. But both the pithiness of the *sūtra* form in which the text is composed and the emphasis on phonetics would suggest a continuing concern with memorising and sound. It is generally believed that his reason for composing the grammar was to systematise the current language of the north-west (which was incidentally not the language of the Vedic texts) and thus perhaps prevent further intrusions of non-Aryan linguistic forms which are apparent in Vedic Sanskrit. The existence of etymological texts was not sufficient to explain the changes inevitable in a language of some common usage. Later grammarians tended to treat Pāṇini's grammar as prescriptive and a sufficiently detailed analysis of grammatical change is rare. Literacy in this case acted almost as a fetter. Nevertheless the existence of a grammar made the language more available to non-Aryan speakers whilst at the same time encouraging the use of the language for more complex thought. It might be interesting to speculate on the direction which Sanskrit could have taken had there been an absence of Pāṇini's grammar.

The use of a script coincided with the increase of trade in northern India and references to promissory notes, letters of credit, records of items produced and exchanged, not to mention usury, are suggestive of the close association of trade and literacy. If literacy began in the culture of cities and commerce, then it would seem that early brahmanical attitudes to literacy were equivocal. The early *dharma-sūtras* are hostile to urban living and cities are visualised as centres of vice where the ritual prescriptions are not observed. This may also have had to do with cities supporting what have been called the 'heterodox sects'. The good *snātaka* therefore is discouraged from going to the *nagara*. Was this also because learning in the *āśramas* was still largely oral and the student, inspite of his long years of training, was not properly equipped to deal with literate activity?

Mauryan administration provides one dimension of the use of

literacy, namely, an aspect of a complex administration and possibly more authoritarian than in situations where a script is absent. Written orders are always less negotiable than oral commands. Rights and obligations also tend to be more clearly stated. It is however unlikely that written orders were issued at all levels of Mauryan administration. Probably these were restricted to the upper levels and more so to orders going from the capital to the provincial centres.

Kauṭilya in the *Arthaśāstra* is clear that the upper levels of the administration should be from the upper castes, preferably *brāhmaṇas* and *kṣatriyas*. Yet the backbone of the administration, the scribes, accountants and record-keepers, had an ambiguous social status. From the first millennium AD, this work began to be manned both by the literate *brāhmaṇas* and by the *kāyasthas* who became a powerful caste in the period after the seventh century AD when scribal functions and the recording of grants and administrative rights increased enormously. There always remained a clear social distinction between the *brāhmaṇa* and the *kāyastha*, even though both were concerned with the function of literacy.[14] Access to literacy and the professional use of literacy was therefore not sufficient to establish social status even at a time when literacy was at a premium. Nevertheless, literacy was associated with levels of power and if the *kāyastha* as scribe was not as respected as the *brāhmaṇa*, his distance from the lower castes was based on both the power of administrative functions and literacy.

One of the most extensive areas for the use of literacy was the writing of inscriptions. These were statements of the present intended for the future as well. The inscription was to be a permanent record, to last, it is said, 'as long as the moon and the sun endure'. Many inscriptions were proclamatory in character such as the votive inscriptions at the sites of many Buddhist *stūpas*, informing us of who were the donors. These were frequently artisans, traders and small-scale landowners. Other inscriptions on copper-plates, or on the walls of temples, were legal documents as they were charters of grants of land. Such inscriptions are very precisely dated in contrast to the rather vague chronology of other texts. The identity of the donor and the donee is established, the location and details of the land donated, the right and obligations of the donee, the witnesses and the sanction of the authority making the donation. Some of the contents refer to technical terms, not only for the measurement of land, but also for precise rights and obligations, on the meaning of which there is still a debate. Such technical terms occur in these charters from various parts of the subcontinent and appear to have been uniformly understood. In some cases the inscriptions are bilingual, where the eulogy on the ruler and the grant is in Sanskrit but the technical data is in the regional language. Literacy by now had not only spread to a wider reach of people, but it had also become an important adjunct to establishing the alienation of property.

Such inscriptions, as documents of contract, seem to draw entirely on a situation of literacy. Yet they also contain a reference to the oral tradition, one that is more fully included in the *vaṃśāvalīs* or dynastic chronicles of the same period. These reflect changing attitudes to the past. The *vaṃśāvalī* reflects a process of state formation with attendant social change.[15] But the past is no longer restricted to legends incorporating change or orally remembered patterns of descent groups. The oral material is restructured into a form which can be used for emerging dynasties, large and small, to assist the process of state formation. New dynasties take pride in establishing their social origins, linking themselves with the established royal lines. The written form, whether as a statement of origins in the inscription or the *vaṃśāvalī*, authored by learned *brāhmaṇas*, makes this link firmer than it was in the oral tradition of the bards. Yet the structure of the oral tradition is retained so that the legitimacy of the earlier and familiar form can also be drawn upon. This is then followed by the inclusion of a record of recent events. Since the written form is relatively less difficult to tamper with, these records come to be treated as historical. The composition of the *vaṃśāvalī* is repeated in the various new kingdoms and becomes a genre on its own.

The transition from oral to literate is also reflected in the teaching of various religious sects. Many started as popular movements using the local language for discourse and worship and the teaching is preserved in that language. Some such as the Śākta sects, often associated with popular cults, composed texts in Sanskrit which may have been an expression of upward mobility. Yet curiously in the Indian religious tradition, even after the recording of religious narrative and discourse in a literate form, the centrality of "the book" to belief and worship is limited. The major departure came late, in Sikhism, and that too probably under the influence of Islam.

Even Brahmanism, viewed later as the religion of the Vedic texts is rooted in *śruti*, that which is heard, and *smrti*, that which is memorised. Some of the Bhakti sects focused on the *Bhagvad-Gītā*, but it was their interpretation of the text rather than the text itself which was of significance. The centrality of the *Gītā* as possibly "the book" of Hinduism dates to recent times. This would at one level have to do with theology and doctrine. But one may also consider the nature of Indian society where the separate identities of social groups were at a premium in various ways, particularly in the link of caste with sect.

Even those Indian religions which used literacy more extensively from an early period, seem to have avoided the centrality of "the book", characteristic of the Judeo-Christian and Islamic religions. The Buddhist canon in particular came to be written as Buddhism gained greater patronage from a variety of social groups. It has been argued that this had to do with the close interaction between Buddhism and its widespread patronage from the trading community with its functional use of literacy. But it also has to do with the nature of Buddhist institutions and organisation. When schisms occurred among the monks on the veracity of the interpretation of the doctrine, a series of councils were called and the interpretation clarified. Since this led to splinter sects in the *saṅgha*, some versions at least of the debated doctrine were recorded in a written form to ensure permanency. These incorporated the justification for particular interpretations as well as the organisation of the *saṅgha*. Inevitably, therefore, they recorded the history of the teaching as viewed by that sect. Such texts, were carefully preserved, copied and handed down through generations of monks. Literacy therefore not only became an important qualification of the monk but was also required for the legitimation of the sect. It became doubly necessary for purposes of record keeping and accountancy, when monastic institutions linked to these sects became property holders through grants of land from royalty and wealthy patrons. Monasteries such as Nalanda were maintained on the revenue of anywhere between a hundred and two hundred villages.[16] The handling of such an income required considerable financial and administrative expertise and it is not surprising that some monks began to specialise in this kind of work. Max Weber has said that the 'rationality' of writing which is an economic rationality, is located in the heart of religious institutions concerned with the non-rational. But it needs to be remembered that the function of literacy in such institutions was not limited to the non-rational.

The period when literacy was beginning to develop from the fifth–fourth century onwards, witnessed a major phase of intellectual speculation. This is not to suggest that the speculation would not have existed without literacy, since the Upaniṣadic thought which preceded it, appears to have been prior to literacy. But the form in which the discussion was recorded suggests the movement from speculation to philosophy. Earlier discussion had emanated from forest retreats, the courts of *rājās* as well as from another institution very pertinent to the times, the *kutūhala-śālās*.[17] These were groves and parks on the edge of the towns where people gathered for amusement as well as to hear the discourses of a variety of teachers, many of them peripatetic. There is a striking similarity to the olive grove of Academus outside Athens, which was frequented by Plato and a variety of Greek sophists. It was in the *kutūhala-śālās* that the views of various teachers were discussed, elaborated upon and refined.

The record of earlier discussions tended to be situational, where narrative often introduced an idea, the narrative acting as a mnemonic device. The gradual change to a literary form encouraged the process of more abstract thought where the construction of ideas and meaning were more carefully analysed. This was similar to the experience of other cultures in the initial stages of literacy.[18] Philosophical interests concerned with theories of knowledge often focussed on rationality and logic, *tarka* and *nyāya*, which although expressed in literary form nevertheless reflect a continued clinging to the earlier oral form.

One of the most interesting aspects of this speculation was the particular patterns of debate and methods of analysis which grew out of both the oral and literary tradition of these times. It has been argued that the evolution of these required literary learning and to that extent moved away from the oral tradition. But this may need reconsideration. The simplest of these forms, the one directly concerned with the philosopher's search for truth, also referred to as *vāda*, was described in later texts as wholesome discussion.[19] In this it was assumed that initially there were two views. That of the proponent was stated and was then countered by that of the opponent. The aim was to find the correct position through the use of reasoning, logic and the accredited means of knowledge. This third position would then approximate to the truth. As a technique of discussion and analysis it permits of arguments from the two opposing positions to be brought into the third position. It concedes that there may be an overlap from either the first or the second position. Was the system of what has sometimes been referred to as a form of dialectic in *vāda,* based on the structure of oral dialogue? Literacy would presume a familiarity with the first statement read prior to its refutation. Oral dialogue requires that the first statement be reiterated even in its refutation. Oral discussion also assumed the possibility of a variety of world views without necessarily declaring one among them as exclusive.

I have so far spoken of texts which reflect a continuity from the oral tradition even if these were converted to literate forms and therefore ceased to be oral. I would like to turn briefly to the other aspect of the link between oral and literate, and look at the kind of knowledge which is initially entirely oral and is regarded with some contempt by at least a section of those who are literate, but which at an opportune moment is converted to literate form. This was evident in areas of applied knowledge, frequently dismissed as technology, and particularly apparent in the two examples which I would like to refer to, the profession of building and the practice of medicine.

Apprenticeship to special professions developed as a parallel stream in the transmission of knowledge. Orally handed down knowledge can perhaps be seen as a form of proto-science. It involved touching, manipulating, observing and systematising. The practitioner began as an apprentice and learnt by practice and application and of course by reflecting on the technique and the problem. The carpenter working on an ox-cart commanded a different degree of knowledge from the carpenter working on a wooden building, where vaulted ceilings were common and which demanded a calculation of stress, durability and structure. A change of medium such as the shift from wood to brick or to stone, required a further reflection, as also the structural changes introduced into a building.

Some craftsmen worked on their own and others belonged to a guild and guilds were common by the Christian era. The technology of the profession was taught through apprenticeship. Recruitment often drew on the children of the craftsmen in the guild, sometimes leading to the guild becoming a *jāti*. The identity of the guild was such that its own social practice, or *śreṇī-dharma*, was a recognised feature.[20] Artisans employed by the state were paid salaries which were barely adequate, being considerably lower than those of soldiers and clerks. This may also have encouraged the formation of guilds. But the prosperity of artisans and guilds underwent a considerable improvement at the turn of the Christian era, when with expanded trade, the guild became a major institution of urban life and artisans and guilds were among the patrons of architecture.

The construction of the earliest buildings are generally associated with Buddhist monuments. Guilds of craftsmen are among those responsible for these structures and on occasion, the guild is also a donor, contributing to the construction of the monument.[21] The builders do not appear to have had manuals. There are however references to Buddhist monks supervising these buildings and the monks would have been literate. In the construction of the early temples use was made of the existing expertise and of artisans who maintained their knowledge through practice.

With the gradual and increasing complexity in the techniques of construction and the structures to be built, two changes become apparent: one is the reference to greater specialisation and the other to texts relating to the profession of building. Specific terms for builders and artisans became more common. Thus there are references to the *śilpin* and the *rūpakāra* and also to the *sūtradhāra* and the *sthapati*.[22] The term *sūtradhāra* had many levels of meaning. Its literal meaning, 'the holder of the thread' can refer to the one who directs an enterprise. It can also be interpreted as the one who knows the *sūtras*, in this case the *śilpaśāstras*, the texts on architecture and the arts. These texts written in Sanskrit, generally date to the early second millennium AD. Some *sūtradhāras* are also described as authors of texts. This would imply formal education as a qualification. They are required to be well-versed in the theoretical aspects of construction. A separation came to be established between the artisan and the one who planned and supervised the building. The *sūtradhāras* are mentioned by name, either individually, such as Sri Yugadhāra at Ajanta,[23] or by family such as the Kokasa family in the Kalacuri inscriptions.[24] The reference to three generations of the same family would suggest that at the level of the *sūtradhāra* and the *sthapati* at least, the guild system was of lesser importance by now and that individuals belonging to established families were employed for the overseeing of major buildings. Were the authors of the texts *brāhmaṇas* who had decided to move into writing books on subjects earlier thought to refer to low status professions, or, did these authors come from artisanal backgrounds of wealth and standing who had had access to formal education and wished to write texts on their professional work? That the writing of a *śilpaśāstra* was regarded as high status activity is evident, else the versatile *rājā* Bhoj would not have associated his name with such a text. That textual knowledge of architecture was required is also evident from the proliferation of temple building at the period when the *śilpaśāstras* appear and the fact that temples were now more complex structures where at least the planning required some knowledge of mathematics and engineering. The separation between the theorist and the practitioner raises yet another question. Where did innovation lie? in the practical work of the skilled artisan or in the theory? Did innovation by-pass the *śāstras* or did the *śāstras* stultify knowledge? Or did the text on professional knowledge act as the means of making this knowledge accessible to many more than in its oral form? Such changes relate both to the technology of the craft as well as the status of the artisan. The *dharmaśāstras* and the *Arthaśāstra* place all artisans in a low status, generally that of a *śūdra* and therefore little detail is available on the transmission of knowledge among such professions. Some of this will have to be reconstructed from the technology. We are told that a *brāhmaṇa* living by a craft is to be treated as a *śūdra* presumably to discourage *brāhmaṇas* from taking up these occupations, and this inspite of the Buddhist *Jātaka* stories referring to *brāhmaṇa* carpenters and weavers. It is not for nothing that Sarasvatī remained a first order deity whereas the pre-eminence of Viśvakarma was gradually lowered. From the perspective of the status of the professions, two interesting developments occur in the first millennium AD. One was the gradual distinction introduced between the artisan and the supervisor and the other was the mention even of craftsmen by name. This first occurs in inscriptions from Mathura referring to Kunika and his pupils.[25] The introduction of a name may suggest a claim for a particular *guru-śiṣya paramparā* or even a guild and where the object produced was of superior quality it would act as an advertisement. As long as the guild was powerful there would be a tendency for knowledge to remain among its members. Were there was a gradual breaking up of guilds the artisan once again was left to his devices. This possibly led to the emergence of the *sthapati* and the *sūtradhāra* as managers and controllers of artisanal activity and this management was further articulated in the authorship of texts relating to the knowledge of building techniques. That the text related to the building and embellishment of temples doubtless gave the activity greater prestige than for example, the scribal work of the *kāyastha*.

This kind of change is also reflected in the practice of medicine. In the social hierarchy endorsed by brahmanism, physicians are rated as inferior for they not only worked with their hands but also handled the pollution of the sick. There might even have been the contempt of the literati for those who claim to cure, to remove disease and to save the dying from death. But the physician in Buddhist texts is often a respected and wealthy man who has been carefully trained in his profession. This training is at least on one occasion associated with the town of Taxila in the north-west,[26] interestingly the same area where, in a later period, was composed the famous medical treatise of Caraka. Both this and the later text of Suśruta, written in Sanskrit, epitomise the current knowledge of medicine and give substantial space to empirical technique and practice. The major contribution of these texts is in the field of surgery. Applied, oral knowledge therefore has a premium in the written form. Putting this knowledge into literate form may have been motivated by the need to control it. It has been suggested that the Buddhist monk as a kind of lay doctor had considerable expertise and some of the theoretical work may have drawn from this expertise.[27] It could also be that in this particular region there was a currency of Greek medicine and the Greeks had well-defined views on medicine with which the Indian views agreed at times and sometimes differed. It could therefore have been an effort to systematise a particular view and give it currency. The classification and systemising of this knowledge in a literary form occurred when control over that knowledge was of advantage to those who had access to a literary form. Resort to a literary form also occurs when knowledge becomes so complex that it cannot be handled by oral techniques. Thus both the social constraints of literacy as well as the nature of knowledge in any field, influence the transition from oral to literate.

My attempt in this lecture is more than merely to state the dichotomy between applied knowledge deriving from an oral tradition and theoretical knowledge based on literacy. It is rather to point to the integration of the oral and the written. I have tried to suggest that in many areas of Indian experience from the early past the literate did not shut out the oral. In fact it often drew from oral sources. Further, that the deliberate insistence on the continuation of the oral tradition, as in the case of Vedic compositions, had a purpose and function quite distinct from the fact that such compositions were also recorded in written from. Ritual language can have a permanence almost akin to literacy. In such a situation the oral tradition had a social and intellectual role other than that of being a system of transmitting knowledge. An understanding of these distinctive roles even within the oral tradition needs underlining.

This may help us to understand a little better the processes involved in educating ourselves, whether it be presuppositions or concerns or techniques and their links with the past. My own experience in pedagogy has been an extremely limited one, that of writing text-books on history for middle schools. I do know however that where these books have been backed by a discussion of the text and by a demonstration of the varieties of evidence used by historians, the impact of the text book has been far greater than where it is treated, incorrectly, as a received text. Where there is an attempt to see the world around one as historically evolved there even history ceases to be viewed as a series of static states into which fresh items are periodically introduced. It takes on a more vibrant character.

Education one hopes should not be a trauma. So, if certain usages drawing from the oral tradition are current then perhaps it would be worthwhile to see if they can be utilised in the process of learning. This requires us to understand that the oral should not be equated with backwardness but should be seen as complementary and in some areas of learning, as essential. Perhaps we need to emphasise the importance of the oral process at particular stages of learning and the difference between what is better learnt orally and what through writing. In a sense the use of the audio-visual mechanism of communication is a partial return to the oral, with however the important difference that there is no dialogue. The usual separation between the literate and the oral where the literate is regarded as the hegemonic learning and the oral as the popular, diluted form, does not necessarily hold. The oral can be as hegemonic when it is legitimising a status or a function as I have tried to show with reference to the *vaṃśāvalī* tradition. There is however the danger that the oral can also descend into a catechism if it is not judiciously juxtaposed with the literate.

In a system where the oral and the literate are seen as complementary, there would perhaps not be the tendency to treat the written invariably as undeniable fact. In a culture where the oral remains strong, if literacy is imposed without integrating it to an oral tradition, the imposition may remain alien. What is required perhaps is a shift from viewing the oral and literate as part of a bicameral mind to seeing it as an integrated cultural expression.

## Notes and References

1. I have found the studies of J. Goody useful in analysing this subject, especially *The Domestication of the Savage Mind*, Cambridge, 1977; *The Logic of Writing and the Organisation of Society*, Cambridge, 1986; and *The Interface between the Written and the Oral*, Cambridge, 1987; as also his edited volume, *Literacy in Traditional Societies*, Cambridge, 1968. A critique of some of these views with reference to early India may be seen in F. Staal, 'The Independence of Rationality from Literacy', *European Journal of Sociology*, 1989, 30, 301–10 and also the discussion in *Rituals and Mantras*, New York, 1990.
2. W.J. Ong, *Orality and Literacy*, London, 1982.
3. M. Parry, *The Making of Homeric Verse*, Oxford, 1971; A.B. Lord, *The Singer of Tales*, Cambridge Mass., 1960.
4. Frances Yates, *The Art of Memory*, Chicago, 1966.
5. A.R. Luria, *Cognitive Development: Its Cultural and Social Foundations*, Cambridge Mass., 1976.
6. P. Kiparsky, 'Oral Poetry: some linguistic and typological considerations', in B.A. Stolz and R.S. Shannon (eds), *Oral Literature and the Formula*, Ann Arbor, 1976. L. Renou, *The Destiny of the Veda in India* (trans.), Delhi, 1965. R.T. Oliver, *Communication and Culture in Ancient India and China*, Syracuse, 1971. J.F. Staal, *Nambudari Vedic Recitation*, The Hague, 1961.
7. Manu 3.156.
8. *Śatapatha Brāhmaṇa* 3.2.1.24; Pāṇini 1.1.1.2.
9. Romila Thapar, *From Lineage to State*, Delhi, 1984.
10. *Arthaśāstra*, 1.12.9; 2.1.34; 2.27.7.
11. Romila Thapar, *Exile and the Kingdom: some thoughts on the Rāmāyaṇa*, Bangalore, 1978.
12. *Rāmāyaṇa* 1.6.14; 1.13.16.
13. Pāṇini 3.2.21.

14. Romila Thapar, 'Social Mobility in Ancient India', in *Ancient Indian Social History*, Delhi, 1978, pp. 129ff.
15. Romila Thapar, 'Society and Historical Consciousness: The Itihāsa-purāna tradition', in S. Bhattacharya and R. Thapar (eds), *Situating Indian History*, Delhi, 1986, pp. 353ff. *See* chapter 7 in this volume.
16. S. Beal, *Life of Hsuan Tsang*, Delhi, 1973 (reprint), p. 212; I Tsing in J. Takakusu, *Records of the Buddhist Religion*, Delhi, 1966, p. 65.
17. Romila Thapar, *From Lineage to State*, p. 153.
18. G.E.R. Lloyd, *Polarity and Analogy: two types of argumentation in early Greek Thought*, Cambridge, 1966. *Magic, Reason and Experience*, Cambridge, 1979; B. Matilal, *Perception*, Oxford, 1986; K.N. Jayatilleke, *Early Buddhist Theory of Knowledge*, London, 1963.
19. S.N. Das Gupta, *A History of Indian Philosophy*, Delhi, 1975, vol. I, pp. 294ff.
20. Manu 8.41; Nārada 10.2–7.
21. As for example, the ivory-carvers guild at Sanchi. J. Marshall, *Monuments of Sanchi*, Cambridge, 1939, vol. I.
22. *Mānasāra* II.11–12; 17–20.
23. M. Dhavalikar, 'Sri Yugandhara — A Master Artist of Ajanta', *Artibus Asiae*, 1969, 31, 4, pp. 301–8.
24. R.N. Misra, *Ancient Artists and Art Activity*, Shimla, 1975, pp. 68–70.
25. Luders List No. 150, *Epigraphia Indica*, 10, 1909–10, p. 25.
26. *Mahāvagga* 8.1.
27. A.L. Basham, *The Wonder That Was India*, London, 1954, pp. 498ff.

# 11

# Dissent and Protest in the Early Indian Tradition*

For many decades now it has been maintained that Indian civilization has shown an absence of dissent and protest. This has become so axiomatic on the Indian past that those who have occasionally questioned it have been labelled as anti-Indian. Such a view stems from a nationalistic over-simplification of Indian society as a vision of harmonious social relations in a land of plenty. Superimposed on this were the preconceptions of idealist philosophy that dissent required materialistic underpinnings, and philosophical themes of materialism in Indian thought have generally received short shrift from contemporary commentators. It is only in recent years that some attempts are being made to suggest that neither materialist philosophy nor dissent were wholly marginal to Indian society.[1] It still remains fashionable in some circles to deny the opposition between forms of orthodoxy and heterodoxy in the ideological traditions of the past, arguing that Indian religions were not based on dogma.[2] Yet the history of groups identified as having a community of religious beliefs, rituals and behaviour, among Buddhists, Jainas, Vaiṣṇavas, Śaivas and Tantrics, is strewn with sectarian dogmatism which found expression not only in inter-religious but also in inter-sectarian rivalries, sometimes of a violent kind.

It has also been argued that there are no words equivalent in meaning to dissent and protest in the early Indian tradition; however there is no shortage of terms connoting what is implicit in the concept. Words for dissent and non-conformity such as *vibheda, vimati, asammati, viparìttā, ananukūla*, are described by modern commentators as negative constructions and therefore alien to the

* *Studies in History*, 1.2.177–96.

language. The same can be said for words such as *dissent* and *non-conformity* which are also derived from negative constructions. What is of historical significance is not so much the syntactical structure of these words but the particular period and the historical context in which they find expression. In any case these terms are new in their specific use in other civilisations as well. The secularisation of the adaptation of terms such as dissent and protest is a relatively recent phenomenon, but this does not preclude the occurrence of actions of dissent and protest in earlier times. Dissenting actions whether symbolic or overt, may not be consciously described as dissent, yet the dissent may be implicit in the nature of the action.

Dissent can be limited to questioning established ideologies or belief-systems, becoming the core of a new ideology. The expression of dissent can thus be relatively confined until such time as it mobilises action. Protest, therefore, involves more than dissent; it requires ideology, mobilisation and clearly defined action. The action has to be legitimate for the groups using it and is often regarded as illegitimate by those whose views are being questioned. The recognition of a protesting group is therefore a gradual process in history and occurs only when such a group has gathered social force and has become, as it were, politicalised. This often coincided with the acquisition of property and the establishment of relations with political authority; which, incidentally, frequently became a point of departure in that it brought about opposition within its ranks to the new situation. Conflicting views over the acceptance of property and involvement in society could be a cause for friction. Among the well-endowed sects, there were rivalries over succession to office which entailed the management of property. Whatever the reasons, breakaway groups justified the schism by appeal to doctrine.

It would seem self-evident that any society which is complex and registers change, as has been the case with Indian society, must also register ideas of dissent, protest and non-conformity; otherwise the very fact of change would be nullified. Protest and dissent are not always expressed through violent action and there is normally a large spectrum ranging from a rather passive non-conformity to violence. Equally essential is the mechanism for containing dissent and protest, which tries to avoid the disruption of society.

During the first millennium BC when the early Indian tradition was being formulated, evidence of overt oppositions is limited. But the expression of dissent through the questioning or even flouting of social norms is conspicuous. Sometimes it took the form of opinion systematised in the views of religious and philosophical sects; but it was also expressed through symbol and action. This often occurred in the form of opting out of society as it were, through various types of renunciation. But not all of these can be seen as protest. Some were attempts at seeking individual salvation and had therefore an other-worldly orientation. Only those forms can be regarded as expression of dissent which satisfy certain criteria. Opposition to existing social norms had to be consciously maintained even if it was expressed at a symbolic level; the new forms could become alternate sources of power; and the attempt was not so much to disrupt the existing system as to set up a parallel or alternate system. These criteria are a necessary pre-condition. Not all renouncers were or are protesters, for there are many in the past and even today, who, rather than utilising renunciation as a technique of dissent, exploited it for mundane ends.

One of the paradoxes of the Indian tradition is that the renouncer, in spite of migrating out of society, remains a symbol of authority within society. An explanation of this paradox may emerge from an analysis of the social role of the renouncer. Apart from those who through austerity and severe discipline, both mental and physical, sought extrasensory power, there were many others who renounced their social obligations, joined an order and far from propagating a life-negating principle, sought to establish an alternate or parallel society. They combined in themselves the charisma of the renouncer as well as the concerns of social and occasionally political dissent. They were neither revolutionaries nor radical reformers; they can perhaps best be described, as I have argued elsewhere, as the makers of a counter-culture.[3] Their migration is symbolic since they re-enter the social arena in a changed guise. Such forms of renunciation were open to all. It was generally assumed however that members of the higher castes and upper levels of society would use this as their form of dissent. For those lower down, migration was rarely symbolic for it carried the bitterness of necessity. Some who joined the renunciatory orders were attempting to overcome the inequities of caste status by joining non-caste groups. Others, such as the peasants, were sometimes forced to migrate to express their discontent. I would like to examine more closely the evidence for the two ends of the spectrum: the open renunciatory groups and their relations with society, taking the case of the Buddhist *saṅgha*, and at the other end the specific limited group of the peasantry who, when they migrated, were articulating a particular discontent.

The first millennium BC is characterised by changes of at least three kinds which had a bearing on the realm of ideas. These changes were the evolving of a recognised social stratification, the emergence of towns and urban centres and, lastly, adjustments to the increasing authority of the state. It is with reference to these that I would like to consider the question of dissent.

Social stratification assumes divergent forms in different systems. In the monarchies frequent reference is made to castes functioning in the framework of the fourfold *varṇa* system. Within the hierarchy of this system the elevation of the *brāhmaṇas* brought, as its counter-poise, the new category later referred to as untouchables. The hierarchy of the fourfold system was based on the distribution of power, authority and access to economic wealth (whether in heads of cattle or in land) and kinship networks. The fact of untouchability highlights an additional feature — the distinction being justified on the basis of ritual purity and pollution which converted the *caṇḍālas* and other such categories into excluded groups. The oligarchies or chiefships do not register a four-caste stratification to begin with, but here the emphasis separated the landowning *kṣatriyas* of the *rājakula* from other clan members[4] and these in turn from the slaves and labourers, *dāsa-bhṛtaka*, who worked the land.[5]

With the extension of agriculture, the growth of centres of craft production leading to networks of trade and the increasing political authority of the state, urban centres became a recognisable feature of the cultural topography. Most of them combined the function of capitals of the newly emergent states, the earlier *janapadas*, as well as centres of trade. Although the rural-urban nexus remained strong, the urban ethos was different. Urban centres provide evidence of a stratification in which the *seṭṭhi*, the merchant and trader was regarded as important. Towns were looked upon with some suspicion by the *brāhmaṇas* who declared that the good *snātaka* should avoid living in such places.[6] Evidently social taboos were liable to be eroded in the flux of urban life. The bulk of urban society consisted of those who laboured either as artisans or as wage-earners in commodity production, constituents of the amorphous category described as *śūdras* in the texts.[7]

This was also the period which saw the establishment of the state as embodying the necessary authority for the maintenance of law and order and for the protection of the people. In theory, the state, whether it took the form of a monarchy or an oligarchy, is an alternative to an otherwise nightmarish chaos. The *Mahābhārata* compares the kingless state to the lawless condition of the desiccated tank in which the big fish devour the little fish.[8] The *Rāmāyaṇa* paints a distressing picture of the afflictions which beset a land without a king.[9] Drought is almost by implication associated with bad government or no government. Buddhist texts are equally graphic in depicting civil strife in the absence of a state.[10] The state was seen as an enforced necessity rather than a naturally evolved institution and the element of contract is implicit to a lesser or greater degree in most of these explanations of the origin of the state, irrespective of whether the state came about through divine intervention or the choice of the people. Whatever its origins, the state as representing political authority was new to the earlier lineage identity now being gradually weakened. In the monarchies the concentration of political authority was strengthened by religious sanction through a range of rituals such as those linked to status and power as in the *rājasūya*, *vājapeya* and *aśvamedha* in particular.

These trends incorporating social stratification, the power of the state and the economic thrust of the extension of agrarian systems and trade, became the substratum of historical activity in subsequent centuries as well. States expanded outwards from geographically nuclear regions, tribes and occupational groups were converted into castes, waste land was cleared for cultivation, new routes were forged and markets for trade, and this process provided a continuing historical momentum in the subcontinent up until recent centuries. This is in part reflected in the constant emphasis on the fear of chaos in the texts of later centuries. The emphasis did not arise from a paranoia regarding disorder but rather reflects the repeated formation of states in new areas which had on each occasion to be justified. State formation is a recognisable feature of historical change in the Indian subcontinent during the millennia AD. This necessitated highlighting the difference between the conditions within a state and non-state societies. Contrasting of chaos with order was part of the required emphasis on the sanction of the state, its legal authority often equivalent to coercion, which was summed up in the word *daṇḍa*. The literal meaning of *daṇḍa*, 'the rod' was not limited in connotation to physical force alone but was symbolic of all authoritarian sanctions which the state could use and which were essential to the functioning of the state. Significantly the legal codes included a comment on all the minutiae of social and political life because the *dharmaśāstras* were again the primary texts of state legitimation. The stress on consensus in matters relating to law was in part due to the continuing authority of customary law and in part the absence of a uniform code. The sanction of the state therefore was endorsed by the appeal to a multiplicity of laws arising out of the separation of *varṇas*, *śreṇīs*, *jātis*, *janas*, which were sought to be ordered within the *varṇa* framework. The emphasis was on the disparate but coherent functioning of these various identities rather than a universal law to cover all identities.

The earliest expression of at least minimal dissent comes to us from the *Upaniṣads* in the earlier part of the first millennium BC. The search for a way to ensure liberation from rebirth and a better comprehension of man in the universe led to a questioning of the efficacy of existing forms such as the sacrificial ritual and a discussion of alternative techniques such as *yoga*, *tapas*, *dhyāna*. These have generally been interpreted as procedures for attaining *mokṣa* or liberation. Yet embedded in this debate is a call away from social mores; a non-conformity which is expressed through renunciation and migration to the forest. That acquisition of knowledge required a distance from society is in itself a rejection of conformity. Those that concerned themselves with such ideas were a restricted group and their autonomy and isolation was respected.

The more apparent social tensions and differences were doubtless resolved more easily in a society which was characterised by a smaller hierarchy of stratification, with fewer economic disparities in a pastoral-cum-agrarian system and with the authority of the over-arching state still to come. The margin for non-conformity in such societies is limited. Migration to the forest was at one level symbolic but at the practical level the absence of a vast social surplus made it easier to live off nature than off the village. This perhaps partially explains why renunciation is by and large alien to the *Ṛg Veda* and becomes important only in the more complex society of the later Vedic period. In the earlier society there is one category of persons who had the licence at least to indirectly comment on conformity; these were the poet-bards. Their expression of dissent took the very subtle form of gentle mockery to which even the gods were not immune. But their power lay in their eulogy of those heroes who were munificent gift-givers and in this the heroic chiefs made every effort to appease them.[11] This relationship is seen even more clearly in the earliest Tamil literature, the Śangam.[12] But the increasing importance of renunciation weakened the freedom of the bards and the renouncer gradually became the key figure associated with dissent.

A concession to these ideas is evident in the theory of the four *āśramas*, the four stages of life, where the dichotomy of observing social norms as symbolised in the householder/*gṛhasthin* is in opposition to the opting out of society, that of the renouncer/*saṃnyāsin*. That the theory of the four *āśramas* functioned to some extent as a safety valve would seem evident from the placing of *saṃnyāsa* in old age, after the completion of social obligations. The symbols of the renouncer such as matted hair, nakedness or the wearing of an animal skin, the breaking of food taboos, celibacy and the discarding of all possessions ran counter to social obligations. The dissenter was thus symbolically placed outside society but was not regarded as an outcast since the act of opting out was believed to imbue him with power. The source of power was the claim to extraordinary bodily control, magical and extrasensory knowledge, heightened energy and philosophical perception. All these went toward creating a charisma around those who practised and claimed these powers and gave them an authority which was difficult to explain in mundane terms. In time, the dissent became muted or even in many cases disappeared, but the authority remained, giving strength to the parallel system. That the actions and views of some renouncers were looked upon as a critique of society is evident from one of the late *Upaniṣads*, the *Maitrāyaṇīya Upaniṣad*.[13] It carries a list of the impediments to knowledge which include mendicants, the pupils of the *śūdras*, those of knotted hair (*cāṭa-jaṭa*), those who wear the red robe and those who falsely argue against the Vedas. Among the renouncers there were dissensions ranging over degrees of conformity. The mere fact of being a renouncer did however imbue the person with authority in the eyes of the others.

The same authority gave direction to the protest at the individual level in later times in the practice of *dharnā*. But behind the act of dissent by the individual lay the sanction of society and tradition. *Dharnā* carries the connotation of a technique of confrontation in which an attempt is made to pressure a person through sheer will, persistence and an appeal to ethics rather than violence. The participants and the desired aim become interlocked in a process of attrition in which the intangible force of the cause can be converted into an ethical issue, a conversion which becomes more successful if it takes on the character of ascetic austerity and practice. The act of *dharnā* carries the suggestion both of confrontation as well as the mobilisation of an ethical appeal. *Dharnā* was used to considerable effect in the second millennium AD by the *cārans*, the bards of Rajasthan. In conformity with bardic tradition they were inviolate as were the *sūtas* of earlier times.[14] A *dharnā* by a *cāran* therefore carried the risk for the king against whom the *dharnā* was directed, of his being held responsible for the *cāran's* death.[15]

Not all the early renouncers chose to remain in isolation. Some among them returned to the margins of society and became the familiar mendicant wanderers, the *parivrājakas*. However, the larger and settled communities of monks emerged in times of a more developed economy, when such communities could be supported by rich villages and urban centres through alms-giving. The earliest monasteries were generally located in the vicinity of towns since the monks lived on alms and donations;[16] some were located along trade routes where travellers and merchants could use them as staging points and donations were again welcome.[17] In still later times when endowments of land constituted the more substantial part of donations, large monastic institutions became common in rural areas initiating a 'monastic landlordism.'[18] It is significant that such institutions were absent in areas of primitive agriculture.

The towns produced their own kind of dissenters, not all of whom became renouncers or monks.[19] Some took to philosophical acrobatics in arguments ranging from the eternalism of the soul and the world, to the notion of a first cause being irrelevant to understanding the origin of the world; the annihilationists supported the destruction of the living being and the hedonists held that the doctrine of happiness brought complete salvation.

Others were recognised by their sharp critique of society and its norms, which on occasion takes on the form of a world view of either sceptical or material philosophy. This was evident in the schools included in the category of Cārvāka and Lokāyata.[20]

These sects drew their audience from the townspeople, not to mention debating opponents among sects similar to theirs. Some opposed not only the observance of social custom and law but the entire structure of explanation. It is this which earned them the disapprobation of those less daring in their views and less willing to give free rein to complete rationalism and unflinching materialist explanations. The teaching of such groups is largely reconstructed from quotations which are referred to as part of the refutation of incompatible views or false doctrines in the literature of the more established sects.[21] That their ideas did attract a following is evident from the vehemence with which they are attacked in this literature. In this the Indian experience was not dissimilar to that of some other early cultures. Despite the sarcasm, the theme of rationality comes through clearly.

To argue that all religious rituals and the existing rules of morality were pointless would attract the wrath of those who accepted the tangibility of these rituals and morals, even though they might have been opposed to the particular forms. Monastic orders were as governed by rites, rituals and laws as was secular society, although they took a different form and catered to different needs. The questioning of the worth of alms and offerings laid the monks as open to attack as any member of society since the monks were dependent on such forms of support. Hence the scathing criticism of such views.

There was also the fear that extreme ideas would disturb the existing order. The logic of rational explanation would have required far more than merely opting out into a parallel system: it would have required changing the very structure of society. Few of these groups established any distinct organisation and the force of their dissent tended to be dissipated in individual enterprise.

Another unchanging feature of the attack on rationalism and materialism was to describe such views as advocating a contingent morality and extreme hedonism. The familiar phrases ring out from the earliest texts with the warning that materialists do not distinguish between actions conducive to merit and those not so, since they are devoid of moral values and argue that all action has material causes and there is no reckoning after death. In spite of these attacks materialist ideas survived. The need for contradicting such views even in the form of ridicule, from time to time, was not merely a literary exercise but reflected the continuity of what were looked upon as unpalatable views. Mahendravarman's play, *Mattavilāsa-prahasana* carried clear attempts at ridiculing heretics. But the tradition of anti-religious philosophical texts survived as is evident from the eighth century work of Jayārasi, the *Tattvopaplavasimha*.[22]

Among the other sects and groups were the Ājīvikas, the Jainas and the Buddhists. These were groups of renouncers for whom the monastery was to become an organisational base. The degree of dissent is determined both by the distance from society and by the symbols of identification. Thus to take the case of the Buddhists, the monastery was a parallel society in that it was totally different from conventional society but was not cut off, being dependent on the lay followers in villages and towns. The natural dichotomy remained that of the householder and the renouncer, expressed much more strongly in the symbols of differentiation, but the interlocking of the two also became essential.[23] This reciprocity was expressed at the symbolic level in the exchange of *dāna* for *punya* — gift-giving for merit.[24] Buddhist teaching lays stress on the distinctive roles of the monk/*bhikkhu* and the householder/*gaha-pati*, and the separate methods of each in the search for liberation from rebirth; but at the more mundane level of the rise of the *saṅgha*, the *bhikkhu* had to be supported by the *gahapati*. The more tangible lay support for the Buddhists came from elite groups such as royal families, landowning clans, merchants and members of the richer guilds.[25]

The negation of social obligations is clear from the encouragement given to enter the monastery as early as possible, some sects arguing that the householder's stage/*gṛhastha-āśrama* should be altogether avoided. The breaking of caste rules lay in recruitment to the monasteries indiscriminately from all castes. The monks were required to live together and eat together thus contradicting the laws of commensality. The requirement that alms must consist of cooked food was again, for the erstwhile upper caste monk, a departure from food taboos where uncooked food was the more acceptable.[26] The taking on of a new name unconnected with caste, reiterated the attempt to negate a caste identity. The new sectarian identity was recognised outwardly by the uniformity of robes and appurtenances carried by the monks. The removal of hair was again in marked contrast to the householder and to the matted hair of the ascetic. These were symbols of an expression of dissent.

The ultimate source of power for such groups came through entry into the parallel society of the monastery. Some of the charisma of renunciation was conceded to the monks but their greater strength lay in the institutional basis of the monastery. Here an emphasis was placed on egalitarianism and the negation of hierarchy although the monasteries were by no means the ideal egalitarian sanctuaries. Ownership of property vested in the monastery and as long as this precluded the individual monk from such ownership, it encouraged a degree of equality. But even the administration of property required an administrative hierarchy which began to erode the egalitarian basis of the institution.[27] The monastery gradually acquired the dimensions of an agency which cut across caste and lineage ties. That this did not lead to confrontation and conflict with social and political authority was perhaps because of the diversion of dissent into a parallel system. But part of the answer also lies in the relationship between the monastery and political authority. Initially, Buddhist monasteries did not open their doors to officers of the state.[28] The Jaina *saṅgha* prohibited friendship between monks and the king and his officers.[29] Doubtless this was to ensure autonomy from political interference as well as to maintain the distance required for independent functioning. However the acceptance of royal patronage became the thin end of the wedge. When the endowments took the form of substantial economic largesse, the monastery was forced to accept a close relationship with political authority.

It is perhaps in this process that the term *pāṣaṇḍa* becomes crucial to the question of dissent and undergoes a change of meaning. The term occurs frequently in the Aśokan edicts where it carries the connotation of a sect with no apparent associations whether orthodox or heterodox (*savve pāsamdā*, *nānā pāsamdesu*, etc.).[30] In one case there is an indirect indication of not merely differences of opinion, which would be expected among sects, but even hostility since there is a plea for tolerance in permitting diverse opinions. Aśoka also refers to *bāmhanā va samanā va aññe pāsamdā* . . .[31] (*brāhmaṇas* and *śramanas* and other sects). The phrase, '*brāhmaṇas* and *śramanas*,' as used in the edicts has generally been taken as a comprehensive reference to a variety of sects. However, another source underlines the implicit hostility of the two by providing the simile of the mongoose and the snake.[32] Megasthenes also divides the caste of philosophers, as he calls them, into two, the Brachmanes and the Sarmanes.[33] Within the Buddhist tradition the fact of sectarian belief and action and false doctrine is very powerful. Those who give false replies — *setakāni vatthāni datvā* — at the Council of Pātaliputra are expelled.[34] In the famous Schism Edict of Aśoka, dissident monks (*saṅghe bhettave*) and those who disrupt the *saṅgha* (*saṅgham bhakkhati*) are made to wear white clothes and expelled.[35] The sectarian developments within Buddhism and Jainism are evident from the history of the two religions, with dissenting sects breaking away and seeking to legitimise the break by arguing that it was sanctioned through a religious council. Thus many of the early major sects trace their origin to a schism at a council, the Theravāda to the Council at Pāṭaliputra, the Śvetambara to the Council at Magadha, and so on.

The antagonism implicit between sects at the intellectual and cult level was doubtless aggravated by the fact of some becoming recipients of royal patronage. This may well have intensified the antagonism into sharp hostility where the brahmanical groups would see non-brahmanical sects as heretics and argue that by not conforming to social mores they were disrupting society and in any case they were identified as the preachers of false doctrines. Dissent declines when protesters become inheritors. Those excluded from the inheritance have to point to the inheritors either as having betrayed the original dissent or as being the perpetuators of false doctrines aimed at the destruction of society. The Puranic literature makes it evident that the term *pāṣaṇḍa* had changed its meaning and in later periods it is used for heretics of all kinds. A late Purāṇa, the *Bṛhaddharma*, illustrates this when it states that the *Pāṣaṇḍas* and *Yavanas* will destroy the *varṇāśramadharma*, create their own gods, write their *śāstras* in Prākrit and teach their own religious ideas.[36] Ultimately in still later usage the word *pākhaṇḍa* came to refer to a fraud as well. It is curious that in the Greek versions of the Aśokan edicts, 'sect' is translated as DIATRIBE, literally a discourse.[37] In its later form this word was also associated with hostility when it meant a discourse directed against a person or an idea.

The developments traced so far, involving the change in a religious group from a small number of adherents to an expansive movement incorporating sectarian growth, property relations and connections with political authority, were not restricted to the Buddhists alone. The same changes were noticeable with some variation at many times and in many areas among sects belonging to the other major religions of India, such as the Jainas, Vaiṣṇavas, Śaivas, Tantrics and still later, Islam. The growth of the sectarian *āśrama*, and *maṭha* or the Sufi *khānqah*, many of which received grants of maintenance and land, became a normal pattern in the historical evolution of such religious sects. The changes which they underwent were, therefore, in many ways similar to those of the Buddhist monasteries of earlier times. Not all of these, however, were dissenting groups. Some attempted to consolidate what they took to be orthodoxy on the wane; but they all included the technique of building an institutional base and this inevitably required them to come to terms with political authority. Theoretically renunciation included the renouncing of material possessions, and therefore there was a necessity for those renouncers who wished to build an institutional base to have to rely on patronage; the most effective form of patronage came from royalty.

The advantage to political authority of such a relationship, quite apart from the theory that patronage bestowed merit on the patron, was that such religious institutions could become centres of loyalty and support in far flung areas. Here they acted as avenues of social acculturation and political legitimation. However, political authority had also to follow a policy of appeasement, since from the late first millennium AD onwards religious establishments also played the role of centres of secular activities[38] and this carried the danger of their becoming the nuclei of popular opposition. Not only were many religious establishments, in effect, landed intermediaries with many fingers in many economic and political pies, but in some areas they almost doubled for the political authority. The relationship between the Jagannath temple at Puri and its political counterparts in the medieval period is an excellent case in point.[39] The geographical distribution of such establishments could also encourage sectarian loyalties cutting across political loyalties. Many religious establishments served functions parallel to the state in their handling of what might be called public welfare. That the Sultans of Delhi were apprehensive of the power of Sufi *khānqahs* was part of the same syndrome. It is also not surprising that the Mughal emperors, including Aurangzeb, made donations to *brāhmaṇas* and Hindu religious establishments in certain parts of the empire.[40]

Religious sects were often the symbolic or potential carriers of dissent. The mobilisation of dissent into protest did on occasion take overt forms, and where it concerned specific issues did not require the legitimation of a belief-system. The right to revolt is central to this question.

The concentration of power in the monarchical states provided the possibility of the counter-weight of protest against such power. Recorded incidents of such protest are not too many, but the evidence does suggest that the notion was familiar. The texts tend to be contradictory on this point. Some negate the right to revolt altogether.[41] Others concede it, provided it is motivated by the desire to terminate the wickedness of the king. Wickedness is defined as acting against the laws of *dharma* and the right is therefore morally justified.[42] The *Mahābhārata* justifies the right to revolt if the king is oppressive, and even permits assassination;[43] but its incidence is such as to suggest that this action would be restricted to *brāhmaṇas*, as in the case of the wicked king Veṇa,[44] suggesting that they alone had the moral right to kill a king. Buddhist *Jātaka* literature has many more references to protest by subjects against oppressive kings (*adhamena*), some of whom are banished.[45] Where a king is put to death for a moral offence, the actual killing is at the intervention of the god Śakra.[46] The right to revolt in Buddhist texts is extended to all subjects of the kingdom, but the context indicates that frequently it was limited to the citizens of the capital.[47] The terms used are *mahājana* — a large crowd which could include the people of the countryside and the town (*janapada negama*), *nagaravāsino* (the inhabitants of the city), *raṭṭhavāsino* (the subjects). Generally the *mahājana* gathers in the capital where the opposition to the king is expressed.

In contrast to the *Jātaka* literature, non-Buddhist sources do not concede the right to revolt to all subjects. Kautilya's perspective reflects the culmination of the state as an agency of control with monarchy as the norm. The citizens cannot revolt, but the king must ensure their welfare. Interestingly, the only revolts which are discussed are palace coups and revolts led by officers, tribal chiefs and vassals, and these inevitably have to be suppressed.[48] There are however two specific references from the Buddhist sources to the citizens of Taxila rebelling against the oppression of the officials of the Mauryan administration.[49] The source of power in this category of protests lay in the fear that the revolt of the subjects would destroy the sanction of the king to rule and would disrupt administration. There was little fear of citizens in revolt taking over the reins of government, and in the Mauryan case it is stated that the objection was to the officials and not to the king.

Peasants are said to have occasionally resorted to migrations to express protest. This would not only disrupt the existing economy because of the desertion of villages and fields but would permit of new settlements if conditions were optimum beyond the boundaries of the kingdom: thus providing an alternative to the existing system. Kings are advised not to oppress their subjects by over-taxing them lest the latter migrate and thereby erode the prosperity of the kingdom.[50] Nor was the migration to new lands a mere gesture. In a period when the population was relatively small and land easily available, the migrations of peasants could well create revenue problems in the smaller kingdoms. It is not surprising that Kauṭilya, jealously guarding the state's control over uncultivated land, prohibits the clearing and settling of forest land without the necessary permission.[51] The Mauryan state also took the precaution of keeping its peasants unarmed.[52]

The threat of peasant migration, consequent to a refusal to pay taxes, occurs in later periods as well. With the establishment of a hierarchy of intermediary landowners, the link between the peasant and the land became more inflexible. In such circumstances, peasant migration, although it did occur,[53] would obviously have been more difficult than in situations where landed intermediaries were absent. Not surprisingly, peasant revolts become an equally effective form of protest, as is evident from at least the sixteenth century. It has been argued that some peasant discontent was spearheaded by the smaller landowners.[54] The migration of the peasantry would have undermined the income of such landowners, while those who espoused the cause of a heavily taxed peasantry would attract discontented peasants. Where the revolt was more than just a local refusal to comply with tax demands, the mobilisation often developed religious overtones. The more organised peasant revolts over larger areas identified themselves by caste — such as the Jāt revolts — or by religious sects, such as the Satnāmis. The latter categories carried obvious influences from the widespread *bhakti* movements in northern India such as those of Kabir, Dādu and Nānak, which were to inspire a variety of social action far beyond the vision of the original teachers. The *bhakti* movement was not a pan-Indian movement, but included various sectarian movements with a flexible range of opposition to Vedic exclusiveness and brahmanical orthodoxy. What gives these movements a pan-Indian character is the broad similarity of their origins, their ideological articulation and the social use to which they were put.

Little is said in the early sources about dissidence or protest among the socially excluded groups, the *dāsa-bhṛtaka* and the *caṇḍālas*. Although some slaves are described as treated ill and others well,[55] there are, in contrast to classical Roman times, no records of large-scale slave revolts. Perhaps the reason was the absence of the employment of slaves on a substantial scale for production. The excluded groups tend to remain excluded in the ideologies of all dissenters, although some are permitted to escape into the parallel society of the monasteries. Even the rationalists, while they do not condemn the excluded groups, do not claim them as part of their audience or encourage opposition to authority among these groups.

Socially excluded groups sometimes express their protest through millenarian movements. Such movements which are common in the Judeo-Christian and Islamic religions particularly in periods of major change, are barely evident within the indigenous religious traditions of India. Two examples of seemingly millenarian ideas are to be found in the coming of Kalkin as the final *avatāra* of Viṣṇu[56] and the Buddha Maitreya, the saviour Buddha yet to come.[57] The social inspiration for such movements is however very different on the Indian scene. The Kalkin *avatāra* is the hope not so much of the down-trodden but of those who believe that Viṣṇu will come to the aid of the righteous to put down the upstart *śūdras* who have been daring to controvert the law of *varṇa*. Kalkin, therefore, is the hope of those who have lost their privileges and feel thwarted by the trauma of the Kaliyuga. The Buddha Maitreya receives a marginal mention in the early Buddhist texts but develops into the saviour figure of the northern Buddhism of Mahāyāna at a time when there is competition from other religions and when Buddhism itself has split into the two major schools of Hīnayāna and Mahāyāna. The coming of the saviour is essentially to re-establish the power and the authority of the Buddhist *sangha*, rather than to help any oppressed group. Perhaps it is not entirely coincidental that the two movements which do in fact come very close to being Chiliastic movements if not millenarian movements in the strictest sense, those of the Satnāmis and the Munda rising under Birsa, were both movements in the proximity of Islamic or Christian ideas. It could be argued that this was less due to the Islamic and Christian religions *per se* and more to the theoretical social egalitarianism claimed by both these religions, and which, at the level of religious sanction to ideas of social equality, was more explicit in these religions than in other earlier indigenous movements in India.

There has been a tendency to view the role of religion and religious sects in the Indian tradition from a limited perspective. Discussion has centred around philosophical intricacies, the 'eel-wriggling' of doctrinal laws and the universe of icons and symbols. Too little attention has been given to the men and women who were the creators, the audience and the continuators of religious cults, sects and organisations. If doctrines and tenets changed it was because human requirements changed, as also the forms of dominant interests.

Religious sects are not static; they change with events. By definition a sect draws upon certain social groups which give it a social sanction and it reflects the changing fortunes of such groups or the incorporation of new groups. Orthodoxy and heterodoxy are never static conditions. Thus Theravāda Buddhism which questioned brahmanical orthodoxy came to be regarded as the orthodox tradition within Buddhism and against which there arose a number of schismatic sects. Other religious traditions in India showed similar distinctions. To the extent that a religious sect articulates social dissent, it reflects the aspirations of the social strata from which it draws its support. Buddhist sects were anxious to win the support of elite groups after a certain point in the history of Buddhism. The degree of dissent was muted by protest taking the form of ethical opposition, and the parallel society became at times almost parasitical. The dissent was further subdued when in the course of time Buddhist institutions began to appropriate the functions of the elite; a pattern of change which was to be repeated frequently in the strategies of many other religious sects. The building of *maṭhas* and *āśramas*, the acquisition of property and status, the manoeuvring of relationships with political authority, and the appropriation of the role of landowners and commercial *entrepreneurs*, converted the religious sect into a recognisable social group often ending up as a caste. Such sects therefore could not have spearheaded a radical change; they remained at best conciliating alternatives.

It is of considerable interest that in the Indian tradition the effective questioning of or breaking away from caste obligations required the form of a religious sect. This may be explained as being substantially due to the logic of caste society in which the non-observance of caste norms would otherwise have resulted in ostracism and low status. Given this basic premise anything short of an overthrowing of the structure of caste society made it necessary to legitimise the breaking of rules by seeking the identity of a religious sect and if possible also by building an institutional base to counteract the charge of losing status. The former was by far the easier way out and was resorted to, times without number. The building of an institutional base required the patronage of the wealthy. This weakened the thrust of dissent and diverted it into the formation of a parallel society rather than strengthening confrontation with the existing system. The parallel society not only legitimised the breaking of caste rules but also provided a mechanism for caste orthodoxy to accommodate this dissent, since the parallel system impinged upon but did not disrupt society.

The weakness of the parallel society is self-evident. It does not provide an alternative system for the entire range of social groups but only for segments; it presupposes the continuation of the existing society which permits a small percentage to opt out. The dissenting group remains enclosed and minimal. This is further emphasised by the fact that the parallel society because of the rules of celibacy perpetuates itself by recruiting members from the existing society. In a caste society each dissident group would tend to be confined to its own social milieu. Even those sects which began by cutting across caste ties would, with the weakening of their dissent and in the process of building institutional bases, tend to work within the confines of caste contours. The dissent has to be viewed not merely in terms of attitudes toward those in power but also toward the socially excluded groups. In the competition for status, even among the parallel systems, the socially excluded groups were only marginally involved and were often left to their own resources for mobilising dissent.

Such considerations were not so primary in situations where the dissenters were low caste groups who by dissenting were not lowering their status any further. If together with this the aim of dissent was not to raise social status or demand the equalisation of status, but to protest against oppression, then the protest could be direct. Hence the possibility of peasant protest not requiring the legitimacy of religious form. In cases where a caste identity or a religious identity was used, as for example in the Satnāmi movement, it was more in the nature of extending the movement rather than acquiring legitimacy or, it could be said, to reflect a movement where differing statuses of peasants were involved. Yet even in these protests, whether migrations or revolts, the aim of the movement was to remove the immediate injustice. To argue that such movements were not protest movements because they did not envisage changing the system is perhaps to demand more from them than what they themselves envisaged at the time. The demand for changing the system as an essential quality of protest movements is not only relatively recent but requires certain historical preconditions which did not prevail in earlier times in India.

That religious sects do often become castes would substantiate the idea that certain forms of religious expression were indicative of dissent. In such cases social discontent was more than merely a marginal factor. Celibate monks cannot constitute a caste; although sometimes, in the transition to becoming a caste, celibacy is dropped, at least among those who are involved in the right to succession in property and office. The lay followers, however, can take on a caste status commensurate with the origins and the ranking of the sect. In such cases the social requirements of building a caste would take primacy over other considerations. Or alternately recruitment to the sect would become restricted to certain castes, and the identity of the sect and those castes would become close where the sect would articulate the ideology of the caste. The effectiveness of dissent lay in bringing about some degree of change in as much as the lay followers were able to either assert their status even if it was low in the *varṇa* hierarchy or on occasion acquire a higher social status. Ivory carvers and corn-dealers, ascribed to *śūdra* status, used Buddhism in their demand for respect from others. But Buddhist lay followers did not aspire to becoming a separate caste and with the decline of the *saṅgha*, they tended to be absorbed without identification, each into his own caste. The Liṅgāyats on the other hand were ultimately successful in asserting a higher status through a judicious use of the religious sect, social dissent and economic potential. In the more remote past the attempt seems to have been to try and bypass the *varṇa* hierarchy. From the late first millennium AD there are more examples of attempts to assert a higher status.

The accommodating of those who opt out is not merely a matter of putting a premium on toleration. To a greater extent it is an indication of a mechanism for containing dissent. Hence the acceptance of *sadhus, fakirs, yogis* and many other 'opters out.' Nor can this be explained in a facile fashion by speaking of the great religiosity of Indian society, for religious expression in itself has to be analysed from a multiple perspective since it performs many functions other than the solely religious.

This interplay of vertical and horizontal structures in Indian society lends it a different complexion and provides it with a logic which has to be understood in relation to its own social context.

Dissent and protest are present in all complex societies and are frequently motivated by attempts at rationalising discontent. The forms which dissent and protest take would naturally vary from one society to another but would be logical within the terms of the structure of each society. Early Indian society was not characterised by absence of striving for material progress accompanied by a decline in ideological evolution. As was the case with many other societies of the ancient world, it neither visualised an ideology directed towards a total change in society nor could it organise such a change. Dissent was resorted to more frequently than protest. The extension of protest to encompass dissent with the aim of restructuring society had to await more recent times.

## Notes and References

1. Such as the studies of D.P. Chattopadhyaya, as for example, *Lokāyata*, New Delhi, 1968.
2. Pratap Chandra, 'Study of Ideological Discord in Ancient India', in S.C. Malik (ed.), *Dissent, Protest and Reform in Indian Civilisation*, Simla, 1977, pp. 85ff.
3. Romila Thapar, 'Renunciation: the making of a counter-culture?', in *Ancient Indian Social History: Some Interpretations*, New Delhi, 1978, pp. 63ff. *See* chapter 40 in this volume.
4. *Pāṇini*, VI.2.34.
5. *Kunāla Jātaka*, London, 1970, pp. 1ff.
6. *Gautama Dharmasūtra*, XVI.43, *Āpastamba Dharmasūtra*, 1.3.9.4, *Vasiṣṭha Dharmasūtra*, XIII.1.

7. Manu VIII.410, 418; IX.334–5.
8. Śānti Parvan, 67.7–24.
9. II.61.7ff.
10. *Dīgha Nikāya*, III.92–3ff.
11. As in the *dānastuti* hymns of the *Ṛg Veda*, V.27; V.30.12–14; VI.63.9; VI.47; VIII.1.33; VIII.5.37; VIII.6.47.
12. K. Kailasapathy, *Tamil Heroic Poetry*, Oxford, 1968.
13. *Maitrāyaṇīya Upaniṣad*, VII.8, S. Radhakrishnan, *The Principal Upanisads*, London, 1953.
14. *Taittirīya Saṃhitā* IV.5.2, *namo sūtāya ahantyāya*.
15. N. Zeigler, 'Marwari Historical Chronicles', *Indian Economic and Social History Review*, April–June 1976, XIII, no. 2, pp. 219ff.
16. Such as those in the vicinity of Rājagṛiha, Śrāvastī, and Kauśāmbi. N. Dutt, *Early Monastic Buddhism*, Calcutta, 1973, pp. 147ff, 167ff.
17. D.D. Kosambi, *The Culture and Civilisation of Ancient India*, New York, 1965, pp. 183ff.
18. The concept of 'monastic landlordism' was used by Max Weber to indicate the change in the function of the monastery: *The Religion of India*, New York, 1958. Of the monasteries endowed with land, Nālandā was among the richest with as many as a hundred or even two hundred villages. S. Beal, *Life of Hsuan Tsang*, London, 1911, p. 212; J. Takakusu (tr.), *Records of the Buddhist Religion*, Delhi, 1966 (reprint), p. 65.
19. Diodorus XVII, 86; Curtius VIII.12.
20. K.N. Jayatilleke, *Early Buddhist Theory of Knowledge*, London, 1963. D.P. Chattopadhyaya, op. cit.
21. *Dīgha Nikāya* I.27, I.55.
22. A.L. Basham, *The Wonder that was India*, London, 1954, p. 297.
23. J.C. Heestermann, 'Vrātya and Sacrifice', *Indo-Iranian Journal*, 1962, VI, pp. 1–37. L. Dumont, 'World Renunciation in Indian Religions', *Contributions to Indian Sociology*, 1960, IV, pp. 33–62.
24. Romila Thapar, '*Dāna* and *Dakṣiṇā* as forms of Exchange', op. cit., pp. 105ff.
25. *Mahāvagga* I.15.1–20; I.9.1–4. *Cullavagga* VI.4.9.
26. Manu IV.205–25, 247–50; V.5–56; XI.153–62.
27. *Vinaya* II.160–75.
28. *Mahāvagga* I.61.1ff.
29. S.B. Deo, *The History of Jaina Monachism*, Poona, 1965, pp. 60ff, 239ff.
30. Rock Edict VII, X, XIII, Pillar Edict VI.
31. Rock Edict XIII.
32. *Vyākarana Mahābhāsyam*, II.4.9. Patañjali explains that they are permanently opposed. I.476: *Yeśām ca virodhaḥ śāśvatikaḥ*.

33. Strabo, XV.I.59.
34. *Mahāvaṃsa*, V.270.
35. Schism Edict. J. Bloch, *Les Inscriptions d'Asoka*, Paris, 1950, pp. 152–4.
36. *Bṛhaddharma Purāṇa* III.19.
37. D. Schlumberger and E. Benveniste, 'A new Greek inscription of Aśoka at Kandahar', *Epigraphia Indica*, XXXVII, part V, no. 35, pp. 193–200. H.W. Bailey suggests a possible Iranian root for the word *pāṣanda* which he argues might have been *fras* + *aṇḍa* meaning the one who asks. This would not be very close to the Greek translation of Diatribe. H.W. Bailey, 'Kuṣānica', *BSOAS*, 1952, XIV, part 3, pp. 420–34.
38. This is apparent from the enhancement of the power of the religious donees to include not merely the right to collecting a large number of taxes, but also to taking over judicial administration. R.S. Sharma, *Indian Feudalism*, Calcutta, 1965.
39. H. Kulke, 'Royal Temple Policy and the Structure of Medieval Hindu Kingdoms', in A. Eischmann, et al. *The Cult of Jagganath and the Regional Tradition of Orissa*, New Delhi, 1978, pp. 125ff.
40. K.K. Dutta, *Some Firmans, Sanads and Parwans*, Calcutta, 1953.
41. *Nārada* XVIII.20–2, *Bhāgavata Purāṇa* IV.13.23, *Arthaśāstra* XI.22–9.
42. *Agni Purāṇa* CCXXV.12.
43. XIII.60.19–20.
44. *Viṣṇu Purāṇa* I.13.
45. *Khandahāla Jātaka*, no. 542.
46. *Manicora Jātaka*, no. 194.
47. *Padakusalamānava Jātaka*, no. 432. In the *Gaṇḍatindu Jātaka*, no. 520, the peasants migrate and desert their villages.
48. *Arthaśāstra* IX.3.
49. *Divyāvadāna* C. 372, p. 234, C. 407, p. 262, P.L. Vaidya (ed.), B.S.T. No. 20, Darbhanga, 1959.
50. *Arthaśāstra* XIII.1.20–1.
51. Ibid., II.17.
52. Arrian, *Indika*, XI.
53. R.S. Sharma, op. cit., p. 268.
54. Irfan Habib, *The Agrarian System of the Mughal Empire*, Bombay, 1961, pp. 303ff. R. Kumar, 'The Transformation of Rural Protest in India', in S.C. Malik (ed.), op. cit., pp. 268ff.
55. e.g. *Jātaka* I.451; I, 402; II.428.
56. *Viṣṇu Purāṇa*, IV.24.
57. *Dīgha Nikāya*, III.74–8; *Mahāvaṃsa* XXXII, 81ff, *Milindapañho*, 159.

# 12

# The Image of the Barbarian in Early India*

'Barbarians' are part of the make up of all early civilisations. It was the way a civilisation demarcated itself from those who were seen as distinctively different. The identification of the barbarian would also change over time. Sometimes the earlier barbarians moved to the core of a culture and were replaced by newer ones. The identification therefore was not invariably a permanent one. Consequently the characteristics of what constituted a barbarian could vary from one civilisation to another or from one period to another within the same civilisation.

The concept of the barbarian in early India arises out of the curious situation of the arrival of Indo-Aryan-speaking pastoralists in northern India who came into contact with the indigenous population (some of whom were the remnants of the urban civilization of the Indus) and regarded them as barbarians. The earliest distinction made by the Aryan speakers was a linguistic and cultural distinction. The Indo-Aryan speakers spoke Sanskrit whereas the indigenous peoples probably spoke Proto-Dravidian and Munda. However the distinction was not one of binary opposition — in fact it admitted to many nuances and degrees of variation, hence the complication of trying to trace the history of the concept. The distinction was rarely clearly manifest and based either on language, ethnic origins or culture. Political status, ritual status and economic power, all tended to blur the contours of the distinction. Added to this has been the confusion introduced by those who tend to identify language with race and who thereby see all speakers of Sanskrit as members of that nineteenth-century myth, the Aryan race.[1]

* From *Comparative Studies in Society and History*, October 1971, no. 4, vol. 13, 408–36.

The Aryans,[2] although unfamiliar with city civilization, did use the central Asian horse and the light, spoke-wheeled chariot which gave them speed and mobility and a military advantage over the people still using ox-drawn carts. Furthermore it is also possible that the Aryans may have assisted in the diffusion of, iron technology, which again was superior to the existing copper technology. It is likely that the cities of the Harappa culture had already declined or at least were in the final stages of decline when the Aryan-speakers arrived as migrants. They were virtually faced therefore with a series of chalcolithic cultures extending from the Indus valley to Rajasthan and across into the Ganga valley. Their association with new technologies would probably explain why the Indo-Aryan language spread through a major part of northern India.[3] The anomaly of pastoralists referring to the inheritors of a high civilization as barbarians can thus be partially explained.

The word most frequently used in Sanskrit to describe the barbarian is *mleccha*. Attempts have been made to derive the etymology of the word from the root *vāc* speech, hence one who is not familiar with the known speech or is of alien speech.[4] This also provides a clue to the early distinction being based on speech which fact is stressed in late works as well.[5] The etymology however is false as *mleccha* represents a cultural event rather than a linguistic fact. It has been suggested that *mleccha* may have been derived from Me-luh-ha, the Sumerian name for an eastern land with which the Sumerians had trading relations, possibly the people of the Indus civilization.[6] The Pāli word for *mleccha* is *milakkha*, which relates perhaps to the Sumerian version.[7] Buddhist sources explain *milakkha* as referring to the Āndhra, Tamil, etc.[8] This is further substantiated by the *Dharmaśāstra* of Jaimini in which he mentions certain *mleccha* words which are Sanskritized versions of words occurring in the Dravidian languages. Thus the etymology of *mleccha* would relate it to the indigenous inhabitants of northern India at the time of the arrival of the Aryan-speaking peoples, a far more plausible derivation than the earlier one. Another attempt derives *mleccha* from the proto-Tibetan **mltse* meaning 'tongue' and the Kukish *mlei*. This would associate the early use of the word with the non-Aryan speaking peoples living close to the Tibeto-Burman area.[9]

*Mleccha* may have been an onomatopoeic sound imitating the harshness of an alien tongue. Retroflex consonants are believed to have been assimilated into Indo-Aryan from Dravidian. The earliest of the better-known grammarians, Pāṇini, gives a form of the word *mliṣṭa* as 'that which is spoken indistinctly or barbarously' and treats it in its noun form as indistinct speech or a foreign language.[10] Used as a noun, the word also has the rather significant association with copper and copper-coloured. This may have had some connection with the Aryan speakers coinciding with the use of iron in Indian cultures erstwhile based on a copper technology.[11] From the early centuries AD onwards the adjectival use of *mleccha* becomes quite frequent.[12]

The gradual emphasis on speech differentiation is apparent in the use of another range of words for barbarians which are clearly onomatopoeic and indicate an incomprehension of the language concerned; words such as *barbara, marmara* and *sarsara*. The first may well be borrowed from the Greek *barabaros*, since it occurs in late works in Sanskrit and refers to people of the north who are said to be sinful, low and barbarous.[13] The word also occurs in Pāli as *babbhara* and means 'people of an unknown tongue'.[14] Further variants in Sanskrit are *bhara-bhara* and *balbala-karoti*, 'to stammer or stutter'. *Marmara* and *sarsara* carry the same meaning and are intended to convey the sounds of a halting and alien speech.

In the *Ṛg Veda*, the earliest of the Vedic texts, there is no mention of the *mleccha* as such but there are references to the Dāsa or the Dasyu, the local peoples who were subordinated and regarded as alien and barbaric. They are compared with demons, with one reference to being black-skinned (*kṛṣṇa-tvach*) and snub-nosed, speaking a strange language or speaking incorrectly (*mṛdhra-vāc*); they practise black-magic and do not perform the required sacrifices; they are treacherous and they live in fortified habitations.[15] The distinction of language and ritual is more frequent than physical appearance. Society is divided into two main groups, the *ārya-varṇa* and the *dāsa-varṇa*[16] suggesting a rather simple division into 'us' and 'them' where political success justifies the superiority of the former over the latter.

That speech was the chief component in distinguishing the Aryan from the others is clearly indicated in a text from the Later Vedic literature. An example of barbarian speech, that of the Asuras, is quoted in the *Śatapatha Brāhmaṇa*[17] and is later quoted and discussed by a grammarian of the second century AD, Patañjali.[18] It is evident from the example that the barbarian speech in this case was a Prākrit dialect of eastern India.[19] This would also suggest that settlements in the middle Ganga valley noticed the difference in speech which was recorded and examined. The emphasis on language was important as the knowledge of correct Sanskrit was crucial to the notion of being an *ārya*, and to the efficacy of the ritual hymns.

Having established a distinction in language, a demarcation was also made with regard to territory. Those areas where a *mleccha bhāṣā* (language) was spoken came to be regarded as the *mleccha-deśa* or country of the *mleccha*, and this in theory at any rate, was clearly cordoned off.[20] The *mleccha* areas were impure lands not only because those who lived there spoke an alien language but what was more important they did not perform the correct rituals. These were lands where the *śrāddha* ceremony (offerings to ancestors on stipulated occasions) was not carried out, and where people did not observe the laws of *varṇa*. The pure land was *āryāvarta*,[21] traditionally the region inhabited by the *āryas*, all else was *mleccha-deśa*. Since the *mleccha* is ritually impure, *āryas* visiting the lands of the *mleccha* must perform *prāyaścitta* or expiatory rites before they can be regarded as cleansed and fit for normal association again.[22] The concept of ritual impurity relates to the functioning of caste and this particular aspect of the image of the barbarian appears to be unique to early Indian culture. It was this dichotomy of purity-impurity which gave added significance to the role and status of the ritually pure — the *ārya* and pre-eminent amongst the *āryas*, the *brāhmaṇa*. If *mleccha* epitomizes the barbarian, then *ārya* includes all that is noble and civilized. It is doubtful that the term *ārya* was ever used in a racial sense. In Sanskrit and Pāli literature it is primarily a descriptive term or an honorific referring to a respectable and honourable man.[23] Ritual purity or its absence was used not to justify aggression against the barbarian, but to justify the laws of exclusion on the part of the *ārya*.

The perspective from the south was rather different. The barbarian was defined as one whose language was incomprehensible. The *ārya* was more often merely the northerner and the word was sometimes used synonymously for Vaḍavar, also a person from the north.[24] Later *ārya* was used in the sense of a noble, respected person. Curiously enough, one of the synonyms given for *ārya* in certain Tamil lexicons is *mleccha*, and it is used for those who cannot speak Tamil, separating them from the northerners — tribes such as the Vaḍukar and the Malavar who live in the forests as hunters and who rob travellers and also steal cattle from the neighbouring settlements. Their language is alien and they use long and unlearned words. Beyond them lies Daṇḍakāranya (in the north-eastern Deccan) which is part of *ārya-deśa*. This attitude compares favourably with modern tribes of the Chota Nagpur region who refer to the neighbouring aryanized Hindus (non-tribals) as *diku*, meaning foreigners, a word which was used to great effect in recent years in the building up of a tribal political movement, which sought to exclude the neighbours.

The relationship between the *mleccha* and the *ārya* was conditioned by all the different facets which went into the making of a caste society. There was, first, a network of exogamous and endogamous kinship relations (*jāti*); second, a hierarchical ordering of occupations and a division of labour which functioned on the basis of service relationships. The third essential was the notion that every social group has a ritual status determined by the degree to which its occupation is clean or polluting. The ritual status need not coincide with the actual socio-economic status. It can be maintained that ritual status is expressed in the notion of *varṇa* with its four categories of *brāhmaṇa* (priest), *kṣatriya* (warrior), *vaiśya* (trader), and *śūdra* (cultivator). But for the purposes of the actual functioning of society, *jāti* (deriving from 'birth') was the more significant unit. Fourth, each group was associated with a geographical location. The *mleccha* had to respond to each of these facets. Kinship relations were excluded and the *mleccha* therefore formed their own *mleccha jātis*. No self-respecting *ārya* would marry into a *mleccha* family. Where the *mlecchas* in question were technologically inferior, their occupation was low and this affected their ritual status which was heavily weighted on the side of impurity and therefore low. Consistency with regard to geographical location is evident from the long periods of designating particular regions as *mleccha-deśa*.

Theoretically this seems to be a fairly clear situation. But in fact there were not only lapses from the theory but rarely did society function in strict accordance with these rules although the façade of the rules was maintained. This has to be kept in mind when seeking information from the sources. Whereas the *Dharmaśāstras*, being legal treatises and social codes, maintain the theory and much of religious brahmanical literature tries to conform to the theory, the non-brahmanical literature, particularly secular literature, and epigraphic evidence provide pointers to the actual situation.

By the latter half of the first millennium BC the picture had become far more complex. The amalgamation of existing local cultures, which was inevitable in the evolution of the culture of the *ārya*, created problems for the theorists of caste society. Not all social groups could be given a precise *varṇa* status. The process of *anuloma* (hypergamy) and *pratiloma* (where the mother is of a higher caste than the father) had to be conceded and a number of new and, inevitably, mixed castes (*saṃkīrṇa jāti*) were admitted to the theory of social order.[25] They were given the rank of *śūdras*. Of these many came to be described as *mleccha* such as the Āmbaṣṭha, Ugra and Niṣādha among the *anuloma*[26] and the Sūta, Māgadha, Caṇḍāla, Ayogava and Pulkasa among the *pratiloma*.[27] Even within the *sankīrṇa jātis* there is a hierarchy of ranking as recorded in the *Dharmaśāstras*.[28] Professionally they followed occupations which were regarded by the theorists as activities associated with unclean tasks such as washermen, fishermen, potters, leather-workers, iron-smiths, basket-makers, hunters and scavengers.

That the members of the *saṃkīrṇa jātis* did not necessarily in fact have a low social status is indicated by the sources. The *Aitareya Brāhmaṇa* mentions an Āmbaṣṭha king.[29] The *Taittirīya Brāhmaṇa* refers to the material well-being of the Ugras, one of whom is mentioned as a king's officer.[30] Similarly the Sūta and the Māgadha were traditionally the bards and the chroniclers, in fact the preservers of the early Indian historical tradition. They were close to the king not only because of their profession, but we are told that the presence of the Sūta was essential to one of the rites in a royal sacrifice.[31] In contrast the case of the Caṇḍālas is exceptional, the emphasis being on impurity and not on a difference in culture. They were regarded as so polluting that they had to live outside the village or town.[32]

One of the most interesting and yet at the same time ambiguous cases of the classification of a people as near-*mleccha* is that of the *vrātyas*. Vedic sources on the *vrātyas* appear confused as to their exact status.[33] Later legal literature uses the word *vrātya* in the sense of 'degenerate'.[34] According to Vedic literature the *vrātyas* were not brahmanical in culture and had a different language; but they did speak the language of the initiated. Yet the *vrātyas* were not dismissed as *mleccha* and considerable efforts were made to try to circumvent this problem, one of them being the famous ritual of the *vrātya-stoma*, the rite by which the *vrātya* was purified and accepted into Aryan society.[35] Clearly the *vrātyas* were a powerful group whose power seems to have emanated from a religious sanction and who were therefore treated with a barely disguised veneration by the authors of the *Atharvaveda*, but with some condescension by the authors of the *Dharmaśāstras*.

The second half of the first millennium BC was also the period which saw the gradual but extensive urbanization of the Ganga valley. The river itself became the main channel of communication and trade with cities rising on its banks. The agrarian settlements had also tended to lie closer to the river. There were still large areas of uncleared forest, especially nearer the hills where the agrarian economy had not reached. It was now possible for the Aryan speakers to assume the role of the advanced urban civilization based on technological and economic sophistication. They could therefore regard with contempt those living in the forests who had remained at the food-gathering and hunting stage. Such technologically backward people as for example the Śabara, Pulinda, Mutība and Kirāta, constituted yet another category which came to be included in the term *mleccha*.[36] The distinction which is made in the epic *Rāmāyaṇa* between the urban culture of the kingdom of Ayodhyā based on a fairly extensive agricultural economy can be contrasted with the hunting and food-gathering culture of the enemies of Rāma, the *rākṣasa* peoples.[37] Very often the latter inhabited the fringes of the agrarian settlements and had to move up into the hills with the gradual expansion of the agrarian economy. By extension therefore those on the frontiers also came to be called *mleccha*, even in cases such as those of the Yavanas and the Kāmbojas who were on par with the *ārya*.[38] Thus the use of the word *mleccha* had now been extended to include speakers of an alien language, social groups ranked as mixed castes, technologically backward tribes and the peoples along the frontiers.

The stabilizing of what was to be the *āryāvarta* and the mleccha-lands took some time. In the *Ṛg Veda* the geographical focus was the *sapta-sindhu* (the Indus valley and the Punjab) with Sarasvatī as the sacred river, but within a few centuries *āryāvarta* is located in the Ganga-Yamuna Doāb with the Ganga becoming the sacred river. Together with the shift eastwards of 'the pure land' the northern Punjab and the trans-Indus region came to be regarded as *mleccha-deśa*. Later Vedic literature speaks of the western Ānava tribes as *mlecchas* and occupying northern Punjab, Sind and eastern Rajasthan, as also the eastern Ānava tribes occupying parts of Bihar, Bengal and Orissa.[39] The peoples of the north were *mleccha* either because they were located on the frontier such as the Gandhāra and Kāmboja and therefore both their speech and culture had become contaminated and differed from that of *āryāvarta*, or else, as in the case of the Madras, they were once *āryas* but having forsaken the rituals were relegated to *mleccha* status. The latter was obviously an attempt to explain the contradiction of the earlier texts mentioning them as *āryas* and the later texts, written when the *āryāvarta* had shifted eastwards, referring to them as *mleccha*.

That the northern region was once the land of 'the pure speech' is stated with reference to the Udicya (northern region) where peoples such as the Uttarakurus and the Kuru-Pañcālas are held up as the model in speech and it is recommended that *brāhmaṇas* be sent there to learn the language.[40] Buddhist literature describes Uttarakuru as a mythical paradise, a land reminiscent of the utopian past when there were no institutions such as private property and the family and when there was no need to work because food was available from the trees and all man's desires were satisfied.[41] The later Puranic tradition echoes this description for we are told that the land is covered with milk trees which eliminate the need for cultivating food, that the women are beautiful like the *apsarās* (celestial nymphs) and that people are born as couples, presumably thereby intensifying sexual pleasure.[42] Possibly the brahmanical conception of Uttarakuru as the land of the purest speech may have symbolized the brahmanical utopia, a land of non-polluting peoples, observing all the required rituals and speaking the purest language. Not surprisingly, of the inhabitants of *āryāvarta* by far the most significant are the Kuru-Pañcāla.[43] They emerge as a confederation of a number of existing tribes earlier associated through war and matrimonial alliances.

The Himalayan region was largely *mleccha-deśa* since it was not only a border region but was mainly inhabited by Tibeto-Mongoloid people and the dissimilarity of language and culture would be indicative of difference. The other mountainous region, that of the Vindhyas and their extensions, is probably the most interesting from the point of view of geo-politics. The Aravalli hills formed the natural watershed between the Indus and Ganga valleys and this would be the natural frontier region between the two valleys. For a long period up to the early centuries AD it was occupied by non-Aryan tribal republics, which survived the general decline of republics in the valley areas, and which were consequently the frontier for the Ganga valley. The central Indian complex of the Vindhya and Satpura ranges with the rivers Narmada, Tapti and Wainganga cutting through them and the plateau areas of Chota Nagpur and Chhattisgarh to the east have formed throughout Indian history an ideal setting for the tribal peoples. This area lent itself easily to a pastoral and food-gathering economy with the possibilities of agriculture in some parts of the river valleys and the rich agricultural areas in the plains being more distanced. With the expansion of agriculture and the clearing of the forest in the Ganga valley the existing population of the valley may have sought refuge in the central Indian highlands. Up to about the middle of the first millennium AD the Vindhyan tribes lived in comparative isolation totally unconcerned with the *mleccha* status conferred upon them by the *āryas*. The Chambal and Narmada valleys being the main route from the urban centres of the Ganga valley to the western ports (e.g. Bhrighukaccha, modern Broach) and the Deccan, the plundering of trading caravans and travellers may well have provided the tribes with extra comforts. Plundering was always a means of livelihood which they could resort to, especially during periods of political disturbance. It is not until the post AD 500 period that they begin to participate in the politics of both northern and southern India.

The settlement of eastern India is attested to by advanced Neolithic cultures and the Chalcolithic copper hoards in Bihar and Bengal.[44] Literary evidence dating to about the middle of the first millennium BC indicates that the people of these areas spoke a non-Aryan language. The initial boundary of control in the Ganga valley is perhaps referred to in a striking story related about king Videgha Māthava, the king of the Videhas, who is said to have travelled with the god of fire, Agni, across the Ganga valley as far as the river Sadānīra. Here he paused as the land to the east of the river had not been sanctified by Agni. Once this was done the king established the Videha people on the other bank and the lands to the east of the Videhas were the *mleccha-deśa*.[45]

Yet it was the *mleccha-deśa* close to Videha, Magadha, which was to play a leading role in Indian history during the subsequent centuries. Magadha is described as the accursed land with a people of mixed caste status. An expiatory rite is required from those who visit it and this injunction is continuously repeated in the *Dharmaśāstras* for many centuries, right through the period when the state of Magadha was the centre of empires and powerful kingdoms, viz., the Maurya and Gupta.[46] The other eastern peoples, those of Aṅga, Vaṅga and Kaliṅga were even more polluting and required more elaborate expiatory rites.[47]

This was not the attitude however among the Jainas and Buddhists since it was in these areas that the heterodox religions first gained ground, as for example, Aṅga, which was an early centre of Jainism. The Jaina texts clearly define the *milakkhu* as the Varvara, Sarvara and Pulinda tribes and discourage monks and nuns from keeping their company.[48] Buddhist sources make no distinction between *ārya* lands and *mleccha* lands when describing the sixteen major states of northern India. Since the Buddha himself preached in Māgadhan Prākrit he would hardly have accepted the term *mleccha* for the people of the region. A late Buddhist work mentions the Magadha *bhāṣā* as the speech of the *āryas* indicating that Sanskrit did finally come to be accepted in Magadha.[49] The word *milakkha* is used in Buddhist writing, and as we have seen, one very reliable definition of it reads *Andha Damil, ādi*, 'Āndhras, Tamils, etc.;' i.e. the people of the peninsula.[50] *Milakkha* is also used to describe those *āryas* who had lost their status and the Kāmboja are quoted as an example;[51] also, foreigners such as the Yavanas or Yonas whose status was high but who spoke an alien language,[52] and finally the tribes of the jungle, such as the Pulinda and Kirāta, where they are not only less civilized but again their language is incomprehensible.[53] It would seem from the Buddhist sources that language was the most important criterion of differentiation. Ritual impurity was not a major item in Buddhist thought, thus discrimination was not as severe as in brahmanical writing.[54] The Buddhists tended to underplay the *mleccha* consciousness probably because of the Buddhist association with the *mleccha* regions, these being the areas where it gained most ground. Nevertheless even powerful rulers motivated by the Buddhist ethic such as the Mauryan emperor Aśoka (third century BC) could not disregard the differentiation. His list of the tribal peoples in his empire recorded in one of his inscriptions agrees closely with the lists of *mleccha* peoples mentioned in other sources, although he does not actually call them *mleccha*.[55]

Aśoka makes a distinction between the tribal peoples and the forest tribes, the latter having to be wooed by his officers in the context of a paternalistic policy where he regards himself in the image of the father and his subjects as his children. It would seem that the forest tribes did not easily reconcile themselves to law and order.[56] The tribal people were those that had a clan organisation and were generally societies without a state system. The same problem is reflected in the *Arthaśāstra*, the treatise on political economy ascribed to Kauṭilya the minister of Aśoka's grandfather (fourth century BC). Kauṭilya also distinguishes between the *mleccha* and the forest tribes (*āranyacārah*, *āṭavikaḥ*). He recognizes the political advantages to be gained from keeping the forest tribes happy since they had their own strongholds and could be used effectively in campaigns. Furthermore it was necessary to pay them off from time to time to prevent their resorting to plundering and pillaging.[57] Another source of the same period, the *Indika* of Megasthenes, the Seleucid ambassador to the Mauryan court, refers to the Indians as surrounded by barbarian tribes, possibly a reference to *āryāvarta* surrounded by the *mleccha-deśa*. Megasthenes adds that all these tribes were indigenous but that they differed in mind and disposition from the Indians.[58]

Although Megasthenes does not describe the Indians as barbarians, the Indians undoubtedly regarded him as a *mleccha*. For the Indians, the Greeks on every count were *mlecchas*. They were referred to by the term Yavana, a back-formation from the Prākrit *yona*, and the Old Persian *yauna*, which is said to derive from Ionia, suggesting that the Ionian Greeks were the earliest to have come into contact with Persia and India. Indian tradition however maintains that the Yavanas originated from Turvaśu the son of Yayāti, associated with one of the very early clans of northern India.[59] But this may well be a late attempt to find the Greeks a respectable ancestry when their role in the history of northern India became more than marginal. For the Bactrian Greeks (or the Indo-Greeks as they are called in Indian history), the Śakas (Scythians) and Kuṣāṇas aggravated the problem of having to concede the existence of *mleccha* rulers. In spite of the dismal prophecies of the ancient seers that the Kaliyuga (the last of the four ages) would initiate the rule of the low-caste, nevertheless the *mleccha* origin of these rulers had to be faced.[60] The problem was further complicated by the fact that these rulers patronized and used Sanskrit as is evident from their inscriptions and coins and they inter-married into the local ruling families. The description of these areas as *mleccha-deśa* was technically also problematical. The inscriptions of the Śaka satraps (rulers and governors of western India from *c.* 100 BC to AD 300) are not only composed in good literary Sanskrit, but also assert with much vehemence that the kings are doing their utmost to prevent the mixing of the castes and are protecting the law of *varṇa*.[61] Thus the two main criteria of barbarism could not theoretically be said to prevail.

The *mleccha* both indigenous and foreign had acquired political power and a new concept was necessary. It was probably largely to circumvent this problem that the term *vrātyakṣatriya* (degenerate *kṣatriya*) became current in describing the origin and status of such peoples. It was maintained that in origin they were of the *kṣatriya varṇa* and that their degeneration was due to the non-performance of sacred rites, or because of the wrath of the *brāhmaṇas* when they ceased to perform the sacred rites.[62] Among the foreign rulers included as *vrātya kṣatriyas* were the Yavanas and the Śakas (Scythians).

The term Yavana was gradually extended to include not only the local Greeks but any group of people coming from west Asia or the eastern Mediterranean. Much the same was to happen to the term Śaka with reference to central Asia, but Yavana remained the more commonly used one. Even in South India, traders from Rome and later the Arabs were called Yavanas. Early Tamil literature has descriptions of a Yavana settlement in Kaveripaṭṭinam. The Yavanas here referred to were also described as *mleccha,* since they spoke an alien language which was so incomprehensible that it sounded as if their tongues were cut off.[63]

Among the tribes of indigenous origin also referred to as *vrātya kṣatriyas* in some sources are listed the Drāviḍa, Ābhīra, Śabara, Kirāta, Mālava, Śibi, Trigarta and Yaudheya. The majority of such tribes tended to be the inhabitants of the Himalayan and Vindhyan region, traditionally called the *mleccha-deśa*. There is evidence from numismatic sources of the increasing political importance of some of these tribes which would explain their elevation to the status of *vrātya kṣatriyas* from being plain *mlecchas*. The period from the first century BC to about the fourth century AD saw the rise of a number of oligarchies in the Punjab and eastern Rajasthan, in fact in and around the watershed between the Indus and Ganga valleys. The

Mālava tribe, mentioned by the Greeks as the Malloi, established themselves in the Jaipur area having migrated from the Rāvi.[64] The Śibi, the Siboi of the Greeks, migrated to north-eastern Rajasthan.[65] The Trigarta, were settled in the Rāvi-Sutlej Doāb. The Yaudheyas moved from Haryana northwards.[66] The fact that these tribes were politically powerful after they had settled in an area is clear from the use of the term *janapada* in the coin legends indicating their assertion over the territory on which they had settled.The Gupta conqueror Samudragupta, campaigning in the fourth century AD, takes great pride in having destroyed the tribal polities which were regarded as poweful.[67] The coin legends also clearly demonstrate that these tribal peoples were now using Sanskrit.

In the middle of the first millennium AD when it was evident that *mleccha* dynasties were dominating politics, the Puranic tradition (as it was then recorded) had much to say on the problem of the *mleccha*.[68] There is a general bewailing of the increase in *mleccha* influence which is associated with the prophecy that the *kaliyuga* will see *mleccha* dominance.[69] This will result in the establishment of the *mleccha dharma*, a barbarous ordering of the universe when vice will be rampant, the authority of the sacred texts neglected, the *śūdras* respected — in short, a complete reversal of the world order as seen by the *āryas*.[70] Passages such as these seem to express the sentiments of a small group fighting to preserve itself and prevent the change which is engulfing its world and its very existence. Not surprisingly the idea of the Saviour Deity is introduced in some of the *Purānas* where it is stated that the god Viṣṇu in his tenth incarnation as Kalkin will ride through the world in an attempt to turn men back to the path of virtue. Some of the *mleccha* peoples such as the Drāviḍa, Śabara and Vṛṣala will be destroyed by Kalkin.[71] But this was a temporary measure as Purāṇic cosmology did not really envisage the coming of the millennium since ultimately the entire universe was to be destroyed at the finale of the *kaliyuga*.

It is curious that in spite of considerably increased communication between the Ganga valley and the peninsula and the spread of Sanskrit and of Aryan culture to the south, there is a persistence in regarding the southern regions as *mleccha-deśa*. The Āndhras, for example, who had ruled the northern Deccan for four centuries, are described as *mleccha* kings and their lands unfit for the *śrāddha* ceremony. At the same time the Āndhra kings were claiming to be the protectors of the *varṇa dharma*, and the destroyers of the Śakas and Yavanas.[72] That less concession was made to the southern kings as compared to the northern kings was partly due to distance and partly perhaps due to the belt of tribes inhabiting the Vindhyas who doubtless acted as a barrier.

However the attitude towards even these tribes was beginning to change and this is reflected partially in the genesis myths associated with their origin. The most frequently referred to are the Niṣāda. References to the four *varṇas* in Vedic literature includes mention of the Niṣāda who appear to have been a non-Aryan tribe who were not assimilated[73] but had a low status in ritual ranking.[74] They are generally located in the region of the Narmada river or among the Vindhya and Satpura mountains.[75] They are described as being dark-skinned, flat-featured with blood-shot eyes and of short stature.[76] A series of myths is related regarding their origin.[77] The variations apart, the main narrative states that they were born from the thigh of king Veṇa. King Veṇa was extremely wicked and flouted the sacred laws and the holy rites. This infuriated the sages who pierced him with the sharp ears of the *kuśa* grass and, according to some versions, killed him. In order to avoid anarchy, since the land was now without a king, they churned his left thigh and from it came a dark, ugly, short man, the ancestor of the Niṣāda, and in some versions, the ancestor of the *mleccha*.[78] Being unsatisfied with this result they then churned the right arm of Veṇa and from it emerged Pṛthu who was crowned king and was so righteous that the earth was named after him, Pṛthivī. Whatever the deeper meaning of these myths may be, it seems obvious that the original Niṣāda and Pṛthu represent two factions which may have fought for power. There also seems to be an association of guilt with the killing of Veṇa and the manner of the birth of Niṣāda suggests that he may have been the rightful heir but was replaced by Pṛthu. The tribes with whom the Niṣāda are associated in these texts such as the Bhīla, Kol, etc., are often the tribes connected with the rise of new dynasties in central India in the period after the eighth century AD.

The Vindhyan region was the locale for the three tribes which came to be mentioned almost as the synonyms for *mleccha*, the Kirāta, Pulinda and Śabara.[79] The Kirāta are described as living in the hills and jungles of Magadha.[80] The *Mahābhārata* describes them as being dressed in skins, eating fruit and roots and inflicting cruel wounds with their weapons. Yet they were not as wild as the text would have us believe because they also brought as gifts to one of the heroes, sandalwood, aloes wood, expensive skins gold, perfume, rare animals and birds and ten thousand serving girls. They arrived riding on elephants.[81] If the gifts amounted to even a portion of what is described then the Kirātas cannot be said to have had a primitive economy. Early texts speak of them as living in the east but later texts give the Vindhyas as their place of residence.[82] Their migration may have been due to the expansion of the agrarian settlements in the Ganga valley. The most interesting reference to them however is the famous literary work, the *Kirātārjunīya* where significantly the Kirāta is identified with the god Śiva and gives battle to Arjuna, one of the heroes of the *Mahābhārata*.[83] South Indian sources as late as the seventeenth century continue to refer to them as living in the Vindhyas in a semi-barbarous condition.[84]

The names Pulinda and Śabara in particular seem to have become generic names for barbarian tribes.[85] Ptolemy uses the curious expression 'agriophagoi', the eaters of wild things,[86] in describing the Pulinda, and locates them to the east of the Malava. The Pulinda may have migrated from the Mathura region to the Vindhyas for the same reasons as did the Kirātas.[87] They too are described as being dwarf-sized, black in complexion like burnt tree-trunks and living in forest caves.[88] The Śabaras were also located in the Vindhyan region.[89] A ninth-century inscription mentions the *mleccha* along the Chambal river and a fifteenth-century inscription refers to the quelling of a revolt by the Śabaras inhabiting the Chambal valley.[90] An early medieval adaptation of the *Rāmāyaṇa* from the south speaks of the Śabara chief as a powerful ruler of *mleccha-deśa*.[91] It is not clear whether this is poetic imagination or whether it reflects a real impression of the Śabaras as seen from a south Indian perspective. As late as the sixteenth century the king Kṛṣṇa Deva Raya of Vijayanagara writes in his manual on government that the Vindhyan tribes must be brought round to accepting the administration by gaining their trust,[92] a sentiment reminiscent of the emperor Aśoka. A Śabara tribe exists to the present day in western Orissa. The Kol tribes preserve a traditional memory of the name Sabara and the Śabari river in Chhattisgarh reflects an association with these tribes.

The authors of the *Dharmaśāstras* continued to prescribe dire punishments for those who travelled in *mleccha* lands, yet this did not deter people. Needless to say Indian traders (*brāhmaṇas* included) did travel extensively and profitably in *mleccha* lands, the performance of the expiatory *prāyaścitta* on returning home providing a convenient solution to the problem.[93] However with the incursions of *mleccha* rulers into *āryāvarta* itself, a new problem arose: the pure land was being turned into a *mleccha* land. This had happened in the case of the Yavanas who had come a fair way into the Ganga-Yamuna Doāb. It was to happen again with the coming of the Central Asian Huns or Hūṇas as they were called in India. The solution to this problem in the words of the medieval commentator Medātithi was that if the *varṇa* laws were introduced into the region (or continued to be maintained) then it would be fit for the performance of sacrifices.[94]

The coming of the Huns was not a traumatic event in the history of India. Its impact has perhaps been exaggerated owing to its continual comparison with the arrival of the Huns in Europe. Even the parallel which is frequently drawn between the Huns dealing a death blow to the Roman empire and the Hūṇas doing the same to the Gupta empire (fourth–fifth centuries AD) is not strictly comparable since the nature of the two empires was different as also the cause of their decline. Northern India was by now familiar with foreign invasions and government under *mleccha* dynasties. The Hūṇas were known to inhabit the northern regions and are sometimes mentioned together with the Cīna (Chinese).[95] The close of the fifth century AD saw the Hūṇa invasions of India under their chief Toramāna. The location of his inscription at Eran (Madhya Pradesh) and the discovery of his seals at Kauśāmbī (Uttar Pradesh) point to his having controlled a substantial part of *āryāvarta*.[96] Hence the problem of living in a region overrun by the *mleccha* referred to earlier. Toramāna's son Mihīrakula lived up to the conventional image of the Hun. He is particularly remembered for his cruelty which has become a part of northern Indian folklore.[97] His violence however was directed mainly against the Buddhists and the Jainas, whose literature is replete with complaints about him.[98] He was however forced back from the Ganga valley and the Hūṇa kingdom after him was reduced to a small area of northern India. The Hūṇa invasion itself did not produce any major changes in the life of northern India, except at the topmost political level. Epigraphical evidence suggests that the feudatories of the Gupta kings continued as the local governors under Hūṇa rule.[99] Hūṇas used Sanskrit as their official language and patronized Hindu cults and sects.

The impact of the Huns was greater in other spheres. Hun activities in Central Asia affected north Indian trade which had close links with central Asia. Furthermore in the wake of the Huns came a number of other tribes and peoples from central Asia jostling for land and occupation in northern India. This led to a migration of peoples in these parts which in turn upset one of the stabilizing factors of the caste structure, the inter-relationship between caste and locality. Some of these movements of peoples from the north southwards can be traced in the place names and the caste names, as in the case of the Gurjaras and Ābhīras.[100]

Politically too the period from the sixth to the ninth century tended to be unstable in northern India, barring perhaps the reign of Harṣa. The kingdoms of the northern Deccan were also beginning to take a political interest in the areas adjoining the Vindhyas, which culminated in the attempts of the Rāṣṭrakūṭa kings to capture and hold the city of Kanauj. In addition to this the system of making land grants to *brāhmaṇas* and to secular officials (to the latter in lieu of salary) was becoming more widespread.[101] In cases where the land was virgin the system resulted in the expansion of the agrarian economy. The tribes of central India were forced to adjust to both the population movements from the north as also to the encroaching agrarian economy often in the form of enforced settlements of *brāhmaṇas* and agriculturalists. That this is also the period in which the areas on the fringes of the Vindhyan uplands give rise to a number of principalities some of which play a major role in the politics of central India is not surprising. Some provided armies to neighbouring states, others became the nuclei of new states which arose on the debris of dynastic changes. The area continued to be a major artery of trade which made it a prey to many ambitious dynasties and the scene of constant battles. This uncertainty benefited the tribal peoples who exploited it to secure power for themselves.[102] However, many parts of central India remained comparatively untouched by either the agrarian economy or the culture of the *āryas* since pockets in this part of the subcontinent still harbour Dravidian and Muṇḍā-speaking tribes existing at a food-gathering stage, or at most, using primitive agriculture.

From the ninth century AD political power moved more recognizably into the hands of the erstwhile feudatories, the recipients of land grants. Some among them in turn became independent kings, granted land and revenue in lieu of salaries to their officers, and to learned *brāhmaṇas* for the acquisition of religious merit. The legal sanction of the grant was generally recorded in an inscription in stone or on plates of copper, and the preamble to the grant contained the genealogy of the kings. The remarkable fact of these genealogies is that most kings claim full *kṣatriya* status on the basis of a genealogical connection with the ancient royal families, the *Sūryavaṃśa* (Solar lineage) and the *Candravaṃśa* (Lunar lineage); or else there is the myth among some Rajput dynasties of the ancestor having emerged from the sacrificial fire, the Agnikula lineage. Such genealogical connections were claimed by the majority of the dynasties of this time though not all.[103] What is even more significant is that most of these families are found on examination to be at least partially of unestablished origin.[104] Thus instead of being described as *mleccha* kings, they claim *ksatriya* status and have had genealogies fabricated to prove the claim. Whereas the Śakas and Yavanas were denounced as *vrātya ksatriyas* and the Āndhras were described as *mleccha* kings, the kings of this period, some of whom came from *mleccha* stock such as the Gonds and Gurjaras, are willingly accorded *kṣatriya* status. Why did the *brāhmaṇas* agree to this validation? It is possible that the distinction between *ārya* and *mleccha* had become blurred in actual practice although the *dharmaśāstras* continued to maintain it. The system of land grants appears to have played a significant part. *Brāhmaṇa* grantees were often given land in virgin areas: thus they became the nuclei of Aryan culture in non-Aryan regions.[105] This process having started in the early centuries AD resulted in more land coming under cultivation and through the intermixing of cultures, the culture even of the *ārya* was being constantly remoulded. The return on the part of the *brāhmaṇa* may have been the fabrication of a genealogy for the new ruler.

The advantage of the fabricated genealogy was that *mleccha* antecedents were soon overlooked or forgotten, particularly in those areas where the *mleccha* had become powerful. In a ninth-century inscription of a Cālukya feudatory of the Pratihāra king great pride is taken in 'freeing the earth from the Hūṇa peoples'.[106] At almost the same time a Guhilla king of the Udaipur region proudly married the daughter of a Hūṇa king.[107] Yet the founder of the Guhilla dynasty claimed to be a *brāhmaṇa*. Marriage alliances broke the kinship barrier and *mleccha* rulers became patrons of Sanskrit learning and culture, so that they were as good as *āryas* for all practical purposes. Ultimately the Hūṇas came to be regarded as on par with the Rajput clans and today the name survives merely as a caste name in the Punjab.[108] The degree of assimilation can be seen in the fact that the accepted lexicon, the *Amarakoṣa*, in its definition of *mleccha* merely lists the three tribes — the Kirāta, Pulinda and Śabara.[109] The names of erstwhile *mleccha* tribes are defined according to occupations. Thus the Ābhīras are herdsmen, the Āmbaṣṭhas physicians and scribes and the Dārada dealers in antidotes. The erstwhile *mleccha-deśa* are described with reference to their produce: thus Vaṅga produces tin and Yavana-deśa horses fit for the *aśvamedha* sacrifice.

The process of sanskritization (the acquisition of Sanskritic culture and higher ritual status) was usually spread over some centuries. The Bedars, a *mleccha* tribe of the Deccan, are recorded in seventh-century AD sources as molesting *brāhmaṇas* who had received land grants and settled in the new areas.[110] It is stated that these plundering raids had to be warded off by the villagers themselves as the king could not enforce law and order in those areas.[111] The situation continued until about the thirteenth century. Gradually the Bedar chiefs themselves were bought off with land grants and other concessions.[112] In periods of political confusion the chiefs began to found independent principalities. Trouble between the Bahmani kings and Vijayanagara was fully exploited and the Bedars not only plundered the city of Vijayanagara in 1565 but strengthened their principalities. Sanskritization continued apace and can be seen in the claim of the Bedar kings to a high ritual status in the use of Sanskrit names such as *mahānāyakācarya*, and also in the endowment made to the temple of Gopāla-Kṛṣṇa by the Bedar chief in 1568 and ultimately in the fact that the famous Śaivite Kannappa was of Bedar origin.[113]

From about the ninth century onwards references to large numbers of indigenous peoples as *mleccha* begin to decrease. Where they are mentioned and are other than the Vindhyan tribes, it is generally for a particular reason. The tenth-century Ābhīra king is called a *mleccha* because he indulges in beef eating and plundering the pilgrims who visit the famous temple at Somanātha.[114] In eastern

India there is the interesting inscriptional reference to the kingdom of Kāmarūpa (Assam) being occupied by a *mleccha* ruler, Śālastambha, who starts a new dynasty.[115] We are not told why he is a *mleccha*. Was he of tribal origin or did he have Tibetan connections?

Among the foreigners with whom there was a fair amount of contact, especially through trade, were the Chinese, the Arabs and the Turks, all of whom were of course considered *mlecchas*. Indirect contact with the Chinese goes back to the third century BC through trade in silk. Although silk was greatly appreciated in India, the Chinese were firmly relegated to the ranks of the barbarians and their land declared unfit for *śrāddha* rites.[116] They are often associated with the Kāmboja and the Yavana (presumably because of the central Asian connection) and with the Kirāta and eastern India — the two regions from which trade with China was conducted in the early period.[117] But the interest in China waned with the arrival of the Turks on the northwestern borders of India and the Arabs in the west.

The Arabs are referred to as Tājiks or as Yavanas and are regarded as *mleccha*.[118] The former relates to the fact that they came from west Asia and were in a sense the inheritors of the earlier Yavana role in India. The Turks are described correctly as Turuṣkas in some cases but more often they too came under the general term *mleccha* or are called Śakas and Yavanas.[119] The latter was probably the result of their coming from the same geographical direction as the earlier invaders. It would suggest that to the Indian mind the Turks represented a historical continuity of the Śakas and Yavanas. It does however point to a comparative lack of interest in events across the frontiers of the subcontinent that the new invaders should not have been clearly demarcated from the old. It is also possible, however, that in using the old terms there was a subconscious attempt on the part of the Indian rulers to compare themselves with earlier kings who had tried to stem the tide of the Śaka and Yavana invasions. Perhaps this degree of romanticism was essential to the medieval ethos.

It was after all the same romanticism which led comparatively minor kings to claim suzerainty over vast areas of the continent. There is a recurring list of places which occurs in many of the inscriptions of this period and becomes almost a convention and which reads '. . . had suzerainty over the *mleccha*, Aṅga, Kaliṅga, Vaṅga, Odra Pāṇḍya, Karnāṭa, Lāṭa, Suhma, Gurjara, Krita and

Cīna . . . .'[120] It is not clear in this case who the *mleccha* were, whether they were the Arabs or indigenous people, although it could well be that the word was used in an adjectival sense to cover these places which were in the earlier tradition regarded as *mleccha-deśa*. A similar convention relates to the conquest of the tribal peoples and the capture of their hill forts such as Ānarta, Mālava, Kirāta, Turuṣka, Vatsa, Matsya, etc.[121] The 'eulogy' style of inscriptions in which these conventions are observed continued to be used even for the Turkish Sultans after they had established their rule.

*Mleccha* as a term of exclusion also carried within it the possibility of assimilation, in this case the process by which the norms of the sub-culture find their way in varying degrees into the cultural mainstream. Assimilation can be achieved at various levels. The obvious forms are noticeable in external habits such as names, dress, eating-habits and amusements. The more subtle forms are those which can be seen in the framework of law and of religious beliefs. The sanskritizing of names was a common feature among both indigenous and foreign *mlecchas* who slowly tried to move away from their status of *mleccha*.[122] Very often in the case of ruling families it took one or two generations to make the transition. In other situations it took a longer time. The importation of foreign fashions is evident from the terracotta and stone sculpture of various periods. The tendency was to follow the dictates of the court circles. The coûture of the deities however was more rigidly bound by conventional forms. Assimilation can also be seen in the appropriation of melodies and musical forms associated with *mleccha* peoples into the mainstream of music.[123] One of the most direct forms of the expression of brahmanical ritual purity was on the form and type of food which the *brāhmaṇa* could eat. He was forbidden to accept cooked food from any non-*brāhmaṇa*.[124] Eatables were ranked in a carefully determined order of priority. Thus when the Punjab became a *mleccha* area, its staple food was given a lower place in the hierarchy of food-ranking. Whereas the Ṛg-vedic *ārya* had a staple diet of wheat and barley, by the twelfth century AD wheat was described in one lexicon as 'the food of the *mlecchas*' (*Mleccha-bhojana*) and rice became the 'pure' cereal.[125] Onions and garlic were also regarded as the food of the *mleccha* and therefore prohibited to the *brāhmaṇa*. One of the habits of the *mlecchas* which seriously defiled them was the fact that they drank alcohol and ate the flesh of the cow, and this in later periods was strictly forbidden to the twice-born.[126]

We have seen that an essential difference between the *ārya* and the *mleccha* was that the latter did not conform to the law of *varṇa*. On one occasion the god Indra is asked how the Yavanas, Śakas, Cīnas, Kāmbojas, Pulindas, etc., can be brought within the social pale, and he replies that if they follow the *dharma* of the *śāstras* (essentially the law of the *varṇa*), they can be admitted.[127] For the laws of the *mleccha* and the laws of the *āryas* were distinct. As was the case with other *jātis*, the *mleccha* appear to have had their own customary laws and functioned within the framework of these. Within the law of the *śāstras* a sharp differentiation was maintained between the status and rights of the *ārya* and the *mleccha*. A significant and relevant example of this is that the *mleccha* is permitted to sell or mortgage his own life and that of his offspring.[128] But an *ārya* can never be subjected to slavery, except for very short periods when he is in adverse circumstances.

An even more subtle form of assimilation was through the incorporation of cults and cult-priests into the religious beliefs and rituals of the established religions of the *āryas*. In the case of the Buddhists the problem was easier since there was not the same stress on ritual ranking as among the *brāhmaṇas*. The Śaka and Yavana rulers and particularly their queens who were patrons of Buddhism were accepted as fully as other Indian ruling families.[129] For the indigenous *mleccha* the acceptance of Buddhism did not necessitate the disavowal of earlier cults, since Buddhism has commonly assimilated local cults in its process of expansion. Buddhism itself arose in *mleccha* areas and it is significant that the main strongholds of Buddhism were in these areas. However, it tended to by-pass the tribes of the Vindhyas probably because the nature of their cults, stressing violence and the shedding of blood at sacrifices, precluded easy acceptance into Buddhism.

The brahmanical religion did not remain rigid either. The Bhāgavata tradition in Vaiṣṇavism and Śaivism which emerged in the early centuries AD stressing the personal devotion, *bhakti*, of the worshipper for an individual deity, made the religion more flexible and more easily exportable. It was this tradition of brahmanism that could and did attract foreign *mlecchas*. The Greek Heliodorus records his devotion to Viṣṇu and speaks of himself as a member of the Bhāgavata sect.[130] The Hūṇas appear to have been quite acceptable to both the major sects of Hinduism. Toramāna was a Vaiṣṇava and was a patron of those who worshipped the *varāha* (boar) incarnation of Viṣṇu. As a royal patron he was the direct successor to one of the Gupta emperors who had earlier donated a cave to this worship at a place not too far from the site of Toramāna's inscription.[131] Mihīrakula was such an ardent Śaivite that he was led to an extreme intolerance of the Buddhists and Jainas, again a tradition which is recorded of earlier rulers of Kashmir.[132] Perhaps the Sun and Fire cults of the Hūṇas acted as a bridge towards their acceptance of and by Hinduism. With the strengthening of the Bhāgavata tradition there was a proliferation of new sects, some of which in their social attitudes were recognizably anti-brahmanical, such as the Śaiva Siddhāntas and others which maintained a flexible attitude to caste such as the Liṅgāyatas. As in the case of the Buddhists and Jainas, such sects did not discriminate between *ārya* and *mleccha* peoples, and for the latter this became an avenue of entry into *ārya* society, since ultimately many of these sects became independent castes within the *varṇa* system.

In the case of the indigenous *mleccha* many of the cults were slowly absorbed into the main cultural tradition. Of these perhaps the most obvious were the fertility cults, especially those devoted to the worship of the mother goddess, and the phallus (*liṅgam*) and snake cults.[133] These cults were not totally foreign to brāhmaṇism, but in the period after the fifth century AD they began to play a more dominant role in the evolution of Hinduism.[134] The mother goddess, Devī, in various manifestations appears to have been the most popular deity among the *mleccha*. Vindhyavāsinī, one of the names for the consort of Śiva, was worshipped by the Śabaras, Barbaras and Pulindas.[135] The name itself means 'she who inhabits the Vindhyas', and clearly she was in origin a mountain goddess. She is said to be commonly worshipped by brigands, and the rites involved the eating of meat and the drinking of wine.[136] In another form she is described as the goddess of the outcastes who bring her oblations of sacrificed animals.[137] Elsewhere she is identified with Nārāyaṇī and Durgā, both well-known manifestations of Śiva's wife and both repeatedly associated with the *mleccha* tribes in early literature.[138] The name Śavari, meaning a Śabara woman, occurs as the name of a goddess in a medieval work.[139] The Śavarotsava or Festival of the Śabaras was a bacchanalian gathering, as well it might have been with a fertility cult as its focus. The Kirāta worshipped the goddess Candikā, yet another manifestation of Śiva's wife Durgā, a more fearsome form of the goddess being responsible for the destruction of the buffalo-demon Mahiṣāsura. The *Devī Māhātmya*, one of the more important sources on the mother-goddess cult, suggests an eastern if not Tibetan origin for the birth of the goddess Caṇḍi.[140] By the medieval period the cults of Durgā and Caṇḍi had been absorbed into classical Hinduism. In fact, a substantial part of Hinduism itself had undergone transformation with the popularity of the Śakti-Śākta cults and Tantricism.

Nor were the cult priests left behind. Depending on the status of the cult they would enter the hierarchy of Brahmanism. As the cult became refined and found a niche in classical Hinduism the cult priest would also become Sanskritized and be given ritual status in the *brāhmaṇa varṇa*. This would account for the existence of contradictory categories such as the Ambaṣṭha *brāhmaṇa* and the Ābhīra *brāhmaṇa*. It would also explain the gradual evolution in status of the Maga *brāhmaṇas* who are said to have come from Śakadvīpa in the west.[141] They are at first looked down upon and not admitted to all the *śrāddha* ceremonies. This may have been because they were soothsayers and astrologers rather than genuine *brāhmaṇas* or else because of their association with the sun cult, which, being a more powerful religious force in western Asia, may have been regarded as somewhat foreign.[142] But gradually their position improved when they were patronized by the royal courts, especially at Thānesar and Kāmarūpa, and they were regarded as the proper people to install and consecrate images of Sūrya and the sun-god.[143] Their association with the sun cult remained constant. However they still married into non-*brāhmaṇa* castes such as the Bhojas and the Yādavas. By the medieval period however they were treated with considerable respect. The curious legends which are told about the origin of certain *brāhmaṇa* families such as those of the Chitpavans who are said to have virtually walked in from the sea,[144] would also suggest that these were families of cult priests who were gradually assimilated into the Hindu social structure.

There was however one facet in the concept of the barbarian which was absent — the notion of the pagan. This did finally arrive in India but never became an intrinsic part of the Indian notion since Indian religions had no use for this concept. It was applied by the Muslims who came to India to the non-Muslim inhabitants of India. They were regarded as pagans and by extension less civilized and the Muslims in turn were described as *mleccha*. From about the fifteenth century onwards, when Turkish and Afghan rule had been established in many parts of the subcontinent, Muslims at all levels of society came to be described more extensively as *mleccha*. They were *mleccha* partly because some were foreign in origin, although the majority were locally born and bred; but what was more important they were associated with an alien language (either Arabic, Turki or Persian) although here again the majority spoke the local language; and they could not in theory conform to the laws of *varṇa* since Islamic laws demand an egalitarian society. Certainly they did not observe the rules of ritual purity. Gradually however the social organization of the converted Muslims began to retain many of their caste mores prior to conversion. It is also possible that since a sizeable proportion of conversions to Islam in India were from the lower castes (conversion to a non-caste religion being one of the traditional methods of trying to by-pass caste), this also encouraged the use of the description *mleccha*.

The most significant clue to assimilation lies not so much in the loss of ethnic identity as in participation in the sense of the past. There is the mutual appropriation of the past on the part of two groups where the group with the weaker historical tradition accepts the stronger tradition. This was certainly the case with foreign peoples who settled in India and with the indigenous tribes. Sanskritization implied the acceptance of the historical tradition to the same degree as the organization of the tribe according to the laws of *varṇa* and *jāti*. Hence the importance of genealogies in the process of both historical and social validation. Yet this sense of the past was in itself the result of assimilation at various points in time and was given direction by the elements which went into the making of the social fabric. Islamic historiography brought with it its own highly developed philosophy of the past which had little in common with traditional Indian historiography except that they were both powerful traditions within the culture.

It is perhaps the very contradiction in the Indian concept of the barbarian which makes it distinctively different from that of Europe. The perception of differences — linguistic, cultural and physical — set the barbarian apart. The separateness was seen not so much in terms of what the barbarians did as in the fact that they did not observe the norms of ritual purity and were to that extent polluted. The lack of description of the *mleccha*, comparatively speaking, was based on the assumption that no self-respecting man would associate with them as long as they were designated as *mleccha*. In a sense, this was the ultimate in segregation. Theoretically this position was maintained throughout. Yet in practice not only were concessions made, as for example, in the notion of the *vrātya-kṣatriya*, but large numbers of *mleccha* peoples were incorporated into the social, political and religious system and were in fact the progenitors of many of the essentials of Indian culture. It would be a moot point as to whether this could be called a culture which entirely excludes the barbarian.

## Notes and References

1. E.g. Caldwell, *A Comparative Grammar of the Dravidian or South Indian Family of Languages*, London, 1875. Thus, all south Indian *brāhmaṇas* who use Sanskrit were seen as originally Aryan.
2. The use of the word 'Aryan' in this article refers to those peoples who spoke an Indo-Aryan language. It has no ethnic connotation and is merely used as a more manageable form than the phrase 'Aryan-speaking' with which it is synonymous.
3. For a discussion of the nature and impact of Aryan culture on existing cultures in northern India, *see* the section on Archaeology and History in this volume.
4. Categories of speech are demarcated in Vedic literature, reflecting a considerable concern for the correctness of speech. *Śatapatha Brāhmaṇa*, IV, 1, 3, 16; *Taittirīya Samhitā*, VI, 4, 7, 3; *Maitrāyaṇī Samhitā*, III, 6, 8.
5. The *Nyāyamalavistāra*. *Manu*, X, 45, distinguishes between *mleccha-vāc* and *ārya-vāc*.
6. Recent exponents of this view are the Finnish scholars, Parpola et al., who have made this identification basic to their reading of the Harappa script as Proto-Dravidian, *Decipherment of the Proto-Dravidian Inscriptions of the Indus Civilisation*, Copenhagen, 1969. An even more recent reading is that of I. Mahadevan who reads two Harappan pictograms as **mil-ey* which becomes **mil-ec* which in turn becomes *mleccha* in Sanskrit, all of which mean 'the resplendent ones' — the assumption being that this was the name by which the Harappan people called themselves. *Journal of Tamil Studies*, II, no. 1, 1970.
7. *Vinaya Piṭaka*, III, 28.

8. Buddhaghoṣa's commentary explains it as *'Andha Damil, ādi'*. The *Jaimini Dharmaśāstra* gives a short list of *mleccha* words, 1, 3, 10.
9. R. Shafer, *Ethnography of Ancient India*, Wiesbaden, 1954, p. 23.
10. *Aṣṭādhyāyi*, VII, 2, 18.
11. N.R. Bannerjee, *The Iron Age in India*, Delhi, 1965.
12. Such as *mleccha-deśa* (country), *mleccha-bhāṣā* (language), *Mleccha-nivāha* (horde), *mleccha-bhojana* (food — used by rice-eaters for non-rice eaters, particularly those eating wheat), *mleccha-vāc* (speech).
13. *Mahābhārata*, XII, 200, 40.
14. *Majjhima Nikāya*, I, 128.
15. *Ṛg Veda*, III, 12, 6; II, 12, 4; III, 34, 9; V; 29; 10; IV, 16, 9; I, 33, 4; X, 22, 8; II, 20, 8.
16. *Ṛg Veda*, III, 34, 9; II, 24, 4; I, 104, 2. The word '*varṇa*' literally means 'colour' and came to be used for *varṇa* society or caste society. With the exception of the *brāhmaṇas* and the *kṣatriyas* the precise status of the other two was never uniform.
17. *Śatapatha Brāhmaṇa*, III, 2, 1, 23; which reads *te'surā ātta-vacaso he'lavo he'lava iti vadantaḥ pārābabhūbuḥ*. The Kaṇva recession has a variant reading (Sacred Books of the East, XXVI; p. 31, n. 3) but the end result is similar.
18. *Vyākaraṇa Mahābhāṣya*, I, 1, 1, which reads, *te'surā helayo helaya iti kurvantaḥ pārābabhūbuḥ*. In both cases the word for enemy, *ari*, uses 'l' instead of the more general Indo-Aryan 'r'. The Asuras here referred to are a puzzle. They are described as demons, but also as a maritime people whom the Aryans of the *Ṛg Veda* had to contend with. Archaeological remains in Chota Nagpur are associated by the local tribes with the Asuras. Banerji Sastri, *Journal of the Bihar Oriental Research Society*, XII, part ii, 246ff.
19. A characteristic of the Prākrit of eastern India attested by the inscriptions of Aśoka is that the 'r' sound changes into 'l', J. Bloch, *Les Inscriptions d'Asoka*, Paris, 1950, p. 112.
20. *Manu*, II, 23; X, 45.
21. *Āryāvarta* was traditionally the region inhabited by the *āryas*. Its precise geographical area is difficult to define as the concept was not static in history. Broadly speaking, however, the Ganga-Yamuna Doab and the plain of Kurukshetra to the north of Delhi would roughly correspond to *āryāvarta*, in the earliest sense. Some texts extend the definition to include almost the entire Indo-Gangetic plain, e.g., *Manu*, II, 17–74.
22. *Viṣṇu*, LXXXIV, 1–4.
23. *Manu*, X, 45, 57; speaks of *ārya-vāc* and *ārya-rūpa* (noble speech and noble visage) where *ārya* is used in an adjectival form. The Pāli *ayya*

or *ajja* carries the same sense. The antonym of *anārya*, *dāsa* or *dasyu* again carries the meaning of lacking in worthiness and respect and cannot be taken in an ethnic sense alone.

24. S.K. Aiyangar, *Some Contributions of South India to Indian Culture*, Calcutta, 1923, pp. 1–42.
25. *Manu*, X, 10–12; 16–17.
26. Others included the Āndhras, Ābhīra, Pulinda, Khāsa, Magadha, Kirāta, Malla. *Gautama Dharmaśāstra*, IV, 4; *Baudhāyana*, I, 9, 3; *Vasiṣṭha*, XVIII, 9.
27. *Gautama*, IV, 15ff; *Baudhāyana*, I, 8, 8; *Vasiṣṭha*, XVIII, 1–6.
28. *Manu*, X, 39.
29. *Aitareya Brāhmaṇa*, VIII, 21; The Āmbaṣṭha tribe is frequently identified by modern scholars with the Ambastanoi of Arrian and the Sambastoi of Diodorus. H.C. Raichaudhury, *Political History of Ancient India*, Calcutta, 1952, p. 255.
30. *Taittirīya Brāhmaṇa*, III, 8, 5.
31. *Taittirīya Saṃhitā*, I, 8, 9, 1–2; The *sūta* was one of the *ratnins* at the rites of the *vājapeya* sacrifice.
32. Pāṇini, II, 4, 10. R.S. Sharma, *Śūdras in Ancient India*, Delhi, 1958, p. 125, suggests that originally they may have been an aboriginal tribe using their own dialect, the *cāṇḍāla-bhāṣā*.
33. *Pañcaviṃśataka Brāhmaṇa*, XVII, 1, 9; 53, 2. *Āpastambha Dharma-sūtra*, XXII, 5, 4.
34. As for example the use *Manu* makes of the term *vrātya-kṣatriya* or 'degenerate *kṣatriyas*' when describing the Greeks, or *vrātya* for those who have failed to fulfil their sacred duties, X, 20; II, 39.
35. *Atharvaveda*, XV.
36. Also included were the Bedar, Daśārna, Mātaṅga, Pundra, Lamba-karṇa, Ekpāda, Yakṣa, Kinnara, Kīkata, Niṣāda. Some of these are fanciful names — Long-ears, Single-footed; some were celestial beings; but in the main both literature and epigraphs record the names of many of these peoples.
37. D.R. Chanana, *Agriculture in the Rāmāyaṇa*, New Delhi, 1964.
38. Yāska in *Nirukta*, II, 2. *Atharvaveda*, V, 22, 14; *Chāndogya Upaniṣad*, VI, 14, 1, 2.
39. The western Ānavas were the Yaudheyas, Āmbaṣṭha, Śibi, Sindhu, Sauvīra, Kaikeya, Madra, Vṛsadarbha. The eastern Ānavas were the people of Aṅga, Vaṅga, Kaliṅga, Pundra and Suhma. It has been suggested that the names ending in *aṅga* are of Muṇḍā origin and these tribes would therefore be pre-Aryan. P.C. Bagchi (ed.), *Pre-Aryan and Pre-Dravidian in India*, Calcutta, 1929.
40. *Aitareya Brāhmana*, VIII, 14, 23; *Śatapatha Brāhmana*, III, 2, 3, 5.
41. Atanatīya Sutta, *Dīgha Nikāya*, III, pp. 199ff.

42. *Brahmāṇḍa Purāṇa*, II, 19, 24; III, 59, 46, *Vāyu*, 91, 7; *Matsya*, 83, 34; 105, 20.
43. The Kuru tribe had a well-known status and antiquity. They acquired fame through the epic *Mahābhārata* which concerns a family feud between the Kauravas and the Pāṇḍavas, both members of the Kuru lineage. The Pañcālas were a confederation of five tribes. According to bardic tradition the royal family of the Pañcālas was an off-shoot of the Bharata family.
44. B.B. Lal, 'Further Copper Hoards from the Gangetic Basin . . . ', *Ancient India*, no. 7, 1951, pp. 20ff. S.P. Gupta, 'Indian Copper Hoards', *Journal of the Bihar Research Society*, XLIX, 1963, pp. 147ff.
45. *Śatapatha Brāhmana*, I, 4, 1, 10.
46. *Atharvaveda*, V.22.14. *Baudhāyana Dharmasūtra*, I, 1, 32–3; *Manu*, X, 11.
47. Texts as late as the *Mārkandeya Purāṇa* and the *Yajñvalkya Smṛti*, III, 292, repeat the need for the *prāyaścitta*.
48. *Prajñapana Upaṅga*, p. 397; *Ācāraṅga Sūtra*, II, 3, 1; II, 11, 17.
49. *Aṅguttara Nikāya*, I, 213. The sixteen *mahājanapadas* or major states are listed as Gandhāra, Kāmboja, Kuru, Pañcāla, Śūrasena, Matsya, Kośala, Kāśī, Malla, Vṛjji, Magadha, Aṅga, Vatsa, Cedi, Āvanti, Asmaka.
50. *Sammoha-vinodini*, Vibhaṅga commentary, 388; *Manoratha-purāṇi*, Anguttara Commentary, I, 409; *Apādāna*, II, 359; *Sutta Nipāta*, 977.
51. *Jātaka*, VI, 208, 210. Cf. *Manu*, X, 44.
52. *Summaṅgala Vilāsinī*, I, 276; *Sammoha-vinodini*, 388.
53. Ibid.; the ancestry of the Pulinda located in Ceylon alone, according to the Buddhist sources, derives from the marriage of prince Vijaya with the demoness Kuveni.
54. The *Caṇḍāla* is known and mentioned in Buddhist sources but usually in the context of his overcoming his low status although this is often done through the acquisition of some spiritual power.
55. Major Rock Edict, XII. J. Bloch, *Les Inscriptions d'Asoka*, pp. 130ff. Aśoka lists the Yona, Kāmboja, Nābhaka, Bhoja, Pitinika, Āndhra and Pālida.
56. The Second Separate Edict. J. Bloch, *Les Inscriptions d'Asoka*, pp. 140ff.
57. *Arthaśāstra*, II, 1; III, 16; VII, 8; VIII, 4; IX, 1; IX, 3; X, 2.
58. McCrindle, *India as Described by Megasthenes and Arrian*, pp. 20–1; McCrindle, *India as Described by Ktesias*, pp. 23–4, 86. Earlier Greek writers such as Ktesias, the Greek physician at the Persian court in the sixth century BC, referred to the Indian king trading cotton and weapons for fruit, dyes and gum with the Kynokephaloi or Kynomolgoi, a barbarian tribe. The identity of this tribe has not been conclusively established as yet.
59. *Matsya Purāṇa*, 34, 30; 50, 76.

60. Utpala's commentary on the *Bṛhatsamhitā*, XIII, 3, describes the Śakas as *mleccha-jātayo-rājanas* and adds that the period of their destruction by Vikramāditya would be known as *Śaka-kāla*.
61. A large number of early Sanskrit inscriptions come from the *mleccha* areas of northern and western India. *Corpus Inscriptionum Indicarum*, vol. II. The Greeks had used Greek and Prākrit or Sanskrit bilingually as on their coins: Obverse — *Basileus Suthos Menandros*, Reverse — *Mahārājas Trādarasa Menamdrasa*. Smith, *Catalogue of Coins in the Indian Museum*, Calcutta, vol. I, pp. 22ff. Kuṣāṇa coins show a slow but increasing adoption of Indian deities particularly of the Śaivite family. The Śaka kings not only affirm their protection of the law of *varṇa* but even record large donations of cows and villages and wealth to the *brāhmaṇas*. Rudradāman's Junāgadh Inscription, *Epigraphia Indica*, VIII, no. 6, pp. 44ff.
62. *Manu*, X, 43–4; *Mahābhārata*, Anuśāsana Parva, 35.17ff; Vana, 48.20ff; Śānti Parva, 65.13ff.
63. Kanakasabhai, *The Tamils Eighteen Hundred Years Ago*, Madras, 1904, pp. 37ff. M. Subramaniam, *Pre-Pallava Tamil Index*, Madras, 1966, p. 618.
64. McCrindle, *Invasion of India by Alexander*, p. 234; *Mahābhārata*, Sabhā Parva, 29.5ff; *British Museum Catalogue of Indian Coins*, p. cv. The legend reads, *mālava-gaṇasya-jaya*.
65. McCrindle, *The Invasion of India by Alexander*, p. 232; *Mahābhārata*, Sabhā Parva, 29.5ff; *Journal of the Numismatic Society of India*, IX, p. 82; *British Museum Catalogue*, p. cxxiv; the legend reads *sibi janapadasa*.
66. *Aṣṭādhyāyi*, V, 3, 116; *Mahābhārata*. Sabhā Parva, 29.5ff; the legends reads, *trakaṭaka janapadasa*. *Aṣṭādhyāyi*, IV, 1, 178; *British Museum Catalogue*, pp. cxlix–cl. The legend reads, *yaudheya-bahū-dhānyake*, and a fourth-century coin-mould reads, *yaudheya-gaṇasya-jaya*.
67. The Allahabad *praśasti* of Samudragupta. *Corpus Inscriptionum Indicarum*, III, pp. 66ff.
68. The eighteen major *Purāṇas* were recorded from about the third century AD onwards. They claim to be compendia of information orally transmitted over a period going back to *c.* 3000 BC. The texts deal with the mythologies of the creation of the universe, genealogies of kings and sages, social custom and religious practices generally pertaining to a particular sect of which each *Purāṇa* claims to be the sacred book. In fact much of the material reflects contemporary attitudes at the time of the composition of the *Purāṇa*. The genealogical sections are in the form of a prophecy, an obvious attempt to claim antiquity.
69. Puranic cosmology envisages a cyclical movement of time and the world goes through a period of four ages with the golden age at the

start and an increase in evil through the duration of the cycle. The last of the four is the Kaliyuga at the end of which evil will be prevalent and the *mleccha* all-powerful. Ultimately the entire universe will be totally destroyed after which a new universe will be created and the cycle will start again.

70. *Vāyu Purāṇa*, 99; *Bhāgvata*, XII, 2, 1–16; 44–51; II, 38; XII, 3, 25; 3, 35–6. Deprived of sacrificial activities the world will be reduced to *mleccha*-hood.
71. *Matsya Purāṇa*, 47, 252; *Vāyu*, 98, 114; *Brahmāṇḍa*, III, 14, 80; 22, 22; 73, 108; 35, 10; IV, 29, 131.
72. *Viṣṇu Purāṇa*, IV, 24, 51; *Brahmāṇḍa*, II, 16, 59; III, 14, 80; IV, 29, 131; *Manu*, X, 8–38; *Yājñavalkya smṛti*, III, 292; *Smṛti-candrikā*, I 22–4. This is particularly contradictory in the case of the *Purāṇas* where a number of *mleccha* cults and rites had become incorporated into the recognized religion, especially rites associated with the mother-goddess. For the reference to the Śakas and Yavanas see, e.g. Nasik Cave Inscription, *Epigraphia Indica*, VIII, no. 8, pp. 60ff.
73. In the Rudrādhyāya of the *Yajurveda*. Other degraded professions are the nomads, carpenters, chariot-makers, potters, smiths, fowlers, dog-keepers and hunters. In this text as also the *Nirukta* of Yāska they are mentioned as the fifth group after the four *varṇas*, III, 8; X, 3, 5–7.
74. *Manu*, X, 8, 18, 48. They were said to have been descended from the marriage between a *brāhmaṇa* and a *śūdra* woman.
75. *Garuḍa Purāṇa*, VI, 6; LV, 15; *Harivaṃśa*, XV, 27, 33.
76. *Viṣṇu Purāṇa*, I, 13.
77. *Matsya Purāṇa*, 10, 4–10; *Bhāgvata*, IV, 13, 42, 47; *Mahābhārata*, Śānti Parva, 59.99ff.
78. *Matsya Purāṇa*, 10, 7.
79. The *Amarakoṣa*, VII, 21; a lexicon of the post-Gupta period, in its definition of *mleccha* mentions these three tribes and describes them as hunters and deer killers, living in mountainous country, armed with bows and arrows and speaking an unintelligible language — the conventional description of the *mleccha* by the time of the medieval period. Yet the location of *mleccha-deśa* in this text is not in central India but in northern India.
80. *Ṛg Veda*, III, 53, 14; *Mahābhārata*, II.13.19ff; *Bhāgvata Purāṇa*, 11, 21, 8; *Manu*, X, 44.
81. *Mahābhārata*, 7.87.27ff.
82. *Mārkaṇḍeya Purāṇa*, p. 284; *Matsya Purāṇa*, 114, 307; a seventh-century author identifies them with the Bhila and Lubhdhaka tribes of the Vindhyas and also connects them with the Mātaṅga, the lawless hunters of the region, Daṇḍin, *Daśakumārcarita*, III, 104; VIII, 203.

The name Mātaṅga is very curious and suggests a Muṇḍā-Dravidian combination. The twelfth-century *Pampa Rāmāyaṇa* of Abhināva Pampa, VII, 105–55, also refers to them.

83. Bhāravi's long poem, the *Kirātārjunīya*, is based on an episode from the *Mahābhārata* when Arjuna goes into the Himalayas and does penance. He finally meets the god Śiva in the form of a Kirāta with whom he has a protracted fight, but eventually acquires the divine weapons which he is seeking. It is interesting that the Kirāta should be identified with Śiva — perhaps suggesting their worship of Śiva, and also that it is through a Kirāta that the great hero Arjuna acquires the divine weapons.
84. *Pampa Rāmāyaṇa*, Nijagunayogi's Vivekcintāmaṇi, pp. 423–4. Chikka Deva inscription of the seventeenth century in Rice, *Mysore and Coorg from its Inscriptions*, p. 129.
85. Buddhist sources refer to the children of the demoness whom prince Vijaya married on his arrival in Ceylon as the Pulinda and state that they lived in the interior of the island at a place called Sabaragamuva ( = Śabaragrāma, the village of the Śabaras?), *Mahāvaṃśa*, VII, 68; *Vinaya Piṭaka*, I, 168. These have come to be associated with the primitive Veddah tribes of Ceylon. In early brahmanical sources they are mentioned as a wild mountain tribe of the Deccan, *Aitareya Brāhmaṇa*, VII, 18; *Mahābhārata*, Ādī Parva, 165.3ff. Later sources connect them with the Bhillas, *Kathāsaritasāgara*, II, 12; *Amarakoṣa*, II, 20–1.
86. Ptolemy, VII, 1, 64; Ptolemy's phrase brings to mind the use of the *Piśāca* in Indian literature which also carries the meaning of those who eat raw flesh. Its most obvious connection is with the famous *Bṛhatkathā* of Guṇāḍhya which was written in a *Piśāca* or goblin language, and the location was the Vindhyas. Possibly the *Piśāca* language was that of these *mleccha* tribes. Interestingly, it is often associated by some scholars with the north western areas which may suggest a migration of some at least of these peoples from the northwest to the Vindhyas. Keith, *A History of Sanskrit Literature*, Oxford, 1928, pp. 266ff.
87. *Rāmāyaṇa*, I.54.1–3; *Kathāsaritasāgara*, IV, 22.
88. *Nāṭyaśāstra*, XXI, 89; *Bṛhatkathāślokasangraha*, VIII, 31.
89. *Rāmāyaṇa*, Ādī Kāṇḍa, I, 47ff; Araṇya Kāṇḍa, LXXVII, 6–32. Bāṇa, *Kādambari*, p. 12.
90. Dholpur Inscription, *Indian Antiquary*, XIX, p. 35; Khadavada Inscription of the time of Gyas Sahi of Mandu, *Journal of the Bombay Branch of the Royal Asiatic Society*, XXIII, p. 12.
91. *Rāmāyana*, IV, 37–8.
92. *Amuktamālyada*, IV, 206.

93. *Viṣṇu Dharmasūtra*, 71, 59, 84, 2–4; *Vasiṣṭha*, 6, 41; *Gautama*, IX, 17; *Atri*, VII, 2. The *śrāddha* ceremony was an essential rite for the *ārya* since it concerned the offering of food to the spirits of the ancestors and thereby strengthened and re-affirmed kin-ties. It is clearly stated in the above texts that the *ārya* is prohibited from speaking with the *mleccha*, from learning their language or from making journeys to a *mleccha-deśa* since contact with the *mleccha* was polluting. The journeys were regarded with particular disapproval since the *śrāddha* ceremony could not be performed in such areas.
94. *Medātithi*, a tenth-century commentator, on *Manu*, II, 23.
95. *Mahāvastu*, I, 135, *Raghuvaṃśa*, IV, 67–8.
96. Eran Stone Boar Inscription, *Corpus Inscriptionum Indicarum*, vol. III, p. 158; G.R. Sharma, *Excavations at Kauśāmbi*, pp. 15–16.
97. *Rājataraṅgiṇī*, I, 306–7; Kalhaṇa calls him the 'god of destruction', I.289.
98. E.g. Hsüan Tsang's descriptions: S. Beal, *Buddhist Records of the Western World*, I, London, 1883, pp. 177ff.
99. Dhānyaviṣṇu the brother of Matṛviṣṇu (*viśayapati* of the Gupta king Budhagupta) became the feudatory of Toramāna. Cf. The Eran Inscription of Budhagupta, *Corpus Inscriptionum Indicarum*, III, p. 89 with the Eran Stone Boar Inscription of Toramāna, op. cit., p. 158. Budhagupta in his inscription is referred to merely as *bhupati* (king), whereas Toramāna takes the full imperial title of *Mahārājādhirāja* and is described as 'the glorious', 'of great fame and lustre' and 'ruling the earth'.
100. It was believed that the Gurjaras came from central Asia after the sixth century AD and were of Tocharian extraction, D.R. Bhandarkar, *Indian Antiquary*, January 1911, pp. 21–2; A.C. Bannerjee, *Lectures in Rajput History*, p. 7; P.C. Bagchi, *India and Central Asia*, Calcutta, 1955, p. 17. But this view is now being replaced by their being of north Indian origin. Place names in the Punjab — Gujrat, Gujeranwala, etc., — suggest a settlement there as do the presence of the Gujjar herdsmen in Kashmir. The Gurjara Pratihāras ruled in western India, and there is the more recent Gujarat as a name of western India. The existence of the Gujjar caste in Maharashtra points to a further movement towards the south; I. Karve, *Hindu Society*, Poona, 1961. The Bad-Gujar clan survives among the Rajputs as also the *brāhmaṇa* caste, Gujar-Gauḍa.

    The Ābhīra are nomadic herdsmen who are believed to have migrated into India with the Scythians. Some of them very soon rose to importance, such as the general Rudrabhūti, Gunda Inscription of AD 181 in *Epigraphia Indica*, VIII, p. 188. They are located in the lower Indus and Kathiawar region, *Bhāgvata Purāṇa*, 1, 10,

35; *Periplus*, 41; *Ptolemy*, VII, 1, 55. The Ābhīras are described as *mlecchas* and *śūdras* in status, *Manu*, X, 15; *Mahābhāṣya*, I, 2, 72. They gradually took over political power from the Śakas and the Sātavāhanas and spread down the west coast of India where there is mention of the Konkanābhīra, *Bṛhatsamhitā*, 14, 12; 5, 42; 14, 18. Samudragupta in the Allahabad *praśasti* refers to the conquest of the Ābhīras, *Corpus Inscriptionum Indicarum*, III, 6ff. A tenth-century Pratihāra inscription speaks of removing the menace of the Ābhīras in western India, Ghatiyala Pillar Inscription, *Epigraphia Indica*, IX, p. 280.

101. This situation is discussed by R.S. Sharma in his book, *Indian Feudalism*, Calcutta, 1965.
102. Ghatiyala Pillar Inscription, *Epigraphia Indica*, IX, p. 280.
103. The Gaṅga and Caṇḍella dynasty claim Candravaṃśi descent, the Gurjara-Pratihāras Sūryavaṃśi descent and the Parmāras regard their ancestor as having emerged from the Agnikula. The Guhilas, the Cālukyas of Veṅgi, the Cālukyas of Bādāmi and the Cālukyas of Kalyāni all claim solar descent, D.C. Sircar, 'The Guhila Claim of Solar Origin', *The Journal of Indian History*, 1964, no. 42.
104. An example of this, which was a common condition, is discussed in D.C. Sircar, *The Guhilas of Kishkinda*, Calcutta, 1965. Even the Khaśa chiefs claim *kṣatriya* status in the Bodh Gaya inscription, *Epigraphia Indica*, XII, p. 30. The Pratihāra claim to descent from Lakṣmaṇa the younger brother of Rāma who acted as a door-keeper (*pratihāra*) also leads to a suspicion about their origins, *Indian Antiquary*, January 1911, p. 23.
105. R.S. Sharma, 'Early Indian Feudalism', in S. Gopal and R. Thapar (eds), *Problems of Historical Writing in India*, New Delhi, 1963, p. 74. These ideas are further worked out in his *Social Changes in Early Medieval India*.

    The same policy was adopted by the Mughals who located colonists in these areas partly to encourage them in the ways of Islam and of 'civilization' and partly to keep a check on them, particularly at the time of the Maratha-Mughal conflict when the Vindhyan tribes occupied a strategic geographical position. It is not surprising that, during the period of British rule in India, Christian missionaries were extremely active in these regions.
106. Una Pillar Inscription of Avantivarman II dated AD 899, *Epigraphia Indica*, IX, pp. 6ff.
107. Atpur Inscription of Śaktikumār, *Indian Antiquary*, XXXIX, pp. 191ff.
108. *Kanhadeprabandha* of Padmanābha, a fifteenth-century work, mentions a Hūṇa among the list of Rajput *jagīrdārs*, *The Journal of Indian History*, XXXVIII, p. 106.
109. *Amarakoṣa*, II, 10, 2.

110. Rice, *Mysore and Coorg from the Inscriptions*, London, 1913, p. 5.
111. *Epigraphia Carnatica*, VII, p. 188; VI, pp. 113–14.
112. The Gaṅga king Koṅgunivarman gave a grant in AD 887.
113. B.N. Saletore, *Wild Tribes in Indian History*, Delhi, 1936, pp. 81ff.
114. Ray, *Dynastic History of Northern India*, II, Calcutta, 1936, p. 941.
115. Bargaon Copper-plate of Ratnapāla, *Journal of the Asiatic Society of Bengal*, p. 99; Pārbatiya plates of Vanmālaverrāmadeva, *Epigraphia Indica*, XXIX, pp. 145ff. It has been suggested that the name Śalastambha approximates a Sanskritized version of the name of the Tibetan king, Sron-bstam-sgam-po.
116. *Manu*, X, 43–4; *Matsya Purāṇa*, 16, 16.
117. *Bṛhatsamhitā*, V, 80; *Mārkaṇḍeya Purāṇa*, 57, 39. Chinese interest in eastern India during the seventh century AD is attested to in the reign of Harṣa and by his contemporaries in Assam. The pedestal inscription on the tomb of Tai Tsung mentions a diplomatic connection with eastern India.
118. Gwalior Inscription of Nagabhaṭṭa I; Sagar Tal Inscription, *Epigraphia Indica*, XVIII, pp. 107ff. An Arab attack in the eighth century is mentioned in the *Rājataraṅgiṇī*, VIII, 2764.
119. Māhamadi Sāhi Inscription, *Epigraphia Indica*, I, p. 93; Jaitrasiṃhadeva grant, *Epigraphia Indica*, XXXII, pp. 220ff; Chitorgarh *praśasti*, *Journal of the Bombay Branch of the Royal Asiatic Society*, XXIII, p. 49; Madras Museum Plates, *Epigraphia Indica*, VIII, p. 9; Bhilsa Inscrip tion of Jayasiṃha, *Epigraphia Indica*, XXXV, p. 187; Danteswara Inscription of AD 1703, *Epigraphia Indica*, IX, p. 164.
120. Bhatūrya Inscription of Rajyapāla, *Epigraphia Indica*, XXXIII, p. 150; Chitorgarh *praśasti* of Rana Kumbhakarṇa, *Journal of the Bombay Branch of the Royal Asiatic Society*, XXIII, p. 49; Bālaghāta Plate of Prithviśena II, *Epigraphia Indica*, IX, p. 270.
121. Sāgar Tal Inscription of Mihīra Bhoja, *Epigraphia Indica*, XVIII, pp. 107ff.
122. Śaka inscriptions reveal this very clearly as also the names of the Indo-Greeks, *Epigraphia Indica*, VII, pp. 53, 55; *Epigraphia Indica*, VIII, 90; *Archaeological Survey of Western India*, IV, pp. 92ff.
123. Mention is made of the Gandhāra and Kāmbhoja melodies as also of Śaka and Ābhīra melodies, *Pañcatantra*, Apanikṣetakanakam, 55.
124. From this point of view at least Indian eating habits and rituals would form an ideal subject for structuralist analysis, along the lines of the theories developed by Lévi-Strauss. See *Manu*, IV, 205–25; 247–53; for laws regarding the acceptance of various kinds of food.
125. Trikāṇḍaśesa in *Nāmalinganuśāsana* of Amarakoṣa.
126. For the prohibition on onions and garlic, *Manu*, V, 19; for references to eating the flesh of the cow, *Jaimini*, I, 3, 10 and *Rājataraṅgiṇī*, VII, 1232.

127. *Mahābhārata*, Śānti Parva, LXV, 13–15.
128. *Viṣṇu Dharmaśāstra*, 84; *Arthaśāstra*, III, 13–15.
129. Mathura Lion Capital Inscription, *Epigraphia Indica*, IX, p. 141; Mandasor Inscription, *CII*, III, p. 81; Viṣṇudatta Inscription, *Epigraphia Indica*, VIII, p. 88. Śaka kings often refer to themselves as *dhārmika* on coin legends with the symbol of the *Dharmacakra* on the coin.
130. *Journal of the Royal Asiatic Society*, 1909, pp. 1053ff.
131. Eran Stone Boar Inscription. The *varāha* cave is at Udayagiri.
132. As for example the reference to Jalauka in the *Rājataraṅgiṇī*, I, 108–52.
133. The snake cult or worship of the Nāga is attested to in literature as well as in the archaeological remains of a multitude of *nāga* shrines. It is frequently seen as the symbol of the chthonic goddess, of the ancestors and of lunar and fertility cults, and is commonly found even to this day in the Himalayan and Vindhyan regions. In the historical period it gained considerable respectability particularly in the peninsula.
134. There is mention in the *Ṛg Veda* of the pre-Aryan cults such as the worship of the phallus, *śiśnadevāḥ*, and the existence of sorceresses, *yātumati*, practising magic. The Harappan evidence supports the worship of the mother goddess which was not predominant in the Ṛgvedic religion.
135. *Harivaṃśa*, II, 22, 59.
136. Ibid., II, 22, 53–4.
137. Ibid., II, 3, 12. She is sometimes described as *kṛṣṇacahvisāma*, *kṛṣṇa* (as black as can be), adorned with peacock feathers and with dishevelled hair. Bāṇa, writing in the seventh century AD when speaking of the *mleccha* tribe of the Vindhyas, describes a Durgā temple, *Kādambari*, 417–26. Of the Pulindas said to be living in the Vindhyan region, an eleventh-century text states that their king adores the cruel Devī, offers her human victims and pillages the caravans, *Kathāsaritasāgara*, IV, 22.
138. *Harivaṃśa*, II, 58; *Daśakumāracarita*, I, 14; VI, 149; VIII, 206.
139. Vākpati, *Gauḍavāho*, V, 305.
140. *Mārkaṇḍeya Purāṇa*, LXXXII, 10–18.
141. *Bhaviṣya Purāṇa*, II, 26; I, 39. *Samba Purāṇa*, 27, 28.
142. *Mahābhārata*, Aṇu Parva, XC, 11. *Manu*, III, 162.
143. *Bṛhatsamhitā*, LX, 19.
144. Maureen Patterson, 'Chitpavan Brahman Family Histories', in *Structure and Change in Indian Society*, Milton Singer and B. Cohn (eds), Chicago, 1968.

# III

# *Archaeology and History*

I have had some hesitation in including these papers since the evidence for the interpretation of archaeological data changes, sometimes radically, with new excavations. These papers were written a long time back and some of the archaeological evidence quoted has now been superceded by more recent evidence. Some of the arguments therefore would now have to be different. My eventual decision to include them was because each of them has a methodological base which might be of interest to historians.

The first paper included in this section is an attempt at integrating a large range of archaeological and literary evidence to suggest the location of three place names mentioned in Mesopotamian sources as being regions of the Indus valley and western India in the Harappan and Post-Harappan period. As is often the case when the range of data are so wide, the intention becomes over ambitious. This paper was 'critically reconsidered' in *JESHO*, 1978, XXI, ii, 113–45, to which my equally lengthy reply was published as, 'The Dravidian Hypothesis for the Identification of Meluhha, Dilmun and Makan', in *JESHO*, 1982, XXVI, ii, 178–90. I have nevertheless included the paper since methodologically the use of archaeological and literary data for place-name studies has considerable potential.

The subsequent papers are attempts at looking afresh at the period 1500–500 BC relating to what is commonly referred to as 'the Aryan hypothesis'. These again attempt a co-relating of archaeological and literary data, suggesting various possibilities and some caveats. A historiographical approach to the concept of Aryan race and its appropriation by various groups of Indians, is discussed in the final paper in Section IX.

1. A Possible Identification of Meluhha, Dilmun and Makan (1978)
2. Society in Ancient India: The Formative Period (1969)

3. The Archaeological Background to the Agnicayana Ritual (1983)
4. Archaeological Artifacts and Literary Data: An Attempt at Co-relation (1987)

# 13

# *A Possible Identification of Meluhha,* Dilmun and Makan***

The identifications of Dilmun, Meluhha and Makan have been subject to considerable controversy. Recently however some consensus seems to have developed. Meluhha, it has been forcefully argued by Leemans in more than one place, was probably the western sea-board of the Indian subcontinent and more specifically the region which is known today as Gujerat.[1] Makan has been identified either with Oman or with Baluchistan and the Makran coast. Kramer on the other hand has argued for the identification of Makan and Meluhha with Egypt and Ethiopia.[2] The Indus Civilisation was suggested for a possible identification of Dilmun, but recent views have tended to support its identification with one of the Persian Gulf islands, either Bahrain or Failaka,[3] possibly the first. The arguments used so far have relied on archaeological data and cultural similarities but these have not provided any evidence which can be regarded as conclusive.[4] An attempt is being made in this paper to add a further dimension to these arguments by using linguistic evidence as well. The result seems to confirm the

* The transcription of Meluhha is incomplete because of the non-availability of type. [RT.]

** *JESHO*, 1978, 18, 1, 1–42.

*Acknowledgements:* I would like to acknowledge assistance received on the linguistic analysis suggested here. For information on the linguistic structure of Sumerian I am grateful to Prof. S.N. Kramer and Dr J.V. Kinnier Wilson. As regards the linguistic evidence from Indian sources I have discussed my views with Prof. Bh. Krishnamurti, Prof. P.B. Pandit and Mr I. Mahadevan. The latter two, not always in agreement with my analysis, have offered useful critical comments. To Prof. Bh. Krishnamurti I am particularly grateful for discussing each entry included here and for finally giving me clearance as regards the linguistic validity of the proposed reconstructions.

identification of Meluhha with Gujerat and Makan with Sind and Baluchistan. Furthermore Dilmun may also have been a part of western India.

That the western sea-board of the Indian subcontinent played a major role in the maritime commerce of Mesopotamia is apparent for a number of reasons both geographical and archaeological. The nature of the land along the west coast — the presence of havens, creeks and a narrow hinterland with frequent and well-defined routes into the plateau inland, a ready availability of a variety of raw materials and the fact of its facing the inter-continental nodes of south-west Asia — would all point to this area being active in maritime trade from very early periods.[5]

When looking at the evidence from this period it is as well to keep in mind that the geographical contours of western India were different from what they are in the present day. There is little doubt that the peninsula of Kathiawar was an island. The same was true for Kutch which was not submerged, as has been the view in the past, because it has yielded numerous Harappan settlements some of which were fortified and of substantial size.[6] Both Kutch and Kathiawar are regarded as semi-insular even today. It has been maintained that the delta of the Indus was further north and the coastline was proximate to the present day sites of Karachi, Ibrahim Hydari, Tharri Gujo, Tatta and Pir Patho.[7] Harappan sites have not as yet been found in the delta of the Indus south of Tharri Gujo. The coastline from the Indus delta to Gujerat would thus have bye-passed the islands of Kutch and Kathiawar. It has also been suggested that the Gulf of Cambay may have extended further to the north in earlier times and that it may have been connected with what are today called the two Ranns. The existence of a salt water lake, the Null, in the isthmus of Kathiawar is suggestive of an earlier stretch of sea in this area. In the third millennium BC, the period with which we are concerned, north-western and western India was in addition, the location of the Indus Civilisation. It would seem logical that this being the major contemporary civilisation in geographical proximity and to the east of Sumer, the latter could have had its major maritime contacts with the Harappa culture. Not surprisingly archaeological evidence has revealed contacts between the two areas both overland and via the Persian Gulf.[8]

That the historical context of the third millennium BC and the geographical frame of reference to these contacts was the area which stretched from the Tigris and Euphrates to the Indus valley and included Iran, is becoming clear from the archaeological evidence from sites in the southern half of Iran which suggests parallels with the pre-Harappan and the Harappan culture of north-western India. The steatite objects from Tepe Yahya are a case in point.[9] The close parallels for bunshaped copper ingots, copper amulets and a copper animal figurine from both Susa and Lothal during the third millennium BC has already been pointed out.[10] The presence of Harappan artifacts at Mesopotamian sites particularly at Akkadian levels was noticed some decades back.[11] The objects were mainly pottery, beads, shell inlays and seals of the Indus style. Similarities in male figurine shapes has also been noticed.[12] The presence of the 'reserved slip ware' noticed at Ur and Brak and also in the early levels of Mohenjo-daro and Lothal, at various sites in Baluchistan, and more recently in Kutch,[13] suggest possible pre-Akkadian contacts. The origin and distribution of the Ubaid culture is also beginning to be seen from a rather new perspective involving the Persian Gulf and its coastal areas, with recent exploration in the Saudi Arabian part of the Gulf.[14] The close relations between south Iran and Baluchistan in the pre-Harappan period may have permitted some Sumerian contact with western India, possibly not a direct link but a communication of goods and ideas through the intermediary communities in southern Iran and the Persian Gulf region. The later role of the Gulf in trade relations may well have had its antecedents in these earlier cultures.

The generally accepted Carbon-14 dates for the Harappa culture of 2300–1750 BC are doubted by some archaeologists such as Wheeler who prefers an earlier start of *c.* 2500 BC.[15] The recent debate on Carbon-14 dating suggests that with calibration the beginnings of the Harappa culture may have to be dated to the earlier half of the third millennium BC. This would lead to a fairly close synchronism in the chronology of the Indus civilisation with that of Sumer.[16] However, it is quite possible that Sumerian contacts with these areas could date to the pre-Harappan period. The nature of the earlier trade may not have required the entrepreneurship of the Harappan merchants. The presence of pre-Harappan levels in the Harappan cities indicate the possibility of pre-Harappan contacts whose economic significance would be of a different kind as compared to the later Harappan contacts.

For the linguistic identification of the place names assuming that they are in north-western and western India, there are four possible alternatives: that the names are Sumerian, or that they conform to one of the two language groups associated with this area in the historical period — Indo-Aryan or Proto-Dravidian, or that they belong to some other language group hitherto unassociated with the linguistic area of north-western India. Dilmun, Meluhha and Makan appear to be non-Sumerian as they have no recognisable meaning in Sumerian. The last alternative also seems doubtful since there has not been to-date, any evidence of a language other than the two referred to, in this part of the subcontinent. Of the two languages, which could possibly have existed historically in north-western India in the past, Indo-Aryan provides neither any meaning for the place-names nor can the names be traced to Sanskrit sources. We are thus left with the only alternative, that of testing the hypothesis of proto-Dravidian, which is what is being explored in this paper.

For the linguistic and cultural basis of the identifications I have used two theories recently put forward regarding the existence of languages in India from the third to the first millennia BC. Various scholars working in the field of Indo-European and Dravidian linguistics, have suggested on the basis of the influence of Dravidian phonology and vocabulary in Vedic Sanskrit, that there was originally a Dravidian language foundation, and at the time of the expansion of the Sanskrit speakers (from the mid-second millennium BC onwards) there was a substratum of Dravidian speakers and a period of bilingualism, which would account for the Dravidian intrusions into Sanskrit.[17] As regards the priority in time of a non-Sanskritic language in this region there is the evidence not only of Brahui in the north-west but pockets of other languages of the Dravidian group elsewhere in northern India, as also, the relatively late arrival and diffusion of languages of the Indo-European group in west Asia and Iran where the earliest evidence for these dates from the Kassites, Mitannis and Hittites to the second millennium BC. Recently an attempt has been made on the basis of the linguistic structure of Dravidian to provide a chronological context to its spread where it is suggested that the highland folk in north-eastern Iran were using Proto-Dravidian in *c.* 4000 BC. From here they travelled south-eastwards to the Indus plains and western India from the fourth millennium BC onwards and later to the peninsula of India.[18] Another suggestion is that given the substratum of Dravidian speakers and a period of bilingualism, then some at least of the words used in Sanskrit for names, objects and places would tend to be either transliterations or more often, translations from the original proto-Dravidian. There would thus exist a linguistic and cultural parallelism where some Dravidian culture concepts would get translated into Sanskrit.[19] This parallelism would extend from language to mythology and custom, although the inclusion of it within the corpus of Sanskritic tradition may well be partial.

It can, therefore, be assumed as an hypothesis on the basis of the arguments suggested above, that a form of proto-Dravidian was the earliest language stratum of north-western India. It would then be possible to argue that the Sumerian place names Meluhha, Dilmun and Makan — if situated in the area of the proto-Dravidian language — are renderings of Proto-Dravidian names and that once their geographical identification has been ascertained, the later Sanskrit names for these same geographical areas could well be translations of the Proto-Dravidian name. This would have been a likely step on the part of the Sanskrit speakers when they came into contact with these areas and their inhabitants. The geographical identification would have to be established on both linguistic and archaeological grounds and the Sanskrit translation would act as an additional crosscheck on the geographical identification. The situation would be similar to the process of later centuries when Sanskrit-speaking peoples arrived in various parts of South India and in some cases made literal Sanskrit translations of the non-Sanskritic place-names, sometimes even misunderstanding the original meaning. Thus the Ezhimalai area of north Kerala was understood by the Sanskrit speakers as *ezhu-malai/eli-malai* ('the seven hills' or 'the rat hill') and translated into Sanskrit as *Sapta-Śailam* and *Mūṣika-śailam*.[20] In areas where Sanskrit was not well-established during the early historical period, the Sanskrit place-names would tend to be renderings of the original.

Language affinities being as fluid as they were (and are) it is difficult to give precisely defined geographical boundaries to language areas, more so in a period as early as the one under discussion. In suggesting the Proto-Dravidian reconstructions which follow, our primary concern is with their validity as reconstructions, irrespective of whether or not they occur in these forms in the Dravidian languages of the historical period.

Sumerian and Akkadian sources mention the names of a large

number of places with which the Sumerians traded and the products obtained from these regions. Among the place-names mentioned most frequently and which it would seem were in close proximity since they are often mentioned as a cluster, are Meluhha, Dilmun and Makan.[21] As regards the phonetic values of these names the following points may be worth noting:[22]

i. t- and d- sounds are often interchangeable in Sumerian writing as also are -k- and -g- in several cases. Hence the variant readings of Tilmun and Dilmun and Makan and Magan.
ii. Vocalic height is not clear in several cuneiform signs and readings vary, especially those relating to *e* and *i*. Thus Dilmun can as well be read as Delmun, or Telmun.
iii. Sumerian does not appear to have retroflex consonants.
iv. The change from -kk- to -hh- is uncommon in Sumerian, and the reading of the second syllable of Tilmun seems to be ascertained by the written form *Til-mu-nu*, but if the toponyms Meluhha and Tilmun are borrowed from another language, change of these sounds could well have been possible.[23]

Of the three place-names, Meluhha is among those which although mentioned frequently by Sumerian sources is mentioned far less in late sources.[24] In one of the Sumerian myths, the god Enki blesses the prosperous land of Meluhha and its *dar* birds. There is also a reference to the *magilum* boat of Meluhha which transports silver and gold and brings them to Nippur for Enlil. Judging from the hymn on 'Enki and the World Order', Meluhha was closely connected with Dilmun and Makan. It is said that Meluhha was conquered by Rimush (2315–2307). In the reign of Naram-Sin (2291–2255) we are told that the people of Meluhha, the men of the black-land bring to Naram-Sin all kinds of exotic wares. These included carnelian and lapis lazuli. In the period of Gudea of Lagash (*c.* 2100 BC) it supplies a red stone (carnelian?) and wood for his temples. Gudea speaks of Makan and Meluhha as if they were situated at the geographical extremity of the then-known world. It would seem that western India was probably the eastern extremity of Mesopotamian geography. The products of Meluhha are listed as carnelian, which appears to have been a major export, mes-magan-na wood and fine sea(?)-wood. It is also noted for its sailors and its people are described as maritime people. Economic documents of the Third Dynasty of Ur (2113–2006) refer to the import of copper, ivory, carnelian and onions from both Meluhha and Makan. Subsequent to this, mention of Meluhha declines noticeably. It then appears to be outside the area of actual contact. Unlike Dilmun for example, no wars are mentioned, no names of its kings and its traders. It remains a supplier of copper, stone, timber and plants as also some porphyry, marble and gold-dust.[25]

Meluhha was apparently a coastal area, hence the reference to sailors and maritime people. The fine sea-wood probably meant a quality of wood which is resistant to weathering by sea water. This may well have been teak, referred to in the earliest Indian sources as the prime wood for ship-building and commonly used in the historical period for this purpose in western India and the Persian Gulf.[26] The reference to carnelian would suggest Gujerat on the west coast of India which has access to the rich carnelian deposits of Rajpipla and the Narmada region. Kidney-shaped carnelian beads are specially associated with the Harappa culture and are listed as imports from Meluhha.[27] The major centre for lapis lazuli has been generally located in Badakshan (northern Afghanistan) which would involve the transportation of the lapis lazuli from there to the coastal parts of Iran or western India. It is possible however that there may have been another source for lapis lazuli in the Satpura range of western India. The northern half of the Western Ghats, known to later Sanskrit sources as the Sahyādri range, was also associated with the Vaidūryaparvata, *vaidūrya* being the Sanskrit name for lapis lazuli.[28] The Vaidūryaparvata is generally identified with the Oroudian of Ptolemy which would again suggest the northern part of the western Ghats. Initially in the early third millennium BC, the northern sites of Mesopotamia seem to have been active in the lapis trade, but later it declined in the north and became more active in the southern sites.[29] The excavation at Lothal has yielded two beads of lapis lazuli suggesting that either it was locally obtained or that the traders of Lothal had access to the Badakshan sources.[30] The *Periplus* lists lapis lazuli as among the exports of western India.[31] However, the lapis lazuli found in Mesopotamia appears to have been obtained from Badakshan.

The name Meluhha suggests a possible Proto-Dravidian (P.Dr.) original of **mēlukku* (DED 4173) meaning 'up, high, the extremity' and by extension 'superior' and also 'western'. The latter, occurring in a more limited number of Dravidian languages would derive from the root **mēl* by the addition of *-ukku* indicating direction as in the case of other words of direction, viz. **kīẓ*: **kīẓ-a-kku* 'east, place below' (DED 1348), **teṉ-kku* 'south' (DED 2839) and **vaṭ-a-kku* 'north' (DED 4267). A possible alternative in Dravidian would be *mēl-kku*; *mēl-u-kku*, meaning 'high place, west extremity'. **mēl* means 'high, excellent, eminent'. The *-kk-* could have been transliterated into *–hh–* in Sumerian, the word being non-Sumerian. There is a close translation of P.Dr. **mēlukku* in Sanskrit, namely *aparānta*, which also means 'the extremity' and 'western'. Aparānta in most of the *Purāṇas* was the name of the western sea-board and more specifically of southern Gujerat and northern Konkan.[32] There is one Purāṇa however in which Aparānta is located as north of the Sindhu-Sauvīra region.[33]

There could be two possible identifications for Meluhha. One would be to the north or north-west of Sind[34] allowing access to the lapis lazuli trade, but at the same time reducing the possibility of its being a coastal region, unless it came as far south as the Makran coast. Alternatively it could be identified with the sea-board of western India. If it was the former, then it would be approximately to the west of the Harappa culture, whereas if it was the latter, it would not be to the west but would certainly be at the extremity of the area of distribution of Harappan sites. Perhaps the association of the word with the west was a later addition and referred to the fact that in the lay-out of the Harappan cities, the higher mound, which was the location of the elite groups and therefore associated with superiority and excellence, was invariably to the west. From the point of view of later geographical nomenclature, Aparānta would certainly conform more readily to the western sea-board. The reference to the land of the black people also suggests Gujerat.[35] Alternatively, Meluhha may originally have been situated further to the west, but from the time of Sargon of Akkad it appears to have been identified with Gujerat (i.e., the estuaries of the Sabarmati, Mahi, Narmada, Tapti) and the northern Konkan.[36] The *Periplus* (of the first century AD) describes the people of present-day Gujerat as being dark in complexion and tall in stature.[37] It refers to the interior part of Ariake (Aparānta) as Aberia, doubtless named after the Ābhīra tribe settled there and to its sea-board as Syrastrene (Surāṣṭra). In this connection it may also be pointed out that the region adjoining the Konkan (on the west coast of India) was known in historical times as Karnāṭaka which some scholars derive from the Dravidian *kar-naḍu* meaning 'the black country'.[38]

During the Akkadian period contact with Meluhha was evident. In the country of Meluhha the centre for carrying on trade with Sumer may perhaps have been Lothal, which according to its excavator was a village site and from *c.* 2450 BC with the arrival of the Harappans, developed into an urban settlement with the characteristics of the settlement pattern of other Harappan cities.[39] The evidence of Harappan objects at Akkadian levels in Sumer further endorse the contact between at least one Harappan city and Sumer. In the early levels at Lothal there is evidence of 'the reserved slip ware'[40] which also occurs at Ur and Brak and was found recently in the early levels at Surkotada in Kutch.[41] The jewellery hoard from Lothal including nine circular beads with axial tubes, reminiscent of the royal cemetry at Ur, further strengthens the evidence for contact.[42] The discovery of a Persian Gulf seal at Lothal indicates contact with the major arteries of trade in the Persian Gulf.[43] A substantial bead factory was also located at Lothal for the production of carnelian, agate, opal, crystal and stone beads.

There is evidence from Lothal of copper-smiths' workshops and the discovery of a bun-shaped copper ingot similar to those found at Susa. The excavator of Lothal suggests therefore that the ingot was imported from west Asia. But it could as well be argued that the ingots were exported from Lothal. It has been argued that the constituents of the ore do not agree with that of Khetri, possibly the major copper-mining area of Rajasthan, since the Khetri ore has 0.06 per cent arsenic, the latter being totally absent from the ingot. Mohenjodaro copper objects do indicate the presence of arsenic. However, the presence of arsenic in such a minute quantity does not really allow a firm conclusion since even the copper analyses from Sumerian city-sites vary. The copper from Khafaje and Ur contain arsenic, whereas that from Kish has virtually none.[44] A recent analysis of the metallurgical content of Khetri ore and artefacts from the Ahar excavations has led to the conclusion that there is reasonable ground to believe that Rajasthan copper was used at Ahar in *c.* 2000 BC There is also evidence of contact between settlements in Saurashtra at this time and the Ahar culture.[45] This would suggest, contrary to the view stated above, that the people of Saurashtra may have used Rajasthan ores. (The question of metallurgical analysis needs to be examined further with the investigation of the total impurity pattern of copper from artefacts from the sites in Mesopotamia, the Indus Civilisation and ores available in northern and western India). The ingots from Lothal and Susa are similar in size (10 × 4 cms) whereas those from Mohenjo-daro are larger (15 × 24 cms).[46] The provenance of the ingots remains uncertain. It is worth noting that copper is not easily available at Susa; that there are substantial copper-smiths' workshops and furnaces at Lothal and Harappa suggesting a considerable manufacture of copper with the proximity of copper in Rajasthan and the Kirthar Range of Sind; and perhaps most significantly the thick, terracotta, bowl-like crucible found at the copper-smiths' workshops at Lothal would result in the production of a bun-shaped ingot.[47] The period of maximum activity in the copper-smithies appears to coincide with that of the import of 'the reserved slip ware' and the beads of Mesopotamian origin. Given the limited evidence there seems little reason to doubt that the ingots were produced at Lothal (and possibly other sites of the Indus civilisation) and exported to west Asia. If the theory of the dock at Lothal is acceptable then it could have been a major centre trading with Mesopotamia. In any case there is little doubt that it was among the major centres of production.[48] Harappa culture sites located in the estuarine regions as far south as the Tapti delta have been described as late Harappan by one archaeologist, but another view believes them to be earlier and suggests that it would not be surprising to find occasional Harappa sites even further south.[49] Traders and sailors from Gujerat would have to move southwards along the west coast to acquire supplies of timber. Further inland along the Tapti river, late Harappan sites have been found as far as the Dhulia District.[50]

The alleged conquest of Meluhha by Rimush raises a problem since there does not appear to be any archaeological evidence for such a conquest.[51] It can, however, be suggested that the conquest was nominal, and possibly indicated an extension of control over raw materials. The date of Rimush is close enough to the suggested date of the Harappan settlement at Lothal. 'Conquest' and 'tribute' in the ancient world did not always refer to actual conquest. Even diplomatic missions and trade relations were often included in such terms, frequently occurring in royal inscriptions. Sources referring to the Old Babylonian period include among imports from Meluhha, blackwood — presumably ebony or alternatively the dark-hued rosewood. Both of these could have been locally available or else brought from the southern regions of the Western Ghats, where they grow to this day. The esu-wood (Akkadian *ešû* or *ušû*) imported from Meluhha and mentioned in an inscription of Gudea has been identified as ebony because of the association of the word with stone in Sumerian and the mention of the blackwood of Meluhha.[52] The habitat of *Ebenaceae*, the order familiar to western India, is the western Ghats, north Konkan and parts of Rajasthan, an area which would to a large extent coincide with the location of Meluhha.[53] Wood remains from Lothal have been identified as Acacia Speciosa (khair), Albizzia Speciosa (sirissa), Tectona Grandis (teak), Adina Cordifolia (haldu) and Soymida Febrifuga (rohan).[54] Teak wood specimens were found in the dockyard at Lothal and it is stated that teak grew in abundance in the Panchmahals District of Gujerat at that time.[55] Timber was brought from the Rajpipla forests and the more southerly regions of the Western Ghats to the port of Broach for export as recently as the last century.[56] The sissoo tree grows in Baluchistan, Sind and the Deccan plateau. There is some controversy however as to whether it is indigenous to Baluchistan and Sind.[57] Multi-coloured birds of ivory are also listed as imports from Meluhha. Gold it is thought may have been brought from the Kolar area of Mysore, although more likely, given the technology of the time, it was alluvial gold washing carried in the sands and gravels of the rivers of Madhya Pradesh. Porphyry and marble would be easily available from Rajasthan and the Baroda District of Gujerat.

The declining years of Lothal are dated by its excavator to the period of *c.* 2000–1900 BC owing to large scale floods.[58] Ultimately by about 1600 BC it had ceased to be a centre of trade. These dates would conform to the Sumerian and Akkadian evidence. Archaeological evidence from Gujerat further suggests that after *c.* 1900 BC the centre of interest in the area seems to shift to Kathiawar where there are many late Harappan sites.

Two areas mentioned frequently in Mesopotamian sources are Dilmun and Makan. Dilmun had a special place in Sumerian life being the land of the immortals with an elaborate mythology woven around it.[59] It is mentioned with affection and reverence, yet at the same time both Dilmun and Makan are said to look up to the Sumerian god Enki. In one text, Dilmun is referred to as the 'land of the crossing'.[60] After the great flood, the hero Ziusudra is transplanted by the great gods to the land of Dilmun, the place where the sun rises — suggesting that Dilmun was to the east of Sumer. It is repeatedly described as 'the pure land', 'the clean land, the bright land', in short, the paradise land.[61] Its bitter and brackish water is changed to sweet on the pleading of its titulary goddess with the sun-god. The role of water and cleanliness is stressed in the life of its people. It is the home of the water-god. If Meluhha is blessed, Dilmun is doubly blessed.

Early sources, one of which mentions the reign of Ur Nanshe of Lagash, refers to the ships of Dilmun bringing tribute of timber.[62] Sargon (2371–2316 BC) boasts of heavily laden ships from Dilmun, Meluhha and Makan docking at his new capital at Agade. He also claims to have taken an expedition into the Lower Sea and into Dilmun.[63] Could the Lower Sea have included the Gulf of Oman as well, rather than just the Persian Gulf? Gudea of Lagash refers to ships bringing him timber from Dilmun. Texts from the Old Babylonian period are replete with descriptions of the extensive and important copper trade with Dilmun. Items imported from Dilmun included[64] copper and timber, and on a lesser scale, stone, ivory, tortoise-shell, white coral, 'fisheyes' (generally taken to mean pearls)[65] and some items which have defied translation such as *arasum*, *ẖulumum* and *meraẖdu*. Items of export to Dilmun are listed as wool, garments, sesame oil, skins, barley, and occasionally cedar. In later periods the copper was exchanged for silver. The Dilmun trade appears to have petered out by *c.* 1700 BC after which for some centuries, Dilmun is associated with the sporadic export of dates.

However Dilmun remains in the sphere of interest of Mesopotamia. In the Kassite period and during the reign of various Assyrian kings, political relations with Dilmun are mentioned.[66] Thus Tukulti Ninurta I (1244–1208 BC) took the title of 'King of Dilmun and Meluhha' and claimed overlordship over these lands. Some centuries later Sargon II (721–705) claims tribute from Uperi the king of Dilmun. Sargon's successor Senacherib (704–681) refers to soldiers from Dilmun armed with bronze spades and pikes assisting him against Babylon. He is also believed to have planted Indian cotton in his garden.[67] Ashurbanipal (668–631) mentions Hundaru the king of Dilmun and lists the booty taken from Dilmun as bronze ingots, copper and bronze objects, sticks of precious wood and *kohl*. Nabonidus (556–539) the last of the kings of Babylon prior to its overthrow by the Achaemenids, mentions a governor of Dilmun. In spite of these claims to overlordship, evidently the control of the Assyrians over Dilmun was somewhat tenuous, given the continuance of kings at Dilmun.

It cannot be denied that several of these texts contain arguments strongly in support of the identification of Dilmun with some part of the Persian Gulf and the island of Bahrein has provided archaeological evidence which has strengthened the suggested identification with this island. In particular two letters from the Kassite period seem to argue for placing Dilmun in a Semitic context in that period. Nevertheless there are also several points which seem not to be compatible with this identification.

The identification of Dilmun from Sumerian sources appears to relate to the oft-repeated description of it as 'the pure land'. The P.Dr. equivalent for the pure land could be, *teḷ* meaning 'clean or pure' (DED 2825) and *maṇ* meaning 'earth or land' (DED 3817), the compound of which could read *teḷmaṇ*, meaning 'the pure earth' or 'the pure land'. Voiced and voiceless consonants do not contrast in the initial position and most Dravidian languages show evidence of secondary voicing initially. Sumerian also shows a similar interchange of voiced and voiceless stops initially and intervocalically. Hence the alternation in the name between Dilmun and Tilmun. Generally *t-* is preferred in the initial position in P.Dr., therefore, the correct form would be Tilmun. The vowel change from *e* to *i* and from *a* to *u* (under the influence of the preceding bilabial *m*) are again not unknown to the rules of Dravidian linguistics and the reading of vowels is uncertain in Sumerian in several cases; in particular it is not known whether in the logogram Tilmun and in the syllabic sign TIL, the vowel should read *i* or *e*. Retroflex *ḷ* and *ṇ* are deretroflexed and changed to dental/alveolar in central and north Dravidian languages.[68] Since Sumerian has no retroflex consonants, the P.Dr. *ḷ* and *ṇ* could justifiably be represented by dental/alveolar *l* and *n*. Admittedly there is a substantial time difference between South Dravidian and P.Dr., but the deretroflexing process is difficult to explain from the available evidence. Thus Teḷmaṇ could become Tilmun. The location of such a 'pure land' on the west coast of India immediately suggests Kathiawar,[69] a more recent name for an area known traditionally to Puranic geography as Surāṣṭra or Saurāṣṭra, the literal translation in Sanskrit for the 'good land'. The name Surāṣṭra and its recognisable variants such as Syrastrene occur in the *Periplus* and other texts of this period and the area continues to be called Saurashtra to this day. Interestingly, there is no convincing explanation in Sanskritic sources as to why it was called so. In later periods Surāṣṭra also included parts of the mainland of Gujerat. There may have been some overlap in the area included in the two terms, Meluhha and Dilmun. Aparānta in later sources was often used for the western region in general. Possibly by the end of the second millennium BC Meluhha was also being used in a general sense to include western India which may account for its infrequent reference in Mesopotamian sources, where particular areas are mentioned in connection with trade. Dilmun may now have included parts of the adjacent mainland to the north and east of Kathiawar. By the time of the *Periplus*, Surāṣṭra included parts of the maritime tracts of the mainland.

The peninsula of Surāṣṭra stood lower than its present level in earlier periods and was semi-insular until as late as the seventeenth century AD. The northern marshes are inundated during the rains leaving a minute stretch of land connection with Gujerat. On the northern side is a stretch of salt land, linking, in the dry season, the Rann of Kutch with the Gulf of Cambay, the remnants of an area once covered by the sea. For all practical purposes Surāṣṭra is an island for most of the year. The water in the northern area and along the Cambay coast is largely brackish and saline, whereas inland and along the south coast the water is sweet and the soil very fertile. The easy availability of fresh, sweet water must, many centuries ago, have required considerable labour, if not the assistance of a god. Sumerian texts suggest the insular character of Dilmun and suggest the presence of saline and brackish water in some parts. The Urjayant peak mentioned in inscriptions and Sanskrit texts has been identified as the Girnar hill near Junagadh,[70] a place of considerable historical importance from at least the Mauryan period onwards and generally revered as a sacred place as well. Surāṣṭra plays a significant role in traditional accounts of the early history of the pre-Mauryan period as the land where many of the important tribes of the *Mahābhārata* had settled such as the Andhaka, Vṛṣṇi, Yādava etc. The Chinese Pilgrim Hsüan Tsang visiting the area in the seventh century AD mentions the thick forests in the vicinity of Girnar.[71] A later text, the *Viṣṇu Dharmottara*[72] refers to the extensive forests of Surāṣṭra.

Archaeological evidence indicates the presence of a few Harappan settlements of the mature phase, although there is a predominance of late Harappan sites all over Kathiawar.[73] The chronological sequence from archaeology would suit the late Akkadian period but it does seem problematical to locate Harappan settlements as early as the date of Ur-Nanshe. It is possible however that more extensive excavation along the southern coast of Kathiawar may reveal pre-Harappan and early Harappan settlements.[74] Recent archaeological exploration and excavation in the adjoining area of Kutch have revealed a large number of Harappan sites and some evidence of what appear to be pre-Harappan settlements.[75] It has been suggested that the evidence for early Harappan sites may have been washed away by a flood which seems to have devastated Kathiawar and Kutch in *c.* 1500 BC or somewhat earlier.[76] This might in turn account for the falling off of trade in this period. It is worth noting however that references to Dilmun in the Akkadian period suggest essentially an area of raw materials with not much in the way of indigenous organized trade. It is only in the Old Babylonian period that Dilmun emerges as a major trading area with the economic underpinnings required for large scale commerce. The chronology of the Old Babylonian period (*c.* 1900 to *c.* 1600 BC) conforms to the approximate period of the mature Harappan settlements and those of the late Harappans in Surāṣṭra.

Surāṣṭra lay to the east of Sumer thus making it the place where the sun rises. The association of the water god with western India is evident at least from the historical period, since in Sanskrit sources, Varuṇa, the god of the sea and of the water, has his location in the western region and is specifically linked with the Indus river and with Kuśasthali or Dvarkā,[77] the small peninsula abutting on the western end of Kathiawar. *Periplus* mentions Syrastrene as lying on the Gulf of Kanthi (Rann of Kutch).[78] Surāṣṭra being a forested area and in close proximity to the forests of Gujerat and the Konkan, could well have supplied shiploads of timber. The break in trade between Dilmun and Mesopotamia could have coincided with the decline of the Harappan cities. However, the break could have been temporary and with the establishment of stability in both regions it was likely to have been resumed. The demand for the products of Dilmun in the first millennium BC on the part of the Assyrian rulers would have been sufficient incentive to resume the trade. According to early Jaina sources Surāṣṭra had a long tradition of trade and was much frequented by merchants.[79]

The alleged conquest of the region by an Assyrian king is not evident from Indian sources.[80] According to Buddhist sources, Aparānta was so-called because it was settled by the Aparagoyāna people, who came from the west, after their lands had been conquered by the primeval king Mandhāta.[81] The references to Dilmun in the sources of the Assyrian period would require further analysis. It may suffice at this stage to highlight a few striking points in this connection. The later reference in three letters and in an inscription of Ashurbanipal to Hundaru the king of Dilmun[82] can perhaps be explained as a somewhat modified transcription in Assyrian of 'Andhra' with an aspirated initial sound (not uncommon in Semitic and also known to the Brahui branch of the Dravidian languages).[83] The *u* and *a* sounds could have been interchangeable as we have seen. The equation of Hundaru with Āndhra would imply that in the seventh century BC a king of the Āndhra tribe was ruling in Surāṣtra. This is not a proposition which is historically impossible or improbable. The *Mahābhārata* refers to various tribes migrating and settling in Ānarta (the region adjoining Kathiawar) and Surāṣtra and among these tribes were the Andhaka and the Vṛṣni.[84] Pāṇiṇi, the earliest of the Sanskrit grammarians and generally dated to the fifth century BC, also mentions the Andhaka and the Vṛṣni people.[85] Early Buddhist sources locate the Andhaka in western India, mention them together with the Ḍamilas and describe their language as a *milakkha* language.[86] The *Aitareya Brāhmana* also refers to the Āndhras as the outcasts among tribes.[87] It would seem that they were a non-Aryan people. The edicts of the Mauryan emperor Aśoka, dating to the third century BC mentions the *amdhra* among a list of peoples.[88] The Āndhra dynasty of kings in the historical period are associated with western India. There is some debate as to whether they originated in the western Deccan and later settled on the east coast or vice versa. Of the objects taken from Dilmun, the sticks of precious wood may refer to sandalwood, available in the vicinity, and *kohl* of course was a local product. The mention of bronze and objects of bronze once again suggests access to copper producing areas. That Surāṣtra had close ties with Iran at least in the next few centuries is evident, for even as late as the reign of the Mauryan king Aśoka (third century BC) his governor in Surāṣtra had an unmistakably Iranian name, Tuṣāspa and is described as a west Asian-*yonarāja*. Archaeological evidence suggests that Saurashtra links up in the post-Harappan period through, what Wheeler has called the Sub-Indus variants, with, 'the chalcolithic cultures of central India, and, through them, ultimately with the central and southern Iron Age'.[89] It is not surprising therefore that Dilmun is again mentioned as an area of contact in the Mesopotamian sources of the first millennium BC. That Ashurbanipal would want to retain control over the Dilmun trade is evident from the fact that in the first millennium BC it is once again a major supplier of the much-needed copper and bronze to Mesopotamia. Any link between Dilmun and the other states of west Asia with access to the Persian Gulf and in opposition to Ashurbanipal could have had serious repercussions on the availability of copper to the Assyrians.

Another place name listed in association with Dilmun, Makan and Meluhha was Gubin/Kupin. Gudea describes it as a source of timber.[90] The above mentioned inscription of Ashurbanipal refers to a place called Kuppi. The word *kuppam* in P.Dr. is generally a place-name suffix (DED 1441). Indian sources refer to a place on the west coast of India as Kupaka. In one text it is described as among the seven Konkans,[91] possibly the coastal area of Karnataka (Mysore State), and in another source it is located in north Malabar.[92] There is also a reference from a much later period inscription, to the Kupalakaṭa-deśa in the western Deccan, for which a possible identification has been made with an area within the present day territory of Goa.[93] Either of these two areas would have been rich sources of timber. The possibility of Kuppi being Kupaka would conform to the geographical direction of places mentioned in the list. The inscription of Ashurbanipal also states that the name of the king of Kuppi is *-ra-a-mit-te* alternatively read as *-ra-a-bat-te*. This sounds fairly similar to the name of a clan which is later known to have provided a Chera dynasty, the Irumporai/Irumpotai. The initial syllable in the name cannot be deciphered and could have been an *a* or *i* and the phonetic value of *-p-* and *-h-* is interchangeable. Sangam literature maintains that the later Irumpotai ruled along the Malabar coast[94] (northern Kerala). The Cheras are mentioned in the inscriptions of Aśoka[95] as Keralaputras. Their capital Vañji has been identified with the inland city of Karur by some scholars and with a coastal location near Cranganore by others.[96] The Cranganore location would place it in north Malabar (Kupaka).

After Kuppi a reference is made in Ashurbanipal's inscription to Padê the king of Qadê. Padê immediately brings to mind the Pāṇḍya kings as they are called in Tamil sources of the early historical period. In one of the inscriptions of Aśoka there is a reference to Pāṇḍya as Paḍā.[97] Qadê suggests Kūḍal, believed to be the earliest of the Pāṇḍya capitals,[98] which was situated on the coast and submerged by the sea, after which it is said, the capital was shifted to Madurai. Ashurbanipal's inscription mentions Qadê as a place and Iske as the city. But it is possible that there might have been some confusion or that the territory of the Pāṇḍyas was referred to by the name of the capital at that time. Of both Kuppi and Kadê it is said that the journey from these places to the Assyrian capital took six months, suggesting that these places were at some considerable distance, and further that their kings had not in earlier times 'trodden the boundary of Assyria . . . .'[99]

The last of the places mentioned in this list is Hazmani, described as an island alongside Dilmun and from which messengers travel a long way across the sea and over land to Assyria — obviously it was even further away than Kuppi. Assuming that Dilmun was by now the general name used for western India in Assyrian documents, being the area with which there was maximum familiarity it may have tended to cover other parts of the sea-board as well with which there was less contact. In this case it is possible that the island referred to could have been Ceylon. The general geographical direction also seems appropriate, moving from Surāṣṭra to the Karnataka coast and north Malabar, then overland (perhaps through the Palghat gap, so frequently used in historical times) to the Pāṇḍyan kingdom on the east coast, from where Ceylon would be just across a narrow sea. In the earliest Tamil literature Ceylon is called Iram (DED 469). The etymology of the word is not clear since the noun form refers to toddy or arrack. The Dr. ṛ has a phonetic value approximating *zh*, thus *iṛam* would be pronounced *izham* which to the Assyrians could well have been converted to *Azham* and given the initial aspirated sound of Semitic would be pronounced as Hazham. It has been suggested that the earlier form of *īram* would have been **cīram* and from which the Sanskrit name for Ceylon, Simhala, was derived.[100] P.Dr. **c* became **h* before it was reduced to zero (or lost). The evidence of Gondi dialects as well as the development of *s* into *h* in Old Sinhalese supports this. However, the P.Dr. **i* being converted to **a* in Assyrian is hard to explain except by recourse to the earlier idea that in pronouncing an alien name the vowel sound may have changed in Assyrian. The termination *-ani* could mean adornment, **ani* (DED 98) so that the original name could have been *iramani* meaning 'the place adorned with toddy (palms)'.[101] Obviously, this reading is more tentative than the other identifications suggested. The need for making contact with Ceylon was doubtless for the same reasons as attracted later traders from the west, the abundance of large pearls, ivory, tortoise-shell and semi-precious stones.[102] Archaeological evidence indicates the existence of a developed megalithic culture in the vicinity of Anurādhapura dating to about the fourth century BC.[103] It would not be unlikely that less developed megalithic settlements along the coast may have existed in the seventh century BC which could well have been the suppliers of the items mentioned earlier. The identifications would suggest that the passage in the Ashurbanipal inscription refers to a group of places in geographical proximity to each other. If this is so then Dilmun would be better located in western India than in the Gulf. In the earlier Gudea inscriptions, the references to Dilmun, Meluhha, Makan and Gubin appear to be one cluster of place names grouped separately from other clusters and could be viewed as areas generally towards the east.[104] However, if Dilmun is taken to be either Bahrein or Failaka then obviously the identification of Hazmani with Ceylon will not be tenable.

The land of Makan brings to Sumer copper, diorite, *u*-stone and *shuman* stone. Alabaster vases inscribed with the phrase 'booty from Makan' date to the reign of Naram-sin the grandson of Sargon of Akkad, who also mentions his attack on Makan.[105] The import of diorite for making statues is recorded by Gudea the governor of Lagash.[106] In the trade between Makan and Ur, Makan exported copper, stone, ivory, beads of precious stones, timber, onions and perfumes and Ur exported to Makan garments, wool, perfumed oil and leather goods — the latter being all perishable commodities (as in the case of exports to Dilmun) and therefore not likely to leave any trace in the importing area.[107]

Makan is continually mentioned together with Dilmun throughout this period until the first millennium BC and therefore was obviously somewhere close to Dilmun. There is no indication in Sumerian sources as to the meaning of the word Makan. Working on the P.Dr. hypothesis two alternative readings are possible. In the first reading the initial syllable could be derived from *Mā* (DED 3917) meaning a large animal such as an elephant combined with *kaṉ* (DED 975) meaning a site or place. Thus Makan could mean a place frequented by elephants. The *-g-* and the *-k-* being interchangeable both in P.Dr. and Sumerian the variation of Makan and Magan would thus be accounted for. A possible Sanskrit association could be with Sindhu, which is associated with the elephant's spray or ichor and is a less familiar meaning of the word but nevertheless known and used and would refer geographically to the lower Indus region.[108] However *kaṇ* (DED 975) occurs in only a limited number of languages and this weakens the possibility of the P.Dr. reconstruction. In Jaina sources, Sindhu is generally described as a *mleccha* region to begin with although the people of this area were later declared to be *ārya*.[109] They refer to frequent flooding in the area and describe the land as full of water because of the breaches in the earth. This may have been due to the ecological change which the lower Indus valley underwent during the second millennium BC and which partly accounts for the decline of the Harappan cities in this area. This identification would also be more suited for the import of Magan-reeds into Mesopotamia than a location on the dry Arabian and Persian coasts.[110] It has been suggested that Makran is a memory of the earlier Makan.[111] The alternative reading for Makan has been suggested to me by Prof. Krishnamurti where the word may be associated with *maka* (DED 3768) meaning a child or young one. The word for 'a male child, an exalted person or warrior' would be **makanṯ* in origin, but with the loss of the terminal *-t* remains as *makan* (qv. DED 3768). If the name Makan was derived from this, then there is an even closer Sanskrit parallel in the name Suvīra, which means 'very manly, heroic, warlike.' The *prefix su* denoting excellence is added to *vīra,* which is also used to mean 'a male child, a husband' in addition to the more general meaning of a brave man, an eminent person, a hero.[112]

The people and the territory of Suvīra in Sanskrit sources are associated with Sindhu and the two together are often used in the compound form *Sindhusauvīra*, and referred to as a single people.[113] Brahmanical texts again refer to the Sindhusauvīra as being a *mleccha* people.[114] Buddhist sources mention Roruka as its capital and Bharata as one of its ancient kings.[115] According to the Jaina sources its capital was Vibhaya, also called Kumbhakārapakkheva, a port town perhaps on a river.[116] The location of Sauvīra is generally placed in Sind.[117] One of the sources states that the Sindhu country lay to the west of the Indus river in which case if Sauvīra adjoined Sindhu it could well have included the Baluchistan hills[118] or else have been located just to the east of the lower Indus. The distribution of the Brahui speakers may reflect what might once have been Makan and which later came to be called Sindhusauvīra. They are located in the Larkana District of Sind, along the Kirthar Ranges, and in the Kalat area.[119] As late as AD 1800, the region between Multan and Tatta was called Mekran/Mehran.[120] As regards Naram-sin's claim to having attacked Makan (*c.* 2291–2255) the only possible evidence could be the conflagrations and indication of some destruction at Amri and Kot Diji.[121] Mesopotamian sources also suggest the attack of barbarians, the Gutians and others, who over-ran various parts of west Asia as also Tilmun, Makan and Meluhha towards the end of Naram-sin's reign.[122] References to Makan decrease appreciably after the Old Babylonian period, i.e., after *c.* 1700 BC,[123] the period of decline of the Indus cities.

In the Old Babylonian period trade seems to have been in the hands of the Dilmun merchants although the raw materials may have in some cases been supplied by Makan. The reference to 'fisheyes' (? pearls) is specific to Dilmun. This would again suggest Surāṣṭra since the pearl fisheries off the coast of Kathiawar were well-known until recent times. Both coral and pearls from western India were in great demand and highly prized by west Asian traders in the early centuries of the Christian era.[124] As late as the sixth century AD the *Bṛhat-Saṁhitā* of Varāhamihira lists Surāṣṭra as one of the eight major areas from where pearls are obtained.[125] The pearls are said to have been medium-sized and butter coloured. The tortoise was well known to the Harappans having been depicted on both seals and pottery.[126] Tortoise-shell could therefore have been an item of trade. Among the unidentified items is the mention of *merahdu*, an item traded in small quantities and measured by weight, which Prof. Krishnamurti has suggested may be a transcription of the P.Dr. *mizaku/mezaku* from which evolved the later Dravidian form of *miḷaku* (DED 3986) the name for black pepper. This was native to the south-western coast of India and in later centuries was a major item of trade between western India and west Asia. The production and popularity of dates in the area of the Indus civilisation is attested to not only by the frequency of the date-palm as a decorative motif on Indus pottery, but also by the datestones discovered in excavations.[127] Doubtless the production of dates continued into the post-Harappan period. The dates of Makran (Kej and Panj-gur) have been and continue to be renowned for their superior quality. These form an important item of trade in the neighbouring areas. It would appear from late texts that the Dilmun date was used for ritual purposes and is distinguished from ordinary dates and this would also help explain the need for the continuing importation of the Dilmun dates.[128] The reference to the Ahlamu destroying the Dilmun dates appears to be to the destruction of the cargo of dates rather than the groves.[129]

By far the most important item of trade was copper, in Sumerian *urudu*, in Akkadian *(w)erûm*.[130] (It might be worth noting that although the P.Dr. word for copper i.e., *eruvai* (DED 700), [*kan* (DED 1180) and *cempu* (DED 2282) both appear to be late], bear little resemblance to the Sumerian word nevertheless the P.Dr. word for smelting, *uruka/urukku*, etc. (DED 569) bears a distinct resemblance to the Sumerian word for copper *urudu*, although of course this may be accidental). The major copper trade was conducted by merchants from Dilmun although the copper was mined initially at least in Makan. So lucrative was the copper trade that the *alik Tilmun* were merchants trading only with Dilmun and paying the substantial customs duty charged on copper. At first Makan appears to be the more important source for copper, particularly in the Ur III period (2113–2006 BC) when there is also a reference to the native of Great Makan. But subsequent to this in the Larsa period (2025–1763 BC) Dilmun emerges as the main centre of the copper trade, although it did not actually produce the copper. Was this due to the ecological changes in the lower Indus valley and the possible diversion of the copper trade to Surāstra associated with the expansion of late Harappan settlements in this region, as a consequence?[131] Apart from traders from Ur going to Tilmun, such as the major importer of copper Ea-nāṣir, mention is also made of traders from Tilmun coming to Ur.

The main copper producing areas in the north and west of the Indian subcontinent are Baluchistan, Sind, Rupavati (Amreli District of Kathiawar) and Rajasthan. Slag heaps in Baluchistan point to the presence of copper. Afghanistan also has copper deposits. The availability of copper in Seistan would also be a source for Makan. The Baluchistan sites of Nal and Kulli are rich in copper although its presence decreases in the plains. Perhaps the diffusion of copper technology from west Asia was first made manifest in Baluchistan as far as the north and west of the Indian subcontinent is concerned. In Sind the valley of Kanrach (thirty miles west of the Saruna valley) has yielded lead and copper in considerable quantities.[132] The main routes from the Kanrach valley to the Indus plains (the vicinity of Amri) were via the Saruna valley and Lake Manchar, which are attested by the numerous Harappan settlements in these areas, apart from the topographical features. In Rajasthan copper is available in Alwar, Khetri and Ajmer. The first two places in particular could well have been sources for this trade since there is a close similarity between the Khetri ore and the copper artifacts of the Banas Culture.[133] Both Harappa and Lothal as we have seen have remains of copper smithies. The low nickel content of the copper found at Sumer 0.2 to 0.3 per cent approximates the low nickel content of Indian copper although this similarity has recently been questioned on the basis of an individual component content being insufficient evidence to posit similarities in ores, in spite of the findings of the Sumerian Committee.[134] The Dilmun standard of weight, using a unit of approximately 1.7 grams, which differed considerably from the Ur standard, agrees very closely with the standard of weights found in the Harappan cities.[135] Since the copper was traded in ingots (*gubarum/kubarum*) it is likely that the standard of the place of manufacture would be the current standard. It has been argued that there was no independent origination of metallurgy in the Harappa Culture, yet the Harappa period shows an appreciable increase and improvement in copper technology. Could the impetus for this have come from the Mesopotamian trade? This situation interestingly continues in post-Harappan Saurashtra and in the Banas Culture of Rajasthan — both areas of Harappan contact. But at the other post-Harappan chalcolithic sites the technological standard in copper technology registers a decline as compared to the Harappan.

Another important commodity was ivory. The ivory trade is noticeable in the Ur III period and continued in the Larsa period with the import from Dilmun of ivory combs, breast-plates, boxes, spoons, inlaid furniture etc. Mention is also made of rods of ivory.[136] Such ivory objects were familiar to the Harappan cities. Here again the elephants of Sind and Saurashtra may have provided the raw material. The elephant is frequently depicted on the Indus seals. Ivory was used in large quantities in the temple workshops both of the woodcutters and the carpenters in Ur in the time of king Ibbi-Sin.[137] But the ivory trade via the Persian Gulf began to decline in the Old Babylonian period, and later.

Of the stone imported from these lands there would be a wide variety to choose from. Deposits of limestone occur in the Vindhyas and in Kathiawar. Sandstone was available in Kathiawar, laterite in the north-west Deccan, gneiss, feldspar and steatite in Rajasthan. Both Kathiawar and the Kirthar Range have deposits of alabaster and gypsum. These could have been the supplies referred to by Naram-sin. Seated male figures in alabaster have been found at Harappan sites.[138] Evidence of black diorite is suggested by the Siyah Sang, the Pass of the Black Stones, near Mundigak.[139] In addition to the Narmada valley, Sind too has deposits of carnelian, agate, chalcedony and steatite and[140] these are known to have been used by the settlers of the Pre-Harappan and Harappa Cultures.

Timber exported from Makan, Dilmun and Meluhha would in the main have consisted of sissoo, ebony, rosewood and teak. As has already been suggested, the Makan reed was probably bamboo. Ktesias, writing in the fifth century BC also refers to the huge reed growing along the Indus river and this has been identified as bamboo.[141] Wood remains from the excavations at Harappa have been identified as, Cedrus Deodara — cedar (or deodara); Dalbergia Latifolia — rosewood; a species of Zizyphus — ber-wood and Ulmus — elm.[142] The discovery of cedar is of some interest. It could have been brought from the Western Ghats or alternatively from the northern mountains. It was used in one of the rare coffins which would not exclude the possibility of its having been imported. Cedar wood is one of the items exported to Dilmun from Mesopotamia in the Old Babylonian period. The white cedar (*dysoxylum malabaricum*) is to this day a large tropical evergreen found in the forests of the Western Ghats.[143] An alternative identification of the Sumerian reference to white cedar is *Juniperus Oxycedrus*[144] and this is known in Baluchistan. Strabo, many centuries later refers to the use of pine, cedar, etc., for the boats built by Alexander when moving down the Indus and states that the timber came from the forests of king Poros (in the northern Punjab).

The Dilmun trade was evidently a major economic undertaking, particularly in the case of the copper trade. It involved merchants from Dilmun visiting the Mesopotamian cities, and well-established merchants from these cities going to Dilmun. It was evidently a large market with the goods coming from Makan and Meluhha as well. That there was a substantial element of risk in this trade is suggested both by the nature of the investments and contracts among the merchants as well as the frequency of tithes and thanksgivings to the deities and temples on the successful completion of a voyage to Dilmun and back. Such thanksgivings are not known in the Mesopotamian trade with other regions to the west and the north, there being no mention of them, neither in the Ur and Larsa texts, nor, for example, in the Mari texts and the innumerable texts from the Assyrian settlements in Anatolia referring to trade. It would also suggest that Dilmun was far away.[145] This is further supported by the complaint about the difficulties of an expedition to Dilmun from Mari. If Bahrein was Dilmun it would have been close enough for trade and probably firmly under the control of the Mesopotamian merchants. It would hardly have had a different weight standard from the Mesopotamian cities.[146] The Harappan weight standard occurring at Bahrain could suggest that Bahrain was an intermediary point in the overall trade. That the Indian weight standard was used as far west as Bahrain would not have been so unlikely as there was undeniably a strong Indian influence in the Persian Gulf, attested too by the style of the seals. (Even in more recent times the Indian monetary units — *annas, paise* and *rupees* — were in use on the Arabian coast as far as Kuwait until 1961). The reference to Dilmun being thirty double-hours away is ambiguous since the point from which the distance was being measured is not clear.[147] Furthermore in one text, Dilmun and Makan are placed *beyond* the Lower Sea.[148]

The copper trade with Dilmun was on a huge scale, certainly far larger than the trade with Susa, and appears to have been the monopoly of the few, both individuals and institutions, obviously those who could afford the investment required. If Bahrain was Dilmun, there would be little point in shipping the copper first to Bahrain and then to Mesopotamia. Since it was mined in Makan and Dilmun, it could as well have gone directly to the Mesopotamian cities. Transportation from Dilmun only makes sense if the Dilmun merchants were the entrepreneurs collecting the merchandise and for this Surāṣtra would have been a better base than Bahrain. Dilmun and Makan are both mentioned as places trading directly with Ur. This does not preclude Bahrain, Failaka and other places along the Persian Gulf from being ports of call for taking victuals, with intermediate markets handling the luxury trade which was smaller in bulk and probably distributed among a larger number of merchants. Evidently Dilmun merchants had also settled in these places as is clear from the objects inscribed with the Harappa script and more importantly, the temple to Enzak the titulary deity of Dilmun at Failaka.[149] The Persian Gulf seals found in these areas at the head of the Gulf also bear the strong influence of Indus seals. This would again point to an area of mixed culture with influences from both the Indus civilisation and Mesopotamia. It is relevant perhaps to distinguish between the bulk trade in copper, timber and stone and the trade in luxury articles the two categories of commodities possibly being under the control of different groups of merchants, though with some overlap. If Bahrain or Failaka were Dilmun one could expect more detailed accounts of Dilmun in the sources of the Assyrian period. There would also be a likelihood not only of conquest but of firm political control over the area. The intermittent references to the rulers of Dilmun, even if tribute bearing, suggests an area outside direct Assyrian control.

The earlier identification of Makan and Meluhha with Egypt and Ethiopia for the entire period under discussion, requires a fresh investigation. A recent survey of the problem endorses the theory of a shift in toponym in the second half of the second millennium BC and this appears more acceptable.[150] Neither of the names Makan and Meluhha can be recognized as place names from Egyptian or Ethiopian sources. Of the items imported from these lands into Mesopotamia, Egypt had access to copper from the Sinai and Libya and to alabaster and diorite, but lacked timber and to such an extent that she had to import vast quantities for her own needs.[151] This would hardly suggest that Makan was Egypt. Ethiopia lacked copper and is generally not associated with the export of timber on a large scale. It is only if the identification of Ethiopia with the Land of Punt is accepted that it can be referred to as an exporter of timber, and this identification is by no means certain.[152] Nor is Ethiopia known for carnelian and lapis lazuli. Gold and ivory seem to be the only two items which, even if not primary products of Ethiopia, could have been brought from Nubia and East Africa and marketed through Ethiopia. There is at the same time a noticeable absence of items generally associated with Ethiopia, such as incense and herbs, being mentioned in Mesopotamian sources referring to Meluhha.[153] Both Makan and Meluhha are linked with maritime trade. The sea voyage from Egypt to Mesopotamia would be extremely lengthy and inconvenient as compared to the far shorter over land route to the Tigris-Euphrates valley. Ethiopia was also at some considerable distance by sea. Further-more, if there was such an extensive trade between Mesopotamia and Egypt and Ethiopia, it is indeed surprising that archaeological evidence of any significant contact between the two areas is absent. There is in fact little evidence to suggest that Ethiopia in the Sargonid period (*c.* 2300 BC) had a material culture sufficient to support the building and despatching of large ships to Mesopotamia or to explain the developed craftsmanship of the exported goods.[154] Such a material base in Ethiopia seems to emerge much later at the end of the second millennium BC. On the basis of the political and economic developments in Egypt and Ethiopia in the second millennium BC this would be regarded as a period of expanding trade for the two countries. Yet, this is precisely the time when Mesopotamian sources record the decline and petering out of the trade with Makan and Meluhha. One of the reasons for identifying Meluhha with Ethiopia is that it is described as 'the black land' and the people are called the black Meluhhaites.[155] But this as we have seen could as well apply to western India. At most it can be suggested that Makan and Meluhha were situated elsewhere in the third millennium BC and that there was a shift of toponym in the first millennium BC when Egypt and areas close to it were called by these names. However there remains some ambiguity regarding the precise geographical definition of Makan and Meluhha in view of the various other names which are also used for Egypt, Nubia and Ethiopia such as Miṣri, Muṣur, Kashi and Kush. If it is true that the Egyptians referred to Ethiopia as the land of Punt, with which they were familiar over the centuries with the many expeditions sent there, then it is surprising that the Assyrians should refer to it by a totally different name. An Assyrian claim to the conquest of Punt would have been far more impressive to the west Asian world of that time than the renaming of Punt as Meluhha. Reminiscences of early relations with Makan and Meluhha persisted in the Mesopotamian mind and the names were included in references to conquest irrespective of political changes and to trade in the context of other places supplying the same items as the earlier ones.[156]

If the geographical identifications suggested in this paper are acceptable, it would be quite feasible that the decline of the Harappan cities and the advent of the Kassites resulted in economic instability which led to a break in the trade relations. When the situation was stabilised in both areas by the beginning of the first millennium BC, trade was resumed. That the west coast of India at this time was in trading contact with west Asia is evident from a variety of sources such as the use of Indian teak in Mesopotamia and the reference to ships going east to Ophir during the reign of Solomon.[157] Ophir is often identified with Sopara or the Sanskrit Surpāraka, a port on the west coast in the Thana district near Bombay. It has also been suggested that this might be the Aberia of the Periplus, the land of the Ābhīra, or even a reference to Sauvīra.[158] Continuing contact is apparent from Achaemenid sources, from Greek accounts prior to Alexander's campaign and contemporary with this event, from Indian references to Babylon as Baveru and not least of all, the detailed information on trade and ports contained in Ptolemy's *Geography* and the *Periplus of the Erythreaen Sea*.

In his discussion on the dating of the Indus civilisation, Wheeler has analysed the chronology of the Indus type seals found in various sites in southern Mesopotamia.[159] He maintains on this basis that by the end of the Early Dynastic III and the beginning of the Sargonid–Akkadian period, *c.* 2400–2300 BC there is evidence of contact between southern Mesopotamia and the Indus coast. The occurrence of the seals further indicates emphatic contact during the Sargonid-Akkadian period and continuing but less emphatic contact in the subsequent Larsa period, after which the Indus type seals cease. During the Larsa period there is the occurrence of the Persian Gulf Type III seal. This would support the evolution of the trade pattern discussed here.

Of the three places referred to, Meluhha, Dilmun and Makan, the Mesopotamian attitude to Dilmun in particular changed considerably over the centuries. The references to Dilmun suggest a number of interesting possibilities which need to be investigated further. For the moment it is enough to draw attention to some of these. There is a remarkable similarity in the origin myth as preserved by both the Sumerians and the early Indians (assuming of course that certain traditions recorded in the Vedas and the *Purāṇas*, go back to an earlier pre-Vedic phase). Ziusudra, the Sumerian Noah, closely resembles Manu in the Indian version of the Flood Story and the events connected with the flood are similar.[160] There is a close parallel in the structure of the Sumerian and Indian king-lists. The pre-Deluge dynasties have mythical kings with long reigns. The Deluge is a major point of change. The post-Deluge dynasties are less mythical with more acceptable lengths of reign. In this context the date of 3102 BC the equivalent in the Christian era for the start of the post-Deluge dynasties and of the Kaliyuga, assumes greater significance. There are echoes of similarities in certain legends and references to deities.[161]

A gradual change can be perceived in the attitude to Dilmun in the Akkadian and Babylonian period. The respect with which Dilmun was held in Sumerian sources, suggestive of a rather special relationship, now begins to decline. Its richness of resources were known and now its potentialities both for trade and conquest were recognised. With the rise of the Assyrians, who had their base in northern Mesopotamia and had no Sumerian tradition, there is a disappearance of the special relationship. It is replaced by an interest motivated entirely by trade, profits and the desire for conquest. The claims to conquest or the exacting of tribute from the rulers of Dilmun increase in the first millennium BC. It is hard to believe that Assurbanipal for instance could ever have thought of Dilmun as the paradise land.

This paper is essentially in the nature of a tentative hypothesis. It does not as yet permit of any generalisations on a wider scale since the investigation contained in this paper has only been applied to a few words. It will be enough if this paper should arouse the interest of specialists in linguistics and of archaeologists, who together might examine sources from Mesopotamia and other parts of west Asia for references to place-names, commodities and names of people which, when taken together with the archaeological evidence, may throw further light on the culture of this period in northern and western India

## Notes and References

1. W.F. Leemans, 'The Trade Relations of Babylonia . . . ', in *JESHO*, III, 1960, pp. 27–30; W.F. Leemans, 'Old Babylonian Letters and Economic History', in *JESHO*, XI, 1968, pp. 215–26; W.F. Leemans, *Foreign Trade in the Old Babylonian Period*, pp. 159ff; Cf. also B. Landsberger, *Welt des Orients*, III, 1966, pp. 261–2 and I.J. Gelb, *Revue d' Assyriologie*, 64, 1970, pp. 1–8, who agree in the main with the identification of Leemans; I. Gershevitch, 'Sissoo at Susa', in *BSOAS*, 19, 1957, p. 317. The most recent summary of these views is found

in J. Hansom, 'A Periplus of Magan and Meluhha', *BSOAS*, XXXVI, 1973, pp. 553–4.

2. S.N. Kramer, *The Sumerians*, pp. 276–80.
3. S.N. Kramer, 'Dilmun, Quest for Paradise', *Antiquity*, XXXVII, 1963, pp. 111–15; G. Bibby, *Looking for Dilmun*.
4. For the archaeological evidence around the Persian Gulf see also C.L. During Caspers, *Journal of Near Eastern Studies*, XXIV, 1965, pp. 53–6; *Origini*, IV, 1970, pp. 205–76; *East and West*, New Series 21, 1971, pp. 21–44 and 217–23.
5. O. Spate, *India and Pakistan*, p. 596.
6. O. Spate, op. cit., p. 598; Meher D.N. Wadia, *Minerals of India*, p. 43n.1; S.R. Rao, 'Shipping in Ancient India', in Lokesh Chandra (ed.), *India's Contribution to World Thought and Culture*, p. 88. The *Periplus* also indicates that what is now the Rann of Kutch was an open sea and ships going to the north of Kathiawar had to be careful of shallow waters (cited Rao).
7. Lambrick, *Sind*, pp. 100ff.
8. C.C. Lamberg–Karlovsky, 'Trade Mechanisms in Indus-Mesopotamian Interrelations, *JAOS*, vol. 92, no. 2, April–June 1972; G. Bibby, 'Ancient Indian Style Seals from Bahrain', *Antiquity*, XXXII, 1958, pp. 243–4.
9. C.C. Lamberg–Karlovsky, 'The Proto-Elamite Settlement at Tepe Yahya, *Iran*, IX, 1971, pp. 92–4.

10 S.R. Rao, 'Contacts between Lothal and Susa', *PCO*, 1964, pp. 34ff.

11 J. Marshall, *Mohenjo-daro*, pp. 102ff.

12. G.F. Dales, 'Of Dice and Men', *JAOS*, 1968, vol. 88 (1), pp. 14–23.

13 J.P. Joshi, 'Exploration at Kutch and Excavation at Surkotada . . . ', *JOI*, XXII, 1–2, Sept.–Dec. 1972, pp. 98–144.

14. Burkholder, 'Ubaid Sites and Pottery in Saudi Arabia', *Archaeology*, XXV, 1972, pp. 264ff. G. Bibby, *Looking for Dilmun*, pp. 393–5.
15. R.E.M. Wheeler, *The Indus Civilisation*, pp. 110ff. Wheeler adheres to his earlier date of 2500 BC as the approximate beginnings of the Harappa Culture. (Foreword to S.R. Rao, *Lothal and the Indus Civilisation*, 1973).
16. G.F. Dales, 'Archaeological and Radio Carbon Chronologies for Protohistoric South Asia', in N. Hammond (ed.), *South Asian Archaeology*, pp. 157ff.
17. M.B. Emeneau has discussed this view in an essay entitled 'Linguistic Pre-History of India' in his *Collected Papers*, pp. 155ff. Other scholars holding similar views are referred to in a bibliographical foot-note in the same essay, p. 156, n. 8; T. Burrow, *The Sanskrit Language*, pp. 373ff also discusses the interaction of the two languages in the Vedic period. T. Burrow, *Collected Papers on Dravidian Linguistics* and S.K. Chatterjee, *Dravidian*, contain further details.

18. K.V. Zvelebil, 'The Descent of the Dravidians', *IJDL*, vol. I, no. 1, June 1972, p. 57.
19. I. Mahadevan, 'Study of the Indus Script Through Bilingual Parallels', *Second Conference of Dravidian Linguistics*, Tirupati, June 1972.
20. E.K. Pillai, *Studies in Kerala History*, p. 51.
21. S.N. Kramer, *The Sumerians*, pp. 276–84; W.F. Leemans, *Foreign Trade.*
22. This information was supplied to me by Prof. S.N. Kramer, Dr Kinnier–Wilson and Dr W.F. Leemans.
23. Cf. with regard to vowels in modern times: Arabic Mosqat is rendered in English by Muscat, in old Dutch by Muskate or Moskate; Ceylon is Ceylan in French; and with, at the same time, an interchange of hh in kk: Macha-Mokka.
24. S.N. Kramer, *The Sumerians*, pp. 276–9.
25. A.L. Oppenheim, 'Seafaring Merchants of Ur', *JAOS*, 74, pp. 6–17; W.F. Leemans, *Foreign Trade.*
26. See G.F. Hourani, *Arab Seafaring*, pp. 89–91.
27. B. and R. Allchin, *The Birth of Indian Civilisation*, pp. 270–1; W.F. Leemans, *Foreign Trade in the Old Babylonian Period*, pp. 32–4 and 163.
28. B.C. Law, *Historical Geography of Ancient India*, pp. 20–1; 300; Some scholars however translate *vaidūrya* as beryl or cat's eye.
29. *Cambridge Ancient History*, vol. I, part I, p. 454.
30. S.R. Rao, *Lothal and the Indus Civilisation*, p. 116.
31. *The Periplus of the Erythreaen Sea*, 56.
32. *Cambridge Ancient History*, vol. III, pp. 389–90.
33. B.C. Law, op. cit., p. 13; *Mārkaṇḍeya Purāṇa*, 58. If Meluhha was derived from Mēlukku and this was the later Aparānta, it would be interesting to speculate whether this might not also provide the clue to the origin of the word *mleccha*, a connection which has been suggested in the past but its precise derivation not known. (Asko Parpola et al., *The Decipherment of the Indus Script*, 1969, pp. 3–4; Leemans, *Foreign Trade in the Old Babylonian Period*, pp. 158ff; *JRAS*, 1900, p. 535; *JRAS*, 1943, p. 38). The Prākrit and Pāli words for *mleccha* are *milakkhu* and *milakkha* suggesting an aspiration to indicate the voiceless -k- and a change of the *u* to *a*. P.Dr. does not have phonemic aspirates therefore this would be a feature of the introduction of a new phonetic system. In the relationship of *milakkha* to *mleccha* the occurrence of the -kkha- is unexplained in most lexicons. (e.g. R.I. Turner, *A Comparative Dictionary of Indo-Aryan Languages*, p. 600). The association of *milakkhu* in Buddhist sources is with Andhras and Tamils (*andha-damilādi*, *Samantapāsādikā*, I.255). The earliest reference to *mleccha* in Sanskrit sources is in connection with the Asuras who cannot speak Sanskrit correctly. (*Śatapatha Brāhmaṇa*, III, 2, 1, 18–28). The *Jaiminī Dharmaśāstra* (I.3.10; T. Burrow, *The Sanskrit Language*, pp. 373ff)

gives a list of *mleccha* words — *pika, śata, tamaras*, etc., which are evidently Dravidian words given in a slightly Sanskritised form. Could the original *mleccha* then have been the P.Dr. speakers of Melukku/ western India who were either mispronouncing Sanskrit or were continuing to speak their own language?

34. *Mārkaṇḍeya Purāṇa*, 58.
35. It is curious that in the Kaira district of Gujerat (the area of Lothal), social divisions among the people hinge on two groups, the Kaliparaj 'the black people' who provide the large substratum population living in hamlets and the Upaliparaj who are the smaller but socially superior group occupying the small village nuclei. Spate, op. cit., p. 606. In this connection it may be pointed out that in a text from Susa a child, born with a dark skin is called a *meluhhanu* (cf. R. Labat, *Bibliotheca Orientalis*, XXVIII, 1971, p. 363). Cf. also W.F. Leemans, *JESHO*, XI, 1968, pp. 225–6.
36. The list of regions included in Aparānta as mentioned in Puranic sources generally starts with the Sabarmati region and includes all the coastal people and those close by in the hinterland of northern Konkan, as well as the Saurāṣṭras and the Ānartas of Kathiawar. (M.R. Singh, *A Critical Study of the Geographical Data in the Early Puranas*, pp. 313ff). The area may well have been more limited in the Harappa period since the term Aparānta was widely used for the western sea-board in later periods. Incidentally, the tribes listed as inhabiting this area are not always referred to as *āryas* in brahmanical sources. The Saurāṣṭras for instance are described as *sankīrṇa yonayaḥ* (*Baudhāyana Dharma Sūtra*, 1.1.13).
37. *The Periplus of the Erythreaen Sea*, 41.
38. P. Gupta, *Geography in Ancient Indian Inscriptions*, p. 48. Incidentally, the alternative reading is *kara-nadu*, meaning 'great country', which may have been the source for the name Mahārāstra.
39. S.R. Rao, *Lothal and the Indus Civilisation*, pp. 54ff, 166.
40. Ibid.
41. J.P. Joshi, op. cit.
42. S.R. Rao, *Lothal and the Indus Civilisation*, pp. 57–68.
43. B. and R. Allchin, op. cit., p. 141.
44. D.P. Agrawal, *The Copper Bronze Age in India*, p. 132.
45. H.D. Sankalia, 'The Beginnings of Civilisation in Rajasthan', III, *Indica*, vol. X, March 1973, no. 1.
46. S.R. Rao, *Lothal and the Indus Civilisation*, p. 81.
47. Ibid., p. 68.
48. An interesting suggestion was made to me by Prof. Jaini of the Dept. of Buddhist Studies, University of California, Berkeley, that the place-name Lothal could have been derived from Loha-sthala, meaning in Sanskrit 'the place of metal'.

49. S.R. Rao, *Ancient India*, nos 18 + 19; Fairservis, *The Roots of Ancient India*, p. 309.
50. Allchin and Joshi, 'Malwan', *JRAS*, 122, 1970, p. 28.
51. S.N. Kramer, *The Sumerians*, p. 280.
52. Leemans, *Foreign Trade in the Old Babylonian Period*, pp. 9–11.
53. D. Brandis, *Indian Trees*, pp. 428ff; W. Rosburgh, *Flora Indica*, p. 413.
54. K.A. Chowdhury, 'Wood and its Use during Pre- and Proto-Historic Times', *IJHS*, v, 1970, pp. 141ff. Identification mine, based on Hooker, II, 298; III, 24; I.567.
55. S.R. Rao, 'Shipping in Ancient India', op. cit., pp. 84–8.
56. Incidentally, a common name for rosewood in P.Dr. is *punku/punti*, DED 3561 which raises the question of whether the Egyptian reference to the Land of Punt may not have been the west coast of India with its rosewood forests? Leemans (*JESHO*, III, 1960, p. 29) has argued that Punt could not be the west coast of India because it also supplied frankincense and there is no mention of frankincense in the imports from Meluhha, nor is it grown in India. J. Inner Miller, *The Spice Trade of the Roman Empire*, pp. 102ff has pointed out that one variety of frankincense, the *Boswellia Serrata*, grows in India. Further that Socotra was the main supplier obtaining supplies from Arabia. Is it possible that the frankincense was picked up from Socotra on the journey back from Punt and therefore got associated with the products of Punt?
57. D. Brandis, *Indian Trees*, pp. 233ff; *Gaz. Prov. of Sind*, 1907, pp. 44–6.
58. S.R. Rao, 'Shipping in Ancient India', op. cit., pp. 84ff.
59. S.N. Kramer, *Antiquity*, XXXVII, 1963, p. 111.
60. G. Bibby, *Looking for Dilmun*, pp. 93–5.
61. S.N. Kramer, *Sumerian Mythology*, pp. 54–9.
62. Kramer, *The Sumerians*, pp. 53, 61, 67, 172.
63. *Cambridge Ancient History*, vol. I, part 2, p. 738.
64. Bibby, op. cit., p. 205.
65. R.C. Thompson, *DACG*, p. 53n.2.
66. G. Roux, *Ancient Iraq*, p. 285; Oppenheim, op. cit.; P.B. Cornwall, *Bulletin of the American Schools of Oriental Research*, 103, 1946, pp. 1–3 and *Journal of Cuneiform Studies*, VI, 1952, pp. 137–45.
67. Oppenheim, *Ancient Mesopotamia*, p. 94.
68. Bh. Krishnamurti, *Telugu Verbal Bases*, I.93.
69. It is perhaps worth recalling Allchin's account of how a sailor from Kathiawar told him that they used to call it Dilmun until recent times. (*Antiquity*, XLIII, 1969, p. 315); Kuda near the port of Hathab (Kathiawar) where a Harappan settlement was found recently is known locally as Dilmun. (S.R. Rao, *Lothal and the Indus Civilisation*, p. 118).
70. B.C. Law, op. cit., p. 300.

71. Cunningham, *Ancient Geography of India*, p. 273.
72. II.251.34–5.
73. S.R. Rao, *Ancient India*, nos 18 + 19, pp. 5–207.
74. The *Mahābhārata* (XVI.8.20; XVII.1.43) contains the tradition that the city of Dvarkā, the home of the Yādava tribes was submerged in the sea. The location of Dvarkā is debatable but most authorities suggest that it was along the coast of Kathiawar possibly near the modern Dvarkā. Should the tradition reflect an historical event, then such disturbances may have affected other sites along the same coast.
75. J.P. Joshi, 'Exploration in Northern Kutch', *JOIB*, XVI, 1966, pp. 62ff.
76. S.R. Rao, ibid., p. 187.
77. *Mahābhārata*, II.9.19; II.13.49.
78. *Periplus*, 41.
79. J.C. Jain, *Life in Ancient India* . . . , p. 211; *Kāvyamimānsa*, p. 281.
80. Unless the earlier suggestion be revived that the references to and the fear of the Asuras in the later Vedic Literature carried a memory of the worshippers of Ashur, the Assyrians. S.K. Chatterjee, *Iranianism*, pp. 21–2.
81. *Dictionary of Pali Proper Names*, G. Malalasekara (ed.), I, p. 117.
82. Ashurbanipal's inscription in the temple of Ishtar at Nineveh. Thompson, *AAA*, XX, pl. XCf, pp. 80ff.
83. T. Burrow, 'The Primitive Dravidian World for Horse', *IJDL*, vol. I, no. 1, 1972, pp. 1ff.
84. III.20.25–6; III.21.1ff. Andhaka is a prakritised form of Āndhra.
85. *Aṣṭādhyāyī*, IV.I, 114.
86. *Dictionary of Pali Proper Names*, G. Malalasekhara (ed.), I, p. 106.
87. *Aitareya Brāhmaṇa*, VII.18.
88. Third Major Rock Edict, Girnar version. Bloch, *Les Inscriptions d'Asoka*, p. 131; T. Burrow, *Collected Papers on Dravidian Linguistics*, p. 335.
89. Wheeler, *Indus Civilisation*, p. 133.
90. Leemans, *Foreign Trade in the Old Babylonian Period*, pp. 12ff; Oppenheim, *JAOS*, 1954, p. 17.
91. *Prapancahṛdayam*, pp. 3–4; quoted in B.A. Saletore, *Ancient Karnataka*, vol. I, p. 29.
92. *Keralolpatti*; quoted in Gopinath Rao, Travancore Archaeological Series, II, pp. 106ff.
93. *Epigraphia Indica*, XXXIII, pp. 62, 64; quoted in P. Gupta, *Geography in Ancient Indian Inscriptions*, p. 44. By way of an aside it may be added that the *Acalypha Indica* whose local names are Kuppai-meni, Kuppe, Kuppi (DED 1414) is native to the Konkan-Travancore region. Prof. R.S. Sharma has drawn my attention to the *Kupādhyakṣa* mentioned in the *Arthaśāstra*, generally taken to be a superintendent of forest produce, although the etymology of the Sanskrit word is difficult to locate.
94. K.A. Nilakantha Sastri, *A History of South India*, pp. 112ff.

95. J. Bloch, *Les Inscriptions d'Asoka*, p. 93.
96. K.A. Nilakantha Sastri, *A History of South India*, p. 119.
97. Second Major Rock Edict, Girnar version, Bloch, *Les Inscriptions d'Asoka*, p. 93.
98. N. Subramaniam, *Pre-Pallava Tamil Index*, p. 310. This identification for Qadê was suggested to me by Dr R. Champakalakshmi.
99. R. Campbell Thompson and M.E.L. Mallowan, 'The British Museum Excavations at Nineveh 1931–32', *AA*, 20, 1933, p. 96.
100. N. Subramaniam, *Pre-Pallave Tamil Index*, p. 127. For the identification with Simhala see T. Burrow, 'The Loss of Initial c/s in South Dravidian', *BSOAS*, XII, 1947. Bh. Krishnamurti, 'Comparative Dravidian Studies', in T.A. Sebeok (ed.), *Current Trends in Linguistics*, vol. 5, p. 316.
101. The meaning of *aṇi* was suggested to me by Dr Champakalakshmi.
102. McCrindle, *India as Described by Megasthenes and Arrian*, pp. 62–3, 169–72.
103. S. Deraniyagala, *Ancient Ceylon*, Dec. 1972, no. 2, p. 50.
104. J.M. Price, 'The Topography of the Gudea Inscriptions', *JAOS*, 43, 1923, pp. 45ff.
105. Kramer, *Antiquity*, XXXVII, 1963, p. 111; Kramer, *The Sumerians*, p. 276.
106. Ibid.
107. G. Dales, *JAOS*, 1968, no. 88, p. 22.
108. Monier Williams, *Sanskrit-English Dictionary*, qv. *Sindhu.*
109. J.C. Jain, *Life in Ancient India as Depicted in the Jaina Canon*, p. 335.
110. W.F. Leemans, *Foreign Trade*, p. 26.
111. Leemans quotes the very plausible argument of W. Eilers in *JESHO*, III, 1960, p. 29.
112. The Ṛgvedic meaning is specifically that of the male offspring and the heroic man. *Vedic Index*, II, p. 317.
113. Pāṇini, IV.1, 148; IV.2, 76; *Bṛhatsaṁhitā*, XIV, 17, 33; R.K. Singh, op. cit., pp. 149ff.
114. *Baudhāyana Dharma Sūtra*, I, 1/9–14; *Viṣṇudharmottara Purāṇa*, I.4.7.
115. *Mahāgovindasutta*, II.235; *Aditta Jātaka*, III, p. 280; *Milindapañho*, II, pp. 269, 296.
116. J.C. Jain, *Life in Ancient India as Depicted in the Jaina Canons*, p. 302.
117. E. Sachau (ed.), *Alberuni's India*, I.302; S.B. Chaudhuri, *Ethnic Settlements of Ancient India*. Most sources would place it west of the Indus river and in Sind although Alberuni describes it in the Multan area, which location may date to a very much later period. There is a curious reference in a seventeenth century AD text, the *Śatpañcasaddeśavibhāga* quoted in D.C. Sircar, *Studies in the Geography of Ancient and Medieval India*, pp. 75ff, 114; to the Saindhava territory

extending from Lankapradeśa to Makka. Sircar has identified Makka with Mecca, but it may be possible to suggest that Makka was a memory of Makan and referred to Sind and Baluchistan.

118. A.M. Shastri, *The Bṛhatsaṁhitā of Varāhamihira*, pp. 99–100.
119. Al–Qadri, 'All About Brahui', *IJDL*, I, no. 1, 1972, pp. 160ff.
120. W. Vincent, *Periplus of the Erythreaen Sea*, London, 1800, p. 345n.8.
121. Allchin, *Birth of Indian Civilisation*, p. 113.
122. *Cambridge Ancient History*, vol. I, part I, p. 454.
123. Oppenheim, op. cit., p. 17.
124. *Aelian*, XV.C.viii; *Pliny*, VI.20, IX.34.
125. LXXX.4.
126. S.R. Rao, *Lothal and the Indus Civilisation*, p. 97.
127. Marshall, *Mohenjo-daro*, pp. 27ff; Wheeler, *Indus Civilisation*, p. 67.
128. *ANET*, p. 343. For a discussion of the date crops of Baluchistan, Sind and Panjab, see O.K. Spate, op. cit., pp. 75, 219, 427, 457, 477.
129. P.B. Cornwall, 'Two Letters from Dilmun', *JCS*, 6, 1952, pp. 137ff.
130. Oppenheim, op. cit.; Leemans, *Foreign Trade in the Old Babylonian Period*, pp. 18–55.
131. R.L. Raikes, The End of the Ancient Cities of the Indus, *American Anthropologist*, 1964; 'The Mohenjo-daro Floods', *Antiquity*, 40, 1965.
132. Lambrick, *Sind*, pp. 65–6.
133. Agrawal, op. cit., pp. 120ff.
134. Ibid., pp. 171ff.
135. G. Bibby, 'According to the Standard of Dilmun', *Kuml.*, 1970.
136. Oppenheim, op. cit.; Leemans, 'Old Babylonian Letters and Economic History, *JESHO*, XI, 1968, p. 216; Mackay, *Early Indus Civilisation*, pp. 106ff.
137. Cf. *Ur Excavations, Texts*, III, 1498.
138. R.E.M. Wheeler, *Indus Civilisation*, pp. 68ff.
139. J.M. Casals, 'Mundigak as a Link Between Pakistan and Iran in Prehistory', *JASP*, 1957, vol. II, p. 3.
140. Lambrick, *Sind*, p. 61.
141. Leemans, op. cit., p. 26; Ktesias, I.6.
142. K.A. Chowdhury and S.S. Ghosh, 'Plant Remains from Harappa', *Ancient India*, no. 7, 1951, pp. 3ff.
143. K.P. Segreiya, *Forests and Forestry*, p. 233; D. Brandis, *Indian Trees*, p. 138.
144. Information supplied by Shereen Ratnagar.
145. Leemans, *Foreign Trade in the Old Babylonian Period*; and 'Old Babylonian Letters and Economic History', *JESHO*, XI, 1968, pp. 215–26.
146. Bibby has argued that this is additional proof that Bahrain is Dilmun since the Dilmun weight is found at Bahrain, *Looking for Dilmun*, p. 377.

147. Luckenbill, *AR*, II, p. 40; *AJSL*, XXXV, pp. 182–5.
148. W.F. Albright, 'A Babylonian Geographical Treatise on Sargon of Akkad's Empire', *JAOS*, 45, Sept. 1965, pp. 193–245.
149. G. Bibby, *Looking for Dilmun*, pp. 59–60.
150. J. Hansom, 'A Periplus of Magan and Meluhha', *BSOAS*, 36, 1973, pp. 553ff. Cf. W.F. Leemans, *Foreign Trade*, p. 165 and *JESHO*, XI, 1968, p. 220.
151. M. Murray, *The Splendour that was Egypt*, pp. 98–9, 226, 256.
152. J. Doresse, *Ethiopia*, pp. 16ff.
153. Leemans, op. cit., pp. 158ff.
154. Ibid.
155. S.N. Kramer, *The Sumerians*, p. 278.
156. Cf. in the same sense Leemans, *Foreign Trade*, p. 165 and *JESHO*, XI, p. 220; I.J. Gelb, *Revue d' Assyriologie*, 64, 1970, p. 3.
157. McCrindle, *Ancient India as Described by Ptolemy*, pp. 39ff.
158. A. Cunningham, *Ancient Geography of India*, pp. 420, 473.
159. Wheeler, *Indus Civilisation*, pp. 117ff.
160. *Śatapatha Brāhmaṇa*, I.8.1, 1–10; S.N. Kramer, *Sumerian Mythology*, pp. 97–8.
161. Gilgamesh has to find the flower of immortality from the sea bed and in the *amṛtamanthana* legend the elixir of immortality has to be churned out of the ocean. The Sumerian sources when describing the religion of Dilmun refer to the great mother, the goddess Ninhursag, giving birth to eight deities some of which become the titular gods and goddesses of Dilmun, Makan and Meluhha. This recalls the story of Aditi in Sanskrit texts (*Ṛgveda*, X.63; X.72); Aditi was the daughter of the great patriarchal deity Dakṣa and was the *deva-matri* in addition to being the earth goddess. She gave birth to eight sons, among them the major deities of the early vedic pantheon, Indra, Varuna, and Mitra. Curiously, among these, the Lord of Dilmun was Enshagag/Enzak, whose wife Ninsikilla was particularly reputed for her chastity. The latter would certainly apply to Indrani, the wife of Indra who was also a model of chastity. Would the proto-types of these deities have to be sought in pre-Vedic mythology, some of which could later have been appropriated by the Vedic Mythology? The association and the stress on cleanliness among the people of Dilmun has already been noticed as indicating a connection with Indian ritual and practice. (Kramer, *Antiquity*, XXXVII, 1963, pp. 111ff).

# 14

# Society in Ancient India: The Formative Period*

I would like to take as my theme an exploration in the study of society in ancient India and to deal with the period from *circa* 2500 BC to 500 BC in northern India, treating it principally as an occasion to demonstrate what I mean by a reorientation of perspectives.†

The beginnings of Indian history have been projected for decades now in the supposed invasion of northern India by the Aryans and the establishment of Aryan culture as a result of this conquest. The projection was that of a racially superior people. The study of both the Sanskrit texts and of ethnology went into the making of this theory.[1] Let me say at the outset that I am not concerned with 'the Aryan problem' *per se*. It is perhaps the biggest red herring that was dragged across the path of historians of India.[2] What I am concerned with is the need to understand the evolution of society at this time. This is a crucial period not only because it saw the initial pattern of Indian culture take shape, but also because it can provide clues to a more analytical understanding of subsequent periods of Indian history. As it happens, the more important and controversial announcements pertaining to ancient Indian studies made during the year also relate to this period. The most serious of the many claims to have deciphered the Harappa script, in terms of the methodology used and the discussion it has provoked, is that of the Finnish scholars, who read the script as proto-Dravidian.[3] An interesting facet of the controversy has been the vehemence of

* Presidential Address, Ancient Indian History Section, XXXI Indian History Congress, 1969, Varanasi. Published in Proceedings of the Indian History Congress. 1970. 15–39.

† Owing to the shortage of time I have confined myself to general remarks and observations in the text of this Address. Further discussion and references are included in the notes at the end of the Address.

the loyalty to the respective Indo-Aryan and Dravidian language groups, with undertones almost of an Aryan and a Dravidian nationalism! This, in spite of the fact that specialists in both languages have for many years been suggesting that although linguistically distinct, at the cultural level at least this dichotomy is false.[4]

Our starting point could be the fact that we have two types of evidence, archaeological and literary. The literary sources are well-known and comprise the corpus of Vedic literature. The archaeological evidence consists of a number of cultures, most of them seemingly disparate. The earliest are the pre-Harappan cultures; the Sothi culture[5] of the Sarasvati valley and the Chalcolithic village sites of Baluchistan and Sind. These were the precursors of the Harappa culture (*c.* 2300–1750) which extended from southern Punjab and Sind to the Narmada delta largely following the coastal region, and eastwards as far as the upper Ganga-Yamuna Doāb.[6] Of the post-Harappan cultures there is evidence from both the Indus and Ganga valleys. In northern Punjab the Gandhara Grave culture[7] (*c.* 1500–500 BC), using a red ware and a plain grey ware, shows evidence of copper in the early stages and later an iron technology, and contacts with Iran and central Asia. The Banas culture of southern Rajasthan (*c.* 2000–1200 BC, with possible extensions in the Ganga valley coming down to 800 BC) with its characteristic white-painted black-and-red pottery and its probable internalizing of certain Harappan forms, possibly acted as a bridge between the Harappan and post-Harappan cultures.[8] In the upper Ganga valley the earliest remains belong to the culture represented by the Ochre Colour Pottery which is post-Harappan in time range (*c.* 1400–1200). This has been associated sometimes with the Copper Hoard Culture[9] found both in the Doāb and in southern Bihar and West Bengal, and whose authors were perhaps the Muṇḍā speaking peoples. At some sites in Bihar there is evidence of the black-and-red ware (occasionally white-painted and similar to that of the Banas culture) forming the earliest level. In parts of the Doāb it succeeds the Ochre Colour Pottery and precedes the predominant culture of the region. The latter is the Painted Grey Ware[10] (*c.* 1100–400) an initially agrarian culture familiar with iron technology and the horse. Finally, the Northern Black Polished Ware culture (*c.* 500–100) is associated with urbanization in the Ganga valley.

The archaeological picture therefore shows a large variety of cultures, none of which can be identified as specifically Aryan.[11]

Nor does the evidence suggest that there was a single dominating culture which slowly spread throughout northern India bringing the various diverse cultures into its fold, which is what one would expect if the popular notion of the spread of Aryan culture be accepted. In comparing the Indian and west Asian material there is again little consistent evidence of a dominant culture recognisably coming from west Asia to India, or for that matter going from India to west Asia, though there are certain similarities of techniques, such as the socketed axe and in ceramics. This would suggest migrants carrying aspects of technology and probably the language in both directions.

In comparing literary and archaeological evidence it is important to determine the nature of the society concerned. In the case of the *Ṛg Veda* the geographical focus is that of the *sapta sindhava* roughly from the Kabul river to the Sarasvatī river.[12] Ṛgvedic society is essentially a pre-urban society with a copper and possibly iron technology.[13] It is evolving from nomadic pastoralism dependent on cattle to an agrarian form with more settled communities. Barley (*yava*) appears to have been the staple food. There is a strong sense of tribal identity and the basic social unit is the patriarchal family. Close linguistic connections with Iran are evident. The important deities are Indra, Mitra, Varuṇa, Savitṛ, Soma and Agni. There is a distinct feeling of cultural exclusiveness and separation from some local people who are both feared and disliked and with whom relations are frequently hostile (e.g. the Dasyus and the Paṇis).

The Later Vedic literature depicts a recognizable change in material culture. The geographical focus includes the Punjab and the middle Ganga valley in the main, with a more marginal familiarity with the Indus area, western and eastern India and the Vindhyas. The society is essentially agrarian culminating in a series of urban centres. There is a considerable acquaintance with iron technology. Frequent mention is made of rice (*vrīhi*) which is not mentioned in the *Ṛg Veda*. The clan identity continues and in many cases is extended to territorial identity. The Ṛgvedic deities do not have the pre-eminent position which they had had earlier since equal importance is now given to more recently incorporated deities. The fourfold *varṇa* structure mentioned only once in the *Ṛg Veda* is now a recognized feature. The geographical and philosophical connections with west Asia have weakened. There appears to be a greater assimilation with local cultures. In comparing the early and late

Vedic literature it would seem that the major characteristic of continuity remains the language, Sanskrit.

Whatever our cherished notions about the Aryans may be, the archaeological evidence does not suggest a massive invasion or a massive migration.[14] Even if it be conceded that the presence of Indo-Aryan in the *sapta sindhava* region can be attributed to invasion, which is at times suggested in the *Ṛg Veda*, the same reason cannot be given for its presence in other parts of northern India. At most it can be said that the Indo-Aryan speakers were small groups of migrants with a strong adherence to a linguistic equipment deriving from Indo-European. Both linguistic evidence and the literature point to the Indo-Aryan speakers living in the vicinity of those who spoke an alien language (*mṛdhra vāc*) and those later called the *mlecchas*.[15] Were these the Muṇḍā or Dravidian speakers? Were they also the authors of pre-iron Chalcolithic cultures? In the Ganga valley archaeological evidence does not suggest that the earlier inhabitants fled or migrated. Therefore their continued presence must have necessitated a process of acculturation. What then was the nature of the impact of these Indo-Aryan speakers? Perhaps it would make greater historical sense if we see it not as the imposition of Aryan culture on the existing Indian cultures, but rather, as the diffusion of Indo-Aryan. The new language could have been accepted for various reasons without necessitating the imposition of a totally new culture.[16]

In the study of the inter-action of cultures there are many facets which require investigation. Let me start with the most primary, the question of the numbers of people involved. This would imply demographic studies of various sites and settlements. Comparative assessments of population figures from the sites of varying cultures could be helpful, as also the detailed charting of the location of sites — whether they are superimposed or adjacent. Would there be a greater possibility of cross-cultural assimilation if the numbers are consistently small and equally matched?[17] A demographic analysis, even if impressionistic, studied together with the nature of the terrain and technology and facilities for transportation would provide indications of the pace and flow of migration. The Painted Grey Ware settlements being generally small, the nature of the terrain being thick jungle, the pace of migration would be slow even if the river was used as the main channel of communication. It should not be forgotten that in spite of a time-span of about six hundred years the geographical distribution of the Painted Grey Ware remains broadly the Ganga-Yamuna Doāb and the Sarasvatī valley. However, acceleration in the pace of communication seems to accompany the development of an urban culture as it would appear from the distribution of the Northern Black Polished Ware.

Even a rough demographic picture will introduce an element of reality into the study. If the settlements of a particular culture are small then production is also likely to be small. A comparison between such data and literary descriptions of extravagant wealth may lead to a correcting of the poetic licence implicit in great works of literature. Estimates of production are relevant to the study of towns owing to the interdependence of towns and villages.[18] More mundane factors such as food habits have their own significance. The Ṛgvedic people had a diet substantially of barley and wheat, and the Later Vedic literature introduces rice. From the archaeological evidence we know that the Harappans were mainly barley and wheat eating, whereas the Ganga valley, the Banas valley and probably a part of western India was predominantly rice eating.[19] This points to a major difference of staple diet between the Ṛgvedic and Later Vedic people. If they were the same ethnically then they must have rapidly adjusted to a change of diet. However the Painted Grey Ware levels in the Doāb suggest a people long accustomed to rice. It is interesting that in later Sanskrit literature wheat is sometimes referred to as *mleccha-bhojana*.[20]

Another aspect in the process of acculturation is the role of technology. A language which is associated with an advanced technology can often make a very effective impact. The use of the horse and of iron would point to an advanced technology. The acceptance of the Indo-Aryan language would therefore not require the physical conquest of the areas where it came to be spoken but rather the control of the advanced technology by the speakers of Indo-Aryan.[21] The horse-drawn chariot seems to have swung the balance militarily in favour of the Indo-Aryan speakers, judging from the hymns of the *Ṛg Veda*. The horse as compared to the ox was a swifter means of transportation as also was the chariot as compared with the cart.[22] The introduction of iron did not mean totally new technological implements. It was more a qualitative improvement of existing forms particularly in relation to the ecological conditions of the region. The hafted copper axe gave way to the socketed iron axe, the wooden plough had an iron tip added to it and the stone hoe was replaced by the iron hoe (or it was introduced where the hoe was not known before), not to mention adzes, arrow-heads, spear-heads, knives, daggers, nails, etc.[23] The technology of the Painted Grey Ware culture seems to support this assessment. The question of who first used iron technology in India has its own importance, but for our purposes it is more relevant to enquire as to whether the speakers of Indo-Aryan exploited the knowledge of iron technology to their advantage. That the new technology was essentially the improvement of existing forms is supported by the use of certain significant words in Vedic literature which appear to have a non-Indo-Aryan origin. Thus the most frequently used word for plough is *lāṅgala* which is of Muṇḍā origin and the word for rice *vrīhi* is believed to be of Dravidian origin.[24] Could there have been a correlation between the degree of technological change and the utilization of Indo-Aryan? That the caste status of iron smiths ultimately became low would accord with the probability that as long as the control of the technology lay with the higher status groups, the actual working of the technology could remain with low status groups.[25]

In ancient agricultural societies, apart from agricultural technology, another factor of some consequence would be the knowledge of the calendar. It is thought that the earliest calendar used in India was the lunar calendar. Yet the solar calendar was more efficient in its application to agriculture and astronomy (and thereby to astrology). The discovery and use of the solar calendar would require more advanced knowledge in mathematics and astronomy. A basis of mathematical knowledge must be assumed in order to explain the construction of the Harappan cities. Was this knowledge continued in some tradition? If the Harappans had used a binary system (by and large) then the decimal system referred to in the Vedic literature would have been an improvement.[26] The essential geometrical knowledge necessary for evolving a solar calendar may have been inherent in the geometry required for the construction of complex sacrificial altars.[27] There appears to be a groping towards understanding the principles of the solar calendar in the Vedic literature. The year of 360 days (30 × 12 months) was known to be defective and attempts were made at intercalation in which the 366-day year was not excluded.[28] It is true that the widespread knowledge of the solar calendar is associated with Greek contacts at a later period. It is not to be ruled out however that a secret knowledge or a restricted knowledge of it may have existed earlier. The appropriation of such knowledge by certain groups may well have given them access to power and influence. A scientific study of the application of astronomy and mathematics to activities such as agriculture and astrology within the context of contemporary society might be revealing: as also the transmission of mathematical ideas between Babylon and India.

In the post-Harappa period the centre of historical activity moved away from the Indus valley towards other directions: to the Ganga valley with Magadha eventually emerging as a nuclear region, to western India, and later, to the coastal regions of the peninsula. Part of the reason for the movement away from the Indus valley was the break-down in the Harappan economic system.[29] The post-Harappan sites in western India appear to have re-introduced the earlier maritime contacts with Mesopotamia, from at least the first millennium BC. As such, western India would have acted as a point of communication for goods and ideas between India and west Asia. A further archaeological investigation of the west coast and routes from here to the Ganga valley may prove worthwhile.[30]

Another aspect worth considering in assessing the reasons for the spread of Indo-Aryan is the interrelationship between language and society. The fact that the earliest Sanskrit grammars were written in the north points to a greater use or longer tradition of the language in this region. By contrast the lower Ganga valley retains a Prākṛt tradition for a longer period.[31] Was this distinction due to the linguistic differences in Indo-Aryan itself or was it due to a greater influence of non-Indo-Aryan languages in eastern India? Magadha is described as an impure land and the people of Aṅga, Vaṅga and Kaliṅga are referred to as *mleccha*.[32] It is also worth examining why certain important words relating to technology were introduced from non-Indo-Aryan sources and retained in Indo-Aryan. We have already noticed the case of *lāṅgala* and *vrīhi*. The Indo-Aryan for horse is *aśva*, yet *aśva* was never as commonly used in the Late Indo-Aryan languages as *ghoṭa* and its derivatives. That this could happen with items as important as the plough, rice and the horse, makes one wonder whether the question of loan words from Muṇḍā and Dravidian does not call for a co-ordinated study by the specialist in linguistics and the historian, which would not merely trace the loan or the etymology of words, but would also throw light on the cultural context of their incorporation. The etymology of technical and professional words in their historical context would alone be worth a study.

It is historically well-known that in the spread of a language associated with an advanced technology it is often the dominant groups in the existing society which take up the new language first. This would be easier to understand in our period if we had some concrete evidence on the origin of the caste structure. It is curious that although the origin of the caste structure is frequently associated with the Aryan speakers it occurs only in India and not in other societies which were also recipients of Aryan culture. It may therefore have been a pre-Aryan system which was reconstituted somewhat, and described in Later Vedic literature. To see caste as the distinction between fair Aryans and dark-non-Aryans is to over-simplify a very complex system. In the study of social structure the historian of ancient India must of necessity now take the help of social anthropology. The essentials of a caste society are, firstly, marriage and lineage functioning through exogamous and endogamous kinship relations (*jāti*); secondly, the integration of the division of labour into a hierarchical system which eventually takes the form of service relationships; thirdly, the idea of pollution where some groups are seen as ritually pure, others less so and yet others totally impure or polluting; and finally the association of castes with particular geographical locations. All these factors could have been present in the Harappa culture where social stratification can at least be surmised.[34] If a similar system prevailed in the Banas culture and those of the Ganga valley, then the spread of a new language could be achieved through influencing the groups which held high status and by rearrangement of endogamous groups.[35]

Ascribing caste status did not merely depend on the occupation of a group. In some cases an entire tribe was ascribed a particular rank. Those speaking a non-Indo-Aryan language were frequently given a low rank and described as *mleccha*. In the case of the *caṇḍālas* there is reference to a *cāṇḍāla-bhāṣā*.[36] Some of these tribes remained consistently of low status over many centuries, such as the Kirāta and the Pulinda;[37] others acquired political power and thereby higher status. Even today there are pockets of Muṇḍā and Dravidian speaking people in areas of Indo-Aryan languages. This is not due to any historical oversight. The Muṇḍā-speaking groups until recently were hunters and pastoralists with, at most, digging-stick agriculture. In contrast to this the Indo-Aryan speaking people are, by and large, plough and hoe-using agriculturalists. Were the *śūdra* tribes those who in the initial stages either did not accept the new agricultural technology or did not apply it? Did the Aryanization of language accompany the expansion of the iron-using agrarian village?

This village was not the neolithic village growing essentially in isolation, nor the chalcolithic village with restricted trade inter-relationships. It was the prosperous iron-using village whose prosperity increased with easier access to both iron ore and more land for cultivation. This prosperity could not only give these villages a political edge over the others but also provide a larger surplus for those in control. At one level this became the stable base for the growth of towns;[38] at another level it strengthened the language, Indo-Aryan.

With the change from nomadic pastoralism to settled agrarian villages, tribal identity was extended to territorial identity, as is reflected in tribal names being given to geographical areas. This in turn gave rise to the concept of the state with both monarchical and non-monarchical forms of government. Woven into this concept were the institutions of caste and private property.[39]

Even among those tribes who had accepted the new technology and language, the priests — the ritually pure groups — would have resisted the new culture unless their own status was safeguarded. Was this done by allowing them to preserve their ritual purity through the caste structure and by their continuing to hold a priestly status, and also by incorporating much of their religion into the new culture? The assimilation of a tribe into the caste structure would also require some assimilation of its religion. The religious aspects of Later Vedic literature, inasmuch as they differ from the *Ṛg Veda*, include a large amount of non-Aryan practice and belief — both at the level of ritual and of deities.[40] It is indeed a moot point whether this literature can be called the religious literature of the Aryans alone.

Every society has a method of remembering what it regards as the important aspects of its past and this is woven into its historical tradition. For our period it is the *itihāsa-purāṇa* tradition which sets out to record the past. The most significant section of this tradition is the preservation of the royal genealogies and the myths associated with them. The royal genealogies (*vaṃśāvalī*) may not be historically correct but when studied carefully they indicate the pattern of the migration and spread of various peoples. Such an analysis can be more useful than the repeated but so far unsuccessful attempts to identify the tribes as either Aryan or non-Aryan. Genealogies have played a noticeably important part in the Indian historical tradition, even when they are known to be fabricated. This is surely the clue to understanding the role of the genealogy, not necessarily as an authentic dynastic chronicle but rather as a social document. Similarly, what is important about the myths is not whether they are historically authentic, but the cultural assumptions of the society which are implicit in the myth.[41]

The questions which arise in the study of the proto-historic period have a relevance to later history. It would seem that in northern India the expansion of the village economy based on iron technology accompanied the diffusion of Indo-Aryan, judging by the archaeological evidence for the distribution of iron in association with literary evidence for Indo-Aryan. Indo-Aryan therefore would not be widely accepted in those areas where iron technology was already known. In the peninsula the area covered by the iron-using Megalithic settlements roughly coincides with the area of the widespread use of Dravidian languages.

If we can explain the reasons for the shift in focus from the Indus valley to the Ganga valley in proto-historic times, then we can also throw some light on one of the more interesting facets of ancient Indian history, namely, the geographical shift in the nuclear regions which were the matrices of large states and empires. At least three regions come immediately to mind: Magadha, the Raichur-Bijapur districts, and the area between Kanchipuram and Tanjore. Why did these regions give rise to a series of politically dominant states and then go into quiescence?[42] Was it due to the fertility of the region yielding large revenues, or the abundant availability of iron, or access to trade routes, or the exploitation of a new technology or the rise of ideologies motivating political action? Or was it merely the strange but happy coincidence of a series of strong rulers, which is the explanation generally offered?

In the analysis of social structure there is a need for redefining social relationships. To see caste only in terms of the four-fold *varṇa* does not take us very far. One would like to know how tribes and social groups were adjusted into the caste hierarchy and assigned a caste status. The theory that the caste-structure was initially flexible but gradually became rigid and allowed of little mobility, is now open to question. There is enough evidence to suggest that there have been in all periods deviations from the theoretical concept of caste.[43] We also know that there was a continual emergence of new castes for a variety of reasons. Furthermore social change presupposes social tension and at times even conflicts between groups, and these are referred to in the sources. The origin, nature and consequences of these tensions constitutes another significant area of study.

The history of religion, apart from its theological, philosophical and iconographical aspects, also has a social aspect, since religion has to be practised by people in order to be viable. The interrelation therefore of religious cults and movements with social groups is very close. What were the social roots of Buddhism and Jainism? Why were certain cults assimilated and others left out in what later came to be called Hinduism? What accounts for the remarkable popularity of the mother-goddess cults in various forms in the post-Gupta period? More precise answers to such questions would help us ascertain with greater accuracy the nature of the 'brahmanical renaissance' as it has been called in the Gupta and post-Gupta periods.

It will be evident that I am making a plea for more intensive studies of the nature of society in ancient India: and by this I mean an integrated understanding of the many facets which go into the functioning of a society. Such a study involves not merely additional dimensions in terms of methods and sources, it also means, if need be, altering the perspective from which we view the past. New perspectives, although they may initially appear whimsical, often provide new insights. The immense labour and scholarship of our predecessors has provided us with a firm foundation on which to base our studies of ancient Indian history. We can with confidence, therefore, explore new perspectives. Ultimately as historians we are concerned not merely with attempting to discover the past, but with trying to understand it.

## Notes and References

1. T.R. Trautmann, *The Aryans and British India*, Delhi, 1997.
2. The Aryan problem arose out of a series of philological studies in the eighteenth and nineteenth century which recorded the similarities

between a number of languages of Asia and Europe and postulated a common ancestry in Indo-European. (T.R. Trautmann, *The Aryans and British India*, Delhi, 1997). Max Müller's statement about the Aryan nation as the physical manifestation of Aryan culture lent support to the search for the Aryan race. His later repeated attempts to deny the existence of an Aryan race were often ignored (*Biographies of Words and the Home of the Vedas*, 1887, p. 90). Incidentally, it is conceivable that Max Müller's Aryan-Semitic dichotomy may well have influenced the Aryan-Dravidian dichotomy. The real damage was caused by his assertion of the superiority of Aryan culture over all other cultures, which has been made axiomatic to the study of the Indian past (*Chips from a German Workshop*, 1867, I, p. 63. '. . . In continual struggle with each other and with Semitic and Turanian races, these Aryan nations have become the rulers of history, and it seems to be their mission to link all parts of the world together by chains of civilisation, commerce and religion . . .'.) Aryan culture is often taken as the starting point of Indian culture and is projected both backwards (in attempts to prove the Aryan basis of the Harappa culture) and forwards in time. It is also sought to be associated with every worthwhile achievement in early India.

In his enthusiasm for the Aryan way of life (as he saw it), Max Müller further depicted Aryan society as an idyllic society of village communities where people were concerned not with the mundane things of everyday living but with other-worldly thoughts and values (*India, What can it teach us?* pp. 101ff). This has also acted as a check on the more realistic study of the actual conditions of life in the Vedic period. That the motives of Max Müller and other Indologists of his views in acclaiming Aryan culture derived from a genuine admiration for Aryan society as they saw it, has to be conceded, but this does not exonerate them from gilding the lily. Max Müller's attempt to link India and Europe via the Aryans was in part to connect the origins of Indian culture with the founders of European culture. Thus Indian culture could acquire status in the eyes of Europe and, at the same time, early Indian nationalism could exploit this connection to combat the cultural inferiority complex generated among Indians as a result of British rule. In fact early Indian nationalism gave greater attention to extolling the Aryans in India rather than to the connection with Europe. Historical scholarship has now moved beyond the needs and confines of nineteenth century nationalism and a re-evaluation of Max Müller's theories is necessary.

Even some modern sociological theorists have made sweeping generalisations on contemporary India and Indian society on the basis of the nineteenth century understanding of Indian history. Max Weber in his study, *The Religion of India* (New York 1967 reprint) used fairly uncritically much of the writing of Orientalists such as Max Müller. A more recent example of the acceptance of this tradition, without a sufficient investigation of the alternatives, is Louis Dumont's *Homo Hierarchicus* (1967). That the influence of such thinking, stressing the other-worldly character of Indian society, is apparent even on economic historians is evident from Gunnar Myrdal, *Asian Drama* (1969), where the Weberian thesis is given considerable emphasis to explain the failure of the development of capitalism in India.

3. Asko Parpola et al., *Decipherment of the Proto-Dravidian Inscriptions of the Indus Civilisation*, The Scandinavian Institute of Asian Studies, Copenhagen, 1969.

   Asko Parpola, *Progress in the Decipherment of the Proto-Dravidian Indus Script*, 1969.

   Asko Parpola, *Further Progress in the Decipherment of the Proto-Indus Script*, 1969.

   A less publicised attempt was made by a number of Russian scholars. Y. Knorozov, *Proto-Indica*, 1968. Two other recent attempts, those of Dr Fateh Singh and Mr Krishna Rao, are generally not acceptable to scholars.

   Owing to a lack of a bi-lingual inscription most attempts so far have used a system of intelligent (and in some cases not so intelligent) guesswork. Using the inconographic representation as the starting point attempts have been made to try and read the script as that of an Indo-Aryan language (Wadell, S.K. Ray, Krishna Rao). Those who have used the script as their starting point have more often arrived at Proto-Dravidian (Hunter, Heras, the Russians and the Finns). The Finns read it as a largely logographic script based on the principles of homophony. The advance made by the Finnish scholars and to some extent the earlier Russian studies is that they have placed greater reliance on linguistic and mathematical techniques rather than on historical guesswork. Any claims to decipherment must satisfy certain preconditions. The decipherment must conform to a grammatical and linguistic system and cannot be arbitrary (this being the major objection to the attempt by Krishna Rao); it must conform to the archaeological evidence of the culture and to the chronological span of the Harappa culture; the reading of the inscriptions must make sense in terms of the context of the culture. Of the recent attempts, the Russian and the Finnish conform most to these preconditions. However even their readings present problems which they have not satisfactorily overcome. As to whether the Finnish claim is justified will depend on the publication of their readings of complete texts, which are still awaited.

4. As for example in the essays of Sylvain Levi, Jean Przyluski and Jules Bloch, translated and published by P.C. Bagchi in *Pre-Aryan and*

*Pre-Dravidian in India*, 1929, and more recently in the writings of S.K. Chatterjee, T. Burrow and M.B. Emeneau.

5. A. Ghosh, 'The Indus Civilisation — Its Origins, Authors, Extent and Chronology', in V.N. Misra and N.S. Mate (eds), *Indian Pre-history*, 1964. An attempt has been made to try and identify the Sothi Culture with the Ṛgvedic people by A.D. Pusalkar, 'Pre-Harappan, Harappan and Post-Harappan Culture and the Aryan Problem', *The Quarterly Review of Historical Studies*, VII, no. 4, 1967–68, pp. 233ff. Apart from the problem that the geographical extent does not coincide since the Ṛgvedic culture included northern Punjab and excluded Sind and western India, there is also the problem of chronology. Attempts to date the *Ṛg Veda* to the fourth and fifth millennia BC are based mainly on references to astronomical positions mentioned in the texts, viz., Tilak, *The Orion* . . . ; Jacobi, 'On the Date of the *Ṛg Veda*', *Indian Antiquary*, June 1894; and Bühler, *Indian Antiquary*, Sept. 1894. Such evidence is not conclusive, since references to astronomy could have been incorporated from the traditions of an earlier people. The parallels with Gāthic Avestan and with Kassite and Mitanni inscriptions which are very close, would date the *Ṛg Veda* to the middle of the second millennium BC.

6. The attempted identification of the Harappa culture with the later Vedic society on the basis of both being agro-urban societies is again controverted by the differences not only in the total culture but also in the geographical nuclei. The Harappa culture is located in the Indus valley and western India and its urbanization is based on a chalcolithic system with an absence of iron. Later Vedic society centering on the Ganga valley from which the Harappa culture is largely absent (except for a few minor sites in the upper Doāb) owes its gradual urbanization to iron technology. The technology of the two cultures is different. The pre-eminent role of the fertility cult among the Harappans is absent in Vedic society. The Harappans buried their dead, the Vedic people largely cremated their dead. (It is interesting that so far no graves have been found in association with the Painted Grey Ware cultures, which may suggest that they cremated their dead.) The horse so characteristic of Vedic society is not associated with the Harappans. The Harappa culture from the very beginning used a script whereas references to writing in Vedic society come at a later stage. If, finally, the Harappan script is read as Proto-Dravidian then there will be hardly any possibility of identifying the Harappa culture with Indo-Aryan speakers.

7. A.H. Dani, 'Gandhara Grave Culture', *Ancient Pakistan*, III, 1967.

8. B.B. Lal, *Indian Archaeology — A Review*, 1959–60 (for the site of Gilund); D.P. Agarwal, 'C-14 Dates, Banas Culture and the Aryans', *Current Science*, 5 March 1966, pp. 114ff; H.D. Sankalia, 'New Light

on the Indo-Iranian or Western Asiatic Relations between 1700–1200 BC', *Artibus Asiae*, XXVI, 1963; H.D. Sankalia, S.B. Deo, Z.D. Ansari, *Excavations at Ahar*, 1969.

9. B.B. Lal, 'Further Copper Hoards from the Gangetic Basin and a Review of the Problem', *Ancient India*, no. 7, 1951, pp. 20ff; S.P. Gupta, 'Indian Copper Hoards', *Journal of the Bihar Research Society*, 49, 1963, pp. 147ff.
10. B.B. Lal, 'Excavations at Hastinapur', *Ancient India*, nos 10 and 11, 1954–55, pp. 5ff; T.N. Roy, 'Stratigraphical Position of the Painted Grey Ware in the Gangetic Valley', *Bharati*, no. 8, II, 1964–65, pp. 64ff.
11. A recent summary of attempts to identify the Aryans with archaeological evidence is that of Dilip K. Chakrabarti, 'The Aryan Hypothesis in Indian Archaeology', *Indian Studies*, IX, no. 4, July–Sept. 1968, pp. 343ff. The more recent evidence of the Gandhara Grave Culture has been interpreted by Dani as representing perhaps, the early Indo-Aryan migration identified with the Ṛg Vedic literature. The linguistic theories of Hoernle and Grierson, suggesting that there were two bands of migration and therefore of language, have been used in the argument that the first band settled in the *sapta sindhava* region, and the second, skirting round the Indus, perhaps settled in the Banas valley. From here there was a movement both along the northern slopes of the Vindhyas to Bihar and also into the Doāb. Incidentally, in the latter case it would have followed a route which was frequently used in historical times to connect the Doāb with the west coast.
12. There are incidental references to migration in the *Ṛg Veda*, in verses such as I.30.9; I.36.18; and they read clearly as for example, VI.45.1, '. . . *ya ānayat parāvataḥ sūnīti turvaśam yaduṁ indraḥ sa no yuvā sakhā* . . . '. Furthermore it must be remembered that the *nadī stuti* hymn which is often quoted to contradict the theory of migration is in fact from the tenth *maṇḍala* of the *Ṛg Veda* which is later than the other sections.
13. The element of doubt arises because of the meaning of the word *ayas*. It is possible that it originally meant copper, as it seems to in some contexts, but later with the introduction of iron it was qualified by the terms *kṛṣṇa ayas* and *śyāma ayas*. When the association of *tāmra* with copper became common, then *ayas* may have been reserved for iron. It has however been argued that *ayas* originally meant iron and that the earliest knowledge of iron in India has therefore to be associated with the Ṛgvedic people. L. Gopal, *Uttar Bharati*, IV, no. 3, pp. 71ff and N.R. Banerjee, *The Iron Age in India*, pp. 158ff. The Indo-European root of *ayas* and its consistent use as iron in other Indo-European languages (*aes, ais, aisa, eisarn*) is a strong argument in favour of this view.

14. The migration theory would seem more acceptable than the invasion theory. The association of the Cemetry H evidence with the Aryans and the supposed massacre at Mohenjo-daro has been doubted. B.B. Lal, 'Protohistoric Investigations', *Ancient India*, no. 9, 1953, p. 88; G.F. Dales, 'The Mythical Massacre at Mohenjo-daro', *Expedition*, VI, no. 3, 1964, pp. 36ff; A. Ghosh, 'The Archaeological Background', *M.A.S.I.*, no. 9, 1962, p. 1; G.F. Dales, 'The Decline of the Harappans', *Scientific American*, vol. 214, no. 5, 1966. There is no evidence of Kalibangan having been attacked and it is unlikely that it would have been spared, being so close, if Harappa had been attacked. Post-Harappan cultures rarely build directly on the debris of Harappan sites except at Rupar and Alamgirpur. The extremely interesting discussion by Burrow on the significance of the terms *arma* and *armaka* in the Vedic literature and Pāṇini (*Journal of Indian History*, XLI, 1963, part 1, pp. 159ff) suggests that the references to ruins were to the Indus Civilization cities. What is curious however is that in some cases it would appear that Indra and Agni were responsible for the destruction of these cities, whereas in other cases they appear already to have been in ruins. It would seem that most of these cities were in the Sarasvatī and Punjab region. It is stated that the dark inhabitants fled and migrated. This would agree with the archaeological evidence that the cities were deserted and not occupied by the new arrivals. They were regarded as places of evil and the haunt of sorceresses (*yātumatī*) and therefore to be avoided. This would hardly be the attitude of a conquering people who had actually destroyed the cities. Could the cities have been deserted owing to a natural calamity before the arrival of the Indo-Aryan speakers, who associated the ruins of cities with evil, perhaps set fire to the remaining ruins and ultimately attributed the destruction of the cities to Indra and Agni? This would also explain the chronological gap, i.e., the Harappa culture having declined by 1750 BC and the Ṛgvedic Aryans being dated to *circa* 1500 BC.

Recent skeleton analysis of the Harappa culture sites are tending to puncture the theory of the Indo-Aryan speakers representing a large and separate racial group. S.S. Sarkar, *Ancient Races of Baluchistan, Punjab and Sind*, maintains that the Harappans were the same as the present-day predominant ethnic types living in these areas, which would contradict the theory of a large scale Aryan invasion or migration. Dr K. Sen, 'Ancient Races of India and Pakistan, a Study of Methods', *Ancient India*, nos 20 and 21, 1964–65, pp. 178ff, has suggested that the ethnic stock of Cemetry R 37 and Cemetry H appears to have been the same although there are cultural differences.

15. In describing the *dāsa* the references to their being conquered in battle are only a few among a large number of other references to the

differences between the *ārya* and the *dāsa*. These differences emphasise the fact of the latter having an alien culture. Thus the *dāsa* are described in the *Ṛg Veda* as *hatvī dasyūn pura āyasīrni tārit* (II, 20.8); *yo dāsam varṇam* (II.12.4); *hatvī dasyūn prāryan varṇam āvat* (III, 34.9); *ayajvānaḥ* (I.33.4); *māyāvān abrahmā dasyurarta* (IV.16.9); *anāsa* (V.29.10); *akarmā dasyūr abhi no amantur anyavrato amānuṣaḥ tvam tasyāmitrahan vadhar dāsasya dambhaya* (X.22.8); *mṛdhra-vāc* (V.29.10), etc.

The word *mleccha* occurs in Later Vedic literature, e.g. in the *Śatapatha Brāhmaṇa*, III.2.1.23–24, and is essentially a term of contempt for those who cannot speak the Aryan language and only gradually comes to acquire the meaning of a barbarian in a cultural sense. The etymology of the word is uncertain and does not appear to be Indo-Aryan, although it is said to derive from *vāc*. It is also said to be onomatopoeic, based on the strange sounds of an alien tongue. A reference to *milakhukā* (from Pali *milakkhu*, Sanskrit *mleccha*) in the *Vinaya Piṭaka*, III.28 is explained by Buddhaghoṣa as, *Andha-Damil ādi*.

16. It is not surprising that elsewhere too where Indo-European speakers have migrated and settled, the evidence for their presence is largely the Indo-European base of some of the languages of those areas. Greek contains elements of pre-Greek languages and the culture of classical Greece is rooted more in the pre-existing cultures of the region than in Indo-European culture (Luigi Pareti, *The Ancient World*, part I; Moses Finlay, *The Ancient Greeks*; George Thompson, *Studies in Ancient Greek Society*). The culture of the Hittites is derived from the Hattians and only the language is Indo-European. The Mitannis worshipped 'Aryan' gods and used technical terms for chariotry which are Indo-European, but their language Hurrian is not included in the Indo-European group. Similarly some Kassites had Aryan-sounding names but only their ruling class seems to have been familiar with the Indo-European language. The idea of a common culture of the Indo-European speakers grew out of philological evidence. Archaeological evidence does not support such an idea. It might be worthwhile for philologists to reconsider the question of how common in fact was the culture of the Indo-European speakers. Clearly there was an early stage when certain ideas and perhaps some institutions were common to the Indo-European speakers. This stage is reflected in, for example, parts of the *Ṛg Veda*, the Avestan *Gāthās*, the inscriptions of the Mitanni and passages of Homer. This forms the starting point of the ideas on comparative mythology developed for instance in the Kuhn-Müller theory and more recently in the writings of George Dumezil and Paul Thieme, which theories were applied to other areas on the basis of philological evidence. Had the spread of the language also

resulted in the spread of similar ideas and institutions then there would have been a far greater identity in the subsequent development of the cultures of the regions where Indo-European languages were spoken. S.C. Malik in *Indian Civilisation, The Formative Period* (1969), p. 144, refers to the Aryan superstructure of ideology being imposed upon the earlier socio-economic organization. 'Hence, it was contrary to the general opinion, not the Aryanisation of India, but rather the Indianisation of the Aryan nomadic pastoralist hordes.'

17. The large concentration of people in the Harappan towns immediately indicates a different type of organization from the smaller settlements of the Painted Grey Ware. Even when describing the Harappan cities it is sobering to remember that Kalibangan for instance could hardly have had a population larger than 5,000. In cases where a series of trenches have been cut across a mound it is possible to assess the increase or decrease of population in an area of habitation at particular periods by comparing the stratigraphy. For example, a comparative study on these lines of P.G. Ware levels and N.B.P. levels could provide considerable information. Population estimates are, of course, best carried out from the evidence of burials and of habitation sites uncovered in a horizontal excavation. Where the latter is not possible, a controlled series of soundings may help. Palaeo-demography has already attracted the attention of scholars after the pioneering work of Matiga half a century ago. Attempts have been made to compute population by studying the relative density of remains, by estimating the mean number of individuals in a village site through the habitations and the burials, the land-man ratio in the context of the technology of the period, the estimated number of persons required for a co-operative effort, the setting-up of menhirs, and by a variety of statistical methods.

18. Attempts can be made to estimate the nature of food production by calculating the area of land required to feed a given number of people on the basis of the agricultural technology and possible soil conditions of the time. The inter-relation of town and village raises the question of the precise use of the term 'urban'. Does it refer to a fortified village, a town or a city? The Indo-European root of *pura* means a wall or a rampart, therefore although in later periods the word *pura* referred to a town, in the early period it could have been a fortified village. A distinction has also to be maintained between the village which becomes an important market and thus the focus of the region, and the town. These distinctions in the degrees of urbanization are relevant not only to the study of prehistory but also in historical periods.

19. The words *dhānya* meaning corn or grain, and *yava* barley or grain, occur in the *Ṛg Veda* and in Later Vedic literature. Specific words for rice, of which the most frequent is *vrīhi* and others are *taṇḍula* and

*śāli* occur only in the Later Vedic literature, e.g., *Atharvaveda*, VI.140.2, etc.; S.K. Chatterjee suggests a possible Dravidian origin for *vrīhi* in *arichi* (History and Culture of the Indian People, vol. I, *The Vedic Age*, p. 1449). Wheat is referred to as, *godhuma*, in Later Vedic literature. It is still not certain whether the rice remains at Lothal indicate rice cultivation or merely a wild variety growing in the marshes (Visnu Mittre, unpublished paper read at Patna 1969, 'Environmental Background to the Neolithic-Chalcolithic Complex in North-Western India). Archaeological evidence suggests that rice was the staple food in a major part of the subcontinent during this period. The use of the word *dhānya* for paddy is late.

20. As for example in the *Trikāṇḍaśeṣa*, a supplement to the *Nāmaliṅg-ānuśāsana* of Amarsiṁha, by Puruṣottamadeva, who is said to have flourished in the court of Lakṣmaṇasena in the twelfth century AD.
21. It is not entirely coincidental that the spread of Indo-European elsewhere is frequently associated with the arrival of the horse-drawn chariot and on occasion with iron technology.
22. It is curious that there should be no substantial remains of at least the metal parts of the chariot in various excavations, and particularly at Harappa and Mohenjo-daro if we are to accept the theory that these cities were invaded by the Ṛgvedic people. This is in striking contrast to the evidence from Egypt where the new arrivals in their horse-drawn chariots are depicted clearly in reliefs and engravings on stone. The Aryan chariot was lighter, had spoked wheels, could accommodate three persons and was horse-drawn. It was therefore speedier, had greater manoeuvrability and consequently the two combatants had a vantage position (O.R. Gurney, *The Hittites*, pp. 104ff and S. Piggott, *Prehistoric India*, pp. 273ff).
23. The significance of these improvements is that the socketed iron axe is more efficient in a heavily forested region, the iron hoe makes a substantial difference in rice cultivation where more continual weeding is necessary than in other crops. This is also suggested in one of the frequently used words for 'hoe' in Vedic literature, *stambhaghna*, literally that which destroys clumps. The importance of the iron hoe has not received sufficient attention in the evaluation of technological change during this period.
24. The Muṇḍā derivation of *lāṅgala* is discussed by J. Przyluski in Bagchi (ed.), *Pre-Aryan and Pre-Dravidian in India*, pp. 8ff; also in T. Burrow, *The Sanskrit Language*, p. 379. It occurs as *nāngal* in Dravidian (Dravidian Etymological Dictionary, No. 2368). An attempt to associate it with the Indo-European *leg/leng* as in J. Pokorny, *Vergleichens des Worterbuch der Indo-Germanischen Sprachen* and thereby to link it with *Nirukta*, VI.26 of Yāska has not been accepted for linguistic reasons (S.K. Chatterjee, 'Non-Aryan Elements in Indo-Aryan',

*JGIS*, III.42). It could be added that even from the point of view of the technology of the plough, the ploughshare is the central object and not an attachment.

The early occurrence of the word for 'plough' in non-Indo-Aryan languages would invalidate the suggestion that the Aryan speakers introduced the plough. The possibility that the plough may have been known to the Harappans on the basis of a particular sign in the script resembling the Sumerian sign for plough has now been confirmed by the last season's excavations at Kalibangan which uncovered the furrow marks in a field outside the city's fortification which date to the pre-Harappan period. On a purely impressionistic view it seems unlikely that a sufficient food surplus could have been produced to maintain the cities without plough agriculture.

25. In the *Saṁhitā* literature the *karmāra* is respected, but gradually his status becomes low. *Ṛg Veda*, X.72.2; IX.112.2, *Atharvaveda*, III.5.6. Ultimately the *karmāra* is ranked with the *Niṣāda* and the *kulāla*. *Manu*, IV.215; Kane, *History of the Dharmashastras*, II, p. 73. The lowering of the status may have had to do with the fact that the smiths were possibly non-tribal artisans, (it has been suggested that the copper-smiths were itinerant smiths) who would be allowed commensality and participation in the ritual, but not marriage relationships with the tribe. The social rights and obligations of such professional groups would be worth examining.

26. The Harappan system of weights has been described as binary in the lower weights — 1, 2, 8/3, 16, 32, 64 . . . and decimal in the higher weights. The decimal basis of counting is referred to in the *Taittirīya Saṁhitā*, IV.40.11.4; *Maitrāyāṇīya Sam.*, II.8.14; *Kāṭhaka Sam.*, XVII.10 and XXXIX.6; *Vājasaneyi Sam.*, XVII.2. There are references to ten raised to the power of twelve. The existence of the earlier binary system suggests that calculations may have been on the basis of the square. The commonly used cosmology of the Babylonians and Sumerians is believed to have had the mathematical base of the square. The use of both the square and circular cosmology in Indian sources at this time does suggest that new ideas on astronomy may have been in the air. There is a great likelihood that the circular theory was first developed among navigators, perhaps the Phoenicians, and would have then travelled to those in contact with the Phoenicians. C.P.S. Menon, *Early Astronomy and Cosmology*, pp. 36ff, makes an interesting correlation between the prevalence of the square cosmology and the circular cosmology in early India.

27. The need for exact geometrical knowledge arose in part because, although there were a variety of shapes permitted for altars such as the falcon, the chariot-wheel, the tortoise, the triangle, etc., their area had to be identical. The number of bricks was also prescribed. The

geometrical principles involved in both creating precisely measured forms and converting one form into another are described in detail in the *Śulva Sūtras*. Admittedly most of these texts belong to the end of the Vedic period or even to the immediately post-Vedic period. Nevertheless they contain the developed and classified knowledge of geometry which must certainly have had earlier beginnings. This geometrical knowledge would be of use in other spheres of life as well, as for example in measuring land.

28. One year of twelve months comprising 360 days is frequently referred to in the *Ṛg Veda*, I.164.11; I.164.48. A year of 366 days has been suggested on the basis of the Ribhus in *Ṛg Veda*, IV.33.7. An intercalary month in a five-year circle finds mention in a late section of the *Ṛg Veda*, X.85.13. An intercalary thirteenth month of 30 days in a five-year circle occurs in the *Atharvaveda*, IX.9.19.

    A primaeval element in Vedic society is indicated by the fact that magic is a substantial feature in both religious and technological concepts. It would be expected therefore that mathematical and astronomical knowledge would tend to be hidden in a mesh of symbolism and magic. That this element persists is apparent from the consultations with the village pandit which are still a part of the rural scene for determining the 'right day' for important agricultural activities such as sowing and harvesting. This has implications relating to the calendar as well as the notion of the auspicious day. The latter almost certainly derives its sanctity from the former.

29. In the Indus valley this would be caused by any or all of the following factors: the geological uplift at Sehwan resulting in the excessive flooding of the Indus near Mohenjo-daro, the salination of the soil, deforestation causing soil erosion and decrease in natural irrigation and thereby rendering agriculture difficult, and finally, the termination specifically of the Harappan trade with Sumer in the eighteenth century BC; apart from a possible attack on the cities of Harappa and Mohenjo-daro. Some of these factors are discussed by R.L. Raikes, 'The End of the Ancient Cities of the Indus'. *American Anthropology*, 1964 and 'The Mohenjo-daro Floods', *Antiquity*, 40; G.F. Dales, 'New Investigations at Mohenjo-daro', *Archaeology*, 18, 1965; H.T. Lambrick, 'The Indus Flood Plain and the Indus Civilisation', *Geographical Journal*, 133, 1967. Detailed discussion of the Sumerian trade is available in L. Oppenheim, *Ancient Mesopotamia* and W.F. Leemans, *Foreign Trade in the Old Babylonian Period*. The breakdown in trade is supported by the fact that the dockyard at Lothal had fallen into disuse by *circa* 1800 BC (*Ancient India*, nos 18 and 19, 1962–63, p. 213).

30. The trade with Ophira during the reign of Solomon, the obelisk of Shalmanesar III depicting Indian elephants, the evidence of Indian teak at Mugheir and in the palace of Nebuchadnezzar and a variety

of linguistic evidence (some of which is discussed in Rawlinson, *Intercourse between India and the Western World*) would attest to trading contacts between India and the Near East. The *brāhmī* script may have originated in western India as a kind of merchant's code partially associated with the Semitic script and in course of time and use in commerce travelled to the Ganga valley and to north India where it was perfected for use with Sanskrit and Prākrit. The *aramaic* adaptations in *kharoṣṭhī* clearly arose from commercial and administrative needs.

31. In the *Śatapatha Brāhmaṇa*, III.2.3.15 and the *Kauṣītaki Brāh.*, VII.6, the speech of the Kuru Pañcālas and the north generally is extolled and made a model for study. This ties in with the fact that Pāṇiṇi is associated with the north. Yet the Punjab had been relegated to the status of a *mleccha-deśa* in the *Atharvaveda*, V.22.14.

    The linguistic differences between the Punjab and the middle Ganga valley were earlier sought to be explained on the basis of the theory that there were two bands of Aryan speakers and this theory was developed by Hoernle, *A Grammar of the Eastern Hindi Compared with the Other Gaudian Languages*, 1880, and by G. Grierson, *Languages*, I.G.I., vol. I, 1907. More recently, S.K. Chatterjee and S.M. Katre in *Languages*, G.I. 1965, have preferred the argument that the differences are due to many more groups mutually interacting. What is perhaps called for at this stage is a comparative study of the linguistic structure of the various Prākrits and the pre-Aryan languages.

32. *Atharvaveda*, V.22.14; *Gopatha Brāhamaṇa*, II.9; *Vājasaneyi Sam.*, XXX.5.22; *Taittirīya Brāh.*, III.4.1.1; *Baudhāyana Dharma Sūtra*, I.1.14.

33. Jules Bloch, 'Sanskrit and Dravidian', in Bagchi (ed.), *Pre-Aryan and Pre-Dravidian in India*, pp. 46ff. The use of the word *ghoṭa* in Sanskrit is late occurring in such texts as the *Āpastamba Śrauta Sūtra*, XV.3.12; *ghoṭaka* in *Pañcatantra*, V.10.4; *Vikramādityacarita*, etc. An early use of *ghoṭaka* in Pāli occurs in *Jātaka*, VI.452.

    A micro-study of the etymology of place-names, even contemporary place-names, would be revealing particularly in the context of early Muṇḍā and Dravidian settlement in northern India. Names such as Gaṅgā, Kaliṅga, Aṅga, Vaṅga, etc., have already been discussed as probable Muṇḍā names, Bagchi, *Pre-Aryan and Pre-Dravidian in India*, pp. 72ff.

34. The pattern of settlement at Harappa, Mohenjo-daro, Kalibangan suggests an elite in residence on the citadel mound; the large and separate residential area to the east of the citadel occupied by lesser status groups; and the single or double-roomed 'workmen's quarters' indicating a third-level of stratification. The question has often been

asked as to who was in authority in the Harappa culture and how was authority maintained? The answer could lie in the existence of a kind of caste structure, where a small group preserving itself through strict endogamous marriage and organizing its authority through a hierarchy of service relationships in which it was assigned a high status, and stressing its ritual purity, could have held power. The great Bath at Mohenjo-daro is now almost universally recognized as being indicative of an ablution ritual which could have been central to a notion of ritual purity.

35. All tribal societies have a social organization based on kinship relations deriving from rules of exogamy and endogamy. Family structure, whether matrilineal or patriarchal, lineage and tribal identity are some of the features which might be ferreted out of the references to the earlier populations. Chalcolithic cultures invariably indicate a division of labour, and where there is trading activity as well, the division of labour is intensified. Nor would identity with a particular geographical location be precluded. The evidence of the notion of pollution in non-Aryanised societies has been noticed by anthropologists and some would regard it as essential to the development of religion and society in India (e.g. M.N. Srinivas, *Religion and Society among the Coorgs*). Thus the pre-requisites for a caste structure were available. It could be suggested that a rudimentary form of the caste structure existed in the pre-Aryan Ganga valley cultures and perhaps a better defined form in the Harappa culture. The Ṛgvedic people show an unfamiliarity with this structure which is not surprising if they regarded the non-Aryan culture as alien. The division of society into four groups has a single reference in the Puruṣasūkta hymn in the late tenth *maṇḍala* of the *Ṛg Veda* (X.90.12). The logic implicit in this particular myth regarding the origin of the castes would in itself suggest the re-arranging of endogamous groups into a carefully worked-out pattern. The word *varṇa* with the connotation of caste is used in the *Ṛg Veda* to differentiate between two groups, the *ārya* and the *dāsa*. The later literature clearly refers to the *catvāro varṇāḥ* (*Śatapatha Brāh.*, V.5.4.9; VI.4.4.13). The expansion to four categories would be necessary once society became more complex and endogamous groups were incorporated and had to be arranged in a pattern. The *jāti* structure may well reflect a pre-Aryan aspect of the caste structure.

36. e.g. *Chāndogya Upaniṣad*, V.10.7; Manu (X.45) makes a distinction between the Dasyus who speak the Aryan language and those who do not.

37. The Kirāta are referred to as low status tribes in the *Vājasaneyi Sam.*, XXX.16; *Taittirīya Brāh.*, III.4.12.1; *Atharvaveda*, X.4.14; *Manu*, X.44;

*Raghuvaṁśa*, XVI.57. The Pulinda are similarly referred to in the *Aitareya Brāhmaṇa*, 7.18; Aśoka's Thirteenth Major Rock Edict.

38. The urbanization of the Ganga valley in the first millennium BC is often referred to as the second urbanization. A crucial factor in this urbanization was iron technology as is evident when one compares the N.B.P. levels with P.G.W. levels or black-and-red ware levels. Surplus produce and the specialization of crafts both utilizing the *dāsa-bhṛtaka*, increase in trade based on production as well as improved communication (both by land and through the use of river navigation) all combined to make urbanization possible. This in turn produced the characteristics associated with urban culture — the building of fortified cities, the introduction of a script (*brāhmī*), the use of coinage (punch-marked coins for example), a wide range of intellectual and metaphysical speculation (from the Cārvākas to the Ājīvikas), some of which reflected the requirements and aspirations of the new urban groups — the artisans and the merchants and traders.

    Unlike the first urbanization in the Indus Valley, we have for the Ganga valley enough evidence to be able to trace its gradual evolution. The quality of the early urbanization of the Ganga valley as compared to that of the Indus valley was less impressive in terms of material culture. But there seems to have been a more even distribution of the characteristics of urbanization, suggesting perhaps that the perquisites of urban living were concentrated and centralized to a lesser degree than in the Indus civilisation.

39. The origin of the state is ascribed to a number of interesting factors in early literary sources. We are told, for example, that the surplus production of rice led to the emergence of the institution of family and private property (initially connoting fields). The state arose because both of these had to be protected as also because of the need to prevent conflict between castes (*Vāyu Purāṇa*, VIII, 128–61; *Mahāvastu*, I, 342ff; *Mārkaṇḍeya Purāṇa*, 49, 74ff). The literature of the mid-first millennium BC indicates the beginning of political concepts. This is in contrast to the Ṛgvedic period where loyalty is primarily to the clan and where, therefore, government is seen in more simplistic terms, namely, authority invested in the chief or leader whose main function is to protect the clan. This concept is assumed in the various stories regarding the appointment of Indra as the *rājā*, which stories are elaborated upon with the growth of the contractual element in the notion of the state in Later Vedic literature (*Ṛg Veda*, VIII, 35, 86; *Aitareya Brāh*., I.14; *Śatapatha Brāh*., III.4.2.1–3). The purpose of the contract gradually changes from protecting the clan militarily, to the king maintaining the order of the castes and also protecting private property (*Arthaśāstra*, III.1; *Manu*, VII.

17–35; *Śānti Parva*, 75.10; *Manu*, X.115). The contract is complete when the *rājā* is paid one-sixth in tax as his wage for services to the people (*ṣadbhāgbhṛto rājā rakṣet prajām*, *Baudhāyana Dharma Sūtra*, I.10.6). The *rājā* is associated with divinity which permits of a different perspective on the notion of contract.

Buddhist texts however indicate the contractual basis of the concept of the state, more clearly as the association with divinity is absent (*Dīgha Nikāya*, III, 84–96; *Mahāvastu*, I.338–48). It was more suited to the context of the non-monarchical systems of government.

40. At the level of ritual there was the incorporation of prayers, spells and magic, as for example in the *Atharvaveda* and the *Yajurveda*. At the level of deities the acceptance of the erstwhile distant Rudra and the growth of the Rudra-Śiva concept for instance. The recruitment of local priests into the *brāhmaṇa* fold can be seen not only in the various purification rites for those of degenerate castes, such as the *Vrātyastoma*, but is also perhaps reflected in the mysterious origin of many *brāhmaṇa gotras*. The concession to the worship of the mother goddess, to any appreciable extent, is a later phenomenon as also the acceptance of phallic worship.

41. Pargiter's attempt to sort out the genealogies on the basis of Aryan and non-Aryan has been criticized. It is possible that, eventually, the Puranic genealogies will be found to be more true to the essence of the history of this period since they are not concerned with the Aryan problem as such but with the activities of a large number of clans and kings in northern India. It is interesting that the two royal lineages, the Ailas and Ikṣvākus are both based in the Ganga valley, from where various lineages move in various directions.

The *vaṃśāvalī* tradition has as its genesis the myth of the Flood and this agrees in many particulars with the Sumerian Flood legend. Indeed it is the agreement in details which is so striking. What is even more interesting is that the traditional date of the *kaliyuga* according to the astronomical tradition of Āryabhaṭa works out to about 3102 BC, which agrees with the archaeological date ascribed to the flooding of Shuruppak in Sumer which is probably the genesis of the Sumerian Flood legend (C. Leonard Woolley, *The Early Periods — Ur Excavations*, vol. IV, 1956; M. Mallowan, 'Noah's Flood Reconsidered', *Iraq*, XXVI, 1964). The reference to this legend in Vedic literature is late, in the *Śatapatha Brāh.*, I.8.1.1 and the *Kāṭhaka Sam.*, XI.2. Had the legend been of Aryan origin, one would expect it to occur in the *Ṛg Veda* or be associated with the Avestan tradition rather than the Sumerian. The legend relating to the genesis of a people is after all of prime importance. Considering the close contacts between the Harappa culture and the Sumerians, it is possible that the same legend may have been used as a genesis in both cultures and the Puranic genealogies may therefore contain a pre-Aryan tradition. R.C. Hazra's very able studies of the Puranic sources point to some non-Vedic religious contents in the *Purāṇas*.

As regards the mythological sections, the initial legend alone raises a host of interesting ideas: the concept of the Flood as genesis, the use of the sun and the moon as the symbol of the two royal lineages, (*Sūryavaṃśi* and *Candravaṃśi*) and the association of these in the tribal mythology of India and elsewhere; the fact that the Aila lineage derives its name from the sole daughter of Manu, Iḷā who married the son of the moon deity (Soma), suggests a matrilineal-cum-mother goddess tradition.

42. Magadha in the period from 400 BC to AD 400 saw the rise of the Mauryas and the Guptas; the Raichur-Bijapur region in the period from 500 to 1200 was the nucleus of Cālukya and Rāṣṭrakūṭa power and the Kanchi-Tanjore region in the same period was the homeland of the Pallavas and Colas. Other areas also gave rise to important dynasties, but generally to only a single dynasty in a shorter period, e.g. Kannauj under Harṣa, Bengal under the Pālas, etc.

43. We know that various groups were recruited to the *brāhmaṇa varṇa* and that their status within the *varṇa* could change; thus the Kuru-Pañcāla *brāhmaṇas* looked down upon the Magadha *brāhmaṇas* (*Jātaka*, I.324, II.83; *Aitareya Brāh*., VIII.14), the Gandhāra *brāhmaṇas* are described with contempt in the *Rājataraṅginī* (I.306ff) yet are regarded as respectable in the *Bhaviṣya Purāṇa*. It is also evident that families of non-kṣatriya origin became rulers or were given *kṣatriya* status through fabricated genealogies. Thus the Nandas are described as *śūdras* in the Purāṇas. The Candella kings claimed Candravaṃśi lineage and *kṣatriya* status in spite of obscure origins and having acquired the status continued to marry into the local Gond families. There is an absence of any reference to the *vaiśya varṇa* in certain parts of India. The composition of the *śūdra varṇa* varied from region to region and its role was different in south India as compared to the Ganga valley. When we cease to look at early Indian society as a static, rigid structure stratified into immobile castes, we then begin to see considerable evidence to suggest the contrary.

# 15

# *The Archaeological Background to the Agnicayana Ritual**

For many decades now scholars have been waiting expectantly for archeology to reveal a culture that can be definitively labeled as 'Aryan,' but the Aryans remain elusive. It is likely that they will continue to remain so until a new definition of the term Aryan can be suggested. Such a clarification would not be entirely out of the question, considering that we are still working with a definition that derives essentially from information and concepts prevalent during the nineteenth century. Now that there is a relatively full picture of the succession of archaeological cultures in northern India for the period with which the emergence of Aryan culture is associated, the continuing absence of a clearly identifiable Aryan culture may suggest that Aryanism is not an isolated, uniform culture but a system that draws on a multiplicity of cultures that remain crucial to the manifold forms it takes in time and space. In such a system, facets of what have been called Aryan culture may find correlates in archaeological artifacts and assemblages, and these correlates may help us to redefine Aryan culture. The purpose of this essay is to consider whether the description of the Agnicayana in the Vedic corpus and its present-day survivals are reflected in the archaeological remains of the proto-historic period.

Any attempt to correlate the Agnicayana as an Aryan ritual with archaeological data would require an initial assessment of the possibility of identifying the 'Aryans' in the various archaeological cultures known to the northern part of the Indian subcontinent during the first three millennia BC. The earliest evidence of the

* In F. Staal (ed.), *Agni*, vols I and II, Berkeley, 1983, 1–40. The *yajña* described here was performed in April 1975 at Panjal at Kerala.

Aryan-speaking peoples is available in the *Ṛgveda*. The geographical area was that of the 'Sapta Sindhu,' generally taken to be a reference to the Indus, its five tributaries, and the Sarasvatī River, which would comprise the Indus and the Sarasvatī valleys (extending to the Indo-Gangetic divide) and include the northwestern borderlands. The archaeological cultures of this region and its fringes and the evidence of material remains from these cultures will have to be compared with descriptions from the *Ṛgveda* and from other later Vedic literature generally dated to the first millennium BC. In the absence of an identification of Vedic culture with any specific archaeological culture, the next step would be to try and correlate aspects of the Agnicayana with archaeological data and see whether such correlations can be made. This essay is an attempt to examine these two questions.

A point that needs to be emphasized is that in speaking of the 'Aryans,' the historical reference is to the establishment of a language, Indo-Aryan, over areas of the Indian subcontinent that were earlier linked with non-Aryan languages. Who the Aryans were racially is not under discussion — nor is the question of whether they were a distinct racial entity, which seems unlikely and uncertain. The only certainty is the occurrence of the language. The mechanism by which the language was introduced and gained currency is also unclear. It was earlier believed that the Aryan speakers invaded northern India, but the evidence for this is now doubted. Migration would seem a more feasible postulate, though here too a question remains as to why there was a migration, or what form it took.

A further complication is that the presence of speakers of languages derived from Indo-European is not limited to the Indian subcontinent but is intimately concerned with activities in western Asia. The area from the Tigris-Euphrates to the Indus valley forms the geographical context of the folk movements, linguistic intrusions, and cultural changes that were the mise-en-scène of the Aryan question in India (although in this essay the discussion will be limited to the Indian context). Admixtures and borrowings from local cultures are evident in all the areas where the Indo-European-speaking peoples settled, and it is possible that some aspects of the later cultures derive from a community of ideas going back to the pre-Indo-European period in the third millennium BC when western Asia constituted an area of cultural interaction.

The chronological frame goes back to West Asian connections. The earliest recorded appearance of the Indo-European speakers associated with the horse and the chariot dates to the second millennium BC in the Boghaz Keui records from Anatolia, the Tell-el Amarna tablets from Egypt, and to the arrival of the Kassites in Mesopotamia.[1] The linguistic proximity of Indo-Aryan to Avestan and Old Persian would suggest a close relationship between Iran and northern India.[2] The linguistic bifurcation between India and Iran and the growing dissimilarities between Zoroastrianism and the Vedic religion might date to the late second or early first millennium BC. Beyond occasional similarities in the typology of pottery or of metal artifacts, there is little evidence to support an archaeological counterpart to the linguistic data. Another area associated with the Indo-European speakers is central Asia. Links between central Asia and northern India, which go back to the third millennium BC, also tend to be sporadic.[3]

A more substantial connection, although isolated, has been recently found in the excavation of a Chalcolithic cemetery and settlement at Sibri Domb at the foot of the Bolan pass. The site indicates a settlement of people from Central Asia, probably dating to the third millennium BC, and suggests links with late Namazga V and early Namazga VI.[4] The period is of course prior to that of the *Ṛgveda*, and there is no indication of a sustained migration. Links with Central Asia are now known to go back to the Harappan period from other evidence as well — namely, the Harappan settlements in the Shortughai plain in Badakshan, where it is thought that Harappan traders may have been anxious to obtain the local lapis lazuli.[5]

If Aryan culture is viewed as a well-defined system uniformly spread over the Sapta Sindhu region, then only the Harappan culture provides a geographical equation.[6] Pre-Harappan cultures of the fourth and early third millennia BC differ, in that the Baluchistan peasant communities are distinct from the pre-Harappan settlements on the plains of the Indus system, such as the Mehrgarh or Kot-Dijian or those sometimes referred to as the Sothi culture, although there may well have been contact between them.[7]

The former evolved from a series of Neolithic settlements of the fourth millennium BC along the Baluchistan borderlands. Many were abandoned during the Harappan period when the focus of settlement shifted to the Indus plains and the Sarasvatī valley, although some sites in the Zhob valley were reoccupied in the post-Harappan period. Uniformity is recognizable only with the emergence of the Mature phase of the Harappan culture, which would broadly date to the second half of the third millennium BC. The declining phase of the Late Harappan extends into the early second millennium BC and in some areas, such as the Punjab and Gujarat, continues to the middle of the second millennium.

Attempts to identify the Harappan culture with Vedic Aryan cultures raises major problems. The chronology of the Harappan culture precedes by some centuries the presence of Indo-European speakers in west Asia and is therefore much earlier in time. In the absence of a conclusive decipherment of the Harappan script, it could be argued that the Harappans were Aryan speakers and spread westwards, but the work done so far on the script suggests the probability of a non-Aryan language.[8] Equally significant is the divergence in the kind of society depicted in the two types of evidence. The Harappan was essentially an urban culture with a commercial orientation, whereas the Ṛgvedic peoples were primarily pastoralists and generally unfamiliar with urban living. The characteristics associated with the latter, such as the domestication of the horse, the use of the spoked wheel and the chariot, and possibly later the use of iron (*kṛṣṇa āyas*) are absent in the Harappan sites. There are a very few remains of what are believed to be bones of horses prior to the second millennium, and even these are controversial.[9] Horses are also conspicuously absent in the symbolism and designs on Harappan seals and pottery, where other animals abound. If the Aryans are to be sought in archeology, then, the search must be conducted in the post-Harappan cultures.

It is sometimes said that perhaps the Ṛgvedic culture may be identified with the pre-Harappan, which would make it indigenous to India and date it to the fourth millennium BC.[10] This would imply that the Harappans, whose culture as we have seen was dissimilar to the Ṛgvedic, came in from elsewhere as an advanced and intrusive culture, and dominated the main Indus valley until such time as the cities declined. The Ṛgvedic people would then have formed a substratum culture, and the later Vedic literature would reflect an amalgam of the previous cultures. This raises a number of problems that cannot be solved with the existing evidence, such as the conflicting chronology of the *Ṛgveda* and the pre-Harappan settlements, the links with Iran, and the correlation of Indian evidence with the data from West Asia that attests to the presence of Indo-European speakers. The pre-Harappan settlements of the Sapta Sindhu region are again not part of a uniform culture.

The decline of the major cities did not bring the Harappan culture to a close, since Late Harappan sites flourished in some areas on the peripheries of the Harappan heartland.[11] In the Indo-Gangetic divide and the upper Ganga-Yamuna Doab, Late Harappan sites were contemporary with other cultures such as the Ochre Colour Pottery culture dating to the early second millennium BC. Recently sites from this area have provided evidence of what has been described as an overlap phase between the Late Harappan and the major archaeological culture of this area, the Painted Grey Ware culture.[12] In Gujarat, Harappan survivals continued into the second millennium.[13] Some degree of continuity is also indicated by the contemporaneity of the Black-and-red Ware cultures with the Mature Harappan sites in Gujarat and their apparent spread to Rajasthan and central India in the second millennium BC. Harappan sites have recently been found in Maharashtra, at Daimabad in the Ahmednagar District, and at Varsus in the Dhule District. The overlap of C-14 dates from the former suggests that it was contemporary with the central Indian and northern Deccan Chalcolithic. A few Harappan survivals may also be identified in the Megalithic culture of the peninsula, as for example, in the graffiti on some of the pottery.[14]

It is evident that the hiatus that was believed to exist between the end of the Harappan cities and the cultures that followed is now being gradually eliminated, and that the probability of survivals from the Harappan tradition into later centuries is being strengthened. These survivals and the contemporaneity of Late Harappan with other cultures lend some support to the theory that linguistically there might have been a period of bilingualism[15] between the earlier non-Aryan and later Aryan speakers, and that the widespread adoption of Indo-Aryan was a gradual process extending over many centuries.

The theory of an Aryan invasion finds little support in archeology.[16] The famous 'massacre' at Mohenjo Daro has been questioned, as has also the notion that Indra and his hosts destroyed the cities.[17] The decline of the cities is now more frequently attributed to ecological changes and the termination of trade relations with western Asia. The references quoted from the *Ṛgveda* in support of the invasion theory refer more often to settlements that had long been deserted and were already in ruins.[18] One may well look in vain for evidence of Aryan war chariots devastating the land, for so far they have failed to materialize.

It has been argued that there is some evidence at sites such as Rana Ghundai III and Sohr Damb for attacks from the Baluchistan borderlands on existing settlements in the mid-second millennium BC. New artifacts appear in this area suggestive of forms known to West Asia.[19] The shaft-hole axe, for example, extends from Baluchistan to the Jhukar culture sites in lower Sind. Other artifacts include circular stamp seals of copper, a flat copper celt with lateral lugs, spiral-headed pins, and a cast-bronze macehead. Most of these are single items not located in a context of related artifacts or along specific routes, and they are therefore not of much value as evidence of invasions.

Quite distinct from this is the Cemetery H culture at Harappa,[20] which is alien to the earlier Harappan culture and yet in a limited way suggests some echoes of Harappan typology, the affinities extending both to the Bahawalpur region and to the Indo-Gangetic divide. The integration is suggested through the pottery, which combines some West Asian with some Harappan elements but is at the same time a distinctive pottery despite its restricted distribution.

Further north, in the Swat valley area, a large number of graves were excavated at Ghaligai, Timargarha, and other sites.[21] The earliest graves date to the mid-second millennium BC and are differentiated from those of Period II by the presence of copper objects and various burial forms. Period III, dated to the early first millennium BC, provides evidence of iron and the domestication of the horse. The ceramic industry consists of a red ware and a more extensive grey ware. The identification of the Gandhara Grave culture (as it is called) with the Aryan speakers would limit the area of their distribution to the Swat valley and its environs, which from the evidence of the *Ṛgveda* forms only a small part of the vast Sapta Sindhu region known to its authors. The grey ware of this culture is also limited to this area and as yet has not been found to be connected with other grey wares in the Indian subcontinent. The Swat valley sites do show some connection with the Gurgan valley sites in northeastern Iran at Tepe Hissar, Turang Tepe, and Shah Tepe, and with other sites in Iran.[22]

Another possible point of entry for migrants from West Asia

could have been western India along a route following the coastal areas of Makran into the Indus delta and Gujarat. The Banas culture[23] of the second millennium BC in Rajasthan is characterized by copper technology and the use of a white-painted Black-and-red pottery, which as we have seen occurs earlier in Gujarat contemporary with the Mature Harappan phase. From Rajasthan this culture appears to have spread to the fringes of the Ganga-Yamuna Doāb. The Banas culture occupies an area without Harappan connections, lies outside the Sapta Sindhu region, and shows hardly any trace of connections with West Asia.

The Black-and-red Ware culture[24] is in some ways the most significant of the post-Harappan cultures. Its genesis remains unknown. Its characteristic pottery was produced as a result of inverted firing at progressively lower temperatures, resulting in the double color of black and red. By the first millennium BC it is also linked with the diffusion of iron into central India as well as with certain categories of megalithic burials, such as cairn burials, cairn circles, and cist burials, that are particularly associated with the peninsula. Whether the more complex Megalithic monuments of the peninsula with their Black-and-red pottery, iron artifacts, and widespread use of the horse are also to be traced to the more northerly Black-and-red Ware cultures remains uncertain. In terms of correlating this culture with the evidence from literary sources, its distribution carries echoes of the spread of the Yadava lineage, a lineage that is claimed by both Aryan and Dravidian speakers in later periods.[25]

The Chalcolithic cultures of central India and the northern Deccan of the second millennium BC are too far removed from the geographical horizon of the *Ṛgveda*, but one of the excavators of these sites maintains that the ceramic industry shows some links with forms from West Asia,[26] indicative perhaps of a folk movement from West Asia that brought people to western India and Rajasthan, whence artifactual traits may have traveled to central India and the northern Deccan.

The nucleus of the Sapta Sindhu region in the *Ṛgveda*, where are located the more important tribes such as the Pūrus and the Bharatas, was the Sarasvatī valley and the Indo-Gangetic divide, an area that was later to form the territory of the famous Kurus, in fact the heartland of Vedic culture. It registers an extremely complex topography because of the major changes in river courses and the drying up of the Sarasvatī.[27] The resulting ecological change does little to clarify the archaeological picture, which is further complicated by the many cultures that appear to have coexisted and overlapped in this area.

Late Harappan sites extend from the water shed into the upper Ganga-Yamuna Doāb, where the Ochre Colour Pottery culture,[28] also of the second millennium BC, has been variously identified with Harappan refugees migrating eastwards or with incoming Aryans, neither of which identifications has been widely accepted. This culture is sometimes associated with the caches of copper implements found in the Doab,[29] but the association is tentative.

The dominant culture of the region is the Painted Grey Ware variously dated to the late second millennium or the early first millennium BC and continuing at least to the middle of the first millennium.[30] Possibly there was an earlier phase when it was restricted to the Sarasvatī valley and sites in the watershed that is reflected in the suggested overlap with the Late Harappan at some places,[31] such as Bhagwanpura, Dadheri, Katpalon, and Nagar. Its extension into the Ganga valley may date from the early first millennium BC. This would also be the period when it could have been in contact with the Black-and-Red Ware cultures in the vicinity of the western Ganga valley, as is evident from some sites that have Black-and-red Ware levels preceding the Painted Grey Ware or overlapping with it, as for example Jodhpura, Noh, and Atranjikhera. The material culture of the Painted Grey Ware in fact shows some affinities with textual descriptions from the Later Vedic literature. It was a society of pastoral cum agricultural people who were dependent on cattle for both dairy products and meat, who grew wheat and rice,[32] who were familiar with the domestication of the horse and who have left evidence of the use of iron weaponry; the absence of burials at their sites suggests that cremation was their common practice. There is a problem in the identification of the Painted Grey Ware with the Aryan-speakers. There are no links between these settlements and those along the Indo-Iranian borderlands, or with cultures in West Asia. The gray ware of the Swat valley was unconnected with this pottery. The evolution of the Painted Grey Ware culture, and of its pottery that is distinctively different from all that went before, remains unexplained.

Thus efforts to identify the Aryans with a variety of archaeological cultures remain inconclusive. There is no uniform distribution of a single culture that coincides with the entire area associated with the early Aryan speakers of the *Ṛgveda*. There are instead a number of overlapping but differentiated cultures in this region. Those that come closest in characteristics and form to what is described in the texts appear to have little connection with western Asia, which would tend to contradict the linguistic evidence. The areas where there are seeming affinities in pottery and artifacts are beyond the geographical horizon of the early texts.

The attempt to identify the Aryan-speakers with archaeological remains is perhaps a pointless exercise. The Aryans were not a distinct racial group with a recognizable assemblage of material culture carefully carried across mountain and desert in the process of migration. It would seem that the most tangible characteristic of their presence was their language. What was therefore being diffused was the language. This would not necessarily have required a chain of artifacts belonging to a uniform culture. Nor would language diffusion necessarily be registered in a uniform material culture. This is apparent from the spread of the Indo-Europeans in Iran and Afghanistan, a development that is recognized not by an identical ceramic or artifactual industry but by the introduction of Indo-European languages.

The pertinent question therefore is that of the mechanism of language diffusion. Conquest and the subsequent imposition of the language of the conquerors would be the simplest method and would bear archaeological traces. But the evidence for conquest is limited, and if it exists, is largely confined to the Indo-Iranian borderlands. In the plains migration would perhaps be a more feasible proposition.

At a hypothetical level a possible reconstruction could be suggested. The earliest Aryan speakers, as pastoralists, could have moved across the Indo-Iranian borders, settling temporarily in the interstices of cities. If the movement across the borders was regular, they might have provided transportation for small items of trade, as is often the case with pastoral groups involved in either transhumance or seasonal migrations.[33] Possibly small settlements may have remained on the Indian side and maintained relations with the existing population in the second millennium BC.[34] That the main period of settlement came after the decline of the Harappan cities would seem likely from the absence of descriptions of cities in the *Ṛgveda*. The occasional references to the destruction of the 'purs' could as well refer to the fortified settlements of the borderlands.

The decline of the Harappan urban centers would have reduced the incentive to pastoral groups as carriers of trading items. This may have encouraged a more permanent type of settlement with seasonal camps turning to agriculture, and the settlements may well have extended to the 'two grassy banks of the Sarasvatī', as one of the hymns of the *Ṛgveda* states.[35] Since Iran was coming under the influence of the Assyrian political system, bifurcation of the Iranian and Indian groups would be natural. Assyrian sources refer to Indo-European speakers in the Zagros area by the early first millennium BC.[36] Were the Asuras, who were once friendly and then became the enemies, the worshippers of either Asura or of Ahura? Such settlements would initially make little impact on the existing culture apart from marginal changes with the introduction of new items brought from elsewhere. Their archaeological identification would be equally difficult. (If the West Asian evidence is a fair parallel, then we can posit that nomadic pastoral groups tend to appropriate the material culture of the more settled agrarian communities). Evidence for the appearance of nomads in West Asia generally takes the form of the introduction of new names, the use of a different language, and the intrusion of new deities.[37]

Their survival would hinge on their maintenance of their own language and oral tradition. Linguistic purity can be maintained in an oral tradition up to a point, but the influence of the bilingualism necessary to a migratory pattern would also come to be reflected in certain linguistic changes. In the juxtaposition of Aryan-speakers with descendents of earlier cultures, there could be either the conquest of the existing population, for which the archaeological evidence is limited, or else the assertion of power by the Aryan-speakers over the settled population, through a mutual acculturation resulting in new cultural forms and the acceptance of the Aryan language. It is legitimate to ask how the language came to be accepted if there is such negligible evidence for invasion. One possibility may have been the gradual introduction of iron technology,[38] together with such innovations as the use of the horse, the spoked wheel, and the chariot, which may have acted as technological levers to give an edge to the culture of the Aryan speakers. The spread of the language would in any case have been a gradual process. This admixture of cultures and languages is perhaps what is reflected in the later Vedic texts and their possible archaeological correlation with the Painted Grey Ware.

The *Ṛgveda* would then represent the erstwhile migratory pastoralists now settled, still largely tribal, holding cattle as their main wealth, practicing religious rites with a component of shamanism, alienated from some indigenous groups but affiliated with others, and possibly appropriating into their tradition some of the past of the land they had come to. The first millennium BC saw a movement southwards and eastwards attributable to ecological changes in the watershed to interaction with existing cultures, and possibly to demographic and economic pressure that favoured settling in new lands. The most fruitful interactions appear to have been at the meeting point of the Painted Grey Ware and the Black-and-red Ware cultures.

The form that Vedic culture took in the first millennium BC, the period of the descriptions of rituals such as the Agnicayana, would seem to be an amalgam of existing cultures. Possibly the comprehension of ritual and symbol was blurred as much by the distance in generations from the earliest practice of these rituals as by the incorporation of originally alien systems. The ritual of the Agnicayana would then have to be seen as symbolizing this amalgam of cultures, going back to the shamanism of Indo-European days, the sacrificial cult of Ṛgvedic practice, forms of possible Harappan survivals, and the accretion of more recent practices, perhaps taken from the Black-and-red Ware cultures. That there is an elaboration of some significance between the rituals as described in the *Ṛgveda* and the same rituals as described later in the other Vedic texts is apparent if a comparison is made of references to the *aśvamedha*, for example. The *Ṛgveda*[39] describes a relatively simple ritual in which the horse is sacrificed for the acquisition of wealth, prosperity, and magical power. In the later texts it becomes an elaborate ritual incorporating the fire altar and consisting of many levels of activities spread over many months.[40] The ceremonies come to include fertility rites and the notion of a potlatch. The latter is as much a declaration of political ascendency and social status as the sending forth of the horse, and this becomes even more evident in the descriptions of the *aśvamedha* in the *Mahābhārata*[41] and the *Rāmāyaṇa*.[42] The *yajña* (sacrificial ritual) would represent the coming together of many rituals of diverse origins.

The search for the remnants of the Agnicayana ritual in archaeological data is made more difficult by the fact that the structures associated with the ritual, sheds with thatched roofs supported by wooden posts, are made of perishable materials. The only exception is the altar, which was built of bricks. Was this done because the initial ritual was connected with migratory groups? Or because it did not require permanent sacred centers? Or was it done deliberately so that the area demarcated as sacred space could be desanctified at the termination of the ritual to leave only the altar? Equally striking is the fact that the objects used are primarily of clay and wood, so there is an absence of utility metals such as copper or iron. Yet copper, at least — and to a lesser extent iron — was familiar to first millennium people. The offerings of ghee, curd, milk, grain, *soma*, and domesticated animals would have been available to pastoralists and agriculturalists.

That the building and worship of fire altars may have gone back to the Harappan period remains a hypothetical suggestion. Brick altars have not been found in association with Harappan sites, nor are they represented symbolically on the Harappan seals. It has been suggested, however, that fire altars may have been known to the Harappans, or more correctly to those living in Lothal and in Kalibangan.[43] A number of rectangular or tub-shaped earthenware structures were found inside the houses in the residential area as well as on a platform of the citadel area. In the latter case they were placed five in a row near a well, but a cut had been made through them at some later period by the construction of a brick-lined drain. The structures were approximately three to four feet in length and about half that in width. In the center of each was an upright stone cylinder with a series of terracotta cakes arranged around it. Traces of ash were visible on the inner side of the structure. These structures are clearly very different in concept and form from the Vedic, even if it is assumed that they were fire altars. The resemblance would at best be symbolic, and even then rather farfetched. It is also curious that these structures should be found only at a couple of Harappan sites. At most it can be argued that some rudimentary ritual connected with fire altars was known at this early period, and that this may have survived in altered garb when incorporated into the highly complex ritual connected with the Agnicayana.

Many decades ago a seminal idea was mooted by Caland in a comment on an excavation by Bloch of a mound at Lauriya Nandangarh,[44] a site better known for an Aśokan pillar located in the vicinity. The site contained three rows of five mounds between twenty and fifty feet high. They were cone-shaped but may originally have been hemispherical. The mound was built up of layers of yellow clay interspersed with layers consisting of straw, leaves, and burnt bricks made from the same clay. Since this was not local clay, it was specially brought, probably from the Gandak river, which is now at a distance of about ten miles from the site. The first mound revealed human bones, animal bones, burnt wood, and a gold plaque of a female figure. A large opening farther down and in the center appears to have held a wooden pillar; the stump of the pillar on excavation was found to be of sal wood and to have a girth of four feet four inches. The second mound contained animal bones. The third contained human bones, the jaw of a teenaged child, and another golden plaque of a female figure.

Bloch thought these mounds to be the *śmaśānas* or burial places referred to in the Vedic texts, possibly royal burials, but Caland argued that *śmaśānas* are generally not round.[45] More pertinently, Caland questioned the placing of animal bones and the plaques of females in the human funeral mound. He suggested that these might instead have been Agnicayana altars, arguing that according to the texts they could have been of various shapes — hawk-shaped, square, round, and so on. They were to be built in five layers interspersed with sand. In the lowest layer was placed the golden form of a man symbolising Puruṣa or Prajāpati, who is sometimes depicted with milk-giving breasts.[46] (In the case of the Nandangarh plaques however, the female genitalia are unmistakable.) In this layer were also to be placed the head of a man, a ram, a goat, a bull, and a horse; they could either be natural or made of clay. He was puzzled, however, by the wooden post in the center of the mound.

Kane has drawn attention to the statement that those who had performed the Agnicayana were permitted a structure of bricks or clods at burial, suggesting an association of ideas if not a clear link between the *śmaśāna* and the Agnicayana.[47] This in turn suggests a link between the terms *citi* and *caitya*.[48] *Caitya*, a form of *cetiya*, is ultimately derived from *citi*, the etymology of which refers to the act of 'heaping up.' A *citi* is a structure that results from a piling up of material in a particular form. Where the piling up was of bricks, the form would be more precise, and where it was of earth or clods of earth, the tumulus and the cairn would be 'natural' in form. The *cetiya* would then be either a sacred enclosure marking a sacred spot or, when it contained the relics of those who had died, a sepulchral monument. Buddhist literature refers to it in both these senses.[49] Mus has suggested that the Vedic altar was the starting point of what developed into the Buddhist *cetiya* and *stūpa*.[50] Presumably the *yūpa* associated with the altar may have become the central pivot in the raising of a tumulus. A distinction is made between the *śmaśāna*, which is essentially a funerary marker, and the *caitya*, which is a sacred enclosure. In the latter capacity the site could presumably be of a sacrifice or ritual, or even of an object of worship that had been cordoned off, such as the *aśvattha* tree. The earliest reference to a *caitya* appears to be in the *Āśvalāyana Gṛhyasūtra*.[51] The epics also indicate familiarity with the worship of *caityas* in various forms.[52] In the *Rāmāyaṇa* *caityas* are mentioned more frequently in connection with the *rākṣasas*. Hanumān takes great pride in destroying the tall *caitya-prāsāda* in Laṅka and uprooting its massive pillar.[53] That this was not regarded as an act of desecration would suggest that *caityas* were perhaps linked with heterodoxy by this time.

Because of the etymological link between the words, it is assumed that the *cetiya* is a later form of the *citi*. It is possible, however, that the two, the Vedic altar and the tumulus, were parallel forms indicating places requiring veneration, and that the difference in form related to differences in the cults and rituals followed by different social groups. The *stūpa* becomes a more elaborate form of the tumulus with a variety of symbolic embellishments. It is curious that in the listing of forms which the *citi* can take, mention is made of the *rathacakra* and the *samūhya* or *dhānyarāśi*,[54] which occur in *stūpa* construction respectively as the spoked-wheel foundation and the paddy-heap shape.

Such burial mounds are generally dated to the first millennium BC on the basis of archaeological evidence and references in both Vedic and Buddhist literature. The worship of *caityas* and *stūpas* is regarded as customary even before the rise of Buddhism. Although *stūpa* architecture was made more elaborate in the Mauryan period[55] and later, the structure existed earlier, as shown for example in the record of Aśoka Maurya visiting and enlarging the Konakamana *stūpa*.[56]

It is significant that there is no mention of the *citi* as an altar of bricks in the *Ṛgveda*.[57] The development of the idea therefore may date to the period of the later texts, which represent the assimilation of Aryan and non-Aryan practices. In this connection a recent suggestion deserves some consideration.[58] It has been pointed out that the burial practices of the Asuras, Prācyas (easterners), and others described in the *Śatapatha Brāhmaṇa* bear a close resemblance to the Megalithic remains from the Jungal Mahal area, that is, to the Vindhyan outliers in the districts of Banda, Mirzapur, and Varanasi. The monuments are basically cairn circles and cist circles constructed of stone, and the dominant feature is the piling up of stones into a cairn. There is, however, no use of bricks anywhere, presumably because stone was easily available. The cairns enclose a pit that in most cases contains some human bones indicating postcremation burial and some animal bones associated with ritual killing, and there is one in which the bones of a tortoise and a rodent were found. The pottery is of various kinds ranging from an ill-fired red ware to the technically more sophisticated Black-and-red Ware. These monuments date to the first half of the first millennium BC. Megalithic monuments serve the function in some cases of memorial monuments,[59] and in others of funerary monuments, a combination that appears to be reflected in the *caityas* of a later period. From both points of view these Megalithic monuments would be regarded as sacred enclosures. There may possibly have been some connections with these monuments in the fashioning of the forms and the symbolism of the Agnicayana.

By the first millennium BC there appears to have been a bifurcation in the rituals relating to death. The Harappans and most of the post-Harappan Chalcolithic cultures buried the dead with a predominance of urn burials or graves of various kinds. The Painted Grey Ware culture registers a noticeable absence of burials, suggesting that possibly cremation was the more regular form and was also legitimized in the Vedic texts. Given the social stratification that had emerged by this time, graves would almost certainly have been linked to persons or families of high status. However, the bifurcation is cultural and ethnic rather than social, since the Asuras and others are generally said to have had graves and burial mounds. The burial of the golden man, identified at some points with Prajāpati, who then passes to the invisible world of immortality to become the symbol of the immortal self and of the attainment of immortality by the *yajamāna*, indicates that burial rites may be woven into the Agnicayana. The fact of the altar being a fire altar obliquely introduces the notion of cremation. The extent to which the Agnicayana uses both burial and fire as symbols was perhaps a concession on the part of those who cremated the dead to the alien but older ritual of burial.

The Agnicayana altar, as it is most frequently described, was a large construction of brick requiring a substantial output in time and energy and a fair knowledge of geometry, since the bricks are of various shapes and sizes.[60] The unit is a square, one-fifth of the length of the sacrificer, and hence called the *pañcami* brick. Another tradition states that it should be one-fourth of the length of the *yajamāna*. Other shapes are variations on this, the basic measurement being subunits of one-half, one-fourth, and one-eighth. A large-sized brick, the *adhyardha*, is rectangular in shape with the longer side measuring one and one-half times that of the *pañcama* and the short side equal to that of the *pañcama,* which in turn is subdivided to accommodate the long and the short quarter. The *sapāda* brick is again rectangular, with the long side being one and one-quarter the length of the *pañcama*. Subdivision of the squares and the rectangles results in triangular bricks of various shapes, which are particularly handy in shaping the pointed contours of a hawk altar. The thickness of the brick is described as being one-fifth of the distance between the *yajamāna*'s knees and the ground. This measurement is ambiguous, since the ratio of this distance to the full length of the *yajamāna* is not given.

Hyla Converse has drawn attention to the fact that brickmaking was a Harappan activity, and the details given for the making, shaping, and firing of these bricks may have derived from Harappan survivals.[61] The ratios of sizes of bricks from pre-Harappan and Harappan levels tends to be 1 : 2 : 3 and 1 : 2 : 4 in terms of thickness, breadth, and length. The size of the brick for the fire altar, i.e., 1 : 1 or 1 : 1.5, is also known from protohistoric sites, but it is not common. Since the ratio of the thickness of the brick to its breadth and length is of uncertain measurement, if the first ratio is deleted, then the size of the pre-Harappan brick would conform to 1 : 1.5, the size of the *adhyardha*. The sheer number of the bricks is also of some consideration. Most texts agree that the number should be 1000, with 200 bricks going into each of the five layers; but some texts mention the figure of 10,800.[62] The size of the brick as defined by one-fifth of the length of the *yajamāna* would under any circumstances be large. Such an effort would require the labor of a settled population over some months and is unlikely to have been easily carried out by groups of nomadic pastoralists. This might in part explain why fire altars of packed earth are permitted in some texts, although the Yajurveda requires it to be built of brick.[63]

Among the other objects that suggest some echo of Harappan affiliation are the discoid wheels of the carts. These consisted of the *śakaṭa*, the large cart for transporting the *soma*, and the *ratham*, the small cart used for oblations. (The *ratham* used at Panjal had a small copper pipe fitted to it, but this could be a recent innovation.) The Harappans, it is thought, were unfamiliar with the spoked wheel, which is first mentioned in the *Ṛgveda*.[64] Toy carts in terracotta from Harappan sites invariably have disc wheels. The recent cache of bronzes from Daimabad has one model of what appears to be an intermediate form between a cart and a chariot, and its wheels are also discoid.

Among the most obvious of the material objects that can be compared with archaeological remains is the pottery used in the ritual. A distinction can be made between the pots as described in the literature and those actually used at Panjal. The pottery vessels required in the Agnicayana ceremony are the *ukhā*, in which the fire is deposited and maintained for many months;[65] the *mahāvīra*, which is used in the Pravargya rite associated with the *soma* sacrifice; and a few other pots used in the ritual.[66]

The making of these pots is described in detail in the texts. The clay has to be mixed with a large number of other things — varieties of earth, pieces of animal hair, plants, fragments of potsherds from deserted places (*armayāni kapālām*), and powdered pebbles. In the case of the *ukhā*, the water used for moistening the clay has to be boiled with the resin of the *palāśa* tree, and the ingredients mixed into the clay include iron rust. The technique suggested is that of coiling and dabbing to produce the actual shape of the pots. In one text this is to be done by a skilled potter, but in most other texts it is done by the *yajamāna* or his wife, or by members of the three *dvija* castes. The potter's wheel is in any case prohibited. The same clay mixture was to be used for making certain other pots, such as those used for milking, the vessel for ghee, and the disclike potsherds for keeping certain offerings. The pots were first to be sun-dried, then 'plastered over' (perhaps the application of a slip). The *mahāvīra* has to be smoothed by using *gavedhuka* grass. The pots are then well fumigated (*dhūpayati*) in horse dung before being fired (*pacati*) in a pit or open-hearth kiln, where they are to be placed in an inverted position.[67] In the description given for the firing of the *ukhā*, a four-cornered pit is dug in which fuel is laid. On it are placed some of the bricks and the *ukhā*, the latter in an inverted position. Above this comes another layer of fuel. The fuel is then kindled for the firing, which lasts the length of the day, and the fuel is replenished when required. If any of the pots crack in the process, they should be repaired, and if they break, then new ones are to be made to replace them. Preparations for the making of some of the bricks were to take place at the same time as the making of the pots.

The *mahāvīra* should be one span high with a broad base and narrowed in the middle.[68] Another text describes it as being the shape of a wooden cup with either three or five elevations.[69] The top of the cup seems to have had a spout that would facilitate pouring. The *ukhā* should be one span high and a little more than a span in width, with a girdle around it and vertical strips.[70] The girdle is decorated with two to eight udders (breasts) with nipples. This would suggest an open-rimmed, oval pot. The pots used for milking are described as having the shape of the lip of the elephant, with a beak-like form for pouring similar to a ladle without a handle.[71]

The potter and the potter's wheel are known both from the literary and the archaeological sources of this period. The insistence that the pots be hand-made may have been an attempt to distinguish ritual pottery from that for daily use; this was doubtless to remove ritual pottery from the pollution of the potter and the potter's wheel, assuming of course that the potter's status was already low, and perhaps also to invest ritual pottery with an ancient tradition by debarring the use of the wheel. The injunction against the use of the potter's wheel is stated in one text with reference to the making of the milking pots.[72] The fact that such specific directions are given for the making of these pots may suggest that there might also have been a functional reason for using this technique.

The admixture of material to the clay would have produced a coarse-grained pottery more akin to early Neolithic handmade pottery than the finely levigated ceramics of the Chalcolithic period. The purpose of the mixture is explained in ritualistic terms, and various deities are invoked, which suggests shamanistic survivals.

Technically, the use of what modern potters call 'grog' as a filler, which produces a clay mixed with crushed potsherds and small particles of pebbles, results in a mixture that is difficult to throw on a wheel because of the meagerness of levigated clay; it is more likely to be successful if the pot is handmade. Wheel-thrown pots require well-levigated clay, the finer the better. The advantage of using grog is that such pottery is less likely to crack when it comes into direct contact with fire. Thus, for the purposes for which the *ukhā* was made, i.e., to be used as a fire pan, a mixture with the clay would be essential. That the same technique was extended to other pots used in the ritual would suggest that there was some attempt at archaicizing the process.

The use of grog would also ensure less shrinkage at the green-hard stage when the pot is dried before firing.[73] The inclusion of hair, which would burn up in firing, served the same function. Iron rust may have acted as a fluxing agent to prevent the pot from collapsing when fired. Water boiled in resin may have assisted in providing an adhesive texture. The fumigation of pots before firing is a recognized technique in making primitive handmade black pottery; it fills in the pores with the soot particles that darkened the pot.[74] Such pottery is generally fired below sinter point, often because the use of a crude kiln does not permit a high enough temperature and results in a porous fabric. Grog was probably also necessary because the firing was done in a pit rather than a regularly built kiln, with no separator between the actual pot and the fire, unless the layer of bricks fired with the pots acted as a separator. In any case, an open-hearth kiln can only fire to low temperatures, and the clay would have to be porous to prevent cracking.

The archaeological correlations of this pottery remain enigmatic. Neolithic potting techniques would go back to the fourth millennium BC in the Indo-Iranian borderlands and to the third millennium in the Deccan. But clearly the potter's wheel and more advanced techniques of kiln firing were also known; therefore the technique for making pots other than the *ukhā* seems to have been deliberately archaic. There are no clear parallels to the shapes described, merely some suggestive similarities. There is one pottery form, referred to as having been found at Dabar Kot in the Loralai area, that is described as a cup with a channel spout,[75] and it does suggest a beak-like spout resembling the lip of an elephant! Pottery with udderlike elevations is rare in the ceramic assemblage of protohistoric India. A reference has been made to such a find at a site on the bank of the Tungabhadra at Itgi in Belgaum district, where a black oval pot was found with the required nipple-like decoration and with the prescribed two holes in the base through which a cord could be passed to enable the *yajamāna* to carry the pot.[76] However, the excavator dates this pot to the first century BC or AD, a period much later than that of the texts.

The statement in the texts that the pots have to be placed in an inverted position for firing in the pit kiln has been interpreted as a possible reference to the inverted firing technique common to the widespread pottery of the Black-and-red Ware culture.[77] But if the intention was to produce a double colour, then it is likely that the texts would have referred to this as a mark of distinction of the ritual pottery. Hyla Converse has argued that this was perhaps the secret technique that receives an ambiguous mention in the text. Reference to the colour of the pottery is limited to one text that stipulates that the pots be fired to a red colour.[78] To produce a black-and-red colour would require controlled firing. Dry fuel and a good draft produce the oxidizing atmosphere necessary to make red pottery, whereas damp fuel and an obstructed draft are required to prevent oxidation and provide the reducing atmosphere necessary to make black pottery. A pit kiln such as the one described would have resulted in an indiscriminate mixture. The inversion of the pot may have had to do with ease of placing the pot in the pit. Pots are often placed in an inverted position in an open-hearth kiln, and the black and red tones that result can be accidental. The depth of the open-hearth kiln would also be significant. A deep pit would obstruct the flow of air. The reference in the texts to the bamboo handle of the spade disappearing in the pit would indicate a deep pit. In the description given for the making of the *mahāvīra*, there seems to be less admixture of grog, perhaps because unlike the *ukhā* this pot was not used for carrying fire. The *mahāvīra* is smoothed, perhaps to facilitate its handling. Curiously no reference is made to digging a pit when the pot is fired in an open-hearth kiln. This may be assumed, but it is worth noting that a shallow pit or a surface-level hearth would encourage a freer flow of air than a deep pit, thus permitting oxidation and resulting in a red-colored pottery. One text states specifically that the fuel to be used, including dry herbs, wood, etc., should be such as would produce a red-coloured pottery.[79]

If the reference to inverted firing had to do with the Black-and-red Ware culture, then it poses another problem. A reference to *nīla-lohita* in the *Atharvaveda*[80] is taken by some scholars to refer to the Black-and-red pottery. If this be so, then the text disapproves of the practices of those who use this pottery, giving it an Asura connection. But this connection is also hinted at in the statement that the *ukhā* is born of the *asuri māyā*.[81] The Ṛgveda links Asuras with the Angirasas, who are believed to be the priests of the fire cult.[82]

To add further complications, the texts also speak of the 'smoothing' of the pots. It has been assumed that the outer surface of the pottery was black, and that therefore the reference to the polishing of this pottery may hint at a relationship with the Northern Black Polished Ware of the mid-first millennium BC.[83] The latter is late on the ceramic scene, has its provenance in the middle Ganga valley, and was made possible through development of a highly evolved technique of firing at temperatures, that, it has been suggested, were probably attainable only after the invention of iron smelting. The nomenclature is deceptive, since the polish is not due to any post-firing technique but probably results accidentally through the interaction of natural constituents of the clay, or the addition of some special ingredient. It is generally associated with the luxury ware of the urban centres in the pre-Mauryan and Mauryan periods. In fact, the method for polishing pots described in the texts could more correctly be interpreted as a form of burnishing, a method used for the smoothing of the exterior surface of handmade pottery and already a common practice in the making of Neolithic pottery. This is further supported by the fact that the burnishing of pottery is usually done at the green-hard stage prior to firing, and polishing is a post-firing technique. The texts are clear that the 'smoothing' is to be done prior to firing. The purpose of burnishing was literally to smooth the exterior surface, but it was also employed to make the pot less porous or to add a decorative feature.

As regards the pottery actually used in the ritual at Panjal, there are some similarities, admittedly very vague, with forms current in the proto-historic period. The *ukhā*, if visualized without the udders, suggests a pedestaled dish, the earliest examples of which go back to the Harappan period, and the form of which, with some variation, has a continuity into the Megalithic and central Indian

Chalcolithic cultures of the peninsula. However, the stand in this case would seem not to match the textual description, which makes it sound like a cauldron. The *mahāvīra*, inasmuch as its shape resembles the bowl-on-stand, would carry traces of some forms from the Gandhara Grave Culture and from post-Harappan pottery, particularly of the central Indian Chalcolithic. The latter cultures also provide evidence of vessels with a tubular spout. However, none of these resemblances are in any way close. The most that can be said is that the pottery used in the ritual at Panjal, if it has any archaeological analogies at all, would seem to come nearest to shapes found more often in the post-Harappan Chalcolithic cultures. Its immediate ancestry in terms of form, texture, and technique is suggestive of a later period, possibly the early first millennium AD. This is not surprising considering that what is under investigation is a living tradition that would doubtless be influenced by late forms and techniques.

In the ceremonial space used for the performance of the Agnicayana, there is only one structure that is likely to survive, namely the altar. Consequently, the presence of an altar is the only major clue to the site of an actual performance of the ritual. Claims to have identified such sites from archaeological remains are extremely few, and of these only one is accepted as genuine, since it carries an inscription describing it as an altar. This extreme paucity of evidence may have to do with the fact that such altars are required to be constructed on ground that has been sanctified and demarcated, and that therefore inevitably has to be at some small distance from settlements. Archaeological excavation is primarily of settlements, and it is largely by chance that such an altar may be found in the process of exploration.

Controversy still swirls around the identification of a *śyenaciti* on the outskirts of the ancient city of Kauśāmbi dating to the mid-first millennium BC.[84] The *śyenaciti* is located on the outside of the eastern gate, but close to the defence wall of the city, and it is bounded by the revetment of the rampart and its returning wall. The altar, in the shape of a bird (eagle?) with outstretched wings, faces southeast. It has a length of 49 feet 8 inches and a width of 33 feet 6 inches. In the construction of the altar the first layer of bricks was sealed by a sand deposit of 6 inches. In its center was a gravel (kankara) nodule — with small cavities enclosed by a circle of 10 bricks — that the excavator takes to be the *svayamātṛṇṇā*.

The most noticeable pottery object was shaped like an offering stand with a broken top approximately 5 inches high. In the same layer was included a terracotta female figurine, stylistically datable to about the second or first century BC. The excavator also describes a brick with an engraving of a man tied to a stake who is about to be beheaded. There is a scatter of animal bones — a horse skull, tortoise shell, the jawbone of a pig, and the bones of elephants, bovines, and goats, the last three having been verified as such. Also included in this layer was an iron model of a snake. Layer II seals off the jawbone of a buffalo and bricks of various shapes. Layer III produced three complete human skulls and some skull fragments, and also hipbones, ribs, and long bones. Some bones bearing incision marks were arranged in a V-shape or were enclosed in brick structures suggesting careful placement and some ritual function. Layers IV and V were badly damaged by a pit from a later period that had been dug into these layers, but they nevertheless provided evidence of human bone fragments. There were also a human skull and some pots placed in the tail section of the altar.

The identification of the site as a fire altar does raise some problems. The location of the altar so close to the ramparts of the city seems unusual. Given the fact that the altar is part of a ritual that requires the demarcation of sacred space, it seems strange that it should not have been placed farther from the city wall. The excavator quotes a reference in the *Kandahāla Jātaka* to a king digging a sacrificial pit just outside the eastern gate of the city.[85] It could be argued that the site was away from the original wall of the city but that the later extension of defences and the building of revetments resulted in encroachment on the altar space. This would depend on the date of the altar. If the terracotta figurine is not a stray from a later period, then the altar may well date to a period subsequent to the reinforcing of the city walls. The shape of the bird as presently reconstructed appears to be rather curvilinear, whereas the bricks used for the altar would indicate a more rectilinear form. The interpretation of the objects found is also not convincing.[86] The engraving on the brick of a man tied to a stake would seem to appear to be such only in the eyes of the excavator, if one can judge by the photograph; nor is the iron model of the snake recognizable. The pottery object described as an offering stand bears greater resemblance to a wide-mouthed jar. The frequency of human skulls and bones would also seem to suggest a ritual different from that described in the texts and it certainly is in excess of what is required. The texts refer to the burial of the head of a man, ram, goat, bull, and horse. The skulls of all but the human are absent in this *śyenaciti*, although their bones are there.

Whether or not the *śyenaciti* is in strict conformity with the descriptions of the fire altar in the literary sources, and whether or not the interpretation of objects as given by the excavator is acceptable, there can be little doubt that the structure did represent some kind of sacrificial or funerary site. The brick structure was built to some specification. The large number of human bones and the associated animal bones would point to a ritual connection. If the site is as late as the first century BC, then it is possible that some pragmatic changes were introduced into the rituals described in the texts. The site was evidently disturbed in later periods, and this may have been accidental, although the possibility that such sites were believed to contain treasure may account for many tumuli having been broken into.

Another place with far less evidence was also rumored to have provided an altar site. This was the town of Nagarjunakonda in the Paland taluka of Guntoor District. The inscriptions of the Ikṣvāku kings who ruled here in the second and third centuries AD refer to the performance of *yajñas* such as the *aśvamedha*, and this encouraged the search for the sites of the rituals.[87] Two structures were interpreted as altars, but recent opinion has rejected such interpretations.[88] Had there been any fire altars in the vicinity of the city, it is most likely that they would have been discovered, since the original location of Nagarjunakonda at a lower elevation in the valley was carefully and systematically explored, the excavation being part of a project of 'salvage archeology' carried out before the site was submerged on completion of the Tungabhadra dam.

By the early centuries AD the Vedic sacrificial rituals, inasmuch as they were performed by monarchs, appear to have acquired another dimension. They became a legitimizing ritual for kings, particularly for those seeking connections with the two royal lineages of *kṣatriya* ancestry, the Sūryavaṃśa and the Candravaṃśa. This may also in part explain the bifurcation of royal patronage to religious sects, where the women of the royal families — as, for example, the Iksvākus — were equally zealous in their support of Buddhism, which support is amply reflected in the monuments and inscriptions of the time.

The one site that can be described without hesitation as that of a fire altar is at Jagatgram.[89] It was discovered in the course of exploration in the Dehra Dun district where the Yamuna River descends from the Siwalik hills to the plains. It lies in the vicinity of Kalsi, better known as the site of a series of rock edicts of the Mauryan emperor Aśoka. Three sites were exposed where a king had performed *aśvamedhas*. Each site consisted of an eagle-shaped altar. Inscribed bricks from the first site provide the information that a king, Śīlavarman, performed four *aśvamedhas* at Jagatgram. One inscription reads:

*siddham aum yugeśvarasyāśvamedhe yugaśailamahipate iṣṭakā vārṣaganasya nṛpatesīlavarmaṇa*

'Hail! Brick from the altar of the *aśvamedha* of the king Śīlavarmaṇa of the Varṣagana, the lord of Yugaśaila, the Yugeśvara.'

Another brick inscription reads:

*nṛpatervarṣaganasya ponaṣaṣṭhasya dhīmata caturatthasyāśva medhasya citoyam śīlavarmaṇa*

'Altars of the four *aśvamedhas* of the renowned king Śīlavarmaṇa of the Varṣagana, sixth in descent from Poṇa.'

It has been suggested that the Varṣagana-gotra may be the same as that referred to by Pāṇini as the sixty-ninth *gotra*, Vṛṣagana,[90] and the word *yugeśvara* suggests 'the lord of the lustrum' described in the *Bṛhatsamhitā*. The latter might indicate that the repeated performance of the ceremony had to do with the purification of the king or the people. The identity of Śīlavarman remains obscure, as also does his line of descent from Poṇa. He may have been associated with the rulers of Lakha-maṇḍala in this area. Paleographically the inscription written in Brāhmī dates to the third century AD. The bricks bearing the inscription are of two sizes, 1 : 2 : 3 and 1 : 2 : 4. The area obviously had settlements during the Mauryan period for there to have been a set of edicts inscribed nearby. Excavations in the neighborhood indicate more evolved settlements dating to the start of the Christian era.[91]

The Agnicayana altar as a structure is proceeded with, layer by layer, and in a sense the same pattern of construction may have gone into the ultimate form of the ritual. Archaeologically there is no clearly defined culture or period to which it can be related. The pottery-making techniques suggest Neolithic practices, the forms of the pottery carry traces of Chalcolithic types, the bricks are strongly reminiscent of a Harappan urban culture, the hawk shape of the altar echoes shamanistic ideas, and the inclusion of both human and animal bones suggests analogies with Megalithic funerary monuments. The increasing emphasis on a form of potlatch included within the rites points to a people probably no longer nomadic and with enough wealth to be distributed and consumed on a ritual occasion. The Agnicayana ritual was gradually put together, modified, adjusted, and elaborated upon in the course of centuries. Not only was it extended by additional rites, taken perhaps from a variety of cultures, but the additions were interlocked in a vast edifice of ritual. In this process its purpose and function also underwent change. Beginning as a ritual performed for the acquisition of magical power linked to the concept of an immortal self and for the expression of communion between men and gods, it incorporated in its development notions of fertility, wealth, and power, and emerged as a ritual of legitimation and social validation. Its very survival into the present takes on yet another dimension, the historical dimension, that is different from those with which it started.

Abbreviations

| | |
|---|---|
| AŚS | Āśvalāyana Śrautasūtra |
| BhŚS | Bharadvāja Śrautasūtra |
| BŚS | Baudhāyana Śrautasūtra |
| KŚS | Kātyāyana Śrautasūtra |
| M | Mahābhārata |
| MS | Maitrāyaṇī Saṃhitā |
| R | Rāmāyaṇa |
| RV | Ṛgveda |
| ŚB | Śatapatha Brāhmaṇa |
| TS | Taittirīya Saṃhitā |
| VS | Vājasaneyi Saṃhitā |

Notes and References

1. V.G. Childe, *The Aryans*, London, 1926.
2. L. de la Vallée Poussin, *Indo-Européens et Indo-Iraniens . . .*, Paris,

1936; A.B. Keith, *The Religion and Philosophy of the Vedas and Upaniṣads,* Harvard Oriental Series, vols 31–2, Cambridge, Mass., 1925; G. Cardona (ed.), *Indo-European and Indo-Europeans,* Philadelphia, Pa., 1970.

3. V.M. Masson and V.I. Sarianidi, *Central Asia: Turkmenia Before the Achaemenids*, London, 1972, pp. 113ff.
4. J.F. Jarrige and M. Lechevalier, 'Excavations at Mehrgarh, Baluchistan: Their Significance in the Prehistorical Context of the Indo-Pakistan Borderlands', in M. Taddei (ed.), *South Asian Archaeology: 1977*, Naples, 1979, pp. 463–535.
5. H.P. Frankfort and M.H. Pottier, 'Sondage preliminaires sur l'etablisement protohistoriques Harapéen et post-Harapéen de Shortugai (Afghanistan du N-E)', *Arts Asiatiques*, 34, 1978, pp. 29–79.
6. A survey of the problem of identifying archaeological cultures with the Aryans can be found in 'Society in Ancient India: The Formative Period', *see* chpater 14 in this volume; and B.K. Thapar, 'The Archaeological Remains of the Aryans in North-western India', unpublished paper read at the Doshambe Conference, 1977.
7. W. Fairservis, *The Roots of Ancient India*, 2nd ed., Chicago, Ill., 1975.
8. A.R.K. Zide and K.V. Zvelebil (eds), *The Soviet Decipherment of the Indus Valley Script*, The Hague, 1976.
9. J.P. Joshi, 'Excavation at Surkotada', in D.P. Agrawal and A. Ghosh (eds), *Radio-Carbon and Indian Archaeology*, Bombay, 1973, pp. 173ff.
10. A.D. Pusalkar, 'Pre-Harappan, Harappan and Post-Harappan Culture and the Aryan Problem', *The Quarterly Review of Historical Studies*, 7.4, 1967–68, pp. 233ff.
11. B.K. Thapar, 'The End of the Indus Civilisation and its Aftermath', in Udai Vir Singh (ed.), *Archaeological Congress and Seminar: 1972*, Kurukshetra, 1976, pp. 1–4.
12. J.P. Joshi, 'Interlocking of Late Harappan Culture and Painted Grey Ware Culture in the Light of Recent Excavations', *Man and Environment*, 2, 1978, pp. 100–3.
13. G.L. Possehl, *Variation and Change in the Indus Civilisation: A Study of Prehistoric Gujarat with Special Reference to the Post-Urban Harappan*, Ph.D. dissertation, University of Chicago, 1974; S.R. Rao et al., 'Excavations at Rangpur and Other Explorations in Gujarat', *Ancient India*, 18–19, 1962.
14. B.B. Lal, 'From the Megalithic to the Harappa: Tracing Back the Graffiti on the Pottery', *Ancient India*, 16, 1960, pp. 4ff.
15. B.M. Emeneau, *Collected Papers*, Annamalainagar, 1967.
16. For arguments in support of the theory, see B. Allchin and R. Allchin, *The Birth of Indian Civilisation*, Harmondsworth, Eng., 1968, pp. 126ff. Other alternatives for the decline of cities have been suggested by R.L. Raikes, 'The End of the Ancient Cities of the Indus',

*American Anthropology*, 66.2, 1964, pp. 284–99. See also R.L. Raikes and G.F. Dales, 'The Mohenjo-Daro Floods Reconsidered', *Journal of the Palaeontological Society of India*, 20, 1977, pp. 251–60.

17. G.F. Dales, 'The Mythical Massacre at Mohenjo-Daro', *Expedition*, 6.3, 1964, pp. 36–43.
18. T. Burrow, 'On *arma* and *armaka*', *Journal of Indian History*, 41.1, 1963, pp. 159ff.
19. B. Allchin and R. Allchin, pp. 144ff; B.K. Thapar, 'The Aryans: A Reappraisal of the Problem', in Lokesh Chandra (ed.), *India's Contribution to World Thought and Culture*, Madras, 1970.
20. H.D. Sankalia, *Prehistory and Protohistory of India and Pakistan*, Poona, 1974, pp. 392ff.
21. M. Antonini, 'Preliminary Notes on the Excavation of the Necropolis Found in West Pakistan', *East and West*, 14.1–2, 1964, pp. 13–27; G. Stacul, 'Excavation Near Ghaligai (1968) and Chronological Sequence of Protohistorical Cultures in the Swat Valley', *East and West*, 19, 1969, pp. 44–92; A.H. Dani, 'Timargarha and the Gandhara Grave Culture', *Ancient Pakistan*, 3, 1967, pp. 1ff.
22. R.H. Dyson, 'Archaeological Evidence of the Second Millennium BC on the Persian Plateau', *Cambridge Ancient History*, II.1, pp. 686–716; C. Young, 'The Iranian Migration into the Zagros', *Iran*, 5, 1967, pp. 11–34.
23. H.D. Sankalia et al., *Excavations at Ahar (Tambavati)*, Poona, 1969.
24. N.R. Bannerjee, *Iron Age in India*, Delhi, 1965; B.K. Gururaja Rao, *The Megalithic Culture in South India*, Mysore, 1972; A. Sundara, *The Early Chamber Tombs of South India*, Delhi, 1975.
25. R. Thapar, 'Puranic Lineages and Archaeological Cultures', in R. Thapar, *Ancient Indian Social History*, pp. 240ff.
26. H.D. Sankalia, 'New Light on the Indo-Iranian or Western Asiatic Relations Between 1700 BC–1200 BC', *Artibus Asiae*, 26, 1963, pp. 315ff.
27. H. Wilhemy, *Zeitschrift für Geomorphologie*, Sup. Band, 8, 1969, pp. 76–91, argues for the change in the Sarasvatī-Hakra and the diversion of water to the Yamuna during this period, the total ecological change having perhaps been due to tectonic disturbances.
28. B. Allchin and R. Allchin, p. 200.
29. B.B. Lal, 'The Copper Hoard Culture of the Ganga Valley', *Antiquity*, 46, 1972, pp. 282–7; S. Piggott, *Prehistoric India*, Harmondsworth, Eng., 1950, pp. 237ff.
30. B.B. Lal, 'Excavations at Hastinapura', *Ancient India*, 10–11, 1954–55; V. Tripathi, *The Painted Grey Ware*, Delhi, 1977.
31. J.P. Joshi, 'Interlocking of Late Harappan Culture and Painted Grey Ware Culture in the Light of Recent Excavations', *Man and Environment*, New Delhi, 1978, II, pp. 100–3.

32. K.A. Chaudhuri et al., *Ancient Agriculture and Forestry in Northern India*, Bombay, 1977, p. 58.
33. A clear case of transhumance being tied into trade is that of the sheep and yak herders along the Himalayan borders who became the backbone of what has been called a 'vertical economy' — in this case, between Tibet and India.
34. M. Rowton, 'Enclosed Nomadism', *JESHO*, 17, 1974, pp. 1–30.
35. RV, 7.96.2; 7.8.4; 7.18.3.
36. Rene Labat, 'Elam and Western Persia, *c.* 1200–1000 BC', in *Cambridge Ancient History*, II.2, p. 506.
37. A. Goetze, 'The Struggle for the Domination of Syria (1400–1300 BC)', in *Cambridge Ancient History*, II.2, pp. 1–8, 109–10.
38. Iron occurs at sites in central India and the Ganga-Yamuna Doāb by the end of the second millennium BC. At sites in the Gandhara Grave Culture and in Megalithic sites in Karnataka it occurs at the start of the first millennium BC. After the eighth century BC it becomes more noticeable. If it was one of the technological levers in the acceptance of Indo-Aryan, then it might have been introduced in the north in association with speakers of Indo-Aryan. Its use in the peninsula would then have had an independent entry, since most scholars tend to identify the Megalithic builders with Dravidian speakers (B.K. Gururaja Rao, pp. 330ff). For a discussion on iron, see D. Chakraborty, 'The Beginning of Iron in India', *Antiquity*, 50, 1976, pp. 114–24.
39. RV, 1.162, 1.163.
40. KŚS, 20.1; ĀŚS, 10.6.1ff.
41. M, 14.90.
42. R, 1.12, 1.13.
43. B.K. Thapar, 'Kalibangan: A Harappan Metropolis Beyond the Indus Valley', *Expedition*, Winter, 1975, pp. 19–32. Cf. *Agni*, vol. I, p. 154.
44. Th. Bloch, 'Excavation at Lauriya', *Annual Report of the Archaeological Survey of India: 1905*, 1906, pp. 11–15; W. Caland, *De Archaeologische vondsten in de heuvels van Lauriya*, Amsterdam, 1912. I am grateful to Professor Staal for drawing my attention to this discussion, and for translating Caland's paper for me.
45. A point that incidentally seems to be contradicted in the ŚB, 13.8.1.5, refers to the *devas* making their burial places four-cornered, whereas the Asuras, Prācyas, and others make them round.
46. ŚB, 2.5.1.3; *Sacred Books of the East*, XII, p. 385.
47. *History of Dharmaśāstra*, IV, pp. 246ff, n. 559; ŚB, 13.8.1–4; KŚS, 28.4.4. A. Parpola, *South Indian Megaliths*, Madras, 1973, pp. 30ff. Professor Staal informs me that there is a rather vague tradition among the Nambudiris that in the past some had the practice of the *yajamāna* or his wife (whoever died first) being cremated on his Agnicayana altar.

48. V.R. Ramachandra Dikshitar, 'Origins and Early History of the Caityas', *Indian Historical Quarterly*, 14, 1938, pp. 440–51.
49. *Majjhima Nikāya*, I.20; *Jātaka*, I.237; VI.173; *Dhammapada*, 188.
50. *Borobudur*, Paris, 1935.
51. 1.12.1–4.
52. M, 1.102.12, 6.3.37. R, 5.10.15.
53. R, 5.41.10ff.
54. TS, 5.4.11; KŚS, 16.5.9. Also BŚS, 17.29, below, pp. 668–71.
55. B. Rowland, *The Art and Architecture of India*, Harmondsworth, Eng., 1959, p. 254.
56. J. Bloch, *Les Inscriptions d' Aśoka*, Paris, 1950, p. 158.
57. The references appear to be to the piling up of wood, RV, 1.112.17, 1.158.4.
58. P.C. Pant, 'Megaliths of Jangal Mahal and Vedic Tradition', paper read at Post-Conference Session at Deccan College, Poona, Dec. 1978. See also *Indian Archaeology — A Review*, 1963–64, pp. 40–1.
59. As for example among the Khasi tribes of Meghalaya and other parts of north-eastern India, where this tradition has continued up to recent times.
60. The details regarding the bricks have been discussed in Volume I.
61. H.S. Converse, 'The Agnicayana Rite: Indigenous Origin?', *History of Religion*, 14.2, 1974, pp. 81–95.
62. Ibid., p. 83.
63. Ibid., p. 84.
64. S. Piggott, pp. 273ff.
65. ŚB, 6.5.4; BŚS, 10.1–8.
66. ŚB, 14.1.2; C.G. Kashikar, 'Pottery in Vedic Literature', *Indian Journal of the History of Science*, 4.1–2, 1969, pp. 15–26; W. Rau, 'Vedic Texts on the Manufacture of Pottery', *Journal of the Oriental Institute*, Baroda, 23.3, 1974, pp. 137–42; Y. Ikari, below, pp. 168–77.
67. ŚB, 6.5.4.4, 14.1.2.21; KŚS, 16.4.11.
68. ŚB, 14.1.2.17; BŚS, 9.4.
69. BŚS, 11.1–4.
70. BŚS, 10.1–8.
71. BŚS, 11.1–4; Kashikar, p. 20.
72. MS, 1.8.3.
73. For some of this information on potting techniques and the firing of pottery, I am grateful to a modern potter, Gouri Khosla, with whom I discussed the details given in the texts.
74. Henry Hodges, *Artifacts*, London, 1964, pp. 20ff.
75. R. Mughal, 'Explorations in Northern Baluchistan, 1972: New Evidence and Fresh Interpretations', *Proceedings of the Second Annual Symposium on Archaeological Research in Iran*, 1973, p. 278.

76. Kashikar, p. 26n.23; R.S. Panchmukhi, *Progress of Kannada Research in Bombay Province from 1941–46*, Dharwar, 1948, I–II; pp. 2.63–5.
77. Converse; Kashikar; Rau.
78. Kashikar, p. 20.
79. ĀŚS, 15.3.20, quoted in Eggeling, *Sacred Books of the East*, XLIV, p. 456n.3.
80. 4.17.4, 5.31.1.
81. ŚB, 6.6.2.6; VS, 11.69; TS, 4.1.9. See volume I, pp. 136–8.
82. ṚV, 3.53.7, 10.67.2. Cf. volume I, pp. 138, 162.
83. Kashikar, op. cit.
84. G.R. Sharma, *The Excavation at Kausambi* (1957–59), Allahabad, 1960, pp. 87ff.
85. *Kandahāla Jātaka*, no. 542.
86. G.R. Sharma, Plate 31B, Fig. 18.4 facing p. 89; Plate 32A, Fig. 18.1 facing p. 89.
87. T.N. Ramachandran, *Nagarjunakonda*, Calcutta, 1938. M.A.S.I. No. 71.
88. H. Sarkar and B.N. Misra, *Nagarjunakonda*, New Delhi, 1972, p. 20.
89. *Indian Archaeology — A Review* (1935–54), pp. 10–11; T.N. Ramachandran, 'Aśvamedha Site near Kalsi', *Journal of Oriental Research*, 21, 1953, pp. 1–31.
90. Pāṇiṇi, 4.1.105.
91. N.C. Ghosh and R.P. Sharma, 'The Cultures of the Early Historical Period in the Siwalik Ranges Between Ganga and Yamuna', paper presented at the Archaeological Society Conference, Chandigarh, 1975.

# 16

# *Archaeological Artifacts and Literary Data: An Attempt at Co-relation**

Attempts at co-relating archaeological artifacts and literary data can sometimes be misleading in that tangible objects and literary descriptions can be reliably compared only if the context of their occurrence can also be examined. The point can perhaps be illustrated by the problem of co-relating the pottery used in the *agnicayana* sacrifice with archaeological evidence. The *Śatapatha Brāhmaṇa*, generally dated to the first half of the first millennium BC, is one of the texts which provide some details on the ritual of the *agnicayana*. The material objects referred to in the text can be compared with the predominant archaeological cultures of the period and the region, namely, the Painted Grey Ware culture, the Black-and-red Ware cultures, and possibly by extending the date, the Northern Black Polished Ware culture. The geographical region associated with the text and the archaeological cultures is that of the western and middle Ganga valley.

Among the ritual objects is a series of pots of which the most important are the *ukhā* and the *mahāvīra* and others in which milk is kept. The initial igniting of fire churned on the *arani* and used for the sacrificial fire is first placed in the *ukhā* in which it is continually carried. This indicates its ritual importance as the fire-pan.[1] The *mahāvīra* also has a considerable ritual significance pertaining to the *soma* ritual in particular as it is used in the *pravargya* rite.[2] The text states that the *ukhā* should be one span

* In B.M. Pande and B.D. Chattopadhyaya (eds), *Archaeology and History*, Delhi 1987, 411–19.

Professor K.T.M. Hegde was kind enough to comment on this paper and I found his comments so useful that I have incorporated them in the notes.

high and a little more in width suggesting an oval, open-rimmed pot. It should be surrounded by a girdle and a series of vertical strips.[3] A breast-and-nipple design should decorate the girdle. The *mahāvīra* is also described as being a span in height with a broad base and contracted in the middle.[4] Elsewhere it is said that it should resemble a cup with three to five elevations.[5] The rim of the cup appears to have had a spout to facilitate the pouring of liquids. This facility is made more explicit in the pots which are to be used for milk about which it is said that they must have the shape of the lip of an elephant with a beak-like form for pouring! These would have resembled a deep ladle but without a handle.[6] It is also said that the size of the pots could be larger should that be thought necessary.

The shapes have their own symbolism but what is even more curious is the detailed description of the method of making these pots in which processes of the potter's craft are referred to but relate generally to those of the more primitive techniques of making pottery. In the first place a large number of items have to be added to the clay when it is prepared for the making of the pots; these consist of various kinds of earth, pieces of animal hair, bits of plants, tiny fragmented potsherds (but only those collected from deserted places) and pebbles which have been powdered. The references to deserted places recalls the mention of these in the *Ṛg Veda* which are said to have been the haunt of sorceresses (*yātumatī*) and magical activities.[7] In the case of the *ukhā* the clay is kneaded with water which has been boiled with the resin of the *palāśa* tree and iron-rust is also mixed into the clay.[8] The same mixed clay was to be used for making the other pots including the disc-like potsherd for keeping specific offerings.

The technique for making the pots was that of coiling and dabbing to produce the desired shape. Coiled pottery is generally thought to be an earlier technique, prior to the use of the potter's wheel. Most of the texts which refer to the making of these pots for the ritual insist that the pots be made by the *yajamāna* and his wife[9] or by members of the *dvija* caste. This is curious in the light of there being professional potters functioning at this time. Perhaps this in part explains the technique although coiled pottery if it is to be successful requires its own expertise. The pots were first to be sun-dried followed by what appears to be the application of a slip. The *mahāvīra* is further treated by its surface being smoothened through rubbing it with *gavedhuka* grass. The pots are then well fumigated (*dhūpayati*) in horse-dung before firing (*pacati*) in a pit or an open-hearth kiln.[10] It is also stated that the pots are to be placed in an inverted position for firing.[11] For the firing of the *ukhā* a four-cornered pit is to be dug in which fuel is laid. On this are placed some of the bricks used for the construction of the *agnicayana* fire altar as well as the *ukhā* in an inverted position. This is covered by another layer of fuel. The firing lasts for a full day and fresh fuel is added when necessary. The bricks and pots were to be prepared in the same way. The depth of the pit was to be such that the bamboo handle of the spade should disappear into the pit, suggesting a depth of about a metre.

The mixture added to the clay would have resulted in coarse-textured pots similar to those of Neolithic cultures rather than the fine ceramics known to Chalcolithic cultures. Although coarse pottery continues from the Neolithic to the Chalcolithic period, the ceramic industries used by archaeologists to identify the Chalcolithic cultures tend to be those of the finely made potteries since they are more impressive both in appearance and in number. In the text the purpose of mixing ingredients into the clay is explained in symbolic terms and is associated with the invoking of various deities and in safeguarding the ritual. Some of this may reflect shamanist survivals such as the reference to potsherds from deserted places and ruined settlements. Nevertheless it remains a curious feature that in a period and culture familiar with the technique of fine, wheel-thrown pottery (as were the ceramic industries of these times and places) there should be a harking back, as it were, to a more primitive technique. It may therefore be worth examining the degree to which the technique may have been necessitated by the actual function of the pottery in the ritual.

Up to a point the technique appears to have been functional. The use of what modern potters call a 'grog' as a filler, i.e., clay mixed with particles of pebbles and potsherds, makes it difficult to throw such clay on a wheel since the levigated clay which is contained in the mixture is of a small quantity and the pot is better if made by hand. Wheel-thrown pottery requires well-levigated clay. However the use of 'grog', according to some potters, reduces the chances of pottery cracking when it comes into direct contact with fire. Thus the function of the *ukhā* as a fire-pan may have necessitated the addition of 'grog'. The technique for making the *mahāvīra* is less clearly described and there seems to be less of 'grog' in the clay. This is likely since the *mahāvīra* and the pots used for milk did not come into direct contact with fire.[12] Furthermore, the surface of the *mahāvīra* is specially smoothened perhaps to make it less porous and to facilitate its handling.

The 'grog' would also ensure less shrinkage at the green-hard stage when the pot is sun-dried prior to being fired. The hair of animals which would be burnt in firing would assist this process. The resinous water may have provided an adhesive texture. A well-known technique in hand-made black pottery involves the fumigation of the pots before firing since the pores of the pot then get filled with particles of soot.[13] 'Grog' may also have assisted in the process of firing in a pit or an open-hearth kiln rather than a properly controlled kiln in that there was an absence of a separator between the pots and the fire. Firing in open-hearth kilns is generally only at low temperatures and the clay would have to be porous to prevent cracking. It would seem likely that the making of the pots, whatever the ritual demands may have been, was such as to ensure a minimum of cracking else the very ritual itself would be negated.

The texts also speak of the smoothening of pots either before or after they have been fired. On the assumption that the outer surface of the pottery was black it has been suggested that this process may reflect a relationship with the Northern Black Polished Ware,[14] a luxury ware of the second half of the first millennium BC. The date of this ceramic industry would be later than the generally accepted date for the composition of the *Śatapatha Brāhmaṇa* and the pottery has its early provenance in the area between Varanasi and Patna which is not an area central to the geography of the *Śatapatha Brāhmaṇa*. The label is deceptive as the pottery derives its quality more from the ingredients of the clay and from firing temperatures and admixture of chemicals[15] rather than from a process of polishing. The clay is finely levigated and the pottery is wheel thrown as is also the case with the Painted Grey Ware and the Black-and-Red Wares. The method described in the texts would in any case suggest a burnishing process rather than polishing, a method used as early as Neolithic times to smoothen the exterior surface of pottery. Burnishing is usually done at the green-hard stage prior to firing in order to make the pot less porous and as a decorative feature.

Polishing is more often a technique associated with a post-firing stage.

The reference in the *Śatapatha Brāhmaṇa* to placing the pots in an inverted position for firing in the pit has inevitably linked the idea with the inverted firing technique believed to be the basis of the Black-and-red effect in the ceramic which carries that name. It has been argued that this was perhaps the secret technique indirectly mentioned in the literature.[16] The argument draws from the theory that the distinctively black and red combination would have required carefully controlled firing in a kiln the temperature of which could also be controlled. On this basis firing in a pit such as the one described in the *Śatapatha Brāhmaṇa* would have resulted not in the distinctive effect but in an indiscriminate mixture of colour. The depth of the pit would also have made a significant difference in terms of easing or obstructing the flow of air for the deeper the pit the more the air would have been obstructed. The firing of the *mahāvīra* however is not specially associated with firing in a deep pit and may have been fired in an open-hearth kiln.

The method of producing the distinctive Black-and-Red Ware pottery and the question of whether it was the result of inverted firing has recently been re-examined and the association of the technique with this pottery is again an open question.[17] K.T.M. Hegde maintains that Black-and-Red Wares cannot be produced by the simple process of inverted firing. The resulting pottery would be red. If the firing is done at a low temperature in a smoking flame then the pottery will be inadequately baked and entirely black. He argues that the special effect is the result of the presence of haematite in the slip and a special baking technique (which is not the so-called 'inverted firing') which leads to Black-and-Red Ware becoming black inside and near its rim and red outside. He also maintains that Black-and-Red Ware does not necessarily require a kiln since the same effect can be produced in an open-fire-baking.

If the ritual pottery was intended to be double coloured it would certainly have been described as such. Instead it is said that the pots should be fired to a red colour[18] although in one case where an excavation has revealed what appears to be a ritual pot associated with the *agnicayana* the colour is black.[19] The inversion of the pot may have had more to do with the packing of the pots into the pit and the resulting tones of colour may have been accidental. If however the reference to inverted firing is to be linked to the Black-and-red Ware there remains a further problem. The *Atharvaveda*[20] refers to a kind of pottery which it describes as *nīla-lohita* and which some scholars have taken to be the Black-and-Red Ware. Curiously the text appears to disapprove of the practices of those who use this pottery and seems to connect it with witch-craft and with the Asuras. But this connection is also hinted at in the statement that the *ukhā* is born of the *asurimāyā*.[21] The *Ṛg Veda*[22] links the Asuras with the Aṅgirasas who are believed to be the priests of the fire cult.

What is equally curious is the general exclusion of the potter and the potter's wheel from association with the pottery made for the ritual.[23] The existence of both is evident from the archaeological data of the period and the region. Even if it be argued that the ritual itself goes back to earlier times, there is strangely enough no attempt to tamper with the technology and associate it with the more advanced pottery techniques contemporary with the period of the *Śatapatha Brāhmaṇa*. Apart from its functional purpose, perhaps the primitive quality of the potting technique is to be explained by an attempt to keep the pottery which was used in rituals quite distinct from that used in daily and mundane routine. Since it is stated that the ritual vessels had to be made by the *yajamāna* and his wife or persons of the *dvija* caste it seems that the professional potter was excluded from this activity which would in itself be a comment on the status of the potter. Had the potter already been ascribed a slow ritual status in the *varṇa* hierarchy and did the avoidance of the potter's wheel derive from the same idea? This would mean that a deliberately archaicising technique was adopted for the pottery used on ritual occasions even though more advanced techniques were used for normal pottery.

It would seem that the pottery used in the *agnicayana* ritual as described in the *Śatapatha Brāhmaṇa* did not conform to any of the dominant ceramic industries of the first millennium BC: neither the Painted Grey Ware nor the Black-and-Red Ware and not even the Northern Black Polished Ware or the Black Slipped Ware. The potting technique goes back to Neolithic times and also relates to the hand-made pottery of what might have been the substratum culture of the Chalcolithic society. The latter would however be curious in view of the ritual itself being the concern of and conducted by members of the *dvija* castes, the elite groups of the society. Ritual pottery appears to have been a distinct category with its own method of manufacture, the difference emphasising the ritual function of the object. In co-relating the description of ritual objects with archaeological data and in using such co-relations to date the texts from which the descriptions come some caution has to be exercised in dating the text from the archaic quality of the object. Rituals and ritual objects may remain relatively unchanged from the earliest rites. Although the material artifacts used in the ritual may seem archaic the texts may be of periods later than that of the technology relating to the ritual, since the sanctity of the ritual often demands the continuation of a primitive technology. Clearly there was a far more complex interplay of priests, rituals and artifacts than a simple co-relation of archaeological and literary evidence would allow.

Notes and References

1. *Śatapatha Brāhmaṇa*, VI.5.3.4; VI.6.4.8. *Baudhāyana Śrauta Sūtra*, X.1–8.
2. *Śatapatha Brāhmaṇa*, XIV.1.2; C.G. Kashikar, 'Pottery in Vedic Literature', *Indian Journal of the History of Science*, May–Nov. 1969, IV, nos 1 and 2, pp. 15–26; W. Rau, 'Vedic Texts on the Manufacture of Pottery', *Journal of the Oriental Institute*, Baroda, March 1974, XXIII, 3. p. 137.
3. *Baudhāyana Ś.S.*, X.1–8.
4. Ibid., IX.4; *Śatapatha Brāhmaṇa*, XIV.1.2.17.
5. *Baudhāyana Ś.S.*, XI.1–4.
6. Kashikar, op. cit., p. 20.
7. T. Burrow, '*Arma* and *Armaka*', *Journal of Indian History*, 1963, XLI, I, pp. 159ff.
8. The term in the text for this is *ayorasa* (*Śat. Brāh.*, VI.5.1.6 which J. Eggeling translates as 'iron rust' (*SBE*, Śat. Brāh., III. p. 231). Professor Hegde suggests that this is probably iron oxide which occurs in natural sources as limonite (hydrated oxide of iron) the colour ranging from orange to yellowish-grey or haematite (without hydration) of a deep red colour. Haematite was used as a pigment in the painted designs decorating the Painted Grey Ware, in the burnished slip on the Black Slipped Ware, in the glossy slip glaze on the Northern Black Polished Ware and in the slip on the Black-and-Red Ware.
9. *Śatapatha Brāhmaṇa*, VI.5.3.1.
10. Professor Hegde suggests that this was open-fire baking.
11. *Śatapatha Brāhmaṇa*, VI.5.4.1; XIV.1.2.21; *Kātyāyana Śrauta Sūtra*, XVI.4.11.

12. Professor Hegde however is of the opinion that the addition of 'grog' would encourage cracking since the coefficient of expansion of the various components in such a clay would differ. One may suggest that perhaps the components indicated in the text were in effect more homogeneous than one assumes.
13. H. Hodges, *Artifacts*, London, 1964, pp. 20ff.
14. Kashikar, op. cit.
15. K.T.M. Hegde, 'Analysis of Ancient Indian Deluxe Wares', *Archaeo-Physika*, Rheinisches Landismuseum (Bonn), 1979, pp. 141–55.
16. H.S. Converse, 'The Agnicayana Rite: Indigenous Origins?', *History of Religion*, Nov. 1974, vol. 14, no. 2, pp. 81–95.
17. K.T.M. Hegde, op. cit.
18. Kashikar, op. cit., p. 20.
19. Ibid., p. 26n.23.
20. *Atharvaveda*, IV.17.4.
21. *Śatapatha Brāhmaṇa*, VI.6.2.6; *Vājasaneyi Saṁhitā*, 11.69; *Taittirīya Saṁhitā*, 4.1.9.
22. *Ṛg Veda*, III.53.7; X.67.2.

# IV

# *Pre-Mauryan and Mauryan India*

The analysis of state formation has entered history and particularly the study of the histories of various early societies largely through Marxist analyses of pre-capitalist societies and through anthropological interpretations of the functioning of early societies. These introduce models different from the more static one used in earlier studies of the Indian state and its origins.

There has been some change in my understanding of the nature of the Mauryan state over the years. This can be seen in a comparison between the essay entitled, 'Asokan India and the Gupta Age' in A.L. Basham (ed.), *A Cultural History of India*, Oxford, 1975, which proposes a largely, centralised state as also explored in *Aśoka and the Decline of the Mauryas* (1961 ed.), and differs from the concept of empire as developed more recently in *The Mauryas Revisited*.

A specific focus on more limited themes of the Mauryan period are included in the remaining essays. Aśoka's endorsement of Buddhism is also discussed in an early essay not included in this collection, 'Aśoka and Buddhism', in *Past and Present*, 1960, 18, 43–51, which is a forerunner of the paper 'Aśoka and Buddhism as Reflected in the Aśokan edicts', in this section.


1. The Evolution of the State in the Ganga Valley in the Mid-first Millennium BC (1982)
2. The Early History of Mathurā: Up to and Including the Mauryan Period (1989)
3. State Weaving-Shops of the Mauryan Period (1955)
3. Aśoka and Buddhism as Reflected in the Aśokan Edicts (1994)
5. Literacy and Communication: Some Thoughts on the Inscriptions of Aśoka

6. Epigraphic Evidence and Some Indo-Hellenistic Contacts During the Mauryan Period (1987)
7. The Mauryas Revisited (1987)

# 17

# The Evolution of the State in the Ganga Valley in the Mid-first Millennium BC*

The Ganga valley in the mid-first millennium BC provides a useful case for the study of state formation in early India. There are data from archaeology, especially in relation to the western Ganga valley, and from literary sources for both the western and the middle Ganga valley. It is possible to compare the conditions in the western region with those of the contiguous area in the central region and see the gradual change towards the coming of the state. In the absence of a firm chronology for the literary sources it is not possible to date the changes in a precise manner, but the trends towards change can at least be recognised and discussed. The mid-millennium may be taken as an approximate dividing line between non-state and state systems and it is argued here that the evidence of the western Ganga valley indicates the continuity of a non-state system whereas that of the middle Ganga valley suggests the start of the process towards state formation. Added to this is the very considerable literature which now exists on the theoretical discussion on state formation.[1]

The significance of this process in the Indian subcontinent is that it was a continuing one in different regions until recent centuries. The emphasis in the sources on the need for a state in the absence of which there would be chaos arose from the constant need to justify new states. Erstwhile frontier zones of uncertain control would gradually evolve into states. The emergence of the state was not a terminal point since pre-existing states would tend to change their character with the juxtaposition of new states. This requires a typology of state systems which has yet to be worked out.

* *Studies in History*, 1982, IV, 2, 181–96.

This paper is concerned with the change from what has been called a lineage system to a state system. The lineage system is characterised by a distinctive social structure.[2] With marginal variations it may broadly be said to consist of a corporate group of unilineal kin held together by bonds of genealogy which is generally regarded as authentic but may be fictive. Stratification is essentially among lineages and there can be in some cases a separation between the senior lineage which holds power and the lesser or junior or cadet lines who are the providers of tribute and prestations to the former, which is then redistributed by the senior lineages through rituals and gifts. The family and its household is the unit of production. Ownership is a limited concept and applies at most to animals. Lineage rights of usage extend to pastures and to arable land. Ritual occasions are mainly sacrificial ceremonies when the lineage is present. External to the lineage are non-lineage groups which are generally small in number to begin with but depending on their function can become very powerful. Thus the shamans and priests, tend to be powerful. Those captured in inter-tribal raids would have to work as slaves and labourers and would be deprived of power.

The state[3] is characterised by a concentration of political authority generally in the hands of an erstwhile senior lineage of which one family claims complete power, a claim which is legitimised by the priests as being based among other things on agencies other than human, such as an association with the gods. This authority is delegated to functionaries who constitute the administration. Legitimacy is also claimed on the basis of myths of origin. These, at a later stage, allow powerful families from groups not recognised as the earlier lineages, to assert authority. The state claims control over a well-defined territory which is defended by a standing army. The revenues for the state are collected through a system of taxes and consist of a contracted amount collected regularly by the officers of the administrative system. The revenue is directed towards a treasury which is the basis for the redistributive system organised by the ruler. The office of the latter is defined as that of protection both against external enemies and against internal disorder. The state also recognises the importance of external relations i.e. relations with other states and these may be hostile or friendly.

The lineage system and the state in the Indian context should not be seen as two sharply demarcated dichotomies. Although clear examples of both are evident in the sources nevertheless the process of state-formation is a gradual one and there are many overlaps from one system to another. It is part of the intention of this paper to suggest that the overlaps are as significant as the changes.

The *Ṛg Veda* and the later Vedic literature provide evidence of the lineage system. The *jana* constitutes the tribe which is made up of a number of clans, the *viś*. There is a demarcation between the senior lineages, *rājanya* and the lesser lineages which continue to be called the *viś*. *Rājanya* derives from *rājā/rājan*, which refers to the chief. Although some texts explain its etymology as the one who pleases,[4] this etymology is unacceptable and the derivation is more likely to have been from the root **raj* to shine or to lead and direct.[5] There is some controversy as to whether the chief was elected by the *viś* or was selected by his peers in assembly.[6] Possibly the idea of election was an earlier process and may well be reflected in the traditional meaning for the term. The word *viś* refers to a settlement and would therefore point to the lineages which settled on the land and were responsible for cattle-raising and agriculture. There are references to the *viś* of the *āryas* as well as the *dāsas* and some of the chiefs among the latter are said to be wealthy.[7] Land was held by the clan and could not be bestowed on anyone without the permission of the *viś*.[8] Pastures and grazing lands were plentiful but seem to have required some transhumance or migration judging by the distances travelled by some of the *janas* such as the Pūrus. Wealth was computed in the form of cattle, horses, chariots, gold and slaves, the latter being primarily female slaves doubtless captured in raids.[9] The importance of cattle wealth is suggested in cattle being listed as wealth and in the use of terms such as *gaviṣṭhi*, the search for cattle, which becomes synonymous with the term for a cattle-raid. The Paṇis who are described as cattle-lifters are also the most feared enemies. The evidence on what constitutes wealth is indicated in the famous *dāna-stuti* hymns of the *Ṛg Veda*, the eulogies by bards and priests on the magnanimous gifts bestowed on them by the *rājanyas* after successful cattle-raids and skirmishes.[10] In the division of wealth a major share would go to the *rājanya* and to the *brāhmaṇa*. The *rājanya* claimed it on the basis of being the protector of the settlement and the *brāhmaṇa* on the basis of his *mantras* and rituals ensuring a successful raid as well as his eulogies ensuring immortality in the land of the living. The *rājanya* became the symbol of the clan's prosperity. The *brāhmaṇa* claimed to be the intermediary between men and gods. The redistribution of wealth between these two categories led to a re-inforcing of the status of each. The gift-giving and the redistribution took place at the time of the major *yajña* sacrificial rituals and these were not only the occasions for offering oblations to the gods but also the occasions for establishing the superior status of the *rājanya* and the *brāhmaṇa*. The Ṛgvedic chiefs based their power and wealth primarily on pastoralism although agriculture was known to the *Ṛg Veda*, and from archaeological evidence which goes back to pre-Harappan times. It is possible that the agricultural niches were cultivated by the non-lineage groups who were also the earlier settlers and who perhaps remained in these areas and did not migrate when the pastoralists arrived.[11] They would then have subordinated themselves to the pastoral chiefs, in a situation of what has been called environmental circumscription,[12] since the niches provided good agricultural land and migration away would have required an effort in clearing the waste land and forests before cultivation could be started. This would have led to a symbiotic relationship between the pastoralists and the cultivators and a situation of bilingualism, should the two have been speaking different languages, as is suggested in the fact of Vedic Sanskrit incorporating non-Aryan linguistic elements.[13] With the gradual but increasing emphasis on agriculture the society of the cultivators although subordinate would have come to play an important role in Vedic society.

The later Vedic literature sees the gradual transition from an essentially pastoral economy to one where pastoralism continues but agriculture begins to supersede it. This is in part reflected in the offerings at the *yajñas* which still include the best livestock but also a variety of items made from grain. The geographical focus of this literature moves from the *sapta sindhu* (the seven rivers of the Indus) of the *Ṛg Veda* to the western Ganga valley and its eastern fringes. The archaeological culture of the Painted Grey Ware appears to coincide in terms of chronology and geographical distribution with the later Vedic literature. This is a culture with a mixed pastoral and agrarian economy with evidence of the cultivation of wheat and barley and probably of rice.[14] The latter has been found at a few sites and may have been locally grown or else imported from the area to the east of the Ganga-Yamuna *doāb*. Its increasing use in rituals suggests a gradual familiarity. There is evidence of the horse which is also attested to in the literature. Iron technology at this early stage seems to have been restricted to arrow-heads, spear-heads, blades and knives.[15] It may well have been used in clearing waste land although literary sources refer more frequently to clearing by burning.[16] In any case the clearing of land points to an increase in agricultural activities. There is a scatter of fairly closely placed small settlements in the upper *doāb* mainly following the river courses. The confederacy of clans known as the Kurus and the Pañcālas emerges as the dominant group in the western Ganga valley. The territories where such clans settle are referred to as the *janapada*, literally where the tribe places its feet. Each *janapada* is identified by the ruling lineage whose name is given to the territory. This is indicative of greater authority invested in the ruling lineage and such lineages gradually drop the term *rājanya* and take on the designation of *kṣatriya*, from the root* *kṣatra* meaning power. The *Śatapatha Brāhmaṇa* provides a wealth of evidence on this process.[17] We are told that the *kṣatriya* and the *viś* were originally close as reflected in the statement that the *kṣatriya* and *viś* once ate from the same vessel, which for a society concerned with the rules of commensality was a substantial indication of social proximity. In describing the relationship between the two, the analogy is often to superior and inferior categories within the same species, thus, the *kṣatriya* is the *soma* and the *viś* the *surā*, the *kṣatriya* is Varuṇa or Indra and the *viś* are the Maruts, and so on. But in addition to this it is also stated that the *kṣatriya* eats the *viś* as the deer eats grain. The superiority of the *kṣatriya* is always stressed. Furthermore it is said that whatever the *viś* produces in that the *kṣatriya* has a share. The differentiation of status between the two is much sharper now although the common origins would still seem to be recognised. The fact of the *viś* providing prestations for the *kṣatriya* is made very evident. The prestations are referred to as *bali*[18] a voluntary tribute which in the Ṛg Vedic context referred to tribute from defeated foes as well as prestations from the *viś*; *bhāga*, which was a share of the produce or a share of the booty from raids;[19] and *śulka* which has the meaning of value or price and is used in the sense of a dower or a tribute.[20] It has been argued that these might have been taxes, as they were in later periods. It is however difficult to accept this argument since there is at this time no reference to *bali*, *bhāga* and *śulka* being of a specific amount, or paid regularly, or to there being special officers to collect these amounts; all of which are characteristic of a revenue system. The content suggests that they were still prestations and not taxes.

In addition to the *kṣatriya* and the *viś* there are two other groups which emerge as professional groups in this period. The *brāhmaṇas* in addition to being controllers of ritual and magic and legitimisers of those in power also register a range of categories as priests. This was required by the change in the *yajña* rituals which had now become elaborate ceremonies sometimes extending over more than a year. Apart from the consecration and rejuvenation ceremonies for the *rājā* the *yajñas* included fertility and prosperity rituals for the *jana* or for the family (*kula*) and these were held frequently in accordance with seasonal and calendric requirements. The *yajña* gradually became the central activity of Vedic society deriving its sanction from religious functions. But it was also the occasion for reiterating the status of the more powerful groups through gift-giving to the priests as well as establishing by the same process the status of those new to the higher reaches of society. Since the success of the *yajña* requires a large investment of animal and agricultural wealth the ritual can also be said to have had embedded in it an economic role.

The other professional group was that of the *śūdras*. The word itself is of uncertain origin and may be derived from **kṣudra* meaning small or low. It has been linked to the Sodroi tribes mentioned in classical sources,[21] but references to *śūdras* in Vedic literature do not suggest any particular tribe. The *śūdras* are mentioned only in the later Vedic literature (except for the single reference in the late hymn of the tenth *maṇḍala* of the *Ṛg Veda*) and clearly emerge as a separate group in this period. They are associated with agricultural labour and with craft and artisanal activities.

The recognition of increasing stratification is reflected in the change from the dual *varṇa* system (*ārya* and *dāsa varṇas*) to the four *varṇa* system (*brāhmaṇa*, *kṣatriya*, *vaiśya* and *śūdra*) which is the accepted system in the later Vedic literature. This was not just a division of two into four, but in fact the recognition of the further stratification in the *ārya varṇa* and a more specific connotation for the *dāsa varṇa*. The *brāhmaṇa*, *kṣatriya* and *vaiśya* were regarded as *āryas* or *dvijas* and the *śūdras* were separate. The *āryas* traced descent and were organised on a lineage system with exogamous *gotras* characterising the *brāhmaṇa* descent groups and the endogamous *vaṃśa* being frequently a feature of the *kṣatriyas*. The *śūdras* on the other hand are specifically said to have no lineage ancestry, only the *varṇa* of their individual parents determining their status. Thus the *śūdras* by being described as such were excluded from those who claimed lineage origin. The concept of *varṇa* was therefore a system for interlocking various types of stratification and its use was more theoretical rather than a description of ethnic or class groups. As a theory it is rooted in lineage-based society and acts as a carry-over from this in later times as well.

Embedded in this stratification are two groups which were later to take the form of what might be called class functions or of incipient classes. One of these was known to the *varṇa* system in the category of *śūdras*, where the negation of a distinct lineage and the nature of occupation were the qualifying factors. In the post-Vedic period the *śūdras* were increasingly cultivators and artisans. As a counterpoise to this group was the category referred to as the *gṛhapatis*. These were the heads of households and could belong to any of the *dvija varṇas*. Initially they seem to have been mainly of the *kṣatriya varṇa* but gradually *vaiśya gṛhapatis* are mentioned. It is possible that the basic unit of Vedic society was a householding economy in which a household, consisting of three or four generations of the family together with some labourers and slaves, constituted the producing unit particularly when agriculture became the dominant economic activity. The *gṛhapatis* may well have been the entrepreneurs in the new settlement and those belonging to the lineages of the *viś* would have moved into *vaiśya* status. From cultivating allotted lands the family units would gradually have begun to claim permanent usage on the lands which they cultivated, usage rights which in the post-Vedic period could have constituted the basis to claims of family ownership over such lands. The increasing demarcation of function between the *kṣatriya* and *viś*, led to the emergence of the *vaiśya gṛhapati* in the post-Vedic period as the main landowning group but not excluding *gṛhapatis* of the other two *dvija varṇas*.[22] The wealth of the *gṛhapatis* supported the *kṣatriya* bid for greater power for the latter would take on the functions of protection at all levels and the former would remain the providers of prestations.

It is a debatable point whether the *rājā* of the later Vedic period remained a chief or became a king. In any case the transition was very gradual and even if kingship had evolved by this time it incorporated much of the tradition of chiefship. Two developments which assisted this process of change were the association of the office of the *rājā* with divinity[23] and the occasional reference to hereditary succession.[24] It is significant that the *rājā's* association with divinity came about not through any claim to divine origins but through the rituals performed after he had been declared a *rājā*. A distinction has also to be maintained between the office of the *rājā* in the Vedic period and the emergence of the state. Very few of the characteristics of the state were apparent at this time. Strikingly absent is the mention of a standing army for protection against external aggression. Battles and campaigns are few and far between, the more frequent conflicts taking the forms of raids and skirmishes in which the *rājanya* would mobilise the clan. Similarly there is no mention of a legal sanction invested in the *rājā*. The symbolic *daṇḍa* is handed to him but without the backing of a *dharma-śāstra*. Social pressure remains the most effective means of redressing wrongs and expiation is often resorted to. Even more fundamental is the lack of a systematised revenue collecting administration. It could be argued that rather than encouraging state formation there was a series of factors which militated against the emergence of the state.

A state requires a considerable outlay of wealth to finance the institutions which are a part of its infrastructure. The wealth which was circulating in Vedic society was distributed and consumed in a manner which was not conducive to encourage the formation of a state system. There were two sources of wealth, one being the booty from raids and the other being the prestations deriving from cattle-rearing and agriculture made by the *viś* and the *gṛhapatis* to the *rājā*. The wealth was redistributed at the gatherings of the *rājanyas* or of the entire clan.[25] Gatherings such as the *sabhā*, *samiti* and *vidatha* take on a further meaning if they are seen as the occasions when redistribution of wealth was also carried out. Such occasions were given a certain ritual form and this in turn bestowed sanctity and legitimacy on the distribution. The redistribution was confined to prestations moving from the *viś* and the *gṛhapatis* to the *rājanyas* and *kṣatriyas* and then circulating among the *kṣatriyas* and the *brāhmaṇas*. Therefore power remained concentrated in the hands of the *kṣatriyas* and was legitimised by the *brāhmaṇas* through rituals such as the *rājasūya*, *aśvamedha*, *vājapeya* and so on. These extended sacrificial rituals were the other occasion on which wealth was distributed in the form of *dāna* and *dakṣiṇā* by the *kṣatriyas* to the *brāhmaṇas* reinforcing the status of each. The *yajña* was also the occasion when a substantial amount of wealth was consumed literally in the sacrificing of the choicest animals of the herd and in the burning up of the produce from dairying and agriculture. To that extent the *yajña* takes on some aspects of the potlatch. This destruction of surplus wealth is related to an absence of a sense of accumulating wealth, and accumulation, so necessary for state formation, is hardly evident. The archaeological evidence of the Painted Grey Ware does not indicate the kind of material evidence associated with societies accumulating wealth. In this the contrast with Northern Black Polished Ware levels of the subsequent period is noticeable. The later Vedic texts do not refer to monumental structures and even references to treasuries or store-houses of the *kṣatriyas* are infrequent. The power of the *kṣatriya* as the recipient of prestations and the distributor of wealth was not questioned and a change of political form was not required. Those who did question the sacrificial ritual opted out of society in the form of renouncers and forest hermits and did not encourage the challenging of the existing system at this stage. Their questioning related more to metaphysical concerns although their disenchantment with the existing system cannot be ignored.

A further mechanism for avoiding too great a tension from developing within the settlement, such as would require changing the system, was that clans in confrontation often migrated to new areas where the same structure was repeated and internal conflict was avoided. Such a 'fissioning off' of clans is clearly stated in the origin myths of many descent groups referred to in the Buddhist tradition.[26] Earlier, the archaeological evidence from the late second to the mid-first millennium BC relating to the Indo-Gangetic watershed and the western Ganga valley also reveals a very intensive pattern of migration. The spread of the Painted Grey Ware sites from a heavy concentration in the upper Ganga-Yamuna *doāb* to lesser concentrations in the central and southern *doāb* and the area east of the *doāb*, would point to migratory patterns. The symbolic meaning of the theme of exile so frequently occurring in epic literature and often associated with a crisis in political succession, would corroborate this trend. The avoidance of internal conflict in turn suppressed the tendencies which might otherwise have forced an authority system conducive to the emergence of a state.

The theme of migration introduces the new geographical location of the middle Ganga valley. This is made explicit in the description of Videgha Māthava migrating to the area east of the Sadānīra (Gandak)[27] river which is referred to as marshland; migration is also implied in the scatter of Painted Grey Ware sites along the northern fringe of eastern Uttar Pradesh as well at the confluence of the Ganga and Yamuna in Allahabad district. Black-and-red wares sites occur more frequently along the southern fringes of the Ganga valley and up along the Gandak suggesting a migration from central India, although the earlier provenance of the Black-and-red wares is western India.[28] The routes of migration therefore from the western Ganga valley were along the Himalayan foothills of the *terai* region or skirting the Vindhyan outcrops towards south Bihar and then north along the rivers.

The middle Ganga valley was substantially marshy land and monsoon forest which would have been difficult to clear by burning except along the fringes. Clearing of the interior areas would have required better tools and considerable labour. Possibly it was in this area that iron technology for clearing land was more effective than in the western Ganga valley. Apart from Kośala, the ecological conditions were not very conducive to the breeding of cattle or the cultivating of wheat. Although cattle herds were still maintained the ideal pasture lands remained those of the western Ganga valley. Wheat cultivation appears fairly soon to have given way to rice which was the natural crop in this area. Thus Kośala was suited for the cultivation of rice and wheat whereas Magadha was especially suitable for the cultivation of rice.

The cultivation of rice (wet rice cultivation which was the more feasible form in this area) was the most productive but it required certain changes in the relationship towards land and agricultural technology[29] as compared to the western Ganga valley. With pastoralism becoming a subordinate economy settlements become more permanent. This was also a precondition to the increase in labour to clear marsh land and to manage rice cultivation. In normal circumstances rice was dependent on rainfall and therefore in an area of just the summer monsoon it would become a single crop cultivation. Rotation is only with leguminous plants. To obtain more than a single crop, irrigation would be necessary and this took the form of tanks, embankments and channels taken off streams.[30] Alternatively a larger area of land would have to be brought under cultivation. Both of these meant an intensification in the employment of labour even though the area of land under rice produces a larger yield than the same area under wheat. The cultivation of rice together with irrigation and the extension of the cultivated area doubtless provided a surplus in excess of what was available in similar acreages in the western Ganga valley. However this in itself was not a sufficient cause for major social changes and there were other factors influencing change.

The lineage system was continued in the middle Ganga valley in the *gaṇa-saṅghas* or chiefdoms but it developed rather differently from its form in the western Ganga valley. The controlling lineage claimed *kṣatriya* status with the head of each family constituting the *rājā* who together sat in an assembly and claimed ownership of land as well as political control.[31] The land was not worked by the members of the *rājā-kula* but by the *dāsa-bhṛtaka* (slaves and labourers) and the distinction between the two categories was sharp.[32] Participation in ownership was by birth and therefore lineage connections were crucial. The worship of ancestral tumuli and memorials in the form of *stūpas* and *caityas* was part of the ritual to establish connections. The Vedic sacrificial ritual was not encouraged. There was therefore no private ownership of land by individuals in these societies and the power of the *gṛhapati* as a separate entity was reduced not only because of the insistence on the common ownership of land but also because of its being worked directly by labour. References to land revenue are absent although some taxes are said to have been collected from traders coming to the cities[33] associated with the *gaṇa-saṅghas*. The residences of the *rājā-kula* were nucleated settlements which often evolved into towns. Sources of a later period refer to officers of an administrative category[34] but these were either anachronistic references or else the officials were part of a rudimentary administration which had not as yet taken on the characteristics of a full-fledged state system. The *gaṇa-saṅghas* consisted either of a single clan such as those of the Śākyas, Koliyas and Mallas or else could be a confederation of clans as in the case of the Vṛjjis who incorporated the Licchavis and various others and had their settlement at the town of Vaiśāli. The distribution of the *gaṇa-saṅghas* in the middle Ganga valley was largely in the area of present day north Bihar and the adjoining areas of eastern Uttar Pradesh.

The highest status in these societies was given to the *kṣatriya*.[35]

In the absence of large-scale *yajñas* the function of the *brāhmaṇa* would be limited. The *varṇa* system is referred to although more often in a theoretical sense as when the Buddha is describing the stages by which government was instituted together with social stratification.[36] Actual social distinctions relate more closely to the *jātis* which are generally divided into two categories, the high and the low.[37] The emphasis on birth continues in the *jāti* system and becomes even more specific in the reference to the *ñāti* which has been rendered as, the extended kin-group.[38] References to *gṛha patis/gahapatis* occur more often in the context of Kośala, Kāśī and Magadha, recognised as kingdoms.

The *gaṇa-saṅgha* system cannot be referred to as a non-state system since it has some of the germinal forms which were a precondition to the state, nor can it be called a state since the institutions associated with the infrastructure of a state are not present. It can perhaps best be described as representing a point along a continuum towards state formation, what Morton Fried,[39] has called stratified societies prior to the emergence of states.

The state emerges together with a monarchical system in Kośala and Magadha and the factors which led to this change relate to the lineage system and its transmutation into a state system. The continuation of the lineage system is perhaps most evident in the establishing of the *varṇa* status as a complementary system to whatever other changes took place. The essentials of a lineage society such as control over marriage alliances within a careful grid of hierarchy and social distance, the maintenance of lineage connections, commensality and occupational activities were in form at least adhered to in the *varṇa* system. Parallel to this there emerged another stratification where the dual division into the *gṛhapatis* and the *dāsa-bhṛtakas* was the main feature. The *gṛhapatis* could be of any of the three *dvija varṇas* and the *dāsa-bhṛtakas* were of the *śūdra varṇa* which by now had multiple sub-sections relating to cultivators, artisans and subordinated tribal groups. The role of the *gṛhapati* as reflected in the *sūtra* literature of the post-Vedic period was of central importance and related both to the changes in agriculture and the beginnings of trade. The intensification of agriculture meant the production of a larger surplus. Not all of this was given in prestation or consumed in the sacrificial ritual. What remained in the hands of the *gṛhapati* became his personal wealth and this was particularly the case with the *brāhmaṇa gṛhapatis* who are described as *mahāśāla* or very wealthy.[40] With the claim to family ownership over the land cultivated the notion of private ownership became current. The rise of ideologies questioning the sacrificial ritual such as the discourses of the *Upaniṣads* and *Āraṇyakas* to begin with and subsequently the teachings of Mahāvīra and the Buddha loosened the ties of the *gṛhapati* to the prestation economy. This enabled him to use his wealth not only to enhance his status but also to invest in trade when the commercial economy became viable. In the latter situation it was the wealthy *gṛhapati* who became the *śreṣṭhin*[41] (he who has the best).

The roots of trade doubtless go back to the local circuits of exchange. These would arise from villages specialising in particular professions and products[42] such as the salt-makers village and the potters village and the carpenters village. Such villages would have supplied the local markets or *nigama* of the Buddhist texts.[43] (The *nigama* seems to have been a market centre rather than a town since the commercial areas of towns are sometimes called *nigamas.*) Added to this were the itinerant herders and professionals who worked a regular circuit and complemented their basic activities with itinerant trade. Ironsmiths would have played a major role in fostering links along local circuits as they do to this day. The major iron deposits being limited to south Bihar, the peripatetic smith became a necessity. The routes of migration into the Ganga valley were to develop into regular trade routes. Thus the northern route along the Himalayan foothills, the Uttarapatha, linked the upper Ganga-Yamuna *doāb* via Kośala and Vaiśāli with Magadha. The southern route followed the right bank of the Yamuna and the Ganga past Magadha and into the adjoining region of Aṅga (Bhagalpur). This route was also linked through the Chambal river and the Malwa corridor to Ujjain and continued across the Narmada to the upper Godavari valley and came to be known as the famous Dakṣiṇāpatha (the southern route). The river system of the Ganga in itself provided a circuit of communication with major settlements at nodal points along the rivers which were to grow into the *mahānagaras* or the great cities of the later period. Kośala controlled a vital segment of the Uttarapatha and this may explain why the capital was shifted to Śrāvastī in the north. Its earlier capital at Ayodhyā remained important however as it lay on the route to Kauśāmbi whose importance was based on its control of the southern route along the Ganga valley and its access to the main Dakṣiṇāpatha. Magadha lay as it were, at the confluence of the two routes and its extension eastwards to Aṅga and the Ganga delta. Magadhan antagonism towards Vaiśālī was almost inevitable since Vaiśālī was crucial to the control of the Uttarapatha as also was Kośala which Magadha eventually annexed. Magadha also controlled the Vindhyan route to central India via the Son valley. The eventual shift of the Magadhan capital from Rājagṛha to Pāṭaligāma on the Ganga river was again to enable it to control the terminal point of these routes.

Routes and itinerant traders do not in themselves lead to the development of commerce. The larger circuit of trade was developed on the basis of exchange between areas more distant. Such exchanges may have been initiated by marriage alliances among the *kṣatriya* families and exchanges of prestigious goods. Such alliances were frequent in the middle Ganga valley but were also known to extend further in contacts between the *kṣatriya* families of Kośala and Kekeya for instance. These alliances would have fostered an elite trade in luxury goods acting as a counterpart to the more mundane but necessary exchanges involved in the circuits of iron-smiths and salt traders. Salt, metals, textiles and pottery were the standard items of trade at this time.[44] The distribution of the Northern Black Polished Ware with its provenance in the area between Varanasi and Patna is an indicator of the gradual rippling out of trading circuits. That there may have been some demands on Indian goods from areas within the Indian subcontinent but included in non-Indian states, such as Gandhāra would have to be examined. Gandhāra was a part of the Achaemenid empire and items of Indian manufacture are said to have been used in west Asia.[45] Similarly the possibility of a sea trade between Mesopotamia and the west coast of India to which there are tantalisingly ambiguous[46] references may have provided a further incentive to trade within the northern part of the subcontinent.

That the trade was based on a recognised medium of exchange would seem clear from the discovery of punch-marked coins in silver and copper from various urban sites going back to levels of the mid-first millennium BC. This evidence is corroborated by the descriptions of coins in the grammar of Pāṇini.[47] Although there is some controversy[48] as to who issued the coins it would seem that they are in the main local issues since the combination of designs punched on the coins tend to relate to particular areas. This would suggest that the mechanism of trade was relatively decentralised although the state derived a revenue from it.

The trading community of *vaṇijas* and *seṭṭhis* (traders and merchants) came from the ranks of the *gṛhapatis* and by now the activities of the *vaiśya* are also described as cattle-rearing, agriculture and trade. The *gṛhapatis* as landowners experienced further changes. The private ownership of land resulted in some very rich households of landowners. But it also led to the subdivision of landholdings and the cultivation of land by tenants some of whom as cultivators had *śūdra* status. Mention is also made of revenue collected from those who cultivated land. Assessment officers measured the land and its produce and calculated the taxes.[49] The king's share was later said to have been one-sixth *ṣaḍ-bhāga* of the produce and this was collected at regular intervals.[50] That these were not prestations but a range of taxes is clear from the fact that in each case it was a contracted amount, stipulated in advance, regularly collected and channelled through an administrative hierarchy of officers. The justification for tax collection is explained in the theory that when stratification became intense and disorder prevailed in society, it was decided that one person should be selected or nominated to maintain law and order and to protect society; and the wages for both these functions were to be gathered as taxes by the ruler.[51] With the establishment of a revenue collecting system political authority began to see the additional advantage of opening waste land to settlers.[52]

These changes brought about the presence of two new groups, the traders and the peasants. Since there was no separate identity for them in the *varṇa* system they were included, together with other groups in the *vaiśya* and the *śūdra varṇa* respectively. Furthermore both indicated the weakening if not the breaking in some areas of the prestation economy as the main economic force. In this they were assisted by the new ideologies of Buddhism and Jainism which, even though they arose among the *kṣatriyas* of the *gaṇa-saṅghas*, were more vigorously preached in the cities of the kingdoms of Kośala, Kāśī and Magadha. The new ideologies were not in favour of burning wealth in the *yajñas* but rather in accumulating and investing it.[53] That accumulation required austerities is fully supported in the exhortation to the lay-followers to refrain from indulgences of various kinds and lead a balanced and generally puritanical life. Brahmanical sources were suspicious of those who lived in cities and objected on principle to the investment of wealth and the earning of interest on investment.[54] Buddhist sources on the other hand, eulogise the *seṭṭhi*, encourage usury and are generally sympathetic to the urban dwellers. With the weakening of clan ties the monastic institutions provided new networks of relations and this was strengthened in the idea of the lay-follower and the monk being interdependent. Many of these new ideologies harked back to the values of the lineage society in as much as social groups were more egalitarian and the individual had a predetermined niche. These values were sought to be resurrected or continued in the monastic institutions. But the contradiction in the situation was that in order to maintain the monasteries the new religions required, in the initial stages, both the direct patronage of the state as well as a society rich enough to support the monks through alms. Such a society would presuppose at least the rudiments of a state, and to that extent a decline in lineage society.

Theories of the origin of the state shift the focus from the *rājanya* who protects the *jana* to the *kṣatriya* who both protects as well as maintains law and order and whose control grows out of a notion of sovereignty. Ultimately even the *kṣatriya* is not sufficient and the state is visualised as the intermeshing of seven elements or limbs (*prakṛtis* or *aṅgas*) among which the king is one of the elements.[55] The others are *amātya* (ministers and administration in general) *janapada/rāṣṭra* (territory) *durga* (fortified settlement or royal capital) *kośa* (treasury) *daṇḍa* (force, army or the right to coercion) and *mitra* (external ally). With the discussion of the *saptāṅga* theory in the Kauṭilya *Arthaśāstra* the concept of the state can be said to have arrived. The prestation economy of the lineage society was now, in the middle Ganga valley, largely a formal ritual of legitimation which was performed by some kings. Thus Pasenadi of Kośala had all the required *yajñas* performed when he became king.[56] But the *yajña* consumed only a part of the wealth. On a lesser scale this was also true of the *gṛhya* sacrifices which in terms of economic outlay did not consume the substantial part of the household's wealth. It is significant that the most powerful monarchies of the middle Ganga valley, namely, those of the Nandas and Mauryas, ignored Vedic rituals, supported the 'heterodox' sects and not surprisingly are described in brahmanical sources as *śūdra* and *adharmaḥ*.[57]

This attempt at examining the process of state formation in the middle Ganga valley suggests a complex process involving a series of inter-related changes. It is also a gradual process and even when the state is established it is not a unitary, monolithic, centralised state to begin with nor do the earlier forms totally disappear: in fact there is an overlap which continues for sometime. This overlapping situation accounts in part for the complicated stratification registering caste groups and also the movement towards incipient classes, the two systems sometimes converging. The mobility of the group and its ability to migrate in a condition of tension reduces the trend towards state formation since migration enables groups to readjust without changing their social forms. The amount of wealth produced and the direction given to the use of wealth is also crucial as a factor inhibiting or encouraging the formation of a state. Ideologies have also to be considered central to frustrating or developing the notion of the state. As a continuing historical process state formation requires an analysis not merely of the transition from non-state to state but also the typologies of states as they take form under varying circumstances.

## Notes and References


1. R. Cohen and E. Service (eds), *Origins of the State*, Philadelphia, 1978; H.J.M. Claessen and P. Skalnik (eds), *The Early State*, The Hague, 1978; L. Krader, *Formation of the State*, New Jersey, 1968; M. Fried, *The Evolution of Political Society*, New York, 1967.
2. I. Goldman, *Ancient Polynesian Society*, Chicago, 1970; J. Middleton and D. Tait, *Tribes Without Rulers*, London, 1964; *Political Systems and the Distribution of Power*, ASA Monographs 2, London, 1965.
3. L. Krader, *Formation of the State*; *Arthaśāstra*, I.8.
4. *ranjitaśca prajāh sarvastena rājeti śabdyate . . . Mahābhārata*, Śanti Parvan, 59, 127ff.
5. Cf. Proto-Dravidian *vel.* DED 4562 and 4524. For a discussion on the etymology of *rex* and *rājā* see E. Benveniste, *Indo-European Language and Society*, London, 1975, pp. 311–12.
6. *Rg Veda*, X.173.1; X.124.8; J.P. Sharma, *Republics in Ancient India*, Leiden, 1968.
7. *Vedic Index*, II, p. 305; I. p. 356.
8. *Śatapatha Brāhmaṇa*, VII.1.1.4–8; *Aitareya Brāhmaṇa*, VIII.21.8.
9. Romila Thapar, '*Dāna* and *Daksiṇā* as Forms of Exchange', in *Ancient Indian Social History: Some Interpretations*, New Delhi, 1978, pp. 105ff. *See* chapter 24 in this volume.

10. Ibid.
11. Suraj Bhan, *Excavation at Mitathal (1980) and other Explorations in the Sutlej-Yamuna Divide*, Kurukshetra, 1975; Suraj Bhan and J.G. Shaffer, 'New Discoveries in Northern Haryana', *Man and Environment*, 1978, II, pp. 59–68; K.N. Dikshit, 'Exploration along the Right Bank of River Sutlej in Punjab', *Journal of History*, 1967, 45, part II, pp. 561–8; J.P. Joshi, 'Interlocking of Late Harappan Culture and Painted Grey Ware Culture in the Light of Recent Excavations', *Man and Environment*, 1978, II, pp. 100–3.
12. R.L. Carneiro, 'A Theory of the Origin of the State', *Science*, 1970, 169, pp. 733–8.
13. M.M. Deshpande and P.E. Hook, *Aryan and Non-Aryan in India*, Ann Arbor, 1978.
14. K.A. Chaudhuri, *Ancient Agriculture and Forestry in Northern India*, Bombay, 1977; V. Tripathi, *The Painted Grey Ware, an Iron Age Culture of Northern India*, Delhi, 1979.
15. R. Pleiner, 'The Problems of the Beginning Iron Age in India', *Acta Praehistorica et Archaeologica*, 1971, 2, pp. 5–36.
16. e.g. The Khāṇḍava-vana which was cleared to establish the settlement of Indraprastha, *Mahābhārata*, Ādi Parvan, 199.25ff, 214–19.
17. IV.3.3.15; XII.7.3.8; III.3.2.8; II.5.2.6; II.5.2.27; VII.1.1.4; III.1
18. *Ṛg Veda*, VII.6.5; X.173.6; *Atharvaveda*, III.4.2.3.
19. *Taittirīya Samhitā*, I.8.9.2; *Taittirīya Brāhmaṇa*, I.7.5.
20. *Ṛg Veda*, VII.82.6; VIII.1.5; *Atharvaveda*, III.29.3.
21. *Curtius Rufus*, IX.4; cf. *Mahābhārata*, Sabhā Parvan, 48.14; *Pāṇini*, II.4.10.
22. As is clarified in the *Gṛhyasūtras* which provide for a variation in the domestic ritual depending on the *varṇa* of the person, e.g., *Āśvalāyana Gṛhyasūtra*, I.19.
23. J. Gonda, *Ancient Indian Kingship from the Religious Point of View*, Leiden, 1969.
24. Hereditary succession is emphasised in the two epics but is infrequently referred to in Vedic literature.
25. The function of these assemblies have been discussed at length by various scholars whose views have been summarised and added to in R.S. Sharma, *Aspects of Political Ideas and Institutions in Ancient India*, Delhi, 1968 and J.P. Sharma, *Republics in Ancient India*, Leiden, 1968.
26. Romila Thapar, 'Origin Myths and the Early Indian Historical Tradition', in *Ancient Indian Social History: Some Interpretations*, pp. 294ff. *See* chapter 34 in this volume.
27. *Śatapatha Brāhmaṇa*, I.4.1.14–17.
28. D.P. Agrawal and S. Kusumgar, *Prehistoric Chronology and Radio-Carbon Dating in India*, New Delhi, 1974, pp. 138ff.

29. E. Boserup, *The Conditions of Agricultural Growth*, London, 1965; M.R. Haswell, *The Economics of Subsistence Agriculture*, London, 1967.
30. W.B. Bollee, *Kunāla Jātaka*, London, 1970, pp. 1ff.
31. *Dīgha Nikāya*, II.73ff.
32. N. Wagle, *Society at the Time of the Buddha*, Bombay, 1966, pp. 134ff.
33. This reference is from a much later text the *Sumaṅgalavilāsinī*, I.338.
34. Ibid., II.59; II.673.
35. *Dīgha Nikāya*, I.97–107.
36. Ibid., III, 80–98.
37. *Aṅguttara Nikāya*, I.162.
38. Wagle, *Society at the Time of the Buddha*, pp. 122ff. V.S. Agrawala, *India as Known to Panini*, Varanasi, 1963, p. 93.
39. M. Fried, *The Evolution of Political Society*, pp. 185ff.
40. *Saṃyutta Nikāya*, I.74.
41. *Aṅguttara Nikāya*, IV.282; *Mahāvagga*, I.7.4; *Cullavagga*, VI.4.1.
42. *Vinaya Piṭaka*, I.207; *Aṅguttara Nikāya*, II.182.
43. *Dīgha Nikāya*, I.7; *Majjhima Nikāya*, I.429; I.488.
44. Agrawala, *India as Known to Panini*, pp. 240ff.
45. E.J. Rapson, *The Cambridge History of India*, Cambridge, 1922, vol. I, 1935, pp. 391ff.
46. Ibid.
47. *Pāṇini*, V.1.19–37.
48. D.D. Kosambi, *Indian Numismatics*, New Delhi, 1981.
49. *Jātaka*, III, 376.
50. Manu, 7.131; 8.305–8. *Arthaśāstra*, II, 15; *Baudhāyana DS*, I.10.6.
51. Ibid.
52. *Dīgha Nikāya*, III.80–98.
53. Ibid., III.188.
54. *Baudhāyana Dharmasūtra*, I.5.10.23–25; *Vasiṣṭha Dharmasūtra*, II.40–42.
55. *Arthaśāstra*, VI.1.
56. *Saṁyutta Nikāya*, III.1.9.
57. F.E. Pargiter, *The Purana Texts of the Dynasties of the Kali Age*, Oxford, 1913, pp. 25ff.

# 18

# The Early History of Mathurā: Up to and Including the Mauryan Period*

The history of Mathurā covered in this paper relates to the earliest period and concerns the region, the people and the city. The evidence for the earlier part of the paper comes in the main from traditional accounts as given in Vedic literature, the Epics, the *Purāṇas* and the Buddhist and Jaina sources. These sources are often of controversial date and the discussion in this paper therefore inevitably relates more to the traditional accounts of Mathurā and events associated with it rather than to the hard facts of ascertained, dateable, historical evidence. This raises the general question of the reliability of tradition for historically authenticated evidence and the use of sources which although compiled as late as the first millennium AD purport to describe events which occurred earlier. Traditional history of this kind has to be used cautiously and, where possible, with recourse to cross-evidence from other sources; furthermore the analysis of such traditions demands its own contextual framework. The latter part of the paper dealing with the Mauryan period moves to firmer ground with evidence from a variety of contemporary sources.

Vedic literature makes no mention of Mathurā nor of its variants such as Madhurā. The Yādava are not associated with this region as they are in other sources, but the Yadu as a clan are mentioned frequently.[1] If Yakṣu is read as Yadu (as some scholars do) then they participated in 'the battle of the ten kings'.[2] They are also said to be involved in raids across the Sarayu[3] but at this early date this was more likely the river in Afghanistan. The Yadu had considerable

* In D.M. Srinivasan (ed.), *Mathura*, New Delhi, 1989, 12–18.

wealth in livestock and were generous donors.[4] The Śūrasena, also associated with Mathurā elsewhere, are not mentioned in Vedic literature. The word *Śūra* has in some instances been interpreted in the sense of a warrior or hero.[5] The name Kṛṣṇa occurs for various teachers but none have pastoral associations.[6]

Other literary sources link the region of Mathurā with the Yādavas and the Śūrasena. The Yādava association is stressed in the *Harivaṁśa* and the *Purāṇas*, more especially the *Viṣṇu* and *Bhāgavata Purāṇas*. These are all texts composed much later than the events which they claim to describe. An indirect Yādava connection can be suggested on the basis of the account of the expulsion of Yadu the eldest son of Yayāti from the *madhya-deśa* owing to his inability to comply with his father's wishes.[7] The Yādavas are said to have been banished to the southern direction. *Madhya-deśa* was then bequeathed by Yayāti to his youngest son Pūru. But the association of the Yādava lineage with Mathurā does not appear to have been terminated, assuming that Mathurā was included within the *madhya-deśa*.

The association of the Yādavas with Mathurā is based on the account related in many of the *Purāṇas* regarding the founding of the city. This is ascribed to Śatrughna, the younger brother of Rāma, who attacked and killed the *asurā/rakṣasa* Lavana, the son of Madhu, who had held sway over the area.[8] Śatrughna cleared the forest of Madhu-vana and celebrated his victory by founding the city of Mathurā.[9] This name is thought to be a variant of Madhurā from Madhu. The building of a city by Śatrughna would suggest that Mathurā began as a royal capital and later developed into a commercial centre. It is curious though that Śatrughna should have named his city after his defeated enemy. We are further told that Śatrughna had two sons, one of whom was Śūrasena and his descendants ruled at Mathurā, thus making the Śūrasenas members of the Sūryavaṁśa or Ikṣvāku lineage and therefore quite distinct from the Yādavas who belonged to the Candravaṁśa or Aila lineage.

This version is contradicted in other sources where the Śūrasenas as descendants of Śūra of the Vṛṣṇi clan are part of the Yādava lineage. The Yādavas are also called Mādhavas[10] which would link them with Madhu and thus make them the original settlers of the region. They incorporated the Andhaka-Vṛṣṇi segment and evidently regained the territory because the struggle between Kaṁsa and

Kṛṣṇa was an internal struggle between members of the same lineage segment, as well as kin group, since Kaṁsa was the maternal uncle of Kṛṣṇa. The *Bhāgavata Purāṇa* narrates the story of Kṛṣṇa in detail starting from the episode of his birth to the eventual migration away from Mathurā.[11] Here the portrayal is that of a pastoral hero and the incarnation of divinity. The episodes thread together the topography of the region. The story does not end with the defeat of Kaṁsa but continues to the animosity of Jarāsandha who seeks revenge. There is considerable elaboration on Jarāsandha's attacks on Mathurā, the city being subjected to eighteen campaigns before it is conquered. Ultimately the Yādavas led by Kṛṣṇa flee to the south-west, to Dvārakā in Saurashtra. A variant of the Kṛṣṇa-Kaṁsa episode also occurs in the *Ghaṭa Jātaka*[12] suggesting that it was a well-known theme among the traditional narratives on the past of Mathurā.

It would seem that we have here a condensation of various traditions which do not provide an authentic history but which do suggest some assumptions to which attention may be directed. It is significant that both the major lineages, the Sūryavaṁśa and the Candravaṁśa, are sought to be associated with the rise of the city of Mathurā, even though this results in a contradiction in explaining the origins of the Śūrasena. This points to the importance of the city from various perspectives. Would it then be legitimate to argue that the association of these traditions with the city of Mathurā also date to the period when it became an important urban centre around which traditions would tend to accrete, that is, in the post-Mauryan period?

Whether or not the original settlers were of the Yādava lineage, there is a pattern of the original settlers being ousted by a power based in the middle Ganges valley to the east, be it Kośala or Magadha, which results in the original inhabitants of Mathurā migrating to Saurashtra. Irrespective of whether the lineage was ousted or not, a migration is implied. There could of course be an ambiguity with regard to the identity of Mathurā for there is always the possibility that the original Yādava settlement of Madhu-vana may have been located elsewhere, but there is no evidence for this. Some sources, admittedly of a later period, distinguish between the northern and the southern cities of the same name, which might indicate a different location for yet an earlier city. (Considering the large number of places with the name Dvārakā/Dvāravatī, such a possibility cannot be ruled out for other cities associated with the Yādavas, given their links with a major part of western and southern India.)[13]

The geographical link between Saurashtra and Mathurā is certainly feasible, even though there is little historical or archaeological evidence to support such a movement at this time. The major structure line in the area runs from Mathurā along the Aravallis to Cambay dividing the arid area to the north from the more hospitable and forested area to the south of this line.[14] The line of migration probably skirted south of the Aravallis and was possibly linked across the river valleys of the Sabarmati and the Banas. If the area was sparsely forested as it is thought to have been, then it would have provided good pasture land for cattle. The Mathurā-Saurashtra connection may have originated as a route of transhumance which later became incorporated into the tradition. The movement of the Ābhīra tribes tended to follow this direction and it has been argued that the Ābhīra pastoralists contributed towards the creation of the pastoral aspects of the Kṛṣṇa cult.[15]

Information on the Yādavas as a political force tends to be vague. They were evidently a pastoral-cum-agricultural society observing what appears to be a segmentary lineage system.[16] An attempt has been made to try and identify their settlements with those of the Black-and-red ware cultures from the archaeology of the second and first millennia BC but the identification remains extremely tentative.[17] Archaeological co-relations with migrations raise the problem that the white-painted Black-and-red ware moved from Gujarat towards Rajasthan and to the west of the Yamunā, and not in the other direction.[18] The Yādava lineage is projected as one of wide ramifications, both of segmenting and assimilating. Its prestige whether real or imagined, is clear from the number of dynasties of the subcontinent who in later periods claimed descent from the Yādavas. Some of the major segments of the Yādavas, such as the Andhaka-Vṛṣṇi followed the *gaṇa-saṅgha* system which is attested to by both Pāṇini and Kauṭilya.[19]

A major problem in the search for historicity in the traditional accounts lies in the biography of Kṛṣṇa which appears to indicate both a contextual and chronological collation. It is plausible that there were perhaps two or more Kṛṣṇas who were knit together in the texts of later periods. The Vṛṣṇi chief who expounds the Gītā appears to belong to the Vedic tradition of teachers who sometimes carry the epithet Kṛṣṇa.[20] As Vāsudeva, he is included in the *pañca-vīra* group of the Vṛṣṇis who were known to have been worshipped in the Mathurā region in the post-Mauryan period.[21] There is also the more centrally pastoral deity in an area with distinct pastoral associations. The miracles, the battles, the dalliances all relate to groves, forests, hills and pastures located in an area known as Vraja (on the western bank of the Yamunā), the cycle of pilgrimage involving *vanas* and *upavanas* each with its tutelary deity and place names frequently carrying cattle connotations, such as Gokula and Govardhana. Possibly there was the emergence of a hero cult focusing on the figure of a pastoral hero who was ultimately merged into a Vaiṣṇava incarnation, a procedure not unknown in other areas such as the Viṭhobā cult in Paṇḍharpur.[22] A further dimension was added to this with the arrival of Rādhā at a later stage. With such an involved series of linkages the Purāṇic tradition would have had no choice but to collate them into a single biography. The determining of the historical stratification of this collation would cover a span extending from the first millennium BC into early medieval times. For the Yādava connections with Mathurā it is perhaps best to leave the discussion in the realm of speculation until such time as there is further historical evidence to substantiate historical reconstruction.

The history of Mathurā as the focus of Śūrasena activity moves from the realm of speculation to a little more certainty, since it is referred to in a wide variety of sources. The *Mahābhārata* mentions the Śūrasenas as among those who fled from Jarāsanda, Śūra being the father of Vāsudeva[23] and Kunti and therefore an elder kinsman of Kaṁsa and Kṛṣṇa. Sahadeva is said to have conquered the Śūrasena in his *digvijaya* to the southern regions.[24] A statement in Manu implies that the Śūrasena were good warriors and the same text includes the Śūrasenaka with the Matsya, Pañcāla and Kurukṣetra as constituting the contiguous territories of the Brahmarṣi-deśa.[25]

Jaina and Buddhist texts also refer to Mathurā and although these references are not contemporary, nevertheless what is said about the city has some significance. Jaina sources describe Śūrasena as one of the *ārya-janapadas* lying to the south of the Kuru and to the east of the Matsya.[26] Its capital was at Mathurā which was listed among the ten most important capitals of *janapadas*. The statement that Mahāvīra visited Mathurā may be an attempt to give added prestige to the city once it had achieved a status in its own right.

Buddhist texts list the Śūrasena as one of the sixteen *mahājanapadas* and state that it had close links with Maccha/Matsya.[27] The capital of the Śūrasena was the city of Madhurā and was situated on the Yamunā. It was visited by Mahākaccāna who stayed at the Gundāvana. It is sometimes referred to as Uttara-Madhurā to distinguish it from Dakṣiṇa-Madhurā.[28] Mahāsāgara was the king of Uttara-Madhurā. Kaṁsa is described as ruling in the city of Asitāñjana and the story of his enmity with his sister's son Kṛṣṇa is repeated but with certain differences of detail. Devagabbha (Devakī) is said to have had ten sons brought up by the lowly servant Andhakavenhu and therefore called the *Andhakavenhu-dāsaputtas*. The link with the Andhaka-Vṛṣṇi is thus established. The sons take to plundering and ultimately succeed in defeating Kaṁsa. They conquer many cities and eventually settle at Dvāravatī. The hostility between Kaṁsa and Kṛṣṇa is referred to in many sources of a diverse kind,[29] and may to that extent have had some basis in actuality. The two names are invoked together in the *Arthaśāstra*,[30] in the curious context of a *mantra* relating to the preparation of a medicine.

In another Buddhist text the king of the Śūrasena *janapada* is called Avantiputta and is described as sympathetic to Buddhist teaching.[31] Mathurā is said to have been visited by the Buddha even though it suffered from five major disadvantages — uneven ground, dust, fierce dogs, *yakkhas* and difficulties in obtaining alms — all of which would have discouraged *bhikkhus* from going there. A post-Mauryan Buddhist text referring back to an earlier period describes Mathurā as the place of residence of a famous courtesan, and a city of rich merchants.[32]

In some Purāṇic sources we are told that twenty-three Śūrasenas will rule as contemporaries among a large number of other ruling families including the Śiśunāgas and their successors until the period of the Nandas.[33] Pargiter has taken an average length of reign of eighteen years and has attempted to reconstruct the chronology with the Śūrasenas ruling from the ninth century BC until they were conquered by the Nandas in the fourth century. But such a calculation seems arbitrary given the variability of lengths of reign. The *Viṣṇu Purāṇa* links Śūrasena with the Yādava lineage as one among the hundred sons of Kārtavīrya.[34] The Śūrasena may well have been a segment of the Yādava lineage who came to power and established a state in the Mathurā region.

The historicity of the Śūrasena is further attested by Greek and Latin writers quoting Megasthenes. Arrian writes that the god Herakles was held in special honour by the Sourasenoi, an Indian tribe who possess two large cities, Methora and Cleisobora and through whose country flows a navigable river called the Iobares.[35] He adds that Herakles had a single daughter called Pandaia and he bestowed the land by the same name on her and adorned her with pearls from the sea. Pliny writes that the river Jomanes flows through the Palibothri into the Ganges between the towns of Methora and Carisobora.[36] Ptolemy refers to a Modoura,[37] the city of the gods, which sounds closer to the southern Madurai, but the context suggests that it might be the northern Mathurā.

The identifications of Sourasenoi, Methora and Iobares/Jomanes do not present any problem. But the identification of Cleisobora or Carisobora or the other variants suggested such as Cyrisobores remains uncertain. An attempt has been made to identify it with Vṛindāvana, the forest of Vṛindā/tulsī or basil whose earlier name is believed to have been Kalikavartta, the pool of Kalika.[38] Other suggestions include reading the name as Kṛṣṇapura and Kalisapura.[39] Pliny's statement is ambiguous as it is not clear whether the two towns are on either side of the river or whether they are on the same side but at some distance from each other. A town on each side of the river would suggest a crossing point, ford or ferry point, possibly linking Mathurā to towns in the *doāb* such as Hastināpura and Kāmpilya with routes going further afield from there.[40]

The reading of Cleisobora as Kṛṣṇapura has not yielded any firm identification. A possible indirect connection could be suggested with Keśavadeva on the basis of this being an alternative name for Kṛṣṇa and there being archaeological evidence of a settlement at the site of Keśavadeva during the Mauryan period.[41] If the original Mathurā is to be identified with Madhuvana, which more recent local tradition identifies with Mahōlī,[42] then both cities would have been on the same bank of the Yamunā and in any case there would have to be some explanation for the shifting of the site to the location of present-day Mathurā and the engulfing of the one city by the other. The identification of Madhuvana with Mahōlī is not only very late but also carries no archaeological support since the only excavation conducted at the site so far has produced sculpture not earlier than the Kuṣāṇa period.[43] A major hurdle in identifying the location of such sites is ascribed to the shifting of the river course and its giving rise to river channels. The tradition of the two cities associated with the Śūrasena is perhaps also reflected in the reference in the *Ghaṭa Jātaka* to the two cities of Uttara-Madhurā and Asitañjana.

The link with Pandaia has led to the idea that perhaps the northern Mathurā had been confused with the southern Madurai ruled by the Pāṇḍyas, and which would have been familiar to Classical writers because of the Roman trade with south India. It was the Pāṇḍyan state in the south which was known to trade in pearls and was famous for its pearl banks. However there is also a tantalizingly vague connection between the Śūrasena and the Pāṇḍavas. The *janapada* of Śūrasena was visited by the five brothers and it lay in the proximity of the Kuru-Pañcāla and Matsya region.[44] The Pāṇḍavas had very close connections with Virāṭa, and passed through Śūrasena on their way from Pañcāla to Virāṭa suggesting that the alleged crossing over the Yamunā was somewhere in Śūrasena territory.

The connection of the Śūrasena with Herakles has also been the source of some discussion. Herakles is generally identified with Kṛṣṇa. An identification with Indra has also been suggested,[45] but (apart from other objections to this identification) the fact that Herakles is described as being held in honour by the Sourasenoi, would make the identification with Vāsudeva-Kṛṣṇa seem more appropriate. If Herakles refers to Kṛṣṇa then it would point to the Vāsudeva-Kṛṣṇa cult being popular in this region at least as early as the fourth century BC. Confirmatory evidence of this comes from Pāṇini where reference is made to the worship of Vāsudeva and to the *dvandva* compound of Saṅkarṣaṇa-Vāsudeva. The identification with the cult is made even more explicit in Patañjali.[46] The earliest epigraphic evidence for this cult dates to about the second century BC.[47] The Vāsudeva-Kṛṣṇa cult not only served to underline the Vṛṣṇi-Yādava identity of the region but it is also worth noting that as a more personalised cult, with its sharper definition in the worship of a deity associated with the same lineage, the cult comes to the fore in the period of incipient state formation under the Śūrasena. Among the indigenous cults centering on the worship of the *yakṣas*, *nāgas* and the like, the Vāsudeva-Kṛṣṇa cult had the maximum potential to encourage wider networks of kin ties which could perhaps be welded into a politically unifying factor.

The Bacchanalian sculpture at Mathurā has been identified with the inebriated Kubera and it has been argued that there might be a connection with the classical iconography of the drunken Hercules.[48] But the notion of the *yakṣa* goes back to earlier periods and there is within the *pañca-vīra* cult of the Vṛṣṇis, known to have been prevalent in the Mathurā region, the theme of Saṅkarṣaṇa-Baladeva given on occasion to drunkenness. The theme of inebriation may well have been evoked by the names *madhu* and *saura* as intoxicants. The cult of Saṅkarṣaṇa-Baladeva is also linked with the *nāgas*, the worship of which is known in this region.[49]

The *yakṣa* figure from Parkham is thought to be dated to the Mauryan period though some would date it later.[50] If the *yakṣa* images are also linked with the concept of the *pañca-vīras*[51] then the finds at Mathurā would endorse the link, but the earliest evidence for the latter is post-Mauryan.

There is a surprising lack of evidence associating Mathurā with the Mauryan period, other than that from excavations. There are no Aśokan inscriptions in the vicinity which is admittedly negative evidence, but nevertheless telling. Archaeological data suggests a transition to urbanism during this period and it is therefore possible that some inscriptional evidence may yet appear. It is difficult to be dogmatic about precisely when Mathurā became an urban centre as urbanism is a gradual process. Since the pre-Mauryan evidence does not indicate an urban settlement and the post-Mauryan evidence does, it may be assumed that the transition to urbanism took place in the Mauryan period.

Of the sites excavated within the limits of what is thought to have been the city of Mathurā, that of Kaṭrā is described as the most imposing.[52] An early report stated that Painted Grey Ware was obtained from the lowest levels, a statement which has led to some controversy. More recently Painted Grey Ware has been found in the locality of Amabarisha.[53] This would make it clear that there was a pre-Mauryan settlement at the site of Mathurā. Both Painted Grey Ware and Black-and-red ware have been found in the vicinity of Mathurā at Sonkh.[54] Such sites could perhaps provide the archaeological co-relation for a settlement of the Śūrasena period.

Excavations at Kaṭrā Keśavadeva[55] have provided evidence at Mauryan levels of a transition from rudimentary structures to well-defined buildings of fired bricks and all the appurtenances of urban living in the form of floors, walls, drains, and ring-wells. The earlier excavation unearthed a coppersmith's furnace and workshop. These finds would endorse the probability of a demographic increase with a concentration of population as well as some evidence of craft production, both of which would point to a process of urbanism. More recent excavations have yielded terracotta figurines associated with this period and animal figures, especially the elephant. The early settlement appears to have made use of a chain of natural mounds perhaps resulting from successive flood deposits and would recall one of the disadvantages of the city of Mathurā as listed in Buddhist sources, namely, its uneven ground.

Excavations in the Dhulkot[56] area have revealed a mud-fortification around the city which dates to the Mauryan period or just prior to it, judging by the characteristic remains from the core of the fortification, such as Northern Black Polished ware sherds and terracotta animal figures. The fortification was strengthened in later periods. Fortification in itself need not imply an urban centre, but continued fortification of an effective kind would indicate the beginnings of urbanism. Where fortification is accompanied by other characteristic features, of what later come to be recognised as urban settlements, there the function of the fortification vis-à-vis the urban settlement is more obvious. There is also the distinction between urban activity within the fortified area (as is frequent in settlements moving towards becoming urban centres), and activities outside the area of fortification which is more common in cities of some standing.

The excavation at Sonkh unfolds a similar sequence. The Painted Grey Ware levels with an admixture of Black-and-red ware preceding the Mauryan provide evidence of post-holes and reed impressions and mud-plaster. The PGW sherds frequently carry the *nandipada* symbol. The Mauryan phase at Sonkh indicates a better quality of mud-plaster to begin with and at a later stage there is a change to mud-brick. The artifacts associated with these levels include NBP ware and terracotta figures of characteristic Mauryan design; silver punch-marked coins and uninscribed cast coins occur at these levels. Among them are some which carry the crescent-on-hill and the tree-in-railing symbols, associated with the Mauryas.

The occurrence of coined money would indicate an incipient

commercial economy more complex than either barter or the direct exchange of goods. That Mathurā had the potential of an important commercial centre in the Mauryan period can be gathered from the references to it as a centre of cotton production and of northern trade in texts such as the *Arthaśāstra*[57] and the *Divyāvadāna*.[58] The latter, in particular, would suggest that Mathurā could slowly have been developing as a distribution point for items coming from the north. Connections between Mathurā and Taxila could date to the Mauryan period since Marshall maintains that Mathurā sandstone was found at Bhir Mound, Stratum III.[59] Chunar sandstone is also attested to for this period at this site. Mathurā's eventual emergence as a sacred centre not merely for the Vāsudeva-Kṛṣṇa cult with which it appears to have had earlier connections but also for the Buddhists and the Jainas, would have lent additional support to its strategic, political and commercial status.

Nevertheless, the question as to why Mathurā does not have any direct evidence of Mauryan control remains, and a number of partial answers can be put forward. The important administrative centres were Pāṭaliputra, Taxila and Ujjain and the latter doubtless overshadowed Mathurā. It was perhaps too close to the centre of power to develop as a provincial capital. Alternatively it may still have nurtured a lineage autonomy to a larger extent than the other cities and managed to maintain this autonomy. It is significant that the Classical accounts refer to Methora as a town of the Sourasenoi and do not connect it with the Mauryas although it is likely to have been under Mauryan control and that the Sourasenoi are described as an Indian tribe and not merely as a territorial unit. This may also suggest that state formation in this region was less well-developed and it was only after the hegemony of the Mauryas that it matured. The *gaṇa-saṅgha* system may have had a strong base in the area.

In the earlier period the major routes appear to have by-passed Mathurā, the more important places being Bairat and Kauśāmbī. This might explain the early location of Buddhist centres at both these places, with the Aśokan inscriptions indicating their importance in the Mauryan period. A major crossing point over the Yamunā river at Delhi is suggested by the nature of Mauryan remains recently discovered.[60] It probably needed the more enveloping control of an imperial administrative and political system to extend the routes from localized circuits to long-distance connections. The counterpart to this is seen in the comparative rapidity with which the Vāsudeva cult restricted to the Śūrasena region in the Mauryan period, spread to parts of Rajasthan, central and western India within a couple of centuries.

The traditional evidence on Mathurā suggests a process of historical change from a lineage based society with a prominence of the Yādava lineage to the emergence of a *janapada* that of the Śūrasena, who, in spite of contradictory statements seem to have been a segment of the Yādava lineage or at any rate sought a connection with them. The Śūrasena *janapada*, as a territorial unit, claims historical recognition and was counted among the important states of northern India. Its status was determined not only by its being listed among the sixteen *mahājanapadas*, but also by the reference to its political centre at Mathurā. Furthermore, it provided a base for a religious cult which was initially specific to the region, but was soon to attain a far wider geographical and social circumference. The identity of Śūrasena was not totally submerged when it came under Mauryan control. With the advent of urbanization during the Mauryan period, a new dimension was added to the importance of Mathurā as it incorporated the role of a commercial centre which reached its full growth in the post-Mauryan period.

## Notes and References

1. A.A. Macdonell and A.B. Keith (eds), *Vedic Index*, II, reprint, Delhi, 1967, p. 185.
2. *Ṛgveda*, VII.18.6.
3. *Ṛgveda*, IV.30.18.
4. *Ṛgveda*, VII.1.31; 6.46.
5. Macdonell and Keith, *Vedic Index*, II, p. 392.
6. Macdonell and Keith, *Vedic Index*, I, pp. 183–5.
7. *Viṣṇu Purāṇa*, IV.10.
8. *Viṣṇu Purāṇa*, IV.4.101; *Bhāgavata Purāṇa*, IX.4.30–1.
9. *Viṣṇu Purāṇa*, IV.4.11. The story is repeated in a late book of the *Rāmāyaṇa*, VII.61 and 62.
10. *Bhāgavata Purāṇa*, IX.23.30; *Brahmāṇḍa Purāṇa*, III.63.186; 71.145–60; *Vāyu Purāṇa*, 88.105; 96.143–59; *Harivaṁśa*, 35.
11. X.1.27–34; X.50 to 54.
12. *Jātaka* no. 454.
13. C.T. Maloney, *The Effect of Early Coastal Sea Traffic on the Development of Civilization in South Asia*, University of Pennsylvania, 1968 (Unpublished Ph.D. thesis).

14. O.H.K. Spate, *India and Pakistan*, London, 1964, p. 148.
15. As for example in Suvira Jaiswal, *The Origin and Development of Vaisnavism*, Delhi, 1967, pp. 80ff.
16. Romila Thapar, 'Genealogy as a Source of Social History', in *Ancient Indian Social History: Some Interpretations*, New Delhi, 1978, pp. 326ff.
17. Romila Thapar, 'Puranic Lineages and Archaeological Cultures', in *Ancient Indian Social History: Some Interpretations*, pp. 240ff.
18. As a society given to some pastoral activity, the Yādava clans could have also been itinerant traders on a small scale with routes of transhumance becoming important as trade routes with the development of trade. The thrust from Gujarat towards southern Rajasthan may well have been connected with the availability of copper near Udaipur known to have been worked in the second millennium BC from the site of Ahar. From here the route along the Aravallis would lead to Bairat and further to the Indo- Gangetic watershed. The route skirting south of the Aravallis would arrive at Bharatpur and Mathurā.
19. *Pāṇiṇi*, VI.2.34; *Arthaśāstra*, XI.1.4.
20. Macdonell and Keith, *Vedic Index*, I, pp. 183–5.
21. As evidenced from the Mora well inscription, *Epigraphia Indica*, XXIV, p. 194. Another reference to the *pañca-vīra* comes from the Ghosuṇḍi inscription near Udaipur, *EI*, X, Appendix, p. 2. There is a curious parallel to the concept of the *pañca-vīra* in the reference to the five great *velir* chiefs — the *aimperumvelir* — in the Śangam literature. The *velir* also claim to be of Yādava descent. (*Pattinap.* 282; *Puram* 201, 202; N. Subrahmanian, *Pre-Pallavan Tamil Index*, Madras, 1966, p. 110.) If both traditions derive from a common ancestor then perhaps the concept of the five heroes may be very much earlier and may also have some connection with that of the *pañca-janāḥ*.
22. G.A. Deleury, *The Cult of Vithoba*, Poona, 1960; S.G. Tulpule, 'The Origin of Vitthala: A New Interpretation', *ABORI*, 1977–78, LVIII–LIX, pp. 1009–15.
23. III.13.26; 22.10ff; 287.20ff.
24. II.28.2.
25. VII.193; II.19.
26. J.C. Jain, *Life in Ancient India as Depicted in the Jaina Canons*, Bombay, 1947, pp. 308–9.
27. *Aṅguttara Nikāya*, I.213; IV.252.
28. *Ghaṭa Jātaka*, no. 454.
29. H.C. Raychaudhury, *Materials for the Study of the Early History of the Vaishnava Sect*, Calcutta, 1936.
30. XIV.3.44.
31. *Majjhima Nikāya*, II, 83–90.
32. *Divyāvadāna*, C. 353.

33. F.E. Pargiter, *The Puranic Text of the Dynasties of the Kali Age*, Oxford, 1913, pp. 21–4; *Ancient Indian Historical Tradition*, London, 1922, pp. 181–2.
34. IV.11.
35. *Indica*, VIII. Herakles is mentioned frequently in the accounts of Alexander's campaign in India. However, since the Greeks seem to have been in the habit of bestowing the name on a number of diverse gods in various parts of the then-known world, there is some confusion about the identification of Herakles. J.W. McCrindle, *The Invasion of India by Alexander the Great*, Westminster, 1896, p. 70, n.2; The rock Aornos is said to have been impregnable since even Herakles failed to conquer it (p. 70). An image of Herakles was carried into battle when Alexander faced Poros (p. 208).
36. *Hist. Nat.*, VI.22.
37. Ptolemy, 50.
38. A. Cunningham, *The Ancient Geography of India*, reprint, Varanasi, 1963, pp. 315–16.
39. J.W. McCrindle, *India as Described by Megasthenes and Arrian*, London, 1877, p. 140.
40. There is, however, little evidence for such a crossing point. Whereas the Pāṇḍavas go through Śūrasena when traveling from Pañcāla to Vairāṭa, the account of Hsüan Tsang (admittedly many centuries later), takes the route from Vairāṭa to Mathurā but travels north again along the western side of the Yamunā to Thanesar and from there he goes to the upper *doāb*. This may have been due to his having to return to Thanesar to meet Harṣavardhana. T. Watters, *On Yuan Chwang's Travels in India*, I, reprint, New Delhi, 1973, pp. 301ff.
41. A. Cunningham, *ASI Report*, XX, 1909, p. 45; *Indian Archaeology — A Review*, 1973–74, p. 31.
42. F.S. Growse, *Mathurā: A District Memoir*, reprint, Ahmedabad, 1978.
43. H. Waddington, 'Preliminary Report on the Excavation of a mound at Meholi near Muttra, U.P. 1940', *JUPHS*, XV, part II, 1942, pp. 135ff.
44. *Mahābhārata*, IV.1.9–10; IV.5.1–4.
45. A. Dahlquist, *Megasthenes and Indian Religion*, Uppsala, 1962.
46. Pāṇini, IV.3.98; VIII.1.15. Patañjali, III.43; I.426; I.436.
47. The Besnagar Inscription of Heliodorus, *EI*, X, p. 63; Ghosuṇḍi Inscription, *EI*, X, Appendix, p. 2; The Nānāghāṭa Cave inscription, *EI*, X, p. 121. Epigraphic evidence is supported by literary data in Patañjali's *Mahābhāṣya*.
48. B. Rowland, 'Gandhara, Rome and Mathurā', *Archives of the Chinese Art Society of America*, X, 1956, quoted in J.M. Rosenfield, *The Dynastic Arts of the Kushans*, Berkeley, 1967, pp. x, 248.
49. Ph. Vogel, 'Nāga Worship in Ancient Mathurā', *Archaeological Survey*

*of India, Ann. Rep.*, 1908–09, p. 162; H. Härtel, 'Some Results of the Excavations at Sonkh', in *German Scholars on India*, II, Bombay, 1976.

50. Rosenfield, *Kushans*, p. 302; N.R. Ray, *Maurya and Sunga Art*, Calcutta, 1945.
51. J.N. Banerjea, *Development of Hindu Iconography*, Calcutta, 1956, pp. 92–4.
52. B.B. Lal, 'Excavations at Hastinapur . . .', *Ancient India*, nos 10 and 11, p. 140. *Indian Archaeology — A Review*, 1954–55, pp. 15–16; 1973–74, p. 31.
53. Personal communication from Shri M.C. Joshi, *ASI*, New Delhi.
54. Härtel, op. cit.
55. *Indian Archaeology — A Review*, 1974–75, pp. 1–114 (cyclostyled copy).
56. *Indian Archaeology — A Review*, 1974–75, pp. 1–114.
57. II.11.115. The name is given as Madhurā and could be either the northern or the southern city.
58. *Divyāvadāna*, C. 353.
59. J. Marshall, *Taxila*, I, Cambridge, 1951, pp. 108ff.
60. The Mauryan levels at the excavations at the Purana Qila are substantial. *Indian Archaeology — A Review*, 1969–70, pp. 4ff and 1970–71, pp. 8ff. A version of the Minor Rock Edict was found in a Delhi suburb and goes by the name of the Bahapur inscription; see, *Journal of the Royal Asiatic Society*, 1967, pp. 67ff.

# 19

# State Weaving-Shops of the Mauryan Period*

The date of the *Arthaśāstra* has been argued over among scholars of Indian history. Suggested dates range from the Mauryan period (third century BC) to the Gupta period (fourth century AD).[1] Majority opinion is now coming round to the view that a part of the text was originally written during the Mauryan period, but was edited with interpolations of various kinds in the centuries following. The original text was written by Kauṭilya[2] or Cāṇakya as he is sometimes called, who was the minister of the first Mauryan emperor, Candragupta. It was expanded and edited by various writers, until it was rewritten in *sūtra* form by Viṣṇugupta in the fourth century AD.[3] This is the form with which we are familiar today.[4]

The *Arthaśāstra* is not, as is often mistakenly believed, a text on Hindu political thought. It does not concern itself with the development of political ideas or with discussing the validity of various political institutions. It assumes that monarchy is the most superior form of government and proceeds to explain how best a monarch can govern. It is in fact a text-book on administration in a monarchical system. The work is divided into fifteen sections, of which the most detailed is the second, which deals with the organisation of various administrative departments. The work as a whole reflects a period of economic development, when the idea of obtaining a national income via taxation from various urban and agrarian sources, had just emerged. Consequently there is an insistence on state supervision of all activities. The purpose of this was both to control production and to derive an income from taxation at various stages. Thus not only had the cultivator to pay a tax on the land he cultivated, and a percentage of the grain he harvested, or the

* *Journal of Indian Textile History*, 1955, vol. I.

merchant a percentage on the goods he sold, but even prostitutes and the keepers of gambling houses paid a regular part of their income to the treasury.[5]

Activities concerned with spinning and weaving would thus fit into this category of production, whether supervised by the state or carried out privately, which was in both cases taxable. One of the chapters in the second section of the work deals with the duties of the government superintendent (*adhyakṣa*) of weaving. His duties consisted of distributing the raw material to qualified weavers and other persons whom he thought suitable, and supervising the work in the government weaving house. Two types of weavers are mentioned. The first were those who worked privately either at home or by renting looms at the weaving house. Secondly there were guilds of weavers.[6] Those individually employed were either professional weavers working independently of the guilds, or non-professionals with special permission to work because of hardship or other causes, which were specified.

References to women who could earn a livelihood through weaving, contain revealing indications of the social relationships between men and women in Mauryan society. It is significant that the profession of weaving was one of the few open to women. Generally it would seem that a woman who was not respectably married, was regarded with some suspicion, since the only other activities open to her were employment in the palace as a servant of the king, prostitution, joining the flower and perfume trade or belonging to a theatrical troupe. Even in connection with weaving, only women in certain conditions were permitted this activity. These conditions are clearly specified.

Widows were allowed to work. This category included women whose husbands had died, as well as those whose husbands were living or travelling in a distant place. In view of the fact that the profession of a merchant or trader was a popular one in urban society, there must have been a fair number of women whose husbands would be away periodically. Owing to the uncertain nature of speculative business at that period, the additional income from occupations such as weaving may have been essential to the livelihood of these women. Young women who were cripples could also support themselves from weaving. Strangely enough women ascetics and nuns were not debarred from this activity. This is surprising, as usually men or women who forsake society and devote themselves fully to a religious life are expected to support themselves through charity or alms. Perhaps it was difficult, if not impossible for a woman ascetic to wander through the country, begging alms. Women who had committed offences and had therefore to pay fines, could earn the money for the fine by working as weavers. Mothers of prostitutes, retired women servants of the king, and retired temple prostitutes were all permitted this occupation. Clearly these were women who were too old to continue in their profession and had no means of sustenance. Housewives or women who had decided to remain unmarried, other than those listed above, were not permitted to work.

Furthermore, women were only given that type of work which could be done at home. This could be either the processing of certain types of raw material, or spinning. Any process which required equipment not available to the women in their homes, was prepared by men in the state weaving house, under the supervision of the superintendent. This was no doubt partly to avoid employing women in the weaving house, and partly to keep a check on the material and thus prevent theft.

Instructions on dealings with women workers are very precise. In the case of women who could not leave their homes, each one was to send her maid-servant to collect the raw material or return the completed work, the superintendent thus being unacquainted with the actual person who worked for him. Women in a position to leave their homes had to call at the weaving house early in the morning at dawn, when the yarn could be exchanged for wages. The author adds that the light in the room should be subdued and only sufficient for the superintendent to examine the work and asses its value. Presumably the subdued lighting prevented the superintendent from recognising the face of the woman concerned. On no account was the superintendent to engage in conversation with the woman on any subject but that concerning the work, otherwise he would be severely punished. This implies rigid segregation between the two sexes, which was not a characteristic of social life as described in other contexts in the same work.[7] Perhaps strictness in this case was to ensure honesty amongst the officials. The punishment for cheating on the part of the worker was extremely severe, and if actually observed would indicate an excessive harshness on the part of the state. Possibly therefore, it was more in the nature of a deterrent.

The raw materials mentioned consisted of wool, cane and bamboo bark, cotton plants and cotton, hemp, and flax. Apart from the weaving of piece-goods, blankets, ropes, armour and girths are also mentioned. The inclusion of armour is puzzling. It is possible that apart from chain-armour, corded armour was used by those who could not afford the former. The reference here may have been to corded armour. The girths were used on domestic animals and those drawing chariots, etc. The cloth girths were probably similar to modern webbing belts, which are used to this day as an essential part of the horse's harness.

The system of wages is explained in great detail. Both guilds and private weavers were given work on the basis of fixed wages. Payment was determined by the quality of the work done and the amount of time taken over it. In the case of the guild-worker payment was made through the guild. Technical efficiency naturally played an important part in assessing payment. Threads spun from raw material were divided into three categories, fine, medium and coarse. The fine thread was more highly valued. Similarly in the weaving of cloth, the finer weaves fetched a higher wage. A careful check was kept on the raw material provided, which was weighed and recorded. A calculation was made as to how much could be expected in thread or cloth. When the completed work was brought back, it was measured and compared with the calculation. If it was found to be short, then the value of the missing amount was cut from the wages of the weaver. It is stated however that blemishes in the raw material were to be taken into account when the calculation was made. Natural loss of weight or length through processing was also noted. We are told for instance that in woollen threads there is a loss of one-twentieth of the total weight when the hair falls in the process of threshing.[8] Women were paid according to the amount of work completed and payment was to be made only on completion. If any weaver took payment in advance and failed to complete the work commissioned, the punishment was severe.

Encouragements in the way of prizes are suggested for fast workers. These could consist of oil and cakes (the latter were made with dried fruit and were obviously regarded as delicacies). Special rewards of perfumes and garlands of flowers are also mentioned, which could be made to those who worked on holidays.[9] These were in addition to the normal wages. Unfortunately no indication is given of the actual amount paid for a particular piece of work.

Fraudulent practices of various kinds were apparently well-known. One section of the work warns the citizen against the trickery of artisans, and weavers are listed as among the more unreliable of artisans.[10] Kauṭilya advises that wherever possible work should be commissioned through a guild, as the responsibility then lay with a recognised group and not with a single person. Severe penalties are suggested if weavers were caught cheating the superintendent or any person who had commissioned work from them. The usual penalty was a fine and this was cut from the wages. Weavers who defaulted by failing to produce work in the agreed time had to forfeit a quarter of their wages and in addition were fined twice the amount of the commission agreed upon. If goods were damaged by the weavers, then they had to pay compensation. Those who produced what was not asked for, had also to pay a heavy fine and in some cases forfeit their wages. If the length of the cloth was short, then the value of the missing length would be deducted from the wages and a fine would be imposed, equivalent to twice the value of the loss. If the finished article was short in weight, then the fine would be as much as four times the value of the loss. The offence of substituting yarn of inferior quality was to be punished by a fine of twice the value of the original.

One of the better known methods of cheating practised by weavers is described. By soaking yarn in rice-gruel, weavers could increase its weight by ten per cent.[11] In this way, the weight of finished linen or silk cloth would be increased by fifty per cent, and of blankets and woollen garments by one hundred per cent. Such practices were punishable by a fine equivalent to twice the total value of the yarn provided, in addition to forfeiture of any advance payment made.

Strangely enough mutilation of the thumbs is not suggested as punishment in any of these cases. Yet this is regarded as normal punishment in the case of women who have received wages in advance and fail to complete a commission. To disable a woman worker was obviously considered above reproach. Apart from emphasising a prejudice against women, it seems a self-defeating punishment. Generally fines were regarded as the usual form of punishment in any offence. Mutilation is suggested by Kauṭilya only in the case of serious crimes. He lists three categories of punishment in relation to various types of offences. The first category was always the highest.

The various stages, from raw material to textile, entailed a series of taxes, which were paid by the cultivator, the weaver and the merchant or the textile guild. All cultivators paid a land tax, and a further tax on their produce, irrespective of whether this produce was a food crop or a cash crop.[12] Both these taxes varied according to the quality of the land and the facilities for irrigation, etc. The tax on the produce ranged from a quarter in the more fertile areas to one-eighth or less elsewhere.[13] (The average tax is thought to have been one-sixth.) In a period of emergency an additional one-sixth could be demanded from the cultivator.[14] The weaver, unless he worked in a guild, was taxed for hiring a loom if he worked in the state weaving house. This worked out to 1½ *paṇas* per loom per annum. The exact value of the *paṇa* remains uncertain, but some indication of the amount may be arrived at through the fact that artisans were paid a salary of 120 *paṇas* by the state. This is listed together with the salaries of other state officials. Presumably this was the salary per year.[15] No commodity could be sold other than in the government controlled market. Here toll dues were paid either by the weavers if they were selling the articles or by the merchants. Work commissioned by merchants or citizens was paid for separately to the guild or to the individual weaver. Undoubtedly this too must have been taxed. Toll dues amounted to one-tenth or one-fifteenth on the following textiles, linen, cotton, silk, curtains of any kind, carpets and woollen goods. Clothing, cotton yarn and fibre were taxed at the rate of one-twentieth or one-twenty-fifth of the total value.[16] In addition to toll dues (*śulka*) there was a gate-tax (*dvārādeya*) of one-fifth of the toll dues.[17] In times of national emergency, weavers could be asked to pay an additional tax of one-sixth and merchants trading in textiles, an additional tax of ten *paṇas*.[18]

In another section of the work, relating to products from various parts of the country, a fairly detailed mention is made of textiles.[19] However this section refers only to those products which are sent to the state treasury as part of the tax. The list of textiles is as follows.

### Blankets

These were generally made of sheep's wool. They could be white or various shades of red. The main techniques are those of *khachitam* (tightly woven woollens), *vānacitram* (loosely woven), *khaṇḍasanghātya* (various pieces joined together), and *tantuvicchannam* (woven with uniform threads). Many varieties of blankets are listed: *kambala, kaucapaka, kulamitikā, saumitikā, turaṅgāstaranam, varnakam, talicchakam, vāravānah, paristomah, samanbhadrakam*. These are thought to be coarse blankets, such as those used by herdsmen and farmers, blankets spread on the backs of animals such as bullocks, horses, elephants, and woollen material woven to the size of blankets. Of these the best quality blanket is that which is slippery and soft.

Nepal is said to have produced blankets known as *bhiṅgisī* and *apasāraka*, both of which were black in colour and water-proof.

Blankets were also made from wool gathered from other animals and described as *samputikā, caturaśrikā, lambarā, kaṭavānaka, prāvaraka* and *sattalikā*.

### Other Textiles

Vaṅga (Bengal) produced a soft white bark-cloth called *dukūla*.[20] From the Puṇḍras came a smooth black cloth, described as being as smooth as the surface of a gem. Suvarṇakuḍya[21] produced a bright golden yellow cloth with a smooth glossy texture, woven while the yarn was damp. Linen (*kṣauma*) came from Kāśī (Banaras) and the Puṇḍra country. Fabrics of bark-fibre were especially woven in Māgadhikā (Magadha), the Puṇḍra country and Suvarṇakuḍya. The trees giving fibre included the *nāga* tree, which produced a yellow fibre; the *likuca* (*Artocarpus Lakucha*), the colour of wheat; the *vakula* (*Mimusops Elengi*), white; and the *vaṭa* (*Ficus Indica*), the colour of butter. Of the cloths made with these fibres, the best came from Suvarṇakuḍya. Silks from China are described as *kauśeya* and *cīna-paṭṭa*.[22]

The finest cotton textiles came from Madhurā (south India), Aparānta (western India), Kaliṅga (the coastal region between the Mahānadi and the Godāvari rivers), Kāśī (the neighbourhood of Banaras), Vaṅga (Bengal), Vatsa (the region around Kauśāmbi, near Allahabad) and Mahiṣa (the region of the Narmadā).

### Summary

The state must have derived a fairly large profit from the manufacture of textiles. This was one of the rare industries which in

Mauryan times employed both men and women. The type of work given to both is of some interest. Women were only permitted to do the lighter work, the processes that could be carried out at home, without elaborate equipment. The weaving house, organised by the state or by a guild, where the greater part of the work was done and probably that of a more arduous kind, appears not to have employed women. The average wage of the weaver (120 *paṇas*) seems small when compared to that of the superintendents which ranged from 4,000 to 12,000 *paṇas*. The manufacture of textiles was clearly one of the foremost industries. They are mentioned among the more lucrative articles of trade. Textiles were regarded as valuable enough to be stored in the national treasury, and are described in the same section of the *Arthaśāstra* as that referring to the various kinds of precious stones and gems.

## APPENDIX

### The Superintendent of Weaving

*A Revised Translation of the Arthaśāstra, II, 23*

The superintendent of weaving shall be responsible for the production of articles such as yarn, outer garments, clothing and ropes, by persons qualified to do so.

Widows, young women who are cripples, women ascetics and nuns, women seeking work in order to pay off fines, mothers of prostitutes, retired women servants of the king, retired temple *deva-dāsis*, may all be employed in the processing of wool, bark, cotton plants, cotton, hemp and flax.

The quality of the threads produced, whether fine, of medium quality or coarse, should determine the amount to be paid. The quantity manufactured should also be taken into consideration. On ascertaining the quality of the thread, special rewards consisting of oil and myrobalam fruit should be made to those producing the most amount of fine threads.

On holidays too, work may be encouraged by giving special rewards (to those who work).

If, after taking into consideration any fault in the raw material, the yarn is found to be short, then payment may be cut accordingly.

Artisans who are qualified to produce a fixed quantity of yarn within a given time and at a settled rate, may also be given work. The superintendent should however remain associated with these artisans.

Those weaving linen, *dukūla*, silk, woollen cloth and cotton cloth should be encouraged by gifts of perfume, garlands of flowers and similar things.

The manufacture of garments of various kinds, curtain materials and blankets, should also be established.

Those proficient in the making of armour[23] shall be engaged in doing so.

Women who are not permitted to leave their homes, widows living away from home, and crippled women, may be permitted to work. Their maid-servants can bring the raw material to them and take the finished work back to the office of the superintendent.

Those women who are in a position to call at the weaving house may do so at dawn, in order to exchange their completed work for wages. There should be only enough light for the superintendent to examine the work. If he should wish to see the face of the woman or converse with her on subjects other than those relating to the work, he shall be punished with the first category of punishment. Neglect in the payment of wages should be punished by the second category of punishment; the same penalty shall obtain in cases where wages are paid for work which has not been completed.

Any woman who refuses to complete a commission, having received wages in advance, shall be forced to restore the amount, and be penalised by the mutilation of her thumbs.[24]

Any person who appropriates, steals or makes off with the material supplied by the weaving house shall be punished in a similar manner.

Weavers must pay fines for faulty weaving, which fines shall be taken from their wages.

The superintendent of weaving should remain in close touch with the rope makers and those manufacturing armour, and should supervise the manufacture of girths and similar articles. He should supervise the production of ropes and girths, used for tethering animals, and made from materials such as cane and bamboo.

NOTES AND REFERENCES

1. *Arthaśāstra*. Preface to Shamasastry's translation (5th ed.), pp. vii–xxxiii; Jolly, *Kauṭilyam Arthaśāstram*, Panjab S.K. Series, No. IV; R.P. Kangle, *The Kauṭilīya Arthaśāstra*, Bombay, 1965–72. Jayaswal, *Hindu Polity*, Appendix C, p. 364; D.R. Bhandarkar, *ABORI*, vii, 1926, pp. 80ff; Raychaudhuri (HCIP, i), *The Age of Imperial Unity*, p. 285; Kalyanov, XXIII Orientalists Congress, Cambridge, August 1954.
2. There has been much discussion on the name of Kauṭilya and its grammatical derivation. (Jolly, *Arthaśāstra of Kauṭilya*, pp. 1–47 and Kane, *JBOR'S*, vii, 1926).
3. Book XV, I.
4. I have used the edition of T. Ganapati Sastri, Trivandrum, 1924.
5. II, 24; II, 22; II, 27.
6. II, 23; IV, I. The guild system was by now a regular feature of urban life. It appears from the *Arthaśāstra* that skilled workers generally preferred to work in guilds, since this system had commercial advantages. In certain trades however it was equally lucrative to work as a private individual.
7. For example, the rights and duties of a married woman, laws of inheritance, etc.; III, 2, 3, 4, 5, 6.
8. IV, I.
9. The calendar of a working year (from the month of *āsādha* to *āṣādha*) omitting the intercalary months, was 354 days.
10. IV, I.
11. IV, I.
12. The *bhāga* and the *hiranya* (Ghoshal, *The Agrarian System of Ancient India*, p. 6). This seems to be confirmed by the Aśokan inscription at Rummindei. Bloch, *Les Inscriptions d'Asoka*, p. 157.
13. One-quarter is stated in the account of Megasthenes. Quoted, Strabo, XV, I, 40; Arrian, *Indica*, XI.
14. V, 2.
15. V, 3.
16. II, 22.
17. Ibid.
18. V, 2.
19. II, 11.97ff.
20. A fine quality cloth made from the inner bark of a delicate plant.
21. The identification of Suvarṇakuḍya (literally, 'golden wall'), is uncertain. *Suvarṇa* was a fairly common prefix in a number of place names. Suvarṇabhumi was the name for Burma and at a later period Suvarṇadvīpa was the term used for the South East Asian islands. Suvarṇakuḍya may have been on the east coast and connected with

the eastern trade, or else it may even have been an alternative name for Suvarṇagiri, the Mauryan provincial capital in the south (Mysore).

22. The reference to *cīna-paṭṭa* was one of the reasons why the *Arthaśāstra* was dated to the early centuries AD, since there were no contacts with China in the Mauryan period, which would permit the importation of Chinese silk via eastern India. However there is evidence to prove that silk was used in Bactria, which was imported from India in the second century BC if not earlier. (Ssu-ma-ts'ien, *Shi-ki*, 123; translated by Hirth. *JAOS*, xxxvii, 1917, pp. 89ff). Chang K'ien in about 129 BC found the Bactrians using Chinese silk, which according to the inhabitants came from India. The interesting point is that it is referred to as silk coming from the province of Szechuan. This province has been known as the area where the silk worm flourished. Thus it would appear that Chinese silk was available in India at an early period and that it came from Szechuan.

    The identification of China with *cīna*, may be a reference to the feudal state of Chin (during the Chou period), before the reign of Shi Hwang Ti (cf. Kosambi, *Introduction to the Study of Indian History*, p. 202).

23. Shamasastry translates *kankaṭa* as 'mail-armour'; but as I have explained, this seems more likely to have been cord-armour in this context.

24. Shamasastry translates *anguṣṭhasandanśam* in the sense of thumbs being cut off. The sense of mutilation seems to me more likely.

20

# *Aśoka and Buddhism as Reflected in the Aśokan Edicts**

In the Puranic texts, Aśoka occurs merely as an undistinguished name in a list of Mauryan kings. From the brahmanical point of view the Mauryas were patrons of heretical sects such as the Jainas, Ājīvikas, and Buddhists and therefore little time and space was wasted on them. But in the traditions of the so-called heretical sects, these kings are depicted as major patrons. Thus the Jaina tradition associates Candragupta Maurya with the major events of the early history of the Jaina *saṅgha*. A parallel portrayal is given of the association of Aśoka with the Buddhist *saṅgha* in the Buddhist tradition. The latter is however more detailed and makes of Aśoka an exemplar for all kings who were patrons of the Buddhist *saṅgha*. Implicit in this portrayal is the question of the relation between temporal and sacral power: a subject which has been analysed extensively by both historians and anthropologists in recent years.

In the nineteenth century the inscriptions of Aśoka were deciphered and by the early twentieth century the identity of Aśoka was established. Because of the portrayal of Aśoka in the Buddhist tradition, historians initially tended to read the edicts merely as documents asserting his belief in Buddhism. But if the edicts are examined more analytically they not only reflect a more complex situation but one that is also enriched by reference to the preoccupations of the contemporary scene. I would like to propose therefore that an assessment of the impact of Buddhism on the Mauryan emperor Aśoka requires analyses from many perspectives. Since he was a person of considerable public importance, such an assessment would have to consider both his personal beliefs as well as his public use of an ideology drawn from the ethical

* A. Seneviratne (ed.), *King Asoka and Buddhism*, Kandy, 1994, 11–26.

perspectives of religion — a consideration which would necessitate a familiarity with the contemporary situation in the third century BC in India.

It is rare in Indian history to have access to the personalized edicts of a king. In this we are fortunate in the corpus of Aśokan inscriptions, which are substantially of this nature. These inscriptions can be categorized as those which are directed to the Buddhist Sangha and which are fewer in number, and those which are addressed to the people at large and which constitute the majority of the edicts. The latter category includes what are referred to as the Minor Rock Inscriptions, the Major Rock Inscriptions, and the two Separate Edicts at Kaliṅga. It is from these that we can gather his definition of *dhamma*. What is even more fortunate in some ways is that we have versions of some of these edicts in Aramaic and Greek. These are significant not only in themselves but also in the fact that they provide us with another perspective on the concepts which he uses. It is my intention in this paper to base myself largely on the inscriptional data and to try to determine from this what might have been Aśoka's relation with Buddhism.

I would like to begin by looking at the evidence which we have for arguing that Aśoka was a Buddhist. Buddhism in this period has often been referred to as a heterodoxy in relation to Brahmanism. There was certainly a clear-cut distinction between the two. This is reflected in the quotation from Megasthenes which refers to the category of philosophers being divided into *brāhmaṇas* and *śramaṇas*, the term *śramaṇa* referring not only to Buddhists but to the large range of non-brahmanical sects. It is also reflected in a passage from Patañjali which indicates the hostility between the two by comparing their relationship to that of the snake and the mongoose. Nevertheless, as far as the middle Ganga valley was concerned, where the state of Magadha was located, the question may well be asked as to whether in this area Buddhism was a heterodoxy or whether it was the dominant sect. Candragupta Maurya is strongly associated with the Jaina tradition and Bindusāra, the father of Aśoka, with the Ājīvikas. It would seem therefore that in this area all these religious ideologies were prevalent and popular and therefore Aśoka's exposure to them may not have been an exposure to heterodoxy but to current religious ideas. His support of any of these sects need not therefore be seen as a major departure from the norm.

Possibly his first close association with Buddhism in an administrative capacity was when he was viceroy at Ujjain. This region was developing as a major centre of Buddhist activity, which is also attested in the brief inscription preceding the Minor Rock Edict at the site of Panguraria near Hoshangabad in Madhya Pradesh. According to the Buddhist tradition it was also here that his son Mahinda was born, and Mahinda's mother Devī is said to have been an ardent lay follower, thus introducing a very private element into his association with Buddhism. However, whatever this association may have been, it is not referred to in his edicts.

Eight years after he had been crowned, Aśoka campaigned in Kaliṅga. The Major Rock Edict XIII records his remorse at the suffering caused by this campaign. He mentions in this edict that after Kaliṅga had been annexed he came close to the practice and teaching of *dhamma*. This is often taken to be a dramatic conversion to Buddhism. However, it should be kept in mind that in the Minor Rock Edict issued in his thirteenth regnal year, i.e. five years after the Kaliṅga campaign, he states that 'I have been an *upāsaka* for more than two and a half years, but for a year I did not make much progress. Now for more than a year I have drawn closer to the Saṅgha (*saṅgham upagate*) and have become more ardent.' The Ahraura version of the Minor Rock Edict refers to the placing of the relics of the Buddha on a platform. In Major Rock Edict VIII he states that after he had been consecrated ten years he went to the Bodhi Tree, the Buddha's tree of enlightenment (*ayāya saṃbodhiṃ*). His statements suggest that there was no sudden conversion but rather a gradual and increasingly closer association with Buddhism.

This is somewhat different from the treatment of the conversion in the Buddhist tradition. No mention is made of the campaign in Kaliṅga in spite of the dramatic and narrative potential of such an event. Instead the conversion significantly relates to close relatives, a younger brother in one case and a nephew in another, who are responsible for showing the way to the king. There is the well known story of the wicked Caṇḍāśoka who changes to the pious Dharmāśoka which is, of course, a familiar stereotype in many such sudden conversion stories. Once the king is associated with the *saṅgha*, the relationship matures and reaches its fruition, as it were, in the decision to call the Third Council at Pāṭaliputra. Here the doctrine is clarified and the Theravāda position is established as the correct doctrine. What is of significance in this event is the mutual legitimation of the emperor and the *saṅgha*. Temporal power is legitimized by a religious assembly and the latter is in turn legitimized by the authority of the king. One of the outcomes of the Council is missionary activity. Missions are sent not only within the subcontinent but also to the northwest, the Hellenized states in the trans-Indus region, and of course to Sri Lanka.

The later years of the emperor, according to the tradition, were filled with palace politics. Subsequent to the death of Asandhimittā, the pious chief queen of Aśoka, there are a number of episodes involving her successor, Tissarakkhā. Her machinations lead to the blinding of the king's son Kunāla, to the king's being cured of a peculiar disease, and to the harming of the Bodhi Tree. Ultimately, Tissarakkhā's evil ways are exposed and she is removed from the scene. In the last phase of his reign the king is said to have made a number of donations to the *saṅgha*, some of which are so magnanimous that they embarrass the ministers of state, and others which are so paltry that they suggest that the income of even the mightiest of kings can be reduced to a pittance. In the inscriptions, donations by the king are referred to only indirectly. One inscription states that the donations of the Queen Kāruvākı, the mother of Tīvara, are to be recorded. The donations of the Barābar caves to the Ājīvikas are engraved in the vicinity. But there is a striking absence of any record of direct donations to the *saṅgha*.

The inscriptions addressed specifically to the Buddhist *saṅgha* carry an echo of some of these events. In the Bhabra inscription the king seems to speak as an *upāsaka* and takes the unostentatious title of *rājā māgadhe*, the king of Magadha, in addressing the *saṅgha*. He states his faith in the Buddha, the Dhamma and the Saṅgha and in the teachings of the Buddha. He goes on to list the particular teachings which he thinks are important and which he wishes monks and nuns to hear frequently and meditate upon.

Even more forceful is the Schism Edict issued at three major monastic centres, at Kosamb, Sanchi and Sarnath. It has been argued that this edict was issued after the Council of Pāṭaliputra. The king takes it upon himself to order the expulsion of dissident monks and nuns. It certainly is suggestive of an attitude towards dissidents subsequent to the correct doctrine being established. But, on the other hand, it does go rather contrary to his appeal for tolerance among all sects and opinions, which is voiced in the Major

Rock Edicts. Possibly a distinction has to be made between the king in his role as a patron of the *saṅgha*, even though an *upāsaka*, and the king as a statesman governing an empire. As a royal patron he rises above sectarian rivalries and donates caves to the Ājīvikas even though there was hostility between them and the Buddhists. Interestingly, these donations are made in the thirteenth and twentieth year of his reign when at the same time he was travelling to places sacred to Buddhism.

The Rummindei Pillar Inscription records a visit of the king to Lumbinī. This has been associated with the statement in the tradition that he made a pilgrimage to places sacred to Buddhism. Curiously, he exempts the village from *bali*, the land tax, and reduces the *bhāga* to one-eighth, but even his piety does not permit him to totally exempt the village from all taxes, the revenue demands of the empire receiving priority. The Nigalisagar Pillar inscription records his enlargement of the *stūpa* of Konakamana and his pilgrimage to the site. This is the nearest that we get in the inscriptions to a direct reference to his embellishing a *stūpa* and thus making a donation at the site. These inscriptions are specific to the concerns of the *saṅgha* and to places of Buddhist pilgrimage. They are to that extent affirmations of his adherence to Buddhism.

The Minor Rock Inscription, raises a number of interesting questions. There are some seventeen versions either exact or approximate of this edict and doubtless more will be discovered. Unlike the Major Rock Edicts there is a greater variation in these texts: some are shorter, some are addressed to local officers, some occur only in certain places and even the language varies. The question of why certain sections were omitted in certain places remains unanswered and suggests that some sections were considered more important than others and were perhaps issued separately although within a brief time span.

The earlier part of the inscription occurs at all the sites. The latter half occurs only at seven sites and that too in a cluster in three districts of Kurnool, Bellary and Chitradurga in Karnataka. The third segment occurs only in the sites in Chitradurga. Strangely, these do not even occur across the Tungabhadra in the sites of the Raichur district. It is possible that these segments were issued by Aśoka when he was actually touring in this area and were issued as after-thoughts.

The first segment is in some cases addressed to the officers of the area and the inscription therefore becomes one which is intended for the general public. This becomes clear in the statement that the officers are to make public its contents. He describes himself as a Buddhist *upāsaka*. It contains the controversial statement, . . . *yā imāya kālāya jaṃbudipassi amissā devā husu te dāni missā kaṭā* . . . This has been interpreted either as a reference to true and false gods (if *amissā* derives from *amṛṣa* meaning false) or that the gods who did not associate with men now do so (deriving *amissā* from *amiśra*, not mingled). If *devā* can be taken in its wider sense of things celestial then the second meaning seems more correct. The plural form *devā* would suggest superhuman beings. Taken in a metaphorical sense it could mean that Aśoka believed that by following the injunctions of *dhamma*, the righteousness so generated would attract even celestial beings. This is further suggested in the next few sentences where he explains the required behaviour according to the precepts of *dhamma*; and that it is open to both the humble and the mighty.

In the second segment he again calls upon the officers and particularly the *rājūka*, the rural officers, and the local chiefs to instruct the people of the countryside, assembling them with the sound of the drum. The virtues of *dhamma* are explained as obeying mother and father, obeying teachers, having mercy on living beings and speaking the truth. These precepts are so broad-based that they did not require any religious sectarian identification. Such virtues were common to a large number of religious sects. The third segment reiterates these virtues and particularly calls on professional groups such as elephant-keepers, scribes and fortune tellers, as well as *brāhmaṇas*, to instruct their apprentices that they must honour their masters and that within a family relatives must treat each other with respect. This is described as an ancient custom conducive to long life. At the site of Brahmagiri the name of the engraver, Capaḍa, is written in *kharoṣṭhī* and not in the script of the inscription, *brāhmī*.

The basic edict was presumably issued at the same time — namely, the 256th night on tour — and was engraved at a number of places. Why nights are mentioned rather than days remains unclear unless the computation was lunar or was connected with the worship of the relics. The locations of the inscriptions are also not consistent. He states that it is to be inscribed on rocks and stone pillars all over his kingdom. Existing stone pillars would certainly be associated with a site and probably a site of religious importance. Were the rocks also in the vicinity of sacred sites or of populated centres? Not all these inscriptions are at important Buddhist monastic centres and some seem to have been located close to megalithic settlements. The later imposition of Buddhist centres at certain megalithic sites (such as Amarāvatī) suggests an association which may have been evolving at this time. However, the presupposition of a sacred site is not necessary to the location of these inscriptions since the text itself makes it clear that the prime purpose was to reach large numbers of people.

What is perhaps more significant about the locations of this edict is that it occurs in large numbers in the peninsula and in the north along routes leading into the peninsula. The dominant culture of the peninsula at this time was the megalithic culture. It is generally agreed that the megalithic culture was either prior to state formation or consisted of incipient states. Chiefdoms therefore would have been the recognized political forms and doubtless it was these that were gathered up into the net of Mauryan conquest. The imperial administration would thus use two avenues of control: one would be through its own officers, the *āryaputras*, *kumāras*, *mahāmātras* and *rājūkas*; the other would be through local chiefs. The reference to officers and local chiefs would point to the ethic being propagated through these channels. Interestingly, the definition of *dhamma* in this edict is rudimentary and carries none of the refinements evident in the Major Rock Edicts. Possibly the reference to elephant-keepers was to chiefs who rode on elephant back and the scribes would of course be the officials.

The reference to scribes raises another set of interesting questions. The Mauryan inscriptions in the peninsula are composed in Prākrit and inscribed in *brāhmī*. Numerically the cluster in the south is in areas which were Dravidian-speaking but had no script. Mauryan *brāhmī* was subsequently adapted to suit Tamil and the earliest post-Mauryan inscriptions in the area are in Tamil *brāhmī*. The inscriptions of Aśoka would therefore have had to be read out to gatherings and possibly translated, since it is unlikely that people other than the elite would have followed Prākrit. The royal scribe Capaḍa was clearly from the northwest as he signs himself in the script of the northwest, *kharoṣṭhī*. Possibly local officers were being trained as scribes by the Mauryan administration. The additional segments to the original edict were obviously intended for the local situation. The Mauryan official was playing the important role of the intermediary between the imperial power and the local chiefs. The sites in the Karnataka were crucial to the Mauryas since this was the major gold-bearing region of the subcontinent and the Raichur doab is proverbial for its agricultural fertility.

In the first section of this edict a reference is made to people who live in the neighbouring areas also being made familiar with these ideas. It was perhaps in this context that a possible version of the Minor Rock Edict was issued in both Aramaic and Greek and was inscribed at Kandahar in southern Afghanistan which was then a centre of Iranian and Hellenistic settlement. The local population here spoke Aramaic and Greek. In this case Aśoka took the trouble to render his inscription into the local language. The edict was issued in the eleventh year of his reign. He claims that men have become more pious since he showed them the way and the world has prospered. In explaining this he emphasizes the restraint on the killing of animals, self-control, and obedience to parents and elders. The Aramaic version carried a statement that there is no judgement for pious men. This is almost certainly a reference to the Zoroastrian concept of a final judgement when the good and evil of an individual's actions will be weighed, as part of the Zoroastrian eschatology. The Aramaic-speaking population at this time was largely Zoroastrian and therefore this statement becomes significant in terms of an appeal which emphasizes the piety of the present and its merit, rather than the agony of waiting for the final judgement. The Greek version uses the term *eusebeia* for *dhamma*, the literal meaning of which is sacred duty and can include piety or pious conduct. It was a general term and had no link with any specific religious or philosophical school.

It is curious that Aśoka makes no reference to the teachings of the Buddha particularly in an area where Buddhism had hardly reached and where therefore a specific reference would have made his intentions very clear. It does raise the question of whether he was intending to propagate Buddhism in his reference to *dhamma*. This question is perhaps better answered by looking at the larger corpus of edicts, namely, the Major Rock Edicts and the Pillar Edicts in which he defines in greater detail his understanding of *dhamma*. In order, however, to clarify the context of these edicts it is perhaps necessary to look at the historical situation in Mauryan India. In the larger corpus of edicts he was more clearly identifying himself as the ruler of an empire and speaking to his subjects. The implicit audience of these edicts is therefore far wider than that of the inscriptions discussed so far.

We are used to treating the Mauryan empire as undifferentiated territory extending over almost the entire subcontinent excluding only the area south of Karnataka. In effect, however, as I have argued elsewhere, the empire has to be seen in terms of differentiated political control. This is also partially reflected in the location of the inscriptions. There were some areas which had experienced state systems prior to the rise of the Mauryas such as the Ganga valley, Gandhāra and Malwa. Magadha in particular had been the nucleus of political power controlling the Ganga valley in the preceding period under the Nandas and it continued to play that role under the Mauryas. It emerged therefore as a metropolitan area within the empire. That Aśoka referred to himself as *rājā māgadhe* was not altogether an act of humility. Earlier states which had been annexed provided the core areas of the empire and tradition has it that Aśoka while still a prince was placed in charge of the administration both at Taxila and at Ujjain. The agriculturally rich regions of Kaliṅga, Saurashtra and Raichur with their potential as states can also be viewed as core regions. Intermediate areas were probably regarded as peripheral. The degree of political control would vary in these regions. The metropolitan area was under a highly centralized system of administration and this was doubtless what Kauṭilya had in mind when he wrote of the political economy of a state.

It was to this region that the revenue was directed and it was regarded as economically the most developed area. The set of seven pillar edicts are addressed to this region. The core areas had the potential of becoming metropolitan areas, which many of them did in the post-Mauryan period. The Major Rock Edicts are largely located in such areas. The ones at Kalsi and Sopara indicate not so much the importance of agriculture as the importance of trade, the first being on the *uttarapatha* or the long-established northern route and the second being the emerging port for trade along the west coast and possibly with Arabia. The revenue from these core areas was again directed to the metropolitan state and the economy of these areas may have been reorganized for this purpose. The locations of the Major Rock Edicts also point to their becoming nuclei of trade centres. The peripheral regions would be those least tampered with by Mauryan administration as long as the revenue from them could be creamed off. There is little evidence of the Mauryan presence at megalithic sites in the peninsula except for the area of Raichur and the adjoining districts where the inscriptions are located. Western Rajasthan, Sind and Punjab do not provide Mauryan associations.

This differentiated political control is also suggested by the variations in the major economic activities of these regions. The metropolitan and core areas drew their revenue from agriculture and commerce. Mention is made of state-supervised agriculture but this did not preclude landowners and a variety of peasant tenures. Megasthenes' account suggests a fairly secure peasantry kept unarmed. Artisanal production and trade also provided revenue in taxes. It is likely that in the peripheral areas Mauryan control was concentrated on keeping the trade routes open and encouraging trade. The Kauṭilya *Arthaśāstra* indicates a concern by the state to derive the maximum revenue from commerce, which if it reflects actual practice, may almost have had a suffocating effect. Where peripheral areas provided lucrative resources such as the gold-bearing regions of Karnataka, there the Mauryan pressure is apparent. Such areas were largely the domain of forest tribes and pastoral groups with pockets of agriculturists. Forest tribes are referred to in the edicts and in relation to these Aśokan paternalism was at its maximum.

Mauryan society shows a wide range of diversity which is reflected both in the archaeological picture and that available from literary sources. The Greek and Aramaic-speaking peoples of the northwest would have appeared as alien to those of the Ganga valley as were the megalithic peoples of the peninsula. The governance of such a diversity required both political control as well as persuasive assimilation. The machinery of political control had to be backed by force and finance. Persuasive assimilation required an ideology which would appeal to this diversity at all levels. The question then is whether Aśoka's concept of *dhamma* provided such an ideology.

The corpus of Major Rock Edicts (hereafter RE) and Pillar Edicts (hereafter PE) provide us in some detail with a picture of what Aśoka meant by *dhamma* or what has since been referred to by historians as his policy of *dhamma*. Those who observe the precepts of *dhamma* are said to be people of few faults, many good deeds, mercy, charity, truth and purity (PE 2, 7). Where he refers movingly to having given a gift of insight, *cakkhudāne*, to people through *dhamma* he describes it as an awareness of the sins of cruelty, harshness, anger, pride and envy. Elsewhere he mentions the behaviour required of those who observe the *dhamma*. This consists of obedience to parents, elders and teachers; concern for friends and relatives; gifts to *brāhmaṇas* and *śramaṇas*; abstention from killing; good treatment towards slaves, servants and the poor; and moderation in attachment to possessions (RE 3, 9, 1). Perhaps to this can also be added his negative attitude to rituals, ceremonies and assemblies (RE 1, 9) and his suggestion that behaviour in accordance with *dhamma* was preferable to the performance of ceremonies.

Repeated emphasis is given to tolerance of all sects (RE 6, 7, 12). True tolerance lies in honouring another's sect and his aim is the progress of the essential doctrine of all sects. This sentiment is in strong contrast to the Schism Edict in which he demands the expulsion of dissident monks and nuns. Whereas dissidence was not to be tolerated within the *saṅgha*, for the world at large dissident sects were as important as any other. He states that his concern for tolerance arises out of his involvement with the welfare of the whole world and helps him discharge his debt to his people, presumably in his role as emperor. The ultimate purpose of this is the attainment of heaven (RE 9; PE 3; Separate Edict 1). Even the officers who function well will attain heaven as will the frontier people if they follow *dhamma* as explained by Aśoka. It is curious that there is repeated reference to heaven (*svarga*) but no reference to *nirvāṇa* or to transmigration. He argues that the purpose of the edicts is to elevate people through the observance of *dhamma* and he calls upon his specially appointed officers, the *dhamma-mahāmattas*, to explain *dhamma* to the people.

The propagation of *dhamma* is such a central concern that he denounces any interest in fame and glory and wishes only that his sons and grandsons will also advance *dhamma* (RE 4, 5, 6, 13; PE 7). It is when people follow *dhamma* that celestial beings and supernatural phenomena appear on earth (RE 4), a statement which is reminiscent of the earlier one referring to the gods associating with the people of Jambudvīpa when *dhamma* is prevalent. In the same edict where he expresses his remorse over the Kaliṅga campaign he expresses the hope that all future conquests will be by persuasion and *dhamma* and not by force and violence, a hope which is extended to the activities of his sons and grandsons; but he adds that should they have to use violence, their punishments should be light (RE 13). By the time of his twenty-seventh regnal year, when he issued the first Pillar Edict, he seemed fairly satisfied with the increase in the observance of *dhamma* and states '. . . For this is my principle: to protect through *dhamma*, to administer affairs according to *dhamma*, to please the people with *dhamma*, to guard the empire with *dhamma*.' This is the sentiment of a statesman and emperor, a man of power. His gradual obsession in the pillar edicts with what he was able to establish through *dhamma* begins to carry traces of what might have developed into an imperial cult.

The edicts are not concerned only with *dhamma*. There are substantial references to the administrative acts which bear on his perceptions of the state. He mentions the frequency of his going on tours so as to be in touch with his people (RE 8). His officers similarly have to travel and to make reports back to the king (RE 3). He declares his availability to the administration at all times irrespective of what he is doing (RE 6). He emphasizes judicial procedures and the need for impartiality before the law and introduces a respite of three days for those condemned to death. Doubtless the administrator in him did not permit the abolition of capital punishment in spite of the precepts of *dhamma*. His concern for the welfare of his subjects leads him to establish medical centres and to build an extensive network of roads lined with shady trees and interspersed with resthouses and wells (RE 2; PE 7).

The famous thirteenth Major Rock Edict, which carries his statement of remorse at the suffering caused by his campaign in Kaliṅga, is interestingly omitted in Kaliṅga itself. This and the fourteenth edict are replaced by two separate edicts which make no reference to his remorse. Possibly it was not considered politically apposite to make this confession to the people of Kaliṅga. Recently another discovery of the Separate Edicts was made at the site of Sannathi near Gulbarga in Karnataka. It remains unclear as to why this site was chosen for these edicts. The Separate Edicts are addressed to the officers of the Mauryan administration and call upon them to concern themselves with the welfare of the people. Tours of inspection are initiated and judicial officers are required to be impartial. The well-known statement that 'all men are my children' occurs in these edicts as well as the simile that the officers of the state are to the subjects as nurses are to children, looking after their well being.

The rock and pillar edicts also refer to a new category of officers instituted by Aśoka, whom he referred to as the *dhamma-mahāmattas* or officers of *dhamma* (RE 5, 12; PE 1, 7). Their functions were again linked to the welfare of his subjects. They were in part concerned with what would today be called 'the weaker sections of society' — the aged, the infirm, women and children. They were also sent on diplomatic missions to the neighbouring Hellenistic kingdoms of west Asia, for their major function was the propagation of *dhamma*. In this connection they were also required to attend to the welfare of various religious sects and among these are mentioned the *saṅgha, brāhmaṇas,* Ājīvikas and Nirgranthas. There is an insistence in the inscriptions that donations are to be made to all religious sects (RE 8, 12; PE 7). Royal patronage, it is generally assumed, if it is to be politically effective, should be impartial. Such an attempt at impartiality is suggested by the making of donations to religious sects without attention to the hostilities prevailing among them. The *dhamma-mahāmattas* appear to have been powerful officers with special privileges, possibly fully aware of their role in propagating an imperial ideology.

Historians over many decades have debated the question whether the *dhamma* of Aśoka amounted to a propagation of the Buddhist religion. Some have argued that it was because of the imperial patronage extended to Buddhism that it became a major religion. They argue that the teachings of the Buddha were referred to as the Dhamma and that Aśoka was using the word in the identical sense. Others have taken a different position arguing that there is nothing specifically Buddhist in the *dhamma* as defined by Aśoka, for the same ethical teachings are to be found in various brahmanical Hindu sects.

To narrow the meaning of Aśokan *dhamma* to the teachings of a single religious sect is perhaps to do an injustice both to Aśoka and to the concept of *dhamma* as it prevailed at that time. The general code of ethics and rules of behaviour as defined by Aśoka are certainly familiar to Buddhist teaching and occur in Buddhist scripture. However, it needs to be kept in mind that such ideas are not unknown to Jaina teaching nor to various other śramanic sects which were popular during that period. Aśoka may well have used the phraseology from the teachings which he knew best, but at the same time it was part of the currency of ethical norms propounded by various teachers. The Aśokan *dhamma* not only addressed itself to a large spectrum of opinion but drew its inspiration from an equally large body of ethical doctrine. His insistence on the honouring of all sects and his careful withdrawal from specifying particular loyalties would be an indication of this. This becomes even more pertinent in a situation where there were sectarian hostilities and antagonisms. His repetitive emphasis on the need for tolerance is suggestive of a situation where such tolerance was largely absent. The phrase that donations were to be made to *brāhmaṇas* and *śramaṇas* is not a restrictive request referring only to the *brāhmaṇa* caste and the Buddhist monks. The compound was probably used to cover a variety of brahmanical and śramanic sects. That he himself made such donations is clear not only from the references to donations in the edicts but also from the fact that he made a major donation to the Ājīvika sect even though the relations between Ājīvikas and the Buddhists were not cordial. His references to heaven rather than to *nirvāṇa* or to transmigration were also addressed to this larger body of belief.

The functions of *dhamma-mahāmattas* are a further indication of this wider concern. They are instructed to look to the welfare of all sects and the ones listed are quite diverse and some such as the Jainas and Ājīvikas were disapproved of by the Buddhist *saṅgha*. The Jainas on their side included the *Buddhasāsana* among what they regarded as the products of false knowledge. The *dhamma-mahāmattas* are also expected to explain *dhamma* to the various people in whose welfare they are involved. The officers of the administration are given the same instructions. It is curious that no mention is made of *bhikkhus* being associated in this work. If it had been the intention of the emperor to propagate the teachings of a particular religious sect then surely the functionaries of that sect would have been associated with explaining its teachings. Even more telling is the fact that in the Aramaic and Greek inscriptions the word *dhamma* is translated as 'good conduct' in the one case and as 'pious conduct' in the other with no reference to Buddhist doctrine. Aśoka informs us that there are no *brāhmaṇas* and *śramaṇas* among the Yona (RE 13), the Hellenized kingdoms. If he was concerned with the propagation of Buddhism it would have been more effective to have specifically stated this.

The discussion on what constitutes *dhamma* was at this time the prevailing concern among a variety of religious and philosophical sects, which are referred to in the Aśokan edicts as *pāsaṇḍa* or *diatribe*. The brahmanical concept of *dharma* in the sense of sacred duty included the observances of rituals and sacrifices as well as social conduct in accordance with the rules of *varṇa-aśrama-dharma*, where the notion of the separate rules of caste activities was clearly delineated. The ascetic sects of the *śramaṇas* either questioned these rituals or substituted others for them. Thus many disapproved of animal sacrifice but the worship of trees was regarded as appropriate. Behaviour according to the rules of the four castes received scant attention among the śramanic sects, where the rules of social class were seen as the actual ordering of society relating as they did more closely to kinship and occupation. The śramanic sects favoured a universalizing ethic which cut across caste demarcations. The wandering ascetics, drawn from both brahmanical and śramanic sects, taught the importance of *dāna-dhamma* (charity) and *soca-dhamma* (purity), the precise terms referred to among the requirements of Aśoka's definition of *dhamma*. It would seem therefore that Aśoka was participating in the wider discussion of what constituted *dhamma*, was providing his own views in the edicts, and was clearly more sympathetic to the general śramanic definition, although at the same time emphasizing that as the ruler of a vast domain his patronage extended even to sects such as some of the brahmanical ones which did not necessarily endorse this definition. Aśoka's *dhamma*, it would seem, provided an ideology of persuasive assimilation. It arose as much from his personal conviction of Buddhist teaching as from the wider discussion of ethical precepts and from the demands of imperial policy.

That the larger corpus of edicts were the pronouncements of political authority is also evident from the title used by Aśoka. He does not refer to himself as *rājā* of Magadha but calls himself *Devānampiya*, 'the Beloved of the Gods.' The notion of a connection between divinity and kingship was familiar to brahmanical thinking particularly in the tradition of major sacrificial rituals associating kingship with divinity. It was, however, alien to much of the śramanic notions associated with political power. The indirect legitimation which Aśoka seeks from deities and celestial beings would have had a popular comprehension but may have been difficult to justify in the ideological framework of those sects for whom deities were irrelevant.

In arguing that we have to distinguish between Aśoka as the individual with his personal beliefs and Aśoka performing the function of a royal statesman, the attempt is not to reduce the importance of the former but to insist that his policies, even if motivated by personal reasons, would have had a public repercussion and would have to be conditioned by public reaction. Aśoka used the symbols of Buddhism but saw his role in the context of a broader ideology. Such an argument requires the historian to look beyond the symbols. Thus donations, *dāna*, are at one level voluntary offerings made out of a sense of piety for the acquisition of merit, *puṇya*. At another level donations build institutions. In the context of governance, institutions can become centres of loyalty or otherwise, depending on the nature and the recipient of the donation. Welfare can also relate to piety but an imperial concern with welfare in the context of differentiated identities and economies can also speak to ideological concerns.

Aśoka's personal commitment to Buddhism and the royal patronage which he extended to it doubtless helped to establish it in various parts of the subcontinent and in the neighbouring areas. The association with Sri Lanka was not only personal but very close, both in the sending of Mahinda and in his relations with Devānampiya Tissa. But even royal patronage has its limitations. It is interesting that in the post-Mauryan period both Buddhism and Jainism were evident in Karnataka and Tamil Nadu, but despite the strong Mauryan presence in Karnataka, Jainism was the more dominant of the two. Elsewhere, as in northwestern India and the western and eastern Deccan, it is Buddhism which more rapidly becomes the established religion. In such areas Buddhist sacred centres develop along trade routes and in urban settlements linked to commerce. Inscriptional evidence points to the fact that the establishment of Buddhism in these areas probably owes more to the *seṭṭhi-gahapatis*, the merchants, traders, landowners and the artisanal guilds, who were all dedicated supporters of the religion and the more significant donors to the embellishment of the sacred centres.

It was during this period that the Buddhist tradition began to reflect on the relationship between Aśoka and Buddhism — a reflection which, as has been rightly pointed out, endorsed the *cakkavatti* ideal of universal kingship in Buddhist thought. Possibly the political role of Aśoka was appropriated by the tradition to a greater degree than historical reality permitted. But at the same time this reflection did underline the social idealism of Aśoka's policies, which however were set within an imperial framework. Ideology can be a driving force of history but it is not a sufficient cause of history. Nevertheless, Aśoka's ideology did make of him an emperor of rare quality in as much as he reached out to more than mundane politics.

# 21

# *Literacy and Communication: Some Thoughts on the Inscriptions of Aśoka*

Given the absence of an acceptable decipherment of the Indus script, the inscriptions of the Mauryan ruler Aśoka are the earliest documentation which can be described as contemporary written historical evidence. It has become conventional now to treat the Vedic corpus as marking the beginning of Indian history in the sense that it is a documentation of a period prior to that of Aśoka, even though it began as an oral tradition and claimed to have remained so until the second millennium AD. Whether this was actually so is controversial, and no documentation has survived from this early period. The Brahmanical tradition emphasises *śruti* and *smṛti*, orality and memory, and has little place for the written word. In terms therefore of an actual text in writing, the earliest evidence is that of the Mauryan period.

The inscriptions mark the transition from orality to literacy although the precise point at which this actually happened remains somewhat uncertain. One view maintains that the use of a script goes back to the fifth century BC with a reference to writing in Pāṇini,[1] but another view holds that the script was invented by the Mauryas to facilitate administration. Inevitably the answer is not a simple one. What is clear is that the invention of a script precedes the reign of Aśoka in the third century BC, and that it is connected with the use of writing both in India at that time and in the neighbouring areas. Without going too far back in time, we know that the Achaemenids were using Aramaic and that various Semitic scripts were also current in west Asian and eastern Mediterranean trade. Parts of north-western India were included in the Achaemenid empire prior to their inclusion in the Mauryan empire and would therefore have already had some familiarity with both the Aramaic language and the script. A script facilitates the administration of an empire as it enables faster communication with officers and subjects in distant places and frontier zones. Similarly the use of a script by traders encourages long distance trade as well as more complex mechanisms of exchange given that literacy allows of the use of promissory notes and letters of credit.

The Aśokan inscriptions use four different scripts and three different languages. The larger number of inscriptions, composed in Prākrit are inscribed in *brāhmī* and these are found in various parts of the subcontinent. A smaller number of inscriptions in Prākrit are also inscribed in *kharoṣṭhī*, and are concentrated in the north-western part of the subcontinent. Scattered in this area are also a few inscriptions in Greek and Aramaic, in both the script and the language. This familiarity with specific scripts for particular areas points to their use in this region prior to Aśoka and in the case of Aramaic we know that it was used prior to the Mauryas. However Greek sources are divided in their ascription of literacy and non-literacy to Indians. Greek observers who either accompanied Alexander such as Nearchos or else visited India as envoys of the Hellenistic kingdoms such as Megasthenes, have made contradictory statements. The former speaks of processed cotton as a surface for writing whereas the latter states explicitly that the Indians do not know the art of writing.[2] A number of suggestions can be made. Could it be that north Indians were using *kharoṣṭhī* and this was not regarded as an Indian script since it was derived from Aramaic. The widespread use of *brāhmī* for official purposes may have occurred after the visit of Megasthenes, particularly if his visit can be dated to the decade after the accession of Candragupta Maurya as has been suggested.[3] This would provide a time span of two generations for the propagation of *brāhmī* at least among the Mauryan officials. It could also have been picked up from trading groups who might have been using it on a lesser scale which would however suggest an earlier date for the script. Since the Separate Edicts of Aśoka mention the reading out of the edicts to the public by officials, such facility with literacy may well have required two generations or more. The question still remains as to whether *kharoṣṭhī* was adapted for the north-west where there was a familiarity with Aramaic or whether the evolving of *kharoṣṭhī* preceded *brāhmī* which then came to be used in other areas?

Some of the Aramaic inscriptions were probably composed well into the reign of Aśoka. These have been read as incorporating Aramaic glosses which refer to the subject matter of the Prākrit inscriptions. Words which earlier had been thought to be Iranian were later read as renderings of Prākrit expressions with cross-references to Prākrit inscriptions.[4] If these readings are acceptable then it would suggest that those who composed the Aramaic inscriptions, were familiar with or had a master copy of both the Major Rock Edicts and the Pillar Edicts. Such Aramaic inscriptions would therefore be partially bi-lingual. This would not be surprising in an area where Prākrit and Aramaic were both spoken and possibly some of the urban population was bilingual in these languages. Those likely to be bilingual would be either employees of the state or those belonging to more outgoing professions such as commerce.

There is a long gap between the use of the Harappan script (incidentally also as an inscription at Dholavira), and the inscriptions of Aśoka. The systems on which the two scripts are based are quite different. The Harappan is probably pictographic and possibly also logographic and homophenous. The scripts used for the Aśokan inscriptions are all phonetic. A pictographic script has the advantage that it can carry a meaning for speakers of more than the single language, provided that the interpretation of the pictograms is clear. A phonetic script relates to a single language. The shift then is from the graphic to the abstract. Perhaps this is reflected in the use of the two words referring to writing in the inscriptions. The term *lipi* from the root * *lip-* 'to smear', carries the connotation of the visual, whereas * *likh-* 'to scratch or scrape', is more suggestive of writing and has also been associated with the Old Persian *ni-pish* 'to write.'[5] The *kharoṣṭhī* inscription at Shahbazgarhi in the north-west replaces the usual Prākrit word *likha* with *nipesa*.[6]

*Kharoṣṭhī* is written from right to left and *brāhmī* from left to right. This might suggest two different sources for these scripts. The former is confined to the north-west where it seems to be the normal script for Prākrit. The recently found fragment of an Aśokan edict in *brāhmī* from Buner, which, if it is not a fake, provides evidence of the use of *brāhmī* in the area, although probably on a limited scale.[7] That *brāhmī* was not unknown here is evident from the coins from Taxila bearing legends in *brāhmī* and *kharoṣṭhī*.[8] If *kharoṣṭhī* had originated in being a Mauryan adaptation of Aramaic for purposes of administrative efficiency or, that the Aśokan edicts had been merely an imitation of the Achaemenid inscriptions, then it is likely that it would have been used throughout the Mauryan empire. The use of Greek and Aramaic was even more limited to areas where it would seem there were either bi-lingual populations as suggested by the bi-lingual inscriptions at Kandahar, or at least substantial numbers speaking and possibly reading, the two languages. In the borderlands between the Achaemenid and Mauryan empires it was important to address subjects in their own languages. Furthermore an attempt was also made to use the idioms and metaphors of the particular language speakers.[9] This concession may have been made because these were regions with established states and a tradition of literacy going back to the earliest Achaemenid inscriptions of the sixth century BC. Juxtaposed with this was the use of Greek in the Hellenistic kingdoms which succeeded the Achaemenid empire.

This concession is in striking contrast to the uniform use of Prākrit in peninsular India. Prior to and in some cases perhaps contemporary with the inscriptions of Aśoka, was the occurrence of Megalithic graffiti, occasionally reminiscent of the Indus script, on pottery from Megalithic sites.[10] This does not appear to have been a phonetic script and may have therefore been ignored, a phonetic script having now become the hallmark of culture. Aśokan *brāhmī* would nevertheless have been an intrusion here. The cluster of inscriptions in Karnataka were in Dravidian-speaking areas yet the inscriptions are in Prākrit and no concession is made to the local language. The inscriptions were therefore probably only accessible to the officials who were required to read them out and doubtless translate them to the local population. The population in these areas did not belong to pre-established states or kingdoms and the intention was not to communicate directly. More likely the intention was to make a statement of power in an oral society and this is perhaps how the inscriptions were also viewed. This was inspite of the contents of the inscriptions focussing on the well-being of the subjects and the teaching of *dhamma*. That the *brāhmī* script could have been adapted to a Dravidian language was demonstrated soon after the reign of Aśoka in the multiplicity of Tamil-*brāhmī* inscriptions. In fact the borrowing of *brāhmī* for both Tamil and for inscriptions in Sri Lanka appears to have been a parallel to the borrowing from Aramaic in the creating of *kharoṣṭhī*.

The use of Prākrit and *brāhmī* in other parts of the Mauryan empire conformed to the locally spoken language. The inscriptions even if not directly read by the population would not have required translation by those reading them.

The extensive use of *brāhmī* in the subcontinent did not follow a rigidly composed original. The language and the script was pliant and reflected to some degree the influence of local dialects. The edicts were issued by the king, either from the capital or from the royal camp wherever he might have been, but were adapted to some manifestations of local language use. This is seen most evidently in the alternative use of 'l' for 'r'. The north-west dialect retains 'r' as do some inscriptions elsewhere, but at Kalsi and in eastern India 'l' replaces 'r'. Dialect variations in a script would suggest that there was some care taken with transcribing local forms and possibly the Prākrit language and the *brāhmī* script were more familiar to central and eastern India than, for example, to Karnataka. At the latter place the dialect forms suggest variant master copies of the texts. The Major Rock Edicts at Yerragudi and Sannati replace 'r' by 'l', and since Prākrit was not the local language, this would suggest that the engraver of the inscription was from eastern India. But the Separate Edicts at Sannati retain the 'r'.[11] Was the engraver of the Separate Edicts different from the one who inscribed the Major Rock Edicts even though the texts are placed on different sides of the same stone slab? It has been argued that the Separate Edicts at Sannati may have been based on a different master copy of the text from that used for Dhauli and Jaugada in eastern India.[12] The incorporation of dialect variations, suggesting a certain confidence in registering such variations, would point to an earlier use of the script.

Three inscriptions in this area — at Brahmagiri, Siddapur and Jatinga-Rameshwar — give the name of the engraver as Capaḍa. Doubtless he added his name in order to underline his own identity and importance, anticipating a formula which was to become common in inscriptions of a later period. He added the word, *lipikareṇa*, thus confirming his profession, but interestingly this word is engraved in *kharoṣṭhī*, whereas the inscriptions are in *brāhmī*. At Yerragudi, where there is no mention of Capaḍa, some of the lines are written from right to left. Was this an attempt at boustrophedon or was it a moment of lapse on the part of the engraver, more proficient in *kharoṣṭhī* than in *brāhmī*? Were the engravers brought from north-western India or was this an accomplished engraver who was showing his knowledge of *kharoṣṭhī* as well?

The inscriptions in *brāhmī* have occasional linguistic mistakes or variations, perhaps arising from having to copy a written text.[13] Letters which get missed out are inserted in an obvious way, later. There are minor variations in spelling, or in words, as for example, *peteṇika, pitenika, pitinika*; or where *rāño* in the Shahbazgarhi versions occurs as *lājine* in the Kalsi version. Syllables get obliterated or else superfluous strokes are added to the letters. Some variations occur in constructions, as for example where *so sukataṃ kāsati* (Girnar) occurs as *se sukaṭaṃ kacchaṃti* (Kalsi), or as in the Minor Rock Edict, *pākāsa ke* (Rupnath), *budhaśake* (Maski), *upāsake* (Brahmagiri, etc.). The Prākrit of the north-western inscriptions is not identical with that of other regions. Such changes could suggest that the engraver was not as literate as the scribe who wrote the original text, even if the text was dictated by the king, or that the local scribe was incorporating changes which would make the text more familiar to those who either read it themselves or had it read out to them. Kauṭilya insists on high qualifications for the scribe who should not only be quick in composing but should have a clear handwriting, and should give appropriate attention to the format of the contents.[14]

It would seem that an entire set of inscriptions need not have been always engraved by a single person as there is occasional variation in the style of writing, as has been noticed for the Major Rock Edicts at Girnar.[15] This is more evident in the Delhi Topra Pillar Edicts where the seventh edict appears to be an addition recorded only on this pillar. The pillar inscriptions however, engraved later in the reign of Aśoka, show a distinct improvement in the script which would indicate either a greater experience by now of engraving the script or the polished sandstone pillars providing a better surface for engraving. The angular forms of the Rock inscriptions now gave way to the more rounded letters of the pillar inscriptions. The Pillar Edicts were engraved either on pre-existing pillars *in situ* and therefore from an earlier period or else recently worked monoliths.

The locations of the inscriptions could provide some clues as to their function. Would familiarity with literacy be a factor in choosing a location? Or were the inscriptions intended for public readings in which case they would be located where people would gather?

The positioning would have to be prominent in either case so as to draw adequate attention to them. Locations commemorating an event would be neutral to literacy or orality, as for example, the Rummindei inscription at the site of the Buddha's birthplace and the Nigalisagar inscription at the site of the Konakamana *stūpa*. These were records of actions intended to enhance the merit gained by the king and to impress the Buddhist fraternity. Similarly edicts at monastic sites, such as Sarnath, Kosam and Sanchi and at Bairat, carried a specific message for the Buddhist Saṅgha and were statements on how the king viewed his relationship with the Saṅgha both at a personal level and as the reigning monarch.

The inscriptions are often clustered in what may be called the core areas of the empire, as for example, the region of Gandhāra in the north-west and Karnataka in the south. These were areas distinct from the nucleus or the metropolitan state of Magadha, but nevertheless potentially important and administratively more complex than the peripheral areas. There are to date fewer inscriptions in Magadha, perhaps because it was small enough and administered under the direct control of the court so that communication was closer. The more scattered inscriptions appear to have been at nodal points along routes such as the ones in north Bihar, or the ones at Ahraura, Rupnath and Panguraria along the route continuing to either Sopara or Amarāvatī. The location of inscriptions on pillars was also in part determined by the use in some cases of pillars which already existed. Such pillars were viewed as significant in themselves and may even have been under worship in association with *stūpas* and *caityas*.

Both locations and pillars also came to acquire a certain reverence as documents from the past, even if in later times the script could not be read. Girnar in the vicinity of Junagadh is an example of locational importance. Girnar was the site of a set of the Major Rock Edicts inscribed with care and a good balance of space on a rock face. Later inscriptions from the time of Rudradāman and of Skandagupta inform us that the Mauryas had constructed a dam at the site, which had twice been breached and the repairs occasioned the later records.[16] The later inscriptions do not refer to the Aśokan edicts but evidently some information on the building of the dam was recorded locally and the dam provided a link with earlier administrations. The Allahabad-Kosam Pillar, shifted from the ancient site of Kauśāmbi to the fort at Allahabad, is almost a notebook of historical records with later inscriptions, some interlinear. Of major significance is an important statement on the conquests of Samudragupta[17] and still later a brief inscription associated with Jahangir. The historical importance of the pillar was recognised irrespective of whether the earlier inscriptions could be read. Possibly the pillar attracted a more complex symbolism than just a document from the past. The Sarnath Pillar also has later inscriptions but one pertains to a Buddhist sect probably resident at the monastery and another to a king whose identity remains obscure.[18] The Lauriya-Nandangarh Pillar carries a brief inscription in Persian giving the titles and a date for the Mughal emperor Aurangzeb. The Barabar Caves donated to the Ājīvika sect, appear to have been used regularly by other sects in later times and carry inscriptions of the seventh century Maukhari rulers. Inscribed surfaces attracted curiosity and even reverence on occasion, as the inscriptions on these pillars would suggest. But this did not preclude the deliberate vandalising of Aśokan inscriptions in later times, as is indicated by the stone-slab inscription at Sannati. This was cut and used as a *pīṭha* for an image in a temple. Given the destruction of the Buddhist site at Sannati, it is thought that there was a confrontation between the Buddhists and the Śaivas.

Whether or not the script could be read in later centuries, some associations with the inscriptions appears to have been known. The pillars with their various capitals seem to have constituted a form of visual literacy. The symbolism of the capitals would have been recognised, particularly where Buddhists in the neighbourhood would have claimed to know the explanation. What then was being encoded in this pictorial form? The intentions of the author may have been forgotten when the script could no longer be read. But the change of surface from rocks to finely polished pillars is not unconnected with the intentions of the author. Whereas earlier Aśoka was anxious to propagate his ideas and have his edicts inscribed on whatever surface was available, the Pillar Edicts coming towards the latter part of his reign suggest a concern with providing an appropriate form for the propagation of his ideas. The specially constructed pillars conveyed the authority of the emperor, which is doubtless what later rulers recognised when they used the pillars for their own inscriptions. But at the same time, the symbols were pointing to the authority of the message as well. The Pillar Edicts are in part a retrospective on Aśoka's activities in which the effectiveness of his endorsement of *dhamma* was a central issue. It becomes almost like the transmission of a code.

The intentions of the author were doubtless many. At one level it was a wish to speak to his subjects and this involved a recognition of the power of orality. The edicts are couched in a spoken style. There is both a repetition of phrases as well as of the structure of ideas. The essential message for a literate audience reading the texts could have been considerably reduced in length, but for an audience listening to these edicts, it was necessary to repeat the essential ideas. The formulaic opening, *devānampiyo piyadassi rājā evam āha . . .* (Thus speaks the Beloved of the Gods, the King Piyadassi . . . .) stresses the orality of the texts. The Achaemenid kings also 'spoke' to their subjects through their inscriptions, but their style was formal and their claims somewhat forbidding. The tone of the Aśokan inscriptions is more conversational and they could have been a bridge from the oral to the literate. This is also suggestive of the idea that Aśoka was dictating the edicts to a scribe. Yet his use of the written form is so pertinent that it would be hard to believe that he himself was not literate. This is demonstrated in the Fourteenth Rock Edict where he mentions that the message of *dhamma* has been inscribed in various lengths and forms, and states that because his realm is vast there is much that has already been engraved but also much that is yet to be engraved.[19] This awareness of the importance of literacy may also have been due to the ambience of Buddhism which recognised the function of literacy. The Brahmanical insistence on *śruti* and *smṛti* could have had the effect of discouraging literacy among those who were not the keepers of the tradition but the receivers of the tradition. The concern of the Buddhist Saṅgha to record the teachings of the Buddha and maintain a tradition, made literacy a significant component of the qualifications of a respected monk. How literate the average monk or nun may have been remains uncertain. In the Bhabhra Edict where Aśoka recommends certain segments of the Buddhist teaching he requires both the religious orders and the laity to *hear* these sermons and meditate on them.[20]

The various audiences to whom the edicts are addressed is apparent from the statements in the text. The major part of the edicts are addressed to the public at large, but a few have more specific audiences. One category is addressed to the Buddhist Saṅgha and these are exhortations, sometimes seeming to be orders. In the

Sarnath Pillar edict, dissident monks and nuns were to be expelled and interestingly copies of this edict were made available to the *upāsakas* or lay followers who were required to endorse the order. This would suggest that some at least of the lay followers were sufficiently literate to be able to act on the order.

The Separate Edicts are addressed to the senior officials, the *kumāras* and the *mahāmattas* of specific places such as Tosali and Samāpa in Kaliṅga and perhaps to the *kumāras* of Ujjain and Taxila.[21] The contents of these inscriptions are instructions to the officers not only to proclaim the edicts, but also to ensure the well-being of the people under their care. Until recently the Separate Edicts were thought to be located only in Kaliṅga and this made a neat argument, since Kaliṅga was the location of a major campaign and the Separate Edicts seem to register concern for the people disrupted by the campaign. Recently a version of these edicts was also found on the stone-slab at Sannati. Was there also a campaign in this region, (perhaps to annexe the lucrative Raichur doab), which required the comforting message of the Separate Edicts? But there is no reference to such a campaign in any of the inscriptions. Or was this the result of a *faux pas* on the part of an official who unwittingly had these special edicts inscribed at Sannati? It could also be suggested that perhaps the Separate Edicts were sent to the southern province, irrespective of their actual relevance to a campaign. Their function was to provide the necessary assurances of good government and welfare from the distant monarch in an area where the existing society of chiefdoms and peripheral economies may have sometimes obstructed the thrust of the imperial system aiming at controlling resources.

That the edicts are required to be read out to the public is stated unambiguously. This is part of the attempt of the author to 'speak' to the people where the officer is the proxy for the king. This would be an attempt at explaining the benefits of Mauryan rule to the local population as well as empowering them to appeal to the distant monarch should these benefits be denied them, an empowerment which probably remained at the level of intention and was obviously ineffective in practice. Nevertheless the physical fact of a royal edict was still more tangible than the assurances of an official. The edict transmitted the king's view more fully, and was regarded as more authentic. In the constructing of an empire from diverse groups, and where campaigning has been forsworn, the alternative is persuasion. The Separate Edicts are a further extension of a propagation through persuasion. The ideology of this persuasion can be used to soften the peripheral areas and to align the core areas to the objectives of the metropolitan state.

Edicts in the form of inscriptions are also conducive to a certain universalism and continuity. Inspite of the diversity within the Mauryan empire, a diversity which is reflected in the language and script of the inscriptions themselves, the fact that a body of texts were available in every part of the empire would at least have encouraged the notion of a common ideology of persuasion. The *mahāmattas* who were accustomed to explaining the edicts in one part of the empire would have been adept at doing so in another area as well. This may have been required of the *yuttās*, *rājūkas* and *prādeśikas* when they went on their quinquennial tours.[22] In such a context, the uniformity of judicial proceedings and punishments, referred to in the Fourth Pillar Edict, may not have been totally unrealistic.[23]

The factor of continuity relates both to a sense of time and to the perception of the future. The edicts introduce a new form of time reckoning when they speak of the number of regnal years that have passed. The dating of the Major Rock Edicts and the Pillar Edicts is accurate on this count. Reckoning in regnal years is seminal to the notion of an era and this in turn is necessary to a linear concept of time. Cosmological time in both the Brahmanical and Buddhist tradition was cyclic. The introduction of even an element of linear time was a departure. Possibly this departure was not unrelated to the simultaneous use of literacy in proclamations. Linear time in turn emphasises the distinction between the past and the future, a distinction which is constant in the edicts. The activities of past rulers are found to be wanting and are replaced with activities associated with the *dhamma*. Virtually the last statement available to us is the wish of Aśoka that his sons and great grandsons follow the *dhamma* and act accordingly as long as the sun and the moon endure.[24] Their knowledge of the *dhamma* could have come to them from the easily accessible oral tradition filtered through the thoughts of those maintaining the tradition. That it was now also available in a corpus of texts as constituted by Aśoka's edicts, would ensure that this knowledge as perceived by Aśoka would also be accessible to them, even if filtered through their reading of the texts.

Literacy therefore was not a common qualification during the Mauryan period. It was required of certain categories of people such as the officers of the Mauryan administration and the more learned monks and *brāhmaṇas*. The *brāhmaṇa* learned in the *Vedas* continued to be described as a *śrotriya*. The Buddhist tradition appears to differ from the Brahmanical in its endorsement of literacy. However such traditions were not uniform. If the Brahmanical texts had strong links with orality, there was also the grammar of Pāṇini which, it has been argued by some scholars, could not have been composed in a non-literate context. But this remains a controversial question. Inscriptions as a different body of texts were not only an indication of literacy but the sheer fact of literacy combined with their authorship carried another message relating to state power.

This introduces another dimension to the meaning of texts as is further evident in post-Mauryan inscriptions. Because inscriptions are documents, some of which record the acts of a king and others the bestowal of patronage of various kinds, the nature of the document becomes an adjunct to the fact of literacy. Frequently, royal inscriptions are the official version of royal activities and as such the notion of state power is closely integrated into the text. The intention of relating the substance of the text to the power and authority of the author continues in later inscriptions, although the forms diversify, ranging from *praśastis* or eulogies on particular kings to recording the grant of land to a *brāhmaṇa*. This more specific function is evident through a change of tone in the text where the king is no longer 'speaking' to his subjects but is recording an action. This is re-iterated by a change in the language. The commonly spoken Prākrit gives way to the more formal Sanskrit and gradually even the Sanskrit is of such complexity that the usual literacy would not suffice in understanding it. These inscriptions were not intended to be read by the populace or even be read to them: they were intended as documentary records. Such documents were doubtless an administrative necessity but they were perhaps also motivated by concerns with perceptions of the past and continuity in the future.

## Notes and References

1. V.S. Agrawala, *India as Known to Panini*, Varanasi, 1963 (2nd ed.), 312ff, 469. A recent excavation at Anuradhapur in Sri Lanka brought

up pot sherds with *brāhmī* graffiti from a level which has been dated to the fifth century BC. This would suggest a far earlier date for *brāhmī* than has been considered so far. Some maintain that the date of the layer from which the sherds were obtained is not certain.

2. L. Gopal, 'Early Greek Writers on Writing in India', *Proceedings of the Indian History Congress*, 1976, 544–52.
3. A.B. Bosworth, *A Historical Commentary on Arrian's History of Alexander*, Oxford, 1995.
4. W.B. Henning, 'The Aramaic Inscription of Aśoka found at Lampāka', *BSOAS*, 1949, 13.1.80–8; E. Benveniste et al., 'Une Inscription Indo-araméenne d'Aśoka provenant de Kandahar (Afghanistan)', *Journale Asiatique*, 1966, vol. 254, Fas 3–4, pp. 437–70.
5. E. Hultzsch, *Corpus Inscriptionum Indicarum*, I, London, 1888–1925, p. xxx.
6. J. Bloch, *Les Inscriptions d'Asoka*, Paris, 1955, 133.
7. K.R. Norman, 'A Newly Found Fragment of an Aśokan Inscription', *South Asian Studies*, 1988, 4, 99–102.
8. J. Allan, *A Catalogue of the Indian Coins in the British Museum*, Coins of Ancient India, London, 1967, cxxv ff, 214–15.
9. Romila Thapar, 'Epigraphic Evidence and Some Indo-Hellenistic Contacts during the Mauryan Period', in S.K. Maity and V. Thakur (eds), *Indological Studies*, Professor D.C. Sircar Commemoration Volume, New Delhi, 1987, 15–19. *See* chapter 22 in this volume.
10. B.B. Lal, 'From the megalithic to the Harappa: tracing back the graffiti on the pottery', *Ancient India*, 1962, 16, 4–24.
11. K.R. Norman, 'Aśokan Inscriptions from Sannati', *South Asian Studies*, 1991, 7, 101–10.
12. K.V. Ramesh, 'The Aśokan Inscriptions at Sannathi', *Indian Historical Review*, 1987–88, 14, 1–2, 36–42.
13. E. Hultzsch, *Corpus Inscriptionum Indicarum*, I, London, 1888–1925, see Major Rock Edicts V, X, XIII, XIV, Minor Rock Edicts, Pillar Edict II. Bloch, op. cit., 102, 103, 125, 145.
14. *Arthaśāstra*, 2.10.
15. C.S. Upasak, *The History and Palaeography of the Mauryan Brahmi Script*, Nalanda, 1960, 132, 195ff. It is possible that used as we are today to the print medium, we expect far greater uniformity than would normally occur in an engraved text of an early period.
16. Junagarh Rock Inscription of Rudradaman, AD 150. D.C. Sircar, *Select Inscriptions . . .*, Calcutta, 1965 (2nd ed.), 175ff. Junagarh Rock Inscription of Skandagupta, Fifth century AD, ibid., 307ff.
17. Allahabad Stone Pillar Inscription of Samudragupta, Fourth century AD, D.C. Sircar, op. cit., 262ff.
18. Epigraphical Discoveries at Sarnath, *Epigraphia Indica*, VIII, 171ff.

19. Bloch, op. cit., 133.
20. Bloch, op. cit., 154–5.
21. Bloch, op. cit., 136ff. K.V. Ramesh, op. cit.
22. Bloch, op. cit., 96.
23. Bloch, op. cit., 164.
24. Seventh Pillar Edict, Bloch, op. cit., 172.

# 22

# Epigraphic Evidence and Some Indo-Hellenistic Contacts During the Mauryan Period*

Contacts between the Mauryas and the Hellenistic world require renewed scrutiny in the light of fresh evidence and argument. The campaign of Alexander of Macedon in northern India marks a turning point not in terms of conquest but rather in the changes which brought Hellenistic West Asia into dialogue with India. Overland links with Persia and maritime links via the Gulf go back to earlier times, at least to that of the Achaemenids as evident from literary and epigraphical sources and still further back as attested by archaeology. Such links were probably not sporadic and even if the evidence remains restricted it is possible that they were maintained at a substratum level until they surfaced in the post-Alexander period.

Close contacts in the historical period begin with the Achaemenids who claimed the trans-Indus region of the Indian subcontinent as part of their empire and received a tribute in the form of gold dust from these areas.[1] This is reflected in the association of the contiguous regions with *yona rājās* in the Aśokan inscriptions. Achaemenid sources claim to include Sind as well.[2] The evidence of Indian soldiers and of Indian elephants in the army of Darius III at the famous battle of Arbela would point to some control over Indian territories. Curiously however the excavation of Bhir Mound at Taxila does not provide any major evidence of an Achaemenid presence. That there was a presence is however suggested by the Aramaic inscriptions of Aśoka.[3] On the other hand, a senior dignitary of Saurāṣṭra in the Mauryan period carries the unmistakably

* From S.K. Maity and U. Thakur (eds), *Indological Studies*, New Delhi, 1987.

Persian name of Tuṣāspa, suggesting that the Achaemenid claim to Sind may have included Saurāṣṭra.

The potentiality of India as an area of resources and raw materials conducive to trade was recognized by the Achaemenids. The expedition of Skylax was not motivated only by military concerns.[4] It established the route down the lower Indus and Skylax might have sailed as far as the southern end of the Red Sea. That it took thirteen months might have been due to a long wait at the Indus delta for favourable ocean currents and winds. Nearchus, returning with some of Alexander's forces, is said to have waited for some time, prior to sailing, suggesting that at least those navigators who sailed to the Gulf may have known of the monsoon.[5] Possibly the use of it for the south Arabian ports was also known, but came to be used more extensively at a later period. Herodotus adds that subsequent to the voyage of Skylax, Darius conquered India and made use of the sea in those parts.

Mauryan contacts with the Hellenistic kingdoms of West Asia and North Africa are of course well known. Greek sources refer to the confrontation between Candragupta Maurya and Seleukus Nikator, the founder of the Seleukid dynasty. By a treaty in *c.* 303 BC the Mauryas acquired territory in Afghanistan and possibly a wider area including Baluchistan and Makran and became the neighbours of the Seleukids.[6] Aśoka in his Thirteenth Major Rock Edict refers to the missions which he has sent to the five *yona rājās*, the Greek kings of the area. The mention of these five kings has its own historical interest.[7] Three among them were major powers, namely, Antiochus the Seleukid, Antogonus of Macedonia and Ptolemy II Philadelphus of Egypt. What remains a puzzle are the lesser two, Magas of Cyrene and Alexander of either Korinth or Epirus and the reason why they, from among the many states of the eastern Mediterranean were included. Perhaps the answer lies in the marriage relations among them, which gave them the appearance almost of an extended family! The five kings were also part of a political network and were not just a casual collection of neighbours to the west.

Antiochus I, the son of Seleukus was related to both the Macedonians and the Ptolemies. His half-sister was married to Antigonus and his daughter-in-law was the daughter of Ptolemy Philadelphus. Antigonus of Macedon had a sister-in-law from Cyrene and a brother-in-law from Korinth. His daughter-in-law on the death of his son, married Alexander of Korinth who was also the nephew of Antigonus. Ptolemy Philadelphus' son married the daughter of Magas of Cyrene. These marriage links might explain the importance to Aśoka of Cyrene and Korinth where Cyrene was in the Ptolemaic area of influence and both Korinth and Epirus in the Macedonian. It is likely that the Alikaṣudala of the Aśokan inscription was Alexander of Epirus since Alexander of Korinth did not come to the throne until 252 BC and therefore after this particular edict had been issued.[8]

Partly because of the hostility between the three major Hellenistic kings there was a tendency for their power to wax and wane. Thus the marriage of Berenike, the Ptolemy princess, to Antiochus II buttressed the weakening Seleukids with financial support from the prosperous Ptolemies: a prosperity which increased subsequently with the exploitation not only of peasant labour for agriculture in the Nile valley but also the expeditions along the Red Sea and links with Ethiopia and southern Arabia if not even further.[9] The closeness of the Ptolemies and the Mauryas may have had to do with some incipient trade relations. A version of the Major Rock Edicts of Aśoka has been found at Sopara in the Thana District near Bombay. So far this is the only evidence of these edicts at any port on the west coast. The importance of Sopara is due to its being a port and to trade. Had this been restricted to trade with the Gulf or coastal trade along the west coast then it is probable that the edicts would have been inscribed at a more important port such as Bhṛghukaccha or else in the Indus delta.

The location at Sopara may point to a direct route to southern Arabia or the southern end of the Red Sea. Given the Ptolemaic interest in trade with the East and the establishing of the ports of Myos Hormus and Berenike in the third century BC such a possibility cannot be discounted. The attack by Ptolemy Philadelpus on the Nabateans was probably motivated by the wish to capture Nabatean trade with the East and edge them out of the southern Arabian ports, as well as from their control over the routes from southern Arabia along the coast to Petra.[10] The initial maritime link between the west coast of India and the Red Sea might have been limited to the southern Nabatean ports but possibly extended north towards Egypt under the Ptolemies. If the ports of southern Arabia had had direct contacts with Sopara there might have been an interest on the part of the Ptolemies to visit these ports.

As early as the fourth century BC the Egyptians brought back cinnamon believing it to be a product of southern Arabia whereas it came from India.[11] Even in a later period when Pliny describes the Red Sea trade,[12] the route to India took more time and required both powerful vessels and a high capital investment which would have been better achieved with more extensive patronage.[13] Pliny refers to four phases in the trading contact between Egypt and India in which the south Arabian ports as entrepôts are important just prior to the direct mid-ocean links.

The exchange of envoys and gifts between the Mauryas and the Ptolemies would be a case of value goods exchanged at elite levels, which could have acted as forerunners to commercial exchange. The interest in trade may also have been encouraged by the demand for elephants for the armies of the Hellenistic kingdoms. Seleukus received five hundred elephants as part of his treaty with Candragupta Maurya. That elephants were a prized commodity is indicated by their use as far afield as the campaigns fought by Pyrrhus of Epirus against the Romans in southern Italy.[14] The Ptolemies may also have been anxious to import Indian elephants into Egypt, even though they had access to African elephants, because it was widely believed that Indian elephants were stronger and tougher and therefore superior in battle, particularly those from Taprobane or Sri Lanka. Given the frequency of wars among the Hellenistic kingdoms elephants would have been an important asset. The African elephants used by the Ptolemies were either from Libya or from the region of Ethiopia and were brought along the Red Sea to Berenike. There was, therefore, some expertise in the shipping of elephants. The description left by Callixeinus of the grand procession in honour or Ptolemy Philadelphus sometime in the 270s BC mentions Indian women sitting in carts and elephants from India.[15] Admittedly much of the Ptolemaic interest was with what was referred to as 'the southern trade', that is, with the Horn and East Africa but the appointment of a special officer in charge of the trade with the Red Sea and the Indian Sea in the second century BC[16] would suggest an interest in the Indian trade starting in the previous century. The evidence of Strabo regarding the expedition of Eudoxus of Cyzicus indicates that by the second century BC[17] Indian goods were part of the royal monopoly of trade of the Ptolemies.

That Cyrene comes into the Mauryan horizon doubtless has to do with its links with the Ptolemies. But it raises another point of interest. Cyrene was renowned for its production of a special herb, the silphium plant, used in a variety of ways and exported to various parts of the then known world which could have included India.

It was earlier assumed that the contact between the Red Sea and western India had to await the discovery of the monsoon winds by Hippalus and thus was dated to the first century BC. This in any case does not preclude coastal or looping trade and possibly the presence of new ports along the Red Sea may have pushed the coastal trade further down from Bhṛghukaccha to Sopara if not even further south to the coastal area of Karnataka where inscriptions of Aśoka have been found inland in the Bellary District at Niṭṭūr and Uḍegoḷam.[18] Given that ports in the Indus delta may have been familiar with problems of sailing during the south-west monsoon it is likely that mid-ocean routes from the west coast to the Arabian coast or the Red Sea were also treated with the same caution. The periodicity of both winds and ocean currents in the Arabian Sea may well have been noticed by early mariners and the conducive coinciding of the two, favouring east-west voyages and vice versa, at specific times of the year need not have remained undiscovered. Even navigators using coastal routes would be affected by wind and current and would soon learn to recognize the prime times. The development of the eastern trade was clearly to the advantage of the Hellenistic kingdoms whether it was a maritime trade as with the Ptolemies or an overland trade as with the Seleukids.

Epigraphical evidence on the proximity of the Greeks to the Mauryan empire is available from the Greek inscriptions issued by Aśoka and found in the environs of Kandahar in southern Afghanistan. A recently discovered pre-Aśokan Greek inscription of the early third century BC has added to our knowledge of Kandahar as a Greek settlement.[19] In the course of excavation a stone threshold turned out to be the base of a statue inscribed with two elegaic couplets referring to the now absent statue. Paleographically the inscription, though badly worn, is similar to the Hellenistic Greek of the Aśokan inscriptions from Kandahar. The inscription refers to a temenos or sacred precinct and to the son of Aristonax. It has been argued that this and other evidence points to Kandahar having been a regular Greek settlement along the lines of other major centres such as Ai-Khanum on the Oxus. Kandahar has been identified by some scholars with Alexandria in Arachosia. This may well be so given the strategic location of Kandahar as the meeting point of routes going to Herat, Kabul and Seistan and linked with India via the Gomal and Bolan passes.[20] There is also evidence to suggest that the site of Shahr-i-Kohna, which later developed into Kandahar, was earlier an Achaemenid fortress.[21] That Aśoka issued edicts in Greek and Aramaic in this area is therefore not surprising.

A version of Aśoka's Minor Rock Edict in a bilingual Greek and Aramaic, refers in a general way to some of his ideas.[22] This inscription as well as the Greek version of a part of the Major Rock Edicts Twelve and Thirteen[23] are important, both in providing additional evidence and in giving contemporary Greek and Aramaic translations of Prākrit words and concepts which have earlier been debated by scholars. In the two versions of the Minor Rock Edict the king states that ten years after his coronation he was drawn to *Dhamma* and its propagation. This would refute the idea of a conversion to Buddhism at the end of the Kaliṅga campaign. Aśoka emphasizes his vegetarianism, non-killing of animals and emphasizes the need for harmonious relations between people, particularly between the young and the old. The reference to expired years of his reign is extremely significant and has helped sort out Mauryan chronology.[24] The terms used for various concepts also have their importance.

*Dhamma* is translated as *eusebeia* in both the Greek inscriptions. It carries the general meaning of piety, reverence for gods and parents as well as loyalty.[25] It is curious that the translation is of a generalized concept and no mention is made of the teachings of the Buddha in particular. Had the king meant Buddhism when he refers to *Dhamma* then he would most likely have made a specific reference to these teachings since they were not well known in this region as he himself states in the Major Rock Edict Thirteen. The use of *eusebeia* does suggest that it was more his understanding of *Dhamma* that the king was anxious to convey and not merely the propagation of Buddhism.

Similarly in the Aramaic version at Kandahar and in other Aramaic inscriptions, *Dhamma* has been translated by modern scholars as Truth and as 'the conduct of the good'.[26] The latter phrase is suggestive of Zoroastrianism in which a contrast is drawn between the conduct of good and evil. An intriguing statement in the Aramaic version reads: 'and there is no Judgement for all pious men'. This has been interpreted in the context of Rock Edict Four, i.e., the officers of the law who have the power to judge.[27] However, it may be suggested that in the same way as the Greek translation draws on terms familiar to Greek philosophy such as *eusebeia* and *diatribe*, the Aramaic translation uses terms derived from Zoroastrian thought. Perhaps the judgement in this case referred not to officers but to the Zoroastrian belief in a judgement after death. This concept being unfamiliar to Greek thought it was not used in the Greek version. What the king might have been saying in effect was that those who observe the *Dhamma* or the conduct of the good would be regarded as pious and therefore exempt from judgement after death. Such an interpretation would in principle be perfectly logical. The Aramaic inscription was intended for those familiar with pre-Hellenistic ideas and practices and its appeal was to the Iranians settled in the region. Aśoka's familiarity with Zoroastrianism probably derived from his period as viceroy at Taxila before he became king. That he had this degree of sensitivity to the religious beliefs of those within his empire, enhances one's assessment of him as an administrator. There is also no mention of *brāhmaṇas* and *śramaṇas* in this inscription presumably because, as he states in his Thirteenth Rock Edict, these two categories are absent in the land of the *Yonas*.[28] The above reading would further endorse the suggestion of an Iranian population in the north-west of India.

The more recent discovery of Greek versions of the Twelfth and Thirteenth Rock Edicts are not complete translations of the Prākṛt texts but are adapted from these. It is unfortunate that only the terminal part of the Twelfth and the initial part of the Thirteenth are available since if the complete texts had been found then a comparison between the Greek and Prākṛt versions would have added considerably to our information about the king's policy towards these areas. Among the more interesting Greek words in these texts is the use of *diatribe* as the translation for *pāsaṃḍa*. Both words in their earlier use referred only to philosophical and religious sects or doctrines.[29] Gradually the notion of hostility came in. Thus they seem to have evolved in a similar pattern. *Pāsaṃḍa* in the later texts came to mean heretical groups and heresy, and was used especially of Buddhists and Jainas in Brahmanical literature. The transliteration of *brāhmaṇa va sramaṇa* as *bramenai-sramenai* is reminiscent of the quotation from Megasthenes where, in describing the philosophers, he divides them into two groups, the Brachmanes and the Sarmanes.[30] This dual division was evidently the form in which religious groups were perceived at this time. That the hostility between the two grew fairly rapidly after this period is clear from the reference in Patañjali to innate enmity, which he illustrates by referring to the enmity between the snake and the mongoose, the cat and the mouse and the *brāhmaṇa* and *śramaṇa*.[31] Aśoka's plea for tolerance between the *pāṣaṇḍas* and the acceptance of each other's teachings does not seem to have taken root.

The Greek version of the Major Rock Edicts focuses on those sections which deal with Aśoka's concern for the *Dhamma*, the well-being of various sects, non-violence and the desire for harmony in society. References to the work of officers have curiously been omitted.[32] Was this because they were irrelevant to this area which was possibly only loosely under Mauryan control, if at all, as some have argued? Or was it because the lands of the *Yona* were as yet comparatively unfamiliar with the teachings of various Indian sects and the king was primarily interested in proclaiming their virtues as well as his own in the propagation of *Dhamma*?

## Notes and References

1. Arrian, *Indica*, 1.2–3.
2. S. Chattopadhaya, *The Achaemenids and India*, Delhi, 1974, pp. 15ff.
3. H. Humbach, 'The Aramaic Aśoka Inscription from Taxila', *Journal of Central Asia*, Dec. 1978, I (2), pp. 87–98.
4. Herodotus, *Histories*, IV.44.
5. Arrian, *Anabasis*, VI.21.1–3.
6. V. Smith, *Early History of India*, Oxford, 1924, p. 159; E.R. Bevan, *House of Seleucus*, London, 1902, I, pp. 296–7.
7. Romila Thapar, *Aśoka and the Decline of the Mauryas*, London, 1961, pp. 40–1.
8. Ibid.
9. M. Rostovtzeff, *The Social and Economic History of the Hellenistic World*, Oxford, 1967 (revised), pp. 267ff.
10. Ibid., pp. 404ff.
11. G.W. Van Beek, 'Frankincense and Myrrh in Ancient South Arabia', *JAOS*, July–Sept. 1958, 78, pp. 141–52.
12. Pliny, *Natural History*, VI.100–1.
13. L. Casson, 'Rome's Trade with the East: The Sea Voyage to Africa and India', *TAPA*, 110, 1980, pp. 21–36.

14. H.H. Scullard, *The Elephant in the Greek and Roman World*, London, 1947, pp. 32ff.
15. Athenaeus, V.197–208.
16. J.D. Thomas, *The Epistrategos in Ptolemaic and Roman Egypt*, part 1, Opladen, 1975.
17. Strabo, II, 3.4ff.
18. D.C. Sircar, *Aśokan Studies*, Calcutta, 1979, pp. 123ff.
19. P.M. Fraser, 'The Son of Aristonax at Kandahar', *Afghan Studies*, 1979; 2. pp. 9–21.
20. L.W. Adamec (ed.), *Historical and Political Gazetteer of Afghanistan*, vol. 5, *Kandahar*, Graz, 1980, pp. 238ff.
21. Ibid.
22. U. Scerrato, G. Tucci, G. Pugliese Carratelli, G. Levi della Vida, *'Une Editto Bilingue Greco-aramaico di Aśoka . . .*', ISMEO, Rome, 1958, pp. 35ff; D. Schulumberger, L. Robert, A. Dupont–Sommer, E. Benveniste, *'Une biligue greco-arameena d'Aśoka'*, *Journal Asiatique*, 1958, 1, pp. 1–48; J. Filliozat, 'Graeco-Aramaic Inscription of Aśoka near Kandahar, *Ep. Ind.*, 1961–62, xxxiv, pp. 1–8.
23. D. Schlumberger and E. Benveniste, 'A New Greek Inscription of Aśoka at Kandahar', *Ep. Ind.*, 37, part v, pp. 193–200.
24. Romila Thapar, op. cit., pp. 31–2.
25. Liddel and Scott, *Greek-English Lexicon*, p. 731.
26. J. Filliozat, op. cit.; H. Humbach, op. cit.; A. Dupont–Sommer, 'Une Novelle Inscription araméene d'Aśoka trouve dans la vallée du Laghman', *Academie des inscriptions et belles-lettres*, 1970, pp. 158–73.
27. A. Dupont–Sommer, ibid.
28. J. Bloch, *Les Inscriptions d'Aśoka*, Paris, 1965, p. 128.
29. Liddel and Scott, *Greek-English Lexicon*, p. 416.
30. Strabo, XV.1.59.
31. *Vyākarana*, *Mahābhāsyam*, II.4.9 (I.476).
32. K.R. Norman, 'Notes on the Greek Version of Aśoka's Twelfth and Thirteenth Rock Edicts', *JRAS*, 1972, 2, pp. 111–18.

# 23

# *The Mauryas Revisited**

## I Towards the Definition of an Empire: The Mauryan State

Many states in India are casually given the label of 'empire' by historians. There have been few attempts to define an empire. It remains unclear as to where a kingdom ends and an empire begins. The Sātavāhanas and the Guptas are said to have ruled empires and more recently Vijayanagara has been elevated to the same status. With the increasing interest in regional history there has been a flowering of empires. It might therefore be useful to pause and consider what qualifies a state to be called an empire.

It was once maintained somewhat tautologically, that he who takes the title of emperor rules an empire, the Latin *imperium* suggesting this definition. An empire would then have to do with the self-perception of its rulers. Therefore when a king takes a title such as *mahārājādhirāja* (king of kings) there the historian would understand that an empire was meant. But this argument would not hold in the case of the Mauryan king Aśoka who sometimes refers to himself merely as, *rājā magadhe* (the king of Magadha)[1] or as *devānaṃpiya* (the beloved of the gods) leaving it to relatively small kings of later times to take the more grandiose title. Epigraphic evidence from the latter provides a rhetoric of high-sounding phrases. On the analogy of the Roman empire which was often taken as a model, historians have implicitly accepted two features as characteristic of an empire. One is extensive conquest and territorial control. The other, sometimes a corollary of the first, is the domination over people who were regarded as culturally different if not inferior and who were seen initially as aliens. Both these characteristics which may well have been consequential also to nineteenth

* Sakharam Ganesh Deuskar Lectures on Indian History, 1984, Centre for Studies in Social Sciences, Calcutta. Published as *The Mauryas Revisited*, Calcutta, 1987.

century European colonial experience, further subscribed to the notion that a certain association with 'glory' was expected of ancient empires: that these were high periods of art and of literature and of monumental buildings.

Territory is often presented as the primary feature but territorial control by itself is not sufficient, as even this is related to other aspects. The territory of an empire covers a variety of regions including geographically nuclear ones and those more isolated. The political importance of nuclear regions is not constant and the areas defined as such change over time, the change being dependent on ecological, technological and economic factors. A region is not necessarily just a smaller area for there is a certain interplay between a region and the totality of an empire which defines the nature of a region. It is relevant to ask whether an imperial system silts up regional features or whether it intensifies them through the exploitation of resources. This does not apply only to economic resources but also relates to patterns of acculturation and of religious expression.

The phrase 'control over territory' remains ambiguous, for such control can be of various kinds. The most direct is conquest and the induction of territory into the existing administrative structure of a state. Less direct is the mere capturing of the capital of another state and using the existing system as a channel for drawing on economic resources and cultural ties. Further removed from direct control would be a quick campaign and nominal subjugation, or, the control over a particular route without necessarily conquering its hinterland. Territory therefore is only one among the factors defining a state or an empire. Historical tradition has also to be treated with caution on the question of territory for sometimes a later tradition associates an area with a well-known king as part of a process of legitimation. Thus Aśoka is said to have visited Khotan and the founding of the kingdom is attributed to Indians and Chinese who came there during his reign.[2]

Conquest is also linked to the notion of the demarcation of territory. In the absence of cartography there can be no boundary lines bilaterally agreed upon. Frontiers are at best natural boundaries or else buffer zones.[3] Such frontiers were often kept deliberately under-developed with an emphasis on indigenous defences. These were frequently areas where the intention was not to maintain a firm control but rather to leave it pliant. Frontier zones such as pastoral areas, forests, uncultivated uplands helped keep political boundaries flexible. Attitudes to territory therefore were not uniform and depended on how the state visualised its advantage from the area.

The acquisition of territory or political glory were among the lesser purposes of conquest and war. There are many other reasons why states go to war.[4] Self-defence would seem the most evident. But for those more aggressive, there was the lure of booty and plunder, the capturing of prisoners-of-war to be used as labour, imposing of taxes, tributes and levies on the conquered and the exploitation of new lands and fresh resources. Where the acquisition of revenue was the primary motive there the conquest of fertile areas under cultivation and trade routes would be resorted to. Where territory was to be exploited it tended to be lands not fully utilised and thinly populated which could be subjected to colonisation by cultivators from other parts of the state or where raw materials would be appropriated. These were all conducive to increasing the wealth of the elite groups in the victorious state. Consolidated booty came to those in power whilst the ordinary soldier contented himself with plunder. An empire would then encourage wars and generate an income from them. If war has economic advantages then the economy of empires would be tied to war and conquest.

Studies of empires in Asia have tended to highlight these aspects but within a different context.[5] Empire it has been argued emerges as a result of a monopoly of force based on kingship. It controls an extensive territory which it has acquired through conquest. It appropriates on a large scale revenue from agriculture and trade. It is enabled to do this partly through a control over the hydraulic machinery and a network of administration. Religion functions as an expression of the state. Size is commonly characteristic of the definition and applies to all early empires, Achaemenid, Han, Roman. Some have argued that Asian empires were characterised by Oriental Despotism or its theoretical reincarnation, the Asiatic Mode of Production. All this implies a centralised control of all functions down to minutiae. Each unit, usually the village, was isolated but identical. Such a beehive structure has dominated much of our thinking on the functioning of Asian empires. This view is from above and suggests a uniform development of all areas included within the empire.

I would like to argue a different proposition.[6] In the typology of states, empire may be seen as a complex form of the state since it includes differentiated political and economic systems. Perhaps the component units within an empire can be listed as, firstly, a metropolitan state which initiates conquest and control, secondly core areas, and thirdly a large number of variegated, peripheral areas. The metropolitan state which historically evolves from a small kingdom and becomes the nucleus of the empire, is ultimately a highly developed state and in the case of early periods, an area of primary state formation, as was Magadha in the Mauryan empire. It spread its hegemony over other areas initially through conquest. The seemingly simple title of *rājā* of Magadha was in fact a significant indicator of where the power lay. The rest of the empire could be divided into core regions and peripheral regions. Core regions were either existing states such as Gandhāra with the city of Taxila which had been incorporated into the empire, or regions of incipient state formation such as Kaliṅga and Saurāṣṭra. Or, they were existing centres of exchange such as Ujjain, Amarāvatī or Bhṛghukaccha whose hinterlands were less important than the actual centre. Core regions are in a sense submetropolitan and on the disintegration of the empire can develop into metropolitan areas. The peripheral regions have further differentiated political and economic systems in that they range from hunting and gathering to producing societies and are areas which have not known a state system. A large part of the peninsula in the Mauryan empire would have constituted such regions as also some parts of the northern subcontinent. Peripheral regions are often located in the interstices between rich agricultural belts.

It should be obvious that such a pattern does not conform to the model of the 'segmentary state'. The differentiation here is not based on ritual control nor on the initiative being with the local society. What is being proposed is control by the single state over the territory claimed; but the form of control would vary according to the resources being tapped and the administration involved in obtaining these resources or their revenues. The crucial feature therefore, is the category of resources and their appropriation by the state. The variation in the pattern is dependent on the resource, the mechanism through which it provides a revenue and the manner in which the state appropriates the resource or the revenue. The initiative for this remains with the state. These are substantial differences between the model of the segmentary state and what I am proposing.

Relations between the metropolitan state and each area would vary. The primary interest of the former was dominance and exploitation, often expressed through revenue collection and the appropriation of resources. If this could be easily tapped without too much interference with the existing channels then the area would be left relatively untampered with. Where this was not possible there the economic restructuring of the area would be carried out by the metropolitan state. In part this also depended upon the nature of local resources. Thus in many areas of the peninsula where the resources were semi-precious stones, gold, elephants and timber, the tapping of these appears to have been left to local agencies as long as the Mauryan state could supervise this process and acquire the resources. Since efforts were directed at enriching the metropolitan state the degree of restructuring would relate to the needs of this state and the contribution of local resources towards these needs as well as the ability of the state to draw upon these resources.

In the case of the Mauryas it seems to have been more limited than one would expect although by no means absent. The major resource to be restructured would have been agriculture for purposes of revenue. Since the metropolitan state received the revenue and organised administrative control there could be imbalances between the metropolitan state and the other regions, particularly the peripheral ones and this imbalance is reflected in the pattern of disintegration of the Mauryan empire.

Magadha was almost predictably likely to emerge as a metropolitan state. It is associated with the formation of the earliest states in the Ganga plain and under Ajātaśatru became the foremost among these. The Nandas added to its stability not only by administering the Ganga plain as an area of effective revenue collection, which would account for their fabled wealth[7] but also by the conquest of Kaliṅga and the building of a canal suggestive of further efforts at extending agriculture.[8] The Nandas are reputed to have had a vast army, so large that it daunted the Greeks and led to the retreat of Alexander. Such an army would be required not only for conquest but also to defend the conquered territory. That some territories slipped out of control might explain Aśoka having to reconquer Kaliṅga in spite of the Nandas having held it in the previous century. Magadha did not have to rely on other areas for its wealth. It was agriculturally rich with a relatively high population density to work the land; it controlled the trade on the rivers of the Gangetic system particularly after the capital was shifted from Rājagṛha to Pāṭaliputra on the Ganga; it had access to iron ore to the south and to timber and elephants in the forests of the Rajmahal hills. With such a potential, any additional wealth in the form of annexation of rich neighbouring lands would provide it with the essentials for a metropolitan state.

For the Mauryas the need to conquer undoubtedly arose due to the necessity to extend the availability of resources from the more limited Ganga plain to the wider arena of the subcontinent. But other considerations were also important. The initial Mauryan expansion may have been justified as a defence of the Ganga valley against the successors of Alexander in the north-west, which situation was brought to a head in the hostilities between Candragupta Maurya and Seleucus Nicator. The north-west gave access to routes through the Hellenistic kingdoms to the markets of the eastern Mediterranean. The lower Indus region bred fine quality horses, an asset to any imperial army. The Mauryan movement into central India was almost certainly an attempt to control the route to the peninsula, the *dakṣiṇāpatha*. Further south, beyond the trade route to Sopārā in the vicinity of Bombay, lay the gold bearing areas of Karnataka, which could be approached from two directions: south of Sopara on the west coast and along the Krishna valley on the east. The latter route may also have tapped the diamond mines of the peninsula. The reconquest of Kaliṅga may well have been to recover lost territory, particularly one that was rich in agriculture, trade and elephants, as well as to defend Magadha from the south-east and to protect the coastal route down the east coast. Thus the need for the Mauryas to conquer was in part to extend the availability of resources.

As compared to other early empires, such as the Achaemenid, Han and Roman, the Mauryan was short-lived. Rising with the conquests of Candragupta and reaching its peak with his grandson Aśoka, it seems to have declined rather rapidly after this. As an imperial structure it survived at most for a century. This may well have had to do with what seems to have been a relatively limited economic restructuring of the area under its control.

A differentiation of politico-economic systems is reflected in

Mauryan sources. Reference is made to the hunters and gatherers and to forest tribes (*āṭavika* or *āraṇyacara*) settled both in the interior regions as well as along the borders.[9] Royal policy tends to treat them with a certain paternal sympathy except that stern action is also threatened if they fail to obey. The containment of forest tribes at the borders may have had a variety of reasons. They generally formed the buffer zones separating well-developed areas. The fear that they could act as predators on core areas incorporating agrarian settlements and caravan routes, could have encouraged their isolation by the state. The officer in charge of the border in the *Arthaśāstra* is also the one in charge of pasture lands suggesting that forests and grasslands were seen as border lands between core areas.[10]

The segregation of core areas was also in the interests of imperial policy and would be one way of keeping them under control without too great an input of army and administration. The chiefships of the *gaṇa-saṅghas* which could in some cases be classified as core areas find mention in the *Arthaśāstra* where it is suggested that they should not be conquered and annexed outright but should be weakened by dissensions and gradually brought under control.[11] In agriculturally rich areas which constituted core areas there was a range of agrarian tenures as is indicated by the listing of taxes such as *bhāga*, *bali*, *piṇḍa-kara* (accumulated), *ṣaḍbhāga* (one-sixth), *kara* and so on. In some cases land was privately owned and taxes were paid to the state. Such areas were generally associated with earlier states in the Ganga plain. Some lands were crown lands (the *sītā* land) where cultivators were given the right to work them under the supervision of the *sītādhyakṣa* or superintendent of agriculture.[12] The *sītā* lands were again worked on a variety of tenures: the employment of hired labourers and slaves, the *dāsa-bhṛtaka* or the *dāsa-karmakara*; or the employment of those who were serving a penal sentence, or share-cropping or the payment of a share of the produce. Exchange systems also ranged from barter to the more complex commercial transactions involving not only markets and trade but also production centres as exemplified in the activities of the guilds or *śreṇīs* and the traders or *seṭṭhis*.

This diversification was not limited to any one part of the empire but lay juxtaposed in various regions.[13] Nor was any attempt made to reduce the range to a uniform system, for example to convert pastoralists to agriculture or to encourage them to change from itinerant to commercial exchange. Possibly there were ecological constraints on such change and the technology of the time could not overcome these constraints. The state was primarily concerned with the extraction of revenue from all kinds of activities, if the advice of Kauṭilya was to be followed (as given in Book II which is believed to be of the Mauryan period).

It has long been a puzzle as to why, if Kauṭilya had known a large imperial state, his work should be concerned with a smaller state. He may well have been describing the functioning of a metropolitan state given his near obsession with the assessment and collection of revenue. He has much to say on the cultivation of *sītā* lands. The settling by the state of new areas or deserted areas is advised.[14] Peasant migrations from other states or from elsewhere in the same state are encouraged so that new lands can be settled. Peasant migration when not initiated by the state was a common form of peasant protest and there is a fear of peasants migrating from their lands when regimes become oppressive.[15] The reference to deserted areas could be to such lands. That peasants were encouraged to migrate from neighbouring states was because they then became an agency of revenue for the state where they settled. This advice to the ruler to encourage such migrations would suggest that there might perhaps have been a shortage of manpower to develop new agricultural resources on a large scale. Flood plains might also constitute deserted areas since floods often led to a shift in cultivation. But such shifts were generally temporary and even archaeological evidence of the Ganga flood plain in western Uttar Pradesh suggests the reoccupation of deserted land.[16] Deserted lands may also refer to those once under swidden agriculture from where earlier settlers had moved or to conquered lands from where the previous peasants had fled because of the campaign. However Megasthenes does make a point of stating that even when battles are raging, peasants in the vicinity continue to cultivate the land, since soldiers were forbidden from molesting peasants. This probably had more to do with the fact that the Mauryas did not conscript the peasantry but relied on a standing army rather than that Indian soldiers were not given to plunder.[17] The lack of conscription might again have been conditioned by the need to keep as much manpower as possible on the land. Cultivators are described as the largest segment of society by Megasthenes. Peasants from one's own state brought to settle such lands would be a shift of the excessive population from one area to another as advised by Kauṭilya. This would more likely refer to a shift of those working on *sītā* lands. It has been argued that the prisoners taken after the Kaliṅga campaign of Aśoka were deported to new agricultural settlements.[18]

Prisoners-of-war are listed as a regular source for the supply of slaves.[19] Some were undoubtedly used as labour to cultivate the *sītā* lands. However slaves were not the only source of labour and hired labourers and share croppers are also referred to. There is unfortunately virtually no evidence on how and when agrarian tenures were changed after the conquest of an area during this period. That Kauṭilya advises the settling of *śūdra* cultivators by the state is not without interest. Even if it is not taken literally the intention of using the pressures of caste to contain cultivators is clear.

Where arable land was allotted by the state to cultivators it was only for a lifetime. Therefore the state had complete control over such land. This was a very different system from that of the land grants of the later period which were permanent and revenue free. Such grants are suggested by Kauṭilya limiting them to *brāhmaṇas* and to those associated with the administration and such grants although heritable could not be sold or mortgaged. The boundaries of fields brought under cultivation were carefully fixed, doubtless for reasons of assessment and collection. The state was also required to assist with seed, irrigation water and adjustments of revenue demands in the initial stages. Clearly good land had to be intensively cultivated and a revenue derived from it. Did the Mauryas follow this advice? There is little evidence from other sources on the settling of new land. The reference to the deportation of prisoners-of-war after the Kaliṅga campaign may have led to the cultivation of waste land but references to colonies and settlements of this kind are rare. A passing reference to land revenue is made in one of the inscriptions of Aśoka. In the Rummindei Inscription located at Lumbinī, the king states that because it was the birthplace of the Buddha he is lifting the *bali* and reducing the *bhāga*,[20] both of which were taxes, the former probably associated with the area of land under cultivation and the latter being a share of the produce. It is curious that the king does not exempt the village entirely from taxes as one would expect given its association but doubtless revenue demands could not be dismissed so lightly. In case it was privately owned land, state legislation on tax exemption would have been limited.

Intensifying agriculture would have required some state interest in irrigation or what has been described as the hydraulic machinery. To date there is only a single large-scale irrigation work which is attributed to Mauryan enterprise, the dam on the Sudarshan lake at Girnar.[21] From the evidence of archaeology this would be regarded as a core area. The absence of large scale irrigation works elsewhere may suggest that there were not many extensive areas brought under state agriculture. More frequently the reference is to small scale privately organised irrigation. Kauṭilya refers to water taken from rivers, pools, tanks, wells and springs.[22] These water works and the channels used with them were constructed through local enterprise and were individually maintained or through a pooling of the resources of local people. State assistance is mentioned in connection with the cultivation of *sītā* lands. Where the state provided irrigation it also charged a higher cess for water (*udaka-bhāga*). Irrigation allowed of double cropping with summer rice and winter wheat and barley in areas where both these crops could be grown. Megasthenes writes that double cropping was possible because of the natural fertility of the soil and the abundant and regular rainfall.[23] But then he is also quoted in another passage (the authenticity of which has been doubted) as having said that a special category of officers was responsible for controlling the supply of water to cultivators by keeping a check on the sluices.[24] If this was in practice in Mauryan India it probably applied only to the *sītā* lands. That the need for and the nature of irrigation, would vary from crop to crop is not reflected in these texts.

The other source of revenue which was beginning to be tapped at the state level in the Mauryan period and which was to grow considerably in the post-Mauryan period, was trade. The superintendent of trade, the *panyādhyakṣa*, and the director of tolls and customs duties are given carefully worked out instructions and this is corroborated by the account of Megasthenes.[25] (If these instructions were followed then the picture suggested is that of administered trade in the sense in which Polanyi uses the term). The state was required to keep a check on the items brought for trade and to direct the profits as well, so that the state may derive an advantage from the sale. The superintendent of trade was to be familiar not only with the provenance of goods traded, but also their mode of transportation, supply and demand and their price. He is also instructed to create a rise in price if need be. Customs houses at the gates of the city were to stamp the passes of traders bringing in goods and check the goods brought in. An elaborate list of penalties is included for any attempt at fraud or hoodwinking the state. Items such as weapons, armour, coats-of-mail, metals, chariots, gems, grain and cattle are not to be included as items of exchange and the state clearly had a monopoly over these. The list is somewhat unrealistic since cattle and grain would certainly have been traded in village marts. But presumably these restrictions apply to the bringing in of such items into the cities. Goods were to be sold only by authorised persons at authorised places.

Traders are treated with an element of suspicion and artisans and guilds are also to be under constant scrutiny. In the lay out of the city a part of the non-residential area near the city wall, was kept for the dwellings of the guilds and foreign merchants.[26] Craftsmen involved in the same or similar professions lived together and could sell their goods only at authorised places.[27] In the absence of an open general market, sale and purchase of items was doubtless to be carried on in that part of the city where these items were produced. Thus the trading nuclei of the city were to be kept distinct from other functional areas. Marshall's interpretation of the data from Bhir Mound at Taxila would support this picture. The workshops and presumably the shops seem to have been located along the exterior walls of houses with no direct access to the house.[28] There is also an absence of any central market similar to the agora of the Greek cities.

Artisans and traders are discussed in further detail in the section of the *Arthaśāstra* which deals with the suppression of criminals: the assumption being that both categories flourish through cheating and the state has to intervene to prevent this.[29] Artisans cheat by undercutting on the quality of the items and traders by selling these as prime quality goods. Also thieves in the guise of artisans can oppress people. There is a preference for the guild rather than the individual artisan since the guild would be more responsible and easier to negotiate with. Fines for late delivery or liabilities for loss or destruction were more easily imposed on guilds then on individuals. That artisans were regarded as low on the social scale is indicated by the inclusion of various low castes in the same chapter such as washermen, tailors, attendants, physicians and wandering minstrels and mendicants. Presumably those artisans who worked directly for the state such as armourers would have had a higher status and been treated with greater respect. In the scale of salaries of perhaps a later period, that of artisans employed by the state was a hundred and twenty *paṇas* which is not a particularly high salary considering that the foreman of labour received sixty *paṇas* and the soldiers and clerks, five hundred *paṇas*.[30]

Traders were to be subjected to massive fines if their goods were found to be below standard. Thus there was support for the idea of a quality control enforced by the state. This was different from the system of barter where quality control is implicit in the exchange. If such fines were actually in operation they may well have acted as a disincentive to trade. As a further disincentive, the text argues for a fixing of the permissible profit at five per cent above the permitted sale price of local goods, and ten per cent on foreign goods. An excessive profit was also subjected to a fine. There was not only a suspicion of traders but perhaps also a fear that a large amassing of wealth by guilds and traders would encourage their becoming alternative sources of power to the state. The *brāhmaṇa* animosity to traders and the city which is expressed in early *dharmasūtra* literature may well have been responsible for these statements in the *Arthaśāstra* although one wonders whether Kauṭilya would give priority to being a good *brāhmaṇa* rather than an astute advisor on revenue. Whether these injunctions were adhered to closely can only be gauged when we have more evidence on urban conditions in the Mauryan period: evidence which can be best obtained from horizontal excavations. The rise to importance of guilds and traders in the post-Mauryan period is noticeable, where not only was there more trade but the traders and the guilds were wealthy enough to become major patrons of religion and did assert a social identity which contradicted their low status as maintained in the *śāstras*.

Political suzerainty implied control over economic resources. This varied according to the resource and its function in the Mauryan economy. The major agricultural regions were the Ganga plain, Saurāṣṭra in the west, the deltas of the Mahanadi, Krishna and Godavari in the east, and the Raichur doab in the south. The latter is rich in megalithic sites often succeeding chalcolithic cultures and therefore pointing to a pre-Mauryan settlement. There are Aśokan inscriptions in the vicinity of places such as Maski and Brahmagiri, and the important Mauryan administrative town of

Suvarṇagiri was located in this area. That Maski was not an isolated settlement is clear not only from the clusters of sites in the vicinity, but also, by a large number of beads including some of lapis lazuli found in Period II of the excavations,[31] contemporary with the Mauryan which must have travelled a long way to get there (the nearest source of lapis being Badakshan in Afghanistan or the mountains of south-eastern Iran). There is ample evidence of gold working, this probably being the primary motivation for Mauryan control over the area, its agricultural produce forming a secondary interest. The gold was doubtless sent back to Magadha, for its occurrence in the habitation sites or burials is not common. What is found in the megalithic burials is a fraction of what would have been available from the region. Nor is there much evidence at this time of the prosperity associated with a wealthy area, if it is argued that the gold was recycled locally. There is much on the technology of working gold in the *Arthaśāstra* and the careful supervision of its production.[32] The obtaining of gold was the main concern for there does not seem to have been a significant attempt on the part of the Mauryas to change the economy of this region. In fact the Mauryan presence is difficult to ascertain from excavations alone. The inland sites of the peninsula contrast noticeably with those of the coastal areas where at Amarāvatī for instance there is greater evidence of NBP and punch-marked coins. The eastern deltas appear to have been more directly under the control of Mauryan administration although the Aśokan inscriptions do refer to the officers of the southern region. The existence of megalithic burials prior to the Mauryan period indicates that the organisation of labour in some form was in practice and this organisation would have been adapted to imperial requirements.

Access to raw materials appears to have been the prime motivation for the conquest of the peninsula where timber and semi-precious stones — quartz, agate, carnelian — were easily available as also were elephants. Indian elephants, believed to be invincible in battle, were in great demand both by the Seleucids in west Asia and the Ptolemies in north Africa. Control over trade routes and trading points was equally important. This would have taken the Mauryan armies into north-western India with the focus on Gandhāra and the city of Taxila providing access to overland routes to Hellenistic west Asia. The treaty with Seleucus provided the Mauryas with the valuable province of Arachosia and the city of

Kandahar which was a nodal point in Hellenistic trade. The locations of inscriptions other than the ones at specifically Buddhist sites points to trade routes having been a significant consideration. Mansehra and Shahbazgarhi were not only linked to the north-west but probably also to the Gilgit-Chitral area as has been revealed in the recent discovery of *kharosthī* inscriptions of the Kuṣāṇa period along the Karakoram highway.[33] Indraprastha and its vicinity controlled routes to the Ganga river system as well as the *dakṣiṇāpatha* going to the peninsula. The sites along the Gandak river follow the well-established northern route or *uttarapatha*. A major central Indian route from Pāṭaliputra passed through the Mauryan sites of Sahasram, Rupnath and Hoshangabad (Panguraria) and proceeded to Sopara on the west coast. Sopara in all likelihood had a coastal-cum-inland link with the Bellary district (where Aśokan inscriptions have recently been discovered at Nittur and Udegolam) with links to the Raichur area. The eastern route from Pāṭaliputra with a branch perhaps to Mahasthan developed further into the maritime route along the east coast touching the Mahanadi delta and continuing to the Krishna delta from where the route turned inland and continued to Yerragudi, Jatinga Rameshwar and other sites located again in an area of megalithic sites and sources of gold.

The location of the Mauryan inscriptions found so far is suggestive of a pattern which follows the known routes and skirts around what might be called the peripheral regions of this period. The northern Deccan remains relatively secluded. Similarly Sind, the confluence of the rivers of the Punjab and north-western Rajasthan are devoid of Mauryan remains. This raises the question of whether it is legitimate to argue for the presence of a political control in areas where there is no evidence of a Mauryan presence. Was the control geographically selective?

Yet, some of these areas were actively involved in the campaign of Alexander which preceded the rise of the Mauryas and also in the hostilities between the Mauryas and the Seleucids. It is unlikely that the Seleucids would have ceded Arachosia and Gedrosia (southern Afghanistan to the Makran) if they were not contiguous to Candragupta's domain. The Aśokan inscriptions refer to the Yona, the Kamboja, the Gandhāra, the Risthika or Rathika and Pitinika as of the west.[34] In the south the Cola, Pāṇḍya, Satiyaputra and Keralaputra as far as Tāmraparṇi are mentioned as inhabiting the land on the frontier (*aṃta*) and this is made more explicit by reference to Antiochus the Greek ruler as being also at the frontier.[35] Those within the empire (*idha rājaviṣayam*) are the Yona, Kamboja, Nābhaka, Nābhapankti, Bhoja, Pitinika, Āndhra and Parinda.[36] There is a distinction between those within the empire and those at the frontier. There is also a distinction between the south Indian neighbours who are referred to by their lineage names and the Hellenistic neighbouring states, the names of whose kings are mentioned. A recurring pattern in the Mauryan inscriptions, it suggests a pre-state system prevalent in the southern regions. This would not contradict the evidence from either archaeology or the early Śaṅgam literature.

The routes linking the location of the Mauryan inscriptions often developed into major routes and centres in the post-Mauryan period. It is interesting that the Major Rock Edicts are located at important nodal points along routes and at centres associated with trade. The pride which Aśoka took in the building of roads was legitimate since these served administrative requirements but at the same time facilitated trade. For purposes of revenue the control of routes and of major trading centres would have been sufficient without the need to control the umland of these centres. If the Mauryas took the advice of Kauṭilya then the suggestion of administered trade might have been almost stifling for the possible development of trade during this period. It would seem that the Mauryas were content to tap whatever revenue they could from the existing commercial activities and did not perhaps exploit this potential to its full extent. It is curious for example that they do not appear to have issued coined metallic money of a distinctive kind, for this in early societies is generally a pointer to the state intervening in urban trade. In spite of arguments in support of certain categories of punch-marked coins being issued by the Mauryan rulers,[37] it is still generally accepted that these coins were issued by guilds or other local bodies and date to a period prior to the Mauryas and continuing to the end of the millennium. This would point to the continuing importance of trade centres rather than the state fully controlling trade in spite of the advice of Kauṭilya.

Conquest and control over such distant areas even if only partially direct and concentrated only on routes and centres of raw material would have required a considerable financial outlay in terms of military and administrative organisation. Greek and

Latin sources refer to the enormous army maintained by the Nandas and Mauryas. The figures mentioned by Plutarch and Pliny were doubtless exaggerated in order to justify Alexander's retreat, arguing that he would have faced a formidable force had he ventured into the Ganga plain. Plutarch's reference to an army of six hundred thousand[38] seems highly exaggerated considering that this was double the figure for the entire infantry of the Roman empire before Diocletian increased it in the third century AD thereby shaking the economy of the empire.[39] Since the Mauryan empire did not have access to the same economic base as the Roman empire and there was no conscription this figure hardly seems tenable. If the size of an army has any relation to population size as is argued by some scholars, then even from this perspective the figures are exaggerated. (Incidentally the calculation of the population of the Mauryan empire as one hundred and eighty one million is based on the figures for the army quoted in Greek and Latin sources and the basic evidence therefore is not reliable).[40] It is also unlikely that there would have been a substantially larger population in the Mauryan period as compared to the Mughal period. Furthermore the entire arming of the soldiery was the responsibility of the Mauryan state since private arms were not permitted.[41] If Megasthenes was right then not only the armour but even horses and elephants for the other wings of the army were a monopoly of the state,[42] the maintenance of which would certainly have added up to a major financial burden. In addition there was a comfortable salary for soldiers.[43] The *Arthaśāstra* suggests a smaller army since it refers to the induction of a variety of paramilitary groups at the time of a campaign.[44] The financial involvement in maintaining a large army may have been one among other reasons for pursuing a policy of non-violence subsequent to effective control over major areas of resources. However, the reconciling of non-violence with imperial demands may have been a difficult proposition. The concept of aggressive expansion was familiar to *brāhmaṇa* ideology with the central role of sacrificial rituals such as the *aśvamedha* and the *rājasūya* eulogising such expansion. Significantly the Mauryan kings in spite of their impressive conquests are not associated with these rituals. Buddhism on the contrary emphasised the role of the *dharma rāja* which made such rituals irrelevant. Whether the Buddhist concept of the universal monarch or *cakkavattin* pre-dated Aśoka or developed after the reign of Aśoka remains a controversial point. Territory although important as the area where the wheel of the *cakkavattin* rolls is nevertheless subservient as a concept to the notion of the *cakkavattin* being defined as a just ruler and one who rules in accordance with the *dhamma* for if he fails to do so then the wheel sinks into the ground and disappears. Aśoka may well have seen himself as a *cakkavattin* and hence his insistence on ruling in accordance with *dhamma* even if the latter was of his own defining. What is often forgotten is that there was also a hierarchy of *cakkavattins*: the *cakkavāla* or *cāturanta cakkavattin* who ruled over the four quarters, the *dīpa-cakkavattin* who ruled a single quarter and the *padesa-cakkavattin* who ruled over only a part of one.[45]

Administrative organisation seems to have been divided into those who functioned in an advisory and supervisory capacity and others at a lower level who carried out the routine requirements. The distance between the two was extreme where the ratio of the salary of the clerk to the minister was one is to ninety-six.[46] The upper ranks were well-paid. The *samahartṛ* or chief collector received half the salary of the *mantṛ*; the *rāṣṭrapāla* and the *antapāla*, provincial and frontier officers received a quarter; the *pradeṣṭṛ* received one-sixth; and the superintendents of the various wings of the army, received one-twelfth. After this comes a sudden decrease with the salary of other superintendents in the ratio of 1:48. The clerks, accountants and the foot soldiers all received the same salary which works out to 1:96. Admittedly this information comes from what may be a post-Mauryan section of the book. Furthermore these were obviously not exact salaries and there is a certain play on numbers — 2, 4, 8, 12, 48, 96. Nevertheless what is of interest is the demarcation and disparity between the higher ranks and the lower where in the case of the lower there is a substantial drop in the salary.

It is difficult to ascertain the value of these salaries as we do not have evidence of prices. The *Jātaka* literature informs us that a pair of oxen could be purchased for twenty-four *paṇas*, a slave for a hundred *paṇas* and a thoroughbred horse for a thousand *paṇas*.[47] As against this the salary of the soldier and the clerk in the *Arthaśāstra* is listed as five hundred *paṇas*, assuming that the same coin is being referred to in both sources and that it had identical value. Given the statement of Megasthenes that the soldiers lived very well on their salaries, it would seem that the salaries of the upper levels of the administration were excessively high. If taken literally this in itself may well have caused a severe financial drain on the resources of the empire. Even if it is not taken literally the salary scale suggests that the ruling elite had access to a large income.

In a chapter on the activity of the *samāhartṛ* or chief collector we are told that his work was largely that of maintaining the records of revenue.[48] The actual recovery of the revenue was the work of the *gopa* and the *sthanika* probably under the supervision of the *pradeṣṭṛ*. Whereas the latter is listed among the recipients of a high salary (1: 6) the former two are not listed at all. This may suggest that the *gopa* and the *sthanika* were locally recruited persons who were permitted to keep a portion of the revenue collected in lieu of a salary, or, as is stated in another section of the text, are given grants of land without the right of sale or mortgage and therefore their salaries were low or omitted from the list.[49] If the *pradeṣṭṛ* was the same as the *pradeśika* mentioned in the Aśokan inscriptions[50] then his functions involved tours of inspection and presumably in that capacity he had a higher status than the local officers. In the absence of any central recruitment to administrative office it is likely that the higher officials came from the metropolitan state or the core regions, toured their area of jurisdiction and ensured the channelling of revenue to the capital. There is however the problem of Tuṣāspa who had a high office in Saurāṣṭra and yet seems to have been a local person unless he was recruited from the north-west (as his Iranian name suggests) and was posted to Saurāṣṭra. The actual collectors at the level of village and town may have been local appointees. In the peripheral areas some of these were likely to have been clan chiefs. The post-Mauryan period sees the rise of the Mahābhoja, Mahārathi, Mahatalāvara and so on, suggestive of chiefs acting as intermediaries between clan and empire. With the breakdown of empire and the rise of local states around the core regions these intermediaries would continue to be important in relations between the new states and what were earlier peripheral areas. If such a system prevailed there would be a greater uniformity of administration at the upper levels and local administration would be more decentralised. The administrative organisation when seen from the upper levels would suggest a centralised, uniform administration geared to the requirements and functions of the metropolitan state. But when seen from the lower levels it would be far less uniform. The high salaries of the upper levels would have been possible if the revenue was in large part taken back to the metropolitan state and then redistributed according to administrative and state requirements. The fact of listing salaries is suggestive of such a system. However what is not certain is whether such salaries were actually paid in money or merely computed in terms of money but paid in kind.

The emphasis on uniformity in empires is sometimes reflected in symbols and at ideational levels. The exploitation of an alien people with an alien culture as part of the definition of an empire becomes significant in this context. The more obvious symbols are of course monuments which encapsulate both the authority of the state and the stamp of the state. Of these there is a conspicuous absence in the Mauryan empire other than in the capital at Pāṭaliputra. None of the cities which are associated with provincial government such as Taxila at Bhir Mound or Vidiśā, Tosali and Suvarṇagiri (Kaṇakagiri) display structures characteristic of the Mauryas; nor for that matter are there such indications at other towns where inscriptions have been found. Possibly Mauryan monuments were engulfed in post-Mauryan reconstruction. Aśoka may well have constructed *stūpas* at places of Buddhist worship even though surprisingly he nowhere claims to have done so beyond the repair and reconstruction of a couple. The structures even if symbolising considerable piety must nevertheless have been simple. It was in the post-Mauryan period that the *stūpas* were enlarged, encased in stone and embellished with sculpture. The patronage involved in making these monuments memorable came not from imperial monarchs but in the main from the community of monks, nuns, artisans and small-scale land owners. The description of Pāṭaliputra given by Megasthenes is impressive and the Persian parallels of what emerged from the Kumrahar excavations would suggest that the city was built by Candragupta. Did Aśoka lack the public finance to continue such building or did he prefer to build rest houses and wells along the highways which no longer survive? The excavating of caves at Barābar did not require a major financial outlay judging by the frequency with which this was done in the post-Mauryan period. The pillars with their elaborately sculpted capitals and finely polished shafts are the contribution of Aśoka to public structures and these again did not require extensive financing.[51] Some pillars were especially made others were already in existence. Some labour and money would have been expended in transporting the sandstone from Chunar to various sites in the Ganga valley where they have been found. The pillars are located either within reach of Chunar or with access to the river system suggesting transportation by river. The increase in the number of pillars from the pre-Mauryan to the Mauryan period points to an enhancement in the making and placing of pillars. Yet the increase in numbers is small and is restricted to the Ganga river system and would not have required a major financial investment. The polishing and sculpting of these is impressive, yet when compared to other imperial monuments in various parts of the contemporary world they do not suggest a spectacular use of wealth and labour. The major monuments were restricted to the capital of the metropolitan state indicating again the channelling of wealth to the capital. Yet even these when imaginatively reconstructed remain a pale second to the grandeur of Persepolis or the almost incredible concept of the burial mounds associated with Shi Huang Ti at Sian.

One may well ask where did the wealth go in the Mauryan period? Where then are the villas of the rich or the physical manifestation of a high standard of material prosperity? Was the wealth consumed in a manner which left few traces? Did status still lie in the holding of lengthy sacrificial rituals where large amounts of wealth were offered, distributed, destroyed, leaving virtually no trace? Or it may have been expended on good living involving destructible items. Buddhist ethics during this period may have discouraged the conspicuous display of wealth. Was the Buddhist ethic on the importance of investment taken seriously and did this form the bed rock of the evident prosperity of the post-Mauryan period? This ethic was supported by Aśoka's *dhamma* where in his inscriptions he advocates a moderated life free from excesses of any kind. This was to change in the post-Mauryan period when donations to the *saṅgha* and the embellishments of the *stūpa* were encouraged. Was the wealth conserved and buried in the form of treasure? Hence perhaps the frequency of references in theoretical works to the king's claims on the discovery of treasure troves which are listed as part of legitimate revenue.[52] Or do we have to concede that the amount of wealth generated during the Mauryan period was less than what the idea of empire conveys.

An attempt at uniformity at the ideational level is emphasised in the rock inscriptions and pillar inscriptions set up by Aśoka in various parts of his territory. His definition of *dhamma* as an ethical principle was an attempt to provide a common factor even if only of an abstract kind. That it was not meant as an imposition of Buddhism seems evident. In the Greek and Aramaic versions the idiom is that of Greek and Iranian belief. Thus *dhamma* is not translated into Greek as the teachings of the Buddha but as *eusebeia*[53] which refers to sacred and filial duty and ethical values. The Aramaic version makes a reference to the pious not being judged suggestive of the Zoroastrian idea of a Judgement after death.[54] The attempt then was to appeal to a broader spectrum of belief and behaviour emphasised by most of the religious teachers of that time without necessarily associating this idea with any single one of them. Discussions on the meaning of *dharma/dhamma* were current among the major religious and philosophical sects and by providing his own definition Aśoka was participating in the debate. Moving away from the requirements of confrontation, conquest and hegemony associated with imperial systems he was emphasising the process equally important to imperial needs of acculturation and this he sought to encourage through a policy of persuasive assimilation in which conforming to the broad ethical ideals of *dhamma* was central. His ideas on *dhamma* therefore borrow from the current debate but are set within an imperial framework. That ultimately these ideas did not work at a political and social level was partly because ideology can be a driving force of history but is not a sufficient cause of history. The cultural norm of the Mauryan state would have been the culture essentially of the middle Ganga plain. The culture of the north-west and the peninsula would be seen as different if not even a little alien. This is suggested by one of the cultural signals of the Mauryan empire, that of language. The inscriptions of the north-west use Greek, Aramaic and Prākṛit but the latter written in the Aramaic-influenced *kharoṣṭhī* script. The need to inscribe in Greek and Aramaic may suggest the rather tenuous hold of the Mauryas in Afghanistan. Prākṛit with some regional variations and written in the *brāhmī* script is common elsewhere and in the peninsula. The inscriptions in the southern areas were in Prākṛit in spite of its not being the current language and this was a manifestation of imperial culture: so different from Afghanistan where the edicts were rendered into the local language and idiom. Śaṅgam literature which is generally not dated earlier than the Mauryan period and may well be later, refers to the Velir chief of Erumaiyur, (the Mahiṣayur or Mysore of later times).[55] This would point to the area being Dravidian speaking at this time. Prākṛit, although the official language, was alien. Perhaps the local language could not be used for inscriptions since it does not seem to have had a script (other than the as yet undeciphered graffiti on the pottery). This probability is further endorsed by the evolution of the Tamil-brāhmī script in the post-Mauryan period. The Mauryan presence in Tamil sources is largely restricted to descriptions of the conquerors whose chariots thundered past. Despite the cultural differences however, the ruling elite would have shared, or at any rate been aware of, a common culture, language and to some degree religion, all deriving from practices prevalent in the metropolitan state. The perception of distinct cultural expressions was significant in demarcating the metropolitan state from other areas.

The ideational search for uniformity on the part of Aśoka has to be explained. At one level it was the personal vision of a single individual but its genesis and articulation would relate to this individual's historical role as well. The Mauryas as a dynasty are implicitly given the status of *śūdras* in the Purāṇic texts perhaps because they were supporters of Jainism and Buddhism.[56] In the texts of these latter religions they are given high status. The Buddhists refer to them as a branch of the Śākya clan,[57] the highest possible status, although this may have been an attempt to link Mahinda the son of Aśoka who brought Buddhism to Sri Lanka with the family of the Buddha. The Mauryan support of non-brahman sects requires an explanation. Was the family really of low origin and therefore required legitimation through patronising those sects which paid little attention to *varṇa* status? Alternatively were they merely being conventional in patronising the dominant sects of the region which was the base of their empire — the middle Ganga valley? The universalistic ethic of these sects as opposed to the caste-based ethic of brahmanical teaching suited the needs of empire since it could forge new ties across clans, tribes and castes. The *rājā* and the *bhikṣu* had a polar relationship in Buddhist thought,[58] yet the *saṅgha* prospered on royal patronage and at the same time, where such patronage was available, it provided networks of loyalty which would be supportive of political needs. The importance to the state of monastic organisation was that renunciatory orders cut across both caste and clan and weakened existing identities. Thus in the metropolitan state and the core areas where caste society was established, the *saṅgha* provided another centre of identity. Where it also supported the state this alternative identity was useful to the state. Renunciatory orders broke caste obligations and even if this applied only to the monks the fact that the monks lived in the vicinity of settlements meant that there was a continual presence of a group respected in society but not observing social obligations.[59] In the peripheral areas the *saṅgha* would again have acted as an alternative form of coalescing identity and weakening clan ties. That the latter might have been initiated in the Mauryan period is suggested by the patronage to the Buddhist and Jaina monastic complexes by ruling dynasties in these areas just after the decline of the Mauryas.

The universalising of *dhamma* by Aśoka went further than merely patronage to a particular sect. Interestingly none of his inscriptions are direct votive inscriptions to the Buddhist *saṅgha*. References to his donations come from Buddhist texts and inferentially from his repairing certain sacred monuments. On the evidence of epigraphy, the grants to the Ājīvikas were recorded on site. The *dhamma-mahāmattas* however are required to make grants to the *saṅgha*, *brāhmaṇas*, Ājīvikas and Nirgranthas. Yet the edicts addressed to the concerns of the *saṅgha*[60] do point to a close relationship between the king and the *saṅgha*: a relationship which is picked up in Buddhist historiography and which is depicted as an inter-locking of the two. His espousal of the *dhamma* initially weakened the notion of divine kingship so often resorted to by the founders of empires. But in the pillar edicts issued towards the end of his reign[61] there is an uncomfortable hint of what might have been an incipient cult of the king, doubtless also fostered by the continuing use of the title *devānaṃpiya*.

Differentiations within the empire of a kind which I have been arguing for are also suggested in the pattern of the break-up of the empire and in the successor states. The metropolitan state of Magadha continued as a political entity with monarchy so firmly established that the successors to the Mauryas were unrelated to them and did not claim dynastic continuity. The Śuṅgas were *brāhmaṇas* and the founder was a professional soldier, the commander of the Mauryan army who assassinated the last of the Mauryas. The control of Magadha continued to extend over the

Ganga plain and adjoining parts of central India. Mauryan investments in Magadha doubtless laid the foundations for its survival as a major state for some time, even if it ceased to be the nucleus of an empire. Gandhāra as a core region reverted back to monarchy although drawn into the orbit of west Asian politics. The lower Indus plain and Saurāṣṭra also had less to do with the Ganga valley. Saurāṣṭra is described in the *Arthaśāstra* as a *gaṇa-saṅgha*.[62] Doubtless the building of the dam by the Mauryas would have brought about major economic changes. Kaliṅga probably experienced an independent monarchy for the first time. The *gaṇa-saṅghas* of north Bihar failed to survive and were incorporated into the adjacent Ganga plain. Doubtless the fertility of these areas led to their being merged into the substantial agricultural economy of the larger plain. The lineage-based societies of Rajasthan however seem to have survived the Mauryas. This was ecologically not such a fertile region, its main resources being copper and a heavy dependence on pastoralism. This area was probably not brought into the agricultural vortex of the Mauryan economy. Trade routes in the western Deccan seem to have been the prime movers in the emergence of the Sātavāhanas as the ruling dynasty where the state came into existence in what was earlier an area of lineage-based societies. Some of the peripheral areas of the peninsula continued as such, whereas others emerged as core regions which gradually became the base of monarchical states. The centrality of trade in such places as a factor in the rise of monarchies, needs to be examined.

These patterns do not indicate a uniform development of all areas held by the Mauryan state. Trade was stimulated but its potential does not seem to have been fully realised. Whereas there may have been an increase in trade and a higher standard of material prosperity reflected in Mauryan levels at excavated sites, the picture is not as rich as that of the post-Mauryan period particularly in terms of a larger community participating in this prosperity. *Sītā* lands were cultivated but probably not as a major enterprise in every part of the empire. Apart from ecological constraints this would also have required colonies and settlers on a wider scale than the evidence suggests. If the recent identification of the dam on the Sudarshan lake is accepted[63] and the size of the dam calculated as given in the inscription[64] the area impounded and the area irrigated remains not too large. The use of iron technology in agriculture was effective in the Ganga valley but perhaps less so in the peninsula. Iron hoes have been found at megalithic sites many of which date to the pre-Mauryan period. There is little evidence however of any noticeable change in agricultural technology introduced during the Mauryan period at these sites. Artefacts generally associated with the Mauryan period (which are in any case not specifically Mauryan) suggest a concentration in the Ganga valley and its fringes and in central India with a scatter elsewhere. Distinctive cultures existed at the same time in the north-west and in the peninsula. The Mauryan stamp on many of these is not easily discernible from archaeological evidence. Nor do the artefacts from the limited excavations conducted so far point to any major new colonies being established at this time.

Access to labour may have created a further problem. Where slaves were not being used on a massive scale for production there was resort to using *śūdras* and low castes as hired labour. It is sometimes argued that because of the reference to *dāsas* in the sources, the Mauryan economy was dependent on slavery. It needs to be pointed out therefore that a distinction should be maintained between domestic slavery which was generally prevalent at this time and slavery for production which was not the basis of the Mauryan economy. The term *dāsa* is often used both for pledged slaves serving a temporary term and those who were regular lifelong slaves. The former are sometimes differentiated by the word *ahitaka*. The compound phrase *dāsa-bhṛtaka* or *dāsa-karmakara* is more frequently used for labour in production. This makes it more difficult to subtract the degree of slave labour from general labour. Kauṭilya states that the *dāsa* and *karmakara* are to be paid one and a half *paṇa* per month that is eighteen *paṇas* per annum and they and their families were fed.[65] The payment to slaves, however low, would make labour more expensive than the use of unpaid slaves. Tribes inhabiting border lands and forests, the more likely deportees (other than prisoners-of-war) appear to have been left alone and not used as labour. The availability of labour also has to do with the size of the population. Unfortunately this is impossible to estimate in the absence of reliable evidence. It would require far more archaeological excavation and survey for evidence from this source to be used. An impressionistic view suggests a disparity in population distribution.

Since the slaves and hired labourers came substantially from the lower castes the question then arises as to whether it was labour that was not forthcoming or whether it was caste that made it geographically immobile. Low status in caste ranking was based on tribal identities, occupation and also location; and above all status was relative to other groups in the area. Low castes could more easily be put to enforced labour in their own localities, where their subordinate status because of caste was easily accepted. The sharp, clear-cut, universally recognisable distinction between citizen and slave as prevailed in the Graeco-Roman world was not possible in a society where some *āryas* could never become *dāsas* whereas others could, even temporarily. The *dāsa* and the *karmakara* were not a universal category easily identifiable because of being aliens as was the case with slaves in the Mediterranean world. The forceable deportation of people from other lands advised by Kauṭilya was easier as a consequence of war as in the Kaliṅga campaign than as an economic policy. Was it possible then that prisoners-of-war converted to slavery and used as labour were more productive as an economic input than the enforced migration of low caste groups? If so, then with the ceasing of campaigns the availability of labour would also undergo a change.

All this is not to suggest that the Mauryan economy was static. It was a period of substantial economic change in that both agriculture and trade were stimulated. The formation of new states and the commercial prosperity of the subcontinent from the first century BC onwards was founded on the developments of the Mauryan period. But the growth required for sustaining an empire or even the reproduction of the existing resources appears to have been limited. When to this were added other factors of a different kind the empire declined.

In a definition of an empire of the ancient world, the two features of extensive territorial control and the governance of peoples of a different culture — what used to be called euphemistically 'other nations' — remain valid. But to these may be added the further dimension of the relation between the metropolitan state and other areas. An empire would require that revenue, labour and resources from other areas should enrich the metropolitan state and its relation to the other areas was therefore exploitative. An empire should register a range of difference in the manner in which the metropolitan state seeks to integrate the various areas which it controls. The variations are significant, for imperial policy was not necessarily trying to plane them but rather to exploit them. The intensity with which a variety of economies were restructured to the needs of the metropolitan state would be an important consideration in the survival of empires. Often these variations and the degree of restructuring is more visible in the forms of the successor states than in the empire, for empires do encourage at least the pretense of uniformity.

The Mauryan state was an empire to the extent that it did control a large territory with culturally differentiated peoples and its nucleus, the state of Magadha, was enriched by the flow of revenue and resources from other regions. That it was unable to restructure to a greater degree the economy of the core and peripheral areas would perhaps explain why it was short-lived. Its primary concern was with extracting revenue from existing resources and probably not to the same extent with creating new resource bases. This might in part also explain why the imperial idea never really took root in the Indian subcontinent in early times in spite of the rhetoric of texts and inscriptions; where exploitative states were plentiful but where the overwhelming power of metropolitan states remained curtailed.

## II Text and Context: Megasthenes and the Seven Castes*

Despite the proximity of the Hellenistic Greeks there is little that Indian sources have to say about them. If the Mauryas sent ambassadors to the courts of the Seleucids, Ptolemies and Macedonians there are no ambassadors journals; nor are there any records of enterprising merchants who may have travelled to and traded at the markets of Antioch and Alexandria. There is a curious lack of interest in exterior landscapes of other regions which pervades the Indian ethos of earlier times. This is in strong contrast to the Greeks who were not only anxious to explore but also to describe what they had seen, even to the point of being accused of having invented the marvels which they associated with India. Admirals, navigators and ambassadors from west Asia have left narratives of their travels and observations.

* I am grateful to the late Lillian Jeffry for reading the Greek texts with me and to Peter Fraser, Sally Humphreys and Simon Price whose comments on an earlier draft led to useful revisions. I am also grateful to Anthony Michaelis for help with the German texts.

Among the latter was Megasthenes who came from the Seleucid court and is believed to have visited the Mauryan capital and other parts of the state and has recorded his impressions in an account entitled, *Indica*. This work unfortunately has been lost and what survives of it is in the form of what are generally referred to as 'quotations' from later writers concerned with the Hellenistic world. Since the quotations are not invariably in agreement their reliability becomes uncertain. Further those who quote these passages with reference to India are authors whose interest in India is relatively marginal and is an appendix to a broader and more central concern with west Asia and the eastern Mediterranean. Nevertheless the quotations from Diodorus, Strabo and Arrian have been used extensively by scholars in studying the Mauryan period and have raised a large number of controversies. I would like in this lecture to consider a small segment from these quotations, the passages referring to the so-called seven 'castes' of Indian society and re-examine these passages. Such a re-examination raises a number of questions. Were the passages in the later authors quotations from the original or were they a paraphrased version? Was Megasthenes referring to caste when describing Indian society? How reliable are his descriptions of the royal ownership of land? Were the accounts of India influenced by the historiography and the perceptions of Hellenistic culture which formed the intellectual background of these authors? Equally pertinent is the question of the modern interpretation of these texts. There has been a tendency to regard classical authors writing on India as largely reliable perhaps because of the sparseness of Indian descriptive sources. Such questions require attention even if they cannot be conclusively answered.

Megasthenes is quoted as having listed the following seven divisions of Indian society: philosophers, cultivators, herdsmen, artisans and traders, soldiers, overseers and councillors. The divisions are referred to in the Greek texts either as *merē* or *genē* and these terms have been variously translated as 'division' 'class' or 'caste'. Altheim uses 'class' for both *meros* and *genos* (the terms used in the original Greek).[66] Oldfather translating Diodorus renders *merē* as 'castes'[67] as also does Jones translating Strabo,[68] whereas Brunt uses 'classes' for *genea* in Arrian.[69] McCrindle translating Strabo refers to *merē* as 'parts' and *genē* as 'castes' both in the case of Strabo and Arrian. Because of its being a description of Indian society perhaps the term 'caste' has been commonly and arbitrarily used and there is now an established reference to the seven 'castes' of Megasthenes.[70]

According to R.C. Majumdar, 'His (Megasthenes) description of the seven castes which are unknown to Indian literature or tradition may be cited as an example where, on a few basic facts he has reared up a structure which is mostly inaccurate and misleading'.[71] This statement results from a lack of careful reading and understanding of the text. If Majumdar had been sufficiently meticulous he would have realised that not every translation of the original texts uses the word 'caste'. As has been pointed out in a rejoinder to him[72] it is not justified to berate Schwanbeck, who put together the fragments relating to India, because even he cautions against an indiscriminate use of the text. In the introduction to Oldfather's translation of Diodorus the translator makes it clear that he is uncertain whether Diodorus is paraphrasing directly or indirectly. The more significant question it would seem is, why was there this confusion?

The question of how Megasthenes arrived at these seven 'castes' has now become a hardy perennial among the controversies relating to early Indian history. Many suggestions have been made on the interpretation of the seven but there is no general agreement. If Megasthenes was referring to the *varṇa* organisation of Indian society then he should have listed only the four castes of *brāhmaṇas*, (priests), *kṣatriyas* (warriors and landowners), *vaiśyas* (traders and artisans), and *śūdras* (artisans and cultivators) and possibly should also have mentioned the fifth group, that of the untouchables, or at least the Caṇḍālas. If however he was referring to the *jāti* organisation then the number of castes would be innumerable and would certainly exceed seven. They might even have had to be divided into the high and the low as is common in Buddhist texts. Why then did Megasthenes give a precise list of seven? Was he merely repeating what Herodotus earlier had said about there being seven major divisions of Egyptian society as some scholars have argued?

Among those who have written at length on this theme are Otto Stein,[73] B.C.J. Timmer[74] and B. Breloer.[75] Stein doubts that Megasthenes had discussions with Indians on caste since his information does not conform to what we know about caste in the Mauryan period or to the statements in the *Arthaśāstra* of Kauṭilya, some sections of which are of the Mauryan period. Timmer was of a different opinion and felt that Megasthenes did have some familiarity with Indian theories about caste to which he probably added some oral information. Breloer makes the interesting observation that the list given by Megasthenes differs from those of Pliny and Solinus both in sequence and in number since the latter two do not refer to overseers/spies as a separate group. Breloer makes a worthwhile distinction between the division according to *merē* which he argues related to fiscal units and the reference to *genē* which were concerned with the social ordering of the community. He argues that it was Arrian's confusion between the two which resulted in fiscal divisions being seen as castes by modern scholars. This suggestion requires that there be some analysis of the concepts of *merē* and *genē*. Van Buitenen has argued that the seven divisions should be seen as forming three groups, each determined by services to the state and fiscal requirements, what he calls, tax categories.[76] Thus the philosophers do not serve the state nor do they pay taxes. The soldiers, overseers and councillors are paid by the state and therefore do not pay taxes. The cultivators, herdsmen, artisans and traders do not perform services for the state but pay taxes. The seven divisions therefore were essentially fiscal and were listed so by Megasthenes from observation and from information relating to the treasury. The argument is plausible to some extent but one wonders why then did Megasthenes not list them as three distinct groups rather than seven. The distinctions also do not always hold since in some cases the philosophers do serve the state in that they are supposed to foretell weather conditions and events and some among the artisans also served the state and paid no tax.

In taking up this question again I am proposing a change of focus rather than an attempt to solve the problem and the change of focus may help eventually in arriving at a solution. The question is generally analysed by comparing the text of Megasthenes, or rather the variant texts purporting to be quotations from Megasthenes, with contemporary Indian sources, especially the *Arthaśāstra* of Kauṭilya. I would like to argue that there is also a need to look more analytically at the Greek texts and at Hellenistic historiography which forms their ideological context.

The earliest quotation comes in the writings of Diodorus Siculus who, as his name indicates, was a resident of Sicily but visited Egypt in the mid-first century BC. His description of India is part of a larger work, *Library of History*, which was substantially concerned with the eastern Mediterranean and whatever was known of neighbouring north Africa and Asia and which he based on earlier Greek accounts such as that of Megasthenes. This is not regarded as a highly scholarly work but more as a summary of contemporary knowledge about these regions.

Diodorus quoting Megasthenes writes that the Indian people (*plethos*) are divided into seven *merē*.[77] The word *meros* (in the singular) refers to a share or a portion, a heritage, a part, a lot. The sense of a part is in contrast to the whole and also carries the meaning of a branch. Diodorus then goes on to state that no one is allowed to marry a person of another *genos* or follow another calling or trade. Interestingly the word used in this section of the passage is not *meros* but *genos* which has a different meaning.[78] *Genos* means kind or variety and is largely used of divisions relating to race, stock, family, direct descent and birth and has a common usage in Greek as 'clan'. Where Herodotus in his *History* refers to the seven *genē*[79] in Egypt the word has been variously translated into English as nation, tribe, class and clan: a sad reflection on the vagaries of translation. Herodotus lists the seven *genē* as priests, warriors, cowherds, swineherds, tradesmen, interpreters and boatmen. Curiously cultivators are absent which is particularly strange for Egypt. Diodorus therefore uses one word for the general divisions of society which he refers to as the *merē* and another for the rules of marriage and hereditary occupation which derive from *genos*, although he illustrates it by reference to the *merē*, giving the example of a soldier not becoming an artisan or an artisan a philosopher.

As regards the seven divisions, the first is described as the order of the *philosophoi*, a general term translated as philosophers and the description seems to refer to *brāhmaṇas* (and that too the more learned or *śrotriya brāhmaṇas*). They are small in number but have a high status. They are exempt from all public duties and are neither the masters nor the servants of others. They perform sacrificial rituals and live off gifts and honours, suggestive of the *dāna* and *dakṣiṇā* given to *brāhmaṇas*. They make predictions about climate and weather for the state and those who err in their predictions are thereafter silent. This was an important public duty in an economy dependent on agriculture. It is curious that there should have been no reference to the *śramana* sects associated with Buddhism, Jainism, the Ājīvikas and other such religious and philosophical movements of the period, as there is in other works quoting from Megasthenes. Perhaps this section was deleted by Diodorus; for it is hard to explain why the term *philosophoi* was used when the functions described relate more closely to those of the priests, *hiereis*.

The second division is that of the *georgoi*, the cultivators who are exempt from public service and from war. They stay on the *chora*, the rural area and do not go to the *polis* or city. For cultivating the land they pay a *misthos* to the king since all of India is royal land and no private person can possess land. Apart from the *misthos* they pay one-forth (of the produce) to the treasury. *Misthos* is generally regarded as a wage or payment for work done or hired service, or allowance for public service but can also be translated as rent. There are therefore two payments made by the cultivators, one on the land cultivated and the other a share of the produce. This would appear to agree with the two taxes mentioned in Indian sources, the *bali* and the *bhāga*. The Rummindei inscription of Aśoka mentions both.[80] *Bhāga* is clearly a share of the produce and is normally stated to be one-sixth in Indian sources. Thus one-fourth would be higher. *Bali* may have been a tax on the area of land cultivated although it does not indicate a connection with a wage nor does it necessarily imply royal ownership of land. That all land is royal, i.e., owned by the king is contradicted by Indian sources.[81] Possibly the statement was derived from the notion of the *sītā* or royal lands also referred to in the *Arthaśāstra*.[82] The *sītā* lands would be similar to the *chora basilīke* of the Seleucids and the Ptolemies. The word *misthos* however seems ambiguous when referring to what the tenants pay to the state. If the cultivators were working the land owned by the state as labour then the state would have been paying the cultivators a wage or *misthos*. The closest equivalent in Sanskrit would be *bhaṭa* or *vetana*.[83] *Misthosis* however can mean letting for hire or lease and may refer to the state leasing land. The cultivators in this case would be tenants of the state and paying a rent.

The category of *boukoloi* and *poimenes*, herdsmen and shepherds, appear to be a nomadic group as they live in tents and include hunters. These are suggestive of pastoralists not quite settled and of their closeness to forests which often formed the major grazing grounds as Kauṭilya suggests.[84] Interestingly Diodorus does not use the word *meros* for these nomadic groups but refers to the *phylon* of shepherds and herdsmen, a word generally used for tribe. Grazing in forests would require pastoralists to be hunters as well in order to clear the area of predators before their animals could safely graze. Forests located on the borders between kingdoms acted as frontier zones and their inhabitants would tend to be left alone. If they were not incorporated into caste society, they would generally be regarded as different. The term *phylon* does suggest this. The nomadic nature of such groups may have been due to their practice of transhumance in many areas or to the circuits of grazing which required seasonal shifts.

The category of artisans, the *technitai*, are described as implement makers who are exempt from taxes and receive maintenance from the royal treasury. Presumably they work for the state but this is not the same as required service or labour in lieu of tax as is suggested by the Sanskrit *viṣṭi*.[85] The *Arthaśāstra* refers to certain categories of artisans such as armour makers being employed by the state[86] but the major part of the artisans work independently.

The soldiers, *polemistai*, refer to the standing army. If the figures given for the Mauryan army in other Greek and Latin sources are to be believed then the soldiers would have constituted a substantial number.[87] The *ephoroi* were the overseers and the term since it implies secrecy, is also translated as spies whose function was to enquire into and inspect all sections of government work and report back to the king, or in the case of kingless states, to the archons or senior administrators. *Ephoroi* was the standard Spartan term for officials and they were required to make reports to the king. This group is familiar from Indian sources where the *Arthaśāstra* refers to the *adhyakṣas* or superintendents of various departments[88] and Aśoka refers to the *pulisā* in his inscriptions.[89] Their presence in the kingless states, presumably the *gaṇa-saṅghas* or the *gaṇa-rājyas* points to a more sophisticated concept of administration which is corroborated by the association of a hierarchy of officials in the state of the Vṛjjis but mentioned in Buddhists texts of a later period.[90]

The reference to the seventh category as the *bouleuon* and *sumedreuon* underlines Diodorus' statement that they were not ordinary advisors but were members of recognised administrative bodies of high status. The Boule was a formally constituted body of advisors or any council of a Greek city as also was the Synod. Both the Boule and the Synod were well-established institutions in the Greek states of Asia Minor as well. The nearest equivalent would be the *sabhā* or *pariṣad* of Mauryan times and this category probably referred to the *amātyas* and *mahāmātras* of the Mauryan administration.

Our second author Strabo, also quotes from Megasthenes in his famous work, *The Geography*.[91] Strabo was born in Pontos in Asia Minor and was therefore even closer to the Hellenistic world and was a slightly later contemporary of Diodorus having written his book at the turn of the Christian era. His father and grandfather were involved in the politics of Roman generals and he himself was not only familiar with Rome but had also worked at Alexandria in Egypt. His book is knowledgeable on the eastern Mediterranean though doubtless the interest in Asia increased with the spurt in the Roman trade with the east. Strabo was writing at the peak period of the trade with India and one would therefore expect fuller information as compared to earlier texts.

Strabo refers to the people (*plethos*) of India being divided into seven *merē* and lists these in much the same way as Diodorus although with some variants. However when speaking of marriage and occupation he refers to the groups as *genē* and repeats the information regarding the restrictions of marrying within the *genos* and keeping to the same occupation. However he adds that only the philosophers can marry outside their *genos*.

Strabo's description of the *philosophoi* refers to the *brachmanes* but also includes another quotation from Megasthenes which Strabo reads as *garmanes*.[92] This seems to be a mistaken reading for *śramaṇas*. The dual division of the *brāhmaṇas* and the *śramaṇas* is corroborated in the inscriptions of Aśoka.[93] Strabo's description of the *brachmanes* carries hints of the system of the four *āśramas* which was considered as the ideal curriculum for a *brāhmaṇa*; that of the *garmanes* ranges over what would be identified as forest ascetics, *saṃnyāsins*, shamans and *bhikṣus*. Elsewhere in the text Strabo mentions the *brachmanes* and those opposed to them as the *pramnae*, 'a contentious and disputatious sect', of whom there are many varieties.[94] Possibly *pramnae* was a garbled version of *parivrājaka* which the various categories seem to resemble.

As regards the *georgoi* or cultivators, he repeats the statement that the *chora* or countryside is *basilīke* or royal and that the farmers cultivate it for a *misthos* and also pay one-fourth of the produce. The statement that the *chora* is royal implies ownership by the king but Strabo does not explicitly state the absence of private property in land as does Diodorus. H.L. Jones translating this passage has glossed it as, 'the farmers cultivate it for wages on condition of receiving a fourth part of the produce'. This reading makes it a very different statement from that of Diodorus and the gloss is not acceptable to many scholars. It would suggest exceptionally well-paid cultivators since they would keep one-fourth of the produce and be paid a wage for their labour on the land. This was unlikely at the time. One may well ask whether it was necessary to attract cultivators to the state lands in order to extend agriculture? This may be compared to Kauṭilya's advice to the king to bring families of *śūdra* cultivators to settle on waste land or deserted land.[95] The *Arthaśāstra* mentions share-croppers *ardha-sītaka,* in the cultivation of *sītā* lands. Reference is also made to those who give their labour to cultivate land for a share (*bhāga*) of a fourth or a fifth but they do not receive a wage as well.[96] Those that receive a wage do not have to pay a part of the produce. The problematic word in the Greek texts is *misthos* with its meaning of both wage and rent and either meaning would change the premises of taxation. Perhaps Megasthenes did not think it necessary to comment on privately owned land with its range of tenures and therefore confined himself to discussing only the royal land which as a legal form was in any case both familiar and of greater consequence from his Hellenistic experience. Possibly royal land or the *chora basilīke* had a different revenue demand in the Hellenistic states and therefore Megasthenes felt it necessary to comment on the Indian system.

Strabo then refers to the herdsmen (*poimenes*) and the hunters (*thereutai*) where only the first term is the same as that used by Diodorus. The description of this group is similar to that of Diodorus except that Strabo adds that no private person is permitted to keep a horse or an elephant. Both of these were rare commodities. Horses had to be imported into India and elephants could not be bred but had to be captured, the procedure having been described by Megasthenes.

In his fourth category Strabo includes those that sell their physical labour, that is hired labourers and the retail traders or petty traders in the market place, the *kapelikoi.*[97] Some among them adds Strabo are employed by the state alone such as the armour makers and ship builders and they receive a *misthos*/wage and provisions from the king. Other artisans pay a tax, *phoros*, to the state and render prescribed services to the state, (*leitourgiai*). These services may be compared to the *viṣṭi* referred to in the *Arthaśāstra*.[98]

The soldiers (*polemistai*) are described as in Diodorus, so also are the overseers (*ephoroi*). The details of the work of the latter are however spelt out more fully and in this the text of Strabo differs from the others. We are told that they keep the rivers in proper condition, inspect the canals and sluices from which water is distributed, measure the land as in Egypt, collect the taxes, superintend the crafts, as well as the building of roads, and the work of the city commissioners and those in charge of armaments. Strabo's experience of administration in Egypt seems to have influenced this description and some scholars doubt that it was included in the original text of Megasthenes.[99] Its general tenor however is also suggestive of the work of the *adhyakṣa* in the *Arthaśāstra*. The rendering by some scholars of the *ephoroi* solely as spies would seem from this text to be exaggerated. Some overseers would certainly have used spies as part of their system of work but that does not justify translating the term *ephoroi* as spies. The seventh category about which Strabo has little to say are listed as the *sumbouloi* and the *sunedroi*, both terms again connected with the Boule and the Synod and suggestive of advisors of high rank. He adds that their work covers the entire range of administration since they hold the chief offices of state.

The third text which drew on the original of Megasthenes was the *Indica* of Arrian.[100] The author was a native of Bithynia (Asia Minor) and wrote in the early second century AD about four hundred years after Megasthenes. He held high offices under the Romans largely because of the patronage of Hadrian but eventually retired to Athens. He wrote extensively on a variety of subjects but was more centrally a historian and deeply influenced by Xenophon. He was easily the most scholarly of the three authors under discussion. Arrian was also involved in the intellectual movement of the early centuries AD which has come to be called the Second Sophistic.[101] This expressed itself in a nostalgia for the classical period of Athens recalling the achievements of Athens in the fifth century BC by imitating Attic prose and literary forms and often writing in what was by now the archaic Ionian Greek. This movement was in part the result of the prosperity of the Hellenised cities of the eastern Mediterranean in the face of what was seen as subservience to Roman power. Arrian's major work was a history of Alexander of

Macedon, the *Anabasis*, and this in a way led to a number of accounts of regions such as Parthia and India where Alexander had campaigned. Arrian used as sources for the *Anabasis*, Ptolemy as well as a large number of contemporary accounts of Alexander such as those of Nearchos, Onesicritus and Aristobulus. The *Indica* is however only a coda to the *Anabasis* since this was not the primary interest of Arrian. As has been rightly said, for Arrian, India had a marginal role between the Macedonians and the Persians who in his perception were the dominant powers at the time of Alexander.[102]

Quoting from Megasthenes he states that all the Indians are divided into seven *genea*.[103] This is different from the earlier two authors who refer to these divisions as *merē*. Was he quoting more precisely from Megasthenes or, was he merely copying Herodotus? Was he substituting a term which he thought was closer in meaning to the concept of caste? Alternatively he may have argued that since the crucial unit involving marriage and occupation was termed the *genos*, it would be more logical to use the same word for the seven divisions as well.

The first category he labels as *sophistai* and therefore differs from the earlier authors. His description is close to that of the *philosophoi* and the *brachmanes* of the earlier authors yet the choice of the word *sophistai* is curious. It refers to philosophers and teachers, especially peripatetic, and those skilled in art. The religious connotation is less evident in this term. He may have had in mind also the renewal of interest in the sophists as the wise men of a society, during his lifetime. This would agree with his statement that anyone in India can become a sophist, but few do because they have to lead such a hard life. Yet in the *Anabasis* he refers to the *brachmanes* as Indian *sophistai* and at another point refers in a general way to Indian sophists.[104] But his description of the sophists has less of brahmanical belief and practices and more of an extensive range of renunciatory sects: in fact more of the *śramaṇas* than of the *brāhmaṇas*.

The cultivators (*georgoi*) according to him pay *phoros* to the kings and the cities which are self-governing. *Phoros* literally refers to payments of tribute. Arrian makes no reference to ownership of land or to royal ownership. Interestingly in the case of the third category that of the herdsmen and pastoralists (*boukoloi, poimenes* and *nomeis*) they are again described as nomadic but are said to pay a *phoros* from the produce of their animals. The same term *phoros* is used even though the animals are not state owned. This would suggest that in the context of land, *phoros* was a tax and not a rent and was probably a share of the produce. The statement is again repeated for the fourth category described by Arrian as the *demiourgikon* and the *kapelikon*, the artisans and traders. Interestingly *demiourgikon* was the term used for artisans and traders in classical Athens. This category are also said to have paid a *phoros* to the state. The only exceptions are the armourers, shipwrights and sailors employed by the state who are paid a *misthos*. *Misthos* in this case was the wage paid by the state to those whom it employed.

The fifth category of soldiers of *polemistai* are paid so well by the state that they can afford to maintain others on their pay. Again the word *misthos* is used here. In place of the *ephoroi* Arrian uses the term *episkopoi* which has a stronger sense of inspecting and overseeing. The seventh category are the *bouleuomenoi* who deliberate on state matters with the king and with the archons in the autonomous cities. It is from this group that the officers of state are selected and the list of functions given by Arrian would again point to the *mahāmātras* of the Mauryan state, although such functions would be performed by senior officers in any well-developed administration.

Arrian concludes with the statement that to marry out of any *genos* is unlawful as also to change professions from one *genos* to another. This is permitted only to the *sophistai*. The consistency of the statement relating to marriage and occupation in all three texts makes it clear that this at least was common to all and undoubtedly went back to Megasthenes. The listing of seven divisions was also common although the element of variation in the terms used suggest that it was more an adaptation from Megasthenes than an actual quotation. Only the terms for cultivators (*georgoi*), herdsmen (*poimenes*) and soldiers (*polemistai*), are common to all three versions. The other terms generally occur in two out of three texts and not always consistently. There are as we have seen discrepancies on the question of agrarian revenue. Similarly the details regarding the first category differ. The crucial term used for the seven divisions varies and two authors use *merē* and *phylon* and the third uses *genē*. All three however use *genos* with reference to marriage relations. Thus the quotations from Megasthenes are only approximate quotations or paraphrased versions. Arrian's style is recognisably different from that of Diodorus and Strabo and his version attempts to give perhaps only the gist of what Megasthenes may have said. The difference may partially also be due to his writing in the Ionian dialect. Clearly the meaning of 'quotation' should not be taken in the more modern sense of stating the actual words of the source. Each author seems to have paraphrased Megasthenes in his own words.

On the question of editing and paraphrasing Megasthenes, Arrian would have had no qualms since he was convinced that most accounts of Alexander's activities and subsequently of his dominions were exaggerated in order to flatter the Macedonian.[105] Onesicritus was generally held in better esteem perhaps because he was a philosopher and a pupil of Diogenes and because he was a contemporary of Alexander. That he influenced Arrian is suggested for example by his consistent use of the term 'sophist' for what might be called Indian 'holy men' which usage was followed by Arrian.[106] Another source regarded as reliable by Arrian was the account of Nearchos who wrote not in Ionian Greek but in a *koiné* requiring Arrian to paraphrase his views.[107] Arrian in any case had his doubts about the reliability of the text of Megasthenes on areas of India beyond the north-west which Megasthenes may possibly not have visited.

Modern historians have debated the veracity of Megasthenes and it is as well to remember that he was regarded with suspicion even by his contemporaries. We are told that he was sent by Seleucus Nicator on an embassy to Sandrocottos (Candragupta) who had his capital at Palibothra (Pāṭaliputra).[108] The book would then have been a description of his visit to India at the time of Candragupta the first Mauryan king. Strabo adds that Deimachus was sent on a similar mission to the son of Sandrocottos, Amitrachades, (i.e., the son of Candragupta, Bindusāra), and he too left an account and goes on to say that the accounts of Nearchos and Onesiciritus were however more truthful.[109] Dionysius is believed to have been sent by Ptolemy Philadelphus of Egypt to ascertain the truth of the account given by Megasthenes. Eratosthenes maintains that Megasthenes and Deimachus accused each other of falsehood.[110] Arrian states that Megasthenes lived with Sibyrtius, the satrap of Arachosia (in modern Afghanistan) and Gedrosia and often visited Sandrocottos.[111] He may thus have spent most of his time in Kandahar and his perspective on India may therefore have focussed more on north-western India than on the Ganga valley. That Kandahar was an important Greek city, possibly the Alexandria in Arachosia, is suggested by recent excavations and finds.[112] Megasthenes was familiar with the Seleucid satrapy and kingdom and if he resided in Arachosia then there would be some Seleucid influence in his picture of India. Among later authors Clement of Alexandria[113] refers to Megasthenes as an historian and Pliny disapproves of both Megasthenes and Dionysius.[114] Thus the veracity of Megasthenes' account may well have been tempered by his inability to obtain detailed information and therefore the Hellenistic and Seleucid imprint may have been greater than has been recognised so far. The quotations from Megasthenes if seen in the light of this as well may not have been taken too literally. They may have been introduced and amended by each author partially to give legitimacy to his own descriptions.

The historiographical ancestry of the *Indica* of Megasthenes is linked to similar writing in Egypt and Babylon as has been pointed out. In the Hellenistic world the account of Egypt written before the end of the fourth century BC by Hecataeus of Abdera, was widely read and respected and treated as a model.[115] The state of Egypt was idealised and projected as a new kind of society which had earlier even excited the interest of Plato. Hecataeus though apparently concerned with Pharaonic ideas and the antiquity of Egypt, was at the same time eulogising the Ptolemies. Manethon, an Egyptian writing in Greek in the early third century BC reiterated these ideas.[116] The challenge was taken up from another direction when Berossus the Chaldean wrote a history of Babylon which he dedicated to Antiochus I and which was partially a Seleucid reply as it were, to Hecataeus, suggesting that there were systems other than the Egyptian considered worthwhile as forms of government and society.

Megasthenes it has been argued, was doing the same in writing on India.[117] He was also seeking a utopian society and was projecting India as such. The magic and the marvels were somewhat reduced especially when compared to the discredited earlier account of Ktesias. But the exotica remained. At another level it was a society which gave maximum honour to philosophers, which insisted on the hereditary nature of occupations and which did not require slaves; all these ideas evoked the interest of contemporary Greeks.[118] Nevertheless in the actual structure of the *Indica*, the account of Hecataeus seems to have been the model in as much as it was divided into sections on cosmology, geography, king-lists (of a sort), the organisation of society and social customs.[119] This format was to be frequently used by Hellenistic writers. Historiographically Arrian is the most important of the three authors quoting from Megasthenes and was influenced by the structure of the earlier *Indica.*[120] His account is also divided into similar sections and he is even more determined to leave out the marvels and the curiosities with which descriptions of India abounded, what he refers to as the gold-digging ants and the gold guarding griffons.

Apart from the historiographical context there is also the question of the influence of prevalent forms in the Seleucid and Ptolemaic systems which may have coloured the perception of India. The Hellenistic imprint can probably be seen more clearly in the statement on land ownership and agrarian revenue. The economy of the Seleucids, the neighbours of the Mauryas, based largely on agrarian revenue listed as the most important categories of land, the *chora basilīke* or the private estates of the king, and the land owned by the independent Greek cities.[121] The king assigned land from the *chora basilīke*. But the existence of royal estates did not preclude ownership of land by the temples or tribes or even private ownership. The *chora basilīke* was cultivated under the supervision of officials by hereditary tenants who paid in cash or kind and the payment could also be in the form of a part of the harvest. The payment was for the use of the land which was said to belong to the king, and was based on earlier prevailing systems. Megasthenes would therefore have been familiar with the notion of the *chora basilīke* and the Mauryan *sītā* lands may have seemed to him to be the exact counterpart of the Seleucid system. The cultivation of land by the state even if not to the exclusion of private ownership of land, is referred to in the Kauṭilya *Arthaśāstra*, where the king is advised to settle new land or deserted land with *śūdra* cultivators.[122] This would have been a major change in the economic picture from earlier times and may have been much talked about; hence suggesting to Megasthenes that the *sītā* lands were far more important than any other system of tenure. The statement regarding cultivation and the payment of a *misthos* may well have been confined to such lands and was not meant to exclude private ownership.

The reference to self-governing cities is puzzling. Although a familiar feature of Hellenistic Asia Minor they are not referred to in Indian sources, unless Megasthenes had in mind a vague notion of the *gaṇa-saṅghas* each of which had an urban centre as its nucleus. The *polis* system of self-governing cities has been described as a pillar of Seleucid power. Lands were assigned to the cities from the estates of the king's land. The cities had considerable autonomy in issuing coins and collecting taxes. The advantage to the Seleucids was that such cities paid a *phoros* or tribute to the ruling family.

The reference to taxes paid to the king and to the self-governing cities in the same passage is so characteristic of the Seleucid system that one may be justified in arguing that this statement could have been taken from the Seleucid system and applied to the Mauryan. Interestingly it is only Arrian, with his experience of Asia Minor who mentions the self-governing cities. Neither Diodorus nor Strabo refer to these, perhaps because they were more familiar with the Ptolemaic kingdom where such cities did not exist.

For both Diodorus and Strabo it was the Ptolemaic state that was possibly the model for systems relating to the Orient, particularly with the increasing communication between the Red Sea and the Indian subcontinent at the turn of the Christian era. The prevalent view in Egypt had been that the gods were the owners of the land and since the kings were their descendents this enabled them to claim ownership.[123] The *chora* was the estate of the king. Political philosophy was dominated by the idea that the king owns and manages the land and has the right to compulsory labour. Agriculture under the Ptolemies was carefully controlled by a large body of officers who assessed and measured the land and managed the distribution of water, all of which was geared to the goal of revenue collection. Land owned by the king, royal land, was cultivated by peasants under royal control, the *georgoi basilikoi*,[124] who were under contract to the king by which they paid a share of the produce to the king and cultivated according to instructions. This did not exclude other categories of ownership such as temple lands, service tenures and privately owned land, although royal ownership was the predominant form. Could this have influenced the comprehension by Diodorus and Strabo of agriculture in India as described by Megasthenes and led to the confusion between the two senses of *misthos*?

In Hellenistic states taxes were paid to the king only from the *chora basilīke*. Other categories of land owners such as temples, autonomous cities and individuals, received the contracted amounts from the peasants and had their own arrangements with the king. Since the major land revenue was from the *chora basilīke* Megasthenes may have assumed that the same was applicable in India and that there was no need to mention other tenurial arrangements. By the time that Arrian was writing, the economy based on the *chora basilīke* had ceased to exist in both the erstwhile Ptolemaic and Seleucid areas. This might in part account for his not referring to the royal ownership of land but merely to the *phoros* paid by the cultivators.

The historiographical context is equally important on the question of social divisions. The term *meros/merē* is familiar to Greek thought particularly through the writings of Aristotle, who would also have had an intellectual influence on Megasthenes. Aristotle's ideas appear to have been known in the centres of Hellenistic activity. It has been suggested that one of his more celebrated disciples, Klearchus, was active at Ai-Khanum the Greek city on the Oxus.[125] Furthermore that he drew attention to the religion and philosophy of the Persians and the Indians. The Hellenistic cities were doubtless the meeting point of a variety of ideas and theories. In his *Politics*, Aristotle refers to various concepts which seem also to be reflected in the views of Megasthenes. Thus he states that each citizen body was composed of a number of *merē* or parts having widely varying characteristics.[126] He then lists the parts of the citizen body as the *georgoi* or cultivators, the *banausoi* or artisans, the *agoraioi* or traders (including the *emporoi* or inter-state merchants and the *kapeloi* or petty traders) and finally the *thetikon* or labourers working for a wage. In some places soldiers are added as a fifth group.[127] All these are said to constitute the larger mass of people, the *plethos*. Interestingly both Diodorus and Strabo refer to the *plethos* or people of India being divided into seven *merē*. Aristotle adds that in every city there are three *merē* — the rich, the poor and those of the middle group.[128] He emphasises the difference between the rich and the poor and an important element in this difference is honour or *timē* which also bestows status on a person. He states that the rich are armed and the poor are unarmed.[129]

In the general discussion on the constitutions associated with oligarchies and democracies, numerous divisions of people are listed as the *merē*. Generally these include farmers, artisans, traders, seafarers, labourers and servile groups. The classification of the *merē* was a matter of considerable debate at this time and presumably Megasthenes was aware of this debate and perhaps had it in mind when composing the *Indica*. In discussing the important officers of government, Aristotle heads the list with designations which are included in the list of *ephoroi* in Strabo.[130] Similarly in passages referring to the requirements of a state the responsibilities of those concerned with food, handicrafts, arms, wealth, religion and decision-making are again suggestive of the divisions listed by Megasthenes although such divisions are so general that they could apply to virtually any society.[131] According to Aristotle the divisions into *merē* are necessary in order to separate functions and that this was established long since in many areas such as Egypt and Crete.[132] It has recently been argued that the Aristotelian concept of *merē* virtually means class since property qualifications and the functions they perform in the productive process are an important aspect of a *meros*[133] Aristotle ends up with a basic division between the propertied and the propertyless and takes a man's economic position as determining his behaviour. But the *merē* as listed by Aristotle or Megasthenes do not have distinct property qualifications. The *merē* of Megasthenes can perhaps be better explained as being linked to production although even this is not an exhaustive criterion for each category. To use class in the modern sense for *meros* would also be misleading as the groups mentioned by Megasthenes do not constitute classes. Megasthenes also mentions that the category of philosophers and of councillors are regarded with respect and have high status or *timē*. The property qualifications or role in production of the former at least would be unimportant to their status. The *georgoi* or peasants, presumably making up the poorer sections of society were kept unarmed. Doubtless the importance of this statement also relates to the argument in Aristotle that arms should be restricted to the rich. That the peasants could continue working in their fields whilst a battle raged in the vicinity, seems to have impressed the Greeks, particularly as the latter had often to resort to conscription.

The seven *merē* of Megasthenes if seen from the perspective of the Aristotelian concept of *merē* make good sense. They are a list of the important divisions of the population involved in the functioning of society. They can be further divided into three broad groups: the first, the philosophers and sophists are those with the maximum honour or *timē* and prescribe on matters religious; the next three constitute a second group concerned with economic production since they consist of cultivators, herdsmen, artisans and traders; and the last three constitute the third group that of persons responsible for administrative functions, namely, soldiers, officials and councillors.

Why did Megasthenes choose the number seven for the *merē* of India? This may have been based on the seven divisions in Egypt as listed by Herodotus. But it is equally possible as it has been argued that a current Indian concept may explain this number. With the gradual evolution of the monarchical state in India, there emerged by the late fourth century BC the notion of the constituent elements of the state. This concept was referred to as the *saptaprakṛti* or more commonly later as the *saptāṅga*.[134] These were the seven elements or the seven limbs of the body politic. The listing of the seven elements was of course different from the *merē* of Megasthenes. The *saptāṅga* consisted of the king, the ministers, the capital, the treasury, the army or a form of authority, territory and allies. Possibly when enquiring about notions regarding the polity and the state, the seven elements were quoted to Megasthenes and he remembered the figure but reconstructed the elements on the principles of the *merē* which were more familiar to his own intellectual background.

It is possible therefore that the original text of Megasthenes may have used the word *merē* and have derived the number seven from the *saptāṅga* theory. Arrian perhaps then replaced *merē* by *genea* and retained the term *genos* when it came to marriage and occupation. He may also have seen in this description a similarity in the use of *genos* with the meaning given to it in the classical period of Athens.

The reference to *genos* states the two important characteristics of caste as marriage rules and restrictions and those relating to occupation. Here again Megasthenes picked up the salient points about caste organisation but perhaps confused caste with *meros*. It is also important to consider whether he was referring to *varṇa* or *jāti*. It would seem that he was not referring to *varṇa* for a variety of reasons. *Varṇas* were four in number, possibly five, but never seven. The seven categories are described by Megasthenes not by special names but in general descriptive terms. Where *brachmanes* may well refer to the first *varṇa*, *brāhmaṇa*, there is no further mention of the remaining three. Of the latter the *kṣatriyas* and the *śūdras* as names of ethnic communities were familiar to the Greeks since they are mentioned in the accounts of the campaign of Alexander in the form of Xathroi and Sydracae.[135] There is curiously no mention of the untouchables or even the Caṇḍālas or the concept of pollution which should have been a strikingly new feature to an observer from another society. (This could be attributed not to a lack of observation but to the influence of a Greek model of social divisions). The occupational groupings are also not suggestive of *varṇa* since it would not have been common to find hired labourers, artisans and traders listed as belonging to one *varṇa*; the former were frequently of *śūdra* status and the latter *vaiśya*. Had Megasthenes been reflecting the dominant ideas of the middle Ganga valley it is possible that he would have listed the *kṣatriyas* as first which was the case in Buddhist and Jaina writings. High status being given to the *brāhmaṇas* might suggest the influence of brāhmaṇical thinking, except that the compound of *brāhmaṇa* and *śramaṇa* occurs in the Aśokan inscriptions as a general category and included those in a religious vocation or renouncers and teachers and therefore of high status. The joint mention of *brāhmaṇas* and *śramaṇas* would again suggest a category other than that of the *varṇa* since the *brāhmaṇas* and the *śramaṇas* (in many cases) regarded each other with considerable hostility.[136]

Whereas the *dharmaśāstra* texts give priority to *varṇa* as the pattern of social organisation, it has been argued that this was more in the nature of a theoretical model or norm or reflective of ritual status; and, that, as is evident from Buddhist sources, *jāti* organisation was the more recognisable and effective social form, in which both kinship and marriage as well as occupation were important factors of identity. The term *genos* which implies a blood/kin connection would be more indicative of *jāti*. Interestingly *genos* is regarded as a cognate of the Sanskrit *jana* which shared the root *ja* with the word *jāti*.

*Genos* has its own history.[137] Fustel de Coulanges has argued that *genos* was a corporate group with common 'property' and collective activities as well as symbols of unity. Later writers have argued that it was a form of grouping to which only some families belonged and it developed particularly in Athenian aristocracy. The rich encouraged a pride of lineage to symbolise superior status. Originally they were of the noble *eupatridai* order but gradually families began to claim rights to certain offices and this became parallel to property and each such group of families constituted a *genos*. One family reiterated this right by insisting on a rule of endogamy. The right also constituted its identity as a corporate group.

If we argue that Megasthenes was revised by Arrian as is suggested by Breloer then the explanation for Arrian having replaced *meros* by *genos* would require a finer linguistic analysis of the use of *genos* in the Greek context and its various meanings. Recent studies of *genos* do not help us in arriving at a more precise definition of its use either by Megasthenes or Arrian.

It could of course also be argued that *meros* and *genos* were used arbitrarily, if not interchangeably, in descriptions of alien societies; and that there was no technical meaning attached to either of them since both Herodotus and Arrian use *genos* for social divisions in societies as distinct as those of Egypt and India. One would then have to look for the specific description of Indian society which might suggest something distinctive, namely, caste. Megasthenes understood the essentials of a caste society when he emphasised the importance of endogamy in marriage, all except for the *brāhmaṇas*; and of course the principle of hereditary caste status as well as the association of caste with occupation and the restrictions on changing occupation. In this passage from Megasthenes as it has come to us in the three versions which have been discussed, there is a juxtaposition of two statements. First, that Indian society was divided into seven parts. Secondly, that Indian society had specific rules of marriage and occupation. These rules were then illustrated by reference to the seven parts resulting in perhaps an incorrect merging of the two ideas by Megasthenes. His confusion lay in identifying his divisions, the *merē*, with the notion of social divisions in India constituting an endogamous unit and governing hereditary occupations.

The utilisation of texts from the ancient period remains a complicated process and requires the removing of many veils of obscurity. With greater research into the precise meaning of terms and inevitably therefore of historical interpretation, the translations made in the nineteenth century of such sources have often to be re-examined. There is also the need to be aware of the perceptions of the original authors and of those who in later periods paraphrased the original. This I have tried to demonstrate in arguing that references to the agrarian structure owe more perhaps to the imprint of the Seleucid and Ptolemaic systems than to an authentic description of the Mauryan. Whereas Diodorus and Strabo mention the *chora basilīke* and refer to the payment of a *misthos*, Arrian makes no mention of royal ownership of land and refers only to a *phoros* or tax. The *chora basilīke* was the most important agricultural land in the Seleucid and Ptolemaic states and it was the equivalent of this which Megasthenes was seeking and to which he refers. The phrase *chora basilīke* is so closely linked to those two states that its use for Mauryan India echoes the other two.

The importance of crown lands to the Mauryan economy has been argued on the strength of references to *sītā* lands in the *Arthaśāstra* and to Megasthenes' statements regarding the *chora basilīke*. I have tried to show that it is necessary to examine the context of such descriptions before taking them as factual. If the Kauṭilya *Arthaśāstra* was in fact a text concerned primarily with the revenue of the metropolitan state, the discussion on *sītā* lands would have to be central. The same would be true of Megasthenes if he was describing the *sītā* lands when referring to the *chora basilīke*. My problem is with the statement that there were only crown lands. This seems to be both partial and influenced by conditions prevalent elsewhere, as I have tried to argue. That there is disagreement in the three texts following Megasthenes on the ownership of land would point to Megasthenes not having made a clear statement. Was this because the incidence of crown lands was not as extensive as Diodorus and Strabo would have us believe? The confusion in these two authors over whether *misthos* refers to rent or tax or whether it was a wage would indicate that the text of Megasthenes was not categorical on this crucial matter. Or, that the confusion has arisen because there were other tenures which have not been listed by Megasthenes, but whose contractual conditions had entered the original discussion.

The seven subdivisions of Indian society as listed by Megasthenes which doubtless drew on some observation, present features of Indian society which require attention. Clearly the definition is in terms other than *varṇa* and is most likely *jāti*. The two characteristics on which there is complete agreement are those referring to endogamous marriage and hereditary occupation. (This is so firmly stated that one almost suspects Megasthenes of having read modern Indian ethnography!). It would seem that a certain parochialism in the functioning of caste is indicated and here I would like to repeat what I said in the first lecture, that there is a need to look at caste along its vertical axis first when trying to assess its role in production.

The Greek in Megasthenes saw these subdivisions as universal categories, but he lists them in no known order. If he began with the *brāhmaṇas* and *śramaṇas* because they are the most highly respected, he should have proceeded to the next most highly respected group, that of councillors and advisors. But the latter come last and instead the second category are the cultivators because they are the largest in number. He nowhere mentions that they are regarded as of low status. That they are the largest in number would bear out the dependence at this time on agricultural revenue.

Herders and huntsmen which even in Buddhist sources are listed as low, are not referred to as such. But significantly they are identified by *phylon* or tribe, suggesting that they might have been regarded as somehow outside the usual framework of caste society. Were these the *āṭavika* or forest tribes mentioned by both Aśoka and Kauṭilya?

If they were outside the caste structure then they would have been more mobile. Why then were they not deported and used as labour? Was it because it was thought safer to leave them in their forests, so that resources from the forests could be more easily tapped through them? That they did provide revenue in kind is explicitly stated. This may have led to these areas being deliberately cordoned off, to prevent interference. Or was it because hired labour and the large number of cultivators sufficed for Mauryan economic ambitions?

The commercial economy is neatly tied up in one package which binds together hired labour, artisans and traders, suggestive of the urban guild which in the post-Mauryan period was to integrate all three groups.

Megasthenes elsewhere, makes an important statement which has been dismissed by historians as it appears to conflict with Indian sources. He states that there were no slaves in India and in this respect draws on the similarity with Sparta.[138] Perhaps the clue to his meaning lies in the reference to Sparta. Spartan helotage was very much a Spartan phenomenon in the Greek world and there was some discussion as to whether helotage was the same as the more general form of slavery, that of the doulos. These were individual slaves and unlike the helots were not an enslaved community owned by the state. What Megasthenes was probably commenting on was the absence of a doulos type of slavery with slaves used on a large scale in both agricultural and artisanal production. Indian sources do provide evidence of slaves of the doulos variety i.e. men and women owned outright as property, with no legal rights or status and not receiving a wage. However such slaves although used in production, appear in large numbers as domestic slaves. What is interesting is that Megasthenes although aware of the issue, does not notice the use of either slaves or hired labour in agricultural production. This may have been because if they were paid even a minimal wage as some slaves were, they would not strictly speaking qualify as doulos.

There was a time when it was argued that the most reliable source material on ancient India was the literature which emanated from Hellenic and Hellenistic authors. Modern scholars were imbued with the notion that somehow the Greek tradition because it had what Europe recognised more easily as, 'a sense of history' could therefore be depended upon by historians. The world of Vincent Smith may have ended but its resonances still reach out to us as do those of scholars who vehemently insist that such sources by virtue of being 'foreign' cannot be relied upon. Because of the paucity of descriptive narrative sources from the Indian tradition for the first millennium BC, the Greek texts also came to be regarded as more reliable than the Indian in depicting the actual conditions of society, rather than the theory behind the institutions. Hence the acute problem over the 'seven castes'. I have tried to argue that even these texts and their context require a more critical investigation before their statements can be taken as fact. This is not an attempt at Orientalism in reverse, for this exercise would be necessary in using any textual material, no matter what its authorship or content.

I have tried to show that the need to consider the ideological influences on the authors of texts becomes significant in that authors are given to ideological positions whether they are aware of these or not. It would be as well to keep in mind Arnaldo Momigliano's assessment of the ancient historians when he writes, 'Greek and Roman historians in fact, after Herodotus, did very little research into the past and relatively seldom undertook to collect first-hand evidence about foreign countries. They concentrated on contemporary history or summarised and reinterpreted the work of former historians'.[139] The use of such literary sources then becomes an enterprise in going beyond the obvious: a process which requires of historical study a proximity both to the comparative method and to historiography.

NOTES AND REFERENCES

1. Bhabra Edict, J. Bloch, *Les Inscriptions d'Asoka*, Paris, 1950, p. 154.
2. Romila Thapar, *Aśoka and the Decline of the Mauryas*, London, 1961, p. 130.
3. A. Embree, *India's Search for National Identity*, New York, 1972.
4. W.V. Harris, 'On War and Greed in the Second Century BC', *The American Historical Review*, Dec. 1971, 76, 5, pp. 1371–85. A.N. Sherwin–White, 'Rome the Aggressor?', *JRS*, 1980, 80, pp. 177–81. M. Finley, 'Colonies — an Attempt at Typology', *Trans. R. Hist. Soc.*, 5th Series, 1976, 26, pp. 167–88; 'Empire in the Greco-Roman World', *Greece and Rome*, 1978, NS 25, pp. 1–15; P.D.A. Garnsey and C.R. Wittaker (eds), *Imperialism in the Ancient World*, Cambridge, 1978.
5. K. Wittfogel, *Oriental Despotism*, New Haven, 1957; K. Polanyi (ed.), *Trade and Markets in the Early Empires*, Glencoe, 1957; S.N. Eisenstadt, *The Political System of Empires*, New York, 1969.
6. Romila Thapar, 'The State as Empire', in H. Classen and P. Skalnik, *The Study of the State*, The Hague, 1981, pp. 409–26.
7. H.C. Raychaudhuri, *Political History of Ancient India*, Calcutta, 1972 (Revised ed.), p. 203.
8. B.M. Barua, 'Hathigumpha Inscription of Kharavela', *IHQ*, 1938, XIV, pp. 259ff.
9. Major Rock Edict (MRE), XIII, Bloch, op. cit., p. 129; *Arthaśāstra (hereafter Artha)*, 2.1.6; 2.34.11.
10. *Artha.*, 2.34.
11. *Artha.*, 11.1ff.
12. Ibid., 2.24; 2.6.
13. The use of the term *ahāra* for a unit of administration is of some interest. *Ahāra* literally means food and it may be suggested that by extension therefore it referred to the agriculturally rich and revenue yielding core areas or else regions where revenue was computed in foodgrains.
14. *Artha.*, 2.1. Diodorus, II.40.
15. *Artha.*, 13.1.20–1.
16. The repeated occurrence of PGW sites on flood plains suggests this.

B.B. Lal, 'Excavations at Hastinapur', *Ancient India*, 1954 and 1955, nos 10 and 11, pp. 5ff.

17. Diodorus, II.40; Arrian, XI.
18. D.D. Kosambi, *An Introduction to the Study of Indian History*, Bombay, 1956, p. 196. The word used in both sources is the same, *apāvahana*.
19. *Cullanārada Jātaka*, no. 477; *Artha*, 3.13.
20. Bloch, op. cit., p. 157.
21. Junagadh Inscription of Rudradāman, D.C. Sircar, *Select Inscriptions*, Calcutta, 1965, p. 175. *Ep. Ind.*, 8, pp. 36ff.
22. *Artha.*, 2.24; 3.9; 6.1.
23. Strabo, XV.1.20; Diod., II, 35–6. K.A. Chaudhuri, *Ancient Agriculture and Forestry in Northern India*, Bombay, 1977.
24. Ibid., XV.1.50.
25. *Artha.*, 2.21; 2.22; Strabo, XV.1.50–2.
26. *Artha.*, 2.4.16; See R.P. Kangle, *The Kauṭilīya Arthaśāstra*, II, Bombay, 1972, p. 69.
27. Ibid., 2.36.6–7.
28. J. Marshall, *Taxila*, I, Cambridge, 1951, pp. 103ff.
29. *Artha.*, 4.1; 4.2.
30. Ibid., 5.3.14–17.
31. B.K. Thapar, 'Maski 1954', *Ancient India*, 1957, 13, pp. 86–7; R.E.M. Wheeler, 'Brahmagiri and Chandravalli 1947', *Ancient India*, 1947–8, 4, 180ff.
32. 2.13 and 14.
33. A.H. Dani, *Chilas*, Islamabad, 1983. Engravings of ibexes and other animals on the rocks point to an early settlement of the area.
34. MRE, V, Bloch, op. cit., p. 103.
35. MRE, II, Bloch, op. cit., p. 93. Epigraphic confirmation of the Satīyaputra has recently come from a post-Mauryan inscription at Jambai.
36. MRE, XIII, Bloch, op. cit., pp. 130–1.
37. D.D. Kosambi, *Indian Numismatics*, New Delhi, 1981.
38. Pliny, *Hist. Nat.*, VI.21–2; Plutarch, *Life of Alexander*, LXII.
39. M.I. Finley, 'The Question of Population', *The Journal of Roman Studies*, 1958, 48, pp. 156–64. 'Manpower and the Fall of Rome', *Aspects of Antiquity: Discoveries and Controversies*, New York, 1966.
40. J.M. Datta, 'Population of India about 320 BC', *Man in India*, Oct.–Dec. 1962, vol. 42, no. 4.
41. 5.3.38.
42. Strabo, XV.1.41.
43. Arrian, XII.
44. 2.33.8.
45. *Dīgha Nikāya*, 1.88ff; 3.156.

46. *Artha.*, 5.3.
47. *Nanda Jātaka*, no. 39; *Gāmani-caṇḍa Jātaka*, no. 257.
48. 2.35.
49. 2.1.7.
50. MRE, III, Bloch, op. cit., p. 96.
51. John Irwin however maintains that some were pre-Aśokan. 'The True Chronology of Asokan Pillars', *Artibus Asiae*, 1983, XLIV, 4, pp. 247–65.
52. *Artha.*, 4.1.52–5.
53. J. Filliozat, 'Graeco-Aramaic Inscriptions of Aśoka near Kandahar', *Ep. Ind.*, 1961–2, XXXIV, pp. 1ff.
54. Romila Thapar, 'Epigraphic Evidence and some Indo-Hellenistic Contacts during the Mauryan Period', in S.K. Maity and U. Thakur (eds), *Indological Studies, D.C. Sircar Commemoration Volume*, Delhi, 1988, pp. 15–19. *See* chapter 22 in this volume.
55. N. Subrahmanian, *Pre-Pallava Tamil Index*, Madras, 1966, p. 163; *Aham*, 253: 19; 115: 5; 36: 17.
56. F.E. Pargiter, '. . . *Dynasties of the Kali Age*, London, 1931, pp. 26ff.
57. *Dīgha Nikāya*, II.166; *Mahāvaṃsa*, V.16; *Dīpavaṃsa*, VI.19.
58. S.J. Tambiah, *World Conqueror and World Renouncer*, Cambridge, 1976.
59. Romila Thapar, 'Renunciation: the Making of a Counter-Culture?', in *Ancient Indian Social History: Some Interpretations*, New Delhi, 1978, pp. 63ff. *See* chapter 40 in this volume.
60. The Kosam, Bhabra, Rummindei and Nigali-Sagar edicts, Bloch, op. cit., pp. 152ff, 154, 157, 158.
61. Bloch, op. cit., pp. 161ff.
62. 11.1.4.
63. R.N. Mehta, 'Sudarshan Lake', *JOI*, Baroda, 1968, XVIII, 1 and 2, pp. 20–8.
64 Junagadh Rock Inscription of Rudradaman, *Ep. Ind.*, 8, pp. 36ff.
65. 2.24.28.
66. F. Altheim, *Weltgeschichte Asiens in Griechischen Zeitalter*, I, Halle, 1974, pp. 257–64.
67. C.H. Oldfather, *Diodorus of Sicily*, II, Cambridge, Mass., 1979.
68. H.L. Jones, *The Geography of Strabo*, Cambridge, Mass., 1966.
69. P.A. Brunt, *Arrian*, II, Cambridge, Mass., 1983.
70. J.W. McCrindle, *Ancient India as Described by Megasthenes and Arrian*, London, 1987, pp. 83ff.
71. R.C. Majumdar, 'The Indica of Megasthenes', *JAOS*, 1958, 78, pp. 273–6.
72. K.D. Sethna, 'Rejoinder to R.C. Majumdar', *JAOS*, 1960, 80, pp. 243–8. The question of the reliability of Megasthenes has been under discussion since Schwanbeck put together the fragments. For more

recent views, see, T.S. Brown, 'The Merits and Weaknesses of Megasthenes', *Phoenix*, 1957, XI, pp. 12–24; 'The Reliability of Megasthenes', *American Journal of Philology*, 1955, 76, pp. 18–33; A. Zamarini, 'Cli *Indika* di Megasthenes', *Annali di lettere et Filosophia*, Series III, XII, I. Pisa, 1983, pp. 73–149. J.D.M. Derrett presents an interesting case of the transformation of a theme in, 'The History of "Palladius on the Races of India and the Brahmans" ', *Cl. Med.*, 1960, 21, pp. 64–135.

73. O. Stein, *Megasthenes und Kautilya*, Wien, 1921.
74. B.C.J. Timmer, *Megasthenes en de Indische Maatschappij*, Amsterdam, 1930.
75. B. Breloer, *Kautilya Studien*, Bonn, 1927–34.
76. J.A.B. van Buitenan, 'The Seven Castes of Megasthenes', *AOS*, Middle West Branch Semi-centential Volume, D. Sinor (ed.), Bloomington, pp. 228–32.
77. II.40. F. Jacoby, *Die Fragmente der Griechischen Historiker* (FGrH), Leiden, 1958, 715 F4 (35–42).
78. Liddell and Scott, *Greek-English Lexicon*.
79. *Histories*, I.56.101; II.164.
80. J. Bloch, *Les Inscriptions d'Asoka*, Paris, 1965, p. 157.
81. *Arthaśāstra*, III.9 and 10; *Uvāsagdāsao*, II.52–4; *Baudhāyana Dharma Sūtra*, I.5.11.11ff; II.2.3.3ff. *Vasiṣṭha Dharma Sūtra*, XVI.13.
82. *Arthaśāstra*, II.24.
83. Ibid., II.29.1–3 of wage to *dāsa-karmakara*, II.24.28.
84. Ibid., II.34.6.
85. Ibid., II.1.33–7; VIII.1.19–20; II.35–1–4; X.1.9; 17.
86. Ibid., II.18.1.
87. Romila Thapar, *Aśoka and the Decline of the Mauryas*, London, 1961, pp. 118–20.
88. *Arthaśāstra*, Book II.
89. Pillar Edict, IV, J. Bloch, op. cit., p. 164.
90. *Sumangalavilāsinī*, II.673.3; *Kunāla Jātaka*, 536.
91. XV.1.39–41, 46–9. FGrH, 715 F 19.
92. XV.1.59ff; FGrH, 715 F.33.
93. J. Bloch, op. cit., pp. 97, 99, 115.
94. XV.1.70, FGrH, 721 F 15.
95. *Arthaśāstra*, II.1.
96. Ibid., 4.1.10ff, 2.29.2.
97. M.I. Finley, 'Aristotle and Economic Analysis', *Past and Present*, 1970, 47, p. 16.
98. See, f.n.20.
99. F. Jacoby, FGrH, 715, suggests that 715 F 19, p. 624 is an addition from F 31 (52).

100. A.B. Bosworth, *A Historical Commentary of Arrian's History of Alexander*, I, Oxford, 1980.
101. E.L. Bowie, 'Greeks and their Past in the Second Sophistic', *Past and Present*, 1970, 46, pp. 3–41; G.W. Bowersock (ed.), *Approaches to the Second Sophistic*, University Park, 1974.
102. P. Vidal–Naquet, *Flavius Arrian Entre Deux Mondes*, Paris, 1984, p. 383, in Arrien, *Historie d' Alexendre*, traduit par Pierre Savinal.
103. *Indica*, XI and XII.
104. *Anabasis*, VI, 16.5; VII.1.5–6.
105. L. Pearson, *The Lost Histories of Alexander the Great*, Oxford, 1960, pp. 5ff. T.S. Brown, *Onesicritus, A Study in Hellenistic Historiography*, Berkeley, 1949.
106. Onesicritus in Strabo, XV.1.58–66; Plutarch, *Alex.*, 65; Arrian, *Anabasis*, 7.3.6; *Indica*, XI.7.
107. P.A. Stadter, *Arrian of Nicomedia*, Chappel Hill, 1980, pp. 112ff.
108. Strabo, XV.1.36.
109. Ibid.
110. *Exp. Alex.*, V.vi.2 (2).
111. *Anabasis*, V.6.2; *Indica*, V.3.
112. P.M. Fraser, 'The Son of Aristonax at Kandahar', *Afghan Studies* (p. 80), 1979, 2. pp. 9–21.
113. *Sylb.*, pp. 132–42.
114. *Hist. Nat.*, VI.21.
115. O. Murray, 'Hecataeus of Abdera and Pharaonic Kingship', *JEA*, 1970, LVI, pp. 141–71.
116. P.M. Fraser, *Ptolemaic Alexandria*, I, Oxford, 1972, pp. 505ff.
117. O. Murray, op. cit., 'Herodotus and Hellenistic Culture', *CQ*, 1972, XXII, pp. 200–13.
118. P.M. Fraser, op. cit.
119. Ibid.
120. P.A. Stadter, op. cit.
121. M.I. Rostovtzeff, *The Social and Economic History of the Hellenistic World*, Oxford, 1967, pp. 464ff. E. Bikerman, *Institutions des Seleucids*, Paris, 1938, Domenico Musti, 'Syria and the East', in *The Cambridge Ancient History*, VII, 1, pp. 175–220. S.M. Burstein, *The Hellenistic Age . . .*, Cambridge, 1985, No. 19, pp. 24–5. C. Brunner, 'Geographical and Administrative Divisions: Settlements and Economy', in E. Yarshater (ed.), *The Cambridge History of Iran*, 3 (2), Cambridge, 1983, p. 713.
122. *Arthaśāstra*, II.1. A similar description of the founding of a colony is referred to in a letter of Antiochus III dating to the late third century BC. S.M. Burstein, *The Hellenistic Age . . .*, No. 29, pp. 37–8.
123. M.I. Rostovtzeff, *The Social and Economic History of the Hellenistic World*, pp. 255ff. H. Kreissig, 'Landed Property in the Hellenistic

Orient', *Eirene*, 1977, 15, pp. 5–26. Eric Turner, 'Ptolemaic Egypt', in *The Cambridge Ancient History*, VII, 1. pp. 118–74. M.I. Rostovtzeff, *A Large Estate in Egypt in the Third Century BC*, Madison, 1922.

124. Rostovtzeff, *SEHHW*, pp. 272ff.
125. L. Robert, 'De Delphos a l'Oxus . . . ', *Compte Rendus des Seances de l'Academie des Inscriptions et Belles-lettres*, Paris, 1968, pp. 416–57. S.M. Burstein (ed. and trans.), *The Hellenistic Age . . .* , Cambridge, 1985, p. 67.
126. *Politics*, IV.3.4.
127. Ibid., VI.7.
128. Ibid., IV.11.
129. Ibid., II.8.
130. Ibid., VI.8.
131. Ibid., VII.8, 9.
132. Ibid., VII.10.
133. G.E.M. de Ste Croix, *The Class Struggle in the Ancient World*, London, 1983, pp. 77ff; 'Karl Marx and Classical Antiquity', *Arethusa*, Spring, 1975, 8.1. pp. 7ff.
134. *Arthaśāstra*, VI.1. This idea is touched upon in a paper by H. Falk, 'Die Sieben "Kasten" des Megasthenes', *Acta Orientalia*, 1982, 43, pp. 61–8.
135. Arrian, XV.4; Quintus Curtius Rufus, 9.3; Strabo, XV.8; XV.1.33.
136. Patañjali, *Vyākaraṇa Mahābhāṣyam*, II.4.9 (I.476).
137. S.C. Humphreys, 'Fustel de Coulanges and the Greek *genos*', *Sociologia del Diritto*, 1982, 3, pp. 35–44; *Genos* has been interpreted in a multiplicity of ways from family and birth to clan, lineage and caste. In each case a kin or blood tie is important and a distant ancestor, real or fictive, is involved. F. Burriot, *Recherches sur la nature de Genos*, Paris, 1976.
138. Diodorus, II.39.
139. A. Momigliano, 'Herodotus in the History of Historiography', in *Studies in Historiography*, New York, 1966, p. 130.

# V

# *Forms of Exchange*

This set of papers focuses on the concept of exchange taking a variety of social forms. Sacrificial fees and donations are a form of exchange where sometimes the tangible is exchanged for the intangible. There are also recognised items of trade in other situations although the use made of these items may vary and include more than the obviously economic. Perceptions of the 'Other' can also form part of an exchange between those who make contact. The motivation for this may differ from group to group dependent on differing functions and negotiations.

# 24

# Dāna and Dakṣiṇā as Forms of Exchange*

In the study of the society and economy of ancient India information has often to be ferreted out from seemingly unlikely sources. What is often associated with apparently non-economic activity such as religious rituals, can sometimes provide insights into social and economic concerns. It is intended in this paper to examine the custom of *dāna*, the act of giving, in its major forms, from this point of view. The earliest literary sources refer to the giving of *dāna*, *dakṣiṇā*, etc. to priests and *brāhmaṇas*. The occasions for making these gifts are mentioned and there is generally an itemization of the objects considered appropriate for each occasion. Gradually gift-giving ceased to be something arbitrary and became systemised. This is evident from the discussion in some of the *smṛti* literature on the elements and aspects involved in the concept of *dāna*. Reference is made to six distinct elements and these include the *dātā* (donor), the *pratigrahītā* (recipient), *śraddhā*, the appropriateness of the gift, and the place and the time, for making the gift.[1] Gift-giving gradually evolved its own rules and requirements and can therefore be examined as an important aspect of the social and economic life of the early period.

Gift-giving has been seen largely in the context of its association with religious ritual and symbolism. There are however at least two other aspects which will be explored in this paper. Firstly, there is the obvious one of the changing items included in the listing of *dāna* and the correlation of these items with economic change. Secondly, the degree to which the nature of gift-giving reflects the socio-economic structure of the society: this hinges on the question of whether *dāna* and *dakṣiṇā* can be regarded as

* From *Indica*, vol. 13 (1976), nos 1 and 2, 37–48.

forms of gift-exchange and, if so, at what point do they cease to perform this function. Needless to say, gift-giving in this connection refers to major gifts given on particular and special occasions and not to the daily or routine ritual of small-scale *dāna*.

In the Vedic texts the two more commonly used words for gift-giving are *dāna* and *dakṣiṇā*. The two words are by no means synonymous. The first is the generic word for gift with its etymological root in √*dā*, to give. *Dāna* therefore refers to the act of giving, bestowing, granting, yielding and prestation, irrespective of what is being given and when. *Dakṣiṇā* has a more specific connotation although its meaning remains a little ambiguous. It is a gift by extension of its meaning. The etymon refers to the right side, the side of purity and of respect. It also carries the meaning of invigorating or strengthening the sacrifice for which purpose the gift is made to the performer of the sacrifice.[2] By extension therefore it came to mean either a gift or a donation made to a priest or a sacrificial fee.[3] The *dakṣiṇā* to the gods can be symbolic but that to the priests must consist of actual objects. It has been argued that the *dakṣiṇā* was never a salary or a sacrificial fee, but has to be seen as part of the economic system of Vedic times, that of gift-exchange.[4] It is possible to argue that it was not a sacrificial fee to begin with but came to be regarded as such by the time of the *Manu Dharmaśāstra* when gift-exchange was no longer an important aspect of the economic system.[5]

The concept of gift-exchange (particularly with reference to early Indian texts) was formulated at length by Marcel Mauss in his now well-known work, *The Gift*. Mauss argued that the earliest forms of exchange were those of total prestation between clan and clan and family and family. Subsequent to this stage comes that of gift-exchange in which certain categories of people are involved in almost ritualised exchanges which are embedded in the larger continuum of social and economic relations.[6] This stage precedes the change to individual contract and the money-market with fixed price and weighed and coined money. Gift-exchange would therefore tend to become less embedded in those primarily agricultural societies which experienced the gradual impinging of changing attitudes to land and the ownership of land and where land slowly emerges as the major economic unit. Literary sources which relate both to societies with a base in primitive agriculture and to societies with more complex social stratification based on advanced plough agriculture would reflect this change.

Mauss maintains that gift-exchange is not arbitrary but is based on the notion of value. What is exchanged is a token of wealth and this is different from money as it is imbued with a magical power. It is not an impersonal gift as it is linked to an individual or a particular group. Thus utility alone is not the motivating force in this exchange. The accepted token of wealth is significant since wealth is a demonstration of status; it is a means of controlling others by winning followers and by placing those who accept the gift under obligation. The exchange is essentially of consumable items and luxuries — food and clothing for example. The gift is not one-sided and implies a return gift, although the return of the actual gift presented was forbidden. The symbolic motivation in making the gift was the belief that it is reproductive and that the donor would receive the same in larger quantity. More recent studies of the system of gift-exchange have pointed to the functional aspect as well. The system of gift-exchange kept goods and people in circulation in a particular pattern and also acted as a means of maintaining political relationships and ranking.[7]

The earliest references to *dāna* as a distinct function in society come from the *dāna-stuti* hymns of the *Ṛg Veda*, hymns in praise of those who make generous and handsome gifts.[8] The subject of these particular hymns is either the donor or the event which occasioned the gift. Thus in one of the hymns Kaśu, the Cedi king is honoured and in another the victory at Hariyūpīyā.[9] The *dātā* (donor) can be a deity — primarily Indra and occasionally Soma, with Aśvins, Viśvadevas and Sarasvatī also included — but is frequently a king/chief or hero. The *pratigrahītā* (recipients) are the hymnodists, the priests or the bards who have composed the verses in praise of the person or the event. The gift comes from human hands but sometimes via the mediation of a god.[10] Thus the god is requested for favours and if these are granted then the kings bestow gifts on the priests who immortalize them in verse.[11] The event is generally a successful battle or cattle raid or victory over the enemy or the destruction of the enemy. In these the role of Indra is preeminent: he destroys the forts of the enemy, he attacks the Dāsas jointly and individually.[12] The gift is made therefore not so much in the spirit of charity but as symbolic of success and as an investment towards further success on future occasions. The appropriateness of the gift is exalted but the time and place are rarely mentioned. The association with Soma may imply that it was made on the occasion of the soma-pressing ceremony. Evidently the purpose of *dāna* in the Ṛgvedic age was different from what it was to become in later times.

The *dāna-stutis* have a fairly uniform format. The composer's *gotra* is usually mentioned early on so that his social bona fides are established. The deity is invoked, the exploits of the deity are lauded and an appeal is made to the deity for aid. Frequently, parallel situations are described which in the past had a successful outcome and were followed by generous gift-giving. Reference is made to the giving of gifts by human heroes. The gifts are unambiguously objects of wealth and are recorded in what can only be, on many occasions, exaggerated figures. The most prized gift and object of wealth is cattle with figures ranging from a hundred cows to sixty thousand head of cattle.[13] Horses come next in priority and although smaller numbers are listed they are often described in greater detail than the cows. Ten horses is a common figure although thousands of steed are also mentioned and, in one case, sixty thousand.[14] There is a preference for stallions over mares, whereas in bovine wealth the preference is for cows. Other gifts include wagons, chariots, maidens, camels, treasure-chests, garments and robes, measures of gold and, infrequently, cauldrons of metal.[15] Perhaps the epitome of the *dāna-stutis* is the paean to *dakṣiṇā* itself where the liberal bestowers of *dakṣiṇā*, the *yajamānas* are described as immortals inhabiting the highest heaven, secure from harm, victorious in battle and living with their brides in eternal bliss — the vision of a hero's paradise.[16]

The *dāna-stuti* hymns are expressions of heroic poetry. The givers of *dāna* are the heroes of the clan, sometimes equated with the larger body, often carrying its name in place of the individual name. The listing of the wealth was an indication of status, for those who gave large gifts such as Kaśu the Cedi king, Divodāsa, Pṛthuśravas or the Yādavas were acknowledged as being more powerful and wealthy than those who made lesser gifts such as Asaṅga or Saṇḍa. The gifts were functional items of wealth and not tokens of wealth. In this case, what was probably the implicit token was not the actual item but the exaggerated quantities in some of the figures.

Among the gifts there is a noticeable absence of the mention of land and, quite evidently, as has been pointed out, it was cattle that was synonymous with wealth.[17] This is also evident from the frequency of words and phrases incorporating cattle as synonyms for other aspects of material life, as for example in the extended meaning of words such as *gaviṣṭhi*, *gopati* or *gomat*. Even grain is rarely listed as an item of *dāna*. This is indicative of the relative unimportance of land as an economic unit.

It has been argued that the Ṛgvedic evidence suggests that the king was essentially a protector of cattle and not of land; consequently it is cattle which is a source of inter-tribal conflict and not land.[18] This may well indicate that land was owned jointly by the clan and, furthermore, despite the references to agricultural activities scattered throughout the *Ṛg Veda*, land was still seen in essence as territory encompassing both fields and grazing ground. The lifting of cattle was a more serious economic problem than trespassing into fields. The Paṇis are feared for they are both rich in cattle as well as being stealers of cattle. Wealth (*rayi*) was computed primarily in cattle.[19] It is also of some interest that male slaves are rarely mentioned as constituting *dāna*, whereas *dāsīs*, if understood as being female slaves were known. This would suggest that perhaps domestic slavery as a source of luxury among the wealthy was evident but the use of slavery in economic production was not the prevalent system.[20] That the possible clan ownership of land continued awhile is reflected in the story of the king Viśvakarman Bhauvana who is rebuked by the earth when he tries to gift the earth he has conquered through his *aśvamedha* to Kaśyapa.[21] But other sections of the Later Vedic literature include land as part of the recognised *dāna*.

The purpose of extensive gift-making in early societies is threefold. Ostensibly it serves a magico-religious function where the gift is symbolic of communion with the supernatural. In effect it also has two other less evident functions: one is that the donor and the recipient confer status on each other, although the source of the respective status may be different in each case, and secondly gift-giving acts as a means of exchanging and redistributing economic wealth.

In the *dāna-stutis* of the *Ṛg Veda* the two groups involved in conferring status on each other are the *brāhmaṇas* and *rājanyas/kṣatriyas*. The former mediate with the gods on behalf of the latter and ensure success in battle and cattle-raids, which success invests the latter with power and political status. The latter bestow wealth on the priests, thus providing them with their major source of income as well as conceding to them charismatic powers inherent in the process of ensuring success. By the time of the composition of these hymns a limited social group was involved in the exchange. However, the existence of a more extensive exchange can be postulated for an earlier phase.[22] A successful battle or cattle-raid resulted in an enforced acquisition of wealth on the part of the victorious tribe.

The process of gift-exchange was however more equitable if it occurred through the performance of the *yajña*, which in turn may be seen as a variant on the potlatch. As far as the redistribution of wealth was concerned, even at the *yajña* it seems by now to have been limited to the same two social groups, the *kṣatriya* and the *brāhmaṇa*. Thus, wealth acquired through the labour of the *viś*, whether in war or in peace, was channelled via the *rājā* to the priests either through *dāna* or through the *dakṣiṇā* at the *yajña*. In earlier periods, when it is presumed that the tribe participated in the *yajña*, some of the wealth may have been redistributed among a wider group. But, by the time of the composition of the *Ṛg Veda*, both the redistribution as well as the participation of the clan in the *yajña* was more limited.

In such a situation there must have been a distinction between those who were the possessors of wealth and the rest of the tribe. Was this distinction expressed in the term *ārya* which Bailey has analyzed in considerable detail and which analysis leads him to state that *ārya* referred to the owner or possessor of wealth?[23] This is also suggested in the *Nighaṇṭu* which equates *ārya* with *īśvara* (owner/master) and in Pāṇini, who explains it by the phrase *aryaḥsvāmi-vaiśyayoḥ*.[24] The *āryas* as possessors of wealth were gradually distinguished from the *viś*, the rest of the tribe, who by then were no longer equal partners in joint wealth. As Bailey states, the association of wealth and ownership suggests nobility of class and not an ethnic group. The significance of birth into the *ārya-varṇa* relates an *ārya* to social status and wealth and not to race.

The literature of the Later Vedic period gradually introduces a change in the concept of *dāna*. It is no longer the arbitrary liberality of a generous patron celebrating his success. It is now less a channel of redistribution of wealth and much more pointedly a channel of deliberate exchange. The changing concept is expressed in the more frequent use of the word *dakṣiṇā*. The strengthening of the notion of exchange is perhaps best summed up in the statement, *dehi me dadāmi te ni me dehi ni te dadhe.*[25] The donor and the recipient remain the same. The appropriateness of the gift and the faith with which it is given are emphasized and the place and time are made much more precise. This is done by a closer linking of gift-giving with the sacrificial ritual via the *dakṣiṇā*. The justification for *dāna* is also spelt out. We are told that there are two kinds of *devas*, the gods and the *brāhmaṇas* learned in the *Vedas*: both have to be propitiated, the former through *yajñas* and the latter through *dāna*.[26] It is also at this point that there is mention of fields and villages as appropriate items of *dāna*, although these references are as yet infrequent.[27] Although *paśu* or animal wealth is still very significant there are some texts which disapprove of the acceptance of animals as *dāna* and presumably preferred gold and land.[28] This is not surprising since by the mid-first millennium BC animal wealth as an economic asset was gradually giving way to land. An interesting indication of the shift in the items gifted is evident from the study of the *rājasūya* sacrifice. The concept of *iṣṭi-pūrta* becomes more central to the procedure with a distinction being made not only between *iṣṭi* and *pūrta* but between *iṣṭi* and *dakṣiṇā*. This is a ritual distinction but not altogether unrelated to the relative decline of livestock breeding and increase of agriculture. The *iṣṭi* which is the offering made to the gods during the performance of the sacrifice is almost invariably a mixture or a cake of some form of cereal, the most frequently used cereals being varieties of rice. The *dakṣiṇā* on the other hand is in most cases an ox, cow or bull, generally a single animal with specified markings, or else a unit of gold.[29] The number of animals is considerably less than the numbers listed in the Ṛgvedic *dāna-stutis*. Sometimes for the seasonal sacrifices the *dakṣiṇā* may include a chariot and mares or stallions.[30] The more spectacular *dakṣiṇā*, which, for instance, is given during the soma rituals of the *rājasūya*, continues however to be in the form of livestock. The list ranges from one thousand to four thousand cows adding up to a total of ten thousand in some texts — a reasonable figure for a wealthy king, to five thousand to thirty thousand cows with a total of a hundred thousand in other texts — an evidently exaggerated figure.[31] Nevertheless the number of cows listed continues to be less than the figures given in the *Ṛg Veda*. Since many of the higher figures in both the earlier and later texts were in any case exaggerated, their significance symbolizes the use of animals rather than the actual numbers involved.

*Dakṣiṇās* associated with particular royal rituals as part of the major sacrifices often consisted of gifting to the priest the most valuable objects used in the ritual. Thus in one text we are told that the *adhvaryu* receives the chariot of the *yajamāna* and the golden dice used in the symbolic game. The carts are distributed among other priests as are also the one thousand cows used in the mock cattle-raid.[32] The *adhvaryu* and the *hotṛ* who recite the legend of Śunaḥśepa at the *rājasūya* are given the golden seats on which they sit for the recitation in addition to a certain number of cows.[33] It is also in connection with this sacrifice that one of the forms of *dakṣiṇā* listed is that of *catuṣpat kṣetra* (field with four parts) which is given to a priest.[34] It has been suggested that this was the land used in a royal ploughing rite as part of the *rājasūya*, being the survival of a rudimentary agrarian fertility rite.

In all these cases the *dakṣiṇā* is specifically linked to a particular ritual or a ceremony. Heesterman has argued at length that the *dakṣiṇā* is not a sacrificial fee or salary; it forms a part of the bigger sphere of gift-exchange.[35] His main point is that the *dakṣiṇā* is given to both the *ṛtvij* or officiating priests and to others such as the *brāhmaṇas* of the *prasarpaka* category whose role is essentially that of observers sitting in the *sadas*. In one of the texts it is specifically stated that the *dakṣiṇā* to the *sadasyas* is to buy them off from drinking the *soma*.[36] Another text maintains that the *yajamāna* by giving *dakṣiṇā* buys himself loose from obligations to the priest.[37] The ritual link is broken or is at least replaced by a status link. Not all texts however accept that the link is broken. The *dakṣiṇā* is seen as a bond between the donor and the recipient, if not as an act by which the recipient is placed under an obligation to the donor. This implies a danger and the danger can only be averted by careful consideration of the propriety of the gift, the place and the time.[38] It is a moot question as to whether the notion of the implicit danger arose from the ritual connection or whether it was a means of diverting attention from regarding the *dakṣiṇā* as a 'fee'.

Heesterman suggests that the *dakṣiṇā* may reflect an earlier stage when the entire clan took part in the ritual and the wealth was shared. This would be more characteristic of the potlatch. In course of time the ritual may have moved into the hands of the sacrificial priests and the others may have become observers. The symbolic nature of the *dakṣiṇā* is evident from the continued gifting of cattle in a society where land was becoming increasingly more lucrative. Clearly, golden seats and golden dice would have to be converted into more mundane objects for the priests to derive a livelihood from these gifts. The question is whether the *dakṣiṇā* was over and above the normal livelihood of the priest or was it his main source of income. Given the nature of later Vedic society where there are not too many references to *brāhmaṇas* owning land or large herds of cattle it is likely that the *dakṣiṇā* from the king would often be the basic source of livelihood for those performing the rituals.

The collection of *dakṣiṇā* was not restricted to the large-scale *yajñas,* for the life of the *ārya* was now beset by *saṃskāras* — the rituals of the individual biography, the prescription and practice of which ensured well-being. The definition of donor gradually began to include more than just the king or the chief, for others were also required to perform *saṃskāras*. This widening definition of the donor in terms of social categories reaches a qualitative change in Manu, where logic takes it to the point of stating that it is the duty of the *gṛhastha* (the householder) to be concerned with *dāna*.[39] The relevance of gift-exchange in a tribal context of potlatch activities seemed to be receding.

Marcel Mauss in his discussion of gift-exchange maintains that the *Mahābhārata* is the story of a tremendous potlatch.[40] He has particularly pointed to the *Anuśāsana-parvan* as the section par excellence devoted to gift-giving. Here we find a further elaboration of the categories of *dāna*. The distinction for example between *iṣṭa* and *pūrta* is emphasized. The *iṣṭa* is that which is offered into the *gṛhya* and *śrauta* ritual fires. *Pūrta* is a larger enterprise and consists of the donation of wells, tanks, temples, gardens and lands.[41] The donation of immovable property as a special category is a relatively new concept. Hitherto donations were of animals, gold, food, clothing, chariots and so on. The listing of what is included in *pūrta* has its own significance since it points clearly to the establishment of an agricultural economy where wells, tanks, gardens and land have a utility which they would not have had in a pre-eminently pastoral economy. Another interesting aspect to this distinction which develops in the legal literature is that the *iṣṭa* can only be handled by the ritually pure but the *pūrta-dāna*, which in economic terms was the more effective, can also be made by *śūdras*.[42]

Not only in the items listed but in spirit too the notion of *dāna* had by now undergone further changes. It was no longer given merely in celebration of an event or a heroic personality or in connection with a ceremony. It was now associated with a new idea which in part derived from the concept of *dakṣiṇā*, namely, the ethical aspect of performing an action such as giving a gift. The notion of exchange remains central, but in return for tangible wealth the donor acquires merit. Not that all exchange discussed in the *Anuśāsana-parvan* is motivated by the acquisition of merit. We are told that *dāna* increases one's material wealth; nevertheless, in every act of giving, whether it be the *pañcadakṣiṇā* service of host to guest or offerings at a ritual, there is merit to be acquired as the ultimate aim.[43] Gift-giving almost develops its own ritual in which the six-fold definition of *dāna* as stated in *smṛti* literature is given due emphasis. The definition of the *pratigrahītā* is further refined and it is stated that the recipient must be deserving of the *dāna*.[44] This has relevance not only to the fact that the acquisition of merit can only accrue if the *dāna* is given to a deserving person but also carries a hint of competition among potential recipients for the acquisition of economic status in a system where, perhaps, more attention was being paid to economic status than in earlier times. *Dāna*, therefore, is not to be given to those *brāhmaṇas* who are physicians, image-worshippers, dancers, musicians; who perform ceremonies for the *śūdras* and who practise usury. The deserving *brāhmaṇas* are those who perform the required ceremonies as indicated in the texts, who are of noble birth and who live off alms. Even if any among this category have had to take to professions such as agriculture and soldiery, they still qualify for *dāna*. The emphasis on the time and place for gift-giving is accompanied by threats that untimely gifts are appropriated by the *rākṣasas*. The emphasis on the recipient being a deserving person may also be a reflection of competition for *dāna*-bestowing patrons, a competition extending not only to brahmanical sects but including Buddhist, Jaina and other heterodox sects as well, many of the latter claiming to have wealthy patrons.

The exchange of *dāna* for merit echoes the Buddhist notion of charity or *dāna*. The idea may therefore have come from Buddhist sources or may have grown independently as a result of changing social forms. For Buddhism the stress on *dāna* was essential; for, even at the mundane level, the Buddhist religious order — the *saṅgha* — was required to subsist on the alms and the charity of the lay followers. All that the *bhikṣu* or the *saṅgha* could provide to the donor in exchange for *dāna* was *puṇya* or merit, since exchange was between economically unequal sections of society. In the early stages, when Buddhism was not a powerful religious movement, it could neither provide social status to its lay supporters nor did its doctrinal teaching promise immortality or heavenly abodes. At most it could maintain that a material gift would be reciprocated with preaching the Buddhist ethic which in turn might provide the gift of vision or enlightenment to the donors. Puranic texts are unequivocal in making promises: thus we are told that the acquisition of merit through *dāna* can release one from the chain of rebirth.[45]

The reciprocity of *dāna* with *puṇya* may also have been conditioned by the fact that in the larger towns, where there was a Buddhist following, the gift-exchange economy was on the decline and was being gradually replaced by an approximation to the impersonal market economy of commerce, where the unit of money was the currency of exchange. In such an ethos gift-exchange made little sense and the *dāna-puṇya* reciprocity held out some compensation for the donor. It is significant that among the non-deserving *brāhmaṇas* listed in the *Anuśāsana-parvan* are those who practise usury and those whose occupation is trade, both activities closely related to a market system. In contrast to the market system, *dāna* is not an impersonal exchange. It involves two parties in a clearly defined relationship, which relationship is affected by the giving of *dāna*. It is also accompanied by an elaborate etiquette, much more elaborate than the frank appeal for *dāna* in the *Ṛg Veda* or the partially disguised *dakṣiṇā* of the *yajñas* and the *saṃskāras*.[46] It would almost appear that by insisting on the institution of *dāna* and the ensuing nexus there was an attempt to invert the values of the market system and to reincarnate those of the gift-exchange.

It is also at this time that attention is given to the acceptance of food as *dāna*. Manu lists the categories of food, chiefly uncooked, which are regarded as legitimate *dāna* for the *brāhmaṇa*.[47] If a *brāhmaṇa* unwittingly accepts forbidden food he has to fast for three days as expiation. Among the types of uncooked food, it is the produce of agriculture, grain, which is the most acceptable. Manu repeats the dictum that the giver will be rewarded many-fold but also adds that he who gives and he who receives, both, go to heaven. The eulogizing of the *dāna* of food, especially to *brāhmaṇas*, continues in the later literature of the *Purāṇas* where *annadāna* is sometimes referred to as the highest form of *dāna*.[48] The relative purity of uncooked food is in contrast to the practice of sects of Buddhists and Jainas among whom cooked food is regarded as the most acceptable.[49] In terms of conferring status via exchange, the *dāna* of food has a direct relation to caste status, where the acceptability of particular types of food is dependent on social ranking. The discussion therefore of food as *dāna* is also an indication of the extension of caste society.

The gifting of land and the precedence which this began to take over other items reflects the increased interest in agriculture and the fact that land was more lucrative than heads of cattle. This would certainly conform to the known extension of the agrarian economy during the Mauryan and the post-Mauryan period. The general decline of pastoralism is evident from the fact that cows were still gifted but not as major items of *dāna*. Their gifting was to become almost a symbolic gesture of the process of making a gift. The gifting of land brought its own problems since land was both immovable and indestructible. It could not be transported as could a herd of cattle or other objects, nor did it get consumed or die during the lifetime of the recipient. Land was inheritable and alienable and this brought it under the purview of the legal system relating to inheritance and sale of land. A land-gift had therefore to be recorded so that it would remain with the recipient or his family even if he changed his domicile or after his death. A gift of land was even further removed from gift-exchange since it could help establish the family of the recipient for many generations and, to that extent, it was not a momentary episode but an investment for the future.

A discussion on the necessity to record a gift of land suggests that the record should act as the legal claim of the grantee and his family before future kings.[50] Hence the record should be a permanent, signed, sealed edict referring to the lineage of the king, the identity of the recipient, the extent and characteristics of the land gifted, the nature of the gift, the seals of the officials concerned with the grant and, according to some texts, a declaration to the effect that it was not to be resumed at a later date. That these instructions were meticulously observed is evident from the copperplate and other charters recording such gifts of land from the Gupta period onwards.[51] The granting of land and villages to *brāhmaṇas* became so institutionalized that it was referred to by the special term of *agrahāra* and later an officer was appointed to look after such grants, the *agrahārika*.

With the granting of land other gifts assumed lesser importance with the exception, of course, of gold which retained its economic value. A special category of gifts was evolved based on gold and referred to as the *mahādānas*.[52] These were made on very special occasions such as can hardly be listed in the normal course of gift-giving. Among the more commonly referred to *mahādānas* were the *tulapuruṣa* (weighing a man against gold) and the *hiranyagarbha* (the symbolic rebirth through a golden womb often performed during coronations). It is significant that this latter ceremony is particularly associated with those who were claiming *kṣatriya* status. Usually sixteen objects are listed among the *mahādānas* including trees, cows, horses, chariots, vessels, all made of gold, and such objects were gifted to the priests on the conclusion of the ceremony. A golden cow studded with precious stones was a long way away from the ten thousand head of cattle which the Ṛgvedic priests acclaimed as a gift. The *mahādānas* are clearly of another category and another time.

Land grants constituted the germ of what was later to develop into a new agrarian structure with its own implications for social and economic formations.[53] For our purposes, suffice it to say that the extensive granting of land as *dāna* changed the comprehension of *dāna* as part of gift-exchange. A new institutionalizing of *dāna* took place, reflecting both a departure from the earlier socio-economic system as well as the evolving of a changed metaphor for both the donor and the recipient.

## NOTES AND REFERENCES

1. P.V. Kane, *History of Dharmaśāstra*, Poona, 1941, vol. II, part 2, pp. 843ff.
2. *Śatapatha Brāhmaṇa*, II.2.2.1–2; IV.3.4.1–2.
3. *Manu*, III.128–37.
4. J.C. Heesterman, *The Ancient Indian Royal Consecration*, p. 164.
5. *Manu*, XI.38–40.
6. *The Gift*, London, 1954, pp. 45ff, 53ff, 71ff.

7. J.P.S. Uberoi, *Politics of the Kula Ring*, Manchester, 1962.
8. *Ṛg Veda*, VI.63.9; V.27; V.30.12–14; VI.47; VIII.1.33; VIII.5.37; VIII.6.47.
9. *Ṛg Veda*, VIII.5; VI.27.
10. *Ṛg Veda*, VIII.46; X.93.
11. *Ṛg Veda*, VI.47.
12. *Ṛg Veda*, VI.47; VIII.1.
13. *Ṛg Veda*, VI.47; I.126.
14. *Ṛg Veda*, VI.33.1; VI.63.9; VIII.46.21–4.
15. *Ṛg Veda*, V.30.15; VI.47.
16. *Ṛg Veda*, X.107.
17. R.S. Sharma, 'Forms of Property in the Early Portions of the Ṛg Veda', *Proceedings of the Indian History Congress*, 1973.
18. Ibid.
19. *Ṛg Veda*, I.33.3; IV.28.5; V.34.5; VI.13.3; VIII.64.2–4.
20. R.S. Sharma, op. cit.
21. *Aitareya Brāhmaṇa*, VIII.21. *Śatapatha Brāhmaṇa*, XIII.7.1.13–15.
22. As has been suggested by K.P. Jayaswal, *Hindu Polity*, in arguing that perhaps the *vidatha* was a tribal assembly, pp. 69–70.

    This has been further discussed by R.S. Sharma, *Political Ideas and Institutions in Ancient India*, Delhi, 1959, pp. 63–80 and J.P. Sharma, *Republics in Ancient India*, Leiden, 1968, pp. 70ff. See also *Ṛg Veda*, I.24.3; I.27.5ff; I.31.6; I.102.4; I.141.1; II.2.12; VII.76.4–5; IX.81.5.
23. H.W. Bailey, 'Iranian Arya and Daha', *Transactions of the Philological Society*, 1959, pp. 71ff.
24. *Nighaṇṭu*, 2.6; *Pāṇini*, 3.1.103.
25. *Taittirīya Saṃhitā*, I.8.4.1.
26. *Śatapatha Brāhmaṇa*, IV.6.6.1ff.
27. *Aitareya Brāhmaṇa*, VIII.20; *Chāndogya Upaniṣad*, IV.2.4–5.
28. Kane, op. cit., pp. 837ff.
29. *Taittirīya Saṃhitā*, I.8.9; I.7.3. Heesterman, op. cit., pp. 49, 174.
30. *Āpastamba Śrauta Sūtra*, 5.23.5; 6.30.7.
31. Heesterman, op. cit., p. 162.
32. *Baudhāyana Śrauta Sūtra*, 12.7.95.15ff.
33. *Aitareya Brāhmaṇa*, VII.18.
34. Heesterman, op. cit., p. 166.
35. Heesterman, 'Reflections on the Significance of the Dakṣiṇā', *Indo-Iranian Journal*, 1959, no. 3, pp. 241–58.
36. *Kātyāyana Śrauta Sūtra*, 28.5.
37. *Āpastamba Śrauta Sūtra*, 13.6.4.
38. *Śatapatha Brāhmaṇa*, IX.5.2.16; *Āpastamba Śrauta Sūtra*, 13.6.4–6; *Kātyāyana Śrauta Sūtra*, 28.158.4; 159.16.
39. *Manu*, III.78.

40. M. Mauss, *The Gift*, London, 1954, pp. 53ff.
41. Kane, op. cit., p. 844.
42. Ibid., p. 845.
43. *Anuśāsana-parvan*, II, VII, VIII, IX.
44. Ibid., XXIII.
45. *Agni Purāṇa*, 209.1–2.
46. *Anuśāsana-parvan*, LXXII.
47. *Manu*, IV.205–25; 235–50.
48. *Agni Purāṇa*, 211.44–6; *Padma Purāṇa*, V.19.289–307; *Brahmāṇḍa Purāṇa*, 218.10.32.
49. As for example in the *Ācārāṅgasūtra*, II.1.1–10. Manu does however insist that the *saṃnyāsin* must only accept cooked food (VI.38) and the reason for this may well have been that he was outside the norms of social regulations.
50. *Yājñavalkya*, I.318–20.
51. Inscription of Śivaskandavarman, *Ep. Ind.*, I. p. 7; Maitraka Vyāghrasena, *Ep. Ind.*, XI. p. 221; pp. 107.111.
52. *Agni Purāṇa*, 209, 210; *Matsya Purāṇa*, 274–89; *Liṅga Purāṇa*, II.28.
53. D.D. Kosambi, *Introduction to the Study of Indian History*, Bombay, 1956, pp. 275ff; R.S. Sharma, *Indian Feudalism*, Calcutta, 1965.

# 25

# *Indian Views of Europe: Representations of the Yavanas in Early Indian History**

I would like to thank the South Asia Institute of the University of Heidelberg and Professor Lutze in particular, for extending to me the invitation to give a lecture in the series, 'Indian Views of Europe'. Having agreed happily to speak on Indian views of Europe and assuming that I was expected to relate this subject to my own field of work, namely, early Indian history, I discovered however that there were no readily available views on Europe from sources pertaining to early India. This then raised the interesting question of why was it that Indian travellers, merchants, officers, and monks who are known to have spent time in areas other than India, have left us no record of their impressions of the lands and peoples which they visited. It is therefore in many senses that I am using the word 'other' in this lecture.

The evidence that Indians visited and even settled in various parts of the then-known world is plentiful. This is so in spite of the injunction in the normative texts on social duty, the *dharmaśāstras*, against crossing the seas or living among those who do not practice the required rituals. Many of the cultural idioms of central Asia and south-east Asia are a clear manifestation of the transgression of this injunction. There is also evidence, although more scattered, of Indians in west Asia and the Mediterranean world.[1] Mention is made of embassies to Rome, of wealthy-merchants in Alexandria as well as of slaves,[2] and there is evidence of Indians at a Red Sea port.[3] Yet there is no attempt on the part of visiting Indians to describe what must have been alien worlds or at least narrate some fanciful stories

* Lecture delivered at the South Asia Institute, at Heidelberg University, 1987 in the series entitled 'Indian Views of Europe'.

of their adventures. This becomes all the more strange given the frequency with which those from the Greco-Roman world, or the Chinese for that matter wrote at length on India; and in their accounts there is an evident change from fantasy to more accurate description, although fantasy never fully falls away. Not only is there an absence of descriptions of others, but often the term used for a variety of other peoples remains the same, as we shall see. Indian interest in 'the other' seems to have been limited.

It becomes necessary therefore to ask the question why, for in the answer to this question something of the 'otherness' of both India and Europe might become more evident. Given the frequency of visitors from foreign lands to India, were they so taken for granted that accounts of such peoples seemed somehow redundant? Was there such a deep concern with the interior landscape that it annulled any curiosity about one's surroundings? Did it result from viewing the world as the geography of the isolate? Did the lack of an aggressive religious sense of mission and conversion, with an absence of the notion that the pagan and the infidel are inevitably damned, dull the enquiry about others? Did the cosmology of rebirth, open to all humans, blur the definitions between them? Or can one argue that the gradation of otherness is so implicit within the formulations of a caste society that distinctions even of a different kind carry less meaning? I would like to explore some of these ideas, keeping in mind our particular concern with Indian views of Europe.

Traditional views on the shape of the world are discussed in some detail in the *Purāṇas* and the *Mahābhārata* and the Buddhist texts, the relevant sections probably dating from the early centuries AD. These are largely fantasies, cosmographies, visions of the universe. Essential to the picture is the notion of the *dvīpa*, the term used for the four or the seven or the nine continents. The word literally means 'an island' and is used sometimes by extension to refer to a defined settlement such as a city or a country which need not actually be an island but where the sense of being apart is crucial. The notion of an island and of circularity governs the description of the universe. In one representation the central point is Mount Meru around which spread the four continents like the petals of a lotus, and these in turn are surrounded by oceans. This image incorporates the four quarters with the fifth point being in the centre. Later the number of continents was increased to seven.[4]

Conventionally, views of the universe envisage a concentric series of continents, *dvīpas*, separated by concentric oceans. Mount Meru lies at the core of the central continent, that of Jambūdvīpa (generally assumed to be referring to India) of which in some texts, Bhāratavarṣa is a part. The sense of a circular symmetry is predominant in such a 'map' and this is important to the world view of the *Purāṇas*, since these texts are concerned with cosmology, geography, narratives of creation and the genealogies of those who have ruled. In one of the versions we are further told that whereas the four *varṇas* or castes inhabit the centre of Bhāratavarṣa, there are other categories of people, other than *varṇas*, on the outskirts of the area: the *mleccha* are to be found all over and are therefore contrasted with the concentrated *varṇa* society in the centre; there are the mountain tribes of Kirātas on the east and on the west are the Yavanas.[5] The feeling of an island is reinforced not only by placing Jambūdvīpa and Bhāratavarṣa in the centre but also by describing it as surrounded by those who are outside the pale of caste society, such as the *mlecchas*. It is in this sense that the vision of the universe supports the notion of Indian isolation.

The term *mleccha*, is crucial to the understanding of attitudes towards others. Such attitudes are often expressions of self-perception. An important dichotomy in social classification was the division into *ārya* and *mleccha*. This was not a dichotomy based on notions of biological race but essentially on language, although some Indologists, like others, have confused the two and race has now become the popular explanation. The fundamental differentiation was that of language.[6] Given the obsession with the power of sound in Vedic thinking, it was believed presumably that alien speech is incapable of capturing this power. It is described as the speech of the incoherent even if the difference is small. The *mleccha* therefore were those living along the frontiers of Indo-Aryan speech whose language was referred to as *mleccha-bhāṣā* because it was either mixed or different. But it also included those within the Indo-Aryan speech area who nevertheless spoke a different language or spoke an incorrect form of the Indo-Aryan language. The cultural frontier was therefore not a geographical one but demarcated by language.[7] Thus Patañjali, in the second century BC, stated in the introduction to his Sanskrit grammar that the study of the language prevents one from becoming a *mleccha*. As the spread of the language widened, the geographical definition of the land of the *āryas*, changed. Initially it was just the Ganga valley but later it came to include all the land between the Himalayas and the Vindhyas, wherever the black buck roamed.[8]

*Mleccha* also carried the connotation of impurity. Since they were unable to speak Sanskrit correctly, their recitation of the *mantras* was ineffectual and therefore they were unable to perform the required rituals. Lands and peoples not performing the rituals were unacceptable and those Indo-Aryan-speakers who visited such lands had to perform an expiatory rite on their return. This incidentally, did not inhibit large numbers from going to distant lands. In addition to being distinguished by their language, they were recognised by the organisation of society along the lines of the *varṇāśrama* ideal, i.e., observing the four orders of castes and the four stages of life. The *āryāvarta* is generally described as the land where the four *varṇas* are to be found. The *mlecchas* are often located outside this area in geographical terms and seen as forming parallel societies with their own language, ritual and custom. In some other contexts they were also ranked within the *varna* hierarchy as *śūdras* in the lowest rank.[9] Customary law as seen in the *dharmaśāstras* related to time, place and social status, and an impersonal code of laws applicable to all was not visualised. If anything laws and social obligations were a method of differentiating groups. Thus an *ārya* could not be sold into permanent slavery, whereas a *mleccha* could.[10] The *mleccha* therefore, was not primarily the object of aggression but of exclusion. The *mleccha* was the contrary of what constituted the *ārya*.

Among the *mleccha* are listed the Yavanas, a term used originally for the Greeks and later for all manner of people coming from west Asia — Hellenistic Greeks, people from the Greco-Roman Mediterranean, and eventually even the Arabs and the Europeans.[11] This makes it difficult to pin-point the references except that the earliest among them referred to the Greeks and Hellenised west Asians. To that extent they may be taken as a perspective on a culture which was significant to the evolution of Europe. The term Yavana appears to have its root in the Greek *Ione*, the Iranian *yauna*,[12] and the Prākṛit *yona*, which according to some gave rise to the Sanskrit *yavana*. Others with whom the Yavana were frequently associated are the Kamboja and the Śaka (Scythian), both geographically contiguous on the one hand, and the Kirāta, Śabara and other *barbara* or barbarian peoples who were included among the *mleccha* on the other.[13] Nevertheless a subtle distinction is maintained between the first category and the second. The Yavana and the Śaka are said to observe a limited *dharma* and some rules of purity and are not therefore totally excluded from contact with the higher castes.[14] The Yavana are complimented not only on being valiant but very knowledgeable and therefore different from the other *mleccha*. But *mleccha* they remain,[15] and this despite the gradual and growing proximity with the Hellenistic Greeks and those of the Mediterranean.

The earliest close experience which the Indians had of the Greeks began badly with the campaign of Alexander of Macedon in north-western India, accompanied by the brutalisation inherent in such campaigns particularly in the repression of resistance.[16] Alexander's hostility towards the *brāhmaṇas* is mentioned more than once, for he believed that they were responsible for instigating opposition to him.[17] A result of this campaign was the rise of Hellenistic kingdoms in west Asia and the opening of commerce between these areas and India. The Mauryan emperors received ambassadors bringing gifts of sweet wine and dried figs.[18] In return Aśoka states that he sent his missions bearing the message of *dhamma* to the Greek kings, the *yona rājās* on the frontiers.[19] The proximity was strengthened by the inclusion in the Mauryan empire of parts of Afghanistan where Greek and Aramaic speaking populations necessitated versions of the Aśokan edicts in these languages.

Observations on Hellenistic society are few but these are of some interest. Aśoka in his edicts refers to the absence of *brāhmaṇas* and *śramaṇas* in the Yona country.[20] We are told elsewhere that the first Buddhist missions were sent to these kingdoms during the reign of Aśoka.[21] Equally significant is what appears to be Aśoka's interest in the religion and ethics of these societies.[22] The use of the word *eusebeia* for the Prākṛit *dhamma* (Sanskrit *dharma*) in the Greek version of the Major Rock Edicts at Kandahar, is also suggestive of a sensitivity to the use of the appropriate term and of some familiarity perhaps with Greek thought, even if the rendering into Greek was done by a local scribe.[23] Yet there is no evidence of the learning of Greek by Indian scholars. Yavana is mentioned in the grammar of Pāṇini and is later glossed as a reference to the Greek script.[24] Curiously none of the Indian grammarians seem to have been interested in the Greek language, or else we might have had a theory of parallels and Indo-European origins many centuries prior to William Jones and Max Müller! This reticence seems strange given the centrality of language and grammar in the intellectual discourse of learned Indians at that time. Possibly it was because Greek was regarded as the language of the impure in the social hierarchy and the study of such languages was discouraged.[25] Since the Yavanas were anyway using Prākṛit there was perhaps no great necessity for Indians to learn Greek. Yet prior to this Aśoka Maurya felt it necessary to issue versions of his edicts in Greek and Aramaic for the people of the north-west. The familiarity with Aramaic seems to have been greater, the *kharoṣṭhī* script having evolved from Aramaic.

The Yavanas, however, became problematical for the theory of identity within a social hierarchy, as it was worked out in the Sanskrit normative texts. Subsequent to the Mauryas, in the second century BC, the Hellenistic Greeks of west Asia, conquered and briefly ruled over north-western India and inched their way to areas regarded earlier as the heartland in the Ganga plain.[26] Referred to by present-day historians as Indo-Greeks, they established centres at cities such as Taxila, Kandahar[27] and Sagala (modern Sialkot?). Indo-Greek coins carry bilingual legends in Greek and Prākṛit with symbols attesting the faith of the rulers in Buddhism and the newly emerging Śaiva and Bhāgavata cults. Inscriptions were issued in Prākṛit by the Indo-Greeks: one from Madhya Pradesh was inscribed by Heliodorus, the Greek ambassador from Taxila to a local court, in which he records his devotion to the Vaiṣṇava cult of Vāsudeva.[28] The text of this inscription is influenced by Sanskrit, suggesting that the Indo-Greeks did make an attempt to use the local language but failed to communicate in Sanskrit as the normative texts would have preferred. However the distinction of language seems by now to have been largely a notional divide which probably would have persisted even if the Greeks had used Sanskrit. Sanskrit had itself undergone change and this would have raised the question of which variety of Sanskrit was to be considered the hallmark of the *ārya*. Patronage of Buddhism, regarded as heretical by *brāhmaṇas* and of the Bhāgavata cult of Vāsudeva, may have been largely political since these were popular religious sects in that part of the country. If coinage is to provide clues then it would seem that the Indo-Greeks were anxious to incorporate Indian cultural signals, even if some kings assumed a predominantly Greek identity in giving prominence to the royal portrait, the monogram and other Greek features.[29]

The art which emerged by the turn of the Christian era, commonly referred to as Gandhara art, draws on these relationships. If art expresses an identity, then Gandhara art has to be seen not only as the fusion of styles — Greco-Bactrian, Roman, Indian — but also as an experiment in identity: an experiment in seeing one's own culture as the other. From the Indian perspective the themes and their meanings were familiar, the representation was different. But since culture is not static, this very representation became a legitimate part of the self-perception of the Indian. To the citizen of Taxila there would be little that was alien in this art.[30]

Although they were rulers, there was a problem about fitting the Yavanas into the caste hierarchy. From the perspective of the normative texts, the *dharmaśāstras*, in terms of the social hierarchy of *varṇa*, the Yavanas as a *mleccha* people had to be given the status of the low caste, the *śūdras*. There was a concession, however, in that they were not the lowest among these. The sop to the Yavanas is the statement that they were originally *kṣatriyas* but because they omitted to perform the sacred rites prescribed by the *brāhmaṇas* they had had to be lowered to the status of *śūdras*, or of *vrātya-kṣatriyas*, literally degenerate *kṣatriyas*.[31]

This in turn required some narration of their supposed Indian origin. Lineage ancestry was invented when it was said that the Yavanas were the descendents of Turvaśa, a son of Yayāti.[32] Even though little is said about this son, Yayāti himself, being a major ancestral figure, gave some credibility to the ancestry of the Yavanas. The other sons of Yayāti were the famous Yadu, from whom the important *kṣatriya* families of the Yādavas were descended, and Pūru, who was the progenitor of the Pauravas whose line terminated in the heroes of the *Mahābhārata*. These were well-established *kṣatriya* lineages; they were the stock from which the earliest ruling clans claimed kinship and from which later dynasties were to seek genealogical links. However, the statement that Turvaśa was the ancestor of the Yavanas was not so complimentary. Turvaśa, who refuses to give up his youth in exchange for his father's old age, is cursed by his father to produce offspring who will face extinction, but before which they will rule over people whose customs are corrupt, who contradict the rules of caste, who are eaters of flesh, who lust after the wives of their *gurus* and who couple with beasts — in short the worst of the barbarians.[33] Later the same text states that the Yavanas were degraded as *śūdras* together with the Drāviḍas, Kaliṅgas, and Śakas.[34] It adds that they can be admitted to 'the society of the *ārya* only if they follow' the *varṇāśramadharma*. Some *dharmaśāstras* maintained that the Yavanas were the progeny of a *kṣatriya* male and a *śūdra* female and being of mixed caste, were therefore of low status.[35] Clearly there was a problem about status and Yavana was not easily to be placed in the caste hierarchy. The definition of the term, either as part of the *varṇa* hierarchy or as an ethnic group, remained ambiguous, perhaps largely because the same term was applied to so many categories of people.

Texts dealing with subjects at a technical level indicate an interest in Greek ideas among professionals. That there was a familiarity with Greek astronomy and astrology, for example, is evident from the titles of the texts referred to.[36] Varāhamihira, a sixth-century astronomer, is appreciative of Greek astrology even if he holds different views and remarks that although the Yavanas were *mlecchas*, nevertheless they should be regarded as sages in this study, if not even as *brāhmaṇas*.[37] It is interesting that the Hellenistic Greeks were seen as more proficient in astrology rather than astronomy.

A notable exception to accommodating the Yavanas was one category of texts which is both aggressive and uncompromising in its depiction of them. The *Purāṇas*, compiled much after the rule of the Yavanas although incorporating earlier material, are generally hostile to the Yavanas. Historical events are often narrated in them in the future tense although they may refer to events which had already taken place. Thus the *Yugapurāṇa*, a work on astrology dating to the turn of the Christian era, states that the Yavanas will conquer the Ganga plain, causing disorder and extensive warfare, and according to one reading, will oppress the people and massacre women and children. They will however, not remain in the area because of internal strife among them.[38] Other *Purāṇas* of a later period, echo this sentiment and state that the Yavanas, although not legitimate kings, will nevertheless rule because of the evil accruing in the last of the four ages, the Kaliyuga, the age of ethical and moral decline. One text has a millennarian message in stating that they will be annihilated by the last of the incarnations of Viṣṇu, Kalkin, at the end of the Kali age, although by now the term Yavana included people other than just the Indo-Greeks.[39]

Yet another text projects an altogether negative image of the Kālayavana, the Black Greek.[40] The Black Greek was born of an *apsarā* or celestial maiden and a *ṛṣi* or sage: the archetypal parentage of many Indian heroes. But the Black Greek, together with his allies of the north-west, attacked the city of Mathura, gave chase to Kṛṣṇa, and impetuously kicked a sleeping sage, who on thus being rudely woken up reacted angrily and reduced the Black Greek to ashes. A variant on this story is narrated in the *Viṣṇu Purāṇa*.[41] The association is with violence and there is a death wish directed towards the enemy. It has been argued that the story of Kālayavana is an attempt at Indian self-definition and the expression of neo-brahmanism which was to be the consensual basis of subsequent kingdoms.[42] Perhaps it would be more precise to describe it as brahmanical self-definition in the light of the Kṛṣṇa cult associated with Mathura and soon to become important. In the story there is hostility between the Yavanas and Kṛṣṇa, whereas in fact some Yavanas were patrons of the Vāsudeva cult.

Was this also a telescoping of the past, where perhaps the social memory of Alexander's campaign was collapsed into the more recent events associated with the Indo-Greeks? Or was it a fulsome resentment against the *mleccha* conquerors on the part of the *brāhmaṇa* authors of these texts, the resentment being in part a memory of Alexander's reputed hostility to the *brāhmaṇas*.[43] This was compounded by the brahmanical suspicion of urban traders and Yavanas who were not rulers or administrators but were city dwellers occupied in commerce. There is also implicit in these statements a sense of hopelessness that the world did not function according to the social rules promulgated by the *brāhmaṇas*. As long as the Yavanas remain along the borders they are tolerated, but when they enter the heartland, then the resentment is uncontrolled. There is the inevitable wish for the coming of the millennium, when the mythical figure of Kalkin will destroy the *mleccha*, the upstarts, and the low castes, and restore the order of *varṇa* and the rules of the normative texts. The alienation of language and custom was evidently deeply resented by brahmanical authors even though in terms of geography the definition of Bhāratavarṣa now included the north-western region of Gandhāra.[44] By now the term Yavana referred not only to the Greeks but also to other peoples beyond the north-west of India.

Implicit in the *brāhmaṇa* hostility to the Yavanas was also the fact that the Yavanas were substantial patrons of the various Buddhist sects who by now were regarded as heretics by the *brāhmaṇas*. Doubtless a mixture of contempt and envy governed this attitude, a particular irritant being that Buddhism was receiving support from the *mleccha* elite which helped consolidate its strength. Similarly patronage of Śaiva and Bhāgavata sects was also a new feature. The polemic against the Yavanas by *brāhmaṇa* authors can therefore be seen as a part of the polemic against dissidents in India.

Not surprisingly the Buddhist view of the Yavanas was rather different, a view which perhaps goes back to the Buddha's attitude to Yavana society, which was one of curiosity and interest. A comment attributed to the Buddha, states that the society of the Yona and the neighbouring Kamboja was constituted of only two *varṇas*, the *ārya* and the *dāsa*. The former term has been variously rendered as master or citizen and the latter as slave. The Buddha adds that individuals could change their status from one to the other.[45] The Buddha uses this information to question the social superiority claimed by the *brāhmaṇas*. Was this his perception of Hellenistic society or was it a reflection on descriptions of the Greek city state? Either way it may suggest that there was a deeper familiarity with things essentially Greek than is ostensibly expressed in the Indian sources. The definition of *ārya* in this case is different from that of brahmanical thought for here, as in Buddhist texts generally, it refers to those who were worthy of honour, or thought of with respect. Again the connotation is not racial. That the *ārya* and the *dāsa* were changeable statuses and were not dependent on birth emphasises that this society was not a caste society. Where references are made to Yavanas as *mleccha* (or *milakkha* in Pali), they are said to be of high status even though they spoke an alien language.[46] Buddhist texts seem unconcerned with emphasis on ritual purity or status determined by *varṇa* ranking.

The Yavana patronage of Buddhism in the north was that of kings who bestowed largesse on the Buddhist *saṅgha* or Order, and assisted in the building of monasteries, *stūpas* and other places of worship. Apart from this there were extensive trading networks which were furthered by the co-operation between merchant and monk and which used the protection of political authority. The epitome of the relationship between Buddhism and Yavana royalty lies in the famous text, the *Milindapañha*, in which the Greek king

Menander is supposed to have posed questions to the monk Nāgasena on Buddhist doctrine. This was an oral discourse which it is claimed led to the conversion of Menander. Menander was chosen doubtless because he was the most powerful of the Indo-Greek kings. The text was meant to demonstrate ascendancy not only over the Yavanas but over a man with an enquiring mind. Menander is said to harass the brethren by putting puzzles to them of a heretical kind.[47] There is little evidence that Menander was regarded as a *mleccha* and therefore to be treated as an inferior. The questions posed are those of the intelligent layman, but interestingly Menander asks for the physical manifestation of the Buddha whereas Nāgasena keeps discussion at the level of the abstract. This could be the layman's problem of belief and proof of belief, but could it also be read as an indication of a Greek interest in empirical evidence? Menander however, when quoting evidence in support of his *kṣatriya* ancestry, which in this text is never doubted, refers to symbols of power which were recognisably Indian.

References to the Yavanas in the Deccan register a shift from political authority to a concentration on trade. This in part may be because most of these Yavanas were traders from the Mediterranean and likely to have come from centres such as Petra, Coptos, Alexandria, Myos Hormuz, Berenice and other places along the Red Sea, and to a lesser extent traders from the north-west with links to Palmyra and other commercial entrepôts overland and further west. The trade was largely maritime. The sailing of ships was dependent on the monsoon winds which carried them along mid-ocean routes across the Arabian Sea instead of the earlier and lengthier coastal looping. Sailing with the summer monsoon winds required returning with the winter monsoon and this in turn necessitated having to live for a few months in India awaiting the winter monsoon. Indian ships, it has been suggested, sailed only to Arabian ports and east Africa.[48] Consequently the merchandise from the Mediterranean came, when sent by sea, in ships from the Red Sea. The ship would be manned by a crew likely to have come from the eastern Mediterranean or picked up from the ports of the Red Sea. Some of such crews may have settled in various parts of the Indian peninsula.

Mention is made of wealthy Yavanas who appear to have been traders and their votive inscriptions are recorded at various Buddhist sacred centres. Some, at sites in the western Deccan, are referred to by their Indian names, which indicate that they were Buddhists.[49] It is unlikely that these were wealthy Indian merchants living in west Asia, as has been suggested,[50] for Indians of standing would not have accepted the label of Yavana, which would have reduced them to *mleccha* status. That some Greeks took Indian names is evident from an inscription which refers to a Theodorus Datiaputra.[51] The rock-cut monasteries at Nasik also record handsome donations from the Yavana, Indragnidatta, the son of Dhammadeva, who is further described as the northerner from Dattamitri, perhaps the Demetrias in Arachosia.[52] At Junnar in the same area, Yavana donors are said to come from Gata, which could be a Prakritised version of Coptos.[53] It has been argued that these donations by the Yavanas were attempts to participate in the cultural distinctiveness of the Buddhist trading diaspora on which the Yavanas were dependent.[54] That Yavanas were converted to Buddhism is claimed by the Ceylon Chronicles, which speak of Buddhist missionaries going to the Yona country and mention that thirty thousand monks came from there to attend the foundation ceremony of a major *stūpa* in Sri Lanka.[55] The number of monks seems exaggerated, but there must have been some ministering to the needs of Buddhists in the Yona country. It is curious that a Yona/ Yavana monk was sent to Aparānta, the western extremity of India, where presumably Greek was spoken, yet a non-Yavana monk was sent to the Yavana country.

Further south, Tamil Sangam literature has references to the Yavanas with whom the people of south India came into contact. These give a rather different picture from the previous two. We are told of the flourishing port at Muciri/Muziris on the Kerala coast, where the large, beautiful ships of the Yavanas dock, laden with gold, and from where they return home with pepper, which the Yavanas loved.[56] Mention is also made of the cool, fragrant wine brought by the Yavanas in elegant jars,[57] an item which was to become a regular import into India from the west. Other verses carry a more hostile tone: the local Cera king is said to have captured the barbarous Yavanas of harsh speech, tied them up and taken away their elegant jars and their wealth.[58] Perhaps it was because of the harshness of their language that they were on occasion referred to as the *milecchar*, evidently a form of *mleccha*.

On the opposite coast, in Tamil-nadu at Kaveripattinam, the Yavanas were not just passing visitors picking up items of trade, but had settled in ports and towns practising a variety of professions. The Pandyan ruler was said to employ the Yavanas as body-guards because they were sharp-eyed, of fearsome appearance, strong, and used to cracking whips.[59] Were these the weather-toughened sailors off the Yavana ships who had decided to abandon sailing on the monsoon-tossed seas and settle in the tropical lands where they had been beached? Yavanas seemed to have been preferred as body-guards, perhaps because they were not embroiled in local factions. It is thought that even in the sculpture of later centuries at temples in the Deccan, the guardians at the gateways were sometimes depicted as Yavanas.[60]

Perhaps emphasis was laid on physical prowess in the Śangam literature in part because heroic poetry eulogises such attainments. Literature, of a somewhat later period, describes a variety of Yavana craftsmen making lamps, boxes, flowers of gold, and items of carpentry, in all of which the craftsmanship is extolled: a compliment indeed coming from a society with high standards of craftsmanship.[61] But above all it is the wealth of the Yavanas which is commented upon: they live in a separate section of the city in houses which are easily distinguishable.[62] Doubtless the impression of wealth can be traced back to the circulation and later hoarding of large numbers of gold and silver coins of the early Roman emperors, which had been brought to south India as part of the trade — coins which were used as bullion, as high-value currency and possibly also as part of a system of gift-exchange among those groups where such exchange was still more significant than trade.[63] The tenor of these descriptions is matched by the excavation at Arikamedu near Pondicherry. Here a settlement of the earlier period and manufacturing site linked to the Roman trade, carries traces of a variety of objects from amphorae to pottery, glass, beads, lamps and other items, some of which had Indian imitations. Among the many items brought in from the Roman trade was the valuable red coral of the Mediterranean which was believed to be a talisman against ill-health and dangers in the Greco-Roman world and was used in India for the same purpose.[64]

The context of trade and of Buddhism provides a different perspective on the attitude to the Yavanas. They may be referred to as socially excluded even in the early Buddhist texts before there was much contact with them,[65] but with the growth of trade relations they are, on the contrary, considered people of status, especially where they make lavish donations. The votive inscriptions and Indian names suggest, of course, that the earlier statement about their alien language was no longer entirely true. Tamil sources comment on the language but otherwise are even less concerned about Yavana ritual status or caste and merely describe the people as they saw them. There are therefore, distinctly different attitudes towards the Yavanas depending on who is viewing them and in what context. Where the Yavana is a symbol of political authority and there is competition for this authority, and where the arena is one in which the society is visualised in terms of caste categories closely deriving from notions of *varṇa*, there the Yavana is an excluded group in spite of periods of successful political control. Interest in the 'other' is absent when the Indian is on the homeground of the other, but when the 'other' comes to India there is a range of comment.

The term Yavana was not, however, restricted to the Greeks, and the people of the eastern Mediterranean. It continued to be used for others who came from the west — for the Arabs, and for those from the direction of Afghanistan, and sometimes even for those Indians who had converted to Islam.[66] Was this due to a lack of interest in political changes in north-west India and west Asia? Or was it that, with the gradual decline of Buddhism and Jainism the ideologies of brahmanism gained ascendancy and all those who were outside the language and caste identity were described as *mleccha* while those who came from the western borders and regions were automatically regarded as Yavana? Thus the sense of the term was extended over time to include more recent people, an extension which might even have continued into our times, but for the intervention of the colonial experience which among other things, fractured the past.

It was the colonial experience which also led to variant modern views on how the Indians saw the Greeks. This further endorses the point that all such views depend on who is speaking to whom about what. The European perception of the Yavanas was different from the Indian nationalist perception. W.W. Tarn for example, compares the Indo-Greeks to the British administering an Indian empire.[67] In his theory of partnership between the Greeks and the Indians he is almost echoing one strand of late British colonial policy in India, which also harped on partnership when the empire was visibly coming to and end. A contrary view is presented by

Radha Kumud Mukherjee. When assessing Alexander in India he writes that his campaign resulted in 'untold sufferings inflicted on India — massacre, rapine, plunder on a scale till then without a precedent in her annals, but repeated in later days by more successful invaders like Sultan Mahmud, Tamerlane and Nadir Shah.'[68] At a subconscious level the list is a recitation of the evil Yavanas in keeping with the image projected in the *Purāṇas*.

The Indian experience of the Yavanas and perspectives on them however, should obviously not be compared to those of European colonialism. Unlike the Yavanas, European colonialism did not involve settlement in India, and the Europeans did not attempt to integrate themselves with things Indian, their primary purpose being to exploit the economy through political ascendancy. The British did not come to India from a contiguous state, but from a geographically distant area. The frontier therefore was a distant one. Difference in speech and custom was recognised but colonialism required that the colonised speak the language of the colonial power. In the dichotomy of Indian and European there are some echoes of *ārya* and *mleccha*, but the adoption of English as the elite language and, subsequent to the emergence of the Indian middle class, the observance of 'western' social custom and law, inverted its form. This inversion may be at the root of many tensions in contemporary perceptions of modernisation where new ideologies which question earlier dichotomies are either appropriated in such a way as to create new dichotomies or else are used as a polemic against dissidents in Indian society.

Whatever the reality may have been, early Indian writers persistently called those who came from the west, Yavanas. This then became a code name, encapsulating a long tradition of attitudes, of acceptance and rejection at various levels and in various ways among various groups of Indians. It was not that the differences between the Greeks, the Arabs and the Europeans were imperceptible or unclear to Indian thought, but that there was a deliberate use of a label, a category which identified such peoples along a social continuum which did not have to be worked out each time. That the Yavanas were *mleccha* meant that they spoke a different language and were assigned a low or an ambiguous caste as far as the *brāhmaṇas* were concerned but were acceptable to the Buddhists and assimilated into Buddhist society. The predicates which constituted such a name and the codes underpinning it would remain constant, even if the actuality of relations changed.[69]

I have tried to suggest that the *brāhmaṇas* and the Buddhists constructed the Yavanas in different ways and have offered possible explanations. The brahmanical view would prefer to see the Yavanas as the opposite of their own status and culture yet at the same time they were required to see the Yavanas within a framework of a social continuum — a gradual gradation of castes and customs — which is inimical to polarities. The view may therefore be intended to be hostile but has to be nuanced as well. Whereas formally the dichotomy between *ārya* and *mleccha* and therefore between the *ārya* and the Yavana is stated, in effect it was often eluded. Even the switch from a geographical identity to a cultural one is not consistent and often wavers between the two. There was an ongoing need for the image of the alien. This could be notional — hence the recurrent Yavana and *mleccha*. The 'other' is not necessarily confrontational, but is a part of a continuum and therefore needs to be demarcated.

The brahmanical polemic against the Yavana is not directed only against what we today see as the alien; it is as much a part of the polemic within Indian society and thought directed by those anxious to acquire and maintain power against those in opposition.[70] Representations of the Yavanas as the other were also representations of some Indians in early historical times.

## Notes and References

1. A very late tradition refers to an Indian gymnosophist at Athens in conversation with Socrates, but this, as has been pointed out, is a quotation twice-removed and historically uncertain. J. Sedlar, *India and the Greek World*, New Jersey, 1980, pp. 14ff; K. Karttunen, *India in Early Greek Literature*, Studia Orientalia No. 65, Helsinki, 1989, pp. 108ff.
2. W. Schmitthenner, 'Rome and India: Aspects of Universal History during the Principate', *The Journal of Roman Studies*, 1979, LXIX, pp. 90–106. S. Levi, 'Alexander and Alexandria in Indian Literature', *Indian Historical Quarterly*, 1936, XII, 1, pp. 121–33.
3. D. Whitcomb and J. Johnson, *Quseir al-Qadim*, Princeton, 1979, p. 18. S.E. Sidebotham, *Roman Economic Policy in the Erythra Thalassa, 30 BC–AD 217*, Leiden, 1986.
4. Rai Krishnadas, 'Puranic Geography of the Cātur-dvipas', *Purana*, 1959, 1, pp. 202ff; B.H. Kapadia, 'The Four World Oceans and the Dvipa Theory of the Middle Ages', ibid., 1961, 3, 2, pp. 215–21;

*Mahābhārata*, 12.14.21ff; *Matsya Purāṇa*, 113.43–4; 114.121–3; *Vāyu Purāṇa*, 34.45–6; 42–5; *Viṣṇu Purāṇa*, II.2; II.3.1–19.

5. *Matsya Purāṇa*, 114.11; V.S. Agrawala, *Matsya Purana, a Study*, Varanasi, 1963, p. 193.
6. The earliest reference to *mleccha* in the *Śatapatha Brāhmaṇa*, 3.2.1.23–4 makes this clear where it states that they were unable to pronounce Sanskrit correctly, *te'surā āttavacaso he'lavo he'lava iti vadantaḥ pārābabhūbuḥ* . . .
7. This can be compared to the Greek reference to *barabaros* as being those who spoke an incomprehensible language, therefore the barbarian was demarcated by language. Sanskrit also has a phrase, *barbara/balbala karoti*, to signify those who speak indistinctly. Romila Thapar, 'The Image of the Barbarian in Early India', in *Ancient Indian Social History: Some Interpretations*, New Delhi, 1978, pp. 152–92. *See* chapter 12 in this volume.
8. P.V. Kane, *History of Dharmasastra*, vol. II, 1, pp. 11ff; see also *Matsya Purāṇa*, 114.10ff; *Viṣṇu Purāṇa*, 2.3.2–5; A.M. Shastri, *India as seen in the Bṛhatsamhitā of Varāhamihira*, Delhi, 1969, pp. 45ff.
9. Manu, 2.23; 10.45; Gautama, *Dharmaśāstra*, 4.4–21; Baudhāyana *Dharmaśāstra*, 1.9.3–15; Vasiṣṭha, 18.1–18.
10. *Arthaśāstra*, 3.13.3–4.
11. The same term is used for those of African descent except that they are called *kālayavanas* or black Yavanas as in the reference to people from the island of the black Yavanas, possibly a reference to Madagascar. Dandin, *Daśakumāracarita* (ed. G. Buhler, BSS X), Bombay, 1887, p. 8.
12. As in the Behistun Inscription of Darius, 522–486 BC, D.C. Sircar, *Select Inscriptions*, I, pp. 4–5; A.K. Narain, *The Indo-Greeks*, Delhi, 1980 (reprint), pp. 165–9; W.W. Tarn, *The Greeks in Bactria and India*, London, 1951 (reprint, 1980), pp. 416ff; C. Tottossy, 'The Name of the Greeks in Ancient India, *Acta Antiqua Hungarica*, 1955, 3, pp. 301–19.
13. *Mahābhārata*, 7.95.37–9.
14. Patañjali on Pāṇini, 2.4.10.
15. *Mahābhārata*, 8.30.80.
16. Arrian, *Anabasis*, 4.27.3ff; 5.24.5–8; 6.11.3ff.
17. Arrian, *Anabasis*, 6.7.4–6; 6.16.5; 6.17.2. That *brāhmaṇas* could take up arms to protect themselves is evident from the *Baudhāyana Dharmaśāstra*, 2.2.4.16–18.
18. Romila Thapar, *Aśoka and the Decline of the Mauryas*, Oxford, 1961, pp. 17–18.
19. J. Bloch, *Les Inscriptions d'Asoka*, 1950, Paris, pp. 130ff.
20. J. Bloch, op. cit., p. 128.
21. *Mahāvaṃsa*, 12.4–5. The monk Yona Dhammarakkhita was sent to

Aparānta, the western extremity of India and the monk Mahārakkhita to Yonadesa. Interestingly, the Yona has an Indian name, presumably in this case because he was a Buddhist monk trained in India.

22. D. Schlumberger, L. Robert, A. Dupont-Sommer, E. Benveniste, Une bilingue gréco-araméenne d'Asoka. *Journale Asiatique*, 1958, i, pp. 1–48ff; J. Filliozat, *Epigraphia Indica*, 34, pp. 1ff; In the Aramaic version of the inscription at Kandahar, Aśoka refers to what has been read as the Day of Judgement, a notion associated with the Zoroastrians at that time.
23. D. Schlumberger, 'Une nouvelle inscription grecque d'Asoka', *Comptes rendus des seances de l'Academie des Inscriptions et Belles-Lettres*, 1964, pp. 1–15; E. Benveniste, 'Edits d'Asoka en traduction grecque', *Journal Asiatique*, 1964, pp. 137–57; *Epigraphia Indica*, 37, pp. 193ff.
24. S.C. Vasu (ed.), *The Aṣṭādhyāyī of Pāṇini*, 4.1.49. The text of Kātyāyaṇa glosses it as *yavanānilipi*.
25. Vasiṣṭha, 6.41; Gautama, 9.16–17.
26. *Mahābhāṣya* (ed. Kielhorn), 2.118–19.
27. Kandahar has been variously identified with Dattamitri/Demetrias in Arachosia or as the Alexandria in Arachosia. Dattamitri is mentioned as a town in the Sauvira region in the *Mahābhārata*, 1.139, 21–3, but this is believed to be a later interpolation and has therefore been omitted from the Critical Edition of the text. The identity of Kandahar with the town of Demetrias is discussed in P.M. Fraser, 'The Son of Aristonax at Kandahar', *Afghan Studies*, 1979 (1980), 2, pp. 9–21.
28. D.C. Sircar, *Select Inscriptions . . .*, Calcutta, 1965, pp. 88–9, 100–11.
29. R. Audouin and P. Bernard, 'Tresor de monnais indienns et indo-grecque d'Aï Khanoum (Afghanistan)', part I, *Rev. Num.*, 1973, XV, pp. 238ff; ibid., part II, *Rev. Num.*, 1974, XVI, pp. 7ff.
30. Lolita Nehru, *Origins of the Gandharan Style*, Delhi, 1989, pp. 65ff, although not centrally concerned with the question of identity, does discuss the differences between artistic expression in Hellenistic west Asia, Bactria and Gandhara, in terms of the inheritance from the past.
31. Manu, 10.43–4.
32. *Mahābhārata*, 1.80.26.
33. *Mahābhārata*, 1.79, 11–13.
34. Op. cit., 13.33.19–21.
35. Gautama, 4.21.
36. Such as the Romaka (Rome) and Pauliśa (Paul of Alexandria?) systems and the *Yavana-jātaka*, P.V. Kane, *History of Dharmasastra*, V, pp. 563ff.
37. *Bṛhatsamhitā*, II.15.
38. The *Yugapurāṇa* is a section of the *Gargīya-jyotiṣa*, and the manuscripts have variant readings. These have been discussed by D.C. Sircar, 'Problems of the Yugapurana', in D.C. Sircar, *Studies in*

*Yugapurana and Other Texts*, Delhi, 1974, pp. 1–17; and more recently by J.E. Mitchner, *The Yuga Purana*, Calcutta, 1986.

39. *Vāyu Purāṇa*, 1.58.81–3; 2.37.106–9.
40. *Harivaṃśa* (ed. P.L. Vaidya), BORI, Poona, 1969, 25.8–27; 80.1–8.
41. *Viṣṇu Purāṇa*, V.23–4.
42. N. Hein, 'Kālayavana, a key to Mathura's cultural self-perception', in D.M. Srinivasan (ed.), *Mathura*, Delhi, 1989, pp. 223–35. Alberuni in the eleventh century refers to Kālayavana as an era associated with oppressive rule. E.C. Sachau, *Alberuni's India*, Delhi, 1964 (reprint), II. p. 5.
43. Plutarch, 69.
44. *Vāyu Purāṇa*, 1.45.80–3; *Mārkaṇḍeya Purāṇa*, 57.7–9.
45. *Majjhima Nikāya*, 2.149–50. In the Greek cities of west Asia, citizenship was open to the Greeks and to Hellenised non-Greeks both of whom formed the upper levels of society. Less privileged persons tended to use their own language and religions and formed a different community. R.J. van der Spek, 'The Babylonian City', in A. Kuhrt and S. Sherwin–White (eds), *Hellenism in the East*, London, 1987, pp. 57–74.
46. *Sumaṅgala-vilāsinī*, I.276ff.
47. *Milindapañha*, 1.14.(1.29). W.W. Tarn suggests that this text is based on a number of Greek accounts of Alexander's dialogues with Indian sophists and a proto-type of such texts was the *Letter of Pseudo-Aristeas*, involving Ptolemy II in a discourse with Jewish Elders. *The Greeks in Bactria and India*, Delhi, 1980 (reprint), pp. 424ff. To argue for such a proto-type seems unnecessary given that most proselytising religions have such catechismal texts.
48. I. Miller, *The Spice Trade of the Roman Empire*, Oxford, 1969, pp. 180ff.
49. J. Burgess and B. Indraji, *Inscriptions from the Cave Temples of Western India*, Varanasi, 1976 (reprint), nos 7, 10. pp. 31–2. *Epigraphia Indica*, VII, nos 7 and 10, pp. 53–5.
50. W.W. Tarn, *The Greeks in Bactria and India*, Delhi, 1980 (reprint), pp. 371ff.
51. S. Konow, *Corpus Inscriptionum Indicarum*, II.1, Kharoshthi Inscriptions, Varanasi, 1969 (reprint), no. 24, p. 65.
52. *Epigraphia Indica*, 1905–6, VIII, no. 18, pp. 90–1.
53. Burgess and Indraji, op. cit., nos 4 and 33, pp. 42 and 55. Gata has generally been identified with Trigarta in northern India, either Jallandhar or Kangra, neither of which however have produced much in the way of evidence of Greek settlement at this time. On the analogy of Sandracottos and Candragupta, it may be possible to suggest that the Prākṛit form Gata, could be derived from Coptos.
54. Himanshu P. Ray, 'The Yavana Presence in Ancient India', *JESHO*, 1988, XXXI, pp. 311–25.
55. *Mahāvaṃsa*, XII.34–5; 39–40; XXIX.39. *Dīpavaṃsa*, VIII.7.

56. Akam, 149.v.7–11, trans. K. Zvelibil, see also N. Subrahmanian, *Pre-Pallavan Tamil Index*, Madras, 1966, p. 716.
57. Ibid., Puram, 56.16–21; Puram, 343.1–10.
58. Ibid., Patirrupattu, II, patikam, v.4–10.
59. Ibid., Mullaippattu, v.59–61.
60. J.C. Harle, 'Two Yavana Dvarapalas at Aihole', in the *K.A. Nilakantha Sastri Felicitation Volume*, Madras, 1971, pp. 210ff.
61. *Manimekalai*, XIX, v.108.
62. *Silappadhikaram*, 5.10; 14.67.
63. M.G. Raschke, 'New Studies in Roman Commerce with the East', in H. Temporim and W. Hasse (eds), *Aufsteig und Niedergang der Romischer Welt*, Berlin, 1978.
64. G.W.B. Huntingford (ed. and trans.), *The Periplus of the Erythraean Sea*, London, 1980, chs 28, 39, 49, 56.
65. G.P. Malalasekhara, *Dictionary of Pali Proper Names*, II, p. 636; *Sammoha-vinodani*, Vibhanga Commentary, 388; *Suttanipāta*, 977.
66. As for example, the reference to Hushanga Gori as a Yavana-Śaka, or to Behari as a Yavana, since he was the adopted son of Salaha, originally a *brāhmaṇa* but converted to Islam. D.R. Bhan, 'Khadavada Inscription of the Time of Ghiyas Shah Khilji of Mandu', *Journal of the Bombay Branch of the Royal Asiatic Society*, XXIII, pp. 12ff; see also Kalhaṇa, *Rājataraṅginī*, 8.2264.
67. Op. cit., p. 181.
68. *The Age of Imperial Unity*, History and Culture of the Indian People, II, Bombay, 1951, p. 51.
69. F. Hartog, *The Mirror of Herodotus*, Berkeley, 1988.
70. Such polemics are of course frequently found in many societies. Thus the accounts of Alexander's dialogues with Indian gymnosophists was a recurring theme in Greek and Latin texts. Given the paucity of authentic evidence for such a dialogue, it has been plausibly argued that these 'events' were used and re-used for purposes of local polemics pertaining to the discussion on relations between the king and the philosopher, to the debate touching on the Cynics and the Stoics as well as the later one on the life-style of the Christian monks. Sedlar, op. cit., pp. 68ff, 279ff. Karttunen, op. cit., pp. 108ff.

26

# *Black Gold: South Asia and the Roman Maritime Trade**

The writing of the early history of South Asia has been largely land-locked. Major studies of the Indian Ocean or the lesser seas generally begin with the rise of Islam. In choosing to speak on an earlier period my intention is not only to underline the continuity of maritime contacts, but also to go behind the artefacts, as it were. The significance of trade lies not only in the items exchanged but also in the nature of the exchange and the mutation of the cultures communicating through the trade. Trading diasporas, where traders as a distinct quasi-cultural group provide channels for the movement of goods between disparate societies, is one aspect of trans-cultural trade,[1] but interventions in the evolution of societies are equally significant. A diversity of items changed hands; some as objects of simple exchange or of purchase, others perhaps as fetishised commodities. The same cargo may play multiple roles. My endeavour in trying to shift the focus in these directions is necessarily hedged in by the limitations of the current evidence which may involve asking more questions than providing answers.

Roman maritime trade was the first extensive contact between Europe and Asia. The geographical pattern of the contact — the foci of maritime trade, the locations of harbours, the routes using monsoon winds and ocean currents — recurred in later centuries with similar overlaps of traders, commercial interests and cargoes. But those who provided its investment changed over time as also did the economic relations between traders and host countries. Trade with Asia remained, as an activity, somewhat distant to the Romans

* This is an expanded version of the South Asia Lecture given at the South Asian Studies Association Conference at Armidale in July 1992. *South Asia*, n.s. 15, 2, 1–28.

themselves, except that with the exotica which the trade brought to them they fantasised about the east, a fantasy which is encapsulated in the phrase, *ex oriente lux*. The actual merchants were mainly Greek or Jewish from Egypt and the eastern Mediterranean as well as Palmyrene and Levantine from the Hellenised world. The financial outlay appears to have been largely from this area although it has been argued that wealthy Romans invested in this trade.[2] But increasingly these traders had the backing of local Roman administration and among others, catered to the expensive tastes of Roman patricians. Although the eventual market was Rome, the actual functioning of the maritime trade focussed on Egypt and to a lesser extent on the eastern Mediterranean. From the South Asian perspective one could as well use the nomenclature familiar from those times and refer to it as the Yavana maritime trade.[3]

The commonly used phrase, 'Roman maritime trade with India', refers to the categories of trade and exchange through maritime channels between the eastern Mediterranean as a part of the Roman empire and various regions of the Indian sub-continent. The term 'Roman' is not intended to suggest that Rome itself conducted the trade but refers rather to the fact that the administration of the trade and the profits thereof in the eastern Mediterranean were within the control and jurisdiction of the Roman imperial system. The volume of trade and its impact on Indian centres varied; but where it was substantial there the Roman maritime trade can be viewed as a significant factor of economic and social concern. It speaks for the profits of the trade that in spite of difficulties it was pursued for so long. The Indian markets supplied exotic and aromatic plants and spices — nard, bdellium, costus, aloes, and pepper; semi-precious stones — chalcedonies, beryls, and pearls; a variety of textiles — silk, fine linens and cotton; timbers such as teak and ebony and fragrant sandalwood; all from different parts of the subcontinent, and even tortoise shell and perhaps cinnamon from Sri Lanka and south-east Asia. The traders from Egypt brought to South Asia a range of goods but most frequently lead, tin, coral, glass, wine and above all in the largest number, Roman coins in gold and silver, used in varying ways in different parts of the subcontinent. Judging by the presence of coins in South Asia, the trade commenced on the cusp of the Christian era, with the earliest major collections of coins being those of imperial Rome, reaching its peak in the first century AD. Recent finds of coins of the Roman Republic in south India, antedating the imperial issues, may point to a possibly earlier start to contacts, and this has also been argued from archaeological and palaeographical data.[4] It has however also been argued that the coins of the Republic could have been circulating together with early Imperial coins and do not therefore indicate an earlier start to the trade. The Ptolemies had some idea about the potentials of such a trade even if they did not fully explore it.

Roman maritime trade in the Indian Ocean makes a neat arc from Alexandria to Malacca and if I may borrow a phrase, it was held together by the 'urban gravitation'[5] of Coptos on the Nile, Barygaza in western India, Sopara in the western Deccan, Muziris on the Malabar coast and Kaveripattinam in the Kaveri delta, and their expansive hinterlands. As it inched its way eastwards it threaded through these distinct segments often underlining diverse socio-economic patterns. The sea creates its own frontiers and zones of activity and these do not invariably coincide with the boundaries of land-based territories. Just prior to the Roman trade the Hellenistic kingdoms, motivated by politics and commercial interests, began to re-explore earlier links. By the third century BC, Mauryan contact with the Hellenistic kingdoms of the Seleucids, Ptolemies and their neighbours are well-established.[6] The Roman maritime trade extended the geographical area of these contacts and realised the potential of economic activities.

Localised circuits of exchange and trade, linking ports and extending into hinterlands sometimes quite far into the interior, existed prior to the Roman trade. Among these were those from the Mediterranean towards the Red Sea pursued by the Phoenicians; the two coasts of the Red Sea involving local seafarers as well as the Ptolemaic search for elephants, which extended this circuit to east Africa and more hesitantly perhaps to south Asia; the caravan trade of southern Arabia with the eastern Mediterranean; the commerce between Syria and the Arab Persian Gulf with the Seleucids encouraging Indian commercial links;[7] the ports in western India drawing on the prosperous commercial centres in the hinterland of northern India and maintaining contact, probably through a looping trade, with ports along the coast of the Arabian peninsula many of which were dependent on this trade for import of food, especially rice, sugar, sesame oil and *ghi*, as well as cotton cloth; the circuits of the Megalithic people of the Indian peninsula and of Sri Lanka further underscored by Mauryan intervention;

possible east coast connections with areas across the Bay of Bengal; and the exchange networks within the islands of Southeast Asia extending to southern China.

Trade in consumables and food items could well remain a down-the-line coastal trade. But the trade in luxury items, as well as the availability of a large fleet of ships financed by commerce from Egypt and the eastern Mediterranean, encouraged greater risks. A faster mid-ocean route, regularly using monsoon winds, becomes more attractive for such trade. Ideally it was limited to a brief period of the year when the harbours of the west coast of India are serviceable in September and which enables a return to the Red Sea in October with the start of the north-east monsoon. The return journey had to be undertaken by December or at the latest, January. Setting out too early, even with using the south-west monsoon, was not only hazardous but entailed a longer wait in an Indian harbour before returning.[8] The gradual emergence of the Red Sea as the main artery of Roman maritime trade to the east dislodged the pre-eminence of the Arab Persian Gulf. The Red Sea route avoided the hostile Parthians closer to the Persian Gulf, required negotiation with the more malleable Arab traders and brought the west coast of India into quicker contact. The Red Sea route did however require the taking on board of archers as a protection against piracy.[9] Cargo arriving at the ports of the Red Sea was transported overland to Coptos and from there taken down the Nile to Alexandria. Such transportation was familiar to the Egyptian administration and economy since grain had been regularly transported down the Nile from Upper Egypt to Alexandria under the Ptolemies. The small-scale canal transportation was in Egyptian hands but the large-scale grain business on the Nile was controlled by the Greeks from Alexandria. The Levantines also participated in this trade.[10] The earlier transportation formed an important circuit and was doubtless easily adapted to include the cargoes from the east. Roman trade over-arched some of the existing circuits but this did not result in their termination, in fact to the contrary it could act as an incentive to increasing their activity. A fuller assessment of this trade would require a view beyond the circuits to their hinterlands and these differ widely, but in attempting to analyse the trade these differences have to be considered.

Discussions on the Roman economy have generally projected a predominantly agricultural economy with trade playing a marginal role in what has been referred to as the presumed cellular self-sufficiency of the ancient economy. This view is now changing as it is taking cognisance of the nature of the role of trade.[11] Whereas in its social attitudes Roman patrician society was prejudiced against trade and traders, as an economic activity it was significant not only to the Roman economy but also to the patrician life-style.[12] The question has been posed as to whether the Roman empire constituted a world-system in terms of the World Systems Analysis[13] where Roman trade would be an important manifestation. As an area of investigation within this theory, the Roman trade with Asia would be additionally significant if in fact there was an imperial policy towards it as well as imperial investment, as has been suggested.[14] The theory assumes a differentiation between two social systems: one was the small, subsistence economy, largely autonomous and not part of a tribute demanding system; the other was the large state containing a multiplicity of cultures and a division of labour related to the most efficient form of production. Of the latter kind there are two categories: the world empire and the world economy. The world-empire is linked by a uniform political system which dominates the various interrelated societies within its boundaries and with enough agricultural surplus to maintain artisans and the administrative stratum. The world-economy is fundamentally different with no political unity and with the redistribution of the surplus via the market. It is divided into core states and peripheral states where the former extracts the surplus from the latter in the form of resources. The frontier between the two is the semi-periphery which can also act as a link. The operation of the system revolved around two dichotomies based on unequal exchange: control over production and the appropriation by the centre of the produce of the periphery.[15] The theory concedes that some pre-capitalist world economies may be postulated, such as in China, Persia and Rome, but these changed into world empires.

Relating primarily to capitalism and excluding the pre-capitalist world, the theory appears nonetheless to have caught the fancy of archaeologists and has been used to investigate centre-periphery relations in various sectors of the Roman empire and in other areas of the ancient world.[16] Whereas the Roman empire may or may not confirm to the world-empire model, the world-economy model seems inapplicable to Roman trade with Asia. Trade alone does not necessarily define centre and periphery nor result in a hegemony of the centre over the periphery even if the trade in pre-capitalist societies was more extensive than is envisaged in the theory. However trade can act in some places as a catalyst whereas in others it is subordinated to local economic patterns. Some of the questions which the World Systems Analysis and its critique have raised, such as the nature of centre-periphery relations, could be pertinent to the changes which occurred in the areas involved in the trade. Perhaps the nature of a centre-periphery relationship can be sought in the smaller circuits where new forms of economic and political power emerged in association with the changes brought about by the trade, but these would not necessarily conform to the model. Thus in the context of the Roman trade the dominance of the Cambay region in western India suggests a pattern almost of a centre-centre trade. As a contrast the Malabar coast remains ambiguous and does not conform to an easily recognisable pattern.

What is of greater significance is an assessment of conditions in areas to which the trade reaches out, the differences from region to region and the perception, both cultural and economic, of the foreign traders among those with whom they trade. Mechanisms of exchange were neither uniform nor universal. They included barter, gift-exchange, formalised trade and monetised commodity exchange involving markets. Some of these categories co-existed in the same region but there was usually a priority among them which differed among different cultures. Each had its own complexities, even barter, which is generally dismissed as simple.[17] Barter could occur in the absence of money or in a condition of paucity of coins or even as a form of social distancing from commercial activities. The social back-up of barter was frequently the larger group of the family or the clan. A backing for the exchange of commodities came from more impersonal organisations such as guilds or corporations of traders. Gift-exchange underwrites social relations but also requires strategy and calculation.[18] Where a trade item is converted into a gift, even money can be absorbed as a valuable rather than a currency. Cargo can also consist of fetishised objects. It is thus as well to remind ourselves that, 'A commodity appears at first sight an extremely obvious, trivial thing. But its analysis brings out that it is a very strange thing, abounding in metaphysical subtleties and theological niceties.'[19] To assess the value of an item therefore involves looking at many dimensions of a society.

This in turn relates to the items exchanged and the mechanism of obtaining these. Raw materials are extracted from some areas, while in others trade demands sophisticated production. Exchange involved a series of transactions, some between the foreign trader and the local middleman or the merchant and some between the latter and the supplier of cargoes. Such transactions would register a regional divergence. Hinterlands are governed by varying characteristics and changed over space and time. Existing economies influenced the nature of the trade, and changes in the pattern of trade are pointers to social change. Activities under the rubric of trade are of many kinds and these are linked to itinerant pastoralism, travelling pedlars, clan chiefs, middlemen, traders. These may exist separately or be knitted together in an overarching trade. Thus whereas peddling is an occupation, trade requires an investment.[20]

Traders and ships crews are carriers of a particular culture. Their initial incursions have to be backed by a political interest if a literate high culture is to be introduced. From the western perspective the trade acted as a link between exchange nodes, ports of call and perhaps the mobile settlements of the traders from the west. From the perspective of those on whom the Roman traders called, the view is different. Within the boundaries of the Roman maritime trade in Asia there is the striking difference between the rather limited Mediterranean cultural imprint on India, and on the other hand, what has been called the 'indigenisation' of Indian culture in Southeast Asia. Yet both were not unrelated to the initial demands of the Roman trade.

The interpretation of Roman maritime trade with South Asia has moved from listing items and claiming cultural influences to assessing social and economic patterns.[21] At first studies remained close to the texts, usefully identifying ports and items. The focus shifted with the introduction of archaeological and numismatic data. The argument was frequently posed in terms of Roman influence on India. Viewed from the Indian perspective, the widespread distribution of Roman gold and silver coins in peninsula India would superficially suggest that the trade had overwhelmed Indian networks of exchange. However the complaint of Pliny that the oriental trade was draining the finances of Rome[22] was read as a statement of the economically superior position of India. But the impact of the trade and the imprint of wealth varied in different parts of India largely because of the dissimilar conditions in the subcontinent, which makes generalisations about India as a whole in relation to this trade, questionable. The evidence of coins alone suggests a pattern which points to divergences in different areas. Backed by other evidence the variation stands out even more strongly. Given this, neither barter nor market exchange appears to have been universal.

Western India, including the ports of Barbaricon and Barygaza (Bhṛgukaccha, Bhārukaccha/Bharuch) was known not only to the maritime traders of west Asia but also as an extension of the overland trade from west Asia to India. Barygaza is mentioned more frequently than any other emporium and inevitably had an important role in the Roman trade. Barbaricon was the port to the capital further up the river. The silting up of Barbaricon, known to happen in the Indus delta, may have ended its existence as a port and led to a convergence on Barygaza coinciding with the inclusion of central India as an area of production and internal trade. At the other end of this circuit there is little evidence of Indian ships docking in the northern ports of the Red Sea and this may have been partly because Indian ships were not permitted beyond Ocelis.[23] The Sabaeans in southwest Arabia are said to have acted as middle-men between India and the Mediterranean world, prior to the development of the Roman trade.[24] Perhaps the coral reefs made it dangerous and only the local seamen could handle these conditions.[25] The *Periplus*, a traders manual probably dating to the mid-first century AD, states that Aden declined as a port after Ptolemaic times and this doubtless coincided with the growth of the Red Sea ports such as Berenice, Myos Hormus and Leucos Limen (Quseir-al-Qadim).[26] Strabo refers to a fleet of a hundred and twenty ships sailing from Myos Hormus to India.[27] This was a radically different situation from the coastal voyages of the earlier trade. It suggests considerable control over shipping in the Red Sea and raises the question of who administered the control — local Arab interests or the Roman administration. The appointment of an official, the *epistrategos,* in charge of the Red Sea and the eastern desert of Egypt which was a Roman continuation of a Ptolemaic practice, would suggest that the local Arabs were edged out of the major trade. The inability or the prevention of Indian ships moving freely in the Red Sea might have been one of the reasons for the initiative of the Indian trade going into Egyptian hands. Indians as individual merchants are however listed as among those who trade in Egypt and are known at Alexandria.[28] Ostracon inscriptions in Prākṛit at Quseir have been read as referring to merchants[29] and graffiti in Tamil Brāhmī on potsherds from the same area could be Tamil names.[30] The connections appear to have been with south India.[31] A much-discussed Greek inscription found closer to the Nile refers to an Indian, Sophon (probably Subhānu) who addresses a prayer to the god Pan and was evidently a Hellenised Indian.[32]

Western India shows a familiarity with more than one pattern of exchange. The Ābhīras who were initially itinerant pastoralists but later took to other occupations give their name to the coastal area which was now associated with a sophisticated commerce. Barygaza was also a manufacturing centre and therefore imported some raw materials as well as commodities such as silverware, wine and perfume not to mention slave girls and musicians.[33] The hinterland of Barygaza from Saurashtra to central India included more distant areas from where silk and Kashmir nard was brought to be exported to the west. The rich trading centres of this hinterland such as Mathura and Ujjain, were familiar with monetary media and had used local high value coins contemporary with the arrival of the traders from the eastern Mediterranean. The paucity of Roman gold coins in northern India may not have been because the Kuṣāṇas melted the metal to mint their own coins, but because there was little need for yet another monetary medium in the area, although there may be more grounds for suggesting that the Ksatrapa silver currency of western India re-used Roman originals.[34] Many parts of the Indian subcontinent, including western India, had known the circulation of punch-marked coins. Although this coinage is distinct from that associated with the Roman trade, nevertheless some familiarity with monetary exchange has to be assumed for the areas where the punch-marked coins circulated. In the first century AD there is an import of Roman *denarii* into western India which, it is said, can be exchanged with much profit for the local currency,[35] but this declines. The Roman trade at Barygaza appears to have been handled by local merchants. Given the variance in forms of trade and the circulation of coins in the area, it is unlikely that the nature of this exchange was limited to barter rather than commerce as has been suggested by way of an explanation for the lack of Roman coins. The nature of the commercial exchange in itself may have precluded the presence of Roman coins although indigenous coins are available.

Further down along the west coast were the port of Suppāra, (Suppāraka/Sopara) and the city of Kalliena (Kalyāna). The importance of the former dates to the Mauryan period. In a Buddhist *Jātaka* story it is linked to Bhārukaccha and associated with mariners and seamanship.[36] The hinterland of the two ports fanned out to central India and the Deccan, the network of which can be mapped by epigraphic references at Buddhist sites to donors from various places.[37] The resources of this hinterland had been earlier tapped by the local Chalcolithic and Megalithic people. The Mauryas in turn had sought access to timber, a large range of semi-precious stones such as carnelian, quartz and agate used for making beads and other forest produce. Processes of exchange were therefore a familiar activity moving towards more complex forms of exchange, but there was a continuity in the items sought by the western trade. The tapping of resources was juxtaposed with centres of production and with towns controlling a sophisticated trade along the routes to the ports. Paithan and Ter in the western Deccan are said to send textiles along almost impassable routes to Barygaza. Bhokardan in the same area was a bead-making centre.[38] The nexus between elite politics and mercantile communities is evident from royalty investing sums of money in craftsmen's guilds by way of a donation, with the interest on the investment going to the Buddhist monasteries.[39] Cash donations involving large sums of money are again indicative of the widespread use of monetary exchange in western India and the western Deccan. The distribution of Satavahana coinage in the Deccan confirms the same. Although some rulers built rest-houses along the longer routes, nevertheless the monasteries must have acted as staging points as they do elsewhere. At those where the halt was necessary prior to facing the difficult terrain of the *ghats* such as at Nasik, Junnar, Karle, Bedsa and Kolhapur, or at terminal points such as Barygaza or Sopara, the endowments in the vicinity were impressive.[40] Even the monastic complex at Kanheri near Sopara was associated with what has been called a 'sub-urban complex'.[41] Frequent and sizeable donations by traders and artisans point to a growth in the commercial economy as compared to the earlier period and in the general expansion of subcontinental and trans-Asian trade, the maritime trade with Egypt played no small role in these parts. A significant body of donors were women — wives of traders, artisans and small-scale landowners as well as nuns.

Inscriptions refer to a large range of professions involved in the production of a variety of commodities. Among these, goldsmiths and workers in semi-precious stones are prominent and this is backed by archaeological evidence of bead working in the western Deccan.[42] Donors at Buddhist sacred sites, identify themselves with towns in the area. Guilds of ivory-carvers, weavers, potters, oil-pressers, bamboo workers and corn dealers are also mentioned.[43] Categories of persons involved in trade include the *seṭṭhi* or financier, the *vanij* or merchant, the *sārthavāha* or transporter and the *negama* who is associated with the market. Other sources describe ships arriving in port with merchants bidding for cargo, of merchants at border towns or in dialogue with producers.[44]

Not surprisingly a large range of items associated with the eastern Mediterranean surfaces at sites in the western Deccan.[45] Some were imported and others were local imitations. Smaller objects, such as bronze figures and Roman lamps, had their local imitations. Clay bullae suggest the same. Roman amphorae, generally containing wine or oil, were bulk items and may well have doubled as ballast. Judging by the distribution of the sherds there appears to have been a brisk market for wine. It has been argued that luxury trade required bulk goods as an economic balance since bulk goods with a saleable value maximise cargo space and freight revenue.[46] The large number of items from the Mediterranean which turn up in western India may also have come through the overland trade although coastal sites appear to have been quite active. More specific to the western Deccan are items such as clay seals of Roman design, double-moulded terracotta figurines, bronze statuettes — appropriately of Poseidon, Eros and Atlas, household objects such as metal cups, mirrors, a wine jug, a candlestick stand and a variety of Roman glass.[47] Were these the belongings of visiting Yavana merchants or, of Indian merchants who had brought them back as souvenirs from their travels west? These were not invariably bulk items but markers of gracious living. Given the frequency of local imitations, Roman objects were prized and may have even been purchased for money. Thus coral brought from the west was valued for the same reason as in the Mediterranean lands: it was a talisman against illness and evil. Imported coral was doubtless thought to be more effective than that available close by.

Roman trade with Barygaza and the western Deccan was therefore conditioned by a locally well-established economic exchange. The commercial advantages outweighed the navigational difficulties of a bad anchorage at Barygaza and the former assumed a familiarity both with local commerce as well as its extensive hinterland. In political terms this implied reasonably powerful states with some concern for the furtherance of the trade. A recognition of the economic importance of the Roman trade would explain why ships arriving at Kalyāna were escorted under guard to Barygaza, given the hostilities between the Śakas and the Sātavāhanas.[48] Clearly the profits from the Roman trade were highly attractive, hence the competition between local powers to capture the trade. This was not a profitable barter or a localised exchange but included a transit trade as well since the destinations of the items were often quite distant, as is frequently so with luxury goods.

Further south the picture changes. In most parts of south India barring the major settlements registering the presence of the Yavanas, there are fewer Roman artefacts but a strikingly larger number of coins, particularly in hoards. This is suggestive of a different dialogue underlying trade. Roman trade with the Malabar coast, focusses on a new item much in demand namely, black pepper. So profitable was this trade to the suppliers of pepper that this item could indeed be called 'black gold', the pepper being exchanged for gold.[49] The volume of black pepper exported must have been enormous because it was the cheapest of the peppers according to Pliny[50] and was paid for in coin. Possibly the pepper was also used as ballast on the journey back.[51] Pliny mentions a price for the pepper, early Tamil sources refer only to exchanging it for gold. Pliny adds that the pepper grew extensively in the area to the east, Cottonara, and was collected and sent in canoes made of hollowed out tree-trunks, to the emporium at Muziris.[52] That it was extremely valuable is also clear from Pliny who states that it was easy to adulterate it with locally available mustard seeds at Alexandria.[53] The demand for other items included semi-precious stones and the popularity of beryl is indicated by Roman coins which tend to cluster around the beryl mines near Coimbatore, a location which was also on the overland route to the east coast. Those who grew the pepper were likely not to have been the same as those who mined the beryl.

The presence of semi-precious stones and their distribution again goes back to Chalcolithic and Megalithic sites in the peninsula prior to the Roman trade. Megalithic exchange networks also carried a range of metal artefacts which have been found in burials. These were mainly weapons, agricultural implements such as hoes, and horse-bits, generally of iron. Also included as grave furnishings were carnelian and gold beads and jewellery. The exchange could have been an itinerant pedlar's exchange but more likely it was an exchange among the elite of goods which conferred status. The proximity of the Kolar gold-fields and auriferous veins in Karnataka, where numerous Aśokan inscriptions were located, also provides evidence of the Megalithic people and the Mauryan administration working these sites.[54] Spectacular remains of gold objects in Megalithic burials are few and possibly the gold was sent back to the Mauryan capital. The working of gold mines and veins would have added to the importance of gold in the local system of exchange and perhaps encouraged its hoarding when available.

The discovery of a sizeable amount of high value silver and gold Roman coins, occurring as stray finds and in hoards, in the peninsula, raises many questions relating to the Yavanas and to the local persons involved in the exchange. It has been argued that the silver *denarii* found in larger numbers were widely used in the transactions of the earlier period of the trade and the introduction of gold coins came later and that the silver coins were tied to the trade in beryl and semi-precious stones.[55] Interestingly Tamil sources associate pepper with gold. However the basic question remains that of explaining why the coins were found mainly in hoards. The explanation may cover more than a single function for the coins and the need to hoard them may have been due to a coinciding of various factors.

Were the coins hoarded against brigandage or alternatively paid as protection money to ensure the safe passage of goods from one coast to the other? Could it be that the hoards were intended as investments in further trade on the part of visiting traders? Were the coins in southern India and the western Deccan indicators that larger quantities of merchandise were bought for the Roman markets?[56] Roman coin hoards in India tend to be of specially selected coins with a high degree of metal purity.[57] Minted in the context of market exchange, they could become a measure for the commoditisation of other items. It has been suggested that Roman coins were used as bullion. This is more likely to apply to silver coins for if the high point of gold mining in Karnataka was during the period from 200 BC to AD 200,[58] there may not have been a need to use gold coins as bullion.

Gold and silver coins as items of consumption outside the context of market exchange could be linked to status hierarchies in which those who had access to these coins were in positions of dominance. Although some items are both necessities and luxuries, their particular role can be differentiated according to the circumstance in which they occur. Luxuries have been described as goods whose principal use is rhetorical and social, they are incarnated signs and respond to political necessity.[59] Commodities subsume value and labour value and value arises from the social context of the object. The intention of exchange can be the enhancement of status or of economic profit and this would be decided by the category of exchange — barter, gift-exchange or commodity trade.

Could the hoards be evidence of a system of gift exchange among indigenous chiefs and ruling families which might have continued from the chiefships of the earlier period? Gift-exchange does encourage the accumulation of wealth up to a point. If so then coins would not be used as high value currency but would be regarded as symbols of status. The political hegemony of the Cēras, Cōḷas and Pāṇḍyas in south India, in competition with the chieftains — the Velir, is evident by the turn of the Christian era from Tamil sources. Even Pliny makes a distinction between the king of Muziris, Caelobothra (the Latin for Cēraputra? echoing an earlier clan identity), and the tribe/*gentis* Neacyndi controlling the port at Porakud, a port also used by the Pāṇḍya king whose capital was further inland.[60] Chiefships and kingships co-existed. Pliny also states that local conditions were changing as reflected in the changing names of tribes, ports and towns. Power was garnered in the traditional manner through marriage alliances and conquests, hence the poems of love and war in the Śangam anthologies.[61] Wealth had earlier been collected but periodically distributed in the holding of great feasts which took on the character of a potlatch. The politics of monarchies was relatively recent in these kingdoms. As they moved towards consolidating kingdoms, the expenses of maintaining both kingship and the state increased. The availability of wealth became imperative. Prestige goods in order to be effective have to be circulated and the hoarding of these would have another meaning. If the coins did not circulate as wealth, their possession may have been of symbolic importance. Control over prestige goods is an enabling factor providing social and economic power useful to negotiating alliances. It is assumed that it was the families of the chiefs and the emergent royal families who, constituting the elite, controlled the goods. They not only had the will and the ability to accumulate wealth but could do so cutting across the identity of the clan. The ready availability of high value coins as prestige goods may have encouraged this process. The intrinsic value of the early imperial Roman coin was obviously recognised. Does the presence of Roman coin hoards suggest that in addition to an established commercial system in the coastal areas of south India, there was also in the hinterland, the prevalence of forms of barter? The coin therefore did not have the single function for which it was minted but could be used variously in accordance with the activities of the recipient and the nature of exchange.

What then was the impact of the Roman trade on such a society? Were the coin hoards seen as status symbols representing an accumulation that was not put to an economically productive use? Or did they contribute to the accumulating activities of the elite groups through whom the local resources were gathered and exchanged and which accelerated and intensified hierarchies. Such groups may eventually have indulged in some entrepreneurship themselves. The exports local to the region were mainly natural resources and not crafted products. The *Periplus* refers to villages and marts along the Malabar coast rather than urban commercial centres with the exception of Muziris and Nelkynda.[62] It records the import of wheat into Muziris presumably to feed the Yavana merchants negotiating with local middlemen or the crews of the ships waiting for the north-east monsoon in order to sail back to the Red Sea. Muziris as an emporium draws for export, cargoes from the east coast, including Chinese silk, Gangetic nard and tortoise shell from south-east Asia. Its imports are a great amount of money and other items not too different from elsewhere. But its hinterland is different from that of Barygaza. The activities at Muziris may not initially have been all that integrated with the hinterland and this may have changed gradually. The change is reflected in Tamil sources. The earlier Tamil source, the *Śaṅgam* literature has a larger space for chiefdoms and the Yavanas are alien, whereas the somewhat later Tamil epics, the *Śilappadikāram* and the *Maṇimēkalai*, assume monarchy to be the more familiar system with cities as centres of commerce in some of which the Yavanas have settled. Transactions within the trade would have moved from the one to the other.

Roman trading contacts on the eastern coast of south India were with a society familiar with commercial exchange although perhaps not as sophisticated as the markets of Barygaza and the western Deccan. Punch-marked coins circulated in Tamil-nadu[63] and may have come as a result of increased trade in the post-Mauryan period. Tamil Brāhmī votive inscriptions found in greater profusion to the east of Coimbatore, suggest the presence of professionals and craftsmen but even in their Buddhist and Jaina identity they do not carry the power and the patronage of the community associated with the monastic centres of the western Deccan. The wharf at Kāveripaṭṭinam and the presence of Yavanas at the port in later times points to the continuing importance of the area. Roman traders located their bases at Arikamedu and Kāveripaṭṭinam, both of which, prior to this, may have been collection points for goods.[64] The location of Arikamedu has been associated with one of the strongholds of the Velir chieftains.[65] As bases, these would have been linked to resources both from Sri Lanka to the south and from the east coast of India along the major river deltas to the Ganga and possibly south-east Asia.[66] Earlier excavations at Arikamedu yielded Roman artefacts and what was interpreted as evidence for the manufacture of textiles.[67] A more recent excavation suggests that the settlement in the previous period had links with local exchange networks.[68] What is also of interest is that the amphorae sherds indicate that they were containers of wine, oil and garum, the latter two suggesting the presence of foreign consumers.[69] The presence of foreign merchants who brought their goods to Kāveripaṭṭinam and who had left their homes and settled there and who spoke a variety of languages is mentioned in the *Śilappadikāram*[70] although the text is later than the first century AD. Recent excavations as Alagankulam suggest a possible trading-station in the Vaigai delta servicing the Pāṇḍyan territory.[71] It has been plausibly argued that Roman ships did not initially round the Cape because of navigational problems and thus the overland route from near Coimbatore — the Palghat gap — to the east coast became the regular route. Furthermore Indian seamen, using indigenous boats, fetched and carried cargo between the two coasts.[72] Payment for this trade may have required a large monetary outlay which could have been delivered to merchants and middlemen along the safer land route. Hence the location of major coin hoards along this route.

Settlements of Yavana traders were not colonies since that would imply that there was an appropriation of resources, land and labour and some degree of permanency which was not the case. The nature of the settlements were by no means identical. Some might have been trading stations with a quick change of visiting traders using local agents as mediators in the trade. The emporium at Muziris may have been one of these. The manufacturing of items locally which were specific to this trade, such as textiles, may have encouraged merchants to live more permanently in the settlements as at Arikamedu and Kāveripaṭṭinam. It is possible that Paithan and Ter in the western Deccan which are also associated with the production of textiles for this trade may have played a similar role given the Yavana settlement at Dhenukākaṭa. This would point to a more-than-casual lateral intervention in the production of items.

In the eastern Deccan, at one site Roman pottery and other artefacts have been found together with Megalithic pottery pointing to an interaction between the two.[73] The area had been under Mauryan administration, had coastal links with ports along the deltas as far north as the Ganga and was also linked to the routes going inland to central India and to the western Deccan. Khāravela in Kalinga, generally dated to about the first century BC, boasts of conquering a confederacy of the Tamils which may be just a boast but could reflect an east coast network.[74] He also refers to defeating the Sātavāhana king at the Krishna river and to receiving pearls from the Pāṇḍyan king. Important Buddhist centres with votive inscriptions, such as at Bhaṭṭiprolu and Amarāvatī, indicate organised mercantile activities involving market centres and towns as well as agrarian prosperity and some date to the period just prior to the Roman trade.[75] Substantial Roman coin finds occur in Andhra Pradesh, particularly in and around the Krishna valley.[76] The *Periplus* has a sparse reference to ports in this area — the region of Masalia — but gradually, judging by coin finds and the more detailed references in Ptolemy to Maisolia (Masulipattam),[77] Roman trading interests appear to have increased. Ptolemy provides details of urban activity and the sources agree that it was a production centre for cotton fabric. The wharf at Dharanikota (ancient Dhānyakakaṭa), the port of the settlement at Amarāvati, continues to be used until it is silted up in the third century AD[78] by which time Roman coins become scarce.

Coin hoards from the region around the Krishna valley contain high value coins. As is also the case in some south Indian hoards, a few are defaced either by a bar or slashed and others carry small punch marks.[79] There appears to be a greater frequency in slashing gold coins than defacing silver coins and the latter seem to be restricted to the Krishna valley. The defacing of these coins is unlikely to have been because of Hīnayāna Buddhist iconoclasm as has been suggested, since Buddhism by now had its own icons and had not objected to royal portraits elsewhere in India. It was more likely to do with differentiating between those coins minted prior to Nero's debasement of coins or with an attempt to prevent these coins from being sent back to Egypt.[80] The defacement ensured that their currency was restricted to the Indian circuits of the trade and particularly along the east coast. This might further relate to Yavana interest in resources from south-east Asia and the need for readily available specie in areas which had links with these resources. (Ptolemy mentions in his discussion of Maisolia that the point of departure for ships going to the Khryse or south-east Asia was on this coast). Yet it is curious that only a small percentage of the coins are defaced. High value coins in the Krishna valley are unlikely to have been used only as symbols of status, as might have been the case in some parts of south India, since there was a familiarity with monetary exchange based on a system of indigenous coins. The use of punch marks may even suggest an attempted continuity from earlier practice.

The lure of trade further east was possibly because of the fabled lands of gold, the *suvarṇa* prefixes in the Sanskrit place names and the possibility of an alternate route to Chinese silk and other items not easily available in India. The *Periplus* gives few details of ports and harbours along the northern half of the east coast. A major commercial port called Ganga, on the delta, was evidently the point at which the trade along the Ganga valley came to settle. Its identity remains uncertain although it has been linked to Tāmralipti (Tamluk)[81] the most active port in the delta going back to the Mauryan period with an extensive hinterland of the Ganga plain. Eastwards the picture is vague for the *Periplus* refers only to Thina as the silk producing land. However the geographer Ptolemy, writing at a later date in the second century AD (and with possible interpolations), provides more details of the ports and produce from the Ganga delta to the Gulf of Siam, a circuit which gradually comes into greater use. This circuit continues to be referred to as 'India', suggesting the strong imprint of Indian trade at these ports.

There has been much discussion on the mutation in some parts of south-east Asia initiated by incidental and later more organised exchange with Indian traders.[82] The process remains elusive but hypotheses can be suggested. In clan-based societies reciprocal relations are achieved through maintaining the status quo or allowing only a limited deviation. Exchange activities with those outside the clan would introduce social imbalances and alter the existing economic forms. Such changes would encourage the accentuation of political control by those already in some positions of authority. A link between alien traders and emergent chiefs would have enhanced the power of the latter and might possibly have impeded the growth of indigenous traders. Initially at least the items traded would tend to be redistributed except where they were regarded as prestige goods. With the emergence of states, however, relations between Indian traders and local royalty in the kingdoms drew on a variety of cultural elements as well. Among the cultural imports into south-east Asia were the coming of Buddhism and Brahmanism, where both were to provide ideologies of political control to the local elite. Buddhism tends to be less acceptable to clan-based societies for whom Brahmanical sacrificial rituals were easier entry points into an imported ideology and could be more comfortably adjusted to local mores and beliefs. When exchange turned into trade, however, Buddhism perhaps became more attractive because of its social ethic which included a partiality for the accumulation of wealth and investment in commerce. But there was an increasing tendency for the two to fade into each other.

Unlike the Indian Ocean trade of later times when Islam and Christianity provided a religious backing to the trading networks, the Roman trade did not carry a religion. Those that came from the Mediterranean were largely worshippers of Greco-Roman and Egyptian deities, with possibly some early Christians. There is an absence of recognisable representations of such deities in India.[83] Nor is there a presence of Christianity at this time although the picture changes by the middle of the millennium.[84] Christian texts written in the eastern Mediterranean begin to mention Christian missions from the second century AD and the establishment of the Church in south India and Sri Lanka by about the sixth century AD.[85] The council of Nicea in AD 325 lists an Indian connection and there is later evidence of a Nestorian mission. Still later, Syrian Christians are said to have settled in Kerala.[86] If at all a wide-ranging religious ideology is to be associated with this trade, then it seems to have been Buddhism which spread along the trade routes and where possible provided an ideological infrastructure which helped to integrate a diversity of mercantile and political interests with religious concerns. These were possibly germane to the almost contradictory tradition of the Christian hermits in Syria and Egypt[87] and the royal cults of Cambodia and Indonesia.

Indian perceptions of those that came from the west, the Yavanas, varied.[88] The north Indian experience of the Yavanas was initially in the context of aggression and military hostility: the campaigns of Alexander and later of the Indo-Greeks. Consequently in some Brahmanical texts, the Yavanas are reviled and regarded as oppressors.[89] When the Indo-Greeks ruled in northern India there was a problem about giving them a rank in the hierarchy of caste and they were slotted as *vrātya-kṣatriyas* or literally, the degenerate *kṣatriyas*. Yavanas arriving as peaceful traders do not find an entry in Brahmanical texts. This was in part because the good *brāhmaṇa* was told to avoid the cities, the traders and their means of livelihood such as usury, and to refrain from crossing the seas. Needless to say few *brāhmaṇas* paid attention to these injunctions. *Brāhmaṇa* hostility to the Yavanas also derived from the fact that the latter, both as royalty and as traders, were substantial patrons of the various Buddhist sects who by now were regarded as heretics by the *brāhmaṇas*. This did not however preclude more than just a passing interest in some categories of technical knowledge. Familiarity with Hellenistic ideas on medicine and horoscopy is evident from various texts. The *Yavanajātaka*, a text on horoscopy is believed to be based on a Greek text from Alexandria and dates to the early Christian era and was probably written in western India.[90] It would seem that a few Greek-speaking persons may have been settled in western India and had a high status since they use the title of *rājā*. The text has a brahmanical idiom and perspective and is contemptuous of other religious sects which it describes as *pāṣaṇḍas* or heretics.[91] The use of such a text may not however have been limited to the *brāhmaṇa* elite.

The Buddhist view of the Yavanas was different. There was a curiosity about Yavana society and there is a tradition of Buddhist missions having been sent to Yavana lands to proselytise. Buddhist texts respect traders and merchants, and Buddhism derived a considerable patronage from the support of mercantile groups in Indian society. Consequently traders and commercial centres were not treated as marginal. Wealthy Buddhist Yavanas are mentioned in the votive inscriptions at Buddhist sacred sites in the Deccan.[92] Some have Prākritised Indian names but were not Indians else they would not have claimed to be Yavanas.[93] In one case the donor describes himself as a northerner but in most instances the term Yavana alone is used. As worshippers of Isis or Poseidon, their 'pagan' beliefs would not have stood in the way of an acceptance of Buddhism. If anything, it would have admitted them to the dominant religious idiom of the traders of western India. If an early reading of these inscriptions is correct that some among the Yavanas came from Gata, then it may be suggested that this should not be identified with Trigarta or Jallandhar in northern India, but could be the Prākṛit form of Coptos (Coptos>Gapta>Gata). However recent readings have related the suffix *gata* to *saṇgata* as in a corporation[94] or else interpret *gata* as part of the Yavana name and not a place.[95] But it is unlikely that the suffix *gata* was a recognised Yavana name-ending. There are references in Greek and Latin sources to persons from Egypt being in India and Coptos was the emporium which handled the trade from India.[96] That a merchant from Coptos could declare himself a Buddhist and be involved in the maritime trade with the western Deccan, also provides a logical context. The inscriptions mention that some of these Yavanas were associated with Dhenukākaṭa which has been variously identified but was probably close to Karle in the western Deccan.[97] That Dhenukākaṭa was a commercial centre is suggested by its description as a *vaniya-gāma*.[98] It is not surprising that the maximum integration between Yavanas and Indians was in an area where commerce was developed. One expression of this integration appears to have been a bi-lingualism in Hellenistic Greek and Prākṛit although there must have been a bi-lingualism in Greek and Tamil as well.

Tamil Śangam literature provides yet another facet of Indian views of the Yavanas. There are descriptions of the beautiful ships of the Yavanas, laden with gold which they exchange for pepper.[99] Mention is also made of the cool fragrant wine brought by them in elegant jars.[100] Sometimes the tone is hostile as when a Cēra chief is said to have captured the barbarous Yavanas and divested them of their wine and their wealth.[101] Cēra hostility towards the Yavanas is repeated in the epics of the subsequent period.[102] To the Tamil speakers of the south, Yavana speech was a harsh and barbarous language. In the Tamil epics the relationship seems to have changed as they describe the Yavanas in the port of Kāveri-paṭṭinam not as passing visitors but as resident craftsmen or even employed as city guardsmen.[103] They are said to live in a separate section of the city and are distinguished by their wealth. This remains a more distanced view of the Yavanas than in the western Deccan. In spite of the presence of Buddhists in the area there are no Yavana Buddhists. Thus the difference in the nature of the trade and exchange is also reflected in these facets of the Yavana relationship with the people of the subcontinent.

The Roman trade may not have bestowed a common belief system on the lands which it touched, but Roman coins became legal tender in large parts of the Indian Ocean. The role of the trade in the Roman economy is significant and has been commented upon both by contemporaries and by modern historians. The starting point of what has become a debate are the statements by both Pliny and Tiberius that the wealth of Rome was being drained by the purchase of articles of feminine vanity and of luxury from the east.[104] Tiberius, in a letter to the Roman senate objected to the conspicuous consumption of Roman patricians in the grandeur of their villas, their numerous slaves, their silver, gold and objects d'art, their fine clothes and the jewels of the women, many of these items coming from distant lands. Pliny at one point mentions a drain of fifty-five million sesterces; and elsewhere he assessed the drain of wealth to India, Arabia and China as one hundred million sesterces.[105] Such statement were taken literally and it was argued that this trade contributed to the economic pressures on the Roman empire which facilitated its decline.

An early attempt at refuting this view[106] pointed out that there was a rigorous control over *ad valorem* customs duties of up to twenty-five per cent on imports from the east into Egypt and the re-exporting of such goods from Alexandria. The actual loss of gold was not high because of the supply from the gold mines of Spain and treasure captured in campaigns. In fact, the price of gold on the Roman market dropped somewhat at the end of the first century AD just after the period of the maximum despatch of gold coins to the Indian trade. Another argument rejecting the fleeing of gold from Rome in the eastern trade maintains that the Romans exported wines, tin, and lead and that the Indians exchanged goods for goods, not having a sufficient monetary outlay.[107] The latter statement is open to question since, as we have seen, a uniform pattern of exchange did not prevail in every part of India. The monetary outlay in northern and western India appears to have been sufficient for the trade. Coin hoards in themselves are not the sole evidence of a financial drain, for the nature of the exchange would have to be examined. The total number of Roman coins in India is small as compared to those found in hoards on the northern frontier of the Roman empire[108] where money was used to buy off the barbarians and therefore played a different role from that of the hoards in the Indian peninsula. A further perspective on this question argues for looking at other features unconnected with maritime trade which contributed to a decline in the Roman economy. These include the over-expansion of global consumption in the Antonine age, the economic pressure on the state arising out of the system of doles, the fiscal pressures on medium and small scale landowners and the evasion of taxes by large property owners as well as the increased expenditure on the army and the bureaucracy and on keeping the barbarians at bay.[109] A more recent debate focuses on doubts regarding an economic decline.[110]

Egypt was the focal point of the eastern maritime trade in the Roman empire.[111] It attracted a larger volume of trade from the east than from the cargoes of the Mediterranean.[112] The initial thrust of the Ptolemies in the eastern direction was extended when Egypt became a province of the Roman empire.[113] Shipping was largely controlled by wealthy Alexandrian merchants who had a monopoly over the Red Sea trade. The Roman administration continued the Ptolemaic office of the *espistrategos* of Thebaid, the prefect of the Red Sea, who had command over the eastern desert and controlled the caravan routes and customs dues levied at Coptos.[114] He also kept a check on the tariffs collected on this route and the tariff rates suggest that small-scale transportation was as frequent as the larger caravans. Heavy fees were charged for the use of these routes which had to be kept well-guarded to ensure a safe passage for the trans-shipment of cargo.[115] The maintenance of a garrison at Coptos may have been required for this purpose as well.[116] The caravan routes from the Red Sea ports to inland centres in Egypt were run by private companies.[117]

A papyrus document containing a contract between a merchant and a ship's captain refers to shipments of goods from India and dates to the second century AD.[118] Views differ as to where exactly the contract was drawn up, either in Muziris or Alexandria or at a port of the Red Sea where the cargo was off-loaded. The contract relates to cargo from Muziris and its transport from the port to the Nile and its safe arrival in the warehouse of the merchant in Alexandria. The cargo which is the subject of this contract consisted of 700 to 1,700 pounds of Gangetic nard, about 4,700 pounds of ivory and a variety of textiles totalling about 790 pounds — all luxury goods and subject to a twenty-five per cent customs duty on import. Curiously pepper is not included in the list. The contract points to a very large capital investment and this had to cover not only the cost of the cargo but also the maintenance of a crew and its stay in India while waiting for the return monsoon, and protection of the cargo from brigandage en route. Possibly Pliny was troubled by such large investments of capital. Yet if one voyage was so costly, the drain of fifty-five million sesterces does not seem totally out of proportion. What the Muziris contract does underline is that the trade with south India was substantial in the second century AD with Muziris continuing to be the emporium for goods even from the east coast. The enormous financial outlay required in this trade as is evident from the contract, does rather diminish the importance of the quantitative aspect of the Roman coin hoards in peninsular India.

Bullion was sold in the open market at Coptos and Alexandria where the former is particularly associated with silver bullion.[119] That Coptos was extremely important to this trade is evident from the large numbers of Greek *ostraca* recording accounts and receipts.[120] These receipts and the evidence of the Muziris contracts point not only to the outlay on this trade but also to complex banking systems in Egypt. High taxes were levied on the various processes of textile production,[121] presumably to encourage the import of textiles rather than raw material. Perhaps this accounted for the vats at Ter and Arikamedu.

Coptos was the bustling business centre and was sufficiently cosmopolitan for Greek families and others such as Hellenised Egyptians, Levantines, traders from Palmyra to be the main actors in the Indian trade.[122] That women were also representatives of trading houses and were ship-owners and merchants goes back to Ptolemaic times.[123] Coptos was the centre for collecting and handling cargo to be forwarded either eastwards or to Alexandria. The ultimate control lay in the hands of the merchants from Alexandria whose representatives were resident at points along which the cargo moved. Alexandria was the centre financing the trade, organising the sale and purchase of cargoes and arranging the trans-shipment of large quantities to Rome. It would seem that although the tastes of the Roman patricians were met by this trade, its commercial base remained in the Roman province of Egypt. Egypt therefore can be viewed as the periphery to the centre at Rome, or else as the centre to the periphery in the eastern Mediterranean.

The spectacular profits of the trade for Mediterranean traders encouraged the fabulous in descriptions of Asia. What is perhaps curious is that despite the close contacts resulting from the trade with the Yavanas and the visibility of the transactions, the Indian world has left us no descriptions of places and peoples visited in the course of this trade.

And what of Rome and its citizens whose demands sustained this trade? Rome, it has been said, was a consumer city par excellence, and the eastern luxury trade was crucial to its life-style. This was recognised in more than just the complaints of Tiberius and Pliny. In what has been referred to as the apocalyptic cartoon language of one book of the Bible — *The Revelations of St John* — Rome is projected as the 'scarlet harlot' and its opulence and evil ways are denounced.[124] The denunciation coincided with the peak period of the eastern trade. St John prophesies doom on the death of Rome and adds that, ' . . . merchants the world over have grown rich on her bloated wealth, but when she dies they will mourn, as no one will buy their cargoes of . . . jewels, pearls, silks and fine linen, of scented woods, ivories . . . cinnamon and spice . . . ' But trade falsified the dire prophecies of St John. The regular visits of merchant ships to India continued into Late Roman times.[125] Given the author of the prophecy, it was all the more ironic that in the fourth century AD Constantine donated to the eastern churches vast quantities of incense, perfume, nard, balsam and pepper.[126] It is not clear as to what the churches would have done with these donations. They may have used a small amount in church rituals but probably sold the bulk on the market, deriving a substantial revenue from the sale.

The cargo listed by St John had a constant market in the Mediterranean, providing a continuity to the trade with South Asia well after Roman times. And in later centuries there were to be, many more cities in Europe emulating the 'scarlet harlot'.

## Notes and References


1. P. Curtin, *Cross-cultural Trade in World History*, Cambridge, 1984.
2. M.G. Raschke, 'New Studies in Roman Commerce with the East', *Aufsteig and Niedergang der Romischer Welt*, Berlin, 1978, p. 646.
3. *Yavana* from the Prākṛit *yona*, was initially the term used for Greeks but soon came to be applied to all those who came from west Asia and even further west.
4. P. Turner, *Roman Coins in India*, London, 1989, pp. 6–7, 42–3, 90. V. Begley, 'Arikamedu Reconsidered', *American Journal of Archaeology*, 87 (1983), pp. 261–482. See also, R. Nagaswamy, 'Alagankulam: An Indo-Roman Trading Station', in C. Margabandhu et al. (eds), *Indian Archaeological Heritage*, Delhi, 1991, pp. 247–54.
5. K.N. Chaudhuri, *Trade and Civilisation in the Indian Ocean*, Cambridge, 1985, p. 165.
6. Romila Thapar, 'Epigraphic Evidence and some Indo-Hellenistic Contacts During the Mauryan Period', in S.K. Maity and U. Thakur (eds), *Indological Studies, Prof. D.C. Sircar Commemoration Volume*, New Delhi, 1988, pp. 15–19.
7. J-F. Salles, 'The Arab Persian Gulf under the Seleucids', in A. Kuhrt and S. Sherwin–White, *Hellenism in the East*, London, 1987, pp. 75–109. F. Millar, 'The Problem of Hellenistic Syria', ibid., pp. 110–33. D.T. Potts, *The Arabian Gulf in Antiquity*, vol. II, Oxford, 1990.
8. L. Casson, 'Rome's Trade with the East: The Sea Voyage to Africa and India', *Transactions and Proceedings of the American Philological Association*, 110 (1980), pp. 21–36. Pliny, *Natural History*, 6.26.106.
9. Pliny, op. cit., 6.26.101.
10. D.J. Thompson, 'Nile Grain Transport under the Ptolemies', in P. Garnsey, K. Hopkins, C.R. Wittaker (eds), *Trade in the Ancient Economy*, London, 1983, pp. 64–76.
11. K. Hopkins, 'Introduction', in P. Garnsey et al., op. cit., pp. ix–xxv.
12. R. Duncan–Jones, *Structure and Scale in the Roman Economy*, Cambridge, 1990, pp. 29, 46ff. H.W. Pleket, 'Urban Elites and Business in the Greek Part of the Roman Empire', in P. Garnsey et al., op. cit., pp. 131–44. J.H. D'Arms, *Commerce and Social Standing in Ancient Rome*, Cambridge, Mass., 1981.
13. G. Wolf, 'World Systems Analysis and the Roman Empire', *Journal of Roman Archaeology*, 3 (1990), pp. 44–56.

14. S. Sidebotham, *Roman Economic Policy in the Erythra Thalassa, 30 BC to AD 217*, Leiden, 1986. But see also L. Casson, *Periplus Maris Erythraei* (hereafter *PME*), New Jersey, 1989, pp. 32–3, for the more generally accepted view that the trade was in private hands.
15. E. Wallerstein, 'A World-System Perspective on the Social Sciences', in *The Capitalist World Economy*, Cambridge, 1979, pp. 152–64.
16. M. Rowlands, M. Larsen and K. Kristiansen (eds), *Centre and Periphery in the Ancient World*, Cambridge, 1985. P. Kohl, 'The Use and Abuse of World Systems Theory', *Advances in Archaeological Method and Theory*, 11 (1987), pp. 1–35. C. Edens, 'Dynamics of Trade in the Ancient Mesopotamian World System', *American Anthropologist*, 94, 1 (1922), pp. 118–39. T. Champion (ed.), *Centre and Periphery, Comparative Studies in Archaeology*, London, 1989. J. Schneider, 'Was there a Pre-capitalist World System?', *Peasant Studies*, 6, 1 (1977), pp. 20–9.
17. C. Humphrey and S. Hugh–Jones, *Barter, Exchange and Value*, Cambridge, 1992, Introduction.
18. C.A. Gregory, 'Gifts to Men and Gifts to God: Gift Exchange and Capital Accumulation in Contemporary Melanesia', *Man*, n.s. 15, 4 (1980), pp. 625–52. *Gifts and Commodities*, London, 1982.
19. K. Marx, *Capital*, I, Harmondsworth, 1976, p. 163.
20. J.C. Van Leur, *Indonesian Trade and Society*, The Hague, 1967.
21. H.G. Rawlinson, *Intercourse between India and the Western World, from the Earliest Times to the Fall of Rome*, Cambridge, 1916. E.H. Warmington, *The Commerce between the Roman Empire and India*, London, 1928, 1974 revised. J.I. Miller, *The Spice Trade of the Roman Empire*, Oxford, 1969. R.E.M. Wheeler, A. Ghosh and Krishna Deva, 'Arikamedu: An Indo-Roman Trading Station on the East Coast of India, *Ancient India*, 2 (1946), pp. 17–125. R.E.M. Wheeler, *Rome Beyond the Imperial Frontier*, London, 1955. 'Roman Contact with India, Pakistan and Afghanistan', in W.F. Grimes (ed.), *Aspects of Archaeology in Britain and Beyond: Essays Presented to O.G.S. Crawford*, London, 1951, pp. 345–81.
22. Pliny, op. cit., 6.26.101.
23. *Periplus*, pp. 25–6. Motichandra, *Sārthavāha*, Patna, 1953, pp. 119ff.
24. P.M. Fraser, *Ptolemaic Alaxandria*, I, Oxford, 1972, p. 543.
25. K.N. Chaudhuri, op. cit., p. 130.
26. *Periplus*, pp. 18–19, 26. Strabo, 16.4.22–4.
27. Strabo, 2.5.12; 2.118.
28. W. Scmitthammer, 'Rome and India: Aspects of Universal History During the Principate', *Journal of Roman Studies*, 69 (1979), pp. 90–106.
29. R. Salomon, 'Epigraphic Remains of Indian Traders in Egypt', *Journal of the American Oriental Society*, 3, 4 (1991), pp. 731–6.

30. Two pot-sherds with Tamil Brāhmī inscriptions — *catan* and *kapan* — were found at Quseir-al-Qadim, a port on the Egyptian side of the Red Sea, D.S. Whitecomb and J.H. Johnson, *Quseir-al-Qadim 1978: Preliminary Report*, Cairo, 1979; *Quseir-al-Qadim 1980: Preliminary Report*, Malibu, 1982.
31. Tamil Brāhmī graffiti on pot-sherds also occurs at Arikamedu. R.E.M. Wheeler, A. Ghosh and Krishna Deva, 'Arikamedu: An Indo-Roman Trading Station on the East Coast of India', *Ancient India*, 2 (1946), 109ff.
32. Salomon, op. cit.
33. Casson, *PME*, pp. 22ff.
34. P. Turner, *Roman Coins from India*, London, 1989.
35. *Periplus*, p. 49.
36. *Suppāraka Jātaka*, 11.463.
37. Romila Thapar, 'Patronage and Community', in B. Stoler Miller (ed.), *The Powers of Art*, Delhi, 1992, pp. 1–34. *See* chapter 27 in this volume. Vidya Dehejia, 'Collective and Popular Bases of Early Buddhist Patronage: Sacred Monuments, 100 BC–AD 250', ibid., pp. 35–45.
38. S.B. Deo and R. Gupte, *Excavation at Bhokardan*, Nagpur, 1974.
39. *Epigraphia Indica*, 8 (1905–6), pp. 82ff, 89ff.
40. *Epigraphia Indica*, 5, Luders List nos 1131, 1133, 1099. K.L. Mahalay, 'Rise and Fall in the Commercial Significance of the Deccan Caves', *Deccan Geographer*, 11 (1973), pp. 1–17. C. Margabandhu, 'Trade Contacts Between Western India and the Greco-Roman World', *Journal of the Economic and Social History of the Orient*, 8 (1965), pp. 316–22. H.P. Ray, *Monastery and Guild*, Delhi, 1986.
41. M. Meister, 'Sub-Urban Planning and Rock-cut Architecture', in *Madhu: Recent Researches in Indian Archaeology and Art History*, Delhi, 1981, pp. 157–64.
42. H.D. Sankalia, S.B. Deo and B. Subbarao, *Excavations at Maheswar and Navdatoli, 1952–3*, Poona, 1958; B.K. Thapar, 'Prakash 1955: A Chalcolithic Site in the Tapti Valley', *Ancient India*, 20, 21 (1964–5), pp. 5–167. S.B. Deo and R.S. Gupte, *Excavations at Bhokardan, 1973*, Nagpur, 1974; B.N. Chapekar, *Report on the Excavation at Ter*, Poona, 1969.
43. J. Burgess and B. Indraji, *Inscriptions from the Cave Temples of Western India*, Delhi, 1976 (reprint), pp. 47, 54.
44. *Cullaka-seṭṭhi Jātaka*, 1.4; *Akatannu Jātaka*, 1.90; *Makasa Jātaka*, 1.44; *Sussondi Jātaka*, 5.360.
45. C. Margabandhu, 'Two Clay Bullae (medallions) from Junagarh', *Visvesvaranand Indological Journal*, 8, 2 (1975), pp. 1–7. *Archaeology of the Sātavāhana Ksatrapa Times*, Delhi, 1985.
46. K.N. Chaudhuri, op. cit., pp. 184ff.
47. H.D. Sankalia and S.B. Deo, *Report on the Excavations at Nasik and*

*Jorwe, 1950–51*, Poona, 1955. H.D. Sankalia et al., *From History to Prehistory at Nevasa, 1954–56*, Poona, 1960. B. Subbarao, *Baroda Through the Ages*, Baroda, 1953. R.N. Mehta and S.N. Chowdhury, *Excavations at Devnimori*, Baroda, 1966. R.N. Mehta and D.R. Shah, *Excavations at Nagara*, Baroda, 1968. S.B. Deo and R.S. Gupte, *Excavation at Bhokardan*, Nagpur, 1974. Relevant reports in *Indian Archaeology — A Review*. M. Dikshit, *History of Indian Glass*, Bombay, 1969.

48. J.A.B. Palmer, 'Periplus Mari Erythrae, the Indian Evidence as to the Date', *The Classical Quarterly*, 41 (1947), pp. 136–40. D.W. Macdowall, 'The Early Western Satraps and the Date of the Periplus', *The Numismatic Chronicle*, 4 (1964), pp. 271–80. G. Mathew, 'The Dating and Significance of the Periplus of the Erythreaen Sea', in N. Chittick and R.I. Rotberg (eds), *East Africa and the Orient*, London, 1975, pp. 147–63. See also L. Casson, 'Sakas versus Andras in the Periplus Mari Erythrae', *Journal of the Economic and Social History of the Orient*, 26, 2 (1983), pp. 164–77, for a different reading of the text.
49. *Akam*, 149.7–11.
50. Pliny, op. cit., 12.14.28. Four *denarii* per pound for black pepper and seven and fifteen respectively for white and long pepper.
51. K.N. Chaudhuri, op. cit., p. 191.
52. Pliny, op. cit., 6.26.105. L. Casson, *PME*, p. 221. *Periplus*, p. 56.
53. Pliny, 12.14.28.
54. F.R. Allchin, 'Upon the Antiquity and Methods of Gold Mining in Ancient India', *Journal of the Economic and Social History of the Orient*, 5, 2 (1962), pp. 195–211. 'Antiquity of Gold-mining in the Gadag Region — Karnataka', *Madhu*, Delhi, 1981.
55. Turner, op. cit., p. 16.
56. Warmington, op. cit., Delhi, 1974, pp. 277, 292.
57. D.W. Macdowell, 'Indian Imports of Roman Silver Coins', paper read at the Third International Colloquium, Nasik, 1990.
58. Allchin, op. cit.
59. A. Appadurai (ed.), *The Social Life of Things: Commodities in the Cultural Perspective*, Cambridge, 1988, Introduction.
60. Pliny, op. cit., 6.26.105.
61. K. Kailasapathy, *Tamil Heroic Poetry*, Oxford, 1968. A.K. Ramanujam, *Poems of Love and War*, New York, 1985. K.V. Zvelebil, *Tamil Literature*, Wiesbaden, 1974. *The Smile of Murugan*, London, 1973.
62. *Periplus*, pp. 53–6.
63. K.V. Raman, Presidential Address, Numismatic Society of India, Visva Bharati, 1990. A recent report of finds said to be of indigenous coins of the Cēras, Cōḷas and Pāṇḍyas of this period, with one coin at least showing a trace of Roman numismatic influence, suggests fresh dimensions to the numismatic evidence and the exchange systems should these be found to be authentic. R. Krishnamurthy, 'Sangam

Period Chera Silver Coin with a Portrait and a Legend', paper read at the First Oriental Numismatic Congress, Nagpur, 1990. See also the publications in Tamil by the same author on Cōḷas and Pāṇḍyas and Malaiyamān coins, 1986–90. R. Champakalakshmi, pers. com.

64. R.E.M. Wheeler, *Ancient India*, 2 (1946), pp. 17–24. Begley, op. cit.
65. The identification is with Virai and has been discussed in R. Champakalakshmi, 'Archaeology and Tamil Literary Tradition', *Puratattva*, 8 (1975–6), pp. 117ff. I. Mahadevan, 'The Ancient Name of Arikamedu', in N. Subrahmaniam (ed.), *Surya Narayana Sastri Centenary Volume*, Madras, 1970, pp. 204ff.
66. The *Śilappadikāram*, 14.116. Refers to aromatic wood and camphor being brought to the port of Kāveripaṭṭinam and this, it has been suggested, may have been cargo from south-east Asia. V.R.R. Dikshitar, The *Śilappadikāram*, Madras, 1939, 14.116n. I. Mahadevan has read the graffiti on one potsherd as a name in Old Sinhalese.
67. R.E.M. Wheeler, A. Ghosh and Krishna Deva, 'Arikamedu: An Indo-Roman Trading-station on the East Coast of India', *Ancient India*, 2 (1946), pp. 17ff.
68. Begley, op. cit.
69. Casson, *PME*, pp. 228–9.
70. *Śilappadikāram*, 6.128–44; 5.7ff.
71. Nagaswamy, op. cit.
72. L. Casson, 'Rome's Trade with the Eastern Coast of India', *Cahiers d'Histoire*, 1988, pp. 3–4, pp. 303–8.
73. H. Sarkar, 'Kesarpalle 1962', 22, *Ancient India*, 22 (1966), pp. 37–74.
74. Hathigumpha inscription. D.C. Sircar, *Select Inscriptions . . .* , I, Calcutta, 1965, pp. 213–20. An early second century inscription at Guntur could be that of an Aira Mahāmeghavāhana ruler, thus lending some credence to Khāravela' claim. Velpuru inscription, *Epigraphia Indica*, 32, pp. 82–7.
75. *Epigraphia Indica*, 2, pp. 323–9; 15, pp. 258–75.
76. P.L. Gupta, *Roman Coins from Andhra Pradesh*, APGMS, No. 10, Hyderabad, 1965. Turner, op. cit., pp. 29ff.
77. *Periplus*, p. 62. Ptolemy, 7.1.15–93.
78. K. Raghavachari, 'Dharanikota', in A. Ghosh (ed.), *An Encyclopaedia of Indian Archaeology*, II, Delhi, 1989, p. 126.
79. Turner, op. cit., pp. 32–6.
80. Ibid., p. 41.
81. Casson, *PME*, p. 236.
82. I.W. Mabbett, 'The "Indianisation" of Southeast Asia: Reflections of the Prehistoric Sources', *Journal of South East Asian Studies*, 8, 1 (1977), pp. 1–14; H. Kulke, *The Devaraja Cult*, Cornell, 1978; H. Kulke, 'The Early and the Imperial Kingdom in Southeast Asian

History', in D.G. Marr and A.C. Milner (eds), *Southeast Asia in the 9th–14th Centuries*, Singapore, 1986.

83. R. Fynes in his unpublished D.Phil. thesis, 'Cultural Transmission between Roman Egypt and Western India', Oxford, 1991, argues that the evolution of the goddess Pattini in south India was deeply influenced by the cult of Isis. This is a plausible idea but the evidence is not wholly convincing. Isis was of course the major deity at Coptos. W.M.F. Petrie, *Koptos*, London, 1986, pp. 17ff.
84. A.E. Medlycott, *India and the Apostle Thomas*, London, 1905. E.O. Winstedt, *The Christian Topography of Cosmas Indicopleustes*, Cambridge, 1909. S. Neal, *A History of Christianity in India: the Beginnings to AD 1707*, Cambridge, 1984.
85. Winstedt, op. cit.
86. S.G. Pothan, *The Syrian Christians of Kerala*, Bombay, 1963, pp. 101ff. In the second millennium AD there is a Christian diaspora which links the Christians of south India to those in the eastern Mediterranean trade, a reversal of the situation of the Yavanas who became Buddhists.
87. P. Rousseau, *Ascetics, Authority and the Church*, Oxford, 1978.
88. Romila Thapar, 'Indian Views of Europe: Representations of the "Other" in History?'. See chapter 25 in this volume.
89. J.E. Mitchner, *The Yuga Purāṇa*, Calcutta, 1986; D.C. Sircar, *Studies in Yugapurāṇa and Other Texts*, Delhi, 1974.
90. D. Pingree, *The Yavanajātaka of Sphujidhvaja*, I, Camb. Mass., 1978, Introduction and Text.
91. Chapters 21 and 22.
92. G. Buhler and J. Burgess, 'Report on the Buddhist Cave Temples and their Inscriptions', *Archaeological Survey of Western India*, 4 (reprint), Varanasi, 1964, pp. 82–140. *Epigraphia Indica*, 7 (1902–3), pp. 47–74; 8 (1905–6), pp. 59–96; 18 (1925–6), pp. 325–9.
93. J. Burgess and B. Indraji, *Inscriptions from the Cave Temples of Western India*, nos 7, 10 (reprint), Varanasi, 1976, pp. 31–2; *Epigraphia Indica*, 7, pp. 53–5. See also the discussion on a possible rock-cut Buddhist temple at Petra, H. Goetz, 'An Unfinished Early Indian Temple at Petra, Transjordania', SD aus, *East and West*, n.s. 24 (1974), pp. 245–8.
94. Pingree, op. cit.
95. S.C. Laeuchli, 'Yavana Inscriptions of Western India', *Journal of the Asiatic Society of Bombay* (1981–4), pp. 56–9, 207–21.
96. Strabo, 2.3.4; 17.1.45. Pliny, op. cit., 6.26.101. Raschke, op. cit., p. 241. Scmitthammer, op. cit.
97. D.D. Kosambi, 'Dhenukākata', *Journal of the Asiatic Society of Bombay*, n.s. 30, 2 (1955), pp. 50–71.
98. *Epigraphia Indica*, 18 (1925–6), p. 326.

99. *Akam*, 149.7–11.
100. *Puram*, 56.16–21; *Puram*, 343.1–10.
101. *Patirrupattu* II, patikam, pp. 4–10.
102. *Śilappadikāram*, 28.142; 29. Usal's song.
103. *Maṇimēkalai*, 19, 108. *Śilappadikāram*, 5.7ff; 14.62.
104. Tactius, *The Annals*, 3.52–4. Pliny, op. cit., 6.26.101; 12.41.84.
105. Pliny, op. cit., 6.101; 12.84.
106. Miller, op. cit., pp. 222ff.
107. P. Veyne, 'Rome devant la prétendue fuite de l'or . . . ', *Annales*, 34, 2 (1979), pp. 211ff. A detailed picture of the items which travelled within Egypt as part of this trade is provided by A.C. Johnson, *Roman Egypt to the Reign of Diocletian*, Baltimore, 1936.
108. Raschke, op. cit., p. 673.
109. A. Bernardi, 'The Economic Problems of the Roman Empire at the Time of its Decline', in C.M. Cipolla, *The Economic Decline of Empires*, London, 1970, pp. 16–83. R. Duncan–Jones, op. cit., pp. 172–3.
110. G. Gunderson, 'Economic Change and the Demise of the Roman Empire', *Explorations in Economic History*, 13, 1 (1976), pp. 43–68. J.L. Anderson and T. Lewit, 'Contact with the Barbarians? Economics and the Fall of Rome', ibid., 29, 1 (1992), pp. 99–115.
111. In AD 297 Coptos was destroyed by Diocletian and in AD 273 Palmyra was sacked by Aurelian.
112. J. Paterson, 'Salvation from the Sea . . . ', *Journal of Roman Studies*, 2 (1982), pp. 146–57. That there was a trade with the western Mediterranean is indicated by the stamps on the amphorae. Other items traded in the Mediterranean such as timber and marble are not part of the Egyptian economy.
113. R.P. Duncan Jones, *The Economy of the Roman Empire*, Oxford, 1974. P.A. Brunt, *Journal of Roman Studies*, 71 (1981), pp. 162ff.
114. Petrie, op. cit., pp. 26–7.
115. S.L. Wallace, *Taxation in Egypt*, Princeton, 1933, p. 253.
116. Petrie, op. cit., pp. 32–3.
117. Johnson, op. cit., pp. 400ff.
118. L. Casson, 'P. Vindob. G. 40822 and the Shipping of Goods from India', *Bulletin of the American Society of Papyrologists*, 23 (1986), pp. 73–9. L. Casson, 'New Light on Maritime Laws: P. Vindob. G. 40822', *Zeirschrift fur Papyrologie und Epigraphik*, 84 (1990), pp. 195–206. The document was earlier published by H. Harrauer and P. Sijpesteijin, 'Ein neues Dokument zu Roms Indienhandel, P. Vindob. G. 40822', *Anzeiger der Osterreichischen Akademie der Wissenschaften*, 122 (1985), pp. 124–55.
119. L.C. West and A.C. Johnson, *Currency in Roman and Byzantine Egypt*, New Jersey, 1944, pp. 180ff.

120. J.G. Tait, *Greek Ostraca in the Bodleian Library at Oxford, and Various Other Centres*, I, London, 1930.
121. S.L. Wallace, *Taxation in Egypt*, Princeton, 1938, pp. 181ff.
122. Tait, op. cit.
123. D.J. Thompson, 'Nile Grain Transport under the Ptolemies', in P. Garnsey et al., op. cit., pp. 64–76. D. Meredith, 'The Roman Remains in the Eastern Desert of Egypt', *Journal of Egyptian Archaeology*, 38 (1952), pp. 94–111; 39 (1953), pp. 95–106. This point has been discussed in some detail by Richard Fynes in his unpublished Oxford D.Phil. thesis, op. cit.
124. T.F. Glasson, *The Revelation of John*, Cambridge, 1965, chapter 18. Babylon in *The Relevations* was the code name of Rome. The phrase 'scarlet harlot' was used by Keith Hopkins who drew my attention to this passage.
125. C.R. Whittaker, 'Late Roman Trade and Traders', in P. Garnsey et al., op. cit., p. 167.
126. L. Duchesne, *Le Liber Pontificalis: Texte, Introduction et Commentaire*, I, Paris, 1955–7, p. 174: III, p. 177 and p. 194. The amounts referred to were aromate 200 pounds, nardinum 200 pounds and balsam 35 pounds. I am grateful to Simon Price for help in locating the references and to Keith Hopkins for referring me to the text.

# Patronage and the Community*

The concept of patronage is usually restricted to the relationship between the patron and the recipient of patronage — often visualized for early times as the king and the artist who works for him. But the relationship created through the act of patronage can vary considerably according to the form of patronage. The patron, the artist and the object are pointers to each other and are deeply interlinked. Art historians of India generally looked for an individual patron and this in part explains the frequency with which monuments are labelled by dynasty and rarely by the name of the architect even when this is known. Further, the recipient is often regarded as subservient to the patron since the former is dependent for his livelihood on the latter. This focus obstructs the consideration of what the patron receives in return for extending patronage.

The act of patronage is initially an exchange. Over time the categories of persons involved in this exchange as well as the objects may change. Often the exchange involves intangibles such as status and legitimation or the acquisition of merit, in return for tangible wealth. The activity involved in patronage includes a number of concerns such as, the occasion, the formal relationship by which it is recognized, the patron, the recipient, the object which encapsulates the acts and the function of the act. Among these the relationship between the patron and the recipient sets the tone as it were, for acts of patronage. Such a relationship can perhaps be categorized into at least four significant forms.[1] Firstly, patronage which is embedded in a society and where the patron and recipient are built into the system as it were, as for example the chief and the bard in chiefdoms or early forms of kingship. Secondly, patronage as a deliberate act of choice can be seen when a community decides to donate wealth and labour towards the building of a monument which encapsulates its religious beliefs, social values and activities and where the patron is not a single person but a

* B. Stoler Miller (ed.), *The Powers of Art*, Delhi 1992, 1–34.

recognizable group. Thirdly, the most familiar form of patronage is where it becomes a service, where the recipient is either a retainer or is commissioned by a patron and this form is frequently found in the relations between a court, a religious institution or a powerful household, each of which may commission an individual or a group to produce an object generally of artistic value. Finally, in more recent times patronage can be seen as a public activity where, for the world of art, the object becomes an investment and artists are more evidently changing style and aesthetics but the material value of the object is still determined by the patrons.

This essay is concerned primarily with the second form of patronage, namely that which involves a community donating wealth towards the building of monuments and their adornment as acts of piety. However since the first of the four categories listed above, that of embedded patronage, contains elements of community patronage, although not particularized as such, it might be useful to consider the difference between the first and the second forms if only to focus on their social concerns.

Embedded patronage can be of at least two varieties. One is the relationship of the bard to the *rājā*/chief and the other is that of the *yajamāna* — the one ordering a sacrifice, to the priests. The first can be relatively more focussed on social and political relationships or on occasion tied to a ritual but where the ritual aspect is not dominant. The occasion for the second has to be a ritual. The bard performing multiple roles acted as the legitimizer of power, the moral conscience of those in power and the 'historian'. This is demonstrated in the *dāna-stuti* hymns (in praise of gift-giving) of the *Ṛg Veda*[2] where the bard composes eulogies on the prowess of the *rājā* in cattle raids and skirmishes with other chiefs and in return for his compositions receives cattle, horses, chariots and gold as wealth. The occasion could be the *vidatha* or any other clan assembly with some degree of ritual connotation, the patron was the *rājā*, the recipient was the bard or the *brāhmaṇa* hymnodist, the object was the gift given by the *rājā* and the purpose or function of this exchange was the eulogizing of the *rājā* which acted as a form of validation and of historical memory. This form of patronage is more commonly found in lineage-based societies prior to the emergence of the state or in what are sometimes called early states (Thapar 1978, pp. 105ff, 1984). However it does not die down completely with the establishing of the monarchical state. At least one aspect continues into the new system. Poets attached to a court and composing eulogies on the king were in a sense continuing this tradition. Thus, much of the *carita* literature of later times, where it relates to royal biographies, such as the *Harṣacarita* of Bāna-bhaṭṭa or the *Vikramānkadevacarita* of Bilhaṇa were, as literary forms, descendants of the *dāna-stutis*.

The *yajamāna* on a ritual occasion is also performing an act of patronage and to that extent Vedic texts as ritual texts are also, in certain passages, manuals of patronage. The word *śilpa* in the Vedic context meant a skill and even the performance of a *yajña* could be seen as a *śilpa*. The occasions are the major ritual sacrifices, such as the *cāturmāsya* and the seasonal sacrifices, as well as the *mahāyajñas* linked to the status and power of the *rājā*, such as the *abhiṣeka*, *rājasūya*, *aśvamedha* and *vājapeya*. The seasonal rituals held in households were essentially domestic where the *gṛhapati* or the head of the household was the patron and the *brāhmaṇa* performing the ritual was the recipient. The object encapsulating patronage was the cow or the gold given by the *gṛhapati* to the *brāhmaṇa* and the exchange ensured the well-being of the *gṛhapati* and his family and reiterated his status.

In the case of royal rituals, the *yajña* itself constituted the form with the *rājā* as patron, the categories of priests — *hotṛ*, *adhvaryu*, *netṛ*, *brāhmaṇa*, and so on — as recipients; material wealth such as cattle, horses, and gold was the tangible exchange for ensuring the well-being of the clan and the power of the *rājā* and of intervening with the gods to make certain of this function. Gift-giving, together with the display and destruction of wealth became a means of claiming status and marginally redistributing wealth.

The system as such continued into later periods with some adaptations. The *mahārājādhirājas* of the centuries AD performed the *mahāyajñas*, the elaborate, large scale sacrificial rituals. This was particularly the case where there might have been a disputed succession or where a family of obscure origin aspired to dynastic status, claimed to be *kṣatriyas* and established kingdoms, practices which are more easily recognised from the post-Gupta period. It is not altogether unexpected that when later the *jajmāni* system of service relationships came into being in some areas, the pattern was similar. The occasion was calendrical services in the form of routine functions, the patron was the *jajmān/yajamāna* or landowner, the re-cipients were those who performed largely routine services for him, the object was payment in kind and the function was production and consumption. When the pattern of the latter was altered the system also changed. The *jajmān* could be an individual landowner or a temple or institution holding property in land. *Jajmāni* also referred to a method of organizing skills, relationships and wealth. The skills would centre around services, the relationship around protection by the *jajmān* and the legitimizing of the *jajmān* by the recipients. The term *jajmān* evokes the flavour of ritual which is extended to the notion of service, the interdependence of patron and recipient, the perception among his peers of the recipient being a model, the possible exploitation of the recipient by the patron and the occasional manipulating of the patron by the recipients as innovators and conservers of skill.

In all these situations the act of patronage not only creates a new (often tangible) object, but it also creates an institution, irrespective of whether it is minuscule or on a grand scale. The legitimation of political authority for example, also gives rise to the question of politically acceptable channels of dissent and political opposition. Thus in the second millennium AD, the bard in Rajasthan was also the articulator of political protest against the *rājā*. This was expressed in a *dharnā*, in this case a fast unto death. The guilt associated with the death of the bard would be so extreme that kings tended to negotiate an agreement before this could happen (Ziegler 1976).

Embedded patronage therefore has a further life in various forms, some overt and some subordinated. As such it constitutes a counterpart to the more apparent community patronage which becomes evident at the turn of the Christian era in some parts of the subcontinent. Here, the act of patronage is a freshly thought out, conscious act, initially regarded as extraneous to other social and religious activities. There is nevertheless a link between the two which lies in the act of making a gift — *dāna* — although the context of the gift is very different in each case. *Dāna* in the earlier system is a gift made from one person to another, not necessarily in a personal capacity since it was often determined by the status of the two persons and the occasion when it was given.

Community patronage in the early period took the form of *dāna* given by a group of people who came together primarily because of a common and closely defined religious identity and a more loosely defined social identity. That the social identity could assume an importance was always possible and in some cases evident, especially where it coincided with particular religious manifestations. The gift was therefore initially made for personal reasons and because of requirements of status or function. Once the institution emanating from this form of patronage was established and began to indicate a social role, at that later stage the making of donations may have taken on the function of a social statement. The *dāna* given by the *yajamāna* was an individual's gift but not necessarily personalized. With community patronage, the gift is neither destroyed in a potlatch type of ritual nor does it go directly towards enhancing the personal wealth of the religious intermediary. The gift in the system under discussion here is appropriated by the *saṅgha*. Another major difference is that in the earlier system the patron and the recipient were in a condition of reciprocal dependence and the objects exchanged tended to be inalienable (Gregory 1982). In the case of *dāna* to the *saṅgha*, the gift took the form of money or labour, both of which were alienable and the relation between the donor and the *saṅgha* was voluntary.

Community patronage involves social relations and a conscious act of exchange. The act of patronage asserts the status of the patrons and in addition articulates the cohesion of the community making the donation. Examples of this category of patronage become evident during the period from the second century BC to the fourth century AD in the patronage extended to the building of *stūpas* such as those at Sanchi, Bharhut and Amaravati and the rock cut caves of the Western Deccan, all of which had at source donations to the Buddhist *saṅgha*.[3] The donations came substantially from artisans, guilds of craftsmen, traders, monks and nuns, small scale landowners and to a lesser extent from royalty and families in high political and administrative office. In some cases this form of patronage becomes unique, where the craftsmen who actually work on the object of patronage are themselves the patrons, as in the case of the ivory carvers guild from Vidiśā who sculpted a part of the gateway at Sanchi (*Ep. Ind.* II, p. 378, No. 200). Such monuments stand in contrast to many of the *stūpas* of north-western India of approximately the same period which were more frequently built with royal patronage.

Artisans as patrons indicate social mobilization in a period of social change with possibilities of upward mobility. Such patronage reflects the respect meted out to artisans who were wealthy as is also indicated in Buddhist texts where a *gṛhapati/gahapati* even in an artisanal profession would be given the status of *ucchakula*, or high family (*Aṅguttara Nikāya* III, 363). This, notwithstanding that in contemporary brahmanical *dharmaśāstras* they are ranked low (Gautama X.60; Manu X.99–100; or even the *Arthaśāstra* 1.3.8). Weavers for example in later texts, were regarded a *antyajas*, lower than the *śūdra* (Alberuni I, pp. 101–2). Is this to be explained by the argument that when weaving declined as a trade, the impoverishment of weavers led to a lowering of their status, or, was the lowering of the status due to the weavers supporting religious sects which the *brāhmaṇas* regarded as heretical?

The establishment of artisan guilds becomes a noticeable feature of urban life from the Mauryan period onwards. The evolution of guilds/*śreṇīs* can be traced to settlements in the proximity of raw materials and villages of craftsmen concerned with a specific craft such as weaving or carpentry, some of which villages grew into *nigamas* or market centres. Specialized areas demarcated for particular crafts remained the norm in urban settlements as well. The structure of the guild as it gained importance was further emphasized by its increasingly hereditary nature. Where endogamous marriage was encouraged it led ultimately to the *śreṇī* taking on some of the functions of caste and some *śreṇīs* came to be viewed as *jātis* in the first millennium AD. Guild donations were therefore up to a point caste donations as well and the *jātis* which collectively donated to the building of a monument did not see themselves as sharply differentiated in social terms.

Patronage is indicated either directly through votive inscriptions which identify the donor and his or her contribution or indirectly in the sculptured panels of donors as for example the *daṃpati* groups at Karle. Buddhist monuments, be they *caitya*-hall, *stūpa*, cave or cistern at a monastery site, are the objects of patronage. The patrons consist substantially of the *gahapati/gṛhapati* and the *seṭṭhi/śreṣṭhin* (families of wealthy landowners and traders), of artisans, of the guilds or *śreṇīs* and just occasionally a *rājā* or his wife and a high status officer and/or his wife. Apart from this there is also a large body of monks and nuns. The recipient is the Buddhist *saṅgha*. The medium is presumably a monetary contribution or a voluntary contribution in labour which helped in the making of the monument as the object encapsulating the act of patronage. The function is the acquisition of merit or *punya* which helped to bring individuals closer to *nirvāṇa*.

The purpose of gift-giving was in part concerned with personal salvation and not altogether uninfluenced by material benefits (*Mahāvastu* II, 363–97). *Dāna* is referred to as the most meritorious act, the other two being *sila* and *bhāvanā*. *Dāna* is particularly meritorious when given to a *bhikkhu* or to the *saṅgha*. Ideally *dāna* consisted of those items of food, clothing and daily life which would meet the *bhikkhu's* minimum requirements (*Dīgha Nikāya* 3.218; *Aṅguttara Nikāya* 4.239, 246). The act of gift-giving therefore was imbued with a sacred quality in addition to its function in maintaining *bhikkhus*. When the act of *dāna* consisted of money or labour to embellish a *stūpa*, then obviously it underwent a change from its earlier function and became less an act of maintaining a monk and more that of faith in the *saṅgha*, for the *stūpa* was seen as one of the physical symbols of the *saṅgha*.

The *stūpa* becomes the symbol of the power of the *saṅgha* in relation to the patron. It emerges as a major symbol when the worship of sacred sites *per se* gives way to monuments as the physical manifestation of the *saṅgha* as an institution. Whereas in the early Pāli canon the *vihāras* or monasteries are more frequently mentioned, the archaeology of the post-Mauryan period refers to the *stūpa* and the *caitya* as the major edifices. The *vihāras* which have survived from these times tend to be rock-cut monasteries. Here the *caitya*-halls are the most spectacular expression of patronage often surrounded by clusters of contrastingly bare rock-cut cells and the occasional water cisterns. The free-standing *stūpa* becomes a focal monument which is adorned and enclosed within a railing demarcating the sacred from the profane. There is a distinction between those objects of patronage which are intended to benefit both monks and nuns and the laity and those intended only for the former. Contributions towards the construction of the railings and the adorning of the gateways and pillars of the *stūpa*, was an act of piety involving the entire community of believers. The rock-cut *vihāra* intended only for monks was a particularized act of piety. The patrons, both in the *Jātaka* stories and in the votive inscriptions tend to come from the same social groups and there is therefore a considerable reinforcing of the identification of these patrons.

The location and symbolism of the *stūpa* has its own importance. There has been some debate on the question of whether the *stūpa* was worshipped as a symbol of the *mahāparinirvāṇa* or whether it was the *nirvāṇa* body of the Buddha. The cult of the *stūpa* came into prominence after the death of the Buddha and it has been argued that this was more conducive to Mahāyāna than to Hīnayāna Buddhism (Ebert 1980). The early tradition suggests a funerary connection, the location being marked by a man-made tumulus. In peninsular India Buddhist sites often occur on or near megalithic burials as at Amaravati, pointing to continuity in areas regarded as sacred and associated with the dead. This sense of continuity also extended to the community which in the first instance built the megalithic structure and later to the Buddhist religious community. This might be a clue to the origin of the inexplicable word *eḍuka/eluka* believed to be of Dravidian etymology and used for *stūpa* in some Sanskrit and Pāli sources (see discussion by B.N. Goswamy in Dallapiccola 1980). The association of the *stūpa* as a symbol of the Buddha when he is described as a *cakkavati* provides yet another level of meaning. Possibly the *stūpa* also symbolized an alternative source or centre of power. Thus when those in political authority were patrons of the building of a *stūpa* they would be subsuming this alternative power; and when the community as such helped build the *stūpa* it would be calling on this alternative source of power for protection. Implicit in the gift therefore is not only the seeking of merit which is the more obvious reciprocation but also the calling upon the Buddha for protection.

The intention of the patrons is at one level clearly stated. The contribution was an exchange of *dāna* for *punya*, a gift for the acquisition of merit. This could be either individual or collective as in the case of the guild and ultimately a collaborative act if the end result was the building of a *stūpa* or *caitya*-hall. There were also a variety of subsumed intentions and some degree of social mobilization can be inferred. Here local chiefs were involved, such as the Mahābhoja or the Mahatalāvara; these were also persons who occur in the Sātavāhana inscriptions as high-ranking officers suggesting a transfer of chiefly authority to administrative purposes (Ray 1986). The most frequently mentioned groups are of course the *seṭṭhi-gahapati* families obviously of some standing as landowners and traders. The emphasis in some cases on the donation of a family where the kin relations are specifically stated as in some Amaravati inscriptions is of interest. Does this reflect the reinforcing of the family as a relatively new unit of social identity in areas of erstwhile clan domination? Equally important are the contributions of monks and nuns mentioned by name. This is surprising in a community where monastic rules tended to blur individual identities and where monks and nuns were not expected to have access to wealth. Was this the wealth which accompanied them on entry into the monastery and which they donated to the *saṅgha*? Or did they continue to hold shares in family property and were therefore permitted to maintain a private income? Or did they invest this income in the trade which passed along the routes on which their monasteries were situated arguing that the profits from such investments would be donated to the *saṅgha*?

The identification of the donor is not necessary to an act of piety or of worship. It becomes necessary when such an act is a public declaration of belief and incidentally also a statement on wealth and status. Were votive inscriptions also inspired by a desire to be known to posterity particularly in a culture which did not commemorate the ordinary mortal through grave-stones or memorial stones? This is in part suggested not only by the close association of some Buddhist sites with megalithic burial sites but also by certain aspects of the Buddhist sites as well. For instance there is a burial gallery at Kanheri where small votive *stūpas* were built to commemorate dead *theras* believed to have achieved a high state of realization (Gokhale 1985). Even for the living, votive inscriptions were advertisements of the status of individuals and families or the status of professions when guilds were constituted, drawing attention to the skills and the quality of craftsmanship. Urban professionals such as ivory-carvers, weavers, potters, perfumers, bead-makers and garland makers are often mentioned. More specifically Ānanda, the foreman of the artisans of Siri Satakani, the Sātavāhana king, states that he carved the top architrave of the south gate at Sanchi (Lüders 346;[4] Cunningham p. 264, No. 190) or the *rūpakara* Buddharakhita of Bharhut (Lüders 857) or the *vadhaki* Svamin of Dhenukākaṭa (Burgess and Indraji p. 30, No. 6). In parallel situations mention is made of an actor's sons, the Candaka brothers, involved in the temple of Dadhikarna Nāga (*Ep. Ind.* I, p. 390, No. 18). Even better known is the reference from Mathura to Gomataka a pupil of Kunika, the sculptor of the famous Parkham *yakṣa* image (Lüders 150). This might also signify a break away from the guild to the setting up of a family identity of craftsmen or at least a *guru-śiṣya paramparā* which possibly evolved from the guild and was the dominant institution in the artistic achievements of a later period. The inscriptions are not limited to recording donations by *gahapatis, seṭṭhis* and artisans, but the broad social stratum of the donors was largely that of individuals belonging to these categories.

The inscriptions also provide evidence on the networks of geographical contacts providing yet another dimension to the concept of community. Traders from Dhenukākaṭa made donations at Karle and other caves of the western Deccan (Burgess and Indraji p. 29, No. 4; p. 30, No. 6; p. 31, No. 7; pp. 32ff, No. 11; Lüders 1020, 1121). Traders and artisans from elsewhere in the Deccan and western India made gifts at places in the western coast such as at Kanheri (Lüders 986, 988, 995, 998, 1000, 1001, 1005, 1013, 1014). The incidence of donors from clearly identifiable towns is smaller in number and the majority may have come from *nigamas* or market centres and villages linked to them. The location of the monuments on trade routes would point to market connections such as the *nigama* of Karahakaṭa (Lüders 705).

Inscriptions from Bharhut included donations from persons residing in Vidiśā, Pāṭaliputra, Bhojakaṭa, Bhogavardhana and Nasik (Lüders 712, 719, 723, 797, 799) indicating an extensive geographical reach. A text of the period refers to merchants and artisans from Bactria, China and Alexandria (*Milindapañha* 4.8.88; 5.4; 6.21). Yavana donors are referred to in cave inscriptions such as the one at Nasik which mentions Indrāgnidatta, the son of Dhammadeva *yavana* (*Ep. Ind.* 8, p. 90, No. 17) the northerner from Dattamitri, believed to be the town of Demetrias sometimes identified with Kandahar although the identification is not certain (Fraser 1979). Yavana donors also identify themselves with Gata/s which has been taken as a reference to Trigarta in northern India but would perhaps make greater sense if identified with Coptos near Alexandria in Egypt.[5]

That Yavanas did take to indigenous Indian religions is attested to not only in these inscriptions but also in the well-known Heliodorus column at Besnagar where the Yavana ambassador from Taxila declares his faith in the cult of Vāsudeva (Sircar I, pp. 100ff). In the neighbourhood of this inscription monks are recorded as gifting pillars and railings to a Buddhist monument (Lüders 671–4). Buddhism in any case had by now spread way beyond the Indian heartland. As for Yavana traders who claimed to be Buddhists, a common Buddhist identity with local traders would have been of immense help in trade relations.

The reference to *nigamas* raises the question of whether ceremonial centres led to the growth of market activities or vice versa. In cases where a *stūpa* was built over a locally venerated megalithic site, there Buddhist ritual may have assimilated the local cult. There are other settlements such as Veerapuram and Kaserpalle which are not associated with Buddhist monuments. The building of a *stūpa* requires raw materials, financial resources, commissariat arrangements for the builders and co-ordination between architects, builders, masons and so on. That there was an existing lay community which supported the activity is evident from references in the inscriptions to members of the *goṣṭhi* and *nigama* (Bhattiprolu Casket Inscriptions, *Ep. Ind.* II, 327–8, Nos 3, 5, 6). Did this community become established after the site acquired importance? It is more likely that sites acquired sanctity (perhaps inherited in some cases) and as the community in the area grew and prospered, it began to contribute towards the building of a monument at the site. This would have brought both pilgrims and traders to the settlement. The geographical location of the *stūpas* was often on trade routes which may earlier have been used in local circuits of exchange by the people of the megalithic settlements.

The patrons see themselves in various ways: as individual donors, as families making donations, or as a community of donors, whether as groups of *seṭṭhi-gahapatis* or *śrenīs* or even members of a village, as for instance Kalavaira-gāma: as a community of worshippers but differentiating between *bhikkhus* (monks), *bhikkhunis* (nuns) and *upāsakas* and *upāsikās* (lay-followers), which would seem to cut across social identities or at any rate not make sharp distinctions: as a community of monks and nuns who have renounced social ties but whose donations still link them to such ties. This is particularly noticeable in the donations recorded from sites in the Ganges plain which follow a somewhat different pattern. Inscriptions at Sarnath and at Saheth-Maheth of the time of Kaniṣka record gifts made by a monk together with his parents, pupils, companions and teachers, suggesting a co-operative donation. (*Ep. Ind.* VIII, pp. 179–81; VIII, pp. 173ff, No. 3; IX, p. 241; IX, pp. 290–1). Probably the monk in question, Bala, was a particularly important member of the *sangha*. A somewhat unusual inscription at Bedsa in the western Deccan records the gift of a pupil in honour of his teacher who is described as a hermit at the site (Burgess and Indraji p. 26, No. 1).

Social distinctions among the donors are not reflected in the location of the inscription on the monument, where the visually more dramatic parts of the *stūpa* could have been reserved for those of high status. Thus, a *torana* or gateway at Bharhut carries an inscription from a family of chiefs — Dhanabhūti Vācchiputa, the grandson of Visadeva Gāgīputa, dating to the Śuṅga dynasty (Hultzsch 1885 and 1892), but other inscriptions on the same *torana* are of lesser persons. Donations for pillars, coping-stones and parts of railings come from *nigamas, seṭṭhis,* lay-women, nuns, *gahapatis* and preachers (Hultzsch 1892, pp. 225, 228, No. 16; p. 229, Nos 22, 27, 28, 31; p. 230, Nos 33, 36; p. 232, No. 67; Lüders 705, 712, 718, 719, 723, 725, 728, 763, 804, 812). Similarly at Bedsa the gifts of *seṭṭhis, mahārathinīs* (women of chiefly families) and pupils of monks are juxtaposed (Burgess and Indraji, p. 26, Nos 1, 2; p. 27, No. 3; Lüders 1109, 1110, 1111).

A more direct form of patronage points to other links. Members of the royal family were known to invest money in guilds, the interest from which went towards financing some aspect of the functioning of the Buddhist *saṅgha*. For example, Usavadāta of the Kṣaharata Kṣatrapa family gave a permanent endowment of three thousand *kahapaṇas* to be invested in two weavers' guilds dwelling in Govardhana. The interest from the larger investment was to be used for purchasing the cloth for the robes of the monks (Nasik Cave Inscription No. 10, *Ep. Ind.* VIII, pp. 78ff). Here a different kind of nexus is established which still draws on patronage but of a less obvious kind. It is also a nexus which brings together royalty, commercial interest and the *saṅgha*. The status of a weaver's guild was clearly high at this time. Elsewhere an official of the Kuṣāṇa government made an endowment to a guild of flour millers, the interest from which was to be used to feed a hundred *brāhmaṇas* per day (*Ep. Ind.* XXI, p. 60). Investments in guilds are also referred to in inscriptions from Nagarjunakonda where *akṣaya-nīvi* or permanent endowments are made of as much as a hundred denarii (*Ep. Ind.* XX, pp. 16ff). Four guilds were involved in this transaction. Perhaps some of these endowments are actualized in the hoards of Roman coins from this area. Gift systems can co-exist with commerce, the gift economy and the market economy not necessarily being in conflict but juxtaposed. The gift can play a dual role of a donation as well as an investment. The geographical network may not be an arbitrary one and can constitute a network of markets and trade as well.

A striking aspect of these donations is the number of women donors. Donations from queens and women of the royal families are of course known from Buddhist sites. Aśoka Maurya orders the recording of the donations of his queen Kāruvākī (Bloch p. 159). Sātavāhana and Ikṣvāku inscriptions also record such donations. Royal patronage was generally extended to more than a single religious sect since in theory at least it was expected not to be partisan. The political and social dimensions of royal power often made it necessary for there to be a range of patronage and this could be more easily handled along gender lines, although it may not have originated in this form. Thus the Ikṣvāku and Sātavāhana rulers presided over brahmanical *yajñas* whilst their wives and sisters made donations to Buddhist monuments (*Ep. Ind.* XX, pp. 1ff; Rosen in Dallapiccola). This was one way of balancing socio-political factions and pressures. Within this category may also be recorded the donations of the wives of local chiefs in the western Deccan. This is not to preclude the importance of the wishes of individual women making donations to particular religious sects, but rather to suggest that the support given to religious sects may also have been encouraged by other considerations, however conscious or subconscious.

What is more striking however are the donations of ordinary women contributing to the building and adornment of *stūpas* and *caityas* and the cutting of cells and cisterns in the rock monasteries. These come in larger numbers from the *seṭṭhi-gahapati* and artisanal families. This is in conformity with the Pāli canon where women from wealthy *gahapati* families are listed as donors. There is also a close relation between the *sangha* and women donors at *stūpa* sites where many such donations come from nuns. This may have been because such donations were small. Generally the contributions are linked to individual names. However in the case of a land donation, the names are often mentioned as part of a family. In family donations women are given equal importance with men. Frequently the donations are made by a husband and wife. This raises the question of whether women in the *gahapati* group shared in rights to their husbands' property. In some cases the donations are from widows together with their sons. The recording of such joint donations may be due to Buddhist women having a better status or else, local inheritance systems being different from those described in the *dharmaśāstras*.

These inscriptions are in sharp contrast to the statements of the Manu *Dharmaśāstra* on the position of women (5.148–56; 9.2–7). Where the donation is by a single woman there it could be argued that it was part of her *strī-dhana*, the wealth given to a woman by her parents, more specifically by her mother, over which the woman theoretically had complete rights of disposal. However it does remain curious that such records are more frequent in Buddhist and Jaina contexts than those of other religious sects. Devotion to the Buddhist teaching on the part of women from royal families and those of merchants and financiers, is not unknown in Mahāyāna texts of this period, some of which are thought to have been compiled in the eastern Deccan. A well-known section of the *Prajñāpāramitā* narrates in detail the story of the daughter of the merchant who assisted the *bodhisattva* Sadāprarudita to realize the *dhamma* (*Aṣṭasāhasrikā-prajñā-pāramitā- sūtram*, quoted in Paul pp. 115ff).

As an economic activity patronage can be seen as the redistribution of wealth, in this case from the individual or the family to the *saṅgha*, or from one group of professionals to another as for instance in the donation made by the guild of corn dealers which doubtless went to finance the guild of stone carvers working on the monument. The ivory workers guild have not told us in their inscription whether they worked on the *stūpa* in their spare time or whether they dedicated their time as wealth. Possibly the idea of time as wealth was not one readily recognized by that society. The overlap of patron and craftsman or artist in this situation enhanced the status of the craftsman. This overlap is an inversion of the pattern of patronage as it is generally defined where the patron is distinct from the artist and of a higher social status. The patron as the donor is materially richer than the recipient, but in this case the recipient is the *saṅgha* whose wealth theoretically is non-existent since the monks and nuns have renounced wealth. Nevertheless the *saṅgha* even as recipient has a higher moral authority than the patron. This may point to a characteristic of at least some other patterns of patronage as well. In the embedded patronage of the lineage-based societies (or what have more commonly been called 'tribal' societies), the bard as the genealogist of the chief had in some respects an authority higher than the chief even though the chief was his patron. The legitimation by descent of the chief so crucial to such societies lay in the hands of the genealogist. This relationship has been characteristic even of later day smaller kingdoms until recent times.[6]

The economic structure of patronage to the *saṅgha* did not remain the same over time. Contributions to the building of *stūpas* changed from a larger number of small donations to a fewer number of large donations. This may have had to do with a greater economic consolidation of traders and prosperous artisans (*Dīgha Nikāya* 1.51; *Majjhima Nikāya* 1.85; *Mahāvastu* 3.113.443; *Milindapañha* 5.4.331). Inscriptions refer to a variety of professions which earlier were regarded as not very lucrative such as timber merchants, cloak makers, blacksmiths, masons and builders. Contributions to the cutting of caves come less often from professional groups and more frequently from rich donors, specifically *seṭṭhis*, apart from royalty and high status officers.

The actual process of collecting contributions in money or in kind was probably through itinerant monks doing the rounds of their parish, demarcated by the boundary of each monastic institution. Alternatively donations could be collected when lay followers and others came on pilgrimage at special calendrical events. The urban organization of guilds and the concept of shares in a guild may have been the prototype for such a collection. This probably also led to monks taking on a supervisory role in the construction of the monument which may gradually have included the more technical aspects of architecture and sculpture; hence the references to the *navakamika*/builder, Damaguta, the pupil of Aya Pasanaka (Lüders 154). Another inscription (Lüders 155) refers to a monk Saṅgharakhita, who was also a pupil or *atevāsin* of Aya Pasanaka. If pupilage here referred merely to Buddhist teaching from a monk, then the word *śisya* is more likely to have been used. The term *atevāsin* is often used for apprenticeship. A large-scale monument would obviously require planning, phasing and over-seeing which may originally have been left to the guild of builders but which eventually went into the making of the profession of *sūtradhāras* so central to the architecture of the post-Gupta period.

Community patronage of this kind began to decline from the mid-first millennium AD with the increase in royal patronage and still later that of wealthy landowners. Some of this had to do with the decline of Buddhism in northern and western India when with the slowing down of trade the usual patronage to Buddhist monasteries also decreased. Decline in trade meant the decline of the guild as an important urban unit. The guild sometimes evolved into a *jāti*, functioning therefore both as a guild and as a caste, but its economic power is likely to have been curtailed or diffused. Where the patronage to the *saṅgha* came from royalty as in the case of some Kuṣāṇa rulers its demise accompanied that of the dynasty. The rise to power of the Gupta dynasty supporting Vaiṣṇava worship diverted royal patronage. Increasing royal patronage to monuments dedicated to Purāṇic deities, which monuments grew from small shrine rooms to complex cosmic representations on a grand scale, further eroded the earlier pattern. The survival of Jainism in India continued the tradition of community patronage in areas where commerce flourished although some of the more spectacular monuments were funded by royalty.

There are however some examples of the continuation of community patronage in the idiom of Purāṇic Hindu religious sects. Among these is that of the guild of silk weavers who migrated from the district of Lāṭa in western India to the town of Daśapura (Mandasor) in Malwa in AD 436 and financed the building of a temple to Sūrya, the sun god (Mandasor inscription, Fleet p. 79). Only some members of the guild continued as silk weavers whereas others took to a variety of professions such as archery and astrology and some became *kathākāras* and so on. Yet they retained their earlier identity as members of a guild and jointly financed the temple.

The migration was doubtless necessitated by the gradual fall in the silk trade between western India and the eastern Mediterranean. Earlier the routes from northern India passing through Taxila, Mathura and Ujjain and terminating at Barbaricum and Barygaza/Bhṛgukaccha were the conduits of Chinese silk being taken to Alexandria and the eastern Roman empire. The Parthians had obstructed the overland route between Palmyra and central Asia. Both Chinese silk routed through India and Indian silk were prized items in the Roman trade with India (Raschke 1978). The Sino-Indian trade reflected an intermeshing of some varieties of Buddhist ritual with commercial commodities (Liu 1987). However by the mid-first millennium AD not only had the Huns begun to threaten the availability of Chinese silk in northern India but Roman trade itself had declined and what remained of it had moved further east. This shift would also have affected the production of silk in western India.

There are some noticeable differences in guild patronage to the *stūpa* and to the Sūrya temple. The inscription recording the latter is more than just a statement of fact. In commissioning the poet Vatsabhaṭṭi to compose the inscription commemorating the temple and the guild, the guild was performing a further act of patronage. Vatsabhaṭṭi, as has been pointed out, was a hack poet who plagiarized liberally from the *Meghadūta* and the *Ṛtusaṃhāra* of Kālidāsa and who used, predictably, all the conventions of Sanskrit poetics (Basham 1983). He gives precise dates for both the building of the temple and its renovation thirty-seven years later, mentioning the *tithi*, *pakṣa*, season and era, in this case the Mālava era of *c.* 58 BC. Such precise dating is more often associated with the inscriptions recording grants of land, which, being legal charters of ownership had to be carefully dated. The details of the date may also have been linked to the notion of choosing the most auspicious moment for commencing the building of the temple. It forms an interesting contrast to the votive inscriptions from Buddhist monuments which are generally not dated although Buddhist textual sources more conscious of chronology than those of a Purāṇic provenance, date major events in years from the death of the Buddha. That the same guild members repaired the temple after thirty-seven years points to their continuing identity and to their economic prosperity in spite of their varying professions.

Brahmanism established status through the ritual of sacrifice, the *yajña* (among other things) which was tangible in performance but its tangibility evaporated after the ritual was completed. In Purāṇic Hinduism, which increased in popularity from the Christian era, the temple housing an image came to symbolize the sacred place and worship and these in turn were the manifestation of Purāṇic Hinduism initially at élite levels. The sculpting of images and the building of temples initiated a new pattern of patronage. Gradually the donation came to include not only the concept of *dāna* or gift offered to the deity through the representative of the deity, but also that of *bhakti* or devotion to the deity which was essentially a relationship between the worshipper and the deity.

The act of patronage, seemingly isolated, in fact links up many facets of society. It can be functional in as much as, in one of the aspects under discussion, it makes possible the construction or the embellishment of a monument such as the *stūpa*. As an object of worship the *stūpa* carries a magico-religious meaning which is extended by some of the forms of embellishment as for example, the *yakṣīs* and the *śāla-bhañjikās*. In the making of the object there is also the aesthetic consideration which draws upon both local perception as well as more universally established aesthetic norms as is so evident in the differing styles of Sanchi and Amaravati. Both social relationships and notions of aesthetics are embodied in the *stūpa* and to that extent it becomes a cultural symbol.

Community patronage raises the question of the definition of the community. There are no tangible boundaries which define a community. Often the bonds are of various kinds — language, religion, observance of social customs, acceptance of political authority — and these would constitute intersecting communities. The definition of community in the context of the discussion in this chapter, identified by religious observances and language, cuts across geographical regions. In the case of the silk weavers guild making donations towards a Sūrya temple, the sense of community was narrower and largely coincided with the identity of a particular guild excluding other silk weavers guilds or any guilds for that matter, as also other worshippers of Sūrya, not to mention such categories of people settled in more distant regions.

Community patronage as discussed here points to a cultural and social innovation for that period. It indicates the emergence of new social groups which, apart from other features, also identify themselves with a particular kind of patronage and with new aesthetic forms. The later association with a temple to Sūrya is a redefinition of the same social category but with enough flexibility to identify with a new idiom. In both cases the act of patronage introduces changes in cultural forms. The object chosen is associated with worship and it is curious that this new social group made no apparent attempt to contribute towards the construction of a secular building or perhaps such attempts have not survived. One expects that there might have been an impressive meeting hall for the guilds. This absence has often been explained as deriving from the essentially religious nature of Indian society. It would be equally valid however to turn the argument inside out as it were and suggest that the nature of early Indian religion in the context as discussed here was closely tied to social identity and perhaps more so than to individual worship. In such a situation a religious movement tends to become a cultural signal with an extensive social dimension.

Bibliography


Alberuni, E.C. Sachau, *Alberuni's India*, Delhi, 1964 (reprint).

*Aṅguttara Nikāya*, R. Morris and E. Hardy (eds), PTS, London, 1885–1900.

Basham, A.L., 1983, 'The Mandasor Inscription of the Silk Weavers', in B.L. Smith (ed.), *Essays on Gupta Culture*, Delhi, pp. 93–105.

Bhandarkar, D.R., 1918, 'Besnagar Vaisnava Column . . .', *Journal of the Bombay Branch of the Royal Asiatic Society*, 23, pp. 104ff.

Bloch, J., 1950, *Les Inscriptions d'Asoka*, Paris.

Burgess, J., 1883, *Report on the Buddhist Cave Temples and their Inscriptions*, ASWI, IV, Varanasi, 1964 (reprint).

Burgess, J. and Indraji Bhagwanlal, 1881, *Inscriptions from the Cave Temples of Western India*, ASWI, X, Varanasi, 1976 (reprint).

Cunningham, A., 1960, *Bhilsa Topes*, Varanasi (reprint).

—— 1879, *The Stupa at Bharhut*, London.

Dallapiccola, A.L. et al., 1980, *The Stupa, Its Religious, Historical and Architectural Significance*, Universitat Heidelberg, Band, 55.

Dehejia, V., 1972, *Early Buddhist Rock Temples*, London.

Deo, S.B. and J.P. Joshi, 1972, *Pauni Excavations 1969–70*, Nagpur.

Deo, S.B. and M.K. Dhavalikar, 1968, *Paunar Excavations (1967)*, Nagpur.

Deo, S.B. and K. Paddayya, 1985, *Recent Advances in Indian Archaeology*, Poona.

Dhavalikar, M.K., 1965, *Sanchi: A Cultural Study*, Poona.

*Dīgha Nikāya*, T.W. Rhys Davids and J.E. Charpentier (eds), PTS, London, 1890–1911.

Ebert, J., 1980, 'Parinirvāṇa and Stūpa', in Dallapiccola, pp. 219–28.

*Epigraphia Indica (Ep. Ind.)*, Archaeological Survey of India, New Delhi.

Fleet, J.F., 1970, *Inscriptions of the Early Gupta Kings and their Successors*, Corpus Inscriptionum Indicarum, III, Varanasi (reprint).

Fraser, P.M., 1980, 'The Son of Aristonax at Kandahar', *Afghan Studies, 1979*, 2, pp. 9–21.

*Gautama Dharmaśāstra*, trans. G. Buhler, Sacred Books of the East, II, Oxford, 1879.

Gokhale, S., 1985, 'Recent Epigraphical Discoveries at Kanheri', in S.B. Deo and K. Paddayya (eds), *Recent Advances in Indian Archaeology*, Poona.

Gregory, C.A., 1982, *Gifts and Commodities*, Academic Press, London.
Hivale, S.R., 1946, *The Pardhans of the Upper Narmada Valley*, Bombay.
Hultzsch, E.A., 1885, 'Bharhut Buddhist Pillar Inscription', *Indian Antiquary*, XIV, pp. 138ff; 1892, loc. cit., XXI, p. 227.
*Jātaka*, V. Fausboll (ed.), PTS, London, 1877–97.
*Kauṭilīya Arthaśāstra*, R.P. Kangle (ed.), Bombay, 1965.
Liu, X., 1987, *Ancient India and Ancient China*, Delhi.
Lüders, H., 1963 (reprint), *Bharhut Inscriptions*, Corpus Inscriptionum Indicarum, II, 2, Ootacammund.
—— 1909–10, 'A List of Brahmi Inscriptions from the Earliest Times to About AD 400', *Ep. Ind.*, X, Appendix.
*Mahāvastu*, trans. J. Jones, PTS, London, 1973.
*Majjhima Nikāya*, V. Trenckner and R. Chalmers (eds), PTS, London, 1887–1902.
*Mānava Dharmaśāstra/Manu Dharmaśāstra*, J.R. Gharpure (ed.), Bombay, 1922.
Marshall, J. and A. Foucher, 1940, *Monuments of Sanchi*, Calcutta.
*Milindapañha*, trans. T.W. Rhys Davids, New York, 1963 (reprint).
Paul, D., 1984, *Women in Buddhism*, Berkeley.
Raschke, M.G., 1978, 'New Studies in Roman Commerce with the East', in H. Temporim and W. Haase (eds), *Aufstieg und Niedergang der Romischen Welt*, Berlin.
Ray, H.P., 1986, *Monastery and Guild*, Delhi.
Rosen, E.S., 1980, 'Buddhist Architecture and Lay Patronage at Nagarjunakonda', in Dallapiccola, pp. 112–26.
Sircar, D.C., 1965, *Select Inscriptions . . .* , Calcutta.
Thapar, R., 1978, *Ancient Indian Social History: Some Interpretations*, Orient Longman, New Delhi.
—— 1984, *From Lineage to State*, Oxford University Press, New Delhi.
*Ṛgveda*, F. Max Muller (ed.), Oxford, 1890–92.
Williams, R., 1984, *Culture*, London.
Zeigler, N., 1976, 'Marwari Historical Chronicles', *Indian Economic and Social History Review*, April–June, XIII, pp. 219ff.

## Notes and References

1. These categories are in part based on those discussed by Raymond Williams in *Culture*, London, 1984.
2. For example, 6.63; 5.27; 5.30; 8.5; 8.6.
3. The basic archaeological and epigraphic data has been gathered from the following sources: J. Burgess, *Report on the Buddhist Cave Temples and their Inscriptions*, ASWI, IV, Varanasi, 1964 (reprint); J. Burgess

and Bhagwanlal Indraji, *Inscriptions from the Cave Temples of Western India*, ASWI, x, 1881; A. Cunningham, *The Stupa of Bharhut*, London, 1879; A. Cunningham, *Bhilsa Topes*, Varanasi, 1960 (reprint); H. Lüders, *Bharhut Inscriptions*, CII, vol. II, Ootacammund, 1963 (reprint); J. Marshall and A. Foucher, *Monuments of Sanchi*, Calcutta, 1940; M.K. Dhavalikar, *Sanchi — a Cultural Study*, Poona, 1965; V. Dehejia, *Early Buddhist Rock Temples*, London, 1972; *Epigraphia Indica*, vols II, V, X, IX–XII; S.B. Deo and J.P. Joshi, *Pauni Excavation 1969–70*, Nagpur, 1972; S.B. Deo and M.K. Dhavalikar, *Paunar Excavation (1967)*, Nagpur, 1968; S.B. Deo and R.S. Gupte, *Excavation at Bhokardan*, Nagpur, 1974.

4. These numbers refer to Lüders' List in *Epigraphia Indica*, vol. X.
5. Trigarta, identified in the past with the region of Kangra or of Jallandhar was not an important enough trading centre at this time to attract traders from west Asia although it lay along the Himalayan route. On the analogy of Sandracottos being equated linguistically with Candragupta, Coptos or even Aegyptos could have been rendered as Gutas or Gatas in Prākṛit. Admittedly this is not a definitive reading, but given the references to trade between western India and Egypt via the Red Sea during this period, such an identification of Gatas is at least plausible. For references to Gatas see Burgess and Indraji, 1976, Junnar inscriptions, Nos 5 and 33, pp. 43, 55; Lüders, 1154, 1182.
6. This continues to be true even in this century as is evidenced by the relationship of the Pardhans to their patrons, the Thakurs, in the upper Narmada. S.R. Hivale, *The Pardhans of the Upper Narmada Valley*, Bombay, 1946.

# VI

# *Of Heroes and History*

The first three papers use historical methods in investigating epic literature and suggesting the role of such literature in historical reconstruction. The focus has shifted from attempting to derive chronological information from the epics, the *Mahābhārata* and the *Rāmāyaṇa*, to investigating the kind of societies which the epics depict. This becomes particularly complex in the *Mahābhārata* since it was added to at various times and does not present a socially homogeneous society. Nevertheless what it does depict is useful to historical reconstructions of the early past.

The last two essays discuss local heroes, the heroes of the hero-stones, which are memorials found in various parts of the subcontinent, and which are now being recognised as an important source for regional history as well as the history of those sections of society who would claim that their function pertained to the *kṣatriya* model.

# 28

# *The Historian and the Epic**

The historian's interest in epic literature arises from the argument that epic literature generally documents a period which is prior to that of early recorded history. The epic does not exclude other data where it may be available but tends all the same to intrude on the consciousness of the historian claiming to be the primary source. However, the epic is essentially a literary crystallisation of the heroic ideal. By its very nature, therefore, it is not to be taken as factual evidence but as the representation of an ideal — a caution which some historians either ignore or forget when using the epic as source material.

Epic literature is intrinsically a part of the oral tradition, composed, compiled and collated over many centuries from bardic fragments and enriched with interpolations of later times.[1] In the Indian tradition, shorter compositions such as the *gāthās*, *dānastutis*, *nārāśaṁsīs* and *ākhyānas* were the precursors of the epic. That the *Mahābhārata* was put together at various times is clear from the internal evidence, for in one case it commences with Vaiśampāyana, the disciple of Vyāsa, reciting the epic at the Janamejaya sacrifice and in another with the recitation by the *sūta* Ugraśravas at the sacrifice of the *ṛsi* Śaunaka which took place a generation later than the first occasion. An earlier and shorter text than the present one also appears to have been known.[2] The Araṇyaka-parvan provides an excellent illustration of the adding on of bardic episodes to the main narrative. Ultimately the entire collection was redacted, probably by Bhṛgu authors, and this imbues the text with a relative unity of theme and literary form.

The making of the epic inevitably creates problems for the historian, who, in the past, has tended to treat the epic as a single

* Bhandarkar Anniversary address delivered on August 27, 1979. *ABORI*, LX, i–iv, 199–213.

text of a particular period and has attempted to test it for historical authenticity. Epic events can rarely be precisely dated nor can one speak of an epic period nor indeed can the narrative of the epic be treated necessarily and without cross-evidence as authentic history. What is of significance to the historian are the assumptions made about the past in the epic and about the changes which earlier societies have undergone, assumptions which eventually will lead us to understand the historical function of the epic rather than to limit our exploration to its historicity. This is especially relevant with the Indian epics since one of the characteristics of Indian social history is the extensive range of social formations which co-existed in all periods, even to the present. The appeal of the epic varies in accordance with the particular society to which it relates at particular points in the text, and it is in the sifting of these segments that the historian can contribute. In such a situation even the critical edition may eventually be found to require some further pruning.

Historians have made many attempts to date the culminating event of the epic, the war between the Pāṇḍavas and the Kauravas. The suggested dates range from the fourth millennium BC to the seventh century BC and the evidence for these draws on a variety of sources, astronomy, archaeology and genealogical history; but none of these dates are universally acceptable. To search for a conclusive date is in a sense to search for the impossible since the purpose of epic literature is not a concern with a chronological sequence of events. Even the central event may not be historical since it is pivotal to the action of the epic but not necessarily to the reconstruction of history. In the vision of the bard, the event, which may once have been historical, can transcend its historicity and become symbolic. It would seem to me, therefore, that it is more relevant for the historian to analyse the assumptions of the epic which would undoubtedly provide an insight into the society of a people, which insight may not be chronologically exact but which would nevertheless enrich our understanding of the past.

Many decades ago scholars argued that there were at least two traditions incorporated into the epic, the original epic and the pseudo-epic.[3] One was the earlier, narrative layer reciting a series of stories based on bardic material. The other consisted of a number of didactic sections relating to the *rāja-dharma*, *mokṣa-dharma* and the practices of different sections of society, which drew ostensibly on the *dharma-śāstra* literature and which were interpolated into the epic at later periods. The rationale for these interpretations would be that with the conversion of the epic into sacred literature, it was necessary that it also incorporate discussions on ethical norms and the definitions of authority both temporal and sacred. I would like to support this distinction and argue that there is a difference in the depiction of society in these two layers and that difference is important to the historical understanding of the epic.

The narrative sections seem to depict societies of tribal chiefships moving towards the change to a state system with monarchy as the norm. There is a strong emphasis on lineage rights and functions and a fairly flexible inclusion of a variety of kinship forms. The economy tends to be pastoral-cum-agrarian in which cattle raids and gift-exchange are important components. Heroism is wrapped up in the defence of territory and the honour of the kinsfolk. The didactic sections in contrast assume a highly stratified society with frequent reference to caste functions rather than lineage functions. The political system assumes well-established monarchies and an increasing concentration of authority in the hands of the king. The economy is essentially agrarian with a familiarity with urban centres as commercial units. Gift-giving involves the granting of land in addition to other forms of wealth. In contrasting the differences between the two sections it can be argued that since the evidence from the narrative section is drawn from the actual happenings as described and the information which they provide on social formations is gathered through inference by the historian, there is, therefore, less likelihood of deliberate interpolation in the text. The didactic sections concentrate on the legalities of social functioning and leave little to historical inference. I would like to examine what appear to me to be two diverse traditions in the light of archaeological, anthropological and historical evidence.

Although the epic story finally involves the clans and kingdoms of virtually the entire northern half of the subcontinent, the core of the narrative focuses on the Gaṅga-Yamuna *doāb* and its vicinity and more particularly the upper *doāb*. The territory of the Kurus extended from the Indo-Gangetic divide into the upper *doāb* with capitals at Hastināpura and Indraprastha. That of the Pañcālas, who play an important part in the narrative, lay in the adjoining areas to the south-east. The proximity of the Kuru and Pañcāla would suggest both hostility and close alliances and the later Vedic texts speak of an eventual alliance. This would not be incompatible with the evidence of the epic in that the Pāṇḍavas were the successors to the Kuru realm and had a marriage alliance with the Pañcālas.

The geographical location provides another possible dimension of evidence which is gradually being brought into the discussion in the form of archaeological data. The earliest settlements in the area date to the start of the second millennium BC. There is evidence now to argue that the Harappan tradition did bequeath some survivals to the later cultures as seen at sites with late Harappan and Painted Grey ware settlements.[4] The earlier Ochre Colour Pottery Culture although indigenous to the region is by all accounts a relatively primitive culture of small settlements and inferior living standards. Its connections with the Copper Hoards which would indicate a more advanced society are by no means established. Undoubtedly the dominant culture of the region is the Painted Grey Ware or PGW variously dated from the late second or early first millennium BC. Attempts have been made to identify this culture with later Vedic literature[5] on the basis of common features of material remains as well as with the *Mahābhārata* by referring to common geographical locations.[6] Excavations at Hastināpura and Indraprastha show a flourishing PGW level which in the case of the latter is also the earliest occupational level. It has further been argued that there is evidence of a flood at Hastināpura which terminates the PGW level (which at this site dates to about 800 BC) and that this may be the flood referred to in the epic as having occurred during the period of Nicakṣu when the city was deserted and the capital shifted to Kauśāmbī.

The distribution of the PGW generally conforms to the core areas occupied by the clans and kingdoms who participated in the events of the epic. There are a noticeably larger number of settlements and the demographic increase may have had to do with an improvement in material culture.[7] The settlements are clearly pre-urban, consisting of huts of wattle and daub with rarely any structural remains of a substantial quality. Of the material remains the most striking is the occurrence of iron artefacts, mainly items of warfare and a few used in agriculture. The presence of weights would point to some minimal degree of exchange other than primitive barter. There is a profusion of animal bones particularly of horse and cattle which judging from the literary data formed the major units of wealth. The widespread occurrence of horse bones is new to the Indian scene since horse bones from late levels of Indus civilization sites are scant. The quantity of cattle bones is also larger for this period. Many which come from domestic contexts often carry marks suggestive of the eating of cattle flesh for food. There is a striking absence of graves or burials which is in sharp contrast to the earlier Indus civilization as well as the contemporary megalithic cultures. It would seem that cremation was the normal form of disposing of the dead in the PGW culture.

The culture which succeeds the PGW is the Northern Black Polished Ware culture or the NBP, dated to the sixth century BC and continuing into the Mauryan period. Here there is evidence of a qualitative and quantitative change from the preceding PGW culture.[8] The demographic picture shows larger concentrations of populations at single sites. The mud plaster huts are replaced with well-defined structures of mud-brick and burnt brick. Brick lined drains, soakage pits and terracotta ringwells indicate a civic life of no mean proportions. There is a substantial increase in the use of iron artefacts many of which are now employed commonly in domestic use. Above all there is also the presence of punch-marked as well as uninscribed cast coins indicating a major change in economic exchange relations involving the use of coined money and an incipient commercial economy.

For the historian, the archaeological co-relation poses a dilemma. If the material culture of the epic is co-related with the earlier PGW culture with which the narrative sections of the epic seem to agree to a large extent, then the date of these sections can be placed between the mid-second and the mid-first millennia BC but the culture will have to be described as pre-urban, transitional between pastoralism and an agrarian economy and probably supporting tribal chiefships on the edge of change to state forms and monarchical systems. The excavated evidence of these levels at Hastināpura and Indraprastha in neither case suggest the splendours of great kingdoms with wealthy capitals; rather, they were people with a technologically unsophisticated culture. The elaborate descriptions of material culture with references to a developed agrarian economy and prosperous towns as given in the didactic sections of the epic would perforce have to be dated to periods later than the mid-first millennium BC in any co-relation with archaeological evidence.

Archaeological continuities can, in some instances, be connected back to the Harappan period in the area under discussion. This makes it possible to suggest that some at least of the traditions recorded in the epic could also, in origin, go back to this period. But this does not mean that the epic or the main events date to the Harappan period.

It would seem apparent, therefore, that the historian would have to argue for different parts of the epic having been composed at different periods and integrated into the text at a relatively late point in time. The basic question is again not that of the date of the epic but the elucidation of the fragments which have been stitched, as it were, into the epic.

Attempts have also been made to try and date the epic using the information provided on the genealogies and lineages of various clans. It has been argued that if an average length of anywhere between fourteen and twenty-two years is taken for each generation, it is then possible to work out a chronological scheme by adding up the number of generations listed in a genealogy. However, anthropological research on lineage data over the last few decades proves that such data for purposes of chronological reconstruction is notoriously unreliable. The chronological function of genealogies is primarily as time-fillers or as bardic mechanisms for suggesting continuities and at best genealogies can provide clues to relative time in terms of some events being earlier or later than others. The kind of information for which genealogies can be used with greater reliance is in locating the geographical distribution and migration of clans, and in the degree to which they reflect descent patterns and kinship relations among clans and individuals. Genealogies are sometimes deliberately forced into patterns to indicate either allegorically or actually a particular view of the past. Such patterns are not historically factual although they are of value in analysing the social assumptions made by the authors. The Indian genealogical tradition is not lacking in consciously patterned genealogies.

The genealogies as given in the epic provide a series of lineage patterns which raise a number of problems. Of the two major lineages epic events involve only the clans of the Candravaṃśa or Aila lineage, the Ikṣvāku lineage being the concern of the other epic, the *Rāmāyaṇa*. Within the Candravaṃśa lineage there is a clear separation between what might be called the nuclear clans and the peripheral clans. The essential narrative involves the descendants of Pūru and Yadu and those of the other three brothers play a marginal role. Clans unconnected with the Candravaṃśa lineage are also introduced into the peripheral sections where possibly these stories were in origin part of a separate bardic tradition. The final battle serves the function of drawing together all the disjointed fragments since both the nuclear and the peripheral clans participate in the war, contributing to making the event in effect the end of an epoch.

The central events of the epic revolve around the conflict between collateral cousins on the succession to a political inheritance. A seemingly simple conflict turns out to have many layers of contradictions. The descendants of Pūru, the youngest son of Yayāti, are in any case not the rightful rulers of *madhya-deśa*, for the kingdom should have gone to Yadu, the eldest son. This change in the law of succession suggests either that primogeniture was not sufficiently well-established or, what is more likely, that the infringement of the rule required an explanation — and this was the story of Yayāti seeking to exchange his old age with the youth of one of his five sons, an exchange which is ultimately conceded by the youngest,[9] leading to the disinheritance of the eldest. That the father had the right to make this change in succession points to the power of the patriarch. The right of primogeniture was still in a state of flux judging by the many instances of what has been called the 'disqualified eldest', the eldest son being debarred from his patrimony.[10]

In a sense the epic events are at one level an exoneration of the descendants of Yadu. The most important Yādava in the epic is the Andhaka-Vṛṣṇi chief, Kṛṣṇa the son of Vasudeva. The honouring of this Yādava at the *rājasūya* of Yudhiṣṭhira sets off a series of hostilities which aggravate the antagonism to a point of no return. Kṛṣṇa's role as the charioteer is crucial to the outcome of the battle. Even if it is argued that this was a later interpolation and may have had a surreptitious Bhṛgu motivation, there is little doubt that the ultimate victory of the Pāṇḍavas is also the victory of the Yādava chief.

Among the many lineage patterns perhaps the most curious is the repeated occurrence of the groups of five-brothers, which turn up at many points in the Candravaṃśa lineage. Sometimes the five are split into three and two, being born of two wives. Vedic literature refers to the *pañcajanāḥ* or five clans which phrase has been variously translated.[11] Its persistence as a lineage pattern does suggest a five-clan classification. In terms of the narrative, the lineage opens with Yayāti and his five sons, born of two wives.[12] At various points in the genealogy and particularly where new geographical areas are brought in, the five-clan classification seems to reoccur. Thus when the Ganga valley is settled it is mainly by Uparicara and his five sons. The same pattern is repeated in eastern India with Bali and his five sons. The closing of the lineage also occurs with the five Pāṇḍavas and significantly there is a repetition of the pattern of three and two almost as a mirror image of the three and two pattern of the sons of Yayāti.

In this connection it may be mentioned that the etymology of the name Pañcāla remains obscure. It is believed to have a confederacy of five clans. The termination *āl* has been linked linguistically to various words indicating a household or a clan. The five-brother classification cannot be coincidental and carries a meaning which has yet to be unravelled. If it reflects some connection with the concept of the *pañcavīra* as prevalent among the Vṛṣṇis, it still speaks of attempts to fit the genealogy into a pattern.

Among the major puzzles of the lineage is that which concerns the immediate ancestry of the protagonists. In the Pūru line of succession, the eldest son Devāpi retires to the forest and the kingdom is inherited by his younger brother Śantanu who marries Gaṅgā and has by her a son, Bhīṣma, the rightful successor. But Śantanu also marries Satyavatī who bears him two sons and demands that Bhīṣma remain celibate so that her sons inherit the kingdom, to which demand Bhīṣma readily agrees and remains true to his word. Neither of Satyavatī's sons by Śantanu can procreate. Therefore, Kṛṣṇa Dvaipāyana, her son by Parāśara and born out of wedlock, is required by the law of levirate to procreate sons on his step-brother's wives. This accounts for the birth of Dhṛtarāṣṭra and Pāṇḍu. In terms of blood ties therefore, the Pūru lineage terminates with Bhīṣma for neither Dhṛtarāṣṭra nor Pāṇḍu carry any blood connection with the lineage. For a society in which kinship ties are crucial this seems to be a strange situation. The fight for succession is entirely among affinal relatives, since neither Dhṛtarāṣṭra nor Pāṇḍu are agnatically related to the lineage. It is also strange that Kṛṣṇa Dvaipāyana should play the dual role of being both the progenitor of the Pāṇḍavas and the Kauravas as well as the compiler of the epic. Was this a pun on authorship taken to a logical extreme where the author of the epic projected himself as the progenitor of the protagonists as well? Or can this be taken as a veiled statement that the events involving the Pāṇḍavas and the Kauravas were added on at a later point? The legitimacy of the claim of the sons of Pāṇḍu is further weakened by their having been fathered by various gods, although at the symbolic level this adds to the allegorical dimension of the epic.

Political events arise out of lineage confrontations and lineage forms are closely related to marriage systems. Three totally different marriage systems occur within the same family in the generations after Bhīṣma and this seems highly improbable in a society where marriage rules were generally very carefully observed. The marriages of Dhṛtarāṣṭra to Gāndhārī and of Pāṇḍu to Mādrī and Kuntī are quite normal, following the usual pattern of clans marrying out to extend alliances and marrying among those who would be regarded as equal in status. In the next generation the five Pāṇḍavas accept the system of fraternal polyandry which is clearly alien and remains unexplained except at the level of a misunderstanding on the part of Kuntī and some rather involved stories of previous births. Curiously the five sons of this marriage play a distinctly subordinate role in the epic. Each of the five Pāṇḍavas marries other women and it is the sons of these which are central to the story. The ultimate line of succession goes through the son of Arjuna by Subhadrā, the sister of Kṛṣṇa. Apart from the fact that in systems of fraternal polyandry other marriage alliances are not permitted, this particular marriage was a cross-cousin marriage, Arjuna marrying his mother's brother's daughter, which in itself is disapproved of in the later didactic sections of the epic.[13] Cross-cousin marriage was acceptable to the Yādavas and this may explain why it was permitted in the narrative. Diverse forms of marriage suggest that there may have been conflicting kinship systems associated with different clans and these were sought to be adjusted in the narrative. The Pāṇḍavas are not only flexible in their marriage alliances but seem to have generally functioned in a manner which seems opposed to the conventional patriarchal modes. The dominating figure in the Pāṇḍava household is that of the matriarch, Kuntī. Apart from her the other person on whom the five brothers are heavily dependent is Kṛṣṇa Vāsudeva, who is their maternal uncle's son. Possibly the objection to honouring him at the *rājasūya* ceremony may have been a much more fundamental objection to the continuation of a particular kinship system rather than the declared reason of his being of lower status than other guests present at the ceremony. The eventual succession of Abhimanyu and his descendants to the Kuru realm doubtless had an unqualified approval from the Yādavas since he was Kṛṣṇa's sister's son which was a recognised relationship in the order of succession. It is ironic that in spite of the war, the succession was not by primogeniture.

Lineage links had a direct connection with two aspects of political power, legitimacy and territory, claims to both being largely based on proving kinship connections — hence the importance of continual reference to genealogies and the possible manipulating of genealogies in favour of political adjustments. Political forms in the epic are not sharply differentiated but they tend to move from tribal chiefships or oligarchies to kingdoms. The epic seems to veer from one to the other indicating that the initial composition may have been in the transitional period of change from tribal chiefships to monarchies. The hidden antagonism between the two is reflected in Kṛṣṇa Vāsudeva's explanation for the hostility between his clan and its allies and the ruler of Magadha, Jarāsandha.[14]

Clan based territories are of various kinds and the most frequent reference is to the eighteen *kulas* of the Andhaka-Vṛṣṇi *saṅgha*.[15] In the later didactic sections such territories become the exception and kingdoms are the norm. The crux of the political functioning of the *gaṇa-saṅgha* system was the smooth working of the assembly, where the senior kinsmen met and took decisions. This was in contrast to the declining role of the assembly in monarchies where it was gradually reduced to an advisory body whose views had customary sanction but were not binding on the king. To the extent that the role of the senior kinsmen was crucial to the narrative of the epic, as for example in the decision to challenge the Pāṇḍavas at a game of dice, it can be argued that the political form was closer to tribal chiefships than to absolute monarchies.

Central to the argument of the distinction between lineage-based societies and kingdoms is the definition of the term *rājan*. This has generally been translated rather casually as 'king' in the sense of a monarch, but the terms used for a king have to be examined more closely. It has recently been suggested that the etymology and context of the word in Vedic sources at least would suggest a tribal leader rather than a king.[16] The territorial link becomes more apparent in later texts with the use of terms such as *rāṣṭra*, and *janapada*. Similarly, terms incorporating *bali* (tribute) are more common in the earlier texts and terms such as *bhāga* (share and therefore tax) occur later.

Clearly defined descriptions of monarchical functioning occur in the didactic sections as in the Śāntiparvan. Theories explaining the origin of kingship are characterised by the loss of utopia.[17] The earliest time is the pristine golden age before the manifestation of pride, arrogance and oppression which results in a condition of evil. This is sometimes symbolised as a condition of drought echoing the earliest stereotypes linking rainfall with good government. A king is appointed by the gods in order to terminate the state of chaos.

Such an appointment inevitably carries with it the sanction to use authority. The legitimacy of kingship now extends from birth and lineage to include the wielding of *daṇḍa*, literally a rod, symbolising the coercive authority of the state. A *kṣatriya* without *daṇḍa* is incapable of enjoying the earth.[18] The abolition of *daṇḍa* would lead to total chaos and destruction. Such passages invariably draw on the *rāja-dharma* sections of the *dharma-śāstras*. The king has rights which place him above his kinsmen but he also has to perform an elaborate number of duties. Significantly the citizens of the state are now described euphemistically as the children of the king, (*prajā*), but they are no longer treated as a vast array of kinsmen. To back up the moral sanction of authority there is the reality of the king performing the role of the ultimate tax-collector, where the right to tax is the complement to the right to wield authority.

Not surprisingly, the didactic sections also include at this stage elaborate rules regarding the functioning of the various castes. It is conceded that *varṇa* was not something which existed from the start but began with the decline of *tapas* and by way of explaining the origin of the caste, the *puruṣa-sūkta* story is repeated.[19] Since the original epic had as its central point the ethos of the *kṣatriya*, this continues to be the main concern of the didactic sections, but the code has clearly changed. Heroic sentiments relating to the protection of the honour of the clan and feats of personal valour in battle, give way to the more familiar duties of the *kṣatriya* as listed in later texts, the giving of *dāna* or gifts in charity, the ordering of sacrificial ceremonies and the study of the Vedas.[20]

The giving of gifts or *dāna* did not mean as it once did at the time of the *rājasūya* ceremony a general liberality to all assembled;

but it now meant specifically the making of liberal gifts to *brāhmaṇas* as these alone were believed to be deserving.[21] This was just one aspect of the wider assertion of the superiority of the *brāhmaṇa* which reads like a chorus in the didactic sections.[22] The emphasis on gift-giving introduces the connection between kingship and wealth, the latter being essential to and an indication of good government. But the role and computation of wealth also changes as between the narrative and the didactic sections of the epic.

The first big occasion for gift-giving in the epic is the *rājasūya* sacrifice to be performed by Yudhiṣṭhira, described in the Sabhāparvan. On the announcement of the *rājasūya*, various tribes and peoples bring their gifts, the nature of the gift indicating status.[23] Another method of ranking the gift-bearers is whether or not they are admitted to the ceremony in the first round, some having to enhance their gifts before admission. The ranking showed whether the gift was to be treated as political tribute, although the nature of the *rājasūya* being what it was, the assumption was that all gifts are tribute and are therefore referred to as *bali*. The elaborate ceremonies required of the *rājasūya* ritual were a means of distributing the accumulated wealth.

The list of items included gold, horses, elephants, slaves and textiles. The first three items could come from relatively less complex societies. Slaves would indicate a greater degree of stratification unless they were prisoners of war. Textiles are associated mainly with central Asia in this list. There is little mention of commodities suggesting specialisation of labour and craft production such as would be associated with developed urban centres and trade. Another definition of what constituted wealth can be culled from the sequences in the game of dice in which Yudhiṣṭhira stakes his wealth.[24] This consists of gold, pearls, chariots, horses, slaves (both male and female) for the entertainment of guests, cattle, sheep and goats. Finally he stakes his city (*pura*), his territory (*janapada*), the wealth of his citizens barring that of the *brāhmaṇas* and ultimately himself and his family. Here again the emphasis is on gold, animals and slaves. The latter are clearly domestic slaves working in the household and not slaves involved in agricultural or craft production which is a significant distinction.

Perhaps the most striking aspect of the listing of wealth is that no mention is made of any privately owned land. The staking of the *janapada* or territory over which Yudhiṣṭhira ruled was of course quite distinct from any reference to cultivated agricultural land. By way of contrast the importance of livestock is highlighted in the list. The pastoral economy finds repeated reference both directly and indirectly in the narrative sections. The Kauravas, for example, organise a *ghoṣa-yātrā*, a cattle expedition to the *Dvaita-vana.*[25] This was obviously a regular procedure since it is the occasion for counting the cows and branding the calves, with the forest pastures providing the possibility of hunting. A vast expedition sets out consisting of the younger Kauravas and their friends and retainers together with horses, elephants, soldiers and hunters. That the permission of the *rājā* had to be obtained and that the young men were personally involved in supervising the expedition indicates that it had an important function in the economy and also suggests that they were more in the nature of chiefs rather than well-entrenched monarchs. That the *ghoṣa-yātrā* carried an element of the potlatch is evident from the distribution of presents and gifts to the cattle herders by the princes. The battle between the Kauravas and the Gandharvas on this occasion is doubtless a reflection of the cattle raids which must have occurred as part of these expeditions. Rights over grazing lands and hunting lands would be territorial rights, the infringement of which would be opposed as strongly as the infringement of cultivated fields in later times. What mattered in the former situation was the prohibition on trespass rather than on the fear of being dislodged from the land.

It has been argued that there is an indirect reference to primitive agriculture in the episode of the burning of the Khāṇḍavavana, where the forest in the vicinity of Indraprastha was burnt and the land cleared for cultivation.[26] The burning of a forest is indicative of the early stages of an agrarian economy when population groups are relatively small and can survive on this low yielding method of cultivation. References to agriculture and agricultural processes are comparatively infrequent in the narrative sections of the text. A well developed agrarian economy would compute wealth in terms of fields and stocks of grain apart from other items such as livestock and gold. It would reflect some differentiation in land ownership and among those working on the land and would make some reference to rainfall and irrigation. Such references occur in the didactic sections such as in the description given by Nārada of a properly governed state.[27] Cultivation was probably still within the confines of the clan since agricultural slaves and peasant cultivators are absent in the narrative sections. Slaves are generally said to be those captured in war or born of slave mothers or reduced to slavery as a result of loss in gambling. Female slaves generally outnumber male slaves and are described as doing domestic chores and entertaining guests.

Epic society as depicted in the narrative sections has little use for the storing of wealth and there is a constant urging that it be distributed. This would prevent the growth of the kind of economic surplus associated with intensive agriculture, well-established monarchical systems using this revenue and professional priests entirely dependent on the community for a living. But this picture derived from the narrative sections gives way to what appears to be a new economic situation in the didactic sections of the text. The change from a pastoral-cum-agricultural economy to one more intensively dependent on cultivation is most clearly seen in the pattern of gift-giving classified as *dāna*, and discussed in detail in the didactic sections, as for example in the Anuśāsana-parvan. Two features are particularly noticeable: the material content of *dāna* changes from animal wealth and gold to include land and secondly there is a shift from a widescale distribution of wealth to the bestowal of wealth solely on the deserving *brāhmaṇa*. This may have been linked with the growth of professional priests who had little means of support other than *dāna* and even their professional fees are preferentially described as a form of gift-giving than as wages. This is, indeed, a contrast to the distribution of wealth during the *rājasūya* which involved feeding the many thousands present at the ceremony, and the generous giving of gifts.

The growing importance of agriculture becomes apparent from the late part of the text when in addition to land the donating of a tank is also mentioned.[28] The ideal tank, it is said, is one where the water fills during the rains and remains available throughout the year. The mention of tank irrigation would in itself make this passage fairly late. Ultimately there is a section eulogising the gifting of land in which *pṛthivīdāna* is described as the best form of *dāna*. It is equivalent to all other gifts and to sacrificial rituals. The rewards are multiple: a heaven full of *apsarās*, rebirth as a king and the transcending of all sins. Land is superior we are told, because it is immovable and indestructible, its value is enhanced each time there is a crop and it can yield other kinds of wealth.[29]

From what I have said so far it should be apparent that for the historian analysing the epic there still remain some fundamental problems. There are as yet very few means of identifying epic events with archaeological evidence. The most useful comparative study would be one focusing on detailed analyses of the socio-economic culture both from excavations and the narrative sections of the epic. This would at least help towards clarifying our understanding of segments of epic society.

The reconstruction of history from genealogy has to be treated with great caution, for, as I have tried to show, genealogical data can be pushed into a deliberately designed pattern as in the frequency of the five-brother or the five-clan pattern or in the attempts to balance senior and junior lineages. But the information, which genealogies provide on kinship systems and on the basis of which social forms can be projected, may perhaps be more reliable. Such information does at any rate suggest fresh possibilities of examining the nature of social relations although, here again, as I have indicated in the example of the putting together of a variety of contradictory marriage systems among the Pāṇḍavas, this information should not be taken literally but as a pointer to co-existing systems. The sifting of economic and technological data could also be of help in separating various sections of the text, now that we have a rudimentary background for such data from other historical sources.

In the past decades the *Mahābhārata* has been the source of an infinite number of studies relating to religion and ethics. This is perfectly legitimate in view of the unusual role of the epic as sacred literature in the Indian tradition. Yet often, embedded in sacred literature is a vast amount of information on what might be called the backbone of a society — its social and economic structure: more so, in literature which has been recognisably sacralised. It is this which now calls for the attention of the historian.

The distinction between the narrative and the didactic sections of the *Mahābhārata* can perhaps be explained if the text is seen as reflecting the transition between two kinds of societies, a new age reflecting on an age that has ended. The heroic world of chiefships had faded out and dynasties had taken over. But the latter were still seeking legitimisation from the world of the heroes and some of the new deities were the associates of the heroes, hence the need for the epic to continue into later times.

The epic is historical to the extent that it presents a view of the past not necessarily in sequential order and frequently with many layers so compressed as to seem contradictory, which we today seek to explain as allegory. The complexity of this historical perspective has first to be determined before it can be regarded as factual data. What is required is perhaps an endeavour to understand the nature of the epic and its historical function rather than its historicity.

## Notes and References

1. R. Finnigan, *Oral Poetry*, Cambridge, 1977; M.B. Emeneau, 'Oral Poets of South India — the Todas', in Dell Hymes (ed.), *Language in Culture and Society*, New York, 1964.
2. *Aśvalāyana Gṛhya Sūtra*, III.4.4.
3. E. Washburn Hopkins, *The Great Epic of India*, New York, 1901; V.S. Sukthankar, *On the Meaning of the Mahābhārata*, Bombay, 1957.
4. J.P. Joshi, 'Interlocking of Late Harappan Culture and Painted Grey Ware Culture in the Light of Recent Excavations', *Man and Environment*, 1978, vol. II, pp. 100–3, New Delhi.
5. R.S. Sharma, 'The Later Vedic Phase and the Painted Grey Ware', *Proceedings of the Indian History Congress*, Calcutta, 1974.
6. B.B. Lal, 'Excavations at Hastinapur . . .', *Ancient India*, nos 10 and 11, 1954–55.
7. Ibid., see also V. Tripathi, *The Painted Grey Ware*, Delhi, 1976.
8. B. and R. Allchin, *The Birth of Indian Civilisation*, pp. 207ff, Harmondsworth, 1968.
9. Ādi-parvan, 70–80.
10. J.A.B. Van Buitenen, *The Mahābhārata*, Chicago, 1973, vol. I, p. xviii.
11. A.A. Macdonell and A.B. Keith, *Vedic Index*, Delhi, 1967, vol. I, pp. 466ff.
12. Ādi-parvan, 57.27ff, 70.31ff; The analysis of the symbolism of the five Pāṇḍava brothers has been made by Stig Wikander but he restricts it to just these five in, 'Pandavasagen och Mahabharata mythiska förutsänniger'. *Religion och Bibel*, VI, 1947. (pers com. B.L.S.)
13. Anuśāsana-parvan, 44–6.
14. Sabhā-parvan, 13.7ff.
15. Ibid., 13.35ff.
16. R.S. Sharma, 'From Gopati to Bhupati', IV World Sanskrit Conference, Weimar, 1979.
17. Śānti-parvan, 259.7ff; 283.5ff.
18. Ibid., 14.14.
19. Ibid., 285.3ff.
20. Ibid., 60.8ff; Anuśāsana-parvan, 127–33.
21. Śānti-parvan, 20.10.

22. Anuśāsana-parvan, 137.
23. Sabhā-parvan, 47.
24. Ibid., 47, 48.
25. Āraṇyaka-parvan, 227–9.
26. D.D. Kosambi, *The Culture and Civilisation of Ancient India in its Historical Outline*, London, 1965, p. 117.
27. Sabhā-parvan, 5.
28. Anuśāsana-parvan, 99.1ff.
29. Ibid., 61.2ff.

# 29

# *Some Aspects of the Economic Data in the Mahābhārata**

Epic literature emerges out of 'heroic ages' and often retains the flavour of such an age in spite of repeated redactions of the text and the interpolation of later ages. This lends to the text elements of internal contradictions as well as a compendium-like quality. The *Mahābhārata* is no exception. The range of time over which the interpolations have been added reduces the flavour of the original. Nevertheless one method of attempting to do the virtually impossible in trying to reach out to the original is to examine the text from the perspective of one theme and ascertain the dominant form. An attempt is being made in this paper to try and locate the predominant economic structure which forms a background to the events described in the early sections of the story. Some distinction between early and late may perhaps be allowed in terms of the context of the evidence quoted. If an action is part of the intrinsic narrative of the epic, it may be taken as belonging to an earlier stratum than a situation which is being described at an abstract level in the many didactic portions of the text.[1] There is a greater probability of the latter being interpolations.

A study has already been made of the geographical and economic data available in at least four sections of the text — the Ādiparvan, Sabhāparvan, Araṇyaparvan, and Bhīṣmaparvan.[2] The intention of this essay is to examine the data and compare it with other parts of the text and to suggest that the predominant economy of the epic is a mixture of pastoralism and agriculture with an earlier emphasis on the former (as evidenced in the narrative sections) gradually changing to the latter which is more apparent in the didactic sections. The epic in origin relates to clan-based society

* *ABORI*, 1977–78, LIX, 993–1007.

with effective power invested in chiefships and where the structure does not preclude social stratification: a society which gradually gave way to monarchies of the more conventional type based on developed agriculture.

Among the more interesting and perhaps lesser known studies of the *Mahābhārata* are two which have for many years been neglected by Indologists but which are now coming into notice again. Marcel Mauss in his study of gift-giving and gift-exchange devotes a substantial part of the book to a discussion of *dāna* in the Anuśāsanaparvan.[3] G.J. Held took as his cue a statement from this book in which Mauss asserts that, 'Le Mahābhārata est l'histoire d'un gigantesque potlatch'.[4] Held has argued that the Kauravas and the Pāṇḍavas were two phratries involved in a potlatch competition: the latter being symbolised in the two major events of the epic — the game of dice and the war.

Both potlatch and gift-exchange as economic systems generally relate to chiefships. Traces of the system very often continue into later times when chiefships have given way to kingdoms and the traces are particularly evident in ritual situations. But their economic function begins to decline when the economy of the society changes. The potlatch is a ceremony in which property is lavishly given away or even destroyed in order to acquire or to maintain social status, the distribution of wealth being symbolic of status.[5] The wealth is often a ceremonial gift/gifts given by a chief acting as the host to other chiefs and their kinsmen: the gathering of chiefs thus becoming a kind of council of both appeal and approval. The potlatch is also often the occasion when an event of importance is announced such as a birth or a marriage or the acquisition of office or of territory and sanction is given to the event by those present. The giving of gifts on such occasions is strictly in order of precedence and priority, as is also the seating arrangement of those present which in turn reinforces social rank and social solidarity. Gift-giving is not a one-way process since it is assumed that at some later date the invitees will also have a potlatch, and this keeps goods in circulation. A rival potlatch can be held if there is an alternate claimant to the title. This results in a competition with even more wealth being distributed or, if need be, destroyed. A further form is what has been called 'a face-saving potlatch, where if an indignity has occurred, the potlatch is the means of wiping it off. (Here perhaps, the closest Indian equivalent might be the *prāyaścitta*.)

Gift-exchange is characteristic of societies which have passed the stage of clans and families making exchanges but have not arrived at the stage of the money and market economy. It involves individual gift-making at two levels: one is largely to ensure the circulation of goods and the other is where the gift is substantial enough to serve the purpose of acting as a symbol of status and recognition. Gift-giving revolves around the notions of obligation, of purchase and of sacrifice.[6] The spirit of the person is attached to the gift and a return gift of equal value becomes obligatory. In the form of sacrifice, the secular notion underlying a gift is the need to circulate and distribute wealth which is emphasised by the belief that if wealth is distributed it returns in a larger amount. Gift-giving has many dimensions. There is the ceremonial exchange among kinsmen on ritual occasions, particularly birth and marriage. There are payments in the form of gifts for services where the actual transaction is disguised as a gift. There are exchanges of material goods against privileges and non-material possessions. There may be the exchange of material goods of little value merely to assert a social and ritual relationship. The most directly functional form of gift-exchange is, of course, barter.

In the *Mahābhārata* the first big occasion for gift-giving is the *rājasūya* sacrifice to be performed by Yudhiṣṭhira and the details of which are described in the Sabhāparvan. The *rājasūya* is in some ways a combination of potlatch and gift-exchange. On the announcement of the *rājasūya*, various tribes and peoples bring their gifts, the nature of the gift indicating a status of equality or subordination. Another method of ranking the gift-bearers is whether or not they are admitted to the ceremony in the first round, some having to enhance their gifts before admission.[7] The ranking showed whether the gift was to be treated as political tribute, although the nature of the *rājasūya* being what it was, the assumption was that all gifts were tribute and are therefore referred to as *bali*. The elaborate ceremonies required of the *rājasūya* ritual were a means of distributing the accumulated wealth. After Yudhiṣṭhira had successfully completed the *rājasūya* in spite of the crisis over the status of Kṛṣṇa, Duryodhana as a matter of rivalry wished also to perform a *rājasūya*. However, he was discouraged from doing so and it was suggested that he substitute a Vaiṣṇava sacrifice for the *rājasūya*.[8] Was this perhaps to avoid a rival potlatch which would have meant a rapid consumption of wealth quite apart from the sharp and immediate tension among the kinsmen and the clan chiefs? The Vaiṣṇava was clearly a lesser known rite and consequently its rewards were not widely publicised. To give it status it was said that it had previously only been performed by Viṣṇu himself.

Held has pointed out that there is a link between the *rājasūya* ritual and the game of dice since the latter is one of the ceremonies in the sacrifice.[9] The importance which the game of dice takes on in the epic makes it a substitute for the rival *rājasūya* as potlatch: the end result of which is to divest the Pāṇḍavas of their wealth and that too at their own volition. Dicing certainly carries non-heroic undertones for the kingdoms of heroes should be lost in battle and combat and not at the throw of dice. Yet neither with the Pāṇḍavas nor with the story of Nala[10] is any condemnation attached to the losing of wealth, territory and family in gambling. Perhaps the cosmological parallels of dicing with ritual and fate (as for example in the names used for the game and the throws) exonerated the heroes.[11] A more immediate association could be with the distribution of grazing land which often required the drawing of lots or the throwing of dice. Thus the throwing of dice could have symbolised the distribution of wealth.[12] Curiously, winning at dice would have made the Kauravas the legitimate heirs and the epic could well have terminated at this point. But the interposing of other claims, some even negative such as the blindness of Dhṛtarāṣṭra disqualifying him from succession, introduces new concerns of legitimacy and the story continues.

If potlatch and gift-exchange involve concepts of wealth it would be worth examining the tangibles which are included in the definition of wealth. In the geographical sections of the Bhīṣmaparvan where Bhāratavarṣa is being described, the rich areas are said to possess gems, metals and fruit-bearing trees.[13] More specific descriptions of wealth are available elsewhere, as for example in the details of the items brought by various peoples as tribute to Yudhiṣṭhira.[14] These may best be tabulated as follows:

| *Source* | *Items* |
| --- | --- |
| Kāmboja | Fleeces of sheep, gold-embroidered fur, deer-skin jackets, 300 horses, camels, varieties of nuts |

| *Source* | *Items* |
|---|---|
| Govāsana<br>Dāsanīya | Golden jars |
| Bhārukaccha | 100,000 slave-girls from Kārpāsika, deer hides, horses |
| Vairāma<br>Pārada<br>Kitava | Goats, sheep, cows, donkeys, camels, gems, gold, blankets |
| Bhāgadatta | Horses, jade vases, swords with ivory carved hilts, gold |
| Barbarians | Silver, horses |
| Chinese<br>Hūnas<br>Śakas<br>Oḍas, etc. | Textiles, wool, deer-hides, silk, cotton, skins, thousands of asses, swords, spears, lances, battle-axes, gems, perfumes and wine |
| Tukhāra<br>Kaṅka<br>Romaśas<br>Śṛṅginonarāḥ | Many thousand horses, gold, palaquins, beds and chariots, gems, javelins, iron arrows and shafts |
| Khaśas<br>Ekāśanas<br>Jyohas<br>Pradaras<br>Dīrghaveṇu<br>Paśupas<br>Kunindas<br>Taṅgana | Gold produced by Pipīlaka ants,[15] yak-tail plumes, honey and herbs |
| Mountain tribes:<br>Vāriṣenā<br>Lohitya | Sandalwood, aloeswood, hides, gems, gold, perfumes, rare birds and slave-girls |
| Vaṅga<br>Kaliṅga<br>Tāmralipta<br>Puṇḍraka | Dukūla cloth, silk, cloaks and elephants |
| Gandharva | 500 Horses and gold harness |
| Śūkara | Hundreds of elephants |
| Virāṭa | 2000 elephants |

| *Source* | *Items* |
|---|---|
| Pāṁśu | 26 elephants and 2000 horses in gold trappings |
| Yajñasena | 14,000 slave-girls, 10,000 slaves with their wives, 26 elephants |
| Siṁhalas | Elephant trappings, pearls, beryls and conches. |

And also a long list of other peoples who brought unspecified wealth.

From this list it would seem that the major wealth consisted of gold, horses, elephants, slaves and textiles. The first three items could come from relatively less complex societies such as livestock breeders and trappers, unless as in the case of the Śūdras of Bhārukaccha the items were imported from elsewhere. Slaves could indicate societies with some stratification unless they were mainly captives as in the case of the mountain tribes. In any case the numbers of slaves may well have been exaggerated. From societies with a greater specialisation of labour and craft production the expectation would be the inclusion of more items as finished products showing the expertise in the craft: thus, varieties of woollen material rather than fleeces of sheep, finely worked objects of gold rather than mere gold, jewellery rather than gems. The list of tributes is more suggestive of tribal chiefships rather than areas of commodity production. The variety of the textiles and weaponry coming from central Asia however indicates something of the latter. There is a surprising absence of any reference to high-quality grain which in small quantities would not have been difficult to transport. Possibly the notion of tribute was more attuned to raw materials than to finished products.

Another definition of what constituted wealth can be culled from the sequences in the game of dice in which Yudhiṣṭhira stakes his wealth.[16] This consists of pearls set in gold, a hundred jars each full of a hundred gold pieces, a special chariot and eight steeds, a thousand elephants with eight cow-elephants each, a hundred-thousand slave girls and a hundred-thousand men slaves who fed and entertained the guests, a hundred-thousand chariots and warriors, Gandharva horses, sixty-thousand broad-chested men selected from each *varṇa* and fed on rice and grain and milk, four hundred coffers of gold, cattle, horses, cows, sheep and goats. When he has lost all this wealth he then stakes his city (*pura*), territory (*janapada*) and the wealth of all his people barring the *brāhmaṇas* and ultimately himself and the family. Here again the emphasis is on gold, animals and slaves. Those clearly mentioned as slaves are domestic slaves working in the household and are not slaves used in herding or agricultural activities. This is an important distinction. The sixty thousand broad-chested men are puzzling. They are associated with rice and grain and draught animals so they could be cultivators. If so, why would they be specially selected from each *varṇa*? Had they been slaves working in the fields or with the herds they would have been described as such by the use of the word *dāsa* or *bhṛtya*. They are not described as soldiers nor as warriors. They appear to be a specially selected body of retainers. In the computing of his wealth Yudhiṣṭhira makes no mention of any private land owned by him or his family. His staking of the wealth of his people is in a sense a rhetorical way of staking his right to rule.

The importance of livestock to the concept of wealth is further demonstrated in the description of the city of Girivraja which is said to be rich in cattle, always flowing with water and with fine houses.[17] It is almost as if livestock had become synonymous with wealth. In the alternative sacrifice of the Vaiṣṇava which Duryodhana is encouraged to perform, the main rituals consist of a large feast (which is characteristic of a potlatch) subsequent to the central rite of ploughing the land with a golden plough, the latter being made out of the tribute brought by various peoples to the ceremony. There is no mistaking the agricultural emphasis of this ceremony, yet it is regarded at best as a substitute for the better known *rājasūya*.

The objects brought are seen either as gifts or as tribute and not as taxes, whether they come from close neighbours or distant people. The term used in most cases is *bali*, even for the gifts from the central Asians. *Bali*, therefore, did not imply any regular tax as in later periods. The gifts were occasional and symbols of goodwill and were eventually to be distributed as part of the largesse associated with the ritual. Even the listing of these gifts as tribute was the momentary vision of the heroes and their bards. The bringing in of gifts does not appear to take the form of any regular trade, else mention would have been made of traders accompanying the gifts. There is also a noticeable absence of reference to coins in the listing of wealth. An itinerant or peddling trade must certainly have been a common feature with probably a series of sporadic markets dependent on availability of produce.

Passages containing lists of tribute-bearers would be among those to which in epic style additions could be made quite easily. Thus as the geographical and economic reach widened fresh names and items could be added on. It has been argued that the inclusion of the central Asians in this list would date this passage to the second century BC.[18] The names and the items may well have been added at this period or possibly even somewhat later, but the structure of the relationships implied belongs to an earlier period. The items listed as coming from these areas may well have been the cargo of the regular trade between north India and central Asia in the post-Mauryan period. What is significant is that they are not mentioned as trading cargo but as tribute for a specific occasion. Poetic fancy apart, many of the items listed as tribute were probably familiar to the trading network of the late first millennium BC and the early centuries AD yet the trading network is kept out of this section of the text. During the Mauryan and post-Mauryan period there were exchanges of royal envoys bearing gifts between Indian rulers and those of west Asia and the Mediterranean. The items included as gifts — rare species of fauna, special varieties of food or fruit, objects of craft specialisation — are very different from the items listed in the epic.[19]

Some of the items from the latter are the natural produce of the forests such as fragrant wood, honey, herbs, furs, and deer-skins. These are valued both in themselves and because forest produce was appreciated by the host society. Association with the forest is indicated by other features as well. Although life in the forest is contrasted with that of the court, the physical entity of the forest was not clearly demarcated or segregated.[20] It was land beyond the village and evidently not much acreage had been cleared for fields since forests seem to have been easily accessible to village dwellers. Forests were often regarded as sacred groves and said to be protected by supernatural beings both kindly and malevolent. The Saugandhika-vana was protected by Kubera, the king of the Yakṣas, and the Hiḍimba-vana was the haunt of the *rākṣasa* Hiḍimba.[21] These were substantial forests and not just a small clump of trees. The heroes could walk for some distance before meeting the protector and the uprooting of trees was common during the conflicts which sometimes occurred within the forest. The association of deities or demons with the forest was an archaic practice which survived into the ritual of the sacred grove.

The Khāṇḍava-vana was protected by Indra, and Agni had to appeal to Kṛṣṇa and Arjuna for assistance before the forest could be destroyed. The burning of the Khāṇḍava-vana is a vast conflagration involving a large area. It has been suggested that this event refers to the burning of forests to clear land for agriculture.[22] The burning of a forest is indicative of the early stages of an agrarian economy when population groups are relatively small and can survive on this low yielding method of cultivation. In the case of the Khāṇḍava-vana it may be argued that, although there was a familiarity with the more advanced plough agriculture, a primitive method of clearing land was used because of the extent of the area which had to be cleared, an area large enough for the Pāṇḍavas and their followers to establish the hub of a *janapada*.

In Vedic literature the *araṇya* often symbolises that which is alien as compared to the *grāma*.[23] In the *Mahābhārata* however the purity and the sanctity of the forest receives greater emphasis. The theme of exile in the forest is also a theme of penance and purification for ultimately the forest is not only the sacred grove but also the natural habitat of the ascetic and the location of the hermitage. The forest is not an alien place. The gathering economy imposed by life in the forest was regarded as an almost ideal way of living in its self-sufficiency. Even if the forest was introduced as a deliberate literary device in order to contrast it with life at the court, the idealisation of the forest reflects a relatively familiar way of life. It could be argued that the mere fact of idealisation indicates a changed environment in which the forest is an archaic symbol. However, the inter-linking of the forest with pasture lands would suggest the continuing economic function of the forest.

The pastoral economy finds repeated reference both directly and indirectly. Some pasture lands are included in forest areas such as the Dvaitavana, and the Kauravas organise a *ghoṣayātrā*, a cattle expedition to this area.[24] Karṇa suggests that he and Duryodhana should take permission from Dhṛtarāṣṭra and go on an expedition to visit the cowherding stations in Dvaita-vana. Karṇa, spoiling for a fight, knew that the Pāṇḍavas were in the vicinity and therefore trouble might ensue. The cattle expedition was obviously a recognised procedure since the *ghoṣayātrā* is the time for counting the cows and branding the calves and incidentally the forest also provides the occasion for hunting. A vast expedition sets out consisting of the scions of the clan and their friends and retainers, an army of eight thousand chariots, thirty thousand elephants, one thousand soldiers and nine thousand horses, together with many hundreds of hunters and womenfolk. It is specifically mentioned that traders also follow in their wake suggesting the organisation of temporary cattle fairs. That the permission of the king had to be obtained and that the young men were personally involved in supervising the expedition indicates that it had an important function in the economy and also suggests that the Kurus were more in the nature of chiefs rather than well-entrenched monarchs. That the *ghoṣayātrā* also carries an element of the potlatch is evident from the distribution of presents and gifts to the cattle-herders by the princes. The battle between the Kauravas and the Gandharvas[25] on this occasion is doubtless a parallel to the cattle raids which must have occurred as part of these expeditions. Rights over grazing lands and hunting lands would be territorial rights the infringement of which would be opposed as strongly as the infringement of cultivated fields in later stages. What mattered in the former situation was the prohibition on trespass rather than on the fear of being dislodged from the land. It was the trespass on the part of the Kauravas which the Gandharvas were opposing.

Meat-eating as a regular part of the diet would reinforce the dependence on hunting and pastoralism. Thus the Pāṇḍavas hunt deer to feed themselves and the *brāhmaṇas* who had followed them into the Kāmyaka forest.[26] Draupadī offers a meal of fifty deer together with rabbit, boar and buffalo meat to the kings of Sindhu and Suvīra.[27] It was not only in the privation of forest life that meat was eaten. Even in the didactic sections the practice cannot be condemned out of hand. It is said that under the constellation of Rohiṇī one should gift meat, rice, *ghi*, milk, etc., to *brāhmaṇas*.[28] Although there is a plea in support of *ahiṃsā* and therefore an attack on the eating of animal flesh, nevertheless it is said that meat if sanctified in accordance with the *Vedas* can be eaten since animals were created for sacrifice.[29] A list of food items for *śrāddha* is given arranged in increasing proportions of gratification to the *pitṛs* as follows: sesame, fish, mutton, hare's flesh, goat, pork, fowl, venison, buffalo, cow, *pāyasa*, the meat of *vadhrināsa* (?), and rhinoceros meat.[30] The rewards for performing the *śrāddhas* are also listed and among these are the obtaining of beautiful wives and children, horses, cattle and other animals, silver and gold, profits in trade, splendour and fame. Curiously land does not figure in the list of wealth and rewards.

In another part of the epic there is a discussion of the places to which pilgrimages should be made.[31] There follows a list of rewards which a person acquires on making such pilgrimages. Most of the rewards are, not surprisingly, intangible, such as going to the worlds of various deities — Soma, Sūrya, Mitra, Viṣṇu, Manu Prajāpati, Varuṇa, Brahmā, Śakra, etc. Others are equivalence rewards, where a particular pilgrimage has the same merit as the performance of a sacrifice such as the *agniṣṭoma, aśvamedha, rājasūya*, etc. Such equivalences were perhaps necessary when geographical mobility improved and cult deities had to be accommodated into religious ritual. As far as the more tangible rewards are concerned they relate mainly to the acquisition of cows and gold and to longevity.

References to agriculture and agricultural processes are relatively infrequent in the narrative sections of the text. In one passage we are told that the peasant ploughs, sows and then waits for the rain to fall. Should the rain fail there is nothing that the peasant can do.[32] The lack of mention of any methods of irrigation connected with agriculture is surprising. Elsewhere there is a specific mention of the need for keeping a sufficient number of tanks full of water in case of drought affecting the harvest, and in times of scarcity providing the farmer with a loan.[33] This latter passage is from a section in which Nārada is defining a well-run state and it would appear to be a didactic section on statecraft. A well-established agrarian economy would compute wealth in terms of fields and grain apart from other items such as animal livestock and gold. There would be references to methods of irrigation to supplement years of poor rainfall. It would also reflect some differentiation in land ownership and among those working on the land. The *Rāmāyaṇa* has many passages referring to the agricultural wealth of Ayodhyā, Kośala and Mithilā, and where the definition of wealth itself refers to grain, orchards and ponds full of water.[34] The early Buddhist literature also includes cultivated fields and grain as wealth and describes methods of irrigation.[35]

It also draws a distinction between the owners of land and the cultivators of land where the latter include independent cultivators, hired labourers and slaves. The category of *dāsabhṛtaka* is mentioned both in the context of the household as well as in agricultural work.

Slaves referred to in the *Mahābhārata* are generally said to have been those captured in war or those reduced to slavery as a result of loss in gambling or those born as such from slave mothers. The overwhelming number appear to have been domestic slaves used for running the household or more often entertaining guests. These are the slaves mentioned in large numbers without name or identification. Those reduced to slavery through gambling or loss of a bet are mentioned by name, as in the story of Kadrū and Vinatā or Devayānī and Śārmiṣṭhā.[36] Some seem to serve joint masters such as the couple Gaṇḍā and Paśusakha serving the seven *ṛṣis*.[37] Slaves given as part of a gift or tribute on special occasions are often described in exaggerated figures. Thus Yudhiṣṭhira boasts of a hundred thousand slave girls and the same number of slave men, all employed in entertaining his guests.[38] It is unlikely that he would have had resources sufficient to maintain them. Slaves as tribute are only listed a couple of times and the fact that there were more slave girls than men would emphasise the use of slaves in domestic functions rather than slavery for production whether in agriculture or in mines. The slaves given with their wives may have been used to clear land and bring it under cultivation. However the use of slaves in this capacity is not alluded to. Even Yudhiṣṭhira when staking his wealth, item by item, does not mention any slaves used on the land. Cultivation was probably still under the control of the clan and the internal stratification within the clan would demarcate the categories with some use of *śūdra* labour. One of the occasions when a distinction is made between the *dāsa* and the *rājanya* is at the *rājasūya* of Yudhiṣṭhira when the Cedi king accuses Kṛṣṇa of being the former and not the latter.[39] But the identification of Kṛṣṇa with his clan is not in doubt. The incidence of debt bondage involving land seems rare, the main forms of recruitment to slavery being by capture or by birth. The intensification of agriculture with the use of slaves appears to have been absent. The terms *dāsa*, *karmakāra* and *bhṛtya* are used as a phrase in one part of the text but in a general sense without specifying the functions of these categories.[40] The context suggests 'dependents' rather than any specific function.

By and large the general hesitancy to store wealth and the constant urging that it be distributed would result in an absence of the kind of surplus associated with intensive agriculture, long-established monarchical systems and professional priests entirely dependent on the community for a living. But this picture begins to give way to a changed economic situation. The gradual change from a pastoral-cum-agricultural economy to one more intensively dependent on land is perhaps most clearly seen in the pattern of gift-giving classified as *dāna*. The pattern is recognisable from a wider range of sources and has been analysed elsewhere,[41] but it becomes apparent even within the confines of a single text. Two features are particularly noticeable. One is that the material content of *dāna* changes from livestock wealth and gold to land. The second is that the emphasis shifts from widescale distribution of wealth to the bestowal of wealth on deserving *brāhmaṇas* alone. This may be linked with the growth of professional priests, a body of people exclusively concerned with religion and religious ritual who have little means of support other than *dāna*. Even their professional fees are preferentially described as a form of gift-giving than as wages.

The distribution of wealth during the *rājasūya* of Yudhiṣṭhira took the form of feeding the many millions present at the ceremony, of a generous giving of alms, the supporting of eighty-eight thousand *snātakas* each with thirty maidservants and the feeding off gold plate of ten thousand ascetics.[42] In contrast to this, in a later part of the epic, the distribution of wealth is strictly limited to deserving *brāhmaṇas*. The duty of the king is to recite the *Vedas*, acquire wealth and with this wealth perform sacrifices, since wealth is created for the performance of sacrifices and must be given only to those who are deserving of it.[43] This is a modification on the emphasis on the act of giving with a stress on the legitimacy of the person to whom the gift is made.

Not only is the deserving *brāhmaṇa* now the sole recipient of *dāna* but the amount of *dāna* to be given to him also increases enormously. At the inauguration of the *sabhā* of the Asura Māyā, Yudhiṣṭhira gave to each of the ten thousand *brāhmaṇas* present a sumptuous meal, a new set of clothes and a thousand cows.[44] The Pāṇḍavas performed the sacred rites at the *tīrtha* on the Gomatī and gave cows and wealth to the *brāhmaṇas*.[45] For the attainment of various heavens the gift of a cow or an ox was necessary.[46] But in the Śāntiparvan and the Anuśāsanaparvan various kings are eulogised for their generosity and the figures mentioned are quite staggering. Thus, Bhāgīrathi gave a million women covered with gold ornaments, the same number of chariots each with four horses, a hundred elephants, a thousand horses, a thousand head of cattle and a thousand goats and sheep.[47] Śaśabindu bestowed on the *brāhmaṇas* at his *aśvamedha*, a hundred elephants, ten thousand chariots, one million horses, a hundred million cattle and ten billion sheep and goats.[48] Gaya performed the *aśvamedha* and donated a hundred thousand cattle, many hundreds of mules and covered an area of a hundred cubits by fifty cubits with gold which gold was then given in *dāna*. Sagara gave mansions with golden columns and golden beds and beautiful women.[49] *Dāna* was efficacious not only in ensuring heaven but also in cleansing one of sins. Thus a hundred thousand cows compensated for a *brahmahatyā* and twenty-five thousand Kapilā cows in calf or a hundred Kāmboja horses would cleanse one of all sins.[50] The excessively large figures need not be taken literally. They appear to be stereotypes in the definition of great wealth. What is significant is the increase in the numbers and the constant listing of animal wealth, female slaves and gold. There was also the added emphasis on the appropriateness of the occasion — *śrāddhas* or *yajñas* — when the gift was to be made.

The gradual but growing importance of agriculture becomes more apparent from a late part of the text where a new type of *dāna* is mentioned, that of donating a tank.[51] It is stated that such a gift merits respect in all three worlds and pleases the gods. The construction of tanks containing water at different times of the year is said to be as meritorious as the performing of sacrifices such as the *agnihotra*, *agniṣṭoma*, *atirātra*, and *aśvamedha*, and some are also equivalent to a *dāna* of kine or gold. Associated with the gifting of tanks and water is the merit of planting trees, indicating an increase of agriculture on cleared land with a concern for the availability of water for irrigation during the different seasons. The ideal tank is one in which the water fills during the rains and remains available throughout the year. The intrusion of this type of *dāna* may well be a later interpolation in the text. If this is so then it is more likely to have been an interpolation from areas requiring the use of tanks. It is curious that the building of wells or of *bunds*, both common sources of water supply, are not listed in this important category of donation.

Ultimately there is a section eulogising the gifting of land in which *pṛthivīdāna* is described as the best form of *dāna*.[52] It is equivalent to all other gifts of tanks, trees and sacrifices. The rewards are multiple: a heaven full of *apsarās*, rebirth as king and the transcending of all sins. Further, there is an explanation for why land is so superior as a gift. Land is immovable and indestructible, its value is enhanced each time there is a crop (therefore cultivable land is preferable) and it can yield other kinds of wealth such as grain, the nurturing of animals and possibly mineral wealth. It is repeatedly said that only the *kṣatriya* can gift land.

Significantly the gifting of land is included in the didactic section of the text suggestive of the custom being relatively recent and requiring strong moral and religious sanction. That the *kṣatriya* alone could donate land might indicate that the period was one when the *kṣatriyas* were landowners by virtue of being members of landowning clans. The donation of land by the individual king points to the emergence of the king's rights over land although there is scant evidence of land having become a salable commodity. Even in the gifting of land the element of potlatch is by no means absent as is clear from the following verse:[53]

> *māmevādatta māṁ datta māṁ dattvā mām avāpsyatha /*
> *asminlloke pare caiva tataś cājanane punaḥ //*

## Notes and References

1. I am using the terms 'narrative' and 'didactic' as defined by V.S. Sukthankar in *On the Meaning of the Mahābhārata*, Bombay, 1957.
2. Moti Chandra, *Geographical and Economic Studies in the Mahābhārata*, Lucknow, 1945.
3. Marcel Mauss, *Essai sur le don, forme archaïque de l'echange*, Paris, 1925; translated into English, *The Gift*, London, 1954.
4. G.J. Held, *The Mahābhārata: An Ethnological Study*, London, 1935.
5. Philip Drucker, *Cultures of the North Pacific Coast*, New York, 1965, pp. 55–66. In G. Dalton (ed.), *Tribal and Peasant Economies*, New York, 1967, pp. 481–93.
6. M. Mauss, op. cit.
7. II.47.5.
8. III.241.27–34.
9. G.J. Held, op. cit., pp. 74ff.

10. III.56.5–18.
11. Held, op. cit., pp. 243ff.
12. Graziers in Tibet until very recently settled the divisions of grazing grounds by a throw of dice, the highest throw enabling the grazier to choose his area for a period of three years. Charles Bell, *The People of Tibet*, Oxford, 1968, pp. 49ff.
13. VI.7–13.
14. II.47 and 48.
15. The reference to ants is reminiscent of Herodotus and other classical writers who mention the 'gold digging ants' of India's northern border. Herodotus, III.102–26; Strabo, XV.1.37; Arrian, *Indica*, XV.6. The items listed in this group seem almost certainly to have come from the high northern borders en route to Tibet from where yak-tails were obtained even in later periods.
16. II.53.22–5; 54.1–29; 58.1–43.
17. II.19.1. The most admirable piece of architecture by far in the entire epic is the palace of the Pāṇḍavas which curiously is built by an *asura*, Māyā, helped by the Kiṁkara Rākṣasas or through *asura māyā*. The palace carries a greater aura of magic than of reality. J.A.B. van Buitenen, *The Mahābhārata*, Chicago, 1975, vol. ii, pp. 6–9.
18. Moti Chandra, op. cit., p. 30.
19. For the exchange of items through envoys during the Mauryan period, Romila Thapar, *Aśoka and the Decline of the Mauryas*, Oxford, 1961, pp. 17–18. E.H. Warmington, *The Commerce between the Roman Empire and India*, Delhi, 1974, pp. 261–72, lists the items which were exported from the Mediterranean and west Asia to India in the Mauryan and post-Mauryan period. These include slave girls (in small numbers), horses, red coral, flaxen clothing, papyrus, storax, clover, dates, frankinsence, lead copper, tin, antimony, realger, vases and lamps, silver vessels, amber and glass objects. Very few of these items feature in the tribute brought to the *rājasūya*.
20. Van Buitenen, op. cit., p. 175.
21. III.151.1ff; 152.3.
22. D.D. Kosambi, *The Culture and Civilisation of Ancient India in Historical Outline*, London, 1965, p. 117.
23. C. Malamoud, 'Landscape and Religion in the *Arthaśāstra*. A Note on Bhūmicchidra'. Paper read at the I.C.O. Mexico, 1976.
24. III.227.19 to 229.10.
25. III.230.1–31.
26. III.47.1–12.
27. III.251.11–12.
28. XIII.63.6ff.
29. XIII.116 and 117.13–14.

30. XIII.88.
31. III.80–9.
32. III.33.44–5.
33. II.5.67–8.
34. Dev Raj Chanana, *The Spread of Agriculture in Northern India*, New Delhi, 1963, pp. 6–8. *Rāmāyaṇa*, II.6.11ff.
35. *Cullavagga*, V.17.2; VII.1.2; *Vinaya Piṭaka*, I.287 are some of the references to irrigation for fields. *Mahāvagga*, III.11.4; *Jātaka*, III.293; IV.276, 281 refer to categories of ownership and the use of *dāsa* and *karmakāras* on the land.
36. I.14.5ff and I.73.
37. XIII.94.5.
38. II.54.12.
39. II.42.1–4.
40. V.132.17.
41. Romila Thapar, '*Dāna* and *Dakṣiṇā* as Forms of Exchange', *Indica*, vol. 13, 1976, nos 1 and 2, pp. 37–48. *See* chapter 24 in this volume.
42. II.48.35–42.
43. XII.20.10.
44. II.4.2–3.
45. III.93.1–3.
46. III.184.7–11.
47. XII.29.56ff.
48. Ibid.
49. XII.2.9.122–6.
50. XIII.24.1ff.
51. XIII.99.1ff.
52. XIII.61.2ff.
53. XIII.61.32.

# 30

# The Rāmāyaṇa: Theme and Variation*

The epic can be seen as the expression of a certain historical consciousness, even though the events which it describes may not be historically authenticated. The epic form is in origin part of an oral tradition and comes to be 'frozen' into a literary form at a date subsequent to that of the oral composition. It reflects a changed historical situation in which the new is looking back on the old and often doing so nostalgically. The nostalgia is, however, circumscribed by new demands. The continuity of the epic is not merely due to a love for mythology and legend in a particular society. Undoubtedly, the appeal of the narrative, the literary form, the evocation of imagery and symbolism and the ethical emphases, all ensure continuity: but the role of the epic in the making of a historical tradition relates more closely to its potential function in such a tradition.

The popularity and the function of the epic *Rāmāyaṇa* in the Vālmīki version are manifest at many historical levels. As a poetic expression it had a literary appeal which, with the spread of Sanskrit, was introduced into new areas at specific times. In turn it became the model for the development of epic genres associated with Sanskritic culture. The literary currency of the epic is apparent from allusions in inscriptional records. As a theme it incorporates the great universal ethic of the battle between good and evil with a large number of subsidiary themes relating to ethical behaviour in a range of human relationships. At a wider level it functions as a link between the classical tradition and local culture where the epic form facilitates assimilation from one to the other, for

* In S.N. Mukherjee (ed.), *India: History and Thought*, Calcutta, 1982, 221–53.

what is pertinent to the local culture can be incorporated into the epic through fresh episodes. In the same way, the geographical horizon of the epic can be extended through the inclusion of local places as the locations of events. An even more significant development in the *Rāmāyaṇa* is its function as a text to propagate Vaisnavism, with the transformation of the hero-prince into an *avatāra* of Viṣṇu. To all these may be added yet another aspect: that the *Rāmāyaṇa* symbolizes the triumph of the monarchical state, and the epic therefore becomes a charter of validation for the monarchical state. As such it can either be used directly where validation is required by groups seeking kinship links with the hero, or else can be virtually reversed if the validation is required for those who were considered the enemies in the original story.

The present paper is concerned with this latter aspect of the role of the epic, and attempts an analysis of three major and different versions of the narrative of events included in the *Rāmāyaṇa* and the degree to which they can be seen as charters of validation referring to distinct and separate groups. The three versions are first, the parallels to the *Rāmāyaṇa* themes in the Buddhist *Jātaka* literature, second the Vālmīki *Rāmāyaṇa* and, finally, the Jaina version of the story, the *Paumacariyam* of Vimalasūri. Irrespective of when the earliest oral tradition was current, these three versions were composed and compiled in the period approximately between the fifth century BC and mid-first millennium AD. What seems significant therefore is the question of the need for these versions and the reasons for the dissimilarities in treatment.

References to the *Rāmāyaṇa* as such in Buddhist sources are met with in the commentaries and in the texts of the later period such as the *Cūlavaṃsa*.[1] The former dismiss the epic with the uncomplimentary remark that it is 'purposeless talk'. But the *Jātaka* literature has many scattered fragments which echo episodes from the story. It has been suggested that these fragments or *ākhyānas* may have been put together in the larger epic, the implication being that both *Jātaka* stories and the *rāma-kathā* derive from a common oral tradition. That the *Jātaka* versions were not an attempt at an alternative version of the *Rāmāyaṇa* seems evident from the absence of any rewriting of the epic as such in the Buddhist tradition. The stories merely illustrate certain actions by recourse to tales familiar to a wide audience, although the details of the stories often differ from the episodes in the *Rāmāyaṇa*. These differences are important.

The *Jātaka* stories associated with the *Rāmāyaṇa* consist either of those which relate events parallel to the events of the *Rāmāyaṇa* or which contain verses alluding to the narrative of the *Rāmāyaṇa* or personalities involved in the story. The selection is therefore not arbitrary. There are some *Jātakas* where the reference is indirect but quite clearly to the *Rāmāyaṇa* itself as when a verse describes the emotion of Rāma's mother on his exile to Daṇḍaka[2] or the reference to Sītā's devotion to Rāma as reflected in her accompanying her husband into exile.[3] Rāma is described as *daśaratha-rājaputta* in the commentary to this *Jātaka*.[4] There is also a reference to a *Rāma-mātuposaka*, an inhabitant of Varanasi who went to Daṇḍaka, a country which was being destroyed by the wickedness of the king.[5] Other *Jātakas* refer to places, persons and episodes which are also mentioned in the Vālmīki *Rāmāyaṇa* or can be associated with this text. Thus Daṇḍaki is referred to as the king ruling over Daṇḍaka which is associated with the area extending down to the Godavari river[6] and his capital is at Kumbhavatī. In the *Ayodhyākāṇḍa* of the Vālmīki *Rāmāyaṇa*, Daśaratha is forced to agree to the exile of Rāma because Kekeyi invokes a boon which he had given her and the exile of his son is explained by his having to undergo the same fate as the blind parents of the young ascetic whom he had accidentally killed whilst on a hunt.[7] This episode has its parallel in the *Sāma Jātaka*.[8]

The town of Ayodhyā is known but not very clearly located. On one occasion it is said to have been attacked by the Andhavenuputta, who besieged and subjugated the city and then returned to Dvāravatī.[9] This reference to the Andhaka-vṛṣṇi clans of the Yādava lineage is echoed in Puranic records where mention is made of the Haihayas, a segment of the Yādava lineage, attacking Kośala.[10] The city of Sāketa which arose on the decline of Ayodhyā is more frequently mentioned in Buddhist sources and is often associated with the Śākyas.[11]

Mithilā and Videha are mentioned more frequently in the *Jātaka* literature.[12] A prince of Mithilā studied together with a prince from Varanasi at Taxila.[13] King Videha ruled at Mithilā and was instructed in the law by four sages.[14] Suruci is referred to as the king of Mithilā in Videha.[15] Similarly, Makhadeva ruled for eighty-four thousand years and became a monk when he saw the first grey hair on his head[16] — a theme often repeated in Buddhist texts. The story is further elaborated upon in the *Nimi Jātaka* where Makhadeva is reborn as Nimi and acquires renown as one who practises all the Buddhist precepts and virtues.[17] He is therefore invited to visit Indra's heaven which he does for seven days making a detour via hell. Nimi also renounces the world on sighting the first grey hair on his head and his son Kalāra-Janaka becomes king. The *Mahājanaka Jātaka* has a long account of the ancestry and tribulations of Mahājanaka who, having lost his right to accession at birth, manages to regain his kingdom but eventually renounces his princely existence and becomes an ascetic.[18] The descriptions of Mithilā in this *Mahājanaka Jātaka* are reminiscent of the descriptions of Ayodhyā in the Vālmīki *Rāmāyaṇa* as a city of considerable splendour and wealth.[19] Elsewhere too, Videha is described as a rich land of sixteen thousand villages and with well-filled granaries and storehouses and sixteen thousand dancing girls.[20] Names such as Nimi and Janaka occur in the Puranic genealogies of the Videha branch of the Ikṣvāku lineage.[21] The religious and philosophical activities of these kings are not dissimilar to the descriptions of Janaka in the later Vedic literature except that in those texts the connections are with the performance of Vedic *yajñas* and the pre-occupation with Upanisadic discourses.[22]

The *Jātaka* story which comes closest to the theme of the *Rāmāyaṇa* is, of course, the *Daśaratha Jātaka* and this has been commented upon at length.[23] Daśaratha is described as the king of Varanasi. He has two sons, Rāma-paṇḍita and Lakkhana, and a daughter, Sītā-devī, from his eldest queen. After her death he raises another wife to the status of queen consort and she demands that her son Bharata be made the heir-apparent. The king, frightened that the new consort will harm the elder sons suggests to them that they flee to the neighbouring kingdom and claim their rights after Daśaratha has died, it having been prophesied that Daśaratha would die after twelve years. Sītā accompanies her brothers and the three go to the Himalaya. Daśaratha dies after nine years. Bharata, refusing to become king, goes in search of Rāma and tries to persuade him to return. Lakkhana and Sītā, on hearing of their father's death, faint, but Rāma preaches to them on the impermanence of life. Rāma insists that he will return only after the twelve years have been completed and therefore gives his sandals to Bharata to guide him in taking decisions. Finally, Rāma returns to his kingdom, makes Sītā his queen consort and rules righteously for sixteen thousand years.

This is in essence the story of the *Ayodhyā-kāṇḍa*, the second book of the Vālmīki *Rāmāyaṇa*. But it also carries traces of the origin myths of various *kṣatriya* clans, pre-eminently the Śākyas and Koliyas, described in other Buddhist sources.[24] King Okkāka, the founder of the Okkāka or Ikṣvāku lineage and the ancestor of the Śākyas, banished the children of his elder queen to the Himalaya and made the son of the younger queen his heir. The exiled children, four sons and five daughters, paired off and became the ancestors of the Śākyas, founding a city at Kapilavastu. The origin of the Koliyas is linked to this story and is traced back to Rāma, the king of Varanasi who was exiled because he had leprosy. He cured himself as well as the eldest daughter of King Okkāka, whom her brothers had left in the forest. They lived together in a *kol* tree and became the parents of sixteen twins, the ancestors of the Koliyas. Koliyanagara was built at the site of the *kol* tree. The thirty-two Koliya princes abduct the daughters of their maternal uncles, the Śākyas, in the accepted manner of certain cross-cousin marriage systems.

The link between Okkāka and the northern region is emphasized in both these stories as also in a *Jātaka* story which states that Okkāka sent for a Madra princess for his son Kuśa.[25] On this occasion Okkāka is said to be the king of the Mallas ruling from Kuśavatī. The princess curiously has a hunchbacked nurse. The Madras were the neighbours of the Kekeyas in northern India. That the Ikṣvākus were originally based further to the west and appear to have migrated eastwards to the middle Ganga valley is implied in certain references to them in Vedic literature.[26] In case of such a migration the shorter and more likely route was probably along the foothills of the Himalaya and the northern fringes of the Ganga valley.

At some point the lineage of Okkāka was connected with that of Ikṣvāku. The name Okkāka is said to derive from *Okkamukha* because when he spoke light seemed to come from his mouth.[27] The Northern Buddhist tradition equates Okkāka with Ikṣvāku and derives the etymology from *ikṣu*, sugarcane, the usual etymology in Puranic sources.[28] Was the association with the Ikṣvākus a later attempt to link the *kṣatriya* clans which supported Buddhism with one of the two major royal lineages of the Puranic *kṣatriya* tradition? This may explain why these clans are given no importance in the Puranic accounts. The relevance of Buddhist origin myths to the epic has to do with the association of these clans with the *janapada* of Kośala.[29]

The theme of exile occurs more than once in the *Jātaka* literature, but of these the *Sambula Jātaka*[30] is the closest in detail to the *Rāmāyaṇa* story. A prince exiles himself on account of leprosy and his wife accompanies him. She is kidnapped by a *rakkhasa* in the forest, but Śakra comes to her aid and she returns to her husband. In spite of her many efforts to reassure him he remains suspicious of her chastity. Ultimately they are reconciled. It is, however, the *Vessantara Jātaka* which is most frequently quoted in connection with the exile theme.[31] Vessantara, the son of the ruler of Sivi, is the epitome of the gift-giving prince since he bestows his wealth in the form of *dāna* on all who ask for it. Finally, he goes to the extent of gifting his famous rain-inducing elephant to the king of Kaliṅga who asks for it in order to terminate a prolonged drought in Kaliṅga. This incenses the subjects of Vessantara who banish him from the kingdom, the loss of this particular elephant symbolizing the loss of prosperity. His wife, in emulation of Sītā, accompanies him into exile. He travels to the Ceta/Cedi kingdom and lives in the Gandhamadana forest. Even here he is beset by greedy *brāhmaṇas*. His children are taken away by a *brāhmaṇa* from Kaliṅga and another asks for his wife to work as a slave. Eventually Śakra appears and it turns out that the tribulations of Vessantara are a test of his generosity.

Underlying the many stories there are some themes which appear to be significant not only in themselves but also as suggestive of some of the ideas which might have gone into the shaping of the Vālmīki *Rāmāyaṇa* as well, although from a non-Buddhist perspective. There is first of all the extension of the geographical circumference. Mention is made of the links and alliances between the *janapadas* of the middle Ganga valley with *janapadas* in two different directions. One appears to have been along the northern route, the *uttarapatha,* to the *janapadas* of the Indo-Gangetic divide, Punjab and the north-west — that of the Kurus, the Kekeyas, the Madras, Gandhāra and Kāmboja. The other went in a southerly direction via Cedi to Kaliṅga. The route from Kāśī to Cedi is said to have been infested with robbers.[32] But Cedi and Kaliṅga seem closely associated with a frequency of safe travelling.[33] The geographical dimension is emphasized in the theme of exile where banished princes go either to the Himalaya or southwards, as for example to Cedi.

The Cedi *janapada* is clearly an important area. The *Cetiya*

*Jātaka* gives the lineage of the Cedi kings who ruled from the capital of Sotthivatinagara in Bundelkhand.[34] They were descended from Mahāsammata and the succession is given as far as the famous Upacara, so named because he travelled through the sky. After him the lineage was segmented and his five sons ruled in five different regions, a statement which is confirmed in the *Purāṇas*.[35] The *Vessantara Jātaka* mentions that the Cetarattha/Cedirāṣṭra was full of meat, wine and rice, and inhabited by sixty thousand *khattiyas* who lived there as *cetiya rājās*. The Cedi-Kaliṅga link indicated in this *Jātaka* is historically attested in the Hathigumpha Inscription.[36] Khāravela, the king of Kaliṅga, describes himself as a descendant of Uparicara Vasu, the Cedi king, and takes the title of Mahā-meghavāhana, as do other kings of Kaliṅga of this period. It would seem that the Cedis migrated or conquered the land to the south-west as far as Kaliṅga, thus extending their control from their original base in Bundelkhand.

Exile in these stories often seems to symbolize migration and settlement and even if the exiles return to their original homes, a connection with the area of exile is established. Colonization was probably expressed in the form of exile, perhaps to provide a dramatic context to the theme and an explanation for migration. Where new land was conquered and colonized the justification for the conquest was given in the theme of exile. The actual process of colonization would be similar in each case, irrespective of the story narrated for its justification. The process is described in the *Jayadissa Jātaka* where fresh land is settled by the king through clearing the land, building a lake, preparing the fields, bringing in one thousand families and founding a village such as will support ascetics by giving alms. New settlements result in the establishment of cities which become the capitals of new *janapadas* such as Kapilavastu and Koliyanagara. The city in turn symbolizes the spread of a particular cultural system.

Legitimacy is bestowed on the new settlement not by the area having been conquered but by the settlers being linked to the appropriate established lineages. Segments of the existing land-owning *kṣatriya* lineages migrate to new areas and in settling there claim ownership by virtue of kinship links with the established lineages. The connotation of *kṣatriya* in the Buddhist texts was evidently more that of a landowning group than of a warrior. Thus, those who go into exile are members of the *rājakula* and not commoners. In some cases, as in that of the *Cetiya Jātaka*, fragments of their genealogy are given to indicate their status; in other cases it is enough to say that they belong to the Ikṣvāku lineage. The repeated occurrence of sibling incest (brother-sister) may symbolize marriage between two exogamous phratries or tribal subdivisions from the period of the original settlement and the emphasis on cross-cousin marriage which, whether actual or not, does indicate the adoption of a system different from that described in non-Buddhist literature. It has also been argued that this type of incest is a method of stressing purity of lineage, where ancestry is traced back to a single set of parents. Purity of lineage would again reinforce status.[37] The theme of sibling incest may suggest some traces of a system of succession where a brother and sister rule as king and queen but without incestuous relations. It appears to have been symbolic unlike the Ptolemies of Egypt.

In terms of political sanction, these stories reflect a mixture of the *gaṇa-saṅgha* system of chiefships or oligarchies and the early stages of monarchy. There are references to the many thousand *khattiyas* or *rājās* ruling in certain *janapadas,* such as Cedi, which would indicate a *gaṇa-saṅgha* system. In other cases individual kings are referred to, but in contrast to the two other versions, kingship is still a relatively unstable feature in these stories. Kings can be removed by angry subjects as in the case of Vessantara. Even though he was removed while yet a prince, his father could do nothing to prevent his being exiled. Other *Jātakas* refer to kings being removed by their subjects as also to kings being elected by popular opinion, or situations of crisis where kings are called upon to abdicate.

These concerns are in turn enveloped in a Buddhist ethos. There is an emphasis on *dāna* where gift-giving becomes a major criterion of morality, as also the emphasis on *karuṇā* or compassion, so clearly expressed in the treatment of the story of the young ascetic killed by the king but revived by the faith of the blind parents. The benevolent and helping hand of Śakra assists in this. Central to this ethos is the *bodhisattva* ideal with the notion of rebirth to help in the salvation of others. In later times the ideal of the king and the *bodhisattva* were to merge, but at this point there is only the occasional king who is in fact a *bodhisattva.*

These four themes — the extension of the geographical area, migration and settlement, social and political legitimacy, and religious sanction — are recognized components of charters of validation and occur, as we shall see, in other versions of the *Rāmāyaṇa* story as well. In the *Jātaka* literature they are not integrated into a single text but remain as isolated episodes. There was evidently a floating oral tradition of such stories, probably a range of oral epics, and episodes from these were consciously worked into the text of the Vālmīki *Rāmāyaṇa*. That references are made to the text in the *Jātaka* stories would reflect the wide currency of the text at a period subsequent to the mid-first millennium BC.

It would be worth examining the way in which these four themes run parallel in the Vālmīki *Rāmāyaṇa*. This raises the problem of indicating at least some of the interpolations in the text, as also of sorting out the fragments which went into its making. There are two easily recognizable foci to the story, the events which centre on the kingdom of Ayodhyā and those which concern the period of exile.[38] Within each of these a number of subfragments can be detected.[39] It is also generally agreed that apart from specific interpolations, which are many, there are two substantial additions, namely, the *Bāla-kāṇḍa* and the *Uttara-kāṇḍa*, the first and the seventh books. These additions are largely extraneous to the story and appear to have been added mainly for didactic purposes. Both books carry many of the stock-in-trade myths from the *vaṃśānucarita* sections of the *Purāṇas* and from the *Mahābhārata*. In the case of the *Rāmāyaṇa* these are primarily the myths connected with the Ikṣvāku lineage. The first and the last books are again the ones in which the role of Rāma as the *avatāra* of Viṣṇu is highlighted, suggesting that these sections may have been introduced to convert the epic into a part of the Bhāgavata literature.[40] The justification for the killing of Rāvaṇa is sought in the appeal to Viṣṇu to incarnate himself and eliminate evil from the earth. Another aspect of the rise of Viṣṇu is the demoting of Indra, which is apparent in some sections of the seventh book in particular.[41] Indra, who in the Vedic literature is said to have been the protector of the Bharatas and the Cedis and various other clans, was both a warrior-deity as well as a practitioner of magical power as conveyed through *yātu* and *māyā*.[42] The use of his *vajra*, thunderbolt, is symbolic of this. The introduction of Sītā as a fertility goddess and the testing of her chastity and ultimate return to the earth are also included in these additions. It may be suggested that the conversion of Rāma from hero to deity has as its counterweight, the dethroning of Sītā as an independent goddess in her own right.

Apart from these obvious indications of later additions, there are other features which would further support this argument. The first and last books display a heightened consciousness regarding caste differences as compared to the earlier sections. This is particularly noticeable in the insistence on the elevated status of the *brāhmaṇa* in contrast to the *śūdra* and the prohibition on the mixing of castes.[43] Although *kṛṣi*, *gorakṣā* and *vāṇijya* are mentioned as the three main occupations, it is clear that herding and agriculture continue to be important.[44] The plough is referred to only in the later books and, curiously, throughout the period of exile no mention is made of anyone ploughing.[45] Merchants adorning the city and the complexities of occupations required for trading societies in the context of developed urban cultures are again features restricted to the first and last books, although references to shops, markets, etc. are made in connection with commerce in other sections of the text.[46] Similarly, in the process of gift-giving on various occasions, cattle, horses and gold take precedence over other forms of gifts. The gifting of villages, although known, is less frequent and is associated with Kośala.[47] A reference to *sāmanta* in the *Bāla-kāṇḍa* would also indicate a late date for this section.[48]

One may therefore assume the validity of the theory that the original text consisted of what are now books two to six and that the first and seventh are later additions, quite apart from specific interpolations in the earlier texts as well. In the earlier sections the societies of both Kośala and the Rākṣasas are relatively less complex and the Rākṣasas approximate to human society to a far greater extent than in the later sections. The Rākṣasas are seen more as enemies than as demons; they perform ceremonies deriving from Vedic sanction and Rāvaṇa's wife refers to him as *ārya-putra*.[49] The impression is one of fairly equally matched societies but with different ways of life.

Going back to the themes emerging from the *Jātaka* literature, perhaps the most problematical is the question of the extension of the geographical circumference as it has to do with what seems to be the insoluble question of the location of Laṅkā. The geographical horizon primarily from the middle Ganga valley, Kośala, is extended into central India. The northern links are implicit in the Kośala-Kekeya alliance and are referred to marginally as when Bharata visits his maternal uncle. The major part of the narrative is located in central India and the Daṇḍaka forest. Those who argue for Laṅkā being identified with Sri Lanka (Ceylon) would extend the horizon south of the river Godavari;[50] those who support the identification of Laṅkā with either the vicinity of Tripuri, Amarakantaka or the Mahanadi or Godavari deltas would restrict the events of the exile to the Vindhyan region and what is sometimes called Gondwana.[51] The geographical directions listed in the epic appear to have been borrowed from other sources, mainly the *Purāṇas*, since the geographical order is sometimes confused and places at great distances from each other are juxtaposed.[52] Since the *Purāṇas* were composed later than the earliest version of the Vālmīki *Rāmāyaṇa* these geographical sections may well be later interpolations. Megasthenes refers to Sri Lanka under the name of Taprobane, presumably the Tāmraparṇi of the *Ceylon Chronicles*. What is uncertain is the date at which the name Laṅkā became more current. The *Dīpavaṃsa* seems to suggest that this name was later than others.

By about the mid-first millennium BC the frequently referred to route to the peninsula from the Ganga valley was the *dakṣiṇāpatha* which would have involved a journey from Kauśāmbi to Pratiṣṭhāna via Ujjayini and Mahiṣmatī — a route considerably further west than the one taken by Rāma. The journey from Citrakūṭa into the Daṇḍakāraṇya as indicated in the *Rāmāyaṇa* points to a more easterly route, perhaps via Tripuri south to the Wainganga and Godavari valleys, a route which is not frequently mentioned but for which there is some evidence at this time.[53] Alternatively, the Cedi-Kaliṅga connection suggests a link emerging between Bundelkhand and the Mahanadi valley.

Perhaps a clue to the area of exile is provided by the reference to a new settlement resulting from the events of the epic and this was the kingdom of Dakṣiṇa Kośala (generally identified in the first millennium AD with the upper Mahanadi valley, the area of Bilaspur, Sambalpur and Raipur on the borders of present-day Madhya Pradesh and Orissa). We are told in the *Purāṇas* that after the area had been cleared of the *rākṣasas*, a kingdom was founded and was ruled by Kuśa, the son of Rāma, and his descendants.[54] Was this an attempt by the later dynasties of Dakṣiṇa Kośala to seek lineage links with the Ikṣvākus/Sūryavaṃśa or does it refer to the actual conquest of the area by an Ikṣvāku? Had this been an area of Ikṣvāku activity then the route to it in terms of geographical feasibility could have been from Bundelkhand to Tripuri and along the upper reaches of the Narmada to the watershed around Mandla and Amarakantaka overlooking the plains of Chhattisgarh and Dakṣiṇa Kośala. References to Dakṣiṇa Kośala in other historical sources are later and can perhaps be dated to the early centuries AD. The *Purāṇas* refer to a dynasty called Megha ruling over Kośala at a period contemporary with that of the Andhras.[55] The name Megha can perhaps be identified with the Megha dynasty of the early centuries AD whose seals and inscriptions have been found in the districts of Allahabad, Fatehpur and Rewa, and who are said to have had their base in the Kauśāmbi area.[56] Were these the descendants of a once-powerful dynasty ruling in both the Bundelkhand and the Dakṣiṇa Kośala area? The entity of the latter as a separate region is recognized in the Gupta period.[57] The historically attested dynasties of Dakṣiṇa Kośala do not however always claim Ikṣvāku descent in spite of the statement to the contrary in the *Purāṇas*;[58] unless of course the area was initially conquered by members of an Ikṣvāku lineage and later gave way to others such as the Cedis but retained a memory of the initial conquest.

The condition of exile also serves to highlight the contrast between the kingdom and the forest. The demarcation between the Kośalan way of life and that of the *rākṣasas* is accentuated in the later books with weird and lurid descriptions of the *rākṣasas*. The lineages of the two groups are kept quite distinct. The royal families of Kośala and Videha are segments of the same descent group and can perhaps be seen as phratries with a common ancestor in Ikṣvāku and both being identified as Sūryavaṃśī.[59] The lineage of the *rākṣasas* is quite separate. Puranic sources refer to them as being of the Paulastyavaṃśa, which originated in Vaiśālī.[60]

The emphasis on primogeniture which is the pivot of the story in so far as the *Ayodhyā-kāṇḍa* is concerned reflects a well-established system of kinship in which hereditary authority has passed into the hands of a particular family whose legitimacy is based on descent — hence Daśaratha's anxiety at not having a son to succeed him.[61] The legitimacy is further emphasized by the introduction of Puranic legends relating to the lives of the royal ancestors even though the actual order of descent in the *Rāmāyaṇa* does not tally with those given in the Puranic literature.[62] Whereas the prince Vessantara in the *Jātaka* was exiled by the angry subjects of his father, in this case even though the subjects of Daśaratha were unhappy at the king's decision to banish Rāma, they could do nothing to change it.

A subtle but important distinction between the two societies, that of Kośala and that of Laṅkā, lies in the emphasis on the monarchical state in the one and its absence in the other. The kingdom of Kośala is well-defined and it takes three days from Ayodhyā to reach the border.[63] The *rākṣasas* do not seem to be limited by any political identity with a particular state. There are no boundaries and they seem to wander freely and interminably. The city of Laṅkā has a boundary by force of being an island and the area of Rāvaṇa's control is never clearly defined. *Rākṣasa* lineages seem to be distributed over a very wide area with kinship ties rather than territorial proximity linking them. In place of a strongly monarchical system, the *rākṣasas* seem to function as an oligarchy and the term *gaṇa* is often associated with them.[64] Even the hierarchies within society so evident in Ayodhyā are absent in Laṅkā, suggesting perhaps that the apportioning of wealth was on a less complex but more equitable system. And there was certainly no shortage of wealth in Laṅkā; nor is there any mention of castes among the *rākṣasas*. It could well be argued that the *rākṣasas* of Vālmīki are fanciful beings and would not conform to any particular social category, but since they are described as having the appurtenances of a human society the assumptions implicit in these descriptions can with justification be analysed.

Perhaps the distinction can be more easily seen in the economic activities of the two groups as highlighted in the later sections of the text. The state of Kośala is associated with plough agriculture and its wealth is described in terms of store-houses well stocked with grain and the bustle of traders and merchants and commercial wealth.[65] In contrast to this the wealth of the *rākṣasas* seems to derive primarily from forest and mineral resources. Plough agriculture is not mentioned in connection with Laṅkā nor does it boast of traders and merchants. Yet it is a city of fabulous wealth and literally glowing with trimmings of gold and gems — an almost unreal city. Clearly, it must have had an agricultural hinterland but this is not highlighted as in the case of Kośala, the agricultural economy perhaps playing a lesser economic role in Laṅkā.

The eulogy on the monarchical state is evident in the definition of kingship as it occurs in the *Rāmāyaṇa*. Kingship involves nurturing the sources of wealth and the administration of wealth, maintaining the distinctions of caste and hierarchy and supporting those who were the legitimizers of the systems.[66] None of this appears to have been of much concern to *rākṣasa* society. It would seem that the *Rāmāyaṇa* was juxtaposing two systems, the monarchical state and chiefships or oligarchies with an unflinching endorsement of the former.[67] To this extent the Vālmīki *Rāmāyaṇa* can be seen as a charter of validation for monarchies established in areas of erstwhile chiefships. This may be one partial reason for a possible geographical extension of the area of exile with every recession of the text, as well as the repeated adaptations and translations of later periods.

There was, however, yet another major theme introduced into the *Rāmāyaṇa* largely by way of later additions to the text and this was the theme of Vaiṣṇava *bhakti*. The text now became a necessary component of the literature used in the propagation of Vaiṣṇavism. It helped to popularize the ethic of the new cult of Bhagavatism. The mode of worship gradually changed from sacrifice to *bhakti*, but sacrifice was not debarred, since Rāma had protected the hermitages in the forest so that the sacrificial ritual should not be disturbed. The *avatāra* theory brought a new dimension into religious belief and in some ways paralleled the notion of the *bodhisattva*. It assisted in the process of acculturation both in channelizing Vaiṣṇava beliefs and values into new areas and in assimilating new cults.

The Vālmīki version of the *Rāmāyaṇa* story is significantly different in detail and construction from the *Jātaka* stories although thematically there is a parallel. The story as current at the time seems to have stimulated yet another version, namely, the Jaina text of Vimalasūri entitled the *Padmacarita* or, as it is called in Prākṛt, the *Paumacariyam*. The date for this text as given by Vimalasūri is 530 years after the death of Mahāvīra, which would make it the first century AD, but most scholars prefer a later date ranging from the third to the seventh centuries AD.[68] The *Paumacariyam* was the earliest among a long line of Jaina versions of the story suggesting that the rewriting of this story was of considerable importance to the Jaina tradition. If the Vālmīki text was redacted by Vaiṣṇava propagandists, the Jaina version is even more didactic in its support of the Jaina religion. But at the same time it carries certain reversals of the story as discussed so far, which are of considerable historical interest.

We are told that the *Paumacariyam* is part of the *ācārya-paramparā* and it would be expected therefore to incorporate much of what might be called the prehistory of the Jaina tradition in the form of cosmology, creation legends and early mythological material. The *Rāmāyaṇa* story is introduced in a provocative manner. The initial scene is that of Magadha, a prosperous kingdom with its capital at Rājagṛha and ruled by king Śrenika (Bimbisāra).[69] Śrenika doubts the authenticity of the story as told in the existing versions of the *Rāmāyaṇa* and asks for the correct version. Most of his doubts centre round the characterization of the *rākṣasas* and in particular Rāvaṇa.[70] It is clearly stated that the *rākṣasas* were not demons and that the name comes from the root *rakṣa* (to protect).[71] Rāvaṇa was neither ten-headed nor a meat-eating fiend and all that has been said about him by foolish poets (*murkhakukavi*) is untrue.[72] The *Paumacariyam* is a conscious and deliberate attempt at rewriting the existing version of the *Rāmāyaṇa* story and depicting the *rākṣasas* in a better light. The story opens with a description of the land of the Vidyādharas of whom the *rākṣasas* and the Vānaras form a part. The early chapters provide a detailed account of the *rākṣasa* and Vānara lineages and it is not until well into the story that the Daśaratha episode is introduced. All the main characters involved in the story are pious Jainas, and therefore try to avoid violence: nevertheless, the heroic values cannot be entirely subdued and kings and princes do show their valour in combat and victory in arms through violence.

The geographical focus is essentially that of the Vindhyan region with its circumference extending south to the Godavari. There is a distinctly westward shift in the initial route taken by Rāma since it involves the Gambhīra river (a tributary of the Chambal) and the towns of Avanti and Daśapura before reaching the Narmada. The narrative then moves in a more easterly and southerly direction. Most locations are in relation to the Vaitāḍhya mountain, also referred to as the Veyaddhagiri. Another Jaina text states that this mountain lay near Gandhamadana-vakkara (echoing the *Vessantara Jātaka*).[73] It is also said to be a very long range touching the Sindhu and the Ganga at each end.[74] If the Sindhu is the Kāli Sindhu then this would be the Vindhya range, with which it is often identified. Laṅkā is located at the base of the Trikūṭa mountain (the location of which is not given) on an island.[75] It would seem from the events of the exile that the location is somewhere in the Daṇḍakāraṇya.[76]

In the genealogical sections we are told that the four best known lineages are the Ikkhaga/Ikṣvāku, Somavaṃśa, Vijjaharana/ Vidyādhara, and the Harivaṃśa.[77] The Ikṣvāku is also called the Adityayaśa, presumably a version of Sūryavaṃśa and companion to the Candravaṃśa/Somavaṃśa. Though not given priority in the list, the most important was the Vidyādhara since it is described in maximum detail. Even the etymologies of the names are sometimes included.[78] The Vidyādharavaṃśa traces its ancestry back to Ṛṣabha who in his later years becomes a monk and divides his kingdom of the Vindhyas between his two sons Nami and Vinami. Being the recipients of many *vidyās* they are called Vidyādhara. The most important among them is Meghavāhana who because of certain complications has to flee to Laṅkā where he establishes the Rākṣasavaṃśa.[79] Many of the names in the long lists seem to have been arrived at through free association although the immediate forefathers of the main personalities are given correctly. The Vidyādhara list has a large number of names connected with *vajra, vidyuta* and *megha*.[80] Yet another segment of the Vidyādharavaṃśa is the Vānaravaṃśa, which is again founded by a Vidyādhara prince who is exiled to Vānaradvīpa which lies outside the Vindhyan region and where at Kiṣkindi he establishes his kingdom. It is called the Vānaravaṃśa because the prince takes a monkey emblem for his standard.[81] This is another point of contention with the Vālmīki *Rāmāyaṇa*. Vānaradvīpa is distinct from the Vaitāḍhya region but too far away, and is the habitat of monkey-like humans whom the prince has to train and discipline.[82] There are both conflicts and marriage alliances between the segments of the Vidyādhara lineage. Thus, although there is tension between the Rākṣasavaṃśa and the Vānaravaṃśa, Rāvaṇa, who is of the Rākṣasavaṃśa, is married to Śrīprabhā of the Vānaravaṃśa.[83] The Harivaṃśa, to which Janaka the father of Sītā belongs, is relatively minor and is not connected with the Ikṣvākuvaṃśa of Daśaratha. Of the earlier Ikṣvāku kings the *Paumacariyam* gives prominence to Sagara of Sāketa, who is said to have married a Vidyādhara princess.[84] The previous births of Sagara are given as well as the story of his sixty thousand sons, echoing the Puranic tradition.

Rāvaṇa is described as an ardent Jaina and a protector of the Jaina shrines. He is brave and handsome and woos many *apsarās*. He has the ability to fly and is therefore called *akāśamārgi*, and in addition he owns a *puṣpavimāna*, an aerial chariot which he uses on occasion.[85] (Strangely enough, Vimalasūri does not see this as an exaggeration.) Rāvaṇa therefore is no less of a hero than Rāma. His relationship with Sītā is sensitively delineated.

Rāma's first major exploit is the expulsion of the *mleccha* threatening the kingdom of Janaka,[86] an exploit similar to that of Sagara of earlier times expelling the Haihayas. Daśaratha's desire to renounce the world on the teaching of a Jaina *muni* leads Kekeyi to demand that her son succeed to the throne.[87] Daśaratha had granted a boon to Kekeyi because of her skill in driving his chariot when he was contesting for her hand. Kekeyi tries to dissuade Rāma from going into exile, since she merely wishes her son to be king. This would suggest that it was not the rule of primogeniture which was being transgressed but merely a matter of which son should succeed the father. The exiles set off for the Vindhyas and there could hardly be a greater contrast in the description of exile between the Vālmīki *Rāmāyaṇa* and the *Paumacariyam*. Whereas in the former it was the *āśramas* of the *ṛṣis* which had to be protected, it is now predictably the Jaina shrines which replace the *āśramas*. The period of exile includes innumerable small episodes involving the princes and princesses of the region. Exile is hardly a condition of long periods of austerity in the forest. It is more frequently spent in setting right the manifold political problems of the many small courts scattered in the area. Austerity is frequently punctuated by prosperous villages, beautiful cities and royal palaces.[88]

In many ways the *Paumacariyam* is the mirror image of the Vālmīki *Rāmāyaṇa*. This is so not merely in its Jaina didactic context which has been commented upon before, but even in the thematic structure of the text in terms of the themes which have been examined so far in relation to the other texts.

The theme of exile occurs at two levels. One is the familiar exile of Rāma. The other is exile as migration and the settling of new areas which is referred to not in connection with the Ikṣvāku lineage but with the Vidyādhara lineage. Meghavāhana establishes himself at Laṅkā and gives rise to the Rākṣasavaṃśa and another prince founds the kingdom of Vānaradvīpa. There are close similarities to the Buddhist origin myths. In each case there is a new settlement demarcated by the term *dvīpa*, with its capital city and some distinguishing topographical feature, often a mountain. Exile is caused by some conflict with the established lineage and the rulers of the new settlement derive their status through kinship connections with the older and original lineage.

Unlike the vast wilderness through which the Vālmīki *rākṣasas* roam, the territories of the Vidyādharas are more clearly defined in the *Paumacariyam*. In the latter text it is the northern kingdoms which are vague and undefined. Many northern towns are referred to such as Hastināpura, Ahichhatra, Kāmpilya, Mathurā, Kauśāmbi, Prayāga and Varanasi, but these references occur more often in connection with the earlier *tīrthaṅkaras* than with the narrative of the story. The area of exile, the Vindhyan region and the Daṇḍakāraṇya, is no longer the forest haunt of demons extending over vast expanses for it now boasts of cities and kingdoms with only the occasional forest areas. The wilderness is evidently gradually being settled. Inevitably, the monarchical state is the accepted norm as much among the *rākṣasas* as among the Ikṣvāku. Not only this but even the institution of *sāmantas* or feudatory chiefs is also known. When Daśaratha decides to renounce his kingdom he invites his *sāmantas* to a consultation.[89] Similarly, when there is a political crisis in Kṣemāñjalipura in the Vindhyas, the *sāmantas* are consulted.[90] However, the alternative, earlier meaning ot *sāmanta*, a neighbour, could also apply here.

Another striking difference is the absence in the *Paumacariyam* of the need to uphold the *varṇāśramadharma* and the status of the *brāhmaṇa*. The *brāhmaṇas* are here the heretics and the preachers of false doctrines who acquired their status through fraud.[91] The most respected social groups other than princes are the merchants, and princes are said on occasion to have been merchants in their previous births.[92] Maximum reverence is naturally given to the Jaina *munis* who weave their way through the narrative. It is they who often relate the stories of the previous births of various persons since they have access to such knowledge. Resort to such stories would not only enrich the narrative but could also be used as a technique to explain away problematical situations, and at the same time underline the concept of transmigration. Although there is no well-defined *avatāra* theory as in Vaiṣṇava Bhāgavatism, the tripartite complex of Vāsudeva, Prati-vāsudeva and Baladeva serves a similar function,[93] and the inevitability therefore of the predetermined relationship between Rāma and Rāvaṇa erodes some of the brutality of the conflict and reduces thereby the occasions for heroic stances. The Jaina *muni* is frequently found to be preaching renunciation. Finally, both Daśaratha and Rāma renounce the world and the Jaina ethic triumphs over the traditional *kṣatriya* ethic.

There is a wide divergence in style among the three versions of the *Rāmāyaṇa* story as examined here. Yet the thematic concerns seem very similar. The vehemence with which the *Paumacariyam* denounces the known versions of the *Rāmāyaṇa* and sets out to give a different version does suggest that there may have been a historical need for such a treatment. Could it be argued that the *Paumacariyam* was attempting to legitimize the Vidyādhara lineage and act as a charter of validation for the kingdoms which arose in the Vindhyan region and its fringes in the early first millennium AD?[94] The major kingdoms were those of western India such as the Traikūṭakas, rising on the decline of the Sātavāhanas and the Ābhīras; the Bodhi dynasty in the region of Tripuri and Bundelkhand, which area later saw the rise of the Kalacuris; the Bhojas and the Vakāṭakas ruling in Vidarbha; Dakṣiṇa Kośala and the Cedis of Kaliṅga. Linking many of these dynasties was what appears to be a Cedi connection with some among them using the Cedi era of AD 248–49 in their records.[95] Most of these dynasties do not publicize any substantial patronage to Jainism although Jainism was becoming more popular in this region during the early centuries AD. Many of them were seeking legitimation through the performance of Vedic sacrifices and *kṣatriya* lineage links. Those claiming Haihaya origins would probably have encouraged the questioning of the authenticity of the Bhārgava versions of the tradition, the Haihayas having been major enemies of the Bhārgayas in the past.[96] Was the *Paumacariyam*, therefore, intended primarily to question the Bhārgava version of the *Rāmāyaṇa* story and thus make it acceptable to the dynasties of Haihaya descent? Were the dynasties which claimed Cedi connections somehow linked in origin with the *rākṣasas* of the *Paumacariyam* if not of the Vālmīki *Rāmāyaṇa*?

It could be argued that the connection was fabricated and that the dynasties claiming Cedi ancestry in the first millennium AD were merely being invested with antiquity by being linked with the pre-eminent lineages of the region, the Haihayas and the Cedis. The search for such genealogical links was common to many dynasties of the first millennium AD and later. But the endorsement of these links with the *rākṣasas* of the *Rāmāyaṇa* story, which is what appears to be suggested in the *Paumacariyam*, is problematical. If this was merely a search for lineage connections then they would hardly choose to be linked with a defeated king and, more likely, the entire story would have been reversed to make Rāvaṇa the victor, or to link the new dynasties with the triumphant Ikṣvākus. The fact that Rāvaṇa is killed and that the main thrust of the *Paumacariyam* is to state that the *rākṣasas* have received prejudiced treatment at the hands of the authors of the *Rāmāyaṇa* and the many other versions of the story current at the time, lends greater credence to the possibility that they might have been the Cedi ancestors of the new dynasties. Were the *rākṣasas* of the Vālmīki version exaggerated to such an extent that the memory of their Cedi identity was pulverized? And yet not completely, for the strange ability of Rāvaṇa to travel through the sky and his aerial chariot has strong associations with the founder of the Cedi lineage, Vasu. The use of the term *meghavāhana*, both as a lineage name as well as a royal title, would help in maintaining the myth that it was derived from an earlier ability to 'ride the clouds'.[97]

The Jaina background to the *Paumacariyam* would not be averse to Cedi connections. Among early royal patrons the Jainas claim Candragupta Maurya during whose reign it is said that Magadha was a centre of Jaina activity.[98] In suggesting that Śrenika was conversing with Jaina teachers, Vimalasūri was merely projecting the association with Magadha to an earlier period. Puranic sources endorse an earlier link between the Cedis and Magadha. That the Kaliṅga Cedis were patrons of the Jainas is stated in their inscriptions. At about the same time Mathura emerged as an important centre of Jaina worship.[99] By the early centuries AD Vidiśā had Jaina centres and gradually such centres were established in Bundelkhand and Rewa as well.[100] The Jaina context of the *Paumacariyam* is therefore as much of a localized phenomenon as the lineages. The need to use the *Rāmāyaṇa* story may also have had to do with competition with other religious sects for patronage.[101] The inscriptions from western India suggest a partiality among royal families for patronage to Buddhist institutions. The decline of the Sātavāhanas and the Kṣatrapas may have provided an opportunity for the rise of Jainism in central India, as indeed the inauguration of the Cedi era may have heralded the rise of those claiming Cedi connections.[102]

With the increasing influence of Sanskritic culture the Vālmīki version seems to have gained wider currency as compared to that of Vimalasūri. By the end of the first millennium AD the later Kalacuris, although of Cedi association, take pride in their Haihaya descent and refer in their inscriptions to the defeat of Rāvaṇa at the hands of the Haihaya hero Arjuna Kārtavīrya.[103] There is also a linking of the Mahanadi area with place names from the *Rāmāyaṇa* story.[104] An inscription of the medieval period locates Dakṣiṇa Kośala to the west of Laṅkā which appears to have been the hinterland of the Mahanadi delta. The site of Sonepur is described as part of *paścima* Laṅkā and an island on the Mahanadi nearby (present-day Laṅkeśvarī) is referred to as Laṅkāvarttaka. Curiously, the sixteenth-century dynasty of Baudh (adjoining Sonepur) claims Sūryavaṃśa origin and descent from an ancestor who came from Ayodhyā. But this is so many centuries after the *Rāmāyaṇa* story that it is hardly feasible to regard it as evidence. This group of inscriptions does indicate that there was a tradition at least in medieval times of locating both the areas of Dakṣiṇa Kośala and Laṅkā on the route from central India to Kaliṅga, a likely battleground for those wishing to control the route. It should however be kept in mind that by now ties between Kaliṅga and Sri Lanka (Ceylon) were very close, to the extent of including dynastic links as well.[105] The use of the place name Laṅkā, therefore, may by now have had some connections with the island of Sri Lanka.

By the mid-first millennium AD the *Rāmāyaṇa* story had moved far away from its initial beginnings. Over the centuries it had also provided the base for a number of literary forms, preeminent among them being the plays of Bhāsa, *Abhiṣeka* and *Pratimā*, and the narrative poem of Kālidāsa, *Raghuvaṃśam*. With each of these literary excursions into the elegant refinement of courtly circles, the original epic receded further into the past. To search for the original epic would require the identification of the *rākṣasas* and the cause for the conflict, which continues to be a matter for speculation.

If the genesis of the conflict in the *Rāmāyaṇa* story lay in an antagonism between chiefships, then the Puranic sources suggest various possibilities. The *rākṣasas* of the Vālmīki story are linked with the Paulastyavaṃśa originating at Vaiśālī. The *aindra mahābhiṣeka* of one of the kings of Vaiśālī, Marutta, was interrupted by a Rāvaṇa.[106] One of Marutta's seven wives was a Cedi princess.[107] Tṛṇabindu, a later king of Vaiśālī, appears to have had some links with the Ikṣvākus.[108] His daughter Ilavilā (alternatively called Iḍaviḍa, Drāviḍa) married a *brahmarṣi* Pulastya and their son Viśravas was father to both Vaiśravaṇa Kubera from one of his wives and from another to Kumbhakarṇa, Daśagrīva, Vibhīṣaṇa and Śūrpaṇakhā.[109] It was in this generation that some of the Ailavilas migrated from Vaiśālī to the Vindhyan region. The relationship with Kubera has influenced the notion that Daśagrīva Rāvaṇa had a Nāga identity. The kidnapping of princesses by *rākṣasas* was not an uncommon story in the Vaiśālī of these times[110] and one among these many stories may have been the prototype for the narrative of the kidnapping of Sītā. Was there a conflict between Kośala and Vaiśālī over the kidnapping of a princess? Or did the proximity of Kośala and Vaiśālī lead to warfare over claims to territorial rights for which the kidnapping of a princess provided an excellent excuse?

The continuing and more frequently mentioned antagonism was between the Haihayas and Ikṣvākus. Prior to this, Arjuna Kārtavīrya, a Haihaya, is said to have imprisoned Rāvaṇa of Laṅkā at Mahiṣmatī on the Narmada and later released him.[111] The thousand-armed hero of the Haihayas claims boons from the *ṛṣis* and is among the most powerful of the *kṣatriyas*. The description given in the *Purāṇas*[112] is reminiscent of the description of Rāvaṇa in the epics. The enmity between the Bhārgavas (whose descendants are said to be among the major redactors of the Vālmīki *Rāmāyaṇa*) and the Haihayas is expressed in the killing of Arjuna Kārtavīrya by Rāma Jamadāgni and this event may well have been one of the layers which went into the making of the *Rāmāyaṇa* story. The Haihayas attacked and captured Ayodhyā and it was not until the rise of Sagara that the Ikṣvākus were able to reestablish themselves.[113] This major conflict would have extended the geographical area of the conflict into the Vindhyan region. The earliest Cedis were linked to the Yādava lineage and would therefore have had a connection with the Haihayas apart from being based in the Vindhyan region as well.[114] The later Cedis, claiming ancestry from the Kuru prince Vasu, controlled the southern bank of the Yamuna and the Ganga from Matsya to Magadha.[115] In a period of expanding territories and the forging of trade routes this would inevitably have brought them into conflict with kingdoms such as Kośala in the middle Ganga valley, also perhaps aiming at expanding southwards or capturing routes going south.[116] These episodes, the material of bardic tradition, would tend to be combined or sifted in accordance with folk memory and can therefore only be regarded as the possible fragments which went into the making of the epic.[117] It would seem though, that there might have been some association in folk memory between the Haihayas, the Cedis and the *rākṣasas* of the *Rāmāyaṇa* story.[118] Unlike the *Mahābhārata* where the theme of conflict, among chiefships, is very apparent, the Vālmīki *Rāmāyaṇa* papers it over in the fanciful descriptions of the *rākṣasas*. Significantly, where the *Mahābhārata* is classified as *itihāsa*, the *Rāmāyaṇa* is generally referred to as *kāvya*.

The epic forms a saga of heroes and focuses on chiefships and newly emerging kingdoms in competition over land, status and rights, although the ostensible reason in the narrative might well be the kidnapping of a princess or the losing of a game of dice. The rewriting of the story in a literary form often takes place at a time when the institution of the state is impinging on tribal chiefships or has already been established. In either case the emergence of the state requires a legitimization from the past through legends and stories justifying its establishment. This takes at least two forms: first, there is the incorporation of new territory into the geographical circumference of epic events, where the territory on which the new state has been founded has to be described as having been rightfully conquered or settled; secondly, the legitimacy of the new rulers has to be ensured through mythology, genealogical links and events held to be significant in the tradition. Mythology is used to draw the territory and the personalities into a circle of known and familiar forms, kingship is used to establish links between the new rulers and the territory which is to be incorporated. The religious background is provided by those religions — Buddhism, Bhagavatism and Jainism — which presuppose the emergence of the state and whose spread coincides with the establishing of monarchies, each with its court and capital and its access or aspiration to royal patronage.

In analysing the three versions of the *Rāmāyaṇa* story it may be suggested that they seem to reflect, among other things, the evolution of the state from tribal oligarchies and tribal chiefships to monarchies. The *Jātaka* stories appear to refer to an early period in that the geographical circumference is more restricted and the symbolic representation of social institutions carries traces of early forms. These stories do not develop into a Buddhist version of the *Rāmāyaṇa*. Probably such a version was not required if the context was one where origin myths sufficed and the absence of an established monarchical state did not demand an epic as a charter of validation. Although the *Jātakas* do describe monarchies, the flexibility of the system stands in contrast to that of the other texts and points to the *Jātaka* stories showing a greater familiarity with the *gaṇa-saṅgha* system. Most of the oligarchies in the Ganga valley with which Buddhism was associated declined as oligarchies and were converted or incorporated into monarchies. Even when Buddhism came to be linked with the monarchical system in its maturest form, the epic was not required since the Buddhist *saṅgha* had its own version of historical events to provide the validation, and association with the *saṅgha* became a form of legitimation: a case in point being the Buddhist version of the reign of the Mauryan king, Aśoka.

The transformation of the episodes into an epic probably coincided with the emergence of the monarchical state in Kośala. A distinction would then be drawn between the acceptability of the monarchical state and a degree of antagonism towards chiefships which were seen as a threat to the growing concentration of power in monarchical systems. The acceptability would then be endorsed by increasing emphases on the forms and stratification inherent to monarchy, as is evident from the Vālmīki *Rāmāyaṇa* as *kāvya*.

The main interest in the *Paumacariyam* from this point of view would then lie in its depicting the acceptance of monarchy in those very areas where previously there had been chiefships or at most the early and faltering forms of monarchy. There is a much sharper and stronger assertion of identity among the *rākṣasas* in this text than in the previous two. In the *Jātakas* they are primarily demons, goblins and magical beings and their role is minimal in the *Rāmāyaṇa* stories. The Vālmīki *Rāmāyaṇa* describes them both in terms of a normal human society as well as lurid creatures of the imagination. The *Paumacariyam* has no doubts about their being a recognizable human group with rights over a specific geographical area, governed by the institutions of a monarchical system. The conflict is a conflict among equals. This new identity in all its facets would have required a rewriting of the story to incorporate these changes.

The historical necessity of each version, therefore, would in turn reflect its function as a form of validation for a changing historical situation.

Notes and References

1. *Sumaṅgala Vilāsinī*, I.76; *Papañca Sudānī*, I.163; *Cūlavamsa*, 6.42; 48.20; 75.59; 83.46. An earlier association of Rāvaṇa with Laṅkā occurs in the *Lankāvatārasūtra* but no mention is made of the *Rāmāyana* story. It has been suggested that this text may have been prior to the fifth century AD when portions of it were translated into Chinese. D.T. Suzuki, *The Lankāvatāra Sūtra*, London, 1932, p. xlii.
2. *Jayadissa Jātaka*, no. 513.
3. *Vessantara Jātaka*, no. 547.
4. V. Fausboll, *The Jātaka*, London, 1896, vol. VI, p. 558. The commentary describes Sītā as Rāma's sister who became his queen. But this is ambiguous for the reference to her being his sister is omitted in other commentaries.
5. Ibid., V.29.
6. *Sarabhañja Jātaka*, no. 522.
7. *Rāmāyana*, II.57.
8. *Sāma Jātaka*, no. 540.
9. G. Malalasekera, *Dictionary of Pali Proper Names*, London, 1960, vol. 1, p. 165.
10. F.E. Pargiter, *Ancient Indian Historical Tradition*, London, 1922, p. 153.
11. G. Malalasekera, op. cit.
12. *Sadhina Jātaka*, no. 494.
13. *Suruci Jātaka*, no. 489.
14. *Mahā-ummaga Jātaka*, no. 546; *Vinīlaka Jātaka*, no. 160.
15. *Mahāpanāda Jātaka*, no. 264.
16. *Makhadeva Jātaka*, no. 9.
17. *Nimi Jātaka*, no. 541; *Kumbhakāra Jātaka*, no. 408.
18. *Mahājanaka Jātaka*, no. 539.
19. *Rāmāyaṇa*, I.5; I.6; 65.18–20; 69.2–3; II.61.6; 77.12–15.
20. *Gandhāra Jātaka*, no. 406.
21. Pargiter, op. cit., pp. 145ff.
22. Ibid., pp. 328–9.
23. *Dasaratha Jātaka*, no. 461; V. Fausboll, *The Dasaratha-Jataka, being the Buddhist Story of King Rama*, Copenhagen, 1971.
24. Ambattha Sutta, *Dīgha Nikāya*, I.92; E. Senart (ed.), *Mahāvastu*, I, Paris, 1882–97, 348–52; *Sumaṅgala Vilāsinī*, I. pp. 258–62.
25. *Kuśi Jātaka*, no. 531.
26. P.L. Bhargava, 'The Original Home of the Ikṣvākus', *Journal of the Royal Asiatic Society*, no. 1 (1976), pp. 64–6.
27. *Sumaṅgala Vilāsinī*, I.248. ' . . . *kathanakāle ukkā viya mukhato pabhā niccharati* . . . '

28. S. Beal, *Romantic History of Buddha*, London, 1907, pp. 18ff. This is also suggested in the *Cūlavaṃsa*, 87.34. This text also refers to Sagara and his 60,000 sons as among the descendants of Okkāka.
29. V. Pathak, *History of Kośala*, Varanasi, 1963, pp. 238ff. The Śākyas claim the Gautama *gotra* and the Mallas the Vasiṣṭha *gotra*. *Dīgha Nikāya*, II.160, 164ff. Manu refers to them as *vrātya-kṣatriyas*, X.22; XII.45.
30. *Sambula Jātaka*, no. 519.
31. *Vessantara Jātaka*, no. 547. The elephant and the cloud are regarded as synonymous, hence the elephant symbolizes rain. H. Zimmer, *Myths and Symbols in Indian Art and Civilisation*, Princeton, 1972, pp. 102ff.
32. *Vedabbha Jātaka*, no. 48.
33. *Vessantara Jātaka*.
34. *Cetiya Jātaka*, no. 422.
35. Pargiter, op. cit., pp. 118ff.
36. D.C. Sircar, *Select Inscriptions*, 2nd edn, Calcutta, 1965, pp. 214ff. One view argues for a first century AD date for Khāravela. T.P. Varma, 'The Date of Kharavela and the Early Satavahanas', *Sri Lanka Journal of South Asian Studies*, I. no. 1 (June 1976), pp. 77–8. For the general use of the term *meghavāhana* by the Kaliṅga kings, see B.M. Barua, 'Minor Old Brahmi Inscriptions in the Udayagiri and Khandagiri Caves', *IHQ*, XIV (1938), pp. 158ff.
37. S. Falk Moore, 'Descent and Symbolic Filiation', *The American Anthropologist*, no. 66, part 1 (1964), pp. 1308–20.
38. H. Jacobi (tr.), *The Rāmāyaṇa*, Baroda, 1960; A.K. Warder, *Indian Kavya Literature*, Delhi, 1974, vol. II, pp. 76ff; Romila Thapar, *Exile and the Kingdom: Some Thoughts on the Rāmāyaṇa*, Bangalore, 1978.
39. C. Bulcke, *Rāma-kathā*, Allahabad, 1971.
40. *The Mahābhārata*, Critical Edition, XII.57.40.
41. E.g., VII.30.
42. S. Bhattacharya, *The Indian Theogony*, Cambridge, 1970, pp. 249ff.
43. I.6.16ff; the killing of Śambuka by Rāma, VII.65; 67.
44. In the giving of gifts animal wealth takes precedence, as for example, in I.71.21.
45. I.38.19; VII.17.30.
46. I.5; I.6; I.65.18–20; I.68.2–3; I.31.4–7; II.61; II.77.12–15; VII.70.
47. E.g., II.64.16; II.28.7; VI.113.41; subsequent to Rāma's victory the gifts distributed are jewels, ornaments, gold and other precious gifts, VII.3.9–10.
48. I.5.14.
49. J.L. Brockington, 'Religious Attitudes in Vālmīki's *Rāmāyaṇa*', *JRAS*, no. 2 (1976), pp. 108–30.
50. A. Guruge, *The Society of the Rāmāyaṇa*, Saman Press, 1969.

52. Critical Edition, vol. IV, pp. xxxvi, xlviii–lxiii.IV.40.10–11 places Utkala, Avanti, Matsya and Kaliṅga in the southern region (Matsya/Vaṅga).
53. S.B. Deo and J.P. Joshi, *Pauni Excavation (1969–70)*, Nagpur, 1972, pp. 9ff.
54. Pargiter, op. cit., p. 279.
55. F.E. Pargiter, *Dynasties of the Kali Age*, Oxford, 1913, p. 51.
56. *The History and Culture of the Indian People*, vol. II, pp. 175–7. K.D. Bajpai, 'New Light on the Early Pandava Dynasty of Southern Kosala', *Annals of the Bhandarkar Oriental Research Institute*, vols LVIII–LIX (1977–78), pp. 433ff, summarizes the early evidence on Dakṣiṇa Kośala before the detailed discussion on the Pāṇḍava dynasty. The Cedi era has also been associated with the Megha dynasty which would place them in the third century AD. K.D. Bajpai, 'The Meghas of Kauśāmbi and Southern Kośala and Allied Problems, *Indian Numismatic Chronicle*, part 1, vol. III, pp. 18ff.
57. The Allahabad *praśasti* of Samudra Gupta. J.F. Fleet (ed.), *Inscriptions of the Early Gupta Kings*, vol. 3 of *Corpus Inscriptionum Indicarum*, Varanasi, 1970, pp. 6ff. Arang copper-plate inscription of Bhimasena, *New History of the Indian People*, VI, pp. 85ff.
58. *The History and Culture of the Indian People*, vol. III, *The Classical Age*, pp. 177ff, 190ff, 217ff. V.V. Mirashi (ed.), *Inscriptions of the Kalachuri-Chedi Era*, in 2 parts, vol. IV of the *Corpus Inscriptionum Indicarum*, Ootacammund, 1955, part 1, pp. xxxiff.
59. *Rāmāyaṇa*, I.69.17; I.70; Pargiter, *Ancient Indian Historical Tradition*, p. 145.
60. *Rāmāyaṇa*, VII.2–5; 9; Pargiter, op. cit., pp. 241ff.
61. *Rāmāyaṇa*, I.8.
62. Cf. Pargiter, op. cit., pp. 145–7; *Viṣṇu Purāṇa*, IV.5; IV.2.
63. *Rāmāyaṇa*, II.43.7ff.
64. Ibid., V.41.12; 46.14.
65. Ibid., I.5; II.17; V.16.5; VI.24.20. The difference in the economic base between Kośala and Laṅkā has been discussed in Devaraj Chanana, *The Spread of Agriculture in Northern India*, New Delhi, 1963, pp. 27–9.
66. Ibid., I.8.11ff; II.61.7ff; II.94; II.73.8; 95.2; 102–30.
67. I am using the term chiefship here not in the sense of a primitive society, but as a stratified society with social and economic differentiation and ruled by an oligarchy. The differentiation would not be as marked as in a monarchical system nor would there be the same concentration of power in the hands of the king.
68. V.M. Kulkarni, *Vimalasūri Paumacariyam*, Varanasi, 1962, Introduction; 'Origin and Development of the Rama Story in Jaina Literature', *Journal of the Oriental Institute*, IX, no. 2, pp. 189–204; H. Jacobi,

'Some Ancient Jaina Works', *Modern Review*, December 1914; *Pariśiṣṭaparvan*, Introduction, p. xix, Bib. Ind., no. 96, Calcutta, 1932; K.H. Dhruva, 'Jaina Yuga', I, part 2, 1981, V.S. pp. 68ff, part 5, pp. 180–1.

69. *Paumacariyam*, II.1–20.
70. Ibid., II.104–16; III.7–8.
71. Ibid., VII.1–13.
72. Ibid., III.14–15.
73. J.C. Jain, *Life in Ancient India*, Bombay, 1947, pp. 354–5; B.C. Law, *India as Described in Earlier Texts of Buddhism and Jainism*, London, 1941, pp. 106ff.
74. Hemacandra, *Tṛṣaṣṭiśalākāpuruṣacaritra*, vol. VII, pp. 173ff. The Vindhyacala hill is located in Mirzapur and is crowned by the temple of Vinduvāsinī. The town of Vindhyacala also known as Pampāpura lies near Mirzapur. B.C. Law, *Historical Geography of Ancient India*, Paris, 1954, p. 134. Ptolemy refers to the Vindhyas as Oiundon. The range includes Ṛkṣavat (the Ouxenton of Ptolemy), Vindhya and Pāripātra, ibid., p. 301.
75. *Paumacariyam*, V.126.
76. Ibid., XLIII–XLVI.
77. Ibid., V.1–2.
78. Ibid., V.14–46.
79. Ibid., V.126ff.
80. Ibid., V.14–46.
81. Ibid., VI.70–92.
82. Ibid., VI.42. '*vānaragaṇa sadatto mānuṣāyāre* . . . '.
83. This is also suggested in the *Rāmāyaṇa* where the *rākṣasas* and the *vānaras* are said to be like brothers, V.49.2–3.
84. V.50–168. The Jaina version of the Puranic legend states that Sagara and his 60,000 sons dug a ditch to protect certain Jaina shrines and the sons were burnt to ashes whereupon Sagara became a *muni*.
85. *Paumacariyam*, XII.143; XLIV.29.
86. Ibid., XXVII.
87. Ibid., XXIX–XXXI.
88. As for example, ibid., XXXIV, XXXVII.
89. Ibid., XXXI.40–53.
90. Ibid., XXXVIII.51ff.
91. Ibid., IV.64ff.
92. Ibid., V.81–92; VI.1–45.
93. Ibid., V.154–6.
94. The *Paumacariyam* does not link the *rākṣasas* with the Paulastyas as in the *Purāṇas* and the *Rāmāyaṇa* unless it can be suggested that the name Vidyādhara is indicative of magical power and knowledge,

generally associated with the *ṛṣis*. Vidyādhara does echo the epithet of *yātudhāna* used for the *rākṣasas* in the *Rāmāyaṇa*, III.25; VI.60.

95. V.V. Mirashi, op. cit., part 1, pp. iff.

96. F.E. Pargiter, *The Ancient Indian Historical Tradition*, London, 1922, pp. 197ff.

97. Aerial chariots are part of the dream world of many cultures, but here a distinction is made between the ability to fly and the possession of aerial chariots and the latter are associated with particular groups of people. Vasu, the Kuru prince who conquered Cedi is called Uparicara because Indra presented him with a celestial chariot which enabled him to move through the sky. *Mahābhārata*, I.63. This gift was made in appreciation of the *tapas* performed by Vasu. Yayāti had a similar chariot and this was acquired by Vasu (*Vāyu Purāṇa*, II.31.18ff). The *Samkicca Jātaka* refers to Cecca/Cedi who once could tread the air. These legends are similar to those of Rāvaṇa and his *puṣpaka vimāna* and may well derive in part from the title Meghavāhana. Another Vidyādhara prince is called Jimutavāhana who also takes the epithet of being 'sky-roaming' (*Kathāsaritasāgara*, XXII.17).

Guṇāḍhya in the *Bṛhatkathā* refers to *vidyādhara* as one who is familiar with magic (A.K. Warder, *Indian Kavya Literature*, II, p. 123) which might also link it with *vijjadhara* meaning a sorcerer. Indra is on occasion also described as *meghavāhana* — he who rides a cloud. Curiously, *meghavaḥni* refers to lightning which would link it up with *vajra* and the association of Indra with *vajra* is well known. The *vajra* in sculpture is depicted rather like a shortened and double-headed *triśūla* with the points curved inwards. In this game of symbols based on lightning and clouds many associations rise to the surface but remain unclear. In one of the Kalacuri Inscriptions, the Haihaya ancestry is written as *Ahihaya* (*Epigraphia Indica*, II. p. 230). Ahi is the serpent in the sky, among other things (Monier–Williams, *Sanskrit–English Dictionary*, p. 125), perhaps a poetic description of lightning as it is depicted on occasions in miniature paintings. The word *airavati* also refers to lightning and Indra's mount is the elephant Airavat, which again would bring in the link with *meghavāhana* /*meghavaḥni*. If there is a link between these, then could one perhaps suggest that the Cedi inscriptions from Kaliṅga where the kings take the title of *aira* may have to do with this symbolism rather than the lineage connections with the Aila or Candravaṃśi lineage as has been suggested, although they did, as descendants of Vasu, belong to the Aila lineage? (B.M. Barua, 'Hathigumpha Inscription of Kharavela', *IHQ*, vol. XIV (1938), pp. 459–85.) What adds to the puzzle is that the etymology of Cedi is uncertain, yet there is a P.Dr. form *ceti*, meaning a bright light [*Dravidian Etymological Dictionary* (DED),

2271], which could perhaps refer again to lightning. Evidently the symbolism of dark clouds, the thunderbolt and lightning had some interconnection in relation to tribal and clan names and titles taken by chiefs and kings, as also perhaps the god Indra. Possibly the denigration of Indra in some sections of the epics had to do with the rise and fall of tribal deities as well.

S.K. Chatterjee suggested that the name Khāravela may be derived from P.Dr. *kār/kar* meaning 'black and terrible' and *vel* meaning 'lance', and the equivalent in Sanskrit being *kṛṣṇa-arṣṭi* (*Vyāsa-saṃgrahama*, 1933, pp. 71–4. Quoted in D.C. Sircar, *Select Inscriptions*, p. 214). The two components of the name in P.Dr. carry the homonyms of 'cloud', DED, 1073, and 'lightning', DED, 4524, as also in the latter case 'chief or hero', DED, 4562. The association of cloud and lightning occurs in the use of names incorporating *megha* and *vajra* among the *rākṣasas* as also the epithet, *nīlameghanimbham* (*Rāmāyaṇa*, VI.70.6). The association with *vel* 'lance'/'spear' or 'chief' may link the name to protection. Curiously one of the Matsya chiefs is called Māvela which would also be translated as *kṛṣṇa-arṣṭi* (*mā* meaning 'black', DED, 3918). If one may further add to the speculation, the name Kalacuri/Katacuri is again of uncertain etymology. Rājaśekhara writes it as Karaculi (Mirashi, op. cit., pp. xliv–lxxi) and also Kalacuri. Could this name also be a variant of 'black' (*kara* or *kala*) 'spear' (*śūli*)? If the compound is meant to convey a spear moving through a black cloud, then the association with lightning would not be unlikely. In the context of the suggestion that the dark, rain-bearing cloud and the elephant are synonymous symbols, it may be worth pointing out that the P.Dr. *mā* means 'black' (DED, 3918), 'a large animal, horse or elephant or deer' (DED, 3917) and 'great, great man' (DED, 3923), though the third meaning is restricted. If the termination *vela* in names such as Khāravela, Māvela, etc. can be regarded as a Prakṛtized form of a P.Dr. word, then it might also have been derived from *vel* (DED, 4524) meaning 'white, shining, light' which could indicate lightning.

It has been suggested that Rāvaṇa is not a personal name but a Sanskritized form of a Dravidian word *ireivan/irauvan* meaning god, king, sovereign, lord. It would thus be a title used by more than one person which might account for the reference to more than one Rāvaṇa in Puranic sources (Pargiter, op. cit., p. 242). A P.Dr. form *iraivan* is listed as no. 448 in the *Dravidian Etymological Dictionary*. Pargiter suggests that Daśagrīva may have been a Sanskritized form of a personal name of such a Rāvaṇa which gave rise to the fable that he had ten heads (op. cit., p. 277). In the context of the symbolism discussed above, could the name Rāvaṇa have derived additional sanction by being linked with the form *airāvan*?

The etymology of *rākṣasa* remains obscure. The root *rakṣ* carries the double meaning of injury and protection and *ārakṣaka* provides the meaning of he who guards or protects. This could be symbolically linked with the association with spears and lances as weapons of protection. The link with lightning remains unexplained as also with flying. In the Indian tradition, the ability to fly perhaps carries a shamanistic connection. (M. Eliade, *Shamanism*, Princeton, 1974.) Thus the *Ṛgveda* mentions the *keśin* flying through the air (X.136). The *Dīpavaṃsa* and the *Mahāvaṃsa* also refer to the Buddha's three flying visits to Sri Lanka prior to the arrival of Vijaya. Did the *rākṣasas* as practitioners of *yātudhāna* carry echoes of shamanistic religious forms?

98. *Pariśiṣṭaparvan*, VIII. pp. lxxi, 415ff.
99. G. Buhler, 'New Jaina Inscriptions from Mathura', *Ep. Ind.*, I, Calcutta, 1892, pp. 371ff; ibid., I. pp. 393ff; ibid., II. pp. 195ff; V.A. Smith, *The Jaina Stupa and Other Antiquities of Mathura*, Varanasi, 1969, rpt.; V.S. Agrawala, 'Catalogue of the Mathura Museum, Jaina *tīrthaṅkaras* and Other Miscellaneous Figures', *Journal of the Uttar Pradesh Historical Society*, XXIII (1950), pp. 36ff.
100. K.D. Bajpai, 'Development of Jaina Art in Madhya Pradesh', *JIH*, LV (December 1977); U.P. Shah, *Jaina Art and Architecture*, vol. 1, p. 128; J.F. Fleet, op. cit., pp. 258ff; V.V. Mirashi, op. cit., pp. clxi–ii.
101. Mirashi, op. cit., pp. clvff.
102. However, the earliest use of an era which is identified later with the Cedi era comes from western India and its use in the Cedi country belongs to a later date. Mirashi, op. cit., viii ff.
103. The Bilhari Stone Inscription of Yuvarajadeva, Goharwa Plates of Karṇa, Banaras Plates of Karṇa, Mirashi, op. cit., pp. 210, 241.
104. B.C. Mazumdar, 'Mahada Plates of Yogeśvaradevavarman', *Ep. Ind.*, XII, no. 25, p. 218; 'Sonpur Plates of Kumara Someśvaradeva', *Ep. Ind.*, XII, no. 29, p. 237; 'Ratnapura Stone Inscription of Jajalladeva', *Ep. Ind.*, I, pp. 32ff.
105. Apart from the controversy of whether Vijaya came to Sri Lanka from Kaliṅga, ties between the two regions were formally mentioned in the sources stating that the Tooth Relic was sent to Sri Lanka from Kaliṅga in the early fourth century AD. This was followed by a series of matrimonial alliances from the tenth century onwards, when some of the most powerful kings of Polonnaruwa claimed Kaliṅgan ancestry. (S. Paranavitana, 'The Kalinga Dynasty of Ceylon', *Journal of the Greater India Society*, vol. III, no. 1, January 1936, pp. 57–64.) The twelfth-century Galpota Slab Inscription of Nissaṃkamalla (*Epigraphia Zeylonica*, II, no. 17, pp. 98ff), combines various claims to legitimacy on the part of this Kaliṅga prince who was called upon to succeed to the throne at Polonnaruwa, claims

which echo many facets of what has been discussed in this paper. He invokes Vijaya as being linked with the *Kaliṅga-cakravarti-kula*, the latter having the ability of travelling through the air (*ākāśa-cāri*) and belonging to the royal line of the Okkāka-rājā. Evidently by now the lineage lines had got crossed! Curiously, the capital from where he ruled, Polonnaruwa, is also referred to as Pulasti-pura. (I am grateful to Dr Sirima Kiribamune for drawing my attention to this inscription.) In the light of the above, could it perhaps be argued that the identification of Laṅkā with Sri Lanka dates to the period of these connections?

It is significant that there are a series of names applied to Sri Lanka which are directly and indirectly referred to in the *Dīpavaṃsa*. In the earliest times the names Oja, Vara and Maṇḍa are used (I.73). The name Sinhala derives from the lion ancestry of Vijaya and his original home (IX). Vijaya and his companions give the name of Tāmraparṇi to the island because of its copper coloured soil and this may have been the origin of the word Taprobane used by the Greeks. (IX.20–30; Pliny, *Hist. Nat.*, VI.24.1.) The *Dīpavaṃsa* also refers to it as Laṅkā, but the date of the text is *circa* fifth century AD so that the name Laṅkā appears to be late. Was the change in name in any way linked to connections with Kaliṅga?

106. *Aitareya Brāhmaṇa*, VIII.21; *Rāmāyaṇa*, VII.18.
107. *Mārkaṇḍeya Purāṇa*, 131.
108. Y. Mishra, *An Early History of Vaiśālī*, pp. 52ff.
109. Ibid., pp. 59ff.
110. Ibid., p. 79.
111. Pargiter, op. cit., p. 266.
112. *Viṣṇu Purāṇa*, IV.11.
113. Pargiter, op. cit., pp. 153ff.
114. Ibid., pp. 102–3.
115. Ibid., pp. 118–19.
116. To search for an archaeological correlation for the events of the Vālmīki *Rāmāyaṇa* is therefore almost a search for a chimera; at most it may be possible to correlate episodes. Conflicts between chiefships would relate to a period of the chalcolithic cultures just prior to the spread of the NBP. But urban centres and royal courts would be of a later date. The description of Ayodhyā in the late sections of the text would be of a later period.
117. The choice of Rāma as the hero of the Ikṣvākus also needs some explanation. Was there already a legend on the heroic exploits of Rāma which was elaborated upon in the epic? Strangely, the *Jātaka* literature does not project Rāma as an epic hero but this may have to do with its Buddhist context. The reign of Rāma seems to mark a terminal point in the history of Ayodhyā and a point of

change in the history of Kośala. Lava succeeds Rāma in Uttara Kośala but the capital is shifted to Srāvastī which then becomes the more important city. It has also been suggested that Rāma's reign marks the terminal point between the Tretā and Dvāpara *yugas* (Pargiter, op. cit., p. 177). It is not until the time of Praśenajit that one hears of Kośala playing a significant historical role again. Was the projection of Rāma as an epic hero entirely imaginary but influenced by the feats of Rāma Jāmadagnya, Sagara and other earlier heroes?

118. More recent claimants to Haihaya descent in the Vindhyan area are the Gonds of Garha-Mandla (C. von Fuhrer Haimendorf, *The Raj Gonds of Adilabad*, London, 1948, pp. 1ff.) A sixteenth-century Gond king also claimed to be of the Paulastyavaṃśa. (J.C. Ghosh, 'Ravana's Lanka Located in Central India', *IHQ*, V, no. 2, June 1928, pp. 255–6.) The parallels between Gond society a nd the descriptions of the Rākṣasas in the Vālmīki *Rāmāyana* have been suggested by various scholars, e.g., G. Ramadas, 'Ravana and his Tribes', *IHQ*, V, no. 2 (June 1929), pp. 281–98; *IHQ*, VI (1930), pp. 284ff.

# 31

# Death and the Hero*

Scattered across the Indian subcontinent are large numbers of memorial stones dedicated to men who have died in an act of heroism such as defending a village against raiders by land or by sea, or defending cattle against cattle-lifters, or who have died on the battle-field. Such stones have come to be called hero-stones and have quite recently attracted the attention of historians, archaeologists and anthropologists. Associated with them are the *satī*-stones, memorials commemorating the wives who have immolated themselves either on the funeral pyres of their husbands or on hearing of the death of their husbands in battle. Both these categories of memorial are in origin associated with the cult of the hero and date back to times when society was suffused with the ethics of the heroic age.

These stones are of more than archaeological interest since the concept underlying the monument not only relates to the changing perception of the death of a hero, but also indicates an important variant of what is generally described as 'the Indian' view of death and the after-life. The latter derives from the high culture of brahmanical texts and practice, whereas the cult of the hero-stone is clearly a substratum cult, but with a widely distributed following. That historians and archaeologists have until recently tended to ignore this cult may also be partially explained by its being culturally a substratum cult and by the fact that it contradicts the neat generalisations culled from the classical Sanskrit texts.

The location of the hero-stones is neither geographically uniform nor arbitrary. They are found in larger numbers in western India (Rajasthan, Gujerat and Maharashtra), central India (Madhya Pradesh and the southern edges of the Ganga valley) and in south India (Andhra Pradesh, Karnataka, Kerala and Tamil Nadu). Northern and eastern India generally register fewer examples. Topographically and ecologically there is a frequency of such

* S.C. Humphreys and Helen King (eds.), *Mortality and Immortality: The Anthropology and Archaeology of Death*, London 1981, 293–316.

memorials in upland areas, in the vicinity of passes across hills, and in areas regarded traditionally as frontier zones which often included primarily pastoral regions, the outskirts of forests and the edges of what have come to be called the 'tribal areas of central India'. Hero-stones are relatively infrequent in the large agricultural tracts of the Indus and Ganga valleys and in the agriculturally rich delta areas of the peninsula.

The origin of the hero-stones remains obscure. They may possibly derive from the menhirs of the megalithic cultures in India of the first millennium BC (Srinivasan 1946; Sontheimer 1976). Their geographical distribution in the Indian peninsula seems to coincide with that of megalithic settlements, but the latter extend further into other areas as well. India is a country of startling cultural survivals: the single menhir of stone or wood is still erected as a memorial (not necessarily over a grave) among the Marias of central India and the Khasis of the north-eastern hills. Another megalithic association is suggested by the occurrence of hero-stones in groups, rather like a graveyard, on the edges of settlements. However, the single stone can be located anywhere. The megalithic necropolis would suggest burials linked perhaps through kinship and possibly associated further by common claims to clan rights and land ownership.

The form of the hero-stone changed through time and the change was related to the status of the hero as well as to the action performed by him. The simplest stone was a flat slab on which was depicted the hero armed with a bow and arrow or a sword. The hero of higher status rode a horse and the trappings of the horse indicate status. The association of cattle or a wild animal such as a tiger would point to the hero dying in a cattle raid or mauled by a tiger. Some stones also depict one or two objects which it is thought had a role in religious ritual, and on occasion a brief inscription is added containing the minimum information on the hero. Such simple stones have been dated to the mid-first millennium AD and continue into later centuries.

Towards the end of the first millennium AD the style of the hero-stone in many areas changed and became far more elaborate. The stone could now be either a slab, as before, or else a square column up to two metres in height with panels sculptured on all four sides. The shape of the stone came to resemble a small shrine with a decorative design on the top (Mate and Gokhale 1971;

Sontheimer 1976). The three or more sculptured panels had a recognisable theme. The sun and the moon were sculpted at the top signifying the eternal character of the memorial and below that the act in which the hero died. Inscriptions of this period recording grants of land often state that the grant would last 'as long as the moon and the sun endure', a phrase which signified that the grant could not be revoked. The symbolism would also relate to timelessness, a condition which the hero, when deified, would share with the gods. The highest panel carried the symbols of the religious sect to which the hero belonged: thus the *lingam* and the *yoni*, indicating phallic worship, were the symbols of a Śaivite sect to which sometimes the bull vehicle of Śiva was added; the standing or seated figure of Mahāvīra would indicate a Jaina devotee. The hero might even be shown worshipping at the shrine. The second panel depicted the veneration of the hero, or else the hero being carried in a palanquin by celestial maidens (*apsarās*), presumably towards heaven. The lower panels provide the narrative of the incident. The hero is shown fighting either on foot or on horseback duly armed with a bow and arrow or a sword, spear and shield. He is frequently surrounded by enemies, some of whom he has killed. In other cases the panels show stampeding cattle. In the coastal areas along the west coast sea battles with ships are more frequent. Except in rare cases of lengthy eulogies, where inscriptions occur on such stones they provide a minimum of information giving the name of the hero, perhaps mentioning the king of the region and a brief word of praise for the action.

The names in the earlier inscriptions suggest persons of lesser status, soldiers and guardians of the village, who died fighting against cattle-lifters, marauders or invading armies on the rampage in the countryside (Vanamamalai 1975). Many of the earlier stones from Tamil Nadu come from North Arcot District which is known to have been at that time an area of livestock breeding where cattle-raiding would be one method of increasing wealth. The change in the style of the hero-stone seems to reflect a change in the status of the hero being memorialised. The elaborate stones commemorated heroes who claimed to belong to the upper caste groups, often claiming *kṣatriya* status — it being the function of the *kṣatriya* in the caste hierarchy to protect the other sections of the society. The indication of the hero's religious sect may have been due to the influence of the *bhakti* (devotional religion) sects which were popular at this time. The hero travelling to heaven and being thus rewarded, was an essential element in the cult of the hero from early times.

The earliest descriptions of hero-stones in literary sources come from the Tamil *Śaṅgam* literature, generally ascribed to the period between 300 BC and AD 200 but possibly including interpolations of a later period. The *vīra-kal* or *Vīra-k-kal* is, literally, hero-stone, and is also referred to as *naḍukal*, the planted stone (Subrahmanian 1966b). The stone, it is stated, commemorates a hero who has been killed in battle. The disembodied soul is regarded as powerful and could use its power for good or ill. It had a tendency to return to its kinsfolk unless it was appeased with rituals and the setting up of a stone, and these in turn were the means by which the power of the soul was appropriated by the kinsfolk. The cutting of a specially selected stone, which was believed to embody the soul of the hero, was begun on an auspicious day (Vanamamalai 1975). When cut it was erected under a shady tree, bathed and purified and then inscribed. It now became an object of worship and the hero was immortalised both in the stone and in the songs and ballads composed about him. The stone was decorated with flowers and peacock feathers. The hero's spear and shield were placed close to it and the whole enclosed in a canopy of cloth. At regular intervals food specially cooked for the purpose was offered at the stone. Those going into battle sought the blessings of the hero by worshipping at the stone.

The symbolism of the objects associated with the ritual suggests various other links. The spear associated with the hero is also the symbol of the god Murugan whose priests carried a spear (Subrahmanian 1966a). Murugan as Kārtikeya was worshipped as the god of war who killed the *asuras* (demons), was the lover and abductor of Valli and was the god of the hill-top.[1] His vehicle was the peacock which was sometimes depicted on his banner, as was the cock. There are two major legends regarding his origin. The *Mahābhārata* (III.213ff) narrates that the gods required a hero to lead them in the war against the demon Taraka and for this purpose Skanda was born as the son of the great god Śiva and his wife Pārvatī (Bhattacharya 1970). Skanda was also known by the names of Kumāra, Mahāsena and Kārtikeya. His vehicle was the peacock. Another version of the story links his birth to those who are associated with the worship of the ancestors. It is said that Agni, the god of fire, dropped his seed on the banks of the Ganga and the six sisters known as the Kṛittikas nurtured it and Kārtikeya was born with six heads. The Kṛittikas are connected with fertility and the month of Kārttika is both the time of the harvest and the time of worshipping ancestors with the lighting of lamps. The ritual period of the *śrāddha*, when ceremonies are performed for the ancestors and for those recently dead, and specially prepared food is fed to selected *brāhmaṇas*, precedes the month of Kārttika. Rituals related to the worship of ancestors and the feeding of *brāhmaṇas* at the time of the *śrāddha* would also involve a display of wealth and of redistributive activities, this being one of the auspicious occasions for making gifts to worthy *brāhmaṇas*, who in turn ensured the well-being of departed souls.

Whereas in south India the references to hero-stones in literary sources seem to be earlier than their archaeological counterparts, in other areas of the country the archaeological finds predate the references in literature which are generally fairly late. Hero-stones in western Rajasthan referred to as *kīrti-stambha* — literally, pillars of fame — go back to the seventh century AD but a larger number are of the eleventh century and later (Agrawala 1963). Many depict cattle raids and cleverly use a well-known legend to symbolise the protection of cattle.[2]

The hero-stones from Saurashtra and other parts of Gujerat are called *pāliya*, the etymology of the word being perhaps connected with *pāla*, the protector or guardian. The *pāliya-bhumi*, the place where several hero-stones are placed together, is often on the outskirts of the village and preferably on the bank of a river (Fischer and Shah 1970). Those linked to the local ruling family may have their stones in the courtyard of the temple. The sculptured side generally faces east. The stones are worshipped annually at the time of Dipāvali, the festival when lamps are lit and which marks the autumn harvest and the start of the winter, which falls in the month of Kārttika. Those who claim descent from the hero also worship the stone on other occasions such as the period of the *śrāddha* and at the time of a marriage in the family. In the ritual connected with the setting up of a hero-stone, peacock feathers are important but the spear is absent.

Associated with the hero-stone are other memorial stones which may be regarded as complementary in some cases and subsidiary in others. Memorials to wives who have immolated themselves on the death of their husbands or have become *satīs* (virtuous ones) are complementary to the hero-stone and sometimes the two memorials are combined in one. Occasionally in one of the panels of the hero-stone, there is a representation of both husband and wife on the funeral pyre (Sontheimer 1976). However, the *satī*-stone is generally an independent memorial.

*Śaṅgam* literature refers to *satī* as the condition of literally falling into flames; it is associated generally with the wife of the warrior, although on occasion other women are also said to have undergone the ritual of self-immolation (Subrahmanian 1966b). The memorial is referred to as the *sati-kal* (*satī*-stone) or the *mā-sati-k-kal* and appears to have been the counterpart of the *vīra-k-kal* of the hero or the chief. The explanation for both kinds of memorials is that they symbolise loyalty to a person, the hero to his chief and the wife to her husband, and the preservation of honour. That it was also considered a possible ritual for the wife of the dead hero is apparent from a different source, the epic *Mahābhārata* where the wives of some of the heroes are said to have immolated themselves on the death of their husbands (Kane 1941: 623ff). A later source refers to all the widows of the Yādava clansmen becoming *satīs*. Texts of the second millennium AD debated whether such an act should be regarded as suicide, and therefore condemned, or as an act of merit, and therefore recommended.

The *satī*-stone depicted the right arm of a woman, bent at the elbow at a right angle with an open hand whose palm faced out. The arm could be shown tied to a post or free. The forearm is covered with bangles and occasionally a lime is held in the hand. The sun and the moon are depicted on either side and signify eternity as in the case of the hero-stone. Sometimes an auspicious symbol such as the *svāstika* is also added. A brief inscription may mention the date and the names of the woman and of her husband. The right arm indicates purity and the condition of *satī*. It has also been suggested that it represents one of the high castes since in some rare cases the left arm replaces the right (Sontheimer 1976). The post probably does not point to the woman having been tied to the post before immolation because the ritual demanded that she sit on the pyre with her dead husband's head in her lap. The post may well signify the act of sacrifice since in the Vedic sacrificial ritual the sacrificial offering was tied to the post (*yūpa*). The open hand and the lime symbolise the absence of evil and tradition has it that they both scare away the demons. A woman normally has to break her bangles on the death of her husband and a widow is recognised by this. The prominence given to the bangles in the *satī*-stone emphasises that the *satī* is not to be regarded as a widow since she remains a wife to her husband, having following him in death. *Satī*-stones were also frequently worshipped, the *satī* being regarded as a deity. She was required to bless the assembly before stepping onto the funeral pyre and her curse was greatly feared. In some cases *satī*-stones have come to be the centre for the sanctum of large temples such as the one of Jhunjhunu in Rajasthan.

As in the case of the hero-stones, the frequency of *satī*-stones also dates to the period after the mid-first millennium AD. Among the earliest epigraphical references to a *satī* is that to the wife of a chief, Goparāja, who died in battle in the early sixth century AD (Fleet 1970). The inscription appears on what seems to be an elaborate hero-stone memorial in the form of a *lingam* (phallus) indicating Śaiva associations. *Satī*-stones increase in number towards the end of the millennium. The largest archaeological finds date to more recent centuries. Where castes are mentioned, the majority claim *kṣatriya* status, and they therefore belong to the landowning castes who linked themselves to the best known lineages of earlier times.

Subsidiary memorials, not unrelated to the hero-stone, are those which are meant to appease the spirit of the dead. The setting up of these stones or wooden memorials follows a pattern similar to that of the hero-stones.[3] The significance of these memorials for this discussion lies in the method of their being made and erected for much the same ritual was probably carried out for the hero-stone and the *satī*-stone. The ritual is performed by the *bhagat* or local cult priest and not by a *brāhmaṇa*, thus emphasising the substratum nature of the cult. The role of the *bhagat* is important since it links the action to the Little Tradition. None of the texts refer to the *brāhmaṇa* performing the ritual for erecting the hero-stone or the *satī*-stone. Doubtless the more elaborate rituals of the high caste *kṣatriya* immortalised in a hero-stone may well have been performed by *brāhmaṇas* but this may not have applied to the more primitive hero-stone.[4]

Echoes of the hero-stone ritual can also be observed in the worship of cult deities such as Iyenar (Whitehead 1921). As the guardian of the village, Iyenar rides a horse and is sometimes represented only by a clay image of a horse, but is invariably surrounded by clay images of the heroes who assist him. The ensemble is placed on the outskirts of a village under a large tree. Offerings of food are made by the villagers to the heroes, the food being eventually eaten by the cult priest who is usually not a *brāhmaṇa*. Sheep, goats and fowls are also offered and after the sacrifice the priest keeps the head whilst the body is taken by the worshipper. At the annual festival the image is washed in a liquid paste made from a number of ingredients and the figure draped in red cloth. The ritual at this time is in imitation of the worship of images in the temples dedicated to various Hindu deities more familiar to the upper castes.

The differentiation between the hero-stone and the memorial to the spirit of a dead man has its counterpart in the death rituals of what may be called the Hinduism of the higher castes. The early texts on domestic rituals mention two categories of rituals for the dead (Ap. D.S. II.7.16.1–3; Apte 1954). The lesser category relates to the *pretas*, those recently dead whose spirits may still be hovering among the living and who have to be appeased and set to rest by a series of ceremonies. The more important rituals are dedicated to the *pitṛs*, the ancestors in the patrilineage for whom rites are performed, particularly during the annual calendrical period of the *śrāddha* when food is offered to the ancestors to nourish them and when *brāhmaṇas* are fed. Whereas the first category of ritual grows out of a fear of the *preta* and the need to propitiate him and convert him into a friendly ancestor, the second is essentially born out of the need to nurture the souls of the ancestors and to maintain a tradition of remembrance. It is assumed that the ancestors are living in heaven, for the dead are nourished in heaven by the food given at the *śrāddha*. Such a concept would seem to conflict with that of a cycle of rebirth and reincarnation. Some texts seek to explain this contradiction by arguing that the food reaches the ancestor whether he be identified with the gods or reborn in some other form. Such rituals seem to reflect an early and continuing belief in heaven and hell which is interwoven into the concept of reincarnation.

Implicit in the notion of the hero-stone is also the interweaving of various customs regarding the disposal of the dead. Both the Vedic texts and the *Śaṅgam* literature assume the coexistence of a variety of methods. The dead can be cremated, buried, cast away or exposed. Gradually cremation became the norm in the high culture. The *asuras*, opposed to the practices of the *āryas* in many instances, were known to bury their dead in stone structures beneath the earth (*Ṛgveda* X.18; *Atharvaveda* XVII.2.34; *Śatapatha Brāhmaṇa* XIII.8.1–4). This may be a reference to megalithic burials in stone cists. The range suggests the continuance of earlier forms of burial together with cremation. The memorials, to the extent that they symbolise a grave, are suggestive of the notion of burial even when the actual disposal may have been cremation.

The firm faith in the belief that the hero lived in heaven after he died suggests the popularity of an alternative to the belief in reincarnation. This is particularly striking in the centuries AD when the doctrine of reincarnation was widely accepted. Living in heaven was in a sense the termination of a cycle of lives, although this is not stated. Heaven was essential in any case if the hero was to be deified, which seems to have been a recognised tradition. The grammarian Pāṇini, composing his grammar in the fifth century BC, states that distinguished *kṣatriya* heroes become the objects of religious devotion (IV.3.99). Deification is perhaps most evident in the concept of the *pañca-vīras* or five heroes of the Vṛṣṇis, a sub-clan of the Yādavas.[5] The pre-eminent family among the Vṛṣṇis was that of Vāsudeva, and three generations of his descendants — sons, grandson and great-grandson — are deified as the five Vṛṣṇi heroes. Among them one, Kṛṣṇa Vāsudeva, was to be identified as the *avatāra* or incarnation of the god Viṣṇu. Tradition maintains that Kṛṣṇa Vāsudeva has a pastoral association, his early life being spent among the cattle keepers of Mathura. It was also around the cult of the *pañca-vīras* and Kṛṣṇa Vāsudeva that there developed the *bhakti* movement of devotional religion which has come to be called Bhāgvatism. There appears to be a curious intertwining of the cult of the hero with pastoralism and with the emergence of some devotional sects.

The transformation of a hero-stone into a deity can be seen in the cult of Viṭhobā at Paṇḍharpur (in Maharashtra), in the suggestion that the image now worshipped was in origin a hero-stone and the hero was gradually changed into a deity and given a new iconography, in keeping with his incorporation into the cult of Kṛṣṇa Vāsudeva (Deleury 1960; Tulpule 1977–8). Paṇḍharpur was located in the pastoral zone of the western Deccan and the pastoral appeal of the Kṛṣṇa cult would have attracted to it the local people. The evolution of the hero-cult, with strong pastoral overtones, into a cult of devotional religion occurred in this area as well, perhaps through the impact of the migration of pastoralists and of religious ideas. By the twelfth century Paṇḍharpur became the centre of the *bhakti* or devotional cult in which devotion was directed to Kṛṣṇa as the cult deity and he was said to have taken the form of Viṭhobā. This deity and the territory in which he was worshipped became crucial in the self-perception of the Marathas when they set up a state in the seventeenth century. The original hero of the hero-stone had undergone a transformation and was now in a world far removed from that of the heroes.

The world of the heroes was steeped in the notion of status by birth, this status being reinforced through the heroic act (*vīrya*) which brought the hero fame (*kīrti*, *yaśa*) (Kailasapathy 1968: 229ff). In a society given to competitiveness, the heroic act was also an act of individual self-assertion and the hero-stone captured the moment of self-assertion for eternity. For the hero's wife to become a *satī* would be in keeping with the values of the heroic cult where the woman was also required to demonstrate an almost aggressive self-assertion through a heroic act, thereby ensuring herself both fame and deification. Together with the stone the ballads and the epics were the means of conveying the renown to later generations. The hero-stone commemorated in form what the epic commemorated in words.

That this changed somewhat in later centuries is suggested by the function of the hero-stone and the *satī*-stone in the second millennium AD. The heroic act became an avenue to status and status in itself required the association with a heroic act. Those of high status were eulogised through hero-stones until finally the mere fact of belonging to a ruling family entitled one to a hero-stone, as for example in the *chhatris* of some Rajput royal families. In the same way the act of self-immolation was no longer a voluntary act of heroic dimensions but was on occasion the sordid detail of a royal funeral or, as some have suspected, the ritual removal of a legitimate heir to an inheritance.

The hero-stone in the earlier periods was the focus of gatherings of kinsmen and a form of ancestor worship, since it was generally the patrilineages which maintained the worship of the stone. This helped to strengthen lineage ties as well as the historical memory of the village and the locality. The rituals emphasised the aggregation of the hero to the community rather than his separation, despite his deification. The memorials provided a different type of continuity from the *śrāddha* ceremonies: it was a political and social continuity, relating to territory and descent groups. In the folk culture the hero-stone replaced the historical text and the tending of the hero-stone was almost synonymous with recording the past. The frequency of hero-stones is greater in areas where the oral tradition was the custodian of history. The incidental echoes of the *śrāddha* rituals would have served to foster communication between the royal and the rural, for the hero-stone represented a substratum cult. Those lacking a sufficiently high status perhaps used the hero as an ancestor and, latching on to his lineage, may well have used this to claim *kṣatriya* status. The hero entered the collective memory and became an ideal. The symbols associated with him raise him, as it were, above the context of family, time and place.

The hero-stone cult had an extensive distribution in India; nevertheless, it manifests local styles and has distinct regional forms. Yet in substance it is similar and much of the symbolism seems to derive from the same sources. Did the cult originate in the widely diffused Yādava clans who, as cattle-herders and early agriculturalists in many regions, carried it with them in their extensive migrations and who continued with the cult even when some of their lineages rose to the status of dynasties (Thapar 1978: 240ff)? Or did it have its origins in a social context which venerated its heroes in a near-identical fashion in many parts of the subcontinent? The association with Kārttikeya and later the assimilation of the Kṛṣṇa Vāsudeva cult were common features over a wide geographical area. Admittedly both can easily be explained since the first is the deity of war, so essential to a hero cult, and the other, being the pastoral god *par excellence*, would be the natural deity in cattle-keeping areas. The elaboration of the cult in its second and later phase does suggest the rise in status of groups lower in the social scale as well as the mingling of local cults with those of what might be called the classical culture.

An impressionistic assessment of the geographical distribution of these memorials (in the absence of careful mapping) suggests that they tend to be concentrated in what have acted as 'frontier zones' at some stage — the peripheral areas of kingdoms and the intersection of ecological zones, particularly where pastoralism separated areas of intensive cultivation or lay close to forested areas. Frontier zones were often maintained as buffer regions where political security was transient and where royal armies did not necessarily guarantee protection to the local inhabitants. They would therefore inevitably have recourse to their own arrangements for protection, in which the village hero or the local chief played a major role. If the 'hero' happened to be a member of the local elite his family may well have emulated the life-style of the royal court and the hero would stake his claim to status by protecting the villagers. In the absence of royal troops this would give considerable credibility to the hero, particularly when the protection may have necessitated defending the village from the pillage of royal armies campaigning in the vicinity. This would suggest a differentiation of military functions in a decentralised political system. The core areas of powerful kingdoms would have had less use for what they would have regarded as upstart heroes. The hero cult therefore also acts as a marker separating those societies in which the significance of the clan and the heroic ideal remain strong from those in which such things are regarded as memories of the past. Peasant protest arising from an inability to pay revenue demands often took the form not of revolts but of migrations. Such peasant groups would tend to settle in the frontier zones in an effort to bring fresh land under cultivation and this would bring them into conflict with the existing population. Alternatively, protesting peasant groups if they failed to find fresh land would take to brigandage, and raiding a village was a relatively easy means of acquiring a minimum livelihood.

The period from the late first millennium AD was characterised by shifting political boundaries in which small states were frequently founded, survived for brief periods and then were either incorporated into a larger state or were readjusted in new alliances. This brought frontier zones into importance either in their earlier role as buffers or alternatively as areas to be settled and developed. The western Deccan around Paṇḍharpur was a clear example of such an area. The gradual conversion of the hero-stone into Viṭhobā and its links with the Kṛṣṇa cult not only demonstrates the process of the mutual assimilation of royal cults and rituals with those of lesser social status, but also marks the acculturation of the frontier zone. Not surprisingly such cults play a significant role in state formation.

But above all the hero-stone gave a different meaning to death. Death is in any case a change in status and the deification of the hero was a distinctive change. That it was not an ordinary death is reflected in the fact that although the death rites may have been restricted to the polluting space of the cremation ground, the event was commemorated in the precincts of the temple or in an area which acquired sanctity because of the presence of the hero-stone. The setting up of the hero-stone echoes the burial practices of earlier times and yet it does not mark the place of relics from the cremation. To this extent it differs from the tradition of building tumuli to the dead in which their relics were enshrined as in some of the *stūpas* and *caityas* adopted in Buddhist ritual.

The heroic act ensured the hero an abode in heaven. The promise of heaven, explicit in the early hero-stones, continued in the later phase as well. Not only did the hero not have to suffer the cycle of rebirth but his reward was immediate in his being taken to heaven. In the absence of an eschatology requiring a judgment day, this was a condition of eternal, timeless bliss. But the ultimate appeal transcended heaven and lay in the fact of deification. In a culture where the bestowal of divinity on animate and inanimate entities is common, deification was in itself perhaps not startling, but that it meant a different level of status for the hero was in effect the prize which made the heroic action worthwhile and placed a premium on a hero's death.

## Bibliography

Agrawala, R.C., 1963, 'Pascami Rājasthan ke kuch Prārambika Smṛiti Stambha', *Varadā*, April 1963, 68ff.

Ap.D.S. = *Āpastamba Dharma Sūtra*, 'The Sacred Books of the East' (M. Müller, ed.), vol. 2, translated by G. Bühler (1879), Clarendon Press, Oxford.

Apte, V.M., 1954, *Social and Religious Life in the Grihya Sutras*, Popular Book Depot, Bombay.

*Atharvaveda–Saṃhitā*, translated by W.D. Whitney, 1971, Motilal Banarsidass, Delhi.

Bhattacharya, S., 1970, *The Indian Theogony*, Cambridge University Press, Cambridge.

Deleury, G.A., 1960, *The Cult of Viṭhobā*, Deccan College, Poona.

*Epigraphia Indica*, 1892, Burgess, J. and E. Hultzch (eds), Archaeological Survey of India, Departments of State and Public Institutions, Calcutta.

Fischer, E. and H. Shah, 1970, *Rural Craftsmen and Their Work*, National Institute of Design, Ahmedabad.

1. Hero-stone from Molcarnem, *c.* 12th century.
*Courtesy:* ASI Museum, Old Goa.

2. Hero-stone from Gatag-Batgeri (Dharwar Distt). *Courtesy:* Director IIAH, Karnataka University, Dharwar.

3. Hero-stone from Holal (Bellary Distt), Karnataka. *Courtesy:* Director IIAH, Karnataka University, Dharwar.

4. Hero-stone from Damkhed (Gujarat), *c.* 12th century.

5. A cluster of hero-stones at Bedsa (Maharashtra).

6. Hero being taken to heaven by *apsaras* from Kadabogere (Bellary Distt), Karnataka. *Courtesy:* Director IIAH, Karnataka University, Dharwar.

7. Sati-stone from North Kerala.

Fischer, E. and H. Shah, 1973, *Vetra ne Khambha — Memorials for the Dead*, Gujarat Vidyapeeth, Ahmedabad.

Fleet, J.F. (ed.), 1970, *Corpus Inscriptionum Indicarum*, vol. III, Indological Book House, Varanasi.

Kailasapathy, K., 1968, *Tamil Heroic Poetry*, Clarendon Press, Oxford.

Kane, P.V., 1941, *History of Dharmaśāstra*', vol. II, part 1, Bhandarkar Oriental Research Institute, Poona.

Mate, M.S. and S. Gokhale, 1971, 'Aihole: An Interpretation', in *Studies in Indian History and Culture* (S. Ritti and B.R. Gopal, eds), Karnatak University, Dharwar, pp. 501–4.

*ṚgVeda*, translated by R.T.H. Griffith (1963, reprint), Chowkhamba Sanskrit Series, Varanasi.

*Śatapatha Brāhmaṇa*, 'The Sacred Books of the East' (M. Müller, ed.), vol. 12, translated by J. Eggerling, 1882, Clarendon Press, Oxford.

Sivathamby, K., 1974, 'Early South Indian Society and Economy: the Tinai Concept', *Social Scientist*, 29 (vol. 3, no. 5), 20–37.

Sontheimer, G.D., 1976, 'Some Memorial Monuments of Western India', in *German Scholars on India* (Cultural Department of the Embassy of the Federal Republic of Germany, ed.), vol. II, pp. 264ff, Nachiketa Publications, Bombay.

Srinivasan, K., 1946, 'The Megalithic Burials and Urnfields of South India', *Ancient India*, 2, 9–16.

Subrahmanian, N., 1966a, *Pre-Pallavan Tamil Index*, University of Madras, Madras.

—— 1966b, *Śaṅgam Polity*, Asia Publishing House, Madras.

Thapar, R., 1978, 'Puranic Lineages and Archaeological Cultures', in Thapar, *Ancient Indian Social History: Some Interpretations*, pp. 240–67, Orient Longman, New Delhi.

—— 1979, 'The Historian and the Epic', *Annals of the Bhandarkar Oriental Research Institute*, 60, 199–213. See chapter 28 in this volume.

Tulpule, S.G., 1977–8, 'The Origin of Viṭṭhala: A New Interpretation', *Annals of the Bhandarkar Oriental Research Institute*, 58–9, 1009–15.

Vanamamalai, N., 1975, 'Hero-stone Worship in Ancient South India', *Social Scientist*, 34 (vol. 3, no. 10), 40–6.

Whitehead, H., 1921, *The Village Gods of South India* (2nd edn), Association Press and Oxford University Press, Calcutta.

## Notes and References

1. In the *tinai* concept, as evident from *Śaṅgam* literature, the hill region is associated with the Kuriñci flower which in turn was the symbol

of Murugan. It is also connected with love in the Akam part of the literature and with cattle raiding in the Puram sections. There is therefore an interlinking of many ideas (K. Sivathamby, 1974).

2. Among the legends related of the cowherd god Kṛṣṇa Gopāla set in the region of Mathura (on the Yamuna south of Delhi) there is one which states that the power of Kṛṣna was challenged by the god Indra who poured down torrents of rain to flood the land and terrorise both men and cattle. Krsna, undaunted, lifted the mountain Govardhana on his finger and the cattle took shelter beneath it and survived the wrath of Indra. The use of this imagery of cattle sheltering beneath a mountain is frequent in these hero-stones where it replaces the depiction of the hero protecting cattle and such stones are therefore called *Govardhana-kīrti-stambha*.

3. The memorial is dedicated to one who has died suddenly or violently and whose spirit is thought to haunt and possibly harass his living kinsmen. The ritual is performed by the *bhagat*, the priest of the local cult, who is not a *brāhmaṇa*. In a version of the ritual prevalent in Gujerat the memorial is cut from a log of teak wood taken after due libations to the tree in the forest and in the presence of family members accompanied by musicians. The assembly travels to the forest in a cart. The carving of the log takes a few days and although women are not permitted on the premises, others can watch the process and feed at the expense of the family whilst doing so. A small stone is taken from the property of the deceased and is said to represent the soul of the person who has died. This is buried either on the property of the deceased or along a road leading to his village. The memorial is placed on the ground above the stone, a ceremony which leads to much festivity. The ritual performed by the *bhagat* requires him to go into a trance and request the spirit of the deceased not to haunt and harass the living. A chicken is beheaded and its blood mixed with alcohol, some of which is sprinkled on the memorial and the remainder drunk by the *bhagat*. The feathers of the chicken are placed on the memorial and its flesh and the alcohol are given to those present. The memorial has a flat surface and is generally of wood. Since stone is expensive, stone memorials are a sign of status. The top is shaped and the symbols of the sun and the moon are shown, with scenes depicted beneath them in horizontal panels. There is usually a bird, generally a peacock or a parrot, a man or a rider with an attendant, a cartful of musicians perhaps assisting in the ritual of cutting the log, and possibly some indication of the situation in which death has occurred, as for example the depiction of a snake or a crocodile. The memorial becomes the permanent resting place of the spirit of the deceased and is named after him. It is worshipped annually by the entire family (Fischer and Shah, 1973).

4. An interesting dichotomy is observed in some cases. In the village of Bedsa (near Poona in Maharashtra) a clear distinction is maintained between the hero-stone depicting a single hero crudely cut in stone worshipped by the Mahar untouchable community with goat sacrifices and alcohol being part of the ritual conducted by Mahar priests, and the elaborately sculpted square columns of the heroes of high status which stand in a row beside the Śiva temple and are worshipped with offerings of coconut and *sindura* (vermilion powder) by the *brāhmaṇas* of the village. The former is described as the guardian of the village by the Mahars and even if it was once a hero-stone it is now serving the function of a cult deity as well. The high status heroes are remembered more precisely as persons who repeatedly defended the village from invaders.
5. The term *pañca-vīra* is reminiscent of the Tamil term *aimperumvelir*, also meaning the five great heroes or chiefs and who are also said to be of the Yādava clan (Subrahmanian, 1966a: 110). The five heroes were worshipped as a group and by the early centuries AD images of the five are also referred to (The Mora Inscription, 'Epigraphia Indica', XXIV: 194; the Ghosundi inscription, ibid., XXII: 204). For the persistence of the pattern of five heroes, see Thapar (1979).

# 32

# As Long as the Moon and the Sun Endure*

I would like in this brief paper to draw on two interests of Gunther Sontheimer. One is his important work on hero-stones.[1] I would also like to bring into the discussion a further aspect of the symbolism of the sun and the moon. The depiction of the sun and the moon is one almost invariable occurrence on hero-stones and *satī*-stones. This can perhaps be linked to Sontheimer's analysis of Hinduism as consisting of five components: the work and teaching of the *brāhmaṇas*, the sectarian movements based on renunciation and asceticism, the tribal, the folk religions where the icon is treated like a living person and the king/hero is identified with a deity, and *bhakti*.[2] The veneration for the hero-stone is rooted in tribal and folk religion but it also has some connections with the other components. The hero-stone is the memory of a living person encapsulated in a *mūrti*. The inter-face of these components seems to be reflected in the cult of the hero-stone, where the symbols set off associations.

The distribution of hero-stones has its own interest and needs perhaps to be plotted with reference to locations, numbers and chronology. This would involve a working out of typologies from the simple depictions of standing figures to those with complex panels in low relief, incorporating among other things, the narrative of the event. This may indicate co-relations between typologies and locations, concentrations in particular ecologies or in the frontier zones of states. Impressionistically, there appear to be fewer hero-stones in agriculturally fertile areas, but this would have to be corroborated. It may also provide evidence as to whether the hero-stones are social markers and relate to clan, status and/ or

* Sontheimer Memorial Seminar, Pune 1993

particular occupations. Are territorial claims and the defence of these associated with the dominant caste in a locality? Are hero-stones making a statement about status? Where religious sectarian identities are indicated, the plotting of these would also provide a different kind of evidence. And finally, do hero-stones refer to groups whose history is not written since they are not part of the royal court of kingdoms and where the oral traditions preserve memories of heroes. It is not my intention to attempt to answer these questions, but the small facet which I propose to discuss touches on many of these questions.

Prior to the setting up of the hero-stone, the hero perhaps represents the aspirations of the local community vis-à-vis the state. Since many of the memorials commemorate cattle-raids one needs to ask, who is raiding cattle? Are there predators — human and animal — or are some of these cattle raids organised by the state wishing to bring pastoralist groups to heel?[3] Predators can be forest peoples, the *āṭavikas*, trying to prevent the encroachment of graziers into the forest lands, or they can be impoverished peasants. They are unlikely to have been hostile pastoralists unless the purpose of the raid was to increase the herd.[4] The hero-stone where it gives expression to the power of the hero could well be a reflection of the stand taken by the local community towards the state, where either the state is the aggressor or as more probable, the state is seen as incapable of defending the local community.

In the setting up of a hero-stone the memorial gives a distinctive status to the hero. Does the memorial restore the power of the hero which had been snatched away in death or does it also restore power to the community of the hero? The appeasing of the spirit of the hero is in part a restoration of power.[5] The stone is also seen as the embodiment of the body of the hero.[6] As one who has been venerated almost to the point of being divinised, the hero could become the mediator between humans and gods, for the memorial not only represents the deity but also evokes the deity. The worship of the stone is therefore the worship of the hero but at a further remove, also the worship of the deity of the hero. The sequence can become merged as in the case of the worship of Biroba as a hero at Vasi near Kolhapur and in Karnataka.[7]

Where the hero is deified, this is related to the manner of his death. It can be either a voluntary death, an act of extreme devotion, frequent among women who become *satīs* and less so among men, or it can be the requirement of a contract with or a vow to, the deity. More commonly however, the death so commemorated results from defence against a raid or in a battle. The hero-stone therefore encapsulates funeral rites. The dead hero is in a sense returned to the community and to his ancestors. If it is treated also as a cult of the ancestors there is a re-ordering of social relationships. The ancestors require the maintenance of a genealogy. Possibly there may also be an emphasis on the need to keep the rites of the *śrāddha*. There is in other kinds of death a dichotomy between body and soul since the soul of the hero goes out of the world of the living and enters another world. But the hero's death seems not to endorse this dichotomy, for he is taken to heaven as himself and not a disembodied soul. In heaven life is timeless. There is no eschatology after the hero has entered heaven and the latter is known by various nomenclatures: Brahmaloka, Sūryaloka, Indraloka, Kailāśa, and so on.

Since it is the heroic death which permits of a distinctive eschatology and on occasion the divinisation of the hero, it is compared to other activities which have a religious bearing and are said to be conducive to the attainment of heaven or of release from rebirth, such as the sacrificial ritual and asceticism. The metaphors which link battle, sacrifice and asceticism are found in various texts, either originally of the brahmanical tradition or appropriated by this tradition. The *Śatapatha Brāhmaṇa* describes the *agnihotra* sacrifice as the heaven-bound boat and compares the two altars to the sides of the boat and the priest who pours the milk to the steersman.[8] The Śāntiparvan of the *Mahābhārata* refers to the best of kings/heroes as the one who protects cows and *brāhmaṇas* (and by implication is willing to die in thus protecting), for he will go to the heaven of Indra.[9] The best of heroes, Arjuna, has Indra for his father and is welcomed in Indra's heaven, the abode of heroes.[10]

In pastoral societies, cattle raids can be one method of increasing a depleted herd. The *dāna-stuti* hymns of the *Ṛgveda*, are eulogies to the successful raider who brings back wealth and wealth is frequently computed in head of cattle.[11] In the *Mahābhārata*, the hero is still a successful raider, but is more often the one who dies heroically in battle. The living hero is eulogised, but so also the one who died in battle. The nobility of heroic death is enhanced when battle comes to be compared with the *yajña*, the sacrificial ritual. The *Mahābhārata* states that the *kṣatriya* should die not at home but on the battlefield.[12] The details of the comparison between the battle and the *yajña* are graphic.[13] The elephants constitute the *ṛtvij*, the horses are the *adhvaryu*, the flesh and blood of the enemy are the libations, the jackals and vultures who consume these libations are the *sadasiyas*, the weapons are the ladles and sticks, the battle-cries are the *sāmans*, the avant-garde in battle array is the *śyenaciti*, the kettle-drums are the *vaṣat* and so on. The continuity of this simile can be seen even as late as the tenth century AD in an inscription of Dhaṅga at the Lakṣmaṇa temple at Khajurāho.[14] Here, in a somewhat gentler rendering of the idea it is said that the king never tired when performing the sacrificial ritual in the form of a battle, where the sword is the ladle, blood is the butter libation, the twanging of the bow-string is the *vaṣat*, the priests are the warriors and the enemies are the sacrificial victims. The hero-stone in a sense negates the idea of the dead being polluting and more so when the act of dying in battle is equated with the performing of a sacrificial ritual, where the patron of the ritual is in a state of purity.

The comparison with asceticism is less dramatic and gory. The austerities and practices of the ascetics are compared to the painful death of the hero in battle or in the severing of his head as part of a voluntary death. Both are seen as superhuman feats.[15] Death is an entry into a different life as also is the act of renunciation. The symbolic death of the ascetic, when the rites of passage of the dead are carried out for him who forsakes his family to become an ascetic, leads him however to a different life from that of the hero in heaven. For instance, the ascetic denies himself sexuality, whereas the hero in heaven presumably lives a life of enhanced sexuality with the *apsarās*. A late text states that two categories of men pierce the orb of the sun, that is attain heaven, the ascetic and the hero who dies fighting the enemy and the latter is waited upon by damsels in heaven.[16] The reward is of course not temporary but for eternity.

On the hero-stones, eternity is symbolised by depicting the full orb of the sun and the crescent moon, usually at the top of the stone. This would seem to reflect a complex inter-twining of sun and moon symbolism with ancestors, gods and the after-life. At one level the representation of the sun and the moon is for obvious reasons. They are the two dominant planets which govern natural laws and above all, which govern time and are perceived as indestructible. An evocative description of time calls it the *sūtradhāra* of the universe.[17]

The sun and the moon are fundamental to time calculations in the various details of the solar and lunar calendar as also in the two systems where the Lunar calendar also draws on planetary positions and the solar calendar refers to other features. This is one area in which the interplay of Indian and Hellenistic astronomy is evident.

So common was its usage for indestructible time, that a phrase incorporating this idea — as long as the moon and the sun endure — occurs repeatedly in inscriptions. Aśoka speaks of his propagation of *dhamma*, so that among his sons and great-grandsons, and as long as the moon and sun endure, people may follow the *dhamma*.[18] As a formula it is frequently found towards the end of inscriptions reading, *a-candrāditya-kāliya* or *candrārka-kṣiti-sama-kālam*.[19] These were generally inscriptions recording grants and were expected to be irrevocable. Sometimes there is a trace of irony perhaps in this reference, since the royal patron making such a grant might also claim to belong to one of the two major royal lineages, the Sūryavaṃśa and the Candravaṃśa. After the two lineages had been plotted in the early *Purāṇas* and further established through the *Rāmāyaṇa* being the text associated with the Sūryavaṃśa and the *Mahābhārata* largely concerned with the Candravaṃśa, it became customary for dynasties to seek links with one of the two.[20]

A text as late as the *Mahānirvāṇa Tantra* also introduces this idea.[21] In yogic practice, the two main nerve centres of the human body, the *nāda* and *bindu* were described as the sun and the moon and their union was sought. Tantric cults give prominence to this symbolism in the *maṇḍalas* of the sun and the moon. The *sādhaka* or the practitioner is referred to as the *vīra*, the hero. The rituals performed by the *vīra* had some items in common with the rituals associated with the hero-stone, such as the sacrificing of a male animal and the use of intoxicants for libations. Alchemical texts also speak of the union of Hara and Gauri — mercury and mica / the moon and the sun — through the two basic processes of sublimation and transmutation, and this union becomes crucial to *rasāyaṇa-vidya* or alchemy.[22]

At the level of folk religion, the area of Sontheimer's interest also reflects the induction of this symbolism into belief. At the Dhangar festival of *somavatī amāvāsya*, Khaṇḍoba is taken in his *pālki* from the temple upto the Karha river where he is said to bathe. This is interpreted today as Khaṇḍoba representing the sun and the river representing the moon.[23] The association of power with the symbols has its own relevance for their use on hero-stones and *satī*-stones. Such examples abound in folk religion.

The presence of these planetary symbols is also evident in the texts of the *brāhmaṇas* and is not unrelated to ideas about the after-life. I would like to trace this primarily through the *Ṛgveda* and the *Upaniṣads*. In a late section of the *Ṛgveda* it is said that the dead travel from this world to the beyond by two paths: the *devapatha* and the *pitṛpatha*.[24] The *pitṛpatha* is open to those who do *tapasya*, to heroes who offer their lives in battle or make large gifts/*dāna*, who follow the *ṛta*/the natural law and to *kavis*/poets skilled in various arts.[25] In the *devapatha*, Agni is the intermediary between men and gods and bears offerings to the gods.[26] However the distinction between the two is not very marked, particularly as there is much detail on the various grades of *pitṛs*[27] and death is sometimes said to have another path from that of the *devayāna*.[28] The *Śatapatha Brāhmaṇa* states that the path on which the offerings are taken to the gods, becomes the path on which the *yajamāna* (the patron of the sacrifice) himself travels to the *devaloka* and that everything that lives here passes onto either of the two ways of the *devas* and the *pitṛs*.[29] The *Mahābhārata* links the two with the two planets when it states that there are two paths, the *devayāna* and the *pitṛyāna* and that the Sun is the gate of the first and the Moon, the gate of the second.[30] This link is developed at length in the *Upaniṣads* where there are elaborations on the earlier ideas as also the introduction of a contrast which derives largely from the way the two planets are perceived. Those living in the forest, meditating on the truth with faith, pass into the light.[31] Meditating in the forest, implying some degree of renunciation, is very different from the hero of the *Ṛgveda* who has to fight, offer sacrifices and make generous gifts. The description of the *devayāna* is that from the light, the soul passes to the day, the *śuklapakṣa* or bright fortnight, the *uttarāyana* or summer solstice to the *devaloka* from where it goes to the sun and eventually the world of Brahmā. From here there is no return, no rebirth. A different path is charted for those who conquer the worlds through *yajña*, *dāna* and *tapasya*. They take the *pitṛyāna*, where the soul passes through smoke into the night, the *kṛṣṇapakṣa* or dark fortnight, the *dakṣināyana* or winter solstice to the *pitṛloka* and on to the moon. Here it becomes food for the gods and then passes into space, air, rain, earth, to become the food of humans and to be born of women. This envisages a cycle of rebirth. The notion of *pitṛyāna* introduces the cult of ancestors, albeit indirectly. The ancestors are differentiated from the gods for they are not immortal; they can and do return to be appeased and theirs is a genealogical identity. The moon and the sun in these descriptions are binary opposites as they were to become in much of the later symbolism. Central to this dichotomy is the question of the knowledge of the self through meditation — *vidyātmanam* — which leads to the *devayāna*.[32] This is to be distinguished from *yajña* which does not lead to immortality because the soul that takes the *pitṛyāna* is reborn. It is not entirely fortuitous therefore that the metaphors of asceticism, sacrifice and battle are sought to be linked in the texts. The hero-stone however does not require the hero to be a patron of the sacrifice: it suffices that he dies in battle.

If an association is postulated between the textual sources and the hero-stones it raises at least two queries for the historian. One relates to the chronological horizon and the other to the agency responsible for the making of an incorporative statement. Chronologically, some texts which carry notions relevant to explaining the meaning of the symbols, are much earlier than the hero-stones but their association with the memorials, if at all, would be of a later date. The linking of the two would have required an agency. Other texts, such as the Tantric, coincide with the time when hero-stones are frequent. The multi-voiced statements of the symbols of the moon and the sun may be seen as an attempt to provide an encompassing tradition or alternatively as reflecting a parallel tradition. If the hero-stone cult was a substratum cult and the symbolic meaning of the sun and the moon was known generally, then the depiction of these planets would be drawing on widely recognised symbols.

The agencies can be multiple. Perhaps the most obvious would be the negotiation between high culture and local cults with a corresponding merging of ideas and practices, what in literary discussion is referred to as *mārga* and *deśi*. This dichotomy would also touch on Sontheimer's use of the contrasting *kṣetra* and *vana*.[33] This separation would also have been encouraged in the diffusion of brahmanism backed by royal patronage and supported through grants of land to *brāhmaṇas*. Such grants generally represent the state and the brahmanical perspective, but to see the outcome of the negotiation it becomes necessary to analyse the religious cults and sects of the time as manifestations of the actual negotiation. This can sometimes be seen in the inter-changeability of local deities and their attributes and forms, as for example in the worship of goddesses or of male deities which are otherwise not central to the pantheon, such as Aiyannar or the various *kṣetrapālas*. Other agencies include the cult of ancestors, the popularity of Tantric practices and sects, the wandering ascetics such as the *Nāthapanthis* and Gosains, as also the migration circuits of pastoralists or blacksmiths who also act as a conduit for beliefs and rituals.

Where locations of hero-stones are relatively close to the land granted to *brāhmaṇas*, as some might have been, there possibly, there may have been an enriching of the bare and simple symbolism of the hero-stone. The change to depicting more complex ideas on the stone appears to be an indication of this. Were the myths of the cattle-raids in the *Ṛgveda* now reiterated in brahmanical circles who were witnessing or hearing about actual cattle raids? Was the society of the hero now becoming familiar with these myths and even indirectly deriving some legitimacy from them? The hero-stones which survive in the largest numbers date to the period after about the ninth century AD. Was there now a growing appropriation of the heroic consciousness from the tradition of the *Mahābhārata*, which in some areas was newly taking root, even if in a local form. Both the textual and oral tradition relating to folk literature indicate this. To this may have been added some distant notion of themes from texts such as the *Upaniṣads*.

Where there might have been proximity between hero-stones and *brāhmaṇa* grantees, there also might have been both assimilation and tension between them. The upwardly mobile family of the hero and the newly settled *brāhmaṇa* grantee may well have had to make major adjustments. In some cases the family of the hero is given a grant which enables it to enter the ranks of the landowning strata or perhaps even claim *kṣatriya* status. If the *brāhmaṇa's* freedom from rebirth lay in knowledge and that of the hero in death on the battlefield or in a skirmish, the two activities would have been sufficiently distanced. The competition for status would however relate to the manner in which they were viewed by the local community, to whom both had to address themselves. The erecting of hero-stones in temple courtyards is a signal of concessions made by the brahmanic, Purānic system to local tradition and such an amalgamation suggests that the dichotomy became less sharp over time. Since the hero-stone did not contain the bodily relics of the dead person it was not polluting and could be erected in the sacred space of the temple. The placement within the precincts of temples maintained by *brāhmaṇas*, although enhancing the prestige of the hero-stone, would at the same time, have required the discontinuing or modifying of those aspects of the rituals connected with the hero-stone which were unacceptable to brahmanical practice. Worship would take the form of *pūjā* and in some cases offerings of blood and alcohol would be replaced by coconuts, flowers, and such like. Consciousness of the brahmanic tradition led to some incorporation of brahmanic ritual in societies otherwise distanced from *brāhmaṇas*. Legitimation is constantly sought, both by those wanting brahmanic rituals and by *brāhmaṇas* reiterating their superior status.

The historical context for such activities is more evident in the post-Gupta period when new states were constantly being created and the process required the appropriation of resources, often through the subjugation of forest peoples and their conversion to caste society and inevitably therefore the incorporation of local religious beliefs and practices into the evolving religious norms. Large numbers of hero-stones seem to coincide with these changes. This is not surprising as it was a time of shifting boundaries which made frontier zones vulnerable. The heroes were also part of the ambience of adventurers attempting to establish small kingdoms.

This is not to suggest that the hero-stone reflects a Sanskritic tradition, but rather, that even a simple symbol on a hero-stone may have touched on more widely ramified cults and associations. The hero-stone and its stance on death and on life after death, does not follow the *pitṛyāna* or the *devayāna*, but refers to a different eschatology. The heaven of the hero is not the abode connected with either the moon or the sun, but that of the deity to which he is taken by the *apsarās* and where he lives to eternity. Nor does the soul have to travel over time, for the heroes reward is immediate. The hero-stone established a distinctly different tradition but one which is suggestive of having some echoes of the others.

Among these could be that if the union of the sun and the moon leads to *mokṣa*/liberation, as in some Tantric traditions then the depiction of the two planets on either side of the hero may also be intended to suggest such a liberation. Where the eschatology is substantially different as in the concept of *nirvāṇa* in Buddhism, presumably the hero attains *nirvāṇa*. This would seem to be so from the unusual tenth century hero-stone from Vilpatta, showing the hero on one face of the stone and on the other a seated Buddha with one hand in the *bhūmisparṣa mudra*.[34] Here there are no *apsarās* taking the hero to heaven.

The implications of the symbolism of the moon and the sun on hero-stones would also include the *satī*-stones. In these the memorial is to an act of devotion, but it is nevertheless a heroic act which, being deliberate and in theory voluntary, is more so in fact than dying on the field of battle. It is the nature of dying which bestows divinity on the woman and makes of her a *satī*.

It is therefore difficult to categorise hero-stones as belonging to either the folk or the high culture. Within the typology of forms there are degrees of difference often expressed in the narration of the episode and recognisable religious identity. The episode becomes an avenue to upward mobility but where the brahmanical model need not apply. The invention of the hero-stone, initially a commemorative memorial, can become the document to claims to higher social status. In the process some elements of high culture are borrowed and some elements of folk culture are elevated and made visible. The audience addressed by these forms recognises the symbols as traversing multiple cultures. This involves the historian in recognising 'codes' which derive not just from textual and ritual sources but also from the wider symbols of variant and relevant cultures. The hero-stone also creates its own community and the study of the memorial needs to investigate what has been so far the invisible community of the hero-stone.

## Notes and References

1. G.D. Sontheimer, 'Some Memorial Monuments of Western India', in *German Scholars on India*, II, Bombay, 1976, pp. 264ff. G.D. Sontheimer and S. Setter (eds), *Memorial Stones*, Dharwar, 1982.
2. 'The Five Components and their Interaction', in G.D. Sontheimer and H. Kulke (eds), *Hinduism Reconsidered*, Delhi, 1989, pp. 197–212.
3. Kil Muttugur insc. *EI*.4.178, 182–3; Naregal insc. *EI*.6.162; Bangavadi insc. *EI*.7.22.
4. The obtaining of meat would have been an unlikely reason. Cattle

herders rarely consume beef indiscriminately as this would damage the lifestock. Meat is eaten only on specific occasions. The predators are likely to have been other organised groups.

5. E. Fischer and H. Shah, *Vetra ne Khambha — Memorials for the Dead*, Ahmedabad, 1973.
6. N. Vanamamalai, 'Hero-stone Worship in Ancient South India', *Social Scientist*, 1975, 34 (3, 10), pp. 40–6.
7. G.D. Sontheimer, *Pastoral Deities in Western India*, Delhi, 1993, 197, 203.
8. *Śatapatha Brāhmaṇa*, 2.3.3.15.
9. 21.18–19; 78.28–31.
10. *Mahābhārata*, Vanaparvan, 43ff.
11. Romila Thapar, 'Dāna and Dakṣinā as Forms of Exchange', in *Ancient Indian Social History: Some Interpretations*, New Delhi, 1978, 105–21.
12. Śāntiparvan, 98.22–4.
13. Śāntiparvan, 99.12ff.
14. *Epigraphia Indica*, I, 126.17.
15. G.D. Sontheimer in *German Scholars on India*, II, p. 268.
16. Parāśara, 3.37–8.
17. Bhartṛhari in *Vākyapadīya*, 3.9.3–5. The *sūtradhāra* is literally the one who holds the string, namely, the manager.
18. Pillar Edict, VII. J. Bloch, *Les Inscriptions d'Asoka*, Paris, 1950, 172.
19. D.C. Sircar, *Indian Epigraphical Glossary*, Delhi, 1966, p. 388.
20. Romila Thapar, 'Genealogical Patterns as Perceptions of the Past', *Studies in History*, ns, 1991, 7, 1, 1–36.
21. 14.66; 14.89–90.
22. D.P. Chattopadhyaya, *Lokayata*, New Delhi, 1968, pp. 468ff.
23. J.M. Stanley, 'Special Time, Special Power: the Fluidity of Power in a Popular Hindu Festival', *Journal of Asian Studies*, 1977, 37, 27–43.
24. 10.88.15; 10.98.11; 10.14.1–10; 10.154; also in 1.162.21; 3.54.5; 7.76.2.
25. *Ṛgveda*, 10.154.
26. Ibid., 1.72.7; 2.2.4.
27. Ibid., 10.14.7–8; 10.16.1; 10.15.1.
28. Ibid., 10.18.1.
29. 1.9.3.2; 12.8.1.21.
30. 12.17.14; 13.16.45.
31. *Bṛhadāranyaka Upaniṣad*, 6.2.15ff. *Chāndogya Upaniṣad*, 5.10.1–2.
32. *Praṣna Upaniṣad*, 1.10.
33. 'The *vana* and the *kṣetra*' in G.C. Tripathi and H. Kulke (eds), *Religion and Society in Eastern India*, Bhubaneshwar, 1986, 117–64.
34. Shown in the Anuradhapura Museum.

# VII

# *Genealogies and Origin Myths as Historical Sources*

Important to heroes and kings were genealogies and origin myths. These again were once regarded by modern historians as significant, if at all, only to chronological reconstructions. As a result of extensive studies of genealogical data from other parts of the world as well, there is a return to these as source materials of a different kind. These papers discuss the variant patterns in genealogies and what these patterns suggest. There is also a continuation from the genealogies of ancient heroes to dynastic lists and some analysis of one origin myth which occurs in association with a number of dynasties quite distant from each other.

1. Genealogical Patterns as Perceptions of the Past (1991)
2. Origin Myths and the Early Indian Historical Tradition (1978)
3. Clan, Caste and Origin Myths in Early India (1992)
4. The Mouse in the Ancestry (1984)

# 33

# *Genealogical Patterns as Perceptions of the Past*[*]

## I

Genealogies have had little respectability among recent historians. It was only with the work of anthropologists and some social historians that what was regarded as fanciful concoction is now being treated more seriously.[1] Genealogies claim to be records of succession in the past although their preservation or even invention can derive from the social institutions of the present for which they provide legitimizing mechanisms. They are rarely, if ever, faithful records of the past reality but they can be memories of social relations. As such they are not records of individuals but of groups and generally those ranked high. Succession therefore also relates to transfer of property and status. They change over time and are rearranged if need be, the rearrangement being in accordance with the requirements of later times. They may or may not record actual migration, fission or assimilation but where they do so, they incorporate such changes in a genealogical pattern. Myth and history in such perceptions of the past, merges, as does the present into the past.[2]

At another level genealogies are a commemoration of those who have passed away and, in some senses they are almost a cult of the dead. They record supposed ancestors, for, the connections do not necessarily have to be biological and are required in order that status be bestowed on those making the claims. Frequently the earlier portions of lengthy genealogies are fabricated. Therefore, the nature of connections sought by those constructing the genealogy are significant.

Genealogies become important at points of historical change,

* *Studies in History*, 7, 1, n.s., New Delhi, 1991, 1–36.

either with the entry of new social groups or factions, or in periods of competition when existing authority feels threatened. Genealogies are legal charters and the rearrangement of fragments of genealogies or the compilation of such fragments into a coherent whole are closely tied to the changing political status of the subject of the genealogies as well as of the authors. The historical reasons for the compiling of genealogies is therefore as significant as the actual pattern of the compilation.[3] Genealogical lists are arranged in a chronological perspective and involve elements of time reckoning. Genealogies therefore do not necessarily reflect the actuality of the past, but claim to represent it and are therefore a perspective of the past. It is in this sense that the genealogical section of the *Purāṇas* are being examined here.

II

At a particular time genealogy comes to be seen as the central component of the past. Among the earlier texts, the *Mahābhārata* opens with the genealogies of the main families and genealogies are also introduced into the first book of the *Rāmāyaṇa*. It gradually became important that the genealogical data be constructed into a pattern and this pattern seems to have taken the shape of the *vaṃśānucarita* section of the early *Purāṇas*. Because the *Purāṇas* were put together at a particular time, this section developed a distinctive pattern and was not just an arbitrary perspective. Since the genealogies of the Vedic texts and the epics and *Purāṇas* do not always tally, they have been dismissed as fabricated. But what is important is to attempt an explanation of the meaning of the final form in which these genealogies were recorded in the *Purāṇas*.

By about the fourth century AD there came to be compiled the earliest of a category of texts called the *Purāṇas*. These drew on materials believed to relate to the past and took the form of cosmology, legends and genealogies. They mark a perspective which is not arbitrary because of their distinctive contents and the fact that they were put together at a particular time. Whether Purāṇic genealogies should be taken seriously as historical material has been controversial. Some have stated that, '. . . to extract either chronology or history from such data, must be an operation attended with equal success as the extraction of sunbeams from cucumbers by the sages of Laputa.'[4] Vincent Smith on the other hand spoke of their dynastic lists as a 'near approach to accuracy', particularly in relation to the Andhra kings, although other historians have been more sceptical.[5] The great defender of the *Purāṇas* was F.E. Pargiter who argued that even as part of the oral tradition some memory of early kings would have remained and that however garbled the genealogies may be, they would still have been based initially on some authentic versions. This provided the *Purāṇas* with some respectability but the debate remained heated.[6] More recently, R. Morton Smith has attempted to streamline the lists into a chronology of kings but not very convincingly.[7]

That there was a tradition of maintaining genealogies in India in early times, is attested to by Megasthenes, who, writing in the fourth century BC, states that upto the time of Sandracottos (Candragupta) the Indians counted 153 kings over 6042 years.[8] Pliny has the figure at 154 kings over a period of 6451 years.[9] The debate among modern historians has hinged on a literal understanding of history as a chronicle of rulers and therefore questioning the genealogies as factual statements, whereas it might be more useful to understand why genealogies, factual or not, came to play such a central role in the perception of the past.

An attempt will be made here to analyse the genealogical chapter of the early *Purāṇas*. This consists of three sections with distinctly different patterns. The first deals with origins and is ensconced in cosmological time. The second constructs a record of what was perceived as the lineages of ruling clans. These include the families and clans which are the subject of the two epics, the *Mahābhārata* and the *Rāmāyaṇa* and appear to reflect clan or lineage-based society prior to, or in transition to, the formation of states. The third section is a listing of kings and dynasties, recording the establishment of the monarchical state. It focuses initially on Magadha in south Bihar and continues upto the Guptas, known from other sources to be reigning from the fourth century AD.[10] These three distinctive patterns would, it seems also reflect a perception of historical change in northern India.

The format of the *Purāṇa* ideally covered the *pañca-lakṣana* or the five facets, of *sarga* or primary creation, *prati-sarga* or secondary creation, *manvantara* which were the major time cycles, *vaṃśa* or succession which is largely material on deities and sages and finally the section which concerns us, the *vaṃśānucarita* or the succession of ruling families. The latter therefore is regarded as an important component of the ideal *Purāṇa* and is set in a context which draws on the past.[11] Needless to say only one *Purāṇa* conforms strictly to this format. Sometimes there is even mention of ten facets and these are even less evident in the texts.[12] Each *Purāṇa* relates to a deity and incorporates the information required by those who worship that deity. The inclusion of rules relating to gift-giving, fasts, pilgrimages, rituals and such like were probably later additions, when the character of the Purāṇic data became more clearly sectarian and religious. The oldest of the *Purāṇas* are the *Matsya*, *Vāyu* and the *Brahmāṇḍa* and for our purposes, the *Viṣṇu Purāṇa*, somewhat later than the first three, is important as incorporating genealogical data.[13]

As a category of texts, the *Purāṇas* also came to include a wide variety of what might be called sub-texts, such as the *Upa-Purāṇas*, texts on sacred topography and places of pilgrimage such as the *Sthala-Purāṇas* and the *Māhātmyas*, the Buddhist and Jaina *Purāṇas* and later the caste-purāṇas as for example those of the Mallas, the Śrimālas, and the Dharmāraṇyas. In each case the attempt is to provide the present with sanctity by drawing upon the past. The earlier *Purāṇas* were composed in Sanskrit and those of a much later period were also written in the regional languages. The tradition therefore did not cease and the texts covered a variety of topics relating to sects, cults, temples, places of pilgrimage and observances in the case of those associated with what has come to be called the Hindu tradition. However our concern is only with the genealogies in the early *Purāṇas* even if embedded in ritual literature. Incidentally, the word *vaṃśa*, literally meaning bamboo or cane, where the joints of the stem are suggestive of generational growth, referred to any list of succession, whether of teachers, sages, ruling clans, descent groups or dynasties.

In claiming antiquity it is stated that the god Brahmā compiled the *Purāṇas* even before the *Vedas* were revealed.[14] This incidentally also emphasises a different origin for the two categories of texts and the difference is further underlined in the fact that each *Purāṇa* becomes a sectarian text focusing on a particular deity. The Vedic link also goes back to the earlier statement that the *itihāsa-purāṇa* was the fifth *Veda*. We are further told that Veda Vyāsa, having edited the earlier Vedic material and authored the *Mahābhārata*, subsequently gathered together the *itihāsa-purāṇa* and compiled the original *Purāṇa*.[15] This story was an attempt to give a higher status to the *Purāṇas*, and the *Vedas* are brought in to sanctify the compilation of the *Purāṇas*. The possibility of such an ur-text has not been accepted by most scholars who hold that there has always been a diversity of Purāṇic texts. Furthermore, before the compilation of the *Purāṇas* as texts, they were probably in the form of oral transmissions and therefore more fragmented.

There is a close parallel in some forms incorporated in the *Purāṇas* and the epics. The *Mahābhārata* also begins with the arrival of the *sūta* or bard in the forest and he is asked to recite the story — *purāṇam* — a story which eventually became the epic. The contents of the *Purāṇas* drew on the hero-lauds and the eulogies of the Vedic texts as well as on the shorter narratives about earlier *rājās* which were incorporated into the *Purāṇas*, although often after some change.[16] There is a controversy among recent scholars as to whether they are intended as commentaries on Vedic texts or as a separate category of literature but drawing on some narratives from the Vedic texts.[17]

The *Mahābhārata* narrates the story of Manu Vaivasvata, referred to as the *matsyakam nāma purāṇam*.[18] There are references in the *Purāṇas* to the use of earlier forms familiar from the Vedic corpus, such as the *ākhyāna*, *upākhyāna*, *gāthā* and others, and the *Viṣṇu Purāṇa* mentions specifically that it was compiled from such earlier material.[19] There appears to have been a gradual process of data accreting to the original bardic narratives which constituted the Purāṇic tradition until, with the *brāhmaṇas* taking over the texts, they became the compendia of sectarian belief, practice, and social observances.

The earlier *Purāṇas* are the most important in terms of the genealogical data. The details of the genealogies again vary from *Purāṇa* to *Purāṇa*. Thus, the *Viṣṇu Purāṇa* has more on the Mauryan dynasty, the *Matsya* on the Āndhras and the *Vāyu* attempts to bring the genealogy upto the Gupta dynasty.[20] The *Purāṇas* did not have the same sanctity as the Vedic corpus, particularly among *brāhmaṇas*, but were respected by other castes and were the focal texts for various religious sects identifying with the central deity of the particular *Purāṇa*. Because they were not regarded as revealed and were to a larger extent explanatory texts rather than ritual texts, they would be changed and brought up-to-date with contemporary social needs. It therefore becomes difficult to date such texts as

The *vaṃśānucarita* section of the *Purāṇa*: The succession of rulers

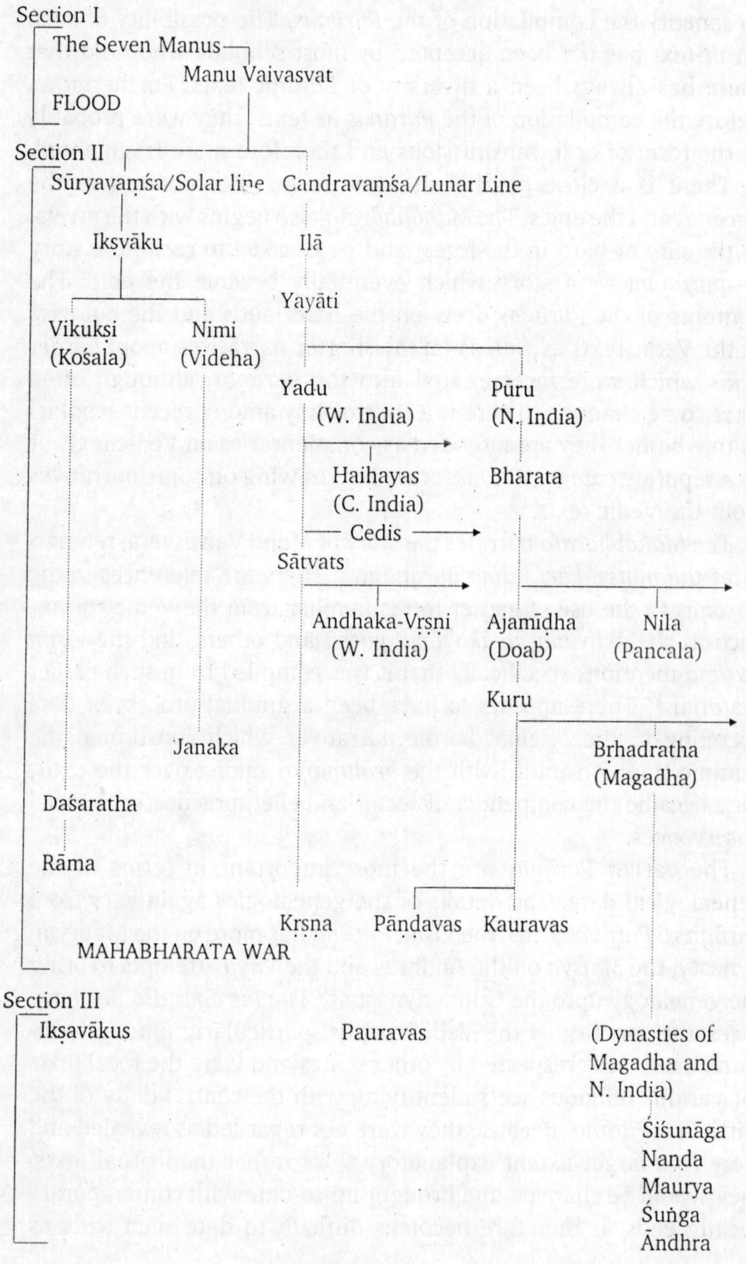

uniform compositions of a particular time. The *Purāṇas* claim that their contents come from ancient times.[21]

From the perspective of the *itihāsa-purāṇa* tradition, the *Viṣṇu Purāṇa* is probably the best example as it is believed to have fewer interpolations, maintains the format of the *pañca-lakṣana* or five facets, and is a reasonably consistent text of the sect worshipping Viṣṇu. It is also referred to, in later periods, as a continuing and important *Purāṇa*. Unlike the *Vāyu* and *Brahmāṇḍa Purāṇas*, which are believed to have been originally a single text and later separated, the composition of the *Viṣṇu* has been consistently that of a single text.[22]

The context of the genealogical section of the *Viṣṇu Purāṇa* within the broader text needs to be noticed. The structure of the *Viṣṇu Purāṇa* which is believed to be a model in that it conforms to the five facets required for a *Purāṇa*, provides an outline.[23] The prelude to the genealogical section includes a description of the creation of the world as well as of the geography of the universe, thus providing both a temporal and spatial context to the central data linked to the construction of the past. The section which deals with primary creation places in context a wide sweep of the past.[24] The world was created by *Viṣṇu* and *kāla* (time) was important as a causal factor in creation. Both *kāla* and *puruṣa* (primeval man) are a part of Viṣṇu. The symbolic measurement of time, both human and divine, described in some detail provides the basis for the concept of cosmological time. The earliest events take place in the first time cycle of the *Kṛta Yuga*, the first of the four which constitute the larger time cycle of the *mahāyuga* and which are the essential components of Purāṇic eschatology.

A number of legends are narrated and these seem to have a purpose in terms of the nature of the text. Thus *Viṣṇu* in his *varāha* or boar incarnation dives into the primeval waters and brings up Pṛthivī, the earth. This is followed by his creating various categories of beings. The *Vedas* are then revealed followed by the creation of the four *varṇas*, the four categories of caste society — the castes of *brāhmaṇa*, *kṣatriya*, *vaiśya* and *śūdra* — created so that sacrifices may be performed. The *varṇas* therefore have, in this case, a ritual context. The centrality of the sacrificial ritual is a form of purification and is contrasted with the third time cycle, the *Treta Yuga*, when sin enters human life.[25] Implicit in this notion is the equation of time with change. The perfection of the golden age of the *Kṛta Yuga* is tarnished when men and women settle in villages and towns.

The story of Pṛthu Vainya, frequently related in many texts, is recounted in its Paurāṇic version.[26] This was important since Pṛthu was a descendent of the earliest rulers, the Manus, and an ancestor of Manu Vaivasvat. We are told that the original ruler was Veṇa, but he became arrogant and refused to offer sacrifices. The *ṛṣis* having initially installed him now had no choice but to decide that he had to be killed. The sages gathered together and pierced him with the stalks of the sacred *kuśa* grass used in Vedic sacrificial rituals. Thus only those who legitimize a ruler have the right to get rid of him and this act is performed in association with a ritual object. On killing him they realized that a society cannot exist without a ruler and therefore a replacement was necessary. They churned his left thigh from which emerged the dark, ugly and quite incompetent man whom they named Niṣāda and whom they banised to the forest. On churning the right arm of Veṇa, there emerged the handsome Pṛthu Vainya, who became the legitimate ruler, introduced cattle-rearing and agriculture and ruled wisely. The earth Pṛthivī, was named after him. Pṛthu is said to have carried the mark of Viṣṇu's *cakra* or disc and is therefore described as a *cakravartin*, the term used later for a universal emperor.

The myth captures many features of the historical perceptions of the time. The disjuncture between *grāma* and *aranya*, the settled village and the forest, is a running thread through the perceptions of Indian social history. The superiority of pastoralism and agriculture over a society drawing on the resources of the forest becomes axiomatic to this idea. Niṣāda becomes a generic term, together with Śabara and Pulinda, for hunting and gathering peoples and those who are indigenous to the forest, almost throughout Indian history.

Multiple myths follow tracing the descent of deities and suggestive of the merging of traditions.[27] Reference is made to the mind-born progeny of Brahmā, among whom are the Bhṛgu and Angiras *brāhmaṇas*,[28] who, as we shall see, play an important role in the historical tradition. The duties of the four castes are given and it is stated that in times of distress the functions may be modified. The four *āśramas* or stages of life (student, householder, hermit, ascetic) are listed as well as the rites of passage for each caste. Other matters pertaining to social obligations are included. This section reads like an encapsulation of the *dharma-śāstras* indicating social and sacred duties, setting forth the normative position.

Secondary creation is essentially concerned with the cosmos and with the geography of the earth and particularly of Jambudvīpa,[29] the land of the rose-apple tree, within which lies *Bhāratavarṣa*, generally taken to be approximately the Indian subcontinent. The universe is projected in the shape of an egg with the measurement of its size running into an infinity of space. The earth lies at the centre with seven nether regions, *pātāla*, below it where the wicked and the sinners are sent after death and which is peopled by demons, whereas above it are another six directions, the *lokas*. At the centre of the earth is Jambudvīpa, circular and surrounded by seven concentric oceans and continents. At the extreme edge is the one which separates the world from the non-world.[30]

Jambudvīpa is divided by mountain ranges into seven parts among which is *Bhāratavarṣa*. The central part is called *Ilāvṛta* which has the mount Meru at its centre, hence Meru is regarded as the centre of the universe. Whereas the wider geography is fanciful, that of *Bhāratavarṣa* is less so, even if it is not precise.[31] Geography is set in a larger canvas of cosmology referring to other continents, nether regions, space, planets and constellations, the movement of the sun and the moon and the seasons. Also included here is the legend of the hero Bharata.

Further along in the text[32] we are told that Brahmā created Manu Svyambhu (the self-born) who was followed by a sequence of seven Manus, each of whose time-period, the *manvantara* is described in detail in the third section of the text. Each is associated with a group of deities, of *ṛṣis* or sages and of sons, culminating in the Manu of the present cycle, Manu Vaivasvat. There are still more *manvantaras* to follow after the destruction of the present. Each *manvantara* is a repetition of an earlier one and the *Vedas* having disappeared at the end of the period, have to be revealed afresh and the four time cycles re-occur. The *ṛṣis* teach the *dharma* and the *Vedas* in each *manvantara*, and continuity is maintained by each group repeating what it has heard from the one in the preceding *manvantara*.[33] But the *manvantara* is not intended as a specific unit of time.

The fourth facet of the text contains the descent lists of the ruling families, the *vaṃśānucarita*. The fifth facet deals with Kṛṣṇa incarnation of Viṣṇu and is replete with all the legends of his biography. A brief sixth section deals with further theories on the four ages and with the ultimate destruction of the world. Thus the text itself completes the cycle and the reader can return to the beginning with the description of primary creation.

III

Tradition has it that the original *Purāṇa* was taught by Vyāsa to his fifth disciple, the bard, Lomaharṣana (or Romaharṣana), who unlike his teacher, was not a *brāhmaṇa*.[34] Lomaharṣana divided the original *Purāṇa* into six parts each of which he taught to each of his six disciples. These six curiously were all *brāhmaṇas*, curious because in later times the high caste *brāhmaṇa* would not have taken instruction from the lowly bard. In addition, Lomaharṣana also taught the entire *Purāṇa* to his son, Ugraśravas, who recited it for a living. Some of the disciples of his son were *brāhmaṇas* and the rest were bards. Clearly there is an ambivalence as to whether the authorship be ascribed to *brāhmaṇas* or to bards. Doubtless this was aggravated by the genealogical material coming from the oral tradition of the bards. Most existing *Purāṇas* claim the stereotyped origin that they were revealed by a deity to a *ṛṣi* who then recited the text at a sacrifice.[35] Many of the early *Purāṇas* suggest that they were first recited in some part of northern India, but this may be just a convention.[36] The *Matsya Purāṇa* seems to refer to the Narbada valley more frequently.[37]

Scholars have differed as to whether or not the genealogical sections of the *Purāṇas* were originally preserved orally in the language of common usage,[38] Prākrit, perhaps by the bards and later rendered into Sanskrit when taken over by the *brāhmaṇas* and edited as texts.[39] The new association would have given them added status. The discussion on the original language of the texts is also tied to the question of whether or not they were in origin texts recording the history of the *kṣatriyas* as preserved by the bards, which were later taken over by the *brāhmaṇas* and re-edited.

The terms used for the bard were *sūta* and *māgadha*, both words of uncertain etymology. If *sūta* derives from the root **su*, it would mean to impel, to consecrate, to give birth to, but the object of this activity is unclear. Could it perhaps have a link with *sūtra*, meaning a thread, where genealogies are seen as threads linking descent, though of course the bard was concerned with more than just genealogies? It might also have been connected to the Prākrit *sutta*, meaning that which is heard and referring to the oral presentation of the data. *Māgadha* is even more obscure etymologically and can only be linked to the region of south Bihar which came to known as Magadha.

The bard had a high status initially, being included among the select group of close associates of the *rājā* especially on ritual occasions. He is included among the eight *vīras* or heroes and the eleven or so *ratnins* — literally jewels — closely connected with the *rājā*.[40] He is described as the *rājakṛt*, the maker of the *rājā* and as *ahantya* or inviolable.[41] The inviolability of the bard remained a continuing feature as late as the nineteenth century. The *sūta* was also the charioteer of the *rājā*, a profession with which he was identified almost exclusively in later times. Presumably at some point both professions had been performed by the same person. He is said to have been honoured by the sages even though he is not entitled to knowledge of the *Veda*.[42] Status in this case seems to have been different from caste since it is said on one occasion that the killing of a *sūta* amounted to the heinous crime of killing a *brāhmaṇa*, yet the same text refers to the bard as being of low caste.[43] By the turn of the Christian era, the Manu *Dharmaśāstra* ascribes a low status to the *sūta* and the *māgadha* who are said to be of mixed caste (*varṇasaṃkara*) with a *kṣatriya* father and a *brāhmaṇa* mother, and therefore born of a hypogamous union (*pratiloma*), regarded as particularly low.[44] Possibly this parentage was to enable the bard to perform functions associated with both these castes. Did this ascription of low status coincide with the taking over of the bardic tradition by the *brāhmaṇas*? The *Artha-śāstra* however does make the distinction between the ordinary *sūta* and the one who recites the *Purāṇas*, but the *māgadha* remains low.[45] In a largely oral tradition, it would be expected that there would be large numbers of persons associated with the profession of reciting narratives and compositions of various kinds, such as, the *gāthakaḥ* and the *gāyanaḥ* both of whom were singers,[46] the *kuṣilavaḥ*[47] and the *vāgajivana*.

The origin of the *sūta* and the *māgadha* as described in the *Purāṇas* is linked to the consecration ritual of the primeval ruler, Pṛthu Vainya. At the consecration of Pṛthu Vainya, supervised by the god Prajāpati, all the creatures of the world gathered for the performance of the sacrifice.[48] Out of the sacrificial fire there emerged two beings, the *sūta* and the *māgadha*, who immediately commenced reciting a *praśasti* or eulogy on the glories of Pṛthu's lineage and the deeds to be performed by him as its founder. The *sūta* and the *māgadha* were then addressed very respectfully and appointed hereditary chroniclers in the territories of Aṅga and Magadha, located on the fringes of the *ārya-varta* (the pure heartland of the *āryas*) which fringes are said to be inhabited by the *mleccha* and the *vrātya*, the impure people of low culture. Curiously in the earlier Vedic texts, Pṛthu Vainya is described as an *aneka-vrātya*, and the *vrātyas* were associated with the region of Magadha. The story was probably intended to provide an exalted status to those who were perhaps the original keepers of the tradition but the association appears to be with a culture regarded as somewhat alien.[49] The *vrātyas* were regarded as beyond the pale yet somehow to be appeased. Later the term was used to mean 'degenerate'. Possibly at this stage the genealogical tradition was a separate one maintained by the bards and may have been later amalgamated with other traditions when taken over by *brāhmaṇa* authors and made a part of the Purāṇic texts. The story also suggests that a bard would have a single king as patron although the patron could change his bard or retain more than one. The taking over of the narratives by the *brāhmaṇas* no doubt tended to curtail the description of the activities of the bards although such activities are retained to a larger degree in the epics. The genealogical tradition was among the major sources taken from the bards.

## IV

From the Purāṇic perspective the genealogical section is a book of genesis. It is linked to the myths on the creation of the world and on the cosmology described in the earlier parts of the text, but concentrates on the genealogical record of those who have wielded power. It assumes for the earlier part the centrality of high status through birth and, therefore, access to power, and provides the descent of those of such status. It claims to provide the genealogies of all the *kṣatriyas* of *Bhāratavarṣa*, although in effect it is largely limited to northern India.

The first section refers to origins. The details having been discussed in earlier parts of the text it acts as preface to the later sections. The narrative, in the form of a dialogue between the bard and the sage, begins with the god Brahmā and descent is traced from the gods via Dakṣa, Āditi and Sūrya to the seven Manus who ruled at the beginning of time. The name Manu, is of course linked to *mānava*, mankind. The seven Manus are associated with enormous time spans. During the reign of the seventh Manu there occurs the great Flood which destroys everything but from which Manu survives to become the ancestor to the two major *kṣatriya* lineages, the Sūryavaṃśa or the Solar line and the Candravaṃśa or the Lunar line.[50]

The story of the Flood is first mentioned in the *Śatapatha Brāhmaṇa*, a part of the Vedic corpus, and is repeated in the *Mahābhārata* and the much later *Matsya Purāṇa*, although the versions differ.[51] The *Śatapatha Brāhmaṇa* version relates that Manu, performing his morning ablutions finds a fish in his cupped hands and rears it until it reaches an enormous size. It divulges the intention of the gods to drown the earth in a deluge for no apparent reason. Wishing to save Manu from this disaster it orders him to build a boat which is tied to the horn of the fish. It then swims through the waters and lodges the boat on a northern mountain.

From here Manu returned when the waters subsided. Being alone and desirous of sons he performed a sacrifice from which however a daughter was born whom he named significantly, *Iḍā/Iḷā*, literally, sacrificial food or a libation. Through her in turn were born his descendants. Thus the restoration of life has to be brought about through ritual and there is an interweaving of sacrifice and procreation.[52] There has also been some discussion as to whether the horn of the fish symbolizes the *yūpa* or the sacrificial post, all of which would have underlined the centrality of ritual to the question of origins. Some texts also speak of the introduction of the plough and agriculture by the gods.[53] In the *Mahābhārata* version, the ship carries not only Manu but the seven *ṛṣis* and the seeds of all creatures, and the fish declares itself to be Brahmā who has ordained that Manu will be the source of all creation. In the *Matsya Purāṇa* the fish becomes an incarnation of Viṣṇu. The deity in this form predicts first a drought and then a flood. The ship is to carry Manu, various deities, some embodied rivers, a sage, the *Vedas* and *Purāṇas* and various branches of knowledge. The inclusion of the Purāṇic texts is of course important to the status of the *Matsya Purāṇa* itself.

Of all the multiplicity of Flood stories from various parts of the world, the versions in the *Śatapatha Brāhmaṇa* and the *Mahābhārata* parallel most closely the story in the earlier Mesopotamian texts.[54] These texts speak of the creation of man, and the reasons for punishing man, both of which as themes are absent in the Purāṇic version. The former refer to the seven prediluvian kings with inordinately long reigns and the survivor who is associated with the descent of kingship onto various cities of Mesopotamia. The seven sages are also mentioned. Regnal years use figures similar to those given in the Purāṇic time cycles, such as 1200, 32,400 and 64,800. The figure of 1200 is mentioned as the last segment of time in which the population increased and became a source of irritation to the gods. Each successive cycle is said to be of 4800 years. These figures are repeated by the Babylonian Berossus with reference to Chaldean chronology where mention is made of 36,000 and 64,800 years. Berossus writes of ten patriarchs from Adam to Noah and of ten kings from the creation to the Flood, ascribing to them a period of 432,000 years.[55] He also mentions eight sages who are involved and the first of these is fish-like in appearance. The Sumerian god Enki who saves mankind is often represented as a fish in later Mesopotamian mythology. Interestingly the reign lengths of the postdiluvian kings drop stunningly to very credible levels such as three or four years. The Flood seems to mark a change from a more mythical past to a more real past.

Given the close connections between the Harappans and the Mesopotamians, the story may have been current in Harappan times and come down as part of an earlier tradition or may have been picked up later from Assyrian sources. What is significant is that the beginning of history in Purāṇic terms is traced to a myth which has links not with Indo-European sources but with those in west Asia. Could the story have travelled from Mesopotamia to India through the traders of the third millennium BC and then have become part of the mythology which was handed down through the generations in northern India? The Iranian variant of the story which one would expect to be similar, given the closeness between Old Iranian and Indo-Aryan, in fact differs considerably and it is not the narrative of a flood but a freeze resulting from endless winters which brings life to a standstill. The earth also suffers from overcrowding, thus echoing the Mesopotamian version. The ark is not a ship but a cubical enclosure which eventually is placed inside a mountain.

The *Śatapatha Brāhmaṇa* version does not describe the creation of man and no explanation is given for why there should have been a flood — unlike the Sumerian version where the Flood is a form of punishment, both to prevent the further growth of population and to stop the rising noise levels resulting from an increase among people. In the Indian version the Flood is not punitive. There is however another story which echoes some strains of a Mesopotamian myth and that is the story of the *Varāha* or boar incarnation of Viṣṇu, in which the earth, burdened by the weight of over population of sinful humans, sinks into the ocean and has to be lifted out on the tusk of the boar. It is possible that the idea of the Flood legend was borrowed from Mesopotamian sources. In both accounts there is the further similarity of the Flood preceding rulership, although it has been argued that the king-list in the Mesopotamian account was added onto the story of the Flood. That the human race was barbarous to begin with and was civilized through the intervention of the gods is an idea common to many origin myths.

The Flood assumes the primary precondition of water from out of which the known creation arises. It is recognised as a stage in the cycle of time, perhaps what Eliade would call the abolition of profane time,[56] where the Flood is a marker, separating a time of origins from later events. The beginnings of history emerge from a condition which has no antecedents. Manu acquires prestige through being chosen to survive. This in turn gives added prestige to those who claim descent from him and who are listed in the second section of the genealogical record.

## V

The second section of the genealogical record introduces the children of Manu. In the Purāṇic version, Manu had ten sons and subsequently one who was a hermaphrodite. These children, particularly the first and the last are eponymous ancestors of the various descent groups listed in detail. The term used is *vaṃśam rājñyam* and this 'succession of *rājās*' is not grouped into dynasties but into lists of lineages, literally claiming a line of descent from a common ancestor and are also referred to as *kṣatriyas*. The descent groups are worked out in a neat structure of genealogical patterns. Interspersed within the lists are legends and myths, sometimes almost at regular intervals, suggesting perhaps points of change or break.

These legends are not arbitrary. Many are variants on what were referred to as *itihāsa* in earlier Vedic sources, their choice thus being deliberate. They provide clues to social custom and define the ethos of the *kṣatriya*. Included among these are the *digvijayas* or world conquests typified by heroes such as Mandhātri and Sagara, and the *svayamvara* or the choice by an eligible *kṣatriya* bride of a husband from among an assembled gathering of *kṣatriyas*. Both these are important to events in the epics, expressive of the character of heroic societies but take on a different connotation in later periods. The *digvijaya* suggests that lands were open to conquest by those who could so organise themselves. This may well have included new clans or the taking over by less established groups who sought legitimacy by claiming to have performed the *digvijaya* and demonstrating thereby that the older line had failed to protect its rights. The listing of areas claimed to have been conquered is also a mechanism of defining one's own territory. The significance of the *svayamvara* was also to underline the importance of marriage alliances to bolster power. To weave such legends into the genealogy is to remind the audience of what is being invoked from the past.

Manu's eldest son Ikṣvāku, the progenitor of the Solar line has three sons, two of whom are important and establish themselves at Kośala and Videha, contiguous territories in the middle Ganga plain and important to the narrative of the *Rāmāyaṇa*. The rulers of Kośala and Videha are therefore seen as belonging to co-lateral lines. The *Rāmāyaṇa* is the epic of the Sūryavaṃśa. The form of this genealogy is the presumed record of descent from father to eldest son. Younger sons are not mentioned barring exceptional cases. Collaterals can be set aside when the purpose is to record the transmission of property and office. The emphasis implies a system respecting genealogical seniority and the list of names come down in parallel columns. Patrilineal descent is heavily underlined as also the unchallenged right to succession of the eldest son. Thus the narrative of the *Rāmāyaṇa* as an epic becomes all the more meaningful in relation to those features of social and political life.

The *Rāmāyaṇa*[57] preserves a list which differs from those in the *Purāṇas* and is shorter by a few generations. Lengthening or shortening within sections of the lists is not uniform and in this process a few relationships may also be altered, others may be omitted and sometimes new names added. Contradictions such as generational differences between the time of Rāma and Sītā in the Purāṇic lists are not corrected. Lengthening either through added numbers or extended father to son succession, is generally associated with more centralized societies. Whereas such succession need not be accurate over an extended period, since it suppresses other categories of succession, nevertheless it does point to a relatively stable political and social situation. The *Purāṇas* appear to have telescoped the earlier generations, a technique often used by genealogists and described recently as 'structural amnesia'. This pattern of linear descent may be an attempt to indicate the more durable polity of a monarchy. The *Rāmāyaṇa* reflects this in the contrast between the kingdom of Kośala and other less developed regions such as Kishkindha and Dandakaranya. The contrast may well have been motivated in part by poetic fancy, but the consistency with which it is adhered to would suggest that it carried some implicit notions of the society associated with the Sūryavaṃśa being better established.

From the female half of Manu's child, Iḷā, are descended a vast spread of clans classified as Candravaṃśa. Women standing at the apex of a clan or myths of celestial women as the mothers of heroes may be suggestive of a different kind of clan organisation.[58] The genealogical pattern of the Lunar line varies from that of the Solar. It records the descent of all the sons, at least in the early part of the genealogy, and each forms a segment of the main lineage. The lists of descent, far from coming down in neat parallels, fan out laterally and inevitably cover a larger geographical space. The obvious suggestion is that segments of these clans were given to migrating, but this pattern may also be seen as attempts to assimilate other groups especially those settled in the areas under discussion. Thus the pattern of the Yādava segments of the Lunar line seems particularly prone to fanning out or incorporating new groups as they are said to have spread over large areas of western and central India. This is a considerable contrast to the static nature of the Ikṣvāku descendants who seem hardly able to move away from the middle Ganga plain. The fanning out of the clans listed as the descendants of Iḷā, involved situations of conflict and these are referred to, such as the attack on Ayodhyā by the Haihayas, a branch of the Yādavas who are said to have had their stronghold at Mahiṣmati on the Narmada river.

Repeated patterns include that of five sons, three from one wife and two from another, which come early and late and often in between. The story of Purūravas and Urvaśī is retold with some variance from the versions in the Vedic corpus and their five sons become ancestral to descendants in the Lunar line. The five sons of the famous Yayāti, and eldest Yadu and the youngest Pūru, are ancestors to the most significant segments of this lineage and form a major part of the Lunar line.[59] Pūru, inspite of being the youngest son, inherits the core of the territory and Yadu migrates to the south-west. A myth is introduced to explain this reversal of primogeniture. The main line of the Pūrus controls the Ganga *doāb*. Their descendants at a much later generational date are contestants in claims to this territory.

However, inspite of the seemingly smooth descent, there are also some barely disguised breaks in succession. An obvious break is the story of Bharata adopting a son, Bharadvāja, since none of his sons were suitable. Further along in the line of descent, Hastin is followed by three sons each of whom have the suffix *mīdha* in their names, suggesting 'spurinyms'. Another break is the story of Devāpi and Śantanu which takes us back to the *itihāsas* of the Vedic corpus. The story is given a new twist in the *Viṣṇu Purāṇa*.[60] For twelve years there was no rain in the kingdom of Śantanu since he had both usurped the throne from his elder brother Devāpi and also married before him. Normally, according to the *brāhmaṇas*, Devāpi should have been recalled from the forest where he was now an ascetic and placed on the throne. But Śantanu had a wily minister who sent a group of heretics to the forest to teach their doctrines to the innocent Devāpi. Thus when the *brāhmaṇas* set out to fetch Devāpi they were appalled by his anti-Vedic views and this was sufficient for them to annual his rights to the throne. The elder brother having thus been disqualified, there was no longer any sin in the younger ruling in his stead. Consequently, the drought ended with Indra pouring down rain.

The *Matsya Purāṇa* clinches the argument further by stating that Devāpi was a leper and therefore had to live in the forest. A physical ailment would automatically disqualify him from ruling. The *Mahābhārata* has a similar version. The significance of the story is of course that it concerns Śantanu, whose son Vicitravīrya had married Amba and Ambālika, the daughters of the *rājā* of Kāśi, but who had died childless. His wives were then required to bear children who were fathered by Kṛṣṇa Dvapāyana (or Veda Vyāsa, incidentally also the supposed author of the *Mahābhārata*). A son each was born, Dhṛtrāṣṭra and Pāṇḍu, the fathers respectively of the Kauravas and the Pāṇḍavas, the two sets of cousins involved in the great battle at Kurukṣetra. Thus neither the Pāṇḍavas nor the Kauravas, the main contenders for power in the *doāb* were actually related by blood to the Pūru line, which in fact terminated with Bhīṣma of their grandfather's generation. Such breaks may be seen as seams in the genealogical stitching. The Candravaṃśa lineages are the ones most substantially involved in the events of the *Mahābhārata* which interestingly is classified as *itihāsa*, claiming that its events may have happened in the past. The genealogical construction in the *Purāṇas* ties together the scattered stories of persons, and places the latter into a framework which draws on the past. This can also be seen as an attempt at unifying the segments. The new entrants can either come in laterally via a marriage alliance or vertically as inheritors and successors.

Artificial lengthening of the descent list is evident from the use of toponyms and geographical names in the list. Thus there is mention of the five sons of Bali as Aṅga, Vaṅga, Kaliṅga, Suhma and Puṇḍra.[61] Some of these names occur as clan names of the peoples of eastern India in the geographical section of the same *Purāṇa*.[62] In other sources they occur as the names of territories. These would also come under the category of what have been called 'spurinyms'.[63] Scattered through the lists are close associations of some clans with geographically identified areas. Mahiṣmati on the Narmada is the location of the Haihayas and Kāśī or Varanasi of the Kasus.

Customs such as bride-price, marriage by abduction, cross-cousin marriage and fraternal polyandry, not entirely approved of in the normative texts, occur in the stories punctuating the descent lists of the Lunar line, reflecting a variety of kinship systems, some dissimilar from those of the Solar line.[64] Could these have been elements of a matrilineal society or more likely, indicative of horticulture and pastoralism rather than a well-settled agricultural community?[65] These clans seem to be much given to political relationships of alliance through marriage. These could be non-lineal and incorporating a wide network over a large geographical area.

The Lunar line does not invariably claim to list a father to son succession. The relationship between generations is frequently left ambiguous with statements such as 'B' followed 'A' or, 'B' was the heir of 'A', or 'B' was of 'A' of 'B' was after 'A'.[66] This is in contrast to the more specific mention of 'B' being the son of 'A'.[67] It is less a list of personal names and more that of clans with some association of territory as well. Many are clan names known from other sources, such as the Cedis, Andhakas, Bhojas and so on.

The geography and migration of the Lunar line and of the Yadus in particular, would include western and central India, the Narmada and the Vindhyas and large parts of the edge of the Ganga plain; a far wider spread than the more concise circuit of the Solar line in the middle Ganga plain and just south of it. This genealogical pattern can be suggestive of either the migration or the assimilation of clans. The inclusion of some geographical locations may well reflect a wish to suggest marriage alliances, so crucial to controlling power in clan-based societies. Alternatively, it could be the attempt of genealogists arbitrarily grouping varieties of peoples into neat genealogical packages except that the packages do not seem to be arbitrary. There appears also to have been a consciousness of geographical space and the attempt to portion out space by locational links among the clans.

## VI

A little digression at this point, touching on aspects significant to the patterns of these two descent groups may be in order. Setting aside the question of the veracity of genealogies, these as a form of remembering the past were central to the society of the Ganga valley and its fringes in the period prior to the rise of states. The oral tradition had, as its repertoire, recitations in praise of heroes past and present. Heroic values were necessary to clans in the context of frequent cattle raids as well as disputes over clearing and settling land. Where agriculture became the rationale for occupying land, settlements would be subject to attack if they encroached on existing habitations.

The clearing and settling of land called for an organised migration often led by *kṣatriya* families. Land thus settled came to be named after the dominant *kṣatriya* clan which ultimately claimed both territorial identity and ownership. This was seminal to the eventual instituting of the state. The clan chief or *rājā* eventually evolved into the king. The lineage claimed by the dominant clan determined the identity of those regarded as the most respected. The major *kṣatriya* clans occupied the area from the watershed to the middle Ganga valley — the clans of the Kuru, Pañcāla, Matsya, Vatsa, Kāśī, Kośala and Videha. Those of lesser status were on the fringes of the area. The Yadus had their base in western India from where they are said to have moved into central India. The picture has some parallels with the distribution of archaeological cultures in the first millennium BC.

In the early half of the first millennium there are two foci. One is the Ganga–Yamuna *doāb*, and its fringes, which coincides broadly with the Kuru–Pañcāla region, incidentally also the core area of the events of the *Mahābhārata*. The archaeology of this region goes back to the late second millennium with the Ochre Colour Pottery and the Painted Grey Ware as the dominant cultures. The second is the middle Ganga region which comes into prominence with the settlements of Black-and-red Ware cultures, with possible connections to proximate places in central India and to an earlier distribution of sites in western India.[68] In both areas new arrivals had to relate to existing populations, albeit small groups. It is only with the growth of urbanization in the mid-first millennium BC that the network of the Ganga plain is drawn closer together and Magadha in south Bihar gradually emerges as the dominant region.[69]

The archaeological picture suggests a demographic change in favour of a rise in settlements. Migrating groups tend to claim high status or to invent links with high status groups where migration involves assimilation with existing populations. Genealogical records were therefore important but could be tampered with as required. Such records assume greater importance when there are tensions over rights to land and political authority in conditions of nascent kingship.

There was now an increasing social distance between those who had access to economic resources and particularly the private ownership of these, and those who worked to produce the resources. Enhanced caste differentiation would also demand a record of the genealogies of those claiming power and ownership of land, and more so where there was competition for both. When claims to territorial identity declined, genealogies still functioned as important indicators of marriage alliances, especially those underwriting political power. Current ideas on the origin of government supported the notion of a single person holding office as king, whether as an appointee of the gods or as elected by the community. The right to collect taxes ensured further power as did the right to coerce, which was given to the ruler on the assumption that it was necessary for the preservation of law and order. Such an accumulation of rights points to the establishment of monarchical states similar to that at Magadha on which there is much evidence. The epics through their later interpolations become charters of validation supporting the legitimacy of such states as a new form of political organisation.

That genealogies were included in ritual texts is not surprising. Attempts were also made in other texts to suggest authenticity by co-relating the succession lists of priests with those of kings performing sacrificial rituals. Sanctification is an obvious means of preservation. But the ritual of sacrifice, apart from its religious meaning, was also the occasion for establishing the social status of a clan chief and for reiterating relations of exchange. It was the occasion when the clan gathered, when social underpinnings were made evident not only by the ritual but also by the display, the consumption and the destruction of wealth; and where the gradually increasing distance between the *rājā* emerging as king and the rest of the clan, the *viś*, was established. The *brāhmaṇas* associated themselves with the focus of power and one form of this association was to gradually appropriate the past of those in power.

The reconstruction of this past in the form of genealogies provides pointers to its social and political concerns. The deeds of individual heroes familiar from the epics are narrated in summary form in the *Purāṇas* as part of a genealogy. What is important therefore is not that the genealogies do not always tally in various sources, but that the function of this data suggests a changed historical situation. Genealogies creating a continuous, seemingly unbroken past relate to societies where descent groups are more central than institutions. This pattern however changes once again in the last section of the *vaṃśānucarita* or narration of succession in the *Purāṇas* when a new form comes to be recorded.

## VII

The second time-marker in the sense of an event indicating a major change comes with the end of these lists when the clans are involved in a war which few survive. Catastrophes are time-markers and initiate new periods. The immensity of the disaster caused by this war is suggested in the attempt to shift the start of the present time cycle, the *Kali-yuga*, from Manu surviving the Flood to the descendants of those who survived the war. The metaphor of water and ocean, reminiscent of the Flood, is used frequently in the description of the battle. As described in the *Mahābhārata*, the war arises out of the hostility between the descendants of the Pūrus but almost every *kṣatriya* clan and *rājā*, are said to have taken sides and are, by and large, wiped out. The war is seen as the end of an epoch, or as the *Purāṇas* put it, the ending of the splendour of the *kṣatriyas*. The world is not the same subsequent to this and politics undergoes a substantial change. This is reflected in distinctly new features of the genealogical record.

Subsequent to the *Mahābhārata* war, statements about what follows are made in the future tense even though the text was compiled centuries later. Thus says the narrator, 'I will now enumerate the kings who will reign in the future periods. . . .'[70] The past lay in events which took place before the war. It imbues the narrator with the extraordinary power of prophecy. The implication also seems to be that those who control the past have access to the future. Happily the switch to the future tense provides us today with a clue as to approximately when the text was compiled since the prophecy has to stop with a contemporary dynasty. The prophetic form did not, however, prevent variations among the *Purāṇas* on what was to follow. A few further descendants of the Sūryavaṃśa or Solar line and the Candravaṃśa or Lunar line, are listed but more now as a rounding off of the descent groups. Among the former, mention is made of the Buddha and his clan, his father and his son; among the latter, the focus shifts from the upper *doāb* to the lower *doāb*, a migration necessitated by the flooding of the Ganga and the destruction of the earlier capital at Hastināpur, leading to a new settlement at Kauśāmbi, near the confluence of the Ganga and Yamuna. These generations are also referred to as *nṛpa*, the protector of men, but are not given any regnal years. Dynastic history is traced through the line of Magadha (in south Bihar) and the first dynasty mentioned together with the regnal years of its members, was that of the Bṛhadratha dynasty of Magadha.

Another change is the statement made by the bard in the preamble to this section, that the kings listed shall include those who are of mixed caste, those regarded as outcaste (*vrātya*), those who are of lower caste (*advija*), the *śūdras*, foreigners and others of impure origin (*mleccha*), and those who are upstarts (*udit-odit vaṃśa*). This was a concession to political power being negotiable and open to those who did not even have to claim to be *kṣatriyas*. As the texts put it, the splendid *kṣatriya* stock is brought to an end. The succession of *kṣatriyas* was replaced by kings listed by dynasty, together with their regnal years and referred to more impersonally as *nṛpa*, the protector of men. Whereas previously the succession was that of the *vaṃśam rājñyam*, the later lists of dynasties are a full account of all the different kings and their successive transactions.[71]

The early Śiśunāga dynasty is permitted a minor concession in that the kings are described as having *kṣatriya* kinsfolk — *rājā-naḥ kṣatra bāndhavah*. Of the Nandas it is specifically said that they will exterminate all *kṣatriyas* — *kṣatra vināsa kṛt*, — therefore subsequent kings will be *śūdras*. Nevertheless the Nandas are described as *eka-chātram*, sole monarchs. The *brāhmaṇa* Kauṭilya, we are told, will uproot the Nandas and anoint Candragupta as king, who will found the Maurya dynasty. Puṣyamitra Śuṅga will uproot Bṛhadratha, the last of the Mauryas. Vāsudeva the minister, will overthrow the last of the Śuṅgas and establish the Kaṇva dynasty, which is referred to as the Śuṅgabhṛtya, literally the servant of the Śuṅga, where the term *bhṛtya* is perhaps better translated as 'in the service of'.[72] This could refer to those in administrative office who, relying on the use of force as well as the authority of office, rose to kingship. The Andhras are also the *bhṛtyas* of the Kaṇvas and are succeeded in turn by their *bhṛtyas*. A long list of successors are then listed. The Guptas, mentioned towards the end of the list, will rule over the *janapadas* (territories) of Gaṅgā, Prayāga, Sāketa and Magadha.

Such statements are new to the account and underline the capturing of political power. (Dynasties described here as evidently foreign, such as the Śakas and Yavanas, do however sometimes add *kṣatriya* suffixes to their names in their inscriptions).[73] The reckoning of kings by regnal years was a concession to a measured concept of time. The exaggerated lengthening of regnal years in the early part of the dynastic section was probably to give the sanctity of antiquity to monarchy. The concept of generations is also different as compared to the earlier section where a generation was counted from birth. Now, a generation was listed when a king assumed office since only regnal periods in each dynasty are recorded.

The third section is essentially one of non-*kṣatriya* kings where dynasties changed with the arrival of new families through conquest and otherwise where the administrators seem to have usurped power. There is a gradual increase in dynasties which do not even claim to have been *dvijas* or twice-born, pointing to a new understanding of political power. Legitimation is not through a ritual sacrifice conducted by *brāhmaṇa* priests but through the assertion of power. This was done either through conquest or through exercising administrative control. This social condition would conform to the statement that in the *Kali-yuga*, caste hierarchies and functions are overturned; inevitably, therefore, those in power would be of lower castes and outsiders. However, in subsequent times, latching onto the *kṣatriya* genealogies was to become one of the methods of legitimizing dynasty. Change in the nature of the polity in the post-Gupta period from about the seventh century AD onwards, led to the emergence of new claims to kṣatriyahood. This is mentioned in the third section of the *vaṃśānucarita* when it speaks of a king of Magadha creating another *kṣatriya* caste.

## VIII

What are we to make of all this information? Attempts at establishing an order in the genealogies was made by Wilson in the nineteenth century and by Pargiter at the start of this century.[74] Pargiter was less interested in the genealogical patterns and what these may be stating and more in trying to identify the different descent groups. This was easier for the third section dealing with dynasties for many of them could be co-related with other sources. Pargiter's plea that the data be treated seriously was well-taken but unfortunately his identifications of the descent groups with the Aryan, Dravidian, and Austro-Asiatic was misleading and his attempt to see Aryan expansion in the genealogies was not tenable, so too similar attempts by later scholars. The *Purāṇas* make no such distinction.

The Pūrus for example, whose 'aryan' identity is doubtful even from other sources since they speak a *mṛdhra vāc* (impure language) and are said to be descended from the *asura rākṣasa*,[75] are given an important status in the genealogies. Those of an equally important Yādava descent — from Yadu — include persons who do not have a high status in some other texts. Thus, the Vṛṣṇis and the Andhakas are referred to as *vrātyas* and the people of Saurashtra, associated with the Yādavas, as belonging to mixed castes.[76] The contradiction between the *Purāṇas* listing them as *kṣatriyas* and *rājās* and other sources referring to their lower status can perhaps be resolved if it is argued that the Purāṇic lists were concerned only with those who constituted the chiefs of clans. Whatever their actual status might have been in the caste ranking given them by *brāhmaṇa* theoreticians, in the historical perspective of the dynastic lists they were seen as societies with *rājās* and included in particular descent groups. The construction of the descent group, therefore, was another kind of statement, setting out the location, alliances and politics of clans as perceived from a later perspective. Inclusion in a particular descent group was also a pointer to the kind of political society associated with the clan. It is significant that the more motley list of clans is included under the Candravaṃśa and not the Sūryavaṃśa.

## IX

Chronologies of Indian history and concepts of time based on these genealogies have not been attempted on the assumption that since many dynasties of the third section are historically attested, the earlier genealogies should also be taken literally.[77] Some historians have tried to compute generational length in India averaging fourteen or even twenty-seven years,[78] going back to 3102 BC, the date calculated from an inscription of the seventh century AD for the start of the Kali-yuga.[79] Reign lengths vary according to the stability of the polity and stable dates tend to support longer reigns.[80] Uninterrupted direct descent from father to son among dynasties rarely exceeds five or six reigns.[81] The Purāṇic lists were not meant to be treated as chronologically precise and although time is important to genealogical reconstructions they were at best approximate.

The dimension of time is inevitably present in all attempts to build an image of the past and time plays a central role in the genealogical patterns as well. We have seen that these are placed within the framework of cosmology and it would seem that varying concepts of time are used to differentiate cosmological notions from those perceived as historical. Included in the *Purāṇas*, therefore, are theories of time where the sequence of time is viewed in different ways, cosmological, genealogical and linear, and this introduces a chronological framework. The grand theory of time, the theory of the *yugas* is a play on the concept of time, a metaphor at many levels.[82] It is used in varying contexts: from the vastness of the aeons running into thousands of years, to the minutiae of the blinking of an eye; from time originating as part of the cosmos to time determining the ethics of an age or to time seen in a spatial form. This is not time which is subject to calibration.

Purāṇic chronology is based on the *manvantara* but also on the calculation of two eras, the *Kali-yuga* of *c.* 3102 BC and the Saptarṣi of *c.* 3176 BC, where the two eras seem to act as a bridge between the infinity of the *manvantara* cycles and the shorter spans of time calculated in the eras. Each major time cycle, *mahāyuga* or great cycle, also referred to as the *cāturyuga* of four cycles, is divided into four cycles, the *yugas* — Kṛta (or Satya), Dvāpara, Treta and Kali — the names (except for one), derived from the numbers at the throw of dice from the highest to the lowest and therefore carrying the suggestion of fate implicit in time. The condition of man and the world has changed from the earliest times which were utopian to the ultimate decline in the fourth *yuga*, the *kali-yuga*, which is the current cycle. *Dharma*, sometimes represented as a bull with four legs, which stood on all four to begin with, has, at the end of each *yuga* lost one leg. Each *yuga* is measured in specific numbers of years and these are 4000, 3000, 2000 and 1000 respectively, interspersed with a dawn and a twilight time which are each one-tenth of the length of the *yuga*, thus, reading as 4800, 3600, 2400 and 1200. The figures for the four decline in arithmetic progression, from 4800 to 1200 divine years, where each divine year has to be multiplied by 360 to convert it to human years. The total cycle of 12,000 divine years is therefore equivalent to 4,320,000 human years. A thousand *mahāyugas* make a *kalpa*, an aeon, each of which is followed by the destruction of the world often through a great deluge. This further underlined the myth of the Flood. The reckoning based on the *kalpa* is also tied to the *manvantara* calculation where the *kalpa* is equivalent to one day of Brahmā in which there are fourteen Manus, so that each *manvantara* is equal to about seventy-one *mahāyugas*. This is truly an infinity of time or almost a sense of time which is without beginning or end.[83]

There appears to have been an attempt to draw on figures from astronomy, perhaps to suggest exactitude, given that the mid-first millennium AD was an active period in Indian astronomy. The *Purāṇas* reflect some of the information on mathematics and astronomy current during this period. The figures also occur as we have seen, in Babylonian astronomy and it has been argued that Indian astronomers were familiar with Babylonian ideas by about *c.* 400 BC.[84] The basic parameter of the *yuga* system was the *Kali-yuga* of 432,000 years, which is the figure for the prediluvian kings in Babylonian sources and which in turn is based on the sexagesimal system ($2 \times 60/3$), a system also in use in India. To this was added the decimal system commonly known to Indian mathematics and a *kalpa* was calculated as 1000 *mahāyugas* or *cāturyugas*. The four *yugas* were then placed in descending order of 4:3:2:1. The cyclic notion was closely related to the idea of the revolution of heavenly bodies and a number of cycles of time were in current use. Among the more popular were the five year luni-solar cycle of the Jyotiṣa-Vedāṅga texts on astrology reconciling the lunar and solar calenders, and the Saptarṣi era, and imaginary cycle of about 2700 or 2800 years, based on the theory that the constellation of the Saptarṣi or Great Bear stays for a hundred years in each of the twenty-seven or twenty-eight *nakṣatras* (asterisms). From the sixth century AD, the cycle of Bṛhaspati or Jupiter became popular and was often computed as a complete cycle of sixty years. That there was some conflict between Purāṇic cosmology and the cosmology of the astronomers is evident from texts by the latter questioning the former.[85]

The notion of this infinite scale of time was an attempt to build it into a concept of cosmology very different from measured time. Was this reflective of a tension between those who sought the sanction of cosmological time for a record of the past and those who wanted a more precise time reckoning? Or was the association of cosmic time with the past yet another device to maintain at one level, the otherness of the past? Cosmological time circumscribes all other time systems, but it does not exclude other time systems such as generational and linear time. The fantasy of numbers in this scheme of cosmological time has been read as a 'refusal of history'.[86] It would seem more appropriate, however, to see it as an attempt at distancing a mythical past by framing it in a time concept which was palpably unreal. Not all the Purāṇic versions agree on the details of the four *yugas*,[87] thus underlining the symbolic character of the idea.

Varying concepts of time can also be used to demarcate historical change. Time cycles of immense scale can also be methods of pushing back the past so that primary creation, as in this case, belongs to a time which is virtually beyond human conception. The Golden Age, located in this early time period, is also easier to handle and describe since it can extend to any limits of fantasy. This may also have had another reason. One of the ways in which conflict between *smṛti* texts was resolved, was to maintain that some, recording customs in contradiction of those currently practiced, were legislating for a bygone age.[88] Such an age would have to be extremely distant in time so that the practice be relegated truly to the past.

Genealogies become a form of sequential reckoning. To record the past in a genealogical form could suggest that there was a core tradition which might have been relatively fixed, but that other material could have been changed. The *Purāṇas* have to change in keeping with changes in every *yuga*. Therefore, the contents of the *Purāṇas* were not sacrosanct in the way the *Vedas* were.

References to regnal years and dynastic time periods suggestive of linear time in the third section of the *vaṃśānucarita*, were of a very different order from cosmic time and genealogical time. This may have had to do with the currency of eras and dates used in other sources in the period when the *Purāṇas* were composed, the commonly used ones being the Kṛta or Vikram Samvat of *c.* 58 BC, the Śaka era of AD 78, and the Gupta era of AD 319–20. Equally popular were the *Kali-yuga* later traced back in some reckonings to the equivalent of 3102 BC and the Laukika era of 3076–75 BC,[89] both of which occur in official records in the post-Gupta period. It may also have had to do with the impact of a culture given increasingly to literacy.

Time as a cycle does not eliminate the past and the future, since the cycle terminates in destruction and a new cycle follows. The inordinate length of the cosmological time cycle is to underline the idea of timelessness. The universe had a beginning in cosmological time which is described as a generative factor. Only later does a different, generationally measured time, under human control come into historical reckoning. Implicit in this is also a distinction between the history of the universe viewed in an infinity of time and the history of man which was subject to exact measurement. The latter was also made apparent in the meticulous measurement of time in astrology which centres on the past and future of the individual.

In terms of eschatology, the Golden Age was in the remote past, in the beginnings of time, after which there has been a steady decline, from *dharma* to *adharma*. The link between time and the moral condition is described in the social decline which will prevail towards the latter part of the *Kali-yuga*. The rulers will be of impure origin, and their subjects will be oppressed; the *varṇa* ordering will be discarded and castes will move away from their allotted functions. Vedic rites will not be observed and even the *brāhmaṇas* will lose their code of ethics. The change in the social condition becomes an allegory of a sense of historical change.

## X

We are told that the *Purāṇas* have to keep pace with changes in every *yuga*. A fixed tradition was not required (which incidentally makes it difficult to date them). Nevertheless something of a tradition does emerge, and in the *vaṃśānucarita* section it indicates changes in the past. The gods and the sages are associated with the beginnings of history. The founder of a descent group has a special relationship with deity which establishes his unique position. Descent from the founder has a noticeable pattern, such as that differentiated in the Solar and Lunar lines, and this pattern presumes a historical condition. The difference possibly points to variant claims to and forms of political power and becomes both the source and the expression of the legitimation of such power. Attempts to chart the major *kṣatriya* clans after the Flood are also attempts to fill in geographical space.

To name the lineages after the sun and the moon seems in no way peculiar. These two planets often have contrasted characteristics such as that the sun is seen as the male symbol and the moon as the female, a contrast which is also suggested in the pattern of the descent groups. Seniority seemed to lie with the Solar line since Ikṣvāku is mentioned as the eldest child of Manu and there is some confusion over the identity of Iḷā. Taken more literally, the sun outshines the moon and this must certainly have been observed by the time that these texts were written. The symbolic frequency of the sun and the moon is noticeable especially in Tantric and Yogic texts, where the sun and the moon symbolize the two main nerve centres to the right and the left in the human body and their unity is sought in certain Yogic practices.[90] This may suggest an interaction with what seem to have been regarded as substratum groups. Taken together, the sun and the moon denote permanency in the iconography of this period, doubtless arising from their association with calendrical time. Both the Solar and the Lunar calendar were in use but associated with different social functions. If the Solar calendar determined the agricultural year, the Lunar calendar set out the rituals.

The difference in the recording of ruling families as dynasties after the *Mahābhārata* war indicates the perception of difference in the nature of power under a system of monarchical states. The *Mahābhārata* war is the watershed in the periodisation of the past as viewed from Purāṇic sources. Whereas earlier all the descent groups were included under the umbrella terms of *rājā* or *kṣatriya* now, on the contrary, the social status of individual dynasties is separately indicated, the assumption being that kṣatriyahood was not a prerequisite for monarchy. The acquisition of power now confers rank, and therefore a dynasty of Hellenistic origin, the Yavana, is described as *vrātya-kṣatriya* or degenerate *kṣatriya*. Dynastic succession is a pointer to the existence of states which now take precedence over nonstate, clan-held territories. The establishment of the monarchical state involved a different set of institutions from those of preceding political forms and, therefore, a different basis of royal power.

If the relationship between descent groups was stated symbolically, that between dynasties is direct and clear. Where a ruling family was subordinate to the previous dynasty it is described as the *bhṛtya*. There are no claims to lineage links connecting dynasties and thereby there is a negation of the importance of lineage in this section. Political power seems to be a sufficient base for claiming legitimacy.

An important and not unconnected statement towards the end of the dynastic section reads that a king of Magadha, having overthrown the *kṣatriya* caste, will create another *kṣatriya* caste,[91] thus conceding that although the traditionally accepted *kṣatriyas* had declined, it was still possible for there to be new *kṣatriyas*: a statement which has interesting consequences, for the future form of the *itihāsa-purāṇa* tradition. Implicit in this statement is the fact that since the dynastic section repeatedly uses the word *nṛpaḥ* rather than *kṣatriya*, any claim to being a *kṣatriya* would have to seek links with the Solar or Lunar descent groups. What is of further interest is that the other *varṇas* listed as being converted to *kṣatriya* status through this new caste are the Kaivarta, Pañcaka and Pulinda, otherwise ranked as low castes. The Pulindas are generally viewed as tribal people outside the pale of caste society. The brahmanical imprint on this section is apparent. As a projection of the decline of an earlier aristocracy and the moving in of upstarts, no statement could be more explicit.

This also raises the question of what the term *kṣatriya* was meant to convey. The earlier function of the *kṣatriya* had been that of the heroic ideal — the warrior, the leader into victory, the successful cattle raider, the clan chief and eventually the king. Were those dynasties which are listed as non-kṣatriya so described because some were patrons of non-brahmanical religious sects, such as the Mauryan kings? Or should this be read as a statement that monarchies as constituted in this early period were disapproved of as political forms by the *brāhmaṇa* authors, who preferred the earlier clan system where the chiefs were dependent on the *brāhmaṇas*? The return to claims to being *kṣatriya* in the post-Gupta period was again a situation of royalty seeking support from *brāhmaṇas* for legitimation. Alternatively, was the term as applied to earlier *rājās* used in the sense of an office or designation rather than as a caste, since some of them were of an ambiguous caste status anyway. The use of *kṣatriya* in later periods appears to have become more closely a caste usage. There is therefore not only a flexibility in the use of the term *kṣatriya*, but possibly also a change of meaning. Disapproval of monarchical states because they encouraged a competition among *brāhmaṇas* and other sects for patronage may partially explain why there is no elaboration on the dynasties in brahmanical literature generally. Even dynasties of *brāhmaṇa* origin such as the Śuṅga royal family, although they feature in the plays of Kalidāsa (probably contemporary with the early *Purāṇas*) are nevertheless not treated at length in brahmanical sources. It is unlikely that the disapproval of *brāhmaṇas* becoming kings would have stood in the way of such descriptions.

## XI

The construction of this genealogical succession may well have been an amalgamation of traditions. The possibility of there having been a distinct *kṣatriya* tradition has been debated.[92] This would not be altogether surprising given the existence of caste *Purāṇas* in many sections of Indian society seeking to provide a history and a status for the caste. Without going over the old debate again,[93] it does seem possible that similar to the succession lists of teachers maintained by *brāhmaṇas*, some *kṣatriya* succession lists were maintained by bards, such as those in the epics. These may well have been taken over by *brāhmaṇa* authors and reconstituted, together with other material into the *vaṃśānucarita* section.

The importance of these activities was recognised by *brāhmaṇa* authors hence the references to *itihāsa* and *purāṇa* in Vedic and other texts. But the fact of controlling the tradition was a later development. The *sūta* and the *māgadha* seemed to have been closely tied to the Vrātyas who were never quite acceptable to the *brāhmaṇas*, even after the performance of the *vrātyastoma* sacrificial ritual. However, one category of *brāhmaṇas* which might in a sense have bridged the differences was the category of Bhṛgu or Bhārgava *brāhmaṇas*. Their role is central not only to the redaction of the epics but also in the writing of texts which were regarded as part of the *itihāsa-purāṇa* tradition. The *Purāṇas* can perhaps be seen as an attempt to appropriate some of the legitimacy of Vedic Brahmanism but at the same time drawing on an equally strong tradition emanating from non-brahmanical sources. Thus, the history of those claiming political power being embedded in the form of a *vaṃśa* in texts on cosmology and sectarian ritual, was in a sense, a continuation of the Vedic tradition of embedding the eulogies on the heroes — the *dāna-stutis* — in ritual texts. The latter provided a legitimacy to both categories of data.

There was the added parallel that dynasties patronizing these sects could be projected in a more favourable light in the construction of dynastic succession, such as the Guptas, whereas those who were not patrons of these sects were described in unflattering terms. The inclusion of succession lists relating to political authority in sectarian texts was a common practice wherever the sect had some links with rulers. It is also worth keeping in mind that the perception of society was not in terms of a universalizing whole, but in terms of sects and castes. Initially the record of the *vaṃśa* or succession would have been orally maintained, hence the possibility of restructuring it at some point. When compiled as texts, then the brahmanical world-view would have entered.

The *brāhmaṇas* most closely associated with the *itihāsa-purāṇa* tradition over time, were the Bhṛgu *brāhmaṇas*. They are linked with the fire cult and hostile to the hero-god Indra and are therefore treated as something of a category apart in the early texts.[94] Gradually they join with the Aṅgirasas and the compound term Bhṛgu-aṅgirasa comes into use.[95] The connection with *yatis* and with *yātu-dhānas* suggests sorcery and magicians or at any rate a group that is somewhat feared.[96] But the *yatis* seem also to have had an earlier association with asceticism. The compilation of the *Atharvaveda* is attributed to the Bhṛgu-aṅgirasa. There is also a link with the Vrātyas where the Bhṛgu-aṅgirasas are said to praise the *ekavrātya*. Sometimes the *itihāsa-purāṇa* as well as the Vedic hero-lauds, the *gāthās* and *nārāśāṃsīs* are all linked to the Vrātyas.[97] This is rather surprising as generally the Vrātyas are regarded as being somewhat deficient in their handling of the Sanskrit language. Did they represent a non-Vedic and possibly a pre-Vedic tradition? This would be significant, particularly if they may have had their origins among priests of lower social groups. The Bhṛgus are recognised as powerful *brāhmaṇas* but their marriages into *kṣatriya* families and some of their activities which deviate from brahmanical norms, sets them apart from other *brāhmaṇas*. The Aṅgirasas are linked to the homeland of the Vrātyas as of the *sūta* and *māgadha* and are also associated with the *itihāsa-purāṇa*. If they were inducted into the *brāhmaṇa* caste then they may have been responsible for bringing the *itihāsa* tradition with them.

It has been argued that certain priest groups among the *dāsas* or existing peoples were adopted by the incoming Indo-Aryan speakers and these groups took on the patriarchal clan groupings from the *kṣatriyas* for whom they officiated. Among such groups were the Bhṛgu-aṅgirasa. The latter were frequently exempted from the usual rules of marriage and hence their alliances with *kṣatriya* women. They are not mentioned along with the seven *ṛṣis* and therefore are not technically *gotras* or exogamous groups.[98] The Bhṛgus are associated with the fire-cult of Agni. That they may have had a pre-Vedic ancestry is suggested by their links with the *yati* or magicians and sorcerers[99] and with the notion of *māyā* or magic. Their eminence is based on their ancestral claim to be the mind-born sons of Brahmā and Manu and who learnt the codes of social and sacred duty from Manu.[100] The Aṅgirasa are linked to the *Atharvaveda*[101] and may well have been shamans originally associated with sorcery and healing and were seemingly semi-mythical. The title Aṅgirasa was taken by many *ṛṣis*. That they were powerful is apparent from the *Atharvaveda* which states that when opposed by the *kṣatriyas*, they ruined the latter.[102] The *Mahābhārata* and the Purāṇic tradition claims that they were among the earliest *brāhmaṇas* and that the Bhṛgus were the priests to the *asuras*, i.e., those who were once powerful and friendly but gradually came to be viewed as hostile.[103] The succession list of the Bhṛgus is given in the earliest *Purāṇas*.[104] Among the more respected Bhṛgus, Uśanas Śakra, is associated with those opposed to the *āryas* and only later does he ally himself with them.

The Bhṛgus are associated with death, violence, sorcery, confusion, *varṇasaṃkara* or the mixing of castes and the violation of the *varṇāśramadharma*, the ordering of society.[105] Their relations with the *kṣatriyas* although close, were ambivalent. In some cases they are hostile to the *kṣatriyas* as in their attack on the Haihaya clans or in the story of Paraśurāma the *brāhmaṇa* who exterminated all the *kṣatriyas*. In other cases they intermarry with the *kṣatriyas* and take *kṣatriya* wives. This makes them degraded *brāhmaṇas*-*brāhmaṇāpasada*.[106] They are also proficient in *dhanurveda*, the science of archery, which is again contrary to the social code since this is the professional expertise of the *kṣatriyas*. They are the great propagators of Viṣṇu as is evident from their redactions of the *Mahābhārata* and the *Rāmāyaṇa*, but at the same time claim to be greater than Viṣṇu in that it is held that Viṣṇu has to be incarnated seven times because of the curse of a Bhṛgu. Interestingly, Paraśurāma finally becomes an *avatāra* of Viṣṇu. The extermination of *kṣatriyas* by Paraśurāma is said to have been repeated twenty-one times. But clearly even then some escaped. The myth revolves around the issue of power and draws not only on the enmity with the Haihayas, a segment of the Yādava descent group, but expands it in the story of Viśvāmitra and Vasiṣṭha.[107] There is a reversal of roles in the activities of Paraśurāma and Viśvāmitra where the *kṣatriya* Viśvāmitra aspires to the powers of the ascetic and the *brāhmaṇa* Vasiṣṭha takes on the role of the warrior. (This is explained by the story of the mixing up of the *carus* or special food, consumed by their respective mothers). Possibly the *brāhmaṇa*-*kṣatriya* hostility reflects two traditions each trying to edge the other out and the myth of extermination is meant to state, as it has been suggested, that the Bhṛgus finally appropriated the *kṣatriya* tradition.[108]

The more interesting question is why the *brāhmaṇas* eventually took over this tradition. This may not have been unconnected with literacy. Literacy and the transmission of the *Purāṇas* in a literate form, made them into texts for reference. They could be recited on ritual occasions, or even as an act of acquiring merit. A more developed historical sensibility required written records. The initial records tend to be texts based on an oral tradition. Writing introduces changes in the transmission of items believed to be significant to a culture. However the form which writing takes and the degree to which it is diffused in society would influence historical sensibility. Further, although an account can be changed, nevertheless the change is less radical in a written than in an oral form.[109] The historical tradition becomes an instrument of control over society, is maintained by a specific category of people whose power derives from their ability to provide those in authority with an identity. A historical tradition, therefore, establishes group consciousness. As a record of the past, transmitting the past in an oral or a literate form, the historian is an informant. Gradually, however, as his control over the past increases, he acquires a patron, and takes on the role of the performer as well.

## XII

The genealogical material could be used to identify groups and provide them with historical antecedents. It could relate traditions about origins and bridge gaps in traditions or separate or amalgamate them. Added to this was some chronological speculation. But above all, the genealogies were crucial to political functions and to legitimize office-holders.[110] Genealogy was the king's legal title to rule and it could include in its patterning, alliances and overlordships. The perception of the past is expressed in the association of places of origin, of links with lineages and the generations accounted for. Newcomers are grafted on or segments detached. The genealogy therefore becomes a useful historical tool. This necessitates that those who keep the genealogical tradition are aware of their closeness to political power.[111]

The reconstruction of the past takes a form very different from that of the nineteenth century interpretation of the earliest Indian past. There is in these texts little which can be construed as an Aryan invasion or even a racial difference between Aryan and non-Aryan. The perception is that of many societies with strong social, linguistic and ritual differentiation, with a variety of mores which seems to have had particular and multiple segmented identities, and did not conform to two confrontational systems. There are many internal dislocations occasioned by these differences. Even the veneer of a certain brahmanical uniformity remains an attempt fostered by the brahmanical perspective, but obviously not adhered to by others. The unifying factors are language and the acceptance of a *varṇa* society.

In the composition of the *vaṃśānucarita* of the early *Purāṇas*, an attempt was made to reconstruct a past, constituted for a purpose. Was this perhaps to establish a brahmanical version of the past, distinct from that put together in other traditions? The oral tradition of the bards was incorporated in this version. Yet the bards were not banished at this point for it is the bard who is said to be foretelling the narrative of dynasties. Nevertheless the perspective neither endorses the bardic view nor that, for instance, of the Buddhists. Thus, the lineage of the Buddha is briefly incorporated towards the end of the Sūryavaṃśa, mentioning Sākyamuni, Suddhodhana, Siddhartha and Rāhula. This was an attempt to subordinate the descent of the Buddha by incorporating it into the line of Rāma. Buddhist texts do maintain that the Śākya clan to which the Buddha belonged had descended from Ikṣvāku, but no reference is made to any link with Rāma as an ancestor. The Ceylon Chronicles written in the mid-first millennium AD as a Buddhist history of Sri Lanka, had much to say on some of the dynasties, as for example, the Nandas and Mauryas because of their links with both the Buddhist Order (the Saṅgha) and with Sri Lanka, but this information is ignored in the *Purāṇas*. Whereas we are told that Kauṭilya will anoint Candragupta, the founder of the Mauryan dynasty, the king Aśoka remains a mere name in a king-list. The *kṣatriya* status of the Mauryas as asserted in Buddhist sources is contradicted in the *Purāṇas*. Nor is there any attempt to incorporate the information on these dynasties given in their inscriptions. Inscriptions were official statements and the authors of the *Purāṇas* maintained their distance from these.

One of the purposes of constructing a view of the past arose from the recognition that religious authority would be considerably enhanced by association with political power and one of the strengths of such an association lay in controlling the construction of the past. This might in part have been the influence of the Buddhist Chronicles and Jaina texts where the association of kings with the Buddhist Councils and the *saṅgha* appears advantageous to the latter. The taking over of the tradition by the *brāhmaṇas*, was not merely an attempt at legitimizing the earlier descent groups and dynasties but the construction of the past was perceived as important to contemporary politics. The genealogical section received attention and was structured to facilitate the claims to legitimacy by a variety of ruling families. The universalizing of the genealogy would be appropriate to historical change, hence the attempt to give it a textual form. This also ensured it a wider audience, than when it was part of an oral bardic tradition. The ideological location of this construction was in the texts of the new Purāṇic religion, particularly of Vaiṣṇavism, also the recipients of royal patronage. This was not only a counterpoint to Buddhism in a period when Buddhism was gradually declining and Vaiṣṇavism was making a bid to take over its role, but it also encouraged the notion of the interface of political power with religious authority.

If situations of tension and confrontation increase sensitivity to historical perceptions, then this would be expected in the mid-first millennium AD. Vedic sacrificial rituals which had earlier been used for legitimizing *rājās* had begun to decline. This was partly due to the popularity of non-Vedic religions such as Buddhism and Jainism and the oligarchic roots of some kingdoms. This change also required the substitution of some other form of legitimation in cases where rulers were not followers of the heterodox sects. Genealogies appear to have provided the answer. These genealogies become part of a historical tradition because they encapsulate the description of processes of change over time. They were relating a historical process in a form which had legitimacy and was an accepted norm of that period. The historical processes to which they point can be reconstructed from other sources.

In the competition between Buddhism and the newly emerged Bhāgavata religion, focusing on the worship of Viṣṇu, the Gupta dynasty as supporters of the latter would have been regarded as appropriate patrons by the *brāhmaṇas* who supported the Bhāgavata religion, such as the Bhṛgu-aṅgirasa. These would then try and construct a past in which there would be a claim to historicity, even if not factually historical, and that this claim took the form of genealogy as a historical narrative. Genealogies therefore become important at a particular point in time because they legitimize power and authority and are closely linked with royal patronage. The social significance of genealogies is demonstrated by the fact that they occur in more than one *Purāṇa*.

Genealogy was the epicentre as it were, of *itihāsa* in the *Purāṇas* and it remained so in many texts of claims to status. It was not arbitrary but embedded in a perspective of the past and, at the same time, was necessary to functions of the present. This is particularly noticeable in the official records of dynasties, namely, the inscriptions in which claims to status are made. Seals of members of ruling families from the fifth century AD onwards, such as that of the Guptas and of Harṣavardhana, carry genealogies.[112] There is a vast spread of families of landowning chiefs and dynasties who, throughout early Indian history, have claimed to belong to the Yadu lineage. This stretches from a ruling family of Uttarakāśi in the Himalayan foothills[113] to the multiple families of the *vels* in Tamil Nadu[114] and to ruling houses in eastern and western India.[115] Lengthy inscriptions from various parts of India carry genealogies and some echo the formula of the *vaṃśānucarita* section. The Pallavas ruling in the seventh century in south India draw on lineage ties in their origin myths. The earlier inscriptions do not refer to their origins, but the later grants in Sanskrit introduce their ancestors.[116] The Pāṇḍyas trace their lineage to the Candravaṃśa.[117] In one inscription it is said that at the time of the Flood, Brahmā appealed to Pāṇḍya to save the world, and Pāṇḍya was therefore born as Budha the son of Soma in the line of Iḷā. The Colas at the end of the first millennium AD claimed descent from the Sūryavaṃśa and this claim was made in the reign of Vijayālaya and of Aditya I who, in one inscription are said to have been preceded by fifteen rulers.[118] Another inscription increases the list to forty-four and, yet another, to fifty-two, where the earlier names draw heavily on Purāṇic lists.[119] The lists do not tally in details but some names are common. The Cedis in central India, claiming association with the Haihayas, describe themselves as of the Lunar line.[120] Dynasties in central India also claim links with the Sūryavaṃśa or the Solar line. Genealogies therefore become agencies of mobilization for lesser families or those of obscure origin. The *vaṃśānucarita* section becomes a political charter for future claims.

As a construction of the past this section of the *Purāṇas* encapsulated a consciousness of history and was used both as such and elaborated upon in the subsequent period. The forms however changed from the bare bones of a genealogical skeleton to the far fuller forms of biographies and chronicles.

## Notes and References


1. J. Vansina, *Oral Tradition as History*, London, 1985; D.P. Henige, *The Chronology of Oral Tradition*, Oxford, 1974.
2. J. Goody and I. Watt, 'The Consequences of Literacy', *CSSH*, 5, 1963, pp. 304–45.
3. M. Fortes, 'The Structure of Unilineal Descent Groups', *American Anthropologist*, 55, 1953, pp. 17–41.
4. V. Kennedy, *Affinity of Ancient and Hindu Mythology*, London, 1831, p. 130.
5. V. Smith, 'Andhra History and Coinage', *ZDMG*, 1902, 56, pp. 649–75; *The Early History of India*, Oxford, 1924, pp. 11–12. H.C. Raychaudhuri, *Political History of Ancient India*, Calcutta, 1923, used the Purāṇic lists for reconstructing early history, particularly dynastic history. For a sceptical view of history in these sources see, D.D. Kosambi, *Ancient India: A History of its Culture and Civilisation*, New York, 1969, p. 174.
6. U.N. Ghoshal, *Studies in Indian History and Culture*, Bombay, 1965, pp. 37–52.
7. *Dates and Dynasties in Earliest India*, Delhi, 1973.
8. Arrian, *Indica*, 9.9. Solinus 52.5.
9. *Hist. Nat.*, 6.21, pp. 4–5.
10. A.B.L. Awasthi, *History from the Puranas*, Lucknow, 1975, maintains that there are references to post-Gupta history in some *Purāṇas*, but these analyses are not very convincing.
11. R.C. Hazra, *Studies on the Puranic Records of Hindu Rites and Customs*, Dacca, 1940; *Studies in the Upa-Puranas*, Calcutta, 1958; L. Rocher, *The Puranas*, Weisbaden, 1986, pp. 115–32.
12. *Bhāgvata Purāṇa*, 2.10, 1ff (trans G.V. Tagare, Delhi, 1976).
13. *Matsya Purāṇa*, Anandasrama Sanskrit Series, 1907; V.S. Agrawala, *Matsya Purana: A Study*, Varanasi, 1963; S.G. Kantawala, *Cultural History from the Matsya Purāṇa*, Baroda, 1964. *Vayu Purāṇa*, R. Mitra (ed.), Bombay, 1988; V.R.R. Dikshitar, *Some aspects of the Vayu Purana*, Madras, 1933; D.R. Patil, *Cultural History from Vayu Purana*, Poona, 1946. *Brahmāṇḍa Purāṇa*, Venketesvara Press, Bombay, 1963. *Viṣṇu Purāṇa*, Venketesvara Press, 1967.
14. *Vāyu*, op. cit., I, pp. 54–5.
15. *Viṣṇu*, op. cit., 3.6.15ff.

16. P. Horsch, *Die Vedische Gāthā und Śloka Literateur*, Bern, 1966, pp. 12–13.
17. For references see Rocher, op. cit., 14ff.
18. 3.185.1ff. Rocher, op. cit., 96ff.
19. A.S. Gupta, 'Purana, Itihasa and Akhyana', *Purāṇa*, 1964, VI.2.451ff. *Viṣṇu*, op. cit., 3.6.15.
20. V. Smith, *Early History of India*, op. cit., 11ff.
21. *Vāyu*, op. cit., 1.203; *Matsya*, op. cit., 53.63.
22. R.C. Hazra, op. cit., p. 18.
23. *Viṣṇu Purāṇa*, Bombay, 1910. H.H. Wilson (tr.), *The Viṣṇu Purāṇa*, reprint with Introduction by R.C. Hazra, Calcutta, 1961. V.R.R. Dikshitar, 'The Age of Visnu Purana', *IHC*, 1950, 13, pp. 46–50.
24. *Viṣṇu Purāṇa*, op. cit., 1.
25. Ibid., 1.6.
26. Ibid., 1.13.
27. Ibid., 1, pp. 14–20. I.13
28. Ibid., 1, pp. 7–15. I.7
29. Ibid., II.2.
30. Rocher, op. cit., pp. 130–1.
31. D.C. Sircar, *Studies in the Geography of Ancient and Medieval India*, Delhi, 1971 (reprint). M.R. Singh, *Geographical Data in the Early Puranas*, Calcutta, 1972.
32. *Viṣṇu Purāṇa*, op. cit., 3, pp. 1–2.
33. J.E. Mitchiner, 'The Evolution of the Manvantara Theory as Illustrated by the Saptarṣi Manvantara Traditions', *Purāṇa*, 1978, 20.1, pp. 7–37.
34. *Viṣṇu Purāṇa*, op. cit., 3.6.15ff. *Vāyu*, op. cit., 1.28–9; 61.55; 103, pp. 58–66. *Brahmāṇḍa*, op. cit., 2.35.63ff. V.S. Agrawala, 'Original Purana Samhita', *Purāṇa*, 1966, 8, 2, pp. 232–45. The caste status of Vyās remains somewhat ambiguous. Although he is universally accorded *brāhmaṇa* status, nevertheless his mother was of low caste, being the daughter of a fisherman.
35. In this connection see G. Bonazzoli, 'Puranic Parampara', *Purāṇa*, 22, 1, 1980, pp. 33–60.
36. G. Bonazzoli, 'Places of Puranic Recitation according to the Puranas', *Purāṇa*, 23, 1, 1981, pp. 48–60. The most popular place was the Naimiṣa forest whose location remains uncertain.
37. S.G. Kantawala, 'Home of the Matsyapurana', *Purāṇa*, 3, 1, 1961, pp. 115–19.
38. F.E. Pargiter, *The Purana texts of the Dynasties of the Kali Age*, Oxford, 1913; for a discussion on the subject see A.D. Pusalkar, *Studies in the Epics and the Puranas*, Bombay, 1955.
39. G. Bonazzoli, 'Composition, Transmission and Recitation of the Puranas', *Purāṇa*, 25, 2, 1983, pp. 254–80.

40. *Pañcavimsa Brāhmaṇa*, op. cit., 1.9.1, p. 4; *Taittirīya Brāhmaṇa*, 1.7.3.1.
41. *Atharva Veda*, 3.5.7; *Taittirīya Samhitā*, 4.5.2, *namo-sūtaya-ahantaya*.
42. Rocher, op. cit., 49ff. He is said to have been addressed as *medhavin*, *vaṃśakuśala*, *Kalpajña*, and *mahābhāga*.
43. *Bhāgvata Purāṇa*, op. cit., 1.18.18.
44. *Manu*, op. cit., 10.11, 17, 47; *Arthaśāstra*, 2.30.42; 3.7.29.
45. *Arthaśāstra*, III.7.27–9.
46. Pāṇini, 3.1.146–7.
47. *Arthaśāstra*, 3.13.30; 2.27.6. The rather uncomplimentary associations were probably because the author of the text treated all professions which were itinerant as suspicious.
48. *Vāyu*, op. cit., 42, pp. 137–48; *Padma*, II.27.
49. The *Mahābhārata* uses the epithet, *vrātyam sūtam*, Anuśāsana Parva, 48.10.
50. See the attached chart for an outline of the genealogical pattern.
51. *Śat. Br.*, 1.8.1, pp. 1–10; *Mahābhārata*, op. cit., 3.185; *Matsya Purāṇa*, op. cit., 1.10–33.
52. J.C. Heesterman, 'The Flood Story in Vedic Ritual', in *The Inner Conflict of Tradition*, Chicago, 1985, 59ff.
53. Ibid.
54. W.G. Lambert and A.R. Millard, *Atra-hasis*, Oxford, 1969.
55. Berossus, *The Babylonica of Berossus*, S.M. Burstein (ed. and trs.), Malibu, 1978, pp. 19–21.
56. M. Eliade, *Cosmos and History*, New York, 1959.
57. *Rāmāyaṇa*, 1, 70–1.
58. This is said to be common in patrilineal polygynous societies. (Personal communication from S.C. Humphreys).
59. Yayāti's five sons — Yadu, Anu, Turvaśa, Druhyu and Pūru — appear almost at the start of the descent list. Towards the end of the list come the five Pāṇḍavas — Yuddhisthira, Bhīma, Arjuna, Nakula and Sahadeva.
60. *Viṣṇu Purāṇa*, op. cit., 4.20.
61. *Viṣṇu Purāṇa*, op. cit., 4.18.13.
62. Ibid., 2, 3.15.
63. Heninge, op. cit., 40ff.
64. T. Trautman, *Dravidian Kinship*, Cambridge, 1981, 238ff.
65. K. Gough, *Matrilineal Kinship*. Berkeley, 1961.
66. Pargiter, *Ancient Indian His cal Tradition*, op. cit., p. 89.
67. *Viṣṇu*, op. cit., 4.16.1ff; 4.19.1ff.
68. Romila Thapar, 'Puranic Lineages and Archaeological Cultures', in *Ancient Indian Social History: Some Interpretations*, New Delhi, 1978, pp. 240–67.

69. For a general discussion of this picture see Romila Thapar, *From Lineage to State*, Delhi, 1984.
70. *Viṣṇu Purāṇa*, op. cit., 4.21.1; 4.24.8.
71. *Viṣṇu Purāṇa*, op. cit., 5.1–2.

    *nṛpānām kathitassarvo bhavatā vaṃśavistaraḥ*
    *vaṃśānucaritam caiva yathāvadanuvarṇitam.*

72. *Bhṛtya*, from the root *bhṛ*, to bear or to carry, means being dependent on, or a servant of, and refers to one who is to be maintained or nourished.
73. *Ep. Ind.*, 8, pp. 59, 86 (ASI, New Delhi), E.J. Rapson (ed.), *The Cambridge History of India*, I, Ancient India, Cambridge, 1935, p. 577.
74. H.H. Wilson, *The Vishnu Purana*, London, 1840; F.E. Pargiter, *Ancient Indian Historical Tradition*, London, 1922; *Puranic Texts of the Dynasties of the Kali Age*, London, 1913.
75. *Śat. Br.*, op. cit., 6.8.1.14.
76. *Mahābhārata*, op. cit., 7.118, pp. 14–15; Baudhāyana, *Dharmasūtra*, 1.1.2.13.
77. S.N. Pradhan, *Chronology of Ancient India*, Calcutta, 1927; P.L. Bhargava, *India in the Vedic Age*, Lucknow, 1956; A.D. Pusalkar, *Vedic Age*, Bombay, 1952, *Studies in the Epics and Puranas*, Bombay, 1958; R. Morton–Smith, *Dates and Dynasties in Early India*, Delhi, 1973.
78. T. Trautman, 'Length of generation and reign in ancient India', *JAOS*, 89, 3, 1969, pp. 564–77; A.L. Basham, *Studies in Indian History and Culture*, Calcutta, 1964.
79. Aihole Inscription, *Ep. Ind.*, 6.1ff.
80. D.H. Jones, 'Problems of African Chronology', *Journal of African History*, 11, 1970, pp. 161–76.
81. Heninge, op. cit., p. 120.
82. C.D. Church, 'The myth of the four yugas in the Sanskrit Puranas', *Purana*, 16, 1, 1974, pp. 5–25.
83. M. Biardeau, 'Etude de mythologique hindoue', *BEFEO*, 54, 1968, pp. 19–45.
84. D. Pingree, 'The Purāṇas and Jyotihśāstra Astronomy', *JAOS*, 110, 2, 1990, pp. 274–80.
85. Ibid.
86. M. Eliade, op. cit., p. 117.
87. *Viṣṇu*, op. cit., 1.3.1–25; *Vāyu*, op. cit., 8.18–63; *Matsya*, op. cit., 142–4.
88. P.V. Kane, *History of Dharmasastra*, Poona, 1947, *et. sq.*
89. The Laukika era was particularly common in Kashmir and Punjab and was also used in Rajasthan towards the end of the first millennium AD.
90. S.B. Das Gupta, *Obscure Religious Cults*, Calcutta, 1946, 235ff.

91. Pargiter, *Dynasties of the Kali Age* . . . , 53, *utsādayitvā kṣatram tu kṣatram anyat kariṣyati*.
92. Pargiter, 'Ancient Indian genealogies and chronology', *JRAS*, 1910, pp. 1–56.
93. L. Rocher, *The Puranas*, pp. 125–9.
94. *Vedic Index*, II, p. 109. Varanasi, 1967 (reprint).
95. R.P. Goldman, *Gods, Priests and Warriors*, Columbia, 1977, p. 146.
96. *Ṛgveda*, 8.3.9; 8.6.18; 10.72.7; *Atharvaveda*, op. cit., 20.9.3; 20.49.6.
97. Ibid., 15.6.4.
98. J. Brough, '*The Early Brahman System of Gotra and Pravara*', Cambridge, 1953, xv, pp. 4–29.
99. *Vedic Index*, op. cit., II, p. 109.
100. Manu, *Dharmaśāstra*, 1, 35; 1, 59; 5, 3; 12, 2.
101. *Vedic Index*, op. cit., I, 11.
102. 5.19.2.
103. Pargiter, op. cit., 186ff.
104. *Vāyu*, op. cit., 65, pp. 72–96; *Brahmāṇḍa*, op. cit., 3.1, pp. 73–100; *Matsya*, op. cit., 195, 11–46.
105. Goldman, *Gods, Priests and Warriors*, Columbia, 1977.
106. Ibid., p. 98.
107. *Mahābhārata*, op. cit., 1.164ff.
108. Goldman, op. cit.
109. Goody and Watt, op. cit.
110. M.D. Johnson, *The Purpose of Biblical Genealogies*, Cambridge, 1969, pp. 77–82.
111. D. Dumville, 'Kingship, Genealogies and Regnal Lists', in P.H. Sawyer and I.N. Woods (eds), *Early Medieval Kingship*, Leeds, 1977, pp. 72–104.
112. Bhitari Stone Pillar inscription of Skandagupta, *CII*, III (revised), 312ff; Nalanda Clay Seals of Budhagupta, Narasimhagupta and Kumāragupta, III, ibid., pp. 350–5; Bhitari Copper-silver Seal of Kumāragupta, III, ibid., 358ff. Sonpat Copper Seal inscription of Harṣavardhana, ibid., 231. The seal inscriptions are close to the minimal genealogical style, obviously for reasons of space.
113. Lakkhamandala Insc., *Ep. Ind.*, 1.10ff.
114. R. Chamapakalakshmi, 'Archaeology and the Tamil Tradition', *Puratattva*, 8, 1975–6, pp. 110–22.
115. Belava Copper-plate of Bhojavarmadeva, *Ep. Ind.*, 12, 39ff; Komarti Plates of Candravarman, lord of Kalinga, *Ep. Ind.*, 4, pp. 142ff, see also pp. 145ff; the inscription of the son of Bhaṭṭārka, king of Vallabhi, *Indian Antiquary*, 10, 283ff. The last of these has been described as a spurious inscription but the claim to *kṣatriya* status is the point at issue.

116. *South Indian Inscriptions*, 2, no. 98, ASI, Madras, 1890.
117. T.N. Subramaniam (ed.), *The Pandya Copper-plates*, Tamil History Academy, Madras, 1961.
118. Anbil Plates of Sundara Chola, *Ep. Ind.*, 15, 44ff.
119. Kanyakumari inscription of Virarajendra–Deva, *Ep. Ind.*, 18, 21ff.
120. Ratanpur Stone inscription of Jajalladeva I, *CII*, IV, 2, 409ff, Ootacammund, 1955.

# 34

# *Origin Myths and the Early Indian Historical Tradition*[*]

The organization of a historical tradition revolves around two related components — the purpose of action and the agency of action. Both of these are implicitly present irrespective of the form which the tradition may take, whether it is expressed as a myth or as an historical narrative. These components are by no means of equal importance but an element at least of each resides in all historical traditions. By the purpose of action is meant that the recording of what is believed to be history has an aim, either to moralize, as was often the case with traditional historical writing, or else to explain why and how past events happened, as is frequently the case with modern historiography. The agency of action is ultimately human (even if sometimes claimed to be divinely inspired); but it is of interest to discover which group of men are regarded as the actors in history and to what extent they function independently of any other agency, as for example, the gods.

Past events have to be related in a chronological order but the time sequence can be part of a much larger concept of time. Events concerning the more remote periods often take the form of a myth. Myth is in a sense a prototype history since it is a selection of ideas composed in narrative form for the purpose of preserving and giving significance to an important aspect of the past. Although myths cannot be used as descriptive sources on the past, their analysis can reveal the more emphatic assumptions of a society. Myths record what a people like to think about their past and to that

[*] D. Chattopadhyaya (ed.), *History and Society*, Calcutta, 1978, 271–94, Essays in Honour of Professor Niharranjan Ray.

My colleagues Dr Satish Saberwal and Dr B.D. Chattopadhyaya read an earlier draft of this paper and discussed it with me.

extent even some modern histories are not always free of an element of myth-making.

*Mythos* is defined as an 'utterance', often a tale recited in association with a religious ceremony. In that sense the narratives of the Puranic tradition were myths, since the *ākhyāna* was recited on ritual occasions and the *purāṇa* is explained as relating to an ancient lore which would tend to be preserved in mythical form. The myth involved archetypal or elemental characters, themes and symbols. It may be differentiated from the folk-tale by its focus on the 'grand events' of the past — the creation of the world, the origin of man and of the gods, the justification of kingship — whereas the folk-tale is concerned with more restricted social pre-occupations generally not involving any grand designs.

The interpretation of myths has resulted in diverse explanations.[1] Early interpreters saw in them symbols of natural phenomena and most myths were nature myths.[2] Others tried to see them as attempts at explaining the real world but couched in symbolic form.[3] Another view held that myths had an intrinsic relationship with ritual and could only be explained in terms of ritual origins, a view which conjured up the world of Frazer's *Golden Bough*.[4] A major re-orientation came about with Malinowski's view that myths were essentially charters of validation in which the aim was very often to provide a sanction for current situations.[5] This analysis encouraged an interest in the social under-pinnings of myth. The notion of myth as charter was reconsidered later when the emphasis shifted to the structural study of myth and the relation of this to the structural study of society.[6] The notion of myth as an archetype and as a primary cultural force has also remained a dominant trend.[7] Partially associated with this is the theory of Mircea Eliade that myths reflect a nostalgia for the origins of human society and try to evoke a return to a creative era.[8] More recently it has been suggested that myths are connected with liminality and arise in transitional situations, thus explaining how one state of affairs became another, or how things came to be what they are.[9] Specific to Indo-European mythology have been the attempts of Georges Dumezil to analyse these myths on the basis of the 'tripartite ideology', a pattern which even for Vedic myths is not always beyond question.[10]

This brief survey of the possible range of paradigms which can provide interpretations of myths is not an attempt to establish any priorities of interpretation. It is provided only to emphasize that in choosing to limit this study to origin myths, and that too in the context of the *itihāsa-purāṇa* and related historical tradition, there will implicitly be a delimiting of the range of interpretation.

Myth is at one level a straightforward story, a narrative; at another level it reflects the integrating values around which societies are organized.[11] It codifies belief, safeguards morality, vouches for the efficiency of the ritual and provides social norms. It is a rationalization of man's activity in the past although the expression may take on non-rational forms. It remains socially important as long as it is a charter of belief, but becomes ineffective when seen as a myth. As a charter of belief it serves to protect cultural continuity and provides through its theme a point of cultural equilibrium. In a historical tradition therefore the themes of myths act as factors of continuity.

The analysis of the structure of a myth can reveal (to a lesser or greater extent) the structure of the society from which it emanates. The analysis may centre on one of two perspectives: either the sequence and the order of events or the schemata and organization of the sequences at different levels. Ultimately the myth is concerned with the quest for understanding the significance of nature and culture. The action of the myth is usually the narration of sacred history which is believed to be a true event which has taken place in the past. Since these primordial events are often associated with supernatural beings they also tend to take on the character of models for action and for ritual. Most myths being explanatory (whether explicitly stated as such or not) they are related to the origin or the commencement of a particular event or action. Myths made the past intelligible and meaningful, but it was intelligibility and meaningfulness which related to the present, for the continuity of myth is largely with reference to the present.

In societies (and this would include most pre-modern societies) where the oral tradition rather than the use of literature is the more functional means of communication on a large scale, myths become one of the means of passing on information. There is therefore a process of constant adjustment, and myths from earlier periods are recast in conformity with the social assumptions of later periods. The repetition of the same myth, with perhaps some modifications, from age to age is partly to ensure 'the message' getting through and partly to indicate new nuances. Myths therefore have a widely over-arching relationship to all aspects of society and each major myth could be the subject of an expansive analysis. The attempt here is not to provide a complete analysis of each myth selected for discussion but to recognize and point up the historically significant aspects of certain myths, i.e., those aspects which had some role in the propagation and continuity of the *itihāsa-purāṇa* tradition and its main concerns. But this is not to deny that even within those aspects there may well be other layers touching on different facets of early Indian society. Further, the attempt is not to ascertain the historical authenticity of the myth but rather to probe the reason for its acceptance in as much as it relates to social validation. As validating charters, myths have a close connections with social organization, not only representing, as they do, the assumptions about the past but also under-pinning the social relationships of the present.

The myths which are the most closely related to the *itihāsa-purāṇa* tradition are available in the core of the tradition, that is, the genealogical sections, *vaṃśānucarita*, of the major *Purāṇas*. A variant of these may be seen from the somewhat different perspective of the Buddhist historical tradition, the sources for which have to be culled from various texts. These will form our primary sources. In both cases the earliest occasion for the recital of these myths would be in association with rituals and ceremonies. The *Purāṇas* were recited over a period of many days in connection with a religious ceremony. The genealogical sections in particular were preserved by the *sūta* and the *māgadha*, the professional bards and chroniclers, who recited them in association with the epics and the heroic ballads at royal courts. In the Buddhist case too the literature would initially be preserved as part of the oral tradition of monastic centres. This does not however imply that there was any integral correlation between the ritual and the purpose of the myth. It seems more likely that the association with ritual occasions would serve to heighten the importance of what the myth was meant to convey, for with the compilation of the texts in a literary form, making them accessible to literate members of society, the association with ritual perceptibly weakens. The texts referred to above were in the main compiled and edited by about the middle of the first millennium AD, but earlier versions of the myths and narrative stereotypes are known from earlier texts, some of which go back to the first millennium BC. There was therefore both time and incentive to recognize the narrative and the symbols of the myths for changing social contexts. The texts drew in the main from the earlier oral tradition and were transferred to a written form in the first millennium AD. In spite of this, *Purāṇas* were frequently treated as part of the oral tradition with the reciting of the texts to large audiences. Both categories of sources came into prominence during the period when Buddhism and Vaiṣṇavism, in addition to their religious role, were performing the function of being agencies of acculturation for those for whom the Great Tradition had hitherto been inaccessible. Such texts reflected the social concerns of the present even though they treated of the social concerns of the past. The significance of this lies in the fact that it is also by the mid-first millennium AD (and in later centuries) that these texts — and the *vaṃśānucarita* section of the *Purāṇas* in particular — are used for the more secular purpose of providing lineage links and genealogical connections for the families which gave rise to the multiple dynasties of the time.

In a historical tradition origin myths play a crucial role as they provide a point of commencement. In the *itihāsa-purāṇa* tradition the origin myth referred to or implied is that of the Flood. It occurs first in the *Śatapatha Brāhmaṇa* and is found again in the *Mahābhārata* and *Purāṇas*, there being a substantial difference of time between the first and the last version.[12] The *Śatapatha Brāhmaṇa* version relates that Manu, primaeval man, was performing his morning ablutions when a fish came into his hands. It asked to be reared and protected and promised Manu safety from the deluge in return, explaining to Manu that the gods had decided to punish mankind by unleashing a massive flood to destroy all creation. The fish grew larger in time. On the eve of the flood it commanded Manu to build a ship for himself, in which Manu escaped from the flood. The ship was tied to the fish who swam through the waters and lodged it on the northern mountain. When the water subsided it glided down the mountain slope and returned Manu to Jambudvīpa. In one account Manu being alone and desirous of sons observed austerities and performed a sacrifice to the gods from which a woman was born and she was called Iḍā (or Iḷā in other versions). Through her Manu generated this race.

The story is repeated in some of the *Purāṇas* but with certain significant additions. In the *Matsya Purāṇa* the fish is described as an incarnation of Viṣṇu — the *Matsya-avatāra*. Iḷā is a hermaphrodite, hence called by the cognate Iḷa-Iḷā, and is the progenitor of one of the two royal lineages, the Candravaṃśa or lunar lineage.

Manu's eldest son Ikṣvāku was the progenitor of the Sūryavaṃśa or solar lineage. In some texts however the male Iḷa is referred to as the eldest son who was inadvertently changed into a woman, Iḷā. To these lineages belonged all those who came to be regarded as legitimate *kṣatriyas*. Manu being the originator of the lineages framed the rules and laws of government and collected one-sixth of the produce of the land as tax. The *Viṣṇu Purāṇa* omits the story of the flood in the *vaṃśānucarita* section but refers to the birth of Iḷā as the daughter of Manu and states that through the goodwill of the gods she was able to switch her form from female to male and back as occasion demanded.[13]

The flood assumes the primary precondition of water from out of which the known creation arises. The great flood caused the total destruction of the world and this is a recognized stage in the cycle of the time concept, what Eliade would call the abolition of profane time.[14] The beginnings of history therefore emerge from a condition which has no antecedents: it is in fact symbolic of the very beginning. However the negation of antecedents is not absolutely total since Manu is not created out of the flood but exists prior to it. Further creation follows from the flood. Repetition occurs frequently in myths of renewal such as the story of the flood and in such cases the abolition of profane time is a marker separating mythical time from historical time. The latter emerges from a condition of renewal where the vestiges of the old have been destroyed.

The choice of the fish as the saviour is obvious since the fish alone could survive the flood and this is used to good effect in the Puranic version where it is referred to as the *Matsya-avatāra*. The myth is brought into service as a means of exalting the deity Viṣṇu and introducing him into what was an old and well-established myth through the mechanism of the *avatāra*. This endows Viṣṇu with antiquity and enhances his image as the deity who was willing to take on the lowly form of the fish in order to save man. It might be worth mentioning in passing that the Sumerian god Enki, who in the Sumerian version of the flood myth saved Ziusudra, the Sumerian counterpart of Manu, is often represented as a fish in later Mesopotamian mythology in which capacity he acts as a saviour deity.[15]

That Manu procreates through his daughter possibly reflects a patrilineal emphasis known from other myths of such societies where an incestuous relationship also occurs in origin myths.[16]

More plausibly it may indicate the symbolic insistence of the purity of lineage, that ultimately the mother-father of the founders of the lineages was the child of Manu and created from a sacrifice. The derivation of the Candravaṃśa lineage from a hermaphrodite suggests a variation on the idea of twins or siblings as parents, stressing again the purity of lineage. It is significant that in the widely accepted description of the utopia, the land of the Uttara Kurus, lineage identities are not required for legitimising procreation.[17] The *Purāṇas* repeat the idea in the story of the evolution of society where it is said that Brahmā created the earth and then four sets of human beings, each consisting of a thousand couples.[18] Life was idyllic and easy. But this did not last, for ultimately decay set in together with the emergence of the four *varṇas* and a general falling off from the utopian beginnings. Yet in a late section of the *Ṛg Veda* the theme of rejecting sibling incest is associated with the god of death, Yama, and his sister, Yami, suggesting that the idea was being questioned by some.[19] However, in Puranic sources Yama is sometimes contrasted with Manu (associated with life), both being sons of Vivasvat.[20] That one of the royal lineages was born from a female form was obviously rather galling in later times when women were of low social status and on par with the *śūdras*. This is sought to be explained away in the *Viṣṇu Purāṇa* by the statement that during the course of the sacrificial ritual there was an inaccuracy and, although Manu had been performing the sacrifice for the obtaining of sons, a daughter was born.[21] The situation was retrieved somewhat by Mitra and Varuṇa permitting the daughter to become an hermaphrodite. In actual fact the male-female distinction was necessary for the purpose of the myth and was required as a distinguishing feature of the two lineages.

In terms of the bi-polarity of symbols the lineages were separated by the one being associated with the sun and the other with the moon.[22] Evidently the lineages had to be kept distinct. This is apparent from the structure of the lineages for the two groups. The Candravaṃśa or Aila appears to be a segmentary lineage system where each male child and his male progeny is treated as a separate segment of the lineage and the descent group of each is recorded.[23] Such a record inevitably covers a wide geographical area — central, western, northern and parts of eastern India. The Sūryavaṃśa or Ikṣvāku lineage on the other hand records only the descent by primogeniture of a few lines and is far more limited in area as well as being confined chiefly to the middle Ganga valley. The difference in the structure of lineages may also indicate the more sedentary settlement of the Ikṣvāku as against a society more given to migrating groups among the Aila.

The choice of the two lineage names, the Sun and the Moon, are significant as the dominant planetary pair. Perhaps the myth refers to a belief in an early division into moieties of the tribes or two rival groups. Alternatively it could have been an attempt at orderliness on the part of the compilers of the *Purāṇas*, to weave the many dynastic strands into two main currents and finally to a single origin. It is not surprising that the word Manu provided the generic base for *mānava* meaning mankind.

The variation between the early and later version of the myth as in the *Śatapatha Brāhmaṇa* and the *Purāṇas* shows the manner in which it was used for two purposes pertinent to the new concerns of the later period. The readjustment of the myth to Vaiṣṇava religious purposes is self-evident in the idea of the *Matsya-avatāra*. The latching on of one of the two royal lineages to Iḷa-Iḷā and Ikṣvāku, the children of Manu, and thereby indirectly to the flood story, was an effective means of giving both antiquity and prestige to the lineages. The historically attested dynasties from the fourth century BC onwards appear to have had little interest in proclaiming their lineage origins. The concern with lineage and genealogical connections involving either the Sūryavaṃśa or the Candravaṃśa are more marked in the early centuries AD and become quite obsessive in some parts of India after the mid-first millennium AD. This concern may have necessitated the adaptation of earlier myths to new interests. Information on what was believed to be the 'history' of the lineages would have been preserved as part of the oral tradition by the *sūta* and the *māgadha*. It is believed that this oral tradition was taken over, probably by priestly authors, in the process of the compiling of the *Purāṇas*, some of which date to the middle of the first millennium AD.[24] The neat arrangement of the lineages and their segments could well have been worked out in the process of adjusting the earlier myth and the new version would then provide the validation for the new lineage connections. The reference to Manu framing the laws and collecting the tax would have underlined the legitimacy of these two functions for those who were the descendents of Manu.

Curiously, there is a striking parallel to this in the Mesopotamian tradition. The story of the flood from Sumerian texts is remarkably similar to the version of the *Śatapatha Brāhmaṇa* in its details. Deluge myths as the genesis of cultures are by no means rare. What is of interest however is the particulars in which the versions seem to agree. It is now well-known that the Sumerian myth found its way via the Babylonian version into the Bible story of Noah's ark.[25] It has also been argued that the Greek version in which Zeus sends a flood to punish mankind and the survivor from the flood is Deucalion, the son of Prometheus (or in later versions Ogygus), is a myth derived from the Mesopotamian original, since the occurrence of the flood and the attitude of the gods towards man are not in keeping with the Greek stereotypes regarding natural calamities and the deities.[26] The Sumerian flood myth is sometimes associated with the archaeological evidence of the massive flooding of a group of cities in the delta of the Tigris-Euphrates valley, an event generally dated to the end of the fourth millennium BC.[27] Is it possible that the Sumerian myth found its way to the Harappans and via the Harappans entered the Vedic tradition? What is even more curious is that in the late third millennium BC the Sumerian flood myth is worked into the story of the king-lists of ancient Mesopotamia.[28] These refer to the mythical seven pre-diluvian kings, then the coming of the flood and the survivor who is associated with the descent of kingship on to various cities of ancient Mesopotamia. Indian sources also refer in sequence to the seven pre-diluvian Manus, the flood and then the royal lineages which succeeded. It would seem that the Mesopotamians made the same use of their earlier Sumerian flood as did the Indians in searching for an earlier sanction to an existing situation of a later period.

The genealogical sections of the *Purāṇas*, with their recital of king-lists and descent groups, are punctuated with myths relating to the supposedly more important personalities. The narration of the Candravaṃśa lineage in the *Viṣṇu Purāṇa* is a case in point and is interspersed with stories. This was in part a mnemonic device as well as an attempt to embellish the otherwise rather dry narration of succession-lists. What is more important from our point of view is the fact that the two ancestral figures from whom the main Candravaṃśa lineage segments trace their origin — Purūravas and, of a later generation, Yayāti — are in each case introduced through a well-known and frequently repeated myth.[29] Purūravas has the female Iḷā as his mother and Soma, the moon-god, as his grandfather. That his descendents were the progeny of Soma would further strengthen the nomenclature of Candravaṃśa. This idea is echoed in at least one Candravaṃśa royal family of the early medieval period, the Candella, who claim the moon god as one of their original ancestors.[30]

The legend of Purūravas and Urvaśī is related in full, following in detail the version earlier recorded in the *Śatapatha Brāhmaṇa* in preference to the variant in the *Mahābhārata*. The earliest version of the myth in the *Ṛg Veda* reads as an inversion of the Cupid and Psyche story.[31] The king Purūravas falls in love with the *apsarā* Urvaśī who has been banished to earth for a temporary period. She agrees to live with him on condition that she should never see him in the nude. After some time the Gandharvas decide to call her back to the celestial regions and arrange one night for her pet rams to be stolen. As Purūravas rushes after the thief there is a flash of lightning which reveals him in his nudity to Urvaśī, whereupon she vanishes. The distraught king wanders for many years in search of her and eventually finds her. She does not return to him but does bear him sons. The Ṛgvedic version appears to be incomplete and there may have been more to the story. In the version recorded in the *Śatapatha Brāhmaṇa*, Purūravas is anxious to join the Gandharvas and thereby live permanently with Urvaśī.[32] The Gandharvas require him to kindle three fires and perform some sacrifices, after which he is accepted into their world. In the *Mahābhārata* the king is killed by the *brāhmaṇas* whom he disturbs during their sacrificial rituals.[33]

The myth has in the past been interpreted as a solar myth with Purūravas representing the sun and Urvaśī the vanishing dawn.[34] A more plausible interpretation suggests that the latter two versions are mythological variants of each other, the significance of the action being that Purūravas is being sacrificed.[35] The sacrifice of the male, symbolized by his kindling three fires and then being taken to the world of Gandharvas, was associated with certain matriarchal mother-goddess cults. The myth therefore would represent the transitional phase to patrilineal society. It is further argued that Purūravas having a hermaphrodite parent is not only an attempt to link him with Manu via Iḷā but is also indicative of a transition to a patrilineal society from an earlier matrilineal one. But as we have seen, the symbolism of a hermaphrodite does not necessarily indicate such a transition. The repeated occurrence of the myth in a variety of texts points to the mythological significance attached to Purūravas as the founder of the Candravaṃśa lineage. Its occurrence in a lineage context as well gives added status to the descent of Purūravas's progeny from an *apsarā*. Of the many sons whom Urvaśī bore to Purūravas, two received particular attention. The eldest was Āyus through whom the main lineages of the Candravaṃśa descended; and the other was Amāvasu whose line included Paraśurāma, the destroyer of the *kṣatriyas*, suggesting thereby a balancing of lineages.

Of Purūravas's sons the main lineage goes via the eldest son Āyus to his eldest son Nahus whose eldest son Yati declined the throne, whereupon it went to his younger brother Yayāti, the emphasis being on primogeniture. At this point there is the famous myth of Yayāti who in old age seeks to exchange his years for the youth of one of his sons.[36] He asks each one in turn, starting with the eldest, Yadu, who refuses, as indeed do each of the next three, Druhyu, Turvaśa and Anu. These three are cursed by Yayāti with the statement that none of their progeny shall possess dominion. The youngest, Pūru, readily agrees to the request of his father and takes upon himself his old age. Ultimately, after many years, when Yayāti is exhausted with his youth, he accepts his old age from Pūru. Before dying he appoints Pūru as his successor and gives him sovereignty over the main kingdom, the *madhya-deśa* (in the main the Ganga-Yamuna Doāb), which should otherwise by rights have gone to Yadu. The eldest son Yadu is sent to the territories to the south-west of the *madhya-deśa*, and the other three to the south-east, the west and the north. The *Viṣṇu Purāṇa* states that Pūru was made the supreme monarch of the earth and his brothers governed as viceroys.[37] The *Mahābhārata* has an elaborate version of the myth and explains further that from Yadu there descended the Yādavas, the Turvaśa produced the Yavanas, the Druhyu produced the Bhojas and the Anu a variety of *mlеccha* peoples, i.e. those regarded as socially inferior.[38] This version takes the story further, involving Yayāti's attempt to enter heaven.

The Yayāti myth has been the subject of a lengthy analysis in which the emphasis has been on an explanation of the symbolism of not only the youth-age syndrome associated with the Yayāti-Pūru relationship but also the expression of values such as valour, sacrifice, riches and, above all, truth.[39] A more narrow interpretation linked to the requirements of the historical tradition indicates two obvious emphases. Firstly, the myth explains the lack of observance of the rule of primogeniture where the eldest son is sent to a distant area and the youngest son succeeds to the throne. Secondly, it highlights the supremacy of the Pūru lineage as being the superior one among the *kṣatriyas* since Pūru inherits the sovereignty. The Druhyu, Turvaśa and Anu lineages tend to die out or else get merged with the Pūru and this takes care, genealogically, of an otherwise impossibly wide distribution of descendants. Significantly, the superiority of the Pūru lineage is contrasted with the low status of the others where in the *Mahābhārata*, as we have seen, they are regarded as *mlecchas*. The Yayāti myth also provides an explanation for why non-*kṣatriya* groups are not recorded in the genealogies. Subsequent to this myth, the narrative of the Candravaṃśa lineage becomes substantially that of the descendents of Yadu and Pūru. In a sense, the events of the *Mahābhārata* war suggest a kind of reversal of the relationship between these two descent groups, where it is the offspring of Pūru who seek the help of the offspring of Yadu and the latter play the dominant role. The myth also serves to explain the migration and settlement of tribes. The Pūrus in Vedic literature are associated with the Sarasvatī region and the Punjab.[40] The Yayāti myth would account for a possible migration into the *madhya-deśa* and perhaps the reorganizing of the settlement in that area. Similarly the Yadus are also associated with the Punjab and their appearance in western India would have to be explained.[41]

The emphasis on primogeniture is continually underlined in many texts. This after all is the crux of the events which form the core of the two epics, the *Mahābhārata* and the *Rāmāyaṇa*. Where the law is not observed the breaking of the law has to be justified. This is clearly set out in an earlier section of the *Viṣṇu Purāṇa* in the myth of Pṛthu the son of Veṇa, a myth which also occurs in other texts.[42] We are told that among the early kings of the earth was Veṇa who obstructed the sacrifices. His opposition to the Vedic *sūtras* and *yajñas* provoked the antagonism of the *ṛṣis* who put him to death by piercing him with stalks of the sacred *kuśa* grass. In the absence of a king there was now a threat of anarchy. So the *ṛṣis* churned the left thigh of Veṇa and there sprang up a short, dark, ugly man whom they called Niṣāda, a name derived from the command of the *ṛṣis* who told him to 'sit down' (*ni-ṣada*). The *ṛṣis* were unhappy with what they had produced so they banished him and he became the ancestor of all the *mlecchas* and the wild tribes such as the Kirāta, Pulinda and Śabara. The *ṛṣis* then churned the right arm of Veṇa and there sprang up a beautiful man whom they called Pṛthu (the broad or expansive one). He was righteous in his manner, introduced cattle-rearing and the plough, and his reign was so prosperous that the earth was named Pṛthivī in memory of him.

The wickedness of Veṇa is ascribed to the usual reason that he objected to the teaching of the Vedas. It is significant that he can be put to death only by the *ṛṣis*, who alone have the power to assassinate kings. His death is caused by the *kuśa* grass used in the sacred rituals of Vedic ceremonies. The fear of revolt against and assassination of legitimate kings is evident from the fear of resulting anarchy. This sentiment is in conformity with the concept of *matsyanyāya* as explained in the *Mahābhārata* where, in a condition of anarchy, the large fish devour the small fish.[43] The legitimacy of succession has to be maintained by producing a successor from the body of Veṇa. It is his left side which produces the ungainly, primitive successor who has to be exiled and the right side which produces the appropriate successor, conforming to the symbolism of the left being impure and the right pure. The association of Niṣāda with the wild tribes, food-gatherers perhaps, is juxtaposed with the introduction of agriculture by Pṛthu and it is through the latter that the earth prospers. That the elder son was banished in favour of the younger could only be justified by pointing to the inadequacies of the elder. The contrast however is so extreme that one almost suspects an association of guilt with the usurpation by the younger son. Could this myth have symbolized the overpowering of the legitimately settled food-gathering cultures by the agriculturalists, in a period which saw the gradual encroaching of agriculture into new lands via the grants of land to religious donees and to officials, when the former cultures would henceforth always be associated with the dark and the ugly and the latter with that which is beautiful and prosperous? Vedic sources mention Niṣāda and Pṛthu but in unrelated contexts. Niṣāda appears to have been a general term used for non-Aryan tribes and Pṛthu was the first of kings and associated with the invention of agriculture.[44] It is from the sacrifice performed at the birth of Pṛthu that there emerged the *sūta* and the *māgadha* who are told that their function is to eulogize the king and praise his actions.[45]

Perhaps historical consciousness (to the extent that this is embodied in bards and chroniclers) was believed to coincide with the development of agricultural society.

Another myth relating directly to primogeniture occurs at a later stage in the Candravaṃśa lineage, in connection with the brothers Devāpi and Śantanu of the Pūru lineage.[46] For twelve years there has been a drought in the kingdom and this is explained as arising from Śantanu, the younger brother, ruling in place of the elder, Devāpi who has gone into the forest. The situation can be righted only if Devāpi can be brought back. When Śantanu's minister hears this he despatches some heretics to the forest who instruct Devāpi in anti-Vedic doctrines. This annoys the *brāhmaṇas* who declare that Devāpi is degraded and unfit to rule, whereupon there is rain. Earlier versions of the myth in the *Ṛg Veda* and *Nirukta* attribute the supercession of the elder brother to his becoming an ascetic or his suffering from a skin disease, both perfectly legitimate reasons for supercession.[47] In these versions Devāpi rejects the throne when offered to him and performs a ritual which results in rain. In the Puranic version the Vedic story is readjusted so as to highlight the importance of primogeniture.

Myths emphasizing primogeniture are relatively rare in the Sūryavaṃśa sections of the genealogies for these record descent only of the eldest son or the legitimate successor. In the Candravaṃśa lineage the stress on primogeniture was required from time to time so that the senior descent group in the segmentary system could be clearly demarcated. Where the procedure was reversed it had to be explained. The myth would serve both to legitimize a junior line which might have become more powerful, as is suggested by the Yayāti myth, and also to ensure that technically at least the core kingdoms remained with the 'senior' lineages.

Mythology in the Buddhist sources relates essentially to two main areas, origin myths of tribes and places and the legend of the life of the Buddha. In later Buddhist texts there are myths connected with the *Theras* and the Saṅgha, but these are often derivative of the earlier myths. The earlier myths tend to be fairly traditional and are often either borrowings from the Puranic tradition or come from a common source of myths which supplied both the Puranic and the Buddhist texts. What is of interest are the similarities in the origin myths as recorded in the two traditions as well as the deviations.

The most important of the clans is of course that of the Śākyas to which the Buddha belonged. The Śākyas are traced back to the Ikṣvāku lineage or the Okkāka as it is called in the Pāli sources.[48] In one text we are told that king Okkāka had five sons and four daughters by his chief queen. On her death the king married a young woman who, when she bore the king a son, wanted her son to be the heir. The king was persuaded to exile his elder children and the five brothers and four sisters travelled to the Himalayan foothills. Here they met the sage Kapila who advised them to build a city and settle in that region. The city therefore was called Kapilavastu. The eldest brother remained unmarried and the other four brothers married their four sisters and from them there descended the tribe of the Śākyas. The *Mahāvastu*, a text of a later period, has a variation on this, in that there are five brothers and five sisters, the name of the king is Sujāta, and it is his concubine who wishes her son to be king.[49]

The Śākyas had a close relationship with the Koliyas according to another version of the origin myth of both.[50] The Śākyas in this case consisted of five sisters and four brothers. Since the degradation of the race had to be prevented it was decided to appoint the eldest sister as the mother and the remaining brothers and sisters paired off. The eldest sister developed leprosy and was therefore put into a deep pit in the forest where she was one day threatened by a tiger. She was rescued by Rāma, the king of Banāras, who had also been exiled because of leprosy but had managed to cure himself. He therefore cured her as well and married her and they lived in a city which they had built. They sent their sons to Kapilavastu so that they could marry their maternal uncles' daughters. The young men kidnapped the Śākya princesses and were not prevented from doing this since they were related to the Śākyas and the kidnapping was almost customary. It was from these marriages that the Koliya tribe descended and was so called because their city of origin was established at a place where a large *kol* tree was growing. The *Mahāvastu* version states that the princess suffering from leprosy was left in a forest where she was discovered by the royal sage Kola who took her to his hermitage.[51] Sixteen pairs of twin sons were born and were called the Koliyas and were sent to Kapilavastu from where they obtained their brides. The settlement of the Koliyas adjoined that of the Śākyas and the two were separated by the river Rohiṇī, the waters of which, used for irrigation, were the cause of dispute between the Śākyas and the Koliyas.[52]

In a late text the Moriyas (Mauryas) were also associated with the Śākyas.[53] They are described as those Śākyas who fled from Kapilavastu when Viḍuḍbha, the king of Kośala, attacked the Śākyas for having deceived him into marrying a maid-servant rather than the princess who was promised to him. This group of Śākyas settled in a *pipal* forest, the Pipphalivana, which abounded in peacocks — *mayura/mora* — from which their name was eventually derived. This appears to have been a later attempt to link Aśoka Maurya with the family of the Buddha.

The origin of the Licchavis again relates them to the royal family of Banaras.[54] The chief queen gave birth to a lump of flesh which was put in a box and floated down the river. It was picked up by a hermit who nurtured its contents until eventually the lump of flesh changed into a twin boy and girl. They had such a translucent beauty that they appeared to have no skin, hence the name, *nicchavi*; or alternatively, everything seemed to get absorbed into them and thus they were called *linacchavi*. Eventually they came to be called Licchavi. The children were adopted by local cowherds but as they proved to be totally undisciplined they had to be abandoned (*vajjitabba*). An area was demarcated and given over to them and this was called Vajji, an obvious attempt to explain the name of the confederacy of eight clans commonly referred to as the Vṛjji or Vajji confederacy. The boy and girl were married and had sixteen pairs of sibling twins. Since the city in which they lived had to be continually enlarged (*viśālikata*) they came to call it Veśāli/Vaiśāli. The Licchavis were to become a powerful tribe and were the main contenders for the control over the Ganga valley against the kingdom of Magadha. Although defeated at this juncture they continued to maintain their status in the Terai-Nepal area, for not only does Candragupta I make much of his marriage to a Licchavi princess[55] but they also provided an early and important dynasty in Nepal. This is assuming that the later Licchavis were descended from the earlier ones and this was not just a political claim. In some of the later *vaṃśāvalīs* of Nepal the lineage of the Licchavis is not only linked to the Ikṣvākus but the actual descent is given via Raghu, Aja, Daśaratha, eight other kings and then the Licchavis, but the Buddhist origin myth is not repeated.[56]

The origin of the Śākyas is related in fuller detail in the biographies of the Buddha from the northern Sanskrit Buddhist texts, some of which have been collated in a Chinese version.[57] This version makes the same points as the earlier one but underlines the emphases more strongly. In the dynasty of the Fish king was born a ruler called Ta-man-tso. Not having a son he became an ascetic and gave his kingdom to his ministers. When he was old and incapable of looking after himself, his disciples, if they had to leave him alone for any length of time, would place him in a basket and hang the basket from a tree. This would safeguard him against wild animals, snakes and the like. One day a hunter shot him by mistake. His disciples, full of grief, cremated his body. But two drops of blood had fallen from the wound onto the ground. Out of these drops of blood sprang up two stalks of sugarcane (*ikṣa*) which on maturing burst asunder and revealed a boy in one and a girl in the other. The children were taken to the ministers who agreed to recognize them as the children of the late king. The boy was called Ikṣvāku and Sūryavaṃśa and the girl Subhadrā. They were married and a son Janta was born to them. Ikṣvāku had four sons by a later, second marriage, all of whom were fine, manly young men. Subhadrā was now concerned that her son, who was not as attractive, would be overlooked for the succession. She therefore plotted to have the four boys banished. They went into exile and travelled north across the Bhāgīrathī and into the Snowy Mountains, accompanied by their four sisters. They arrived in a beautiful valley where the sage Kapila dwelt and settled there. So as not to pollute their race they married their sisters and founded the city of Kapilavastu. Because they were able (*śaknoti*) to govern well they came to be called Śākyas. The story then continues to trace the lineage of descent from the princes down to Suddhodana, the father of the Buddha.

This sample of origin myths indicates certain characteristics which provide some clues to social concerns. In each case the myth attempts to explain not only the origin of the tribe but also the city associated with that particular *janapada* or territory where the tribe eventually settled. The inclusion of the city seems to have almost equal importance as indeed the cities of the *janapadas* in the latter part of the first millennium BC had considerable political and economic importance. In the *janapadas* with the *saṅgha* or *gaṇa* system of government (oligarchic government or chiefdoms), the city was the nucleus of political life and would inevitably be seen as arising almost coterminously with the *janapada*.

The attempt to explain the name of the clan is a striking feature of these myths if only because the etymologies are so patently false. The survival for example of the extremely far-fetched etymology for Licchavi is quite remarkable. It would seem that the original etymology for these names was either forgotten or lost and clumsy attempts were made in a later period to invent an etymology. This would also account for the variation in the explanation. Thus Śākya is derived from *Śaknoti* (to be able), the *śaka* tree and *sakahi* (with reference to their marrying their sisters). Totem worship may be suggested as a possible explanation but this would be a plausible theory only if there had been a consistency of association with a single object in each case.

The selection of clans whose origin and genealogy are considered worthy of record are invariably those which had *saṅgha* and *gaṇa* systems of government. These gave prominence to the *kṣatriya* families since they were the ones who had the right to be represented in the *santhāgāra* or assembly-hall. The *kṣatriya* members of these *janapadas* were frequently inter-related and their territories lay in geographical proximity to each other. The *kṣatriya* families were again those who were associated with the Buddha, Mahāvīra and other heterodox teachers. None of these origin myths are concerned with the genesis of the neighbouring kingdoms where monarchy prevailed, even though the Buddha after his enlightenment preached more frequently in the kingdoms of Magadha and Kāśi.

The insistence on siblings or, even better, sibling twins as the procreators of the *jana* is explained in the myths as necessary for maintaining the purity of lineage, where the lineage can be traced back to those of identical blood. Related to this was possibly also the idea that sibling marriages would be the closest simulation of the situation which prevailed in the Uttara-Kuru utopia, which utopia was equally acceptable to the Buddhists and to the *brāhmaṇas*. Periods of genesis would inevitably be associated with the earliest golden age or utopia from where the origin myth would begin. The occurrence of the sixteen pairs of twins makes a rather special number. It may perhaps be explained as a multiple of two ($2 \times 2 \times 2 \times 2$) where the base of two would again convey the sense of a twin or couple. The sibling marriage symbolism is so strong that in the *Daśaratha Jātaka*, Rāma and Sītā are described as brother and sister and finally reign as consorts, a distinctly Buddhist transformation of the *Rāma-kathā*.[58]

The prevalence of cross-cousin marriage would also seem apparent, especially that involving the maternal uncle's daughter. This may reflect an actual social situation or it may be symbolic. In the Chinese account, the marriage is not only mentioned but is explained as being prevalent by the pointed reference to there being no objection to it. This might perhaps indicate that in later periods the system of cross-cousin marriage had to be explained or that the audience for this particular text was unfamiliar with the system.

The reference to cross-cousin marriage in the Pāli texts and in the epics, *Purāṇas* and other literature, raises the question of the prevalence of the system. These references are a contradiction of the śāstric rules on the observance of *sapiṇḍa* and *sagotra* limitations with regard to marriage. Some late *dharmaśāstras* refer to the legitimacy of cross-cousin marriages by quoting a few ambiguous passages from Vedic literature, but far more forcefully by arguing that where it was a customary practice, as for example in the southern regions, it was a permitted relationship even for *brāhmaṇas*.[59] It has recently been suggested that the references to cross-cousin marriage in texts pertaining to northern India may be traces of an earlier Dravidian substratum culture, particularly as the texts appear to have been composed in areas where cross-cousin marriage was the prevalent pattern, as in the case of the Pāli canon edited and compiled in Ceylon.[60] That the acceptability of the system was doubted in cases other than those occurring in the Buddhist texts is evident from the attempt to find an explanation for it or to treat it somewhat contemptuously.[61] In such cases the reference to cross-cousin marriage may well be a memory of an earlier social custom among some people which gave way later, to the more prevalent disapproval of cousin marriage, at least among the elite groups of northern India.

In the Buddhist tradition however there appears to be more than either the memory of a substratum culture or the influence of southern social usage. There is a deliberate attempt to associate cross-cousin marriage with elite groups. This would heighten the antiquity of the custom as well as the exclusive character of the groups involved. It has been argued that, in order to prolong the relationship established by marriage between kin-groups, two techniques were used to record the relationship.[62] One was that the original relationship could be traced back to sibling incest, thereby emphasizing the close blood tie; the other was the frequent introduction of cross-cousin marriage at appropriate points in the genealogy among the related lineages. It is evident that at least the Śākyas and Koliyas were closely connected by kinship and the use of both these techniques in their records may have been an attempt to emphasize the connection. The techniques would be identical for both matrilineal and patrilineal groups so that cross-cousin marriage need not indicate, as it was once thought to, the precondition of a matrilineal society. At another level incest is a logical explanation of how two people could found a lineage. That the questioning if not the tabu on incest had crept into some of the later Buddhist texts is evident for example from the reference to the Śākyas being rebuked by the Koliyas for cohabiting with their own sisters.[63]

The *kṣatriya* status of the clan is both assumed and made implicit in the fact that the origin is always from an established royal family either of the Ikṣvāku lineage or from the king of Banaras. The Ikṣvāku lineage would make these clans off-shoots of the Sūrya-vaṃśa. The repeated theme of exile would either point to their being dissident groups or else that they migrated from the family base, generally a kingdom along the Ganga river or the middle Ganga plain, to the foothills of the Himalayas. The theme of exile would also become necessary where a major social tabu, that of sibling incest, was being broken even if only symbolically. Possibly, these were groups of cultivators in origin, belonging to the *jana* (but perhaps not to the *rājakula* or the landowning groups), who had migrated in search of new land and, on becoming prosperous, adopted the *kṣatriya* genealogy of the *jana* from which they came. Equally possibly, they could have been local tribes who, on becoming agriculturalists and acquiring landownership and status, sought links with the prestigious Ikṣvāku tradition and invented the myth of exile.

That there was some element of discordance is evident from the fact that, in spite of the Buddhist insistence on their *kṣatriya* status, these tribes are never listed in the Puranic genealogies. If it was merely a question of discounting those who were the fountain-head of heterodox movements, then surely the Puranic genealogies would have deliberately included them and described them either as *vrātya kṣatriyas* or else given them *śūdra* status.[64] The disavowal of monarchy as the accepted political system may in part explain their exclusion from the Puranic lists. In the case of Vaiśāli for example, the period of monarchy is referred to in the Puranic genealogies but there is silence with regard to the period when it was the nucleus of the Vṛjjian confederacy. Even though the Śākyas and Koliyas in their myths emanate from royal families, they do not appear to have repeated the experience of monarchy and their political organization seems more often to have been oligarchic, the emphasis being on political egalitarianism extending to at least the *kṣatriya* families. The reference to sixteen pairs of twins can be interpreted as an attempt at the symbolic diffusion of power within a small but powerful social group. In a monarchical situation, presumably, there would have been a single pair of twins. That substantially the same myth is related for all these *janas* suggests that they formed a separate group; probably in origin an extended kin group settled in geographical proximity of each other. Alternatively, the use of a similar origin myth may have been deliberate; to emphasize a similarity of political and social culture and an exclusivity which separated them from the more common monarchical *janapadas*.

The expanded version of the myth in the *Mahāvastu* seems much more elaborate with an implicit attempt at providing explanations. Thus the name Ikṣvāku is introduced through the reference to the sugarcane stalks and the association with the Sūryavaṃśa lineage is also made clear. The location of Kapilavastu is more explicitly described as being north across the Bhāgīrathī and into the Snowy Mountains, presumably the proximity to the Himālaya. This explanation would be necessary for the new audiences for Buddhist literature who would be unfamiliar with northern India.

The theme of the exile of princes carries echoes of the *Rāmāyaṇa*. It would seem from the frequent references to this theme and to that of the abduction of princesses in Buddhist literature that exiled princes may well have been a stereotype of the folktale. The *Daśaratha Jātaka* suggests the possible existence of an earlier *Rāma-kathā*, the events of the *Jātaka* being a Buddhist version of the story of Rāma. It is not without significance that the events of the *Rāmāyaṇa* also concern the members of the Ikṣvāku-Sūryavaṃśa lineage.

The importance of the *kṣatriya* in society is also apparent from another myth which relates to the origin of government.[65] When the Buddha was asked about the origin of government he explained that to begin with the world was of a utopian order where no one laboured and time was passed in pleasant leisure. Gradually this golden age began to tarnish and evil crept into the ways of man. The cause of the decay was man's desire for possessions and this was reflected in the emergence of the family as a social institution with the possession of woman by man, and in the notion of personal property where fields were demarcated and were claimed by individuals. Ultimately the situation became so chaotic that the people gathered together and elected one from among them (the great elect or the *mahāsammata*) in whom they invested the power to make laws and maintain order and to whom as recompense for performing this unenviable task they agreed to pay a percentage of their produce.

The story apart from its strikingly rational assumptions reflects early thinking on the origin of the *kṣatriyas*. A demarcation is made between the period of common ownership of land and the later evolution of private ownership. Out of a non-stratified society there first arose the stratification of occupations. Subsequent to this, those who owned land were set apart and the establishment of the family is also associated with the cultivation of land. Ownership of land accelerates dispute and disequilibrium which can only be tentatively corrected by the imposition of an authority which lay above and beyond that invested in ordinary persons. The crux of the story relates to the two areas of *kṣatriya* interest, landownership and the exercise of political authority.

The readjustment of the format of the Buddhist origin myth of the Śākyas and the Koliyas to changed social conditions in a later period becomes apparent in the myth regarding Vijaya and the early history of Ceylon as recorded in the *Mahāvaṃsa*.[66] A princess of Vaṅga, too arrogant to accept a human husband, is married to a lion. She gave birth to a son Sīhabāhu and a daughter Sīhāsavalī but remained unhappy and homesick. Ultimately she persuaded Sīhabāhu to kill his father, the lion, whereupon the princess with her two children returned to her father's kingdom. But soon after this the children left her, wandered away to a distant place where they married each other, built themselves a city and established a kingdom. The marriage resulted in sixteen pairs of twin sons. Among these Vijaya was regarded as the eldest. He was however so evil that he had to be exiled but was permitted to take seven hundred attendants with him. He travelled at first to western India and finally arrived in Ceylon together with his attendants on the very day of Buddha's *nirvāṇa*. The island was inhabited only by *yakhas* and *yakhinīs* whom he subdued. He sent to India for wives for himself and his attendants and not only made the island fit for human habitation but became himself a virtuous king.

The myth seeks to introduce all the elements of the traditional origin myth of the Buddhist texts. There are also, underlying the story, many levels of assumptions. The geographical area of the story is very wide, starting with eastern India, moving to western India and from there to Ceylon. This is not the compact region of the earlier myths. At the time of the compilation of the text both eastern and western India were in close contact with Ceylon. The western contact is attested to linguistically, the Pāli of the Chronicles having an affinity with the western *prākṛit* of India. The eastern link may have been introduced to establish as close a connection as possible with the Buddhist homeland. The myth is replete with assumptions regarding the social order. Vijaya's unusual and supernatural origin is amply emphasized: he is the grandson of a lion, the son of an incestuous marriage and the eldest of sixteen pairs of twin brothers. Incest in this case again points to purity of descent. Uniqueness is further stressed by the sixteen pairs of twin brothers, although here the eldest stands out since the context is monarchy and not oligarchy. His social status is indicated by his royal antecedents both in the animal world and in the human. Royal antecedents also provide him with the economic means to travel the long distance from Vaṅga to Ceylon together with his attendants. The story of the exile was necessary to explain why anyone would travel such a distance to an island inhabited only by demons. It is appropriate that the man who founded the first human colony in Ceylon should arrive on the auspicious day of the Buddha's *parinirvāṇa*. Such a connection would be virtually inevitable in the *Mahāvaṃsa* which after all was the Chronicle of the major Buddhist monastery of Ceylon, the Mahāvihāra. The etymological interest is also clear from the attempt to explain the derivation of the name of the island — Sinhala — associated with a lion. The earlier origin myths had by now almost become archetypes. The story of Vijaya does not occur at the start of the *Mahāvaṃsa* but in the sixth chapter. Nevertheless it marks the commencement of the narrative of the history of Ceylon. Earlier chapters relate the story of the Buddha's visit to Ceylon and the conversion of Aśoka which prepares the ground for the arrival of

Buddhism. This structure makes the narrative more purposive and strengthens the notion of the mission of Buddhism to Ceylon.

The social function of these origin myths in the context of the early Indian historical tradition appears to be fourfold: to establish kinship links, to emphasize the legitimacy of succession, to indicate the migration of important groups and to provide social status to those who had acquired political power. The recognition of kinship links among the *kṣatriya* families in the mid-first millennium BC was central to the question of rights of landownership and ultimately political authority. In the first millennium AD, with new claimants to *kṣatriya* status and political power in the many dynasties of the period, the kinship links were revived through the search for actual or fabricated genealogical connections.[67]

The legitimacy of succession was implicit in the genealogical links requiring *kṣatriya* antecedents. In the monarchical system there was the additional need to stress primogeniture. That this was a real concern is evident from other literature which stresses not only the need for hereditary succession but also the rights of seniority within it.[68] It is not surprising that this question crops up repeatedly in the literature of the mid-first millennium AD and later, where in plays such as the *Devīcandraguptam* and in historical biographies such as the *Harṣacarita* and the *Vikramānkadevacarita*, there is an elaborate justification for the transgressing of the rule.[69]

The theme of migration, often disguised as exile, sets the geographical dimensions of the social group and can be used to establish the rights and priority of a particular group over a particular region. This assumes significance in periods when new groups are moving in as entrepreneurs in either previously occupied areas or in newly opened up lands: the entrepreneurs in the mid-first millennium AD being the recipients of grants of land. Those who succeeded in establishing new dynasties would either have to link themselves genealogically with the descent groups, who were already associated with the area or else would have to introduce the idea of migration. The Sisodia Rajput link with the Sūryavaṃśa lineage and the migration of one of their ancestors from Lahore (associated with Lava the son of Rāma) to Rajasthan would form a case in point.[70] Puranic sources refer to the dispersal of the Haihayas (a sub-lineage of the Yādavas). This provided a useful peg for many early medieval dynasties to hang their genealogies on, such as the Kalacuris of Tripuri[71] and the Muṣakavaṃśa of

Kerala.[72] Exiled princes also provide one of the mechanisms by which local tradition can be hooked onto the 'classical' tradition and vice versa.

In both the *itihāsa-purāṇa* tradition and the Buddhist tradition, as far as origin myths are concerned, it is in the main the *kṣatriya* status which is sought to be validated. The origin myths of the *kṣatriya* clans in Buddhist literature are attempts to provide status for those who played an important part in the events relating to the establishment of Buddhism, and are the counterparts to the lineage myths in the Puranic tradition, both sets of myth endorsing the groups in political authority at the time. Nor is it coincidental that this search for validation through myth is systematized and recorded at the time when dynasties claiming *kṣatriya* status rose to political control and, in the Buddhist case, sectarian institutions of the Buddhist *saṅgha* were involved, albeit not always directly, in political authority.

## Notes and References

1. G.S. Kirk, *The Nature of Greek Myths*, Harmondsworth, 1974, pp. 31ff.
2. Max Müller, *Chips from a German Workshop*, London, 1867, 68, vols. I & II.
3. A. Lang, *Custom and Myth*, London, 1884; *Myth, Ritual and Religion*, London, 1887.
4. W. Robertson Smith, *The Religion of the Semites*, London, 1894; J.E. Harrison, *Themis*, Cambridge, 1912.
5. As in *Magic, Science and Religion*, New York, 1948.
6. C. Levi–Strauss, *The Raw and the Cooked* and *From Honey to Ashes*, being the first two volumes of a longer work, *Mythologiques*, Paris, 1964–72. The more successful applications of the structural analysis of myth have been in the myths of pre-literate societies. E. Leach (ed.), *The Structural Study of Myth and Totemism*, London, 1967 and T.A. Sebeok (ed.), *Myth: A Symposium*, Indiana, 1955. Changes introduced in myths over a period of time in literate societies could add a worthwhile dimension even to structural analysis.
7. The notion of the archetype as developed by S. Freud, *The Interpretation of Dreams*, New York, 1965, was of considerable influence. But the names of Jung and Cassirer are more closely associated with the growth of this idea. C.G. Jung and K. Kerenyi, *Introduction to a Science of Mythology*, London, 1963 and E. Cassirer, *The Philosophy of Symbolic Forms*, vol. 2, 'Mythical Thought', New Haven, 1955.
8. Eliade has touched on this theme in many of his writings but more

especially in *The Myth of the Eternal Return, Myth and Reality*, and in *Patterns in Comparative Religion*, New York, 1963.

9. V. Turner, 'Myth and Symbol', in *The Encyclopaedia of Social Sciences*, vol. x.
10. Georges Dumezil's *Mythe et Épopée* in three volumes. An attempt has been made to represent his ideas in C. Scott Littleton, *The New Comparative Mythology*, London, 1973. Dumezil uses the theory of the three functions (which can be approximately translated as sanctity, coercion and fecundity) as the basic pattern of Indo-European symbolism and myth. None of the functions are precisely defined and the overlapping makes for a rather ambiguous analysis at times. Also associated with these ideas are the writings of Stig Wikander, especially the paper entitled 'La Legende des Pāṇḍavas et la substructure mythique du Mahābhārata', in Georges Dumezil, *Jupiter, Mars, Quirinus IV*.
11. K. Thomas, 'Anthropology and History', in *Past and Present*, no. 24, April 1963, pp. 1ff.
12. *Śatapatha Brāhmaṇa*, I.8.1.1–10; *Matsya Purāṇa*, I.11–34; *Mahābhārata*, Vanaparvan, 185ff.
13. *Viṣṇu Purāṇa*, IV.1.
14. M. Eliade, *Myth and Reality*, pp. 5ff.
15. This point came up in a discussion with Professor A. Kilmer.
16. Sally Falk Moore, 'Descent and Symbolic Filiation', *The American Anthropologist*, no. 66, VI, part 1, 1964, pp. 1308–20.
17. *Aitareya Brāhmaṇa*, VIII.14–23; *Śatapatha Brāhmaṇa*, III.2.3.15; Āṭānāṭiya Sutta, *Dīgha Nikāya*, III.199.7ff.
18. *Vāyu Purāṇa*, VIII.176ff.
19. *Ṛg Veda*, X.10.
20. Sukumari Bhattacharji, *The Indian Theogony*, Cambridge, 1970, pp. 217–18.
21. *Viṣṇu Purāṇa*, IV.1.
22. The symbolism of the sun and the moon occurs frequently in Yoga and in Tantric texts although in these the sexual association is reversed: the moon is associated with the male and the sun with the female. M. Eliade, *Yoga*, Princeton, 1971, p. 239.
23. For a description of the segmentary system which fairly approximates some of the features of the Candravaṃśa see Marshall D. Sahlins, 'The Segmentary Lineage: An Organisation of Predatory Expansion', *The American Anthropologist*, vol. 63, no. 2, 1961, pp. 332–45.
24. F.E. Pargiter, *Ancient Indian Historical Tradition*, London, 1922, pp. 15ff.
25. A. Heidel, *The Babylonian Genesis*, Chicago, 1963.
26. G.S. Kirk, *The Nature of Greek Myths*, pp. 261ff.

27. L. Woolley, *Excavations at Ur*, London, 1954, pp. 34–6; *Ur of the Chaldees*, London, 1950, pp. 29ff. *The Cambridge Ancient History*, vol. I, part 1, pp. 353ff. Reliable evidence on substantial floods in India during this period (as available so far) would point to two areas and time brackets. The first would be the flooding of Mohenjo-daro and the lower valley in the early second millennium BC (G. Dales, 'New Investigations at Mohenjo-daro', *Archaeology*, 1965, no. 18). The second would be that of the Ganga-Yamuna Doāb and particularly Hastināpur in the early first millennium BC (B.B. Lal, 'Excavations at Hastināpur', *Ancient India*, 1954 and 1955, nos 10 and 11). The second is certainly too late in time to have been the original of such a myth. More than likely the myth was not referring to any particular flood but rather to the possibility of a flood as a cataclysmic point of time and change and this notion may have arisen from the observation of recurring floods in the area.
28. Th. Jacobsen, *The Sumerian King-List*, Chicago, 1939.
29. *Viṣṇu Purāṇa*, IV.6 and 10.
30. N.S. Bose, *History of the Chandellas of Jejakabhukti*, Calcutta, 1956; E. Zannas and J. Auboyer, *Khajuraho*, The Hague, 1960, pp. 30ff.
31. *Ṛg Veda*, X.95.
32. *Śatapatha Brāhmaṇa*, XI.5.1.1ff.
33. *Mahābhārata*, Ādiparvan, 70.16ff.
34. Max Müller, *Chips from a German Workshop*, IV, London, 1968, pp. 109ff.
35. D.D. Kosambi, *Myth and Reality*, Bombay, 1962, pp. 47ff.
36. *Viṣṇu Purāṇa*, IV.10.
37. Ibid.
38. *Mahābhārata*, Ādiparvan, 80.
39. Georges Dumezil, *The Destiny of a King*, Chicago, 1973.
40. *Vedic Index*, II, pp. 11–12.
41. Ibid., p. 185.
42. *Viṣṇu Purāṇa*, I.13.
43. *Mahābhārata*, Śāntiparvan, 67, 16–24.
44. *Vedic Index*, vol. I, p. 452; ibid., vol. II, p. 16.
45. *Viṣṇu Purāṇa*, I.13.
46. Ibid., IV.20.
47. *Ṛg Veda*, X.98; *Nirukta*, II.10; *Bṛhaddevatā*, VII.155, 156ff.
48. *Sutta Nipāta*, 420ff; *Sutta Nipāta Commentary*, I, 352ff; *Sumaṅgalavilāsinī*, I. pp. 258–60.
49. B.C. Law, *Some Kṣatriya Tribes of Ancient India*, pp. 162ff, Varanasi, 1975, rpt.; *Mahāvastu*, I, pp. 348–52.
50. Ambattha Sutta, I.16 in *Dīgha Nikāya*, I; *Kuṇāla Jātaka*, no. 536, vol. V, p. 219.

51. H.C. Raichaudhury, *Political History of Ancient India*, Calcutta, 1952, pp. 192ff.
52. *Kuṇāla Jātaka*, no. 536.
53. *Mahāvaṃsa Tīkā*, pp. 180ff.
54. Buddhaghoṣa, *Paramatthajotika*, Khuddakapatha, pp. 158–60.
55. S.R. Goyal, *A History of the Imperial Guptas*, Allahabad, 1967, pp. 81ff.
56. Paśupati inscription of Jayadeva, quoted in B.C. Law, *Kṣatriya Clans in Buddhist India*, pp. 28–9; J.F. Fleet (ed.), *Corpus Inscriptionum Indicarum*, III, pp. 133, 136, 155.
57. S. Beal, *Romantic History of Buddha*, London, 1920, pp. 18ff.
58. *Daśaratha Jātaka*, no. 461, vol. IV, p. 78.
59. P.V. Kane, *History of Dharmaśāstra*, II.1, Poona, 1941, pp. 460ff.
60. T.R. Trautmann, 'Cross-Cousin Marriage in Ancient North India', in T.R. Trautmann (ed.), *Kinship and History in South Asia*, Michigan, 1974.
61. *Bhāgavata Purāṇa*, X.54.18.
62. Sally Falk Moore, op. cit.
63. *Sutta Nipāta Commentary*, I.357; *Kuṇāla Jātaka*, no. 536.
64. *Manu*, X.22, does however refer to the Licchavis as *vrātya kṣatriyas*.
65. Aggañña Sutta in *Dīgha Nikāya*, III.93.
66. *Mahāvaṃsa*, VI.
67. For some references to fabricated genealogies see D.C. Sircar, *Indian Epigraphy*, New Delhi, 1965, pp. 24ff.
68. *Arthaśāstra*, I, 17.34; *Majjhima Nikāya*, II.75; *Manu*, IX.105–9.
69. The first of these texts justifies the succession of Candragupta II, who, owing to the cowardly act of his elder brother Rāmagupta, had finally (it would seem from other sources) to kill his elder brother and usurp the throne. Both biographies concern the succession of younger brothers and here again an elaborate argument is produced to prove the justification for the younger brother. In the *Harṣacarita* the elder brother is killed by the enemy so that the justification is not so elaborate. In the *Vikramānkadevacarita* we are told that the god Śiva himself commanded the younger brother to usurp the throne for the sake of the well-being of the people and the prosperity of the kingdom.
70. J. Tod, *Annals and Antiquities of Rajasthan*, I. p. 176.
71. F. Kielhorn, 'Kalachuris of Tripuri', *Epigraphia Indica*, II, pp. 300–5.
72. T. Gopinath Rao, 'Extract from the Mūṣakavaṃśa . . . ', *Travancore Archaeological Series*, II, 1, no. 10, pp. 87–113. M.G.S. Narayanan, 'History from the Mūṣakavaṃśa', *P.A.-I.O.C.*, Jadavpur, 1969

# Clan, Caste and Origin Myths in Early India*

Many years ago, a group of us as young researchers were in conversation with Professor Niharranjan Ray and inevitably asked him how he saw the role of the researcher in the universe of knowledge. Characteristically his reply was that one should be like the fish which lives in water but never drowns. This may not be zoologically exact, but it was characteristic of his own work. Although formally a historian of art, there was in fact no aspect of history and its related disciplines in which he did not show an enquiring interest if not considerable knowledge. But at the same time he did not make a fetish of scholarship. His lively mind was frequently able to pick up the pieces which went into the making of the jigsaw of Indian history and this he did with style and no little degree of panache.

His studies of Indian art were not narrowly limited to art for he was well aware of its social context, a context which tied it to the broader contours of change over time. This in turn involved an analysis of ideology in artistic manifestations, an area which had already begun to be explored through the insights of Coomaraswamy. Niharranjan Ray was a historian of both art and society and therefore looked at them as inter-meshed. Frequently social history was a necessary background to generalizations about art history, but equally often, his work on social history had its own significance.

The involvement with the totality of social knowledge and the encouragement to others to do the same was what made him such a successful director of the Indian Institute for Advanced Study at Shimla, when it was first started. It was a period thick with Fellows who have now achieved distinction, and a frequency of seminars

* Niharranjan Ray Memorial Lecture, Indian Institute of Advanced Studies, Simla, 1992.

on themes which invariably produced some innovative thinking. If the Institute has been unable to take off in the manner in which Radhakrishnan had envisioned it, one major reason has been the unconcern of various governments, which through the years have been largely unaware of the intellectually generative function of such institutes. This lack of concern has expressed itself in the most banal fashion, in the repeated attempts to convert the present historic building in which the Institute has been housed, into a tourist hotel. But even buildings alone do not make an Institute of Advanced Study. The other imperative input, if the institution is to survive is the need for a fully equipped and well-organized library. Unfortunately those that govern us assume that research is born out of the minds of scholars unaided by reading and therefore deny us access to reading. Even if, over the last two decades, whilst the Ministry debated the priorities of tourism over advanced study, an attempt had been made just to finance an up-dated library, the Institute would have determined the choice. But in the vacillation about the future of the building, advanced studies have been the victim. Please forgive this carping. Unhappily scholars comply too easily with 'the authorities' and scholarship goes by the board. If at all an Indian intellectual heritage is both to be preserved and to be developed then scholarship has to be taken more seriously by those who provide the patronage and the wherewithal.

Despite all this, I am deeply appreciative of the honour which the Institute has done me in asking me to give the first Niharranjan Ray Lecture. I would like therefore to speak on a theme which interested him and on which he encouraged investigation. I shall be speaking on one of the major features of Indian history, namely the juxtaposition of clan-based societies to caste-based societies, what are sometimes referred to as *jana* and *jāti*, implicit in much of which is also often the transition from non-state to state systems, the latter generally taking the form of a monarchy. I would like to view it from the perspective of some of those texts which, it seems to me, are concerned with this change although perhaps we as historians have not given enough attention to this concern.

Possibly this neglect arises from the fact that historians have in the past looked only at the elite sections of society and read the texts from this perspective. With reference to early history the major problem is that sources from other levels of society are few and far between. Therefore deduction becomes an important part of historical analysis. Furthermore, the change which I have referred to is not uniform or identical in space and time. We know that it occurred in parts of the Ganga valley by the fourth century BC and occurred elsewhere at other times, in some places quite recently. Therefore, it not only requires us to reexamine our notions of periodisation but it also does not allow of any easy periodisation. The two forms were not dichotomous for the transition often carried over features from the one to the other. It frequently results in overlapping social formations and therefore makes generalizations about the nature of society in any given area very complex.

It was earlier argued that states and castes emerged out of conquest, that the need to suppress the conquered required the infrastructure of a state. It is now being suggested that environmental and ecological features are crucial to some areas rapidly evolving into states and others remaining isolated. This is sought to be demonstrated in the Indian situation where many parts of central India and of the north-east appear to have been by-passed by the transitions taking place in their vicinity. Whether it was actually so remains to be investigated. Where population pressure is intense and segments of a society cannot break away and migrate to fresh lands establishing clones of the earlier society, there the tensions within the original society can lead to change in the direction of a greater centralization of power and resources and eventually to the emergence of a state.

Essential to this process are other requirements. Improved technology often results in the diversification of an economy and this can now be examined with greater precision with the assistance of archaeology. Attempts are made by groups in society to control both resources and production, a control which may have a ritual backing to begin with but which is ultimately institutionalized in the structure of the state. This may take the form of claims over land and revenue accompanied by using the labour of others to work the land. Or it may focus on urban centres as places of exchange and ultimately of commerce, not altogether unaided by being centres of administration and the collection of revenue. Concentrations of populations also grow around ritual and ceremonial centres. Where the system of authority is undergoing change there the legitimation of this change has to be explicit. Ceremonial centres may embody this legitimizing process in the rituals performed for the bestowal of special powers on particular people.

The hierarchy of stratification in a society, whether it be caste or any other form, is a pre-requisite to the formation of a state. Societies in which identity is traced through birth and kinship or territory and where clan and lineage are fundamental to this identity, gradually give way to other identities such as caste, occupation or community. The meshing together of the latter as a process now comes under the purview of more impersonal factors such as institutions. However the change is neither sudden nor total and often the overlaps continue for long periods.

In this survey of features which point to change I would like to suggest that the earliest markets, urban centres, religious monuments in a region may be seen, among other things, as symbols pointing to the direction in which society has been changing. Equally important as symbols are texts which attempt to record this change. Some do so by taking the most significant indices of the identity of a group and show how these have changed, for example, texts which record the movement of political power from those who claim it ostensibly on the basis of birth and kinship to those who claim it actually through economic and administrative control. Other texts add to this the more obvious symbols of cities, revenue, conquest and temples. Some sources even attempt to hide the antecedents of the ruling family in their efforts to prove their legitimacy as rulers. In the change from clan-based societies to state systems, caste identities play curious roles.

I would like to look at the way in which this change is reflected in two categories of literature. One is the genealogical section — which is referred to as the *vaṃśānucarita* — of the early *Purāṇas*, the *Vāyu*, *Brahmāṇḍa*, *Matsya* and *Viṣṇu*, composed around the fourth-fifth centuries AD. The other is the *vaṃśāvalī* style of writing which occurs both as texts and in inscriptions. As an example of this category I shall be referring to those relating to the Candella dynasty and dating to the tenth century and later.

Historians have generally been sceptical about genealogies and have rightly maintained that they are not to be taken literally, unless there is other evidence to support them. Nevertheless modern studies of genealogies indicate that genealogical patterns can be read as ways of representing society. The social assumptions of a society can be prized out of myth and genealogy, and therefore genealogies record social forms. They assume importance at times of historical change and are often used to legitimize the present. They represent therefore a perspective of the past.

The *vaṃśānucarita* section of the early *Purāṇas* is a record of change from clan-based societies to monarchies and this change is set out in the form of genealogical patterns. The data consist largely of skeletal genealogies with occasionally a story about a member of the descent group. These stories generally occur at major points of change. The material was compiled by bards — the *sūta* and the *māgadha* — and these bards also play an important role in the *Mahābhārata* and the *Rāmāyaṇa*. The material was later taken over, it is thought, by *brāhmaṇa* authors, primarily the Bhṛgu *brāhmaṇas*, and reconstituted in the form of the genealogical section of the *Purāṇa*. Clearly control over this data was linked to controlling some aspects of the legitimacy of those in power. To this extent it parallels the resort to history for purposes of legitimacy by many groups in contemporary times.

The texts are ambivalent regarding their authorship which veers from bards to *brāhmaṇas*, an ambivalence which continues to characterize later *vaṃśāvalīs* as well. The tradition of bards, such as the *chārans* and the *barots*, maintaining the genealogies of land owning families has continued unbroken upto present times. A parallel to this is the *pāṇḍas* at important places of pilgrimage, maintaining the genealogies of the dominant castes of the region. It is not my intention to claim that the descent lists from the *Purāṇas* are historically accurate or reliable, but rather to try and examine the social assumptions implicit in this data and the insights which these provide on the nature of social change.

The genealogical chapter in the *Viṣṇu Purāṇa* consists of three sections with distinctly different patterns. The first deals with origins and is ensconced in cosmological time. The second constructs a record of what was perceived as the lineages of ruling clans. These include the families and clans which are the subject of the two epics, the *Rāmāyaṇa* and the *Mahābhārata*. They reflect a clan-based society prior to or in transition to, the formation of states. The third section is a listing of kings and dynasties, pointing to the establishment of the monarchical state. It focuses initially on Magadha in south Bihar and continues upto the period of the Guptas, known from other sources to be reigning in the mid-first millennium AD. I would like to suggest that these three distinctive patterns also reflect a perception of historical change in northern India.

The genealogical pattern begins with the seven Manus who claim descent from the gods and are said to have ruled for long spans of time, but they remain hazy figures. During the period of the seventh Manu there occurs the great Flood, a massive deluge which covers the earth.

The Flood assumes the primary precondition of water from out of which known creation arises. It is recognised as a stage in the cycle of time, perhaps what has been called the abolition of profane time, where the Flood is a marker separating a time of origins from later events. The beginnings of history emerge from a condition which has no antecedents. Manu acquires prestige through being chosen to survive. This in turn gives added prestige to those who claim descent from him.

Manu's children become the ancestors to what is described as the succession of *rājās* also referred to as *kṣatriyas*. The precise meaning of the term *rājā* for the earliest times is controversial and there is a debate as to whether it means 'king', as earlier believed, or whether it means 'chief', or 'head of a clan', as seems more likely from the way the genealogies of this section are set out. The genealogical section then proceeds to give the descent groups in long lists of lineages of these *kṣatriyas*.

There are two major descent groups, the Sūryavaṃśa and the Candravaṃśa. The Sūryavaṃśa is said to have descended from the eldest son of Manu, Ikṣvāku and is therefore also referred to as the Aikṣvāka-vaṃśa. The Candravaṃśa claims its ancestry from the female half of the androgynous Iḷā and is therefore also referred to as the Aila-vaṃśa. The use of the planetary symbols of the sun and the moon, would make the point that these were contrasting symbols and this is borne out in the pattern of the genealogical data.

Incidentally, the term *vaṃśa* is derived from the word for bamboo or cane, with each segment growing out of a nodule. However the analogy is limited, for there is no necessary biological link between the segment of the lineages. The *vaṃśānucarita* should therefore be more precisely translated as 'succession lists', although the pattern in which it is set out endorses the claim to its being a genealogy.

The descendants of Ikṣvāku are said to occupy a clearly demarcated geographical area, that of what is now eastern Uttar Pradesh and the middle Ganga plain. The descent is patrilineal, going from eldest son to eldest son and primogeniture is consequently of the utmost importance, an issue which is central in the narrative of the *Rāmāyaṇa*. As an epic, the *Rāmāyaṇa* focuses on the Sūryavaṃśa since both the families of Kośala and Videha belong to this line. The Purāṇic data does not suggest a monarchy and merely lists the descent, terminating fairly soon after the generation of Lava and Kuśa.

The Candravaṃśa is a complete contrast to this. It begins with a female ancestor. It proceeds to record all the male children of each generation and those females who are significant to marriage alliances. The genealogical pattern therefore fans out and includes a vast geographical area covering most of northern India. This was obviously a much later version when there was a familiarity with most of northern India. The segments claim Candravaṃśa descent suggesting that they were groups which had migrated away from parental groups, but they could equally well have been aliens who had been assimilated and therefore included in the lists of descent. Genealogies can be a mechanism for assimilating new groups where they are recorded as descendants but need not be genetically linked. Among the Candravaṃśa the most important lines were those claiming descent from Yadu and from Pūru. Interestingly there was a reversal of primogeniture here where the youngest son, Pūru, inherited the kingdom. Whereas the Ikṣvākus are said by and large to have observed customs approved of by the *brāhmaṇas*, the Ailas on the other hand had many social observances which were outside the rules of the *dharmaśāstras*. For example, in the case of marriage they accepted both polyandrous and cross-cousin marriages as well as bride-price, all of which were frowned upon by the authors of the *dharmaśāstras*. The epic of the Candravaṃśa was the *Mahābhārata* in which such customs are described at greater length.

Diversities in social patterns are important to kinship rights. The absence of homogeneity, even as a later attempt to synthesize the data, suggests the consciousness that an early society may not have observed caste rules, even if its members were called *kṣatriyas*. That these were also being projected as societies without states is evident from the absence of references to state boundaries or the major infrastructure of a state. Rights are asserted over territory by way of birth and this in turn provides status. Genealogies such as these attempt to create a seemingly unbroken past. This is more frequently the case when descent groups are more central than institutions.

The second time-marker in the *vaṃśānucarita* section is the Mahābhārata war, the cataclysmic battle which terminates the existence of most of the clans. The *Purāṇas* refer to it as the end of the splendid *kṣatriya* families. The genealogical pattern gradually changes and there now follows the record of dynasties. The genealogical pattern not only makes the change very evident but also introduces some curious features.

The record now comes to be written in the future tense, a pointer to a disjuncture in the record. In other words these are supposed to be prophecies of the dynasties which will rule. Needless to say the prophecies have to stop by about the fourth century AD, the date when the texts were probably compiled. The earlier descent lists had recorded the succession of *kṣatriya rājās*. This is replaced by the names of dynasties, some of which are familiar to us from other evidence, such as the Nanda, Maurya, Śuṇga, Āndhra, Gupta and so on. There is little information on the dynasties except that each king is mentioned in succession and the number of years that he is said to have ruled are also listed.

Dynasties point to a monarchy and this in turn means a monarchical state. The genealogies therefore are recording a different political and social system from that of the clan-based society of the earlier lists. Dynasties now take precedence over non-state, clan society. Royal power does not derive its legitimacy from birth and kinship. There is no continuous link between the dynasties and no lineage connections. Some dynasties are said to have been the servants of earlier ones, such as the Āndhra-bhṛtyas, perhaps a euphemism for administrative office. What is however clear is that the relations of power are now more important than kinship links.

Kings are referred to in these texts not as *rājās* but as *nṛpas*, literally, the protectors of men. We are also told that kings will arise from families of *kṣatriyas*, mixed castes, *śūdras*, *mlechhas* and foreigners and some amongst them will not observe the *dharma*. Political power was now open and negotiable. Towards the end there is another statement, that eventually a new caste of *kṣatriyas* will be created when those of various *varṇas* and some such as the Pulindas and Śabaras, who are generally listed as tribal peoples, will claim *kṣatriya* status. This is an important statement in view of the developments after this period when families of obscure origin, or alternatively, of what today are called tribal groups, did succeed in establishing kingdoms and claiming *kṣatriya* status. It is significant that even if the dynasty is not of *kṣatriya* caste, nevertheless the importance of caste is underlined.

The *vaṃśānucarita* section of the *Purāṇas*, it seems to me, is making a statement. In contrasting the earlier genealogical pattern with the dynastic pattern, the underlying assumption is that there has been a change from what we today would call a tribal society to a caste society with a state system. This change appears to have been of major importance to the authors of the texts. Further, there is a change from *kṣatriya rājās* to non-kṣatriya monarchs. Equally significant is the fact that this pattern of genealogies forms a construction of the past and this construction is very different from the narrative which modern historians have put together on the earliest past.

I would now like to turn to the second category of texts, the *vaṃśāvalīs*, literally, the paths of succession. These also reflect directly or implicitly, the change from clan-based to caste society and from non-state societies to state systems. They are frequent in the period from the about the tenth century onwards, occurring both as literary texts and in inscription form. It is fortunately possible in many kingdoms to co-relate these texts with inscriptions. This has an added importance given that inscriptions in this period were often the near equivalent of the annals of dynasties in other parts of the world.

There is some continuity between sections of the *Purāṇas* and the *vaṃśāvalīs* since the latter draw on the former for origin myths and genealogical material. However the *vaṃśāvalīs* register a change from skeletal king-lists to continuous narratives. The family which had acquired power and ruled as an independent dynasty backed up this power by seeking legitimacy. This was frequently in the form of an appropriate story of origin often involving the deities and also the claim to being of *kṣatriya* status. When such a claim is made it is clear that caste society has become established in the region over which the family rules. And if earlier, the family had had connections with what we today call tribal people, then it implies the possible transition to caste.

Other features are also apparent. The geographical area earlier associated with the family becomes the initial territory of the state. The dependence on a revenue paying peasantry or on land-owners is either directly recorded or implicitly so in reference to structures which were intended to change the rural economy. Urban centres develop as commercial centres, some coinciding with those which are the nucleus of state administration. Approximation to Sanskritic culture is expressed in various forms. Acculturation not only means the transition to a caste society or the claim to *kṣatriya* caste but also implies the ideology of a new belief system. Religious manifestations change from local deities to the universalizing deities of the Purāṇic pantheon, generally some form of Viṣṇu or Śiva. Association with a religious sect identified with these deities provides a wider network than just the local territory. In fact the *vaṃśāvalīs* indirectly include those features which were traditionally counted as the seven limbs of the state — the king, the territory, the administration, revenue, the capital city now adorned with temples, coercive authority and allies. Most of these attributes of the state are introduced into the narrative in some form.

The author of the *vaṃśāvalī* is a court poet and not a bard, since the text has to be written in a style which conforms to the best literary tradition. The material is often taken from bardic sources and there may well have been some tension between the bards and the court poets. The *vaṃśāvalī* is the official version of the history of the dynasty. It is therefore of some interest to us today to see whether there were variants and what was said in these.

I would like to take as my example of a *vaṃśāvalī*, the Khajuraho inscription of the Candella ruler, Dhaṅga, which dates to AD 953. The inscription in Sanskrit verse records the installation of an image of Viṣṇu in the Lakṣmaṇa temple at Khajuraho by Yaśovarman, but the record was erected during the reign of his son, Dhaṅga. By this time the Candella dynasty was well-established in the heart of Bundelkhand and the narrative in the inscription is an official version of how the ruler of the time wished the dynasty to be perceived.

The inscription begins with an invocation to Viṣṇu and a reference to the creation of the universe, and various Vaiṣṇava *avatāras* and myths, echoing the *Viṣṇu Purāṇa*. The origin myth of the Candella dynasty states that the family was descended from the *ṛṣi* Atri and his son, Candratreya. The latter name, Candratreya, was presumably the origin for the family name of Candella. This is a way of underlining high brahmanical descent as well as trying to explain, admittedly in a rather garbled way, the etymology of the name, Candella. In the larger canvass the family therefore claimed links with the Candravaṃśa line.

The genealogy of the family is then narrated with some detail about each successor. Of Yaśovarman's father named Harṣa, it is said that he married a Chahamāna princess, both being of the same *varṇa*. This is a curious statement, for the Chahamānas were known to be one of the four pre-eminent Rajput families regarded as *kṣatriyas*. This statement therefore is a Candella claim to *kṣatriya* status. The fact that it contradicts their status as surmised from the origin myth, does not seem to have bothered them. It seems to suggest that this marriage gave them a higher status else it would not have been specially mentioned, yet at the same time they are insisting on their own status as *kṣatriya*.

A longer passage then speaks of the widespread conquests of Yaśovarman, the father of Dhaṅga, which is in the style of the *carita* or biographical literature of the time. He is described as a sword cutting down the creeper of the Gauḍa, the god of death to the Mālava, the bringer of distress on the Cedi and a scorching fire to the Gurjara. The author was evidently using the earlier seventh century biography of Harṣavardhana, the *Harṣacarita* of Bāṇabhaṭṭa, as a literary model. Yaśovarman's campaign against the Cedis, a powerful group of ruling families in central India, is singled out for detailed mention and has a ring of authenticity distinct from the hyperbolic verses referring to other conquests. Yaśovarman was succeeded by his son Dhaṅga, and among other details, the boundaries of his kingdom are given.

Mention is also made by the same ruler in another inscription of the construction of a large tank by his father, which was evidently used for irrigation, as were many others built by the Candellas. This would have changed the rural economy of the neighbourhood. The need to generate substantial wealth was a precondition to many activities, not least the splendid temples which were built as a result of Candella patronage.

The purpose of the Khajuraho inscription was to record the installation of an image of Viṣṇu at Khajuraho, the then capital of the Candella dynasty. We are further told that the image was an old and much travelled icon, its provenance being the Himalaya. This was a statement of identity with the Vaiṣṇavite sect and the claim that the image had been brought from so far, hints at the wide geographical network of the sect. That it is to be installed in a temple in the capital city points to the religious associations encouraged by the dynasty. The inscription concludes with a precise date, stating the day, fortnight, month and year in the widely used Vikrama era. All this points to a clear recognition of linear time. The author and the engraver of the inscription are court appointees. This official version is a reconstruction of the past in which the dynasty comes out as having impeccable antecedents and with no hint of associations other than the highest.

But there are other versions which disagree with this version and which suggest that the Candella family may have had a different origin. These versions rely more evidently on bardic sources. Among them is the sixteenth century epic poem, the *Pṛthvirāja-rāso*, composed by Cand Bardai. This is written in praise of the Cahamānas and since they married into the Candella family, there are references to the latter. But by this time, the two families had witnessed a falling out and the references to the Candella are therefore not very complimentary. We are told that the founder of the dynasty was the illegitimate son of the widowed daughter of a *brāhmaṇa* and the moon-god, Candra, hence the contorted derivation of the name Candella. The young man was an adventurer who fought for control over his village and was ultimately successful. The frequency of the violent wresting of power suggests that acculturation tended to be confrontational.

We are also told that the family worshipped Maniyā Devī, a Gond anionic image which they made into a royal cult. Were they Gonds in origin who were adjusting to Sanskritic culture when they had acquired enough power to declare an independent kingdom? If they were merely associating with local but powerful Gonds it is unlikely that they would have made the worship of Maniyā Devī into the royal cult, for they would surely have had their own claim or family cult. Was the territory of the worship of this deity sought to be incorporated into the area of influence of the dynasty? The acculturation is eventually so complete that there is no mention of Maniyā Devī in the Khajuraho inscription. In terms of social stratification this would be a case of legitimation from below. But at the same time it would seem that the basis of power could well have been the Gond clans.

The association with tribal peoples is not unusual at this time, particularly among those anxiously claiming *kṣatriya* status. Another example is that of the Sisodia Rajputs and the Bhils. The origin myths of and about such dynasties, if analysed may reveal worthwhile facets on actual origins. The claim to the *varṇa* status of *kṣatriya* rather than a specific *jāti* status could have been a means of enlarging power.

There is yet another version of purely bardic origin and partisan to the Candella. This is the epic poem, the *Ālhākhaṇḍa*, which remained part of the oral tradition until it was recorded in the eighteenth century. The Candella family, ruling a much reduced kingdom, is assumed to be of lower caste than in their inscriptions as they are closely linked to the Āhiras in various ways. The Āhiras although claiming to be Yadu-vaṃśis were nevertheless regarded as lower than the Rajputs in the caste hierarchy. They were cattle-keepers and as such not unfamiliar with raiding. The description of royal activities is not only more realistic but also brings the events down to ground level, as it were.

The much eulogized act of *dig-vijaya*, the supposed conquest of the four quarters is here described as a different matter, namely, that of forcing recalcitrant feudatories and tenants, to pay their dues. The *svayamvara*, the assembly of kings at which a princess was supposed to choose her husband, is here reduced to the capturing of the bride after a brutal conflict between the two families involved in the marriage. The capturing of the bride was, in brahmanical texts, associated with the *asura* form of marriage, one which was regarded as distinctly low. The story of Pṛthvirāja abducting Samyuktā at her *svayamvara* has overtones of the same idea. If alliances between militarily equal groups were converted into marriage alliances then they could on occasion take the form of raids.

The hero, Ālhā, prays to his titular deity Maniyā Devī for help. We are told that she is now the goddess Śārada and eventually she bestows immortality on the hero. Interestingly, even though she has been transformed into a Sanskritic deity her earlier association is still mentioned in this version.

From the categories of texts which I have discussed, both pertaining to perceptions of the past, certain aspects of the way society functioned are emphasised. After the break-up of clan-based societies, political power it would seem, was open to those who made a bid for it. Success required both the conquest of territory and the incorporation of existing tribal societies. References to the Niṣāda, the Śabara and the Pulinda, the generic names for tribal peoples in Sanskrit sources, which have tended in the past to be generally dismissed, may have to be seen in a new light. It has been argued that segmentary lineages, even without a central authority can function over large areas very effectively. They would therefore have commanded power of no small consequence. Where power was emanating from such groups, there the model of monarchy was accepted and the required cultural changes were made. The change from clan-based to caste-based social organisation was seen as a form of upward mobility, at least by the families of chiefs and those who were claiming *kṣatriya* status. The colonizing of new areas was also a process of reproducing caste society.

In the transition to caste through acculturation, local customary law and religious cults mediated between the stages of clan-based society and its transformation into a state. Should we see this process invariably as what has been called Sanskritisation, or should we not also recognise situations where the reverse may have happened, where a particular form of Purāṇic Hinduism is a concession to local custom and belief. It has been argued that by continuing to support a religious cult of tribal origin, which initially had a relatively large geographical network, the territory of the cult would be incorporated into the territory of the state. This not only complicates the process of state-formation but has much to contribute to a realistic understanding of the evolution of Purāṇic Hinduism.

Large numbers of grants of land were made to *brāhmaṇas* at this time and these acted as the nuclei of Sanskritic culture in many areas. We tend to observe the impact of these entirely from the official versions of the time. But this was not a one-sided acculturation. Nor was it limited to caste and religion alone. If the economic base of a state requires a developed agrarian economy and substantial commerce, then other transformations were also required. Cultivators would have to be converted into tax-paying peasants. Caste in such situations becomes an adjunct to coercion. New identities also demanded a ranking in the new hierarchy. The integration of society through a state system is in many ways different from the integration of clans into larger units. If the families of chiefs were given *kṣatriya* status, how were the rest fitted in? Were there attempts to resist this hierarchy? There is for example, one inscription from central India which refers to the need to suppress the Śabara, Pulinda, and others.

Ultimately the clan identity did not altogether disappear for some aspects remained essential to the basic unit of caste society, the *jāti*. This seems to take on the role of a bridge in the transition to state systems. The identity conferred by birth, kinship, and marriage relations continues. It has been and is, a source of major social cohesion or of conflict. The study of the process by which clan-based societies changed into caste societies and the transformation of non-state systems into states, was a slow one and needs to bc enquired into in some detail. Such studies would require the utilization of a variety of sources and among them even oral traditions could be helpful. Literature, whether written or oral, when used as a historical source, may not provide what some historians tend to call 'hard facts'. But these sources do illumine our perspectives and our historical assumptions. The categories of texts which I have been speaking of carry the perceptions of the past of their authors and these perceptions frequently indicate contemporary concerns. Analyses of these sources are likely to provide the kind of insights into social history that may enable us to better understand our past and therefore also our present.

# 36

# *The Mouse in the Ancestry**

Historians of India have tended to give little credence to the histories of dynasties and regions as described in the *vaṃśāvalīs* dismissing the texts as being of slight consequence. There is however a pattern to the *vaṃśāvalī* literature which needs to be investigated and which suggests that the texts although in part drawing on mythologized accounts of the past, do however provide certain social and political insights which should be of value to the historian. That these patterns recur with frequency in the literature of various parts of the sub-continent is of course partly due to its being a literary genre in the second millennium AD and therefore observing its own rules of structure and form; but in part it also draws on the *itihāsa-purāṇa* tradition which obviously continued to be meaningful and which provided a common fund of origin myths and genealogical links. An illustration of this is the role of the *mūsaka* (mouse or rat) as a symbol in the origin myths of dynasties as recorded in a number of *vaṃśāvalīs* from geographically unrelated areas.

Most *vaṃśāvalīs* can be fairly clearly demarcated into earlier and later sections. The former draw heavily on traditional material often deriving from Purāṇic sources and the latter reflect historical events suggestive of a more authentic record of what actually happened. The *vaṃśāvalī* of the Himalayan valley of Chamba is a case in point. The gradual but noticeable change of symbols provides indicators in the changing process of those who ruled.

The Chamba *vaṃśāvalī* claims to be a history of the kingdom of Chamba and has been gathered and collated by modern scholars.[1] The earlier part (vs 1–34) shows a familiarity with Purāṇic sources particularly the *Bhāgavata* and the *Skanda Purāṇas* and describes the origins of the earliest ruling family. The later and major

* *Amṛtadhārā*, Prof R.N. Dandekar Felicitation Volume, S.D. Joshi (ed.), Delhi, 1984, 427–34.

portion of the text is a more reliable account of events connected with the Chamba state. The original compilation dates to about the seventeenth century and was probably put together by a *brāhmaṇa* editor emphasising as it does the grants and donations made to *brāhmaṇas* and the religious under-pinnings of the actions of kings.

The dynasty is said to be of the Sūryavaṃśa lineage and the Chamba *vaṃśāvalī* makes the link through a founding ancestor Kuśa, the son of Rāma, but continues the descent to include the Śākyas and Prasenaka (? Prasenajit). The immediate ruling ancestry of the Chamba royal family is traced to Mūṣanavarman, the story of his early life being reminiscent of some other dynastic origin myths. His father, we are told, died as a result of an attack by the Kiras against his kingdom. The pregnant queen, rescued by the ministers and the *guru*, gave birth to a posthumous son who was kept in a cave. Later he was taken to a neighbouring kingdom where he was brought up in a style befitting a prince and given a patrimony at the time of his marriage to his benefactor's daughter. Eventually Mūṣanavarman was able to defeat the Kiras and win back his kingdom.

Epigraphic evidence corroborates some of the terms used in the origin myth as related in the *vaṃśāvalī*. There are references to *āditya-vaṃśa* and *moṣūna gotra*.[2] Given the context in which they occur these references also suggest that the claim to monarchical status involved controlling the *sāmantas* or feudatories. The Gum inscription and the later Proli-Ra-Gala inscription make this apparent in the reference to the title of . . . *mahārājādhirāja parameśvara*. . . .[3] The continuing presence of feudatories into the second millennium AD is also indicated by the 'fountain stones', a form of memorial stones characteristic of Chamba. A further inscription links one of the names with Kishkindha which VOGEL interprets as a location in Chamba[4] state but which may indicate connections further away. Linguistically the earlier inscriptions display a poor knowledge of Sanskrit and a groping from Prākrit to Sanskrit. The quality of the language and style changes noticeably in the Saraham *praśasti*[5] composed in the established tradition of Sanskrit lyrical poetry. This also links the royal family to Kishkindha, the link being through a marriage with Somaprabhā, obviously a woman of great political consequence since the *praśasti* is lavish in her praise. Subsequent to this, the inscriptions are frequently records of donations of cultivated land or terraced fields made to *brāhmaṇas* and temples in the main. The format of these inscriptions follows that of the land grants from the kingdoms in the plains of this period. Clearly the Chamba state in the second millennium AD was taking on the form familiar from the established monarchies of northern India.

The earlier inscriptions are issued chiefly from Brahmapura (Brahmor) the first capital of the state. This was a seemingly inaccessible area but in fact well-endowed with terraced fields and lying on the route over the Kukti Pass to Lahul and Zanskar. In the next phase the issuing of royal inscriptions is from Champakā (Chamba) which was the new capital.[6] However, the connections with Brahmapura were not entirely terminated and there was an element of validation in mentioning the earlier capital in some of the inscriptions. Echoes of the *praśasti* style are also evident in phrases such as, 'Sahilla was a rain cloud extinguishing the Kira forces.' It is curious that in the *vaṃśāvalī* it is only after the moving of the capital to Chamba that the origin myth is narrated. Does this reflect a marriage alliance with the *kṣatriyas* of the plains or the migration of the latter to the hill valleys? If it was the latter there is no clear reason to account for such a migration as the reason which is generally given by modern historians, the invasion by the Turks, would not account for such a migration since the reference to the Turuṣkas is of a later period. Dynastic origin, even in the later phase, is associated with the *āditya-vaṃśa* and the *Mūṣana-gotra*. Legitimation includes the standard formula, . . . *deva-dvija-guru-pūjā paripālam cāturvarṇya vyavasthā* . . . , which was in keeping with the best traditions of *rāja-dharma*.

In analysing the myth of origin it is clear that a link was sought with one of the two major lineages, the Sūryavaṃśa or solar lineage and this was characteristic of claims put forward by many *kṣatriyas* of the post-Gupta period who often sought either Sūrya-vaṃśa or Candravaṃśa ancestry. The former provided associations with the descendants of the Ikṣvākus and the epic hero Rāma, the later *avatāra* of Viṣṇu. All these were impeccable antecedents. However the use of the term *Moṣūna* as a *gotra* name raises another set of questions. In the popular tradition of Chamba this word and its variants *mūsuna/mūṣuna* is associated with *mūṣ/mūṣi* and therefore with a mouse. In fact the king Mūṣana is said to have been guarded by mice whilst taking refuge in the cave.[7]

The story of the founder of the family being born posthumously in a cave on the defeat of his father and the child growing up among people of lesser status and using them to reconquer his father's kingdom in order to reassert his rights, is common to other historical traditions as well. According to Tod,[8] the Guhilas of Mewar are said to have derived the etymology of their name from Goha/Guha the prince being born posthumously in a cave—*guha*. In this case the prince exploited the friendship of the Bhil tribes to regain his kingdom. It could perhaps be argued that this myth encapsulates a process by which tribal resources were used by adventurers in borderlands to carve out kingdoms for themselves where the term *guha*, meaning a cave or to live in a cave, may have been a generic term for tribal peoples (for example, Guha the Niṣāda in the *Rāmāyaṇa*). Elsewhere it has been argued that the term Guhila means a forest and is to be identified with the area between the Guhila-bala and the river Mahī.[9] The birth of a prince in a cave need not therefore be taken literally but may be an oblique reference to tribal connections. The story of the recapturing of the kingdom was to legitimize the formation of a kingdom and may not have referred to the inheriting of a patrimony in literal terms. But the claim to the territory would be strengthened if it could be described as a patrimony. Further sanction is obtained by the child being reared or cared for by the family of a *brāhmaṇa* or a *guru*. In some cases it is hinted that the original caste of the family was *brāhmaṇa*. Thus, in the Guhila ancestry, the Atpur inscription refers to Guhadatta as *viprakulānandaḥ*.[10]

The theme however is not restricted to northern India. A parallel origin myth comes from Kerala in the eleventh century text of the *Mūṣakavaṃśakāvya* composed by the court poet Aṭula.[11] According to this text, Paraśurāma, having slaughtered all the *kṣatriyas* then discovered that he required one for completing a sacrifice. A prince is produced and it is stated that he is the posthumous son of a *kṣatriya* killed by Paraśurāma, that he is of Haihaya ancestry and that his then pregnant mother was rescued by a *purohita* at the time of the killing of the *kṣatriyas* and was taken to south India for safe-keeping. The child was given birth to in a cave, *guha*. The name Mūṣaka was given to the family because of the appearance of an elephant-sized mouse in the cave just before his birth. The lowly status of the mouse is explained by its being in fact the great Parvatarāja, the lord of the mountains, inadvertently converted into a mouse by the power of a *ṛṣi*. The child was reared by the *purohita*. On the successful completion of the sacrifice by Paraśurāma he bestowed on the child the region of Elimallai in northern Malabar as his kingdom and he was consecrated king by Paraśurāma himself who libated him with jars of water, hence his full name, Rāma-ghaṭa-mūṣaka. (It is curious that the play on the word 'mouse' is maintained in this story since *eli* is the Dravidian term for mouse and *mallai* for mountain). The link with the Haihayas locates the ancestry in the Vindhyan region or along the Narbada and therefore the migration southwards has to be explained. A later section of the text clearly refers to Mahiṣmatī as the capital of the Haihayas[12] who are usually listed as a segment of the Candravaṃśa lineage in the Purāṇic sources.[13] In claiming links with the lunar lineage, the *Mūṣakavaṃśakāvya* differs a little from the Chamba *vaṃśāvalī*.

It would seem then that the stereotype of posthumous birth in a cave and an association with a mouse in the founding ancestry were part of a common heritage among some origin myths of families claiming *kṣatriya* status during the second millennium AD. The term Mūṣaka occurs in early sources as the name of an important tribal people[14] and is sometimes also identified with the Musikenoi/Musicanus who opposed Alexander of Macedon when he was campaigning in northern India. STRABO[15] quotes Onescritus in locating the Musicanus in the southernmost part of India. In a later passage however he locates them near Patalene, generally identified with the delta of the Indus and states that they dwelt along the river lands of the Indus. This raises the obvious question of whether a section of the Musicanus migrated from the Indus delta, perhaps along the west coast and settled in the Elimallai area. This would further suggest that the provenance of the origin myth might have been western India and that the people had as their symbol or totem, the mouse. If the identification of Mūṣaka with Musicanus is feasible then they must have been a people of some consequence (as is suggested by the accounts of Alexander's campaigns) and later genealogists would seek links with the name. Or it could be suggested that the bards, who were the keepers of the tradition before it went into the hands of the court poets and the *brāhmaṇas*, had certain stock stereotypes for origin myths and used these indiscriminately, hence the occurrence of parallel stories from areas as far afield as Chamba and Kerala. In the case of Chamba it may be possible to argue that the Guhila tradition had travelled up to the hills with the migration of some Rajput families seeking their fortune in the valleys of the Himalayan foothills and further up. From the inscriptions at Chamba it is clear that the use of terms such as *āditya-vaṃśa* and the Mūṣaka *gotra* are fairly early and if they travelled up from the plains they would date to the post-Gupta period.

It is however worth keeping in mind that the root **mūṣ* can also be used for *mūṣaka*, meaning, a thief and a plunderer. Was the term *mūṣaka* a synonym for clans and families which forcibly seized power or welded lineage based societies into monarchical states in spite of being themselves of uncertain origin? The double meaning of *mūṣaka* would then be the only clue to their less salubrious origins. Such a meaning would strengthen the idea of their being born or raised in a forest cave.

Both the Guhila and Chamba sources make a passing reference to Kishkindha but it remains uncertain whether the reference is to the same place (although unidentified) or to two distinct places both of which can be separately identified one being near Udaipur in Rajasthan and the other in the Curah area of Chamba.[16] In the Chamba inscription it is associated with a marriage where the lady, Somaprabhā, is described as of the house of Kishkindha. That the inscription is substantially a eulogy of the lady in unexpectedly fine Sanskrit may hint at her having come from the plains and having introduced through her presence and her entourage the use of a more literary Sanskrit in Chamba than was usual earlier.[17] Possibly the place-name Kishkindha may also have travelled to Chamba in some such fashion.

Another link between the Guhila tradition as recorded by Tod and the Chamba *vaṃśāvalī* is the role of the *siddha* and of the Tantric cult. In the Guhila story, Bappa, who actually establishes the kingdom is initiated by a Śaiva ascetic, receives his armour from the goddess Bhavānī and at the most crucial point of his career, when making a bid for the control of Chittor, he meets the *yogi* Gorakhanātha, who gives him a double-edged sword.[18] (The anachronism of Gorakhanātha dating to a period after the founding of the Guhila kingdom is ignored). In the rise of the state of Chamba, the Jogi Carpaṭa Nātha plays an important role as the royal advisor. The inclusion of *yogis* as key persons in the story may have derived from the tendency among the record-keepers of the tradition, the genealogists and chroniclers, often being worshippers of the *kula-devas* and the *śakti* and Tantric cults.[19] Their deities and *gurus* would therefore be involved in the successful establishing of power by the clients of the record keepers. Or alternatively, if the new ruling families had local origins then they may have associated local cult figures with the processes of legitimizing their power. In the case of Chamba the association of the Jogi sect would have been an added support for legitimacy since Tantricism was popular in the forthills of the Himalayas with Mandi and Kangra being major cult centres as also parts of the adjoining plains at Jallandhar, not to mention areas further away such as western Tibet.

There appear to have been two levels of sanction derived from religious systems. With the transfer of the capital from the more remote Brahmapura to the more accessible site of Chamba the sanction seems to have come from the Tantric *siddhas* suggesting that they were the more popular. Sahilavarman who worked towards establishing a powerful state and founded the city of Champakā, is clearly linked with Tantric *siddhas* who grant him the boon of ten sons. His preceptor was the Jogi Carpaṭa and the founding of the city is associated with the goddess Champāvatī. Sahilavarman introduces the worship of *lingas*, orders the building of a number of temples and also a sanctuary for Carpaṭa to which he himself eventually retires after installing his son as king. The location of Chamba on a plateau overlooking the confluence of the Ravi and the Saho rivers points to the need for a large and more open location easily accessible to the foothills. The site also provided entry points into the main valleys of the region controlled by the feudatory chiefs or *rāṇās*. The establishing of the new capital probably dated to the end of the first millennium AD since the successors of Sahilavarman are referred to in the *Rājataraṅgiṇī* of Kalhaṇa and would date to the eleventh century AD. The religious sanction is extended to include Vaiṣṇavism as Sahilavarman is also said to have built the important Lakṣmī–Nārāyaṇa temple at Chamba with its special image made of white marble brought from the Vindhyas. A further Vaiṣṇava association is that of a subsequent king Pratāpasiṁhavarman who as a devotee of Viṣṇu wished to build yet another temple but was initially unable to finance it. However the discovery of a copper mine in Chamba helped to overcome his obstacle.

It would seem that the sanction of the *siddhas* may have been politically insufficient and consequently the further sanction of

Vaiṣṇavism was necessary. This perhaps becomes more significant as the powers of the state are further established and the assimilative ability of Vaiṣṇavism becomes an effective agency of social manipulation by the ruling elite. Whatever the personal religious persuasions of a ruler may have been the fact of his giving public expression to them through large-scale financing and monumental structures inevitably draws these persuasions into the social concerns of the state. The influence of Vaiṣṇavism would also have underlined the indenting on the *itihāsa-purāṇa* tradition for links with the conventional roots of *kṣatriya* culture. The claim to Sūrya-vaṃśa connections by the ruling family would have tied in with the worship of Rāma both as an ancestor of the royal family as well as an *avatāra* of Viṣṇu. Vaiṣṇavism was also in part a reflection of other influences from further away, from the cultural norms and life style of the established kingdoms of the plains. It is significant that the white marble for the image of Lakṣmī–Nārāyaṇa has to come from the Vindhyas. The financial cost of temple building could only be met after the discovery of a copper mine which would point to the heavy financial outlay required in imitating the trappings of the larger states as also using this for purposes of legitimation. It could be argued that the introduction of the Vaiṣṇava sanction was an interpolation into the *vaṃśāvalī* by *brāhmaṇa* editors. That this was not merely a matter of recording a tradition in a *vaṃśāvalī* but reflected the growth of brahmanical culture in the region is evident from the epigraphical data registering the granting of land to *brāhmaṇas* which becomes a noticeable feature from this point onwards. That much of the land granted was cultivated land also points to the gradual acculturation of the area with nuclei of *brāhmaṇa* settlements. As was common in many of these kingdoms the *brāhmaṇas* were often invited from sacred centres and in one of the copper-plate grants of Vidagda it is stated that the *brāhmaṇa* Nandu came from Kurukṣetra.[20]

Power relations within the state and with neighbouring states are also reflected in the sources. Thus there are references to close links between Chamba and Kashmir which were initially hostile but later became more amicable with a marriage alliance in the eleventh century,[21] a clear indication that Chamba now had high status and an acceptable culture since the 'high culture' of Kashmir dates back to an earlier period. The acculturation of Chamba is also expressed in the changing forms of the 'fountain stones', the memorial stones erected mainly by the families of the *rāṇās*, in memory of and for the merit of, deceased kinsmen. The earlier stones carry traces of local craftsmanship in the style of carving and the use of space. The later stones depict recognizable deities carved in an elaborate style. There is a noticeable refinement and elegance of all that is included on the stone. The epigraphical data further indicates the administration of the state assuming a form similar to that of other areas of northern India. A large range of feudatories are referred to as well as a hierarchy of administrative officials[22] suggesting that the formalities and embellishments of state functioning were now familiar to the state of Chamba. However the significance of the mouse in the ancestry still remains something of an enigma!

## Notes and References

1. J.Ph. Vogel, *Antiquities of Chamba State*, Calcutta, 1911, ASI, vol. XXXVI.
2. Laksana Image inscription at Brahmor, ibid., p. 144; Gum inscription, p. 146.
3. Ibid., pp. 146–8.
4. Svaim image inscription, ibid., p. 150.
5. Sarahan praśasti, ibid., p. 152.
6. Kulait Copper-Plate inscription, ibid., p. 182.
7. Vs. 49–61, ibid., pp. 91ff.
8. J. Tod, *Annals and Antiquities of Rajasthan*, Oxford, 1920, vol. I, pp. 173ff.
9. J.N. Asopa, *Origin of the Rajputs*, Delhi, 1976, pp. 102ff.
10. *Indian Antiquary*, XXXIX, p. 191.
11. Gopinatha Rao, 'Extracts from the Mūṣakavaṃśam . . . ', *Travancore Archaeological Series*, 1916, II, 1, no. 10, pp. 87–113; M.G.S. Narayanan, 'History from the Mūṣakavaṃśakāvya of Aṭula', *PAIOC*, Jadhavpur, 1969.
12. Ibid., section VI.
13. *Viṣṇu Purāṇa*, IV.11; F.E. Pargiter, *The Ancient Indian Historical Tradition*, London, 1922, p. 266.
14. *Mahābhārata*, VI.10.62.
15. Strabo, *Geography*, XV.1, 21 and 33.
16. Vogel, op. cit., pp. 180–5.
17. Ibid., p. 152.
18. Tod, op. cit., pp. 180–5.
19. Cf. N.P. Zeigler, 'Marwari Historical Chronicles . . . ', *IESHR*, 1979, XIII, no. 2, pp. 319–52.

20. Vogel, op. cit., pp. 255ff.
21. Kalhaṇa, *Rājataraṅgiṇī*, VII.218; 58.
22. Vogel, op. cit., pp. 120ff.

# VIII

# The Renouncer in a Social Context

Among the more central aspects of religion in India is the unusual and paradoxical presence of the renouncer, not just as a marginal feature but as a person of considerable authority. In the early period the renouncer emerges with the coming of sects such as the Buddhists and the Jains, which in turn are tied to some of the departures from Vedic ritual as registered in the major *Upaniṣads*. The renouncer becomes important as the counterpoint to the insistence in other texts on social obligations and also to the limits of political power. That the renouncer has an authority in society reflects on the centrality of the individual, and renunciation becomes the assertion of the individual even in a social context.

The last essay in this group of papers suggests that millennarianism, again thought to be more appropriate to Christianity and Islam, was manifested in some of the beliefs of Buddhism and Vaiṣṇavism.

# 37

# Sacrifice, Surplus, and the Soul*

The sage Yājñavalkya, discoursing on the transmigration of the soul from one body to the next, described it as analogous with the caterpillar who, when it comes to the end of a leaf, draws itself together and moves onto another leaf, or else like the goldsmith, who, taking a piece of gold, transforms it into another shape, more beautiful perhaps than the first.[1] Both analogies are actions that result in change: in the first there is movement from one object to another, and in the second there is a mutation within the same substance. These ideas are crucial to the understanding of the soul and immortality as developed in the *Upaniṣads*, the earliest recorded discourses (as they are often called) of any length in India on theories of the immortality of the soul.[2] The two analogies concretize the essence of the doctrine of transmigration, which was to become culturally hegemonic as the bedrock of religious thinking among many sects in India. It might therefore be worth examining more closely the initial process that enabled this doctrine to take root.

The *Upaniṣads* as a subject of scholarship have generally been left to the domain of philosophers, who see them as fundamental to many philosophical systems, and to grammarians and philologists. However, texts, and especially those with such specific concerns, are anchored in points of time that give them a historical dimension. The historical moment is linked both to the genesis of an idea and to its reception — two aspects with which this lecture is concerned. The *Upaniṣads* are at one level philosophical speculations on an

* This is the text of the Forster Lecture on the theme of the Immortality of the Soul, delivered at the University of California, Berkeley, on April 8, 1992. I would like to thank Frits Staal for his initial encouragement of the idea and Kunal Chakrabarti for his comments on an earlier draft. I remember with particular warmth the long discussions on this subject with the late Barbara Stoller Miller. In *History of Religion*, 1994, 305–24.

abstract theme, but at another they are embedded in the society to which they relate. They encapsulate a process that leads to the formulation of an ideology. The interaction of this ideology with its environment, its source of power, and its historical ambience need to be inquired into.[3] Ideology speaks of and from a social order and ideas can be used to justify or legitimate the particular order. This is not to suggest that there is a simplistic correlation between ideology and society, for ideology is not merely a pale reflection of reality.[4] In many early societies ideology is incorporated into religious beliefs but articulated in ritual. If ritual is tied to the social order, however, then it can also be seen as the questioning of that order. In early Indian thought ritual is viewed as *karman*/action; therefore, it has been suggested that it would be more appropriate in the case of India to speak of orthopraxy than of orthodoxy.[5]

The period of the composition of the early and major *Upaniṣads* is generally taken as from about the eighth to sixth centuries BC.[6] They emerge out of earlier compositions, stemming from the *Ṛg Veda* and the *Brāhmaṇas* in particular but deviating sufficiently from these origins to become foundational to new groups of thinkers, some of whom were to take a conservative perspective and others, such as the Buddhists, who were to be regarded as heterodox. They represent, therefore, a watershed between the Vedic corpus and the new ideologies, epitomizing features of what has often been called an 'axial age'. The earlier texts emphasize the centrality of the sacrificial ritual, whereas the new ideologies move away from this and explore alternative eschatologies with, initially at least, an absence of ritual.

The historian's concern is with why this change occurred. It has been argued that possibly the *Upaniṣads* represent an interaction between Indo-European or Aryan ideas and the belief and practices of the local non-Aryans or pre-Aryans in northern India.[7] However, once it is conceded that we cannot identify any group as specifically Aryan, it becomes difficult to support an argument that insists so precisely on the differentiation of Aryan and non-Aryan.[8] It might therefore be more feasible to look at other aspects of the historical background. This lecture is not intended to explore all the historical changes of the time, but rather to examine more closely the relevance of a few of them.

The contribution of non-Vedic thought to the evolution of the concepts of the *Upaniṣads* remains hypothetical since there are no texts or well-articulated traditions of such thought. That some merging from such sources occurred is very likely given that Vedic Sanskrit itself reflects non-Aryan features suggestive of bilingualism.[9] Nevertheless, the concepts of the *Upaniṣads* addressed themselves to the existing expressions of Vedic belief and ritual, and to that extent they reflect a departure from them. This was a change in the paradigm of knowledge. The nature of the change was a shift from the acceptance of the *Vedas* as revealed and as controlled by ritual to the possibility that knowledge could derive from intuition, observation, and analysis.

The *Upaniṣads* were explorations in the search for enlightenment of the human condition and release from its bonds. This was not a situation involving priest and ritual nor the regular teacher-and-pupil learning of the *Vedas*. This knowledge was part of the oral tradition but was deliberately kept to a limited audience. The teachers were unconventional and those whom they taught were specially selected.[10] The latter could, however, include those who would normally be excluded from Vedic ritual — those of uncertain social origin such as Satyakāma[11] and women such as Maitreyī, the wife of Yājñavalkya. They are included perhaps to make a point.[12] It is sometimes argued that Satyakāma was accepted not because the social status of those taught was irrelevant, but because, having spoken the truth, he was recognized as a *brāhmaṇa*. However, his uncertain origin was sufficient to suggest that the question of his being a *brāhmaṇa* was not central. Where *brāhmaṇas* were the sons of *dāsis*, they were referred to as *dāsyaḥ-putraḥ*, but nevertheless respected.[13] The legitimacy of *brāhmaṇa* teachers was sought to be established by their status in lists of succession relating to their function as priests.[14] In an otherwise patriarchal society it is curious that matronymics are so prominent in these succession lists. The *kṣatriya* teachers have no particular qualifications. They were the *rājās*, the chiefs or oligarchs, *kṣatriya* being derived from *kṣatr*, meaning power. They are not included in the succession lists nor listed separately, although on some matters they instruct the *brāhmaṇas*. The form of dialogue was new, and, in breaking away from ritual and *mantra*, it seemed to be a rationalizing movement. At the same time, however, the mysticism of the doctrine introduced other elements. The location of the discussions were frequently the residences of *kṣatriyas* or occasionally those of *brāhmaṇas*. The *pariṣads*, or assemblies of the *kṣatriyas*, mentioned as locations for these dialogues, included those of Kāśī, Videha, and the Kuru-Pañcāla. Pravahaṇa Jaivali of the Kuru-Pañcāla taught Śvetaketu Āruneya, the son of Gautama, and his father also came to the *rājā* to be taught.[15]

It was understood that the new doctrine was concerned with knowledge not about the mundane world, but with the conceptualization of other worlds,[16] although this exploration helped systematize knowledge about the mundane world. Despite the shift of focus to new methods of attaining knowledge instead of conforming to Vedic ritual practice, sacrificial rituals were not suddenly discontinued. The deities of earlier times were not denied, but rather their role tended to fade. If the sacrificial ritual was limited in its efficacy or ineffective in its purpose, then what were the other forms that could be central to the human condition? These interests revolved around questions of mortality and immortality — the immortality of the soul, the realization of the self, and belief in rebirth and retribution. Much of this was tied into examining the nature of reality: Is reality what we perceive around us or is there a reality beyond this which becomes tangible only through new techniques of perception? These involved control over the complementary categories of body and mind (*yoga*) and meditation (*dhyāna*), both ideally requiring a form of life given to austerity if not asceticism (*tapas*). This centered on the individual as the seeker of immortality through his own effort. Salvation of a limited kind had been present in the ritual of sacrifice, intended, among other things, for the attainment of the heightened pleasures of the heaven of Indra. But now the concern was not for heaven, but for release or liberation, *mokṣa*. This was not initially associated with sin and redemption but was conceptualized as the liberation of the soul.

*Mokṣa* was seen as related to the concept of *ātman-brahman*.[17] *Brahman*, necessary to the creation of the universe that it enters, is manifest in the *ātman*, the soul, which is an essential part of every individual life. *Mokṣa* therefore lies in achieving the realization of the *ātman-brahman*, releasing it from the bonds of the body and from repeatedly having to undergo death and rebirth from body to body. The transmigration of the *ātman* must cease before *mokṣa* is possible. In other words, the caterpillar must stop moving from leaf to leaf. Perhaps because the new doctrine distanced itself from the sacrificial ritual and drew on mystic concepts, claiming almost supernatural powers, it was referred to as the secret doctrine, *guhya-adesa, rahasyam*. One statement actually equates the secret doctrine with the *Upaniṣad — iti rahasyam iti upaniṣad*. The texts tend to retain this character of closed knowledge.[18] The new doctrine questioned the sacrificial cult — it alone could not be a means of liberating the *ātman*. The *Vedas* were said to be inferior to the now more frequently discussed alternative belief systems.[19] Sarcastic references to the greedy behaviour of priests at the sacrificial ritual highlighted doubts about the ritual and its main actors.[20]

Another startling feature is that the exploration of these new ideas was often not by *brāhmaṇas* but by *kṣatriyas*. Thus, the *rājā* of the Kuru-Pañcāla explains to Śvetaketu that his father, though learned, is not familiar with all aspects of the new teaching, and later Gautama is initiated into the teaching by the *rājā*; *brāhmaṇas* who come to Uddālaka Aruni seeking knowledge on *ātman-brahman* are directed by him to the Kekeya *rājā*, Aśvapati; in the dialogue between Ajātaśatru the *rājā* of Kāśī and Dṛptabalaki of the Gārgya clan, it is clear that the former is the more knowledgeable.[21] The noticeably important role of the *kṣatriyas* has been commented upon both in the *Upaniṣads* and by modern scholars.[22] The *rājā* of the Pañcālas says to the learned *brāhmaṇa* Gautama, 'This knowledge has never in the past been vested in any *brāhmaṇa*, but I shall tell it to you.'[23] This is striking coming from the *rājā* of the Kuru-Pañcāla, an area noted for its learned *brāhmaṇas* and frequency of the best sacrificial rituals.[24] Those who discoursed on the doctrine taught it either to their sons or to selected pupils. These *kṣatriyas* included the *rājās* of the Uśināra and Matsya clans and of the Kekeya, Kuru-Pañcāla, Kāśī, Kośala, and above all, Janaka of Videha,[25] substantially of the western and middle Ganga plain.[26] It is impressive that this vast geographical area saw the mobility of *rājās*, *brāhmaṇas*, and ideas at so early a stage.

The interest of the *brāhmaṇas* in the new teaching may have stemmed from dissidents seeking alternative philosophies or the curious exploring new ideas. Those attracted to asceticism would have supported such discussion. However, some *brāhmaṇas* who taught the new doctrine received lavish gifts or charged huge fees,[27] and others, who were by no account ascetics, are ascribed on occasion as extremely wealthy and learned.[28] Categories of knowledge were hierarchical, reflected a spectrum of interests,[29] and incorporated what appears to be a folk or subaltern knowledge.

This is suggested, for example, by the inclusion of Raikva as a teacher. He sits under his cart scratching himself and hardly behaves as would upper-caste teachers.[30] Distinctions were made between knowledge as and for ritual, as intuition, as intellectual speculation that encouraged debate and the dialectical form of argument, and as knowledge of the *ātman*. The participation of some *brāhmaṇas* may have led to the eventual inclusion of this material as part of the Vedic corpus, and it also has occasional references to other earlier Vedic compositions. But the later appropriation of the *Upaniṣads* could also have been an attempt to stem the heresies of the Buddhists and other sects by tracing the origins of their deviation to Upaniṣadic thought. Modern philosophers continue to disagree as to whether Buddhism is to be treated as a part of the spectrum of post-Vedic thought rooted in the *Upaniṣads* or as a radical departure from the *Upaniṣads*.[31]

The new teaching moved away from *brāhmaṇas* as priests to *kṣatriyas* and *brāhmaṇas* as teachers, parallel to the shift away from ritual and religious duties, which required a high degree of specialization in mantras and rites. Max Weber distinguishes between the priest, the magician, and the charismatic prophet. The priest entreats the deity via prayer and sacrifice, whereas the magician coerces the deity via ritual. The priest eventually emerges as a functionary of a social group rather than of individuals, and the office becomes hereditary.[32] The teachers of the *Upaniṣads* do not fall into any of these categories as they are distinct from the priests, and, although their teaching leads to a new belief system of a higher order, they are not prophets. Priests as mediators between men and gods were not required in this system, since in the new teaching each individual was responsible for his or her own salvation and the role of the deity could be absent. Knowledge had earlier included the kinds of questions controlled by the traditional priest, but in effect the new knowledge superseded the old.

The move away from the sacrificial ritual requires some comment. The term for sacrifice, *yajña*, means to consecrate, to worship, to convert the profane into the holy. Sacrifice as a ritual involves the one ordering the sacrifice or the patron of the ritual, the *yajamāna*; the *devatā*/gods to whom the prayer is addressed; the *brāhmaṇa* priests who act as intermediaries and mediate between the *yajamāna* and the gods; and the offering, the *dravya* or *bali*, which is transferred from the ownership of the *yajamāna* and gifted to the gods via the mediation of the priests. There is no countertransfer of any visible equivalent.[33] The concept of *tyāga*/renunciation, became increasingly important in the debate on whether there should be a renunciation of the outcome of the ritual. The sacrificial rituals were of various kinds. The smallest and most compact were the *gṛhya*, or domestic rituals, using a single priest. The *śrauta*, or traditional rituals, were more elaborate, with several priests and altars, and continued for some days.[34] To these may be added the rituals associated with the acquisition of power and fertility where the patron of the sacrifice had to be a *kṣatriya rājā*.

The *yajamāna*, or patron, had first to be changed from a profane condition to a sacralized one. This involved a lengthy purification during which all other activities were set aside, which automatically excluded as *yajamānas* those who were essential to the daily curriculum, such as men who laboured and women. The *yajamāna* was stripped of authority during this process and underwent a change of status through ritual cleansing. The location for the ceremony had also to be purified and demarcated, for, outside this area, all killing was not immolation but murder.[35] The offering could be first fruits, the *bali* and the *bhāga*, or could be specially selected objects, such as animals identified as the victims of the ritual. The offering was owned by the *yajamāna* and was of value, which introduced an element of renunciation. An offering implies an existing asymmetrical relationship whereas a gift creates such a relationship. Theories on the purpose and function of the sacrifice range over many explanations such as homage to and communion with the gods, catharsis, renunciation, rejuvenation, and social legitimacy. The Vedic sacrifice had many functions; what it distinctly was not, however, was a covenant between a man and his jealous God.

Ritual activity, even where it involves a simple, everyday act, must be demarcated from the mundane, sometimes by archaizing its artifacts and its articulation. The demarcation points to the ritual having a different connotation than mundane acts. Nevertheless, ritual is also social action inasmuch as it involves a performer and a professional and therefore becomes symbolic of a social statement. Such a statement has many levels of interpretation, including the religious, the philosophical, the relationship between the performer and the professional, the perception of each of these by the audience — whether physically present or not — and the material objects involved in the performing of the ritual. Rituals therefore carry multiple messages. Even when the ritual was performed by a single household it was a signal to the community. Major ritual occasions, even as early as the *Ṛg Veda*, were community occasions.

The *brāhmaṇa* as priest had a relationship of reciprocity with the *kṣatriya* embodying political power. The sacrificial ritual was an exchange in which the gods were the recipients of offerings, *bali*, the priests were the recipients of gifts and fees, *dāna* and *dakṣinā*, and the *kṣatriya* as the one who orders the ritual, was the recipient of the benevolence of the gods and of status and legitimacy among men. Reciprocity involves an offering, a giving up or 'sacrifice' of something valuable. For the *kṣatriya* this consisted of the visible *bali*, the voluntary tribute in the form of material goods as well as the acceptance of the mediation of the *brāhmaṇa* with the gods, which was to some degree an acceptance of the *kṣatriya's* dependence on the *brāhmaṇa*. The priests were therefore deeply involved in the articulation of power in their relations with the *kṣatriyas* through the ritual of sacrifice. The new teaching, however, had little use for this particular interconnection. Admittedly, the same two social categories, the *kṣatriya* and the *brāhmaṇa*, who were the main participants in the sacrificial ritual, were now involved in the new doctrine, but their roles and purposes were different. The *brahma-kṣatra* hierarchy was reversed in the acquisition of mystical knowledge.[36]

A sacrificial ritual involves resources. It also requires the mobilizing of resources and attention to the social problems posed by the procurement of offerings. The required wealth could be a substantial portion of the *yajamāna's* resources. Not only was the best of livestock sacrificed but the gifts to be made to the priests in terms of cattle wealth and golden objects, if taken literally, would have materially impoverished many a *yajamāna*. When something of value was offered it was in the belief and expectation of receiving in return, at a later point, something of even greater value.

The frequency of the different types of rituals — such as daily, new and full moon, and seasonal sacrifices that increased with the agricultural calendar, rites of passage, and those intended to obtain either a boon or expiation — would be in part dependent on the availability of offerings.[37] The mobilization of resources would initially be the responsibility of the family and clan members, whose resources were limited. The common sharing of offerings enhanced the unity of the participants, making the sacrifice a collective activity. Gradually, the collective element receded and the focus turned to the individual *yajamāna*. This was the price paid by the individual aspiring to status and power and using the sacrificial ritual as a means of claiming legitimacy. The power was intended to assert an authority beyond that of the ordinary authority of the chief of the clan. This authority was to increase over time and become qualitatively different in the claim, not of chiefship but of kingship, with the mutation of chiefdoms into kingdoms.

There was an element of gift exchange involved in the relationship between the *brāhmaṇa* and the *kṣatriya* through the sacrificial ritual. The participants were not of equal status and the *brāhmaṇas*, even when consecrating a *rājā*, stated their independence by their allegiance to Soma.[38] Reciprocity was not always balanced, and the obligation to give was that of the *kṣatriya*; to receive, that of the *brāhmaṇa*. The exchange was not protected by law but was dictated by custom. The acceptance of the gift bound the two participants as partners and reiterated their bonds.

The historical context of the sacrificial ritual is first encountered in the *Ṛg Veda*. The function of the *rājā*, as the warrior chief, was to protect the *viś*, or clan, even if such protection involved skirmishes and raids against other clans, and to augment resources through cattle raids, which in a cattle-rearing culture are imperative. Raiding was a proof of manhood and a matter of honour and assumed the character almost of a ritual process. It is idealized in the heroic qualities of the lifestyle of the god Indra. A successful raid required leadership but also drew on the prayers of priests interceding with the gods. The subsequent ritual was a thanksgiving and a means of distributing the booty. This was the subject of the many *dāna-stutis*, or hymns of praise, in which *brāhmaṇa* poets eulogized the prowess of those *rājās* who had increased their wealth through raids.[39] Wealth was computed primarily in terms of cattle, horses, chariots, and gold. These were often listed in exaggerated amounts — sixty thousand head of cattle and a thousand horses — where the exaggeration was intended as an incentive to those *rājās* who had heard the praise of others and, it was hoped, would emulate them. The availability of resources affected attitudes toward the offering. Because they were herders, animals were normally not killed indiscriminately for food and there was a prohibition on the eating of the animals as daily fare. They were consumed only on special occasions, when a guest visited or after a ritual.[40] This was a mechanism for conserving the herd. However, the archaeological evidence from contemporary sites suggests a larger-than-normal consumption of beef.[41] Possibly the supply of prime livestock diminished until the cow gradually was declared inviolable. The ritual conferred legitimacy on the *rājā*, and the hymns of praise articulated his power. The *rājā* bestowed *dāna*/gifts in the form of wealth on the priests and acquired status in return. This was of central importance in societies that consisted of small, highly competitive groups in which there could be a quick turnover of status, resources, and power.

Subsequently, two trends became evident. One was the concentration of power with the *rājā*, now more frequently mentioned as *kṣatriya*. This was accompanied by a change in the primary resource base from cattle herding to agriculture, and particularly to wet rice cultivation in the middle Ganga plain. The *kṣatriya* was no longer just the cattle-raiding warrior. He augmented his wealth by settling new lands and encouraging their cultivation. The territories where the clan settled, the *janapadas*, were named after the *kṣatriya* ruling clan, such as the Kuru-Pañcāla, Kośala, Videha, and so on. This did not imply their ownership of the land but is indicative of enhanced political power. Cultivation was carried out by the *viś*, or clansmen, assisted by the labour of the *śūdras* and *dāsas* who were outside the clan. The *kṣatriya* demanded and received prestations from them. We are told that the *kṣatriya* eats the *viś*, or the clan, as the deer eats the grain, so the *viś* is subordinate to the *kṣatriya*.[42]

The occasion for making prestations was the sacrificial ritual, and this was the second feature that had changed. There were now a variety of *yajñas*, which ranged from simple daily rituals required of heads of households to more elaborate ones.[43] The most complex were those asserting *kṣatriya* authority, often lasting many months, such as the *rājasūya* and the *aśvamedha* and the *vājapeya*, or rejuvenation ritual. The *rājasūya* involved the conquest of the four quarters and the amassing of tribute before the ritual could begin. *Kṣatriyas* who performed these rites were transformed from *rājās* into *mahārājās*.[44] Such rituals often incorporated the rhetoric and symbols of the raids and skirmishes of pastoral-agricultural societies, even though these were now en route to becoming established kingdoms. Simple rituals could require the gift of a cow to the priest, but elaborate rituals brought in large amounts of wealth as sacrificial fees and gifts.[45] Such rituals were in effect a display, consumption, and destruction of wealth and therefore presupposed the availability of considerable resources to the patron of the ritual.

The specific use to which the wealth was put tended to convert the sacrifice into something of a potlatch. The more the wealth expended on the ritual, the more, it was assumed, would come back to the *yajamāna* through the pleasure of the gods, the discipline of giving, successful warfare, and good harvests; but above all it further raised the status of the *yajamāna*. At the same time, however, it depleted his treasury. The competitive spirit, encouraged by the earlier eulogistic *dāna-stutis*, still persisted and probably resulted, as far as wealth was concerned, in what has been called an 'alternating disequilibrium'.[46] Where the head of the household, the *gṛhapati*, was encouraged to perform frequent calendrical sacrifices, the voluntary tribute to the *kṣatriya* would also decrease because of the demands of these sacrifices. Given the absence of burials in the cultures of the Ganga plain, unlike most other contemporary high cultures in Asia, the utilization of wealth was concentrated on the ritual of sacrifice. The ritual, therefore, combined a testimony of religious affirmation with a claim to status on the part of the *yajamāna*, as well as a demonstration of wealth and resources.

Potlatch, it has been argued, implies maximizing net outgoings.[47] Property is distributed seemingly voluntarily but in fact under compulsion of the ritual. Ostensibly it bears no interest, although a higher return is implicit. This, however, is different from capital accumulation since it cannot be collected on demand or indeed be repaid at all. It is not a series of gifts, but a series of counter gifts. The return gift creates a debt that has to be met in the next ritual. It is an exchange of inalienable objects between people in a state of reciprocal dependence and is particularly evident in societies with a clan structure and a strong kinship organization. The obtaining of gifts and wealth for the ritual is from the labour of the family and kinsmen. When this system changes and the labour of nonclan persons is introduced, with fresh adjustments in relationships between the clans and within the clan, then the handling of wealth also begins to change. Access to wealth begins to require coercive measures. The production of wealth draws on a different kind of impersonal relationship. In such a situation, attitudes of the major *yajamānas*/patrons toward the sacrificial ritual would presumably also change. Reciprocity was between *brāhmaṇas* and *kṣatriyas* and the competition was among the latter, expending their wealth.

The historical background to the *Upaniṣads* depicts a society that was no longer predominantly that of cattle-herding clans. The more common occupation was agriculture with some incipient trade. The frequent and ready violence of raids was now replaced by political control and alliances. Agricultural resources required not capturing and raiding but the availability of regular and coordinated labour. This is reflected in the intensification of the *varṇa* or status hierarchy, where the upper castes claim lineage descent, whereas the fourth caste, that of the *śūdras*, has no lineage base. This was a method of distancing those who provided labour.[48] Claims to ownership of land still lay largely with the clan, although a slow shift is perceptible to claims by families, perhaps as a result of rights of usage.[49] In the middle Ganga region, which included Kāśī, Kośala, and Videha, marshlands and forest were cleared for settlement, assisted to some degree by new iron tools. The cultivation of wet rice led to larger yields and increased wealth. The consumption of wealth in sacrificial rituals may initially have been a stimulus to production, but perhaps when resources could not keep pace with this consumption, the ritual began to have a negative effect. Unlike the produce of herders, grain can be stored for long periods and some accumulation is possible. This may also have resulted in an upward demographic trend requiring more resources. Archaeology provides evidence of increasing numbers of settlements and larger settlements, some of which were to gradually develop into urban centres.[50] *Kṣatriya* rule over these settlements was intended to protect the settlers and maintain minimum laws. For this the *kṣatriya* received a share of the produce in the form of what began as voluntary tributes such as the *bali* and the *bhāga* from the heads of households: such tributes were eventually to evolve into taxes. This encouraged the accumulation of wealth, which ultimately provided resources for the emergence of kingdoms and states. Such wealth was necessary to the new demands of incipient state systems, such as a rudimentary administration, an army, and the expenses of kingship. In addition, the universalizing of religious belief and practice, as in Buddhism, sometimes lent ideological support to the state, as in the Mauryan period.

Let us return to the question of why the *kṣatriyas* explored the doctrines that came to be included in the *Upaniṣads*. Were they moving away from the sacrificial ritual solely because of philosophical curiosity, or was there also, perhaps subconsciously, a search for an alternative that would discourage the expending of wealth — wealth that could be eventually diverted toward maintaining a state system with enhanced powers for the *kṣatriyas* far exceeding those of the earlier chiefships? Such a shift, of course, was not seen in terms of rational well-being or economic theory. The discontinuance of the Vedic sacrificial ritual would break the nexus between the *brāhmaṇa* and the *kṣatriya* and would provide a new role for the *kṣatriya*, more in consonance with the broader changes of the time. While the *brāhmaṇa* and the *kṣatriya* were interlocked in a competition for status, the sacrificial ritual, although seemingly separating their powers, in fact made them interdependent.[51] The *kṣatriya* may have preferred to be released from this dependence. The reality of power was seen now not only as divine dispensation but also in terms of access to resources. The power of the *kṣatriya* did not need to be circumscribed by the sacrificial ritual.

The new doctrine first evolved in areas that had experienced an increase in wealth. The question of whether this wealth would be accumulated as the basis for greater power or be consumed in the sacrificial ritual may have been expressed and considered. Was the break from the prestation economy encouraged as a search for legitimation through other means? Was this tied into an interest in a wider *kṣatriya* identity in areas where there was a perceptible change toward establishing kingship?

The new doctrine required discipline, meditation, and concern with the self alone. It called for neither intermediaries nor deities, which therefore gave it a universalism in the pursuit of *mokṣa*. Whereas the sacrificial ritual required the contribution, to a greater or lesser degree, of the clan and thereby underlined clan identity, the new doctrine moved away from this identity and underlined the separation of the individual from the clan.[52] Meditation and yoga are best undertaken in isolation subsequent to the initial period of training with a teacher. The clan therefore was marginalized, and the individual emerged as the subject seeking knowledge and liberation. This placed a premium on removing oneself from one's society and renouncing social obligations, a sentiment that ran counter to involvement in clan activities required by the earlier rituals. Renunciation is also contrary to the accumulation of wealth, but the notion of such an accumulation was probably necessary for the idea of renunciation to be effective. The focus on the individual highlights the anomie of changing social relations: the breakup of clans as well as the alienation and skepticism was implicit in the new identities emerging in nascent urban centres.[53] This was to be further reinforced by the centrality of individual *nirvāṇa* in subsequent teachings, especially those of Mahāvīra and the Buddha.

If the reasons why the *kṣatriya* was supportive of this doctrine have to do with both philosophical curiosity and changes in social and political forms, these do not entirely explain its attraction for some *brāhmaṇas*. A change in the focus of these ideas was to introduce a substantial Brahmanical concern. It is significant that not all *brāhmaṇas* were familiar with the new doctrine: it was viewed initially as rather esoteric, meant only for the selected few. Those that supported it saw the limitations of the rituals and sought more innovative forms of liberation, even if these ultimately involved renunciation. The use of the vocabulary of release in relation to the soul may have been partially associated with release from social obligations as well. Did *brāhmaṇas* view renunciation with a nostalgia for the nomadic life that was disappearing[54] or with a concern that radical ideas had to be introduced gradually and that renunciation would provide freedom to experiment with new ideas, a freedom not permitted by rigidly controlled rituals?

Sporadic but vague speculation on these matters has been traced to earlier Vedic compositions. The departure from them lay in the forging of a consistent theory for which the observance of the earlier rituals was not required. The construction of this theory has its own history. Shamanistic origins have been suggested[55] in references to *munis, ṛṣis,* and *keśins*,[56] the long-haired ones flying through the air, living in isolation and seeking their own forms of knowledge, which included magic and meditation. They were the forerunners of the renouncers and the ascetics. The *yātudhāna* may well have been shamans and therefore seen as sorcerers and alien by Vedic priests. The lengthy period of training under a teacher as envisaged in the *Upaniṣads* required a desocialization from the family. Thus Śvetaketu left the home of his learned father and went elsewhere to attain knowledge.[57] Together with this, the secrecy of the doctrines is suggestive of shamanistic influence as are descriptions of the journeying of the soul.[58] The soul goes through the air, which opens out like a hole in the chariot wheel; it goes to the sun and moon; it journeys to the world of Brahmā, which is an elaborate movement through many heavens and multiple deities; it enters the clouds and then the rain, then plants and crops, which when eaten take it to the human body. The *ātman* can be larger than the universe and smaller than the mustard seed. The ecstatic state of the *ātman* when released from rebirth echoes shamanistic ecstasy when the spirit is said to be in communion with the divine.

These descriptions of the journeying of the soul and the idea of souls inhabiting plants and animals, were not, as many have pointed out, altogether alien to animistic views on the passage of the spirit.[59] If the archaeological picture of the Ganga plain provides a clue, it is that of a variety of coexisting and overlapping cultures. Fertility cults grew around the worship of trees and female deities often linked to sacred enclosures. The *stūpa* as a tumulus, perhaps with some funerary association,[60] may have drawn on ideas of a soul and an afterlife different from the Vedic. The proximity of megalithic burials in the Vindhyan region and central India indicates further the presence of non-Vedic religion. Cremation encourages a belief in an afterlife rather different from burials, which maintain greater continuity with the mundane. The reduction of the human body to a handful of ashes may have required, by way of a counterpoint, a focus on the disembodied soul and its continual reincarnation. Significantly, some *kṣatriyas* associated with the new doctrine belong to geographical areas often described as outside the boundaries of the *āryāvarta*, the land of the *āryas*,[61] suggesting the need to incorporate other cultures.

The working out of the doctrine involved knowledge which moved from ritual to analytical and speculative argument but included meditation and contemplation.[62] Thus Sanatkumāra asks to be taught the knowledge of the *ātman* — knowledge that later was to be regarded as the higher knowledge as against the lower knowledge of the *Vedas*. The sage Uddālaka Aruni, conversing with his arrogant son, Śvetaketu, provides an explanation of *ātman* which is almost rational in its incorporation of empirical knowledge, of queries, of doubts, and of observation and in its attempts at making categories.[63]

Among the most subtle discussions of the *ātman* is the dialogue between Naciketas and Yama, the god of Death.[64] The *ātman* is described as the charioteer of the body, which is the chariot, a strongly *kṣatriya* symbol.[65] *Mokṣa* was the releasing of the *ātman* from the cycle of repeated death, *punarmṛtyu*, because of being reincarnated in a body.[66] The notion of *mokṣa* as distinct from heaven introduced a change in the meaning of death in which the ideal was not a blissful life in the heaven of the heroes, but the release from being born repeatedly, a release requiring, among other things, an absence of desire. The breaking away from ritual and the search for knowledge about the soul and immortality led to other explorations of the self. But the theory was to be further formulated in a manner that linked it once more with social reality. This lay in the concept of *karma* and *saṃsāra*, the actions of one's life determining the future rebirth of one's *ātman*, an idea further developed by Yājñavalkya, among others.[67]

At death, there are two possible paths that the soul can take. One is the *devayāna*, the path of the gods, taken by the soul of one who meditates, has knowledge of *brahman*, and does not have to undergo rebirth. The soul ascends by stages through the day, the bright fortnight of the month, the six-month period, the year, to the sun, the lightning, and on to *brahman*, never to return.[68] The other path, the *pitṛyāna*, the path of the ancestors, because of the ties to rituals and *karma*/actions, is a temporary residence for the soul, for, remaining on the moon until its *karma* is exhausted, the soul enters a new birth returning via the air, smoke, vapor, clouds, and rain into crops.[69] A mortal ripens like grain and like grain is born again.[70] Repeated rebirth is a form of retribution. And then comes the crucial question: What determines the rebirth of the soul in a particular body? To this the answer is that if the individual's life has been one of good actions then the soul is reborn among the higher castes — *brāhmaṇa*, *kṣatriya*, or *vaiśya* — but if the actions have been evil, then the choice of rebirth is among the lowly: the dog, the pig, or the *caṇḍāla*/the outcaste.[71] (The superiority of the *brāhmaṇa* and the *kṣatriya* and their interdependence is spoken of as epitomized in the relationship between Yājñavalkya and Janaka.[72]) There was a trace in this idea of the element of chance, since the soul entering a new body would have depended on who eats the plant, but this element of chance was denied by the increasing insistence on the ethical imperative.[73]

The answer to the next question, namely, 'Who determines good or bad conduct?' was, in later times and among some important sects, said to lie in the hands of those who prepared the norms of social behaviour — the *brāhmaṇa* authors of the *dharmasūtras*.

According to them release from rebirth was possible only by observing the *dharma* of caste. Those born among the upper castes could claim a virtuous previous life in accordance with the rules of *dharma*. The relegation of the *caṇḍāla* to the status of the despised assumed that the *caṇḍāla* was receiving the just merit of evil conduct in a previous life. *Dharma* now replaced the sacrifice as that which sustains the universe.

The explanation of social inequalities on the basis of transmigration could keep society under the control of those who pronounced on conduct. The irrelevance of *varṇa* status in the new doctrine was nullified by this explanation of social differentiation. At one level, what began as a search for an alternative path concerned with releasing the *ātman* was pursued as such. But in social practice it was also reduced to a means of controlling the less privileged and justifying their condition on ethical grounds of *karma*. Reincarnation and *karma* are logically separable since moral justice can be accorded in other ways, as the eschatology of various religions suggests. At the philosophical and religious level the theory of *karma* was to become a central marker differentiating Indian religions from Semitic religions. Much of what followed in discussions on the soul within the Indian tradition drew on this theory.

The formulation of the notion of *karma* was gradual and doubtless tapped a range of ideas emanating from the societies settled in the Ganga valley. Mention has been made of a tribal origin but this is too vague an entity.[74] The more plausible argument points toward elements of the ritual of *śrāddha*, possibly suggesting the kind of connections that became more evident in the concept of *karma*. The link with the idea of *punaramṛtyu* would have given way to that of the cycle of rebirth. The transfer of merit has also been traced to a variety of origins. Among these is the suggestion that the notion of *tyāga*, renouncing the fruits of activity, which became the essence of the sacrificial ritual, was carried over into the new teaching.[75]

These ideas also helped to marginalize another aspect of the sacrificial ritual. If transmigration included animals as possible recipients of the *ātman*, then the killing of animals in sacrificial rituals could not be approved of.[76] Although this is not made explicit, it is implied in the statements on the forms in which the *ātman* can be reborn. This established a precedent of *ahimsā* and not eating the flesh of animals.

The doctrine did not remain secret for very long. It was carried from place to place by wandering teachers, the *parivrājakas*.[77] Inevitably, much of the post-Upaniṣadic thought traced itself to these teachers, who developed it in variant ways, some endorsing it and others opposing it. Frequently, the more prominent of the new teachers, such as Mahāvīra and the Buddha, were *kṣatriyas*, and the social aspects of the new philosophies were in part circumscribed by their caste concerns.[78] A later *Upaniṣad*, more conservative, is clear in its hostility to the contrary doctrines of those who wear the red robes and are opposed to the *Vedas*.[79] This was the birth of heterodoxy.

The theory of *ātman-brahman*, relating to the immortality of the soul and its release from the bonds of the body, was a philosophical innovation. By implication, it was a negation of the centrality of the prevalent sacrificial ritual. I have tried to argue that the search for an ideology independent of the sacrificial ritual may have had among its many interests the wish to conserve wealth. This was necessary for the transition from clan-based societies to states and kingdoms, in which the relative egalitarianism of the former gave way to social hierarchies and the enhanced power of the *kṣatriyas*. It is interesting that, in the oligarchies and in some kingdoms — the *gaṇa-rājyas*, *gaṇa-saṅghas*, and *rājyas* — of the subsequent period, where *kṣatriyas* were dominant, there is either an absence of sacrificial rituals of the Vedic variety or a decrease in their frequency. Nevertheless, the notion of transmigration as determined by the rules of caste reinstated the authority of the *brāhmaṇa*, even outside the sacrificial ritual, as preeminent among those determining the rules of conduct conducive to an improved rebirth. These were issues widely debated in post-Upaniṣadic times.

Arguing for a correlation between sacrifices, resources, and innovations in belief systems is not just an economic enterprise. It is an attempt to insist that ideologies are not history-free. In the complexities associated with Upaniṣadic and consequent ideas there are earlier features that were transmuted and others that were conditioned by contemporary needs. These may have coincided with the free-floating visions of the sages. Elements of embedded social contours in the sacrificial ritual should not be ignored in the larger explanation of philosophical speculations.

The universalizing of the doctrine influenced many sects and schools of thought that altered the intellectual landscape of early

India. The centrality of the sacrificial ritual was displaced by the centrality of the notion of transmigration. This carried within it both the movement of the caterpillar from leaf to leaf and the mutation of the object of gold. The pursuit of comprehension of the immortality of the soul was intense. It moved from analytical arguments and discriminating discussions to a mystical idealism couched in poetically rich language. A different kind of immortality emanated from the discourses of the *Upaniṣads*, which themselves became a fountainhead for ideologies, some supportive and some dissenting, which fashioned much of subsequent Indian thought.

## Notes and References

1. *Bṛhadāranyaka Upaniṣad* (hereafter cited as *Bṛ. Up.*), 4.4.3–4. Sarvepalli Radhakrishnan (ed.), *The Principal Upanisads*, London, Allen & Unwin, 1953.
2. I am using the term discourse in its literal, dictionary meaning, namely, the discussion on a matter, and without reference to its extended meaning in recent works of critical theory.
3. Marc Bloch, *Ritual, History and Power*, London, Athlone, 1989, pp. 113ff.
4. Jorge Larrain, *The Concept of Ideology*, London, Hutchinson, 1979, pp. 50ff; David McLellan, *Ideology*, Milton Keynes, England, Oxford University Press, 1986.
5. Frits Staal, 'The Meaninglessness of Ritual', *Numen* 26, fasc. 1 (1979): 1–22, and *Rules without Meaning*, New York, North-Holland, 1989, pp. 116–17.
6. For an attempted chronology of segments of the texts, see Walter Ruben, 'Die Philosophie de Upaniṣads', in *Geschicte der indischen Philosophie*, Berlin, Deutscher Verlag der Wissenschaften, 1954, pp. 113ff. There is a distinction between the early and the late *Upaniṣads* and the former include the ones that will be most frequently referred to here, namely, the *Bṛhadāranyaka* and the *Chāndogya Upaniṣads*.
7. Ruben, 'Die Philosophie de Upaniṣads'; Jan Gonda, *Change and Continuity in Indian Religion*, The Hague, Mouton, 1965, p. 37; T.G. Goman and R.S. Laura, 'A Logical Treatment of Some Upanisadic Puzzles and Changing Conceptions of Sacrifice', *Numen* 19, no. 1 (1972): 52–67.
8. Romila Thapar, 'The Study of Society' and 'Puranic Lineages and Archaeological Cultures', in *Ancient Indian Social History: Some Interpretations*, New Delhi, Orient Longman, 1978, pp. 211ff, 240ff.

9. Madhav M. Deshpande and Peter E. Hook (eds), *Aryan and non-Aryan in India*, Ann Arbor, University of Michigan, 1979; Murray B. Emeneau, 'Indian Linguistic Area Revisited', *International Journal of Dravidian Linguistics*, 3, no. 1 (1974): 93ff.
10. *Chāndogya Upaniṣad* (hereafter cited as *Ch. Up.*), 4.1.5.1ff.
11. Ibid., 4.4.5; *Bṛ. Up.*, 2.4.1ff, 4.5.3.
12. Only the *dvija* could perform the Vedic rituals (*Kātyāyaṇa Śrauta Sūtra*, 1.1.1ff).
13. *Bṛhaddevatā*, 4.11–15, 21–5; *Aitareya Brāhmaṇa*, 2.19; *Kauṣītaki Brāhmaṇa*, 12.3.
14. The *vaṃśa*, or succession list, was inflated to give it antiquity. Some of its members are sons, others are pupils, and sometimes the mother's name can provide an identity, as also can the social antecedents of the pupil (*Bṛ. Up.*, 2.6, 4.6.1ff). The line of teachers often traces itself from the present back to Brahmā.
15. *Bṛ. Up.*, 2.1.2, 3.1.1ff, 4.1.1, 6.2.1.7; *Ch. Up.*, 5.3.1.
16. *Muṇḍaka Up.*, 1.1.4–5.
17. *Bṛ. Up.*, 2.4.5, 4.4.7, 4.5.6ff; *Ch. Up.*, 3.14.1ff.
18. *Bṛ. Up.*, 4.4.13.
19. *Muṇḍaka Up.*, 1.1.5
20. *Ch. Up.*, 1.12.1ff; *Bṛ. Up.*, 1.5.16, 3.9.10–26; *Muṇḍaka Up.*, 1.2.9–13. Attempts have been made by modern scholars to argue that Western scholars and some Indians maintain that the *Upaniṣads* do not support the ritual of sacrifice and the worship of the Vedic deities, but that there are passages in the texts to the contrary. See B.K. Chattopadhyaya, 'Upanisads and Vedic Ritual', in S. *Mookerjee Felicitation Volume*, B.P. Sinha et al. (eds), Varanasi, Motilal Banarsidass, 1969. However, such passages are few and far between.
21. *Ch. Up.*, 5.3.1–7, 5.11.1ff, 5.12.1ff; *Bṛ. Up.*, 2.1.14–15ff, 3.1.1ff.
22. *Bṛ. Up.*, 2.1.15; Paul Deussen, *The Philosophy of the Upanisads*, London, Clark, 1906; reprint, New York, Dover, 1966, p. 17; Arthur B. Keith, *Religion and Philosophy of the Vedas and Upanisads*, Harvard Oriental Series, Cambridge, Harvard University Press, 1925, p. 495.
23. *Bṛ. Up.*, 6.2.8; also Ch. Up., 5.3.7.
24. *Bṛ. Up.*, 3.1.1, 3.9.19; *Śatapatha Brāhmaṇa* (hereafter cited as *Śat. Br.*), 1.7.2.8, 3.2.3.15.
25. *Bṛ. Up.*, 3.1.1, 4.3.1ff, 6.2.1; *Ch. Up.*, 5.3.1.
26. Deussen, p. 214.
27. *Bṛ. Up.*, 3.1.1ff.
28. *Mahāśālā mahā śrotriyaḥ*, *Ch. Up.*, 5.11.1ff; cf. *Dīgha Nikāya*, 1.235, Tevijjasutta.
29. *Ch. Up.*, 7.1.2.
30. Ibid., 4.1–3.

31. Buddhism, it has been argued, is a radical attack on the *ātmavāda* of the *Upaniṣads*. It opens up a new tradition by opposing theories of the unchanging, eternal soul, which lead to inaction and a refusal to better oneself. T.R.V. Murti, *The Central Philosophy of Buddhism*, 2nd ed., London, Allen & Unwin, 1960; Pratap Chandra, 'Was Early Buddhism Influenced by the Upanisads?' *Philosophy East and West*, 21 (1971): 317–24.
32. M. Beard and J. North (eds), *Pagan Priests*, London, Duckworth, 1990.
33. Raymond Firth, 'Offering and Sacrifice: Problems of Organisation', *Journal of the Royal Anthropological Institute*, 93, no. 1 (1963): 12–24.
34. Staal, '*The Meaningless of Ritual*'.
35. Henri Hubert and Marcel Mauss, *Sacrifice: Its Nature and Function*, trans W.D. Halls, London, Cohen & West, 1964.
36. *Ch. Up.*, 5.3.7, 5.11.1ff; *Bṛ. Up.*, 2.1.15; *Śat. Br.*, 11.6.2.10.
37. *Ṛg Veda*, 3.21.5; *Śat. Br.*, 3.8.2.26–8; *Aitareya Brāhmaṇa*, 7.3.6.
38. *Vasiṣṭha Dharma Sūtra*, 1.45.
39. *Bṛhaddevatā*, 6.92; Romila Thapar, 'Dāna and Dakṣina as Forms of Exchange', in *Ancient Indian Social History: An Interpretation*, pp. 105–21. *See* chapter 24 in this volume.
40. Yājñavalkya in *Śat. Br.*, 3.1.2.21.
41. B.B. Lal, 'Excavations at Hastinapur and Other Explorations in the Upper Ganga and Satlej Basin', *Ancient India*, 10/11 (1954–55): 115. The formula for begetting learned sons involved eating rice cooked with veal or beef together with *ghī*. *Bṛ. Up.*, 6.4.18. One dreads to think of how few cows would survive in contemporary India should this formula have persisted!
42. *Śat. Br.*, 13.2.9.8, 5.1.3.3, 12.7.3.12, 13.2.2.15. Gradually, this status came to include, although to a smaller extent, another category of *yajamānas*, namely, the *gṛhapatis*, or heads of households, who built their resources largely on the lands which they cultivated (ibid., 4.6.8.5).
43. Such as the *agrāyana-iṣṭi*, *cāturmāśa*, *piṇḍapitryajña*, and so on. Even more complex were the *agniṣṭoma*, *agnicāyana* and the *sattras*.
44. *Aitareya Brāhmaṇa* 7.34.
45. *Śat. Br.*, 1.7.3.28, 4.3.4.7; *Pañcaviṁśa Br.*, 1.8.2ff, 12.8.6; *Bṛ. Up.*, 6.2.7.
46. A.J. Strathern, *The Rope of Moka*, Cambridge, Cambridge University Press, 1971, p. 11.
47. Chris A. Gregory, 'Gifts to Men and Gifts to Gods', *Man*, 15 (1980): 626–52, and *Gifts and Commodities*, London, Academic Press, 1982.
48. Romila Thapar, *From Lineage to State*, Delhi, Oxford University Press, 1984, pp. 51ff.
49. Ibid., pp. 88–9.

50. Ibid. Earlier settlements were of the Painted Grey Ware and the Black-and-Red Ware cultures. The reaching out of the Northern Black Polished Ware, beginning in the seventh/sixth centuries BC, from its provenance between Patna and Varanasi to almost every part of the Ganga plain, suggests contacts, exchange, and increased production as compared to earlier periods. See T.N. Roy, *The Ganges Civilisation*, New Delhi, Ramanand Vidya Bhavan, 1983; R.C. Gaur, *The Excavations at Antranjikhera*, Delhi, Motilal Banarsidass, 1983; George Erdosy, *Urbanisation in Early Historical India*, BAR International Series, 430, Oxford, B.A.R., 1988.
51. *Bṛ. Up.*, 1.4.11.
52. Romila Thapar, 'Renunciation: The Making of a Counter-Culture?', in *Ancient Indian Social History: Some Interpretations.*
53. Ibid., pp. 63ff, and 'Householders and Renouncers in the Brahmanical and Buddhist Tradition', in *Way of Life*, T.N. Madan (ed.), Delhi, Vikas, 1982, pp. 273ff. *See* chapter 41 in this volume.
54. Frits Staal, *Exploring Mysticism*, Berkeley, University of California Press, 1975.
55. Walter Ruben, 'Schamanismus im alten Indien', *Acta Orientalia*, 18 (1940): 164–205.
56. *Ṛg Veda*, 7.22.9, 10.14.15, 10.130, 10.136.
57. *Ch. Up.*, 6.1.1ff.
58. *Bṛ. Up.*, 5.10.
59. Erik af Edholm, 'The Golours of the Soul and the Origin of Karmic Eschatology', in *On the Meaning of Death: Essays on Mortuary Rituals and Eschatological Beliefs*, S. Cederroth, C. Corlin and J. Lindstrom (eds), Uppsala Studies in Cultural Anthropology, no. 8, Uppsala, Univ Acta Univ Uppsaliensis, pp. 95–111.
60. James C. Harle, *The Art and Architecture of the Indian Sub-continent*, London, Penguin, 1986, p. 26.
61. *Śat. Br.*, 1.4.1.10ff.
62. Compare K.N. Jayatilleke, *Early Buddhist Theory of Knowledge*, London, Allen & Unwin, 1963, p. 169.
63. *Ch. Up.*, 6.1ff.
64. *Kaṭha Up.*, 1.1.20–9.
65. *Kaṭha Up.*, 1.3.3.
66. *Bṛ. Up.*, 4.4.3–5; Ch. Up., 5.10.7.
67. *Bṛ. Up.*, 3.2.13, 4.4.1ff; *Ch. Up.*, 5.3–10; *Śat. Br.*, 3.7.4.4.
68. *Bṛ. Up.*, 6.2.15ff; *Ch. Up.*, 4.15.5, 5.10.1ff.
69. *Ch. Up.*, 5.10.3ff. The moon is the lord of seasons, therefore the soul goes beyond the natural rhythms. See Wilhelm Halbfass, *Tradition and Reflection*, Albany, N.Y., SUNY Press, 1991. The distinctive symbolism of the sun and the moon was to remain dichotomous in many spheres of Indian thought.

70. *Kaṭha Up.*, 1.1.6.
71. *Ch. Up.*, 5.10.7.
72. *Bṛ. Up.*, 1.4.11, 4.1.1ff.
73. *Ch. Up.*, 5.10.7.
74. Gananath Obeyesekere, 'Theodicy, Sin and Salvation in a Sociology of Buddhism', in Edmund Leach, *Dialectic in Practical Religion*, Cambridge, Cambridge University Press, 1968, pp. 7–40.
75. Frits Staal, *Agni: The Vedic Ritual of the Fire Altar*, vol. 1, Berkeley, Asian Humanities Press, 1980.
76. This could usefully be compared with the Greek text of Porphyry dating to the third-fourth centuries AD and the discussion of whether animals have souls, a theme and text that were suggested to me by Richard Sorabjee. See Porphyry, *On Abstinence from Animal Food*, T. Taylor (trans.), London, Centaur, 1965.
77. *Bṛ. Up.*, 3.3.1.
78. Of the Buddhas who are said to have preceded Gautama, the large majority were *kṣatriyas*.
79. *Maitrī Upaniṣad* 7.8ff. Interestingly, elsewhere the term for a dissenter is *avaidika*.

# 38

# *Ideology, Society and the Upaniṣads*[*]

The reconstruction of the social and economic history of early India having become an established facet of the discipline, it is feasible for historians to include in their study the analysis of ideology in early society. There has lately been a debate on the placing of ideology in society. Some have defined it as a superstructure linked to the socio-economic base, as socially determined thought. Others have maintained that it is integrated into the larger whole in a way where, at times, ideology may be a catalyst or at any rate so enmeshed as to make its distinct discernment somewhat problematical. This is not a repetition of the Weber versus Marx debate, since there has been a considerable refinement of the concept of ideology in recent years.[1] For the purposes of this paper it is assumed that ideology is not a pale reflection of reality perched on the summit of the superstructure but (if one is permitted to modify Lukacs) can in certain circumstances become a driving force of history. It also assumes, as argued by Gramsci, that there is such a thing as 'cultural hegemony' where the ideology of a dominant group comes to be accepted by lesser social groups in society, sometimes without either of them being overtly aware of this. And further, that when there is a lack of fit between ideology and its affiliation to dominant social groups then there is a potential for social change.

This paper attempts to look at the problem with reference to the first millennium BC in a concern with what might be called the watershed situation as reflected in the Upaniṣadic texts,[2] where the centrality of the sacrificial ritual was conceded as an act of society, but at the same time was doubted as the sole means of

* In D.N. Jha (ed.), *Society and Ideology in India*, Delhi, 1996, 11–28.

self-realization. These doubts had an almost logical culmination in a variety of new belief systems and ritual practices, as for example, that of Buddhism. It is not incidental that it arose at this time because with the wavering of the hold of tradition, ideas were opened to challenge and began to compete. It has in the past been argued that these early philosophical speculations spring from the two cultures of the Indo-European and the pre-Aryan Indian.[3] This may to a limited extent be so. But it is incidental to more fundamental social changes which had to do with features not necessarily deriving from either of the two cultures.

The centrality of the sacrificial ritual has tended to be dismissed by historians of this period since it is seen primarily as an articulation of the religious sphere. To sacrifice is to 'make holy'. The word *yajña* from the root *yaj*, to worship, to consecrate, carries the same meaning of converting the profane into the sacred. The process establishes a union between the human and the divine and this in a sense is a forerunner of one of the essentials of Upaniṣadic thought, namely, the link between the human and that which is beyond, the *ātman* and the *brahman*. The sacrificial ritual involves conciliation which is achieved through the death of the victim expiating evil; communion, where eating the victim sanctifies the consumer; and honorific offerings consisting of first fruits and gifts.[4] The Buddhists were contemptuous of the sacrificial ritual as being futile, incapable of providing effective spiritual benefits, cruel to animals and easy to nullify by power acquired through meditation or resort to the miraculous as is said to have been repeatedly demonstrated by the Buddha.[5]

The sacrificial ritual is the central ritual in the Vedic texts. To the extent that this ritual dominated the social activities of people as indicated by the texts, the historian must analyse the social meaning of sacrifice to such a society in order to understand why it became a pivotal concern in the *Upaniṣads*. Given the absence of burials in the Ganga valley culture, the utilization of wealth concentrated on the ritual of sacrifice. Such wealth was also tied to the notion of status. The ritual therefore is at one level a religious expression, at another the statement of status on the part of the *yajamāna* and, and at a third level, a demonstration of wealth and resources.

The *Śatapatha Brāhmaṇa* contains an elaborate description of the various sacrificial rituals. Among these are the shorter seasonal rituals such as the *āgrāyaṇa iṣṭi* (offerings of the first fruits), *darśapūrṇamāsa iṣṭi, cāturmāsyāni, piṇḍapitṛyajña*; the special *soma* sacrifices of which the *agniṣṭoma* is often mentioned in other sources; the long rituals for prosperity such as the *agnicayana* and various *sattras*; funeral rituals; the *pravargya* sacrifices and the elaborate 'royal sacrifices' where the *yajamāna* was the *rājā* and the ritual had to do with his consecration, conquest and claim over territory and rejuvenation as in the *abhiṣecanīya*, *rājasūya*, *aśvamedha* and *vājapeya* rituals which intermittently lasted for a period of years.

The ritual involves the death of a living being either actually or symbolically and includes gift offerings, consecration and sacred food and drink. Sacrifice means the surrender of something valuable but in the expectation of greater gain. The individual and the community value that which is given up. If it is livestock then the expectation is that of greater fertility of the herd and this in turn meant greater numbers and therefore prosperity. The sacrificial ritual was also a rite through which there was a communication with gods and spirits. The status of the participants was also underlined through the ritual. The group periodically renews the sentiment which it has of itself and of its unity. It hinges on notions of power, force, energy in the philosophy of such cultures. There is therefore a multiplicity of ideas involved in the ritual.

The killing of the sacrificial victim required a special preparation. A location had to be purified and cordoned off since to kill outside this area was tantamount to murder. Within this space was the sacred enclosure, the *vedi*. The killing of the victim should not in any way act adversely on the *yajamāna* so that in the process of sacralization a start was made with the *yajamāna*.[6] One of the methods of purification was fasting, the *upavasatha*, which combined fasting in the proximity of the area where the sacrificial fire was lit.[7] Fasting and asceticism were equivalent in some cases to a sacrificial ritual. Thus the germ of the change was contained in this sentiment. Added to this was the element of renunciation in the giving up of a victim or an offering. The period of purification being long it would exclude those who were essential to the daily activities of life and would require that only those who could set apart these activities or find substitutes for their activities, were eligible to be *yajamānas*. This together with the resources required for the ritual meant that only those with some wealth at their command could be *yajamānas*. At the conclusion of the rite the consuming of the sacrificial victim was shared in by the deities, priests and the *yajamāna*, once again setting these social categories apart.[8] The picking out of these essentials of the sacrificial ritual but placing them in a different context was characteristic of groups such as the Buddhists. The *uposatha/upavasatha* for the Buddhists was not the eve of the *soma* sacrifice but the first, eighth, fifteenth and twenty-third nights of the lunar month. On the fifteenth, the *dhamma* was expounded, the *pātimokkha* was recited and the *sila* vows were taken, the ritual of sacrifice being replaced by a different emphasis on restraint and ethical behaviour.[9]

The sacrificial ritual has also been described as a part of the gift-exchange system.[10] The distinction between an offering which may not be the same as an act of giving is suggested in the terms used in relation to Vedic sacrifices. The offering or the oblation is the *bali* deriving perhaps from the roots *bhṛ* or *hṛ* and meaning, 'to bear' or 'to carry'. *Dāna*, on the other hand, is specifically the act of giving. It has been argued that even an offering is a species of gift because it is personal to the giver and is valued by him.[11] Whereas this is true of *dāna* it is not necessarily true of *bali*. The element of exchange is often absent in an offering whereas it is intrinsic to a gift. An offering, where it is a gift, implies an asymmetrical status relationship. Even if *bali* as an offering does not conform strictly to the role of a gift in a gift-exchange system, the *dāna* which was bestowed on the priests by the *rājā* would have functioned in this manner.[12] Thus there is a touch of renunciation involved in the giving up of something precious to be used in the ritual. The nature and the quality of renunciation changes in the subsequent period when there are a number of shifts in emphases. The notion of gift-exchange is also introduced into the ritual. Buddhism however emphasizes the importance of *dāna* directly. The giving is at some cost to the giver because normally what is given is a scarce resource which has alternative uses.[13] Thus the number of sacrificial rituals may be determined by the availability of such resources. The logic of the latter argument may indicate one of the reasons for lengthy rituals with an ample use of dairy produce but with a smaller destruction of livestock. It has been suggested that Buddhist hostility to animal sacrifice may have had to do with the decline of herding in the middle Ganga valley.[14]

The availability of resources affects attitudes towards the offering.

In herding communities, and particularly among cattle herders, animals are not indiscriminately killed for food. There is often a prohibition on the eating of such animals and the occasions for eating the flesh of these is specially marked out.[15] The eating of the meat of a particular animal is generally limited to the occasion of a sacrifice when the animal is offered as a victim, unless of course the animal dies a natural death after which it may be eaten. This was one way of conserving the herd. Vedic texts maintain that after the victim has been sacrificed, even if it be of the cattle family, its flesh can be eaten. There is the oft-quoted passage in which Yājñavalkya lists his preferences for tender cuts of beef.[16] Similar meat is served to honoured guests, the term *go-ghna*, the one for whom the cow is killed, being used for special guests.[17] In a cattle-herding society this was part of the notion of a gift, the assumption being that one would receive the same in return on a visit to the home of the guest, apart from the host being lauded as both generous and of noble status. That there was not a total prohibition on the eating of beef, but that it is specifically mentioned in the context of special occasions would suggest that the cow was valuable and therefore inviolate and not sacred and therefore inviolate.[18] The conservation of the herd required that a prohibition be placed on the indiscriminate killing of cattle for food which prohibition was sought to be strengthened through giving it a sacred sanction. There is a difference between an offering that can be destroyed and one that can be reserved and eaten after the sacrificial ritual has been completed. Thus *ghī* and milk were destroyed, the *ghī* being burnt in some of the more dramatic rites such as the *vasordhārā*.[19] Animals of the edible kind were consumed after the ritual. That the conventions regarding cattle were not widely observed is evident from the remains at excavated sites. Cattle bones with marks indicating that the meat had been cut with knives or some sharp instrument are often found in the vicinity of hearths at Painted Grey Ware sites[20] (the archaeological culture generally equated with the later Vedic corpus). The incidence of such bones would suggest a higher consumption of beef than that available only from sacrificial rituals or the feasting of guests.

The gradual decline of a cattle economy as is suggested in the later Vedic corpus meant the decrease in raids and skirmishes; hostilities developed into warfare on a larger scale with calculated violence. The synonymity of a warrior with the *rājā* gradually gave way to the *rājā* being associated with the management of land where agriculture superceded cattle herding. The *kṣatriya* became the one who had access to land. To continue to translate the term as 'warrior' and attribute the characteristics of the warrior as the primary characteristics of the *kṣatriya* fails to take account of a fundamental change in the ethos of *kṣatriya* society. The management of agricultural resources required not only the propitiation of a different set of deities but also a new ethic in which violence was to be subordinated. The emphasis on *ahiṃsā* was appropriate to this change. Agricultural resources could not be increased through 'capturing' land, but through using labour on land and through investing wealth in land. The greater the investment of labour and wealth, the larger the return. The social distancing of potential groups as labour had to be created and socially legitimized. The return to a myth of origin involving a primeval sacrifice was used as early as in the *puruṣasūkta* hymn but the outcome of the sacrifice was the assertion of a social hierarchy.[21] The functions associated with the four *varṇas* reflected the social distinction and reinforced it with a religious sanction.

Wealth had also to be accumulated if it was to be invested in the new resource of cultivated land. In the potlatch there is no capital accumulation. Wealth is distributed and although in each case a larger amount is given the increase is not regarded as an interest on the original but as a larger gift.[22] The objection to the sacrificial ritual when reiterated by an institution such as the *saṅgha* is conditioned by the attempt to control or receive gifts. *Dāna* is collected for the *saṅgha* and those that make the maximum donations are important to the *saṅgha* and are remembered in the texts, as was Jīvaka.[23] Gifts to an institution can play the role of commodities. Although the gift is not returned to the donor and only intangible merit — *puṇya* — is returned, the institution can use the gift as a source to be invested in its establishment.

When the means of subsistence was cattle and the productive group was the herding clan led by *rājanya/kṣatriya* warriors, the sacrificial ritual remained central. When the means of subsistence changed increasingly to land and agriculture with cultivators and eventually peasants as the productive groups organized around landowning clans and later landowning families, the centrality of the sacrificial ritual began to recede. However, since it articulated more than just a religious expression, it began to be replaced by many new aspects of social activity and religious articulation. In looking at the underlying features of exchange in society during the transition in the mid-first millennium BC in the Ganga valley, there is a move from a system drawing heavily on gift exchange to one which gradually establishes a redistributive structure to which is added an incipient market exchange. These changes were by no means divorced from those in speculative and religious thought.

Society as depicted in Vedic texts of the earlier part of the first millennium BC was characterized by *viś* and *rājanyas*.[24] Being primarily pastoral with a gradual change to agriculture, cattle-raiding and booty-capturing were major preoccupations. The superior lineages of the *rājanyas* who were eventually to become the landowning elite increased their domination over the lesser lineages of the *viś*, who, through a system of prestations provided whatever wealth was unobtainable from booty and after the change to agriculture came to be the main support of the *kṣatriya*. Social distancing encouraged the crystallization of at least three systems of kinship and descent: *brāhmaṇas*, *kṣatriyas* and *vaiśyas*, and those who were excluded, the *śūdras*. Each group performed services for the other and a hierarchy based on such services was evolved.

A successful raid encouraged the holding of a sacrificial ritual which would be hosted by the *kṣatriya yajamāna* (sacrifiant) and at which the *brāhmaṇa* priests ranging over many categories and each specializing in some aspect of the ritual, would act as intermediaries between the *yajamāna* and the gods, particularly those gods invoked at the ritual. The sacrifice was a prayer for fertility, victories, wealth (computed in cows, horses, chariots and gold) and general well-being. Elements of earlier shamanism were retained in the ritual: the altar was often in the shape of an eagle; pebbles and stones with natural holes and cavities were essential and the sound of the *mantra* or verse carried its own magical power.[25] The Vedic sacrifice was thus not a parallel to the Semitic covenant between a man and his God.

The sacrificial ritual had more than a religious purpose. A spectacular ritual, extending over many days or even months added fame and glory to the *yajamāna* for, the greater the amount of wealth expended the higher would be the status of the *yajamāna*. In the mutual dependence of the *kṣatriya* and the *brāhmaṇa* the former acquired status and the latter wealth, for each such occasion ended with gift-giving to the priests in the form of tangible wealth.

When the *kṣatriya* increased his authority and was regarded as a king rather than a mere chief, this dependence also increased. The *brāhmaṇa* now associated the *kṣatriya* with divinity thus enhancing his legitimacy to rule and in return the *brāhmaṇa* came to possess even greater wealth. The major source of the *kṣatriya*'s wealth was now from the *viś* in the form of first fruits of the harvest and larger ritual prestations, described metaphorically as the *kṣatriya* eating the *viś*.[26]

The sacrificial ritual therefore was to become a major point of controversy in the germination of new ideas as suggested by the evidence of the *Upaniṣads*. It would seem from these texts that a small proportion of the *brāhmaṇas* and *kṣatriyas* came to think about mortality and immortality — a question which also motivated the sacrificial ritual. The efficacy of the ritual as a means to individual's release from rebirth gradually came to be regarded as inadequate and was not the primary concern of the sacrificial ritual. *Mokṣa* becomes important in relation to the centrality of the concept of the *ātman* and of rebirth. It lies ensconced in a shift emphasizing the centrality of the individual. This is given further stress by the association of *prāṇa* or breath with the *ātman*. What might be described as the Upaniṣadic breakthrough was developed by a small group who introduced the notion of the individual soul (*ātman*) seeking union with the universal soul (*brahman*) which was seen as the eventual form of liberation or *mokṣa*. *Ātman* is variously derived from the roots *an*-to breathe, *at*-to move, *va*-to blow, all suggestive characteristics of life and the individual self. *brahman* from the root *bṛih*, expanding and evolving, is suggestive of that which is all-inclusive and which led perhaps to the notion of a universality which is both the source and the destination of the individual soul, an idea not alien to those who saw both time and life as cyclic. Etymologically *brahman* has also been associated with power and magic — an association which may well have had its roots in shamanist sources. As to the definition of the *ātman* and *brahman* there is a continuous bipolarity. The *ātman* can be larger than the entire world but it can also be smaller than a mustard seed or a grain of rice.[27] It remains therefore an abstraction. Release from rebirth, it was argued, could be achieved better through *yoga* (bodily control) and *dhyāna* (meditation) than by the sacrificial ritual. An initial groping towards metempsychosis and the idea of the rebirth of the soul in another body and in accordance with the merits and otherwise of one's present existence (which was to develop into the theory of *karma* and *saṃsāra*) is also discernible although in a seminal form. The fuller discussion of this in the *Kaṭha Upaniṣad*, describes Yama, the god of death, in dialogue with Naciketas and the central question posed is that of *punar-mṛtyu* (the cycle of deaths) and curiously not of *punar-janma* (the cycle of births). The latter was to become the more frequent term in later texts. Conquest over death or over the repetition of deaths and its counterpart, immortality, provides a subtler difference in concern than does the idea of the termination of rebirth. The questioning of the sacrificial ritual and its replacement by *yoga* and *dhyāna* as well as by the secret doctrine[28] (as it is described in the texts) of the *ātman* and the *brahman*, has its own historical value given the role of the ritual in social and economic processes.

That it was a secret doctrine communicated only to the trusted few has its own interest. *Iti rahasyam iti upaniṣad*, suggests confidentiality. The element of secrecy is said to have emerged from the secret explanations of the ritual which are discussed in the *Āraṇyakas* and which grew independently of the ritual. These were the more speculative exercises and were doubtless germinal to the ideas of the *Upaniṣads*. Explicatory manuals were required possibly because of the incorporation of new rituals through the assimilation of new ethnic communities, where these rituals would have to be adjusted to the existing ones. New ideas may well have arisen in the course of such explanations. These would tend to be tied to the rituals until such time as the rituals were either gradually discarded or were openly refuted. Secrecy raises the curiosity of others once they suspect it but, above all, it binds those who are a party to the secret and perhaps encourages a feeling of superiority: they know that which others do not. The emphasis on secrecy also points to some apprehension regarding its widespread knowledge. This may have had something to do with its authors. These consisted of a few *kṣatriyas*, some from the fringe areas of the *āryāvarta*, areas where the sacrificial ritual had declined and which were therefore described in Vedic literature as 'impure lands' (*mleccha-deśa*).[29] But the *kṣatriyas* of these areas, it would seem, discoursed on this doctrine and taught it to a few selected *brāhmaṇas*. The more frequently mentioned of these *kṣatriyas* are Pravāhana Jaivali of the Pañcālas, Aśvapati Kaikeya, Hiraṇya-nābha of Kośala, Ajātaśatru of Kāśī and Janaka of Videha.[30] These *kṣatriyas* are described as teaching the *brāhmaṇas*, and one of the early *Upaniṣads* states that Ajātaśatru commenting on this says, that it is contrary to the usual procedure where the *brāhmaṇa* teaches the *kṣatriya*.[31] Possibly it was embarrassing to the *brāhmaṇas* in the early stages of the new doctrines to openly consider alternatives to the sacrificial ritual. The decline of the sacrificial ritual may have been due to the existence of other cults, such as the worship of ancestral tumuli and sacred enclosures and trees and the *stūpa* and *caitya* cults, some of which may have been earlier than the Vedic sacrificial ritual in these areas.

These *kṣatriyas* although not antagonistic to the sacrificial ritual were probably not too eager to enforce it. This may have derived from a questioning of the ritual but also secondarily from other considerations. The mutual dependence of the *brāhmaṇa* and *kṣatriyas* for power and status could be broken if the sacrificial ritual was discontinued. The reality of power came increasingly to be recognized as lying in access to resources and in some schools of thought the bestowal of divine attributes became more marginal. In any case wealth was necessary to obtaining legitimacy. However since wealth was consumed in the ritual and in gift-giving to the *brāhmaṇas*, the power of the *kṣatriya* was circumscribed. A direct assertion through controlling resources would be one way of conserving power. The 'impure lands' were located either in north-western India where major trade routes were to develop, or else in the middle Ganga valley. Claims to landownership on the part of the *kṣatriya* families and the use of slaves and hired labour to work the land increased the resources at their command permitting accumulation of wealth and sharpening the stratification. Wealth, if it was not to be destroyed in the sacrificial ritual would be a realistic basis for actual power. The temptation to break away from the prestation economy would have been apparent. It is interesting that the new doctrine places a different emphasis on the *kṣatriya*. He is no longer the warrior boasting of heroic deeds and awaiting the heaven of Indra, for he is now also the owner of land, the weilder of power, asserting himself in a new role. The *kṣatriya* identity cut across geographical regions as also did the *kṣatriya* doctrine and its teachers who belonged as much to the Kekaya clan of the north-west as to the Videha of the middle Ganga valley.

The two social categories involved in the reciprocal relationship of the sacrificial ritual were the *kṣatriyas* and the *brāhmaṇas*.

Uncertainty in the initial ranking of each in relation to the other and the interdependence of the two is clearly stated.[32] It is the same two who are now involved in the new doctrine. Thus, the control of what was to emanate from the new doctrine was monopolized by those who had earlier controlled the sacrifice. Janaka of Videha asks Yājñavalkya, when the latter comes to see him, whether he has come to obtain cattle or join in a discussion, to which Yājñavalkya replies that he has come for both purposes.[33] However, since the secret doctrine did not require a ritual which requisitioned resources, the relation of reciprocity was eroded. The boundaries of reciprocity as a system of exchange and control could not continue once the system began to change. If the analogy can be carried further (without sounding facetious) the subsequent redistributive economy found its ideological parallel in the transformation of the secret doctrine into a universal belief system and in the institutionalizing of its rituals in the form of a variety of *saṅghas*.

That some *brāhmaṇas* too were participants in these new doctrines requires an explanation. Some among them who go to the *kṣatriyas* to learn the new doctrine are described as *mahāśālā mahāśrotrīya* (the extremely wealthy and very learned).[34] Elsewhere *mahāśālā* is the epithet for *brāhmaṇas* who owned large acreages of cultivated land which they had received as gifts for the performance of major sacrifices, land having now become a category of wealth.[35] Were these *brāhmaṇas* also anxious to conserve their wealth which otherwise they would be expected to expend on *soma* sacrifices? Or does one look for a less mundane, even if partial, explanation? That there were some who doubted the efficacy of the ritual is evident from the earlier texts.[36] But such doubts were marginal at that time. Now they seem to have become more central. Part of the answer may lie in the early texts being aimed at propitiating the gods, whereas now the aim was to comprehend reality — a distinctly different activity. However, not all the *brāhmaṇas* interested in the new doctrine were *mahāśālā*, some were those who had set up hermitages in the forests, where, surrounded by their disciples, their concern was to try and unfathom the nature of reality, and of mortality and immortality. Not that such *brāhmaṇas* were averse to wealth.[37] The fees that were charged for teaching the new doctrine could be substantial and reference is made to gifts of upto a thousand cows, gold, horses, *dāsīs*, chariots, elephants and land. Nevertheless, there were others who received pupils and taught them free of a fee and passed on their knowledge to them if they felt that the disciple was capable of comprehending it. The latter were among the early groups who opted out of society and sought a distance from social concerns. Their predecessors were the *munis* and *ṛṣis*.

The *munis* not only broke away from social obligations but also claimed extraordinary powers. They are referred to as the long haired ones flying through the air, suggestive of shamans.[38] Elements of shamanism are reinforced in the new doctrine. An early text refers to the soul remaining in plants.[39] In the *Upaniṣads* the soul is described as going through the air which opens out like the hole in the chariot wheel and then it goes to the sun and the moon which open out like apertures in musical instruments.[40] In another passage the soul travels through space, air, cloud, rain, crops and finally lodges in plants where it is eaten and thus reborn,[41] reminiscent of shamanic descriptions of the journeying of the soul. It is interesting that the cycle is an agricultural one. As a shamanistic group they were the forerunners of the renouncers and ascetics. Their techniques involved the demonstration of bodily and mental powers and their theories were in part concerned with the voyaging of the soul. The notion of *brahman* also carries a shamanic trace inasmuch as it is associated with *brahma*, a magical power, equated by some with *mana*. The sheer secrecy of the doctrine handed down from the teacher to a specially selected pupil and not revealed publicly and the fact that it derives from knowledge obtained through the human senses, by intuition, bodily control and meditation, is suggestive of shamanistic techniques. To this may be added other characteristics: the lengthy period of training, fasting and solitude, the need to have a teacher who initiates and guides the acolyte, not to mention the ultimate goal of the soul entering into communion with the divine. The description of the journey to the world of Brahmā is a complex picture of many heavens and crossings involving deities, which is evidently an attempt to reconcile the notion of heaven with the abstract notion of *brahman*, but carries in the description the influence of shamanism.

The social context of the new doctrine is again different from that of sacrifice: whereas the sacrifice required not only the presence of the clan but also the participation of the clan, be it the priests performing the ritual, or the *rājās* as *yajamānas* or the *viś* who brought the prestations, the new doctrine required a distance from social obligations whether of family or of clan. The emphasis shifted dramatically from the clan to the individual, a shift which was symptomatic of some of the anomie of changing social relations. The soul was that of the individual and *mokṣa* was an individual concern. The term *ātman* in itself encapsulates individuality.[42] The sacrifice could not be conducted in the absence of the clan: the comprehension of the *ātman-brahman* relationship was impossible in the presence of the clan, since it grew out of *yoga* and *dhyāna*.[43] It required neither intermediaries nor deities. The uncertainty of one's status after rebirth was in itself a departure from a hierarchical view of the future. The distancing from social obligation is also evident in the implied irrelevance of *varṇa* status in the new doctrine. The story of Satyakāma who, wishing to become a disciple of a teacher is asked to identify his caste, replies truthfully that he does not know his father and his mother is of low caste.[44] He is accepted. Even if it is argued that the fact of his speaking truthfully is taken as an indication of high caste, nevertheless he was born low by the rules of *varṇa* and should have been treated as of a low caste. The caste of the individual, it was implied, was unimportant in the search for salvation. It is not status that is crucial to immortality or rebirth, but one's actions. There is here again a germinal idea towards a universal ethic which was to be taken up by later teachers. But this germinal idea also prevented the notion of negating caste in daily life: the negation only applied to those who lived in hermitages at a distance from society.

These speculations inevitably had an impact on theories of knowledge. Not only was knowledge more important than ritual but it had its own reward, such as the discovery of the concept of immortality.[45] The introduction of doubt and investigation was a departure from the sacrificial tradition which was obsessed with the correct interpretation of ritual actions in a form which hardly encouraged wide-ranging speculations. The new theories on *punarmṛtyu* and *ātman-brahman* grew out of a process of reasoning and were explained through a series of empirical similarities and analyses.[46] The debate on logic (*vākovākya*) did have its origins in sacrificial ritual but was extended via the new theories which came to refer to it as *tarkaśāstra*. These new techniques travelled long distances carried by the *carakas* and *parivrājakas*, terms earlier associated with pastoral nomads but now with the wandering teachers going from one settlement to another, and who were met with even more frequently in the parks and groves on the edges of the new urban centres. The repeated reference to groves makes one wonder whether some of the mysticism involved in the worship of sacred groves did not find its way into Upaniṣadic thought. It is unlikely that those who founded major schools of new thinking were unfamiliar with many of these ideas. The later *Maitri Upaniṣad*,[47] in a spirit quite alien to the earlier *Upaniṣads*, castigates these teachers as a hindrance to knowledge, presumably referring to their complete openness to question and to analyse. It includes them together with the *śūdra* teachers and those who wore the red robe and who attack the *Vedas* through juggling false arguments. It adds sternly that a *brāhmaṇa* should not study what is not included in the *Vedas*! This heralded the coming of heterodoxy.

Among the major sects associated with the emergence of heterodoxy was the one founded by the Buddha. It has been argued that some Buddhist doctrine grew out of seminal ideas from the *Upaniṣads*.[48] This is in part true, but this argument is also an attempt to trace all philosophical and ethical traditions back to the *Upaniṣads* as a mechanism of appropriating heterodoxy should it become necessary. Significantly the Buddha does refer to these earlier teachers but is equally clear that his teaching is a departure from them. The nature of the difference can be seen from a few ideas. Thus the *Upaniṣads* speak of the importance of *kāma* or desire which ties a person to the world.[49] The *Upaniṣad* maintains that the attainment of *brahman* helps to transcend hunger, thirst, sorrow, old age and death.[50] Renunciation according to the *Upaniṣads* is the means of overcoming sorrow and attaining *brahman*.[51] When a person dies his *karma* controls his new existence. The texts speak of two kinds of knowledge, that which is based on knowledge (*vijñāna*) and that which is intuitive (*prajñā*).[52] Equally significant is the notion of the seeker having to overcome temptation. In the *Kaṭha Upaniṣad*, Naciketas has a dialogue with Yama, the god of death, who offers attractive alternatives to the former's search for salvation, but ultimately concedes to the wish of Naciketas and reveals to him the doctrine of *brahman*.

These points of seeming similarity should not however detract from the fact that the Buddha was not merely following through some ideas of the *Upaniṣads* but even where this may seem so, he was transforming them. The Buddha also speaks of desire as the cause of sorrow, but uses the term *tṛṣṇā* which carries a starker meaning of thirst, with an emphasis on the longing for or grasping towards the quenching of thirst, rather than the more ambiguous *kāma*. Hunger, disease, old age and death are familiar to us from the biography of the Buddha which are said to have led him to question the permanence of life. The Buddha, prior to his enlightenment, has a dialogue with Māra, the personification of evil, and refuses the temptations.[53] The god of death is of course the more powerful image but in a system without deities, as was the Buddhist, a deity could not be a teacher and knowledge has ultimately to be discovered by the individual. Naciketas' concern with what happens after the great departure is common to both him and the Buddha. *Tṛṣṇā* (desire) became the central cause of suffering and the elimination of desire the focus of ethical and behavioural norms. The analysis of ethics was in the context of human action with logic, rationality and intuition as major elements of analysis. Central to Buddhist thinking was the emphasis on causality. To this was linked the doctrine of *karma* and the next life. The early *Upaniṣads* are not consistent in their view of the soul after death. The *Bṛhadāraṇyaka* speaks of the *devayāna* or the path of light and the *pitṛyāna*, the path of darkness: whereas in the former there is no rebirth, in the case of the latter, the soul is reborn after a period.[54] The *Kauṣītakī* has a variation on this. It states that all souls go to the *pitṛyāna* from where some move permanently to the *devayāna* and others are reborn.[55] The link between desire and rebirth is expressed more clearly in a later *Upaniṣad*, the *Muṇḍaka*.[56] To the Buddha, transcendental concerns, as e.g. the path to *nirvāṇa*, were also viewed as systems explaining social action and human destiny. However, even the quest for salvation is not the acceptance of the arbitrariness of human actions and social arrangements, but the conscious outcome of these on the basis of human choice. The doctrine of causation was to become central to the teaching of many sects at this time.

Schools of thought evolve from earlier systems. Buddhism was a heterodoxy because it took the structure of the earlier system but gave it a new focus. It is not therefore confined to the boundaries and framework of Vedic and Upanisadic thought. It not only goes beyond but changes the paradigm. If the *Upaniṣads* mark a watershed between the ideologies of Vedic brahmanism on the one hand and the 'heterodoxies' on the other and draw upon the concerns of certain categories of *brāhmaṇas* and *kṣatriyas*, Buddhist ideology changes the paradigm to focus on the concerns of the *gahapatis* and *seṭṭhis*. It abolishes the notion of a secret doctrine and universalizes its teaching.

The growth of Buddhist heterodoxy has to be seen in the various other contexts, the most radical of which have come to be called the doctrines of the Lokāyata. In the Buddhist texts, it is explained as the science of casuistry in which logic was central.[57] This kind of discourse perhaps had its origin in the riddles posed in the course of the sacrifice, since the structure of riddles derives from an abstraction of logic and questions were often put in the form of riddles in the texts under discussion. As such, the technique was not characteristic of heterodox methods of argument and grew within the Vedic practice. However, it was taken over and developed into an intellectual method. Some sects underlined empiricism as the sole source of knowledge, and argued that the soul does not exist since it cannot be perceived or felt, that there is little merit in religious practices and that the only source of knowledge is sense perception. This reduced the importance of inference. The authority of the *Vedas* was denounced as being tainted by untruth, self-contradiction and tautology.[58] These views did make an impact on Buddhist thinking, although by and large the Buddha was contemptuous of these sects. Logic was important to such debates. This was an early occasion when analytical categories were introduced and used in discourse as well as being applied to the comprehension of social reality. Such debates were joined by *brāhmaṇas* as well as non-*brāhmaṇas*. Similar categories of thought were applied to disciplines other than philosophical discourse as is evident from the first grammar of Sanskrit composed by Pāṇini. Within the tradition of analysing language, the form of debate which came to be preferred, *pūrva-pakṣa prati-pakṣa*, carries something of a dialectical flavour.

An important notion common to many of these sects was that the analysis of social action or metaphysical beliefs required a distancing from society and ultimately the path to liberation lay through renunciation. This too germinates from the Vedic concept of *tyāga* or separation, abandonment, resignation. The freeing was both from society and the body. Renunciation for those who followed the precepts of the *Dharmasūtras* was of course very different from what it was for those who were Nirgranthas or Buddhists. Brahmanism supported the notion of the four *āśramas* where any form of renunciation was subsequent to a socially productive life. For others it had the reverse effect of withdrawing from social obligations. For the Buddhists, this led to the dichotomy of preaching to two categories, the *gṛhastha* or the householders who were embedded in society and the *tyāgin* or *parivrājaka* who had renounced their social obligations. The mundane and the transcendental of a different order were thus separated. But unlike the ascetics who were symbolically dead to society and attempted to reduce their dependence on the physical body by mortification, the Buddhist renouncers were to become a parallel or alternative society and were made part of the scheme of things through the argument that they were assisting the *gṛhastha* towards liberation. The contradiction lay in the fact that although the societal order was seen as inferior and incomplete, its continuance and its very incompleteness was necessary for the existence and justification of the renouncers.

The degree to which the Buddhists and other sects were heterodox becomes evident from both their doctrines as well as their social role. If dissent is a characteristic of heterodoxy then there is evidence for it. The Buddhists had a firm doctrinal position in which Vedic theories and practices were either discarded or at least questioned. Even the less orthodox theories of the earlier *Upaniṣads* were merely the starting point for a well-articulated and distinct ideological position. The relationship between the *brāhmaṇas* and the *śramaṇas* was to be characterized later as that between the snake and the mongoose, the cat and the mouse, the venom of opposition being instinctive.[59] Even more significant was the physical form which the Buddhist, Jaina, Ājīvika and some other sects were to take, where, from the start their identity was based on clustering around particular teachers and then building an order (*saṅgha*) and institution around this identity. The differentiation was sharp and clear both between the order and the rest of society as well as between the orders; a differentiation which was to lead to the segmenting off of sects from the main stem on issues involving precisely these questions of identity and doctrinal differences. The institutionalizing of the sects and the competition among them for acceptance encouraged in them both historiographical thinking as well as missionary activities.

The social hinterland of these sects was not immune to these changes and the degree to which they were accepted is also indicative of changed social conditions. Religion as an embedded feature was not prised loose but nevertheless the shift from revelation to analysis did suggest new modes for religious thought. Religious practice did not dominate ethics but ethical emphasis did pervade the concept of social norms. Earlier practices were given a new orientation as is exemplified in the concept of *dāna* and *puṇya*. *Dāna* was gift-giving, what was earlier given at the sacrificial ritual and was now given to the *saṅgha* or the order of the sect; *puṇya* was the merit which accrued from such actions and which contributed towards the donor's proximity to *nirvāṇa*. Prestations were neither prescribed nor hierarchically ordered; they could be a gift from anyone and the merit so accumulated was part of the balance between the individual and the accumulation of merit *vis-à-vis nirvāṇa,* allowing for the fact that *dāna* constituted only one element in the building up of *puṇya*. The essence of religion had begun to change. It was less the ritual act and more the individual concern with release from rebirth, at least in theory. In practice the ritual acts were not altogether forsaken but less meticulously observed. The grander rituals were often performed for reasons of legitimation as was the case with *rājās*. The prestations however were now marginal to the access to economic resources since the economy itself had been transformed from the days of pastoralism mixed with agriculture in the western Ganga valley.

Legitimizing the *rājā* which was a crucial function of the major sacrifices of the Vedic texts was not discontinued, although it became less frequent. The same function was also performed by the Buddhist *saṅgha* in accepting royal patronage and grants. The alternate function of the *rājā* ordering the sacrifice and therefore becoming the initiator of religious action was sought to be paralleled by the insistence in Buddhist historiography on associating kings with the calling of the various Buddhist Councils where doctrinal differences were sorted out. Thus Ajātaśatru of Magadha is associated with the calling of the First Council of Rājagṛha soon after the Buddha's death and Aśoka Maurya with the Third Council at Pāṭaliputra when the pre-eminence of the dominant Sthaviravāda sect was established. The *saṅgha* was thus both above and beyond secular society yet at the same time closely linked to it. What is significant is not the continuity of the religious connection with the political but the change in the nature of the link. The *saṅgha* could be independent of royal patronage or could, if it wanted greater social control, work through royal patronage. The political order as the central locus of mundane society was not regarded as exclusive, for the ideal king as defined by Buddhism was the *cakkavattin/cakravartin,* the just king who rules in accordance with the *Dhamma* or the ethical system as developed by Buddhist thinking.[60] It was not accountability to a higher authority as much as accordance with a higher ethic which governed the making of a *cakkavattin.* The accountability is in any case to society, for kingship according to Buddhist theory evolved out of a situation of disharmony where one person, the *mahāsammatta*, was elected to maintain order. This theory of the origin of kingship presupposes a number of persons in competition and conflict and the need for defining a hierarchy. This may well have been a reflection of competing elites at this time.

The activity of the new sects is also indicative of new social groups. Not only did these ideologies often reinforce the *kṣatriyas* as an alternative focus of power to the *brāhmaṇa* with material wealth in the form of landownership but also provided the backing of an ideology emphasizing the transcendental in a manner which appealed even to some *brāhmaṇas*. This was as it were a logical outcome of the direction taken by the *Upaniṣads*. But the appeal also extended elsewhere and included an entirely new social group, that of the merchants and traders who were essential to the towns of this time. The social genesis of these groups appears to have been in the landowning families for it was from these *gahapatis* or householders that there emerged the *seṭṭhi-gahapatis,* later to become the families of bankers, financiers and traders. In a later period, it was these groups which formed the hard core among the patrons of Buddhism and Jainism, apart from royalty. By the Mauryan period, therefore, the range of elites extended from *brāhmaṇas* to *kṣatriyas* to *seṭṭhis*. In terms of economic classes, the landowning *gahapatis* (which included some *brāhmaṇas* and *kṣatriyas*) and the commercial *seṭṭhis* were clearly dominant. Implicit in this diversification was the idea that there was also a range of ideologies. The political elites remained the landowning groups but could now be drawn from *kṣatriya*, *brāhmaṇa* and even (if *brāhmaṇa* sources are to be believed) from the *śūdra varṇa*. Thus the Nanda and Maurya dynasties are described as being of *śūdra* origin in the Purāṇic dynastic lists. It is however possible that this was intended more as a remark of contempt for dynasties supportive of the new sects rather than as a statement of authenticated social origins.

The existence of new elites has at one level to do with the social and economic changes evident in the middle Ganga valley as compared to the Vedic heartland to the west. The pastoral-agrarian economy of the latter with a premium on the cultivation of wheat and barley and substantially by villages with few clusters of densely populated centres presented a rather different social landscape from that of the eastern area. Here the introduction of wet rice cultivation resulted in a new pattern of settlement. The emphasis was on large areas of land under cultivation, to an exclusion virtually of pastoralism, given the marshlands of north Bihar. Wet rice cultivation and irrigation meant intensive labour controlled by entrepreneurs requiring initially the clearing of the monsoon forest in which the use of new technologies adapted to agriculture were introduced. Once the mechanics were under control then the produce was so substantial that it did open up the possibility of other developments such as incipient trade. The latter used the network of geographically located nodal points connected by the river system of the Ganga plain to evolve into complex circuits of exchange. These changes were not unconnected with the other changes discussed earlier in this paper and an interlinking is necessary although not of a mechanical kind.

The earlier society seems to have expanded less through aggression and more through migration. Cattle raids did give some power over a neighbouring area but this tended to be parochial. The migration and settlement of a segment of a tribe was a more effective way of extending the control of a lineage and this was practised in many areas. With the establishment of the monarchical state raids and migrations gave way to annexation and consolidation of annexed territory. This was necessary in a situation where revenue was beginning to be systematically collected and territorial control provided access to power. The endorsement of the concept of non-violence however militated against aggrandizement and to that extent could act as a theoretical check on untrammeled state power.

There are two evident features in this discussion which need to be reiterated. One is the transformation of earlier traditions into later forms, which change not only in the new context but also in the new network of relations. The second is the attempt of universalizing the ideology and moving away from the ethic of groups and castes to that of society *per se*. This is partly expressed in the marginalizing of *varṇa* functions in some sects and their elimination in the teachings of the Lokāyata sects. Whereas caste as *jāti* remains important in defining marriage and kinship, the actual status of *varṇa* become less significant in the new theories. Social differentiation moves in the direction of economic and professional distinctions in terms of access to resources. Thus the dichotomy between the *gahapati* (householder) and the cultivator (*kassaka*) is more real than between the *kṣatriya* and the *śūdra*.[61] Another dichotomy of a different kind was that between the householder and the monk. In the parallel society of the *saṅgha*, social distinctions are sought to be negated and the doctrine and its laws are universally applicable to all. In the concept of the *cakkavattin* the king dispenses justice and acts righteously irrespective of caste considerations. The law of *Dhamma* was a universally applicable ethic and this places it above any given reality.

This difference is also apparent in the two institutions symbolic of the ideological forms of the doctrines. The Vedic hermitages were *āśramas*, retreats in the forest inhabited generally by *brāhmaṇas* and their wives and disciples, removed from cities and settlements and self-sufficient in their needs. Those living there had fulfilled their social obligations and moved towards renunciation in the twilight of their lives. This was a contrast to the Buddhist *saṅgha*, open even to the young. The *saṅgha* was the assembly or coming together of a number of people drawn from various backgrounds in the common pursuit of a path to *nirvāṇa*. These were located close to settlements and cities from where they drew their sustenance. Both the *āśrama* and the monastery often performed the function of frontier settlements in later periods when the monasteries also become self-sufficient and more distanced from settlements. Travelling monks and renouncers formed a network of communication in which an exchange of ideas was natural. In this earlier period the dependence of the monastery on the settlement was the reversal of the self-sufficient *āśrama*. Since the Buddhist monastic tradition did not have an ecclesiastical parallel or a secular clergy, its relations with the lay community had to be close. The early bifurcation of shaman and priest continues into these times. Shamanistic traces can be seen in the questioning of the sacrificial ritual and the alternate path to liberation in *yoga* and meditation. The concern with individual salvation and *nirvāṇa* was alien to shamanism and can be traced to Upaniṣadic thought. The transformation of this thought into the doctrine of the sect was to become the foundation in turn for other ideologies and belief-systems.

## Notes and References


1. D. McLellan, *Ideology*, Milton Keynes, 1986.
2. P. Deussen, *The Philosophy of the Upaniṣads*, London, 1906; S. Radhakrishnan, *The Principal Upaniṣads*, London, 1953; Hastings, *Encyclopaedia of Religion and Ethics*, see Upaniṣads; W. Ruben, *Die Philosophen der Upanishadan*, Bern, 1947; M. Winternitz, *A History of Indian Literature*, I, 1, Calcutta, 1962, pp. 208ff.
3. Ruben, op. cit., p. 306.
4. Hastings, op. cit.
5. *Mahāvagga*, I.15, 1ff.
6. *Ait. Br.*, 6.3.9; 6.9.6.
7. *Śat. Br.*, 1.1.1.7.
8. Ibid., 3.8.2.28; *Ait. Br.*, 7.3.6.
9. PTS Pali-English Dictionary, sv. *uposatha.*
10. J. Van Baal, 'Offering, Sacrifice and Gift', *Numen*, 1976, 23 (3), pp. 161–78.
11. R. Firth, 'Offering and Sacrifice: Problems of Organisation', *Journal of the Royal Anthropological Institute*, 1963, 93 (1), pp. 12–24. See also H. Hubert and M. Mauss, *Sacrifice: Its Nature and Function*, London, 1964, M.F.C. Bourdillon and M. Fortes (eds), *Sacrifice*, London, 1980.
12. Romila Thapar, '*Dāna* and *Dakṣiṇā* as Forms of Exchange', in *Ancient Indian Social History: Some Interpretations*, New Delhi, 1978, p. 105. *See* chapter 24 in this volume.
13. Firth, op. cit.
14. D.D. Kosambi, *The Culture and Civilisation of Ancient India in Historical Outline*, London, 1965, p. 105.
15. E.E. Evans–Pritchard, *The Nuer*, Oxford, 1940; P.J. Newcomer, 'The Nuer are Dinka: An Essay on Origins and Environmental Determinism', *Man*, 1972, 7, 5–11; M. Glickman, 'The Nuer and the Dinka: A Further Note', *Man*, 1972, 7, pp. 586–94.
16. *Śat. Br.*, 3.1.2.21.
17. Pāṇini, 3.4.73.
18. B. Lincoln, *Priests, Warriors and Cattle*, Berkeley, 1981.
19. *Taittirīya Saṃhitā*, 4.7.1–11, 57.

20. B.B. Lal, 'Excavations at Hastinapur', *Ancient India*, nos 10 and 11, 1954–55.
21. *Rgveda*, X.90.
22. C.A. Gregory, 'Gifts to Man and Gifts to God', *Man*, 1980, n.s., 15, pp. 626–52.
23. *Sumaṅgala-vilāsinī*, I.33.
24. For a survey of social formations pertinent to this paper, see my *From Lineage to State*, New Delhi, 1984.
25. F. Staal, *Agni*, vol. I, Berkeley, 1982.
26. *Śat. Br.*, 5.1.3.3; 8.7.1.2; 9.4.3.5.
27. *Ch. Up.*, 7.25.2; 3.14.3.
28. Ibid., 3.5.2; *Kaṭha Up.*, 1.3.17; *Śvetāśvatara Up.*, 6.22, 5.6; *Veda-guhyam* is a term frequently used.
29. *Śat. Br.*, 1.4.1.10; *Atharvaveda*, 5.22.14.
30. *Ch. Up.*, 5.3.1ff; 5.12.1ff; *Praśna Up.*, 6.1; *Bṛhad. Up.*, 3.1.1.
31. *Bṛhad. Up.*, 2.1.15.
32. Ibid., 1.4.11.
33. Ibid., 4.1.1.
34. *Ch. Up.*, 5.11.1.
35. *Dīgha Nikāya*, 1.136ff; 146; 3.16, 20.
36. *Ṛgveda*, 10.157; 168.4.
37. *Kaṭha Up.*, 1.1.23; *Bṛhad. Up.*, 3.1.1, 6.2.7.
38. *Ṛgveda*, 10.136.
39. Ibid., 10.16.
40. *Bṛhad. Up.*, 5.11.1; cf. *Kauṣītakī Br. Up.*, 1.3–5.
41. *Ch. Up.*, 5.10.1ff.
42. *Ait. Br.*, 6.3.9; 6.9.6; *Śat. Br.*, 3.3.4.21.
43. *Cf. Muṇḍaka Up.*, 2.2.3; 3.2.1–2.
44. *Ch. Up.*, 4.4.1–5.
45. K.N. Jayatilleka, *The Buddhist Theory of Knowledge*, London, 1963, pp. 29ff, 43ff.
46. *Ch. Up.*, 4.1–16; *Bṛhad. Up.*, 3.1.1–9; 4.1–4.
47. 7.8.
48. S. Radhakrishnan, *The Principal Upaniṣads*, London, 1953, Introduction.
49. *Bṛhad. Up.*, 3.2.7.
50. Ibid., 3.5.1.
51. Ibid., 3.2.13.
52. Ibid., 4.1.2.
53. These references come from later texts such as the commentaries on the *Nikāya*, e.g., the *Papañca Sudāni*, I.384.
54. 6.2.2.
55. *Kauṣ. Br. Up.*, I.2ff.

56. 3.2.1.
57. Jayatilleka, op. cit., pp. 46ff.
58. S. Radhakrishnan, *Indian Philosophy*, London, 1948, I, p. 278.
59. Patañjali, *Vyākaraṇa Mahābhāṣyam*, 2.4.9/I.476.
60. *Dīgha Nikāya*, I.88; 3.156.
61. Romila Thapar, *From Lineage to State*, pp. 104ff.

# Ethics, Religion and Social Protest in the First Millennium BC in Northern India*

The first millennium BC witnessed a seemingly spontaneous burst of new ideologies in areas that subsequently became nuclear regions for major civilizations. The impression is one of a chain of apparently similar developments linking the then known world. The geographical reach of these civilizations was relatively confined, and allowed the formation of a network of connections resulting from conquest, trade, and religious missions. The almost simultaneous and sustained period of speculative thought throughout this area resulted either from the juxtaposition of a number of seminal regions and their interconnections or from internal developments within each society that broke the relative quiescence of the earlier bronze-age cultures.

The sixth to third centuries BC in northern India saw the emergence of patterns of thought that were embryonic to the evolution of what was called in later centuries the Indian ethos. This paper is an attempt to observe the historical anatomy of this period and to point up the intellectual processes that gave a legitimacy to these patterns. The focus is narrow and concentrates on Buddhism, seen not merely as the teaching of a single individual but rather as a wider response to a particular doctrine and as a reaction to the changing milieu with which it was associated.

The middle of the first millennium introduces a new ideological perspective, which, although touched upon marginally in Vedic literature, is more fully developed in the teachings of what came to be called 'the heterodox sects'. To the extent that Buddhism

* From *Daedalus*, Spring, 1975, vol. 104, no. 2, 119–33.

subsumes this new perspective, it is convenient to juxtapose the polarity of Vedic thought with that of Buddhism. The primary concern of the new attitude is with the perception of change, the recognition that the context during this period was different from any that had existed before. The outcome of this recognition was the growth of ideologies that were at the same time innovative and germinal to the social and religious philosophy and ethical thought of subsequent periods. This carried within it the elements both of pessimism at the passing of the old order and of optimism in having discovered a way to deal with the changed situation. The 'way' as perceived by the Buddha was arrived at through an innovation in ideology — the notion of causation. Causation in turn highlighted other aspects of innovative thinking, some entirely new, others resulting from the extension of existing ideas.

To understand the perception of change at this time and the need for a new ideology the authors of these ideas have to be seen in a historical context. The priorities in their questions and the kinds of avenues which they explored in a search for answers were not unconnected with the historical milieu in which they lived. They appeared in response to the essentially urban civilization of the Ganga valley. This is often termed the 'second urbanization' of early India, the first having been that of the third millennium in the Indus valley. The antecedents to this second urbanization point to a shift in geographical location from the nuclear area of the third millennium. The Indus civilization had declined by the middle of the second millennium BC, and the new culture of the Ganga civilization grew and matured on the other side of the watershed during the first millennium BC, seemingly unconnected with the earlier copper-age civilization. Technologically the new urbanization was based on the use of iron, the domestication of the horse, the extension of plough agriculture, and a sophisticated agricultural and commercial economy. Until recently it was believed that the new civilization grew under the aegis of nomadic pastoralists speaking an Indo-European language, Sanskrit, who had conquered the existing inhabitants, possibly destroyed the bronze-age cities, and had given rise to the new civilization in the process of settling down in the Ganga valley — thus moving, as it were, from the age of the heroes to that of princes and traders. But fresh evidence has suggested that this discontinuity is more imagined than real: many aspects of the later culture bear the impress of the earlier civilization in spite of the considerable difference in the physical location.[1]

Technological changes were not the only indication of a new historical context, for these changes coincided with various other developments. Clan identity gradually gave way to territorial identity. The territorial units, or *janapadas,* that emerged were named after the *kṣatriyas* and others constituting the *janas* (tribes) settled thereon, such as Gandhāra, Kuru, Pañcāla, Matsya, Cedi, Kāśī, Kośala, Magadha, etc. Lineage, speech, and customary law were the three criteria of identity and status in the earlier society, with lineage being central to political control and landownership. The *kṣatriya* clans were landowning, and some were later assigned to either the Candravaṃśa (Lunar) or the Sūryavaṃśa (Solar) lineages. The location of the two was distinct, with the Candravamśa lineages centered in the Doāb, and extending southward and westward, and the Sūryavaṃśa centered in the middle Ganga plain. The separate identity of the Doāb and South Bihar is evident at every point. Cultivated land was initially owned in common by members of *kṣatriya* lineages — the *khattiyas* of Buddhist literature — although much of the actual tilling appears to have been done by the *dāsas* (slaves) and *bhṛtakas* (hired labourers and servants).[2] Lineage rights thus included land ownership, and lineage connections were carefully recorded. This accounts for the predominantly *kṣatriya* oligarchic political organization in many *janapadas.*

The stress on kinship ties was further emphasized by the use of the word *jāti* ('assigned by birth'). It occurs first in a late text and is used in the sense of an extended family.[3] In time, the references to *jana* decreased and those to *jāti* increased, until in Buddhist literature *jāti* is used in the sense of caste, implying an endogamous kinship group, ranked in a list of specialized occupations and service relationships reflecting an increase in social stratification. The bi-polarity of purity and pollution remained an important characteristic of the classification by *varṇa*, but this classification was of a more theoretical kind involving initially four (*brāhmaṇa*, *kṣatriya*, *vaiśya*, *and śūdra*) and subsequently five (with the addition of the *pañcamma* or 'untouchable') groups in society, and eventually became more closely related to ritual than to social status. *Jāti* slowly became the gauge of a more precise assessment of the socio-economic status of a group, but the criteria of status continued to include ritual status (*varṇa*).

During the time of the Buddha (sixth to fifth centuries BC) a major change in the agrarian structure was the emergence of large estates owned by individual *kṣatriya* clans; the criterion of wealth came to be associated more with land and money and less with cattle, which had been the measure of riches in the earlier society. The transfer of land took place largely within the same social group that had earlier maintained joint ownership. As an adjunct to this development of a landed class, there is a noticeable increase in the categories of wage labourer, hired labourer, and slave. The slave had the *varṇa* status of a *śūdra*, which was particularly necessary for those who worked as domestic slaves, the more common category met with in the Indian sources. A text of the late first millennium BC mentions the price of a slave as being a hundred pieces of money; by comparison, a pair of oxen was twenty-four pieces.[4] Slaves were probably expensive even in earlier centuries and could not therefore be used too extensively in production.

Agriculture provided the economic base for the growth of towns in the Ganga valley. Many of the cities, apart from being important commercial centres, were also the capitals of the *janapadas* such as Kauśāmbi, Kāśī, Ayodhyā and Rajagṛha. These were not the cities of bronze-age civilization, but were the nuclei of the affluent and the natural habitat of the *seṭṭhi-gahapatis,* the immensely wealthy traders and financiers. The flexibility of an urban economy increasingly based on markets was facilitated by three innovations — the use of a script, the consequent issuing of promissory notes, letters of credit, and pledges, and the introduction of money in the form of silver and copper punch-marked coins issued initially, it has been suggested, by traders' guilds. These, in turn, resulted in the new profession of trading in money, and the appearance of the banker deriving his wealth from usury. Unlike the Buddhist texts, the *brāhmaṇa* sources disapprove of usury, although the censure is restricted to *brāhmaṇas*' fraternizing with those who live off usury.[5] Apart from the archaeological evidence, another indication, albeit indirect, of the growth of cities is the rapid rise of Jainism when, with the prohibition on agricultural professions and restriction on ownership of land, trade became the predominant occupation of the Jainas. The discovery of new routes and the revival of old routes were further incentives to trade.[6]

The city produced its own social stratification, where the *śreṣṭhin* ('merchant or banker') was to become powerful and where the institutional base was to be that of the *śreṇī* ('guild'). This explains why various religious sects competed for the patronage of the *śreṣṭhins*.[7] Yet in brahmanical literature the trader is not included among the superior social groups. The *varṇa*-ranking of the *vaiśya* ('trader') in the third position may have been irksome to those who had such access to wealth. Furthermore, power in brahmanical terms was connected with ownership of land; although not ultimately associated with the *śreṣṭhin*, land was by no means his primary source of wealth. Up to a point there was a distinction between the urban and rural élite — the *seṭṭhi/śreṣṭhin* and the *khattiya/kṣatriya* and *gahapatis* — because they derived their income from different sources. But some of the latter who owned estates were also town-dwellers, and thus formed another group alongside the traders and merchants.

The guild was emerging as an essential institution of urban life, acting as a centre of both professional and kin cohesion. The recognition of *śreṇī-dharma* (the customary law of the guilds) as legitimate law by the end of the millennium is another indication of the powerful status of the *śreṇī*.[8] Ultimately it evolved into an agency of caste organization where some of the larger and better established guilds took on *jāti* status; no less important was the role of the guilds in later centuries as patrons of the heterodox sects.

The lower orders of the guild were the *karmakāras* ('artisans') and the *antevāsikas* ('apprentices'), who were nevertheless still superior to the *dāsabhṛtaka* ('slaves and hired labourers'). These, together with the cultivators, were all included in the rank of *śūdras*. In brahmanical texts, their low rank was maintained by the legal fiction that they were of mixed caste origin. The gradation among *śūdras* ran from the *sacchūdra* ('clean *śūdra*') to the edge of untouchability. The untouchables constituted the fifth major group. Their untouchability derived from their being considered polluting either because of their occupation as scavengers, such as Caṇḍālas and Doms and those who maintained the cremation grounds, or because they belonged to primitive tribes. Their speech was alien and their manner of life was strange. Later the Buddhists despised the Caṇḍālas. The inequities of city life further aggravated the degradation of these groups, already declared impure on account of ritual pollution.

The rise of political authority as symbolized in systems of government and the concept of the state were explained in a variety of ways. Vedic literature had connected the emergence of kingship with the emergence of government and stressed that the qualities of leadership in battle and elements of divinity were essential to kingship.[9] By the middle of the first millennium, tribal egalitarianism had surrendered to the evolution of a system of government that, whether oligarchic or monarchical, was explained as concerning itself with the problems of social disharmony, the need for authority, and the justification for revenue collection. The Buddhist theory emphasized the perfection of society in the pre-government age, thus implying that government had become an unfortunate necessity,[10] through the diffusion of social disharmony resulting from family discord and private property. Seeking a solution, people had gathered together and elected a leader — the *mahāsammata* 'the Great Elect' — in whom they invested the authority to maintain law and order; in payment for this service the *mahāsammata* was paid a share of the revenue. Significantly the Buddhist theory emphasizes contract and seems not to have had any notion of royal divinity. The *Mahābhārata* expresses a similar idea, but with a greater emphasis on the notion that societies without governments result in anarchy, the anarchic society is described as a state of *matsyanyāya* 'the law of fish', where the big fish devour the smaller ones.[11] In this theory, the king also contracts to maintain law and order, but an element of divinity is introduced in his actual appointment as king.

These theories reflect an increasing sense of alienation where it becomes necessary to enforce harmony, since the pristine natural harmony of society has disappeared. They also reflect the acceptance of the idea of authority based on power and not necessarily on kinship alone. The *janapadas* were coalescing into territorial states. By the fifth century BC competition for power had already developed among the stronger of the major *janapadas*, such as Kāśī, Kośala and Magadha, where even close kinship ties were ignored to further political gains. Magadha was to emerge as the most powerful, ultimately becoming the nucleus of the Mauryan empire, which was built on the conquests of Candragupta Maurya in the fourth century BC and comprised, during the reign of his grandson Aśoka, almost the entire Indian subcontinent and eastern Afghanistan. With the growth of political authoritarianism and a complicated state machinery, it is not surprising that the justification for the emergence of government came to be based on the necessity for taxation and the need to maintain law and order.[12]

Two co-existing systems of economic redistribution came into being and sometimes into conflict as well. One, at the level of the state, derived its income from taxes, tributes and fines and redistributed it through awards, salaries, grants, and expenditures on public works and ceremonies. But the redistribution was not equitable, and the prestige economy, particularly in the monarchical states, consumed a large part of the income. The second system, on a lesser scale, was confined to the merchants and bankers of the cities; among them the ethic of redistribution was such that substantial sums were retained as capital for further investment.[13] They were doubtless irritated by the economy of demands by the state. That the second system could function in the cities points to their more diffused political authority; this is also suggested by the absence of citadels in these cities. To some extent money liberated the financier from overarching political control.

Caste structure at this time grew out of a variety of interrelationships between groups. The purity-pollution dichotomy, which above all demarcated the *brāhmaṇa* from the untouchable and which was absent in the earlier period, is by now well established. The *ārya-dāsa* dichotomy deriving from, linguistic, and cultural differences was now replaced by the *ārya-śūdra* dichotomy, where the main criteria are the use of Sanskrit and the observance of the *varṇa* rules. Non-*āryas* are *mleccha* ('the barbarians' or 'the impure') and are generally ranked as *śūdras* except in later centuries, when foreign conquerors such as the Indo-Greeks had to be given the dubious status of 'degenerate *kṣatriyas*'. The formation of new castes, theoretically resulting from the intermixing of the original four, was probably a more open system than has hitherto been recognised. The evidence from subsequent centuries suggests that new *jātis* arose as a result of incorporating tribes and guilds and, still later, religious sects into caste society.

The complexity of the new society is clearly reflected in the need for codifying the laws of the various social groups, which is what is aimed at in the brahmanical *dharmasūtras*. The purpose of the laws is to differentiate between the various social groups generally identified as those of *jana*, *jāti*, and *varṇa*. These, however, are made part of a cohesive view of society. There is an implicit belief that the demarcation of differences would lead to a resolution of tensions, an attitude that could only have been feasible in the absence of a situation of conflict. Also implicit in the *dharmasūtras* is the *brāhmaṇas'* claim to being the arbiters of the law. There was no overt challenge to this claim since the codification did not aim at a uniformity of laws, but, on the contrary, to the recognition of their diversity. The Buddhist social code, on the other hand, stressed broad ethical principles of general application to a variety of social groups into the new patterns. The integration was easier at the theoretical level. At the practical level there was a tendency to separate ritual status (*varṇa*) from actual status (*jāti*). Social roles were not entirely dependent on the one or the other. The older traditions and norms were thus placated, and the new entrants into the social hierarchy were not entirely disappointed. However, the demarcation was in fact by no means facile or simplistic. Many of the later subtleties and intricacies of caste relationships emanate from this early attempt at demarcation.

It was apparent that a condition of permanence was neither feasible nor possible in the world of reality where all was flux. Even the above brief survey of the historical scene shows that the condition of constant change could not be ignored.[14] It affected the assumptions of the philosophers of the time and is still reflected in the prevailing intellectual systems. The consciousness of change is perhaps seen most clearly in the fundamental problem of human salvation or liberation in which three interrelated aspects were emphasized — the ethic of the individual in terms of his own moral consciousness and his search for release from the bonds of human existence, the verification of ultimate knowledge so essential to the working out of a means to salvation, and finally the discovery of a path to salvation. The prime motivation was to find an answer that would subsume changing material conditions and yet remain viable. The Buddhist attempt to analyse these problems makes a point of contrasting the attempts of other groups of thinkers similarly involved.

That these concerns were widespread is apparent from the rise of a variety of what have been called 'heterodox sects', among which Buddhism was included. These sects were not merely a reaction to Vedic religion, as is often suggested, because within the Vedic-*brāhmaṇa* framework there had also been a diversification of views as evidenced by the *Upaniṣads* and the *Āraṇyakas*. These were the discourses of a mixed group of some renouncers, some chiefs of clans and a few who lived in forest retreats. They stood apart, disenchanted with existing explanations, seeking ultimate truths. Their discourses show a liberation of the speculative consciousness from the burdens of magical sacrifice and ritual. However, the universalistic basis of their thinking had some limitations. They recognised the need for individual salvation. In isolation and through *saṃnyāsa* ('asceticism'), the individual could find his *mokṣa* ('liberation from rebirth') which would release his *ātman* (individual 'soul') and enable it to unite with the *brahman* ('all-soul'). Asceticism was motivated both by a desire to escape from the insecurity of a changing society and by the conviction that meditation was an effective means of acquiring the knowledge that furthers self-realization as well as the potential (*tapas*) to become superior even to the gods. Gradually asceticism came to be regarded as a more powerful force than sacrifice, thus admitting the ineffectiveness of a community attempt to reach moments of magic and power. Perhaps more important, asceticism resulted in total freedom, a break with family ties and social obligations, provided sexual needs could be sublimated. Hence the correlation between asceticism and asexuality. This freedom insured the renouncer a moral status far higher than that of even a sacrificing *brāhmaṇa*.

Some sects, such as the Ājīvikas, based their thought on determinism and saw renunciation as the only and ultimate path to *mokṣa*. The Buddhists and the Jainas had both philosophical and social concerns. Access to knowledge did not lie through the authoritative voice of the Vedas, for what is not personally verifiable is unacceptable. Nor is skepticism a path to knowledge; the skeptics are described by the Buddhists as 'eel-wrigglers'. Even asceticism was not possible as a path to salvation for everyone. Both the Buddha and Mahāvīra, though seeking enlightenment through isolated meditation, nevertheless returned to the world of the cities and villages to preach the path of salvation to the householder who could not become a monk owing to his social obligations. In the case of the Buddha, the emphasis on 'the middle way', the path devoid of excesses, emphasizing moderation and a moral life, was indicative of his concern that the path suggested by him be compatible with the real problems of social existence. Not surprisingly, the early supporters of Buddhism were not only the ascetics but also, and in larger numbers, the *seṭṭhis* and members of the *kṣatriya* clans. At the other extreme were a number of *lokāyata* sects, particularly the Cārvākas, who were based primarily in the towns and who taught a thoroughgoing materialism, such as the teachings of Ajīta Keśakambalin, which was seen by some others as an idealization of hedonism.

The thread of social protest winding through these heterodox teachings was indicative of a perception of change: of existing change, the recognition that further changes were imminent, and toward change itself. For the Buddhists, change was symbolized in two strands, which occasionally intertwined, the cosmic and the historical. The universe is transient and in a state of continuous flux. Buddhist cosmic time was cyclical, starting with a pristine utopian society, which had gradually decayed and was slowly reaching its nadir of sorrow and suffering — the direction in which contemporary society was moving. Eventually the time cycle would rise upwards again and begin a utopian phase. Brahmanical sources, also positing cyclical time, attempted a mathematical measurement of it, albeit of an infinite magnitude, as did the Buddhists, who indicated infinite eons by spatial descriptions.[15] Time was seen as an unending continuity of which historical time was but a fraction. Within this continuity the individual consciousness also moved unceasingly from one lifetime to the next birth until liberated from the chain of rebirth. It is compared to the flame of a lamp used to light another lamp and so on, *ad infinitum*. In each case the flame of the lamp is both the old and the new flame, and so it is with the perception of change in the continuity of time.

Change, therefore, cannot be seen as a sudden break. But within historical time there is a far sharper awareness of the past and the future. Other 'enlightened ones' have trod the same path in the past as the Buddha. Was this allegorical, or was it a reference to earlier teachers with a similar doctrine? There is also the reference to the Buddha Maitreya, who will reawaken the world to the *Dharma* ('the law') many centuries after the present Buddha.[16] This was to develop in the first centuries after Christ into almost a millennarian movement within Buddhism, no doubt further stimulated by contact with the messianic message of Christianity and Manichaeism. The decline from utopian beginnings is not accidental. There is a concern with moral decay, which, although partially inherent (the very state of nature having evolved from luminosity to dross), is nevertheless caused by changes in the material content of life. It can be circumvented to some extent by the individual's choice in the manner of adapting to changing social situations.

Central to the awareness of change is the law of causality, and it is around this that much of Buddhist doctrine revolves, claiming to derive from rational arguments and examples. At the individual level, the interconnection between desire, suffering, and rebirth is explained by causality. The elimination of *dukkha* ('suffering') lies in the elimination of *tanha* ('desire'), and this can be achieved by observing the precepts of the *Dhamma/Dharma* ('the Law as taught by the Buddha') and the eight-fold path. Social change is also explained by causality and becomes a part of the underpinning, as it were, of the universal applicability of the *Dharma*, for, once the causal connection is known, change comes under human control.

This led to a new perspective on the significance of the individual. The heterodox teaching, and Buddhism in particular, turned the earlier perspective inside out, and the focus shifted to the individual rather than the social group to which he belonged. Up to a point this encouraged a nihilistic trend, as in the case of the Ājīvikas. But nihilism was not characteristic of all sects. On this question the central core of the Buddhist *Dharma* is very clear. Where renunciation or opting out is not feasible, the individual, whatever his social status, had the choice of becoming a lay disciple and observing the rules of 'the middle way'. Furthermore, the moral responsibility of the individual was seen in the choice of action made by him through his chain of rebirth. The *Bṛhadāraṇyaka Upaniṣad* described rebirth as consisting of *saṃsāra*, the transmigration of souls, to which was added the notion of *karma* ('action'), the outcome of the activities of one life affecting the next. The Buddhists modified the notion of *saṃsāra* to exclude the soul and to refer to consciousness as the element that continues, and they appropriated the doctrine of *karma* in its entirety. Thus not only was the individual responsible for the nature and condition of his present and future lives, but the doctrine of *karma* also became a useful means of explaining the origin of social inequality and the creation of caste society.[17] Not only was a man's social condition a reference point in social justice, but disease, physical pain, and even death were seen as aspects of social justice, although the moral responsibility for this condition rested with the individual. Thus the sting of social protest was numbed by insisting that there was no tangible agency responsible for social injustice, or even an abstract deity against whom man could complain, but that responsibility belonged with man himself. This in turn tended to curb non-conformity in behaviour for fear of the consequences in the next life.

It is not altogether fortuitous that Buddhism was popular among the entrepreneurs and the life-affirming groups in Indian society — the merchants and the artisans. Nor should it be forgotten that at the political level Buddhism registered its initial success in the period of the first empire, that of the Mauryas. The life-asserting aspect of *karma* is that, if the rules are observed, the next birth can at least bring a better and more prosperous life, if not freedom from the chain of rebirth. There can be, therefore, considerable motivation for observing the rules. That the onus was on the individual is further emphasized by the necessity of being born a human, rather than any other creature, before release can be attained. Moral responsibility was not developed into a philosophy of radical change, which would have meant challenging the existing system. The Buddha made a distinction between caste as the frame of the socio-economic structure, which he accepted, and the notion of the relative purity inherent in the upper castes, which he rejected.[18] The emphasis was on an individual's choice of an ethic, but the end result of this had its social implications.

Fundamental to Buddhist teaching was the notion of the interplay of acts of merit (*puṇya*) and demerit (*pāpa*, literally 'evil, wickedness'), and *puṇya* becomes central to ethical thought from this time onwards. The constituents of merit for the layman are activities motivated by the need to further social good, such as harmonious social relationships and charity, but, above all, sexual control and non-violence. Harmony in social relationships referred not only to those between parents and children, but also between master and slave, and employer and employee in general. This had a clear correlation with the large estates of the *khattiyas* and the new urban culture. Although the Buddha associates the growth of evil in the world with (among other factors) the institutions of the family and private property, both of which, he argues, encouraged sentiments of possessiveness and consequently aggression, he nevertheless projects an undisturbed continuity for both institutions. In spite of its evils, the family did weaken the sense of alienation, and hence there is a stress on respecting kinship ties. Charity was seen not only as a means of alleviating the suffering of the materially poor, but also as the giving of gifts (*dāna*) especially to the *saṅgha* (the order of monks). This had the additional advantage of strengthening the monastic organization and its relations with the lay community.

Both sexual puritanism and non-violence became controversial issues in the debate among the various sects. The Buddha was not loathe to accept the devotion of the more renowned and accomplished courtesans of the towns, such as Ambapālī, but it took considerable persuasion for him to agree to admit women into the *saṅgha*. Family ties were a major obstacle to renunciation, and women were symbolic of these ties. Yet during this time it was only in the Jaina and Buddhist orders that nuns were permitted, and the women were drawn largely from urban society and the royal households.

Non-violence (*ahiṃsā*), the central focus of Buddhist and Jaina ethics, was less important in other religious sects. Veiled, ambiguous references can be culled from the *Upaniṣads*, but the exposition of the idea as an ethical value was that of Mahāvīra and the Buddha. The Jaina understanding of *ahiṃsā* appears to be an extreme position involving all created beings and the attempt to preserve them from destruction, whether deliberate or accidental.[19] The Buddhists tend to stress the ethical question of man's actions in furthering or preventing violence.

*Ahiṃsā* can be viewed in association with many facets of contemporary life. It has been seen as an objection to the sacrifice of animals during the *yajña*, the sacrificial ceremony essential to the Vedic brahmanical religion. There is repeated mention of the futility of killing animals as a religious ritual.[20] Possibly this coincided with the transformation of pastoral groups into agriculturalists, which resulted in a depletion of animal wealth.[21] The debate on the inviolability of the cow is referred to *en passant* in the *Śatapatha Brāhmaṇa*, but it is again largely due to Buddhist and Jaina disputation that the prohibition is extended from cattle to violence *per se*.[22] *Ahiṃsā* can also be explained as a reaction among the new urban groups to the prestige economy of non-urban societies, who were wilfully destroying wealth to no purpose. Sacrifice, it was argued, is essentially an offering; consequently it lies not in the destruction of life but in the embodiment of moral values that become the foundation for ethical behavior — in honouring parents, in honouring all the members of the household from the highest to the lowest, in having patience, meekness, and self-control. The values listed are both conservative and conciliatory. Yet the element of radicalism in this view is the inclusion of slaves and workmen as deserving of honor. At another level *ahiṃsā* would have suited those who were discouraging inter-tribal warfare and encouraging the expansion of settled agriculture and trade — activities from which both the *khattiyas* and *seṭṭhis* stood to gain.

*Ahiṃsā* also included a discouragement of the use of coercion and violence to justify political authoritarianism — very pertinent to the transformation of the *janapadas* into kingdoms laying political claim to large territories. The suspicion of political authoritarianism may have to do with the fact that the heterodox sects often had their genesis in the relatively more egalitarian tradition of the oligarchies and chiefdoms, such as that of the Śākyas and Vṛjjis. Those most directly affected by war would be the cultivators, whose fields were the prey of marauding armies, and the traders, who would be unable to transport their goods, or, even worse, whose centres of production would be destroyed in the devastation of a town — so often the symbolic final act of a successful campaign. Possibly *ahiṃsā* could also undermine the ritualized wars — the campaigns that were fought subsequent to the *aśvamedha* sacrifice, when a king claiming sovereignty over a region would release a sacrificial horse and would then be duty bound to conquer all the lands over which the horse wandered. Implicit in *ahiṃsā* at the political level is an objection to even the legitimate use of coercion (*daṇḍa*) by the political authority of the state. The king in his role as protector should avoid coercion, modelling himself after the ideal universal monarch, the *cakravartin*, who is *adaṇḍa* 'not having to resort to coercion'.[23]

*Ahiṃsā* might have had an ameliorative influence in situations of tension, which were by no means rare. Ultimately there was also the ethical and philosophical level. Conscious non-violence (not to be confused with cowardice) was expressive of the highest ethical stand. The credibility of non-violence can only stem from a belief in man's innate virtue. It has been argued that the Buddha's *ahiṃsā* represents the negative philosophy of pacifism. To the extent that the Buddha was not preaching rebellion, but rather a conciliatory ethic, as a solution to social ills, the negative aspect of pacifism can be justified. But if *ahiṃsā* arose from an awareness of varying levels of comprehension and reaction, then pacifism alone cannot be the complete explanation. As a method of social protest, the objection even to ritual sacrifice involving the destruction of life takes on an active and affirmative role, as is evident from the continuing debate on this subject up to recent times. It is perhaps also worth remembering that the brahmanical insistence on vegetarianism dates to the post-Buddhist period.

The significance of renunciation has its own role in the Buddhist moral position and relates to the moral and political authority of the renouncer. There has been a tendency to see renunciation as a purely life-denying process. This it may be if the renouncer moves away from society and lives in isolation, though, even here, the negative aspect to the isolation is rarely foremost. But if the renouncer, after a period of isolation, resumes a function in society, in spite of his having renounced his ties, his influence can become both powerful and positive. Moral and political authority are separated and the former becomes the censor of the latter. This separation can be crucial to the establishing of an independent intellectual tradition, as was the case in the lifetime of the Buddha, provided that the independent relationship between the two is not eroded by the requirements of patronage. If the renouncer is also in sympathy with the aspirations of a community and if he comes from a social background not generally associated with life-denial and renunciation, but rather with political authority and social status (such as the *khattiyas* of the time), his moral authority is almost unlimited. In such situations the renouncer forsakes one life-style to take on another.

Recruitment to the heterodox sects was not limited to any particular group. Those who had an organized body of adherents, enlisted monks, and built monasteries, encouraged people of all castes to join the organization and, in theory at least, did not bar any caste. In the Buddhist *saṅgha* the adoption of a new name by the monk was symbolic not merely of a new birth in the *saṅgha* but also of a removal from his caste and status.[24] The proximity of all castes within the monasteries ran counter to the Brahmanical ideas of the segregation of castes in daily living. Commensality among such monks from the lay community broke the food taboos so essential to the *varṇa* system. Outside the monastery and among lay followers the problem of integrating social groups remained.

Each *jāti* had its own religious observances. Religious differentiations were preserved through the mechanism of caste, as were the observance of rituals pertaining to local cults, some of which were assimilated into Buddhist practice.[25] The Buddhist shift of emphasis from deities to the more abstract notion of *dharma* ('the law') was an attempt in part to undermine these religious differentiations. It may be argued that the absence of a deity in Buddhism inherent in the doctrine strengthened the idea of a universal religion. In some ways, however, *dharma* almost took on the characteristics of an omniscient presence symbolized in the turning of the wheel of the law. *Dharma* was the eternal Law — ultimate, timeless, temporal, transcendent, immanent. In spite of changing human society the Law remained changeless. It integrated within itself the ethic of the individual, the verification of ultimate knowledge, and the path to salvation. Change was perceived, recognized, and understood. But it was not the changed situation that was to be subjected to radical social alteration as much as the law that was to be applicable in all situations. The law was above the particular and was universally viable. Enlightenment lay in the discovery of this law and identification with it. But the law was not to be kept to oneself in isolation. The enlightened ones must return to the cities and the villages and preach the law. There is the repeated parable of the raft, where he who has discovered the law (the raft) must leave the raft for others to cross the waters on it.[26]

The arbiters of the *dharma* were the Elders of the monastery. The Buddhist monastery was both a retreat for meditation and an institution for action. The early monasteries had to be located close to large concentrations of population, because of the requirement that the monks feed off alms, since they were forbidden to do any manual labour including cultivating their own food. Begging for alms and preaching the doctrine brought them into contact with the lay community. The *saṅgha* was thus a collection of renouncers but not of ascetics. The monks took on a new way of life based on communal sharing and dedication to poverty, evidenced by the prohibition against personal possessions and by the name they adopted, *bhikṣu* (mendicant). Central to the organization of the *saṅgha* was the emphasis on the equal status of every monk, influenced perhaps by the more egalitarian political organization of the oligarchic *janapadas*, familiar to the Buddha. But this insistence on equality did not apply to the world outside. It was almost as if the creation of a radical, egalitarian society within the monastery exhausted the drive toward such a society in the world outside, or at least weakened the urgency of radical change — assuming, however, that this had been intended. Celibacy and the discouraging of manual labour for the monks point up the bi-polarity between the monk and the householder where the latter qualifies himself in part by his ties to family and property.[27] The monk and the householder lived in worlds apart.

The *saṅgha* gradually acquired a strong sense of mission. This is evident from the frequency of the councils determining the true doctrine and the splintering off of sects within the *saṅgha* after the death of the Buddha, each claiming to represent the true doctrine. Even more significant was the system of maintaining records and historical accounts not only of the major events in the history of Buddhism, but also of the more important sects within the *saṅgha* that encouraged the polemics of Buddhist sectarian thought. The community of renouncers was not altogether unaware either of its political role or of its role in the new ethic that they were promulgating.

The sense of mission was encouraged by the literate monks. The monasteries developed into centres of learning. This was again a point of opposition to the Vedic brahmanical approach for which literacy was the preserve of the socially-determined few and which in any case laid greater stress on the oral tradition. As a part of the appeal to the wider audience, the Buddha preached not in Sanskrit but in *ardha-māgadhi* — a *prākṛit* of the middle Ganga plain. At the same time as brahmanical culture was seeking an *ārya* identity and exclusivity, the Buddha was breaking away from it.

The extension of literacy was symbolic of much that the new ideologies stood for, the insufficiency of faith and ritual and the incorporation of reason and moral action in a manner that would have wide applicability to large numbers of people of diverse social origins. The new teachers arose as individuals and not through an institutional base. But the continuance of the new ideologies required the building of their own institutional base. The perception of change and the need to come to terms with it were not seen as synonymous with a radical ideology in favour of a total change. The Buddhists, for example, were more analytical than earlier thinkers in their views on man and society, but they did not feel it necessary to suggest a complete reorganization of the social structure. To that degree, Buddhism in its historical role touched the chords of social protest but went no further. This was perhaps because the groups for which it was projecting a new ideology ceased to be the protesters at a certain historical point and became the heirs. The element of social protest in Buddhism was therefore limited to providing the intellectual encouragement and justification for the formation of a new elite. It can be argued that in the historical context of those times even this was a radical position and it was not necessary to extend causation to its logical limits. The *lokāyatas* who insisted on natural causation and opposed the doctrine of *karma* were either subsumed into the new system or were left on the fringes as anarchists.

The historical mission of Buddhism took it far afield. The monasteries, irrespective of sectarian differences, acted as networks of acculturation and contact within the Indian subcontinent reaching out into the remotest corners, monks travelling either in isolation or accompanying the traders. In the first millennium AD the significance of the mission of Buddhism was that it acted as a catalyst in many parts of Asia. Its major orientation was in Central Asia, China, Japan, and Southeast Asia. The period when Buddhism took root and prospered in these new areas coincided with its fading in the country of its origin. Can this be regarded as a historical demonstration of the Buddhist notion of change and continuity — the analogy with the flame of one lamp lighting the flame of another before being extinguished?

## Notes and References

1. Archaeological evidence of the post-Harappan period, particularly in Gujarat, Malwa, the Banas valley, and parts of the watershed and upper Doāb, points to some continuities of cultural traits from the Harappa culture. Small settlements of primitive agriculturalists in the Doāb or the western Ganga plain (the Ochre-Colour Pottery culture) were superseded toward the end of the second millennium BC by larger settlements of more advanced agriculturalists gradually taking to iron technology by the earlier part of the first millennium BC (the Painted Gray-Ware Culture). Further east, in the middle Ganga plain and south Bihar, the impetus for using an iron technology is associated with apparently different groups of people (the Black- and Red-Ware cultures), who appear to have had some links with western India via the northern part of the central Indian plateau. The Doāb was the geographical focus of the later Vedic literature and was identified (in the main) in Brahmanical literature with the *āryāvarta* or the land of the *āryas* (the respectable people), those who

spoke Saṇskrit and observed the caste laws. South Bihar, which included the territory of Magadha, was to a greater extent the geographical focus of 'the heterodox sects'. In the Buddhist and Jaina texts, south Bihar was the core of the *āryāvarta*, since these texts tended to give a more easterly location to the 'pure land'. An area of high precipitation, the Ganga plain was at that time covered with forests. It has been argued that settlement on any appreciable scale would have been virtually impossible before the introduction of iron technology, the monsoon forest being relatively impervious to the tools of copper technology. That the introduction of iron could have coincided with an increase in population is also possible judging by impressionistic archaeological data. The iron-age precondition to urbanization is evident from the number of settlements of iron-using cultures that developed into towns. Increase in population not only assisted in the clearing of more land for agriculture in the Ganga plain, but could also have acted as a lever toward encouraging a change to iron technology and more particularly to plough-using agriculture. However a technology by ifself cannot be the causal factor in major historical change and has to be accompanied by other changes in the society and economy. Urbanisation is therefore a more complex process than can be explained by a single technological change.

2. Patañjali, *Mahābhāṣya* on Pāṇini, IV, I.168.
3. *Kātyāyana Śrauta Sūtra*, XV.4.14; XV.2.11.
4. *Nanda Jātaka*, 1.98; *Gāmani Caṇḍa Jātaka*, II.207.
5. *Āpastamba Dharma Sūtra*, I.6.18.22; *Baudhāyana Dharma Sūtra*, 1.5.93–4.
6. Maritime trade with west Asia was revived in the first millennium BC. Close contacts were established between Iran and north-western India. Within the subcontinent, overland and maritime routes to the south (Dakṣiṇāpatha) were being explored.
7. Wagle, *Society at the Time of the Buddha*, Bombay, 1996 (2nd ed.).
8. *Manu Dharmaśāstra*, VIII.41.
9. *Ṛg Veda*, VIII.35.17; 86.10–11.
10. *Dīgha Nikāya*, III.93.
11. *Mahābhārata*, Śānti Parvan, 67.3ff.
12. The words used for the two basic taxes were *bali*, originally meaning a tribute or offering and eventually coming to mean a tax on land, and *bhāga*, meaning 'a share' and applied to the produce of the land, reflecting the more stable distribution of settled times. An early term for the king was *bhāgadugha*, literally, 'he who milks the share'.
13. As suggested by the Buddha in *Dīgha Nikāya*, III, p. 188 (P.T.S. ed.).
14. For a correlation of material conditions with the rise of Buddhism,

R.S. Sharma, 'Material Milieu of the Birth of Buddhism', paper presented to the Twenty-Ninth International Congress of Orientalists, Paris, 1973.
15. *Samyutta Nikāya*, 15.ii.178–93.
16. *Dīgha Nikāya*, III, 76.
17. *Majjhima Nikāya*, I.289; *Aṅguttara Nikāya*, V.288–91. This is made even more explicit in the preeminent text of Brahmanism, the *Bhagavad Gītā*, IV.13, composed in the period after the Buddha.
18. *Aṅguttara Nikāya*, III.214; *Samyutta Nikāya*, I.167; *Majjhima Nikāya*, II.128–30.
19. *Ācārāṅga Sūtra*, II.1.1–4.
20. *Aṅguttara Nikāya*, IV.42–5.
21. D.D. Kosambi, *The Culture and Civilisation of Ancient India in Historical Outline*, London, 1965, p. 105. Cattle provided both labour and fertilizer in agricultural societies, and any depletion was a serious loss. That cattle were singled out for protection is clear from the emphasis in some sections of the Buddhist texts, such as *Majjhima Nikāya*, I.220.
22. The debate is perhaps best symbolized by passages in the early text, the *Śatapatha Brāhmaṇa*, III.1.2.21, where the eating of meat (the flesh of the cow is the case in point) is defended by Yājñavalkya, who represents an important point of view, and the later prohibition on it, as for example in the text of Manu dating to the first century BC.
23. Cakkavati Sinhanādasutta, *Dīgha Nikāya*, III, p. 58 (S.B.B. ed.).
24. *Vinaya Piṭaka*, II.239; *Aṅguttara Nikāya*, IV.202.
25. Dates for important events such as the *vassa* (the rainy season when the monks had to return to the monastery), the *uposatha* (the days for the hearing of the confession of the monks), etc. were calculated on the basis of the lunar calendar, although the solar calendar was also in use at the time.
26. *Majjhima Nikāya*, I.134–5; *Aṅguttara Nikāya*, II.201.
27. S.J. Tambiah, *Buddhism and the Spirit Cults in North-East Thailand*, Cambridge, 1970, pp. 81ff.

# 40

# Renunciation: The Making of a Counter-culture?*

One of the paradoxes of the Indian tradition is that the renouncer is a symbol of authority within society. An explanation of this paradox may emerge from an analysis of the social role of the renouncer. Not many decades ago renunciation was described as a life-negating principle; the fact that it involved an opting out of society led to its characterization as a denial of the need to come to terms with society. But in recent years it has been argued that, far from being life-negating, the techniques adopted by ascetics and renouncers and popularized because of them, have, as axiomatic, the belief that life can be the means of discovering immortality and freedom.[1] An attempt will be made in this paper to argue that the organized groups of renouncers of the post-Vedic period were neither negating the society to which they belonged nor trying to radically alter it: but rather that they were seeking to establish a parallel society. Inherent in this attempt was the notion of dissent; but its articulation was often ambiguous. To the extent that the two societies were kept distinct, there was a tacit recognition of the futility of changing the larger society; that the renouncers had links with this society however, also indicates that there was an equally tacit recognition of osmosis as a process of social change.

Renouncers in any society play a social role. In early India this role is enmeshed with the complexities of caste and with the nature of dissent. The power of the ascetic rubs off onto the renouncer to a far greater degree than, for example, in Christian Europe, and

* From N. Jagadesan and J. Jeyapragassam (eds), *Homage to a Historian* (Dr N. Subramanian Festschrift), Section II, pp. 1–50.

*Acknowledgements*: I am grateful to my colleagues, Drs Suvira Jaiswal, B.D. Chattopadhyaya and R. Champakalakshmi for their comments on this paper.

the renouncer becomes a continuing source of both authority and dissent. In the process of osmosis there is also, unlike as in Europe, provision for temporary periods of renunciation (as among Buddhist Orders) which underlines the central role of the renouncer in society, namely, the relationship between the ascetic, the renouncer and the householder.

The term ascetic refers to a person who has opted out of society, renounced social mores and cast himself away. Ostensibly he has also taken upon himself the goal of discovering the ecstasy (*ānanda*) in the comprehension of the ultimate reality and of characterizing this search by resorting to austerity (*tapas*) and meditation (*dhyāna*) with the aim of union with the ultimate reality (*yoga*). A further distinction is however required for the purposes of this paper. A differentiation must be made between the individual renouncer who isolates himself totally and is thus lost to his kin and his society and to other ascetic colleagues — in short, the ideal ascetic, and the one who opts out of society but joins a group of renouncers. The distinction can perhaps be maintained by referring to the former as ascetics and the latter as renouncers. The term renouncer approximates more closely to the meaning of *saṃnyāsin*. The first category has always been something of a rarity, more frequently described in literature than encountered in reality.

The renouncer is identified not necessarily with a religious sect but with an order constituting an alternative life-style, in many ways contradictory to that of his original social group. Thus he cannot observe caste rules, he must be celibate, he cannot own property, he must carry the distinctive outward symbols of his order and he may be required to break various food tabus. The ascetic on the other hand lived in isolation, observed the food tabus by subsisting on what was naturally available in the forest, stressed the fact of his brahmanhood (where he was, as was often the case, a *brāhmaṇa*) by the austerities which he undertook. A further and fundamental distinction between the two was that whereas the ascetics were figures of loneliness working out their salvation each one for himself, the renouncer was concerned about other people and this concern was expressed in his desire to lead others along the path which he had found. This paper is concerned with the renouncers, who left the society into which they were born and took on the alternative life-style of the sect/order which they joined. At one level the reason for this was that 'the search' required a guide and groups of disciples tended to congregate around individual teachers. At another level there was a conscious attempt to live in a way which would be different from established society.

The focus here is on the social manifestations of these groups and their role in historical change rather than the ideational level and the philosophies which this may have generated. At the ideational level the debate centred on the nature of authority, where the dissenting groups denied the *Vedas* as the source of all knowledge and preferred knowledge acquired through perception and experience.[2] Further, transmigration and notions of salvation were largely acceptable to both the orthodox and the heterodox but the comprehension of these varied. Other matters of controversy related to the nature of the ultimate reality and the juxtaposition of the individual with the universal. The main concern was with the desire for knowledge which in early society was seen as magical power. Initially asceticism arose from groups which questioned the ritual of sacrifice as the means of acquiring magical power. Proponents of asceticism believed that *tapas* and *dhyāna* were more effective. Gradually the idea was extended to more than magical power — to absolute freedom. Primarily this was seen as the freedom of the soul or consciousness to achieve a state of ecstasy. Logically, it also implied freedom from recognizable worldly bonds, of the human body, the mind and of society. By and large there were certain themes which were common to all these groups and which were preconditions to further knowledge: there was a need to comprehend and control the physical body as also the mind, to differentiate between matter and spirit and to derive knowledge from experience and meditation rather than from the claim to revelation.

The initial part of this paper discusses briefly the major groups of renouncers which gained recognition in the early period in the context of the historical background and the social changes which may have encouraged the rise of these groups. The second part is concerned with the bi-polarity of the renouncer and the householder as well as the symbols of difference between the two and among the sects. The last section deals with the element of social protest and concern among these renouncers, and attempts to understand the paradox of their social role.

It has been argued that the term 'sect' is a misnomer for Hindu religious groups since the essential element of a sect — the heretical opposition to orthodox doctrine — is absent among Hindu sects.[3] The argument is based on the use of the term *saṁpradāya* as the nomenclature for sect, but this refers to the transmission of a tradition which can hardly be called a heretical process. However, *saṁpradāya* is generally used by the established religious groups with reference to their own sects, i.e. of the 'received doctrine'. The more frequently used terms for other sects are *śākhā*, *mata*, *samāya*, suggesting a branching off or a schismatic group (which implies heresy) or a coming together of those with a common perspective. The selection of sects discussed in this paper is governed by an inclusion of those which identify themselves with reference to a specific doctrine, specific symbols and rituals and the acceptance of a relationship between the lay followers and the sacerdotal hierarchy: all of which would justify the group being called a sect in the wider sense of the word. The case of Buddhist and Jaina sects is unambiguous since the basis is heresy and false doctrine is manifestly clear from the history of the splitting off of the *saṅgha* into sects. In the Greek translation of one of the edicts of Aśoka, the original word *pāsaṇḍa* is translated as DIATRIBE.[4] *Pāsaṇḍa* was used both of heretics and imposters and the *Purāṇas* describe the Buddhists and the Jainas as such, whilst the latter used the same term to refer to schismatic groups in their own *saṅghas*. It has been further suggested that the ambiguity in the case of the Hindu sects is due to the absence of a centralized institution to control orthodoxy and although caste sanctions often performed this role it was nevertheless not clearly defined. The flexible nature of the Hindu canon also allowed constant and major interpolations which accommodated heresies as well. The assimilative character of Hinduism weakened the idea of false doctrine. Yet the notion of false doctrine was not absent and is apparent for instance in the dissensions of some of the schools of philosophy. In the post-Śaṅkara period it occurs more frequently in the literature. The heresy was often more apparent on the social plane, hence this attempt to view the question from a social perspective.

Asceticism has a historical continuity from the earliest times, although inevitably the role and nature of the ascetic groups has changed over the centuries. It is believed that the earliest representation of an ascetic practice comes from the supposed Paśupati seal of the Harappa culture.[5] A known incipient practice is perhaps that of temporary withdrawals from society during periods demanding a condition of ritual purity. Thus the *yajamāna* of the Vedic sacrifice opts out for the period of the sacrifice. This notion may be extended to a life-time in which ritual purity may result in generating extraordinary powers. Ascetic groups are referred to in Vedic literature, and some texts such as the *Upaniṣads* and the *Āraṇyakas* are largely concerned with asceticism. However a distinction should be drawn between the characteristics emphasised in the Ṛg Veda and other Vedic texts. The terms used most frequently in the former are *yati, muni* and *ṛṣi.*[6] The etymology of these words indicates magic, mystical rites, meditation and the ecstasy which comes with vision and inspiration. In short, the kind of activity which is more often associated with shamanism. The long-haired *muni*, the *keśin*, flying through the air[7] suggests a shamanising technique as also does the reference to magical heat (*tapas*).[8] The shamans would have to be distinguished from the sorcerers and the sorceresses (*yātu-matī*) said to inhabit the ruins of old cities.[9]

Shamanism is often associated with tribal societies surviving on subsistence economies. The attraction of shamanistic practices however continues even when the structure of tribal life undergoes substantial change. In the *Aitareya Brāhmaṇa* Indra is hostile to the *yatis* and on one occasion feeds them to the hyaenas, which possibly led to his being deprived of *soma.*[10] It has been plausibly argued that *soma* was a hallucinogen[11] and this would support the presence of shamanistic activities, incurring the wrath of the tribal deity. Although the shaman was never a renouncer, characteristics of shamanism can nevertheless be seen in the practices of many of the later groups of renouncers. The shaman stood somewhat apart from his tribe, yet was primarily concerned with the well-being (both physical and spiritual) of his tribe. The shaman's norms were a law unto himself, yet at the same time the shaman was dependent on the tribe. His distinctiveness was apparent both from outward symbols of dress and accessories as also by his behaviour. He derived his legitimacy from his claim to superior knowledge acquired through considerable effort involving the claim to magic, meditation and the inducement of visions with the aid of hallucinogens.

In the Later Vedic literature terms such as *tapasvin*, *śramaṇa*, *saṃnyāsin*, *parivrājaka*, *yogi*, occur more commonly. They are suggestive of renunciation, or casting aside one's social obligations, of the taking on of a life of austerity, of controlling the functions of the body (particularly breathing) and above all of wandering from place to place. The *parivrājaka* is sometimes described as a young man who, having finished his education, takes to a life of wandering for a brief period prior to becoming a householder.[12] But more often the *parivrājaka* was a permanent condition. Was this a nostalgia for the nomadic state[13] or was it a flouting of growing authoritarianism which disapproved of wanderers in a society increasingly given to stable agricultural settlements? The mystery surrounding the pre-eminent of wanderers, the *vrātyas*, remains largely unsolved. They appear to have been a group of shamans moving towards ascetic or yogic practices.[14] The *Saṃnyāsa* and *Yoga Upaniṣads* of a later period speak of yogic practices not merely in terms of magical powers (*siddhis*) but also the cultivation of meditation (*dhyāna*) and the control over breathing (*prāṇāyāma*), the ultimate aim of which was in part tied up with the search for immortality — a quest which was to take various forms in later centuries and which ran like a thread through the entire texture of ascetic practices. From visionaries and seers, the ascetic perspective moved to peripatetic teaching and the investigating of man and the universe through a variety of intensive techniques of mental concentration and control over the body.

The mid-first millennium BC sees a proliferation of sects in the Ganga valley.[15] Many of these were *parivrājakas* wandering in groups under the direction of a teacher or others loosely affiliated to sects, but preferring to wander by themselves, alone.[16] Their main function, apart from acquiring knowledge, was to participate in discussion and debate. They were such an established institution that some of the towns and larger villages associated them with *kutūhala-śālas*, literally places for exciting curiosity or interest, i.e., halls for discussion. Many such wanderers lived on the edges of towns and only those of a markedly ascetic disposition retired to places more isolated.[17] Some *brāhmaṇa* ascetics were sedentary, often living in hermitages, sometimes with their families,[18] although claiming to conform to celibacy all the same. These came to be called the Vaikhānasa and later texts mention names such as Saubhari who lived with his fifty wives in a hermitage.[19] *Brāhmaṇa* orthodoxy was averse to city-dwellers and restrictions were placed on *snātakas* visiting cities.[20] The wanderers were often the dissidents. The questioning of the orthodox tradition had started prior to this period, but what was new was the emergence of various sects such as the Nirgranthas, the Ājīvikas and later the Buddhists, not to mention various Cārvāka sects as well. The dissidence of these groups was however qualitatively different since they were not individual dissenters but had organized their dissent into sects whose identity was based on an opposition to the orthodox doctrines as expressed in the notion of the sanctity of the *Vedas*, the authority of the *brāhmaṇas*, *varṇāśrama-dharma* and the worship of the gods.[21] They were seen as a counter- influence on Āryan polytheism, particularly in their recognition of the rule of natural law in the universe. The theory of transmigration, which was the starting point for a number of these sects, may have been developed from older animist theories.

The proliferation of sects has been explained as due to the break-up of tribal society and its consequences.[22] The cushioning effect of kinship ties was declining with the impersonal relations of post-tribal society coming to the fore. The increasingly hierarchical ordering of society would in any case have been hostile to the wanderers. This was further reiterated by the growth of towns and cities during this period with the anonymity and alienation encouraged by urban institutions. Inevitably there was a search for methods of adjustment. It should also be remembered that the introduction of iron technology coupled with urbanization was more traumatic in terms of social change than any experienced earlier. The age of transcendence was not accidental.[23] At the same time it was precisely the economic margin of prosperity made possible by the new situation which allowed for the maintenance of such large groups of renouncers. Supportive evidence for this comes from the literature itself. The new sects of renouncers lived at the edges of towns, drew their recruits mainly from the towns and were dependent for alms on the householders. The Buddha for example spent more years at Rājagriha and Śrāvastī than anywhere else and the early and important monasteries were located at both these towns and at Kauśāmbi.[24] The earlier Jaina *tīrthaṅkara* Pārśvanātha is also associated with towns.[25] It was the towns which provided the renouncers with an audience and later with patronage.

Important towns were capitals of the *janapadas* and were thus either centres of royal patronage or of oligarchic support, depending on whether the state had a monarchical or a *gaṇa* form of government. The support took the tangible form of offerings and of donations of land for monasteries. Patronage at these social levels was equally effective even when indirect. Thus when Khema, a Madra princess and the queen of Bimbisāra accepted Buddhism, the fame of the Buddha spread to the distant land of the Madras.[26] When the Mallas were ordered by their assembly, the *santhāgāra*, to support the Buddha this greatly enhanced the cause of Buddhism in that *janapada*.[27] Both the Buddhists and the Jainas claim the patronage of the kings of Magadha. Apart from royal patronage there were ministers, bankers and merchants, the *seṭṭhis* and the rich *gahapatis*, who provided *vihāras* for the Buddhist monks.[28] The wealthy *mahāśālā brāhmaṇas* who had received land grants from the king, such as Lohicca and Pokkharasati, were influential persons.[29] In the early years of the Buddhist *saṅgha* the conversions which are singled out for mention were those of the richer *seṭṭhis* and the *brāhmaṇas*. The main body of monks was however drawn from the lower social orders such as artisans, fishermen, hunters, basket-weavers.[30] Similarly, the Mathura inscriptions of the pre-Gupta period indicate support for the Jainas from trading groups, artisans and castes low on the social scale.[31]

The Buddha had greater success among the cities of the monarchical kingdoms. The *kṣatriya* oligarchies were not so forthcoming in their support and some were more partial to the Nirgranthas. The general approval of the Buddhists and Jainas by urban groups was also linked with the ethical views of these sects. Rigorous and extreme ascetic practices although indulged in by some monks were on the whole discouraged. Nor were the earlier shamanistic elements regarded as fundamental. Resorting to the demonstration of *siddhis* was not unknown but in both cases it was permitted only on certain occasions and when persuasive means of conversion through logical argument failed.[32] Some of the symbols of earlier practices such as the sacred tree and the *stūpa* and *caitya* were appropriated into the religious cults. But the emphasis was on knowledge and meditation and the observance of the middle-path (*majjhimā paṭipadā*), eminently suitable for urban householders. Furthermore, both the Buddhists and the Jainas had a distinct role for the lay community *vis-à-vis* the monks, and in the case of the former the interaction between the *upāsaka* and the *bhikkhu* was an important aspect of monastic functioning. This was partly a reflection of the doctrine of salvation common to a number of heterodox sects where the concern for the lay community is summed up best in the attitude of the Buddha when he uses the parable of the raft, that those who have discovered enlightenment should not keep it to themselves but should leave the raft for the use of others.[33] The social involvement of groups such as the Ājīvikas, Jainas and Buddhists contributed to the manner in which the *saṅgha* developed in each case. Whatever may have been the primary function of the *saṅgha* as a gathering of persons seeking release from rebirth and which continued to dominate the more sectarian angularities within the institution, it very soon also became the main channel through which the sect communicated with the rest of society.

The history of these sects of renouncers moving into new areas follows a similar pattern. It begins with a handful of monks living singly or in small groups in relative isolation in cave sanctuaries (*leṇas*), as for example the hermitages in the vicinity of Rājagriha or the habitations dotted in the hills of the Tamil country. The isolation was not total since the caves tended to be on major trade routes or in the vicinity of towns. In more arduous terrain these proto-monasteries often provided welcome staging points as did the later monasteries. This is particularly true of hilly country and mountains such as the routes from the plateau to the coast through the Western Ghats or those across Ladakh and Nepal into Tibet. Monastic establishments thrived near urban centres and in rich agricultural regions where there was a surplus to support the monks. It is not altogether accidental that the initial penetration of the heterodox sects into south India coincides with the Roman trade and the trade with south-east Asia. The expansion of the Mahāsaṅghika sect going from Vaiśālī and Pāṭaliputra south to Andhra carefully avoided the tribal belt south of Magadha. Similarly the Sarvāstivāda spread from Mathura northwards to the Punjab and Kashmir but not into the adjoining areas of Rajasthan where there were well-established tribal areas. Apart from the need for a surplus to support the monks, the ethical teaching of these sects was doubtless more appropriate to richer agriculturalists and urbanites rather than to pastoral and hunting tribal people. The worship of tribal deities and the tribal ethic would hardly be conducive to the acceptance of Buddhism.

Gradually commercial patronage and royal support led to the establishment of a full-fledged *saṅgha* with all its physical edifices and accessories. For the mercantile community the Buddhist and Jaina teaching provided the required ethic.[34] Inscriptional evidence witnesses endowments to the *saṅghas* in every region in the first millennium AD. The endowments included land, revenue from villages, shops and residences for the monks.[35] There was a noticeable increase in the number of monks and monasteries. So rich and important were some of these centres that the sects came to be named after the place-names of their residence, thus, the Sandeva *gaccha*, and the Kāñci *gaccha* of the Jainas. Royal patrons were well-disposed to the *saṅgha* since they acted as an instrument of acculturation in the new areas, both introducing the Great Tradition as well as assimilating and focusing on the local culture. But royal patronage was also at the root of the destruction of the social involvement of the *saṅgha* as originally perceived. Lavish endowments of land to the monasteries resulted in a greater secularisation of the *saṅgha*. There was a consequent decline in its concern with providing salvation for the lay community and an increase in its concern for acquiring and maintaining authority.

Individual renouncers and those who joined the 'heretical sects' were in the early stages the chief dissenters. Megasthenes' description of the Brachmanes and the Sarmanes living in the forest across the Taprobane is indicative of this.[36] Through a process of historical change many of these dissenting groups in time took on the role of the establishment. The brahmanical theory of the four *āśramas*, first propounded in full in the late *Jabāla Upaniṣad*, brought asceticism into conventional custom by making it the last stage of a man's curriculum and accessible to the upper castes. By implication however the *gṛhastha-āśrama* was a necessary prior requirement. Thus only those who moved directly from *brahmacarya* to *saṃnyāsa* could be called dissenters. An aging *gṛhastha* taking to *saṃnyāsa* was merely conforming to the ideal vita. The heretical *saṅghas* also took on shades of conformism through the acquisition of wealth and power and by association with the ruling elite. At this stage it was necessary for the orthodoxy to consolidate its views on the renouncers and for new groups of renouncers to emerge as the carriers of heresy.

The new groups were to some extent dissidents from among the renouncers. Both the Buddhist and Jaina sects came under the influence of and incorporated Tantric ideas and practices. Vajrayāna Buddhism with an early nucleus at the Vikramaśīla monastery in

Bihar was a reflection of this. It also represented the minor but consistent trend among some Buddhist monks of dabbling in magic and necromancy.[37] The still later Sahajiyā cult among the Buddhists was a protest against the formalities of the life and religion of earlier Buddhism. It questioned the earlier theories of knowledge and emphasized the practice of *yoga*. It was opposed not only to scholarship but also to monasticism,[38] thereby underlining what it regarded as the social irrelevance of monasticism. Up to a point, the Sahajiyā cult can be seen as a return to the twilight area of the shaman.

After the mid-first millennium AD when the sects associated with the heterodox religions were on the wane in northern India, there appears to have occurred the spectacular rise of Śaiva monasticism especially in the peninsula. Considering that Śiva is projected as the great ascetic, this is not surprising. Hsüan Tsang refers to various groups associated with 'daiva temples' in the vicinity of towns.[39] These sects and particularly the Kapālikas and Pāśupatas are referred to in earlier literature but are more commonly mentioned in sources from about the seventh century onwards.[40] Clearly there was a gestation period for these monastic orders. From the *Pāśupata Sūtras*, the existence of the Pāśupatas has been dated to at least the second century AD.[41] The *Purāṇas* regard such groups with contempt.[42] They are mentioned in the inscriptions of the Jainas of the Karnataka with whom there was a sustained relationship of rivalry.[43] The Digambara Jainas were by now concentrated in the Karnataka, well-esconced in the patronage of traders, merchants and officers of the state.[44] The Kapālikas had their own patrons who endowed them with land and villages. The sect had a strong likeness to many of the activities and practices of the Tantrics and as such came in for scathing attacks from some of the established social groups. Among the more fierce of its opponents was Śaṅkarācārya who accused the Kapālikas of sexual licence and alcoholism. Another influential Śaiva group in the peninsula was that of the Kālāmukhas, sometimes included in the wider category of Pāśupatas. This sect was more sympathetically treated by the orthodox *brāhmaṇas* since it did not question their superiority and, if anything, on occasion subscribed to it. Hsüan Tsang does not refer to distinctively separate monastic organizations associated with these sects although the inscriptions of the subsequent period emphasize this. Possibly this aspect developed after the seventh century AD when the survival and effectiveness of dissenting groups once again required the organization of monastic centres, particularly in relation to the competition for patronage and support where some sects with monastic organization were seen to be successful.

By about the ninth century AD there had emerged a distinctive group of Śaiva renouncers, the Daśanāmi Saṃnyāsis. The sect modelled itself on earlier monastic orders with approximately the same broad rules of discipline — permanent residence in monasteries, austerity, celibacy, subsistence on alms and the study and teaching of prescribed texts. The monasteries (*maṭhas*) were attached to temples and these and other properties endowed to the order were administered by the chief of the *maṭha*, the *mahant*.[45] Śaṅkarācārya further organised the Daśanāmi Saṃnyāsis into categories and hierarchies thus simulating the monastic form of earlier sects.[46] The Śaiva *maṭhas* seem to have played the same role as Buddhist and Jaina monasteries, as instruments of acculturation in new areas, since their early distribution was substantially in the peninsula and on the fringes of the heartland in northern India (e.g. Kashmir, Nepal). Saṅkarācārya's imprint is apparent in as much as the sect took upon itself the defence of the orthodoxy, suggesting perhaps that the earlier heterodoxy had become too influential. The Śaivite tradition appears to have been the indigenous tradition in these areas and Śaiva monasticism grew rapidly. The Daśanāmi sect was organized for deliberate proselytizing, its main competitors being the Buddhists and the Jainas with whom the rivalry was to become acrimonious, and at times violent.[47] Apart from the ideological motives, ambition for power and economic control played its part. It has been plausibly suggested that these monasteries in some ways approximated to feudal authority.[48]

Vaiṣṇavism at this stage did not encourage monasticism. It has been argued that Vaiṣṇavism subsumed *yoga* into the *bhakti* tradition when the *Gītā* speaks of *yoga* as the highest way and the true *yogi* as being one who does not detach himself from society but takes on the suffering of others.[49] Since it is in a sense a salvation religion it did not require the agency of renouncers. The process of *bhakti* in itself offers an alternative to both ritual and asceticism.[50] It may also be suggested that proselytization through monastic groups was not required of Vaiṣṇavism since the theory of *avatāras* acts as an agency of incorporation. Nevertheless, by about the eleventh and twelfth centuries, the Vairāgin or, as it was popularly called, the Bairāgi movement, initiated Vaiṣṇava monastic orders. From the thirteenth century onwards there were violent conflicts between the Saṃnyāsis and the Bairāgis in the competition for status and power.[51]

It was also at about this time that groups of renouncers calling themselves Yogis and propagating the teaching of Gorakhanātha and the Nāthapanthis spread across northern India. The Yogis reflected the growing influence of Tantricism and in their view it was a combination of Haṭhayoga and Tantric practices which were likely to lead to knowledge and fulfilment. The association of Tantricism with Yoga was probably an undercurrent of one strand in the ethos of renouncers since earliest times. Tantricism has to be viewed not as yet another sectarian movement but as a major religious re-orientation, since the fundamentals of Tantricism pervaded the dominant religious forms at many levels. Not only were there Kapālikas among Śaivas and the Rādhā-Kṛṣṇa cult among Vaiṣṇavas, but even the originally more puritanical religious groups, the Buddhists and Jainas, underwent a Tantric phase. Vajrayāna Buddhism acted almost as the harbinger of the arrival of Tantric cults and ideas into the ranks of both established society and the heterodoxy.[52] The Tantric-Yogic combination was predominant in the relatively less Hinduized border regions — the northwest of the subcontinent and Assam, and this may explain it as being a channel by which foreign elements were assimilated into Hinduism coming into importance as it did in the period of such incursions.[53] It may also be said to reflect the rise of the substratum culture coinciding with the social elevation of relatively obscure families and castes in the new areas brought into the political and economic vortex of the Great Tradition via the system of land grants.[54] The *siddhācāryas* of this cult are more frequently of low caste.[55] The substratum culture was opposed to the orthodox tradition, an opposition which came to be symbolically expressed in Tantric ritual, much of which is a reversal of *brāhmaṇa* values.[56]

This all too brief survey indicates that the appearance of renouncers as an organized section of society occurs historically at periods of change when there emerge within society not only religious but socio-economic sanctions to maintain such groups, as for example the growth of urban centres and the expansion of the agrarian economy. The religious impetus may come from the need to institutionalize a way of life that is new (the Ājīvika, Jaina and Buddhist *saṅghas*) or as a strategy for proselytizing (the Daśanāmi Saṃnyāsis and the Bairāgis) or as a means of crystallizing a popular religious ethos and providing it with status (the Tantric sects and the Yogis). Not all such sects were opposed to orthodoxy, but the technique of using social heresy was employed to organize a religious identity, and the sects therefore registered various degrees and stages of non-conformity. The Buddhist, Jaina and Ājīvika monks were opposed to brahmanical orthodoxy but the expression of their dissidence took on a puritanical form, in which certain social mores were ultimately strengthened but the manifestations of brahmanical religion were discarded. The groups influenced by Tantricism accepted some of the religious symbols but discarded many of the social mores. The Daśanāmi Saṃnyāsis supported brahmanical orthodoxy but did not conform to the brahmanical view of *saṃnyāsa* in the setting up of monastic centres.

The historical pattern therefore carries within it a range of divergencies. The ideals of brahmanical *saṃnyāsa* are opposed by the renouncers of various persuasions, such as the Ājīvikas, Jainas and Buddhists, who organize themselves into monastic units and who are characterized by an ethic of moderation in action. The notion of monastic organization is then taken up by other groups when it becomes socially necessary for purposes of recognition and support. Some such as the Daśanāmi orders are created to counteract the growth of other religious sects and to propagate orthodoxy. Others such as the Pāśupata and Kapālika sects retain an extreme stance abhorrent to orthodoxy. It has been suggested that the Pāśupatas were shamans *manqués* with their vows of beast-imitation and sexual practices,[57] a suggestion which has interesting possibilities *vis-à-vis* the tradition of later Tantric cults as well. The Vaiṣṇava monastic orders eventually take on the role of competing with the Daśanāmis. The influence of Tantric beliefs and practices extends to all the religious groups and initially it acts as a dissenting line of thought and action. Eventually, groups such as the Sahajiyās produce their own opposition to the Tantrics.

Cutting across the chronological scheme is the lineal descent of certain trends. The *brāhmaṇa saṃnyāsin* remains largely unchanged, playing a role of social conformism but with a potential of protest should he have wished to use it. The renouncer, associated with an ethic of moderation remains primarily within the order of the Buddhists and the Jainas, which however develop their own orthodoxy and become increasingly less linked with dissent. The more shamanistic groups tend to be those opposed to all forms of orthodoxy and consequently carry an immediate potential of protest. Furthermore, the institution of the monastery acts as a curtailment on dissent. There seem to be two phases in the evolution of such groups: the pre-monastic, where the element of protest is stronger, and the monastic, when concessions have been made to conformity.

To the extent that historical change led to the emergence of these sects, the sect itself underwent transformation reflecting historical change. The holding of Councils, characteristic of Buddhism and Jainism, indicates new regional and social demands and schismatic tendencies pointing to a groping towards adjustment in an effort to stabilize. Most of the issues under debate at these Councils related to the rules of behaviour and the organization of the monastery — food and the acceptance of money offerings for example. Where the nuances of interpreting the doctrine were at issue the problem could often be traced back to a social cause. The rules of almost every sect underwent change with the gradual accretion of rituals, the introduction of new forms of worship, the deification of the founders and, above all, the encroachment of the lay and monastic communities on each other. It is these 'inner contradictions', as it were, of orthodoxy and heresy and schism which develop within each sect and which preclude the historian from describing them as either orthodox or heretical in every situation and for all time.

For our purposes, the most important aspect of the social role of the renouncer is the relationship between the renouncer and the lay community. The initial relationship is perhaps best seen in the bi-polarity between the *brāhmaṇa* and the *saṃnyāsin*.[58] Hinduism, it has been said, is a dialogue between these two, where the *brāhmaṇa* represents the religion of the group, assimilative and well-established, whereas the *saṃnyāsin* represents the liberation of the individual, exclusive and separated from society. This bi-polarity is apparent in much of the symbolism which distinguishes the renouncer from conventional society. The brahmanical ideal of the ascetic was based on a denial of any form of reciprocity between the *saṃnyāsin* and society, thus negating a major focus in Hindu social action, namely reciprocity.[59] But the ideal was rarely observed and more often than not the relationship between the *saṃnyāsin* and *gṛhastha* came to the fore. This was certainly historically the richer and more complex relationship where the bi-polarity of the two takes on a dialectical interconnection. The outward symbols by which the renouncer was recognized were often anathema to brahmanical orthodoxy, but the root of the contradiction of *saṃnyāsa* as a social phenomenon lay in the negation of the social function of *gṛhastha* by the *saṃnyāsin*. The two are polar opposites and yet dependent on each other. The lay community provides material support for the renouncer through *dāna* (gifts and offerings) and alms, and in turn the merit, *puṇya*, accumulated by the renouncer is in part transferred to the lay community. In each case the relationship is initially sharply differentiated and the difference is expressed in the adoption of totally opposite symbols. Gradually the differentiation becomes blurred and, although the symbols may continue, the relationship begins to overlap.

The bi-polarity is made very evident by the totally contradictory rules of discipline as applied to the householder and the renouncer. There is first of all an initiation ceremony at the time of entering *saṃnyāsa*[60] which indicates the renouncing of one's social obligations and ties and opting out of the society into which one was born. Where the entry is according to the ultimate *āśrama*, the *saṁskāra* becomes a life-cycle rite. The concession to *saṃnyāsa* as the ultimate *āśrama* was perhaps to prevent renunciation among young men. To that degree it would also have acted as a check on active dissenters. That *saṃnyāsa* in one's old age, when one's obligations to society had been fulfilled, was gaining the best of both worlds, is reflected in some texts in the debate on the legitimacy of such *saṃnyāsa*, since in old age celibacy and the giving up of property is not too difficult. The true *saṃnyāsin* should avoid the state of *gṛhastha*. The ceremony of the Hindu *saṃnyāsin*, at whatever age he entered *saṃnyāsa*, symbolized his death to society and the acceptance of a life ultimately attached to loneliness and complete self-reliance. He was required therefore to quench the sacrificial fires and perform his own *śrāddha* ceremony. For the *saṃnyāsin* entering an order this was ameliorated as it was in the case of a *bhikkhu* where one life-style, that of the householder, was substituted by that of the community of monks, where the refuge of society was replaced by the refuge of the order and the monastery. The trauma of the change softened by the creation of a new tie, that between the novice and the *ācārya* or *guru*, since in all cases the renouncer had to begin his renunciation under the tutelage of a teacher. The Buddha emphasized that this relationship should be as one between a father and son.

The *gṛhastha* enters his *āśrama* with the reverse values, where he is being introduced to his social obligations and attachment to a family. The procreation of his own family becomes essential to this condition, whereas the renouncer has to remain celibate. Celibacy was a necessary condition to all sects of renouncers although in some of the more extreme Tantric acts ritualized sex was required.[61] The householder concerns himself with the acquisition of material possessions and property for the welfare of the family whereas the renouncer forswears any claims to property or possessions other than a few symbols of his new status.[62] The insistence on the renouncer being a wanderer (a rule which was observed until the sect became prosperous and powerful) was mainly to prevent the development of any attachment, either with the lay community or with fellow monks and *saṃnyāsis*.[63] It also encouraged the notion of individual salvation. The concept of *ahiṃsā* in daily routine was easier in the observance for the renouncer,[64] a case in point being the precautions taken by Jaina monks to clear the ground from living beings before stepping on it and wearing cloth masks to prevent the breathing in of insects. The renouncer was forbidden any kind of profession or occupation and, more particularly, manual labour. This again sharpened the difference between him and the householder. The former was expected to spend his time in study, meditation and the purification of the mind and the body by the practice of *prāṇāyāma* and *yoga*,[65] all of which were, from the material point of view, counter-productive.

Further distinctions were made in the breaking of food tabus. The monks and the *saṃnyāsin* were forbidden from doing their own cooking and could receive only cooked food as alms.[66] This was a contradiction of the *brāhmaṇa* otherwise being permitted to accept only uncooked food from non-*brāhmaṇas* and cooked food only from those of the appropriate caste. The *brāhmaṇa saṃnyāsin*, in one text, is told to avoid food from *śūdra* houses[67] but there was no prohibition on this. Some *brāhmaṇa* ascetic groups however did observe the normal restrictions by living in isolation in forests and surviving on fruit and roots, thus eschewing altogether the acceptance of alms.

But this was possible only to those who lived alone or in small groups, such as the ascetics mentioned by Megasthenes.[68] It is interesting that historical references to such groups become more limited in later periods when monastic orders develop. The Jainas had elaborate rules regarding the acceptability of food even within the limitations of living off alms.[69] Further, the fact that food was eaten together in an assembly (irrespective of whether it was collected through alms or cooked for the monastery as in later times), also undermined the rules of caste commensality. Dietary rules differed among the sects. Generally, animal food and alcohol were forbidden. Some groups deliberately contravened this and the Kānphaṭā Jogis ate meat, drank alcohol and indulged in narcotics. The Aghoris made a fetish of this principle by feeding on human corpses. The eating of meat and fish and the drinking of alcohol were ritualistically prescribed in some of the Tantric sects.

Visual appearance underlined the separation between the householder and the renouncer and was symbolic of the new life-style of the latter. The renouncer was either naked or else wore clothing of a distinctive colour — red, ochre or white — or of a distinctive kind, as for example, unstitched robes. The head was either tonsured or else the hair was unkempt (*jaṭā*). The latter signified a condition of power through danger in as much as hair signified virility and aggression.[70] The Buddhists and the Jainas on the other hand made a ritual out of depilation, perhaps initially to demarcate themselves from *brāhmaṇa jaṭila saṃnyāsins*. Most *saṃnyāsins* carried an alms-bowl and a staff and some identified their sect with a tilak. The *daṇḍa* or staff was so characteristic that the early ascetics were called *maskarin*, i.e. those of the bamboo staff, *maskara*. The later word *daṇḍa* might also have been associated with the extension of the meaning of *daṇḍa*, authority. Living in a monastery again demarcated the habitational area of the renouncer from that of the lay community. The final and most symbolic of the oppositions was that the ascetic among Hindu sects was to be buried in a sitting posture and his *samādhī* came to be regarded as a sacred enclosure, an object of veneration. The householder was cremated in a common cremation ground which has always been a place of great impurity, fit only to be maintained by the *caṇḍālas*. In some cases, the adoption of certain symbols was not merely the breaking of social tabus but also the deliberate cultivation of the horrendous — association with dirt, excreta and corpses — in order to highlight the disassociation with 'normal' society. The courting of dishonour was on occasion deliberately designed to shock the public and attract attention. In the case of the Pāśupatas the justification for this has its own interest.[71] By simulating an anti-social action the Pāśupata was believed to acquire the merit of the observer who unnecessarily reviles him and the bad *karma* of the Pāśupata is transferred to the observer.

The adoption of outward symbols has its own contrapuntal pattern. The *brāhmaṇa* ascetics who kept matted locks, ate uncooked food such as fruit and roots in the forest or accepted alms and ate in the evening, lived beneath trees and emaciated their bodies were directly contradicting the mores of the Buddhist and Jaina *bhikkhus* who demanded depilation, ate only cooked food in the forenoon, and lived in *vihāras*, many among them keeping away from extreme physical austerities. It is only in the acceptance of religious suicide as the ideal manner of dying, and which was abhorrent to the orthodox, that there was agreement, although the particular form in which the suicide was to be achieved differed.

Inherent in the need for this differentiation is not merely the opting out of the existing life-style and substituting it with a distinctively different one but also that the characteristics of the new life-style be seen as a protest against the existing one. To this extent such movements may be regarded as movements of dissent.[72] But the element of protest was muted by the wish, not to change society radically, but to stand aside and create an alternative system. Ideally, liberation lay in joining a sect of renouncers. Some sects such as the Ājīvikas made this conditional. Others conceded that this was not open to everyone and a via media was suggested, as for example the *upāsaka* or periodic renunciation as among the Buddhists. Ultimately, when the renouncers were themselves viewed as having fallen short of the ideal, they were denounced. This could result in the emergence of schismatic groups. Initially, it was dissent which led to a splitting off from society or an established sect and the renouncers formed elements of a counter-culture. Eventually, many became dependent on society. The splitting off was often led by those who, disgruntled with the order/sect, took a lone path in their search for salvation. Nevertheless the sects of renouncers did create a climate of opinion in which the legitimacy of dissidence was conceded. It is a moot point as to whether such sects can be called protest movements *per se* or whether they are manifestations of a sustained counter-culture which, from time to time, reacts to social pressures and throws up movements which carry, among other things, traces of social protest. The ultimate in dissidence was still the *parivrājaka* who did not join any order and wandered alone, or for that matter even the isolated *saṃnyāsin*.

One aspect of the dissidence was that, in theory at least, most sects of renouncers disregarded caste observances. There was a debate on whether the two symbols of brahmanhood, the top-knot (*śikhā*) and the sacred thread (*yajñopavīta*), should be retained by *brāhmaṇa saṃnyāsins*;[73] as also the controversy on whether *śūdras* should be recruited as a separate sect, as in some of the later *saṃnyāsin akhārās*.[74] In the main, the *Dharmasūtras*, the Epics and the *Purāṇas* are averse to the idea of *śūdra* ascetics[75] indicating that renunciation was open only to *brāhmaṇas*. Among the Ājīvikas, Buddhists and Jainas, the sect was open to any caste. The physical proximity of all castes in a congregation was also a contradiction of certain caste restrictions. Among some Tantric sects there were no caste identities since all males were considered as forming one caste and all females another.[76] The Sahajiyā cult was unambiguous in its attack on the status of the *brāhmaṇa* and caste society in general.[77] Nor was it only a protest against caste. The preaching of universal values with universal application and the notion of transcendence in the theories of knowledge of such sects was itself a denial of the dominant social values and was implicitly a questioning of the religious beliefs and groups whose identity focused on caste affiliations.

However, religious universalism was also sometimes used for what appears to be a form of social manipulation. The Kālāmukha Saṃnyāsins, for example, claimed *brāhmaṇa* status and took the name ending of *paṇḍita-deva*, and were often the defenders of *varṇāśramadharma*.[78] One may wonder whether the sect was not used by some non-*brāhmaṇas* to acquire individual *brāhmaṇa* status, since one of the signs of brahmanhood — Vedic and Sanskrit learning — was available to and encouraged among the members of the sect. In this connection it is interesting that the priests of the Yogi caste in Bengal associated with the Nātha cult have been referred to as *rudraja brāhmaṇas*, deriving their origin from Rudra and eventually claiming to belong to a 'Śiva' *gotra*.[79] This would be a case of using the alternative system to acquire status.

The break with society and the anonymity of the new entrant were sought to be established by the taking of a new name. The latter indicated the new identity in terms of the monastery (thus Mahānāma points to a connection with the Mahāvihāra), or the sect (Digvijayanātha indicates a Nāthapanthi), or the desire for the attainment of *mokṣa* (as in the use of *ānanda* as part of the name) or to the degree of attainment (as reflected in titles such as *avadhūta* or *paramahaṅsa*). Each of the *maṭhas* established by Śaṅkarācārya was said to have been associated with a *gotra*[80] (as for example, the *kāśyapagotra* with the Govardhana *maṭha* at Puri) and the members of the *maṭha* would take on its *gotra*, thus subscribing to a form of Sanskritisation.

The negation of the family as a basic unit of society is evident from the opposition to the *gṛhastha* status and especially the insistence on celibacy. This can also be seen as perhaps an avoidance rather than an infringement of the fundamental rule of caste organization, namely, the prohibition on inter-caste marriage. Women, whether as nuns in the Buddhist and Jaina orders or as *parivrājikās*, were on the whole grudgingly accepted. Nuns were always under the jurisdiction of the monks and in both orders were regarded as an inferior category.[81] This was in spite of the fact that occasionally women of the royal families became nuns, although the majority were from less exalted social groups.

The effectiveness of an alternative life-style could not remain an arbitrary process beyond a certain historical point. The *parivrājakas* and *śramaṇas* of the *Upaniṣads* had, for a variety of reasons, to identify themselves as groups rather than move about as individual wanderers. The authoritarian trends in the states emerging in the mid-first millennium BC were not always sympathetic to wanderers.[82] They were often seen as people escaping social responsibility or socio-political demands. Their survival as free thinkers was dependent on their being able to assert the right to an alternative life from a position of institutional security. Only then could they obtain the political rights of passage so essential to their existence. Furthermore, their continuity in an egalitarian parallel system could only be safeguarded if their leaders could confront political authority as powerful heads of sects. The social ineffectiveness of the actions of individuals was demonstrated by the effectiveness of the group. Among the early efforts at assembling groups around specific doctrines were, as we have seen, the sects of the Cārvākas and Ājīvikas.[83] But in order to be effective a name was not enough, a physical habitation was also necessary. This contributed to the evolution of the monastery.

The monastic institution grew out of a need for a permanent residence during the rainy season when mendicancy was difficult. Such seasonal residences (*āvāra*) gradually acquired a longer duration in the *ārāma*, often a park endowed by an individual to the *saṅgha*, such as the Aṁbavana of Jīvaka at Rājagriha. Ultimately, the settlement of monks expanded into a *vihāra*, a regular monastic complex. In the organization of such a monastery the features of the parallel society are apparent. There is an attempt at imitating the structure of the tribal and oligarchic systems. The hierarchy of units in the Jaina *saṅgha* uses a terminology which is reminiscent of the lineage structure of the earlier tribes — *gaṇa*, *kula*, *śākhā*, *anvaya* and *gaccha*. In the Buddhist *saṅgha*, the general assembly of monks was the sovereign authority and even the *saṅghathera* had to abide by its decision.[84] The emphasis on frequent assemblies and unanimous decisions is stressed in the early literature. Every ordained monk was a member of the *saṅgha* and all monks living within the jurisdiction of a particular monastery had to be present at the *uposatha* assembly. Ownership of property vested with the *saṅgha* and never with the individual monk. (In later centuries, however, the shares of the monks in the monastic property led to some of them acquiring a substantial personal wealth.)[85] Grievances against individual monks were discussed at the assembly as also any breach of monastic regulations or the rules of the sect.[86] The ritual of initiation into the *saṅgha* was similar to that of adoption into the tribe, adoption being the only means of entry into both.[87] Underlying the structure of the monastery was the emphasis on conjoint action and discipline and the strict enforcement of monastic regulations. The monastery was not the place for those seeking absolute freedom, for whom asceticism in isolation was preferable. The monastery provided an alternative only to those who opted out of social obligations.

The functioning of the *saṅgha* has been described as an attempt to retrieve the fast vanishing past.[88] It may be argued that the form adopted was also in deliberate opposition to the monarchical system and its centralized power, which system is otherwise seen as ideal for society and to which the lay community is required to give its loyalty.[89] This again serves to underline the distinction between the lay community and the monastic group, where the latter takes on the nuances of a primitive commune, perhaps echoing the utopian egalitarianism of pristine society.[90] Or did the *saṅghas* in newly monarchical societies act as 'safety valves' for the containment of political dissidence, taking on the role of egalitarian sanctuaries?

The relative absence of hierarchy in the monastic structure was however not a permanent feature. The goods and services of monastic living required that some monks be designated the distributors of food (*bhata-uddesaka*), accommodation and furniture (*senāsanagāhāpaka*), robes (*cīvarapaṭiggāhaka*)[91] etc.; with donations and endowments, administrative infrastructures became necessary. The revenue from endowed lands had to be collected, the interest from donations to be recorded.[92] Annual dues had to be shared out among the monks who were resident in wealthy monasteries and the profits from endowed lands distributed after meeting the annual expenses. Repairs to old buildings and the construction of new buildings had to be supervised by those monks appointed as *ārāmapesakas*.[93] Administrative responsibilities not only cut into the normal functions of a monk but also required an administrative hierarchy within the monastery. This increased its participation in the local economic life. The monastic calendar increasingly coincided with the agricultural calendar.[94] Ultimately, the monastery was legitimized as a socio-economic institution through the myths explaining its origin, through the establishment of the Vinaya Laws which became the legal code of monastic groups and through the acquiring of an historical identity.[95]

The establishment of the Śaiva monasteries was not a dissimilar process. Śaṅkarācārya is said to have organized *saṃnyāsi* groups on a functional basis by the arrangement of ten orders among the *saṃnyāsins*[96] and by setting up four major monastic nucleii, the four *maṭhas* at Dvārkā, Badrī, Purī and Sṛngerī, with clearly demarcated territorial jurisdiction. Distinctions of sectarian loyalty within the Daśanāmi Saṃnyāsis were evident from the accessories which they carried such as the design of the staff, the type of *rudrākṣa-mālā* and the *tilak*. Contact within the monastic network throughout the country was maintained by *saṃnyāsins* of the same sect going on regular pilgrimages and visiting other *maṭhas* in different parts of the country. The regular assemblies of Śaiva ascetics at the time of festivals in the major pilgrim centres was another means of intermonastic communication and administration. The proliferation of land grants in the early medieval period accelerated the prosperity of many *maṭhas* as did the donations to the temples attached to these *maṭhas*, converting them into semi-administrative units with a tangible economic viability in agriculture and trade. This prosperity was enhanced by the fact that *saṃnyāsins* and their institutions were free from any taxes,[97] which was a boon in the period after the eighth century AD, when taxes tended to multiply.

Even more far removed from the ascetic ideal was the organization of the *akhārās*, or military wings of the *maṭhas*. The earliest of these, believed to go back to the ninth or tenth century AD, were of the Daśanāmi Nāgas. They were maintained by wealthy *maṭhas* almost as a regiment of mercenary soldiers. Some sources maintain that the *akhārās* were manned by *śūdra* recruits.[98] The emphasis was on physical prowess and skilful weaponry, which were used to full effect in later periods in the battles with the Bairāgis.[99] The para-military basis of the *akhārās* is clear from the fact that they were arranged in a hierarchy of importance, the protocol of which was strictly observed at festivals and *melās* when they assembled. Each *akhārā* had its own banner and insignia of identification. The financial maintenance of the *akhārā* came from the lands and buildings owned by the *maṭha*, the offerings and donations made at the temple, a variety of religious levies and participation by the *maṭha* in local banking and commercial activities.

In the eyes of the lay community, the acquisition of an historical identity was crucial to the transformation of the sect and the monastery into a social institution and to the bestowal of a legitimacy reaching into the past. The historical tradition was put together in various ways. A list of succession of the Elders of the monastery was preserved where each dissident monastic sect would mark its break by maintaining a variant list. Thus the Theravāda and Sarvāstivāda lists vary as can be seen in their respective literatures.[100] Similarly there is mention of the succession in the Kālāmukha *maṭha* attached to the Kedāreśvara temple at Belegave.[101] The lists of succession of the nine Nāthas vary from region to region.[102] Founders of sects and important personalities associated with their growth became the subjects of sections of the *Ācārangasūtra* and *Kalpasūtra* on Mahāvīra, or of Ānandagirī's *Śaṅkaravijaya*. Sometimes the history of an event was sought to be established by associating a known personality, preferably a king, with the event: thus Ajātaśatru features in Buddhist and Jaina literature and Aśoka in Buddhist literature.[103] Even more effective was the attempt to compile the history of a particular monastery and relate it to the state, such as the Mahāvihāra monastery in the *Mahāvaṃsa*. The history of the sect itself could result in a substantial inclusion of the history of the region such as the *Dīpavaṃsa* in Śri Laṇka or Tāranātha's *History of Buddhism in India*. At a more local level, the histories of regions or areas, such as the *Śrimāla Mahātmya* of the Jainas, were collections of information, factual and fanciful, on places of sectarian importance, associating the place with the sect. Such records claiming to be historically valid were also necessary to prove the legitimacy of the institution in disputes over property and juridical rights. With the development of missionary activities, these historical antecedents could be used in the balance of power with secular institutions.

The evolution of the monastic institution (irrespective of the religious sect to which it belonged) into a form where it participated to a substantial degree in secular life was in a sense self-annihilating. This participation, especially in economic life, tended to erode the notion of a counter-culture and strengthen that of a parallel society. In the early stages, the reach of the *vihāra* or the *maṭha* into secular economic life was limited and was related at a simple level to redistribution and reciprocity. Redistribution was enforced by the lay community having to maintain the renouncer on alms and by the making of donations and endowments. For the ordinary householder, the feeding of monks was sufficient. For the rich householder, there was the providing of oil and clothing, the repairing and building of monasteries and, for even wealthier patrons, the endowment of land. Reciprocation lay in the tying of *dāna* to *puṇya*, where, in exchange for alms and donations, the householder acquired merit. But when the *dāna* was of a nature that enabled the monastery to lead its own independent existence, the distance from the lay community increased, the reciprocation of *puṇya* became reduced and the character and the role of the monastery underwent a change. This in turn undermined notions of social protest.[104] This was further intensified in situations where the monastery played a major role in the urban or rural economy.[105]

The reciprocal relationship between the lay community and the *saṅgha/maṭha* was pivotal to the making of a parallel society and can be seen at various levels. Royal patronage was the source of reciprocity at the political level. Patronage was of two varieties: there was the direct endowment of caves, monasteries, residences, the revenue from villages and lands to the sects;[106] and there was the indirect support derived from royal investment in commerce and manufacturing guilds, the interest from which was donated to monastic needs.[107] Thus the nexus of royal patronage and the sect was woven into the rural and urban economy. The monasteries in such situations provided a variety of services. Each sectarian group maintained a network of links and control over a large geographical area and thereby helped to build a political base as well. If the sect was politically loyal to the king the monasteries which they controlled would act as focal points in the diffusion of this loyalty, thus providing a further support for the administration. The interplay between the sect and political authority is reflected in those situations where rules of discipline relating to the former may be modified to placate the latter. This it would seem was the main reason for the Buddha prohibiting the recruitment to the monastery of officers in royal service (*rājabhaṭas*), slaves and offenders against the law.[108] The monasteries had access to a large local base in the lay community and could be mobilised to provide a focus for public opinion and possibly even provide political legitimacy to the king. One of the channels for exercising public opinion was through the educational function performed by the *saṅgha* and the *maṭha*. The orientation of the religious institution would inevitably become at least a part of the subconscious of the lay community. This was further strengthened with the emergence of these institutions as the centres of artistic and intellectual life in the community.

For the more powerful and richly endowed monasteries, a political role became a necessity.[109] The relative independence of the monastic institution was a threat to political authority. At the individual level, monks and *gurus* were influential and many functioned as advisers through the office of the *rājagurus* to kings and administrators.[110] Not all the incumbents of this office were *brāhmaṇas*. Some of the Kālāmukha monks were preceptors to kings. Theoretically, Jaina monks were supposed to preserve political neutrality by refraining from friendship with kings, royal officers and administrators.[111] However in the Gaṅga and Hoysaḷa kingdoms they were active participants in political policies and king-making, and in Rajasthan and Gujarat were closely associated with royalty. They had the advantages both of a high degree of literacy and of close links with the banking and financial groups, both of which the royal family could not ignore. With the patronage of royalty and wealthy citizens providing such an expansive area of social intrusion, it is not surprising that the competition for this patronage among the sects sometimes took a violent turn.

A less quantifiable reciprocity between the monasteries and the lay community related to the former providing an ethic and discipline for the latter. This emerged from and complemented the activities of a particular social group which supported the sect. The Buddhist attitude to the laity illustrates the point most clearly. A distinction was made between the general run of lay followers and those who were especially devoted to and closely associated with the *saṅgha*, namely the *upāsakas*. This rippling out of the degrees of support strengthened the position of the *saṅgha*, *vis-à-vis* the lay community. The majority of the *upāsakas* were *gahapatis* and in the *gahapativagga* sections of some of the *Nikāyas*, their problems in accepting the teaching and discipline of the *saṅgha* are discussed. Central to these was the inability of the *gahapati* to detach himself from worldly possessions particularly the accumulation of gold, property, servants, etc.[112] The category of *upāsaka* seems to have been created to circumvent this problem so that the *gahapati* could be associated with the *saṅgha* as more than just a lay follower without renouncing his attachment to all possessions. Thus the duties of the *upāsakas* were not only to maintain the *saṅgha* but also to look after the welfare of their own families. The moral precepts required of the *upāsaka* focused on the puritan ethic of austerity, saving and investment, as much as on being generous in making donations to the *saṅgha*[113] — the two not being entirely unrelated. Some of the abstinences prescribed for *uposatha* days were required of the *upāsaka* but none of these were especially arduous and the promise of wealth and prosperity (among other things such as attaining heaven) was the reward. The directions given to women lay followers in particular, underline the requirements of a well-to-do housewife attending to the well-being of her husband and his material comfort.[114]

Overt concern with the lay community is not so clearly ascertainable from the literature and practices of sects other than the Buddhists and the Jainas. But, by and large, the providing of an ethic remains an essential part of the relationship. The Daśanāmi sects provide a base for orthodoxy to the same extent as the Tantric sects reversed the ideals of this orthodoxy. The social groups from which they sought their support were of course not the same and, upto a point, the sects were embodying the ethical systems which these social groups found most conducive. The advantage to the lay community, quite apart from the acquisition of merit and other non-material rewards, was that their ethical systems were validated and imbued with moral authority when they were seen to emanate from a body of renouncers.

The moral authority of the renouncers was derived from two sources. One was the non-tangible psychological relationship with the lay community based on the charisma of the renouncer. The other lay in the apparent contradiction of a social nexus based on the repudiation of society which we have been attempting to discuss in this paper.

The charisma of the renouncer has been a continuing feature of Indian society. The great men of the tradition include those who are seen as successful ascetics. There is no limit to their power for even the gods fear them.[115] The authority of the ascetic is not only of parallel stature but often exceeds that of kings, for the ascetic is associated with powers beyond the ordinary, symbolised as magical powers. It is this which attracts the respect and awe of the lay community. Here the achievements of the individual isolated ascetic imbued with mystical powers rub off onto the renouncer in the monastery and add to the prestige of the latter. The charisma is seen at the simplest level in the fact that the renouncer is able to detach himself from material possessions. Furthermore, he is celibate and yet, at the same time, the most virile of men.[116] The ascetic's demonstration of sexual prowess is not a contradiction in terms: it is in fact a demonstration of his complete control over body functions, since ideally the emission of semen is prohibited to him.[117] Sexual practices were associated with this and with magic and both of these became a prerequisite for claims to mystical powers. They were insisted upon even in the ritualized sexual practises of Tantric sects, which practices were essential to detachment from the normal rules of morality.[118] The mystical element was enhanced by the association of fecundity and sanctity with sexual union performed on ritual occasions. This had antecedents in the *aśvamedha* and *mahāvrata* ceremonies.[119]

Celibacy or, alternatively, ritualised sexual practices were not however the main component of the charisma. It lay as much in the magical powers derived from the comprehension of bodily functions and from knowledge ensuing out of prolonged meditation. The search for knowledge often led to non-conformist directions. This involved experimenting with the human body at a physical level, either by using external aids such as hallucinogens or by manipulating the functions of the organs of the body such as breathing, pulse- and heart-beat and either extending or atrophying the muscles. Experimenting with states of mind took the form of exercises in meditation. Some of these practices went back to the shamanistic practices of at least the Vedic period if not earlier. Others evolved with the coming of new knowledge, both genuine and spurious, which tended to gravitate in non-conformist circles.

Theories of knowledge was yet another area in which the renouncers sometimes functioned as dissenters. These ranged from the development of logic and analytical concepts to secret cults antagonistic to orthodoxy. The early groups, as we have seen, objected to Vedic orthodoxy and the tradition of received knowledge. They sought experiential knowledge or tried to understand it as a function of the intellect. Yogic powers achieved through *tapas* were seen as a manifestation of control over the human body extending into the mind. Levitation, flight and invisibility were possible through yogic power.[120] The generally non-conformist trend among such sects was in part a search for a non-orthodox comprehension of knowledge and in part a means of asserting power through claiming to know the incomprehensible. Emanating from this was, on the one hand, the development of philosophical schools and, on the other, the exercise of what was generally regarded as non-conformist knowledge. Among the latter, medicine attracted attention as also did alchemy (*dhātuvidyā*, *rasāyanavidyā*). In neither case was the knowledge tabu in orthodox circles but the investigation was hedged round with social restrictions. The ascetic tradition emphasized experimentation and demonstration which was antithetical to the scholastic tradition.

The interest in medicine can be related to yogic exercises where the aim is to control breathing (*prāṇāyāma*), to understand the structure and inter-connection of various parts of the body, to prolong life by these processes and by the use of certain vegetable and mineral matter, and, in the understanding of the mind, the use of hypnosis, hallucination and meditation. Nāgārjuna in a sense sums it up when he refers to the transformation of *prakṛti* (substance) by the use of *oṣadhi* and *samādhi*.[121] Patañjali in the Kaivalyapada of the *Yogasūtra* states that *siddhi* can be attained by the application of a herb, and the commentators explain this as a reference to *rasāyana*.[122] It is not surprising that the earliest of the major compendia on medicine, that of Suśruta is associated with Nāgārjuna.[123] Nor is it strange that Taxila, apart from being a culturally cosmopolitan town with important Buddhist monasteries, was equally renowned as a centre of medical knowledge. That some form of approximate medicine was practised by ascetic sects is mentioned specifically by Megasthenes in his description of the *sarmanes*.[124] In the Buddhist and Jaina tradition, attending to the medical well-being of the lay community is incumbent upon the monk.[125]

The interest in alchemy developed in the early centuries AD, presumably when both mercury and sulphur were available and their properties familiar.[126] Nāgārjuna, the Buddhist philosopher, is described as being conversant with alchemy.[127] A Chinese source refers to an Indian taken to China by Wan Hsuan Tse in the seventh century AD who claimed that he knew the substance for prolonging life.[128] The early medieval period saw a considerable interest in alchemy among certain Jaina groups and later among Yogi sects associated with Tantricism.[129] The fascination lay in two processes fundamental to alchemy — sublimation and transmutation.[130] Through sublimation the structure of the metal was decoded and could be changed. Transmutation was the actual changing of one metal into another, the most common attempt being to change bronze or copper into gold. Both these processes had an analogy with yoga — the changing of bodily structures to enable the body to be transmuted into one capable of performing feats beyond the normal and gaining new perceptions. The connection with Tantric practice can be subtle but apparent, as for example in the statement that Hara and Gauri (mercury and mica) must combine in order to produce a new substance[131] — a clearly sexual symbolism for the transformation of substances. The close connection of alchemy with medical knowledge was through the use of various metals in medication.

Much of this knowledge remained secret, passed on orally from the *guru* to the novice. Eventually the secrecy became a cult and developed its own language, as for example the *sandhā-bhāṣa*,[132] which helped not only to perpetuate the cult and permit free communication among its practitioners, but also protected the *yogi* from the non-initiate and separated him from the profane universe.[133]

Some Tantric sects do generally stand out as being different and it has been plausibly argued that their materialism contributed to concepts of the physical sciences. The *dehavāda* tradition led to their taking an interest in human anatomy and these sects argued that the brain was the seat of consciousness and not the heart.[134] In their alchemical ideas, emphasis was placed on experiment and observation, as is evident from the eighth century text, the *Rasaratnākara*. (Whether the enhanced interest in the conversion of base metal into gold was motivated entirely by the wish to control the magical alchemical process or whether it was due to a shortfall in the availability of gold still requires to be investigated. The interest seems to coincide with the decline of supplies of gold from Central Asia and the hoarding of golden objects in temples. However, other sources of supply such as west Asia were also becoming available.)

Experimentation in the use of hallucinogens was primarily to achieve heightened perception and these are described in detail in the *Yogasūtra*, the *Abhidharmakoṣa* and certain Buddhist texts. This was also part of the tradition of non-conformist knowledge since hallucinogens change perception even if they do not transmute bodily substances. That these experiments were only for the initiates was clearly stated. The ritual of the use of hallucinogens had moved from the *soma* rites of the Vedic sacrifices, where it was part of the mainstream of orthodox ritual, to the twilight areas of secret, heretical practices, indicating thereby the change which the orthodoxy itself had undergone, particularly in its attitude towards experimentation and perception.

The charisma of the renouncer therefore derived from the practice and pursuit of non-orthodox knowledge, which provided one aspect of the ultimate moral authority of the renouncer. Equally important was the fact of their creating an alternate or parallel society. The renouncers demonstrated their power by maintaining a recognized style of life without resort to any profession. The prohibition on manual labour highlighted their ability to live off society: yet they were not *of* society. The renouncers were above and beyond the conventional laws, for they conformed to their own laws and these were often in contradiction to the accepted social laws. This gave them added prestige as it also gave them the freedom to protest against the laws of normal society. The form which their protest took was the flouting of social convention. The accommodation of this protest, and the investing of it with charisma and moral authority, has been in a sense characteristic of Indian society. But it has also been subject to the fact that, ultimately, the society of the renouncers had to be supported by the lay community. The opposition inherent in the status of *grhastha* and *samnyāsa* remains, but the relationship is essentially dialectical, for the one cannot exist without the other. Changes within the lay community affected the community of renouncers and the lay community was, in turn, influenced by them. The acceptance of the renouncer as a necessary counter-weight to conventional society may account for the continuing authority of the renouncer.

## Notes and References

1. M. Eliade, *Yoga*, Princeton, 1971.
2. K.N. Jayatilleke, *Early Buddhist Theory of Knowledge*, London, 1963; A.L. Basham, *The History and Doctrine of the Ājīvikas*, London, 1951.
3. A. Eschmann, 'Religion, Reaction and Change: The Role of Sects in Hinduism' from, *Religion and Development in Asian Societies*. The Greek root HAIRESIS indicates the choice of a doctrine, again by implication referring to a range to choose from. The Latin root *secta* refers to a body of followers, the heretical element being a contribution from Christian ecclesiastical history.
4. D. Schlumberger and E. Benveniste, 'A New Greek Inscription of Aśoka at Kandahar', *Ep. Ind.*, XXXVII, part v, no. 35. pp. 193–200.
5. J. Marshall, *Mohenjo-daro and the Indus Civilisation*, London, 1931, pp. 52ff.
6. *Ṛg Veda*, VII.22.9; 56.3; 70.4; VIII.3.9, 6.18; X.14.15; 72.7; 109; 136; 130.5.
7. Ibid., X.136.
8. M. Eliade, *Shamanism*, Princeton, 1974.
9. T. Burrow, '*Arma* and *Armaka*', *Journal of Indian History*, XLI.1963.I. pp. 159ff.
10. *Aitareya Brāhmaṇa*, VII.28.
11. G. Wasson, *Soma: Divine Mushroom of Immortality*, New York, 1968.
12. *Bṛhadāraṇyaka Upaniṣad*, IV.4.22.
13. F. Staal, *Exploring Mysticism*, Berkeley, 1975, p. 204.
14. J.W. Hauer, *Der Vratya*, Stuttgart, 1927; M. Eliade, *Yoga*, Princeton, 1971, pp. 103–5.
15. Buddhist sources mention fifty-eight major sects whereas Jaina sources take the number up to three hundred and sixty-three. *Dīgha Nikāya*, Brahmajālasuta, I.12.30; *Sūtrakṛtāṅga* (S.B.E., XIV, pp. 315–19).

16. *Dīgha Nikāya*, Udumbarika-Sihanādasutta, III; N. Dutt, *Early Monastic Buddhism*, Calcutta, 1973, I. pp. 31ff.
17. Strabo, XV.1.60; Curtius, VIII.12.
18. Strabo, XV.1.59.
19. *Viṣṇu Purāṇa*, IV.3.1ff.
20. *Manu*, IV.107; *Gautama DS*, XVI.45; *Baudhāyana DS*, II.46.33.
21. N. Dutt, op. cit., I. pp. 104ff; S.B. Deo, *The History of Jaina Monachism*, Poona, 1956, pp. 60ff.
22. A.L. Basham, op. cit., pp. 4ff.
23. Romila Thapar, 'Ethics, Religion and Social Protest in the First Millennium BC in Northern India', *Daedalus*, Spring, 1975, vol. 104, no. 2, pp. 119–33. *See* chapter 39 in this volume.
24. N. Dutt, op. cit., pp. 147ff and 167ff.
25. S.B. Deo, op. cit., pp. 60ff.
26. N. Dutt, op. cit., I, p. 197.
27. Ibid., p. 183.
28. Such as Anāthapiṇḍaka and Viśākhā (the daughter of a *seṭṭhi* of *Sāketa*). *Mahāvastu*, I.4; *Cullavagga*, VI.4.10; VIII.7.4.
29. *Dīgha Nikāya*, I. Lohiccasutta; Ambatthasutta.
30. D. Chattopadhyaya, *Lokāyata*, New Delhi, 1968, pp. 468ff.
31. S.B. Deo, op. cit., pp. 101ff.
32. Ibid., pp. 420ff; *Ep. Carnatica*, VII.64, 66, 117, 127, 140, 351; *Dīgha Nikāya*, Samannaphalasutta.
33. *Majjhima Nikāya*, I.134–5. The idea was developed further in the notion of the Bodhisattva as the saviour and the compassionate one who defers his own *nirvāṇa* to help others attain it, and also in the concept of the Buddha Maitreya as a chiliastic principle.
34. D.D. Kosambi, *Introduction to the Study of Indian History*, Bombay, 1956; Romila Thapar, *The Past and Prejudice*, New Delhi, 1975, pp. 28ff.
35. S.B. Deo, op. cit., p. 105.
36. Strabo, XV.1.59.
37. A.L. Basham, *The Wonder that was India*, London, 1954, p. 280.
38. S. Dasgupta, *Obscure Religious Cults*, Calcutta, 1946, pp. 35ff.
39. T. Watters, *On Yuan Chwang's Travels in India*, New Delhi, 1973, reprint, I. p. 221.
40. D. Lorenzen, *The Kapalikas and the Kalamukhas*, New Delhi, 1972, pp. 13ff; V.S. Pathak, *History of Śaiva Cults in Northern India from Inscriptions*, Varanasi, 1960.
41. *A Comprehensive History of India*, vol. II, pp. 393ff.
42. *Vāyu*, LVIII.64–5; *Brahmāṇda*, II.31.64–6.
43. Lorenzen, op. cit., pp. 24ff.
44. S.B. Deo, op. cit., pp. 114ff and pp. 568ff.

45. R.N. Nandi, *Religious Institutions and Cults in the Deccan*, Varanasi, 1975, pp. 96ff.
46. G.S. Ghurye, *Indian Sadhus*, Bombay, 1964, pp. 70ff; H. Chakraborty, *Asceticism in Ancient India in Brahmanical, Buddhist, Jaina and Ajivika Societies*, Calcutta, 1973, pp. 178ff.
47. The later rivalry of the Jainas and the Lingāyatas in Karnataka took in its sweep, idol breaking and temple destruction as well. The Buddhist disapproval of Śaṅkarācārya was expressed in a number of Buddhist works. One among these refers to his losing a debate with Buddhist monks and, as a result, being ducked thrice in the Ganga, Tāranātha's *History of Buddhism in India*.
48. R.N. Nandi, op. cit., pp. 65ff.
49. M. Eliade, *Yoga*, p. 153.
50. F. Staal, op. cit., p. 171.
51. G.S. Ghurye, op. cit., p. 177.
52. S. Dasgupta, op. cit., pp. 14ff.
53. M. Eliade, *Yoga*, Calcutta, 1965, pp. 200ff.
54. R.S. Sharma, *Indian Feudalism*, Calcutta, 1965, pp. 263ff; B.N.S. Yadava, *Society and Culture in Northern India*, pp. 375ff, Allahabad, 1973; R.S. Sharma, 'Material Roots of Tantricism', International Orientalists Conference, Canberra, 1971.
55. N.N. Bhattacharya, *Ancient Indian Rituals*, Calcutta, 1975, p. 139.
56. L. Dumont, 'World Renunciation in Indian Religions', *Contributions to Indian Sociology*, 1960, IV. pp. 33–62.
57. D.H. Ingalls, 'Cynics and Pāśupatas: The Seeking of Dishonor', *Harvard Theological Review*, LV, 1962. pp. 281–98.
58. L. Dumont, *Homo Hierarchicus*, London, 1972.
59. J.C. Heesterman, 'Vrātya and Sacrifice', *Indo-Iranian Journal*, 1962, VI, pp. 1–37.
60. *Vinaya Piṭaka Pātimokkha*; *Aṅguttara Nikāya*, IV.202; *Baudhāyana DS.*, II.10.11–30; *Manu*, VI.38; *Yājñavalkya*, III.56; *Visnu DS.*, 96.1.
61. D. Lorenzen, op. cit., p. 97; G. Briggs, *Gorakhanātha and the Kānphāṭā Jogis*, Calcutta, 1930.
62. *Brhadāranyaka Upanisad*, II.4.1; III.5.1.
63. *Manu*, VI.41–4; *Vasiṣṭha Dh. S.*, X.12–15.
64. *Manu*, VI.40, 92–4; *Yājñavalkya*, III.61–6; *Gautama*, III.23.
65. *Manu*, VI.70–5.
66. *Manu*, IV.207ff; V.129; VI.43; *Āpastambha DS.*, I.5.16.21–2.
67. *Vasiṣṭha DS.*, X.31.
68. Strabo, XV.i.59.
69. *Ācāraṅgasūtra*, II.1.1–10.
70. J.P.S. Uberoi, 'On Being Unshorn', in *Sikhism and Indian Society*, Transactions of the Indian Institute of Advanced Study, Simla, no. IV, 1967.

71. D.H. Ingalls, op. cit.
72. It is perhaps worth keeping in mind that the word 'dissent' has only relatively recently been secularised in English. Dissent is embedded in the ecclesiastical history of European Christianity and refers to groups in opposition to the doctrine of (particularly) the Church of England. Until the eighteenth century it referred to Christian non-conformists. It is only when political sectarianism became significant in the nineteenth century that it took on the secular connotation of differences of opinion on politics and society and the articulation of seemingly radical action for change. Etymologically the word is based on the negative prefix and is the reverse of consent. 'Protest' derives from an act of protestation or a formal declaration in legal terms. Its etymological root relates it to being a witness in a court of law or parliament. Again, it is not until the eighteenth century that it comes to be accepted as a formal expression of dissent or disapproval in matters other than the law (O.E.D.).
73. *Jābālopaniṣad*, 5; *Śaṅkara on Bṛhadāraṇyaka Upaniṣad*, III.5.1.
74. Ibid., IV.5.15.
75. *Rāmāyaṇa*, Uttarakāṇḍa, 67.1–6; Kālidāsa, *Raghuvaṁśa*, XV.53; *Viṣṇu Purāṇa*, VI.1.37.
76. Ānandagiri, *Śaṅkaravijaya*, XVII, quoted in D. Chattopadhyaya, *Lokāyata*, pp. 274ff.
77. S. Dasgupta, op. cit., pp. 35ff.
78. D. Lorenzen, op. cit., p. 149.
79. S. Dasgupta, op. cit., p. 198.
80. H. Chakraborty, op. cit., pp. 171–2.
81. S.B. Deo, op. cit., pp. 465ff: A curious feature in Jaina literature is that in listing the number of followers of various *tīrthaṅkaras*, the figures for the number of nuns and women lay-followers is always substantially larger than for the men, *Kalpasūtra*, SBE, XXII, pp. 267–8.
82. A.K. Warder, 'Early Buddhism and Other Contemporary Systems', *Bulletin of the School of Oriental and African Studies*, 1956, XVIII.1, pp. 43ff.
83. A.L. Basham, op. cit., argues that perhaps Ājīvikas were the earliest to evolve a *saṅgha*.
84. *Dīgha Nikāya*, XVI, Mahāparinibbanasutta.
85. Cf. R.A.L.H. Gunawardana, 'Some Economic Aspects of Monastic Life in the Later Anuradhapura Period: Two New Inscriptions from Madirigiriya', *The Ceylon Journal of Historical and Social Studies*, January–June 1972, vol. II, no. 1, pp. 60ff.
86. N. Dutt, op. cit., pp. 290ff and 313ff.
87. D. Chattopadhyaya, op. cit., p. 483.
88. Ibid.

89. *Dīgha Nikāya*, III, Cakkavatisihanādasutta.
90. *Mahāvaṁsa*, II.1ff.
91. *Vinaya*, II.160–75.
92. Fa Hsien in S. Beal, *Chinese Accounts of India*, Calcutta, 1958, I, p. 22; I. Tsing in J. Takakusu, *A Record of the Buddhist Religion*, Delhi, 1966, p. 193.
93. *Vinaya*, II.160–75.
94. R.N. Nandi, op. cit., p. 59; S.J. Tambiah, *Buddhism and the Spirit Cults in North-eastern Thailand*, Cambridge, 1970, pp. 81ff.
95. S. Dutt, *Buddhist Monks and Monasteries of India*, London, 1962, p. 76.
96. G.S. Ghurye, op. cit., pp. 82ff; H. Chakraborty, op. cit., pp. 178ff.
97. *Viṣṇu DS.*, V.132; *Āpastambha DS.*, II.10.26, 14–17.
98. G.S. Ghurye, op. cit., pp. 103ff. In this connection it might be mentioned in passing that there is a curious institution of the *caṭṭas* and *bhaṭṭas* referred to in various sources but whose exact function is not very clear. They occur in the post-Gupta period, are associated with *maṭhas*, were trained in Sanskrit and Vedic studies and in the handling of weapons and arms. They are generally accorded *brāhmaṇa* status but are nevertheless differentiated from the other *brāhmaṇas*. M.G.S. Narayanan, 'Kantalur Salai — New Light on the Nature of Aryan Expansion into South India', *PIHC*, Jabalpur, 1970, pp. 125–36. The epigraphs recording land grants prohibit the entry into the area by these persons in the phrase, '*a-cāta-batta-praveśya*'. They have been described as a para-military vanguard of *brāhmana* settlements or else as a category of semi-officials. Might they have been the precursors of the later *akhārās*, who were not to be encouraged in *agrahāras* and other land granted by the king, since, living off alms as they were (and possibly enforcing the *dāna*) they would be a financial liability?
99. G.S. Ghurye, op. cit., pp. 98, 177; G. Briggs, op. cit., p. 35.
100. As, for example, the variation as recorded in the *Mahāvaṁsa* and the *Aśokāvadāna*.
101. B.L. Rice, *Ep. Carnatica*, VII. J.F. Fleet, 'Inscription at Ablur', *Ep. Ind.*, V.1890–99, pp. 213–65.
102. S. Dasgupta, op. cit., pp. 208–9.
103. Hemcandra, *Triśaṣṭiśalākapuruṣacarita*, pp. 160–4; *Divyāvadāna*; *Aśokāvadāna*.
104. The installation of a *mahant* described by J.C. Oman in *The Mystics, Ascetics and Saints of India*, London, 1903, pp. 253ff, takes on the character of a gigantic potlatch in which the redistribution is limited to the *saṃnyāsis* alone. Such an occurrence indicates a departure from the notion of reciprocity or at any rate the return flow is obscured.

105. R.A.L.H. Gunawardana, 'Irrigation and Hydraulic Society in Early Mediaeval Ceylon', *Past and Present*, November 1971, no. 53.
106. Such as the Baniyan Cave in the Barabar Hills given to the Ājīvikas by Aśoka Maurya and those in the Nagarjuna Hills given by Daśaratha. Romila Thapar, *Aśoka and the Decline of the Mauryas*, London, 1997 (2nd. ed.), pp. 186, 260; Donations of this nature to the Jainas are listed in S.B. Deo, op. cit., pp. 101–35; similarly for Kāpālikas and Kālāmukhas in D. Lorenzen, op. cit., pp. 24–8 and 111–14. The monastery at Nālandā was financed through an endowment of the revenue of two hundred villages according to I. Tsing and J. Takakusu, *A Record of the Buddhist Religion*, p. 65.
107. R.N. Nandi, op. cit., pp. 88ff and 96ff.
108. *Mahāvagga*, I.61.1 to I.72.1.
109. This is perhaps best described with reference to the Mahāvihāra monastery in the *Mahāvaṁśa,* particularly in the period subsequent to Devānampiya Tissa.
110. R.N. Nandi, op. cit., pp. 88, 90.
111. S.B. Deo, op. cit., p. 239.
112. N. Dutt, op. cit., II, pp. 210ff.
113. *Dīgha Nikāya*, III, Sigalovādasutta.
114. N. Dutt, op. cit., II, pp. 217ff.
115. As is evident from the general contempt with which Indra is treated by the great ascetics in the *Mahābhārata*.
116. As for example, Krsna Dvaipāyana in the *Mahābhārata.*
117. W.D. O'Flaherty in *Asceticism and Eroticism in the Mythology of Śiva*, Oxford, 1973, tends to treat it as a contradiction.
118. F. Staal, op. cit., p. 104.
119. M. Eliade, *Yoga*, p. 254.
120. Ibid.
121. Quoted in M. Eliade, *The Forge and the Crucible*, New York, 1971, pp. 127ff.
122. S. Dasgupta, op. cit., p. 193.
123. There is a controversy as to whether this is the same Nāgārjuna as the Mādhyamika philosopher. J. Filliozat in *The Classical Doctrine of Indian Medicine*, Delhi, 1964, pp. 11ff, argues for this identification. It is significant that Hsüan Tsang (T. Watters, op. cit., II. pp. 200–6) refers to the philosopher as being an expert in medicine and alchemy.
124. Strabo, XV.1.59.
125. *Mahāvagga*, I.39.1. Even a monastery as late in date as Nālandā is described as a centre for the study of medicine, astronomy and mathematics (S. Beal, *The Life of Hsüan Tsang . . .* , pp. 112, 153).
126. For a discussion of the pre-Arab date for the use of mercury in India

see P.C. Ray, *A History of Hindu Chemistry*, Calcutta, 1907–25, II, pp. 8ff.

127. T. Watters, op. cit., II, pp. 200–6.
128. J. Needham, *Science and Civilisation in China*, Cambridge, 1954, I, p. 212.
129. The twelfth century text, *Rasārṇava*, is associated with Tantric groups. The highly respectable Merutuṅga wrote a commentary on the alchemical text *Rasādhyāya*, in the fourteenth century.
130. *Encyclopaedia Brittanica*, 1972, qv. ALCHEMY.
131. D. Chattopadhyaya, op. cit., p. 329.
132. The word is probably a mis-reading for *sandhya-bhāṣā*, but it has gained currency as *sandhā-bhāṣā*. qv. Monier–Williams, *Sanskrit-English Dictionary*, although most scholars would accept its meaning as 'intentional language'.
133. M. Eliade, *Yoga*, pp. 251ff.
134. D. Chattopadhyaya, op. cit., pp. 335ff.

41

# The Householder and the Renouncer in the Brahmanical and Buddhist Traditions*

In the discussion on the four *āśramas* as theoretical preconditions to the concept of *puruṣārtha* there has been a tendency to treat the *āśramas* as chronos-free, floating as it were in historical space. The theory has been analysed and its structure viewed essentially from the perspective of belief systems and rituals in a broadly Brahmanical context. It might, however, prove rewarding to consider that the theory has a historical specificity and to view it as an ideology which is pertinent to and is interlinked with a historical situation; that the theory was elaborately formulated long after the idea of *āśramas* was first articulated and in its practice also, historical changes are very noticeable; and that these changes were evident particularly in the institutions which accompanied the theory.

Such an analysis requires that the *āśrama* theory be seen not as an isolate but as one segment in a larger ideological whole. A consideration of its relation to other facets of the perspective on man and his life as viewed by a variety of belief systems would not be out of place. The range of the latter is obviously vast; and two among them have been selected in terms of a methodological exercise for consideration, the Brahmanical and the Buddhist both having been major movements at the time. To see the theory only in Brahmanical terms is to leave out the context within which it developed. To separate the two traditions in viewing the ideological concerns of the mid-first millennium BC is to pull a historiographical

* From *Contributions to Indian Sociology*, (NS) vol. 15, nos. 1 & 2, 1981, 272–98.

situation out of alignment. Historically in the initial stages, the Brahmanical and Buddhist world-views presented both a dialectical and an inter-face relationship. Within this the notion of *āśrama* and its implications read as distinct ideological formulations relating to problems perceived in common by both. Sociological writing on India has drawn heavily on the Indological tradition which in turn has concerned itself substantially with the Brahmanical world-view overlooking the fact that from the mid-first millennium BC to the mid-first millennium AD, the period when theories such as those of the *āśramas* and *puruṣārtha* were expressed and crystallised as ideals, was a period when Buddhism was, if not the dominant belief system in northern India, certainly as important as Brahmanism. The separation of the two stems in part from the decline of Buddhism in India from the second millennium AD and the tendency, therefore, to underestimate its significance for earlier times. An overly synchronic view of Indian society tends to obliterate the strands which go into the weaving of the present from the past.

The two stages of householder and renouncer have been viewed in recent writings as binary opposites (Dumont 1960). It has been argued that whereas *gṛhastha* was oriented to reciprocity viewing life as a series of interactions with others, renunciation denied reciprocity and to this extent it denied a major focus in Hindu social action. Indian society, it is said, constrains the individual and renunciation alone allows the individual to be independent and liberated from the fetters of life. It is said that the renouncer was not concerned with changing the social order but being outside it. In a holistic society individualism has to be a condition of opposition to such a society (Dumont 1980). It is, however, debatable whether the seeming dichotomy between householder and renouncer is as much of a binary opposition as has been made out; or whether the main thrust of the *āśrama* theory was to reduce the absolute dichotomy by introducing an interplay of the dialectic of the householder and the renouncer in each of the *āśramas* but with one being given greater prominence over the other. In other words, the binary opposition was not posed in the formulation of the theory of the *āśramas* but in the content of each of the four. Nor is the dichotomy absolute. The joining of an order by the renouncer often brought him back into performing a social role. This not only reduced the claim to individualism but also involved him in trying to change the social order. It is not accidental that socio-political reformers in India have frequently appropriated the symbols of the renouncer (Thapar 1979).

The debate on renunciation, which is in many ways the focal point in both traditions, has centred on the question of whether the ideal of *saṃnyāsa* and that of the *bhikkhu* evolved independently at a particular historical conjuncture or whether the one was influenced by the other (Jacobi 1895; Varma 1922; Dutt 1924; Bhargava 1968). The counter-posing of the *gṛhastha, gahapati*/householder to the *saṃnyāsin, bhikkhu*/renouncer, is worked out in the form of the four *āśramas* in the Brahmanical tradition. Buddhist views pose the opposition more sharply and in essence it is reduced to two. The counter-position relates to the dialectic of attachment and non-attachment to a worldly life. In the four *āśramas, brahmacarya* is a stage in preparation towards the passage to the other three and swings from *gṛhastha* to *saṃnyāsa* in the symbolism of its rituals. Whereas the guru simulates the renouncer, the guru's house harks back to the setting of the householder. *Gṛhastha* is obviously the stage of the householder, but he has to aid the renouncer with alms and hospitality and is constantly aware of his obligations to the renouncer as indeed the renouncer when he intervenes in social action, as many do on occasion by demonstrating their powers, is reiterating the interplay. The location of hermitages in the vicinity of settlements points to a degree of participation in social life which cannot be taken as the renouncer making a total break from society. *Vānaprastha* is more directly a preparation for *saṃnyāsa*. It could be argued that the choice of four stages was a spelling out of the two, but that this was not entirely arbitrary. It may have been inspired by the need to conform to the four of the *varṇas* particularly useful in the model of the *varṇāśramadharma*; or perhaps that there was symbolic convenience in the number four; or that in the stretching out to four it offered choices of a kind more in keeping with the Brahmanical tradition.

Not only does the Buddhist tradition pose more sharply the dialectic of attachment and non-attachment but encourages a choice between the two, thus laying the emphasis on an implicit opposition. However, even in the Buddhist tradition the interplay is discernible. The *gahapati* has to maintain the *bhikkhu*, a relationship which is echoed in the later *dharmaśāstras*. Even the *bhikkhu* in the monastery had eventually to choose between a greater involvement with the village or a retirement into seclusion. The *āśrama* theory seeks to ameliorate this problem of choice by converting it into a life-cycle within a life-time, thus eliminating the need to choose at an early stage and also permitting the problem of choice to resolve itself into a given curriculum, or else occurring late in life when the extremity of the choice is less severe. The central point of the *āśramas* is not, however, the individual life-cycle so much as the concern with social obligations. The Brahmanical tradition further underlines the priority of social obligations by making *saṃnyāsa* the final stage, subsequent to the performance of social obligations. However this does not preclude the taking up of *saṃnyāsa* at an early stage in life since this is the terminal *āśrama*

The earliest exposition of the *āśrama* ideal as a theory is found in the *dharmasūtras* which although they cannot be precisely dated were certainly texts of the post-Vedic period and composed in a period probably contemporary with, and in some cases subsequent to, Buddhist teaching (Banerji 1962; Lingat 1973). There is no uniformity in the *dharmasūtras* with regard to terms used for the four stages, although a broad conceptual agreement regarding three or four stages in a life-cycle is expressed. Thus Baudhāyana refers to the last two as *vānaprastha* and *parivrājaka* (II.11.14). Gautama refers to *brahmacāri*, *gṛhastha*, *bhikṣu* and *vaikhānasa* (III.2). Āpastamba seems to suggest that after the period of *brahmacarya* it is possible to proceed to any of the following stages, *gṛhastha*, *acāryakula mauna*, *vānaprastya* (II.21.1). The early *dharmasūtras* maintain that there is really only one *āśrama*, that of *gṛhastha*. The others are inferior to it as they do not permit the begetting of offspring (Kane 1941: 422). The usage of describing the four *āśramas* as *brahmacarya*, *gṛhastha*, *vānaprastha* and *saṃnyāsa* took a little time in becoming standardised. Pāṇini, generally dated to the fifth century BC, refers indirectly to the different *āśramas* but not to the theory as an entity (Agrawala 1963: 83).

The notion of renunciation was however prevalent earlier than the period of the composition of the *dharmasūtras*. It has been argued that renunciation may have been common among those not identified with Vedic society and the *yatis*, *munis* and *śramaṇas* are quoted as among the earliest renouncers (Pande 1975: 251–61). The association of renunciation with those who meditated on death and the link between repeated birth and death conditioned by attachment to desire, is a theme familiar to the *Upaniṣads* (e.g. *Bṛhadāranyaka* IV.3.2.2–10) although the link through the soul being reincarnated was not developed until a later period. Renunciation was seen as an important if not necessary precondition to an escape from death and rebirth. In the search for *mokṣa*, the efficacy of *yajñas* was doubted, knowledge, meditation and renunciation being seen as more viable methods. Reference is made to the three *skandhas* which may have been an early groping towards the theory of *āśramas* since they are described as *tapas*, *brahmacarya* and absolute control over the body. Of the renouncers, the *śramaṇas* are frequently mentioned, and often they held views contrary to those of the *brāhmaṇas*. That there was intense hostility between the *brāhmaṇas* and the *śramaṇas* is reflected in the metaphor of describing them as having a natural antipathy such as between the snake and mongoose.[1] The hostility was in part due to the ideological negation of Brahmanical practices by the *śramaṇas* and their opting out of social obligations. The division is also referred to in Buddhist sources where the *brāhmaṇas* are described as being of two kinds, those who perform rites and those who meditate and are renouncers (*Dīghanikāya* III.94). The *śramaṇas* as renouncers were also opposed to the *brāhmaṇas* as performers of the *yajña* and recipients of *dāna*. The *brāhmaṇas* were to develop the notion that in return for *dāna* they took upon themselves the sins of their *yajamānas*, thus entangling themselves further in social obligations. This was anathema to the renouncer, who even when he joined a sectarian order and thereby took upon himself at least minimal social obligations, was never as seeped as the *brāhmaṇa* in such obligations.

A suggestion of another kind, attempting to explain renunciation, has been offered in the argument that some cultures obliterate certain kinds of emotions as, for example, those of intense loneliness, by denying them public expression. It is said that the Indian environment encourages a flight from emotional involvement[2] and withdrawal from entanglements with the world. Asceticism is valued as a condition which denies the expression of passion in any form. Renunciation is born from the need to escape pain (Moussaieff Masson 1980). Such an explanation raises questions of a culture's articulation and would be viable in a few cases of renunciation where this specific reason is given by the individual renouncer. But it would not hold true either for *saṃnyāsa* as the final *āśrama* or for the compulsions which led *śramaṇas* to organise themselves into sectarian orders or indeed which led to the rank and file joining such orders.

Degrees of social obligations were also written into the four *āśramas* by the linking of this theory with that of *varṇa* and the labelling of both as *dharma*. The implication of the latter would suggest that they were regarded partially as incumbent on those *dvijas* who were concerned both with observing social obligations and attempting to attain to *mokṣa*. Alternatively insofar as the *varṇa-dharma* was the theory of the ordering of society, the *āśrama*-dharma was also to be taken not literally, but as a theory towards the ordering of the individual life-cycle. However *āśramas* and *varṇas* do not form a vertical and horizontal grid for the entire range of society since the *āśrama* curriculum is only open to the *dvija* and consequently applies to and is the concern of a relatively smaller segment of the social whole.

Even within the *dvija* its actual applicability is limited almost to the *brāhmaṇa* caste. The *kṣatriyas* are also included within this curriculum but, in fact, the *kṣatriya* had his own *puruṣārtha* as we know from other sources. The ideal life-style of the *kṣatriya* falls back upon earlier heroic models of the warrior and the protector, in short the *vīra* or hero. Even when the connotation of *kṣatriya* changed from warrior to landowner and gift-giving (*dāna*) became as important as protecting, heroism remained an aspect of the ideal *kṣatriya* function. It drew on the pre-*āśrama* period of a lineage-based society in which the mores of the clan chiefs and their families were the norm and these certainly bypassed the *āśrama* theory and continued to be maintained in the widely dispersed and well-attested cult of the hero, as is evident from the numerous herostones (*vīragal*, *pāliya*, *kīrti-stambha*) found liberally scattered in various parts of the subcontinent from the first millennium AD. The 'good' death for the hero was that he should die defending himself, his kinsmen and their property. Such a death ensured eternal life in heaven, accompanied by his wife should she have become a *satī* on his death. In some cases the hero was deified by his kinsmen and community. So consistent is this pattern that it can legitimately be spoken of as an actual *kṣatriya āśrama* and it is curious that it was ignored in the *āśrama* model if the purpose of the model was even minimally to include varying life-styles. This may have been due in part to the model excluding the clan-based society subscribing to heroic values, since the social milieu of the *āśrama* was that of peasant and urban society.[3]

The appeal of renunciation as envisaged in the *āśrama* theory would have been limited to the upper castes. If the texts relating to those who opted out and became renouncers, the *Upaniṣads* and the *Āranyakas*, provide any clues then clearly this option was open to *brāhmaṇas* and *kṣatriyas* in the main. The renouncers were not the sorcerers and the magic men of the earlier pastoral society but were those who had deliberately chosen to dissociate themselves from the beliefs, rituals and social obligations of a complex society with the aim of discovering an alternate path to salvation because of disillusionment with the existing ways.

In analysing the reasons for the growth of renunciation at this time, it has been suggested that it was partially the result of the disorientation which followed on the break-up of clan based society with the emergence of urban centres and the authority of state systems (Warder 1956). Nostalgia for the clan may have led to the particular organisation of Buddhist and Jaina monasteries, where many of the ecclesiastical terms — *saṅgha, kula, gaṇa* — originate in the *gaṇa-saṅgha* chiefships of the middle Ganga valley. Alternatively, the *gaṇa-saṅgha* system provided a model for organising such sects, especially as the founders and other important members of the *saṅgha* were from the Śākya, Jñātrika, Vajji and other such *gaṇa-saṅgha* clans. Parallels are frequently drawn between the structure of the monasteries and that of the *gaṇa-saṅgha* system (*Aṅguttaranikāya* IV.17; *Dīghanikāya* II.72ff). The monasteries were seen ideally as egalitarian sanctuaries in an otherwise increasingly hierarchical society dominated by the monarchical state.

Urbanisation in the Ganga valley in the mid-first millennium BC encouraged the growth of scepticism and sophistry among the wandering renouncers who roamed through the towns teaching their doctrines. This was, however, a later phase of an enquiry which had begun earlier in the variant ways suggested in the quest for mokṣa. Within these suggestions can be traced an element of dissent which was crucial to the comprehension of the role of renouncers in society.

The theme of dissent originates in the questioning of revealed knowledge with a preference for perceived knowledge and in the exploration of other methods of comprehending the universe (Jayatillake 1963). The ritual of sacrifice was found to be inadequate and was substituted by *tapaṣ* and *dhyāna*. The change from *yajña* to *tapas* and *dhyāna* was in itself a shift from participation in a public ritual, meticulously prescribed, to a more personalised quest for an open though arduous method of individual and private articulation. But the very isolation of the renouncer from public performance imbued him with a charisma which was to be most effective in its public role. The liberty given to the renouncer to question the *Vedas* was the thin end of the wedge leading to a much wider range of questioning. The expression of dissent and protest was one element in renunciation but the joining of an order or sect could and did modify if not nullify the social content of the protest (Thapar 1979). Those who joined sects and returned to preach in villages and towns had a social counterpart to their search for release from rebirth as is evident from the Buddhist view of the relationship between the householder and the renouncer. The questioning of revealed knowledge and the dependence on *yajña* for salvation coincided with the gradual erosion of the prestation economy central to the *yajña* ritual. Whereas the protagonists of the *Upaniṣads* merely opted out of the system, those who were members of what have been called the 'heterodox' sects, further threatened the slowly receding faith in the *yajña* ritual among the householders: a faith which was partially restored by the use of the Vedic sacrifice as a ritual of legitimation in the monarchical states. The householder as the performer, preserver and guardian of the sacrificial ritual became the counterpoint to the renouncer who denied both the ritual and the social role of the one who preserved it.

The questioning of knowledge is an enterprise in which few take part. The direction of the quest was more restrictive, focus as it did on doctrines of release — these being essentially metempsychosis and rebirth. The latter is touched upon obliquely in the *Bṛhadāraṇyaka Upaniṣad* as also in references to the idea of birth and death as a repetitive cycle. The concepts of *karma* and *saṃsāra* are developed more fully in Buddhist thought and become central to the Brahmanical tradition in the period after the Buddha had taught, when expiation for the present and preparation for a new birth becomes a major concern. Nevertheless the notion of heaven and hell remain a part of the popular imagery of the after-life and become substratum ideas often interwoven into the overarching theme of *karma* and *saṃsāra*. Renunciation is never aimed at the attaining of heaven, but has as its goal release from rebirth taking the more abstract form of *mokṣa*. Ultimately such an appeal could again be directed only to the limited few.

Renouncers, unconcerned with preaching their ideas to others and content either with a solitary existence or at most the company of others such as themselves, moved to forest retreats away from towns and villages, although close enough for the townsmen to know of their existence and if need be for them to supply alms. That this was not an ideal but an actuality is evident from, among other sources, the descriptions of such groups met with by Greeks visiting India either in the entourage of Alexander of Macedon or as ambassadors of his successors in west Asia (McCrindle 1877: 98–105). The hermitages referred to in Indian sources, set in forest clearings, were often the vanguard of the colonisation of the area by settlers of agriculturists with or without state backing. Such hermitages were often under attack by those who claimed the forest as their territory or hunting ground (Thapar 1978a).

In the dialectical relationship between the householder and the renouncer a crucial question related to when a man could opt out of his social obligations as a householder and become a renouncer. Buddhist and Jaina views did not stipulate *gṛhastha* as necessary. Some among them argued that it was necessary to forego the stage of *gṛhastha* so that renunciation becomes a truly parallel stream. The authors of the *dharmasūtras* insisted on *gṛhastha* as a precondition arguing that this made it more difficult to renounce the worldly life (*Baudhāyana* II.10.17.2–5; *Āpastamba* II.9.21). In these circles the debate hinged on the individual and the problem posed for the individual in the process of renunciation. In the *dharmasūtras* the question of whether *brahmacārin* could proceed directly to *saṃnyāsa* and bypass the stage of *gṛhastha* was linked to the performance of one's social obligations. It may have been for this reason that there was also a difference of opinion as to whether *saṃnyāsa* should be restricted to *brāhmaṇas* (*Manu* VI.1–38). It is frequently stated that *gṛhastha* is both crucial and necessary almost to the point of suggesting that true renunciation can only be attained once one has passed through the stage of *gṛhastha* (*Manu* VI.87ff), which makes renunciation all the more arduous. This insistence may have been an attempt to counteract the entry into monkhood at a young age which was being encouraged by Buddhists and Jainas. Renunciation coming after the completion of *gṛhastha*, would minimally affect the performance of social obligations. The bypassing of *gṛhastha* carried the danger of a decline in the performance of *yajñas* which would have been a serious curtailment of *dāna* for the *brāhmaṇas* and an erosion of the status and power of the Brahmanical tradition. In terms of social dissent too it would be a muffled protest. The possibility of its encouraging an alternate form of social organisation is guarded against by the insistence on celibacy. A curious reference in the *Baudhāyana dharmasūtra* (II.6.11.28) states that the renunciatory stages were the creation of an *asura* who wished to annoy the gods, since if men took to renunciation the gods would lose the offerings of the *yajñas*. This would point indirectly to, perhaps, an initial disapproval of renunciation and the possibility that it had to be conceded somewhat grudgingly. However, once it was conceded, it was taken up with great éclat.

Each of the *āśramas* is characterised by three phases which may be described as initiation, liminality and reintegration. Initiation was into a condition different from the previous one. Liminality related to the current *āśrama* carrying traces of the earlier one and a foretaste of the later. Reintegration completed the process and provided a new context and identity to the individual.

The ritual required for the *brahmacārin* was both a preparation for *gṛhastha* but also a taste for *saṃnyāsa*, thus suggesting that the essential dichotomy was the opposition between the *gṛhastha* and the *saṃnyāsin*. The *upanayana* or initiation of the male child was his formal entry into caste status and reflects an earlier ritual of initiation into the clan. Subsequent to the *upanayana* the boy was introduced to the first *āśrama* where he was placed under the tutelage of a guru or *ācārya* symbolising a spiritual father and reiterating his second birth and thus confirming his *dvija* status (*Āpastamba* I.1.1.16–18; *Vasiṣṭha* II.6). The emphasis therefore was on the transition from one status to another, non-*dvija* to *dvija*. The boy is regarded as a *śūdra* before the *upanayana*, a polluting category from which he emerges into *dvija* status. The *āśrama* theory was therefore also a social marker in which the *dvija* status was continually emphasised and a demarcation made through rituals of the separation from the *śūdras* and others. It anticipates renunciation by removing the boy from his familiar social milieu to the hermitage of the guru. The purification required was partly to do with the fact that biological birth is polluting and the pollution can only be fully removed by a second birth, the initiation into *varṇa* status and *brahmacarya*, an initiation which affected not merely the individual boy but also his place in the social matrix, his social status. The *brahmacārin* stage is a period of preparation requiring a study of the *Vedas* (the corpus of authoritative and revealed knowledge); the precepts of moral behaviour often strikingly similar to those which governed the life of renouncers; and the practice of austerity.

The *brahmacārin*'s vows (*Baudhāyana* I.2.3.7ff; I.2.4.7ff; I.3.5.1ff), such as celibacy, tending the guru and bringing him alms daily, sleeping on the bare ground and strict dietary rules are similar to the rules for novice monks in Buddhist monasteries. Celibacy and the prohibitions regarding the guru's wife emphasise the separation from women and the domestic sphere, which of course is reintroduced by contrast in the *gṛhastha* stage. The begging for alms (*bhikṣā*) would suggest that the guru's hermitage was in the vicinity of settlements and that the latter were in a position to support such hermitages. Evidently the forest here does not refer to the virtually inaccessible deep forest, but rather the *āraṇya* or waste land on the edges of settlements. The *brahmacārin* is invested with a staff (*daṇḍa*) which becomes an essential item for both the *saṃnyāsin* and the *bhikkhu*, so essential that some renouncers are referred to as *maskarin*, the bearers of the staff.

Recognisable differences in clothing and appurtenances as well as the period of stay were stipulated on the basis of caste differentiation (Apte 1954: 170ff, 182ff). To this extent there is dissimilarity with the novitiate period of monkhood. The Vedic texts studied were inevitably those of the *śākhā* to which the guru belonged, the particular *śākhā* thus receiving some secular support in terms of an investment in students who as householders would continue to be well-disposed towards their guru and his *śākhā*. The curriculum is suggestive of preparation for discourse rather than for householding and those who returned to their social obligations terminated the stage of *brahmacārin* earlier than the stipulated number of years. The highpoint of the termination ceremony was the ritual bath, hence the use of the term *snātaka*, and a mock triumphant return to the village and home from where the *brahmacārin* had originally set out. The first *āśrama* is rather like a prolonged initiation ritual with some preparation for the immediate future but with a stronger foretaste of the ultimate goal. It is characterised by separation from the social context, a period of liminality followed by a reintegration into the social context. The preparation provides an understanding of the social role of the householder in upholding the Brahmanical mores and tradition through sacrifices and the maintenance of the *brāhmaṇa*.

Marriage initiates the second *āśrama* of *gṛhastha*. Both Brahmanical and Buddhist sources continually stress the importance of this *āśrama* but for different reasons. The *dharmasūtras* maintain that it is the most important stage because the other three are dependent on it (*Baudhāyana* II.11.27; *Vasiṣṭha* VIII.14; *Gautama* III.3). Its prime function is the continuation of the family and the perpetuation of the *gṛhya* or domestic rituals. It is only the householding stage which permits of offspring and the successful householder provides material support for the others. The fire used for the marriage ritual is maintained without a break throughout the lifetime of the *gṛhastha* or as long as he remains in that condition, a custom which echoes that of the tending of the sacred fire by the kin members in clan based. societies.[4] The family fire was used for the various *yajñas* associated with rites of passage rituals, expiatory ceremonies, seasonal sacrifices, ceremonies dedicated to the ancestors and the worship of the quarters — in short all the rituals of a temporal and spatial context. The life of the *gṛhastha* was punctuated by actions relating to social obligations and few demands of an individual nature.

The two categories of people who can always draw on the householders' respect and hospitality were the *śrotrīya brāhmaṇa* and the guest (*atithi*) (*Āpastamba* II.4.8.1ff; 4.9.1ff; *Gautama* V.43–5), and often the two were identical. Generous hospitality would in such circumstances provide a means of indirect support for the *brāhmaṇas*, as indirect but highly effective as the performance of endless daily and seasonal sacrifices. The *gṛhapati* was the mainstay of the prestation economy in a situation of sedentary agriculture and where not every *brāhmaṇa* had access to the royal court and could enjoy the *dāna* emanating from the performance of royal sacrifices. The necessity of performing the *gṛhya* rituals was emphasised doubtless in part because the system of prestations was required to be maintained since the *brāhmaṇas* at least were dependent on it. Domestic rituals were also closely related to the household as a socio-economic unit, a self-sufficient body in terms of its daily needs since agricultural activities and minimal artisanal needs were controlled by the household. The rituals served to reiterate the status of each person in the household and more particularly the head of the household as indeed the *āśrama* theory served to demarcate the *dvija* family from its *śūdra* servants, slaves and retainers. The *atithi*, the one who does not stay permanently, was honoured as part of the code of honouring guests, but not anyone could claim this status and it was necessary to ascertain the identity of the guest before accepting him into the household. Hospitality to the guest was part of the wider system of being able to support 'the other'.

Buddhist texts focus more closely on the *gahapati*/householder in his social milieu and the householder is perhaps given even greater importance than in the Brahmanical tradition. It often includes the *upāsakas* or lay-followers and these are contrasted with the *bhikkhus* who are the renouncers. The householder is the source of *dāna*, the gift-giving which maintains the *saṅgha*. Since the *saṅgha* is an institutionalised body of renouncers it is dependent for its maintenance on the lay-followers. The householder and the renouncer, therefore, are counter-weights to each other in social balance and there is a clear cut distinction between the two. The institution of the *saṅgha* makes the pendant relationship much sharper than in the Brahmanical tradition. The householder is the source of recruitment to the monkhood since the monks are celibate. Support is extended by giving of alms and of donations of a material kind. This implies that it was the prime duty of the householder to ensure that he had access to wealth at all times. *Dāna* was, therefore, visualised as the giving of gifts but also the observing of certain rules of behaviour which as an ethic provided the basis of the accumulation of wealth.

Because of this it was necessary that the prestation economy in which wealth was destroyed in the rituals or else was given towards the maintenance of *brāhmaṇas*, be substituted by a code in which wealth could be conserved if not enhanced so that it could be donated not only to individual renouncers but to the institution as well. Not only was the conservation of wealth discouraged in the Brahmanical system but commercial wealth was despised since it was based on the repeated investment of wealth. The *saṅgha* on the contrary encouraged commercial wealth and investment, the ensuing surplus being required to support the institution of monks. The *yajña*, therefore, was replaced by an ethical code encouraging austerity and ensuring the conservation of wealth. The *gṛhastha* who opted out and became a monk was in a sense terminating a source of support for the *saṅgha* and this contradiction was sought to be solved by the concession made to the *upāsaka* who could attain merit without becoming a *bhikkhu*, although in the ultimate stage renunciation would be inevitable. The Buddhist tradition demanded austerity from the *gahapati* to ensure the continuance of wealth. Although it nowhere approached the condition of *tapas* it did encourage an empathy for renunciation, since wealth was not to be enjoyed hedonistically but was to be produced in order to provide *dāna* to the *saṅgha* and to meet social obligations. Such austerity is not enjoined upon the *gṛhastha* in the Brahmanical tradition. The good householder was constantly aware of the merit of almsgiving which has priority in the list of exalted qualities (Gahapati vagga, *Aṅguttaranikāya* VIII.3.21–30; X.30ff). The *upāsaka* is one who conforms to the five virtues and abstains from taking life, stealing, lust, lying and intoxicants. He strives for his own welfare and that of others. The Buddha's teaching appeals to one who has few desires, is contented, secluded, energetic, composed and wise. Gift-giving can ensure rebirth in an easier life such as that of a wealthy *kṣatriya*, *brāhmaṇa* or *gahapati*, surrounded by luxury: or alternatively a life in heaven. The threat of rebirth in animal form or the tortures of hell are held out to those who are niggardly in their *dāna* to the *bhikkhu* or the *saṅgha*.

*Dāna* as virtue is clarified in the Buddha's discourse to the householder Sigāla (Sigālovadasutta, *Dīghanikāya* XXXI.4). The replacing of ritual by ethical action is clearly stated when the Buddha tells him that the worship of the quarters does not consist of prescribed rituals but the avoidance of the fourteen evils of life. These are listed as the four vices in conduct: slaughtering life, stealing, lying and adultery; the four evil motives of action, partiality, hate, fear and dullness; and the six channels for dissipating wealth, the taking of intoxicants, roaming the streets at unseemly hours, going to fairs and festivals, gambling, keeping evil friends and idleness. It is significant that these are listed specifically as ways of dissipating wealth. Some of them result in harm to the family and to property and both of these have to be protected by the householder and are of course crucial to the continuity of social obligations and the maintenance of the *saṅgha*.

Family and property are again the crux of the ethic in the details of virtuous behaviour, and social obligations are spelt out in the description of what constitutes the worship of the four quarters from a non-Brahmanical perspective. The west is worshipped through the mutual concern of husbands and wives for each other and where the wife runs the daily business of the household deputising for her husband, and she is enjoined upon in doing so to safeguard the property of her husband. The north relates to clansmen and friends who are to be treated with generosity and benevolence. The eastern quarter is reserved for parents and the wider family. The southern quarter involves the care of one's teacher through respectful behaviour and diligence in learning. The substitute for the worship of the nadir revolves around relations between the master and his servants where the humane treatment of servants encourages them to work fully and loyally. The zenith symbolises the wider relationship between the householder and the *śramaṇas* and *brāhmaṇas* where the central concern is that he is to supply their needs and they in turn will guide him towards meritorious actions and heaven. Family and property are further emphasised when the Buddha states that the amassing of wealth is required of the good layman for it is through this that he benefits his clan. The procedure for amassing wealth is described as, spending a quarter of one's income on daily living, keeping another quarter in reserve and investing the remaining half in an enterprise which will result in monetary profit. Family and private property were believed to be crucial to the evolution of human society and the state according to Buddhist theory and they emerged from a pristine utopian beginning in which both were initially absent. To the extent that the *gahapati* upholds family and property he is in a sense upholding the need for social sanctions and the authority of the state. By the same token the renouncer breaking away from family and private property represents a return to the pristine condition.

The third *āśrama*, that of *vānaprastha*, is referred to by many synonyms such as *vaikhānasa*, *parivrājaka* and *bhikṣu* and probably included the 'hylobioi' of Megasthenes (McCrindle 1877). The use of a number of terms points to a wide variety of renouncers conforming to degrees of renunciation seen as part of the social scene. The differences appear to have been partly doctrinal and partly based on varied observances, both of which overlapped to a greater or lesser extent from one group to another, covering a range from gentle isolation to a fierce regime of asceticism. The category, therefore, seems to refer more to the present of 'opters out' in society than to a specific and identifiable stage in life. The *vānaprastha* is required to live in the forest but can take his wife with him. There is a heavy emphasis on dietary rules which largely confined him to what he could collect in the forest (*Baudhāyana* II.6.11.12ff; III.3.13ff; *Āpastamba* II.9.23.2). He has to avoid living in or near inhabited places except in the period of the rains thus echoing the *vassa* period of Buddhist monks who were also permitted closer contact with settled areas during this time of year. The *vānaprastha* may continue to perform, but in a modified fashion, some of the rituals of the *gṛhastha*, thus requiring in some cases that the sacrificial fire of the household be maintained even in the forest retreat. His clothing was restricted to the minimum. Nakedness or at least a change of clothing is important to all baptismal rituals. His head was shorn according to some texts or, alternatively, he refrained from cutting his hair. He prepared himself for the fourth and final stage through study and meditation, but if this was not his ambition he could terminate his life by living only on water and air and dying of slow starvation — an ideal which recalls the death enjoined upon Jaina monks.

*Vānaprastha*, therefore, was seen as a transition from *gṛhastha* to *saṃnyāsa* and as with all transitional stages is not very clearly defined. True renunciation was seen as *saṃnyāsa*. A distinct ceremony marked the entry into the fourth and final stage and is defined by a complete break of ties with family, property and society and takes on the symbolic form of a death ritual. *Saṃnyāsa*, therefore, is a much more definitive action involving major changes than is *vānaprastha*. In a sense the would-be *saṃnyāsin* undergoes an excommunication ceremony but he is not regarded as defiling because although he breaks all social taboos he does so ritually and he exiles himself not out of having sinned but voluntarily. It was regarded as a worthy end to one who had fulfilled his social obligations. He takes the vows of the ascetic, abstention from injuring the living, from lying, from stealing and conformity to continence and liberality. He is permitted to accept alms from either *brāhmaṇas* or *dvijas* although in some texts even this is not permitted. That the isolation was not total in most cases is suggested by the term used by Pāṇini for ascetics. The *bhikṣu* is distinguished from the *tapasvin* (*Aṣṭādhyāyī* III.22.155, 168; V.2.102ff). Some follow the *bhikṣu-sūtras* and are differentiated from others such as the *maskari parivrājaka* (*Aṣṭādhyāyī* IV.3.110ff; VI.1.). The fact of renunciation did not mitigate the competition among renouncers and their claims to have discovered the true path to salvation. The distinction among ascetic orders had to do with techniques for attaining *mokṣa* and less with ritual status. The initiation of the Buddhist monk was the *pabbaja/parivrājaka* ceremony, literally the 'going out' and since it could be undertaken at any age permission was sought from kinsmen to ensure that social obligations would not preclude the opting out (*Jātaka* IV.119; *Vinaya Piṭaka* I.82).

In the counter-posing of the householder to the renouncer the major obligations and characteristics of the one were deliberately and systematically negated by the other (Thapar 1978b). Initiation into *gṛhastha* was through the marriage ritual which is negated by the insistence of celibacy among renouncers. The *gṛhastha* was expected to build his life around the rearing of a family, observing the social norms required by the fact of living amidst others, worshipping his ancestors at the time of *śrāddha*, protecting and enhancing his property and labouring on his profession. The renouncer denied all this through the ritual by which he entered *saṃnyāsa* which was in effect a death rite. He was required to quench his sacrificial fire and dispose of his sacrificial implements. This is a subtle concession to the act of *yajña* being the stamp of the householder and those functioning within a temporal framework. The permission of the *vānaprastha* to perform *yajñas* indicates the degree to which he is still tied to householdership and removed from renunciation. The *saṃnyāsin* by breaking all taboos becomes ritually impure and cannot either perform the *yajña* or be a *yajamāna*. At the same time, *tapas* and *dhyāna* enable him eventually to reach a state of purity and power which supercede that of the *yajña*-performing *brāhmaṇa*. The renouncer has to foreswear any ties with property, to break any attachment to person or place and in effect take to a life which required wandering from place to place and thereby precluded working at any profession. The break with social attachments was further emphasised by his taking on the outward symbols which made him recognisably a renouncer: being naked or sparsely clothed, either removing his hair or never cutting it, carrying a staff and an alms bowl and living either in a monastery, theoretically cordoned off from secular settlements, or living isolated in a forest.

The insistence that the renouncer was dead to the world was symbolic not merely of the break with society but also because death was seen as a condition in which the social order does not prevail. Although the rituals of death serve to enforce the social order for the living, physical death releases the person from that order. *Śrāddha* rituals were a generalised worship of ancestors, reincarnation involved a fresh entry into society and heaven at least had no social ordering. The performance of death rites negated the individual identity. *Saṃnyāsa* had a character of transcendence over death. The actual death ceremonies for the renouncer had therefore to be different from those of other *dvijas*. Instead of being cremated the ascetic was buried, often bound in a sitting position and his grave became a place of worship. (Curiously burial in the earliest source was associated with *asura* customs and these were regarded as socially alien to the Aryan.) In the case of the more venerable Buddhist monks, even though the body was cremated, relics were collected and buried in the tumulus (*stūpa/caitya*) erected to their memory. Thus even the physical body of the renouncer was treated differently on death. Pollution was not associated with his corpse and bodily relics could, therefore, be preserved. The individual *saṃnyāsin* did not require his descendents or peers to observe the *śrāddha* ritual for him as he was not listed as an ancestor and no continuity was sought. But among the *bhikkhus* and the *saṃnyāsins* who were part of a sectarian order, continuity was maintained though the line of succession in the monastery or the institutional *āśrama*, where both the oral tradition and literate history were the means of doing this. Important as this became to institutional requirements it subtracted from one of the original purposes of *saṃnyāsa*.

Food regulations were also distinctive. In the case of the *gṛhastha* food regulations relating to caste status and purity were worked out with the same theoretical finesse as were regulations regarding marriage. The higher the caste the more restricted was access to cooked food. The Buddhist and Jaina renouncers broke this tabu by insisting that only cooked food was acceptable as alms. *Brāhmaṇa* ascetics were also permitted this concession but it was preferable that they subsist on what they could glean from the forest. Intercaste commensality, prohibited to the *gṛhastha*, was enjoined upon the monk and the ascetic, the justification for this being that neither were regarded as caste members after renunciation. Similarly, regulations regarding flesh foods observed by the *gṛhastha* were not required of the renouncers. The same held true for the consumption of alcohol and intoxicants although Buddhist ethics firmly prohibited these even to the *gṛhastha* as well and unlike the *brāhmaṇas* made no concessions to the taking of intoxicants even on ritual occasions.

The exclusion of women is evident at the stage of initiation and in that of renunciation. Descriptions of the *gṛhastha āśrama* take women for granted speaking of them almost in the tone of sacrificial implements. The descriptions of the *gahapati* in the Buddhist sources certainly makes much more of the role of women in householding. Women *parivrājikās* are referred to, some in their own right and some in the hermitages with their *parivrajika* husbands. The Buddhist concession to women entering the nunnery was a major departure but its origins are concerned probably less with permitting them a search for salvation and more with the logic of permitting them an alternative life. Their necessity to the *gṛhastha* stage was doubtless sought to be reinforced by discouraging them from renunciation.

That the negation of caste implicit in all forms of renunciation raised some problems is evident from the difference of opinion in the *dharmasūtras* as to whether a *brāhmaṇa* alone should be permitted access to *saṃnyāsa* and, if not, whether *brāhmaṇas* should not carry some distinguishing marks such as the *śikhā* (top-knot) to indicate their original status. Buddhist renouncers by taking on a new name when they graduated to monkhood negated or at least disguised their caste origins.

The encouragement to the *gahapati* to enhance his wealth was again in contrast to the vow of poverty which both ascetic and monk were required to observe. Eventually poverty was to be dissociated from life in the monasteries when these ascetic institutions became wealthy property owners. Inscriptions dating to the Christian era refer to extensive donations made by monks and nuns to the *saṅgha* (*Epigraphia Indica* X. Nos.1016, 1020, 1041, 1089). In times when kinship was the major avenue to property rights, the property of the *saṅgha* was jointly owned. When individual property rights prevailed, members of the *saṅgha* claimed similar rights. This change grew to sizeable dimensions by the latter half of the first millennium AD when Buddhist and Jaina monasteries competed for power and property with the *maṭhas* and *āśramas* of various Śaiva and Vaiṣṇava sects of renouncers (Lorenzen 1972; Nandi 1973; Sarma 1966). The accumulation of such property acquired through lavish donations by lay patrons, whether privately held by monks or jointly by the institution was restricted in its ownership to the institution, although shares in the property could be held by individual renouncers who were members of the institution (Gunawardana 1979: 77ff).

This dichotomy in attitudes to property is also linked up in some ways to another dichotomy, that of the village and the forest, the *grāma* and the *vana* or *araṇya*. The word *grāma*, literally a village, refers by extension to all settlements and is, therefore, associated with the householder. By way of contrast, *araṇya* represented the waste land, the wilderness, the forest which lay between settlements. This was the great unknown with all its hazards. It was the symbol of chaos against the known order of all settled society. It would be the natural habitat of those who had broken away from society and who were confident of perceiving order in the seeming chaos which surrounded them. At another level the forest was a place of refuge where those deliberately opting out of society because of their disillusionment with its order, would go as an escape. At yet another level it was the symbol of the start of a new system of an attempt to reorder the universe which was sought to be done by setting up monasteries on the edge of settlements. The forest was the habitat of other groups segmenting off from existing settlements and creating new *janapadas*, founding new political territorial units. Interwoven with the notion of exile and of going out was that of creating or starting a new order, as is evident from the origin myths of the *kṣatriya* clans as described in Buddhist literature. But even in these new units the distinction between *grāma* and *aranya* remained and in the history of Buddhism this was to be a dichotomy between those monks who preferred to preach in villages and remain close to the lay community and those who were concerned with the ultimate aim of monkhood, an aim which had no place for monastic property.

The argument that renunciation denied reciprocity and to this extent it denied a major focus in Hindu social action, would be tenable if renunciation did in fact remove the renouncer from social action. In effect the monastery (whether Buddhist and Jaina to begin with and of the various Hindu sects of a later period) evolves both into an institution within which reciprocity is a fundamental need and into an institution which functions as a major social and political force and has, therefore, to maintain reciprocal relations with society. Whereas an ideal renunciation does deny reciprocity, in fact, the institutions which it spawned were deeply involved with society. The isolated renouncer remained socially marginal if not ineffective, but the image and connotation of the renouncer when it was associated with social movements became a powerful force for mobilisation. The strength of such a force doubtless derived from the fact that renouncers were the only category of persons who could with impunity discard social mores.

In generalising about the renouncer a distinction has to be made between the individual *saṃnyāsin* and the monk who joins an order. Both are concerned with individual salvation and hence remove themselves from the social group to which they belong. Remaining with the social group would involve them in having to observe the *dharma* of the group both because of social obligations and in order to acquire a better *karma*. *Dharma* as viewed in the Brahmanical tradition relates to the *dharma* of each caste and is expressed in the interplay of the individual's *dharma* and that of his caste. The Buddhist concept of *dharma* is that of a universal category which can be subscribed to irrespective of caste. The contrast can perhaps best be seen in the discourse on the duty of the *kṣatriya* in the *Bhagvadgītā* where protection and the unholding of the *varṇāśrama dharma* in its specificity is his concern and that of the king in the Cakkavatti-sinha-nāda-sutta (*Dīghanikāya* III.58) where the *cakravartin*'s duty is to follow the precepts of the universal *dharma* applicable to all and to ensure the well-being of his people.

Renunciation in the Brahmanical tradition was restricted since it was initially open only to the *dvija*, the *śūdras* being excluded. The non-Brahmanical sects were open to *śūdras* as well as other castes. This in itself would require a universalistic *dharma* given the immense social divide between *dvijas* and *śūdras*. By the time of the *dharmaśāstras*, *śūdra* ascetics were disallowed as this would doubtless have upset the social order and would have opened up an avenue of authority to the *śūdra* if not access to some degree of upward mobility. The possibility of renunciation being open to *śūdras* could have been viewed with alarm since it would have resulted in materially the most productive segment in society taking up what seemed to be materially the most counter-productive occupation. The prohibition on *śūdras* ascetics does suggest that at the ideological level renouncers were not viewed as being so far removed from society as to be ineffectual.

The monk as renouncer does raise something of a contradiction. By joining an order he subjects himself to a new set of mores and to obligations to the order which would inevitably modify his personal search for salvation even though ultimately his release from the cycle of rebirth lay in his hands alone. The Buddha tells the monks that each should live as an island unto himself guided by the *dharma* which is common for all. Monastic living would however not have allowed for the full implementation of this position. The emphasis on the individual both in *saṃnyāsa* and monkhood accounts in part for the strengthening of the notions of a person's *punya* and *pāpa* which is apparent in the texts of the time.

The contradiction is evident from the frequency with which there are debates in the *saṅgha* on the issue of whether monks should devote themselves to their own salvation or whether they should be concerned with strengthening the *saṅgha* by attending to the needs of the lay following. The distinction between the *grāma* and the *aranya* are symbolic of this choice and these terms enter the discussion. The care of the lay following required the performing of ceremonies particularly those associated with 'rites of passage' as these were occasions when faith would be strengthened. The dual role of the monk was kept separate in the Brahmanical tradition by the separate functions of the *brāhmaṇa* and the *saṃnyāsin*. In the initial stages when the monks lived in rock shelters and caves the problem was marginal, but later with the establishment of large monasteries close to settlements, the problem became more complex. The solution lay either in monks breaking away and going to forest retreats or in maintaining that both meditation and preaching were required of the monk and that the two should not conflict.

Such a conflict is sought to be partially ameliorated by the emphasis of the Buddhists on the goal being more important than the method. Thus the Buddha argues that austerity for the purpose of self-mortification characteristic of some kinds of asceticism is inadequate: the fundamental question being that of the nature of the goal of self-mortification (*Dīghanikāya* III.2.25). Asceticism by itself is not sufficient. It has to be accompanied by the norm, the *dharma* which ensures escape from the corruption of life and from rebirth. The discipline of living in a monastery is part of the process towards attaining salvation, since the monastic order consists of a body of people all seeking salvation.

It may legitimately be asked why some groups of renouncers sought to organise themselves into orders. This was an increasingly frequent form taken by renouncers from the late first millennium AD 'Hindu' sects of renouncers became common after the initial organisation established by Śaṅkarācārya in the ninth century AD. In subsequent centuries virtually every sect irrespective of its position in the spectrum of beliefs and forms of renunciation, was characterised by an institutional base. The search for individual salvation was not selfish and those who believed that they had found the way wished to enlighten others. The Buddhist parable of the raft where the raft symbolises enlightenment, insists that the raft be left for the use of others. Thus the creation of a sect for preaching the message was necessary. Monkhood obviously had the advantage that it allowed those who were seeking salvation and subscribing to a particular teaching to live together and thus facilitate the search.

That a body of renouncers had to have an institutional base also has to do with the nature of a caste society. Renouncers as we have seen were required, as it were, to 'de-caste' themselves. Having broken the rules of the *dvija* code, had they remained as individuals in society they would logically have been accorded *śūdra* status at best or been regarded as untouchables. Two *brāhmaṇa* novices wishing to become *bhikkhus* inform the Buddha that they are abused and reviled by other *brāhmaṇas* in whose eyes the novices have been lowered to *śūdra* status because of their joining the Buddhist order (*Dīghanikāya* III.81). It was, therefore, necessary that they be organised as a group outside society and yet with some links — as a parallel group with its own norms. The *brāhmaṇas* could well regard them as outcastes and their legitimacy, therefore, depended on their receiving public support in terms of recognition of their parallel or alternate system. The hierarchy of caste society was reinforced by attempting to reverse it in creating an egalitarian society of renouncers: the separation between the two societies was also reiterated. If the monastery reflected a search for an ideal society, its continuation would clearly be limited since it could not reproduce itself and was dependent on fresh recruitment. An unequal, hierarchical society could not be levelled nor opposed individually, but collective retreats based on egalitarian status, in theory if not in practice, were possible. The fear of the parallel society is demonstrated in the hostility in Brahmanical sources towards the heretical sects, whereas the individual *saṃnyāsin* although breaking the same caste rules is, nevertheless, revered.

It is a moot question whether the Buddha was aware of the political potential of the *saṅgha*. Initially the harking back of the *saṅgha* to the clan based societies may have suggested a role of opposition to the emergent monarchies which were feeling their way towards authoritarian state power at the time when Buddhism was beginning to acquiry popularity. The possible opposition gave way eventually to mutual respect which may have been directed by the need to accept royal patronage. The bestowing of patronage was doubtless inspired by the personal religious proclivities of the heads of state but was combined perhaps with a political insight which saw these monastic orders as powerful networks of public opinion. Mutual respect was tempered by mutual adjustments. The monastery although it remained a parallel society was from time to time an accomplice of political authority in supporting the state system. The Buddha advised the monks to obey the king and agreed that royal officers and those who were under a judicial sentence should not be admitted to the *saṅgha* (*Vinaya piṭaka* I: 73–6). Bimbisāra, then ruling Magadha, in turn agreed to declare monks immune from judicial punishment. Monasteries, *maṭhas* and *āśramas* in the later period, even when they were large scale property owners with judicial and fiscal rights over villages, were, nevertheless, declared immune from interference by state officials.

Buddhist historiography tends to associate major changes in the *saṅgha* with heads of state, implying thereby, that changes originated from kings who were patrons of Buddhism rather than from the internal dynamics of the *saṅgha* functioning in changing historical situations. The most obvious example of this is the attribution to Aśoka Maurya of calling the Third Council at Pāṭaliputra (Thapar 1961: 41–5) and of acting thereby as midwife to the birth of the Theravāda sect. The association of political authority with such events could in some cases have been an after-thought on the part of the monk chroniclers who sought to integrate political authority with an event of primarily religious significance: although of course it can be argued that such events were not primarily of religious significance and did have a political repercussion even if not precisely in the manner portrayed by the chroniclers.[5] It is incorrect to maintain that the reign of Aśoka saw the earlier politicisation of Buddhism (Weber 1967: 206ff, 237ff) since this had occurred in the lifetime of the Buddha. The *saṅgha* emerged rather like 'a state within a state'. *Dāna* to the *saṅgha* meant, in addition to religious merit, support to a socio-political institution. The Buddhist network drew in a number of areas in varying stages of state formation, from the more flexible chiefships to the unified state. Where the *saṅgha* was established it rapidly became the focus of community life.

The political role of the *saṃnyāsin* is not without significance. The authority of the *saṃnyāsin* deriving from the fact of renunciation coupled with the powers of *tapas* and *dhyāna* was seen as a parallel authority to that of temporal power. With the decline of *yajña* as the sole source of sacral authority, the *saṃnyāsin* came to personify an even greater authority. The *saṃnyāsin*, if he so wished, could curb temporal power by using the energy which he had acquired through austerity and meditation. The later, didactic interpolations in the two epics raise the power of the ascetic higher than even that of the great deity of the sacrifices, Indra. Kings were fearful of the wrath of the *saṃnyāsin*. The *daṇḍa* carried by the *saṃnyāsin* was not merely a physical staff for it symbolised the power of coercion through an intangible source of strength. Far from being life-negating the renouncer was the symbol of power and was often treated as the counter-weight to temporal authority. It may be argued that by insisting that renunciation come at the end of the life-cycle, a subtle attempt was being made to diffuse a possible concentration of authority. The encouragement of individual renunciation as distinct from joining an order was in itself a form of diffusing the political potential of the renouncer. This is demonstrated in the changed role of the renouncer in the period subsequent to the mid-first millennium AD when the *maṭhas* and *āśramas* of Vaiṣṇava and Śaiva sects were deeply involved in theories of meditation as well as problems of temporal power. The growth of these institutions changed the nature of dissent and conformity and the individual solitary renouncer tended to become a faded image. The increasing numbers of the orders of renouncers was feasible only insofar as they were permitted and protected by society.

The power of the renouncer had also to do with the fact that such groups and individuals were wrapped up in what might be called the non-orthodox understanding of knowledge. The initial absence of deities in this tradition and the break from the sacrificial ritual provided a rationalistic strain to much of their thought. There was, nevertheless, a claim to extra-sensory powers and the *saṃnyāsin* like the gods could conjure up visions of the universe and create the illusion of time, place and person. The Buddha discouraged the notion of *siddhi*, the almost magical power so deeply associated with renouncers, but the literature of Buddhism is replete with resort to such power when all else fails. Even the alchemical process was ultimately brought into such experiments with knowledge and was justified on the analogy that the process of sublimation and transmutation so central to alchemy was after all similar to that involved in the search for *mokṣa*. Besides alchemy was centrally concerned with empirical processes of knowledge.

The more evidently rational theme was directed to the opposition of revealed knowledge and as was often the case with early civilisations (Lloyd 1979: 37ff), to the analysis of bodily functions and experiments with the body — the foundation of *yoga* and *prāṇāyāma* — which encouraged a more empirical understanding of man. Coupled with this empirical knowledge came the notion of causation so skillfully utilised in Buddhist thought. The somewhat primitive magic associated with the performance of *yajña* and the correct recitation of the *mantras* had to make space for the more sophisticated idea of controlling the body and the mind through *tapas*, *yoga*, *prāṇāyāma*, *dhyāna* and other such techniques with the ultimate aim of using this control if need be to perform superhuman feats. The emphasis shifts from man supplicating the gods and the supernatural to man generating the power to comprehend the universe and the supernatural from within himself.

The trend of investigating empirical knowledge received something of a setback in the post-first millennium AD when monastic centres as the nuclei of renouncers became economically self-sufficient through grants and endowments. The initiates, or at least those who were not involved in the arduous task of managing and administering the property owned by the institution and the villages over which it had authority, spent their time in writing scholarly commentaries and treatises on existing philosophical and theological texts. The empiricism of perceived knowledge gave way to hours of scholarly debate. The monastic system of encouraging literacy which was on occasion used by monks of low status to aspire to high positions was now reinforced by the vogue for scholasticism. The plethora of manuscripts which are a hallmark of these times came frequently from monastic or near-monastic centres of various ideological persuasions. As renouncers such groups had moved a long way from the genesis of the *saṃnyāsa āśrama* or *bhikkhu saṅgha*.

Seen from a diachronic perspective the *āśrama* theory was generated from an interaction of social needs, historical processes and ideological concerns. The historical background to the dichotomy of householder and renouncer suggests an initial situation where renunciation was not at the forefront of social consciousness in that the early lineage based society of Vedic times seemed to accept the prestation system centering on the sacrificial ritual. The renouncers were few and were concerned with the quest for comprehending the universe. Thus dissent from the existing systems was essentially an intellectual dissent and a search for alternatives or the articulation of a private world view and did not impinge on the householding society of the majority. Stratification in such a system was less marked since clan and kinship connections were the determinants of status.

The dichotomy of householder and renouncer assumed more serious proportions in the subsequent period when, as a result of various historical changes, sects of renouncers not only became more numerous but began to organise themselves on an institutional basis. The opting out into the forest and the cutting away from society was among many such groups purely symbolic, since the sects remained in the purview of settlements and lived off them. The renouncer had now to seek the aid of the householder and was dependent on the latter. The giving of aid not only encouraged the questioning of the Brahmanical tradition in terms of the inadequacy of *yajñas* but also threatened the very system of ritual and symbol on which the Brahmanical tradition was based. Such a questioning also had a theme of social protest which was not appreciated by those who regarded themselves as the inheritors of the tradition. There was a need, therefore, to clarify the dichotomous relationship by defining its relative functions and by setting limits to the social impact of renouncers. Thus whereas the Buddhist and the Jaina traditions, for example, encouraged the dichotomous categories in the role of the *gahapati* and the *bhikkhu*, the Brahmanical tradition sought to weaken it by weaving it into a single life-cycle.

Within this definition the *āśramas* were linked to the *varṇas* so that caste functions could be continued and dissent made less apparent. The exclusion of *śūdras* from this curriculum was important and telling since it acted not only as a social marker but also guaranteed a marginal change from renunciatory groups who would have to be drawn from the *dvijas*. It also prevented the *śūdra* from having access to the kind of powers associated with renouncers. This was further reinforced by encouraging the notion that ideally only *brāhmaṇas* should be permitted renunciation. It is significant that those who did not conform to the *āśrama* theory opposed all these attempts at circumvention. The actual formulation of the idea of *āśramas* into a theory dates to a period when the strength of renunciatory groups had become noticeable. The linking of the *āśrama* theory to that of *varṇa* ensured that *varṇa* functions would not be neglected. Those who were reluctant to accept or could not accept the *āśrama* ideal could function at least with the *varṇa-dharma*. Thus *śūdras* were required to observe the *varṇa-dharma*. This was in turn subjected to the individual measure of merit and demerit in action leading to the centrality of the notions of *puṇya* and *pāpa*.

The Brahmanical insistence, in the early historical period, that the individual *saṃnyāsin* alone could be regarded as a renouncer was not only an attempt to reiterate the earlier model but also to hold back the tide of the various orders of renouncers who were looked upon by the *brāhmaṇas* as heretics (*pāṣaṇḍas*). What were once marginal dissenters were by now taking on the dimensions of a serious opposition to the Brahmanical world view. Earlier, individual renouncers had not only been accommodated in the Brahmanical tradition but their charismatic power had been accepted as a legitimate source of authority. This concession was born out of a genuine fear that *yoga*, *tapas* and *dhyāna* enabled the renouncer to control the natural and the supernatural world as well as from the reassuring belief that the impact of this power on society has perforce to be limited and cannot undermine the existing system. However, the rapid growth of organised groups of renouncers brought about a qualitative change in the perception of the role of the renouncer. The individual *saṃnyāsin*, although still the ideal, was hedged in by the influence on society by the sects of renouncers. Ultimately the emergence of a Śaṅkarācārya and the organisation of Brahmanical ascetic orders was a logical outcome of this situation. But prior to this, in an atmosphere of a more generalised discussion on the interplay of householder and renouncer and the social obligations of each, the Brahmanical tradition passed through a period of anxiety. The *āśrama* theory may have been less of an idealist abstraction projecting an ordering of the ideal life-cycle for the *dvija* and particularly for the *brāhmaṇa*, and more of the ventriloquism of a Brahmanical perception of a time of troubles.

## Additional Bibliography


Agrawal, V.S., 1963, *India as known to Panini*, Varanasi, Prithvi Prakashan.

*Aṅguttaranikāya*, Morris, R. and E. Hardy (eds), 1885–1900, London, Luzac and Co.

*Āpastamba Dharmasūtra*, Bühler, G. (tr.), 1879, Oxford, Clarendon Press.

Apte, V.M., 1954, *Social and Religious Life in the Grihya Sutras*, Bombay, Popular Book Depot.

Banerji, S.C., 1962, *Dharmasutras*, Calcutta, Punthi Pustak.

*Baudhāyana Dharmasūtra*, Bühler, G. (tr.), 1882, Oxford, Clarendon Press.

Bechert, H., 1978, 'The beginnings of Buddhist historiography: Mahavamsa and political thinking'. In B.L. Smith (ed.), *Religion and Legitimisation of Power in Sri Lanka*, Chambersberg, Anima Books.

Bhargava, D., 1968, *Jaina Ethics*, Delhi, Motilal Banarsidass.

Carrithers, M., 1979, 'The social organisation of the Sinhalese sangha in historical perspective'. *In* Gopal Krishna (ed.), *Contributions to South Asian Studies*, Delhi, Oxford.

de Coulanges, F., 1963, *The Ancient City*, New York, Doubleday and Co.

*Dīghanikāya*, Rhys Davids, T.W. and J.E. Carpentier (trs), 1890–1911, London, Luzac and Co.

*Dīpavaṁsa*, Law, B.C. (ed.), 1959, *The Ceylon Historical Journal*, Colombo, 8, 1–4.

Dumont, L., 1960, 'World renunciation in Indian religions', *Contributions to Indian Sociology*, 4: 33–62.

—— 1980, 'A modified view of our origins: the Christian beginning of modern civilisation', Deneke Lecture, Lady Margaret Hall, Oxford (unpublished).

Dutt, S., 1924, *Early Buddhist Monachism*, London, Trubner and Co.

*Epigraphica Indica*, 1909–10, Luders, H., Calcutta, Government Printing.

*Gautama Dharmasūtra*, Bühler, G. (tr.), 1879, Oxford, Clarendon Press.

Geiger, W., 1908, *The Dīpavaṃsa and Mahāvaṃsa and their Historical Development in Ceylon*, Colombo.

Gunawardana, R.A.L.H., 1979, *Robe and Plough*, Arizona, The University of Arizona Press.

Jacobi, H., 1895, *Jaina Sutras*, Oxford, Clarendon Press.

*Jātaka*, Fausboll, V. (ed.), 1877–97, London, Luzac and Co.

Jayatillake, K.N., 1963, *Early Buddhist Theory of Knowledge*, London.

Kane, P.V., 1941, *History of Dharmaśāstra*, vol. II, 1, Poona, Bhandarkar Oriental Research Institute.

Lingat, R., 1973, *The Classical Law of India*, Berkeley, University of California Press.

Lloyd, G.E.R., 1979, *Magic, Reason and Experience*, Cambridge, Cambridge University Press.

Lorenzen, D., 1972, *The Kapālikas and the Kālamukhas*, New Delhi, Thompson Press.

*Mahāvaṃsa*, Geiger, W. (tr.), 1964, London, Luzac and Co.

Manu, *The Laws of Manu*, Bühler, G. (tr.), 1886, Oxford, Clarendon Press.

McCrindle, J.W., 1877, *Ancient India as Described by Megasthenes and Arrian*, London, Trubner and Co.

Moussaieff Masson, J., 1980, *The Oceanic Feeling*, Leiden, D. Reidel Publishing Co.

Nandi, R.N., 1973, *Religious Institutions and Cults in the Deccan*, Varanasi, Motilal Banarsidass.

Pande, G.C., 1957, *Studies in the Origins of Buddhism*, Allahabad, The University Press.

*Pāṇini Aṣṭādhyāyī*, Vasu, S.C. (ed.), 1962, Delhi, Motilal Banarsidass.

*Patañjali vyākaraṇa mahābhāśyam*, Kielhorn, F. (ed.), 1962, vols I and II, Poona, Bhandarkar Oriental Research Institute.

Perera, F., 1976, *The Early Buddhist Historiography of Ceylon*, Gottingen University (unpublished thesis).

Sarma, S.N., 1966, *The Neo-vaiṣṇavite Movement and the Sattra Institution of Assam*, Gauhati, The University Press.

Tambiah, S.J., 1976, *World Conqueror and World Renouncer*, Cambridge, The Cambridge University Press.

Thapar, R., 1997, *Aśoka and the Decline of the Mauryas*, Oxford University Press, Delhi (rev. ed.).

—— 1978a, *Exile and the Kingdom: Some Thoughts on the Rāmāyaṇa*, Bangalore, Mythic Society.

—— 1978b, *Ancient Indian Social History: Some Interpretations*, New Delhi, Orient Longmans.

Thapar, R., 1979, 'Dissent and protest in the early Indian tradition', *Studies in History*, 1, 2: 177–96. See chapter 11 in this volume.
Upaniṣad, *The Principal Upaniṣads*, Radhakrishnan, S. (tr.), 1953, London, Allen and Unwin.
Varma, V.P., 1972, *Early Buddhism and its Origins*, Delhi.
*Vasiṣṭha Dharmasūtra*, Bühler, G. (tr.), 1882, Oxford, Clarendon Press.
*Vinaya piṭaka*, Oldenberg, H. (ed.), 1879–83, London, Luzac and Co.
Warder, A.K., 1956, 'Early Buddhism and other contemporary systems', *Bulletin of the School of Oriental and African Studies*, 18, 1: 43ff.
Weber, M., 1967, *The Religion of India*, New York, The Free Press.

## Notes and References

1. *Yeśam ca virodhaḥ śāśvatikaḥ*. Patañjali *Vyākarana mahābhāśyam*, I. p. 474, on Pāṇini, II.4.9. Other sources also refer to the dichotomy between *brāhmaṇas* and *śramanas* such as *Anguttaranikāya*, IV.35; Strabo, XV.1.59 in McCrindle. The etymology of *brāhmana* indicates one imbued with divine knowledge which linked to Vedic knowledge. The terms *śramaṇa* and *āśrama* in both cases derive from the root *śram*, to labour or make an effort. The *śramaṇa*, therefore, is one who labours towards an objective and *āśrama* was the process of doing so. Eventually the place where the *śramaṇas* gathered was also called the *āśrama*. The differentiation between the *brāhmana* and the *śramaṇa* was, therefore, clear and unambiguous.
2. By way of an aside one might consider in this context, the centrality of tragic plays in Greek culture. Did the public expression of emotions of sorrow and loneliness through the performance of such plays and through the cathartic experience of the audience prevent the obliteration of such emotions? The essence of Greek tragedy lay in forcing the audience to face emotional situations of a kind which in other cultures may have been treated as personal and private. And curiously the Greeks were not given to renunciation. But such an argument can perhaps be too simplistic.
3. The epic heroes of the *Mahābhārata* and the *Rāmāyaṇa* were, in the interpolated later sections of the text, supporters of the *gṛhastha-āśrama*. They do not contemplate *saṃnyāsa* as a possible condition for themselves. When in exile they come into contact with renouncers and on occasion have to protect the renouncers against their enemies although the renouncers are frequently forest hermits still maintaining the sacrificial ritual and suggesting thereby that they were not *saṃnyāsins*. Only in one version of the *Rāmāyaṇa*, the mid-first millennium AD composition of the Jaina adaptation in the *Paumacariyam*, does Rāma renounce his kingdom in his later years and becomes

Jaina ascetic — and the *Paumacariyam* is already far removed from a heroic ethos.

4. One is here reminded of the discussion in Fustel de Coulanges (1864) on the significance of the sacred fire in claims to kinship and in family cults associated with it.
5. The relationship between the Buddhist *saṅgha* and the political state has been analysed in considerable detail with reference to the situation in early historical Sri Lanka. The Ceylon chronicles, especially the *Dīpavaṃsa* and the *Mahāvaṃsa*, are an invaluable source for indicating this relationship and a number of studies have been based on this (Geiger 1908; Perera 1976; Bechert 1978). Another study treats of this relationship with reference to Thailand (Tambiah 1976). There is undoubtedly a strong tradition in Sri Lanka of associating major changes in the *saṅgha* with political events. Recent attempts to suggest that reforms within the *saṅgha* in the last two centuries were motivated by internal developments within the *saṅgha* and did not seek external legitimisation, fail to explain the departure from tradition and in themselves are not very convincingly argued (see Carrithers 1979).

# 42

# *Millenarianism and Religion in Early India**

Millenarian movements are the outcome of a dissatisfaction with the present expressed in a religious idiom and which focus on a belief that a perfect society will be established through divine intervention. The term 'millenarianism' has now come to include a variety of protest movements. Initial interest in millenarian movements included a perspective which regarded them as the paranoid fantasy of a group unable to accept reality (Cohn 1957). They were viewed with the same suspicion as were shamans, mystics, mantics and ascetics. It was unclear whether the leaders of such movements were the manifestations of a disturbed personality or whether they were attempting to restore normalcy in a disturbed society (Durkheim, Elwin, Bellah, Lewis). It has also been argued that these were revolutionary movements of change, integrating conflict through new ideologies, fostering self-respect and linking religion to a political message (Hill, Worsley). The emphasis in the analysis of such movements has shifted from a concern in the main with eschatology to a recognition of the importance of attitudes to power (Burridge). Whether many of the movements which arose in a colonial context can be called millenarian is a point which has been debated at some length, and alternative labels such as 'nativistic' or 'revitalisation' movements have been suggested (Linton, Wallace, Krader, Jay). If the perspective is widened from just the religious idiom to include the problems which give rise to such movements then millenarianism can be seen as part of a much larger concern with the expression of dissent. The religious idiom draws on what might be called a transcendental sanction but

* Keynote Address to the session on 'Millenarian Movements in Asia', at CISHAAN, Tokyo, 1983.

what distinguishes millenarianism in turn from other movements claiming this sanction is that history is viewed as directed towards a futuristic if not an apocalyptic vision. These movements see themselves as hyphens between the past and the future; and it is the virtual negation of the present which further differentiates them from other movements of protest, dissent and rebellion. The attempt is not to change the present and remove the cause of dissatisfaction but to await the coming of a perfect future.

The millennial idea developed in a Judeo-Christian context although Zoroastrianism provided some seminal thoughts. The Judeo-Christian roots are traced to the Book of Daniel and the Revelations of St John and the apocalyptic texts dating to the late first millennium BC and the early first millennium AD. This was a time of crisis, for Judaism in the earlier period and Christianity in the later. Both were struggling to remain firm in the face of the more powerful religions associated with the four empires, the Assyrian, the Persian, the Hellenistic and the Roman. Messianic hopes for Judaism were therefore prominent. Christian millenarianism had its roots in opposition to the Roman empire but by the second millennium AD hostility was directed against the established Church. Millenarianism was the term used to describe the doctrine or belief in the coming of the millennium, when for a thousand years, Christ would return and preside over the fate of individual men and women. The history of man was seen as a continuum between the pristine utopia of creation and the ultimate return to paradise whether in heaven or on earth.

The concept of the millennial was not entirely absent in other religious traditions. The Mahdi in Islam has distinct millennial overtones and these are evident in the Shi-ite tradition as well. In Buddhism the Buddha Maitreya, the Buddha yet to come was touched upon in the early Pāli texts but the idea was developed more fully in later Buddhism. Among Hindu sects, the Vaiṣṇava carries an element of millennial ideas in the theory of the various incarnations of Viṣṇu which occur in periods of crisis. The human incarnations in particular can be seen, apart from other things, as parallel to figures of redemption. The possibility of multiple incarnations to alleviate suffering would however have weakened the notion of the single messiah and the ultimate redemption. The closest to millennial thought is the coming of Kalki the final incarnation of Viṣṇu, which is yet to be. Thus although the concept is not absent in other religions it has a more central position in the Judeo-Christian tradition. Alternatively it could be suggested that it was expressed in a different way in the religions other than the Judeo-Christian and Islamic, and has yet to be recognised as parallel to Judeo-Christian millenarianism. The elements of eschatology and prophecy, central to millenarianism, would have to be examined in these religions.

Apocalyptic ideas play a crucial role in eschatology. For the historian this has the added interest that it points to a distinct and definitive intervention by God or Deity in human destiny and this intervention is to be recognised by a series of unprecedented events, generally of a catastrophic nature. The influence of Zoroastrianism is evident in the concept of the struggle between the forces of light and darkness, the final judgement of the deity in favour of the forces of light and the condemnation to burning of the forces of darkness. The ultimate intervention of the deity brings the hope of salvation which, in a situation of crisis, could be imminent. The Christian tradition elaborated these ideas and included the resurrection of the dead at the time of the last Judgement and the final Redemption.

Religious movements characterised by a millenarian eschatology therefore expect 'imminent, total, ultimate, this-worldly collective salvation' (Cohn 1962; Talmon). Salvation is thus preordained, is expected at a particular point in time and cannot be thwarted. The linear form of time emphasises the inevitability of the coming of the millennial. The present becomes incidental for time is seen largely as the past and the future. History is important both as the configuration of the past and as the expected form of the future. Salvation is not only collective but a sharp demarcation is made between the followers and the non-followers. Salvation is brought by a redeemer who mediates between the human and the divine and is generally a charismatic leader making messianic claims.

Some of these features present problems to the non-Semitic Asian religions such as Hinduism and Buddhism. The nature of salvation differs. There is an absence of the eschatology of a final Judgement Day for salvation lies in freedom from rebirth. Even at the popular level where the heaven of Indra was sought after death, the notion of a final Judgement Day is absent since entry into Indra's heaven is in itself the final act — a statement which is so vividly portrayed in the sculptured panels of many hero-stones commemorating the death of a hero. Hierarchical tiers of heaven and hell are depicted in some aspects of Buddhist cosmology, but the notion of a Judgement Day is again absent for the ultimate goal for salvation seekers is *nirvāna*. Freedom from rebirth and the attainment of *nirvāna* has led to a wide-ranging discussion on what is meant by *nirvāna* both in the Buddhist texts and in the interpretation of these texts (Radhakrishnan, 446–53, 600–5; Dutt, 187ff; Welbon). What is clear is that *nirvāna* is neither imminent nor collective. Even more important release from rebirth can only be achieved by the individual through his own effort. It involves not a collectivity of behaviour and action but the effort of a lone person often in isolation. Even the theory of the transfer of merit in later Buddhism emphasised the individual as the recipient accumulating merit for his own salvation. In the Hindu tradition perhaps the nearest affinity to the idea of collective salvation comes in the concept of *bhakti* where the individual expresses his devotion, love and loyalty to a particular deity as part of a *bhakti* sect. But this devotion involves him only marginally with others in an identity of worship and the belief that the deity would ensure the salvation of all. However the deity could be incarnated and could provide individual salvation. It is interesting that the period of the rise of the *bhakti* tradition in northern India, coincides with the closest approximation to the millenarian idea in Vaiṣṇavism, namely that of the coming of Kalki.

Differences in time concepts may suggest an explanation for theoretical divergences but the differences decrease on a detailed consideration of the concepts. Hindu and Buddhist time concepts were not linear but there was an inevitability in the pattern of the human condition in time. Time was seen in a cyclic form, with the cycle or *mahāyuga* either terminating in the destruction accompanying the end of the cycle or witnessing the rise of a new cycle when the original had been completed. The measurement of time was outside the bounds as it were, of human computation (MacGovern, 45ff) and was often described spatially (e.g., *Samyukta Nikāya*, XV.1.5–8). Cyclic concepts were not necessarily nihilistic. The upswings of the cycle in Buddhist cosmology were positive in nature and there were certain segments of time which were associated with the appearance of a Buddha. Cyclic movement therefore envisaged a variation in which human suffering could be partially alleviated by the coming of a Buddha. The pursuit of virtue and the discarding of evil actions by men would hasten the coming of better times (e.g., *Dīgha Nikāya*, I.73ff). The awaiting of the utopia was not altogether passive. The moral decline of society inherent in the Hindu notion of cyclic time when the Kali-yuga comes near to a close, was off-set by the appearance of Kalki at the end of the cycle. The actions of Kalki would lead to the rise of a new *mahāyuga*, the initial phase of which would be the utopian conditions prevalent in the first of the time cycles, the Kṛta-yuga. This notion carried an inevitability which was almost parallel to that of the eschatology in linear time, although the inevitability was not of a final and eternal salvation but of a promise of better things to come. The ultimate utopia is to be created on earth and not in heaven. Heaven and hell are in a sense transitional. This is made very explicit in the Jaina tradition where the twenty-four *tirthānkaras* yet to come, headed by Padmanābha, are currently men and women who are fulfilling their *karma* either in heaven or hell and will be reborn to assist in the salvation of all mankind (Stevenson 1915, pp. 275ff).

The historical moment at which a millenarian idea is brought into play and the person through whom it is channelled are both of considerable consequence. In the Pāli texts, the marginal importance of the Buddha Maitreya in the *Dīgha Nikāya* (III.75ff) is developed further in the *Anāgatavaṃsa*. The *Mahāvaṃsa* (XXXII.72ff) weaves the idea closely into Sinhalese politics by associating him with Duṭṭhagāmiṇi who, it is said, would go to the Tuṣita heaven on his death and become the first disciple of the Buddha Metteyya when the latter appears on earth. Duṭṭhagāmiṇi was the hero of the Sinhalese, responsible for establishing a kingdom in Sri Lanka after defeating the Ḍamila king Elāṛa, and even more important was regarded as a great patron of the *saṅgha*. The mythical saviour figure is sought to be linked with a historical person thought to be playing a similar role.

That the presence or absence of millennial ideas is not solely a matter of eschatology and time concepts but has also to be viewed in the light of particular kinds of social organisation, needs to be emphasised. Many societies in their early history expressed social concerns in what we today regard as a religious form: others by the very nature of their social organisation used the idiom of religion as a reference to a wider area of social concern than has been conceded by modern commentators. In the Indian tradition the effective questioning of or breaking away from caste obligations, which were the framework of caste society, often required recourse to religious expression. This derived substantially from the logic of caste society in which the non-observance of caste norms would otherwise have resulted in ostracism and low status. An analysis of dissent in such a society would require a greater co-relating of social norms and the possibility of dissent open to the society, than has been generally recognised (Thapar 1979).

A major requirement of the millenarian movement is the prophet, the redeemer or the charismatic leader who mediates between the human and the supernatural. In a sense religious movements generally require such leadership. What distinguishes the leader of a millennial movement from the others is that he is more of a prophet and his message hinges on prophecy of a particular kind. In the Semitic religious tradition the concept of the prophet is clear and central. By contrast it is largely absent in other major Asian religions. In Hinduism and Buddhism, claims to comprehension of the transcendental or communion with the supernatural require isolation, the virtual opting out of the individual from social obligations and if necessary entry into the alternative or parallel society of the monastery which is built on a contravening of existing social obligations. In such religions the ascetic and the renouncer are more crucial than the prophet. Renouncers, referred to as the *parivrājaka* and the *bhikkṣu*, did not isolate themselves completely as was required of ascetics and often lived on the edges of settlements either individually or in groups, which led inevitably to a nexus between the renouncer and society (Thapar 1978).

Millenarian leaders evoke dedication and a fervour which is expressed either in the abandonment of self-control or in stringent self-discipline (Talmon). The ritual can at times deliberately break accepted social taboos. Renouncers in most cases opted for stringent self-discipline (although examples of the abandonment of self-control are known from later periods and other traditions). This was in part an insistence on a differentiation between themselves and the householders, that is between those who had opted out of maintaining social obligations and those who were at the very centre of social gravity (Thapar 1981). There were differences in visual appearance, an insistence on celibacy and the professed egalitarianism in the orders was in theory at least the opposite of the hierarchically ordered caste society and the political state of monarchy (Thapar 1978). The questioning of the efficacy of the sacrificial ritual was a negation of established religious practices. To the extent that renouncers were protestors, it was protest through withdrawal and not through active revolt or the mobilising of aggression (Cohn 1962).

In the initial phases of many renunciatory movements the renouncer was in a sense a liminal person where liminality represents a threshold condition (Turner) and one which placed the renouncer outside the legally structured society. The authority which he claimed was in part derived from the power of asceticism which over the centuries accumulated its own mythology. Equally important was his role as mediator. Periods of historical change are often characterised by the emergence of mediators. Where the familiar foci of authority was being superceded by other forms, there the presence of the renouncer as a constant factor was reassuring. The ideal of the *bodhisattva* enhanced the notion of mediation, for the *bodhisattva* postponed his own salvation in order to help others towards theirs. The Buddha Maitreya is on occasion described as a *bodhisattva*. The mediational role also required an explanation of social iniquities, the rationale for which was given in the doctrine of transmigration and rebirth which tended to place the responsibility for seeming injustice in the hands of the individual. This sharpened the dependence on the mediator who could help in the acquiring of merit and freedom from rebirth. The mediational role of the renouncers may have partly accounted for the relative marginality of the millennial idea in early Buddhism. As long as the monastic order was secure from competition and had access to patronage in the form of grants of land and interest from monetary investments (*Epigraphia Indica*, 1909–10) invoking the Buddha Maitreya was not imperative. An additional factor may have been that in both Buddhism and Vaiṣṇava Hinduism the ecclesiastical system was nascent at this time. The dues and demands from the ecclesiastical hierarchy on the laity were not strictly prescribed, as they were in Catholic Europe and were not therefore conducive to protest and criticism from lay followers.

Millenarianism derives its strength from those who are socially excluded, those who feel they are deprived of wealth and power and those who are poor and have lost their traditional roots. They can be enthused through apocalyptic visions into protest. But the enthusing has to be done by one who claims to be a prophet or else speaks in the voice of a prophet. For such people the renouncer may not hold sufficient hope even though there is a flavour of the millennial leader in his role. It could perhaps be suggested that the presence of the renouncer weakened the need for a prophet or alternatively that the weakness of the millennial idea in some religions may be partially explained by the absence of the prophet. A distinction has been posited between what has been called ethical asceticism and ethical prophecy (Obeyesekare). The message of the former is derived from meditation and is essentially a precept from which deities are absent. It may remain neutral in relation to the social order, although some scholars do not see it as neutral (Tambiah). Ethical prophecy on the other hand is the vehicle of the transcendental in which the deity is a necessary cause since the message is a proclamation of the Divine Will and may well conflict with pre-existing religions and the secular order.

The association of millenarianism with groups who feel they are deprived is seen as a characteristic of millennial movements. Such groups are naturally attracted to the myth of being the chosen people since it plays to the fantasy of the reversal of roles (Talmon). However it has been argued that deprivation in this case is a relative term and it is not necessarily always those at the bottom of the social hierarchy who are drawn into millennial movements. Nor is it in itself a sufficient cause. Deprivation may relate to those who once had access to power which access is later cut off (Aberle). This would largely explain the notion of Kalki in the brahmanical texts. Kalki was to be the saviour of the upper castes and more particularly the *brāhmaṇas* who felt threatened by the rise to power of lower social groups, such as the *vaiśyas* and *śūdras* (Yadava). In this case there was also the conflict between two kinds of power, the sacerdotal brahmanical status and the *kṣatriya* access to political power which was relatively open to groups considered low in caste ranking.

At the turn of the millennia BC–AD northern India had been subjected to foreign invasions and foreign rule. Even in areas not so subjected families of low status were able to establish dynasties (*Viṣṇu Purāṇa* IV.24; Pargiter), and as yet did not require legitimation through brahmanical ritual. Inspite of the prosperity of many, such as those involved in the manufacture of goods and in trade, from the brahmanical perspective this was a time of troubles registering a decline in traditional social regulations and witnessing the establishing of heretical religions. The brahmanical version of how society should be ordered was upset and even slaves and *śūdras* were said to be resentful of serving the twice-born (*Vana Parvan* 188.64ff; *Śānti Parvan* 254.39ff). The 'heretical' religions because they discouraged brahmanical rituals were regarded as the channel through which the traditional power and authority of the *brāhmaṇas* had decreased. The economy of urban areas based on trade and money and which had encouraged the prosperity of the Buddhist and Jaina *saṅghas* remained largely alien to the *brāhmaṇas* who had derived their wealth substantially from gifts and grants of land as fee for sacrificial rituals. A decline in these rituals led to their fearing an ultimate decline in their wealth. They were apprehensive that their claim to exemption from paying taxes would not be honoured and it was prophecied that they would have to flee from the burden of taxes (*Viṣṇu Purāṇa* IV.24). The *brāhmaṇas* did not espouse the cause of the poor and the most deprived (such as the peasants who were facing a growing range of taxes), for, the resentment was against those of lower status who had used the changed times to improve their status. As one text puts it, 'the despised will rise to the middle and those of the middle will be ranked as the lowest' (*Vana Parvan* 188.18ff). For the *brāhmaṇas* it was indeed 'the world turned upside down'. Needless to say Kalki was to be a *brāhmaṇa* and at the same time a king, resplendent in armour, destroying the lowly barbarians (*mleccha*) and the usurpers of status and power, and was to make over the earth to the twice-born upper castes with appropriate ritual sacrifices (*Viṣṇu Purāṇa* IV.24; *Vana Parvan* 188.85ff). The manifestation of Kalki it is said will purify the minds of people and with the coming of enlightenment the Kṛta age, the start of a fresh *mahāyuga* will be initiated (*Viṣṇu Purāṇa* IV.24).

The inevitability of decline as a process in time is also stressed in Buddhist texts. An indirect reference to the Kali age is made in the *Mahāsupina Jātaka* (No. 77 Fausboll 335ff) where the king of Kosala has sixteen great dreams pertaining to an age to come. The message of the dreams as interpreted by the Buddha is terrifying but the king is reassured that the dreams are prophecies of a time which lies in the distant future. The dreams portend calamities such as drought and the growth of evil and unrighteousness. Those of noble birth will be degraded and the low will rise in status. The peasants will be oppressed and crushed as if in a sugar-cane mill and many will flee to the borders of the kingdom. The desertion of towns and villages implied the decline of the *saṅgha* and this is made more explicit by the statement that the *bhikkhus* will preach not to further the doctrine but for money. Again the fear is not that the lowest and the most deprived will revolt, in fact they are said to be the worst sufferers. The prognosis indicates lower status people being appointed to high office with upstarts claiming the rank and property of the old nobility. The future is envisaged not as a confrontation between the powerful and those without any power but rather the acquiring of greater power by those with relatively less power; a change in the role of intermediary groups competing for power.

Millenarian fantasies do occur in situations of evident social change or of conflicting or discrepant systems in society (Talmon 1966). They suggest an attempt at re-establishing the self respect of groups which feel that they have lost status and wish to establish a new identity in the midst of change and search for a coherent system of values where earlier values have been challenged if not discarded. The projection of the coming of Kalki if carefully analysed tells us much more about social anxieties than many of the texts of the period would allow. For the historian the occurrence of millennial ideas is not merely the indication of a movement, but of wider social changes which can be argued back from the nature of the movement.

The popularity of the cult of the Buddha Maitreya in the northern tradition seems to have derived from a more complex historical situation. The juxtaposition of a number of competing religions along the routes linking India, Iran, central Asia and east Asia — areas where the cult was widespread — provided the historical context. Competition would point to some insecurity in acquiring patronage. Elements of Zoroastrianism, Manichaeism and Christianity doubtless contributed to the form taken by the cult but the germinal idea is traced to the *Dīgha Nikāya* and the prediction of a Buddha yet to come. Maitreya dwells in the Tuṣita heaven and will appear after evil has increased and the time-cycle has neared its end, or, as others maintain, after a lapse of five hundred, a thousand or five thousand years. But the worship of the Buddha Maitreya was not just a millennial cult. Unlike the return of Christ, Maitreya was a different Buddha from Gautama. His future coming was only one aspect of his larger role as the Buddha of love and compassion helping in the liberation of all. The worship of Maitreya before his descent from the Tuṣita heaven was a subtle form of extending the idea of release from rebirth to situations other than the perfect future. The cult of the Buddha Maitreya would not therefore in every case be linked to millenarianism.

Fa Hsien visiting the Indian subcontinent in the fifth century AD records a statement made by an Indian devotee whom he meets in Sri Lanka, that predictions were current at the time, regarding the future of the doctrine. Among these was the prophecy of the Buddha Maitreya. When men become short-lived, evil and start killing one another, those that remain faithful to the teachings of the Buddha will hide in the mountains and will emerge only on the death of the evil ones to re-establish a virtuous society and await the coming of Maitreya. The Buddha Maitreya will appear and assist the faithful to attain salvation and convert others to the doctrine. Fa Hsien makes a special note of the devotee telling him that this information was not written in any of the scriptures and was presumably part of the oral tradition (Legge 1886, pp. 109–10). Hsüan Tsang writing in the seventh century quotes a similar story while visiting monasteries in the middle Ganga valley. It is said that the Buddha had predicted the coming of Maitreya. He would be born in a *brāhmaṇa* family, would preach the doctrine and would hold three great assemblies to ensure the salvation of those then living (S. Beal 1884, I. pp. 30, 78–9, II. pp. 46–7). (In the distinction between pre- and post-millenarian ideology, the Maitreya story would conform to the latter which requires an anticipatory period in which people perfect themselves for the millennial (Shepperson). An echo of the renouncer is introduced into the story when Hsüan Tsang refers to various renowned Elders who lived hidden in the mountains awaiting the coming of Maitreya. The relevance of the millenarian Maitreya in the *madhya-deśa* of northern India by this time may have been due to the gradual decline of Buddhism in this area as is evident from Hsüan Tsang's account. The patronage of the state and of the wealthy having decreased, the doctrine seems to have fled to the more peripheral areas of northern India. The compassionate tone of the Buddha Maitreya story contrasts sharply with the strident voice predicting the coming of Kalki. Perhaps the difference lay in salvation being the primary purpose of the coming of Maitreya whereas Kalki's concern was to restore power and wealth to the upper castes.

The Buddha Maitreya cult however was not as widespread in India as it was in the Buddhism of central and eastern Asia. The political upheavals in the oasis-states of central Asia with confrontations between nomadic and sedentary cultures created a situation of flux and insecurity in which a millennial figure would have provided a much-needed sense of psychological security. The significance of Maitreya in China may have been linked to Buddhism having to compete initially with well-established religious cults patronised by the court. The millennial hope may have been an undercurrent in the effort to attract a following. The peak period of the cult in the mid-first millennium AD appears to coincide with hostility to Buddhism among the Chinese elite (Zurcher, 254ff) and becomes less evident once the religion is firmly established. It might be worth examining possible connections between the Buddha Maitreya cult and the evolution of urban centres in these areas where such centres were also the meeting point of cross-cultural ideas. The anonymity of towns attracts protestors and the activity of itinerant merchants and middlemen encourages the peddling of goods as well as ideas. Initially the notion of the millennial in the Judeo-Christian tradition arose among groups with urban, cosmopolitan associations as is also expressed in the key position of the city, the New Jerusalem, in the vision of the future. The organisation of peasants around millennial ideas in Europe in the second millennium AD was frequently inspired by urban leaders of Christian sects such as the Cathars, Taborites, Anabaptists, which had divergent views from those of the established Church. English millenarianism of the seventeenth century — the Diggers, Seekers, Ranters, Quakers, Muggletonians and Fifth Monarchy Men — had its roots in an urban environment (Hill, Capp, Elliot, Lamont). The rise of such cults among peasant communities and in segmentary or lineage-based societies seems to make its appearance in more recent times.

The term millenarianism has now been extended to include a variety of movements closely related to peasant discontent and to various expressions of antipathy or hostility to colonial rule. Some of these movements may not be strictly millenarian in their ideology although their political and social aspirations are similar. It has been argued that the movements tend to be pre-political in segmentary societies and politically more developed in peasant societies or where the movement arises with the decline of established political power or in confrontation with colonial power (Worsley). Peasants uprooted as a result of changes in agrarian structure introduced by colonialism saw themselves outside the system as did the urban poor. In colonial situations millenarian movements often arose in the intersections of indigenous and colonial cultures and became the means by which aspects of the latter were internalised by the former (Stern). The disruption of the existing patterns of power through colonial interference was often at the root of more recent movements. The criterion of what constitutes power needs to be looked at in greater detail. In a sense all millennial movements have been struggles in the context of power where the struggle is expressed in a cultural idiom which may disguise the crux of the conflict. Claims to mystic visions and communion with the transcendental constituted one kind of power which, as a motivator of social action should not be underestimated. But equally important was the concern with the hard realities of power: the state, and wealth in the form of valued objects, land and money.

The original millenarian movements were hostile to monarchies. Curiously however, the structure of the eschatological vision reflects the imprint of the monarchical state: the vision of the deity in Judgement parallels the monarch in his court, glittering with fabulous wealth and the notion of judgement and the trappings of Judgement Day draw on the working of monarchical administration. The impact of monarchical power as an over-arching political form was undoubtedly substantial. Implicit in the allegory of the Day of Judgement is the transference of that power and its control to those who in reality were without power. The Fifth Monarchy was similar to the first Four but for the fact that the deprived saw themselves as the forces of righteousness and the inheritors of power. Kalki although born a *brāhmaṇa* is envisaged as a *kṣatriya* king, leading warriors and re-establishing the power of the *brāhmaṇas*. The image combines military and monarchical strength. Only the Buddha Maitreya is without the glamour of state power. Millenarian beliefs therefore can be compatible with ideological conservatism (Elliot), and not all such movements are essentially protest movements supporting radical change (Lamont).

Land as a source of both wealth and power is crucial to millennial movements involving peasants. Peasant revolts in India are recorded in the second millennium AD. Prior to that, peasant migration (generally because of oppressive taxes) and peasants deserting their land were the forms of peasant protest (Thapar 1979). The change from migration to revolt has featured in the widely debated theory of the moral economy of the peasant (Scott). Migration to new, cultivable land would in part account for the absence of peasant revolts. With the intensification of agriculture and more land being brought under cultivation the easy accessibility of new land would have declined. Apart from this the agrarian system of the early second millennium AD with its hierarchy of intermediaries, hemmed in the peasant and made it more difficult for peasants to migrate. Peasant revolts in south India in the thirteenth century seem to have been triggered off by excessive taxation within this structure (Karashima). The co-relation of demography to the availability of easily cultivable land might provide an additional perspective on peasant movements. The echoes of millenarianism in the Satnami revolt of the seventeenth century and the Santal rebellions and the Birsa Munda movement of more recent times (Roy; Fuchs) may have been due to the proximity of Islam and Christianity. But the movements attracted low status peasants fearful about the large scale encroachments onto their land, their inability to pay taxes and their observation that money was one of the means by which land was lost or snatched away. Peasant involvement in movements of a millennial nature is historically later in India than the involvement of other social groups. This would suggest a possible corollary to the definition of millennial movements: protesting groups should perceive of their relation with the rest of society as being one where their withdrawal or revolt can affect the well-being of the society. The use of millenarianism by various social groups would therefore require an awareness on their part of their economic and social significance to society, irrespective of their actual status.

Millenarian movements therefore ostensibly involve groups led by persons using an apocalyptic vision and drawing on an ideology which anticipates a perfect future coming at a particular point in time through the intervention of the supernatural. Such groups in effect are dissatisfied with existing conditions, suffer from a sense of deprivation, seek power and status, are conscious of a lack of material wealth or fear its decrease and see their action as having an impact on the well-being of the social whole. It is often these effective realities which constitute the need for protesting and the protest is expressed in a religious idiom. The proto-type draws on the Judeo-Christian tradition but elements of millenarianism appear to be present in societies subscribing to other religious idioms. Where millenarianism is not evident it might be worth investigating whether there are alternate forms of protest which arise from the same causes and achieve similar results but whose apocalyptic allegories might be different.

## References


Aberle, D., 1962, 'On Deprivation Theory', in S. Thrupp (ed.), 'Millennial Dreams in Action', pp. 209ff.

*Vana Parvan*, 1942 (Mahabharata), V.S. Sukthankar (ed.), B.O.R.I., Poona.

Beal, S., 1884, *Buddhist Records of the Western World*, London, I.134, 137, 226–8, II.142–4.

Bellah, R.N. (ed.), 1965, *Religion and Progress in Modern Asia*, Glencoe.

Burridge, K.O.L., 1969, *New Heaven New Earth*, Oxford.

Capp, B., 1971, 'Godly Rule and English Millenarianism', *Past and Present*, 52, pp. 106–17.

Cohn, N., 1957, *The Pursuit of the Millennium*, London.

—— 1962, 'Medieval Millenarianism', in S. Thrupp (ed.), *Millennial Dreams in Action*, pp. 35ff.

*Dīgha Nikāya*, 1890–1911, T.W. Rhys Davids and J.E. Carpentier (eds), London, PTS.

Durkheim, E., 1964, *The Rules of Sociological Method*, New York (trans. S.A. Solavay and J.H. Mueller).

Dutt, N., 1977, *Mahayana Buddhism*, Delhi.

Elliot, J.H., 1969, 'Revolution and Continuity in Early Modern Europe', *Past and Present*, 42, pp. 35–56.

*Epigraphia Indica*, 1909–10, X, Appendix, pp. 1ff.

Elwin, V., 1955, *The Religion of an Indian Tribe*, London.

Emmett, D., 1956, 'Prophets and their Societies', *Journal of the Royal Anthropological Institute*, 86, pp. 13–23.

Fuchs, S., 1965, *Rebellious Prophets*, Bombay.

Gunawardana, R.A.L.H., 1979, *Robe and Plough*, Arizona.

Hill, C., 1975, *The World Turned Upside Down*, Harmondsworth.

Jay, E., 1961, 'Revitalisation Movement in Tribal India', in L.P. Vidyarthi (ed.), *Aspects of Religion in Indian Society*, New Delhi (1984).

Karashima, N., 1984, *South Indian History and Society*, Delhi.

Krader, L., 1956, 'A Nativistic Movement in Western Siberia', *American Anthropologist*, 58, pp. 282–92.

La Barre, W., 1971, 'Materials for a History of Studies of Crisis Cults: A Bibliographical Essay', *Current Anthropology*, 12, pp. 3–14.

Lamont, W., 1983, 'The Muggletonians 1652–1979: A Vertical Approach, *Past and Present*, 99, pp. 22ff.

Lanternari, V., 1965, *The Religion of the Oppressed*, New York.

Legge, J., 1886, *A Record of Buddhistic Kingdoms*, Oxford, pp. 109–10.

Lewis, I., 1971, *Ecstatic Religions*, Harmondsworth.

Linton, R., 1943, 'Nativistic Movements', *American Anthropologist*, XLV, pp. 230–40.

*Mahāsupina Jātaka*, 1877–97, no. 77, Fausboll, 335ff, London.

*Mahāvaṃsa*, 1908, W. Geiger (ed.), London.

McGovern, W.M., 1923, *A Manual of Buddhist Philosophy*, London.

Obeyesekare, G., 1980, 'Rebirth Eschatology and its Transformations', in W. O'Flaherty (ed.), *Karma and Rebirth in the Classical Indian Tradition*, Berkeley, pp. 137–64.

Pargiter, F.E., 1913, *The Purana Texts of the Dynasties of the Kali Age*, Oxford.

Radhakrishnan, S., 1923, *Indian Philosophy*, London.

Rousseau, P., 1978, *Ascetics, Authority and the Church in the Age of Jerome and Cassian*, Oxford.

Roy, S.C., 1921, 'A New Religious Movement among the Oraons', *Man in India*, I, no. 4, pp. 267–324.

*Samyukta Nikāya*, 1884–1904, L. Freer (ed.), London, PTS.

Scott, J.C., 1976, *The Moral Economy of the Peasant*, New Haven.

Shepperson, G., 1962, 'The Comparative Study of Millenarian Movements', in S. Thrupp (ed.), *Millennial Dreams in Action*, pp. 45ff.

Stern, T., 1968, 'Ariya and the Golden Book: A Millenarian Buddhist Sect among the Karen', *Journal of Asian Studies*, 27, pp. 297–327.

Stevenson, S., 1915, *The Heart of Jainism*, Oxford.

Talmon, Y., 1966, 'Millenarian Movements', *European Journal of Sociology*, 7, pp. 159–200.

Tambiah, S.J., 1981, 'The Renouncer: His Individuality and his Community', *Contributions to Indian Sociology* (ns), vol. 15, nos 1 and 2, pp. 299–320.

Thapar, R., 1978, 'Renunciation: The Making of a Counter-culture?', in *Ancient Indian Social History: Some Interpretations*, New Delhi, pp. 63–104. *See* chapter 40 in this volume.

—— 1979, 'Dissent and Protest in the Early Indian Tradition', *Studies in History*, vol. I, no. 2, pp. 177–95. *See* chapter 11 in this volume.

—— 1981, 'The Householder and the Renouncer in the Brahmanical and Buddhist Traditions', *Contributions to Indian Sociology* (ns), vol. 15, nos 1 and 2, pp. 273–98. *See* chapter 41 in this volume.

Thrupp, S.L. (ed.), 1962, *Millennial Dreams in Action, Comparative Studies in Society and History*, Sup. II, The Hague.

Turner, V.W., 1969, *The Ritual Process*, Chicago.

*Viṣṇu Purāṇa*, 1961 (2nd ed.), trans., H.H. Wilson, Calcutta.

Wallace, A.F.C., 1956, 'Revitalisation Movements', *American Anthropologist*, LVIII, pp. 264–81.

Weber, M., 1965, *The Sociology of Religion*, London.

Welbon, G.R., 1968, *The Buddhist Nirvana and its Western Interpreters*, Chicago.

Werner, E., 1960, 'Popular Ideologies in Late Medieval Europe; Taborite, Chilliasm and its Antecedents', *Comparative Studies in Society and History*, II, pp. 344–65.

Worsley, P., 1968, *The Trumpet Shall Sound*, London.

Yadava, B.N.S., 1978–79, 'The Accounts of the Kali Age and the Social Transition from Antiquity to the Middle Ages', *Indian Historical Review*, V, nos 1 and 2, pp. 31–63.

Zurcher, E., 1959, *The Buddhist Conquest of China*, Leiden.

# IX

# *The Present in the Past*

The last group of essays in this collection relates to concerns about the way in which Indian history has been interpreted to encourage communal views of the past. These adhere largely to a nineteenth century historiography. The change in historical perspective reflected in this collection of papers points to a focus which would by its very nature challenge a communal perspective.

Included here are essays not all intended for academic journals, but relevant as explanation of communal interpretations for a wider audience.

An initial attempt at a long-distance view of the Rāma story is available in, 'Epic and History: Tradition, Dissent and Politics in India', in *Past and Present*, 1989, 135, 3–26. This was further explored in various ways as in some of the essays in this section.


1. Imagined Religious Communities? Ancient History and the Modern Search for a Hindu Identity (1989)
2. The Tyranny of Labels (1996)
3. Secularism and History (1995)
4. Syndicated Hinduism (1985/97)
5. A Historical Perspective on the Story of Rama (1991)
6. The Ramayana Syndrome (1989)
7. In Defence of the Variant (1993)
8. The Politics of Religious Communities (1990)
9. The Theory of Aryan Race and India: History and Politics (1995)

# 43

# *Imagined Religious Communities? Ancient History and the Modern Search for a Hindu Identity*[*]

My choice of subject for this lecture arose from what I think might have been a matter of some interest to Kingsley Martin; as also from my own concern that the interplay between the past and contemporary times requires a continuing dialogue between historians working on these periods. Such a dialogue is perhaps more pertinent to post-colonial societies where the colonial experience changed the framework of the comprehension of the past from what had existed earlier: a disjuncture which is of more than mere historiographical interest. And where political ideologies appropriate this comprehension and seek justification from the pre-colonial past, there, the historian's comment on this process is called for.

Among the more visible strands in the political ideology of contemporary India is the growth and acceptance of what are called communal ideologies. 'Communal', as many in this audience are aware, in the Indian context has a specific meaning and primarily perceives Indian society as constituted of a number of religious communities. Communalism in the Indian sense therefore is a consciousness which draws on a supposed religious identity and uses this as the basis for a political and social ideology. It then demands political allegiance to a religious community and supports a programme of political action designed to further the interests of that religious community. Such an ideology is of recent origin but uses history to justify the notion that the community (as defined

* *Modern Asian Studies*, 1989, 23, 2, 209–31. I would like to thank K.N. Panikkar, Neeladri Bhattacharya and B.K. Matilal for their helpful criticism of an earlier draft of this lecture. Kingsley Martin Lecture, Cambridge.

in recent history) and therefore the communal identity, have existed since the early past. Because the identity is linked to religion, it can lead to the redefinition of the particular religion, more so in the case of one as amorphous as Hinduism.

Such identity tends to iron out diversity and insists on conformity, for it is only through a uniform acceptance of the religion that it can best be used for political ends. The attempt is always to draw in as many people as possible since numbers enhance the power of the communal group and are crucial in a mechanical view of democracy. This political effort requires a domination over other groups and where the numbers are substantially larger, there is a deliberate emphasis both on superiority and the notion of majority, a notion which presupposes the existence of various 'minority communities'. In the construction of what have been called 'imagined communities',[1] in this case identified by religion, there is an implied rejection of the applicability of other types of divisions in society, such as status or class.

In the multiplicity of communalisms prevalent in India today, the major one obviously is Hindu communalism since it involves the largest numbers and asserts itself as the dominant group. I shall therefore discuss only the notion of the Hindu community and not those of other religions. Nevertheless my comments on communal ideology and its use of history would apply to other groups claiming a similar ideology. I would like to look at those constituents of Hindu communal ideology which claim legitimacy from the past, namely, that there has always been a well-defined and historically evolved religion which we now call Hinduism and an equally clearly defined Hindu community. Implicit in this are the historical implications of Hindu communalism and I shall argue that it is in part a modern search for an imagined Hindu identity from the past, a search which has drawn on the historiography of the last two centuries. The historical justification is far from being the sole reason for the growth of communalism, but recourse to this justification fosters the communal ideology.

The modern description of Hinduism has been largely that of a *brāhmaṇa*-dominated religion which gathered to itself in a somewhat paternalistic pattern a variety of sects drawing on a range of Buddhists, Jainas, Vaiṣṇavas, Śaivas and Śāktas. The texts and the tradition were viewed as inspirational, initially orally preserved, with multiple manifestations of deities, priests but no church, a plurality of doctrines with a seeming absence of controversies and all this somehow integrated into a single religious fabric. Differences with the Semitic religions were recognized and were seen as the absence of a prophet, of a revealed book regarded as sacred, of a monotheistic God, of ecclesiastical organization, of theological debates on orthodoxy and heresy and, even more important, the absence of conversion. But somehow the logic of these differences was not built into the construction of the history of the religion. Hinduism was projected largely in terms of its philosophical ideas, iconology and rituals. It is ironic in some ways that these multiple religious sects were seldom viewed in their social and historical context even though this was crucial to their understanding. Histories of the 'Hindu' religion have been largely limited to placing texts and ideas in a chronological perspective with few attempts at relating these to the social history of the time. Scholarship also tended to ignore the significance of the popular manifestation of religion in contrast to the textual, a neglect which was remedied by some anthropological research, although frequently the textual imprint is more visible even in such studies.

The picture which emerges of the indigenous view of religion from historical sources of the early period is rather different. The prevalent religious groups referred to are two, Brahmanism and Śramanism with a clear distinction between them. They are organizationally separate, had different sets of beliefs and rituals and often disagreed on social norms. That this distinction was recognized is evident from the edicts of the Mauryan king Aśoka[2] as well as by those who visited India and left accounts of what they had observed, as, for example, Megasthenes;[3] the Chinese Buddhist pilgrims Fa Hsien and Hsüan Tsang;[4] and Alberuni.[5] The Buddhist visitors write mainly of matters pertaining to Buddhism and refer to the *brāhmaṇas* as heretics. Patañjali the grammarian refers to the hostility between Brahmanism and Śramanism as innate as is that between the snake and the mongoose.[6] Sometimes the *brāhmaṇas* and the *śramaṇas* are addressed jointly as in Buddhist texts and the Aśokan edicts. Here they are being projected as a category distinct from the common people. Such a bunching together relates to a similarity of concerns suggestive of a common framework of discourse but does not detract from the fundamental differences between the two systems. It might in fact be a worthwhile exercise to reconstruct Brahmanism from the references to it in Śramanic and other non-Brahmanical sources.

A historical view of early Indian religion would endorse this dichotomy and its continuity even in changed forms. Early Brahmanism demarcates the twice-born upper castes from the rest. The twice-born has to observe the precepts of *śruti* — the *Vedas* and of *smṛti* — the auxiliary texts to the *Vedas* and particularly the *Dharmaśāstras*. *Dharma* lay in conforming to the separate social observances and ritual functions of each caste. The actual nature of belief in deity was left ambiguous and monotheism was not a requirement. The focus of worship was the sacrificial ritual. Brahmanism came closest to having a subcontinental identity largely through its ritual functions and the use of a common language, Sanskrit, even though it was prevalent among only a smaller section of people.

Śramanism, a term covering a variety of Buddhist, Jaina, Ājīvika and other sects, denied the fundamentals of Brahmanism such as Vedic *śruti* and *smṛti*. It was also opposed to the sacrificial ritual both on account of the beliefs incorporated in the ritual as well the violence involved in the killing of animals. It was characterized by a doctrine open to all castes and although social hierarchy was accepted it did not emphasize separate social observances but, rather, cut across caste. The idea of conversion was therefore notionally present. The attitude to social hierarchy in most Śramanic sects was not one of radical opposition. In Buddhism, for example, recruitment to the *saṅgha* and support from lay followers was initially in large numbers from the upper castes and the appeal was frequently also made to such groups.[7] Nevertheless there were no restrictions on a lower caste recruitment and in later periods support from such groups was substantial. The founders of the Śramanic sects were not incarnations of deity. Buddhism and Jainism had an ecclesiastical organization, the *saṅgha*, and in most cases there was an overall concern with historicity.

In terms of numbers there appears to have developed even greater support for the Śākta sects which were in many ways antithetical to early Brahmanism. The essentials of Śāktism are sometimes traced back to Harappan times and some of these elements probably went into the making of popular religion from the earliest historical period. Recognized sects gradually crystalized from the first millennium AD when they come to be referred to in the literature of the period. The centrality of worshipping the goddess was initially new to upper caste religion. Some of these sects deliberately broke the essential taboos of Brahmanism relating to separate caste functions, commensality, rules of food and drink and sexual taboos.[8] That some of the beliefs of the Śākta sects were later accepted by some *brāhmaṇa* sects is an indication of a break with Vedic religion by these *brāhmaṇa* sects although the legitimacy of the Vedic religion was sometimes sought to be bestowed on the new sects by them. Such religious compromises were not unconnected with the brahmanical need to retain social ascendency. However, some brahmanical sects remained orthodox.

As legitimizers of political authority, the *brāhmaṇas* in the first millennium AD were given grants of land which enabled them to become major landowners. The institutions which emerged out of these grants such as the *agrahāra*s became centres of control over rural resources as well as of Brahmanical learning and practice. It was probably this high social and economic status of the *brāhmaṇa* castes which encouraged the modern idea that Brahmanism and Hinduism were synonymous. But that Brahmanism had also to compromise with local cults is evident from the religious articulation of text and temple and from the frequency with which attempts were introduced into Brahmanism to purify the religion in terms of going back to *śruti* and *smṛti*. In the process of acculturation between brahmanic 'high culture' and the 'low culture' of local cults, the perspective is generally limited to that of the Sanskritization of the latter. It might be historically more accurate on occasion to view it as the reverse, as, for example, in the cult of Viṭṭhala at Pandharpur or that of Jagannātha at Puri.[9] In such cases the deities of tribals and low caste groups become, for reasons other than the purely religious, centrally significant and Brahmanism has to adapt itself to the concept of such deities. The domain of such deities evolves out of a span spreading horizontally, moving from a village to its networks of exchange and finally encompassing a region. The focal centre of such a cult takes on a political dimension as well in the nature of the control which it exercises, quite apart from ritual and belief. Pilgrimage then becomes a link across various circumferences.

The increasing success of Brahmanism by the end of the first millennium AD resulted in the gradual displacement of Śramanism — but not entirely. Local cults associated with new social groups led to the emergence of the more popular Puranic religion. Vedic deities were subordinated or ousted. Viṣṇu and Śiva came to be worshipped as the pre-eminent deities. The thrust of Puranic religion was in its assimilative and accommodating processes. A multitude of new cults, sects and castes were worked into the social and religious hierarchy. Religious observance often coincided with caste identities.

By the early second millennium AD a variety of devotional cults — referred to by the generic label *bhakti* — had come to form a major new religious expression. They drew on the Puranic tradition of Śaivism and Vaiṣṇavism but were also in varying degrees the inheritors of the Śramanic religions. Their emphasis on complete loyalty to the deity has been seen as a parallel to feudal loyalties. But what was more significant was that *bhakti* cults and the sects which grew around them sought to underline dependence on and liberation from rebirth through the deity. To this extent they indicate a departure from earlier indigenous religion. These cults were god-centred rather than man-centred. The ritual of sacrifice had been substituted by the worship of an icon. Some sects accepted, up to a point, brahmanical *śruti* and *smṛti* whereas others vehemently denied it, a debate which continues to this day. Those sects in opposition to Brahmanism which sought to transcend caste and differentiated social observances, insisting that every worshipper was equal in the eyes of the deity, often ended up as castes, thus once again coinciding sect with caste. With the arrival of Islam in India some drew from the ideas of Islam. Most of these sects were geographically limited and bound by the barriers of language. Possibly the beginnings of larger religious communities within what is now called the Hindu tradition, date to the middle of the second millennium, such as perhaps some Vaiṣṇava sects, where, for example, the worship of Kṛṣṇa at Mathura drew audiences from a larger geographical region than before. This also heralds a change in the nature of Puranic religion, for Mathura attracts Vaiṣṇavas from eastern and southern India and becomes like Ayodhya (for the worship of Rāma[10]) the focus of a search for sacred topography. It might perhaps be seen as an attempt to go beyond local caste and sect and build a broader community. The historical reasons for its happening at this juncture need to be explored.

Initial opposition from those of high caste status also encouraged *bhakti* sects to inculcate a sense of community within themselves, particularly if they were economically successful, such as the Vīraśaivas. Even when such religious sects attempted to constitute a larger community, the limitations of location, caste and language, acted as a deterrent to a single, homogeneous Hindu community. In the continuing processes of either appropriation or rejection of belief and practice, the kaleidoscopic change in the constitution of religious sects was one which precluded the emergence of a uniform, monolithic religion.

The multiplicity of cults and sects also reflects a multiplicity of beliefs. Even in Brahmanism we are told that if two *śruti* traditions are in conflict then both are to be held as law.[11] This is a fundamentally different approach from that of religions which would like to insist on a single interpretation arising out of a given theological framework. This flexibility together with the emphasis on social observance rather than theology allowed of a greater privatization of religion than was possible in most other religions. Renunciatory tendencies were common, were respected and often gave sanction to private forms of worship. The renouncer opted out of society, yet was highly respected.[12] The private domain of belief was always a permissible area of early Indian religion: a religion which is perhaps better seen as primarily the religious belief of social segments, sometimes having to agglomerate and sometimes remaining sharply differentiated. The coexistence of religious sects should not be mistaken for the absorption of all sects into an ultimately unified entity. But the demarcation was often more significant since it related both to differences in religious belief and practice as well as social status and political needs. The status of a sect could change as it was hinged to that of its patrons. Political legitimation through the use of religious groups was recognized, but the appeal was to a particular sect or cult or a range of these and not to a monolithic religion. Royal patronage within the same ruling family, extended to a multiplicity of sects, was probably conditioned as much by the exigencies of political and social requirements as by a religious catholicity. This social dimension as well as the degree to which a religious sect had its identity in caste or alternatively was inclusive of caste, has been largely ignored in the modern interpretation of early Hinduism. With the erosion of social observances and caste identity, there is now a search for a new identity and here the creation of a new Hinduism becomes relevant.

The evolution of Hinduism is not a linear progression from a founder through an organizational system, with sects branching off. It is rather the mosaic of distinct cults, deities, sects and ideas and the adjusting, juxtaposing or distancing of these to existing ones, the placement drawing not only on belief and ideas but also on the socioeconomic reality. New deities could be created linked genealogically to the established ones, as in the recent case of Santoshi Ma, new rituals worked out and the new sect could become the legitimizer of a new caste. Religious practice and belief are often self-sufficient within the boundaries of a caste and are frequently determined by the needs of a caste. The worship of icons was unthought of in the Vedic religion, but the idol becomes a significant feature of Puranic religion and therefore also in the eyes of contemporary Muslim observers. The consciousness of a similarity in ritual and belief in different geographical regions was not always evident. Thus *bhakti* cults were confined to particular regions and were frequently unaware of their precursors or contemporaries elsewhere. Recourse to historicity of founder and practice was confined within the sect and was not required of a conglomeration of sects which later came to be called Hinduism. This is in part reflected in the use of the term *sampradāya* for a sect where the emphasis is on transmission of traditional belief and usage through a line of teachers. The insistence on proving the historicity of human incarnations of deity, such as Rāma and Kṛṣṇa, is a more recent phenomenon and it may be suggested that there is a subconscious parallel with the prophet and the messiah. The identification of the *janmabhūmis*, the location of the exact place where Kṛṣṇa and Rāma were born, becomes important only by the mid-second millennium AD.

Religions such as Buddhism, Jainism, Islam and Christianity, see themselves as part of the historical process of the unfolding and interpreting of the single religion and sects are based on variant interpretations of the original teaching. They build their strength on a structure of ecclesiastical organization. In contrast to this, Hindu sects often had a distinct and independent origin. Assimilation was possible and was sometimes expressed in the appropriation of existing civilizational symbols. What needs to be investigated is the degree to which such civilizational symbols were originally religious in connotation.

Civilizational symbols are manifested in many ways: from the symbol of the *svāstika* to the symbol of the renouncer as the noblest and most respected expression of human aspirations. The history of the *svāstika* goes back to the fourth millennium BC where a design which resembles it occurs on seals and impressions from northwest

India and Central Asia. In the Indian subcontinent it is not a specifically Hindu symbol for it is used by a variety of religious groups in various ways, but in every case it embodies the auspicious. The Bon-po of the Himalayan borderlands reverse the symbol to distance themselves from the Buddhists. The two epics, the *Mahābhārata* and the *Rāmāyaṇa*, frequently treated as primarily the religious literature of the Vaiṣṇavas, are in origin as epics, civilizational symbols. They were, at one level, the carriers of ethical traditions and were used again by a variety of religious sects to propagate their own particular ethic, a situation which is evident from the diverse treatment of the theme of the *Rāmāyaṇa* in Vālmīki, in the Buddhist *Vessantara* and *Dasaratha Jātakas* and in the Jaina version — the *Paumacariyam* of Vimalasūri.[13] The epic versions were also used for purposes of political legitimation. The primarily Vaiṣṇava religious function of the epics develops gradually and comes to fruition in the second millennium AD with clearly defined sects worshipping Rāma or Kṛṣṇa coinciding with the development of what has been called the Puranic religion. Subsequent to this were various tribal adaptations of the *Rāmāyaṇa*, and these were less concerned with the Vaiṣṇava message and more with articulating their own social fears and aspirations.

Even on the question of beliefs about the afterlife, although the concept of *karma* and rebirth was commonly referred to, there were distinct and important groups who believed in a different concept. The life after death of the hero in the heaven of Indra or Śiva, waited upon by *apsarās*, goes back to the Vedic belief in the *pitṛloka* or House of the Fathers. This belief is a major motivation in the widespread hero cults from the mid-first millennium AD onwards.[14] Here even the concept of afterlife was conditioned by social birth and function. A different idea influences the way in which the ritual of *satī* changes its meaning over time. Initially a ritual which ensured that the faithful wife accompanied her hero-husband to heaven, and therefore associated largely with *kṣatriya* castes and those dying heroic deaths, its practice by other castes in the second millennium AD involved a change in eschatology. Ultimately the *satī* was defied, which meant that she neither went to heaven nor was subjected to the rules of *karma*.[15]

It has been suggested that there was a structural similarity in various rituals practised by people in different regions and therefore shared myths and shared ritual patterns can account for some unity in the varieties of the religious beliefs that we find in India over a long time.[16] This is certainly true. But nevertheless it is different from a shared creed, catechism, theology and ecclesiastical organization.

The definition of Hinduism as it has emerged in recent times appears not to have emphasized the variant premises of Indian religion and therefore the difference in essence from the model of Christianity and Islam. This definition was the result of various factors: of Christian missionaries who saw this as the lacunae of religions in India and which they regarded as primitive; of some Orientalist scholarship anxious to fit the 'Hindu' process into a comprehensible whole based on a known model; the efforts also of Indian reform movements attempting to cleanse Indian religion of what they regarded as negative encrustations and trying to find parallels with the Semitic model. Even in the translation of texts from Sanskrit into English, where religious concepts were frequently used the translation often reflected a Christian undertone. The selection of texts to be studied had its own purpose. The East India Company's interest in locating and codifying Hindu law gave a legal form to what was essentially social observance and customary law. The concept of law required that it be defined as a cohesive ideological code. The Manu *Dharmaśāstra*, for example, which was basically part of Brahmanical *smṛti* was taken as the laws of the Hindus and presumed to apply universally. In the process of upward social mobility during the late eighteenth and early nineteenth centuries, traders and artisanal groups emerged as patrons of temple building activities and the trend to conform to the brahmanical model was reinforced by this comprehension of Hinduism.[17] The growth of the political concepts of majority and minority communities further galvanized the process.

The degree to which castes and sects functioned independently even in situations which would elsewhere have been regarded as fundamentally of theological importance, can perhaps be seen in attitudes to religious persecution and the manifestations of intolerance. Among the normative values which were highlighted in the discussion of Hinduism in recent times, has been the concept of *ahimsā* or nonviolence. It has been argued that nonviolence and tolerance were special features of Hinduism which particularly demarcated its ethics from those of Islam and to a lesser extent Christianity. Yet *ahimsā* as an absolute value is characteristic of certain Śramanic sects and less so of Brahmanism. The notion appears in the *Upaniṣads*, but it was the Buddhists and the Jainas who first made it foundational to their teaching, and their message was very different from that of the *Bhagavad-Gītā* on this matter. That Brahmanism and Śramanism were recognized as distinct after the period of the *Upaniṣads* further underlines the significance of *ahimsā* to Śramanic thinking. This is also borne out by the evidence of religious persecution.

In spite of what historians, ancient and modern, have written, there is a persistent, popular belief that the 'Hindus' never indulged in religious persecution. However, the Śaivite persecution of Śramanic sects is attested to and on occasion, retaliation by the latter. Hsüan Tsang writing in the seventh century refers to this when he describes his visit to Kashmir.[18] That this was not the prejudiced view of the Buddhist pilgrim is made clear by the historian Kalhaṇa in the *Rājataraṅginī*, who even in the twelfth century refers to the earlier destruction of Buddhist monasteries and the killing of Buddhist monks by the Hūna king Mihirakula and other ardent Śaivites.[19] That Mihirakula was a Hūna is used by modern historians to excuse these actions, but it should be remembered that he gave large grants of land, *agrahāras*, to the *brāhmaṇas* of Gandhāra, which Kalhaṇa in disgust informs us they gratefully received. Clearly there was competition for royal patronage and the Śaiva *brāhmaṇas* triumphed over the Buddhists. The Buddhist association with the commerce between India and Central Asia was one of the reasons for the material prosperity of the Buddhist *saṅgha*.[20] The Hūna disruption of the Indian trade with Central Asia may well have resulted in an antagonism between the northern Buddhists and the Hūnas.

Elsewhere there is a variation on this story. In Tamil Nadu, for example, from the seventh century onwards, Śaiva sects attacked Jaina establishments and eventually succeeded in driving out the *śramaṇas*.[21] In neighbouring Karnataka, at a somewhat later date, the Vīraśaivas or Liṅgāyatas acquiring wealth and status in commerce, persecuted Jaina monks and destroyed Jaina images.[22] In some inscriptions the Vīraśaivas claim that the Jainas began the trouble. In this case the hostility can be traced not to competition for royal patronage but rather to control of the commercial economy over which the Jainas had a substantial hold. A further reason may also have been linked to the fact that the Jainas, maintaining high standards of literacy, may have been seen by the Vīraśaivas as rivals in the role of advisers and administrators at the royal court.

What is significant about this persecution is that it involved not all the Śaivas but particular segments of sects among them. The persecution was not a *jehād* or a holy war or a crusade in which all Hindu sects saw it as their duty to support the attack or to wage war against the Buddhists or the Jainas. Nor was there room for an inquisition in the Indian situation, for there dissidents could found a new sect and take on a splinter caste status. The notion of heresy evolved gradually. The term *pāsaṃḍa* in the Aśokan edicts refers merely to any religious sect or philosophical school. By the time of the Puranic literature, *pāṣaṃḍa* quite clearly referred to sects in opposition to Brahmanism and carried with it the clear connotation of contempt.[23] Untouchability was also a form of religious persecution, for this exclusion was common to Brahmanism as well as to some Śramanic sects, the *caṇḍāla* being a category apart. Vaiṣṇavism, although it had its episodes of enemity with Śaivism and others, seems to have been less prone to persecuting competitors. Instead it resorted to assimilating other cults and used the notion of the *avatāra* or incarnation of Viṣṇu to great effect in doing so. But even Vaiṣṇavism was less given to assimilating the Śramanic sects, preferring to absorb tribal and folk cults and epic heroes. Thus in spite of the reference to Buddha as among the ten incarnations, this, interestingly, does not become the focus of a large body of myths or Puranic texts as do the other incarnations. If acts of intolerance and violence against other religious sects reflecting the consciousness of belonging to a religious community did not form part of a Hindu stand against such sects, then it also raises the question of how viable is the notion of a Hindu community for this early period

The notion of a Hindu community does not have as long an ancestry as is often presumed. Even in the normative texts of Brahmanism, the *Dharmaśāstras*, it is conceded that there were a variety of communities, determined by location, occupation and caste, none of which were necessarily bound together by a common religious identity. The term for village, *grāma*, referred to the collective inhabitants of a place and included cultivators and craftsmen. The control of this community lay in the hands of the *grāma-saṅgha*[24] and the *mahājana* and, in some cases, the *pañcakula*. Customary law of the village is referred to as *grāma-dharma*.[25] The sense of the village as the community was further impressed by the grants of land to *brāhmaṇas* and officers in the late first millennium AD when they began to be given administrative and judicial rights over the villages granted to them. Community therefore had one of its roots in location, and the law of the *janapada*/territory is listed among those which a king should observe.

In urban centres, craftsmen of the same profession or of related professions formed organizations and guilds, such as the *pūga*, *goṣṭhi* and *śreṇī*. They were responsible for production and sale and gradually took on a community character. Thus donations were made at Buddhist *stūpas*, as the one at Sanchi, by *goṣṭhis* and *śreṇīs* which identified themselves as such.[26] These communities were part of the larger Buddhist community and the same *stūpa* was embellished from donations by a number of other such communities and by individuals. One can therefore speak of a Buddhist community which cuts across the boundaries of caste and locality. In contrast is the silk-weavers guild at Mandasor which built a temple to Sūrya, the Sun-god, and rennovated it in the late fifth century AD.[27] Even though the members of this guild had taken to a variety of alternative professions they retained their identity as a guild for the purpose of building a temple. This religious edifice was built through the effort of a single group, identified as a guild and worshipping Sūrya, for no other Sun-worshippers were involved nor any other religious group which today would be called Hindu. It is unlikely that such a group saw itself as part of a larger Hindu community as its identity seems to have been deliberately limited. The Hūnas established themselves in the region soon after and were known to be Sun-worshippers. A temple to the Sun was built at Gwalior in the early sixth century AD by a high-ranking individual.[28] Curiously there is neither contribution from nor reference to other Sun-worshipping communities in the area in the later inscription, barring the reference to the Hūna kings.

In urban life the guild was a commanding institution acting as the nucleus of the urban community. The coins and seals of such guilds point to economic power and social status.[29] The *Nārada-smṛti* clearly states that a guild could frame its own laws and these laws related both to administration and social usage.[30] The customary law of the guild, the *śreṇī-dharma*, is particularly mentioned in the *Dharmaśāstras* and to which kings are required to conform. The importance of the guild also lies in the fact that some evolved into *jātis* or castes, becoming units of endogamous marriage uniting kinship and profession. Those not following a Śramanic religion maintained their own separate religious identity. We are also told that the king must respect *jāti-dharma*. The emphasis on the *dharma* of the *janapada* (locality or territory) *śreṇī* (guild) and *jāti* (caste) and the absence of reference to the *dharma* of various religious sects or of a conglomeration of religious sects are a pointer perhaps to what actually constituted the sense of community in the early past.

Identities were, in contrast to the modern nation state, segmented identities. The notion of community was not absent but there were multiple communities identified by locality, languages, caste, occupation and sect. What appears to have been absent was the notion of a uniform, religious community readily identified as Hindu. The first occurrence of the term 'Hindu' is as a geographical nomenclature and this has its own significance. This is not a quibble since it involves the question of the historical concept of 'Hindu'. Inscriptions of the Achaemenid empire refer to the frontier region of the Indus or Sindhu as Hi(n)dush.[31] Its more common occurrence many centuries later is in Arabic texts where the term is initially used neither for a religion nor for a culture. It refers to the inhabitants of the Indian subcontinet, the land across the Sindhu or Indus river. Al-Hind was therefore a geographical identity and the Hindus were all the people who lived on this land. Hindu thus essentially came to mean 'the other' in the eyes of the new arrivals. It was only gradually and over time that it was used not only for those who were inhabitants of India but also for those who professed a religion other than Islam or Christianity. In this sense Hindu included both the *brāhmaṇas* and the lower castes, an inclusion which was contrary to the precepts of Brahmanism. This all-inclusive term was doubtless a new and bewildering feature for the multiple sects and castes who generally saw themselves as separate entities.

The people of India curiously do not seem to have perceived the new arrivals as a unified body of Muslims. The name 'Muslim' does not occur in the records of early contacts. The term used was either ethnic, Turuṣka, referring to the Turks,[32] or geographical, Yavana,[33] or cultural, *mleccha*. Yavana, a back formation from *yona* had been used since the first millennium BC for Greeks and others coming from West Asia. *Mleccha* meaning impure, goes back to the Vedic texts and referred to non-Sanskrit speaking people often outside the caste hierarchy or regarded as foreign and was extended to include low castes and tribals. Foreigners, even of high rank, were regarded as *mleccha*.[34] A late fifteenth-century inscription from Mewar refers to the Sultan of Malwa and his armies as Śakas, a term used many centuries before for the Scythians, and therefore reflecting a curious undertow of historical memory.[35] These varying terms, each seeped in historical meaning, do not suggest a monolithic view, but rather a diversity of perceptions which need to be enquired into more fully.

For the early Muslim migrants Indian society was also a puzzle, for it was the first where large numbers did not convert to Islam. There was, further, the unique situation that they were faced with a society which had no place for the concept of conversion, for one's birth into a caste defines one's religious identity and conversion is outside the explanation of belief.

Historians have posited two monolithic religions, Hinduism and Islam, coming face to face in the second millennium AD. This projection requires re-examination since it appears to be based on a somewhat simplistic reading of the court chronicles of the Sultans. These spoke of Hindus sometimes in the sense of the indigenous population, sometimes as a geographical entity and sometimes as followers of a non-Islamic religion. Such references should be read in their specific meaning and not as referring uniformly to the religion of India. Possibly the germ of the idea of a Hindu community begins when people start referring to themselves as Hindus, perhaps initially as a concession to being regarded as 'the other'. Such usage in non-Islamic sources is known from the fifteenth century. The literature of the *bhakti* sects registers a variation on this. Much that was composed in an indigenous tradition such as the *Rāmacaritamānas* of Tulsidās seems not to use the term Hindu. That which was clearly influenced by Islamic ideas such as the verses of Kabīr refers to Hindus and counterposes Hindus and Turuṣkas in a religious sense. Curiously both Tulsidās and Kabīr belonged to the Rāmanandin sect, yet expressed themselves in very different idioms.

Rānā Kumbha of Mewar ruling in the fifteenth century, on defeating the sultans of Dhilli and Gurjarātra, takes the title of *himdu suratrāna*,[36] *suratrāna*, being the Sanskrit for sultan. In the context of the inscription in which it occurs, it is less a declaration of religious identity and more a claim to being a sultan of *al-hind*, superior to the other sultans. In another inscription the sultan of Gujarat is referred to as the *gurjareśvara* and the *gurjarādhīṣvara*, but the virtually hereditary enemy, the sultan of Malwa, merely as *suratrāna*,[37] a subtle but significant distinction.

It would also be worthwhile to investigate when the term Muslim came to be used in what would now be called Hindu sources. One's suspicion is that Turuṣka and its variants and certainly *mleccha* were more commonly used as they are to this day. *Mleccha* does not have a primary religious connotation. It is a signal of social and cultural difference. Indian Muslims of course did not discontinue caste affiliations, particularly as the basis of marriage relations and often even occupations. Thus the gulf between the high caste Muslims claiming foreign descent, such as the *ashrafs*, and the rest was not altogether dissimilar to the social difference between *brāhmaṇas* and non-*brāhmaṇas*. But the rank and file were often converted from lower castes, where an entire *jāti* would convert. These Muslims retained their local language in preference to Persian, were recognized by minor differences of dress and manner and often incorporated their earlier rituals and mythology into Islamic tradition. Some of the *mangal-kābyas* in Bengali, for instance, are an example of such interlinks in the creation of what might be seen as a new mythology where Puranic deities intermingled with the personalities of the Quran.[38] This becomes even more evident in the folk literature of regions with a large Muslim population. Elsewhere in Tamil-Nadu, for instance, the guardian figures in the cult of Draupadi are Muslim.[39] This is not an anomaly if it is seen in terms of local caste relations.

This is not to suggest that the relationship was one of peaceful coexistence or total cultural integration but rather that the perception which groups subscribing to Hindu and Islamic symbols had of each other was not in terms of a monolithic religion, but more in terms of distinct and disparate castes and sects along a social continuum. Even the recognition of a religious identity does not automatically establish a religious community. Tensions, confrontations and even persecutions at the level of political authority were not necessarily repeated all the way down the social scale nor were all caste and sectarian conflicts reflected at the upper levels. Clashes which on the face of it would now be interpreted as between Hindus and Muslims, would require a deeper investigation to ascertain how far they were clashes between specific castes and sects and to what degree did they involve support and sympathy from other castes and sects identifying with the same religion or seeking such identity.

The nineteenth-century definition of the Hindu community sought its justification in early history using Mill's periodization which assumes the existence of Hindu and Muslim communities and takes the history of the former back to the centuries BC. Its roots were provided by yet another nineteenth-century obsession, that of the theory of Aryan race.[40] It was argued that the Aryans conquered India and created the Hindu religion and civilization. In the theory of Aryan race the nineteenth-century concern with European origins was transferred to India. The theory as applied to India emphasized the arrival of a superior, conquering race of Aryans who used the mechanism of caste to segregate groups racially.[41] It underlined upper caste superiority by arguing that they were the descendants of the Aryans and it therefore became an acceptable explanation of the origin of upper castes, who could now also claim relationship to the European Aryans.[42] The lower castes were seen as the non-Aryan, indigenous people and were said to be of Dravidian and Austric origin. Aryanism was seen then to define the true and pure Hindu community. Other groups recruited into the caste structure at lower levels were regarded as polluting the pristine Hindu community.

Because of its centrality to both the notion of community and religion, the theory of Aryan race requires to be looked at critically by historians working on nineteenth-century ideas as well as historians of ancient India. The earlier evidence quoted in support of the theory as applied to India begins to fade with information from archaeology and linguistics. The notion of an Aryan race has now been generally discarded in scholarship and what we are left with is essentially a linguistic category: the Indo-Aryan speaking people. The archaeological picture takes the foundation of Indian civilization back to proto-history and the Harappa culture. The characteristic features of the latter do not mesh with those of the Vedic texts associated with the culture of the Indo-Aryan speakers.[43] The culture depicted in the Vedic texts seems increasingly to have drawn on local practices and beliefs, some going back to the Harappa culture or earlier, others drawing perhaps from the then contemporary society in India. There is virtually no evidence of the invasion and conquest of northwestern India by a dominant culture coming from across the border. Most sites register a gradual change of archaeological cultures. Where there is evidence of destruction and burning it could as easily have been a local activity and is not indicative of a large-scale invasion. The border lands of the northwest were in communication with Iran and Central Asia even before the Harappa culture with evidence of the passage of goods and ideas across the region.[44] This situation continued into later times and if seen in this light then the intermittent arrival of groups of Indo-European speakers in the northwest, perhaps as pastoralists or farmers or itinerant traders, would pose little problem. It is equally plausible that in some cases local languages became Indo-Europeanized through contact. Such situations would require a different kind of investigation. If cultural elements from elsewhere are being assessed, then during the Harappan period excavated evidence for contact with West Asia via the Gulf was more significant than that with eastern Iran and Central Asia and this raises another set of possibilities.

The more basic question for the historian is to explain the slow and gradual spread of the Indo-Aryan language across a large part of the Indian subcontinet. Here again the evidence from linguistics provides an interesting pointer. The claim that the earliest of the Vedic texts, the *Rg Veda* dating back to the second millennium BC is linguistically purely Indo-Aryan is now under question for it is being argued that the text already registers the presence of non-Aryan speakers. The later Vedic texts show an even greater admixture of non-Aryan and specifically when dealing with certain areas of activity, such as agriculture.[45] The emergent picture might suggest that the speakers of Indo-Aryan may have been in a symbiotic relationship with speakers of non-Aryan languages, with a mutual adopting of not only vocabulary and linguistic structures in a bi-lingual situation but also technologies and religious practices and beliefs.[46] The exclusivity of *brāhmaṇa* ritual does not have to be explained on the basis of a racial segregation, but can be viewed as derived from the will to retain a certain kind of priestly power, which, claiming bestowal by the deities would ensure a separate and special status. Possibly the political hold of priestly power has its roots in the Harappa culture. In charting the spread of Indo-Aryan it is worth remembering that Sanskrit not only underwent change in relation to other languages with which it had to co-exist and in relation to social change but that its use was initially restricted to *brāhmaṇa* ritual and elite groups.

The focus therefore is shifting to an investigation of the many ways in which a language gains acceptability. This would involve detailed studies of the juxtaposition of new technologies particularly in relation to ecological contexts, of demography, of kinship systems and the ways in which social groups interact where stratification relates to lineage rather than to race. So deep has been the modern obsession with race that Pargiter as late as in the 1920s suggested the identification of even the traditional descent groups from the genealogies of the Puranic texts as Aryan, Dravidian and Austric.[47] Thus the spread of the Indo-Aryan languages and the changes they manifest are a far more complicated study than that implied in the theory of spread by conquest. There is also a need to see the evolving of early Indian society as suggested by archaeological evidence independent of the attempt to impose Aryan identities on archaeological cultures. Only then can we hope to understand the social processes which went into the creation of early Indian society. In the text the term *ārya* generally refers to status indicating one who is to be respected. Whereas the connotation of *dāsa* may be said to contain ethnic elements, as for example, in the emphasis on physical characteristics, such elements are not in the forefront of references to *ārya*. Thus in the Vedic texts there are *āryas* of *dāsa* descent, the *dāsi-putrāḥ brāhmaṇas*,[48] or, politically powerful *dāsa* chiefs making gifts to the *brāhmaṇas*.[49] It is interesting that one of the most respected lineages, that of the Pūrus is associated with sub-standard Sanskrit.[50] It is also said that Pūru was descended from an Asura Rākṣasa[51] which can hardly be said to place the Pūrus in the category of the pure Aryans! In the *Dharmaśāstras* it is the observance of the complex *varnāśrama-dharma* which defines the *ārya*. To trace the emergence of caste would also involve a study of access to resources, kinship and clan networks and notions of pollution.

Early history suggests the existence of multiple communities based on various identities. The need to create the idea of a single, Hindu community appears to have been a concern of more recent times which was sought to be justified by recourse to a particular construction of history. The new Hinduism which is now sought to be projected as the religion of this community is in many ways a departure from the earlier religious sects. It seeks historicity for the incarnations of its deities, encourages the idea of a centrally sacred book, claims monotheism as significant to the worship of deity, acknowledges the authority of the ecclesiastical organization of certain sects as prevailing over all and has supported large-scale missionary work and conversion. These changes allow it to transcend caste identities and reach out to larger numbers. Religions indigenous to India which questioned brahmanical belief and practice such as Buddhism and Jainism have been inducted into Hinduism and their separateness is either denied or ignored. Pre- Islamic India is therefore presented as a civilization characterized by an inclusive Hinduism, whereas it would seem that the reality perhaps lay in looking at it as a cluster of distinctive sects and cults, observing common civilizational symbols but with belief and ritual ranging from atheism to animism and a variety of religious organizations identifying themselves by location, language and caste. Even the sense of religious identity seems to have related more closely to sect than to a dominant Hindu community.

The modern construction of Hinduism is often acclaimed as in the following defence of Orientalism: 'The work of integrating a vast collection of myths, beliefs, rituals and laws into a coherent religion and of shaping an amorphous heritage into a rational faith known now as "Hinduism" were endeavours initiated by Orientalists.'[52] Given that religious traditions are constantly reformulated, the particular construction of Hinduism in the last two centuries has an obvious historical causation. Deriving largely from the Orientalist construction of Hinduism, emergent national consciousness appropriated this definition of Hinduism as well as what it regarded as the heritage of Hindu culture. Hindu identity was defined by those who were part of this national consciousness and drew on their own idealized image of themselves resulting in an upper-caste, *brāhmaṇa*-dominated identity. Even the counterposing of Hindu to other religious identities as an essential fact of social and historical reality grew out of this construction. But this construction not only deviates from the history of the religious groups involved but fails to encapsulate the essential differences within what is called the Hindu tradition whose presuppositions were distinct from other religions and closely entwined with social articulation. The search for coherence and rational faith was in terms of a perspective familiar to those who came from a Christian religious tradition and hardly reflected any attempt to understand the coherence of a different, indigenous religious tradition. The shape thus given to the latter has changed what originally existed and has made it difficult to recognize the actual earlier form.

The need for postulating a Hindu community became a requirement for political mobilization in the nineteenth century when representation by religious community became a key to power and where such representation gave access to economic resources. The competition for middle class employment brought with it the argument that in all fairness the size of the community should be taken into consideration. Communal representation of the religious kind firmed up the image. Once this argument was conceded it became necessary to recruit as many people as possible into the community. Here the vagueness of what constitutes a Hindu was to the advantage of those propagating a Hindu community. It encouraged an almost new perception of the social and political uses of religion. Conversion to Hinduism was invented largely to bring in the untouchables and the tribals. The notion of purification, *śuddhi*, permitted those who had been converted to Islam and Christianity to be reintroduced to the Hindu fold. A Hindu community with a common identity would be politically powerful. Since it was easy to recognize other communities on the basis of religion, such as Muslims and Christians, an effort was made to consolidate a parallel Hindu community. This involved a change from the earlier segmented identities to one which encompassed caste and region and identified itself by religion which had to be refashioned so as to provide the ideology which would bind the group. In Gramsci's terms, the class which wishes to become hegemonic has to nationalize itself and the new 'nationalist' Hinduism comes from the middle class.

The change implicit in the various levels of what is called modernization inevitably results in the refashioning of communities. Given that the notion of expansive communities may well be imagined, nevertheless the premises on which such communities are constructed are open to analysis and where they claim an historical basis, there the historian has perforce to be involved. This involvement becomes even more necessary when the concept of communities is brought into play in assigning positions to them in history either close to or distant from what are regarded as national aspirations. Thus the majority community tends to define national aspirations. The minority communities in varying degrees are viewed as disrupting society by their refusal to conform. The projection of such communities historically is that of their always having been alien to the dominant culture and therefore refusing to assimilate with the majority.

Minority communities pick up their cue in a similar reconstruction of history seeking to project a unified community stance in all historical situations. The fear of being overwhelmed by the majority community is expressed even in opposition to the making of homogeneous civil laws. These are treated as threats to a specific culture and practice, and there is a tendency to preserve even that which is archaic in an effort to assert a separate identity.

If the history of religions in India is seen as the articulation not only of ideas and rituals but also the perceptions and motivations of social groups, the perspectives which would follow might be different from those with which we are familiar. The discourse and the play between and among religious sects of various kinds, has been a central fact of Indian religion and would reflect a more realistic portrayal of the role of religion in society. A historically analytical enquiry into the definition and role of religion and the concept of religious communities in pre-modern India could be juxtaposed with the way in which these have been perceived by interpreters of the past in the last couple of centuries. Incidentally such an assessment would be valuable not only to contemporary society in India but also to those societies which now host the vast Indian diaspora. Communal ideologies may be rooted in the homeland but also find sustenance in the diaspora.

It is possible now to look more analytically at the perspectives on early Indian society as available in the sources, keeping in mind the insights which we have, arising from research which, in a sense, is being gradually liberated from the polemics of the colonial age. Where institutions and ideologies of modern times seek legitimacy from the early past, at least there, the dialogue between historians working on these time periods becomes imperative.

## Notes and References

1. B. Anderson, *Imagined Communities*, Vaso, 1983.
2. J. Bloch, *Les Inscriptions d'Asoka*, Paris, 1950, pp. 97, 99, 112.
3. J.W. McCrindle, *Ancient India as Described by Megasthenes and Arrian*, London, 1877; Arrian, *Indica*, XI.I to XII.9; Strabo, XV 1.39–41, 46–9.
4. J. Legge, *Fa-hien's Record of Buddhistic Kingdoms*, Oxford, 1886; S. Beal, *Si-yu-ki: Buddhist Records of the Western World*, London, 1884.
5. E.C. Sachau (trans. and ed.), *Alberuni's India*, Delhi, 1964 (reprint), p. 21.
6. S.D. Joshi (ed.), *Patañjali Vyākarana Mahābhāṣya*, Poona, 1968, II.4.9; I.476.
7. N. Wagle, *Society at the Time of the Buddha*, Bombay, 1966, p. 74.

8. Curiously, the eating of meat and the drinking of intoxicants was part of the rejection by Brahmanism for these were now abhorent to Brahmanism, a rather different situation from that described in the Vedic texts where *brāhmaṇas* consumed beef and took *soma*.
9. G.D. Sontheimer, 'Some Memorial Monuments of Western India', in *German Scholars in India*, II, New Delhi, 1976; S.G. Tulpule, 'The Origin of Viththala: A New Interpretation', *ABORI*, 1977–78, vols 58–9, pp. 1009–15; A. Dandekar, 'Pastoralism and the Cult of Viṭhṭhala', M.Phil. Dissertation, JNU; H. Kulke, *Jagannātha kult und Gajapati Königtum*, Wiesbaden, 1979, p. 227; H. Kulke and D. Rothermund, *A History of India*, London, 1986, pp. 145ff.
10. A. Bakker, *Ayodhya*, Groningen, 1984.
11. Manu II.14–15.
12. Romila Thapar, 'Renunciation: The Making of a Counter-Culture?', in *Ancient Indian Social History: Some Interpretations*, Delhi, 1978, pp. 63–104. *See* chapter 40 in this volume.
13. Romila Thapar, 'The Rāmāyaṇa: Theme and Variations', in S.N. Mukherjee (ed.), *India: History and Thought*, Calcutta, 1982, pp. 221–53. *See* chapter 30 in this volume.
14. Romila Thapar, 'Death and the Hero', in S.C. Humphreys and H. King, *Mortality and Immortality: The Anthropology and Archaeology of Death*, London, 1981, pp. 293–316. *See* chapter 31 in this volume.
15. Romila Thapar, 'Sati in History', *Seminar*, no. 342, February 1988.
16. Personal Communication, B.K. Matilal.
17. H. Sanyal, *Social Mobility in Bengal*, Calcutta, 1981.
18. S. Beal, *Si-yu-ki*, I.xcix. 19. I.307.
20. Xinru Liu, *Ancient India and Ancient China*, Delhi, 1988.
21. Romila Thapar, *Cultural Transaction and Early India*, Delhi, 1987, pp. 17ff.
22. P.B. Desai, *Jainism in South India*, Sholapur, 1957, pp. 23, 63, 82–3, 124, 397–402; *Epigraphia Indica* V, pp. 142ff, 255; *Ep. Ind.* XXIX, pp. 139–44; *Annual Report of South Indian Epigraphy*, 1923, pp. 4ff.
23. Romila Thapar, 'Renunciation'.
24. Manu, VIII.41.
25. *Āśvalāyana Gṛhyasūtra* I.7.I.; *Āśvalāyana Śrauta-sūtra* XII.8; Pāṇiṇi 6.2.62; *Amarakoṣa* 2.3.19; Buddhist texts speak more specifically of village boundaries (*Vinaya Piṭaka* I.109.10; III.46.200). This was necessary in a system where the limits of areas for collecting alms had to be defined for each monastery.
26. See inscriptions from Sanchi as given in J. Marshall and A. Foucher, *Monuments of Sanchi*, Calcutta, 1940; also H. Lüders, *Ep. Ind.*, X.162–907; See also the Bhattiprolu inscription, Luders no. 1332.
27. J.F. Fleet (ed.), *Inscriptions of the Early Gupta Kings and their Successors*, Corpus Inscriptionum Indicarum, III, Varanasi, 1970 (reprint), pp. 79ff.

28. Ibid., pp. 162ff.
29. *Bṛhaspati* I. 28–30; *Kātyāyaṇa* 2.82; 17.18; I. 126; Archaeological Survey of India, Annual Report, 1903–04; 1911–12.
30. *Nārada-smṛti*, X. 1–2; *Ep. Ind.*, XXX, p. 169.
31. The Persepolis and Naqsh-i-Rustam inscriptions of Darius, in D.C. Sircar, *Select Inscriptions*, vol. I, Calcutta, 1965, p. 7.
32. Similarly Muslim women were often referred to as *turuṣki*, as, for example, in Hemādri, *Caturvarga-cintāmaṇi*, Prāyaścitta-kāṇḍa.
33. e.g. Chateśvara temple inscriptions, where in the thirteenth century a reference is made to a campaign against the *yavanas*. *Ep. Ind.*, 1952, XXIX, pp. 121–2.
34. Romila Thapar, 'The Image of the Barbarian in Early India', in *Ancient Indian Social History*, pp. 152–92. A fourteenth-century inscription from Delhi refers to Shahab-ud-din, as a *mleccha*, who was the first Turuṣka to rule Dhillika/Delhi. D.R. Bhandarkar (ed.), Appendix to *Epi. Ind.* XIX–XXIII, no. 683.
35. Udaipur inscription of the time of Rajamalla in *Bhavnagar Inscriptions*, pp. 117ff. And see Bhandarkar (ed.), Appendix to *Ep. Ind.*, XIX–XXIII, no. 862. It is ironic that it was earlier thought that these Rajput ruling families may in some cases have had their origin in the Śakas!
36. Sadadi Jaina inscription of the time of Kumbhakarṇa of Medapata in *Bhavnagar Inscriptions*, pp. 114ff and D.R. Bhandarkar, op. cit., no. 784; D. Sharma, *Lectures on Rajput History and Culture*, Delhi, 1970, p. 55.
37. Kīrtistambha-praśasti, *ASIR*, XXIII, pp. 111ff.
38. Ashim Roy, *The Islamic Syncretistic Tradition in Bengal*, Princeton, 1983.
39. A. Hiltebeitel, *The Cult of Draupadi*, Chicago, 1988.
40. Romila Thapar, 'Ideology and the Interpretation of Early Indian History'. *See* chapter 1 in this volume.
41. H. Risley, *The People of India*, London, 1908.
42. As, for example, in the writings of Keshab Chunder Sen, 'Philosophy and Madness in Religion', in *Keshab Chunder Sen's Lectures in India*, London, 1901.
43. Romila Thapar, 'Society in India: The Formative Period', in *Ancient Indian Social History*, pp. 211–39; also, 'The Archaeological Background to the Agnicayana Ritual', in F. Staal, *Agni*, vol. II, Berkeley, 1983, pp. 3–40. *See* chapters 14 and 15 in this volume.
44. J. Jarrige, 'Excavations at Mehrgarh: their Significance for Understanding the Background of the Harappan Civilisation', in G. Possehl (ed.), *Harappan Civilisation*, New Delhi, 1982, pp. 79ff.
45. T. Burrow, *The Sanskrit Language*, London, 1965, p. 379: M.M. Deshpande and P.E. Hook (eds), *Aryan and non-Aryan in India*, Michigan, 1979.

46. Romila Thapar, *From Lineage to State*, New Delhi, 1984, pp. 21ff.
47. F.E. Pargiter, *Ancient Indian Historical Tradition*, London, 1922.
48. *Bṛhaddevatā* 4.11–15; 21–3; describes the birth of Dīrghatamas and his son Kakśivant as the son of a *dāsi*. The *Aitareya Brāhmaṇa* 2.19 and the *Kauśītaki Brāhmaṇa* 12.3 describe the Ṛg Vedic seer Kavaṣa Ailuṣa as a *dāsi-putra*.
49. Romila Thapar, *From Lineage to State*, p. 43.
50. *Ṛg Veda*. VII. 18.13.
51. *Śatapatha Brāhmaṇa* VI. 8.I.14.
52. D. Knopf, 'Hermeneutics versus History', *Journal of Asian Studies*, 1980, 39.3, pp. 495–505.

# The Tyranny of Labels*

In the writing of Indian history, we have become accustomed to packaging our past and identifying it with labels. Such labels, even where they may include a variety of activity and experience, tend to force interpretations into a single category so that the infinite shades of difference within them, disappear. When this happens, the historical perspective comes to be governed by the tyranny of labels: a condition which requires the historical unpacking of the categories and a redefining of the contents.

I would like in this lecture to explore two of these labels: the Hindu community and the Muslim community, with particular reference to the way they are used in the writing of pre-colonial history. My intention in this exploration is both to question the validity of these as all inclusive categories in historical analysis, and to suggest the need to analyse afresh our historical understanding of what we are referring to when we speak of Hindu and Muslim communities in history. Such labels draw on conventional religious identities, but the form so demarcated is sought to be applied to every other aspect of life, whether applicable or not. It is also used to include a vast spectrum of social groups under the single label.

The viewing of Indian history in terms of these two monolithic, religious communities, has its origins in nineteenth century interpretations of Indian history, where not only were the two communities described as monolithic but they were also projected as static over many centuries. This is of course not to deny that the labels were used earlier, but to argue that they were used in a different sense, and their use has its own history which has yet to be investigated. A small part of this investigation is attempted in this lecture. My intention is to observe how those to whom we give

* This is an expanded version of the Zakir Hussain Lecture, Delhi, 1996.

a primary association with Islam, when they first arrived in India, were initially perceived in northern India, and the way in which such groups were represented as part of this perception. This was far more nuanced than is allowed for in the concept of monolithic communities, and these nuances require further exploration. The representation in turn had an impact on what have been described as the multiple new communities which came to be established. The newness was not because they were invariably alien, but because there was a departure from the existing pattern of communities. The newness of these communities requires investigation and this links the study of the first millennium AD with that of the second. The continuities did not have to be literal but could have been conceptual and while the nature of change in some situations was new in others it could well have followed earlier patterns.

The definition of the Muslim community extends to all those who claim adherence to Islam and the adherence is said to be demonstrated by a clearly stated belief and form of worship, which through conversion confers membership in a large body of believers, a membership which also assumes the egalitarian basis of the association. The perspective of the court chronicles of the Sultans and the Mughals was that of the ruling class and this perspective is now seen as broadly endorsing the above definition and reinforcing the projection of a Muslim community, a perspective in which the Hindu — as defined by such literature — was seen as the counterpart. It is as well to keep in mind that this is the current interpretation of these texts and although some may conform to the view from the windows of power, not all do so. Therefore, although sometimes carrying some political and even theological weight, this view was nevertheless limited. As the articulation of a powerful but small section of society it needs to be juxtaposed with other indicators.

The notion of a Hindu community evolves from a geographic and ethnic description gradually giving way to religious association. The Hindu community is more difficult to define given the diverse nature of belief and worship making it the amorphous 'Other' of the Muslim community in some of the court chronicles. The crystallisation of this perception occurs when erstwhile Vaiṣṇavas, Śaivas, Lingāyats and others, begin to refer to themselves as Hindus. Communities of the subcontinent have in the past been diverse, with multiple identities and the attempt to force them into unchanging, static entities, would seem to contradict the historical evidence. With the modern connotation of a religious community, both terms have come to include even in the interpretation of the historical past, all manner of diverse societies across the subcontinent, for some of whom convergence with the formal religion is of recent origin, if at all.

The idea of two, distinctive, segregated civilisations, the Hindu and the Muslim, in conflict with each other was assumed in colonial scholarship. Thus James Mill, differentiated the Hindu civilisation from the Muslim, which gave rise to the periodisation of Indian history as that of the Hindu, Muslim and British periods. It crystallised the concept of a uniform, monolithic Hindu community dominating early history as did the Muslim equivalent in the subsequent period, with relations between the two becoming conflictual. These notions were in a sense summarised by Christian Lassen who, in the mid-nineteenth century, attempting to apply a Hegelian dialectic, wrote of the Hindu civilisation as the thesis, the Muslim civilisation as the anti-thesis and the British as the synthesis![1]

Part of the insistence on the separateness of the two civilisations was the assumption that those who came with Islam, had been regarded even by earlier Indians as alien, in fact as alien as the Europeans. This however was an erroneous perception of earlier historical relationships. Those associated with Islam had come through various avenues, as traders, as Sufis and as attachments to conquerors. Their own self-perceptions differed as also did the way in which they were perceived by the people of the land where they settled. For a long while in India, they were referred to by the same terms as were used in earlier times for people from west and central Asia, suggesting that their coming was viewed in part as a historical continuity. And there are good historical grounds to explain such a continuity.

The Arabs, Turks, Afghans and Persians were familiar to northern and western India, since they had not only been contiguous peoples but had been linked by trade, settlement and conquest, links which went back, virtually unbroken, to many centuries. Central Asia was the homeland of the Śaka and Kuṣāṇa dynasties which ruled in northern India at the turn of the Christian era and later of the Hūṇas who came as conquerors and became a caste. In Iran, the genesis of the languages spoken there and in northern India, were Old Iranian and Indo-Aryan which were closely related languages as is evident from examples of common usage in the *Avesta* and the *Ṛgveda*. Persian contacts with India were initially through the Achaemenids who were contemporaries of the Mauryas and later through the Sassanids, contemporaries of the Kuṣāṇas and Guptas. Territories in Afghanistan and the north-west were alternatively controlled by rulers from both sides. Aśokan inscriptions in Greek and Aramaic in Afghanistan attest to Mauryan rule and later dynasties with bases in the Oxus region and Iran brought north-western India into their orbit. Trading links were tied to political alliances. Close maritime contacts between the subcontinent and the Arabian peninsula go back to the time of the Indus civilisation and have continued to the present.

There is therefore an immense history of interaction and exchange between the subcontinent and central and western Asia. The change of religion to Islam in the latter areas does not annual the earlier closeness. Interestingly even the Islam of these areas was not uniform for there were and are strong cultural and sectarian differences among the Muslims of central Asia, Persia and the Arab world, differences which can in some cases be traced to their varying pre-Islamic past and which are likely to have influenced the nature of their interaction with the subcontinent.

These were contiguous people whose commercial and political relations with India over a long past, were sometimes competitive and hostile and at other times friendly, but were well recognised. Battles were fought, campaigns were conducted, commercial exchange was encouraged and migrants moved across borders in various directions. Many had settled in India and married locally. One of the clauses of the treaty between Chandragupta Maurya and Seleukus Nikator has been interpreted as a *jus conubii*, freedom for the Greeks and Indians to intermarry. Such marriages doubtless gave rise to mixed communities of new castes and practices, a process that did not cease with the arrival of Muslim Arabs and others. Similarly Indian traders and Indian Buddhist monks who lived in the oasis towns of central Asia and in China, were also to be found in ports and markets in west Asia, and were agencies of cross-cultural fertilisation. Manichaeism for example became a major religion in the early Christian era largely because it drew on Mahāyāna Buddhism, Zoroastrianism, Nestorian Christianity, and elements of central Asian animism. The dialogue between Indians, central Asian Turks, Persians and Arabs was a continuing one, irrespective of changes of dynasties and religions or of trade fluctuations. This dialogue is reflected for example, in Sanskrit,

Greek and Arabic texts relating to astronomy, medicine and philosophy, and in what is said of Indian scholars resident at the court of Harun al' Rashid.

The coming of the Europeans and the colonisation of India by Britain, was an altogether different experience. They came from distant lands, were physically different, spoke languages which were entirely alien and in which there had been no prior communication; their rituals, religion and customs were alien; their exploitation of land and labour exceeded that of the previous period; and above all they did not settle in India. The assumption that the west Asian and central Asian interventions after the eighth century AD and that of the British were equally foreign to India, in origin and intent, would, from the historical perspective, be difficult to defend.

Colonial interpretations of the Indian past were often contested by Indian historians, but the periodisation was accepted in essentials. This was implicitly the acceptance of the idea that the units of Indian society were communities defined by single religions, requiring therefore that monolithic religious identities be sought and established in history. This view coincided with the incubation of the nation-state. All nationalisms use history, some more evidently than others. Essential to nationalist ideology was also the attempt to locate and define a national culture, often equated with that of the dominant group. Inevitably other cultures get excluded in this process. But the historian also acts as a remembrancer, reminding the society of the histories that are not always apparent up front.

When communalisms become visible on the political stage, as they were from the early years of this century, there is not only a contestation between them on the question of identity, but there is also a conflict with the earlier anti-colonial nationalism. The separation of the indigenous and the foreign emerges as a contentious issue and is taken back to the beginnings of Indian history. Communal historiographies attempt to construct a religious majority into a monolithic community, claiming that their interpretations of the past which support such a monolith are the only valid ones. Religion is sought to be restructured in order that it can be used for political mobilisation.[2] There is inevitably a confrontation between historical evidence and its logic, counterposed with resort to a fantasized past, in what are projected as conflicting histories.[3]

I would like to illustrate this by taking up one central issue, now contested, of the period prior to the modern in south Asian history. The question of identities has hinged on the definition of communities as solely religious communities. Hindu and Muslim in the main, the former being indigenous and the latter foreign, and projected as generally hostile to each other. The assumptions have been that the Hindus and the Muslims each constituted a unified, monolithic community, and were therefore separate nations from the start, and that religious differences provide a complete, even though mono-causal explanation for historical events and activities in the second millennium AD. The reconstruction of this history is largely based on particular readings of court chronicles and texts where political contestation is sometimes projected in religious terms, to the exclusion of other categories of texts which allow of a different reconstruction.

My objection to the use of blanket terms such as 'the Hindus' and 'the Muslims', in historical readings, is that it erases precision with reference to social groups and is therefore methodologically invalid and historically inaccurate. It fails to differentiate between that which is more pertinent to religious history and that which relates to other aspects of life even if there had been an overlap in some situations. To explain the events of the time in terms only of an interaction between groups identified either as Hindus or as Muslims, is simplistic as a historical explanation. Some continuities in historical processes are arbitrarily broken by this usage and at the same time it is difficult to observe historical changes. Questioning the existence of such monolithic, religious communities, therefore has extensive historiographical implications.

The argument that the notion of community was always defined by a single religion even in the pre-Islamic past has been countered by the evidence of sources other than Brahmanical normative texts. Such sources relate to diverse social groups and depict a different social scene. Theoretical interpretations emphasising the nature of relationships between socially diverse groups and focusing on access to power, whether through economic or other disparities, have also changed the contours of pre-modern history. The many studies of caste, clan, village, town, language and region, have encouraged a diversified view of past identities. Caste as *varṇa*, earlier thought to be a definitive identity is now being recognised as intersected by identities of language, sect and occupation. Each individual therefore, had varied identities, of which some might over-lap, but which interfered with the consolidation of a single, monolithic, religious identity, even in societies prior to the coming of Islam.[4]

For Orientalist scholarship the construction of what came to be called Hinduism was a challenge, being different from the familiar perspective of religions such as Judaism, Christianity and Islam. The latter were founded on the teachings of historically recognised prophets or of a messiah, with a theology and dogma, a sacred book and some ensuing deviations which took the form of variant sects. Yet the religious articulation which we recognise as constituting the religions which came to be called Hinduism did not subscribe to these features. Of its many variant forms, some were deviations from earlier belief and practice but others had an independent genesis. The juxtaposition of religious sects did result almost through osmosis in similarities which introduced some common features, but the diversities remained. Hence the preference in some recent scholarship for the phrase 'Hindu religions', rather than Hinduism.[5] Because of this flexibility and decentralisation, the religious identity was frequently closely allied to caste identities and since these incorporated occupation and access to resources, there were factors other than belief alone which governed religious identities. This is equally true of other religions in the subcontinent.

The term 'Hindu' as referring to a religion is initially absent in the vocabulary of Indian languages and only slowly gains currency. This is quite logical given that earlier religious identities were tied to sect and caste. Membership was not of a specific religion, binding groups across a social spectrum and a geographical space, as was the case for example, with Buddhism. The use of a single term to include the diversity would have been bewildering, and adjustment to this usage would have required a long period. When and why it came to be a part of the self-perception of what we today call the Hindus, would make a worthwhile historical enquiry. Terms such as 'Muslim' or 'Musalman' are also not immediate entrants into the vocabulary of Indian languages after the arrival of Islam, although these terms occur in the texts of what were initially non-Indian languages. Prior to that a variety of other terms are preferred and these have their own history. The Arabs, Turks, Afghans and others are referred to variously, such as Tājika, Yavana, Śaka, Turuṣka and *mleccha*. There is therefore an attempt to associate the new entrants with existing categories and are therefore expressive of more subtle relationships than we have assumed. The categories gave them an identity which was familiar and interestingly provided them with historical links, emanating from Indian connections with western and central Asia in the past. The use of these terms was at one level a continuation from the earlier past. What is striking is that initially none of these terms had a religious connotation. It would again be worthwhile to locate the point in time when this connotation was acquired in cases such as Turuṣka and its variants, which later included a religious identity.

Inscriptions from the eighth century AD refer to Arab incursions coming from Sind and Gujerat into the Narmada delta.[6] The Arabs are referred to as Tājikas which suggests some complex link to an Arab identity in addition to their being maritime traders. The Rāṣṭrakūṭa kings of the ninth-tenth centuries had appointed a Tājika as governor of the Sanjan area of Thane District on the west coast, whose name is rendered as Madhumati, thought to be the Sanskrit for Mohammed since it also rendered sometimes as Madhumada.[7] He conquered the chiefs of the neighbouring harbours for the Rāṣṭrakūṭas and placed his officers in charge. As governor, he granted a village to finance the building of a temple and the installation of an icon. Arab writers of this period refer to Arab officers employed by the *rājās* and settlements of Arab traders, and in both cases they had to work closely with the existing administration.[8]

The term Yavana was originally used for Greeks and later for those coming from west Asia or the west generally.[9] The Sanskrit word *yavana* is a back formation from the Prākṛit *yona*, derived from the west Asian *yauna*, referring to the Ionian Greeks. It was used in an ethnic and geographical sense. Buddhist texts speak approvingly of the Yavanas. Some became Buddhists or were patrons of Buddhism. There was also a curiosity about Yavana society which it was said had no castes but had a dual division of master and slave.[10] The Greek speaking population of the Indo-Iranian borderlands is familiar from the Mauryan period. For most people the Yavanas were just another people, but the *brāhmaṇas* were initially antagonistic. A text of the early centuries AD — the *Yuga Purāṇa* of the *Gārgi Saṃhitā* — depicts them as unfriendly[11] even though some Yavanas declared themselves to be Vaiṣṇavas. Perhaps this hostility grew out of the memory of Alexander's brutal attack on the Malloi[12] and the later resentment against Indo-Greek rulers in India patronising what the *brāhmaṇas* regarded as heretical sects. The negative image of the Kālayavana reflects a dislike of the Yavanas in another source, the *Harivaṃśa*[13] inspite of the original Kālayavana being of Indian parentage. Nevertheless Yavanas were not only accommodated but accepted as rulers. They were however given the status of *vrātya kṣatriyas* or degenerate *kṣatriyas*: those who were grudgingly given what was an apology for *kṣatriya* status or those who, although born of *kṣatriyas* had not married women of an equal caste.[14] This was an example of providing a caste ranking for what was originally a ruling class which came from outside caste society. Much of the brahmanical hostility was because the Yavanas were seen as upsetting the norms of brahmanical society and not performing the rituals approved of by brahmanical orthopraxy.[15] The didactic section of the *Mahābhārata*, thought to be an interpolation, mentions that the Yavanas fell from status because they disregarded the *brāhmaṇas*[16] and the revenge of the latter led to their calling them *vrātyas*. This hostility was limited to the *brāhmaṇas* for in the narrative section of the *Mahābhārata*, thought to be less tampered with, the Yavanas are given a high status in that they are said to be descended from Turvaśa, one of the five sons of the ancestral hero, Yadu.[17]

Turks and Afghans are referred to as Yavanas in multiple inscriptions.[18] This was an indication of their being from the west and therefore alien, but also of not being all that alien since there was already a status and an identity for them in the existing system. It enabled them to be included later in the scheme of how the past was conceptualised, as for example in one eighteenth century Marathi chronicle.[19] Such texts were partial imitations of the earlier tradition of maintaining king-lists, as in the *Purāṇas* and the *vaṃśāvalīs* or chronicles. With the establishment of Maratha power, there was the need for writing 'histories' to legitimise this power. As has been pointed out, the legitimising of Maratha rule also required legitimising the preceding Mughal and Turkish rule, which these texts refer to as the rule of the Yavanas.

But this was not a simple matter for it had to conform to the *vaṃśāvalī* tradition. The earlier *vaṃśāvalīs* had linked contemporary rulers genealogically to the ancient heroes of the *Purāṇas*. Something similar would have to be done for these more recent Yavanas. It was therefore stated that a certain text, called the *Ramala-śāstra* contained the history of the Yavanas. We are told, in true Puranic style, that this text was first recited by Śiva to Pārvatī and then through Skanda, Nārada and Bhṛgu to Śukra, the last of whom told it to the Yavanas. It is Śiva who sent Paigambar to earth and there were seven *paigambars* or wise men, starting with Adam. This is of course reminiscent of the seven Manus with which Puranic chronology begins. The *paigambars* came to earth during the Kali-yuga. They started their own era based on the Hijri era and different from the earlier Indian *saṁvat* era. They renamed Hastināpur as Dilli and initiated Yavana rule. They are thus located in time and space and provided with links to the past in accordance with the earlier and established *vaṃśāvalī* tradition.

The prime mover in this history is the deity Śiva and this makes any other legitimation unnecessary. Since the Yavanas had the blessing of Śiva, Piṭhor Rājā Chauhana could not hold them back. The establishment of the Maratha kingdom also took place at the intervention of the deity. This kind of adjustment which emerges out of upper caste interests may also have been in part a response to the necessary change in the role model. Those claiming to be *kṣatriyas* were now not approximating the life-style of their ancestors to the same degree as before, but were increasingly imitating the appearance, dress, language and life-style of the Mughal courts, as is evident from painting and literature. The culture of the elite had changed and there was a noticeable degree of accommodating the new. The importance of such accounts lies not in their fantasy on what actually happened, but that they provide us with a glimpse of how a historical situation was being manipulated, in order to correlate a view of tradition with the problems of contemporary change. This might enable us to assess the nature of the ideological negotiation which conditioned such perceptions.

The term Śaka, was the Sanskrit for the Scythians, a people from central Asia who had ruled in parts of northern and western India around the Christian era. The reference to Turkish and Afghan dynasties as Śakas suggests a historical perception of place and people, a perception both of who the rulers were and how they might be fitted into the history of the ruled. A Sanskrit inscription of AD 1276 may illustrate this.[20] It records the building of a *baoli* and a *dharmaśālā* in Palam (just outside Delhi) by Uḍḍhara from Ucca in the Multan district. The inscription, composed by Pandit Yogeśvara, dated in the *vikram saṁvat* 1333, begins with a salutation to Śiva and Ganapati. It then refers to the rulers of Delhi and

Haryana as the Tomaras, Chauhanas and Śakas, the earlier two having been recognised Rajput dynasties and the last being a reference to the Sultans.[21] This is made clear by the detailed list of Śakas, that is, the Sultans of Delhi upto the current ruler Balban, referred to as *nāyaka śrī hammīra* Gayāsdīna *nṛpati samrāṭa*, and whose conquests are described with extravagant praise. His titles mix the old with the new. *Nāyaka* was an earlier title and *hammīra* is thought to be the Sanskritised form of Amir. In the eulogistic style of the earlier *praśasti* tradition, Balban's realm is said to be virtually subcontinental — an obvious exaggeration. This is followed by a fairly detailed family history of the merchant in the traditional *vaṃśāvalī* style. He was clearly a man of considerable wealth. Other sources inform us that Hindu merchants from Multan, gave loans to Balban's nobles when the latter suffered a shortfall in collecting revenue.[22] The identity of the Sultan is perceived as a continuity from earlier times and the identity of the merchant is in relation to his own history and occupation, and perhaps the unstated patronage of the Sultan. The sole reference to religion is oblique, in the statement that even Viṣṇu now sleeps peacefully, presumably because of the reign of Balban.

A Sanskrit inscription from Naraina (also in the vicinity of Delhi), dated *saṁvat* 1384 or AD 1327 follows the same format.[23] We are told that in the town of Dhilli, sin is expelled by the chanting of the *Vedas*. The city is ruled by Mahamūda Sāhi who is the *cūḍāmaṇi*, the crest-jewel, of the rulers of the earth (a phrase used frequently in Sanskrit to describe a king), and is a *śakendra*, the lord/Indra of the Śakas. This may well be the rhetoric of sycophancy, nevertheless the juxtaposing of Vedic recitations to the rule of Mohammad bin Tughlaq carries its own message. The identification with the Śakas is complimentary since the earlier Śakas were associated with the important calendrical era of AD 78, still in official use.

Another term is Turuṣka, and was originally a geographical and ethnic name. An interesting link is made with earlier Indian historical perceptions of central Asia, when Kalhaṇa, in his twelfth century history of Kashmir, the *Rājataraṅginī*, uses the term retrospectively. He refers to the Kuṣāṇas of the early centuries AD as Turuṣkas, and adds ironically, that even though they were Turuṣkas these earlier kings were given to piety.[24] Here perhaps the points of contrast are the references in two twelfth century inscriptions to the Turuṣkas as evil, *duṣṭātturuṣka*, or to a woman installing an image in place of one broken by the Turuṣkas.[25] Familiarity with the Turks was also because they competed with Indian and other traders in controlling the central Asian trade, especially the lucrative trade along the silk route between China and Byzantium and because Buddhism, known to these areas prior to Islam, had been reinforced by missions from north India. The initial attacks of the Turks and Afghans were tied into local politics, what Kalhaṇa refers to as the coalition of the Kashmiri, Khasa and *mleccha*.[26] The entry of the Turuṣkas on the north Indian scene is in many ways a continuation of the relations which had existed between the states of north-western India and those across the borders.

Kalhaṇa writes disparagingly of the Kashmiri king Harṣadeva ruling in the eleventh century who employed Turuṣka mercenaries — horsemen in the main — in his campaigns against local rulers, even though the Turuṣkas were then invading the Punjab. The activities of Harṣadeva, demolishing and looting temples when there was a fiscal crisis, leads to Kalhaṇa calling him a Turuṣka.[27] But he adds that such activities have been familiar even from earlier times. However, the looting of temples by Harṣadeva was more systematic, for he appointed Udayarāja as a special officer to carry out the activities, with the designation of *devotpāṭana-nāyaka*, the officer for the uprooting of deities.[28]

Alberuni writing soon after the raids of Mahmud of Ghazni, states that Mahmud destroyed the economy of the areas where he looted and this accounts for the antagonism of the local people towards the Muslims.[29] This is as much a commentary on Mahmud as a statement of what he perceived. The historical question would inquire into the degree of devastation, the areas referred to and the memory of the disruption. An interesting case is that of Somanātha, particularly associated with Mahmud's destruction of the Śiva temple in the early eleventh century.

Curiously, Bilhana referring to his visit to Somanātha later in the same century makes no mention of Mahmud's raid.[30] An inscription from Veraval in the vicinity of Somanātha and dating to AD 1216 is a eulogy on the town and its temples, the Caulukya dynasty, the local governor Śridhara and the Śaiva priest of the temple and speaks of the heroic Hammīra who was subdued by Śridhara, yet there is no mention of the destruction of the temple or of its restoration.[31] Here the Turuṣkas are a political enemy similar to others against whom the Caulukyas fought. Even more curious is the evidence of another inscription from Veraval also in Sanskrit. It records that during the reign of a Caulukya-Vaghela king a substantial grant of land was made in Somanātha for the construction of a mosque in 1264 to the owner of a shipping company called Noradina Piroja/ Nur-ud-din Firuz[32] the son of Khoja Nau Abu Brahima of Hormuja-*deśa* or Ormuz. The mosque is described as a place for the worship of *rasūla*. It is said that Nur-ud-din had the co-operation of the local *pañca-kula* apart from the king. Among the members of the *pañca-kula* were Śaiva priests (perhaps of the Somanātha temple?), merchants and administrators. Were memories surprisingly short, or was the destruction of the temple by Mahmud highly exaggerated, or were the profits of trade a surmounting concern on the part of the authorities at Somanātha? Or were the Turuṣkas seen as different from the Muslim traders from the Gulf, since the former were political enemies whereas the latter were contributing to local prosperity.

Finally we come to *mleccha*, the most contentious among the words used. It has a history going back to around 800 BC[33] and occurs originally in a Vedic text and is used for those who could not speak Sanskrit correctly. Language was frequently a social marker in many early societies. The use of Sanskrit was largely confined to the upper castes, and gradually the word *mleccha* also came to have a social connotation and referred to those outside the pale of *varṇa* society — those who did not observe the rules of caste as described in the *Dharmaśāstras*, or those who belonged to certain categories of lower castes. When used in a pejorative sense it included a difference of language and ritual impurity. The category of *mleccha* was again a well-established category but used more frequently by upper castes to refer to those from whom they wished to maintain a caste distance.

It has been argued that *mleccha* was essentially a term of contempt for the Muslim, or more recently, that the demonisation of the Muslim invaders in using the term *rākṣasas* for them, and invoking the parallel with Rāma as the protector, was part of the Indian political imagination of the twelfth century.[34] But the '*rākṣasisation*' of the enemy, irrespective of who the enemy was, has been a constant factor with reference to many pre-Islamic enemies and going back to earliest times. Sāyana's commentary of the fourteenth century AD on the *Ṛgveda*, refers to the *dāsas* as *rākṣasas* and *asuras*. An in-scription from Gujarat dating to AD 1253, states that Arṇorāja killed Raṇasimha in battle and the latter was like Rāvaṇa — *rāvaṇamiva* — and the Gurjarra *rājyam* is said to be greater than that of Rāma.[35] The inscription proceeds to mention the attack on the Turuṣka — *rājā* who is described as the lord of the *mlecchas*, but interestingly not as Rāvaṇa. The powerful *gaṇa-saṅgha* or chiefdom of the Yaudheyas issued coins in the early centuries AD, a few of which carry the name Rāvaṇa.[36]

In later centuries, the reference to some Muslims as *mlecchas*, was an extension of the term to include them among the many others who were denied *varṇa* status. This usage is more common in sources which come from the upper castes, such as Sanskrit texts and inscriptions, and was more easily used for the lower castes who were, even without being Muslim, marginalised and moved to the fringes of society. The term itself included a multiplicity of peoples and *jātis* but generally it referred to those who were not members of a *varṇa*.

There is however a marked ambivalence in the use of the term. In another Sanskrit inscription of AD 1328 from the Raisina area of Delhi, reference is made to the *mleccha* Sahāvadīna seizing Delhi. But he is praised for his great valour in what is described as his burning down the forest of enemies who surrounded him.[37] If in this context *mleccha* had a contemptuous meaning it is unlikely that a local merchant would dare to use it for a Sultan.

The same ambiguity occurs in earlier texts. It is in this sense that *mleccha* is mentioned in the narrative sections of the *Mahābhārata* (1.62.5). This is emphasised in the passage which relates that Vidura, the uncle of the Pāṇḍavas, spoke in the language of the *mleccha* — *mlecchavāca* — to a messenger (1.135.6). Vidura was the son whom Vyāsa fathered on a slave woman and was conversant therefore with both Sanskrit and the language of the *mlecchas*. The sixth century astronomer Varāmihira, states that among the Yavanas (referring to the Hellenistic Greeks), knowledge in astronomy had stabilised and therefore they were revered as *ṛṣis*, even though they were *mlecchas*;[38] and a seventh century inscription from Assam refers to one of the rulers, Śālastambha, as the *mlecchādhināthā*.[39] Thus the context of this term varied but it was generally a social marker. The identification of what were regarded as *mleccha* lands and people could also change over time.

Social markers are frequently forged by those who demarcate themselves sharply from others and this tends to be characteristic of the upper levels of society. The usage of *mleccha* is no exception.

Among castes, *brāhmaṇa* identity was created in part out of an opposition initially to the *kṣatriyas* as is evident in the Vedic corpus, an opposition which was extended to the heterodox teachings of the *kṣatriyas* in the Śramanic sects, and then to the non-*brāhmaṇa* in general. The dichotomy of the *brāhmaṇa* and the *śūdra* became common to virtually every part of the subcontinent. References to the coming of the *mleccha* creating a social catastrophe of a kind expected of the Kali age as described in the *Purāṇas*, was frequently invoked when there was a political crisis.[40] The insistence that the brahmanical ordering of the world had been turned upside down on such occasions, was repeated in brahmanical texts each time this ordering was challenged. In the Kali age, which was not a specific historical period but was symbolic of a time when the brahmanical normative order was reversed in practice, *mleccha* rulers were frequent. Alternatively the existence of *mleccha* rulers in itself endorsed the characteristics of the Kali age and required that their rule be described as such.

The social distinctions implicit in these terms applied to people of various religions. The connotation of these terms used in the last thousand years, changed with time, application and context, and the mutation of meaning requires analysis. The less frequent use of Yavana and *mleccha* for Europeans had been pared down in meaning by the nineteenth century. Some uses of these terms were mechanisms for reducing social distance, others for enhancing it. A major indicator of social distance was caste. Among castes which we now identify as Hindu, there was the separation of the *dvija* or twice born from the *śūdra* and even more sharply from the untouchable. Muslim society segregated the Muslim from central and western Asia and the indigenous convert. Even if this was not a ritual segregation, it was an effective barrier, and possibly encouraged the local convert to maintain certain earlier caste practices and kinship rules. At the level of the ruling class, the culture of the court influenced all those who had pretensions to power, irrespective of their religion. Further down the social scale, caste identities often controlled appearance and daily routine. Caste identity, because it derived so heavily from occupation and the control over economic resources, was not restricted only to kinship systems and religious practices. The perception of difference therefore was more fragmented among the various communities than is projected in the image of the monolithic two.

Those from across the Arabian Sea who settled as traders along the west coast and married into existing local communities, the Khojas and Bohras of western India, the Navayatas in the Konkan, the Mapillahs of Malabar, assumed many of the customary practices of these communities, and sometimes even contradicting the social norms of Islam. This was also the case with some communities which had converted to Islam. Because of this their beliefs and practices were distinct even from each other, influenced as they were by those of the host community. Today there may be a process of Islamisation among such communities, encouraged by the politics of communalism, which is ironing out these contradictions, but in the past there has been some uncertainty as to whether some of these practices could be viewed as strictly Islamic.[41] There have been marked variations in the structures and rules governing family, kinship and marriage among communities listed as Muslim in the subcontinent. These have quite often tended to be closer to the rules associated with the Hindu castes in the region.[42]

The process of marrying into the local community is unlikely to have been free of tension and confrontation in the initial stages. The orthodox among both the visitors and the hosts, would doubtless have found the need to adapt to custom and practice on both sides not so palatable, but the presence today of these well-articulated communities speaks of the prevalence of professional and economic concerns over questions of religion. Their continuing historical existence points to the eventual adjustments of both the host and the settlers.

Even on conversion, the link with caste was frequently inherent. A multiplicity of identities remained, although their function and need may have changed. Not only was the concept of conversion alien to Indian society, but conversion to Islam remained limited. Possibly one reason for this was that those who introduced Islam could not break through caste stratification. If conversion was motivated by the wish for upward mobility, then even this did not necessarily follow. Conversion in itself does not change the status of the converted group in the caste hierarchy. Even converts have to negotiate a change, and the potentiality for such negotiation would depend on their original status, or else a religious sect would have to evolve into a new caste: a process which has been observed for the history of caste society over many centuries. At the same time, conversion does not eliminate diversities and there would be a carry over of earlier practices and beliefs. Caste ranking continued to be important to marriage and occupation, for a radical change in ranking would have involved confronting the very basis on which Indian society was organised.

Reports as recent as a century ago point to the continuing role of caste even after conversion. The Gazetteer of Bijapur District in 1884 is an example.[43] The Muslim population was listed as consisting of three categories: Muslims who claim to be foreign, indigenous Muslims but descended from migrants from north India and the local Muslims. Those claiming foreign descent list their names as is usual, as Saiyid, Shaikh, Mughal, Pathan; insist that they are Urdu speaking and strictly Sunni; and many of them held office in the local administration. Like the scribes of earlier times, some sought administrative positions in the emerging kingdoms. The second group, working in a different capacity, claims to have come from north Indian communities such as Jat cultivators, or from the trading communities of the west coast and identified themselves by their earlier caste names. They too maintained that they were Sunnis. Their languages varied with some using Urdu and others Marathi and Kannada, with some even preferring Tamil or Arabic.

The third group, with the maximum number in the district, was in many ways dissimilar. They were local converts, some of whom took on *jāti* names that had come to have a subcontinental status and connotation, such as Momin and Kasab, but many retained their original *jāti* names such as Gaundi, Pinjara, Pakhali, and so on, and identified themselves by the same name which they had used prior to conversion. The *jāti* name was associated with the occupation as had often been so from earlier times. Their occupations ranked them at the lower levels of society as the poorer artisans and cultivators and tended to conform to those which they had performed as members of Hindu castes. Their Urdu was minimal because they used Kannada and Marathi. Most of them are described as lax Sunnis, not frequenting the mosque and instead declaring that they worship Hindu deities, observe Hindu festivals and avoid eating beef. The avoidance of beef may have been to distinguish themselves from untouchables who were not restricted from eating beef. The social and religious identity of this third group would seem to be closer to that of their Hindu caste counterparts than to that of Muslims of higher castes. From the thirteenth century there was intense Sufi activity in the area, nevertheless — or possibly because of the openness of certain schools of Sufi teaching — groups such as these could keep a distance from formal Islam. This was the larger majority of those technically listed as Muslims, who, perhaps because of their lower social status and therefore distance from formal religion, are likely to have been untouched by *fatwas*.

This picture was not unique to Bijapur and can be replicated for other parts of the subcontinent. Such groups can perhaps be better described as being on the intersection of Islam and the Hindu religions. This gives them an ambiguous religious identity in terms of an either/or situation. Were they Hindus picking up some aspects of Islam or were they Muslims practising a Hinduised Islam? Did caste identity have priority in determining the nature of the religious identity and did these priorities differ from one social group to another?

Groups such as the third category mentioned above receive little attention from historians of religion since they cannot be neatly indexed. The same was true of their status in the historical treatment of Hinduism. The study of groups which reflect liminal spaces is recent and here too there is frequently a focus on the curious religious admixtures rather than the social and economic compulsions which encourage such admixtures. But in terms of the history of religion in the subcontinent, such groups have been the majority since earliest times and have lent their own distinctiveness to belief and to the practice of religion. On occasion, when they played a significant historical role, attempts would be made to imprint facets of the formal religion onto their beliefs and practices. History is rich in demonstrating the mutation of folk cults into Puranic Hinduism. For example, the hero who saves cattle from raiders was worshipped by the pastoralists of Maharashtra, but eventually emerges at Pandharpur under the patronage of the Yādava dynasty as the god Viṭṭhala, associated with Viṣṇu.[44] This was also one reason why belief and worship across the subcontinent, even when focusing on a single deity, was often formulated differently, except at the level of the elite who differentiated themselves by claiming adherence to forms approved of by brahmanical orthodoxy.

The evolving of Hindu religions, with specific rituals and practices often emerging from particular castes or regions, was a process which did not terminate with the arrival of Islam, nor did it turn away from Islam. The dialogue between Islam and earlier indigenous religions, is reflected in various Bhakti and Sufi traditions, which have been extensively studied in recent years. Since the indigenous religions did not constitute a monolith and registered a range of variations, there were a range of dialogues. These were partly the result of such movements having a middle caste and *śūdra* following even if some of those who led them were *brāhmaṇas*. Formal religious requirements were often rejected in such groups. But not in entirety. Where a few showed familiarity with philosophic doctrine,[45] others broke away from such a dialogue. The attempts to sanskritise the *bhakti* tradition both in texts recounting the activities of the *sants* and in modern studies, has been cautioned against.

The famous *Hindu-Turk Samvād* of Eknāth written in Maharashtra in the sixteenth century, is the imagined dialogue between a *brāhmaṇa* and a Muslim who seems to have been a *maulāna* and there is an undercurrent of satire in the treatment of both.[46] The language used by each for the other would today probably cause a riot! The crux of the debate states, 'You and I are alike, the confrontation is over *jāti* and *dharma*' (v.60). The attempt is at pointing out the differences between facets of what were seen as Hindu and Muslim belief and worship, but arguing for an adjustment. Kṛṣṇadāsa's *Caitanya-carita-amṛta* reflects similar concerns in eastern India — a different part of the subcontinent.[47] The pre-Islamic interweaving of religion and social organisation was not broken and the process of using new religious ideas to negotiate a social space, continued. At a different level but at about the same time, in the seventeenth century, Shivaji was writing in a political vein to Jai Singh about the grave danger facing Hindus and chiding him for his support to the Mughals and offering him an alliance instead. This would be an indication of the perception at elite levels being different from those at other levels and largely conditioned by factors of statecraft and political policy. Eknāth's reading of the situation stands in strong contrast to this.

This also becomes apparent in common cultural codes symbolising an altogether different level of communication. For example, the imagery and meaning encapsulated in the depiction of riding a tiger and who rides a tiger, becomes a powerful symbol. For those who live in the forests, the tiger is the mount of the forest deity such as Dakhin Rai in the Sunderbans. For caste Hindus, the goddess Durgā rides a tiger. Among Nāthapanthis, the *nātha* was depicted as riding a tiger and using a live cobra for a whip. In Sufi hagiography, the Sufi often rides a tiger and sometimes meets another Sufi riding a wall. At the shrine of Sabbarimala in Kerala, the deity Ayyappan rides a tiger. In many rural areas there is to this day an all-purpose holy man who rides a tiger and is variously called, Barekhan Ghazi or Satya-pir, and is worshipped by all, irrespective of formal religious affiliations.[48] This bond, or even the subconscious memory of a bond binding a range of peoples, had no formal definition. These were not individual deviants from conventional religions. This was the religious articulation of the majority of the people in such areas. When we arbitrarily attach such religious expression to either Islam or Hinduism, we perhaps misrepresent the nature of these beliefs.

The existence of parallel religious forms, some conflicting and others cohering, has characterised Indian society. Some of these distanced themselves from all orthodoxies and attracted those who participated in .what might be called forms of counter cultures, preferring the openness of the heterodox. Their ancestry can perhaps be traced through a lineage of thought and behaviour going back to the wandering *vrātyas*, to the rogues with matted hair and the mendicants of the *Upaniṣad*,[49] to the *siddhas* claiming extrasensory powers, the Nātha *yogis*, and some among the *gurus*, the *pirs* and *faqirs*. This was not invariably a confrontation with those in authority, but it was a statement of social distancing. The power of deliberate social distancing could sometimes help in mobilising popular support, the potential for which was recognised by those in authority. Hence the depiction of rulers paying homage to ascetics in myth, in history and in art. The absence of sharply etched religious identities among such groups, gave them a universality, but was also responsible for history neglecting to recognise their significance. This is turn relates directly to the question of whose history are we writing.

Religious expression, if treated only in formal terms and indexed according to established religions, leaves us with a poverty of understanding. For, together with the formal there is the constant presence of the informal and of beliefs unconstrained by texts. These were often forms of legitimising widespread popular practice which adhered neither to the formal requirements of Islam nor of Brahmanic or Puranic Hinduism. They could be, but were not invariably manifestations of peaceful coexistence or even attempts at syncretism.

It has been suggested that it might be useful to investigate the dichotomy between conversion and syncretism. The question of what historical situations result in the one or the other, needs exploration.[50] Syncretism is often a transitory phase for what might in the end become the continuation of two traditions in an unequal relationship although sometimes it may locate the new religion within the existing range. The locating can be based on metaphor which weaves complexities into the manifestation of a religion. Perhaps a new description should be sought for.[51] The degree of institutional support or its curtailment in relation to religious practice and belief would result in varying patterns in the political impact of a particular religion. These variations become significant to questions of conversion and syncretism.

Concepts such as those of composite culture or syncretism are only partial explanations and refer to particular situations. Syncretism would apply for example, to Akbar's attempts at combining variant religious activities and beliefs by propagating a religion of his own making, or to Eknāth in his formulation of a dialogue between the Hindu and the Muslim, the two remaining distinct. Akbar's efforts were in part a crystallization of the earlier Indian tradition where royalty bestowed patronage on a variety of religious sects, some even hostile to each other. Akbar's acceptance of a religious pluralism, irrespective of how he formulated it, was significant even to the subsequent interweaving of religion and political policy although this was not characteristic of every aspect of religion during this period.

There were aspects of life in which religion was an identifier but there were also many other aspects in which more broad-based cultural expressions, evolving over time and through an admixture of various elements, gave an identity to a social group. It is these which need to be investigated. Associated with this is the exploration of a multiplicity of causes for particular historical events, causes which include or emphasise aspects of political expediency, economic control, ideological support, social associations, religious practices and custom; the exploration of which provide variations in the ordering of priorities among causal connections and historical explanations.

Composite culture also presupposes self-contained units in combination or in juxtaposition. In the history of Indian society such units would be *jātis*, sects, language groups and groups with a local identity and would have a history in many cases going back to pre-Islamic times. The juxtaposition would not have been invariably between formal religions, Hinduism and Islam, as is often argued, since this again presupposes the notion of the monolithic community, but more often between variant articulations among the many constituent units of society. These units would have to be historically identified, an exercise which requires a sensitivity to the problems of writing the history of those on the intersections of varied religious expression.

The concern would be with both social dissonances and social harmonies, and a need for adjustment. Occurrences of religious conflict were not unknown, but were more frequently associated with the attitudes of formal religions for whom the conflict was rarely confined to religious factors. It arose more frequently from competing claims to patronage and resources. Perhaps the existence of the parallel, informal religions played a role, not in preventing conflict, but in ensuring that intolerance was contained and remained at the local level, as it had done even in earlier times.[52]

The relationship between segments of society, even those identified as Hindu or Muslim, would take the normal course of jousting for social space and social advancement. This would have involved diplomacy and management or on occasion conflict of a violent kind, particularly where established statuses were being challenged by newly evolved ones, using the patronage of authority. But the conflict at levels other than those of the ruling class, was localised. Friends and enemies were demarcated less by religion and more by the concerns of social and economic realities. Cultural transactions and social negotiations were common but were bounded by the degree of proximity to the structure of power.

To unravel the creating and modulating of religious identities, is a far more complex process than the chronicling of religious activities. I have tried to argue that it is linked to social identities and historical perceptions, which in turn hinge on access to resources and power, or alternatively, to a deliberate distancing from these. I have also tried to suggest that if we move away from the notion of monolithic communities we begin to see the historical potential of understanding how identities may actually have been perceived at points in time, and their multiple manifestations and functions. Exploring the perceptions which people had of each other in the past is not merely a matter of historical curiosity for it impinges on the way in which current identities are being constructed. An insistence on seeing society as having consisted for all time of monolithic religious communities derives from the contemporary conflict over identities. Yet identities in history are neither stable nor permanent. Inherent in the process of historical change is the invention and mutation of identities. And the identities of the pre-colonial period would seem to have been very different from the way in which they have been projected in our times.

## Notes and References


1. *Indische Alterthumskunde*, Leipzig, 1847–62.
2. R. Thapar, 'Syndicated Hinduism'. *See* chapter 46 in this volume.
3. This was demonstrated in the debate over the history of the Ramjanmabhoomi at Ayodhya, S. Gopal (ed.), *Anatomy of a Confrontation*, Delhi, 1990. See especially, K.N. Panikkar, 'An Historical Overview', pp. 22–37. The pamphlet published by some JNU historians entitled *The Political Abuse of History*, is concerned with the same issue.
4. R. Thapar, 'Imagined Religious Communities? Ancient History and the Modern Search for a Hindu Identity', in R. Thapar, *Interpreting Early India*, Delhi, 1992, pp. 60–80. *See* chapter 43 in this volume.
5. As for example in some of the papers included in G.D. Sontheimer and H. Kulke (eds), *Hinduism Reconsidered*, Delhi, 1989 and V. Dalmia and H. von Steitencron (eds), *Representing Hinduism*, New Delhi, 1995.
6. R.S. Avasthy and A. Ghosh, 'References to Muhammadans in Sanskrit Inscriptions in Northern India', *Journal of Indian History*, 1935, 15, pp. 161–84.
7. *Epigraphia Indica*, 32, pp. 47ff; 64ff.
8. M. Athar Ali, 'Encounter and Efflorescence . . .', *PIHC*, Gorakhpur, 1989.
9. R. Thapar, 'The Image of the Barbarian in Early India', in R. Thapar, *Ancient Indian Social History: Some Interpretations*, New Delhi, 1978, pp. 152–92. *See* chapter 12 in this volume.
10. *Majjhima Nikāya*, 2, 149–92.
11. D.C. Sircar, *Studies in the Yuga Purāṇa and Other Texts*, Delhi, 1974; D.R. Mankad, *Yugapuranam*, Vallabhavidyanagar, 1951; J.E. Mitchner, *Yuga Purāṇa*, Calcutta, 1986, gives a different reading.
12. Arrian, 6.6ff, Plutarch, 69.
13. N. Hein, 'Kālayavana, A Key to Mathura's Cultural Self-Perception', in D.M. Srinivasan (ed.), *Mathura*, New Delhi, 1989.
14. Manu, X.20.
15. Manu, X.43–4.

16. *Mahābhārata*, 13.35.17–18.
17. *Mahābhārata*, 1.80.26.
18. R. Avasthy and A. Ghosh, 'References to Muhammadans in North Indian Inscriptions, 730–1200 AD', in *Journal of Indian History*, 1935, 15, 161–84; 1936, 16, 24–6.
19. The *Cāryugāci-bākhar* discussed in N.G. Wagle, 'Hindu-Muslim Interactions in Medieval Maharashtra', in G.D. Sontheimer and H. Kulke (eds), *Hinduism Reconsidered*, Delhi, 1989, pp. 51–66.
20. Palam *Baoli* Inscription in P. Prasad, *Sanskrit Inscriptions of the Delhi Sultanate 1191–1526*, Delhi, 1990, pp. 3ff.
21. Such a recounting of the rulers of Delhi occurs in inscriptions from elsewhere in northern India as well. Avasthy and Ghosh, op. cit.
22. I. Habib, 'Economic History of Delhi Sultanate', *The Indian Historical Review*, 1978, 4, 2, pp. 291, 295.
23. Naraina Stone Inscription, ibid., p. 22.
24. *Rājataraṅginī*, I.170; VIII.3412.
25. Avasthy and Ghosh, op. cit.
26. *Rājataraṅginī*, VIII.887.
27. Ibid., VII.1095, 1149; VIII.3346.
28. Ibid., VII.1091.
29. E. Sachau, *Alberuni's India*, London, 1910, p. 22.
30. *Vikramānkadeva carita*, XVIII.
31. *Epigraphia Indica*, 2, pp. 437ff.
32. *Epigraphia Indica*, 34, pp. 141–52.
33. R. Thapar, 'The Image of the Barbarian in Early India', *Comparative Studies in Society and History*, 1971, XIII, pp. 408–36. *See* chapter 12 in this volume. A. Parashar, *Mlecchas in Early India*, Delhi, 1991.
34. S. Pollock, '*Rāmāyaṇa* and Political Imagination in India', *Journal of Asian Studies*, 1993, 52, 1.
35. *Epigraphia Indica*, 1, pp. 26ff.
36. M.K. Sharan, *Tribal Coins*, New Delhi, 1972, pp. 122, 127.
37. Sarban Stone Inscription, P. Prasad, op. cit., p. 29.
38. *Bṛhatsaṃhitā*, M.R. Bhat (ed.), II.32.
39. Bargaon Copper-Plate Inscription of Ratnapāladeva; quoted in K.L. Barua Bahadur, *Early History of Kamarupa*, Gauhati, 1966, pp. 66–7.
40. C. Talbot, 'Inscribing the Other, Inscribing the Self: Hindu-Muslim Identities in Pre-colonial India', *Comparative Studies in Society and History*, 1995, 37, (4), 692–715. E. Zelliot, 'Four Radical Saints in Maharashtra', in M. Israel and N.K. Wagle (eds), *Religion and Society in Maharashtra*, Toronto, 1987, pp. 131–44.
41. For example, V.S. D'Souza, *The Navayats of Kannara*, Dharwar, 1955.
42. I. Ahmed (ed.), *Family, Kinship and Marriage among Muslims in India*, Delhi, 1976.

43. Summarised in R.M. Eaton, *Sufis of Bijapur*, New Jersey, 1978, pp. 310ff.
44. A. Dandekar, 'Landscapes in Conflict: Flocks, Hero-stones and Cult in Early Medieval Maharashtra', *Studies in History*, 1991, VII, 2, pp. 301–24.
45. D.N. Lorenzen, 'Social Ideologies of Hagiography', in M. Israel and N. Wagle (eds), *Religion and Society in Maharashtra*, Toronto, 1987, pp. 92–114.
46. E. Zelliot, 'A Medieval Encounter between Hindus and Muslims: Eknath's Drama-Poem Hindu-Turk Samvad', in F.W. Clothey (ed.), *Images of Man: Religion and Historical Process in South Asia*, Madras, 1982.
47. J.T. O'Connell, 'Vaisnava Perceptions of Muslims in Sixteenth Century Bengal', in M. Israel and N.K. Wagle (eds), *Islamic Society and Culture*, New Delhi, 1983.
48. In the Sundarbans the tiger and its manifestations such as Dakhin Rai the tiger-god, Bonobibi the goddess of the forest, or Ghazi Sahib, are universally worshipped by Hindus and Muslims alike and the mythologies which accompany this worship have diverse Hindu and Muslim sources as also does the chanting at the *pūja*. For an account of the continuity of this worship to this day, see S. Montgomery, *Spell of the Tiger*, New York, 1995.
49. *Maitri Upaniṣad*, 7.8.
50. D.N. Lorenzen, 'Introduction', in D.N. Lorenzen (ed.), *Religious Change and Cultural Domination*, Mexico, 1981, pp. 3–18.
51. W.H. McLeod, 'The Problem of Syncretism', in S.S. Hartman (ed.), *Syncretism*, Stockholm, 1969, Quoted in Lorenzen above.
52. R. Thapar, *Cultural Transactions and Early India*, Delhi, 1987.

45

# *Secularism and History**

It was only recently proclaimed that the end of history had arrived with the victory of global capitalism over socialism. Yet within the short span of these last few years we have witnessed and are continuing to witness, the most dramatic resurgence of ideologies and aspirations which have a distinctly nineteenth century feel to them. These have brought back history — if ever it had indeed been ended — with a disquieting resonance. I am not referring only to the ethnic confrontations in former Yugoslavia, but more widely to actions motivated by theories of racism and of ethnicity, and of the permeation of religion into politics. Such actions are more than visible in the heart of global capitalism as they also are in the societies of our subcontinent.

The intellectually fashionable periodisation today, speaks of history in terms of the pre-colonial, the colonial and the post-colonial. The latter two are familiar and subject to much discourse. But pre-colonial history in India, is largely unfamiliar to those who conduct this discourse. Nevertheless generalisations are made about the pre-modern tradition in India and these frequently derive from what is assumed to be the tradition, an assumption often based on the negation of that which is held to be characteristic of modernity. There is little hesitation in using colonial constructions of 'tradition or 'community' or 'culture' in speaking of an earlier historical heritage. A familiarity with the various pre-colonial associations of these concepts is regarded as unnecessary. If, as some historians assert, cultural concepts are to be given priority in historical explanation, then surely these concepts have to be viewed from a historical perspective. It seems to me that this is all the more necessary in a society which even today carries so many 'cultural

* Address to the Fortieth Annual Convocation, Jadavpur University, Calcutta, 24 December 1995.

survivals' from earlier times. Part of the reason for this unconcern with earlier history is the theory, disturbing for the historian, that all historical moments are isolated, fortuitous and contingent. The logic of this would justify even the rejection of history, and if the historical moment belongs to a post-colonial situation, its antecedents or mutations from a pre-colonial or a colonial time would be regarded as irrelevant. From a historian's perspective, this is unacceptable.

We are being encouraged today to take a fragmented view of ourselves and of our past, where the fragmentation follows from the premises of nineteenth century interpretations of our past, and which had hopefully been replaced by a holistic view when we terminated colonial rule. In speaking of a holistic view I am not endorsing the claim of ruling groups to represent the whole, but am insisting that the relationships between various groups which constitute society be included, even where some of these are confrontational. Fragmentation has returned in many forms, the most prominent being religion-based nationalism, the kind of nationalism which we had believed had been laid to rest at the time of independence. Added to this is caste and regional chauvinism. Some would view all these as products of the nation-state and argue that once the nation-state disappears so will these, but how this is to happen and what will replace the nation-state remains unclear. For the moment, the nation at least, is visible and apparent. It is more realistic for us to ensure its well-being through actions which we regard as instrumental for the common good.

The return to a holistic view requires a reassessment of the relation of civil society to the nation-state. In this the secularising of our society as part of the process of change envisioned in modernisation, becomes a central issue. I would like to argue that this is not a matter related only to religious identities and religious nationalism but has implications for the totality of social change. Further, that although it differs from our pre-colonial past, such a secularising is not an attempt at alienating ourselves from our tradition, since the pre-colonial past has, in ample measure, ideas and institutions conducive to the secular.

Secularism in Europe has its own history. Its association with the separating of religion from civic life, is only of recent times accompanying the advent of the nation-state and the historical process of modernisation. The meaning of the word has changed in European intellectual history and therefore its exact translation cannot be sought in non-European languages, but as a concept it can be located in cultures where this historical process is taking place. For the Romans 'secular' meant a specific period of time, generally a hundred years, marked by holding games and worshipping the gods. Because of its association with a long temporal duration it came to be used gradually as a description of the world which had existed for a long period. This was later contrasted with the Church which had a briefer life. Secular was initially taken in this sense as that which pertained to the world and not to the Church.

To speak of secularism as a western concept superimposed on India is historically incorrect, for it is not confined to the question of the relations between religion and the state derived from the experience of the Christian Church. Within the Christian Church there was a substantial difference between the Protestant induction of some aspects of secularism and the Catholic confrontation with it. The Lutheran Scandinavian countries had few problems with secularising their societies, the Catholic priests of Italy and Spain, not to mention Latin America, are still battling with it. The crux of the confrontation is not around the religion of the individual or its negation but over the question of the authority of religious institutions or institutions inspired by religious identities, over civic life.

By the mid-nineteenth century the definition of secular focussed on the question of ethics. It was stated that social morality, central to the secular, should have as its sole basis the well-being of mankind to the exclusion of considerations stemming from a belief in God or in a future condition. The key elements of this morality were legal order, political freedom, individual autonomy and material well-being. These are elements endorsed even by those that find modernisation antipathetic. The emphasis therefore is not on a hostility to religion but on rational and moral principles governing society, principles which oppose the alienation of human beings, or the absence of social ethics. Yet there is a persistence in arguing that the secular hinges solely on the conflict between Church and State. In the definition of secularism, the state is not the arbiter of conflict or co-existence between religions, nor is secularism the ideology of statehood. If we have conceded this to the state then this will need to be corrected by the state having to adhere to the values and ethics of a secularised society.

Where secularism is so interpreted, the evidence from pre-colonial India points to a relationship far more nuanced than it was in Europe and in some ways, dissimilar. This was in part due to the multiplicity of religions from early times and in part to the nature of Indian social organisation which was entirely different from Europe. There were certainly rituals to consecrate a *rājā* and these were moments of intense religiosity. A new Sultan was announced by having the *khutba* read in his name in the mosque. Interestingly however, state patronage was bestowed in substantial amounts to a range of what may otherwise have even been conflicting religious sects and institutions. The Mauryan emperor Aśoka encourages respect for both the *brāhmaṇa* and the *śramaṇa* although elsewhere the relation between the two is compared to that between the mongoose and the snake. There is an on-going controversy, as to whether Harṣavardhana of Kannauj was a Buddhist or a Śaiva, given his endowments and support to both, and this was soon after the time when the Śaiva sects of Kashmir had destroyed Buddhist monasteries and killed Buddhist monks. The Caulukyas of Gujarat built a mosque for the Arabs trading in western India, which mosque was destroyed by the Paramāras of Malwa campaigning against the Caulukyas. Mughal endowments to *brāhmaṇas, jogis,* and temples, are recorded, even those of Aurangzeb.

Cultural pluralism and its protection was accepted as the duty of the king. His protection of *dharma* was not religion in the modern sense for it enveloped the entire range of social obligations of which religious ritual was a part. This however is not what is meant by a secular society. Secularism is not expressed merely by the state protecting and ensuring the co-existence of religions. But, where there is evidence for this from the past, it increases the potential for locating those historical activities which would be conducive to the encouragement of the secular today.

The notion of a state religion in pre-colonial India also becomes somewhat meaningless when it is apparent that political power was relatively open throughout Indian history. Ruling families frequently came from groups ranked as socially low or from obscure families, where some made an effort to cover this up with fancy origin myths and claims to *kṣatriya* status. But in the process of becoming politically established they tended to carry their religious cults with them and these had then to be recognised as part of the established religion. The entry of Śāktism into upper caste practice was in part due to this process. Where such kings could eventually claim to be the *avatāra* of Viṣṇu, the centrality of a God as a focus of power, begins to pale.

Alternatively, an existing state sometimes had to extend its patronage not only to the established religious institutions, but even to a cult of the marginalised groups, in order to strengthen its authority. Although such cults are sometimes brought on par with upper caste religion, their local roots and specific meaning remain, and distinguish them from other such cults. Thus the worship of the hero-stone among pastoralists in Maharashtra was mutated into the cult of Viṭhobā, the Yādava dynasty encouraging its identity with Viṣṇu. This resulted in Yādava control over large tracts of the less fertile parts of Maharashtra. The same process has been sketched for many other areas especially at the turn of the first millennium AD.

If one takes a long view of the past, human societies have moved from the palaeolithic to the neolithic to the chalcolithic to urban civilisations and much more. Each change brought its own anxieties and bewilderments where power and authority were conceded by some and contested by others. As far back as 500 BC, emerging kingdoms in the Ganga plain began to supersede the clans and the beginnings of urbanisation brought further change. There was at this time a strong endorsement of social ethics. Buddhist thought maintained that ethical behaviour was socially determined and did not derive from deity, a clear separation of ethics from religion. The centrality of social ethics is a significant part of our cultural inheritance.

The history of religion in India has generally been viewed from the perspective of both the Hindu and the Muslim upper castes. Such religion was directed to a specific deity or deities and had institutions for channelling worship. Sacred space was demarcated by the temple and the mosque. Sometimes this was extended to the *maṭha* and the *khānqah*. Temples and *maṭhas* were closed to some lower castes and to untouchables, mosques and *khānqahs* were open, but nevertheless the clientele was discrete. There were orders of priests and monks, there were *ulema*, there were texts held sacred, and there was a competition for wealthy patrons, particularly royalty. These were all characteristics of Christian Europe as well. But there, at the lower levels of society there was an enforcing of support for these institutions, whereas in India such support was garnered but did not prevent the existence of alternative religious identities by the same people. The lower castes, viewed as servants of the temple, would have performed the requisite services but would not invariably have been included among the worshippers. Their religious practice lay outside these institutions and was bounded by social codes of behaviour. Since these castes, whom we now arbitrarily label Hindu and Muslim, formed the majority of the population, their religion has to be recognised as distinctive.

The religion of this majority was a mixing and merging of belief and ritual drawn from a variety of religious experiences, in which the formal differentiations of upper caste religions did not generally prevail. Frequently the religious practices of these groups were unacceptable to those who defined Islam and Hinduism. Thus, *brāhmaṇas* shrank from libations of alcohol and offerings of flesh and *mullahs* could not prevent converts to Islam continuing to worship idols. The recognition of these religions as central to the assessment of religion in India, is a recent interest, having been substantially ignored in the Orientalist construction of Indian religion.

The claim that there was religious tolerance in Indian society is defended by recourse to texts. In fact it was the juxtaposition of various kinds of religious practices and beliefs, tied closely to social organisation which was the basis of both a relative religious tolerance and a heightened intolerance based on social outcasting. Religious practices and beliefs could overlap among adjoining castes, but social distinctions were firmly demarcated. Religious tolerance was possible because of the enforcement of social boundaries, but when these were transgressed or seen as competitive, as for example, between the Śaivas and the Jainas in Karnataka, the tolerance disappeared and the conflict took a religious form. Violent forms of religious intolerance were local and did not develop into *jehads* and crusades. The co-existence of religions is again described as secularism but this is not a sufficient description of secularism.

The religious reality in the past for the majority of Indians has been the recognition of a multiplicity of religions drawing marginally perhaps from the established ones, but far more rooted in local cults, beliefs and rituals and identified less by religion and more by *jāti* or by *zāt*. This gave them a certain freedom to worship a stone, an icon or a deity with which they alone had a dialogue. These were groups entwined by social regulations but of a local kind. They maintained a distance from the *brāhmaṇas* and the *ulema* for they were essentially unconcerned with norms of the *śāstras* or with *fatwas*, governed as they were by their own customary observances. This distance was not an idyllic or archaic freedom but resulted from the segmentation of *jāti* which kept them apart. The distancing in religious belief and practice, however, did not prevent an oppressive proximity in areas of civic concern, in the control exercised by those in authority over such groups. Within the *jāti/zāt* there was a degree of egalitarianism. In the absence of democracy the ranking was held together by the coercion of those at the top and the acquiescing of those at the lower end. More often than not, within each broad category there was a certain consensus and some manoeuvrability. With the coming of democracy the coercive aspect should ideally fade away but this will not happen easily and quickly, given the force of historical conditioning.

Caste as *jāti* combined in itself kinship systems, occupation and access to resources, and rituals and beliefs. Further removed socially were the untouchables and the tribals whose religious practices were yet more different. There was therefore an immense diversity even in religions believed to be uniform such as Islam and Christianity. Worship at temples and mosques was formal but the perfect worshipper was the *bhakta* who chose his own deity, his *guru*, his form of worship. Religious belief was bound by individual inclination but religious practice conformed to that of the *jāti*. The pressures to conform were pressures of society and did not emanate from a Church.

As in most pre-modern societies, hierarchy bound the segments into a whole but it was not an immutable hierarchy. Osmosis between close castes did permit of some mobility although this was dependent on the historical situation. Recruitment to upper castes in the case of *brāhmaṇas* and *kṣatriyas* took the form of incorporating new groups and assigning status. Inscriptions of the post-Gupta period from Bangladesh mention an increase of *brāhmaṇa gotras* which have been explained as resulting from the incorporation of people from local societies who were then given *brāhmaṇa* status. This becomes a feature in many areas where there was an expansion of the agrarian economy and state power. In the case of Ashrafs and Saiyyads who claimed higher status because of foreign origins, and frequently had high administrative positions, their ranks could also increase when after a few generations indigenous converts made the same claims. A change of status required a change in the way of life. Therefore only those who could invest in this change were able to make it. Others sought to alter the ranking or express their dissent by initiating a new religious sect which, in negotiating with other social groups, either negated or ignored caste-ranking, but more often than not was transmuted into a caste. Both these features make a consistent pattern throughout the Indian past.

This does not make Indians more embedded in religion. But it requires that we investigate the relation between religion, politics and society in the pre-colonial period in terms different from the established ones. Monolithic, homogeneous, religious communities claiming to represent either the majority or the minority provide little explanation of the antecedents to the present functioning of Indian society. They only foster the aspirations of some present day political parties. But at the same time, the contemporary ideology of religious majoritarianism not only moulds religion into a new homogeneous and militant form to enable it to function as an agency of political mobilisation, but it also makes a mockery of democracy by giving to the majority a pre-determined identity. The fears of those labeled as minorities are also sought to be allayed by encouraging them to resort to uniformity and militancy.

This is not to suggest that there was an absence of communities in the past, but that the community identities were many and drew on caste, location, language, religious practice and belief, some of which intersected. These were not communities identified across the subcontinent by a single, recognised, religious mould. Communities are in any case constructed, which is why there can be intersecting identities and these identities can disappear over time or survive in variant forms. The current recognition of monolithic religious communities is also a construction which grows out of the way Indian society was perceived in the colonial period. Social memory is also influenced by historical perceptions.

The induction of the secular into a society cannot be a partial experience, revolving around religion. It is a component of a bigger change involving primarily the introduction of democracy, but also of new technologies, and the emergence of a new social group, the middle-class, which breaks away from earlier social identities. There is inevitably a search for new identities and in the Indian situation of recent times, encouragement has been given to religious identities, on the basis of a particular interpretation of what is regarded as the Indian tradition and Indian history. Secularism is no more a western concept than is the middle-class or the nation-state, even if all these are changes introduced to the world as a result of capitalism or colonialism.

The recognition of the secular relates to specific historical changes experienced by a variety of societies and may well in the next century result in varied manifestations. In Europe this change was associated with societies which had been confined to a single religion which evolved as a focus of power and therefore came into confrontation with the state. In India there has been a multiplicity of religions and the state did not need to confront these. This pre-colonial experience should make it easier for us to secularise our society provided we can cut our way through the impositions of the last two centuries. Religion in India, even if viewed in terms of Hindu and Muslim, has had a strong personal component and has not been dependent on a Church. It would therefore be regarded as natural that religion be a personal matter, a matter of faith, and neither the concern of the state nor of the self-appointed theologians of any majority or minority community. To draw on a secular tradition from the Indian past would have less to do with religious identities and more to do with the questioning of social boundaries.

The problems of the monolithic religious communities, created and endorsed by colonial and, to some degree, nationalist opinion, remains with us. If the nation-state has accepted these identities, then the failure lies with civil society acquiescing in this acceptance. We are hesitant to recognise the elements of a different tradition which I would argue is the historical heritage and which although not secularism, would nevertheless legitimise a secular social ethic. This in turn would empower civil society to strengthen democracy and prevent authoritarianism by the state. Secularisation creates new categories of cohesive social relationships which can monitor the activities of the state. The monitoring is not necessarily a self-conscious act for it is written into the legislating of human rights. These are opposed to any identity used for constructing monolithic, homogeneous, religious communities, or for that matter even communities identified by race and ethnicity. Such identities are only too present in various parts of the world and are by no means absent in the subcontinent where they have become the major source of opposition to the rights necessary to an enlightened society.

The secularisation of society is neither an easy nor a rapid change. The requirements of social justice and of social welfare, with precedence for subordinated groups and gender justice, have not been given priority in Indian development and are likely to be brushed aside by the demands of global capitalism. To try and hold back modernisation is now a fantasy. But we cannot be passive recipients of modernisation. In the absence of the practice of human rights and social justice, a modernised state can become merely another oppressive state; and where it appropriates the kind of nationalism which creates ghettos, it becomes a fascist state. Ideologies of social welfare and social justice can be effectively put into practice by the state, but their continued existence if not enhancement, should become the essential concern of civil society. This implies not just an expectation from the state, but more importantly, the ensuring of their presence in our institutions. It is only through empowering that which is secular in our society that we can hope to live with dignity.

# 46

# *Syndicated Hinduism*[1] *

The term Hinduism as we understand it today to describe a particular religion is modern, as also is the concept which it presupposes, both resulting from a series of choices made from a range of belief, ritual and practice which were collated into the creation of this religion. Unlike Christianity and Islam (with which the comparison is often made), which began with a founder and structure at a point in time and evolved largely in relation to them, Hinduism (and I use the word here in its contemporary meaning) has been constituted largely through a range of reaction to specific historical situations. This is partly why some prefer to use the phrase Hindu religions (in the plural) rather than Hinduism. Ironically there has been little analysis of the various manifestations of Hinduism from a historical perspective. The normative and the empirical in the analysis of Hinduism are seldom interwoven. Comparisons with Semitic religions — particularly Islam and Christianity — are not fortuitous since these have been catalysts in the search for a structure among contemporary Hindus.

Whereas linear religions such as Buddhism and Jainism or Christianity and Islam can be seen to change in a historical dimension, both reacting to their original structure and the interaction with the constituents of historical circumstances, such changes are more easily seen in individual Hindu sects rather than in Hinduism as a whole. This may be a partial explanation for the general reluctance of scholars of Hinduism to relate manifestations of Hinduism to their historical context and to social change.

The study of what is regarded as Hindu philosophy and religious texts has been so emphasised as almost to ignore those who are the practitioners of these tenets, beliefs, rituals and ideas. The latter

* From G.D. Sontheimer and H. Kulke (eds), *Hinduism Reconsidered*, Delhi, 1997, 54–81.

became an interest of nineteenth century ethnography but this was not generally juxtaposed with textual data. Furthermore the view has generally been from above, since the texts were first composed in Sanskrit and their interpreters were *brāhmaṇas*. But precisely because Hinduism is not a linear religion, it becomes necessary to look at the situation further down the social scale where the majority of its practitioners are located. The religious practices of the latter may differ from those at the upper levels to a degree considerably greater than that of a uniform, centralised, monolithic religion.

Discussions on Hinduism tend to be confined to Hindu philosophy and theory. But the manifestation of a contemporary, resurgent, active movement, largely galvanised for political ends, provides a rather different focus to such discussions. It is with the projections of this form of popular Hinduism and of its past that this article forms a comment. The kind of Hinduism which is being currently propagated by the Sanghs, Parishads and Sammelans, is an attempt to restructure the indigenous religions into a monolithic, uniform religion, paralleling some of the features of Semitic religions. This seems to be a fundamental departure from the essentials of what may be called the indigenous Hindu religions. Its form is not only in many ways alien to the earlier culture of India but equally disturbing is the uniformity which it seeks to impose on the variety of Hindu religions.

My attempt here is to briefly review what might be called Hinduism through history, and observe the essentials of the earliest beginnings and the innovations introduced over time. More recent innovations of colonial times have sometimes provided the possibilities for the directions in which some segments of Hinduism are now moving. The study of Hindu philosophy and thought has its own importance but is not of central concern to this article. Religious articulation in the daily routine of life draws more heavily on social sources than on the philosophical or the theological.

Religions such as Buddhism or Islam or Christianity do diversify into sects but this diversification retains a particular reference point — that of the historical founder and the teaching embodied in a single sacred text or a group of texts regarded as the Canon. The area of discourse among the sects is tied to the dogma, tenets and theology as enunciated in the beginning. They see themselves as part of the historical process and of the unfolding of the single religion even though they may have broken away from the mainstream.

Hindu sects on the other hand generally had a distinct and independent origin related to the centrality of a particular deity and/or to a founder and to a system of beliefs. The latter could, but need not be, related to an earlier system. Only at a later stage, and if required, were attempts made to try and assimilate some of these sects into existing dominant sects through the amalgamation of new forms of recognized deities or, of new deities as the manifestations of the older ones, and by incorporating some of their mythology, ritual and custom. Subordinate sects sought to improve their status by similar incorporation from the dominant sects if they were in a position to do so.

What has survived over the centuries is not a single monolithic religion but a diversity of religious sects which we today have put together under a uniform name. The collation of these religious groups is defined as Hinduism even though the religious reference points of such groups might be quite distinct. 'Hinduism' became a convenient general label for studying the different indigenous religious expressions. This was when it was claimed that anything from atheism to animism could legitimately be regarded as part of 'Hinduism'. Today the Hindus of the Parishads and the Sanghs would look upon atheists and animists with suspicion and contempt, for the term Hinduism is being used in a different sense.

Hinduism as defined in contemporary parlance is a bringing together of beliefs, rites and practices consciously selected from those of the past, interpreted in a contemporary idiom in the last couple of centuries and the selection conditioned by historical circumstances. This is not to suggest that religions with a linear growth are superior to what may apparently be an ahistorical religion or one with multiple historical roots, but rather to emphasise the difference between the two.

In a strict sense, a reference to Hinduism would require a more precise definition of the particular variety referred to — Brahmanism, Bhakti, Tantrism, Brahmo-Samaj, Arya-Samaj, Shaiva-Siddhanta, or whatever. These are not comparable to the sects of Christianity or Islam as they do not relate to a single sacred text and its interpretation. Many are rooted in ritual practices and beliefs rather than in texts and it has been argued that a characteristic difference relates to the orthopraxy of Hinduism rather than to an orthodoxy.[2] Present-day Hinduism therefore cannot be seen as an evolved form with a linear growth historically from

Harappan through Vedic, Puranic and Bhakti forms, although it may carry elements of these. In this it differs even from Buddhism and Jainism leave alone Christianity and Islam.

Its origin has no distinct point in time (the *Vedas* were regarded as the foundation until the discovery of the Indus civilisation in the 1920s when the starting point was then taken back to the previous millennium), no historically attested founder, no text associated with the founder, all of which reduces its association with historicity. This of course makes it easier to reinterpret if not to recreate a religion afresh as and when required.

Many of these features, absent in the religion as a whole, do however exist among the various sects which are sought to be included under the umbrella-label of 'Hinduism' which makes them historical entities. But then, not all these sects are agreed on identical rites, beliefs and practices as essential. Animal sacrifice and libations of alcohol would be essential to some but anathema to others among the sects which the Census of India labels as 'Hindu'. The yardstick of the Semitic religions which has been the conscious and the subconscious challenger in the modern structuring of Hinduism, would seem most inappropriate to what existed before.

We know little for certain about the Harappan religion and guesses include a possible fertility cult involving the worship of phallic symbols, a fire cult, perhaps a sacrificial ritual and rituals to legitimise rulership, some suggestive of an authoritative priesthood. The decipherment of the script will hopefully tell us more. It was earlier thought that with the ascendence of Vedic religion, the Harappan became a substratum religion, some facets of which surfaced in later periods. A different interpretation is now being put forward, and although tentative, is worth consideration. It is being suggested that some important aspects of Vedic religion may in fact have been incorporated from the earlier Harappan religion and this would include, the building of a fire-altar and even perhaps the *soma* cult.[3] The Vedic compositions even if they might incorporate elements of the earlier religion, emphasise the central role of the sacrificial ritual of the *yajña*, are suggestive of some elements of shamanism, include a gamut of deities where the *brāhmaṇa* is the intermediary to the gods and worship focuses on rituals without images. Because of the pivotal role of the *brāhmaṇa* it is sometimes referred to as the beginnings of Brahmanical Hinduism to distinguish it from other important forms of Hinduism. The Vedic compositions and the *Dharmaśāstras* (the codes of sacred and social duties) are said to constitute the norms for Brahmanism and the religious practices for the upper castes.

Brahmanism is differentiated from the subsequent religious groups by the use for the latter of the term Śramanism. The Buddhist and Jaina texts, the inscriptions of Aśoka, the description of India by Megasthenes and the account of the Chinese pilgrim Hsüan Tsang, covering a period of a thousand years, all refer to two main religious categories: the *brāhmaṇas* and the *śramaṇas*.[4] The identity of the former is familiar and known. The latter were those who were often in opposition to Brahmanism such as the Buddhists, Jainas and Ājīvikas and a number of other sects associated with both renunciatory orders and a lay following, who explored areas of belief and practice different from the *Vedas* and *Dharmaśāstras*. They often preached a system of universal ethics which spanned castes and communities. This differed from the tendency to segment religious practice by caste which was characteristic of Brahmanism. The segmenting of sects is of course common even among historically evolved religions but the breaking away still retains the historical imprint of the founder, the text and the institution.

Brahmanism was free of this. The differentiating of Brahmanistic practice for a particular caste makes it an essentially different kind of segmentation. It was this segmentation which some Śramanic religions opposed in their attempt to universalise their religious teaching, as for example in the banishing of those monks and nuns thought to be creating dissension in the Buddhist *saṅgha*.[5] The hostility between Brahmanism and Śramanism was so acute that the grammarian Patañjali, when speaking of natural enemies and innate hostility refers to this and compares it to the hostility of the snake and the mongoose, the cat and the mouse.[6] Literature dating to after the fifth century AD has derogatory statements about the Jainas as heretics and Jaina literature refers to the *brāhmaṇas* as heretics and liars. This indigenous view of the dichotomous religions of India is referred to even at the beginning of the second millennium AD by Alberuni who writes of the Brahmanas and the Shamaniyya.[7]

Within Brahmanism there was also segmentation but seen from the outside it seemed an entity. Brahmanism did maintain its identity and survived the centuries although not unchanged, particularly after the decline of Buddhism. This was in part because it was well-endowed with grants of land and items of wealth through intensive royal patronage, which in turn reinforced its claim to social superiority and enabled it further to emphasise its distance from other castes and their practices. The extensive use of Sanskrit as the language of rituals and learning enhanced the employment of *brāhmaṇas* in work involving literacy such as the upper levels of administration and gave them access to high political office in royal courts. This again supported its exclusive status. The use of a single language — Sanskrit — gave it a pan-Indian character, the wide geographical spread of which provided both mobility as well as a strengthening of its social identity. Since it was also increasingly the language of the social elites and of administration, the establishment of new kingdoms from the latter part of the first millennium AD onwards resulted in an extensive employment of literate *brāhmaṇas* and especially those proficient in the *Vedas*, *Dharmaśāstras* and *Purāṇas*.

The Bhakti tradition of the first millennium AD is sometimes traced to the message of the *Bhagavad-gītā*, which was interpolated into the *Mahābhārata*, to give the *Gītā* both antiquity and currency. The *Gītā* endorsed a radical change in that it moved away from the centrality of the sacrificial ritual and instead emphasised the individual's direct relation with the deity. An earlier formulation of a similar idea was current through the *Upaniṣads* where the sacrificial ritual was questioned, the centrality of rebirth was emphasised with release from rebirth being sought through meditation and *yoga* and the recognition of the *ātman-brahman* relationship. Many of the early *śramaṇa* sects had also opposed the *yajña*. The *Gītā* did however concede that *dharma* lay in observing the rules of one's own caste, *svadharma*, and the arbiters of *dharma* remained the *brāhmaṇas*. Selfless action as projected in the *Gītā* was the need to act in accordance with one's *dharma* which now became the key concept.

This shift of emphasis provided the root in later times for the emergence of a number of Bhakti sects — Śaiva, Vaiṣṇava, Śākta and other — which provided the contours to much that is viewed as 'traditional Hinduism' or Puranic Hinduism as some prefer to call it. The Pāśupatas, the Ālvars and Nāyannārs, the Śaiva-Siddhānta and the Liṅgāyats, Jñāneśvara and Tukārāma, Vallabhācarya, Mīrā, Caitanya, Śankaradeva, Basava, Lalla, Tulsīdās, and so on are often bunched together as part of the Bhakti stream. In fact there are variations among them which are significant and need to be pointed out. Some among these and similar teachers accepted the earlier style of worship and practice, others were hostile to the Vedic tradition: some objected to caste distinctions and untouchability, whereas for others such distinctions posed no problems. Some of the sects opposed to caste discouraged their members from worshipping in temples or going on pilgrimages and from observing the upper caste *dharma*. A few felt that asceticism and renunciation were not paths to liberation whereas others were committed to these. Kabir and Nanak for instance, infused Sufi ideas into their teaching. These major differences are rarely discussed and commented upon in modern popular writing which is anxiously searching for similarities in the tradition. Yet these dissimilarities were to be expected and were in a sense their strength.

The Bhakti sects were up to a point the inheritors of the Śramanic tradition in that some were opposed to Brahmanism and the sacrificial ritual, most were in theory open to every caste and all of them were organised along sectarian lines. They arose at various times over a span of a thousand years in different parts of the subcontinent. They were specific in time, place and teacher, and were constricted in cross-regional communication by differences of language. They did not evolve out of the same original teaching nor did they spread through conversion; they arose as and when historical conditions were conducive to their growth, often intermeshed with the need for particular castes to articulate their aspirations. Hence the variation in belief and practice and the lack of awareness of predecessors or of an identity of religion across a subcontinental plane. Similarities were present in some cases but even these did not lead to a recognition of participation in a single religious movement. With the growth of the Bhakti sects, where many focused on a single deity, the worship of the iconic image of the deity gained popularity, or else a few sects refused to worship an image at all. Image-worship was possibly encouraged by the icons which had been used by Buddhists and Jainas from the Christian era onwards. Whereas Megasthenes visiting in the fourth century BC does not refer to images in discussing the religions of India, for Alberuni, writing in the eleventh century AD, icons are a major feature of the indigenous religions.[8]

This was also the period which saw the currency of the Śākta sects and Tantric rituals. Regarded by some as the resurgence of an indigenous belief associated with subordinate social groups (gradually becoming powerful) it was, by the end of the first millennium AD, popular at every level of society including the royal courts. The attempt in recent times to either ignore it or to give a respectable gloss to its rituals or their manifestation in the art of the period,[9] is largely because of the embarrassment these might cause to middle-class Indians heavily influenced by Christian puritanism and somewhat titillated in imagining erroneously that Tantric rituals consist essentially of pornographic performances. That there has been little effort, except in scholarly circles, to integrate such groups into the definition of Hinduism derives also from the attempt to define Hinduism as Brahmanism based on upper caste rituals and such cults were initially alien to traditional Brahmanism.

Another noticeable manifestation of non-Brahmanic religion is what has recently been euphemistically called 'folk Hinduism' — the religion of the untouchables, 'tribals' and other groups at the lower end of the social scale. This is characterised by a predominance of the worship of goddesses and spirits (*bhūta-preta*) represented symbolically and often aniconically and with rituals performed by non-*brāhmaṇa* priests: the latter for a variety of reasons, not least among them being that since the offering and libations consist of meat and alcohol, these could be regarded as polluting by *brāhmaṇas*. Needless to say, such groups would not be able to afford the costly donations required of a brahmanical *yajña*. For the upper caste Hindus these groups were (and often still are) regarded as *mlecchas* or impure and not a part of their own religious identity. Interestingly attempts by Hindu missionaries to proselytise among such groups, lay particular emphasis on prohibitions on meat-eating and alcohol in everyday life.

The sects included in the honeycomb of what has been called Hinduism were multiple and ranged from animistic spirit cults to others based on subtle philosophic concepts. They were oriented towards the clan, the caste and the profession or else on the reversing of these identities through renunciation. The social identity of each was imprinted on its religious observances. The deities worshipped vary, the rituals differed, belief in after-life varied from the theory of *karma* and *saṃsāra* to that of *svarga* and *naraka*, heaven and hell. In the same *Mahābhārata*, where the characters of the narrative find themselves in heaven and hell at the end of the story, Krṣṇa preaches release from rebirth which is a very different eschatology.

This variance may in part explain why the word *dharma* became central to an understanding of religion. It referred to the duties regarded as sacred which had to be performed in accordance with one's *varṇa*, *jāti* and sect and which differed according to each of these. The constituents of *dharma* were conformity to ritual duties, social obligations and the norms of family and caste behaviour preferably as stipulated in the *Dharmaśāstras* or accepted as incontrovertible rules of behaviour. As has been noticed, theology although not absent, is not to the fore, nor any ecclesiastical authority, both of which again point to the difference between these religions and the Semitic. A major concern was with ritual purity. The performance of sacred duty heavily enmeshed in social obligations was so important that absolute individual freedom only lay in renunciation.[10]

But the significance of *dharma* was that it demarcated sharply between the upper castes — the *dvija* or twice-born — for whom it was the core of the religion and the rest of society whose conforming to *dharma* was left somewhat in abeyance, as long as it did not transgress the *dharma* of the upper castes. The latter were to that extent without *dharma* or had their own. In trying to redefine Hinduism today as a universalising religion, the implicit attempt is to try and include those without the recognised *dharma*, who have in the past been excluded; but the inclusion is not divorced from the terms of the upper caste *dharma* and this raises problems.

Hindu missionary organisations, such as those attached to the Ramakrishna Mission, the Arya Samaj, the R.S.S. and the Vishva Hindu Parishad, taking their cue from Christian missionaries are active among the *ādivāsis*, mainly scheduled castes and tribes. They are converting these latter groups to a Hinduism as defined by the upper caste movements of the last two centuries. Not surprisingly there was a difference of opinion among some members of the upper castes in the early twentieth century on whether such groups can be counted as Hindus even prior to 'conversion'. The proponents of Hindutva have had contrary views about this.[11] What is important for Hindu missionaries is that these communities declare their support for the *dharma* and be ready to be labelled as Hindus in any head count of either a census or a support to a political party. That this conversion does little or nothing to change their actual status and that they continue to be looked down upon by upper caste Hindus is of course of little consequence. This is one reason why some Dalit groups have been confrontational towards caste Hindus.

The origin of the word Hindu is geographical and derives from the Sindhu river, where the Achaemenid Persians used the name Hi(n)du with variants to refer to those that live on the cis-Indus side.[12] Later the Arabs described the area as al-Hind.[13] Initially used in a geographical and an ethnic sense, the term Hindu came subsequently to be used in a religious sense for those who lived in this area but were not Muslims or Christians. Hindus became a term of administrative convenience when the Muslim rulers had to differentiate between 'the believers' and the rest. Hindu therefore referred to the rest.

The first step towards the crystallisation of what we today call Hinduism was born in the consciousness of being the amorphous, subordinate, other. In a sense this was a reversal of roles. Earlier the term *mleccha* had been used by the upper caste Hindus to refer to the impure, amorphous rest. For the upper castes, Muslims and especially those not indigenous to India, were treated as *mleccha* since they did not observe the *dharma* and were debarred from entering the sanctum of the temple and the home. Indigenous converts to Islam also came under this category but their caste origins would have set them apart initially from the amorphous Muslim. Now the upper castes were clubbed together with the indigenous *mleccha* under the label of 'Hindu', undoubtedly a trauma for the upper castes.

This in part accounts for the statements made by upper caste Hindus today that Hinduism in the last one thousand years has been through the most severe persecution that any religion in the world has ever undergone. The need to exaggerate the persecution at the hands of the Muslim is required to justify the inculcation of anti-Muslim sentiments among the Hindus of today. Such statements brush aside the fact that there were various expressions of religious persecution in India prior to the coming of the Muslims and particularly between the Śaiva and the Buddhist and Jaina sects and that in a sense, the persistence of untouchability was also a form of religious intolerance.[14] The authors of such statements conveniently forget that the last thousand years in the history of Hinduism, and more so the last five hundred years, have witnessed the establishment of the powerful Śankarācārya *maṭhas*, *āśramas*, and similar institutions attempting to provide an ecclesiastical structure to strengthen Brahmanism and conservatism; the powerful Daśanāmi and Bairāgi religious orders of Śaiva and Vaiṣṇava origin, vying for patronage and frequently in confrontation; the popular cults of the Nāthapanthis; the significant sects of the Bhakti traditions which are to be found in every corner of the subcontinent; and more recently a number of socio-religious reform movements which have been aimed at reforming and strengthening Hinduism. It was also the period which saw the expansion of the cults of Kṛṣṇa and Rāma with their own mythologies, literatures, rituals and circuits of pilgrimage. The definition of the Hindu today has its roots more in the period of Muslim rule than in the earlier period and many of the facets which are regarded today as essential to Hinduism belong to more recent times. The establishment of the sects which accompanied these developments often derived from wealthy patronage including that of both Hindu and Muslim rulers, which accounted for the prosperity of temples and institutions associated with these sects. The more innovative sects were in part the result of extensive dialogues between *gurus*, *sādhus*, *pīrs* and Sufis, a dialogue which was sometimes confrontational and sometimes conciliatory.[15] The last thousand years have seen the most assertive thrust of many Hindu sects. If by persecution is meant the conversion of Hindus to Islam and Christianity, than it should be kept in mind that the majority of conversions were from the lower castes and this is more a reflection on Hindu society than on persecution. Upper caste conversions were more frequently activated by factors such as political alliances and marriage circuits and here the conversion was hardly due to persecution.[16] Tragically for those that converted on the assumption that there would be social equality in the new religion, this was never the case and the lower castes remained low in social ranking and carried their caste identities into the new religions.[17]

When the destroying of temples and the breaking of images by Muslim iconoclasts is mentioned — and quite correctly so — it should however at the same time be stated that there were also many Muslim rulers, not excluding Aurangzeb, who gave substantial donations to Hindu sects and to individual *brāhmaṇas*.[18] There was obviously more than just religious bigotry or religious tolerance involved in these actions. The relationship for example between the

Mughal rulers and the Bundela *rājās*, which involved temple destruction among other things, and veered from close alliances to fierce hostility, was the product not merely of religious loyalties or differences, but the play of power and political negotiation. Nor should it be forgotten that the temple as a source of wealth was exploited even by Hindu rulers such as Harṣadeva of Kashmir who looted temples when he faced a fiscal crisis or the Paramāra ruler who destroyed temples in the Caulukya kingdom, or the Rāṣṭrakūṭa king who tore up the temple courtyard of the Pratihāra ruler after a victorious campaign.[19] Given the opulence of large temples, the wealth stored in them required protection, but the temple was also a statement of political authority when built by a ruler.

The European adoption of the term 'Hindu' gave it further currency as also the attempts of Catholic and Protestant Christian missionaries to convert the Gentoo/Hindu to Christianity. The pressure to convert, initially disassociated with European commercial activity, changed with the coming of British colonial power when, by the early nineteenth century, missionary activities were either surreptitiously or overtly, according to context, encouraged by the colonial authority. The impact both of missionary activity and Christian colonial power resulted in considerable soul searching on the part of those Indians who were close to this new historical experience. One result was the emergence of a number of groups such as the Brahmo Samaj, the Prathana Samaj, the Arya Samaj, the Ramakrishna Mission, the Theosophical, Society, the Divine Life Society, the Swaminarayan movement, *et al.*, which gave greater currency to the term Hinduism. There was much more dialogue of upper caste Hindus with Christians than there had been with Muslims, partly because for the coloniser power also lay in controlling knowledge about the colonised and partly because there were far fewer Hindus converting to Christianity than had converted to Islam. Some of the neo-Hindu sects as they have come to be called, were influenced by Christianity and some reacted against it; but even the latter were not immune from its imprint. This was inevitable given that it was the religion of the coloniser.

The challenge from Christian missionaries was not merely at the level of conversions and religious debates. The more subtle form was through educational institutions necessary to the emerging Indian middle class. Many who were attracted to these neo-Hindu groups had at some point of their lives experienced Christian education and were thereafter familiar with Christian ideas. The Christian missionary model played an important part, as for example in the institutions of the Arya Samaj. The Shaiva Siddhanta Samaj was inspired by Arumuga Navalar, who was roused to reinterpret Śaivism after translating the Bible into Tamil. The movement attracted middle-class Tamils seeking a cultural self-assertion. Added to this was the contribution of some Orientalist scholars who interpreted the religious texts to further their notions of how Hinduism should be constructed.[20] The impact of Orientalism in creating the image of Indian, and particularly Hindu culture, as projected in the nineteenth century, was considerable.[21]

Those among these groups influenced by Christianity, attempted to defend, redefine and create Hinduism on the model of Christianity. They sought for the equivalent of a monotheistic God, a Book, a Prophet or a Founder and congregational worship with an institutional organisation supporting it. The implicit intention was again of defining 'the Hindu' as a reaction to being 'the other'; the subconscious model was the Semitic religion. The monotheistic God was sought in the abstract notion of Brahman, the Absolute of the *Upaniṣads* with which the individual Ātman seeks unity in the process of *mokṣa*; or else with the interpretation of the term *deva* which was translated as God, suggesting a monotheistic God. The worship of a single deity among many others is not strictly speaking monotheism, although attempts have been made by modern commentators to argue this. Unlike many of the earlier sects which were associated with a particular deity, some of these groups claimed to transcend deity and reach out to the Absolute, Infinite, the Brahman. This was an attempt to transcend segmentary interests in an effort to attain a universalistic identity, but in social customs and ritual, caste identities and distinctions between high and low continued to be maintained.

The teaching of such sects drew on what they regarded as the core of the traditions, where the notion of *karma* and *saṃsāra* for instance, came to be seen as uniting all Hindus, even though in fact this was not the case. The Upaniṣadic idea of the relation between *Ātman* and *Brahman* was seen as a kind of monotheism. The need for a Book, led to one among a variety of texts being treated as such — the *Bhagavad-gītā* or the *Vedas*. The Prophet being an altogether alien idea, could at best be substituted by the teacher-figure of Kṛṣṇa, even though he was neither Prophet nor son of God. Congregational worship, not altogether alien to lower caste forms of worship, was systematised and became the channel for propagating these new versions of Hinduism. The singing of hymns and the common chanting of prayers became an important part of the ritual. The discarding of the icon by both the Brahmo Samaj and the Arya Samaj was like an allergic reaction. It was seen as a pollution of the original religion but, more likely it was the jibe of idol worship from the practitioners of Christianity and Islam which was a subconscious motivation. This was not a new feature, for some Bhakti teachers had earlier pointed out the incongruity of worshipping images rather than concentrating on devotion to the deity. A reaction against the icon, but a substitution virtually for the image by the Book, was and is, the centrality of the *Guru Granth Sahib* in Sikh worship.

Much of the sacred literature had been in earlier times orally preserved and served a variety of social and religious ends. The epic narratives of the *Mahābhārata* and the *Rāmāyaṇa* were converted to sacred literature by depicting Kṛṣṇa and Rāma as *avatāras* of Viṣṇu. The narration then became that of the actions of a deity. Interpolations could also be added as and when required, as for example the *Gītā*. This is a different attitude from that of the Semitic religions to the centrality of the Book, or for that mater, from that of the Sikhs to the single, sacred text. The imprint of the idea of the sacredness of the Book itself, is suggested in some late texts such as the fifteenth century *Adhyātma-Rāmāyaṇa* where it says that the reading of the text is in itself an act of worship.[22] Interestingly interpolations become far less frequent when the text is written. These new religious identities of the nineteenth and twentieth centuries were in part the inheritors of the older tradition of combining social aspirations with religious expression and establishing new sects. But at the same time they were conscious of the attempt to create a different kind of religion from the past and which gave currency to the term Hinduism.

Traditional flexibility in juxtaposing sects as an idiom of social change as well as the basic concepts of religious expression now became problematic. In the absence of a single 'jealous' God, often associated with monotheism and demanding complete and undiluted loyalty from the worshipper, there were instead multiple deities, some of which were superseded over time and others which were created as and when required. Thus the major Vedic deities — Indra, Mitra, Varuna and Agni — declined with the rise of Śiva and Viṣṇu at the turn of the Christian era. The latter have remained major deities supported by sects which are not always in agreement about what the deities represent for them. This has not prevented the creation of an altogether new deity, as has been witnessed in the last half century with the very popular worship in northern India of the goddess, Santoshi Mā.

The attitude to deity would in part support the argument that it is not theology which is important in Hinduism but the mode of worship. The Vedic *yajña* has a carefully orchestrated performance of ritual with the meticulous ordering of every detail including the correct pronunciation of the words constituting the *mantra*. Worship as *bhakti* in Puranic Hinduism is more personalised and informal. The earlier emphasis on oblation and sacrificial ritual was now transformed into sharing in the grace of the deity and devotion to the deity, sometimes even taken to the extreme of ritual suicide.[23] The deity was conceptualised in a variety of ways — abstract, aniconic, an image or an image elaborately sculpted and housed in an equally elaborate temple. Devotion could also be expressed in various ways. There was no requirement of uniformity in methods of worship or in who performed the ritual. There was little ecclesiastical order involved and no centralised church. The caste of the worshipper frequently conditioned the nature of the ritual and the method of worship. This included the caste of the priest, the contents of the offering, the language and form of the prayer and even at times the particular manifestation of a deity. This was evident in even the diversity of shrines and temples in a single village.

Because worship was so closely tied to caste and recruitment to caste was by birth, the question of conversion became irrelevant. In its absence, sects emerged either independently, or through segmenting off or amalgamating with similar sects. The religious sect was also an avenue to caste mobility. Origin myths of middle and lower castes often maintain that the caste was originally of higher status but a lapse in the ritual or an unwitting act of pollution led to a loss of status.[24] Imitation of higher caste norms or the dropping of caste obligations would normally not be permitted unless justified by the creation of new religious sect. The latter would initially be regarded with hostility by the conservative but if it became socially and economically powerful it would be accommodated.[25] The absence of conversion accounted for the absence of distinction between the true follower and the infidel or pagan. Yet, distinctions of another kind were more sharply maintained, particularly among sects with a substantially upper caste following. There was an exclusion of all those who were regarded as outside the social pale and who came under the category of *mleccha* — the untouchables, some lower castes, the 'tribals' and Indian Muslims and Christians. They were segregated because they performed neither the ritual duties nor the social duties required by the *dharma*. That in many cases they were prohibited from doing so, such as entering the temple for worship, did not prevent their being excluded. There was little active attempt to change this and where it was attempted, such as in the *śuddhī* movement of the Arya Samaj, the results were negligible.

It is often said that one is born a Hindu and one cannot be converted to Hinduism, for the caste identity is determined although the sectarian identity can change. The idea of conversion was much debated in the nineteenth century when various organisations wished to both reform and expand the Hindu identity as they saw it. Possibly this was also tied into the increasing consciousness of numbers with the notion of majority and minority communities being introduced into politics. Earlier it had been argued that each sect had its own regulations, obligations and duties which often drew both on religious antecedents and social requirements. Gradually if a sect acquired a large following cutting across castes it tended to become a caste in itself. This further endorses the notion that it would perhaps be more correct to speak of the Hindu religions rather than of Hinduism. Some would argue that the correct term for the latter would be *sanātan dharma*.

There was one agency which had its roots in religious articulation and which could legitimately transgress the rules of caste and this was the range of renunciatory orders. Some of these orders restricted themselves to recruiting only *brāhmaṇas*, but in the main most of them recruited from a variety of castes. Even among the latter, although theoretically the orders were open to all, there was a tendency to prefer caste Hindus. Open recruitment was possible because renouncers were expected to discard all social obligations and caste identities, and were regarded as being outside the rules of caste and *dharma*. Joining such an order was also in some cases the only legitimate form of dissent from social obligations since it required the revoking of these obligations. The multiplicity of renouncers in India has therefore to be viewed not always as inspired by otherworldly aspirations but also by the nature of the links between the social forms and dissent.[26] The Śramanic religions were similar to these sects in that they did recruit members from a range of castes although, as was the case also with Indian Islam, Indian Christianity and Sikhism, converts often retained their original caste identity, especially in the crucial area of marriage connections.[27]

Religious sects battened on patronage, whether royal or from other members of the community. Even the renunciatory orders were not averse to accepting wealth which ensured them material comforts as is evident from the many centres of such orders scattered across the Indian landscape over the last two thousand years. The wealth ranged from small donations of labour and money to extensive grants of land. The pattern of patronage to Buddhism is repeated with other religions.[28] Renunciatory orders were dependent for alms and requirements on stable societies and had therefore to be closer to the patronage of the elite, although some did maintain a reciprocal relationship with the lower castes. The initial radical thought of some of these orders was marginalised by their need for patrons. Where such economic wealth helped these sects to build institutions, whether that of the *saṅgha*, the *maṭha*, or the *khānqah*, it provided them with access to political power with the result that politics and religion were intertwined. The real texture of Indian social history in the second millennium AD has been bye-passed with the obsessive concern with simplistic Hindu-Muslim relations to the exclusion of the pertinent investigation of how politics and religion at some levels were interrelated. A further aspect is that in many cases these sectarian institutions were also centres of literacy and literacy was a powerful mechanism of social control.

Caste identities, economic wealth, literacy, and access to power also contributed to providing the edge to sectarian rivalries and conflicts. Hsüan Tsang and Kalhaṇa record the persecution of Buddhists by Śaivas, and Karnataka witnessed the destruction of Jaina temples in a conflict with the Śaivas.[29] Once the Buddhists and Jainas were virtually out of the way, hostility among the Hindu sects remained, even between ascetic groups, as is evident from the pitched battles between the Daśanāmis and the Bairāgis over the question of precedence at the Kumbha Mela.[30] Antagonism of the latter kind was not that of the Hindu against another religion but that of particular sects hostile to each other. An assessment of the degree of tolerance and non-violence, has therefore, to take into account sectarian aggression. It is true that there were no Inquisitions. This was partly because dissent was channelled into the creation of a separate sect which, if it became a renunciatory order, was less directly confrontational in society. Breakaway sects or new sects, even where they did not form renunciatory orders, found a rung on the social hierarchy of sects and their continuance and status was dependent on the social groups who became their patrons and supporters. Among the Hindu sects there was no centralised church whose supremacy was endangered by the emergence of new sects. However social subordination, justified by theories of impurity, replaced to some degree the inequities of an authoritarian church.

Religious violence is not alien to Hinduism despite the nineteenth century myth that the Hindus are by instinct and religion a non-violent people. The genesis of this myth was partly in the romantic image of the Indian past projected for example, by scholars such as Max Müller.[31] Added to this were the requirements of nationalism maintaining the spiritual superiority of Indian culture of which non-violence was treated as a component. Non-violence as a central tenet of behaviour and morality was first enunciated and developed in the Śramanic tradition of Buddhism and Jainism. These were the religions which not only declined at various times in various regions of India, but were persecuted in some parts of the subcontinent. One is often struck by how different the message of the *Gītā* would have been and how very much closer to non-violence if Gautama Buddha had been the charioteer of Arjuna instead of Kṛṣṇa. Gandhiji's concern with *ahimsā* is more correctly traced to the Jaina imprint on the culture of Kathiawar. Not that the Śramanic tradition prevented violence, but it was a central issue early on in the ethics of Buddhism and Jainism and only later enters the discussion of some Hindu sects.[32]

Sectarian institutions acted as networks across geographical areas, but their reach was limited except among some renunciatory orders. *Bhakti* as a religious manifestation was predominant throughout the subcontinent by the seventeenth century; yet curiously there was little attempt to link these regional movements to forge a single religious identity. Each tradition used a different language and there was no ecclesiastical organisation to integrate the development.

There was however the gradual building up of a network around Kṛṣṇa worship at Brindavana and later Rāma worship at Ayodhya which incorporated teacher and disciples from eastern and southern India, with new foci of worship and the demarcating of a sacred topography associated with the life-cycle of the deity incarnate and a renewed emphasis on the benefits of pilgrimage. One of the side effects of pilgrimage is that it can increase the catchment area of worshippers. Nevertheless even pilgrimage tended to remain largely regional, as for instance in the pilgrimage to Paṇḍharapura in the worship of Viṣṇu as Viṭṭhala which followed a well-defined circuit relevant only to Maharashtrian worshippers. The limitations to pilgrimage lay both in the nature of the cult and also in problems of distance and easy transportation. The Bhakti sects saw themselves as self-sufficient, with religious forms closely tied to local requirements. The closest to ecclesiastical organisation were the *maṭhas* associated with Śankarācārya, but these had a limited religious and social jurisdiction.

A suggested historical explanation for the spread of Bhakti sects links them to the feudalising tendencies of the period after AD 500 and parallels have been drawn between the loyalty of the peasant to the feudal lord being comparable to the devotion of the worshipper for the deity.[33] The Bhakti emphasis on *mokṣa* through devotion to a deity and through the belief in *karma* and *saṃsāra* was a convenient ideology for keeping subordinate groups under control. It was argued that they might suffer in this life, but by observing the *dharma* they would benefit in their next birth. The onus of responsibility for an unhappy condition was therefore on the individual and not on society. This gave the individual an importance which was absent in real life and therefore served to keep him/her quiescent. An explanation which requires lower castes to admit to misdemeanors even in a previous life, would hardly be widely acceptable. Common as was the belief in *karma* and *saṃsāra* it did not preclude the growth at a popular level of the concepts of heaven and hell. The multiplicity of memorials to the dead hero — the hero-stones — which increase in number after AD 500, and are found scattered in many parts of India, make it evident by symbol if not by inscription that the hero on dying a hero's death, was taken up to eternal life in heaven.[34]

The segregation of social communities in worship and religious belief and the absence of an over-arching ecclesiastical structure demanding conformity, was characteristic of the Hindu religions. Attempts at introducing an authority were made on a small scale, such as the Śankarācārya *maṭhas*, doubtless influenced by the model of the Buddhist *saṅgha*. These did eventually become centres of pilgrimage, particularly among caste Hindus who could afford to make the journey and among renouncers. But the important source of funds and concerns related to the upper castes. The segregation led to the possibility of each group leading a comparatively separate existence. The clash could come in the competition for support and patronage. This might partially explain the notion of tolerance with which the nineteenth century invested indigenous Indian religions. However, sectarian rivalries existed, sometimes taking a violent form and the coming of Islam added to the number of competing sects.

It was however within the broad spectrum of what has been called Puranic religion and that of the Bhakti sects that there was a dialogue between these and Islam resulting in some mutual borrowing. Curiously there was little overt interest in Islamic theology among learned *brāhmaṇas*. There are hardly any major studies of Islam in Sanskrit whereas the regional languages do provide evidence of a lively interest, either directly or indirectly, in the religious interface between Hindu and Islamic religions.[35] Interestingly, Muslims were referred to not as such but as either Turuṣka/Turk, Śaka, Yavana or *mleccha*. The first three have a historical ancestry and were used for people coming from central Asia or west Asia and the last referred to social distance. It is strange that what we today see as an essentially religious difference does not get projected in these terms although it was evidently present.

The more learned among Muslim authors such as Abu'l Fazl merely give resumés of Brahmanism when it comes to details about the indigenous religions, presumably because this was the most prestigious and accessible. There is much less detail of the other sects except in a generalised way. Abu'l Fazl refers to the strife among the various indigenous religions which he attributes to diversity in language as well as the resistance of Hindus to discuss their religions with foreigners.[36] He lists four kinds of worship among Hindus: the preeminent is the *pūjā* of the image, the second is the *yajña* or sacrificial ritual, the third is *dāna* or gift-giving and the fourth is *śrāddha* offered in honour of the ancestors.

In the histories of India written in the last two centuries, Islam and Hinduism are generally projected as two monolithic, antagonistic religions, face-to-face. For the conservative in Islam the Indian experience must have been bewildering since there was no recognizable ecclesiastical authority to which it could address itself. It faced a large variety of belief systems of which the most noticeable common feature was idol-worship — but even this was by no means uniform. This may also partially account for the success of the Sufis as agencies of conversion to Islam, their beliefs and religious practices sometimes being more flexible and varying as compared to the Islam of the theologians.

It is often said that the Hindus must have been upset at seeing Turkish and Mongol soldiers in their heavy boots trampling the floors of the temples. This would certainly have been traumatic. But the question arises as to which Hindus were thus traumatized? For the same temple now entered by *mleccha* soldiers was in any case open only to the caste Hindus and its sanctum would have been barred to the larger population consisting of the indigenous *mleccha*. The feelings of the latter were of little concern to the caste Hindus who had worshipped at these temples. The trauma was therefore more in the nature of the polluting of the temple rather than the confrontation on any substantial scale with another religion.

*Brāhmaṇa-Śramaṇa* hostility did not disappear over time. It kept cropping up and books authored by *brāhmaṇas* in the first millennium AD often refer to Buddhists and Jainas as heretics — *pakhaṇḍa* — and the same word is used in some Jaina texts for *brāhmaṇas*.[37] Brahmanism was also distanced from certain Bhakti sects and some Śākta groups, since the latter in particular had rituals offensive to Brahmanism. Inevitably however with the increasing incorporation of Tantric ideas into the religion especially of the elite groups, one expression of the claim to legitimacy was the 'Sanskritisation', literally, of the texts of such sects. This required both the accommodation of some categories of *brāhmaṇa* priests in the performance of the ritual, when with the decline of Vedic ritual by this time other forms of ritual held out a more promising patronage for the *brāhmaṇas*; as well as a process of 'brahmanisation' of the priests who had earlier performed the rituals. The separateness of such sects was forced to narrow though not to amalgamate, when they were all, *brāhmaṇas*, *śramaṇas* and the rest, forced to come under the single label of Hindu. A formal closeness was imposed on them by the coming of Islam and the categorisation for the first time of all indigenous cults as 'Hindu' where the term carried the connotation of 'the Other'.

A further crisis came with the arrival of Christianity riding on the powerful wave of colonialism. This experience of both Roman Catholic and Protestant Christianity was very different from the much earlier arrival of Syrian Christianity which came in the wake of traders and had a limited geographical reach. In the projected superiority of Semitic religions, it was once again the Hindus who were regarded as 'the Other' and this again included both the Brahmanic and Śramanic religions. This time the Christian dialogue was with Brahmanism and this was not altogether unexpected considering that the Indian middle class was to emerge from the ranks of the upper castes, and among these, initially, the *brāhmaṇas*, were the more significant.

Inevitably the Brahmanical base of what was seen as the new or neo-Hinduism was unavoidable. But merged into it were also various practices of upper caste worship and of course the subconscious model of Christianity and Islam. Its close links with certain nationalist opinion gave to many of these neo-Hindu movements a political edge which remains recognisable even today. It is this development which was the parent to what I should like to call Syndicated Hinduism and which is being projected by some vocal and politically powerful segments of what is referred to as the Hindu community,[38] as the sole claimant to the inheritance of indigenous Indian religion.

It goes without saying that if Indian society is changing then its religious expressions must also undergo change. But the direction of this change is perhaps alarming. The emergence of the powerful middle-class with urban moorings and a reach to the rural rich would find it useful to bring into politics a uniform, monolithic, Hinduism created to serve its new requirements. Under the guise of such a Hinduism, claiming to be the revival of an ancient, traditional form, but in effect being a new creation, an effort is made to draw a large clientele and to speak with the voice of numbers. This voice has been created to support claims of majoritarianism based on a religious identity in the functioning of democracy.

The appeal of such a Hinduism to the middle-class is obvious since it becomes a mechanism for forging a new identity aimed at protecting the interests of the middle-class, even if this is not made widely apparent. To those lower down in society there would be the attraction of upward mobility through a new religious movement. Such groups having forsaken some of their ideologies of non-caste religious sects, as from the Bhakti tradition, would have to accept the *dharma* of the powerful but remain subordinate. A change in this direction has introduced new problems. In wishing away the weaknesses of the old, one does not want to bring in the predictable disasters of the new.

Perhaps the major asset of what we call Hinduism of the pre-modern period was that it was not a uniform, monolithic religion, but a flexible juxtaposition of religious sects. This flexibility was its strength and its distinguishing feature, allowing the inclusion even of groups questioning the *Vedas*, disavowing caste and the injunctions of the *Dharmaśāstras*. The weakening or disappearance of such dissenting groups within the framework even of religious expression would be a considerable loss. If Syndicated Hinduism could simultaneously do away with social hierarchies, this might mitigate its lack of flexibility. But the scramble to use it politically merely results in realignments within the hierarchy.

Syndicated Hinduism draws largely on reinterpreting Brahmanical texts of which the *Gītā* is an obvious choice, defends the *Dharmaśāstras* and underlines a brand of conservatism in the guise of a modern, reformed religion. The model is in fact that of Islam and Christianity. There is a search for a central book and recently, on the wave of the Ramjanmabhoomi agitation, there has been a focus on the *Rāmāyaṇa* with the insistence on the historicity of Rāma which makes him into a founder. Ecclesiastical authority is sought for in requesting the Śankarācārya to pronounce upon all matters religious, social and political. Meetings of the *dharmasansads* call upon *dharmācāryas*, *sādhus* and *sants* to give opinions on any matter of importance, which is then said to be binding even if opposed to the Constitution or the rulings of the Supreme Court of India. This is described as the Hindu Vatican. That these persons may be self-appointed *sants* and *sādhus* is of no consequence. Worship is increasingly congregational and the introduction of sermon-style homilies on the definition of a good Hindu and Hindu belief and behaviour, are becoming common at marriages and funerals and register a distinct change from earlier practice.[39] This form of Hinduism ends up inevitably as an oversimplified Brahmanism with garbled versions of elements of Bhakti and Puranic forms of belief and practice, largely to draw in increasing numbers of supporters.

The call to unite under Hinduism as a political identity is if anything, anachronistic. Social and economic inequality, whether one disapproves of it or condones it, was foundational to Brahmanism. To propagate the texts associated with this view and yet insist that it is an egalitarian philosophy is hardly acceptable. Some religions such as Islam are, in theory, egalitarian. Others such as Buddhism restrict equality to the moral and ethical spheres of life. The major religions arose and evolved in societies and in periods when inequality was not only a fact of life but was not questioned as a matter of right. The social function of these religions was not to change this but to ameliorate the reality for those who found it harsh and abrasive. Further, as a proselytising religion, Syndicated Hinduism cannot accept a multiplicity of religious statements as being equally important. Clearly some beliefs, rituals and practices will have to be selected from among an extensive range, and be regarded as essential and therefore more significant. Such an essentialising of scripture invests it with the potentialities of fundamentalism. This is a substantial departure from the traditional position. Who does the selecting and from what sources and to what purpose, also becomes a matter of considerable significance. In the absence of a single, authoritative scripture, those who make this selection will be questioned by others, unless they can back up their selection with the threat of force or control over power. This assertion is also encouraged by the success of comparable organisations in various parts of the world, based on a sharply contoured body of belief and practice backed by scripture emanating from a religious tradition.

Equally important to Syndicated Hinduism is the means of its propagation. It uses a variety of existing organisations from the erstwhile rather secretive RSS to the strident Bajrang Dal. The thrust is aggressive and categorical rather than persuasive. There is an impressive exploitation of modern communication media — audio-visual and print — with a substantial dose of spectacle, drama and hysteria. Television serials on Doordarshan, such as the *Rāmāyaṇa* and the *Mahābhārata* present what is intended to be the received version of these texts and others such as *Chanakya* are an evident underlining of Hindu nationalism with the pretext of using history. Received versions are an attempt to erode variants. Television serials have accelerated the pace of propaganda from the more slow-moving, 'mythological' films of earlier decades. The resort to media presentations gives it a veneer of modernisation, but the essential message remains conservative.

Another factor of increasing importance to this Syndicated Hinduism is the trans-national dimension in what might be called the Hindu diaspora — the dispersal of Hindus in various parts of the globe. In the pre-modern period there were Indians settled mainly as traders in many parts of Asia, but these were small settlements. The large colonies of present times are related to colonial needs. These are the result either of migration in the nineteenth century when immigrant labour was moved by the colonisers to other parts of the British empire such as to Guyana, Surinam, Trinidad, Malaysia and Fiji, or of traders being inducted into east and south Africa, or of the arrival of workers and/or professionals in the United Kingdom, North America, Saudi Arabia and the Gulf, after 1947, in search of better job opportunities. Such communities settled outside India, experience a sense of cultural insecurity since they are minority communities, frequently in a largely Christian or Islamic society. Their search is for a form of Hinduism parallel to Christianity or Islam and with an idiom comprehensible to these other two which they can teach their children (preferably we are told, through the equivalent of Hindu 'Sunday' schools and video films). These communities with their particular requirements and their not inconsequential financial support also provide the basis for the institutions and propaganda for, Syndicated Hinduism.[40]

The importance of this diaspora is reflected not only in the social links between those in India and those abroad supporting this new form of Hinduism, but also in the growing frequency with which the Sanghs and Parishads hold their meeting abroad and seek the support and conversion of the affluent.[41] Conversion often takes the form of re-establishing faith in this new Hinduism and creating a demand for the overt expression of this loyalty as a form of identity. This is not to be confused with the guru-cult in affluent societies where there is little attempt to convert people to Hinduism, but rather to suggest to them methods of 'self-realisation' irrespective of their religious affiliations.

The creation of this Syndicated Hinduism for purposes more political than religious and mainly supportive of the ambitions of an emerging social class, has been a long process during this century and has now come more clearly into focus. Whatever political justification it might have claimed in the past as a form of nationalist assertion against British rule, no longer exists. Its growing strength relates to a number of features which have come to dominate the contours more particularly of urban middle class Indian society today. Changing social mores result in a sense of insecurity, particularly as the move towards a consumer oriented society is now on the increase and keeping up with the consumer market is seen as a necessity. The change in the economy brings in greater scope for individual enterprise, witnessed in the phenomenal expansion of the Indian middle-class, not just since 1947 but more so in the last two decades. But the required competition implicit in a liberalised, market economy also increases the sense of insecurity. The injection of egalitarian ideas into a hitherto hierarchical society creates its own forms of social disequilibrium. The solution is sought in the search for a scape-goat or an enemy within and here the politics of the partition of India in 1947 return forcefully in the building up of hostility against the Muslims, hostility which can easily be extended to Christians and when occasion demands, to Sikhs. This hostility further feeds the insecurity and sense of powerlessness of those communities which are smaller in numbers and often disadvantaged. There is also the tacit recognition that the lower castes cannot be subordinated for long given the use of the ballot and the concession to reservations in the struggle for a place in the corridors of power. But the concern for the lower castes and Dalits is essentially a form of tokenism. The ideology of Syndicated Hinduism remains an ideology endorsing the status of the middle-class.[42]

Social groups in the past have expressed their aspirations in part by creating new religious sects. We are now witnessing a movement that seeks to go beyond sectarian appeal and claims to represent 'the Hindus' and insists on a particular identity for all those who are technically called Hindus, irrespective of whether they wish it or not. In a sense the notion of 'the Hindu' as it evolved in Islamic writing has now come to fruition in this claim. The emergence of Syndicated Hinduism is different both in scale and scope and is not restricted to the creation of a new sect but a new religious form seeking to encapsulate all the earlier sects. The extensive use of the media is a paradigm change in communication and permits of the possibility of reaching an all-India audience. The sheer scale as well as motivation, call for concern. Syndicated Hinduism claims to be re-establishing the Hinduism of pre-modern times: in fact it is only establishing itself and in the process distorting the historical and cultural dimensions of the indigenous religions and divesting them of the nuances and variety which were major sources of their enrichment. The survival and continuation through history of many such religious manifestations was not only through power and dominance but also in many instances through the sense of security that their presence and existence would not be prohibited. There is something to be said for attempting to comprehend the real religious expression of Indian civilisation before it is crushed beneath the wheels of the Toyota-*rathas*.

## Notes and References

1. This article was first published under the title of 'Syndicated Moksa?', in *Seminar*, September 1985, no. 313 and intended for the general reader. It remains substantially the same except for some up-dating and the addition of a few references. I would like to thank Kunal Chakrabarty for his comments on the earlier article.
   Reference is made in this article to 'the Semitic religions', a term used for Judaism, Christianity and Islam. It refers primarily to the fact that their scriptures were written in the Semitic languages, such as Hebrew and Arabic, and to the similarities in their religious tradition. The term is not intended to mean the Semitic race, since this would exclude the major point under discussion which is that their structure of belief and practice, is very different from that of Hinduism.
2. F. Staal, *Exploring Mysticism*, Berkeley, 1975, 65, 173.
3. F. Staal, *Agni*, vol. I, Berkeley, 1982, 27–166. H. Converse, 'The Agnicayana Rite: Indigenous Origin?', *History of Religion*, 1974, 14, 81–95; I. Mahadevan, 'The Cult Object on Unicorn Seals: A Sacred Filter?', *Purātattva*, 1981–83, 13–14, 165–86.
4. Strabo, 15.1.39; Arrian, 11; J. Bloch, *Les Inscriptions d'Asoka*, Paris, 1950, 97, 99, 112; S. Beal, *Si-yu-ki*, Delhi, 1969 (reprint).
5. This is clear from the well-known Schism Edict of Aśoka. Bloch, op. cit., 152–3.
6. S.D. Joshi (ed.), *Patañjali Vyākarana Mahābhāsyam*, Poona, 1968, 2.4.9; 1.4.76.
7. E. Sachau, *Alberuni's India*, Delhi, 1964 (reprint), 21.
8. J.W. McCrindle, *Ancient India as Described by Megasthenes and Arrian*, London, 1877, 98; Strabo, 15.1.59. Sachau, op. cit., 111ff.

9. For a sober and insightful interpretation see the discussion in Devanagana Desai, *Erotic Sculpture of India*, New Delhi, 1975. *The Religious Imagery of Khajuraho*, Mumbai, 1996.
10. Romila Thapar, 'Renunciation: The Making of a Counter-culture?', in *Ancient Indian Social History: Some Interpretations*, Delhi, 1978, 63–104. 'Householders and Renouncers in the Brahmanical and Buddhist Traditions', in T.N. Madan (ed.), *Way of Life*, Delhi, 1982, 273–99. *See* chapters 40 and 41 in this volume.
11. Gyan Pande, 'Which of us are Hindus', in G. Pande (ed.), *Hindus and Others*, Delhi, 1993, 238–72.
12. R.G. Kent, *Old Persian*, New Haven, 1950, 170ff.
13. A. Wink, *Al-Hind*, Delhi, 1990, 10ff.
14. Romila Thapar, *Cultural Transaction and Early India*, New Delhi, 1993.
15. Ashim Roy, *The Islamic Syncretistic Tradition in Bengal*, New Jersey, 1983. H. van Skyhawk, 'Vaishnava Perceptions of Muslims in Eighteenth Century Maharashtra', in A.L. Dallapicola and S. Zingel–Avelallemant (eds), *Islam and Indian Religions*, Stuttgart.
16. S.I. Zaidi and S. Zaidi, 'Conversion to Islam and Formation of Castes in Rajasthan', in A.J. Baisar and S.P. Verma (eds), *Art and Culture*, Delhi, 1992.
17. E.g., R. Eaton, *Sufis of Bijapur*, New Jersey, 1978, 310ff, Bijapur.
18. As for example, K.K. Datta (ed.), *Some Firmans, Sanads and Parwanas* (1578–1802), Patna, 1962. B.N. Goswamy and J.S. Grewal, *The Mughal and Sikh Rulers and the Vaishnavas of Pindori*, Simla, 1969.
19. Kalhana, *Rājataraṅgiṇī*, 7.1081–95; P. Bhatia, *The Paramaras*, Delhi, 1970, 140ff; 269. *Epigraphia Indica*, VI, 38 v. 19.
20. D. Knopf, 'Hermeneutics versus History', *Journal of Asian Studies*, 1980, 39, 3, 495–505.
21. Romila Thapar, *Interpreting Early India*, Delhi, 1993.
22. Romila Thapar, 'A Historical Perspective on the Story of Rama', in S. Gopal (ed.), *Anatomy of Confrontation*, Delhi, 1991, 153ff. *See* chapter 47 in this volume.
23. This is occasionally illustrated in memorial stones dedicated to a person who has committed ritual suicide with a depiction of the act. N.K.L. Murthy, 'Memorial Stones in Andhra Pradesh', in S. Settar and G.D. Sontheimer (eds), *Memorial Stones*, Dharwad, 1982, 212ff.
24. E.g., V. Das, 'A Sociological Approach to the Caste Puranas of Gujerat: A Case Study', *Sociological Bulletin*, 1968, 17, 141–64.
25. An interesting case in point is the history of the Liṅgāyat sect in Karnataka, originally a religious sectarian movement but today a powerful caste as well.
26. Romila Thapar, 'Dissent and Protest in the Early Indian Tradition', *Diogenes*, 981, 113–14, 31–54. *See* chapter 11 in this volume.

27. Imtiaz Ahmed (ed.), *Caste and Social Stratification Among the Muslims*, Delhi, 1973.
28. Buddhist sects initially began with small gifts of cells, cisterns and assistance with building a *stūpa*, or royal investments with guilds of which the interest was donated; and later, as at Nalanda, received the revenue of a hundred or even two hundred villages. Romila Thapar, 'Patronage and Community', in B. Stoler Miller (ed.), *The Powers of Art*, Delhi, 1992, 19–34. *See* chapter 27 in this volume. Nasik Cave Inscription No. 10, *Epigraphia Indica*, 8.78ff. S. Beal, *Life of Hiuen-Tsiang*, Delhi, 1973 (reprint), 112.
29. Romila Thapar, *Cultural Transaction and Early India*, 19ff.
30. These were so endemic that there are miniature paintings of the Mughal period depicting such battles.
31. M. Müller, *India What Can it Teach Us?*, London, 1983, 101ff.
32. Sporadic killing apart, even the violence involved in the regular burning of Hindu brides, does not elicit any threat against the perpetrators of such violence from the spokesmen of Hinduism. Feminist groups are the main agitators against such acts.
33. M.G.S. Narayanan and Kesavan Veluthat, 'Bhakti Movement in South India', in D. Jha (ed.), *Feudal Social Formation in Early India*, Delhi, 1987, 348–75.
34. S. Settar and G.D. Sontheimer (eds), *Memorial Stones*, Dharwad, 1982. Romila Thapar, 'Death and the Hero', in S.C. Humphreys and H. King (eds), *Mortality and Immortality: The Anthropology and Archaeology of Death*, London, 1981, 293–316. *See* chapter 31 in this volume.
35. E.g., N. Wagle, 'Hindu-Muslim Interactions in Medieval Maharashtra', in G.D. Sontheimer and H. Kulke (eds), *Hinduism Reconsidered*, Delhi, 1997, 134–52.
36. Abu'l Fazl, *Ain-i-Akbari*, III, trans. H.S. Jarret, Delhi, 1978 (reprint).
37. E.g., Kṛṣṇa Misra, *Prabodhacandrodaya*, V.L. Pansikar (ed.), Bombay, 1916. Vimalasūri, *Paumacariyam*, H. Jacobi (ed.), Varanasi, 1962.
38. The Rāṣṭra Svāyamsevaka Saṅgha and the Vishva Hindu Parishad in particular, as is evident from a reading of their periodicals and literature.
39. Given today's centrality of the notion of profit and the market and the message of the media, the sale of cassettes and tapes with prerecorded hymns and sermons in support of uniform practice and belief, are often on sale where there are large gatherings, such as at funerals.
40. According to *Fortune International*, Indians in the USA are the richest foreign born group, in Britain they own 60 per cent of all retail stores, and in Hongkong, control a tenth of its exports.
41. The most recent example of this was the convention organised by the

Vishva Hindu Parishad in Washington in 1993 to commemorate the anniversary of Vivekananda's visit to America. Where, a century ago, Vivekananda was virtually introducing Hinduism to an international audience as a religion given to tolerance and religious laissez-faire, what was now being commemorated in his name was an aggressive, assertive, outgoing drive for a religious identity with strong political aspirations for Hindus both in the United States and in India.

42. This was demonstrated for example in the anti-reservation movement by members of the middle-class taking to the streets and to self-immolation, when the V.P. Singh government announced the implementation of the Mandal Commission Report.

# A Historical Perspective on the Story of Rāma[1]*

It is popularly believed today, especially in northern India, that there have been only two important versions of the *Rāma-kathā* or the story of Rāma in Indian civilization: the earliest being the Sanskrit version of Vālmīki, the *Rāmāyaṇa*, and the Hindi version of Tulsīdās, the *Rāmacaritamānas*. However, historically, what is of the greatest interest about the *Rāma-kathā* is its multiple versions. Each major version reflects a substantial change both in how the role of the story was perceived, and in the acceptance of each of these different versions by their audience as the authentic one. This places the Vālmīki and the Tulsī texts in a broader civilizational context rather than solely in a religious one — a context which I hope to explore in this essay.

As each of these many different versions makes a particular statement as part of an ongoing dialogue over time, some versions contradict the others in both narrative and intent. As the same story or a relatively similar story is treated variously in terms of ethics, values, social and political norms and religious identities, the purpose and function of each version are significant and they cannot all be labelled as manifestations of a single religious expression. Even an overview of these variants provides rich material for the historical and cultural understanding of the role of the story. The variations introduced into the story by specific authors are for specific reasons and constitute a debate whose parameters change with historical change. It becomes necessary then to make a distinction between versions which are cultural idioms and those which are essentially propagating a religious sectarian point of view. Historically, the significance of the cultural idiom is in many

* From S. Gopal (ed.), *Anatomy of a Confrontation*, New Delhi, 1991, 141–63.

ways richer, with many more levels of symbolic meaning, than the more narrowly religious, sectarian form. However even among the latter, the contradictions and deviations are in themselves very valuable pointers to the cultural idiom.

The Vālmīki *Rāmāyana*, in its original form, was not a 'sacred book' as we understand sacred books today. It was a narrative, a story, cast in an epic mould. It was not even described as a text on *dharma*. Nor is it generally classified as an *itihāsa* — that which was believed to have happened in the past. It is more frequently referred to as a *kāvya* or an *ādikāvya*, a poetic composition. Unlike sacred books which are rarely questioned or altered (and if they are, the change is marginal) the *Rāmāyaṇa* was refashioned time and again, sometimes to convert it into a religious text and sometimes for other more literary purposes.

That the Vālmīki *Rāmāyaṇa* was not originally treated as a sacred book becomes apparent from the difference between its recording, orally at first and later in writing, and the recording of the Vedic corpus. The hymns of the *Vedas* were meticulously memorized using a range of mnemonic devices taught to and restricted to *brāhmaṇas* performing priestly functions — as they still are. This ensured a remarkable reproduction of the original composition,[2] and the hymns being regarded as sacred, such correct recitation was a precondition to their effectiveness. By contrast, texts such as the *Rāmāyaṇa* had a much more open method of preservation. Its oral memorization did not preclude changes and later interpolations such as perorations on good government and the observance of the rules of *dharma*. In fact that very act of converting the text from an epic poem to the story of Rāma as an *avatāra* of Viṣṇu, required that there be substantial additions.

Literature which is recorded orally in a fashion as free as that of the epics of early India cannot be dated to any one period as it has constantly undergone change. It can only be precisely dated from the time when the earliest manuscripts of the text survive. In the case of the Vālmīki *Rāmāyaṇa* this would be quite late. However, other texts of earlier periods refer to the *Rāmāyaṇa* and we know that at least the oral form was current in earlier centuries. As to when even this originally oral form was composed, remains uncertain and has its own history.

Epics do not date to a particular period for they are in essence the literature of a later age looking back on an earlier one. Events and characters are fictionalized to such a degree that even if there is a kernel of history embedded in them, it is often not in conformity with the narrative. The importance of the epic, for the historian lies not in the narrating of events which may be believed to have happened, but in the perception of the past which is encapsulated in the text, a vision which portrays a society of earlier times and thereby also provides a commentary on the social assumptions of the age when the epic was composed.

Some decades ago historians using the data from the two epics, the *Mahābhārata* and the *Rāmāyaṇa*, argued for what was termed 'the epic age' in Indian history.[3] This age has now been eroded from historical periodization for the original epics are embedded in the versions which have survived. Attempts to find a solution to the date of the Vālmīki *Rāmāyaṇa*, by excavating sites mentioned in the text, have been disappointing for those who believe in the great antiquity of these places. Thus excavations in and around Ayodhyā do not take the settlement back to earlier than the seventh century BC. The artefacts of this period suggest a very simple way of life, which in no way can be regarded as urban living; nor can it be regarded as the archaeological counterpart to the descriptions in the text.[4]

There have been many interpolations over the millennium from 500 BC to AD 500, and therefore only episodes can perhaps be dated on comparative evidence.[5] This would imply that the epics do not belong to a specific period because they are part of an ongoing tradition and that the epic itself is made to change its function over time when it is converted from bardic to religious literature.

Poems as literary forms, even if they should be dealing with historical themes, cannot in themselves be regarded as historical texts. They can at best provide clues to the ways in which people perceived the past or their own times. Such clues are important to the historical reconstruction of ideologies and attitudes, but are not evidence of historical events unless proven to be so from other contemporary historical sources.

Epics are not religious documents in origin. But some versions of an epic story can be transformed into religious statements, as was done in the rewriting of the Vālmīki *Rāmāyaṇa*. The emphasis on the sacred has tended to make this text the preserve of specialists in religion. Some analyses of its religious concepts and philosophical ideas are valuable to the study of Hinduism, as is also the unravelling of its mythology. What has however been neglected is the comparative study of the large range of substantially variant versions. Frequently intended for a popular audience, they incorporate changes which have a significance other than just a sectarian religious statement or a deviation in mythology. The change of function is in itself of historical importance and the range of variations suggests that the historian should view the variants as recounting historical change. I hope to show that this is pertinent even to the contemporary use of the epic, both in defining social attitudes and in manipulating political conflicts.

Epics are frequently an amalgam emerging out of a number of ballads, folk tales and myths. Stories are threaded together by a bardic poet and these linkages give a different form to a literary genre. The *Rāma-kathā*, put together from a number of floating, bardic compositions, is believed to be the first form of the epic and it no longer exists in its original form. Even the earliest surviving versions, dating in their present forms to the turn of the Christian era, have each been worked over from particular perspectives. Among the early versions was the literary epic composed by the poet Vālmīki, the *Rāmāyaṇa*, which has come to be popularly accepted as the standard version. The story incorporates the usual raw material and stereotypes of epic tales: the changing fortunes of the hero, the kidnapping of the princess, the quest for rescuing her, the heroic battle interspersed with flying monkeys, demons and an aerial chariot.

The original epic, composed by bards as part of the oral tradition, was recited at sacrificial rituals, at feasts and at the courts of the *rājās* — the chiefs and kings. Its origin could be seen as a eulogy to a patron or else the eulogistic functions could be seen as a simile. The story involved the families of the *kṣatriyas*, chiefs and warriors, with other social groups playing lesser roles. The hero had often to be distinguished by a special birth. Thus, Rāma and his brothers were born only after the performance of a sacrificial ritual by a particular sage.[6] Exile was a useful device. It gave the bard occasions for fresh incidents if the narrative was wearing thin. Time was not rigid. It could move back and forth with a continuum between mythic, heroic and historical time. Narrating the previous incarnations of various persons was a way of playing with time. The conflict between Rāma and Rāvaṇa has been described as a prototype myth echoing the earlier conflict described in Vedic sources between Indra and Vṛtra, and exalting the heroic ideal. Rāma is the personification of the ideal *kṣatriya*. He is referred to as a human hero and in these references there is no question of his being identified with Viṣṇu.[7] He is however the perfect man.[8]

That the story gained popularity is evident from its inclusion among the narratives, the *ākhyānas*, of the sixteen great heroes as given in the *Mahābhārata*. The 'Rāmopākhyāna' as it is called is not just a summary of the Vālmīki text as is often assumed, but a rendering of the story with distinct changes. Whether it preceded the Vālmīki version or was composed later remains controversial. The popularity of the story has been attributed to various factors such as that it was a compendium of nature myths with Sītā as a fertility goddess and Rāma as the solar deity, given his descent from the solar line. Perhaps it was because of this increasing popularity that the Vālmīki *Rāmāyaṇa* was now converted into a religious text[9] through a new edition which was a refashioning by *brāhmaṇa* authors. Appropriate changes were made in the text and two further books were added at the beginning and the end, the 'Bālakāṇḍa' and the 'Uttarakāṇḍa'.[10] The pre-eminence given to the Bhārgava *brāhmaṇas* is noticeable in both these additions.[11]

The hero Rāma was now said to be an *avatāra* or incarnation of Viṣṇu, one of the two major deities of the emerging Puranic Hinduism. The *Rāmāyaṇa* therefore becomes a text for the propagation of the worship of Viṣṇu with the suggestion that the reading of the story might free one from sin. The additional book at the beginning and end of the text gathered to it a variety of myths, legends, genealogies and changes in the narrative which drew on features of the religious sects of the Bhāgavatas. Furthermore, an elaboration on the character of the protagonists led to an exaggeration of their earlier depiction. Thus Rāvaṇa emerges as a ten-headed monster, and so much the personification of evil as to be almost a caricature. Yet at the same time, in a lengthy interpolation at the end we are told that Rāvaṇa was descended from a line of *brāhmaṇa* seers and was himself an ascetic whose power had to be broken because of his turning to evil actions.[12] Many see it as a battle between good and evil where the narrative encapsulates a theory of ethics. One of the explanations for its popularity originated from a nineteenth century Indologist, Christian Lassen, who argued that the story describes the Aryan invasion of the non-Aryan south, and the conflict is between Aryan and Dravidian culture.[13]

Substantial changes introduced into the story have their own interest, such as those referring to the birth of Sītā. Further, when Rāma and Sītā return to Ayodhyā after the exile, Sītā's chastity is again questioned and on this occasion she is banished and goes to live in the hermitage of the sage Vālmīki. Here twin sons are born to her and named Kuśa and Lava, a curious choice because ***kuśīlava*** came to be used as the technical term for a bard.[14] It is said that Vālmīki composed the *Rāmāyaṇa* and taught it to the sons of Sītā, directing them to recite it on appropriate occasions. This is a curious turn to the story. The main thrust of the Brahminized version which continued to be referred to as the Vālmīki *Rāmāyaṇa* was of course the glorification of Viṣṇu incarnated as Rāma.

The arena was that of clans in conflict, in a situation of new settlements encroaching on forests and the migrations of peoples.[15] The Vālmīki *Rāmāyaṇa* has obscured the identity of the *rākṣasas* by describing them as demons, where the fantasy of the poet has had full play. Nevertheless it is evident that these were not demons but a people with ways of life different from those of Ayodhyā and into whose territory the hermits and the exiled heroes were intruding. The original *Rāma-kathā* probably attempted to describe a conflict between chiefdoms prior to the rise of monarchies. Subsequent rewriting changes the focus to a strong endorsement of the monarchical state. Monarchy is now regarded as the ideal political form and there is an implied disapproval of pre-monarchical or of variant systems such as among the *rākṣasas*.[16]

The *Rāmāyaṇa* repeatedly states that a people without a king is conducive to general anarchy.[17] Ayodhyā is the capital of a monarchical state, Rāma endorses the duties of a king, primogeniture becomes a crucial issue when the eldest son is exiled and debarred from kingship, contrary to the norm. Society in Ayodhyā is ordered according to the rules of caste.[18] Its citizens count their wealth in grain and in valuables which they exchange even over long distances.[19] The *rākṣasa* territory by contrast has no boundaries, lacks the authority of a state and its society is not ordered according to caste. Decisions are taken by Rāvaṇa the *rākṣasa* chief and his kinsmen for there is neither consultation with ministers nor a hierarchy of status. Laṅkā, his island stronghold, is described as a city of gold, gems and untold riches but there is no obvious source of wealth.[20] The luxury may well be an example of extravagant poetic imagination. The *rākṣasas* are unfamiliar with agriculture and know no trade. The hermits are the vanguard, as it were, of encroachment into the hunting grounds and forests of the *rākṣasas*, for they are, in effect, also the precursors of an agricultural society which would clear and settle the forested areas. This may well have occasioned the need for the *rākṣasas* to disturb the rituals of the hermits. The *rākṣasas* were looked down upon. Yet they are also said to have access to magical powers and objects among which the most impressive was the aerial chariot of Rāvaṇa. The demonizing, as it were, of the *rākṣasas*, could be the projection of a feared enemy. There is both a putting down as well as a looking up to Rāvaṇa in the Brahmanical version.

The lesser persons who became the allies of Rāma in exile, such as the Niṣāda chief and the kinsmen of Hanumān, have been viewed as possible hunting and gathering tribes of the forests, who in early myths were expelled to less accessible areas.[21] These were people bound by elaborate rules of gift-giving and reciprocal obligations, more so than in the monarchy. The text therefore might seem to incorporate a continuum of social and economic forms, moving from hunting and gathering peoples to chiefdoms, and reserving the accolades for the monarchical State. With each major version of the text, there is an increasing emphasis on the monarchy as the model, but some of the non-monarchical forms are retained for contrast or else manage to slip through.

The *Rāma-kathā* was part of a floating tradition of bardic stories which were picked up and reworked into variant versions. This is confirmed also by versions which occur in the literature of what are generally regarded as the heterodox religions, Buddhism and Jainism, the heterodoxy being opposition to Brahmanism. From the Buddhist sources comes the story as narrated in the *Dasaratha Jātaka*[22] dating to anywhere between the fourth and the second centuries BC and which is in effect the briefest of summaries of part of the *Rāma-kathā*. Some scholars have argued that this version of the *Rāma-kathā* predates Vālmīki whereas others maintain that it is later.[23] There is a significant change in the story, for here Sītā is not the wife but the sister of Rāma. At the end of the exile when Rāma returns to Ayodhyā, Sītā is made the queen-consort of Rāma and they rule jointly for sixteen thousand years. This version may reflect the tradition of brother-sister marriages in Buddhist origin myths, including that of the Buddha himself.

It can be interpreted in many ways: as a symbol of the purity of blood or, possibly, a demarcation of a distinctive status. A comparison with Buddhist origin myths suggests that Rāma and Sītā may have been seen as the originators of a royal clan and therefore placed in this particular relationship for the ancestry of Rāma is traced back to the eponymous ancestor Ikṣvāku, from whom incidentally the clan of the Buddha also claimed descent.[24] Sibling incest is not to be taken literally but seen as a cultural signal. Written in Pāli for the edification of Buddhist audiences, the function of the story was different from other versions of the *Rāma-kathā*. The Buddhist ethic is underlined in the consolation which Rāma offers to his brother Lakṣmaṇa on the death of their father.

The Jaina version of the *Rāma-kathā*, the *Paumacariyam*, is aggressively different from the others and sets itself up as the counter epic.[25] Composed by Vimalasūri in about the third century AD or a little later, it was written in the popularly used language, Prākṛit. It contradicted the *Rāmāyaṇa* as reworked by *brāhmaṇa* authors and which it describes as part of the false tradition propagated by *brāhmaṇa* heretics, the *brāhmaṇas* being heretical from the Jaina point of view.[26] The Jaina version, framed in the perspective of the Jaina ethic and doctrine, was in a way the mirror image of the Vālmīki version as revised by the *brāhmaṇas*. Vimalasūri naturally claims veracity for his narrative but also introduces a new dimension of historicity in arguing that his version conformed to what actually happened. Historicity is not one of the claims of the Vālmīki *Rāmāyaṇa*.

The Jaina version starts by giving the genealogy and background not of Rāma, as in the Vālmīki version, but of Rāvaṇa and then of Hanumān.[27] We are told that the *rākṣasas* were not demons but normal humans. Rāvaṇa was not a ten-headed monster but was described as such because he wore a necklace of nine large gemstones which reflected his face. Similarly Hanumān was not a monkey but the leader of a clan with a monkey emblem on its standard. His role as mediator rather than one who loyally serves Rāma, is more pronounced in this version. Rāvaṇa, we are told, belongs to the Meghavāhana lineage, the word literally meaning that he was 'cloud-borne', which also links him to his other epithet, *ākāśamārgi*, he who travels through the sky — both epithets are suggestive of aerial chariots.

At the time when the Jaina version was written the Vindhyan region had witnessed earlier settlements growing into trading centres, cities and the nuclei of small kingdoms. Patronage to Jainism came to be associated with some of these. Not unexpectedly, Rāvaṇa in the Jaina version far from being a villain, is a devoted Jaina who practised all the required religious precepts and austerities and acquired considerable ascetic power. At the end of the story, Daśaratha, Rāma and Lakṣmaṇa, all become Jaina ascetics and Sītā takes herself off to a nunnery. The question of self-perception therefore takes on a different definition. The ethic of the warrior so evident in the Vālmīki version now changes to that of the Jaina ascetic. At the same time the Jaina epic is a powerful contradiction of the Brahmanic version.

There now begins a tradition of a series of Jaina versions of the *Rāma-kathā*.[28] These coincide with the period when Rāma as an *avatāra* of Viṣṇu begins to gain popularity, although an increase in the number of Jaina versions dates to the later time when Rāma emerges as the focus of *bhakti* worship. The Jaina texts are composed in various languages: Prākṛit, Apabhramṣa and Sanskrit. The characters are all human heroes but placed in a setting of Jaina ethics. Even within the Jaina tradition there are variations in the story for in some texts Sītā is the daughter of Rāvaṇa but is brought up by Janaka, a theme which was to be popular in other late versions. This makes the abduction doubly heinous but adds a further layer to the symbolic meaning. The accusation that the Brahmanical version of the story was incorrect continues to be made. What the Jaina and Buddhist versions point to is that the *Rāma-kathā* was a popular story which was picked up by a range of sectarian interests for a variety of purposes and at the same time, there was a continuing controversy as to the authenticity of event and character. The historically interesting question is whether Vimalasūri's version draws from an earlier tradition which might explain the contradiction in the treatment of the story, or does it reflect an increasing confrontation between Jainas and *brāhmaṇas*.

The *Rāma-kathā* provided familiar stories to many different audiences. These themes found their way into yet another and entirely separate genre, namely, plays and poems written for the royal courts and the literati. They were reworked into the classics of creative literature in Sanskrit and many underwent major changes conforming to the requirements of courtly literature. Among the better known and more frequently quoted are the narrative poem of Kālidāsa, *Raghuvaṃśam*, the play of Bhāsa, *Pratimānāṭaka* and Bhavabhūti's *Uttararāmacarita*. Some compositions even took the form of a literary *tour de force* as in the ninth century biography of a contemporary east Indian king, Rāmapāla, where the *Rāmacaritam* of Sandhyakaranandin can be read equally easily as the story of Rāma or as the biography of the king. Such compositions were not treating the *Rāma-kathā* as sacred literature but as a source for literary themes and demonstrations of poetic virtuosity.

The emergent regional languages also produced at different times their own versions of the *Rāma-kathā*, such as the Tamil epic of Kamban, *Iramavatāram* or the Telugu, *Ranganātharāmāyaṇa*, or the Kannada *Pampa Rāmāyaṇa*, or the later Bengali, Krittibāsa *Rāmāyaṇa*, or that of Ekanāth in Marathi, the *Bhavartha Rāmāyaṇa*.[29] The writing of the *Rāma-kathā* in regional languages has been a continuing process and many of these versions introduced innovations in response to changes in Indian society and regional perspectives. The innovations were both of event and of character. Thus the treatment of Rāvaṇa in many of these versions is that of a hero in decline rather than a villain and is distinctly different from that of Vālmīki. The Tamil poem draws a little more heavily on the Bhakti tradition of devotion to a deity.

By the early second millennium AD there had been an enormous geographical spread of the Rāma story. This had less to do with *Rāma-bhakti* as such and more with the fact that in its variant forms, local traditions were expressing themselves in a common cultural idiom which was widely dispersed and understood. A distinction therefore has to be made between the story as a cultural metaphor and as sacred literature. In the reworked Vālmīki text it remained the sacred literature of the Vaiṣṇavas, but many other variants were treating it as a cultural metaphor. The latter were popular in central Asia, China and Tibet,[30] sometimes drawing on the Buddhist originals, although these versions had their own variants reflecting the social and cultural norms of the society from which they arose. In south-east Asia there was an avid appropriation of the story frequently drawing on Indian folk and regional versions, with clear variants deriving inspiration from local geography, tradition and events. In one version the area of north Vietnam (Annam) is identified as the Ayodhyā of the text and that to the south of it

(Champa) as Lanka, a considerable shift in geographical identification. In some versions Sītā appears, unknown to him, as the daughter of Rāvaṇa. The more up-to-date versions in south-east Asia incorporate Islamic legends, some even featuring the prophet, Adam.[31] In the Malayan version of the legend, Rāvaṇa is exiled to Serendib, where Adam sees him and pleads for him before Allah, who grants him a kingdom.[32] It has been argued that the sculptured reliefs at major sites in Indonesia are more likely based on folk versions of the story than on any text.[33]

Narrative art in painting and sculpture had also begun to draw on the local version of the story from the middle of the first millennium AD. Gupta period sculpture at the temples of Nachna Kuthara and Deogadh have been interpreted as depicting scenes from the *Rāma-kathā*. The depiction of the *Rāma-kathā* was part of the general theme included among the *avatāras* of Viṣṇu. The treatment of Rāma as an individual deity in his own right, with temples dedicated specifically to him is, however, a much later development.

When we ask why there was this mushrooming of the story in India, the notion of cultural idiom appears to take precedence over the religious text. One obvious reason was that it was a tale well told, personifying the conflict between good and evil with the virtuous eventually triumphant. Equally obvious was the use of the text for the propagation of the cult of Viṣṇu. Specialists in the history of Indian literature have argued that the spread of Sanskrit to new areas which were until then using their own local language, was facilitated by the use of the simple Sanskrit of the Vālmīki epic. This became the model for epic genres in the new regional languages although the narrative was changed in accordance with the demands of popular culture and local tradition. Such explanations are entirely feasible, but perhaps not sufficient. An investigation of the historical background may further fill out the picture.

If the *Rāma-kathā* was also seen as a charter of validation for monarchy then it was an appropriate text for historical changes taking place from about the eighth century AD. There was a noticeable growth of a large number of small kingdoms. Barring a few major dynasties, these were generally short-lived kingdoms of no great pretension to extensive territory but each claiming and indulging in the full panoply of monarchical status. Minor rulers rushed to take grandiloquent titles and did not hesitate to call themselves *mahārājādhirāja*, great king of kings. Local courts boasted large retinues of retainers whose code of behaviour laid emphasis on heroic chivalry combined with blinkered devotion and loyalty to the king. The subsistence of these kingdoms came in large part from the steady encroachment of the agrarian economy into erstwhile forested regions. Waste land was brought under cultivation, not necessarily by the state directly but also through a system of granting land to learned *brāhmaṇas* and those holding high administrative office. The ancestors of many of the lesser kings were such grantees in origin and the more ambitious among them aspired to the monarchical model. Some came from families of tribal chiefs who through administrative office had moved into the hierarchy of the State. In this situation access to economic resources implied increasing the land under cultivation. Forest tribes were under all circumstances to be subjugated, a strategy which has continued through the centuries. The triumph of Rāma over Rāvaṇa therefore provided a powerful metaphor for a process which was actually taking place.

Where royal courts came into existence, there the *brāhmaṇas* legitimized the king by providing him with a genealogy and by performing rituals through which his divine status was proclaimed.[34] There is a frequency in this period to claims to ancestry in the two royal lineages — the Sūryavaṃśa and the Candravaṃśa. By means of the genealogy the status of *kṣatriya*, now seen as that of the landed aristocracy was bestowed on the family irrespective of its actual origins. Those who claimed descent from the Sūryavaṃśa had Rāma as a distant ancestor. The *Rāmāyaṇa* would then become the story of the royal ancestor. That the ancestor was an incarnation of the god Viṣṇu, helped underline the divinity of kingship which by this period was more generally asserted than in earlier times.

The settling of *brāhmaṇas* in areas previously unfamiliar with Brahmanical culture brought about an acculturation through which a familiarity with the Sanskritic tradition was introduced to these areas. But such acculturation increasingly required that the Sanskritic tradition incorporate manifestations of the local culture. Thus new versions of the *Rāma-kathā* were composed in which the ingredients of local culture predominated.

One form taken by these manifestations was the use of historical geography. The geography of the earlier Vālmīki *Rāmāyaṇa* remained confused. Thus, the location of Lanka, never made precise, may have moved from the Vindhyan region south-eastward following a known route of migration and trade.[35] According to popular belief today it could even be the island of Ceylon or Sri Lanka. This geographical flexibility could be put to good use. The theme of exile came in very handy. Originally a bardic device used in virtually all epics to stretch the story or incorporate other fragments, it became, in this case, part of the process of acculturation. Local opinion could claim that exile had actually brought Rāma to that area. Topographical features and local cults were gradually linked to the story. This enhanced the cultural prestige of the site, assisted in the proselytizing of people to the religious cults of Viṣṇu and his incarnations and incidentally also helped to strengthen the theory of the genealogical links of the local ruling family where it claimed descent from Rāma. In a sixteenth century version of the *Rāma-kathā* from Orissa, the exiles are depicted as travelling through the then contemporary kingdoms.[36]

Parallel with these developments but of a qualitatively different kind was the emergence of a specific sect focussing on the worship of Rāma and dating to the early second millennium AD. This was the influential sect of Rāmānandins. For them the worship of Rāma or *Rāma-bhakti* was the most effectual form of devotional worship and ensured the salvation of the individual. *Rāma-bhakti* was of course part of the Vaiṣṇava Bhāgavata tradition even earlier, but the focus which the Rāmānandin sect provided was new. They drew on those versions of the story which emphasized *Rāma-bhakti* and the texts associated with them were distinct. The focus shifts somewhat from Viṣṇu to more specifically Rāma, but the concern of these texts was not so much the activities of Rāma as the prescription for the attaining of *mokṣa* (release from the cycle of birth and death).

Among these texts the *Adhyātma-Rāmāyaṇa*, dating to about the fifteenth century AD[37] carries the notion of *māyā* or illusion to its logical conclusion, when it argues that the very story of Rāma is an illusion and that the importance of the text is less the story and more what the text has to say about devotional worship. The *Rāma-kathā* is set in the frame of Śiva telling the story to Pārvatī for the salvation of all. This is yet another idea which changes the function of the story. There is also a listing of benefits derived from the recitation of the *Adhyātma-Rāmāyaṇa*. This points to a move in the direction of making the text into a sacred book for the *Rāma-bhaktas*, even though at many crucial points there are differences with the

Vālmīki *Rāmāyaṇa*. Echoes of the Kṛṣṇa legend are introduced from time to time as in the description of the childhood of Rāma.[38] The legend of how Vālmīki took to the ways of a low-caste thief but eventually came to compose the *Rāmāyaṇa*, is also related.[39] We are told that Rāma being in fact Viṣṇu, knew that Rāvaṇa would kidnap Sītā, and therefore places her in the safe-keeping of Agni by making her enter the fire and she is replaced by the shadow or *chāyā* Sītā.[40] The real Sītā returns to Rāma after the fire ordeal. Rāvaṇa in turn knows that Sītā is in fact Lakṣmī, therefore, although he kidnaps her, he treats her like his mother.[41] Rāvaṇa also knows that Rāma is an incarnation of Viṣṇu, so, by kidnapping Sītā and being therefore killed by Rāma, he ensures that he will go to heaven. When Sītā is banished for the second time, the author does leave us with the question of how could Rāma, knowing Sītā to be his own Śrī, have banished her? Yet Rāma tells Sītā of his plan to banish her, so that she can return to heaven and he will follow later.[42] This altogether changes the ethical implications of the banishment. The obvious logical inconsistencies in this version of the story are subordinated to the text being sacred and devoted to the worship of Rāma. The problem for the author was to reconcile the story with the necessary religious explanations. Hence the deviations. The importance given to the Rāmagītā recited by Rāma towards the end of the story,[43] would seem to point to parallels with *Kṛṣṇa-bhakti*. Many of these features derived from the differing versions related in the major Purāṇas, which either refer to the story or carry a summary of it. The influence of the *Bhāgavata Purāṇa* is particularly noticeable in the *Bhuśuṇḍi Rāmāyaṇa*, where the treatment of Rāma's early life is modelled on that of Kṛṣṇa, and Sītā is surrounded by *gopis*.[44]

The notion of a shadow Sītā or even a substitute Sītā, was to become extremely popular in the later versions. Sītā's fire ordeal in these is less a test of Sītā's chastity and more a mechanism by which the real Sītā is reunited with Rāma. This idea, apart from its link with the philosophical notion of *māyā* or illusion, was perhaps also a concession to the popular goddess cults of this time which not only insisted on the power and presence of the female principle, but also may not have allowed a goddess of fertility to be subjected to such ordeals.

The influence of the now powerful Śākta tradition on the *Rāma-kathā* is clear from further changes in the narrative and treatment of the story in other texts. Śiva had already been introduced as the narrator of the story. More interesting is the change in the role of Sītā, where she, whether the shadow or the actual Sītā, goes into action single-handed against Rāvaṇa and finally kills him, episodes narrated in the Sanskrit *Adbhut* and *Ānanda Rāmāyaṇas*. Sītā, as an incarnation not of Lakṣmī but of the Śākta concept of Devī, is common to many Śākta versions of the story and does not hesitate to kill the hundred-headed or the thousand-headed Rāvaṇa. From the Śākta tradition such a change in the story is of course predictable, given that the goddess is all-powerful. But it converts the image and role of Sītā into something different from that of even the revised Vālmīki *Rāmāyaṇa*. The relationship between Rāma and Sītā changes, as does the delineation of Sītā as the ideal woman in the earlier version.[45] Some of these versions also retain the story of Sītā being the daughter of Rāvaṇa, a fact not known to him.

The increasing influence of the Rāmānandin sect led to a physical focus being located for the *bhaktas* of Rāma in the city of Ayodhyā, which had over time become the centre for many different religions and sects. The focus on Ayodhyā was directed through the pilgrimage circuit and this in turn required the demarcation of a sacred topography locating the events of the *Rāma-kathā*. The *Ayodhyā-mahātmya* was compiled in the early part of the second millennium AD, one among a genre of such texts which deal with the local history of a sacred site as part of a remembered tradition and which include myth, narrative about the cult and descriptions of the places regarded as sacred and required to be visited by the pilgrim.[46] Pilgrimage to Ayodhyā associated specifically with the *Rāma-kathā*, seems to have begun only at this time.

In the sixteenth century Tulsīdās composed the *Rāmacaritamānas* in Hindi, which became the most popular version in northern India. This was not surprising as the Rāmānandin sect, with which Tulsī was associated, required a text which would be comprehensible to a large audience than the limited one of those who knew Sanskrit. For Tulsī, Rāma was essentially the divine being present among humans. We are continually told that he is adored by all, even by ascetics who gaze on him like 'a bevy of partridges gazing at the autumn moon'. Tulsī's view of the world made such devotion imperative. He saw his contemporary times as a period of declining morality, the fall from the initial golden age to the present age of iron, the Kaliyuga (the age of Kali), accompanied by inevitable decline in social and ethical norms. He states that caste rules are now ignored, upstarts and low-caste people come into prominence and succeed through fraud and cheating. It is indeed a world turned upside down. The only consolation is the worship of Rāma, which alone could bring back the utopian society once ruled by Rāma.[47]

A section of popular opinion today maintains that this picture of decline was Tulsī's protest against the Mughal rulers who were Muslims and that his *Rāmacaritamānas* consolidated and saved the Hindu ethos. But the text does not bear this out. The evils of the Kali age were conjured up repeatedly by *brāhmaṇa* authors whenever they felt that Brahmanical authority was in crisis, and this had happened at various times even before the coming of Islam to India.[48] Tulsī as a *brāhmaṇa* was doubtless disturbed by many of the current religious movements within the fold of what is today called Hinduism, which denied the authority of the *brāhmaṇas* and the texts which they respected, which propagated alternative religious ideologies and attracted large audiences of non-*brāhmaṇas*. Sects deriving from Puranic and Śākta worship were often opposed to the more conservative Brahmanical tradition. Thus, far from seeing the decline of Hinduism, India under Muslim rule witnessed the vibrancy of a large number of Hindu sects. Some of these competed for patronage, a competition which was at times to take violent turns as in the battles between the Bairagis and the Sanyasis. Even among the Vaiṣṇava sects there was some competition for patronage. The Kṛṣṇa cult at Vrindavana was becoming increasingly important. The *Rāmacaritamānas* is not only a Vaiṣṇava text but one which focuses more narrowly on *Rāma-bhakti*. Yet it is not just a Hindi rewrite of the Vālmīki *Rāmāyaṇa* as revised for Bhāgavata worship. It does carry differences of religious meaning. Tulsī's version also gains in importance today because of the status of Hindi in relation to other regional languages.

The popularity of Tulsī's text encouraged a new idiom, that of the *Rāmalīlās*. These were in the nature of folk plays enacting the *Rāma-kathā* and performed in the Hindi-speaking areas of north India. The time of year coincided with the autumn harvest and the worship of the ancestors (*śrāddhas*) as well as the major seasonal worship of the mother goddesses. Possibly the *Rāma-kathā* ousted the worship of the goddess in these areas, for elsewhere the festival continues to be associated primarily with the goddess.

Yet another very different use to which the story was put was the mobilization of peasants in Uttar Pradesh by Baba Rāma

Chander in the early part of this century. Its dual objective was to support the national movement and to oppose the large-scale landlords of the area. Selected verses of the Tulsī version were popularized as part of the resistance to colonial rule. The virtuous characters in the story, Rāma, Lakṣmaṇa and Sītā, were identified with the peasants. The *rākṣasa* who were the villains were identified with the landlords, capitalists and the British.[49] Baba Ram Chander does not speak of the return of the *Rāma-rājya* or the golden age of the reign of Rāma, but since he identified Rāma with the peasants, the fulfillment of the dream of peasants in power would virtually amount to a *Rāma-rājya*.

Local versions of the story differing in narrative and symbolism from the Vālmīki and Tulsī versions have continued to be performed or even read, sometimes as a parallel tradition and sometimes as the central tradition in certain communities. Among these, by way of an example, is the popular Tamil version which was earlier handed down orally, but since the beginning of this century has been made available in printed form. This is the *Chatakantakatai* or the *Story of the Ten-Headed Ravana*.[50] Here once again it is Sītā who, with Rāma as her charioteer, goes into battle against Rāvaṇa and in single combat kills him. Clearly the imprint of the powerful, assertive goddess overrides the more accommodating and gentle image of the Vālmīki or Tulsī versions and follows the narrative of the Śākta versions. These are not marginal traditions for they are central to the societies from which they emerge. In many of the folk versions the role of Hanumān changes. He remains a devotee of Rāma but is in addition associated with popular humour and jokes, and speaks in a more indigenous style suggesting indirectly that he represents the local people.

The popular depictions in the *Rāmalīlās* found a place in the movie industry and since the early 1900s, films have been made on the themes of the *Rāmāyaṇa* and advertised as 'mythological'. The films being largely in Hindi and propagating *Rāma-bhakti*, it was almost inevitable that they would rely on the Vālmīki and Tulsī versions. The films in turn have influenced the most recent form of the *Rāma-kathā* — as the most successful soap opera on national television — again drawing on Vālmīki and Tulsī, now regarded as received versions.

Thus the *Rāma-kathā* in India has had a chequered history and has performed many functions, not all of which were solely religious.

There are parallel traditions of the story which continue to this day and which relate to diverse social perspectives. There was a floating, oral tradition which probably began with ballads and epic fragments, narrating stories which were finally woven together into epic poems or the *Jātaka* stories of the Buddhist tradition. Such forms continue to dominate folk traditions which have on occasion been incorporated into the many manifestations of the *Rāma-kathā*.

The *Rāma-kathā* as a story, important to religious sectarian positions, comes into its own in the second millennium AD. This tradition of *Rāma-bhakti* becomes more focussed and powerful and the new versions are treated fundamentally as the texts of *Rāma-bhakti*. But the variations among religious sects are also reflected in the treatment of the story. Thus the Tulsī version is different from the Śākta version and if the Tulsī version is popular in the Hindi-speaking areas, the Śākta version is popular elsewhere.

There is therefore, no single authentic version of the *Rāma-kathā*, for each version is authentic to the particular sect to which it is addressed or to the local community from which a version may emanate. By and large, and even when it is included in canonical or semi-canonical literature (as in the case of the Buddhist and the Jaina versions), the story is imbued with a sectarian perspective, but is not necessarily regarded as a sacred text. Only a few versions have latterly been treated as sacred. The multiplicity of folk versions in function go back to the epic tradition. These obviously are not regarded as sacred texts but are a significant part of the cultural idiom.

The *Rāma-kathā* has thus itself been through many incarnations and has changed its function in society over time. So no particular version can be treated as a specific sacred book, sacred to all Hindus whether of high or low caste or whether conforming to elite or popular religious traditions and irrespective of region and language. Nor is it possible to argue that the topography of pilgrimage at Ayodhyā goes back to the centuries BC when, it is supposed, the events of the *Rāma-kathā* took place. What is of interest in looking at the historical perspective on the *Rāma-kathā*, is the role which the story has played in articulating a range of dialogue in the context of Indian civilization. This is not to suggest that those who wish to treat any of these many versions of the *Rāma-kathā* as a sacred book should not do so: but it is to insist that those who wish to see the *Rāma-kathā* tradition in its totality outside of a religious context, also have the right to see it that way. The differentiation between a cultural idiom and a religious, sectarian, sacred book should not be ignored. That this distinction was not ignored in the past, also becomes fundamental to our understanding of the role of the *Rāma-kathā* today.

The political exploitation of the worship of Rāma has not only been visible but has been forced to the forefront in recent months, culminating in the fall of a government. This has added yet another dimension to the ways in which the *Rāma-kathā* has been used. Its roots lie in the realization that in the same way as once long ago the story was used to propagate a new religious idea (Bhagavatism and the concept of Rāma as the *avatāra* of Viṣṇu), the worship of that *avatāra* could now be used to build up a political base and political demands. This first required the annulling of different versions and the projection of a single version as the authentic one. In this the media was of considerable assistance.

Because the medium of television is becoming the most powerful in the country, in places superseding even the entrenched oral tradition, its use of this theme has to be seen in context. The versions selected, with no attempt to suggest that there were other versions contradicting it, is a Hindu Vaiṣṇava text, centring on the worship of Rāma, familiar to north Indian Hindi speakers and broadly to the literate few elsewhere. The choice of this version therefore makes a specific social and political statement, becoming all the more significant given that television is part of the Government-controlled media. With such powerful backing the serial comes to be seen as the national culture of the mainstream. This eliminates the range of folk and popular versions or alternative versions even within the same religious tradition. There is a very deliberate choice of one tradition and the elevation of this tradition (remoulded in accordance with contemporary tastes and values) to national status. The differences, the debates, the discussions implicit in the interplay of variants are thus nullified. It is made impossible in the present context even to discuss on television, the specific variants in the Buddhist, the Jaina and the Śākta versions or in folk motifs, leave alone show them as serials. The richness of the themes in contradictory or alternate versions is suppressed and the story is underlined as a sacred story, which therefore cannot be questioned. This is a very different treatment from that given to the *Rāma-kathā* by Indian civilization. The manifestation of diversity and its accommodation was characteristic of Indian culture in the pre-colonial period and enriched every tradition. To accept and conform to a single version erodes cultural flexibility as well as the encouragement to innovate, so necessary to any cultural idiom.

Inevitably this is also part of the attempt to redefine Hinduism as an ideology for modernization by the middle class. Modernization is seen as linked to the growth of capitalism. In terms of its religious associations, capitalism is often believed to thrive among religions such as Christianity and Islam. The argument would then run that if capitalism is to succeed in India, then Hinduism would also have to be moulded to a similar form: although this desired change is often disguised in the theory that what is actually happening in the new resurgence of Hinduism is a return to Hindu traditions.

Characteristic of the Semitic religions are features such as a historically attested teacher or prophet, a sacred book, a geographically identifiable location for its beginnings, an ecclesiastical infrastructure and the conversion of large numbers of people to the religion — all characteristics which are largely irrelevant to the various manifestations of Hinduism until recent times. Thus instead of emphasizing the fact that the religious experience of Indian civilization and of religious sects which are bunched together under the label of 'Hindu' are distinctively different from that of the Semitic, attempts are being made to find parallels with the Semitic religions as if these parallels are necessary to the future of Hinduism.

The parallel can be seen for example in the recent resurgence of the worship of Rāma, where the control of this religious articulation is politically motivated. The characteristics of the Semitic religions are introduced into this tradition. The teacher or prophet is replaced by the *avatāra* of Viṣṇu, Rāma; the sacred book is the *Rāmāyaṇa*; the geographical identity or the beginnings of the cult and the historicity of Rāma are being sought in the insistence that the precise birthplace of Rāma in Ayodhyā was marked by a temple, which was destroyed by Babur and replaced by the Babri Masjid; an ecclesiastical infrastructure is implied by inducting into the movement the support of Mahants and the Shankaracharyas or what the Vishwa Hindu Parishad calls a Dharma Sansad; the support of large numbers of people, far surpassing the figures of earlier followers of *Rāma-bhakti*, was organized through the worship of bricks destined for the building of a temple on the location of the mosque. There has been an only too apparent exploitation of belief. The current Babri Masjid dispute is therefore symbolic of an articulation of a new form of Hinduism, militant, aggressive and crusading, which I have elsewhere referred to as Syndicated Hinduism.[51]

In earlier times a dispute over a location would not have arisen, since the historicity of the deity being worshipped was not a matter of significance. These are new strategies for mobilizing political power by exploiting belief. The dialogue between culture and power is directed towards political purposes although the front of a religious movement is sought to be projected. The worship of bricks is new to Hinduism and has been effectively demonstrated as a form of mobilization in the recent Shila puja. Syndicated Hinduism has little in common with either the openness of philosophical Hinduism or the catholicity of the rituals and beliefs of innumerable sects and cults all labelled as Hindu. These latter groups may eventually protest against a uniform religion imposed on them by those who are in power, but if such a religion becomes essential to upward mobility, then the protest will be muted.

Religious movements, by virtue of being social movements and therefore not limited to the salvation of the isolated individual, have at all times had a social base. Some have been movements of intolerance, excluding particular groups in society, whereas others have been movements of accommodation and have assimilated groups thought to be alien. Some have had a larger degree of religious concern, others have merely been a mask for social and political concerns. The movement which has grown around the demand for the replacement of the Babri Masjid by a temple to Rāma has been of the latter kind. It has not only politicized the worship of Rāma, but has equally unfortunately denied the validity of the variant versions of the story of Rāma.

## Notes and References

1. The earlier part of this essay is drawn from a paper entitled, 'Epic and History: Tradition, Dissent and Politics in India', published in *Past and Present*, November 1989, 125, Oxford, pp. 1–26.
2. L. Renou, *The Destiny of the Veda in India*, Motilal Banarsidass, Delhi, 1965; J.F. Staal, *Nambudri Vedic Recitation*, Mouton, The Hague, 1961.

3. See the discussion in A.D. Pusalkar, *Studies in the Epics and the Puranas*, Bharatiya Vidya Bhawan, Bombay, 1955.
4. B.B. Lal, 'Historicity of the *Mahabharata* and the *Ramayana*: What Has Archaeology to Say in the Matter?', Paper presented at the International Seminar on 'New Archaeology and India', Indian Council for Historical Research, New Delhi, 1988.
5. Attempts to do this have been made and point to various periods of composition and interpolation, as for example in H.D. Sankalia, *Ramayana: Myth or Reality*, Munshiram Manoharlal, New Delhi, 1982.
6. *Rāmāyaṇa*, 1.12.1–34; 13.1–46, Critical Edition, Baroda.
7. H. Jacobi, *The Ramayana* (trans.), MS University Press, Baroda, p. 59; for references also see J.L. Brockington, *Righteous Rama*, Oxford University Press, New Delhi, pp. 218–19.
8. R.P. Goldman, *The Rāmāyaṇa of Vālmīki*, Volume I: Bālakāṇḍa, Princeton University Press, New Jersey, 1984, p. 43.
9. R.G. Bhandarkar, *Vaishnavism, Shaivism and Minor Sects*, Stassburg, 1913, pp. 46ff.
10. A recent discussion of these interpolated layers is to be found in J.L. Brockington, *Righteous Rama*, Delhi, 1984. An earlier and pioneering analysis of the text, is that of C. Bulcke, *Rāmakathā*, Prayaga Vishvavidyalaya, Allahabad, 1950.
11. N.J. Shende, 'The Authorship of the Ramayana', *Journal of the University of Bombay*, 1943, 12, pp. 19–24.
12. *Rāmāyaṇa*, 7.9–34.
13. C. Lassen, *Indisches Alterthumskunde*, Leipzig, 1847–62, I, pp. 596ff. The Aryan is represented by the orderly and advanced society of Ayodhyā and the Dravidian by the uncouth wildness of the *rakṣasa*. This dichotomy was a direct transplant from European ideological obsessions with 'the Aryan' and does not reflect indigenous identifications. This explanation had a politically explosive effect on Tamil nationalism during this century.
14. Kautilya, *Arthaśāstra*, 1.12.9; 2.1.34; 2.27.7.
15. For a discussion on the background to this early society, see Romila Thapar, *From Lineage to State*, Oxford University Press, New Delhi, 1984.
16. Romila Thapar, *Exile and Kingdom: Some Thoughts on the Ramayana*, The Mythic Society, Bangalore, 1979; Romila Thapar, '*Rāmāyaṇa*: Theme and Variation', in S.N. Mukherjee (ed.), *India: History and Thought*, Subarnarekha, Calcutta, 1982, pp. 221–53. *See* chapter 30 in this volume.
17. *Rāmāyaṇa*, 2.16.7ff.
18. Ibid., 1.1.75; 1.6.17; 5.33.11; 6.115.13.
19. Ibid., 2.29.15; 32.6.

20. Devaraj Chanana, *The Spread of Agriculture in North India*, People's Publishing House, New Delhi, 1963, pp. 27–9.
21. Romila Thapar, 'Origin Myths and Early Indian Historical Tradition', *Ancient Indian Social History: Some Interpretations*, Orient Longman, New Delhi, 1978, pp. 307ff. *See* chapter 34 in this volume.
22. V. Fausboll, *The Dasaratha Jataka, Being the Buddhist Story of King Rama*, Copenhagen, 1981; *Dasaratha Jataka*, no. 461.
23. J. Przyluski, 'Epic Studies', *Indian Historical Quarterly*, Trivandrum, 1939, 15, pp. 289–99. C. Bulcke, *Rāmakathā*, pp. 84–105. D.C. Sircar, 'The Ramayana and the Dasaratha Jataka', *Journal of the Oriental Institute*, Baroda, 1976, 26, pp. 50–5.
24. Romila Thapar, 'Origin Myths and the Early Indian Historical Tradition', op. cit.
25. The text has been edited by H. Jacobi, *The Paumacariyam of Vimalasuri*, Prakrit Text Society, Varanasi, 1962, reprint. See also K.R. Chandra, *A Critical Study of Paumacariyam*, Research Institute of Prakrit Jainology and Ahimsa Vaishali, Bihar, Varanasi, 1970; V.M. Kulkarni, Prakrit Text Society, *Vimalasuri's Paumacariyam*, Kasi, 1962.
26. *Paumachariyam*, 2.116; 4.64ff.
27. Ibid., 5.16ff.
28. V.M. Kulkarni, *The Story of Rama in Jaina Literature*, Saraswati Pustak Bandhar, Ahmedabad, 1989.
29. Virtually every regional language had many versions of the story and it is not possible to discuss them all in a short essay.
30. J.W. de Jong, *The Story of Rama in Tibet*, Franz Steiner, Stuttgart, 1989.
31. As in the Javanese version, *Serat Kanda*.
32. W. Stutterheim, *Rama-Legends and Rama-Reliefs in Indonesia*, Abhinav Publications, New Delhi, 1989, pp. 23ff.
33. Ibid.
34. D.C. Sircar, 'The Guhila Claim of Solar Origin', *Journal of Indian History*, 1964, XLII, pp. 381–7. Romila Thapar, 'Genealogy as a Source of Social History', in Thapar, *Ancient Indian Social History*, pp. 326–60.
35. Romila Thapar, 'Rāmāyaṇa: Theme and Variation', op. cit.
36. N.N. Misra, 'Folk Elements in the Jagmohan Ramayana', in A.K. Banerjee (ed.), *The Ramayana in Eastern India*, Calcutta, 1983, pp. 74ff.
37. N. Siddhantaratna, *Adhyātma-rāmāyaṇa*, Calcutta Sanskrit Series, Calcutta, 1935; F. Whaling, *The Rise of the Religious Significance of Rama*, Oxford University Press, Delhi, 1980. B.H. Kapadia, 'The Adhyatmaramayana', *Journal of the Oriental Institute (Baroda)*, 1964–5, 14, pp. 164–70.
38. *Adhyātma-Rāmāyaṇa*, 1.3.54–5.
39. Ibid., 2.6.65ff. This idea catches on in folk versions, as for example

in Maharashtra, where in one version he is a thief of the Koli caste to begin with. G.D. Sontheimer, 'The Ramayana in Contemporary Folk Traditions of Maharashtra', in M. Thiel–Holstmann (ed.), *Contemporary Ramayana Traditions* (in press).

40. Ibid., 3.7.1ff.
41. Ibid., 3.7.65.
42. Ibid., 7.4.32ff.
43. Ibid., 7.5.2ff.
44. Brockington, *Righteous Rama*, Oxford University Press, New Delhi, 1984, op. cit., pp. 257ff.
45. W.L. Smith, *Ramayana Tradition in Eastern India*, University of Stockholm, Stockholm, 1988; pp. 136ff.
46. A. Bakker, *Ayodhyā*, Egbert Forsten, Groningen, 1984.
47. *Rāmacaritamānas*, 7.97–103.
48. *Mahābhārata*, 3.186–8; *Matsya Purāṇa*, 273; *Viṣṇu Purāṇa*, 6.1; *Vāyu Purāṇa*, 58; *Brahmāṇḍa Purāṇa*, 2.3.74; B.N.S. Yadav, 'The Accounts of the Kali Age and the Social Transition from the Antiquity to the Middle Ages', *Indian Historical Review*, 1978–9, 5, 1 and 2, 31–63.
49. Kapil Kumar, 'The Ramacharitamanas as a Radical Text; Baba Ram Chandra in Oudh 1920–50', in Sudhir Chandra (ed.), *Social Transformation and Creative Imagination*, Oxford University Press, New Delhi, 1984. See also M.H. Siddiqi, *Agrarian Unrest in Northern India*, Vikas, New Delhi, 1978.
50. D. Shulman, 'Battle as Metaphor in Tamil Folk and Classical Tradition', in S.H. Blackburn and A.K. Ramanujam (eds), *Another Harmony*, Oxford University Press, New Delhi, 1988, pp. 105–30.
51. Romila Thapar, 'Syndicated Hinduism', see chapter 46 in this volume. See also, 'Imagined Religious Communities? Ancient History and the Modern Search for a Hindu Identity'. See chapter 43 in this volume.

# 48

# *The Rāmāyaṇa Syndrome*[*]

In the opinions that were gathered by newspapers when Ramanand Sagar's serial on the *Rāmāyaṇa* closed, various comments were made. It was stated that its popularity resulted from its being a part of the collective unconscious; that among adults it evoked memories of childhood stories and among children it paralleled the exploits of the hero, Superman, that it was an embodiment of higher values and laid out the quest for *dharma* in a simple, narrative form; that it projected the ideal woman in Sītā; that it appeased the apprehensions and insecurities of a society transiting to modernity; that it gave visual form to the spiritual fountainhead of Hinduism. Those that were unhappy with the rendering complained of the absence of poetry and meaning. It was also described as a folk genre, a small town Ramlila that managed to hit the big lights through projection on television.

Only a few seemed concerned about the long-term effects of such a serial. Were we perhaps witnessing an attempt to project what the new culture should be, an attempt to expunge diversities and present a homogenised view of what the *Rāmāyaṇa* was and is? Can this be seen as part of an increasing trend of treating the state as the arch patron of culture, of state patronage requiring a uniform culture with the state determining the manifestations of culture, whether it be the festivals, the media or the aims behind the cultural zones? The state defines culture, finances culture, is the final arbiter and as the patron, bestows recognition on those whom it regards as creative and worthy. Private initiative cannot compete with the financial outlay which the state can provide and there is not enough public initiative to sustain alternate avenues to support innovatory forms.

The state prefers to endorse a uniform, homogenised culture for

* Seminar, No. 353, January 1989, 71–5.

such a culture would be simple to identify and easy to control. To concede that a nation's culture may be constituted of a variety of cultural systems would require that the functionaries of the state be sensitive to these multiple cultural systems and respond to their political implications. Where culture is taken over by the state as the major patron, there the politics of culture is inevitably heightened. It is therefore often easier for the state as patron to adopt a particular cultural stream as the mainstream: a cultural hegemony which frequently coincides with the culture of the dominant social group in the state.

Some would see this new extension of patronage by the state as legitimate, for the state is now expected to provide for everything. But others would see this as a threat to creativity. The relationship between the patron and the one who creates is delicate, where, although the patron controls finance and recognition, the patron is at best merely the agency for the act of creativity. In earlier times acts of creativity had an audience but could do without a patron, although the more elaborate arts and literature required a patron. That creativity today is far more dependent on patronage, requires the patron to be particularly careful about the representation of culture, particularly where culture is being represented through the authoritative state-controlled media. I would like to illustrate this by reference to the *Rāmāyana*.

The *Rāmāyana* does not belong to any one moment in history for it has its own history which lies embedded in the many versions which were woven around the theme at different times and places, even within its own history in the Indian subcontinent. The Indian epics were never frozen as were the compositions of Homer when they changed from an oral to a literate form. Professional reciters, *kathākāras*, recited the written versions with their own commentary and frequently adjusted the story to contemporary norms. The appropriation of the story by a multiplicity of groups meant a multiplicity of versions through which the social aspirations and ideological concerns of each group were articulated. The story in these versions included significant variations which changed the conceptualisation of character, event and meaning.

Even within the literate tradition there are substantial differences. The now non-existent original *Rāma-kathā* was worked over by Vālmīki. This version was then changed by the Bhārgava *brāhmaṇa* redactors who introduced the concept of Rāma being an *avatāra* of Viṣṇu, thus transforming the epic into sacred literature, a transformation which was resorted to in the past as a means of capturing popular literature for didactic purposes. Parallel to this was the Buddhist rendering in some of the *Jātakas*, where in the *Dasaratha Jātaka*, Sītā inspite of being the sister of Rāma nevertheless becomes his queen consort. This change in the kinship pattern is reflected in Buddhist origin myths and carries its own meaning.

A Jaina version, the *Paumacariyam*, claims to be the authentic version of the story and maintains unequivocally that the *brāhmaṇa* version is a false one. The treatment of Rāvaṇa in this text is much more sympathetic, Laṅkā is as important if not more so than Ayodhyā and the events are coloured by Jaina ethics. Thus Daśaratha and Rāma end up as Jaina *munis* and Sītā gets herself to a nunnery. The earliest Tamil version by Kampan changes the treatment of Rāvaṇa who is here the tragic hero rather than the villainous demon. The religious importance of the story increased in the early second millennium AD with the spread of the Rāmanandin sect who worshipped Viṣṇu in his incarnation as Rāma and their most popular sacred literature was the sixteenth century work of Tulsīdās, the *Rāmacaritamānas*.

Even within the literate tradition the significance of these variations is not ignored. The differences highlight the varying perceptions of ethical behaviour, whether it be the ideal of the *kṣatriya* in the brahmanical version or the ideal of the Jaina ascetic in the *Paumacariyam*; of historicity, where the Jaina version claims it, but the brahmanical ignores it; of the depiction of Rāvaṇa as the personification of evil or as a tragic hero; of the embodiment of women where the role of Sītā varies. These were not simply variations in the story to add flavour to the narrative. They were deliberate attempts at taking up a well-known theme and using it to present a new point of view arising out of ideological and social differences of perspective.

These were acts of deliberate innovation, where the creator of the form felt free to experiment with the story even after the story had been given a sacred character by *brāhmaṇa* authors. These variants were not hidden in some obscure treatise. They took the form of popular narratives, recited and written in Pāli and Prākṛit and therefore available to large numbers of people. If we are to be aware of at least this strand of our cultural tradition then the debate and the dialectic embedded in these various versions should be more openly discussed.

What would happen today if an attempt were made to project on TV the Buddhist version of the story, where Sītā as the sister of Rāma becomes his queen consort? It is likely that Doordarshan would not allow it, arguing that it would hurt the religious sensibilities of the majority community. Even if an attempt were to be made to put it not on the media, but only as a play, the self-appointed guardians of Hinduism, such as the Shiv Sena and similar organisations, would prevent its being staged. The assault by the Shiv Sena on a theatre in Bombay and the beating up of the playwright, where a play was to be performed on the interlocking theme of Rāma and Sītā and Romeo and Juliet, is an indication of what would happen. Unfortunately public protest has been too ineffectual to counteract such attitudes. But if the state claims to be the major patron of culture, such incidents require at least a statement from the patron.

If the state has taken on the role of the main patron of culture and if it should then withdraw from innovations in creativity on the grounds that it will hurt the sentiments of a 'religious community', culture will tend to be reduced to the lowest common denominator. The interface between religion, politics and culture becomes a central issue in this situation. Religious sects in India, even those which draw on Islam and Christianity, are characterised by a relative absence of the equivalent of the fiat from the Vatican. Who then speaks for that nebulous mass which is referred to as a 'religious community'? Those that force the issue on the state taking action on cultural or intellectual items are not the religious functionaries of a community, but the political spokesmen of some groups claiming to represent a religious community.

Thus the Shiv Sena can once again object to the government of Maharashtra reprinting a chapter of Dr Ambedkar's book because it questions the authenticity of the brahmanical version of the *Rāmāyaṇa* among other things, and the government bends. It may not even be a question of objecting to the suppression of the views of Ambedkar *per se*, but of allowing various readings of a cultural tradition. Or a Shahabuddin can demand the banning of Salman Rushdie's book *Satanic Verses*, and again the government accedes to this demand. Predictably the next step is that the government anticipates a demand from some Christian groups to ban *The Last*

*Temptation of Christ*, and yet once more the government bans the film. Are we going to be left then with laundered strips of culture because the patron, the state, cannot distinguish between religious sensibilities and cultural articulation?

Our politics are being increasingly conditioned by appeals to the sentiments of various religious communities resulting in a politicising of religion. But at the same time we insist that religion is sacrosanct and cannot therefore be treated as a political ideology inspite of its having become a political ideology in association with communalism. How long will we continue to use this political blackmail, threatening that something will hurt the religious sensibilities of a community, in order to keep religion as a convenient ploy with which to play politics? This is all the more objectionable in a society which has traditionally been open to intellectual and cultural discourse even where it is conducted through religious texts.

A statement which is repeated *ad nauseum* is that of tolerance being a value characteristic of Indian civilisation. There has been little attempt to analyse the nature of this tolerance. It assumed a segmented society in which each caste functioned in accordance with its own *dharma* and the totality was juxtaposed and co-existed. Intolerance was effective within each caste but by and large other castes were left alone to do and believe as they pleased. There was intolerance at times, even before the coming of Islam, when people were killed and their religious structures damaged, nevertheless intolerance never took on the dimensions of a Catholic Inquisition. Polemics were in fact an essential part of ideology and belief. Now that we are moving away from a segmented society, we have to consciously acquire a concern for tolerance. We can retain tolerance only if we refrain from rushing to censorship of all kinds.

Tolerance does not grow with banning what is thought to be unpalatable; it grows with arguing and talking about it; for that which is unpalatable gets discarded. The banning or not of a book should at least have a minimal debate. There was no attempt to discuss what had actually been said in *Satanic Verses* and the issues involved. Those who demanded the ban blatantly stated that they had not read the book. Presumably those who rushed to ban it had not read it either. To demand the banning of the book immediately was shrewd as it also pre-empted any discussion, even among Muslims, on the issues raised in the book. Such a discussion might have revealed differences of opinion, differences indicating that not every Indian Muslim is an Islamic fundamentalist. And such discussions are imperative even for those who have a strong religious identity of any kind, if, as a society, we are to break the seige of communalism.

Let me return to the *Rāmāyaṇa* and its different versions. The authorship changed from bards to *brāhmaṇas* to monks to local story-tellers. Change in authorship and social setting introduced new features. Even those which are regarded as intrinsic to the story, such as the birth of Sītā from the furrow and the ten heads of Rāvaṇa, were at one point, innovations. So too were other events, as for example, the notion of the shadow Sītā — that the real Sītā was not the one kidnapped by Rāvaṇa but an illusory or shadow Sītā, for the real Sītā returned to Rāma after the *agni-parīkṣā*. This innovation has been explained as deriving from the *advaita-vedānta* philosophy and the doctrine of *māyā*. Possibly a more immediate reason was the influence of the Śakti cults, where woman was viewed as an embodiment of power and the indignity of a fire ordeal to prove chastity would not have been easily accepted. This episode might even reflect the debate on *satī* which was prevalent at the time, since the self-immolation of a widow was supposed to lead to reunion with her husband and the *satī* was regarded as a symbol of chastity.

The gradual diffusion of the story influenced the folk genres and the result was something very different from the literary tradition of upper caste culture. One of the major areas of difference focused on the depiction of Sītā. In many folk versions (such as in Kannada) Sītā is the daughter of Rāvaṇa (as she is in versions from south-east Asia). This carries a very different meaning for the abduction by Rāvaṇa. I have recently been informed that in one tribal version, the fire ordeal is performed not by Sītā or a shadow Sītā; but by another woman substituted for the purpose, the tribal Shabari. This speaks volumes for the way in which a tribal society perceives its relationship with the mainstream culture.

Tamil speaking societies derive their version from Kampan or from a variety of local forms, which were earlier recited but during this century have come to be published and are now read. A recent discussion on this genre focusses on the *Catakantaravana-katai,* or the story of the ten-headed Rāvaṇa. Here it is Sītā who, with Rāma as her charioteer, goes into battle against Rāvaṇa. In single combat she is the one who kills Rāvaṇa. Clearly the imprint of the powerful, assertive, goddess figure overrides the more accommodating and gentle image of the Sanskrit and Hindi texts. These are not marginal traditions for they are central to the societies from which they emerge. If it is claimed that Indian culture as being propagated by the state is representative of the Indian people and not just of a small segment of Indian society, then these variants must also find a place.

The question then is that of whose version of the story are we propagating? What was shown on TV and has now become the received version was essentially the *Rāmacaritamānas* of Tulsīdās. The choice of this version must have a reason: perhaps because it is best known among. Hindi speakers and is therefore familiar to north Indian Vaiṣṇavas? Epics are not religious documents in origin. But some versions of an epic story can be transformed into religious statements and this was certainly the case with the later version of the Vālmīki *Rāmāyaṇa* and even more so with the *Rāmacaritamānas*.

The TV version is not a folk genre. It borrows from the films of the 1940's, the 'mythologicals' and it borrows from the Ramlīlās. The latter are again prevalent in the Hindi speaking region, for in other parts of the country, Dusshera and Divali have other connotations and rituals. But what is absent from the TV version is the incorporation of the folkways and the comedy of the Ramlīlās. Local issues and local commentary gave a flavour and vibrancy to these performances. If the literary version in Sanskrit attempted to freeze the rendering of earlier centuries, the TV version may now have the same effect on future Ramlīlās. Yet these multiple and conflicting versions have a legitimacy since they are statements of a social condition and a historical moment. Received versions deny the legitimacy of others as also the idea that a society does not have a single culture but is a collation of cultural systems.

Culture is not an object. It is among other things a way of conducting social relationships expressed in various idioms. State patronage and direction of culture tends to look for a single 'national culture'. It tends to take on the perspective of the dominant group and the culture of this group is projected as the mainstream national culture. Cultural hegemony requires the marginalising and ironing out of other cultural expressions. Those who complain against this hegemony and argue that to treat Ramanand Sagar's version as the received version is to display a poverty in understanding Indian culture are described as deracinated, westernised Indians, out of touch with the culture of the masses. They are dismissed as 'elitists' seeking to dictate cultural norms, forgetting of course that in the system described, choice is anyway restricted and the so-called 'elitists' are in fact supporting a more extensive choice. What is also surprising in this context is that no comment is made on some of the more glaring examples of deracination and elitism seeking to influence cultural choices, namely, the advertisements which precede and follow the sponsored programmes on TV.

The enthusiasm of the masses has been repeatedly invoked in justifying the TV version as an expression of national culture. Which masses are we invoking? Those below the poverty line who are unable to come within watching distance of a TV set? Or are we referring to the urban underclass who have access to a neighbour's set? Even if it is the latter, one wonders what they made of the commentary spoken by Ashok Kumar, who, like the bard of olden times introduces parallels with contemporary life. When the four young princes of Ayodhyā are sent at a tender age to the *gurukula* for training and their mothers are saddened by their departure, Ashok Kumar introduces the parallel of young children today going to boarding school — hardly an experience with which the masses would be familiar.

When supernatural weapons, swirl and zig-zag across the screen, the commentator compares them to the weapons of Star Wars — perhaps a subtle appeal to the wishful thought that Indian civilisation once might have had space weapons but certainly an endorsement of such weaponry. The depiction of the demons who threaten the noble *ṛṣis* and whom Rāma and Lakṣmaṇa are fetched to destroy, are so evidently the physical type associated with 'tribal peoples' that the message of their being alien and evil hardly needs stating in words. If the TV version is fulfilling the role of the story-teller in the life of the young child then what are the nuances which it portrays? Comics, drawing on these stories and the TV version, are part of an urban child's fantasy. The versions which had a universal appeal also had a different kind of message. Are we really talking about an appeal to the masses or are we talking about the middle class and other aspirants to the same status?

Tulsī's *Rāmacaritamānas* did have an appeal for caste Hindus. As a good *brāhmaṇa* Tulsī complained of the upsetting of caste hierarchics and the rise of the low castes to positions and status (as also good *brāhmaṇas* had complained in earlier times). A return to a *rāma-rājya* would set society on the right course for caste hierarchies would be re-imposed. Each man functions according to his allotted caste and then all is right with the world. The notion of *rāma-rājya* does have a widespread appeal. It is a generalised millennarian dream which envisages the well-being of all. It does not go into the question of social inequities. To romanticise hierarchy is one way of supporting it and the message means different things to those at the upper levels and to those down below. The appeal to the latter is the religious message. The religious wrapping in the past tended to hide the political message. The religious wrapping could not altogether hide the political message on a more recent occasion when the actor cast as Rāma campaigned on behalf of the Congress-I in the Allahabad election. If religion is reduced to a vote-catching mechanism then the consequences can only be very different from the avowed goals of the state.

The religious message of the Tulsī version is stated in no uncertain terms. Tulsī repeats again and again that the only thing of supreme importance is *Rāma-bhakti* — unqualified devotion to Rāma as the incarnation of Viṣṇu and to which his text is dedicated. Clearly this rendering of the *Rāmāyaṇa* theme has to be differentiated from the many others which either identify with other religions and ideologies or else are genuine folk genres where such identities are subordinated or are at any rate less sectarian. The very specific identity of the Tulsī version cannot be extended to include the picking up of the theme and its alteration in other religious traditions (including incidentally Islamic features in Indonesian and Malay versions).

There have been statements by the public, commenting on the serial, in defence of the right of the Hindus to see their religious literature on TV. It is said that the majority of Indians are Hindus and therefore a public broadcasting system and television has a duty to bow to the tastes and preferences of the majority. This is a statement which may be seen as impinging on the government's policy towards programmes on the audio-visual media and would require a response from the government. If the media had been autonomous, as has often been urged by various government appointed committees, then the onus would not be on the government. But since these media are government controlled, the government is responsible for the categories of programmes it is supporting and the influence of these programmes on public issues, not to mention concepts of culture. If the state is anxious to be the patron par excellence, one assumes that it is aware of what it is patronising.

Of course the Ramanand Sagar version has a popular appeal. It is the world of Indian middle class fantasy, in which problems arise but are miraculously solved. Its presentation through spectacular sets, glittering costumes and ham acting, matches up to these fantasies. And we all need fantasies, from those who have avidly watched the serial every Sunday to those who play Dragons and Dungeons with the computer or read science-fiction.

One's anxieties about the *Rāmāyaṇa* syndrome arise from other causes: that the fantasy of one social group should not be projected as the fantasy of the entire society, for the essence of cultural renewal is the freedom to innovate and to use changing idioms even for themes regarded as traditional or sacred — as indeed was done in the past; that culture be treated not as a single, homogenised, national package, but as free intersecting cultural systems reflecting the assumptions of all the constituents of Indian society; and lastly, the question of whether the state realises that behind every fantasy there lies a reality and the fantasies of some can be in conflict with those of others. Is the state aware of the reality behind this fantasy?

# In Defence of the Variant*

In the 1988 Annual Number of Seminar (353), I had written about the variant versions of the Rāmakathā and expressed my fears that the television version as well as the politics of the Ramjanmabhumi would drive out the versions of the story which did not conform to the Vālmīki or Tulsī renderings. I had mentioned specifically that it was unlikely now, that a Buddhist version as narrated in the *Dasaratha Jātaka* would be permitted a public performance, given the facility with which the Sangh parivar has set itself up as the arbiter in matters relating to the sentiments of all Hindus. The validity of this view was recently demonstrated in the reaction to a brief mention of this version in one of the panels of an exhibition on Ayodhya organised by Sahmat: the *Dasaratha Jātaka* has become a *cause celêbre*. If variant versions are going to be objected to, as in the case of the *Dasaratha Jātaka*, then we may well be left with just a single, received version.

What was startling about the denunciation of the brief statement in the Sahmat exhibition was that the entire political spectrum went down like a row of nine-pins. Not a single politician enquired into what this version was and its meaning, but rather they all rushed to join in the denunciation, so as to share in what the Sangh parivar saw as political dividends from the Hindu vote. What was even more appalling was the ignorance about the *Jātaka* stories, about their Buddhist connection and meaning; and this from people who preach to us *ad nauseum* about preserving our cultural heritage and the wisdom of the ancient texts. One politician of considerable standing and said to be familiar with the classical texts, referred to the *Jātaka* as 'some old book'; another wanted to know what the Rāma story had to do with Jakarta; and yet another of a seemingly more liberal bent of mind appears to have felt that

* Seminar, No. 413, January 1993, 31–3.

whereas he himself was above being averse to the story, nevertheless it might embarrass his wife and daughter. Perhaps our politicians need to be familiarised with the cultural heritage which they so glibly refer to on any and every occasion.

The *Jātaka* was a collection of popular stories intended for a popular audience and therefore frequently borrowed themes from stories familiar to the general public. The stories were originally part of an oral tradition and were incorporated into texts at a later date. As an oral tradition they were familiar to large numbers of people and were obviously well-liked or else they would not have been incorporated into the texts. They were not exclusive stories meant for a limited audience. The themes were widely used in the narratives of many audiences and these eventually also went into the making of the *Rāmāyaṇa* and the *Mahābhārata*.

Epics are made up from an oral tradition and frequently fragmentary narratives are strung together. There is also the use of formulaic descriptions. Epic stories, therefore, are constructed, in however loose a manner. The Vālmīki *Rāmāyaṇa* is a construct, as are other narratives which pick up segments of the same story. Some *Jātaka* stories refer to characters and events from the Rāmakathā, such as Kauśalya's grief at Rāma going into exile or Sītā's insistence on accompanying Rāma. Some of the place-names are similar; thus Mithilā is a very prosperous city and Daṇḍaka is a forest. Others have similar narrative themes such as the story of the young ascetic who takes care of his blind parents and is accidentally killed in the *Sāma Jātaka*, or the princess going into exile with her husband who is courted by a rakshasa which leads to the husband doubting her chastity in the *Sambula Jātaka*, or the role of the hunch-backed maid in the *Kusa Jātaka*.

The *Jātaka* stories were eventually collated and included in one of the major texts of Buddhism, the *Khuddaka-nikāya* which is part of the *Suttapiṭaka*, an important section of the Buddhist Pali Canon. The *Dasaratha Jātaka* has been widely commented upon during the last hundred years in the extensive discussion on whether it preceded the Vālmīki *Rāmāyaṇa* or was subsequent to it or whether it drew from the same sources as Vālmīki. Was the essentially Buddhist reformulation of the story incidental or was it making a statement in relation to the other versions? It is again the stories from the *Jātakas* that are depicted in large numbers on the railings and gateways of *stūpas* such as at Sanchi, Bharhut and Amaravati.

Both the narrative and the precept were part of the folk tradition of villagers and townsmen visiting the *stūpa*. Some of the themes of these tales are generic and recur in later collections of stories as well, irrespective of religious affiliations.

The *Jātaka* stories refer to a previous life of the Buddha. It is claimed that they were narrated by the Buddha supposedly at the Jetavana monastery and each is adapted to Buddhist purposes and is used to explain and illustrate an ethical precept; hence their inclusion in the religious texts. Many of the stories which carry parallels to those familiar from the *Rāmāyaṇa*, gloss the *Jātaka* version by a strong moralistic tone. In the story of the young ascetic tending his blind parents and who is killed by mistake, he is revived because of the faith of his parents. The continuity of this function of the *Jātaka* stories can be seen in many parts of the Buddhist world. In Southeast Asia for example, where the *Dasaratha Jātaka* is both popular and highly regarded, the emphasis in its popular presentations has always been on its illustrating the need to be distanced from the illusions of mortal existence and to be concerned with the impermanence of mortal life.

The *Dasaratha Jātaka* belongs to a distinct group of stories which indicate the Buddha's concern with the allaying of sorrow. The story is said to have been narrated by the Buddha to a householder whose father had died and who was therefore inconsolable. The Buddha was explaining the impermanence of life through this story which goes as follows:

In times past, Dasaratha was the *mahārājā* of Banaras and from his chief queen he had two sons, Rāmapaṇḍita and Lakkhana, and one daughter, Sītā. The queen died and Dasaratha grieved for her but eventually raised another to her status. The second queen bore him one son, Bharata. After this she asked repeatedly of Dasaratha that he declare her son the successor. Dasaratha, fearing that she might harm the older children, suggested that they go away to the forest and return to claim the kingdom on his death, which had been predicted for twelve years later. The three travelled to the Himalayas where they built a small hermitage. Rāmapaṇḍita became an ascetic and Lakkhana and Sītā looked after his needs.

Meanwhile Dasaratha grieving for his children died after only nine years. When the queen tried to raise the royal umbrella over Bharata, the ministers objected and said that the rightful successor was in the forest. Bharata went to fetch Rāma and seeing him in the hermitage fell at his feet weeping and informed him of their father's death. Lakkhana and Sītā were uncontrollably upset to hear the news but Rāmapaṇḍita sat quietly. He comforted his brother and sister. When Bharata asked him why he was not mourning, Rāma preached to him on the impermanence of life and the uselessness of sorrow to those who have acquired wisdom. A mortal dies all alone and the wise can see beyond this world to the next.

Bharata then asked him to accept the kingship which Rāma refused saying that he would wait until twelve years had been completed in accordance with his father's wishes. He did however, give his sandals to Bharata saying that they would indicate whether Bharata's decisions were correct or not. After three years, Rāmapaṇḍita, Lakkhana and Sītā returned to Banaras. The ministers anointed Rāma and Sītā was his queen-consort. They ruled for sixteen thousand years.

The Buddha is said to have explained that the various persons in the story were those connected with him who had taken birth as the characters of the story. Thus Rāmapaṇḍita was the Buddha himself, Lakkhana and Bharata were his disciples Sāriputta and Ānanda, Dasaratha was Suddhodana and Sītā was the mother of Rāhula. Of all these, Rāmapaṇḍita as the *bodhisattva* was the most highly respected.

The question arises as to why Rāma and Sītā are described as brother and sister. This has to do with Buddhist origin myths where, in the major clans, descent is traced back to the sibling parent. The implication therefore is that the clans are descended from sibling incest. This is as true of the Śākyas, the clan to which the Buddha belonged as it is of the Koliyas and others who play an important role in the events of the Buddha's life. These myths are narrated not only in the Pāli texts but also in Chinese texts recording Buddhist origin myths. Even the ancestry of Vijaya, who established the first kingdom in Sri Lanka, goes back to sibling incest as described in the famous chronicle of Sri Lanka, the *Mahāvaṃsa*.

The next question then is that of whether these narratives are to be taken literally or metaphorically? In the case of the Ptolemies of Egypt there was in fact the marriage of brothers and sisters among the members of the royal family. This was not the case with the Buddhist origin myths since the reference to sibling incest relates to a remote period prior to the emergence of those who might be historically attested. Subsequently there is no incestuous marriage. This is contrary to the Ptolemies where such marriages are specific to the dynasty. Nor should this be seen necessarily as a memory of an earlier promiscuous society, a theory which once was popular among ethnographers but has since been questioned. Origin myths of this kind are what might be called 'cultural codes', encapsulating extensive concepts symbolically but perfectly understood by the audience.

If these stories are taken as cultural codes, then we have to ask what they are stating. Such narratives clearly are emphasising the legitimacy of a clan, a territory or a kingdom, and such legitimacy is linked to the appropriate descent group. The notion of sibling incest, even when not taken literally, places an emphasis on purity of lineage where ancestry is traced back to a single set of parents and which reinforces claims to high status even if the status is not actually so. It acts as a form of social demarcation. High status groups can deviate from the norm, can break the taboos. The notion then becomes the symbol of origin of a royal or near-royal clan.

For an audience familiar with Buddhist origin myths and their cultural codes, the implication of sibling incest in the *Dasaratha Jātaka* would not have posed a problem since they would have recognised the story as a pointer to the high status of the family. There was also the association of both the Buddha and Rāma belonging to the same descent group since both families were descended from Ikṣvāka, an association which is made even as late as in the *Purāṇas*. This is all quite apart from other analyses which have been made of symbolic incest relating it to kinship, property rights and ritual.

The theme of incest in origin myths or in the mythology of the gods is not limited to Buddhist sources. The earliest Indo-Iranian mythology includes a myth of primeval twins that gave birth to the human race. The *Ṛg Veda* is not unfamiliar with incestuous relationships and not surprisingly these are generally associated with the gods. Later mythology in the *Purāṇas* also on occasion plays with the notion of twins, in that hermaphrodites occur as ancestors to those of high status.

There is however more to the *Dasaratha Jātaka* than merely a matter of understanding a single story embedded in the Buddhist tradition. Throughout history various groups have appropriated the Rāma-kathā and used it to project their own ideological concerns and social aspirations. Some of the versions therefore become dissenting versions. Others are assertions of self-perception and projections of what are culturally significant to a particular segment of society. Still others introduce their own social norms ar' the story becomes an agency of legitimation.

This has led to a multiple variety of renderings and retellings. They concern the cultural heritage not just of India but of many parts of Asia. Are we now going to ban all those versions which carry traces of incestuous relationships on the grounds that these versions are offensive to the sentiments of the Hindus? We are likely in this process to run aground with versions both in India as well as in Southeast Asia. On the theme of incest alone, quite apart from the *Dasaratha Jātaka*, there are strong traditions in many parts of India which maintain that Sītā was the daughter of Rāvaṇa, although he failed to recognise her. This adds another dimension to Rāvaṇa's infatuation with Sītā and to the insistence on her having to prove her chastity.

If the variants are disallowed, the strength of the Rāma-kathā tradition will wither and result in the imposition of a single version. As an intelligentsia we are already impoverished in terms of familiarity with the essentials of what we call our cultural heritage, as was adequately demonstrated in the Sahmat episode. If only a single version is to prevail then we are cutting the ground from under the feet of our own cultural past. The denial of other versions is a mechanism by which other voices are silenced. Do we still have a right in public places to refer to other versions or are we now expected to live with the lie that there is only one version?

It is curious that for centuries the alternate versions of the Rāma-kathā have been known and accepted without objections from Hindus and others. The notion of blasphemy was alien. Suddenly one morning in 1993 it is stated that this one version is hurtful to Hindu sentiment. Those that make this statement then turn out to be party to an earlier statement of some decades ago where this particular variant was seen as merely an appropriation of the Rāma-kathā by the Buddhists (The Sunday Times, 21 November '93). This surely indicates that the hue and cry was part of a political agenda and had little to do with the sentiment of the Hindu community. It was equally odious that in Congress-I politics the episode was used in the struggle between two factions of the party, exacerbated no doubt by the Ministry of HRD having financed the exhibition. The espousal by the Left parties of the condemnation of the exhibit can only be explained by their general confusion over the question of the role of religion in contemporary Indian life.

The existence of the variants and their acceptance by Hindus was possible (and may continue to be possible surreptitiously), because for the true Rāma-bhakta, the version is unimportant as long as Rāma is the focus of *bhakti*. From this perspective the *Dasaratha Jātaka* cannot be faulted, since its focus is on the wisdom and perceptiveness of Rāma and the belief that he was a *bodhisattva*. What will become increasingly impossible will be the other uses of the story as articulating dissent.

The objection to the *Dasaratha Jātaka* is not just a matter of objecting to a particular version of the Rāma-kathā which some people regarded as offensive. It does raise the wider question of the closing of the mind. There was a time when the complex symbolism of such stories was recognised, but today we are sheering the richness of form and meaning and replacing it with a simplistic narrative — presumably because this would be easier to manipulate in the politics of religion. On each occasion when a ban is sought to be imposed, be it on *The Satanic Verses* or on the Sahmat exhibition, or on the scholarly analyses of Sikh scriptural texts, it is invariably argued by a small, politically motivated group of people that the larger community will find it offensive. Is there any mechanism for asking the larger community if this is really so? And are such matters really only limited to one community: do they not have wider repercussions across communities on society in general?

In these situations the media plays a crucial role. The politics can be played up to a point where the ban is projected as inevitable. This also raises the issue of who takes the decision. Is it always the state which has to judge and intervene or is it the community in whose name the decision is being taken? If all such decisions are relegated to the state without an open discussion on the issue, then we are in fact placing more power in the hands of the state than is necessary. And the state has shown itself to be partisan to particular views. Today it is the banning of a book or the tearing down of a panel at an exhibition and these may seem marginal; tomorrow it is the dogmatism of substituting knowledge by political slogans in school textbooks which works towards stunting the mind; and by the day after it will be the assertion of control over citizens which can seriously impinge on the quality of our lives.

# 50

# The Politics of Religious Communities*

There was a popular belief at the time of Partition in 1947, that the division of the country would end the communal tension as those in favour of a separate Muslim state would migrate to Pakistan. This in part accounts for the slogan voiced these days that all Muslims are the progeny of Pakistan and should go there. Such an attitude arises from an erroneous understanding of what the partition of India was about and, more than that, a failure to comprehend the complexities of a multi-religious society. That the solution to communal conflict did not lie in religion-based states was evident from the rapidity with which East Pakistan broke away as Bangla Desh and by the frequency of violent confrontations between variously defined groups in Pakistan. The fact that in every case the involvement is of members belonging to the same religious community, Islam, does not reduce the tension or the violence.

The notion of the religious community being the unit of modern political functioning has its roots in the 19th century. Not only did the British perceive Indian society in terms of religious communities, as is evident also from Indological scholarship on the subject, but this perception was later projected into political representation as well with the notion of separate electorates defined by religion. The acceptance of separate electorates by Indians was an indication of the social and political disparity being by then perceived as a religious one.

For colonial purposes there were two main communities. The larger, which they referred to as the majority community, was an amorphous mass to which they applied the label of Hindu (and this included Buddhists, Jainas and Sikhs), and the others, the minority

* Seminar No. 365, January, 1990, 27–32.

communities, were the more easily defined Muslims and Christians. Included among minorities were what later came to be called the Scheduled Castes and Scheduled Tribes, a nomenclature derived from constitutional usage. The term minority community at that time referred generally to the Muslims. Today we have to speak of minority communities in which the Sikhs also feature.

Societies define themselves by their own perception of what they think constitute social units. In India the notion of religious communities was picked up and reinforced and was graded into majority and minority communities. It is debatable whether what constitutes the Hindu community today was in fact a consciously recognised community in the Indian subcontinent in pre-modern times. It has been argued that the very nature of 'Hinduism' in the past, its flexibility and the identity of belief and ritual with various castes, precluded the idea of a single, closed community characteristic of Semitic religions. There were in pre-modern times a conglomerate of communities, identified by language, caste and ritual, occasionally overlapping in one or the other of these features but rarely presenting a uniform, universalising form. What is often mistaken for uniformity, namely brahmanical culture, was only the culture of the elite.

In the attempt to make inter-caste functioning more cohesive and mould social groups into larger entities, the notion of religious communities has been an acceptable alternative over the last century. The opposition to substituting caste by religious community has been a source of major ideological conflict both within the national movement and since. This is not to suggest that one should return to caste identities, but rather to understand that the notion of the religious community is not embedded in the foundations of Indian civilisation.

The posing of secularism against communalism did not at one level face the issue squarely. It was, and is, not enough to negate the emphasis of religious identity in public life; it is equally necessary to encourage other alternative identities. These can also be sought from more analytical studies of the past where the nuances and sensitivities of a variety of inter-community relationships need to be investigated and understood. There was also a lulling of the fears aroused in the 1940s by communalism with the adoption of a constitution in the subsequent decade where secularism was given importance and by the constant reiterating of the *mantra* of secularism, particularly at the level of the state, without vigilantly ensuring that it was being put into practice.

The centrality of communalism in our lives today, as witnessed in November 1989, is now being more widely discussed than before largely because of the political success of the BJP in the last election. Yet for those who have been stating for some years that communalism is on the rise and who have been dismissed as alarmists in the past, this is not surprising. It has, however, required a political demonstration for there to be a recognition of a change which goes beyond politics. The BJP, as of the recent election, also represents the ideological right wing in politics and it is this combination which is perhaps the more startling although not unexpected. It would, however, be of interest to see whether the BJP will go the whole communal way and continue to support the demands of the Vishva Hindu Parishad or whether the taste of power will encourage it to maintain at least a small distance from the VHP.

What is more disturbing is the increasing communalisation of Indian society where various religious identities are now in confrontation, predominantly Hindu, Muslim and Sikh; where religious identities are being deliberately reiterated, irrespective of whether such a reiteration is relevant or not. The seminal period of these communalisms is not the present, for they each have roots in the immediate past. More evident on the social and political landscape are the various *shakhas, senas, parishads* and *sammelans*, the Leagues, the *Jamats* and Allah's Tigers, not to mention the Damdami Taksal — each of which has at its core an aggressive, narrow, political concern which is articulated in religious terms.

The state, during the last few years, has lent itself to the politics of these groups in attempts to manipulate them, instead of exposing them. Slogans on city walls carry the messages of these groups. Where the more aggressive among them go further and appropriate state space, the state has pretended apathy, where apathy means connivance. The Congress-I is now taking a 'holier than thou' attitude in its public opposition to communalism, but it has failed to explain what it was doing during the riots in Delhi, Meerut, Bidar, Bhagalpur and other places, when it was in control of the state machinery and was unable to protect citizens. When the representatives of the state, who are supposed to be impartial protectors of the citizens, become participants in the riots, then either the state has to take action against them or else it is to be understood that they have the backing of the state.

The growth of communalism is not merely the result of governments which at best have been unable to contain it and at worst have tried to use it to remain in power. As an ideology, communalism has a wider appeal and it is also other situations that have given it encouragement. Communalism has to be seen for what it is: an intermeshing of ideology and power, where groups aspiring to power use a particular religious ideology to subvert a social order and replace it with an order that is based on sharp differentiations between those who accept the ideology and those who do not. It also places power in the hands of the authors of that ideology. This combination of a religious ideology and power enables such groups to define social practice and law apart from symbols and belief, all of which condition the ensuing social order.

In a multi-religious society attempts are sometimes made to introduce ascendancy through other channels, such as claims to racial superiority as among those who claim to be Aryans, or civilisational continuity which is deliberately defined largely in terms of ritual and belief, eliminating or ignoring other aspects which go into the making of a civilisation and thereby also marginalising those who do not observe that particular ritual and belief. Such channels are diversionary for the centrality of action remains the intertwining of the particular religious ideology and power.

The major springs of communal support are from those who are in some ways disembodied from their earlier social moorings: the growing middle class of those whose standard of living materially has risen and who see themselves as having to modernise without being fully aware of the implications of this process; who see modernisation as westernisation and therefore an implicit contradiction between what they have been taught to think of as 'traditional' and what they believe is modern and who therefore think they are establishing a 'traditional identity by supporting the new religious movements. In the same way they adopt the outer trappings of western modes and assume that this makes them 'modern'.

The insistence on a dichotomy between 'traditional' and 'modern' confuses the understanding of tradition, which is, in effect, a continual process of selecting from the past, both consciously and sub-consciously. Part of the flotsam and jetsam which gets carried into the communal stream are the erstwhile princelings who have lost both status and power and seek to find a new status as purveyors of a disappearing world. The leadership of some fundamentalist groups and communal organisations includes smugglers and drug peddlers, the kind of clientele which has also found its way into political parties. Where the religious 'cause' is highlighted, it becomes an attempt at whitewashing other activities. This in turn encourages the criminal elements already present on the political scene, who can be relied upon to start a communal riot as and when required.

Aspirations to wealth and status, whether among lower caste artisans some of whom have improved professional prospects with new openings or among the middle class moving into new professions, bring with them intense competition and consequent insecurity. Apprehensive of how to remain on top, as it were, of these changing prospects, it often becomes necessary to search for either a prescription or a scapegoat. The prescription seems to lie in talismans, in what is depicted even in the most elitist advertisements — the wearing of *mouli* threads and *monga* rings to avert the evil eye; the scapegoat is often found in the members of the other community who are seen as competitors. In the recent riots in the Bhagalpur area, the main victims seem to have been the Muslim weavers.

Added to this is the aspiration to political power. Secularism in India has been converted into a system by which a particular party could draw on the votes of the minority community (initially only the Muslims), and the Harijans as they were then called. In the recent elections the Sikh vote has also become part of this process. Democracy is seen as a numbers game. Mobilisation is therefore crucial and draws on religious communities. The recent mobilisation by the VHP through the making of bricks and the *shila-pujas* and processions where riots became an assertion of power, combined both religious and political mobilisation in a manner which has so far been unprecedented. Should this become the vehicle for political mobilisation then the future is frightening.

If the initial appeal of communal ideology is apparent among the prosperous middle class, it does not rest there, for the politicalisation of religion requires mobilisation on a large scale. Unlike the RSS whose leading figures tended to be from the upper castes, the Vishva Hindu Parishad draws on a wider group for leadership extending to what would earlier have been regarded as middle castes and to professional classes. Its missionary programme of converting Dalits and tribals to Hinduism (inspite of 'conversion' being alien to earlier forms of Hinduism) will serve a double purpose should it succeed: it will increase the numbers of those who can be called Hindus and it will reduce the numbers involved in the policy of reservation.

This policy as applied in education and in employment for Scheduled Castes and Tribes has been a source of considerable resentment on the part of caste Hindus who regard it as a threat to their opportunities for upward mobility. Built into this kind of communalism therefore is the implicit factor of keeping the Dalits oppressed, for even if the policy of reservation is dropped, any concessions made to Dalits will be resented. The fear of the lower castes breaking away from the status defined for them by the upper castes and attaining a better status is endemic to caste society. It has been recorded even in the past in what may be called the crisis of the Kaliyuga. On repeated occasions from the first millennium AD onwards there have been descriptions of the evils of the Kaliyuga where the rise of the lower castes is seen as evidence of the world being turned upside down.

Equally implicit in communalism is the place of women, which, drawing from the conservative interpretation of ancient texts and social codes, such as the *dharmaśāstras* and the *shariat*, forecloses possibilities of independent action. The religious ideology in communalism has to be defined for contemporary times and in its representation of the universal values of ancient times it requires that women be subordinated. Such subordination, often characteristic of those in power, provided the illusion of complete authority. The reality could often be very different in other segments of society, but these realities find no place in communal ideology. Whether it is the endorsement of the ritual death of a *sati* or the denial of maintenance to a divorced Muslim woman, the underlying statement is that of subordination. That a woman must know her place and stay within its bounds, is also seen as the solution to the problem of the independent woman staking new claims of status on a society in the process of change.

The projection of the past in terms of communal history, namely that the history of India is to be seen as the glory of the ancient period when Hinduism was in the ascendant and its decline during the medieval period when that place was taken by Islam, continues to be the simplistic view of Hindu communal groups. The variation is that Muslim communalists see the period of Islamic dominance as the period of glory and Sikh communalists perceive their relations with the Mughal state entirely in terms of the religious confrontation between Muslim and Sikh. The appeal to history for legitimation by communal groups is in effect a red herring. The issue is not that of the historical correctness of the claim, for the claims being made are in fact political and relate to the society of today. But by reiterating a communal history, justification is sought for trying to undo the past by communal actions in the present. A communal interpretation of the past, even where clearly untenable, is useful for whipping up hysteria in mobilising a community.

If, however, history is to be brought into the controversy, then communal interpretations of history have to come to terms with many facts which are now conveniently ignored. It has to be conceded that there has been intolerance and persecution of religious sects not just under Muslim rulers but also under Hindu rulers and by powerful Hindu groups even in pre-Islamic times. The evidence of Shaivite persecution of Buddhists and Jainas is conveniently ignored, even though it involved some killing of monks and the desecration of temples and religious sites. The very notion of untouchability is an extreme form of intolerance and persecution. Will the Hindus of today first come to terms with their own intolerance before rushing to set right the intolerance of others from the past?

The bulk of the conversions to Islam were not by force of arms but under the influence of Sufis and other religious teachers and these conversions were frequently by *jāti* where an entire caste or professional group would convert. This raises questions about the nature of Hindu society and what might have encouraged conversions. Relations between groups in society even if identified by religious practice and belief, are never simplistically black-and-white. The evidence on such relations in the past and the analysis of this evidence by present-day historians suggests a very different interpretation from that which was current fifty years ago. But inspite of historians constantly reiterating this change, the old theories still hold in the popular mind.

The refusal to recognise that historical analyses have changed our image of the past stems from the refusal on the part of the mediators of knowledge (both the educational system and the media) to first read and then pronounce. It is far easier to go on mouthing old ideas even if these are unacceptable to historians. The old cliche of Muslim rulers being bigots to a greater or lesser degree, continues to be repeated despite the work which has been done on their policies, suggesting a far more historically complex context for such policies. This is not a question, for instance, of Hindus being more aware of Aurangzeb but of Aurangzeb being consistently depicted only in one form.

The media is not altogether innocent in fostering communalism. The fashion for glitter and tinsel as news and the underlining of the need for media hype has resulted in an obsession with instant stories focusing on the view of anybody and anything as long as it can be presented as news. Thoughtful commentaries are dismissed as too academic for the press and Doordarshan, with a few exceptions, has been largely concerned only with projecting the lowest common denominator both in politics and in 'culture'. It is therefore not surprising that the definition of culture assumes that Indian society consists in the main of caste Hindus transmuting into a middle class. The success stories of Doordarshan are seemingly endless serials portraying narratives linked to Vaiṣṇava worship which are sought to be projected as the national culture of India. At least if the aesthetic qualities of the original had been sought to be conveyed it might have mitigated the religious propaganda.

The fostering of communalism in some cases requires the issuing of *fatwas* and *hukumnamas*. Alternatively, riots are made the excuse to damage if not destroy the religious sites of those one is rioting against and this ensures a continuing hostility. Frequently such sites or others which become the focus of dispute are in the centre of urban areas and therefore, as property, extremely valuable. The acquisition or control of such sites becomes an economic asset as well. But communalism can also spread in a far more subtle manner in the gradual building up of hostile feelings against other communities which results in a sub-conscious discrimination. It is strange that inspite of the large numbers of educated Muslims, few seem to reach the upper echelons of government. A creeping discrimination against the Sikhs is also becoming noticeable.

There is of course in addition the involvement of the Indian diaspora with some facets of communalism. The Vishva Hindu Parishad receives extensive support, financial and otherwise, from

Indians settled in the United States, Canada and Britain, as indeed do Sikh communal organisations from equivalent bodies in these countries. Centres of the VHP in Britain have received hefty monetary donations from official British agencies on the grounds that the VHP is a purely cultural organisation. Muslim communal organisations are said to receive support from the wealthy in west Asia as well.

Financial support is not, however, the only encouragement to such organisations. The question of identity is crucial to Indians in the diaspora, for in the world of Europe and north America they are the minority groups in an alien culture. Yet they have to come to terms with this insecure situation and their solution is the attempt to assert their identity by recourse to mobilisation on the basis of a religious idiom. Their minority character in foreign lands isolates them and they frequently seek unity in religious organisations, trying to combine a western life-style with 'traditional' religion. Such groups become the role-model for upwardly mobile middle class Indians who, with economic improvement, are in any case able to maintain close contacts with segments of their families who have settled abroad.

The existence of the diaspora has implications for the growth of communalism in India. The obvious form this takes is comments from groups and organisations and even governments outside India. When Muslims outside India and governments of Islamic states condemn riots in India where Muslims are killed, this is objected to as outside interference. However, as long as Indian society continues to define itself only in terms of religious communities, members of such communities living outside India will comment on the situation in India. And perhaps there will be more than comment. In August 1989 a Ram Janmabhoomi *sammelan* was held in London, and bricks intended for Ayodhyā were worshipped by British citizens, both white and those of Indian origin. Such activities, particularly by the former, are seen not as interference but as welcome endorsement.

The Ram Janmabhoomi issue has been in the nature of a time bomb. It has ticked for 40 years, since 1949 when the so-called miracle of the images appearing in the mosque was fabricated, before exploding. This initial step in the drama was taken after communal tension had reached a peak with the creation of Pakistan. The reviving up of the tension towards an explosive climax was encouraged by the general growth of communal identities over the years and by the closeness of the elections.

Are there other similar time bombs still ticking which will explode in the years to come? Such explosions can only be diffused if the state takes a firm stand on the Ram Janmabhoomi issue and does not make concessions to communal politics. The BJP has already declared that, 'Such issues cannot be resolved by court verdicts' (Times of India, 7 December 1989). This inspite of the fact that the site being claimed is located on disputed land. The VHP has announced that its next campaign will be to agitate for the destruction of the mosques at Mathura and Varanasi.

It is therefore now possible for any group to organise itself, gain some political leverage, and proceed to occupy prime urban sites in the name of religion. Once the Muslims, the Sikhs, the Christians, the Jainas and the Neo-Buddhists get into the act, there will be complete pandemonium in both urban centres and at archaeological sites, not to mention those which are also places of tourist interest. This is already beginning with Muslim groups attempting to reclaim for worship mosques which have been desanctified and which are under the protection of the Archaeological Survey. The acquisition of the Ram Janmabhoomi will be quoted as precedent and the outcome can only be violence worse than what has been witnessed so far.

If the redressal of believed wrongs of the past become the right of religious communities, then temples located at the sites sacred to other religions will also have to be destroyed although, with the predominance of Hindu communalism other religious communities might hesitate to make such a demand. What, for instance, is to happen to the temple at the supposed Krishna Janmabhoomi which is built at the site of Katra in Mathura and which, according to one authority, was the site of a Buddhist religious complex and could therefore be claimed by the Buddhists? How far back in history will we have to go in order to satisfy the politics of religious communities?

It is not election results alone which will condition the future of communalism in India. If the reasons for the rise of communalism are understood, then it becomes clear that it is not religious sentiment which is at stake, but the exploitation of this sentiment at a moment in time when there is apprehension about the present and the future. The apprehension has to be reduced and the easy slipping into religious identities as social units has to be questioned.

Alternative identities will undoubtedly emerge with the growing strength of lower caste and Dalit movements as also with the demands of Scheduled Tribes for greater representation and statehood. There are already movements in this direction which tend to be overshadowed by the immanence of communal violence. What Hindu communalism fails to recognise is that at the end of the road there is not going to be a dominance of the majority community because inspite of its supposed uniformity at present, given that the real objective is the acquisition of power, it too will split into contending groups.

The fundamental change which is taking place in the form of Hinduism, which has been variously described as New Hinduism or, as I would prefer, Syndicated Hinduism, will eliminate the very flexibility which allowed the *sanatana dharma* to survive over these many centuries. From a religious form that had the openness of Upanishadic philosophy it is now being reduced to the worship of bricks. Its aggressive militancy belies its earlier claims to tolerance and non-violence. When Hindu *mahantas* refer to themselves as *imams* and talk about issuing *fatwas* as happened recently in connection with the election of a member of the Ramjanmabhoomi Mukti Yajna Samiti, and when reference is made to ostracising non-believers, then the divorce from earlier Hinduism is complete.

The support of a religion as a form of the articulation of religious sentiments, beliefs and practices is not under question. The objection is to the manipulation of such identities for the purposes of political mobilisation, where the manipulation requires violence and aggression and destruction in order to succeed. In this latter sense religious communities are imagined communities and it is therefore possible to change them. In the search for identities as alternative to the notion of the religious community for purposes of political mobilisation, liberalisation in all such communities will have to proceed at the same pace. Minority insecurity underlies their conservatism and hesitancy to change. Civil codes and criminal laws will have to be common.

There is a difference between the communalism of the majority and that of the minorities. The former is often born of an aggressive assertion of power. The latter is born of fear and a sense of powerlessness in the face of the majority. In a society which sees itself as a conglomerate of religious communities, the onus for removing this fear lies with the majority community. Enhanced communalism can make communalism the only form of political dialogue. In each case communalism suppresses the aspirations of other groups as indeed of dissident groups within the community since it is based on the fundamental assumption that the believers are superior to the rest — be it a Pakistan, a Khalistan or a Hindu Rashtra — and the believers are defined by those who have created the communal ideology. Its removal therefore becomes a necessity.

But such qualifications do not mitigate the existence of either the majority or the minority communalisms, for neither is justified. The fight is not only against the dominance of Hindu communalism asserting itself amidst a range of minority communities, but also the need within each community to marginalise the communal elements. This would be imperative if there is to be an alternative to the politics of religious communities.

# 51

# *The Theory of Aryan Race and India: History and Politics**

The invention of an Aryan race in nineteenth century Europe was to have, as we all know, far-reaching consequences on world history. Its application to European societies culminated in the ideology of Nazi Germany. Another sequel was that it became foundational to the interpretation of early Indian history and the there have been attempts at a literal application of the theory to Indian society. Some European scholars now describe it as a nineteenth century myth.[1] But some contemporary Indian political ideologies seem determined to renew its life. In this they are assisted by those who still carry the imprint of this nineteenth century theory and treat it as central to the question of Indian identity. With the widespread discussion on 'Aryan origins' in the print media and the controversy over its treatment in school textbooks, it has become the subject of a larger debate in terms of its ideological underpinnings rather than merely the differing readings among archaeologists and historians.

I intend to begin by briefly sketching the emergence of the theory in Europe, in which the search for the Indian past also played a role. I would like to continue with various Indian interpretations of the theory which have been significant to the creation of modern Indian identities and to nationalism. Finally, I would like to review the major archaeological and literary evidence which questions the historical interpretations of the theory and implicitly also its political role.[2]

It was initially both curiosity and the colonial requirement of

* This is an expanded version of the text of a lecture delivered at the 40th International Conference of Eastern Studies in Tokyo, 26 May 1995. The text is reproduced with the permission of the Toho Gakkai, the sponsor of the Conference.

knowledge about their subject peoples, that led the officers of the East India Company serving in India to explore the history and culture of the colony which they were governing. The time was the late eighteenth century. Not only had the awareness of new worlds entered the consciousness of Europe, but knowledge as an aspect of the Enlightenment was thought to provide access to power. Governing a colony involved familiarity with what had preceded the arrival of the colonial power on the Indian scene. The focus therefore was on languages, law and religion. The belief that history was essential to this knowledge was thwarted by the seeming absence of histories of early India. That the beginnings of Indian history would have to be rediscovered through European methods of historical scholarship, with an emphasis on chronology and sequential narrative, became the challenge.

These early explorations were dominated by the need to construct a chronology for the Indian past. Attempts were made to trace parallels with Biblical theories and chronology. But the exploration with the maximum potential lay in the study of languages and particularly Sanskrit. Similarities between Greek and Latin and Sanskrit, noticed even earlier, were clinched with William Jones' reading of Sandracottos as Chandragupta. Two other developments took place. One was the suggestion of a monogenesis or single origin of all related languages, an idea which was extended to the speakers of the languages as well.[3] The second was the emergence of comparative philology, which aroused considerable interest, especially after the availability of Vedic texts in the early nineteenth century. Vedic studies were hospitably received in Europe where there was already both enthusiasm for or criticism of, Indian culture. German romanticism and the writings of Herder and Schlegel suggested that the roots of human history might go back to these early beginnings recorded in Sanskrit texts.[4] James Mill on the other hand, had a different view in his highly influential *History of British India*, where he described India as backward and stagnant and Hindu civilization as inimical to progress.[5]

Comparative philologists, such as E. Burnouf and F. Bopp were primarily interested in the technicalities of language. Vedic Sanskrit, as the earliest form of Sanskrit, had primacy. Monogenesis was strengthened with the notion of an ancestral language, Indo-Germanic or Indo-European as it came to be called, as also in the origins of some European languages and their speakers being traced back to Iran and India or still further, to a central Asian homeland. Europe was on the edge of an Oriental Renaissance for it was believed that yet another Renaissance might follow, this time from the 'discovery' of the Orient, and thus taking knowledge into yet other directions.[6] The scholars associated with these studies and therefore with interpreting the Indian past, were generally based in Europe and had no direct experience of India.

The latter part of the nineteenth century witnessed discussions on the interrelatedness of language, culture and race, and the notion of biological race came to the forefront.[7] The experience of imperialism where the European 'races' were viewed as advanced, and those of the colonised, as 'lesser breeds', reinforced these identities, as did social Darwinism.

Prominent among these identities was Aryan, used both for the language and the race, as current in the mid-nineteenth century.[8] Aryan was derived from the Old Iranian *airiia* used in the Zoroastrian text, the *Avesta*, and was a cognate of the Sanskrit *ārya*. Gobineau, who attempted to identify the races of Europe as Aryan and non-Aryan with an intrusion of the Semitic, associated the Aryans with the sons of Noah but emphasised the superiority of the white race and was fearful about the bastardisation of this race.[9] The study of craniology which became important at this time began to question the wider identity of the Aryan. It was discovered that the speakers of Indo-European languages were represented by diverse skull types. This was in part responsible for a new turn to the theory in the suggestion that the European Aryans were distinct from the Asian Aryans.[10] The former were said to be indigenous to Europe while the latter had their homeland in Asia. If the European Aryans were indigenous to northern Europe then the Nordic blonde was the prototype Aryan. Such theories liberated the origins of European civilisation from being embedded in Biblical history. They also had the approval of rationalist groups opposed to the Church, and supportive of Enlightenment thinking.

The application of these ideas to Indian origins was strengthened by Max Müller's work on Sanskrit and Vedic studies and in particular his editing of the *Ṛgveda* during the years from 1849 to 1874. He ascribed the importance of this study to his belief that the *Ṛgveda* was the most ancient literature of the world, providing evidence of the roots of Indo-Aryan and the key to Hinduism. Together with the *Avesta* it formed the earliest stratum of Indo-European.

Max Müller maintained that there was an original Aryan homeland in central Asia. He postulated a small Aryan clan on a high elevation in central Asia, speaking a language which was not yet Sanskrit or Greek, a kind of proto-language ancestral to later Indo-European languages. From here and over the course of some centuries, it branched off in two directions; one came towards Europe and the other migrated to Iran, eventually splitting again with one segment invading north-western India.[11] The common origin of the Aryans was for him unquestioned.

The northern Aryans who are said to have migrated to Europe are described by Max Müller as active and combative and they developed the idea of a nation, while the southern Aryans who migrated to Iran and to India were passive and meditative, concerned with religion and philosophy. This description is still quoted for the inhabitants of India and has even come to be a cliché in the minds of many.

The Aryans, according to Max Müller were fair-complexioned Indo-European speakers who conquered the dark-skinned *dāsas* of India. The *ārya-varṇa* and the *dāsa-varṇa* of the *Ṛgveda* were understood as two conflicting groups differentiated particularly by skin colour, but also by language and religious practice, which doubtless underlined the racial interpretation of the terms. The Aryas developed Vedic Sanskrit as their language. The Dasas were the indigenous people, of Scythian origin, whom he called Turanians. The Aryan and the non-Aryan were segregated through the instituting of caste. The upper castes and particularly the *brāhmaṇas* of modern times were said to be of Aryan descent and the lower castes and untouchables and tribes were descended from the Dasas. Max Müller popularised the use of the term Aryan in the Indian context, arguing that it was originally a national name and later came to mean a person of good family. As was common in the nineteenth century, he used a number of words interchangeably such as Hindu and Indian, or race/nation/people/blood/ — words whose meanings would today be carefully differentiated.

Having posited the idea of a common origin for the languages included as Indo-European and among which was Indo-Aryan, common origin was extended to the speakers of these languages. Aryan therefore, although specifically a label for a language, came to be used for a people and a race as well, the argument being that those who spoke the same language belonged to the same biological race. In a lecture delivered later at Strassburg in 1872, Max Müller denied any link between language and race. In spite of this, he continued to confuse the two as is evident from his description of Raja Ram Mohan Roy in an Address delivered in 1883.

Ram Mohan Roy was an Arya belonging to the south-eastern branch of the Aryan race and he spoke an Aryan language, the Bengali . . . We recognise in Ram Mohan Roy's visit to England the meeting again of the two great branches of the Aryan race, after they had been separated so long that they had lost all recollection of their common origin, common language and common faith.[12]

The sliding from language to race became general to contemporary thinking. An equally erroneous equation was the identification of Dravidian languages with a Dravidian race.[13]

This reconstruction of what was believed to be Aryan history, supercedes the initial Orientalist search of Biblical parallels or connections with early Indian history. There was now a focus on common origins with Europe, untouched by the intervention of the Semitic peoples and language. As an Aryan text the *Ṛgveda* is said to be free from any taint of Semitic contact. Nor do the *Purāṇas* which were significant to Orientalist reconstructions of the past, enter Max Müller's discourse for whom they were not only later but were in comparison, second order knowledge. The *Purāṇas*, in their descriptions of the past, do not endorse an *ārya-dāsa* separation in a manner which could be interpreted as different races. There was also an exclusion of anything Islamic in Max Müller's definition of the Indian. He refers to the tyranny of Mohammedan rule in India without explaining why he thought it was so.

The theory of Aryan race became endemic to the reconstruction of Indian history and the reasons for this are varied. The pre-eminence given to the role of the *brāhmaṇas* in the Orientalist construction of Indology was endorsed by the centrality of the *Vedas*. The Aryan theory also provided the colonised with status and self-esteem, arguing that they were linguistically and racially of the same stock as the colonisers. However, the separation of the European Aryans from the Asian Aryans was in effect a denial of this status. Such a denial was necessary in the view of those who proposed a radical structuring of colonial society through new legislation and administration, and in accordance with the conversion of the colony into a viable source of revenue. The complexities of caste were simplified in its being explained as racial segregation, demarcating the Aryan from the others.[14] And finally, it made Indian origins relevant to the current perceptions dominating European thought and these perceptions were believed to be 'scientific' explanations.

Max Müller's books were read in India and his views were endorsed in various influential publications, such as John Muir's *Original Sanskrit Texts* (1858–1863) and John Wilson's *Indian Caste* (1877). Both authors were Christian missionaries and drew attention to the plight of the low castes, oppressed by *brāhmaṇas*, an oppression which they claimed went back to the Aryan invasions. They referred to the conflict of the *ārya* with the non-*āryas*. The term *ārya* was used as a patronymic referring to the Aryan people. They launched an attack on the inequities of caste and therefore of Hinduism and maintained that Christianity alone could bring these to an end.

Missionary views in the later half of the nineteenth century were familiar to many Indians. Among these, Jyotiba Phule provided a radical exposition of the Aryan theory. He viewed caste relations as relations of inequality, where society had been divided into a hierarchy of ranked castes. By emphasising the importance of the non-Aryans he used the theory of Aryan race to argue a different origin and status for the lower castes. Referred to as the *dāsas* and the *śūdras* in brahmanical texts, the lower castes were, according to him, the indigenous people. They were the rightful inheritors of the land, whose rights had been wrongfully appropriated by the invading Aryan, and who had subjugated them and reduced them to a lower caste status.[15] The immediate context was for him the recent Peshwa rule in western India and the confrontation between the *brāhmaṇas* and the non-*brāhmaṇas*. The *brāhmaṇas* were Aryan and therefore alien and the indigenous peoples were the *ṣūdras* and others, whom he labelled as *kṣatriyas*. The argument ran that the golden age was prior to the invasion of the Aryans when King Bali ruled and what are now the lower castes were then in the ascendant. The invasion of the Aryans was crucial to the creation of segregated groups in the form of castes, where the Aryans were the victorious aliens who kept the indigenous people permanently subordinated. He used to good effect the well-known myth of the *brāhmaṇa* Paraṣurāma destroying the *kṣatriyas*, in this construction of the past. Phule's radicalisation of the theory was popular among the lower castes and became central to many non-Brahmin movements in other parts of peninsular India. By stating that the upper castes were not indigenous, the theory was used to exclude the upper caste dominated middle class claiming an Aryan identity. From Phule's perspective, the theory endorsed a confrontation of castes.

The upper-castes had their own use for the theory and it was again given a twist which suited their social aspirations and political needs. The views of Phule were generally ignored. The theory was used to argue the superiority of the upper castes and promote their self-esteem by maintaining that not only were the upper-castes the lineal descendants of the Aryans but that they were also racially related to the European Aryan. Keshab Chunder Sen follows Max Müller and John Wilson in his statement that, '. . . in the advent of the English nation in India we see a reunion of parted cousins, the descendants of two different families of the ancient Aryan race.'[16] B.G. Tilak endorsed the antiquity of the *Ṛgveda* by taking it back to 4500 BC, much earlier than the 1500 BC suggested by Max Müller, basing his argument on what he interpreted as references to planetary positions.[17] Influenced by the theory of a Nordic homeland for the Aryans, Tilak suggested that they had migrated from the Arctic regions in the post-glacial age and then branched off, with one group going to Europe and the other coming to India.[18] The European Aryans according to him relapsed into barbarism but the Indian Aryans retained their original, superior civilisation which they re-established on conquering the non-Aryans of India. The introduction of geology into the argument was also seen as supporting an early date for the *Ṛgveda*.[19] Tilak's view were known to Max Müller who of course did not agree with him but was incidentally, helpful in getting Tilak released from jail when he was incarcerated for nationalist activities.

Dayananda Sarasvati, seeking to return to the social and religious life of the *Vedas*, used the Vedic corpus as the blueprint of his vision of Indian society.[20] But he argued that the *Vedas* are the source of all knowledge including modern science, a view with which Max Müller disagreed. He underlined the linguistic and racial purity of the Aryans and the organisation which he founded, the Arya Samaj, was described by its followers as 'the society of the Aryan race'. The Aryas were the upper castes and the untouchables were excluded. The innovation, or according to some the revival, of, the ritual called *Śuddhi* or purification made it possible for those converted to other religions to be accepted back as caste Hindus. The same ritual, but with less frequency, was also used to 'purify' those outside caste, into being given a caste status. For Dayananda, it was said, castes were merely different professions or guilds established by the state and therefore the *de jure* status could change. A change in the *de facto* status had to be ordered by the state or by society regulating itself.[21] This was his reply to the criticism that he wanted to retain caste as practiced in the *Vedas*, despite its being projected as a rigid system in the *Sūtra* texts.

These views coincided with the emergence of nationalism in the late nineteenth century in India, articulated mainly by the middle class, which was drawn from the upper caste and was seeking both legitimacy and an identity from the past. Origins therefore became crucial. To legitimise the status of the middle class, its superior Aryan origins and lineal descent was emphasised. It was assumed that only the upper caste Hindu could claim Aryan ancestry. This effectively excluded not only the lower castes but also the non-Hindus, even those of some social standing. Aryanism therefore became an exclusive status. In the dialogue between the early nationalists and the colonial power, a theory of common origins strengthening a possible link between the colonisers and the Indian elite came in very useful. For early nationalism, Aryan and non-Aryan differentiation was of an ethnic and racial kind, but was also beginning to touch implicitly on class differentiation.

Sympathetic to nationalism in India were the views of the Theosophical Society which changed the theory to suit its own premises. A prominent member of the Society, Col. Olcott[22] maintained that not only were the Aryans (equated with the Hindus) indigenous to India but that they were also the progenitors of European civilisation. Theosophical views emerged out of what was believed to be an aura of oriental religions and particularly Hinduism, as also the supposed dichotomy between the spiritualism of India and the materialism of Europe. The romanticising of India included viewing its civilisation as providing a counter-point to an industrialising Europe obsessed with rationalism, both of which were seen as eroding the European quality of life.

The theosophical reading of the Aryan theory was echoed in the interpretation of the theory by Hindu nationalist opinion. A group of people, close to and involved with the founding of the R.S.S. (Rashtriya Svayamsevaka Sangha) and writing in the early twentieth century, developed the concept of Hindutva or Hinduness and argued that this was essential to the identity of the Indian.[23] Since Hinduness in the past did not have a specific definition, the essentials of a Hindu identity had to be formulated. The argument ran that the original Hindus were the Aryans, a distinctive people indigenous to India. Caste Hindus or Hindu Aryas are their descendants. There was no Aryan invasion since the Aryans were indigenous to India and therefore no confrontation among the people of India. The Aryans spoke Sanskrit and were responsible for the spread of Aryan civilisation from India to the west. Confrontations came with the arrival of foreigners such as the Muslims, the Christians and more recently, the Communists. These groups are alien because India is neither the *pitṛbhūmi* — the land of their birth — the assumption being that all Muslims and Christians are from outside India, nor the *punyabhūmi* — their holy land. Hindu Aryas have had to constantly battle against these foreigners. Influenced by European theories of race of the 1920's and 1930's, parallels were drawn between the European differentiation of Aryans and Semites with the Indian differentiation of Hindus and Muslims. Justifying the treatment of the Jews in Germany, the threat of the same fate was held out to the Muslims in India.

The Hindutva version of the theory became a mechanism for excluding some sections of Indian society, specifically Indian Muslims and Christians, by insisting that they are alien. Inevitably it also ran into problems with the lower castes and the untouchables, who propagated Jyotiba Phule's view. There was a certain ambiguity among the Hindutva group as to whether or not the untouchables were Hindus and therefore Aryans. This posed the problem that if only caste Hindus are Aryans then the untouchables would have to be excluded, and this reduces the numerical count of Hindus; whereas, if the lower castes and Dalits are included as Hindus, then although this may upset some caste Hindus nevertheless the numbers listed as Hindu increases the Hindu constitution of the majority. The question of numbers also influenced the insistence that the Aryans are indigenous and not invaders. Such an increase in numbers is important to political mobilisation and to the assertion that since Hindus constitute the majority in India, it should be declared a Hindu state. The identity and origins of the

Hindus was seen as crucial to the identity of the nation of the Hindus and of the nation-state. From this perspective, it is emphasised that the national identity has to focus on the antiquity and continuity of the Hindu Arya as the major component of the Hindu nation. This inevitably brings historians and archaeologists into a debate which is at one level about history but also touches on questions of political ideologies and national identities.

Mainstream historians writing on ancient India did not accept the Hindutva version of the theory. Going back to the views of Max Müller they began their narrative with the coming of the invading Aryans. The *Vedas* therefore came to be seen as the foundational texts of Indian civilisation. With the growing influence of nationalism in the writing of Indian history, Max Müller was seen as sympathetic and positive in his reading of the Indian past. The idyllic Indian lost in philosophic speculation could have been viewed as a condescending image, but in fact was appreciated. Indian historians were themselves largely from the upper castes and not averse to the highlighting of their own status. The acceptance of the Aryan theory underlined the Hindu idiom in nationalist historical writing. The Aryans were eulogised for laying the foundation of a civilisation thought to be at least equal, if not superior, to most others.

The discussion on caste as we have seen, also incorporated the Aryan theory. Caste as racial segregation, separating the upper caste Aryans from the lower caste non-Aryans, was viewed as a scientific way of organising society in keeping with modern ideas, but this view was gradually discarded when there was evidence to the contrary. The Christian missionary criticism of caste was partially conceded by referring to the extreme rigidity of caste. This became a way of explaining the weakness of Indian society, particularly in its confrontation with Islam and 'in the face of Muslim invasions', for it was said that caste was divisive and the Hindus could not unite to meet the threat. But it was also argued that caste saved Hinduism from being absorbed into other religions such as Islam and helped maintain its continuing identity. There were only a very few analyses where caste was seen to have its own history of change and adaptation. Moralising on the evils of caste precluded the need to see it as an agency of power, dominance and subordination, or to recognise the large area of flexible negotiation which, to some degree, permitted certain castes to shape their status. For example, families of obscure origin and some even said to be of the lower castes, rose to political power and many legitimised their power by successfully claiming upper caste *kṣatriya* status.[24] To concede these facts would have contradicted the theory that the upper castes are the lineal descendants of the Aryans.

This varied exploitation of the theory received a jolt with the archaeological discovery of the Indus civilisation. The excavation of the cites of Harappa and Mohenjo-daro in the 1920's and subsequent excavations in India and Pakistan, revealing an extensive urban culture in the northern and western parts of the Indian subcontinent, created problems for the Aryan theory. Being predominantly urban, the Indus culture in distinctively different from the pastoral-agrarian society described in the Vedic texts.[25] The *Vedas* are primarily ritual texts and their depiction of society is ancillary to their main purpose. The archaeological evidence, more specific on data relating to the environment, technology and economy, covers a much wider area and goes further back in time. It has become therefore the primary data for the reconstruction of the earliest history of India. But because the Vedic texts were used in reconstructing the past, prior to the availability of archaeological evidence, there is a readiness to read the archaeological data in the light of the literary.[26]

The nature of the literary data is significant to the historical reconstruction of this period. It is virtually impossible to date the Vedic texts with precision since they are essentially ritual texts and in some passages are clearly anachronistic.[27] They are composed in the language of ritual and require explanatory and etymological commentaries. Among those surviving is the *Nirukta* of Yāska, generally dated to 700–600 BC Pāṇini in his grammar differentiates between the language of ritual and the spoken language.[28] The compositions were preserved orally for many centuries through careful methods of memorising. However, the question has been raised as to whether the systems of memorisation were fixed prior to the compilation of the hymns, and further whether this was also prior to the adoption of a script. On this opinions differ. A long period of a few centuries intervened between the composition of the earliest hymns and their compilation into the *Ṛgveda* as we know it. Even within a strictly monitored oral tradition there can be changes and if the memorisation extends over some centuries, then some degree of additions and subtractions may be expected. The use of astronomy in dating an entire text is regarded as unreliable since the references to planetary positions could have been incorporated from an earlier tradition which need not have been Vedic but was known in the area where the hymns were composed.

The *Ṛgveda* has been approximately dated to about 1500 BC by when the Indus cities had declined. Therefore in accordance with this chronology, the Indus civilisation was prior to the Vedic culture and precedes it as foundational to Indian civilisation. If however there is an insistence on 4500 BC as the date of the *Ṛgveda*, (which is unlikely on the basis of linguistic evidence), then the Vedic would precede the Harappan culture. Excavations in Baluchistan indicate that some settlements there go back to the seventh millennium and continue to the first millennium[29] thus vastly preceding even the early date which some have proposed for the *Ṛgveda*. But the pre-Harappan culture of these sites are not present at the same date in the sites of the Punjab and the north-western borderlands of the Indian subcontinent, which is the location of the *Ṛgveda*. It is difficult to find an archaeological counter-part among the pre-Harappan settlements to the material culture as described in the *Ṛgveda*. The mutation to the pattern of the Harappan culture takes place at approximately the same period in both areas.

Pre-Harappan cultures in the areas where eventually the Harappa culture prevailed, are of diverse kinds and distinctively different. The Ghaggar-Hakra river system which some have sought to identify with the Ṛgvedic Sarasvatī and are projecting it as the nucleus of what evolved into the Harappa culture, has a large number of sites but these cannot be regarded as the sole precursors to Harappan urbanisation. The contribution of the sites in the Indo-Iranian borderlands and in Baluchistan as also in the Indus system itself, appear to be more significant. The Harappan sites, although not entirely uniform, do maintain a pattern which is not only recognisable but marks a departure from the earlier cultures. Its major characteristics are the emphasis on an urban pattern with towns laid out on a grid and a rationalisation of streets in terms of direction and size, with an extensive drainage system, distinctive domestic and public buildings, artefacts such as seals and weights and measures associated with developed exchange, a variety of crafts and distinctive pottery. This was a motivated reaching out into a wide area through various networks of settlements. The requirement of manpower and the exploitation of resources was on a scale unfamiliar to preceding cultures. The sheer size of the area tapped by the Harappan culture led inevitably to some regional variation.

The Late Harappan phase, from the early to mid-second millennium BC when the Mature Harappan began to decline, sees a return to a stronger regional articulation and a diversity in archaeological culture which is geographically delimited. Once again there are a variety of cultures which emerge at this time, some with no ostensible links with other regions, some with continuities with the Harappan and some with evidence of the arrival of innovations from elsewhere. Settlements in Baluchistan suggest links with central Asia and Iran in the second millennium BC. Interestingly the overlap between the Late Harappan and a subsequent independent culture — that of the Painted Grey Ware — occurs in Punjab and Haryana. With the decline of the cities there appears to have been a ruralisation in the regions earlier associated with the Harappan culture, since it takes a few centuries before another urbanisation is witnessed and this time in the Ganga valley.

Ṛgvedic references to the grassy banks of the Sarasvatī would predate the hydrological changes which led to the drying up of the Sarasvatī just prior to about thousand BC provided that the Ṛgvedic Sarasvatī is not located in Afghanistan. The geographical location of the Ṛgvedic *saptasindhu* is generally taken to be the Punjab and the adjoining borderlands, although some scholars would place the geographical location of the *Ṛgveda* closer to central Asia and Afghanistan.[30] There is virtually no familiarity in the Ṛgvedic hymns with Sindh and Baluchistan, leave alone Gujarat (all these being areas were Harappan settlements have been found), nor with the middle Ganga valley. The last is part of the geography of the later Vedic corpus, when interestingly, the language of the north is described as superior. Thus the Punjab could have been the geographical overlap between a part of the area of the Harappan culture and the *Ṛgveda*.

Although the earlier notion of a systematic destruction of Harappan sites by Aryan invaders has been questioned from the evidence of archaeology, this does not allow us to maintain that the speakers of Indo-Aryan were therefore indigenous to India. Nor does the evidence support the identification of Vedic culture with the Indus/Harappan culture. That Indo-Aryan has cognates in a few words that occur in texts from northern Syria, and that the links with Old Iranian suggest more than just a linguistic affinity, is well-established. Parallels from Iran occur in rituals, deities and social forms, but these were not imports from India as is also suggested by the deliberate reversal of some associated ideas in the two societies. The cult of *soma/haoma* and the emphasis on the worship of fire were common to Iran and India. The cult of *soma* does not occur elsewhere in the Indo-European speaking world suggesting a particularly close relationship of the Indo-Iranian culture, if not a common source. The ritual of *soma* has also been linked to some proto-type shamanistic rituals from earlier periods in Central Asia. The Indo-Iranian links tie into the chronology of the *Ṛgveda* since the earliest suggested date now of Zoroaster is *circa* 1200 BC.[31] There is also no evidence of a linguistic movement from India to Iran. The Vedic texts indicate to the contrary, that Indo-Aryan speakers moved eastwards from north-western India to the Ganga valley. The problem for the historian then is to try and understand the mechanism by which Indo-Aryan was brought and adopted in India. For this it is necessary to go back a little in time and observe activities in west Asia and Iran since these are closely connected with events in North India.

Archaeological evidence from the third millennium BC confirms wide-ranging, overland contacts between north-western India, southern and eastern Iran and the Oxus region, and maritime contacts with Oman and Mesopotamia.[32] It was clearly a cosmopolitan world with people on the move, making languages mobile too. Traders from the Indus cities would have had to use diverse languages such as Akkadian, Elamite, and possibly Indo-European in the upper Oxus. This further complicates the decipherment of the Indus script, which so far has been divided between two main schools, one reading it as Indo-Aryan and the other as Proto-Dravidian, where the latter reading seems to be based on a greater reliance on the rules of linguistics.[33] One attempt however which remains controversial among linguists is the close connection which has been suggested between Elamite in southern Iran and Proto-Dravidian. The Proto-Elamite script suggests comparison with the Harappan and it was being used in eastern Iran. Elamite was the language known in the area lying between the Harappan culture and Mesopotamia, prior to the arrival of Old Iranian when Indo-European place-names and proper names start being mentioned in cuneiform documents from northern Mesopotamia in the second millennium BC.[34]

The decline of the Indus cities in the early second millennium BC is now attributed to environmental changes, the closing of trade with the Gulf and the collapse of political authority in the cities. However, the decline of the cities is not an abrupt termination of the Indus civilisation as there is some continuity of Harappan traits in post-Harappan cultures and an overlap at some sites in Punjab and Haryana. In relation to cultural traits from Iran and central Asia, the possibilities of small-scale migrations into India and the interaction of peoples and cultures over a long period of time, can be assumed. The emphasis is both on smallness and long duration as there was no massive migration such as to overwhelm the existing cultures. This is also much more likely to have been the mechanism by which the Indo-Aryan language came to be established in north-western India.

If the archaeological evidence is given primacy in establishing the roots of Indian civilisation then it is possible to reconstruct a picture of the evolution of various societies in the northern and western parts of the subcontinent. In this reconstruction, the Indus civilisation/Harappan culture, is a significant landmark and interest is shifting away from futile attempts to identify every new archaeological culture with the Aryans. A close examination of the archaeological evidence in various dimensions permits a comparison of Harappan society with that depicted in the Vedic texts and the two are diverse. The one characteristic which is striking in the archaeology of the Harappan culture is the strength of the urban organisation, reflected in the way the towns were planned and the amenities provided. Urban centres were central to extensive trade in Harappan life, whereas the Vedic society was pastoral and agricultural without descriptions of urban living. There are no references to granaries or large-scale storage systems under administrative authority. Craft production which was an established feature of the Harappan cities is mentioned in passing in the texts. The use of a script is evident from the seals but is absent in the texts. Vedic society gradually becomes more familiar with the use of iron and this is absent in the Harappan culture where the metal technology is of copper and bronze. Other technologies also point to major differences, as for example, the *rājā* in the Vedic texts was equipped with a chariot run on spoked wheels neither or which are to be found at Harappan sites where oxen drew carts and the wheels were discoid. Chariots were drawn by horses but these are late arrivals and there is only sporadic evidence of the horse at the time of the decline of the cities.

Despite these differences, an alternative view is being propagated. This interpretation seeks an unbroken genealogy for the Hindu as Arya and therefore supports the Hindutva reconstruction of events. The argument runs as follows: the Indus civilisation is said to be Vedic and Aryan and this, together with the lack of evidence of a large-scale Aryan invasion from archaeology, is said to further prove that there were people who called themselves the Aryans and who were indigenous to India.[35] The preferred date for the *Ṛgveda* is 4500 BC so that it precedes the Indus cities, but the two can also be made to coincide chronologically.[36] It is claimed that the Indo-Aryan language originated in India and spread from India westwards.

Such an early date for the *Ṛgveda* is untenable on the available linguistic evidence nor is there support for the argument of a westward flow of people from northern India, neither from linguistic nor from archaeological source. Since language cannot be identified by an archaeological culture, the use of the term Aryan in this interpretation refers to a combination of people, culture and language, rather than strictly only to language. We are back once more to Max Müller's confusion over language and race. The attempt to push back the chronology of the *Ṛgveda* is accompanied by the attempt to take the Harappan culture back to the fourth millennium or even earlier and the equating of the Harappan culture with the Vedic texts. There is a focus on those pre-Harappan cultures whose location is along the Ghaggar-Hakra which is identified with the now invisible Sarasvatī river, important to the *Ṛgveda*. It is argued that the number of sites along the Ghaggar-Hakra river system is greater than along the Indus, therefore the former should be seen as the nucleus of the Harappan culture. The claim is then made that the Indus civilisation should more correctly be called the Indus-Sarasvati civilisation.[37]

The theory ignores the existence of a variety of pre-Harappan cultures in other areas, some of which were closely related to the process of Harappan urbanisation. It has also been contested by some archaeologists who disagree with the count and location of sites as with the implicit argument of what constitutes the nucleus of a civilisation. However, there are ideological and political dimensions to this theory which make it acceptable to those seeking origins in what they call indigenous identities. The equating of the Harappan and Vedic culture is not essentially an attempt at co-relating archaeological and literary sources in reconstructing the beginnings of the history of the subcontinent. There are other agendas which are being addressed in this attempt. If it can be argued that the Harappan culture is in fact Vedic or that the *Ṛgveda* is earlier even than the Harappan, then the *Vedas* continue to be foundational to the subcontinental civilisation of South Asia and also attract the encomium of representing an advanced civilisation, superior even to the pastoral-agrarian culture actually described in the Vedic texts. The Vedic culture then, has an unbroken flow, as it were, from the fourth millennium into the historical period, and in terms of the antiquity of civilisations (which was a nineteenth century obsession), places it on par with the earliest. The Sanskritic base of the civilisation is sought to be established by reading the Vedic into the Harappan. The label Indus-Sarasvati civilisation evokes the *Ṛgveda*.

There is also in this interpretation, the advantage that an extensive territory can be claimed for the Vedic culture, since Harappan artefacts and sites are located in a widespread area from Badakshan in Afghanistan to northern Maharashtra and from the Ganga-Yamuna doāb to Baluchistan. This vastly extends the geographical area as described in the *Ṛgveda* and which is much more limited. The discovery of Harappan sites on the Indian side of the border between India and Pakistan, is viewed as compensating for the loss of the cities of Mohenjo-daro and Harappa which are located in Pakistan. By insisting on the Ghaggar-Hakra being the cradle of the Indus civilisation, there is an element of recapturing the civilisation for India. The equation of the Harappan with the Vedic strengthens the notion of an unbroken Hindu Aryan origin for the historical beginnings of both India and Pakistan.

Another curious agenda is that of what is described as 'a critical mass' of Indians and a few others in America and Canada who refer to themselves as the Indo-American school (as against what they call the Indo-European school of scholars who work within the earlier Indian and European scholarship). The Indo-American school, (as they call themselves), according to one of its prominent spokesmen, consists of predominantly American-trained Indian professional scientists researching on ancient India (presumably as a hobby), and using the resources of modern science and technology.[38] Obviously well-endowed, they run their own journal from their main office in Canada. They too are committed to proving that the Vedic and the Harappan cultures are the same and that their antiquity goes back to the fifth millennium BC and therefore the Aryans are indigenous to India and took the Aryan mission westwards from India. Much of their writing contributes to the invention of yet more mythologies about a complex subject. What is striking about their reconstructions is their evident unfamiliarity with the methods of analysing archaeological, linguistic and historical data. Consequently their writings read rather like nineteenth century tracts but peppered with references to using the computer so as to suggest scientific objectivity since they claim that it is value-free. Those that question their theories are dismissed as Marxists! That Indian scientists in America should take upon themselves the task of proving the Harappan to be Vedic, to having influenced other civilisations such as the Egyptian, and to proving that the Aryans proceeded on a civilising mission issuing out of India and going westwards, can only suggest that the 'Indo-American school' is in the midst of an identity crisis in its new environment. It is anxious to demarcate itself from other immigrants and to proclaim that the Indian identity is superior to the others who have also fallen into the 'great melting-pot'.

These reconstructions disregard the linguistic data, probably because it would puncture their argument. It is conveniently stated that the linguistic models arise out of political and cultural factors and presumably therefore may be ignored. Yet linguistics introduces another dimension, other than archaeological, which has a considerable bearing not only on the nature of the Vedic language but also on the reconstruction of the history of this period. Linguistic analyses, subsequent to Max Müller and particularly those of the last few decades have led to the radical revision of many earlier views. The internal evidence of the Vedic texts points to Indo-Aryan travelling eastwards from north-western India to the middle Ganga valley. The *Ṛgveda* has its location in the *saptasindhu* region, but the later Vedic corpus indicates a shift eastwards and the crossing of the river Sādanīra/Gandak is specifically mentioned. Changes are apparent within the evolution of Vedic Sanskrit from the period of the *Ṛgveda* to that of the later *Vedas*.[39] There is also a greater incidence of non-Aryan linguistic elements in the later Vedic corpus as compared to the *Ṛgveda*. There is therefore an induction into Vedic Sanskrit from Indian non-Aryan languages registering an increase over time, and thus suggesting that Indo-Aryan was not indigenous. The recent linguistic analysis therefore is set aside by those who argue to the contrary.

Yet the linguistic evidence cannot be ignored as it forms part of a primary source — the Vedic texts — in the reconstruction of the history of this period. But this evidence has also to be seen in a wider context. Related languages, constituting what is called the Indo-European family are said to go back to an ancestral language spoken in the Indo-European homeland which has generally been located in central Asia and which is referred to as Proto-Indo-European.[40] Such reconstructions previously assumed that a proto form could be arrived at from words taken from later texts. This has been questioned and historical linguistics is now particular about possible changes in the history of words. Linguistics also places an emphasis on the structure of the language and does not limit itself to comparing similar sounding words.

A single homeland would imply a widespread diffusion from a small area, and the explanations for such a diffusion have been speculative. The drying up of the pasture lands in the steppe area has been suggested. In central Asia settlements tend to acquire simple fortifications in the third millennium BC perhaps indicating a more than normal movement of people. An alternative reconstruction might suggest that there was a wide belt of Indo-European speaking peoples inhabiting a large part of central Asia, from the Tocharian speaking region to the Slavonic. These would have moved in different directions and associated with a variety of pre-existing cultures, thus resulting in some similarities among Indo-European derived languages but with variant characteristics as well, the latter deriving from pre-existing languages of these cultures. This would involve some variation in the ancestral languages and a wider spectrum of migrations and movements of peoples. The languages taken to new areas would have changed to some degree on coming into contact with non-Indo-European speakers and establishing of languages related to Indo-European would have taken a few centuries. The imprint of Indo-European would vary from the maximum impact, namely that of gradually establishing an Indo-European language in the area, to the minimum, namely, that of the local language merely incorporating a few Indo-European words. Given the interrelatedness of Indo-European languages and that these languages in contiguous areas have historical roots which are often connected, it is not possible to study the history of any single Indo-European language in isolation. Each has to be viewed in the context of the group with which it is associated. Thus Indo-Aryan has to be examined within the context of links with old Iranian and a possible Indo-Iranian phase at an earlier stage.

Some clarification in the use of these terms is necessary. Indo-Iranian descended from an original Indo-European would have preceded the division into Old Iranian and Indo-Aryan. The early sections of the *Avesta,* associated with Zoroaster provide evidence of Old Iranian. Indo-Aryan is available from the *Ṛgveda* onwards. However, there is another form which some scholars identify with Indo-Aryan and which they argue is perhaps a little earlier and therefore it is called Proto-Indo-Aryan. This would make it possibly earlier than the *Ṛgveda.* Its occurrence is not in south Asia or Iran, but in a few inscriptions from Turkey and Syria. There is however, no evidence of an Indo-Aryan language acting as a connecting link from an earlier location in south Asia towards the area to the west. Furthermore, these inscriptions are firmly dated to the second millennium BC and this has some relevance for dating the *Ṛgveda.*

The term 'Aryan' in the label Indo-Aryan, refers solely to the language and not to the people who spoke it or for that matter to any imagined race. The word *airiia* in the *Avesta* is seen as the same as the *ārya* of the *Ṛgveda.* Its etymology has been discussed at length and has been read as derived from meanings such as companion, enemy-friend, stranger, guest, a person of noble lineage or a person of status and possessions.[41] The inscriptions of the Achaemenid kings of Iran are also quoted where they identify themselves as Aryan.[42] But the earliest of these inscriptions are of the sixth century BC and therefore much later than the *Avesta.* Although the term has been associated with descent, it can also be read as referring to nobility of status. Since Indo-Aryan refers to a language and *ārya* refers to a social status, attempts to identify either with archaeological cultures tend to be meaningless.

Cultural similarities recognised in the various Indo-European languages have given rise to theories concerning the organisation of the societies which use Indo-European. Of these the most influential is that of Dumezil who describes the tripartite function of

Indo-European society as consisting of three categories — priests, warriors and hereditary-cultivators.[43] However, it has been shown that these divisions are so general that they can even be seen in non-Indo-European literature such as the Bible.[44] A similarity of patterns and their traces have also been sought in the mythology and laws of Indo-European speaking societies.[45] The assumption that the speakers of Indo-European became the dominant group in the areas where the language spread, has now been superseded by the recognition that the diffusion of a language introduces some new ideas and institutions in an area, but that frequently there is a restructuring of existing ideas and institutions.

Tentative suggestions from this perspective have been made in relation to rituals. Some rituals characteristic of the Indo-Iranian area, are not practised in other areas where Indo-European in spoken. This may be because of the close connections between north-western India and Iran, even prior to the establishing of Indo-European language in the region. One such ritual is the cult of *soma* (in Indo-Aryan) or *haoma* (in Old Iranian), which involves the consuming of the elaborately prepared juice of a plant with hallucinogenic properties as part of major sacrificial rituals. It has been thought that the tradition goes back to shamanistic practices in central Asia. The plant has been identified by some with the ephedra, found in a ritual context at the site of Togolok 21 in Margiana (Turkmenistan) and by others with the fly agaric, a mushroom which grows in a habitat associated with mountains of Afghanistan.[46] The geographical restriction of the cult may have arisen because the plant was specific to a limited location. A tentative hypothesis takes the cult back to the Harappans.[47] The argument is not that the Harappans therefore were the people of the *Vedas*, but that this cult had pre-Vedic and pre-Avestan origins and was incorporated into the Vedic and Avestan ritual. This underlines the need to examine how a ritual is constituted, and the extent to which it retains archaic features and introduces new ones.

The earliest definitive evidence of Indo-European, apart from a few names in a Mesopotamian source of the nineteenth century BC comes from Hittite and Mitanni inscriptions from Turkey and Syria in the period between about 1750 to 1300 BC and from the names of the Kassites whose short-lived presence in Mesopotamia is dated to the mid-second millennium BC. These data are not texts in Indo-European, but words; names of deities and rulers, and terms used in the training of horses.[48] The occurrence of Indo-European words is striking in an area which was non-Indo-European speaking prior to this and remained the same after this brief intrusion.[49] This does not indicate large numbers of Indo-European speakers, nor a substantial local population taking to the new language. That this form of Indo-European is close to Ṛgvedic Sanskrit has tended to endorse the date of about 1500–1200 BC for the early hymns of the *Ṛgveda*. Linguistic evidence of language or words close to Vedic Sanskrit prior to the second millennium BC in the area between the Indus and Turkey, is not forthcoming. This is also the period when the earlier connections between the Indus and west Asia begin to decline. In the absence of language links in the intervening area, it has been suggested that Proto-Indo-Aryan may have travelled originally from a more central point, perhaps in Iran, westwards to Turkey and eastwards to northern India.[50] Avestan references to the migrations of the *airiia* mention places in northern and Eastern Iran and the direction would appear to be from the north to the north-east.

The assimilation of non-Aryan linguistic elements into Vedic Sanskrit[51] raises the question of whether there was bilingualism between the speakers of Indo-Aryan and of other languages, and if so, then to what degree; and who were the authors of these texts? It could be that groups of migrants over many centuries came from the region of Margiana and Bactria to north-western India.[52] The migrants could have been slow-moving pastoralists, who also functioned as itinerant traders. This is suggested by the centrality of pastoral society in the *Ṛgveda*. They probably settled in places en route, so that those who entered India were already ethnically and culturally mixed and spoke what evolved into Indo-Aryan carrying traces of closeness to Old Iranian, but nevertheless distinct. It would have been more convenient for them to use local artefacts rather than carry items from their earlier settlements. Archaeology therefore would register their presence in indirect forms and not as a major change in material culture. They would have met with non-Aryan speakers in India, using proto-Dravidian, Austro-Asiatic and possibly in some areas even Tibeto-Burman. Bilingualism would have followed, resulting in the induction of non-Aryan traits into Aryan, recognisable in morphology (word formation), phonology (sound), syntax (sentence pattern and grammar), lexical items (vocabulary) and semantics (meaning). Non-Aryan speakers were part of this bilingualism and over many centuries may have become proficient in Indo-Aryan.[53] Apart from elements of language, it is likely that custom and ritual were also incorporated into Vedic practice, amalgamating cultural items from local and distant traditions. This would result in some anachronisms. Bilingualism would have been a necessity. But the motivation for the adoption of Indo-Aryan by non-Aryan speakers may have been encouraged if the language being adopted gave access to artefacts, rituals, status and security.[54]

In order to strengthen this hypothesis, it would be necessary to examine the artefacts which are innovatory towards the early first millennium BC. Was the increasing use of the horse and the spoked-wheel chariot linked to the Aryan speakers? Or the introduction of iron artefacts?[55] The horse is an insignificant animal in the Indus cities and can be said to arrive, at the earliest, towards the decline of the cities and not before the second millennium BC.[56] It is noticeably absent in any ritual context such as a depiction on a Harappan seal or at places thought to be associated with rituals. This is in contrast to its presence in some post-Harappan cultures and its centrality to Vedic ritual and life. This centrality was probably because the horse, and certainly the quality livestock, was imported even in later times from central Asia or from Arabia.

The use of the horse and of the bovine in ritual, especially the ritual of sacrifice, is not identical. The sacrifice of a bovine carries less status than that of a horse. In the *dāna-stuti* hymns of the *Ṛgveda* in which the poets list the wealth they request from their patrons, the number of horses is far fewer than of cattle.[57] Excavated animal bones from Hastinapur in the first millennium BC when the use of the horse was more frequent, indicate that horse bones make up only a very small percentage of the bones, the largest amount being those of the *bos Indicus*, the humped cattle.[58] The horse being more valuable, its association was with the more spectacular sacrifices such as the *aśvamedha*. The eating of cattle flesh was limited to occasions when the animal had been sacrificed or on special occasions. It was not eaten routinely. This is a common feature among cattle pastoralists who thus preserve quality stock.[59] The horse sacrifice is mentioned in the *Vedas* and the number of horses said to have been sacrificed are sometimes excessive. Exaggerated figures may have been intended to suggest power and wealth and need not be taken literally. There is no evidence of the sacrifice of a horse from Harappan sites and even what is interpreted by some as evidence of the sacrifice of an animal is extremely limited.[60]

In the Indo-Iranian borderlands, horse remains date to the second millennium BC. The arrival of the horse in the Swat valley of Gandhāra and in the Ganga valley dates to the first millennium BC. Found in the early part of the millennium at sites such as Atranjikhera, Hastinapur, Bhagwanpura, the remains increase in the subsequent period.[61] From the Vedic texts onwards the horse is symbolic of nobility and is associated with people of status. In the *Avesta* the suffix *aspa* meaning 'horse' is frequent in the names of those claiming status and even as late as the Mauryan period, a high official in Saurashtra carries the Iranian name, 'Tushaspa'.[62] Functionally, mounted herders could substantially improve efficiency in controlling herds grazing in extensive areas, apart from being an important adjunct in combat and in the fast transportation of individual riders or those riding chariots. If the culture of the *Ṛgveda* is to be equated with the Harappan culture, then obviously the horse has to be found in the Harappan cities. But even allowing for a generous time margin, there are no horse remains prior to the second millennium BC some of the earlier suggested identifications of bones being now confirmed as those of the onager and the ass. There is therefore a frantic search for horse bones from archaeological levels prior to the second millennium BC.[63] The point which also needs to be emphasised is that the discovery of a single tooth of a horse at Lothal[64] does not indicate the presence of the horse on the scale described in the *Ṛgveda*. Such single items are a striking contrast to the more substantial bones found at Hastinapur and other sites in the first millennium BC.

Associated with the horse was the chariot and the spoked wheel, appearing on the scene at the same time and with antecedents further west. Prior to this, the ox-cart and the discoid wheel were extensively used in north-western India. Models of actual wheels for toy carts from Harappan sites are generally of the discoid variety. Occasionally there are wheels with four lines radiating from the hub painted over the solid wheel. These have been taken to represent spoked wheels.[65] But the construction of a spoked wheel is different and presumably would be represented with many more spokes and a rim.

Iron weaponry dates to about 800 BC although some iron artefacts from central India are said to be earlier.[66] References to iron therefore in the Vedic texts would date to the first millennium BC. Interestingly in peninsular India, megalithic burials in the first millennium BC reveal the extensive use of iron artefacts as well as the presence of the horse, but such burials are located in areas which are either still proto-Dravidian speaking or else have had a proto-Dravidian substratum. Thus in spite of these innovations, there seems to have been little inclination to adopt Indo-Aryan. Two other non-artefactual innovations may be suggested: the binary system of measurement used in Harappan times may have been replaced by the decimal, more familiar to Vedic texts; and the use of the solar calendar in addition to the lunar calendar would have been a functional advance with the gradual reorganisation or agricultural activities. Did these technological changes provide a lever, giving an edge to the speakers of Indo-Aryan who may have introduced the innovations initially. Possibly the claims based on the power of sacrificial ritual was yet another lever. The redefinitions in culture, social organisation and economy resulting from technological innovations would have been a slow process. They also imply far more complex and varied dimensions of historical change, than the simplistic mono-causal explanations of either conquest or alternatively indigenous origins for everything.

Archaeology and language can provide separate evidence on some essential questions, as for example an enquiry into migrations. This would involve an explanation of why there was a need to move and of the numbers involved. The expending of wealth on the journey would have to be controlled so as not to be counter-productive and this would determine up to a point the goods with which people traveled.[67] Assessing linguistic change would indicate the adoption and modification of the languages of those migrating and the areas to which they migrate. In the case of pastoral migrants, the animals bred might provide clues to travel. The domestication of the *bos Indicus* breed of cattle, evident from excavations, links the Indus valley and Iran. Migrations may have been occasioned by the search for pastures and north-western India may have been familiar to herders from the borderlands. If exchange and incipient trade also featured as they often do with pastoral groups, then the circulation of items may have encouraged a larger circuit of travel and a greater mixing of the populations. Where the migration included farming communities, new agricultural land and the diffusion of crops would be part of the pattern.

If the existing evidence is integrated then the emerging picture is one where the presence of Indo-European in the form of Old Iranian and Proto-Indo-Aryan and Indo-Aryan is registered in the second millennium BC. This period also sees the arrival of the horse, the chariot and spoked wheel, and the use of iron, all of which are more evident in the first millennium. At a few sites in India there is an overlap of Late Harappan with the Painted Grey Ware — the latter dated to the first millennium BC. This makes a more plausible picture for the entry of Indo-Aryan into India than the arbitrary shifting of the chronology of the Harappan culture and the *Ṛgveda* to make them coincide.

Equally important to the question of why Indo-Aryan was a adopted is the nature of the interaction between the speakers of the various languages. I have suggested elsewhere that initially it involved a symbiotic relationship between agriculturalists and pastoralists,[68] a symbiosis which is evident in many such mixed societies. With the decline of the cities of the Indus civilisation and the breakdown of political authority, villages would have been open to predatory raids from various sources. In the collapse of the Harappan system, the erstwhile farmers and craftsmen and particularly those living in villages who had been deeply integrated into the Harappan system, would have been economically rootless. The Harappan agrarian system appears to have been more carefully controlled in the north-west, if the granaries can be regarded as an indication. This was the region which would have received settlers from the borderlands. The incoming groups may not have been averse to controlling what remained of the pre-existing hierarchical structure. Did non-Aryan speaking agriculturalists seek protection from the chiefs of pastoral clans who were Aryan speaking? This does not imply the conquest of the former by the latter, but a system of patronage, which may even have existed in Harappan times except that now the patrons were not from the Harappan cities. The familiarity which these chiefs had with the horse and with new weaponry would have enabled them to provide the required protection as well as place them in a status of superiority. Such a relationship may on occasion have led to localised conflict, but would have soon assumed a symbiotic pattern, involving bilingualism at first and subsequently the adoption of an evolving Indo-Aryan. Linguistic convergence may follow from the meeting of two languages. Curiously, words associated with agriculture in Vedic Sanskrit and as early as the *Ṛgveda*, are often non-Aryan.[69] At some sites of the Painted Grey Ware cultures in northern India, frequently identified as 'Aryan', there is an interesting mixture: the cultivation of rice and the domestication of the water buffalo are associated with developments in eastern India, but the horse is an importation from the west.[70]

The historical reconstruction of this period therefore presents a different picture from that envisaged in existing theories. Given the range of evidence, there can now be a greater exploration of reconstructions rather than an insistence on reconstructing a history for which the evidence has yet to be found. The identification of archaeological cultures as Aryan, which was methodologically untenable, becomes irrelevant. Archaeology does not provide evidence to identify language where there is an absence of a script. Even where languages are related as in Proto-Indo-Aryan, Old Iranian, and Indo-Aryan, the material culture of the societies associated with these languages is dissimilar.

The notion of an Aryan race identified on the basis of an Aryan language has now been discarded. Language and race are distinctly different categories. Perhaps it would be more appropriate to discard the term 'Aryan' as well, using only Indo-Aryan to identify the language, or else staying strictly within the definition of *ārya* from Sanskrit texts where it is a linguistic and social qualifier, without the overlay of nineteenth century theories. The reconstruction of the societies of the period would draw substantially on archaeological data. How and when the Aryan language entered India and the process of its adoption and adaption requires to be investigated as a process in social history and not as providing identities which we today can label as indigenous or alien for purposes of narrow nationalism. A comparative analysis of analogous situations might provide some clues. Interestingly, the Indian experience parallels that of Iran where Old Iranian as an Indo-European language was ancestral to later Iranian languages. This contrasts with the short-lived intrusion of Indo-European in Turkey and Syria.

Such a change of focus would require a search for a graduated interaction over many centuries between various settlements and cultures, where large-scale violent conflict would be limited. The *Ṛgveda* refers to relations between the *ārya-varṇa* and the *dāsa-varṇa*. These are generally identified as distinct peoples, although *ārya* carries the connotation of a person of status and knowing Sanskrit. The presence of non-Aryan speakers are registered in the reference to those of obstructed speech, *mṛdhravāc* and those who could not speak correctly, *mleccha*. The later Vedic texts provide evidence of regional variations. Whereas appeals are made to the gods to destroy to the *dāsas*, mention is also made of the generosity of wealthy *dāsas* chiefs for whom rituals are performed. The hostility of the *ārya* towards the *dāsas*, refers more frequently to differences in worship and rituals, than to physical differences. Nor was the conflict always between *ārya* and *dāsas*. Conflicts also occur between established clans and *ārya* enemies are mentioned.[71] Subsequent Vedic texts also acknowledge that some respected *brāhmaṇas* are *dāsīputra*, the sons of *dāsīs* and this evidence has been used to suggest that Vedic *brāhmaṇas* were, to a large extent, recruited from the priest class of the pre-Aryan population. It has even been hyposthesised that the *dāsas* were the remnants of the Indus civilisation.[72] It would seem then, that the relationship is more ambivalent than has been recognised so far.

This in turn relates to the subordination of the *dāsas* by the *ārya*. This is central to Jyotiba Phule's version of the Aryan theory revived in Dalit politics today and its reversal from the Hindutva perspective. With the emergence of *varṇa*, which some sociologists have described as ritual status, the lowest category came to be called *śūdra* and was expected to be servile. *Dāsa* was not a ritual status and the word eventually was used for a slave or a servant, its antonym being *ārya*. In the post-Rigvedic *Brāhmaṇa* texts, the appeal to the gods to destroy the *dāsas* declines, for by now they are already low in the hierarchy of stratification. In a situation as complex as this, the mechanisms of subordination may be less evident than in the projection of conquest, but nevertheless they cannot be ignored. The presumed identity and lineal descent of the supposed Aryan in this reading of the evidence becomes questionable and therefore, difficult to use for political mobilisation in contemporary times.

The process of the subordination of the *dāsas* by the *ārya* could provide clues to some aspects of relations of dominance and subordination in the social history of later times. Hierarchies, differentiations and regulations essential to caste, exist as part of its stratification and social functioning, irrespective of an Aryan component. The insistence on differentiating between the alien/foreign and the indigenous is historically untenable for earlier times when even the existence of such a differentiation based on the premises being suggested, is questionable. 'Indigenous' and 'foreign' as notions are neither permanent nor unchanging nor transparent. The identities of the indigene and the alien are constantly mutated throughout history. It is more pertinent to analyse the major historical processes of early times, namely, the emergence of dominant groups — the *āryas*, and the subordination of others referred to as *śūdras* and *dāsas*.

I have tried to show that the application of the Aryan theory to Indian history, which began as an attempt to uncover the beginnings of Indian history, to explain the origins of Indian society, and to establish what were thought to be roots of Indian identity, has inevitably become entangled in Indian politics. The emphasis today on a particular kind of Aryanism is also a revival of nineteenth century historiography, moulded by specific ideological concerns of time and place. This historiography has undergone a radical change where the insistence on Aryanism as an essential ingredient of the civilisations of Iran and Greece is now passé, for civilisation is being viewed as a process and not the monopoly of a particular people.[73]

The Aryan theory in India, has been in some ways, a kaleidoscope where scholarly and political concerns have in the past been trying to change the configurations of the pattern. Used in the search for modern Indian identities by drawing on a definition of origins, it sought legitimation from history, and tried to justify the aspirations of one particular group or controvert those of others. In its contemporary incarnation it provides an important element in the search for collective identities in political contestation, quite apart from contested interpretations of early Indian history. I have tried to show that in reconstructing the beginnings of Indian history, the entire complex range of evidence — archaeological, linguistic and textual — has to be brought into play, relating both to India and the neighbouring areas. This is so formidable in itself, that historians have neglected to comment on the political appropriations of the theory in our time. Thus, when the theory is again becoming an agency of empowerment and entitlement, to include some and exclude others, historians will need to challenge spurious history, irrespective of how popular it might be in the politics and ideologies of the present.

## NOTES AND REFERENCES

1. E. Leach, 'Aryan Invasions Over Four Millennia', in E. Ohnuki–Tierney (ed.), *Culture Through Time*, Stanford, 1990; L. Poliakov, *The Aryan Myth*, New York, 1974.
2. I have discussed some of these aspects elsewhere. See Romila Thapar, 'Society in Ancient India: The Formative Period', *Ancient Indian Social History: Some Interpretations*, New Delhi, 1978, pp. 311ff. *See* chapter 14 in this volume; 'The Archaeological Background to the Agnicayana Ritual', in F. Staal (ed.), *Agni*, II, Berkeley, 1983, pp. 1–40. *See* chapter 15 in this volume. 'Archaeology and Language at the Root of Ancient India', *Journal of the Asiatic Society of Bombay*, 1989–91, 64–6 (n.s.), pp. 249–68.
3. J. Majeed, *Ungoverned Imaginings*, Oxford, 1992.
4. J.W. Sedlar, *India in the Mind of Germany*, New York, 1982.
5. Majeed, op. cit.
6. R. Schwab, *The Oriental Renaissance*, New York, 1984 (trans).
7. Isaac Taylor, *The Origin of the Aryans*, London, 1892 (2nd ed.).
8. Used in the *Edinburgh Review* of 1851.
9. L. Poliakov, *The Aryan Myth*, New York. 1974, pp. 233ff.
10. I. Taylor, op. cit.
11. F. Max Müller, *Lectures on the Science of Language*, 1862; *Biographies of Words and the Home of the Aryas*, 1888; *India What Can It Teach Us?*, 1883; *Chips from a German Workshop*, 1884.
12. 'Raja Ram Mohan Roy 1774–1833', in *Biographical Essays*, Oxford, 1884, p. 11. This was an address delivered at Bristol Museum on 27 September 1883 on the fiftieth anniversary of the Raja's death. See also, *I Point to India*, ed. by N. Mookerjee, Bombay, 1970, pp. 24–8.
13. R. Caldwell, *A Comparative Grammar of the Dravidian or South Indian Family of Languages*, London, 1856.
14. An example of this is the influential study by Herbert Risely, *The People of India*, London, 1980.
15. R. O'Hanlon, *Caste Conflict and Ideology*, Cambridge, 1985. G. Omvedt, *Jyotiba Phule: An Incomplete Renaissance*, Surat, 1991.
16. *Keshab Chunder Sen's Lectures in India*, p. 323.
17. *Orion or Researches into the Antiquity of the Vedas*, Poona, 1893.
18. *The Arctic Home in the Vedas*, Poona, 1903.
19. A.C. Das, *Rigvedic India*, Calcutta, 1920.
20. *Satyarth Prakash*, Y. Mimamshak (ed.), Sonipat, 1972.
21. Lajpat Rai, *The Arya Samaj*, Bombay, 1915, p. 46.
22. J. Leopold, 'British Applications of the Aryan Theory of Race to India 1850–70', *The English Historical Review*, 1974, 89, pp. 578–603. 'The Aryan Theory of Race in India 1870–1920, Nationalist and

Internationalist Visions', *Indian Economic and Social History Review*, 1970, VII, 2, 271–98.

23. V.D. Savarkar, *Hindutva. Who is Hindu*, Bombay, written and distributed 1922, published 1969; M.S. Golwalkar, *We or Our Nationhood Defined*, Bombay, 1938.
24. Romila Thapar, *Clan, Caste and Origin Myths in Early India*, Shimla, 1992. *See* chapter 35 in this volume
25. Romila Thapar, 'The Study of Society', op. cit.
26. The tendency to give priority to textual and linguistic data over the archaeological goes back to the earliest major attempts to co-relate the two sources in the writings of G. Kossinna and G. Childe. The more recent attempt of C. Renfrew, *Archaeology and Language*, London, 1987, draws on ideas from processual archaeology which makes it theoretically an interesting departure, but his reconstruction of Aryan origins remains unconvincing.
27. Romila Thapar, 'The Archaeological Background to the Agnicayana Ritual', in F. Staal (ed.), *Agni*, Berkeley, 1983, pp. 1–40. *See* chapter 15 in this volume
28. V.S. Agrawala, *India as Known to Panini*, Varanasi, 1963, 2nd edn., p. 354.
29. J.F. Jarrige, 'Excavations at Mehrgarh–Nausharo', *Pakistan Archaeology*, 1986, 10–22, pp. 63–131.
30. A. Parpola, 'The Coming of the Aryans to Iran and India and the Cultural and Ethnic Identity of the Dasas', *Studia Orientalia*, 1988, no. 64.
31. M. Boyce, *Zoroastrians*, London, 1979, 18.
32. H.P. Francfort, *Fouilles de Shortughai*, Paris, 1989; P.H. Kohl, 'The Balance of Trade in South-western Asia in the Mid-Third Millennium BC', *Current Anthropology*, 1978, 19, pp. 463–92; C.C. Lamberg–Karlovsky, 'The Proto-Elamites on the Iranian Plateau', *Antiquity*, 1978, 52, pp. 114–20. S. Ratnagar, *Encounters, The Westerly Trade of the Harappa Civilisation*, New Delhi, 1981.
33. I. Mahadevan, *The Indus Script*, New Delhi, 1977. S.R. Rao, *The Decipherment of the Indus Script*, Bombay, 1982. A. Parpola, *Deciphering the Indus Script*, Cambridge, 1994.
34. D.W. McAlpin, *Proto-Elamo-Dravidian: The Evidence and its Implications*, Transactions of the American Philosophical Society, No. 71, Philadelphia, 1981. A. Parpola, *Deciphering the Indus Script*, Cambridge, 1994, 128.
35. Swami Sankaranand, *Rigvedic Culture of the Prehistoric Indus*, Calcutta, 1943–4; K.N. Sastri, *New Light on the Indus Civilisation*, Delhi, 1965. A.D. Pusalkar, 'Pre-Harappan and post-Harappan Culture and the Aryan Problem', *The Quarterly Review of Historical Studies*, 1967–8, VII, 4, 233–44. K.D. Sethna, *The Problem of Aryan Origins*, Delhi, 1980.

36. V.N. Misra, 'Indus Civilisation and the Rigvedic Sarasvati', in A. Parpola and P. Koshikallio (eds), *South Asian Archaeology*, 1993, vol. II, Helsinki, 1994, 511–25.
37. S.P. Gupta, 'Longer Chronology of the Indus-Sarasvati Civilisation', *Puratattva*, 1992-3, 23, 21–9.
38. N.S. Rajaram, 'Vedic and Harappan Culture: New Findings', *Puratattva*, 1993–94, 24, 1–11.
39. M. Witzel, 'Tracing the Vedic Dialects', in C. Caillat (ed.), *Dialectes dans les litteratures Indo-AryennesD, Paris, 1989, pp. 97ff.*
40. J.P. Mallory, *In Search of the Indo-European*, London, 1989, provides a useful summary of the evidence.
41. J. Brough, *The Early Brahmanical System of Gotra and Pravara*, Cambridge, 1953, xiii–xv. H.W. Bailey, 'Iranian *arya* and *daha*', in Transactions of the Philological Society, 1959.
42. R.G. Kent, *Old Persian: Grammar, Texts, Lexicon*, New Haven, 1953 (2nd ed.).
43. C. Scott–Littleton, *The New Comparative Mythology*, Berkeley, 1973.
44. J. Brough, 'The Tripartite Ideology of the Indo-Europeans: An Experiment in Method', *BSOAS*, 1959, 22, 69—85.
45. J. Puhvel (ed.), *Myth and Law among the Indo-Europeans*, Berkeley, 1970.
46. F. Hiebert (ed.), New Studies in Bronze Age Margiana (Turkmenistan), *International Association for the Study of the Cultures of Central Asia, Bulletin*, No. 19, Moscow, 1993. G. Wasson, 'The Soma of the Rigveda: What was it?' *JAOS*, 1971, 91, 169–87.
47. I. Mahadevan, 'The Sacred Filter Facing the Unicorn: More Evidence', *South Asian Archaeology, Helsinki 1993*, I, Helsinki, 1994, pp. 435–50.
48. J.P. Mallory, *In Search of the Indo-Europeans*, London, 1989, pp. 24ff, 37ff.
49. Mallory, op. cit.
50. T. Burrow, 'The Proto-Indo Aryans', *Journal of the Royal Asiatic Society*, 1973, 2, pp. 123–40.
51. T. Burrow, *The Sanskrit Language*, London, 1965, pp. 373ff. M.M. Deshpande, 'Genesis of Ṛgvedic Retroflexion', in M.M. Deshpande and P.E. Hook (eds), *Aryan and non-Aryan in India*, Ann Arbor, 1979. F.B.J. Kuiper, *Aryans in the Rigveda*, Amsterdam, 1991.
52. F.T. Hiebert and C.C. Lamberg–Karlovsky, 'Central Asia and the Indo-Iranian Borderlands', *Iran*, 1992, 30. pp. 1–15. F.T. Hiebert (ed.), *New Studies in Bronze Age Margiana (Trukmenistan)*, IASCCA Information Bulletin No. 19, Moscow, 1993; A. Parpola, 'The Coming of the Aryans to Iran and India . . . ', *Studia Orientalia*, 64. Helsinki, 1988. A. Parpola, *Deciphering the Indus Script*, 148ff.
53. M.B. Emeneau, 'Indian Linguistic Area Revisited', *International Journal of Dravidian Linguistics*, 1974, 3, 1, pp. 93ff.

54. Mallory, op. cit.
55. Romila Thapar, 'The Study of Society', op. cit.
56. R. Meadow, 'Continuity and Change in the Agriculture of the Great Indus Valley: the Palaeoethnobotanical and Zooarchaeological Evidence', in J.M. Kenoyer (ed.), *Old Problems and New Perspectives in the Archaeology of South Asia*, Madison, 1989.
57. Romila Thapar, '*Dāna* and *Dakṣinā* and Forms of Exchange', in *Ancient Indian Social History: Some Interpretations*, New Delhi, 1978, 105–21. *See* chapter 24 in this volume
58. B.B. Lal, 'Excavations at Hastinapur . . . ', *Ancient India*, 1954 and 1955, 10 and 11, pp. 109ff.
59. E. Evans–Pritchard, *The Nuer*, 82–3. B. Lincoln, *Priests, Warriors and Cattle*, Berkeley, 1982, 43ff.
60. S.R. Rao, *Lothal*, 218. B.K. Thapar, 'Kalibangan', *Expedition*, Winter, 1975, pp. 19–32.
61. A. Ghosh, *The Encyclopaedia of Indian Archaeology*, I, Delhi, 1985.
62. Romila Thapar, *Aśoka and the Decline of the Mauryas*, Oxford, 1961, p. 128.
63. An example of this is A.K. Sharma, 'The Harappan Horse was Buried under the Dunes of . . . ', *Puratattva*, 1992–93, 23, 30–4.
64. S.R. Rao, *Lothal*, New Delhi, 1985, 641.
65. A. Ghosh (ed.), op. cit., I, 337.
66. D.K. Chakrabarti, 'The Beginning of Iron in India', *Antiquity*, 50, 1976, pp. 114–24.
67. F. Kortland, 'The Spread of Indo-Europeans', *Journal of Indo-European Studies*, 1990, 18, 1 and 2, pp. 131–40.
68. *From Lineage to State*, Delhi, 1984. The symbiosis involved for instance, pastoralists grazing their animals on the post-harvest stubble in the fields and thereby helping to manure the fields. This initial simple, inter-dependence can lead to more complex relationships.
69. Burrow, op. cit. Kuiper, op. cit.
70. D.K. Chakrabarti, 'The Aryan Hypothesis in Indian Archaeology', *Indian Studies: Past and Present*, 1968, IX, 4, pp. 343–58.
71. *Rgveda*, 7, 33; 7.83.
72. D.D. Kosambi, 'On the Origin of the Brahmana Gotras', *Journal of the Bombay Branch of the Royal Asiatic Society*, 1950, 26, pp. 21–80.
73. An example of such a revision, although rather extreme, can be seen in M. Bernal, *Black Athena*, London, 1987. See also M.A. Dandamaev and V.G. Lukonin, *The Culture and Social Institutions of Ancient Iran*, Cambridge, 1989.

# Index